DECISION POINTS AND DECISIONS IN CRIMINAL JUSTICE

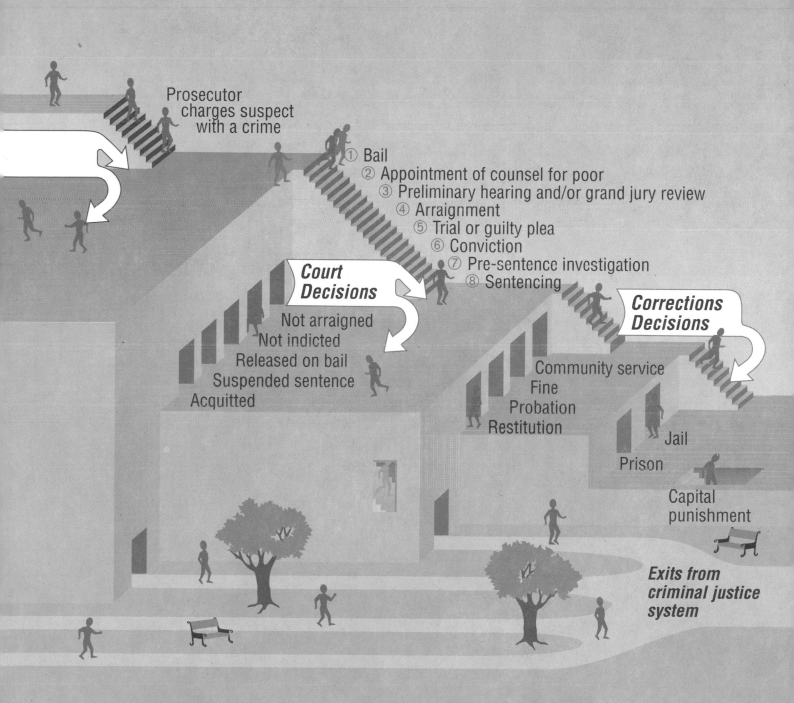

Prosecutor charges suspect with a crime

① Bail
② Appointment of counsel for poor
③ Preliminary hearing and/or grand jury review
④ Arraignment
⑤ Trial or guilty plea
⑥ Conviction
⑦ Pre-sentence investigation
⑧ Sentencing

Court Decisions

Not arraigned
Not indicted
Released on bail
Suspended sentence
Acquitted

Corrections Decisions

Community service
Fine
Probation
Restitution

Jail
Prison
Capital punishment

Exits from criminal justice system

Fourth Edition

Criminal Justice

**WEST
PUBLISHING
COMPANY**

Minneapolis/St. Paul
New York
Los Angeles
San Francisco

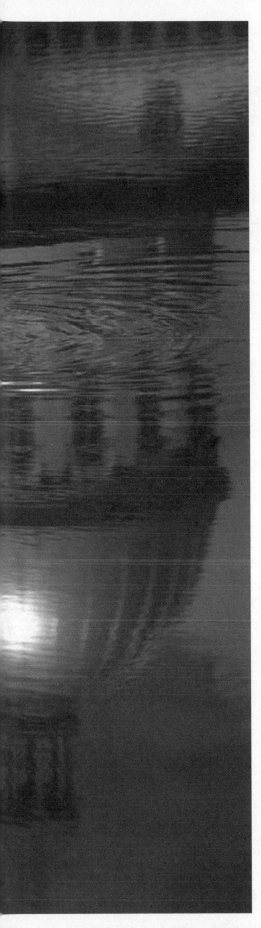

Criminal Justice
Fourth Edition

Joel Samaha
University of Minnesota

West's Commitment to the Environment

In 1906, West Publishing Company began recycling materials left over from the production of books. This began a tradition of efficient and responsible use of resources. Today, 100% of our legal bound volumes are printed on acid-free, recycled paper consisting of 50% new fibers. West recycles nearly 27,700,000 pounds of scrap paper annually--the equivalent of 229,300 trees. Since the 1960s, West has devised ways to capture and recycle waste inks, solvents, oils, and vapors created in the printing process. We also recycle plastics of all kinds, wood, glass, corrugated cardboard, and batteries, and have eliminated the use of polystyrene book packaging. We at West are proud of the longevity and the scope of our commitment to the environment.

West pocket parts and advance sheets are printed on recyclable paper and can be collected and recycled with newspapers. Staples do not have to be removed. Bound volumes can be recycled after removing the cover.

Production, Prepress, Printing and Binding by West Publishing Company.

British Library Cataloguing-in-Publication Data. A catalogue record for this book is available from the British Library.

Text design: *David J. Farr, Imagesmythe*
Indexer: *Erik Larson*
Copyeditor: *Bonnie Goldsmith*
Cover Image: *David Young-Wolff, Photo Edit, Coral Image Library*
Art: *Stan Maddock, Maddock Illustration and Nancy Wirsig McClure, Hand to Mouse Arts*
Composition: *Carlisle Communications*
Production, printing and binding: *West Publishing Company*

Copyright © 1988, 1991, 1994 By West Publishing Company
Copyright © 1997 By West Publishing Company
610 Opperman Drive
P.O. Box 64526
St. Paul, MN 55164–0526
All rights reserved
Printed in the United States of America
04 03 02 01 00 99 98 97   8 7 6 5 4 3 2 1 0
Library of Congress Cataloging-in-Publication Data
Samaha, Joel.
    Criminal justice / Joel Samaha. -- 4th ed.
      p. cm.
    Includes index.
    ISBN 0-314-09624-8 (hardcover : alk. paper) (Student Edition)
    ISBN 0-314-20610-8 (hardcover: alk. paper) (Annotated Instructor's Edition)
    1. Criminal justice, Administration of--United States. I. Title.
HV9950.S25 1997
345.7305--dc20
[347.3055]

Photo Credits

Part opener photo supplied by Comstock (image has been digitally altered) 2 Stock Boston; 4 Joe Sohm, Stock Boston; 5 Akos Szilvast, Stock Boston; 16 Robert E. Daemmrich, Tony Stone Images, Inc.; 30 Tom McHugh, Photo Researchers, Inc.; 37 Mark Richards, PhotoEdit; 44 Savino/The Image Works; 61 Richard Hutchings, Photo Researchers, Inc.; 80 Richard Hutching, Photo Researchers, Inc.; 84 Jeff Greenberg, Photo Researchers, Inc.; 97 Cary Wolinsky, Stock Boston; 110 David J. Sams, Stock Boston; 114 P. Chock, Stock Boston; 118 Bob Daemmrich, Stock Boston; 125 Charles Gatewood, The Image Works; 130 Christopher Brown, Stock Boston; 144 Herb Snitzer, Stock Boston; 150 Tropham/The Image Works; 154 Daemmrich/The Image Works; 163 Stephen Agricola, Stock Boston; 168 B. Bachmann, The Image Works; 173 Christopher Brown, Stock Boston; 178 Bob Daemmrich, The Image Works; 186 Michael Newman, PhotoEdit; 192 Greig Cranna, Stock Boston; 196 Michael Newman, PhotoEdit; 202 Starr, Stock Boston; 206 Richard Pasley, Stock Boston; 208 Robert Daemmrich, Tony Stone Images; 222 L. Mulvehill, The Image Works; 225 David R. Frazier, Photolibrary; 230 Robert Yager, Tony Stone Images; 233 David Frazier Photolibrary; 239 David Frazier Photolibrary; 239 David Frazier Photolibrary; 268 David Frazier Photolibrary; 272 A. Ramey, Stock Boston; 281 R. Sidney, The Image Works; 291 David Guttenfelder, AP/Wide World Photos; 299 David Frazier Photolibrary; 304 Barbara Alper, Stock Boston; 326 David Frazier, Photolibrary; 337 Dawson Jones, Tony Stone Images; 340, Aaron Haupt, David Frazier Photolibrary; 342 Barbara Alper, Stock Boston; 348 Savino, The Image Works; 350 S. Gazin, The Image Works; 356 Jonny Crawford, The Image Works; 362 Steven D. Starr, Stock Boston; 367 Bob Daemmrich, Stock Boston; 377 David Frazier Photolibrary; 385 David Frazier Photolibrary; 392 Bruce Ayres, Tony Stone Images; 398 Billy E. Barnes, Tony Stone Images; 402 Alan Klehr, Tony Stone Images; 410 Jim Pickerell, Tony Stone Images; 416 B. Daemmrich, The Image Works; 421 Billy E. Barnes, Stock Boston; 434 Tony Garcia, Tony Stone Images; 448 A. Ramey, PhotoEdit; 454 Hank Morgan, Photo Researchers, Inc.; 470 David R. Frazier Photolibrary; 486 John Eastcott, Photo Researchers, Inc.; 493 Stock Boston; 499 Spencer Grant, Photo Researchers, Inc.; 510 A. Ramey, PhotoEdit; 513 John Eastcott, Photo Researchers, Inc.; 524 Don Smetzer, Tony Stone Worldwide, Ltd.; 532 David R. Frazier Photolibrary; 534 Jeffrey Muir Hamilton, Stock Boston; 540 A. Ramey, PhotoEdit; 542 A. Ramey, PhotoEdit; 556 A. Ramey, Stock Boston; 572 Robert E. Daemmrich, Tony Stone Images, Inc.; 581 A. Ramey, PhotoEdit; 583 A. Ramey, PhotoEdit; 591 David Woo, Stock Boston; 595 Keith Wood, Tony Stone Images, Inc.; 598 M. Greenlar, The Image Works; 600 A. Ramey, PhotoEdit; 618 Michael Newman, PhotoEdit; 623 Harry Cabluck, AP/Wide World Photos; 626 Bob Daemmrich, Stock Boston; 636 John Coletti, Stock Boston; 646 David Frazier Photolibrary; 656 Michael Newman, PhotoEdit; 662 G. Azar, The Image Works; 665 Blair Seitz, Photo Researchers; 667 D. Green, The Image Works; 669 Bob Daemmrich, Stock Boston; 673 A. Ramey, PhotoEdit; 676 A. Ramey, PhotoEdit.

About the Author

Professor Samaha was admitted to the Illinois Bar in 1962. He taught at UCLA before coming to the University of Minnesota in 1971. At the University of Minnesota, he served as Chairman of the Department of Criminal Justice Studies from 1974 to 1978. Since then he has returned to teaching, research, and writing full-time. He has taught both television and radio courses in criminal justice, and has co-taught a National Endowment for the Humanities seminar in legal and constitutional history. He was named Distinguished Teacher at the University of Minnesota, a coveted award.

Professor Samaha is an active scholar. In addition to his monograph on pre-industrial law enforcement and transcription with scholarly introduction of English criminal justice records during the reign of Elizabeth I, he has written numerous articles on the history of criminal justice, published in such scholarly journals as *Historical Journal, American Journal of Legal History, Minnesota Law Review, William Mitchell Law Review,* and *Journal of Social History.* In addition to *Criminal Justice,* he has written two other successful textbooks, *Criminal Law,* now in its fifth edition, and *Criminal Procedure,* now in its third edition.

Contents

**PART TWO
Police 143**

4 The Missions and Roles of the Police 144

5 Police Strategies 186

6 Police and the Law 222

Preface

Rewarding and daunting—these are the words that come to mind in preparing the fourth edition of *Criminal Justice.* Rewarding because it is testament to the success of the previous three editions. Daunting because both our knowledge and the challenges of presenting that knowledge grows enormously between editions. The fourth edition of *Criminal Justice* builds on the successful foundation laid by the first three editions. The fourth edition accounts for the major new developments in the increasingly vast literature of criminal justice. It also reflects major rethinking about criminal justice theory, policy, and practice. However, this edition remains firmly committed to the approach that proved enormously successful in the first two editions. That is, it organizes the vast and complex subject matter of criminal justice according to the formal legal-bureaucratic and the informal discretionary decision making that occurs in the major public agencies of crime control—police, courts, and corrections. Topics are arranged chronologically according to when decisions are made regarding:

1. The definition, measurement, explanation, and reporting of crime.
2. The investigation, apprehension, prosecution, and conviction of criminal suspects and defendants.
3. The punishment and release of convicted offenders.

The Informal/Formal Perspective

The fourth edition sharpens the focus on the decision making process. This sharpened focus does not radically change the formal/informal perspective followed in the first three editions. After all, the systems approach or paradigm that has dominated criminal justice analysis for the last half century brought the formal and informal dimensions of criminal justice into the forefront of empirical, theoretical, and policy research. The first three chapters introduce students generally to two major themes that run throughout both this textbook and in the day-to-day operation of criminal justice:

1. The nature of formal and informal decision making in criminal justice.
2. The sociology, politics, economics, and law of criminal justice.

The remaining chapters analyze the nature and operation of the principal public agencies of crime control, beginning with the police, followed by the courts, and ending with corrections. A final chapter contains a brief overview of the structure and process of juvenile justice.

Active Learning

Criminal Justice, fourth edition, expands the interactive learning approach taken in the first two editions. Like its predecessors, this edition emphasizes the complexities of criminal justice; it avoids simple answers because they are all too often simplistic. *Criminal Justice* aims both to inspire and to challenge students to participate in the decision-making process. In doing so, students discover that learning criminal justice is a positive experience. Adopters have repeatedly affirmed the success of this aim. It is gratifying to one who has labored hard to present complex matter in an interesting manner that instructors report that their students actually *enjoy* reading *Criminal Justice.* Writing a book of not only substance but also of style, one that both challenges and gives pleasure, and that engages students in active learning, remains a major goal of the fourth edition.

Major Changes and Additions

Writing this fourth edition provided me with the opportunity to keep *Criminal Justice,* fourth edition, abreast of the latest empirical research. In addition to updating the entire text with appropriate new research, I made major additions and revisions in *Criminal Justice,* fourth edition. Highlighted here are some of these major revisions and additions.

Chapter 1

- New section. "Social Structure and Process" treats the role of gender, ethnicity, and race in criminal justice.
- New section: "Controlling Discretion," examines the efforts to control discretion in the past 30 years, relating the changes in position on whether to expand or restrict discretion in criminal justice to shifts between conservative and liberal ideology.

Chapter 2

- A new section, "Situation Theories of Crime" analyzes the theories of crime that focus on the importance of time, place, and opportunity in explaining criminal behavior. This section reflects the new interest in more applied theories that might be more useful in formulating criminal justice policies, such as hardening targets of crime to reduce the opportunity and motivation for criminal behavior.

Chapter 3

- A new section entitled "Causing a Harmful Result," expands on the analysis of the material elements of crimes. No other textbook introduces students to the important distinction between "crimes of criminal conduct" that require only a criminal act and a criminal intent and crimes that require a harmful result beyond the conduct itself.

Chapter 4

- The section "Federal Law Enforcement Agencies" now includes a discussion of the controversial use of federal law enforcement in local areas, using the intervention in the cases of David Koresh and Randy Weaver as examples.

Chapter 5

- New section: "Hot Spots' Patrol," analyzes the implementation and evaluation research re-

garding targeting specific addresses for more aggressive patrol.
- New section: "Assessment of Community Policing," surveys the state of existing empirical research evaluating the effectiveness of community and problem-oriented policing.

Chapter 6

- In order to strengthen the logical organization of materials regarding the enforcement of constitutional safeguards, the material in the section of prior editions entitled, "Enforcing Constitutional Safeguards" is divided in the fourth edition. The discussion of the exclusionary rule is retained in Chapter 6. The discussion of civil lawsuits, internal and external review, and disciplinary actions against police abuse of power now appear in Chapter 7.
- New analysis: This edition includes a discussion of provocative recent empirical research suggesting that the exclusionary rule deters illegal police behavior and that the social costs of the rule (allowing guilty people to go free because the police act illegally) are not nearly so high as once believed.
- New section: DNA testing, includes a discussion of the latest research on its accuracy in identifying suspects and its use by the courts.

Chapter 7

- This chapter includes a new discussion of empirical research regarding the effects of women officers' attitudes on job performance.
- The chapter includes a major new discussion of the *legitimate* use of force as the defining characteristic of police.
- New section: "Policy and Practices Regarding Force," examines existing empirical research regarding the relationship between formal written policies and unwritten rules governing the use of force in day to day police operations.
- The section "Civil Lawsuits" now includes a more thorough analysis of police civil liability, including the doctrines of *respondeat superior,* qualified immunity, and official immunity. It also includes a discussion of the important Supreme Court case of *Anderson v. Creighton* that expanded the immunity of police officers from civil lawsuits under the federal civil rights act.
- The new section, "Internal Review" includes both a description of various internal review

mechanisms and empirical findings regarding their operation and effectiveness.

- The new section, "External Review" describes and analyzes the types of external review, and surveys the empirical research evaluating the effectiveness of external review.

Chapter 9

- The new section "Race and Gender Bias in Bail Decisions," surveys some of the empirical research that suggests race and gender bias in bail decisions.

Chapter 11

- The expanded and revised section, "Sentencing Guidelines," contains major new material on the mechanisms and reasons for departing from guidelines sentences.
- The section, "Mandatory Minimum Sentencing Laws," is almost totally rewritten. It includes a history of mandatory sentencing, a description of its actual operation, and a survey of the empirical evaluations of mandatory minimum sentencing.
- New section: " 'Three Strikes and You're Out' Laws" traces the long history of these "new" laws, and reviews some empirical research on the cost and effects of the current laws.

Chapter 12

This chapter was part of Chapter 15 in previous editions. Part III (Corrections) in previous editions was organized so that prisons were discussed first. The rationale was that prisons receive the most attention and were most familiar to students. However, despite the growing number of prisons and prisoners, most people under correctional supervision are not incarcerated; they are supervised in the community. Therefore, it makes more sense to begin the examination of corrections with sentences to community supervision since it is by far the most common sentence and affects the greatest number of people.

In previous editions, one chapter was devoted to community corrections. In this edition, the subject is divided into two logical sections. This chapter discusses probation and other sentences that are largely *substitutes for* incarceration. The subject of parole and other conditional release *from incarceration* are discussed in a separate chapter (Chapter 15) entitled "Returning to Society."

- New section: "Revocation of Probation," examines the reasons for revocation, the em-

pirical research regarding public safety and violations, and the outcome of probation violation.

- The new section, "Probation and the Law," examines the legal status of probationers, the "diminished rights" of probationers, and the due process requirements for revoking probation.
- The new sections, "Fines," "Community Service," and "Day Reporting Centers," expand the coverage of intermediate punishments. They illustrate the wide variety of possible alternatives to traditional probation. The sections also examine the extent of their use, and the state of empirical research evaluating them.

Chapter 13

- The new section, "Super Maximum Security Prisons," examines the small but growing number of prisons designed to house the most dangerous criminals in both the federal and state prison systems.
- This expanded section, "New-Generation Maximum Security Prisons," examines the growing consensus among reformers and prison officials that prisons should be constructed and managed according to a "confinement model"—sending offenders to prisons *as* punishment, not *for* punishment.
- The expanded section, "New-Generation Jails," includes recent empirical research suggesting that men fare better than women in new generation jails.

Chapter 14

The section "The Constitution in Prison," is a shortened version of a separate chapter entitled "Prisoners and the Law," in previous editions. The trend has definitely shifted away from court intervention in the lives of prisoners and the conditions of imprisonment back to discretionary control of prison life by prison administration. Therefore, it seemed wise to reduce the coverage of prisoners and the law in this edition more in line with the reality of the late 1990s and the early 21st century.

The section on prison programs is considerably expanded. The section includes more analysis of education, vocational training, work release, financial assistance, and prison industries. And, this edition includes entirely new sections on treatment, work, recreation, and religious programs in prisons.

The expanded section on "Evaluation of Prison Programs," includes a survey of the latest research on the nature and effectiveness of prison programs.

Chapter 15

This is an almost entirely new chapter. This edition devotes an entire chapter to the subject of returning to society following incarceration. It fits chronologically and logically after the chapters on probation and prisons. Probation shares much in common with parole but probation is supervision as a *substitute for* incarceration while parole is community supervision *following* incarceration.

Conditional release from prison deserves major treatment in an introductory textbook because contrary to common knowledge and despite some move to abolish parole in a few places, the vast majority of prisoners eventually return to society in one of three ways, all of which are discussed in this chapter: at the expiration of their prison terms, upon a mandatory release with conditions attached to the release, and on traditional discretionary parole.

The chapter includes the following greatly expanded and entirely new material:

- A history of conditional release.
- An examination of the multiple and sometimes conflicting missions of parole—rehabilitation, punishment, politics, and prison management.
- A detailed description and an in depth analysis of traditional parole boards and their membership.
- An expanded description and analysis of parole board release.
- A discussion of mandatory release.
- An expanded discussion of parole supervision.
- A detailed examination of the major empirical findings regarding the effectiveness of conditional release.
- A new description and critical analysis of parole revocation, including the formal legal and informal influences on the decision to revoke.

Pedagogical Aids

The pedagogical aids that reviewers and students found effective in earlier editions continue.

Chapter Outlines consist of a list of the main topics and subtopics in each chapter. They provide a road map of each chapter so that students know where they are going as they read each chapter. Students have found the Chapter Outlines a major aid in organizing the large amount of material in each chapter.

Chapter Main Points sum up the major general points made in each chapter. They tell students what they should look for as they read each chapter. Students report that the Chapter Main Points help them to organize and guide their reading so that they can focus on the important ideas, information, and issues presented in each chapter.

Chapter Key Terms identify and define in the margins important items and concepts that all students should know.

You Decides are unique among criminal justice textbooks. They present several sides to major issues and invite students to participate in decision making. They demonstrate the complexity and difficulty in resolving issues, and in establishing and evaluating the effectiveness of criminal justice policy. Instructors report that the You Decides are successful; students say that they are among their favorite parts of *Criminal Justice.*

Historical Notes are also unique to *Criminal Justice.* They are not mere curiosities and frills. They demonstrate the durability of problems, the persistence of the efforts of reform, and the familiarity of popular perceptions in criminal justice. The Historical Notes appear in the margin near their modern counterparts in the text.

Comparative Criminal Justice boxes provide students with international perspectives on criminal justice. They present contrasting approaches, policies, and practices from a variety of countries around the world, including policing in Japan, criminal prosecution in Germany, criminal defense in Russia, and prison populations in the Scandinavian countries.

Chapter Review Questions test whether students have followed the outline, grasped the main points, remembered the important details, and grappled with the issues in each chapter. Students have repeatedly reported that the Review Questions are a major aid to understanding the large amount of information in each chapter.

Interdisciplinary Influence

Every book to some extent reflects the individual experience and training of its author. *Criminal Justice,* fourth edition, is no exception. My training as a social scientist, historian, and lawyer definitely influenced both the content and the style of *Criminal Justice.* The emphasis on theoretical and empirical research in criminal justice reflects my social science training. The systems paradigm and the view of criminal justice as a series of decisions adopted as an organizing principle of the text stems from social science theory and research. My training as a lawyer has drawn me to issues and the possible alternatives to resolve them. The You Decides and the presentation of varying views, conclusions, and research findings throughout the text reflect the tendency of lawyers to concentrate on issues and argument.

Historians are trained to look for change and continuity in human experience as a fundamental aspect of their discipline. *Criminal Justice* shows some of that training. It emphasizes not only the continuing problems in criminal justice but it also recognizes change and development. Some new programs, policies, and institutions and enhanced training of criminal justice professionals demonstrate the possibility of a fairer, more humane, efficient, and effective criminal justice system. Much remains to be done, of course. These bright spots should not obscure the darkness that remains. *Criminal Justice* aims to strike a balance that acknowledges the shortcomings that make up the present reality of criminal justice and recognizes the hope that new developments promise for criminal justice in the 21st century.

Acknowledgments

Many instructors around the country have reviewed the previous three editions of *Criminal Justice*. The book bears marks of their positive influence, marks that I hope they see and for which I am indebted to them. The list of my debtors is long and the mere mention of their names hardly repays my debt to them. The following instructors reviewed the fourth edition of *Criminal Justice* and provided thoughtful and serious evaluations of it: John S. Boyd, Stephen F. Austin State University; Neil R. Vance, University of Arizona; H. Wayne Overson, Weber State University; Nicholas H. Irons, Community College of Morris; Walter M. Francis, Central Wyoming College; Dave Camp, Georgia State University; Dana C. DeWitt, Chadron State College.

The instructors who contributed their comments on the first and second editions may rest assured that their influence continues. They include James A. Adamitis, Bonnie Berry, Stephen Brown, Paul V. Clark, Walt Copley, Jerry Davis, Marlon T. Doss, Edna Erez, Peter Grimes, John P. Harlan, Vincent Hoffman, Michael Israel, Gary Keveles, Peter B. Kraska, Robert Lockwood, Matthew Lyones, Joseph Macy, Stephen Mastrofski, G. Larry Mays, William Michalek, JoAnn Miller, Robert Murillo, Gordon E. Meisner, Donald R. Morton, Charles E. Myers II, John Northrup, Gary Perlstein, Mario Peitrucci, Harry L. Powell, Joel Powell, Archie Rainey, Christine Rasche, Philip Roades, Ronald Robinson, Glenda Rogers, John Scarborough, William Selke, Edward Sieh, Stan Stodkovic, Kenrick Thompson, Myron Utech, Timothy Vieders, Mervin White, Thomas Whitt, Warren M. Whitton, Keven Wright, and Stanley Yeldell.

In addition to the debt I owe to these instructors, it gives me great pleasure to acknowledge the deep obligation I owe to my colleagues at the University of Minnesota and former students who are now criminal justice professionals generously gave to the improvement of *Criminal Justice*.

Professor David Ward, professor in the Department of Sociology, my loyal friend and colleague, knew all the answers to my questions about corrections research. The book is richer because of his knowledge, his experience and his unlimited generosity in taking the time and energy to share that vast knowledge and experience with me.

Professor Joachim Savelsberg who read the entire book in earlier editions, made copious notes, and discussed his experiences in using *Criminal Justice* as a test in an introductory course in criminal justice. Joachim offered not only editorial advice but he has also continued to engage me in constructive thinking about the theory and sometimes not too subtle biases that appear in the text. I have not always taken his suggestions but the book is better because of his time and effort.

Norm Carlson, former director of the Federal Bureau of Prisons and now my colleague at the University of Minnesota, has facilitated many visits to correctional facilities, helped me obtain information and other materials that I could not otherwise easily find, and praised and helpfully criticized the text. But more than that, he has set an example that we should all follow—he remains generous, optimistic, cheerful, and open-minded in the face of what would have soured many others in less challenging positions. His advice, encouragement, and example have all enriched *Criminal Justice,* fourth edition. His advice to me to "show the positive side of criminal justice," I took to heart. I hope it shows in *Criminal Justice,* fourth edition.

Captain Greg Meyer, Los Angeles Police Department, has graciously read some of the chapters on policing with a critical eye. He has also generously shared with me his extensive knowledge of the use of force in particular and his perspectives on policing generally. His influence has definitely improved the chapters on policing.

Lieutenant Richard Gardell, St. Paul Police department; Sergeant James De Concini, Minneapolis Police Department; Martin Costello, Hughes and Costello; John Sheehy, Meshbesher and Spence; Judge Phil Bush; David Schwab, United States Probation Office; Warden Dennis Benson, Stillwater State Prison, all former students and now experienced professionals, have helped me more than they know or I can recognize. Following their careers, sharing their experiences, listening to their stories, and arguing with their positions, has kept me young in mind, in touch with the "real world," and inspired me to continue in the pursuit of knowledge, understanding, excellence, and improvement in criminal justice.

Stephen E. Brown, East Tennessee State University, has once again written an excellent Study Guide to accompany *Criminal Justice,* fourth edition. His careful, thorough, painstaking efforts have made the ancillaries to this edition a stronger package. Erik Larson, University of Minnesota, has helped me write the Instructor's Manual with Test Bank to accompany this edition. Erik is regarded by hundreds of undergraduates at the University of Minnesota as a demanding but fair, caring, knowledgeable teacher who appreciates the difficulties of students in mastering the enormous amount of information, concepts, and issues in criminal justice. This part of the ancillary package is definitely better for his work.

Criminal Justice, fourth edition owes much to the expertise, devotion, and effort of editors and others at West Publishing Company, who worked so hard to transform the manuscript into a book. David Farr has outdone himself, designing an even more attractive and authoritative book than the third edition. John Tuvey, promotion manager, brought to this project his unparalleled creative ideas and enthusiasm. Stephanie Syata's confidence, efficiency, sensitivity, and even-handed competence were just what I needed to bring *Criminal Justice,* fourth edition, to the satisfying finished book that I believe it is. Mary Schiller for more than fifteen years has kept my eye on the prize—writing not only a successful book but a *good* book. Only her unwavering and deep devotion to both quality and success could have encouraged, inspired, guided, and nudged this—to put it most kindly—mercurial temperamented author to do my best.

The good in the book owes much to the instructors around the country who have reviewed this and earlier editions, to my colleagues at the University of Minnesota, to my former students who are now successful and experienced criminal justice professionals in their own right, and to criminal justice professionals around the country whom I have met over the past thirty years. The book has also profited from the now thousands of students who have taken criminal justice courses from me at the University of Minnesota. Undergraduates, graduate students, and law students have changed in many respects over the years but in one important respect they have remained constant—they have challenged me to give them the most that I can and the best that I have. I hope the book goes some distance to meeting their challenge. I am happy to share what is good in the book with them. The shortcomings are my own.

Joel Samaha
University of Minnesota

PART ONE

Criminal Justice

1 Crime and Criminal

Justice

CHAPTER MAIN POINTS

1. *The answers to most questions of criminal justice policy require a knowledge of the real workings of criminal justice.*

2. *The systems paradigm considers criminal justice as a series of decisions from the commission of a crime to the final release of offenders from state supervision.*

3. *Day-to-day decision making in criminal justice depends on both formal rules and informal discretion.*

4. *Formal criminal justice consists of a range of written rules, including constitutional provisions, court decisions, statutes, and agency rules and regulations.*

5. *Informal criminal justice consists of discretionary judgments influenced by ideology, social structure, and social processes of which criminal justice is an integral part.*

6. *The structure of criminal justice comprises a group of federal, state, and local agencies involved in crime control.*

7. *The process of criminal justice consists of a series of decisions related to the detection, investigation, and apprehension of crime suspects, the prosecution and conviction of criminal defendants, and the punishment of convicted offenders.*

8. *The criminal justice system is made up of a group of agencies linked loosely together by their common crime control functions and the interdependence of their decisions.*

9. *At each stage of the criminal process, some cases are removed and the rest moved further into the process.*

10. *The history of criminal justice consists of a pendulum swing between the competing values of crime control and due process, and of law and discretion.*

ear. Frustration. Anger. Disgust. Strong words but, according to most reliable opinion surveys, these are the words that describe the attitudes of the majority of Americans toward crime and its control. They are also the words that have described attitudes toward crime and crime control since at least the 1960s. They reveal not only powerful negative emotions, but also a definite lack of confidence in the ability of the criminal justice system to control crime. Are people's fear, anger, frustration, disgust, and lack of confidence justified? Television news and documentaries, radio talk shows, politicians of both parties, civic and religious leaders tell us, and we tell each other, that crime, particularly violent crimes and drug offenses, is about to destroy our society. Is it true? Conservatives say that if only the police had more power and criminal suspects fewer rights; if only juries convicted more criminals; if only judges sentenced more convicted criminals to longer prison terms; and if only prison really *punished* offenders instead of coddling them, we could solve the crime problem. Furthermore, the right of people to be free from victimization should take precedence over the rights of a few criminals. Are they right? Liberals maintain that punishment doesn't work. Only by improving the social conditions that cause crime,

Frustration runs high when children are crime victims.

such as poverty, poor education, prejudice, and lack of opportunity; only by preparing people to work and play by the rules so that they will neither need nor want to commit crimes; only then can we reduce crime. Furthermore, say liberals, the rights of all people are too valuable to compromise in the name of controlling crime. Are they right?

These are all questions of great concern, and major public policy decisions depend on complete and accurate answers to them. The best answers require a knowledge of the reality of crime and of the capacity of agencies of criminal justice—police, courts, and corrections—to control crime. The reality of crime and criminal justice—what we actually *know*, as opposed to what we *think* we know—is the subject of this book. Understanding this reality requires answering the following questions as completely as possible:

1. *What are the amounts, kinds, trends, and causes of crime?* Not according to stories and public belief, but in actual statistics.
2. *What are the responses to crime of individuals, legislatures, and public agencies—police, courts, and corrections?* Responses shown by day-to-day behavior and operation, not prescriptions about *desired* responses.
3. *Do the responses to crime work?* That is, do they help to control crime? Responses must be evaluated by careful, empirical research, not by anecdote and wishful thinking.
4. *Even if they work, are they legal?* That is, do crime control policies and practices comply with constitutional protections; the laws of the nation, state, and locality; and, the rules of agencies and departments?
5. *Even if they work and are legal, are current responses to crime wise public policy?* That is, do they match the values of the ideal society in which we all want to live by maximizing individual privacy and liberty to the extent consistent with safety? Is it worth the cost to enforce them?

This book attempts to answer these questions as completely as our existing knowledge allows. This chapter presents concepts and themes common to all of criminal justice. Understanding criminal justice requires knowledge not only of its specific parts, that is, police, courts, and corrections, but also of criminal justice as a whole. Much of the dissatisfaction with the administration of criminal justice—a dissatisfaction almost as old as Anglo-American law—stems from a misunderstanding about how decision making in criminal justice really takes place.

Most people believe that decision making in criminal justice operates—or at least *should* operate—strictly according to the law. In the popular conception, the law prescribes a clear-cut set of decisions required to control crime. Criminal law defines what is criminal and designates appropriate punishment. Police are supposed to catch the criminals and turn them over to the courts for prosecution and trial. Following trial and conviction, criminals get their "just deserts." In the struggle between "good," law-abiding people and "evil" criminals, the good people are supposed to win.

When good does not triumph over evil—as it frequently does *not* in television and tabloid accounts of the Constitution "handcuffing the police," and criminals "getting off" with just a "slap on the wrist"—people feel angry, disgusted, frustrated. These feelings are heightened when it appears that power, money, class, race, ethnicity, gender, ideology, and politics—not the even-handed application of the law—determine who gets caught, who gets punished, and how much punishment they get. The crosscurrents of law, money, race, class, gender, ideology, and politics were dramatically revealed in the trial, "not guilty" verdict, and public reaction to the acquittal of former football hero O. J. Simpson in the murder of his former wife and her friend. All these dimensions of the case were televised for the world to see—from the day of the murders, through the "slow chase" of O. J., the preliminary hearings, trial, and acquittal, to public reaction.

The O. J. Simpson case forced into the open some fundamental questions about American criminal justice. Was this case typical? If so, in what ways? How does criminal justice work in its day-to-day operation? Do criminal justice professionals make decisions according to the law, or according to their individual whims? Are lawyers merely trying to win cases, make money, and further their careers, or are they earnestly searching for truth? Can

The O. J. Simpson murder trial was only one of a long list of sensational murder trials in the history of criminal justice.

money buy justice? Does the criminal justice system treat men who abuse their wives too leniently? What part does race play in arrest, prosecution, conviction, and punishment? Do juries decide cases according to the evidence, or according to their prejudices and public pressures? What does the picture of African Americans cheering and white Americans looking glum following the acquittal of Simpson tell us about racial attitudes and criminal justice? Why do African Americans especially, but other nonwhites as well, tend to have a more negative view of criminal justice than white Americans do?

The following *You Decide,* "Criminal Justice—Equal Justice for All?," introduces you to a prominent feature of this textbook. *You Decide* presents issues in criminal justice that invite you to engage in decision making. There is no single "right" way to resolve the issues presented; one reason for featuring them is to demonstrate how difficult it is to decide these important questions. This first *You Decide* presents two different views of the importance of formal rules of law and informal influences of class, race, power, and ideology in the O. J. Simpson case.

You Decide — "Criminal Justice—Equal Justice for All?"

Consider the decisions made by police, prosecutor, judges, and jury in the O. J. Simpson case, as Scott Turow, the lawyer-turned-novelist, portrays them. Turow, a former prosecutor, wrote *Presumed Innocent* and, most recently, *Pleading Guilty,* two novels about crime and criminal justice. What motivated their decisions? A belief in law? Politics? Conservative ideology? Liberal ideology? Money and power?

"Simpson Prosecutors Pay for their Blunders"

By Scott Turow, New York Times, October 5, 1995
The prosecution of O. J. Simpson was doomed from the start. Not in the sense that the state lacked proof—the case against Mr. Simpson remains compelling. But the prosecution was a low-road enterprise that began with the kinds of ugly tactics that have aroused suspicions about the criminal justice system among members of racial minorities in Los Angeles and elsewhere. The problem was not only the way the police went about gathering evidence at Mr. Simpson's home the morning after the murders, but more important the way the Los Angeles District Attorney's office subsequently defended those arrogant blunders.

At the preliminary hearings, Detectives Philip Vannatter and Mark Fuhrman testified that they and two other detectives traveled to Mr. Simpson's home on Rockingham Avenue to inform him of the murder so he could make arrangements for his children. The detectives testified that after getting no response to the buzzer at the gate, and following their discovery of a small spot of blood on Mr. Simpson's Bronco, which was on the street, they jumped the wall because they feared for Mr. Simpson's safety. It was after this adventure in low-rent rappelling—which was not only a violation of the Fourth Amendment but also criminal trespass—that Detective Fuhrman says he found the famous bloody glove.

The trouble with this testimony, in my view, is that the detectives' explanation as to why they were at the house is hard to believe. At the time of the preliminary hearing, before the DNA results had come in, the bloody glove, which matched one found at the crime scene, was the foremost evidence against Mr. Simpson. So the police were under tremendous pressure to explain their actions in a way that would legally excuse them for violating Mr. Simpson's rights and allow the glove to be introduced as evidence. Thus the dubious claim about fearing for Mr. Simpson's safety. Four police detectives were not needed to carry a message about Nicole Simpson's death. These officers undoubtedly knew what Justice Department statistics indicate: that half of the women murdered in the United States are killed by their husbands or boyfriends. Simple probabilities made Mr. Simpson a suspect.

Also, Mark Fuhrman had been called to the Simpson residence years earlier when Mr. Simpson was abusing his wife. Thus Mr. Simpson was more than the usual suspect husband; he had a known propensity to do violence to his wife. Of course, he is also one of the most exceptional physical talents of his generation, a member of the relatively small class of human beings capable of murdering two persons at once and of wielding a knife with sufficient power to virtually decapitate someone.

If veteran police detectives did not arrive at the gate of Mr. Simpson's home thinking he might have committed these murders, then they should have been fired. The detectives went to Rockingham for one reason: they wanted to question Mr. Simpson before he had a chance to lawyer up. Perhaps he would explain himself, offer an alibi. But it's more likely they were hoping he would confess or tell one of the stupid little lies that so often become a defendant's undoing.

The detectives did not need a spot of blood on the Bronco to have powerful reasons to question Mr. Simpson. But assuming they did see the blood, why were they fly-specking the car if they had come only to deliver tragic news? The cops went over the wall to find Mr. Simpson, not to save him, and anyone who has spent time as a player in the criminal justice system had to recognize that. The fact that the district attorney's office put these officers on the witness stand to tell this story and so that the municipal judge at the pre-trial hearing, Kathleen Kennedy-Powell, accepted it is scandalous. It is also routine.

Everybody hates the Fourth Amendment, of course. What a lamentable concept: the constable blundered so the evidence is lost. But the Fourth Amendment was not added to the Constitution to make most of us happy. It was intended to protect individuals from the state and to insure that political minorities would not be the object of random searches engineered by the political majority. And when the Fourth Amendment and the other constitutional rules restricting police behavior are violated, it necessarily carries with it a strong message to our political minorities—including members of racial minorities, who are more likely to have contact with the police than are whites—that the legal system is a two-faced joker, one which says: We make the rules and we'll follow the ones we like.

I was an Assistant United States Attorney for eight years, and I never had a piece of evidence suppressed in a case I handled. This is not because I am such a great lawyer or mastered any special legal legerdemain. It was because the Federal agents I worked with understood the Fourth Amendment and didn't violate it. Assistant United States Attorneys were available to answer Federal investigators' legal questions 24 hours a day. The agents were forbidden to make an arrest or enter a residence without our approval. They made it their business to follow the law, because they knew we would not put them on the witness stand to play make-believe. We couldn't even if we wanted to because the district court judges turned aside all such efforts with fury and scorn.

A legal system, like any moral system, is a complex and interdependent social arrangement. No one does good on his own. It requires the constant support, reinforcement and allegiance of all players for each to resist the everpresent temptations to let ends justify means. And that system appears to have broken down in Los Angeles. To lambaste only Detectives Fuhrman and Vannatter misses the point. It was the Los Angeles District Attorney's Office that put them on the stand. It was Judge Kennedy-Powell who took their testimony at face value rather than stir controversy by suppressing the most damning evidence in the case of the century. And it was Judge Lance Ito who refused to reverse her decision.

Because the prosecutors routinely accepted even the most unlikely stories from police officers, they were unable to recognize Mr. Fuhrman as a genuinely bad character. By the time news of Mr. Fuhrman's background began to emerge, prosecutors were hip-joined to him, their star witness—a foul-mouthed racist cop, the latest poster boy of the Los Angeles Police Department, his image hanging on the wall of the public mind next to those of the officers who beat Rodney King. The jury made them pay. The jurors were impaneled knowing from the start that this was business as usual in Los Angeles. Nothing the 6 prosecutors could do could convince them that this case was not corrupted by the police department's world-renowned racial hostility.

It is worth thinking about how this case would have developed had the authorities played it straight from the start. If Judge Kennedy-Powell had said: "I know these police officers want to believe what they've said, but that defies the realities of the work they do. This evidence is suppressed." If the District Attorney's office had conceded that the police had violated Mr. Simpson's rights, but tried to have the evidence admitted on the "inevitable discovery" theory, which allows evidence that would have surely been found if the police had gotten a search warrant.

Yes, suppressing the glove would have made headlines. It would have been another black eye for the police department. But it would have been a clarion announcement to the world—and to Los Angeles's black community—that the criminal justice system had mended its ways and was committed to treating all citizens fairly. Paradoxically, it would also have given the district attorney's office its best chance to win this case. It would have relieved the jurors, all but two of whom were black or Hispanic, of the troubling choice they ultimately faced—between convicting Mr. Simpson or vindicating their own rights, which no one else in the legal system seemed to have bothered about. Copyright © 1995 by *New York Times* Co., Reprinted by Permission.

***

Compare Scott Turow's interpretation of the Simpson case with that of George Will, the conservative pundit. Does Will see the case as an expression of the rule of law as it ought to work in our criminal justice system? Does he agree with Turow that the police, prosecutors, and judges caused the government to lose a "good" case against Simpson? Or does he suggest that some sinister influence was at work in the verdict of the jury?

"When Justice is Political, People Get Away with Murder"

By George F. Will, **Washington Post,** *October 5, 1995*
Hyperbole expands in societies where articulateness atrophies, so the circus in Los Angeles was called "the trial of the century," which puts the proceedings at Nuremberg in an interesting perspective. Actually, from the start it was the jury that was on trial. It did not acquit itself well. Incited by Johnnie Cochran—good lawyer, bad citizen—to turn the trial into a political caucus, the jurors did that instead of doing their banal duty of rendering a just verdict concerning two extremely violent deaths. The jurors abused their position in order to send a message about racism, police corruption or whatever.

There was condescension, colored by racism in some of the assumptions that the jurors would be incompetent jurors and bad citizens—that they would be putty in the hands of defense attorneys harping on race, that they would be intellectually incapable of following an evidentiary argument, or, worse, they would lack the civic conscience to do so. But those assumptions seem partially validated by the jury's refusal even to deliberate. Life is full of close calls, but the question of O.J. Simpson's guilt was not one of them. If 90 percent of the evidence against him had been excluded—indeed, if the defense had been allowed to decide which 90 percent would be excluded—the remaining 10 percent would have sufficed. Ten percent of the evidence would have sufficed had evidence been germane, which it was not when the trial was transformed into a seminar on Mark Fuhrman's viciousness and society's defects.

The defense brassily said to the jury approximately what Groucho Marx said in the movie "Duck Soup": "Who are you gonna believe, me or your own eyes?" The result has been a lesson about what happens when the reckless, rampant politicalization of life encompasses even the criminal justice system: People get away with murder.

This case has given a new cast to the familiar question, "Can a black man get a fair trial in America?" And it leaves a debris of disturbing facts: The defense team demonstrated that if you have enough money to throw at the criminal justice system you can tie it up, like Gulliver among the Lilliputians, with a thousand threads of procedural tangles. The incompetence, or worse, of public institutions such as the Los Angeles coroner's office is even worse than you thought. The experience of the African-American community with police departments often is beyond the comprehension of white Americans.

Another chilling residue of this debacle should be the realization that nothing—no institution, no pattern of civility—is spared the ravages of racial thinking. For more than a generation now public policies such as affirmative action, the racial spoils system and the cult of "diversity" have been teaching the nation that groupthink is virtuous. Such policies have taught this by encouraging identity politics—the politics of thinking that you are but a fragment of the racial or ethnic group to which you belong and you have few if any obligations beyond it.

Such policies have taught this by making it admirable—and lucrative—to identify with grievance groups defined by their resentments of the larger society. Such policies have taught this by accommodating the doctrine of categorical representation—the doctrine that the interests of a group can be understood, empathized with and properly represented only by members of that group. Given all this, it is not surprising that the jurors had no pangs of conscience about regarding Simpson merely as a member of a group—and not seeing his victims at all. People who think "race-conscious remedies" for this or that can be benign are partly to blame.

At least there should now be sober reconsideration of the presence of television cameras in courtrooms. One question is whether it is good for society to treat the criminal justice system as a source of entertainment. It simply will not do to chant the mantra about "the public's right to know." The impulse often behind that is just voyeurism stirred up in rights talk. The public's "right" to whatever entertains it is not sovereign over considerations of the moral standing and proper functioning of the criminal justice system.

Cochran himself says that he believes some of Judge Lance Ito's rulings during the trial were made as they were because the world was watching. If so—if cameras are not a passive presence, if the act of observing alters that which is observed—then the case against cameras in courtrooms is irrefutable. And so perhaps it is possible to hope that the Simpson circus—which was without precedent—will not be any similar circus' precedent.

© 1995, Washington Post Writers Group. Reprinted with permission.

---

systems paradigm *special way of looking at criminal justice by focusing on decision making throughout the criminal process.*

There is so much to learn about the agencies of criminal justice—police, courts, and corrections—and their important roles, functions, and day-to-day activities that we often lose sight of the "big picture." This chapter examines a number of elements common to the whole of criminal justice. These include:

1. Criminal justice is a system, that is, a group of agencies related to crime control.

2. Criminal justice is a process, that is, a series of decisions from first reporting crimes to the police to finally releasing offenders from correctional supervision.

3. Criminal justice in a constitutional democracy reflects decision making in the context of the competing values of due process and crime control, and of formal rules and informal discretion.

4. Day-to-day decision making in criminal justice reflects the effects of competing ideologies, economics, and the larger social structure and processes of which criminal justice is an integral part.

Law and Discretion— Formal and Informal Criminal Justice

All disciplines have a special way of looking at their subject matter. Criminal justice is no different. For more than a generation, the systems paradigm has dominated the arrangement of knowledge in criminal justice, the direction of research, and even reform efforts. The **systems paradigm** has several features:

1. It organizes criminal justice according to a series of decisions made in the effort to control crime.

2. It examines decision making throughout the criminal justice system, from the time crimes first come to the attention of the police to the final release of convicted offenders from government supervision.

3. It focuses on what actually happens in the day-to-day operation and activity of police departments, courts, and corrections agencies.

These features have led to research that has greatly enriched our understanding of the reality of criminal justice. First, research has shed light on what are otherwise low-visibility decisions hidden from public view. Research guided by the systems paradigm makes clear that decision making in criminal justice is not simply a matter of learning or researching rules and then applying these rules to specific situations. It is not nearly that open, direct, and simple. According to this research, these decisions involve a lot of **discretion,** that is, they result more from the judgment of individual personnel than from written rules and regulations. Moreover, the reality of decision making in the day-to-day operation of criminal justice is not only its low visibility and discretionary aspects, but also its complexity. The circumstances calling for decisions by criminal justice personnel are frequently extremely complicated, and they are neither categorized nor controlled easily. Criminal justice personnel must respond to an almost endless variety of problems, people, and circumstances.[1]

Important as discretionary decision making is, research since the 1950s has also made clear that day-to-day criminal justice activities and operations do not consist solely of discretionary, low-visibility, complex decisions. According to the late Donald J. Newman, a leading teacher and scholar in criminal justice, criminal justice is not simply a system of informal social behavior without formal control. Criminal justice "rests on, indeed is created and enabled by . . . law." Therefore, understanding the reality of criminal justice requires knowledge of *both* law and other established rules *and* field research into what actually happens on the street, at police stations, in courts, and in corrections agencies. Throughout your study of criminal justice and while reading this book, you should remember these two dimensions: formal law and other established rules, and informal discretion exercised by professionals in their day-to-day actions. Frequently, you will see references simply to informal and formal criminal justice, shorthand terms for these two basic dimensions. The balance of formal and informal decision making is the heart of criminal justice and a central theme of this book.

Rules and Formal Criminal Justice

The law and other written rules make up **formal criminal justice.** They provide the broad framework within which discretionary criminal justice operates. Laws and other written rules define the outer boundaries of permissible actions of professionals and policy makers, but they cannot explain most of the day-to-day operations of criminal justice. Written rules include everything from constitutional provisions to departmental rules and regulations (see Table 1.1). The best known formal rules are the provisions in the Bill of Rights and the rules handed down by the United States Supreme Court in its decisions interpreting these provisions. Perhaps the most famous example of Court rule making is the case of *Miranda v. Arizona* in which the Supreme Court formulated the *Miranda* warnings as specific rules to control police discretion.

The Constitution and the Supreme Court are not the only sources of rules and rule making in criminal justice. In fact, they have received too much attention in the past. In this book you will also learn about the other rules that influence day-to-day operations in criminal justice. These are listed in Table 1.1 and discussed in detail in the appropriate chapters. However, it is worth noting here that administrative rules and rule making in criminal justice agencies are becoming increasingly important as a means to control discretionary decision making.[2]

Table 1.1
Formal and Informal
Decision Making

Formal Rules	Informal Discretion
Constitutional Provisions 1. United States Constitution and Bill of Rights 2. State constitutions and bill of rights **Statutes** 1. United States Code 2. State codes **Court Decisions** Decisions of courts interpreting constitutional provisions and statutes **Rules of Procedure** 1. Federal Rules of Criminal Procedure 2. State rules of criminal procedure **Department and Agency Rules and Regulations** 1. Federal law enforcement agency rules 2. U.S. Attorney General rules 3. Federal Bureau of Prisons rules and regulations 4. State and local police departments rules and regulations 5. County and district attorneys rules and regulations 6. State and local prison and jail rules and regulations	**Police** 1. Do nothing 2. Investigate crime 3. Report and record crime 4. Arrest criminal suspect 5. Search criminal suspect 6. Interrogate criminal suspect 7. Release criminal suspect 8. Verbally warn criminal suspect 9. Use force against individuals 10. Intervene to maintain the peace by giving orders to people to "break it up," "move on," or "keep it quiet" 11. Provide service to people by recommending other social services, helping lost persons find their way, helping parents find their children **Prosecutor** 1. Take no action 2. Divert case or person to another agency 3. Charge suspect with a criminal offense 4. Recommend bail or detention 5. Negotiate a guilty plea 6. Go to jail 7. Recommend harsh or lenient sentence **Judge** 1. Bail 2. Pretrial detention 3. Accept negotiated plea 4. Reject negotiated plea 5. Suspend sentence 6. Sentence to probation 7. Minimum sentence 8. Maximum sentence

informal criminal justice
discretionary decision-making aspect of day-to-day criminal justice operation.

rational decision making
decisions based on alternative choices, information, and defined goals.

Discretion and Informal Criminal Justice

Discretion, or decision making without written rules, determines **informal criminal justice,** that is, the reality of criminal justice in action. Throughout this book, the focus is at least as much on discretionary decision making and informal criminal justice as it is on decisions according to formal rules. Discretionary decision making requires judgments based on experience and training. The range of decisions available to criminal justice personnel is wide. Table 1.1 lists some of them.

Discretionary decision making does not mean illegal action or even action without constraint. Quite the contrary. In the best of all possible worlds, discretionary decision making is rational. **Rational decision making** assumes the presence of three critical characteristics:

1. A choice of at least two alternative decisions—doing nothing or doing something—but probably several more.

Table 1.1

Formal and Informal Decision Making— Continued

Formal Rules	Informal Discretion
	Probation Department 1. Little or no supervision 2. Minimum supervision 3. Medium supervision 4. Maximum supervision 5. Report probation violations 6. Take little or no actions regarding revocation of probation
	Prisons 1. Place minimum restrictions on prisoner liberty and privacy 2. Place medium restrictions on prisoner liberty and privacy 3. Place maximum restrictions on prisoner liberty and privacy 4. Issue disciplinary reports 5. Take disciplinary actions 6. Release prisoners
	Parole Board 1. Grant parole 2. Deny parole
	Parole Department 1. Little or no supervision 2. Minimum supervision 3. Medium supervision 4. Maximum supervision 5. Report probation violations 6. Take little or no actions regarding revocation of probation

2. The availability of information upon which to base decisions and the use of that information to reduce the uncertainty of the outcome of the decision.

3. A specific goal or goals that the decision is supposed to achieve or maximize or minimize.[3]

In the real world, the choices are many, the availability of information often spotty, and the need to make the decision often immediate, not allowing time for reflection and research. The pressure of frequent emergencies particularly in police stations and corrections agencies, adds significantly to the complexity and difficulty of decision making.

As if the need for immediate action were not enough to render decision making difficult, the goals or mission of criminal justice are frequently not stated. Moreover, even if they are stated, they are rarely stated clearly. Perhaps most important, the goals are usually multiple and conflicting. For example, police missions are to enforce the law, keep the peace, and provide services to the public. Police are called on to decide right now, often with little or no guidance, which of these missions to pursue and what actions will best achieve goals. Prosecutors, too, strive to achieve multiple and conflicting goals. They want to win cases, crack down on specific crimes, improve efficiency, save money, and divert cases from the criminal justice system. Judges face the conflicting problems of retribution, deterrence, incapacitation, and rehabilitation, goals impossible to achieve simultaneously. Probation officers are expected to provide both law enforcement and counselling. Corrections officers are supposed to maintain order and prevent escapes,

structure of criminal justice
federal, state, and local agencies of criminal justice.

discipline prisoners, keep their staffs satisfied, and turn prisoners into people who will return to society ready to work hard and play by the rules.

But these are not all the difficulties of decision making in the real world of criminal justice—not just many choices, limited information, the pressure of circumstances, and unstated, unclear, conflicting goals. Politics, budgetary constraints, the existing social structure and processes, shifting ideology, even individual personality, ambitions, and needs also guide, shape, and limit discretionary decision making. Many of the remaining chapters discuss in depth the range of choices, available information, missions and goals, and circumstances surrounding decision making in police departments, courts, and corrections agencies. Here, it is only important to grasp the general significance of this highly complex, difficult job. Remember that there are no easy answers to any of the questions surrounding crime control.[4]

Criminal Justice—Structure and Process

Criminal justice is both a structure and a process. Viewed as a structure, criminal justice consists of a group of agencies. Viewed as a process, it focuses on the people in these agencies who make decisions, on the decisions they make, on the factors that influence their decisions, and on the effects of their decisions. These people include the professional decision makers, including legislators, police, prosecutors, judges, and corrections personnel. Also included are the people whom the decisions directly affect, including suspects, defendants, offenders, and victims. Figure 1.1 depicts the criminal justice agencies, major decisions, and stages in the criminal process.[5]

The Structure of Criminal Justice

Understanding decision making requires a basic idea of the **structure of criminal justice,** that is, of the federal, state, and local agencies within which most of these decisions are made and which employ the key decision makers. Criminal justice is, traditionally, first and foremost *local.* (Local criminal justice agencies employ nearly 60 percent of all justice personnel, most of them local police officers.) The principal types of agencies that make up the structure of state and local criminal justice include:

- *Law Enforcement*—municipal police departments and county sheriff's offices.
- *Courts*—district lower criminal and trial courts and state courts of appeals.
- *Corrections*—county and sometimes municipal jails, and state prisons.[6]

However there is also federal criminal justice.

Federal criminal justice has been growing since the 1960s but especially during the 1980s and 1990s. This growth is due mainly to the creation of many new federal drug, gun, and violent crime laws, sometimes passed in haste and emotion and without regard for local differences. Attempts to meet public demands and to enhance the careers of politicians who want to sound "tough on crime" account in part for this enhanced federal law enforcement. The principal federal law enforcement agencies include the Federal Bureau of Investigation (FBI), the Drug Enforcement Agency (DEA), and the Bureau of Alcohol, Tobacco, and Firearms (ATF).

The large federal court system includes prosecutors, judges, and probation officers. Every region in the country has a United States Attorney's office staffed by United States attorneys and their assistants, nearly all of whom the president appoints and the Senate approves. The federal court system also includes federal magistrates who issue warrants and conduct pretrial court

Figure 1.1

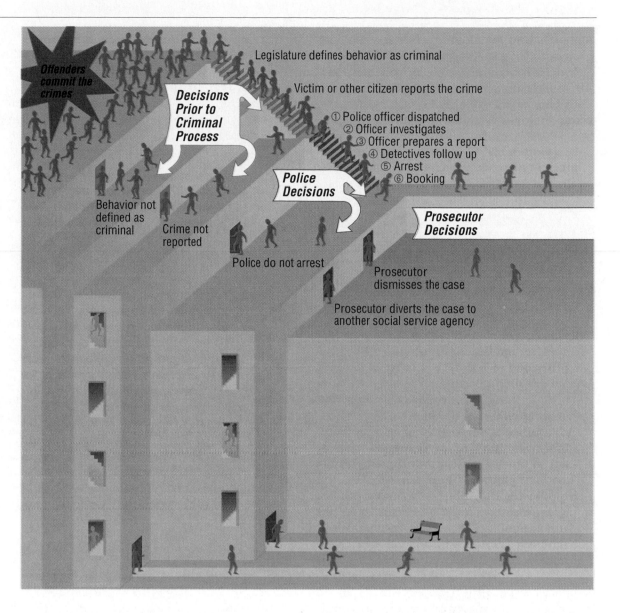

proceedings. The United States District Courts try cases and hear challenges to local and state jurisdictions, such as *habeas corpus* petitions. The United States Courts of Appeals, the federal intermediate court of appeals, hear appeals both from federal district courts and often from state courts involving constitutional questions. The United States Supreme Court, the court of last resort in the nation, finally resolves constitutional questions; no appeals remain from its decisions in criminal cases except for executive clemency and pardons.

The federal correctional system consists mainly of the United States Probation Office and the Federal Bureau of Prisons. These offices administer persons convicted of federal offenses. As its name indicates, the Probation Office administers probation through probation offices and officers throughout the United States. The Bureau of Prisons administers the network of federal prisons throughout the United States.

The Process of Criminal Justice

Criminal justice is not only about structure. It is also about process, that is, the complexity of the decision making that takes place throughout the public agencies of crime control. This book examines the decisions, decision makers, and agencies according to the chronology of criminal justice. It

Figure 1.1

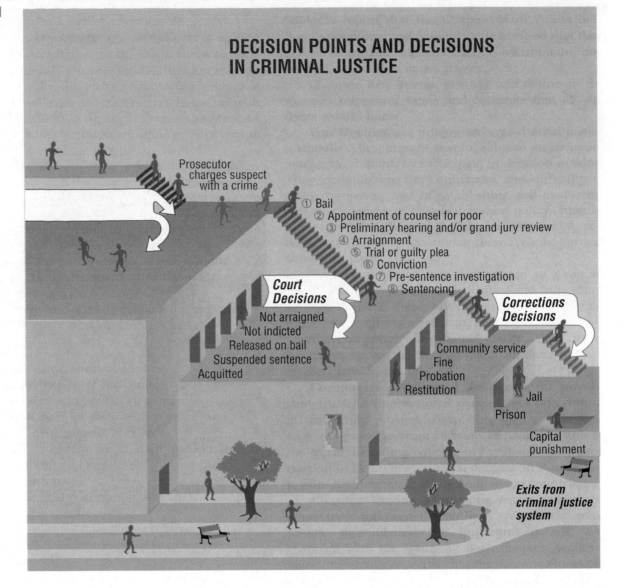

DECISION POINTS AND DECISIONS IN CRIMINAL JUSTICE

Prosecutor charges suspect with a crime

① Bail
② Appointment of counsel for poor
③ Preliminary hearing and/or grand jury review
④ Arraignment
⑤ Trial or guilty plea
⑥ Conviction
⑦ Pre-sentence investigation
⑧ Sentencing

Court Decisions

Not arraigned
Not indicted
Released on bail
Suspended sentence
Acquitted

Corrections Decisions

Community service
Fine
Probation
Restitution

Jail
Prison

Capital punishment

Exits from criminal justice system

criminal justice process *decision making that takes place throughout the public agencies of crime control.*

begins with the investigation and apprehension of suspects by the police. Then it moves to the prosecution and conviction of defendants in court. Finally, it examines the punishment in and release of offenders from corrections agencies.

Most of these decisions take place inside the agencies described in the last section. Many—but by no means all—of the decisions made inside criminal justice agencies have to do with the **criminal justice process,** that is, they involve whether to move people further into the system. But the decisions of criminal justice agencies extend far beyond the criminal process, because the functions of these agencies extend beyond the narrow limits of criminal law enforcement. For just one example, police departments not only investigate crime and apprehend and arrest suspects, but they also maintain public order and perform a range of other public services unrelated to criminal justice.

These order maintenance and public service functions involve decision making no less than deciding whether to move criminal suspects toward charging, conviction, sentencing, and punishment. The roles and functions of criminal justice professionals that go beyond crime control are discussed in detail throughout the chapters on the police, courts, and corrections. Here we briefly identify and describe criminal justice decisions and the functions they are intended to perform, emphasizing the general idea of the systems paradigm with its heavy emphasis on decision making in agencies.

The major steps through the criminal justice system—and the major decisions connected with them—include the following (see inside front cover and Figure 1.1 for a more detailed and graphic depiction of the criminal justice structure and process):

1. *Detection and investigation of crime,* the responsibility of police departments.

2. *Apprehension and arrest of criminal suspects,* the responsibility of police departments.

3. *Charging criminal defendants,* the responsibility of prosecutors.

4. *Detaining defendants prior to trial or releasing them on bail,* the responsibility of judges.

5. *Determination of guilt,* presided over by judges, with prosecutors and defense attorneys participating.

6. *Sentencing,* the responsibility of trial court judges.

7. *Appeal and collateral attack,* an appellate court function.

8. *Punishment,* an administrative responsibility of corrections administrators and officers, with supervisory powers in the judiciary.

The Criminal Justice "System"

As the common phrase "**criminal justice system**" suggests, this collection of federal, state, and local agencies is a *system,* meaning a collection of parts that make up a whole. In important respects, the agencies of criminal justice do make up a whole. They are all public agencies engaged in crime control. They all process people who have come in contact with public efforts to control crime—as suspects, defendants, and convicted offenders. And the result of the process is a "product," subject to statistical measurement at "intake" and "output." The product is a person who begins as a suspect in the police station, then becomes a defendant in court, then an offender in corrections agencies, and finally, when released from supervision by the state, an ex-offender.[7]

Furthermore, because they are so interdependent, the decisions of one criminal justice agency affect other agencies. Lloyd E. Ohlin, a distinguished scholar and teacher who was one of the original designers of field research in the systems paradigm, wrote of this interdependence:

> Discretion denied to sentencing judges by legislatively mandated prison terms simply pushed sentencing choice and variations back to the prosecutors in their bargaining capacity. Early parole release of chronic offenders affected police practices in the communities to which they were returned. In short . . ., [criminal justice is] a system of complex individualization of justice, adaptively balanced, not easily controlled, and certainly not inevitably improved by attempts to mandate choices, remove discretion, or impose well-meaning but simplistic panaceas on such a highly complex process.[8]

This shifting of discretion from one agency to another is called the **hydraulic effect,** meaning if you compress discretion at one point in the system it will inevitably expand somewhere else. This is because managing human behavior under the myriad circumstances of everyday life cannot be reduced to uniform responses.

System is not an altogether accurate description of criminal justice agencies. In some important respects, these agencies are independent bodies. They derive their authority and budgets from different sources. Police departments get their authority and funding mainly from towns and cities. Prosecutors, public defenders, jails, and trial courts are mainly countywide, with separate budgets. Appellate courts and prisons are statewide and funded by state legislatures. In addition to separate sources of authority and financing, these agencies set their own policies and to a large extent do not consciously coordinate their decisions and operations with each other. In day-to-day operations, for example, neither police departments nor individual officers base their actions and decisions on the effect these will have on the "system." The decision is too far down the line to worry about these larger implications. When police officers arrest suspected drunk drivers, child molesters, burglars, and thieves, they are hardly thinking about the impact such arrests might have on prosecutors, courts, and prisons.

The Criminal Justice "Wedding Cake"

The stages and processes of decision making vary from state to state, between states and the federal government, and sometimes between districts in the same state. In addition, the procedures differ for **felonies** (serious crimes with penalties usually of more than one year in prison) and **misdemeanors** (less serious crimes with penalties of fines or less than one year in prison). Trial courts hear felony cases, for which the procedures are usually more elaborate and the punishment more severe—more than one year in state prisons. Lower criminal courts hear misdemeanors, for which the proceedings are less formal and the penalties lighter—fines and up to one year in local jails. Least formal of all are justice of the peace courts, which are not courts of formal record, that is, they do not keep a written record of their proceedings.[9]

Cleaning up and investigating after the Oklahoma City bombing.

Procedures differ in other respects. Systems paradigm research, with its focus on the complexity of discretionary decision making in the actual day-to-day operation of criminal justice, has demonstrated further differences in the processing of criminal cases. Criminal justice officials regularly treat "real" felonies differently from "garbage" or "bullshit" cases. The distinctions lie in the seriousness of the charge; the past criminal record of the offender; the relationship of the victim to the offender; whether the victim was injured; and whether the offender used a gun. "Real" crimes will get more attention at every stage of criminal justice than "garbage" cases, as we will see in detail in later chapters.[10]

Lawrence M. Friedman and Robert V. Percival, in their study of crime and criminal justice in Alameda County, California, between 1870 and 1910, introduced the "wedding cake" idea of criminal justice to describe the different treatment of cases according to their perceived seriousness. Samuel Walker, based on more recent evidence, has elaborated the idea into what he also calls "the criminal justice wedding cake." Wedding cake may seem an odd image for the criminal justice process, but the idea comes more from its shape than its content: a wedding cake is narrow at the top and gets progressively wider toward the bottom (Figure 1.2). Also, wedding cakes usually come in several layers or tiers. The **wedding cake model** of criminal justice divides cases into four types or tiers, the fewest at the top and the most at the bottom, and emphasizes the different decisions required by each.

1. A few "celebrated cases" in the top tier.
2. A somewhat greater number of "real crimes" in the second tier.
3. Most "ordinary felonies" in the third tier.
4. The vast number of misdemeanors in the fourth tier.

"Celebrated cases" are those few that have gained the attention of the public because the crime is particularly grisly, a person involved is famous, or the case raises questions of current social concern. In the 1990s, a number of such cases stand out: Jeffrey Dahmer, convicted in Milwaukee of the cannibalistic murders of young men; William Kennedy Smith, the socially

Figure 1.2

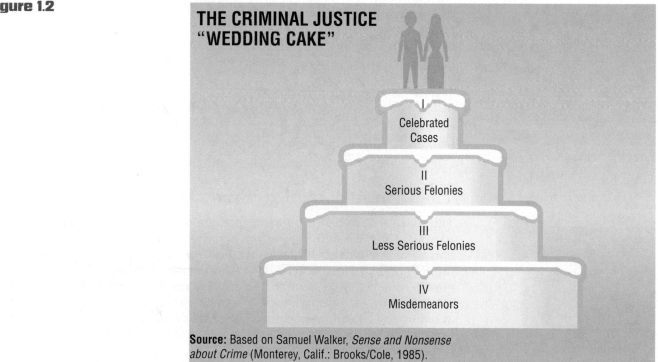

THE CRIMINAL JUSTICE "WEDDING CAKE"

I
Celebrated Cases

II
Serious Felonies

III
Less Serious Felonies

IV
Misdemeanors

Source: Based on Samuel Walker, *Sense and Nonsense about Crime* (Monterey, Calif.: Brooks/Cole, 1985).

prominent young medical student acquitted of date rape in Florida; Lorena Bobbitt, acquitted of cutting off her abusive husband's penis; Susan Smith, convicted of drowning her two young sons because her boyfriend did not want children; and, surely the most celebrated case of the decade, the trial and acquittal of O. J. Simpson. The celebrated cases are also exceptional because they receive full formal processing, including a trial—the rarest event in real-life criminal justice. Surely, one reason why they receive full formal processing is *because* they are celebrated.

The second layer consists of "real crimes"—serious felonies such as rape, aggravated assault, and armed robbery. Crimes are placed in this category especially if they are committed by people who have past criminal records, are strangers to their victims, use guns to commit their crimes, and injure their victims. People charged with "real" crimes are not as likely to go to trial as those in celebrated cases, but are more likely to do so than in ordinary cases and misdemeanors. If cases do not go to trial, defendants are still likely to plead guilty and receive harsher sentences.

The third layer of the wedding cake, more numerous than the celebrated cases and "real crimes," consists mainly of "ordinary felonies." These include most burglaries and thefts, and even robberies if no weapons were used, no one was injured, and the victims were in some way related to the offenders. For example, some cases are, legally speaking, serious felonies, but the event is really a private dispute. Suppose someone asks a friend for $25. When the friend hands over the money, the person believes the friend has given it to her as a gift. A few months later, the friend demands the return of the money. When the person refuses, the friend grabs her purse and takes all the money in it, $40, saying, "The extra is for interest." This kind of case, of which there are many, will probably not be treated as robbery. In most jurisdictions, such cases do not receive full formal processing. They are either diverted out of criminal justice or are determined by pleas of guilty.

By far the greatest number of cases fall into the fourth layer of the criminal justice wedding cake. This layer consists of the most common misdemeanors, such as simple assault, petty theft, and shoplifting. Most of these cases are disposed of informally; they are considered not worth the cost and effort of the formal procedures afforded the celebrated and serious felony cases. Practically none go to trial; most are decided quickly either in preliminary proceedings in the lower criminal courts or in agreements between prosecutors, defendants, and lawyers. Many do not result in criminal charges at all; they are treated more as problems that the parties should settle themselves.[11]

The criminal justice wedding cake is an important dimension of the day-to-day decision making so central to the systems paradigm. It underlies much of the discussion in the remaining chapters of the decisions made both inside and outside the major criminal justice agencies.

The Criminal Justice "Funnel"

The shape of a funnel is opposite that of a wedding cake. A wedding cake is narrow at the top and wide at the bottom; a funnel is wide at the top and narrow at the bottom. But in criminal justice, both the wedding cake and the funnel illustrate the reality of day-to-day decision making. The wedding cake depicts the results of formal and informal decisions that put cases into layers, from the few celebrated cases at the top to the vast majority of misdemeanors at the bottom. The funnel depicts the results of decisions that remove many cases early in the criminal justice process, moving fewer and fewer cases further into the system.

Some decisions remove people from the system either by diverting them into other agencies—such as drug and alcohol treatment, and family counsel-

funnel effect *dwindling numbers of people remaining in the criminal justice system following the sorting decisions that remove some of them and send the rest to the next stage of the criminal process.*

ing—or by releasing them outright. Other decisions send remaining individuals on for further processing. At each stage, fewer individuals remain for sorting. Figure 1.3 depicts the **funnel effect** created by this sorting operation. More people are arrested than are charged with crimes; more people are charged with crimes than are convicted; more people are convicted than are sentenced to prison. Technically speaking, this means that there are more suspects than defendants, more defendants than convicted offenders, and more convicted offenders than prisoners.

The remaining chapters elaborate on the funnel effect. The police function requires decisions about many more people than the courts have to deal with. In fact, when we take into account that the police perform order maintenance and public service functions in addition to law enforcement, the number of people they deal with far outstrips the number encountered by all other parts of the system. The courts deal with far fewer people than police departments do, but the number the courts deal with far exceeds the number of people incarcerated. However, the *costs,* both in time and resources to the public and in invasions of liberty, privacy, and property to suspects, defendants, and offenders, *increase* with each decision to move the process from the police, to the courts, to corrections.

The decisions made prior to the involvement of criminal justice agencies affect vastly larger numbers than those affected by agency decisions. Legislative decisions that define behavior as criminal apply to every person in the state or other jurisdiction. The decisions of offenders to commit crimes, of course, affect fewer than every person in the jurisdiction. But the decision to commit a crime, if it is carried out or even attempted, affects each victim of the crime. The decision of victims to report crimes to the police affects only

Figure 1.3

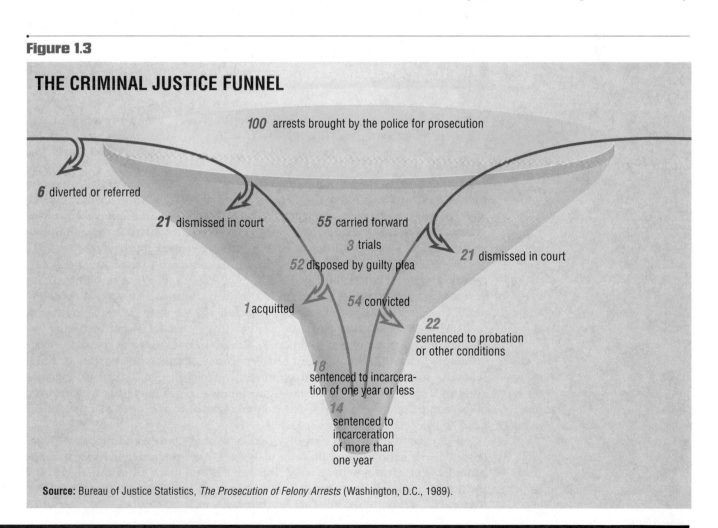

THE CRIMINAL JUSTICE FUNNEL

100 arrests brought by the police for prosecution

6 diverted or referred

21 dismissed in court

55 carried forward

3 trials

52 disposed by guilty plea

21 dismissed in court

1 acquitted

54 convicted

22 sentenced to probation or other conditions

18 sentenced to incarceration of one year or less

14 sentenced to incarceration of more than one year

Source: Bureau of Justice Statistics, *The Prosecution of Felony Arrests* (Washington, D.C., 1989).

International Gender Differences and the Funnel Effect

The funnel effect operates in all countries, according to an analysis of the Second and Third United Nations Crime Surveys. The Secretary-General of the United Nations, through the UN Crime Prevention and Criminal Justice Branch in Vienna, invites all member states to complete extensive surveys detailing statistics concerning criminal justice and to attach commentaries if they wish. The UN has conducted the surveys every five years beginning in 1970; the latest reported survey was for 1985. The data are incomplete because not every state completed the surveys.

All participating states reported a decrease in numbers of individuals at four major decision points in criminal justice: apprehension, prosecution, conviction, and imprisonment. Also of particular interest are these findings:

● In all countries at all times between 1975 and 1985, men greatly out-numbered women among those suspected, apprehended, prosecuted, convicted, and imprisoned.

● In some countries in 1970 and 1975, and in most countries in 1980 and 1985, women were disproportionately filtered out of the later stages of the criminal justice process.

● During the period 1980-1985, women came to represent a higher propor-tion of those suspected, prosecuted, and convicted, but *not* of those im-prisoned.

The result is a reverse funnel effect; that is, as the criminal process progresses, more women are filtered out and more men remain. Figure 1.4 depicts the increasing ratios of men to women in the latest UN survey.

some victims, because many victims do not report crimes, for reasons we will examine in Chapter 2.

The chapters in this book are arranged according to this funnel. The earliest chapters focus on the decisions occurring before the process ever reaches the top of the funnel. Then the focus shifts to the top of the funnel, to police decisions regarding the detection and investigation of crime and the apprehension and arrest of suspects. The police filter some people out of the system because they either cannot or decide not to investigate, apprehend, or arrest them. Next, attention shifts to the narrower part of the funnel, decisions involving the judicial system. Prosecutors eliminate some people by deciding not to charge them with crimes. Judges remove a few defendants because of constitutional violations. Juries remove more by acquitting defen-dants. Judges sentence only some convicted offenders to prison. Finally, the focus shifts to the narrowest part of the funnel, to decisions involving the punishment of convicted offenders. Prison administrators release some offenders before the end of their terms because of good time earned or other reasons, such as overcrowded prisons. Juvenile justice, a separate justice system, requires its own funnel but follows a similar progression from definition through correction. The juvenile justice funnel is the subject of the final chapter in this book.

What accounts for the criminal justice "funnel" and "wedding cake"? Until around 1950, scholars and professional observers took a negative view of the funnel effect. Critics whose ideal was full enforcement of criminal law and the total eradication of crime from society called the funnel effect "case mortality." They believed that corruption, incompetence, and "bleeding

Comparative Criminal Justice

Continued

Figure 1.4

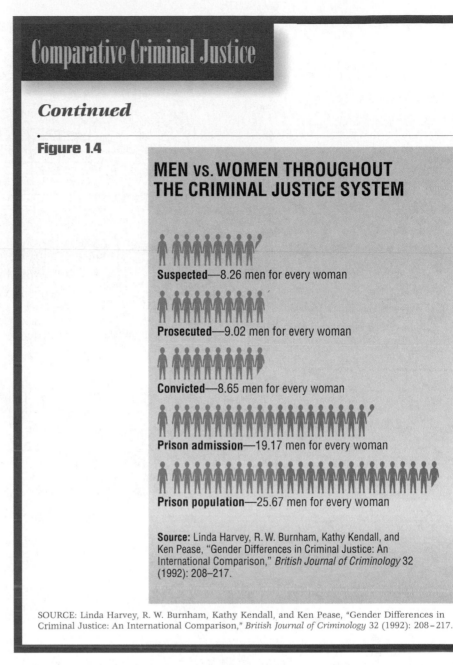

MEN vs. WOMEN THROUGHOUT THE CRIMINAL JUSTICE SYSTEM

Suspected—8.26 men for every woman

Prosecuted—9.02 men for every woman

Convicted—8.65 men for every woman

Prison admission—19.17 men for every woman

Prison population—25.67 men for every woman

Source: Linda Harvey, R. W. Burnham, Kathy Kendall, and Ken Pease, "Gender Differences in Criminal Justice: An International Comparison," *British Journal of Criminology* 32 (1992): 208–217.

SOURCE: Linda Harvey, R. W. Burnham, Kathy Kendall, and Ken Pease, "Gender Differences in Criminal Justice: An International Comparison," *British Journal of Criminology* 32 (1992): 208–217.

case attrition *reduction in numbers of crimes from those reported to those resulting in punishment.*

hearts" in the criminal justice system were responsible for the reduced numbers of cases at each stage. They assumed that every arrest should and—barring corruption, incompetence, and soft-heartedness—*could* result in conviction and punishment. This was a naive view and, after the research undertaken by systems paradigm scholars, a demonstrably wrong assessment of the reality of criminal justice.

Research inspired by the systems paradigm has demonstrated that a variety of influences both inside and outside criminal justice affects the decisions to remove, divert, or continue individuals in the criminal process. One main reason for **case attrition** (the reduction in numbers) from crimes reported to the police to conviction is the law itself. According to the Constitution, which we will examine in detail later, the government has to back up with sufficient facts every invasion of the liberty, privacy, and property of individuals. The greater the invasion, the more facts required. A brief stop on the street requires fewer facts than a full-blown arrest; an arrest requires fewer facts than charging a suspect with a crime. Conviction for a crime requires the greatest number of facts—proof beyond a reasonable doubt.

Crime Control and Due Process Models

due process *requirement that the government cannot deprive people of life, liberty, or property without fair procedures.*

The funnel effect is more complex than suggested by a simple application of the constitutional requirement of backing up government invasions with facts. The law is not applied mechanically. Values underlie application to particular cases. Underpinning all decisions in criminal justice are two basic and competing values: crime control and **due process.** Due process means that the government can only invade the lives, liberty, or property of citizens according to established procedures intended to insure fairness. The tension between the values of crime control and due process is perhaps the single most pervasive influence on the way that Americans think about criminal justice and the way that criminal justice professionals *perceive* their roles.

Most people in the United States deeply desire to reduce and control crime, even if they understand that no society can completely eradicate crime. But most people also reject the idea that we should control crime regardless of the cost in money, privacy, and liberty. Authorities in police states, as history has amply demonstrated, can wield enormous power. They can define crime as anything they oppose, and they can use the power of the state to enforce their will. They have the power to obliterate the security of homes, the dignity of individuals, and the rights of property. Few people in the United States are likely to favor this view of criminal justice.

The definition of crime and the responses to crime must remain consistent with the values of our constitutional, representative democracy. These values mandate not only that crime control policy arise out of the political process, but also that crime control practices respect the property, privacy, liberty, and dignity guaranteed by the Constitution. At her confirmation hearings, Attorney General Janet Reno nicely captured the importance of both crime control and due process. When asked what her priorities would be should the Senate confirm her nomination, she answered simply and directly: "First, to protect the innocent from prosecution. Second, to prosecute the guilty to the fullest extent of the law, according to the due process of law."[12]

Common but Competing Values

Despite differences of opinion about the role of government in defining and responding to crime, some common values underlie American criminal justice. These values stem from assumptions based on the **rule of law,** that is, that there are limits to the power of government to define and respond to crime, and that, therefore, rules limit the discretionary power of decision makers in criminal justice.

First, criminal justice agencies are authorized to respond only to conduct that legislatures define as crimes and for which they prescribe a penalty. Second, once an act is defined as a crime, the formal legal responsibility for enforcing the law belongs primarily to criminal justice agencies. Our constitutional democracy allows only an extremely limited right of individuals to "take the law into their own hands." However, **vigilantes** (individuals and groups who take the law into their own hands) have appeared from time to time throughout American history, whenever some segment of the population believes that the government has not done its job in enforcing the law. Those who engage in and support vigilante action maintain that such action is required to "right" the "wrongs" that government failed to put right itself. The eighteenth-century colonial "regulators" in South Carolina, the "posses" of the western frontier, and the "lynching mobs" of the South in the first half of this century are all examples.

Public frustration, anger, and fear—both real and exaggerated by journalistic hype and opportunistic politicians—has led to some widely reported instances of vigilantism in our own day, some approved and supported by communities. In Detroit in the early 1990s, Angelo Parisi and Perry Kent got tired of the violence, drug dealing, and contempt for the citizenry exemplified by a "crack house" in their neighborhood. They burned it down. "Nobody could sit out on the front porch anymore. The kids couldn't play outside. The police said wait until something bad happened. Well, we couldn't do that." Their actions met with wide public approval. During their trial for arson, they proudly admitted setting the house on fire. The jury deliberated only two and a half hours before acquitting them. One juror said he would have done the same thing. Then he reconsidered. "No—I would have been more violent." Neighbors praised the burning too. "I just wish they'd do it to more houses," one said.[13]

Actions such as these are controversial. Civil libertarians, those who support individual liberty and privacy against both government and "vigilante" groups, deplore the tactics of self-certified "good-guy" citizens like Angelo Parisi and Perry Kent. But according to Professor Hans Toch, distinguished professor at State University of New York at Albany, and J. Douglas Grant, president of the Social Action Research Center:

> The enthusiasm civil libertarians often deplore is essential for citizen groups, particularly in neighborhoods in which a sense of powerlessness or apathy has prevailed, and where activists may engage the

crime control model *model that favors informal, discretionary decision making in order to efficiently, economically, accurately, and swiftly separate the guilty from the innocent.*

due process model *model that puts the formal legal process at the heart of decision making in criminal justice.*

displeasure of violent peers when they embark on their rounds. Citizen groups need to feel militant, they need appreciation and backing from the police, and they need all the help they can get. The last thing they need is to be equated with lynching mobs and lectured to and admonished.[14]

Civil libertarians worry not only about citizen threats but also about government actions that unlawfully invade the privacy, liberty, and dignity of individuals suspected but not convicted of crimes. As James Fyfe, former New York City police officer, now professor of criminal justice, cautioned:

> The question is, What happens when the drug problem goes away or is diminished? Are we still going to be left with this mentality? The founding fathers went to war over the right to privacy.[15]

The late Supreme Court Justice Thurgood Marshall warned:

> Precisely because the need for action is manifest, the need for vigilance against unconstitutional excess is great. History teaches that grave threats to liberty often come in times of urgency, when constitutional rights seem too extravagant to endure.[16]

To the complaints of civil libertarians, Mayor James Moran of Alexandria, Virginia, replied:

> The reality is that the civil rights of the majority of people who live in low income drug-infested communities are being abridged 24 hours a day. [We are only] attempting to respond to the reality that confronts us in a way the court system has failed to do.[17]

In addition to the formal requirement that criminal justice agencies are the only ones authorized to control crime, most people also believe that everybody should "have their day in court." Due process requires that we treat criminal suspects and offenders as people who can force the police, courts, and corrections to prove they have the power to act against them. This obligation can *enable*—but it does not *compel*—the accused to play an active part in the process. It *can*—but it need *not necessarily*—lead to a contest, or adversary process, between the government and the individual. For example, suspects may cooperate with the police and consent to a search, but they can also refuse to allow a search unless the police have probable cause. They may confess to a crime or refuse to speak. They can plead guilty or demand a trial.[18]

Based on these assumptions, Professor Herbert Packer devised two models—the crime control model and the due process model—to describe two competing value systems underlying the criminal process. These models are perhaps the best known and most widely accepted in all criminal justice. Briefly stated, the **crime control model** favors an informal administrative process to discover the facts in order to free the innocent and convict the guilty as quickly, efficiently, accurately, and smoothly as possible. The crime control model deemphasizes the contest or formal legal element of the process, stressing instead the informal or discretionary side. The **due process model** puts the contest—formal legal proceedings—at the heart of the process. Neither model, however, is based wholly on either crime control or due process. Each recognizes the importance of *both* informal discretionary decision making *and* formal legal proceedings in criminal justice. It is, rather, a matter of emphasis.[19]

The Crime Control Model

According to the crime control model, the most important function of the criminal justice process is the reduction of crime. Failure to reduce crime leads to the destruction of a primary condition of a free society—public order.

presumption of guilt *attitude of the crime control model that considers those who remain in the system as probably guilty.*
presumption of innocence *formal legal idea that people are legally innocent until proven guilty according to due process.*

Failure to enforce the criminal laws leads to a disregard for law generally. Law-abiding citizens may then suffer invasions of property, threats to personal security, and finally encroachments on liberty that restrict their capacity to function as contributing members of society. In short, crime control guarantees social freedom by protecting the security of persons and property. To fulfill this high purpose, the crime control model requires that the criminal justice process operate efficiently to screen suspects, determine guilt, and punish offenders.[20]

Since the public demands limited budgets, since criminal law encompasses a broad range of behavior, and since society produces many offenders, the crime control model requires high apprehension and conviction rates, putting a premium on speed and finality. Speed depends on informality and uniformity; finality on a minimum of challenges to decisions. In Packer's words, according to the crime control model, "the process must not be cluttered up with ceremonious rituals" of a formal legal contest. So, for example, the crime control model favors police interrogation because it uncovers facts faster than examination and cross-examination in formal trial proceedings.

Informality is not enough, however; the model also demands uniformity. It requires routine operations to process high numbers. According to Packer, the crime control model operates like

> an assembly line conveyer belt down which moves an endless array of cases, never stopping, carrying the cases to workers who stand at fixed stations and who perform on each case as it comes by the same small but essential operation that brings it one step closer to being a finished product, or, to exchange the metaphor, a closed file.[21]

According to the crime control model, therefore, criminal justice is a screening process that moves cases by routinized operations to a successful conclusion: removing the innocent at the earliest possible stage and quickly convicting the guilty, with minimal opportunity for challenge. Quality control imposed informally at the administrative level assures the release of the innocent and the conviction of the guilty without excessive interference by formal legal proceedings. (See Figure 1.5.)

Confidence in the informal determination of guilt requires the crime control model to operate according to a **presumption of guilt.** The presumption of guilt considers those who remain in the criminal process as probably guilty. (The **presumption of innocence,** or the idea that "you are innocent until proved guilty," is not the opposite of the presumption of guilt, as we shall see in the discussion of the due process model.) The attitude of probable guilt is really a prediction based on the fact that the person held is probably guilty.

The presumption of guilt works efficiently because, the model assumes, informal fact finding by the police and prosecutors obtains the correct result in most cases. Therefore, the criminal process should place few restraints on police and prosecutors. The courts should not "handcuff" the police in their efforts to get at the truth by throwing up too many formal barriers to searches and interrogations of suspects. The crime control model puts most emphasis on the early stages in the process, namely, the role of the police and prosecutor. It places less emphasis on proceedings in court; in fact, these should be as short and simple as possible. In place of all the technical, time-consuming, expensive pretrial and trial proceedings, the crime control model favors the guilty plea.

The Due Process Model

The due process model resembles an obstacle course, rather than an assembly line. Each step in the criminal process, according to this model, should

Figure 1.5

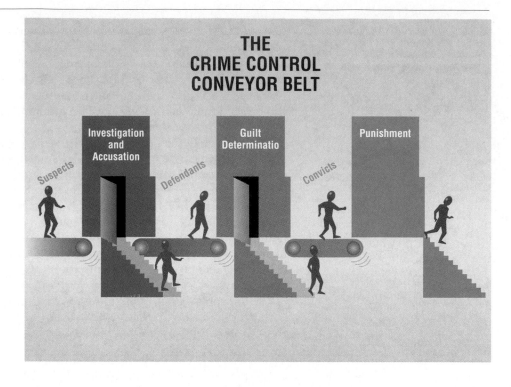

THE CRIME CONTROL CONVEYOR BELT

present as many impediments as possible to further involvement of the accused. These impediments take the form of formal procedural rules. Due process describes the formal structure of the law; the crime control model describes the day-to-day operation of criminal justice. The due process model does not oppose crime control. It does stress the unreliability of the informal fact finding central to the crime control model. The inaccuracy of human observation, the power of emotion, and the influence of bias all stand in the way of getting the truth informally, according to the due process model. Formal, adversary, public proceedings during which experts can examine and cross-examine witnesses before neutral judges and then submit the facts to impartial juries for the final determination of truth reduce the chance of mistake, according to the due process model. (See Figure 1.6.)

The difference between the two models is not simply that each claims its methods lead to the truth. Also important is the value that each places on reliability (obtaining the correct result by freeing the innocent and convicting the guilty) and efficiency (quickly and economically handling large numbers of cases). The due process model puts the premium on reliability; the crime control model accepts the reality of some mistakes (according to the model's adherents, very few occur) in order to achieve efficiency. The due process model rejects the emphasis on efficiency because it holds that criminal justice should aim as much to protect the innocent as to convict the guilty.

The due process model also emphasizes the primacy of the individual. The stigma, loss of liberty and privacy, threats to employment, disruption of family, and general assault on personal dignity that accompany suspected criminal involvement result in the greatest possible deprivations and intrusions the government can inflict. These deprivations and intrusions, according to the model, require strict formal controls at all stages, but especially in the early stages of police investigation of crime and apprehension of suspects.

Controlling the government requires that the criminal justice process operate according to the presumption of innocence. The presumption demands that the process treat all individuals as innocent until the government proves guilt—according to the formal rules of criminal procedure—beyond a reasonable doubt. To punish a citizen, according to the model, the state must

Figure 1.6

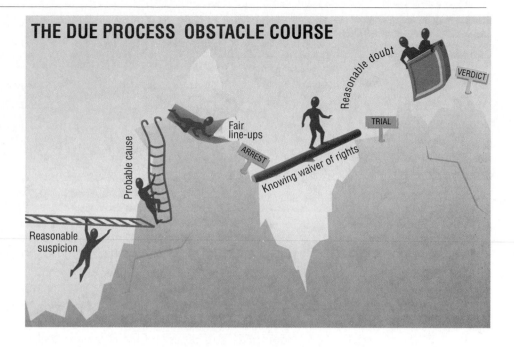

THE DUE PROCESS OBSTACLE COURSE

prove guilt by gathering evidence, admitting evidence, and presenting evidence according to the rules. A person may be guilty in fact, but not legally guilty. For example, if the police seize evidence in an illegal search, the prosecutor cannot use the evidence, however reliable, to prove the guilt of the defendant. The evidence shows that the defendant committed the crime *in fact;* preventing its admission prevents the proof of guilt *at law.* In such cases, juries, contrary to many mispronouncements of journalists, do not find defendants "innocent"; their verdict says "not guilty," meaning not proven guilty according to the rules, but perhaps not innocent either. According to the due process model, the need to control the government and promote the rights of individuals outweighs the importance of obtaining the conviction of a guilty person in a specific case.

Equality is another feature of the due process model. According to the model, sociological influences (discussed in the last section of this chapter) such as race, ethnicity, gender, age, social and economic status, or education should not determine the treatment individuals receive in the criminal justice process. Finally, in contrast to the crime control model which takes a positive attitude toward the discretionary decisions of criminal justice professionals, the due process model adopts a more negative view. In the words of Professor Packer, the due process model harbors a "mood of skepticism about the morality and utility of the criminal sanction." Due process stresses all the imperfections possible in criminal justice—convicting the innocent; allowing racial, ethnic, and other prejudices to influence decisions; and relying on institutionalized punishment to control crime. Professor Paul Bator expresses that skepticism in stark terms: "The criminal law's notion of just condemnation and punishment is a cruel hypocrisy visited by a smug society on the psychologically and economically crippled."[22]

Crime Control and Due Process in Historical Perspective

The tension between the values of due process and crime control is not a recent phenomenon. In the broadest terms, the history of criminal justice in Western cultures reveals a pendulum swing between a commitment to crime control and a commitment to due process. (See Figure 1.7.) At one extreme is

Figure 1.7

THE CRIME CONTROL/
DUE PROCESS PENDULUM

the fear of government abuse of power, which results in calls for formal control of that power. At the other extreme is the public fear of crime and demands for more informal government power to eliminate it. Fear of governmental abuse of power has always resulted in demands for more rules and less discretion. Fear of crime has always produced calls for more discretion to enforce the law. No one has stated more eloquently the problem of crime control in a representative constitutional government than James Madison during the debate over the Bill of Rights in 1787:

> If men were angels, no government would be necessary. If angels were to govern men, neither external nor internal controls on government would be necessary. In framing a government which is to be administered by men over men, the great difficulty lies in this: You must first enable the government to control itself. A dependence on the people is no doubt the primary control on the government; but experience has taught the necessity of auxiliary precautions.[23]

The Early History of Criminal Justice In the early days of the Roman republic, citizens enjoyed strong safeguards against government power. Despite threats of capital punishment, in practice the criminal law of the Roman republic "became . . . the mildest ever known in the history of mankind." Tribune Novius, victimized by a violent criminal, released him because "I will not follow the example of him with whom I find fault, and I will quash this sentence." In reaction to this mildness, during the later years of the Roman Empire, Rome went to the opposite extreme. The Emperor Hadrian boasted that merely sending a suspect to trial constituted conclusive proof of guilt.[24]

Similar developments took place in England. Following the Norman Conquest in 1066, the Norman kings wielded enormous power, which by 1185 the great Angevin king Henry II had consolidated and centralized. In the thirteenth century, a reaction occurred, provoked by Henry II's unpopular, avaricious, and power-hungry son, John. In 1215, John's barons demanded that he accept several restraints on the royal authority. The king conceded much to the barons by signing the Magna Carta, or Great Charter, the famous antecedent to the American Constitution. Among other constraints, John agreed to the restriction that "no freeman shall be taken or imprisoned . . . or in any wise destroyed, nor will we go upon him, nor will we send upon him, unless by the lawful judgment of his peers, or by the law of the land."[25]

These thirteenth-century limits on royal authority emboldened the English nobility to great lawlessness that went largely unchecked for more than two centuries. Finally, royal authority reemerged under the Tudor monarchs in the late 1400s and throughout the 1500s, especially during the reigns of Henry VII (1485–1509) and his son, Henry VIII (1509–1547). Complaints that the ordinary courts afforded criminals, rioters, and fomenters of disorder too much protection led to the creation of special royal courts known as the prerogative courts, the most famous of which was held in the Star Chamber. At the outset, these prerogative courts operated without the rigid rules of procedure that bound the common-law courts that administered the ordinary law of the kingdom. Eventually, however, the prerogative courts produced their own rules of procedure. Throughout the 1500s under the Tudors, these rules and the general commitment to the rule of law provided a sufficient balance against the substantial increase in royal power.[26]

The case in 1575 of George Dibney, an Elizabethan gentleman, illustrates the balance between law and royal discretionary power. Queen Elizabeth suspected that Dibney had published seditious libels against Benjamin Clere. She called on the local constables to go to Dibney's house in the borough of Colchester and search for the libels. When the constables arrived at his door, Dibney demanded to know what authority they had to search his house. They replied, "By the Queen's authority." Not good enough, according to Dibney, who lectured to them that according to the law they needed "probable cause" both to enter his house and to search it. The constables responded that they had probable cause. "Of what does it consist?" Dibney inquired. They answered that they were "credibly informed" that he had the libels in his house. Who credibly informed them? Dibney wanted to know. On hearing the name, Dibney scoffed that he, the constables, and everyone else knew that their informant was a "liar and a knave." Now impatient, the constables replied that they were coming in whether Dibney liked it or not. Dibney demanded to know everyone's name who was about to enter. When asked why he needed to know, Dibney replied so that when he sued them in the common-law courts he would be sure to collect damages for their illegal entry, just as he had done with the "last lot" who had illegally searched his house. Because the record ends at that point, we do not know if the constables carried out their search or, if they did, whether Dibney sued them and collected damages. However, we do know that the Queen's suspicions were not legally sufficient to allow her to send officers into a private home without probable cause to search.[27]

The resurgence of royal authority under the Tudors emboldened the Stuart monarchs in the 1600s to aggrandize their power. The Stuarts upset the precarious Tudor balance between royal discretionary power and legal limits. By the reign of King Charles in the early 1600s, the royal Court of Star Chamber had abandoned procedural safeguards in favor of the royal power to convict the guilty. Furthermore, royal domination of common-law judges ensured decisions favorable to royal interests and to the members of the aristocracy who supported the Stuart kings. This aggrandizement, and the abuses accompanying it, eventually led to the English Civil War, and later to the Glorious Revolution. Both were fought in part to resolve the struggle between those who favored royal discretionary power (some even claiming the monarch had absolute power above the law) and those who maintained that the law, not kings, queens, and their minions, ruled England.[28]

The Colonial American Balance The first New England colonists came to America not only to establish their own church but also to escape the harsh Stuart criminal law and its arbitrary administration. They established the Massachusetts Body of Liberties, which reduced the number of capital offenses and guaranteed defendants several procedural safeguards. John Winthrop, the leading founder of the Massachusetts Bay Colony, devoted a major part of his life to working out the proper balance between the power of the government to enforce the criminal law and the rights of those charged with committing crimes.[29]

James Madison, 18th century proponent of the need for balancing crime control and individual liberty and privacy.

One of the most heated debates in the colony's earliest days was over criminal sentences. All agreed that the law alone conferred the power to punish. Some, however, maintained that the law must prescribe specific penalties, known as fixed or determinate penalties, for every offense, thereby eliminating judicial discretion in sentencing. Otherwise, these proponents of determinate sentencing argued, judges would abuse their authority. Others, Winthrop included, contended that discretion must always temper law in order to provide justice in individual cases. "[A] reproof entereth more into a wise man than 100 stripes into a fool," Winthrop wrote. The supporters of fixed penalties won the day, but the tension between law and discretion did not vanish; it still surfaces periodically, just as does the debate over determinate sentences.[30]

The Influence of the American Revolution   The American Revolution, fought in part over the colonists' perception of George III's tyranny, led to the creation of a government of checks and balances, separation of powers, and constitutionally prescribed limits on government's power over individual citizens. All these actions bespoke a hostility to government power, expressed in Lord Acton's famous aphorism that power tends to corrupt, and that absolute power corrupts absolutely. Recall James Madison's eloquent argument in support of a Bill of Rights, quoted at the beginning of this section.

The authors of the Constitution believed they could create in a written document a perfect balance between liberty and security, summed up in the Preamble: "insure the domestic tranquility" *and* "secure the blessings of liberty." But some did not trust the document unless it included specific limits on the government's power to enforce the criminal law, including the rights against unreasonable searches and seizures, self-incrimination, and cruel and unusual punishment, and the guarantees of the right to jury trial, to confront witnesses, and to counsel (see Chapters 3, 6, 8, 9, and 14). These appeared as amendments, known as the Bill of Rights. The safeguards written into both the Bill of Rights and the similar bills adopted by every state for their own constitutions established a criminal procedure with strong formal safeguards against government power. This structure existed with minimal complaints as long as a relatively homogeneous, widely scattered, mainly agrarian population dominated American society and institutions.[31]

Industrialization, Urbanization, and Immigration

Industrialization, urbanization, and immigration fundamentally transformed American society and its institutions during the last half of the nineteenth century. By 1900, a predominantly manufacturing society created a population of wage laborers from widely disparate cultural heritage, crowded into cities of teeming millions and causing enormous problems of order. In the early years of the twentieth century, many influential Americans believed they were in the midst of an epidemic crime wave. The widespread fear of crime led to the questioning of restrictions on the power of government to establish order, and to demands that police, prosecutors, and judges crack down on crime and criminals. Some, such as Samuel Untermeyer, a prominent New York attorney, advocated the abolition of the Fourth Amendment's protection against unreasonable searches and seizures and the Fifth Amendment's guarantee against self-incrimination. Others demanded more and harsher punishments for even minor offenses, such as life imprisonment and even death for hardened drunkards and prostitutes. This tough stance toward criminals, demands for the use of more government power, and calls for rules to restrain the discretionary power of criminal justice officials largely prevailed throughout the 1920s, 1930s, 1940s, and 1950s when, in turn, the public feared gangsters, mobsters, and juvenile delinquents.[32]

The "Due Process Revolution"

Then came the due process revolution of the 1960s. The U.S. Supreme Court expanded the meaning of many of the rights of criminal defendants. For example, in the famous *Miranda* case, the Court expanded the right against self-incrimination by requiring the police to give specific warnings before they interrogated suspects in custody. Then the Court extended the rights of criminal suspects and defendants in state proceedings. Prior to the 1960s, the Bill of Rights applied only to federal, not state and local, criminal law enforcement. The Court substantially equated federal and state rights of criminal suspects, defendants, and offenders (see Chapters 3, 6, and 14).

During the 1960s, Americans also witnessed a series of challenges to their values, institutions, public policies, and programs. These included soaring crime rates; an increasingly militant civil rights movement; growing discord over an unpopular war in Vietnam; a highly publicized youth counterculture that supposedly glorified promiscuous sex, mind-altering drugs, and rock and roll, and attacked all society's norms; and rioting in the streets and cities that left law-abiding citizens reeling. These events produced a litany of complaints about the administration of justice and prescriptions for its improvement— more power to enforce the criminal law and establish order, and harsher punishments for lawbreakers and rioters.[33]

The Return to Crime Control

One popular interpretation of the crisis in crime, law, and order in the 1960s was that a permissive society, too many safeguards for criminal defendants, and too lenient penalties had emboldened budding criminals to flout the standards of decency, hard work, and compliance with social norms. Instead, these "antisocial renegades" turned to a life of sex, drugs, rock and roll, riot, and crime. The popular and political answer was to declare and fight an all-out "war on crime," consisting of more police, more punishment, and fewer rights for criminal defendants. The consequences of this siege mentality toward crime continued relatively unabated through the 1980s and the 1990s. There is ample demonstration that the fear of illegal drugs and violence have led to a widespread belief that the law-abiding public is still at war with crime, particularly violent crime and drugs.[34]

Controlling Discretion The pendulum swing between crime control and due process is closely connected to swings between rule and discretion, as the history just outlined indicates. However, the swings between a reliance on rules and an emphasis on discretion are neither consistent nor system-wide. That is, they are not based on the broad principle that either discretion or rule is a better way to make criminal justice decisions generally. Those who called for rules instead of discretion in *police* decision making during the 1960s and 1970s *claimed* their stand was based on a general commitment to the value of due process, such as when the U.S. Supreme Court decided *Miranda v. Arizona.* Those who called for the control of police discretion in the interest of due process also *promoted* judicial discretion in sentencing, to accomplish the rehabilitation of offenders.

On the other hand, in periods when the value of crime control prevails, the demands for rules are mainly directed at limiting or even abolishing the discretion of *prosecutors* to plea bargain, of *judges* to sentence convicted offenders, and of *corrections officials* to release offenders before the end of their sentences. Those who favor the restriction of prosecutorial, judicial, and correctional discretion in the name of crime control also call for giving more discretion to the police to achieve the same goal.

It is not quite correct, therefore, to refer to the history of controlling discretion during the last 30 years as if it consisted of "taming the system," as the historian of criminal justice, Samuel Walker, does. To the extent that the description applies to those who wish as a matter of principle to control discretion, it is accurate. However, in criminal justice policy, it is more accurate to see discretion and rules as means to accomplish the ends of crime control and due process.[35]

Informal Influences on Decision Making

Criminal justice does not exist in a legal vacuum, as this brief history of the shifting emphasis on due process and crime control values demonstrates. In addition to the historical context, a number of other influences outside of law determine the outcome of decision making. These include our democratic political system, economy, and society, and the values inherent in each.

Democracy

Decisions affecting crime and responses to it are in part political, and not in a negative sense. As used in this text, political means that decisions depend on public policy. In a democracy the electorate, its elected representatives, and its appointed criminal justice personnel establish and implement public policy. Of course, democracy does not operate in a pure sense. Interest groups and a variety of other pressures shape the "will of the people." Furthermore, in a pluralistic society, consensus does not always exist on the definition of crime and the enforcement of criminal law. The political nature of decisions in criminal justice appears in several ways: in the selection of decision makers, in public opinion regarding the policies and practices of criminal justice agencies, and in the allocation and distribution of resources for police, courts, and corrections.

The selection of decision makers takes place either by election or appointment. In both cases politics, whether for good or bad, affects decisions. Political influences affect the laws legislatures enact; legislators do not, and should not, ignore their constituents. Voters either elect judges directly, or the governors appoint them. During any election campaign, advertisements appear, such as one urging voters to elect a judge because "she was a law enforcement agency's judge." The president nominates the federal judiciary, whose nomination requires the confirmation of the Senate. This has often led to political wrangling over the appointment of judges, particularly justices of the United States Supreme Court. The latest such political wrangling was over the appointment of Associate Justice Clarence Thomas, an avowed and highly political conservative. Only the naive and those ignorant of history recoil at the idea of injecting politics into the selection of Supreme Court justices, but it has a long history. Neither conservatives nor liberals, Democrats nor Republicans, have a monopoly on it. Presidents Franklin Roosevelt and Lyndon Johnson secured a liberal majority on the Supreme Court, and Presidents Nixon, Reagan, and Bush secured a conservative majority. At this writing, speculation has already begun that President Clinton has moved the Supreme Court toward the center. Conservatives lament, and liberals hope, that Clinton will fill the present 100-plus vacancies in the lower federal courts with less conservative judges.

Throughout most of our history, Americans have accepted the political nature of Supreme Court appointments. In 1869, President Grant nominated to the Court two powerful Republicans, Edwin Stanton, Lincoln's secretary of war and Grant's superior during the Civil War, and Rockwood Hoar, Lincoln's attorney general, not because of their judicial philosophy but so Grant "would not have to contend with the overly energetic bustle of Stanton and the superciliousness of Hoar." The Senate confirmed Stanton but rejected Hoar on openly political grounds; while he was Lincoln's attorney general, Hoar had refused to follow the tradition of nominating federal judges recommended by senators. The senators paid him back by refusing to confirm him.[36]

The appointment of Supreme Court justices receives national public attention, but it is only one example of the political nature of selection in criminal justice. Elected officials also participate in selecting police chiefs. Local prosecutors run for election. Elected officials appoint the top corrections officials in the state. Public opinion and community pressure groups also influence the policies and practices of police departments, courts, and corrections. Individual police departments respond to specific crimes in part because the public, or at least the public that speaks out, demands responses to its priorities. If a neighborhood is "up in arms" about prostitution, the criminal justice agencies respond, even if perhaps not exactly as critics might like. Police management and officers listen to civic demands and shape their actions, at least in part, accordingly. They look for and arrest more prostitutes, and sometimes even their "johns."

Prosecutors, partly with an eye on the next election, and perhaps because of their ambitions for higher office, also listen to the active voice of the community. Prosecutors set their priorities, to some extent, based on these voices. If a community demands greater drug law enforcement, prosecutors charge more drug offenses. If a community demands greater action regarding AIDS, prosecutors may charge prostitutes and others with assault or attempted murder for intentionally transmitting the virus. Judges, too, listen to the public, if only indirectly. In these examples, judges may sentence prostitutes, AIDS transmitters, and drug offenders to maximum sentences in order to satisfy the public demand for a criminal justice response.

Corrections officials also listen to the public when they formulate and implement policy. The decision to expand new forms of probation that stress punishment, for example, was not made in the vacuum of official bureaucracy and criminal justice research that suggested it. It also reflected public impatience with "coddling criminals" and its perceived effect on crime rates.

Even the Supreme Court does not escape public pressure. The famous political cartoonist Peter Dunne recognized this in the early 1900s. His character, Mr. Dooley, summed it up: "The Supreme Court, like the rest of the country, reads the election returns." In the 1930s, public dissatisfaction with the Court's obstruction of President Roosevelt's New Deal legislation led in part to the Court's reversal of some of its most controversial decisions. The strong negative public reaction to the *Miranda* decision in the 1960s probably affected subsequent decisions limiting its impact. The growing public support for a limited right to abortion may also have led to the upholding of *Roe v. Wade* in 1992.

Budgets

Budgets, particularly in periods of shrinking funds for public services, also affect most responses to crime. Police departments cannot respond to all behavior that legislatures have defined as crimes; they set their priorities in part according to budget restraints. This may require balancing public demand for action and the availability of resources. Police may, for example, commit more resources to crack cocaine dealing than to marijuana use; more to robbery than to gambling; and more to rape than to prostitution. Judges can only sentence offenders to existing facilities. Laws mandating longer prison terms, and the longer sentences of judges, have filled prisons and jails to overflowing. The political demand for more arrests and convictions and for harsher penalties in the form of longer prison terms does not always meet an equal public willingness to supply the money required. This is particularly true when the public must choose between building prisons and cutting back on other popular public services, such as education, health care, transportation, and housing.

Social Structure and Process

Criminal justice is a part not only of American politics and budgetary realities but also of United States society as a whole. This larger society affects decisions regarding the definition and responses to crime. In the remaining chapters, you will find a heavy emphasis on this sociology of crime and criminal justice. Here it is important to note that all of the following affect the definition, amount, and distribution of crime and the responses to crime:

- *Geography*—the time, place, and opportunity to commit crimes.
- *Demography*—the age, gender, race, and ethnic origins of both offenders and victims.
- *Status*—the social class, economic position, and social relations of offenders.

Table 1.2 depicts how victimization varies according to some of these characteristics.

The debate over whether and to what extent sociological variables affect decisions in criminal justice has always generated controversy. It is not easy to accept hypotheses and research that challenge some of our deepest held beliefs about human behavior and society. If we admit that social structure and processes have determining power, we accept an interpretation of human behavior that seems to negate free will and individual responsibility. After all, if it is neighborhood, job opportunities, and social class that determine actions, then criminals are not responsible for their crimes. Also, if we accept that sociological variables such as race, ethnicity, and gender influence decision making in criminal justice, we offend another deep belief—that Americans are basically fair. If we concede that the demographics of class, gender, ethnicity, and race affect the decisions of criminal justice personnel, we must also accept that the system discriminates against people because of things they cannot control.

Table 1.2
Victimization Rates for Persons Age 12 or Older, by Type of Crime, Sex, Age, Race, Ethnicity, Income, and Locality of Residence of Victims, 1993

	Victimizations per 1,000 persons age 12 or older							
		Crime of violence						
Characteristics	Total	Total	Rape/ Sexual assault	Robbery	Total	Assault Aggra- vated	Simple	Personal theft
Sex								
Male	63.3	61.0	.4	8.5	52.1	16.3	35.8	2.3
Female	45.2	42.6	4.0	4.0	34.5	8.3	26.2	2.5
Age								
12-15	125.3	120.8	4.5	13.6	102.6	23.3	79.3	4.5
16-19	120.7	117.0	7.2	11.7	98.1	30.0	68.1	3.7
20-24	97.7	93.6	5.7	10.5	77.4	27.1	50.3	4.1
25-34	61.2	58.8	2.4	7.4	49.1	15.0	34.1	2.3
35-49	44.9	43.0	1.6	5.1	36.2	8.8	27.5	1.9
50-64	18.3	17.1	.2*	3.0	13.9	4.0	10.0	1.1
65 or older	7.9	5.6	.3*	1.3	4.1	1.1	3.0	2.2
Race								
White	51.8	49.8	2.3	5.1	42.4	11.4	31.1	2.0
Black	72.6	67.0	2.7	13.0	51.3	19.0	32.3	5.6
Other	41.9	39.7	2.0*	8.2	29.5	8.8	20.8	2.2*
Ethnicity								
Hispanic	62.5	59.1	2.1	10.8	46.2	17.2	29.0	3.4
Non-Hispanic	53.2	50.9	2.3	5.8	42.8	11.8	31.0	2.3
Family Income								
Less than $7,500	93.5	89.5	5.5	12.2	71.8	23.0	48.8	4.0
$7,500-$14,999	59.4	57.5	2.7	8.9	45.9	14.4	31.5	1.9
$15,000-$24,999	53.5	50.5	2.5	5.9	42.2	13.0	29.2	3.0
$25,000-$34,999	51.9	50.2	2.3	4.7	43.3	11.6	31.7	1.7
$35,000-$49,999	51.5	49.2	1.9	5.0	42.3	11.8	30.6	2.3
$50,000-$74,999	47.6	45.9	1.1	4.6	40.2	8.7	31.4	1.7
$75,000 or more	40.9	38.2	1.9	4.2	32.1	6.4	25.7	2.7
Residence								
Urban	73.8	69.2	3.4	10.9	54.8	15.2	39.6	4.6
Suburban	47.8	46.0	1.7	5.1	39.3	11.2	28.1	1.7
Rural	43.4	42.1	2.2	3.0	36.9	10.6	26.2	1.3

Note: These data are preliminary and may vary slightly from the final estimates.
The victimization survey cannot measure murder because of the inability to question the victim.
*Estimate is based on about 10 or fewer sample cases.
Source: *Criminal Victimization 1993*

Perhaps no sociological variables have caused more controversy both in explaining criminal behavior and in making criminal justice decisions than the extent and effects of gender, race, ethnicity, and class. Throughout the book, we examine these influences as they affect the following decisions:

● Legislatures in defining criminal behavior and prescribing punishments.
● Offenders before, during, and after the commission of crimes.
● Victims before and after victimization.
● Police officers and departments on the street and in station houses.

racial and ethnic disparities
existence of more nonwhites than whites in the criminal justice system.
statistical discrimination
attributing group stereotypes to individual members of the group.

● Prosecutors, defense attorneys, and judges in and out of court.
● Corrections personnel in probation departments, jails, and prisons.

As an example, let's look here at race and ethnicity.

No serious scholar and no sound research challenges the conclusion that **racial and ethnic disparities** exist at every stage of the criminal process, including street stops and frisks, arrests, searches and seizures, bail, prosecution, trial, conviction, probation, incarceration, parole, and other forms of conditional release from prison. That is, everyone agrees that the percentage of racial and ethnic minorities in the criminal justice system consistently and sometimes greatly outnumbers the percentage of these groups in the general population. Scholars, however, disagree hotly over *why* these disparities exist. Some is surely due to the bigotry of individual police officers, prosecutors, defense attorneys, judges, and corrections officers. However, we have no empirical research to tell us how many racist and otherwise bigoted people work in criminal justice, and how much of the disparity they account for.

But even the absence of conscious discrimination does not mean that all people receive *equal* treatment in criminal justice decision making. Whether consciously discriminatory or not, disparate treatment can inflict considerable harm on those who experience it. African Americans, for example, suffer from what social welfare scholars call **"statistical discrimination,"** that is, attributing to individuals the stereotypes of their group. According to Professor Michael Tonry, who has studied race and criminal justice, statistical discrimination in criminal justice means that "because young black men are members of a group in which crime is high, many people of all races react to the stereotype and unfairly judge individuals." Professor Tonry recounts the following incident:

> Early in 1993, Brian Roberts, a . . . law student in a three-piece suit, visiting a white St. Louis judge as part of a class project, was pulled over by the police soon after his rental car entered the judge's affluent neighborhood. He was then followed, the squad car leaving only after he was admitted to the judge's home.[37]

Many "privileged class" African Americans tell similar stories. Brent Staples, a member of the *New York Times* editorial board, has written of numerous instances where he was stereotyped in college, graduate school, and afterwards. The journalist Ellis Cose, in *The Rage of a Privileged Class,* says he was thrown out of a restaurant because the waiter mistook him for another African American who had caused trouble in the past. In *Race Matters,* the Harvard philosopher Cornel West relates that he was stopped on false charges of trafficking in cocaine while he was driving to Williams College and was stopped three times in his first ten days at Princeton "for driving too slowly in a residential neighborhood."[38]

Newark Judge Claude Coleman, a police officer-turned-judge, tells of how he was arrested while he was Christmas shopping in Bloomingdale's because of mistaken identity. Earlier that day, another African American had tried to use a stolen credit card. Even though Coleman bore no resemblance to the man, the police arrested him.

> When the officers arrived, Judge Coleman protested his innocence, asked to see his accusers, and showed identification. He was nonetheless handcuffed—tightly and behind his back—and was dragged through crowds of shoppers to a police car. At the station house, he was chained to the wall and was prevented from calling a lawyer.

Judge Coleman was eventually released. His response to the incident: "No matter how many achievements you have, you can't shuck the burden of being black in a white society."[39]

Racial disparities exist throughout the criminal justice system but disagreement exists as to whether discrimination is the reason for it.

In addition to such individual cases, some local courts and bureaucracies are systematically discriminatory. Therefore, the general nondiscriminatory decision making that states as a whole enjoy does not mean much to those who meet pockets of discrimination in individual police departments, prosecutor's offices, courts, probation departments, jails, or prisons.

Still, the weight of research on discriminatory decision making in criminal justice indicates that most decisions are *not* based on discrimination. We will examine this research in some detail at appropriate places throughout the book. Here, it is enough to point out that empirical research spanning more than twenty-five years conducted by a wide range of scholars from all parts of the ideological spectrum has repeatedly demonstrated that decisions throughout criminal justice—arrest, charge, conviction, sentence, punishment, and release from custody—are based mainly on three legitimate criteria. Listed in the order of their importance, they are:

1. The seriousness of the crime.
2. The amount of proof of guilt.
3. The past criminal record of the suspect and convicted offender.[40]

To the extent that discriminatory decision making occurs, it takes place most often in minor offenses such as disorderly conduct, public drunkenness, and prostitution. As the seriousness of the offense increases, discriminatory decision making occurs less often and explains less of the racial disparity.

Equally important according to sociologists, social factors—particularly education, job opportunities, families, and class—are strongly related to criminal behavior. So it may be true that legitimate criteria such as seriousness of the offense, criminal history of the offender, and amount of proof—not discrimination—explain most of the decision making that takes place *inside* the criminal justice system. However, the variables of class, family structure and dynamics, job opportunities, and education *outside* criminal justice in the larger society relate both to the seriousness of offenses and the criminal history of offenders. The history of discrimination, poor education, and the lack of good jobs, therefore, must still be accounted for in explaining the disproportionate numbers of minorities compared to whites in the criminal justice system.

Finally, the empirical research concerning discrimination in criminal justice deals with its relationship to formal *decisions*—to stop and frisk, arrest, search, convict, sentence, incarcerate. The finding that discrimination does not account for most of that decision making does not mean that criminal justice professionals are free of race, ethnic, gender, age, and class bias. William Wilbanks has surveyed most of the serious research on racism in criminal justice and has conducted some of his own. Even though he forcefully argues that a "racist criminal justice system" is a "myth," Wilbanks nonetheless concedes,

> To argue that there is no systematic bias against blacks in formal decisions does not speak to the issue of whether the police are more likely to "talk down" to black citizens or to show them less respect. The fact that a police officer may call a 40-year-old black man "boy" [however] does not necessarily mean that the officer will be more likely to arrest that man (or, if he does, that his decision is based primarily on the racist stereotype). Harassment of minorities by system personnel, less desirable work assignments, and indifference to important cultural needs could exist, but not be systematically reflected in formal criminal justice processing decisions.[41]

The following *You Decide,* "Did Race and Class Influence the Decisions?" raises the problems of formal and discretionary decision making. It also brings into relief in ordinary cases some of the problems more dramatically portrayed in the O. J. Simpson case discussed at the outset of this chapter.[42]

You Decide   "Did Race and Class Influence the Decisions?"

A city ordinance makes it illegal to drink alcoholic beverages in city parks. Three Native Americans were sitting in one of the parks eating tuna fish sandwiches and drinking cheap red wine. In another park, a group of people were eating salmon mousse with French bread, and drinking imported French white wine. They were members of a gourmet club that was interested not only in cooking fine food but also in eating it in the "proper atmosphere." Police officers see both of these incidents.

Should the police arrest these people for drinking in the park? These incidents really happened. In one case, the police arrested the Native Americans and took them to jail. They did not arrest the members of the gourmet club. However, the local newspaper society page wrote up the gourmet club luncheon because of the club's interest in combining food with atmosphere. Should the prosecutor charge them with violating the ordinance prohibiting drinking in the park? The public defender representing the Native Americans thought not. He argued that his clients were doing nothing more or less than the gourmet club. They were both eating, drinking, and enjoying themselves in the city parks. They were, after all, even eating food and drink from the "same food groups." And yet, the Native Americans landed in jail while the gourmet club wound up in a favorable article on the society page.

Summary

Understanding criminal justice as it actually operates requires a knowledge of the amounts, kinds, trends, and causes of crime. It also requires a knowledge of the responses of police, courts, and corrections to crime. Furthermore, it demands that we know something about how effectively these responses control crime—the principal object of criminal justice. It is not enough to know what the responses are and whether they work. It is also important to know whether they are legal, that is, whether they comply with constitutional standards and the laws of the nation, state, and locality. Last, understanding criminal justice requires a knowledge of whether the policies and practices of criminal justice agencies are good public policy, that is, whether they are wise, efficient, economical, and humane.

The fullest understanding of criminal justice requires not only a knowledge of the system's specific parts but also an appreciation of criminal justice as a whole. Criminal justice shares several elements common to all crime control agencies:

1. Criminal justice is a system, that is, a group of agencies related to crime control.
2. Criminal justice is a process, that is, a series of decisions, from reporting crimes to the police to releasing offenders from correctional supervision.
3. Crime control in a constitutional democracy reflects the effects of the competing ideologies of crime control and due process.
4. Day-to-day decision making in criminal justice reflects the effects of competing ideologies, economics, and the larger social structure and processes of which criminal justice is an integral part.

Major criminal justice decision points include: (1) the detection and investigation of crime, and the apprehension of suspects by the police; (2) the prosecution, conviction, and sentencing of defendants by the courts; and, (3) the punishment of offenders by corrections agencies. The systems paradigm, dominant in criminal justice for the last forty years, focuses on the day-to-day operations of criminal justice agencies and the decision-making process within those agencies. Most of these operations involve low visibility, highly complex, difficult decisions that must be made with little or no time to reflect.

The systems paradigm examines both the formal rule and informal discretionary dimensions of this day-to-day decision making. Formal rules include constitutional provisions, statutes, court decisions, court rules, and the rules and regulations of criminal justice agencies. Discretionary decision making involves a range of political, economic, and sociological influences. Rational decision making requires three conditions:

1. more than one alternative decision
2. information upon which to base a decision
3. clear goals that the decision is expected to achieve

The real world of day-to-day criminal justice rarely affords purely rational decision making. Goals conflict or are not clear; information is insufficient; circumstances demand immediate action; and the alternatives are often too numerous for calm consideration. Decision making in criminal justice does not lend itself to simplistic, "bumper sticker" prescriptions.

Criminal justice is both a structure and a process. The structure consists of a loose confederation of agencies on three levels—federal, state, and local. The process consists mainly of "processing" free individuals into suspects, then into defendants, then into offenders, and then back into free people who will, we hope, work hard, pay their bills, and play by the rules. The processing involves the critical decision of whether to send individuals further into the criminal justice system, to divert them into some kind of social service, or to release them. The structure and process of criminal justice add up to a system, a collection of agencies with a similar objective— crime control. The decisions of one agency affect the decisions of the others.

Scholars have used two models to illustrate criminal justice decision making. The "wedding cake" shows that cases receive varying degrees of attention. The criminal justice cake has four tiers, each tier representing a different type of case—a few celebrated cases on top, followed by somewhat more cases of "real crime," then a large number of "ordinary felonies," and finally the largest number of misdemeanors. Formal criminal justice characterizes the top two layers; informal criminal justice the bottom two.

The other picture, the "funnel," focuses on the decision to move people further into the system or remove them from it. The top of the funnel—its widest part—depicts all people arrested. The number of cases shrinks as people proceed further into the system. Fewer suspects are charged than arrested; fewer defendants go to trial than plead guilty; fewer defendants are convicted than go to trial; fewer convicted offenders are sentenced to prison than probation; fewer convicted prisoners stay in prison for their full sentence than are released early.

The reasons for either the wedding cake or funnel effect depend on both formal rules and informal discretion. Formal rules have mainly to do with the requirements of proof in order to invade the privacy, liberty, and property of individuals. Discretionary decision making is determined by much more varied influences, including political, economic, social, and ideological.

The widely accepted due process and crime control models explain the predominantly ideological influences on decision making in criminal justice. These models are not new; they form part of the larger history of criminal justice in Western societies, a pendulum swing between the predominance of crime control and then a reaction in the form of a commitment to due process. Crime control, as its name implies, puts the reduction of crime at the heart of the process. The model focuses on informal discretionary fact finding in order to convict the guilty and free the innocent as quickly, efficiently, economically, and harmoniously as possible. The model's adherents have little patience with cumbersome, technical rules that stand in the way of crime control. An assembly line is a good analogy for the crime control model. A conveyer belt moves along smoothly, removing those who do not belong in the system and sending the others on for further processing.

The due process model resembles an obstacle course. Each step should present as many difficulties as possible to moving the accused further into the process. The heart of the due process model is the constitutional safeguards and formal procedures protecting the rights of individuals. The due process model reflects a skepticism about the effectiveness of the criminal justice process in controlling crime and about the wisdom of discretionary decision making. The skepticism arises from the belief that social influences—such as class, education, jobs, neighborhood, family, gender, ethnicity, and race—unduly and perniciously affect discretionary decision making.

Review Questions

1. Identify the five main questions that it is necessary to answer in order to understand the reality of criminal justice.
2. To what is much of the dissatisfaction with criminal justice due?
3. In the popular conception, how is criminal justice supposed to work?
4. Explain the importance of "good" and "evil" in the popular conception of criminal justice.
5. Identify the fundamental questions that the O. J. Simpson case forced into the open about criminal justice in the United States.
6. Identify and briefly describe the four major elements that the whole of criminal justice has in common.
7. Define the systems paradigm in criminal justice and explain its significance.

8. Explain the role of discretion and law in criminal justice decision making.
9. Identify the major sources of criminal justice.
10. Identify and explain the three elements of rational decision making in criminal justice.
11. How does the real world affect rational decision making in criminal justice?
12. Explain how criminal justice is both a system and a process.
13. Identify the principal agencies in the structure of criminal justice.
14. Identify and briefly describe the major steps in the criminal justice decision-making process.
15. Identify and briefly explain the major ways in which criminal justice is a "system."

16. Explain why "criminal justice system" is not a completely accurate description of criminal justice.

17. Identify and explain the four tiers in the conceptual model of the criminal justice "wedding cake."

18. Describe the conceptual model of the criminal justice "funnel." Compare and contrast the model of the funnel with that of the wedding cake.

19. Explain the "funnel effect" in criminal justice.

20. Explain the importance of the values of crime control and due process in criminal justice.

21. Identify and explain the common but competing values in both due process and crime control.

22. Identify and explain the major values in the crime control and due process models of criminal justice.

23. Compare and contrast the values of crime control and due process.

24. Summarize the major "pendulum swings" in the history of criminal justice.

25. Identify and explain the major informal influences on criminal justice decision making.

26. Summarize the state of our knowledge of discrimination in criminal justice, based on the available empirical research.

27. According to the existing state of our empirical knowledge, identify the three major influences on decision making in criminal justice.

Notes

1. Lloyd E. Ohlin, "Surveying Discretion by Criminal Justice Decision Makers," and Donald J. Newman, "The American Bar Foundation Survey and the Development of Criminal Justice in Higher Education"; in Lloyd E. Ohlin and Frank J. Remington, *Discretion in Criminal Justice: The Tension Between Individualization and Uniformity* (Albany: State University of New York Press, 1993), 279–349.

2. Samuel Walker, *Taming the System: The Control of Discretion in Criminal Justice, 1950–1990* (New York: Oxford University Press, 1993), 18–20.

3. Michael R. Gottfredson and Donald M. Gottfredson, *Decision Making in Criminal Justice: Toward the Rational Exercise of Discretion,* 2d edition (New York: Plenum Books, 1988), v–vi.

4. From a memo of Professor Remington quoted in Samuel Walker, "Origins of the Contemporary Criminal Justice Paradigm: The American Bar Foundation Survey, 1953–1969," *Justice Quarterly* 9 (1992): 47.

5. Keith Bottomly, *Decisions in the Penal Process* (South Hackensack, N.J.: Fred B. Rothman & Co., 1973), xiii.

6. *Report to the Nation on Crime and Justice* (Washington, D.C.: National Institute of Justice, 1983), 45.

7. Frank Remington et al., *Criminal Justice Administration* (Indianapolis: Bobbs-Merrill, 1969), 19–20.

8. Ohlin, "Surveying Discretion," 10.

9. Wayne R. LaFave and Jerold H. Israel, *Criminal Procedure* (St. Paul: West Publishing Company, 1984), 1:11–32.

10. Gottfredson and Gottfredson, *Decision Making in Criminal Justice;* Lynn Mather, "Some Determinants of the Method of Case Disposition: Decision Making by Public Defenders in Los Angeles," *Law and Society Review* 8 (1974): 187–216; Cassia Spohn and Jerry Cederblom, "Race and Disparities in Sentencing: A Test of the Liberation Hypothesis," *Justice Quarterly* 8 (1991): 306.

11. Samuel Walker, *Sense and Nonsense about Crime and Drugs,* 3d edition (Belmont, Calif.: Wadsworth Publishing Company, 1994), 29–37.

12. Remington et al., *Criminal Justice Administration* 3–4; Senate Confirmation Hearings for Janet Reno as Attorney General of the United States, 10 March 1993.

13. " 'Crack House' Fire: Justice or Vigilantism?" *New York Times,* 22 October 1988.

14. Hans Toch and J. Douglas Grant, *Police as Problem Solvers* (New York: Plenum Press, 1991), 274.

15. Quoted in Toch and Grant.

16. Quoted in Toch and Grant.

17. Quoted in Toch and Grant.

18. Herbert Packer, *The Limits of the Criminal Sanction* (Palo Alto: Stanford University Press, 1968), 155–57.

19. Packer, Chapter 8, upon which this discussion of the crime control and due process models is based.

20. Ibid., 158.

21. Ibid., 159.

22. Quoted in Packer, 170.

23. James Madison, "The Federalist No. 51," in Jacob E. Cooke, ed., *The Federalist* (Middletown, Conn.: Wesleyan University Press, 1961), 349.

24. Roscoe Pound, "The Future of the Criminal Law," *Columbia Law Review* 21 (1921): 1–16; James L. Strachen-Davidson, *Problems of the Roman Criminal Law* (Oxford, U.K.: Clarendon Press, 1912), 114, 168.

25. Quoted in Theodore F. T. Plucknett, *A Concise History of the Common Law,* 5th ed. (London: Butterworth & Company, 1956), 24.

26. Geoffrey R. Elton, *England Under the Tudors,* 2d ed. (London: Methuen, 1974).

27. Joel Samaha, *Law and Order in Historical Perspective* (New York: Academic Press, 1974); for further development of how the law of criminal procedure afforded safeguards to Tudor subjects, see Joel Samaha, "Hanging for Felony: The Case of Elizabethan Colchester," *Historical Journal* (1979); and Geoffrey R. Elton, *Tudor Police and Policy* (Cambridge, England: Cambridge University Press, 1972).

28. Jack P. Kenyon, *The Stuart Constitution,* 2d ed. (New York: Cambridge University Press, 1986).

29. Samuel Walker, in *Popular Justice* (New York: Oxford University Press, 1980), has written about these and other themes in the history of American criminal justice.

30. Joel Samaha, "John Winthrop and the Criminal Law," *William Mitchell Law Review* 15 (1989): 217–53.

31. Pound, "Future of the Criminal Law."

32. American Academy of Political and Social Science, "Administration of Justice in the United States," *Annals of the American Academy of Political and Social Science* 36 (1910); Frederic C. Howe, "A Golden Rule Chief of Police," *Everybody's Magazine,* July 1910; Walker, *Popular Justice;* Craig M. Brown and Barbara D. Warner, "Immigrants, Urban Politics, and Policing in 1900," *American Sociological Review* 57 (1992): 296–305.

33. Thomas E. Cronin, Tania Cronin, and Michael Milakovich, *U.S. v. Crime in the Streets* (Bloomington: Indiana University Press, 1981).

34. *The National Law Review,* 7 August 1989.

35. Walker, *Taming the System.*

36. William S. McFeeley, *Grant* (New York: W. W. Norton, 1982), 387.

37. Michael Tonry, *Malign Neglect: Race, Crime, and Punishment in America* (New York: Oxford University Press, 1995), 50–51.

38. Ibid., 51.

39. Ibid., 50–51.

40. The literature on discrimination in the criminal justice system is voluminous, and we will refer to it in the chapters on crime, police, courts, and corrections. A few of the best overviews, and those on which I relied in writing this section include: Gottfredson and M. Gottfredsen, *Decision Making in Criminal Justice;* Joan Petersilia, *Racial Disparities in the Criminal Justice System* (Santa Monica: Rand Corporation, 1983); William Wilbanks, *The Myth of a Racist Criminal Justice System* (Monterey: Brooks/Cole Publishing Company, 1986); and Tonry, *Malign Neglect.*

41. William Wilbanks, *The Myth of a Racist Criminal Justice System* (Monterey, Calif.: Brooks/Cole Publishing Company, 1987), 6.

42. Ibid.

Crime, Criminals, a

nd Victims

CHAPTER MAIN POINTS

1. The main categories of crime include crimes against the state, violent crimes, crimes against habitations, property crimes, crimes against public order and decency, and occupational crimes.

2. The three main sources of crimes statistics are official reports, victim surveys, and self-reports.

3. The reasons for measuring crime include assessing the moral strength of society, the effectiveness of crime control measures, the extent of victimization, and the validity of criminal justice theories.

4. The UCR, the leading official source of crime statistics, includes only the crimes that come to the attention of local police departments and which these local departments report to the FBI.

5. The NCVS, the major victimization survey, includes the crimes that victims are willing to report to interviewers from the U.S. Census Bureau.

6. Self-reports of crime ask only specific groups of people, usually convicted prisoners and young people, about their criminal behavior.

7. All measures of crime suffer from the "dark figure in crime," that is, crimes committed but not reported and recorded.

8. Violent crimes are the fewest in number, but they attract attention because of the serious physical and emotional harm they can cause.

9. The vast number of property and other crimes, in relation to the many fewer violent crimes, has led to the conclusion that most crime is "ordinary."

10. Research has not demonstrated that involvement with drugs causes the commission of other crimes.

11. Crime is unevenly distributed geographically, and according to age, gender, class, race, ethnicity, and occupation.

12. Men commit more crimes than women, but it is not clear whether they differ in the kinds of crimes they commit.

13. Research has demonstrated that career criminals commit a disproportionately high number of predatory crimes, but it is not clear how to make policy on the basis of this knowledge.

14. Occupational crime consists not only of crimes committed for material gain and power, but also of crimes that can injure and even kill people.

15. Official reports of crime show an almost steady increase in serious crime while victimization surveys show a higher, although fairly steady rate of crime over the last 20 years.

16. Most explanations of criminal behavior fall into the broad categories of free will and determinism.

17. Determinist explanations of criminal behavior fall into two further categories, individual and societal explanations.

18. Explanations of criminal behavior influence criminal justice policy and decision making, because response to crime depends on the explanation given for its cause.

19. Crime victims have played an increasingly minor role in criminal justice since colonial times.

20. Crime victims suffer not only from their victimization but from their experiences with the criminal justice system.

21. The age, gender, class, race, and ethnicity of victims resemble that of their victimizers.

22. Victims report most of the crime that enters the criminal justice system.

very day I scan several print newspapers and on-line services looking for crime news. The following headlines appeared in the last edition of this book. They depict a frightening array of violence, destruction, and exploitation:

"Mother Faces Charges in Daughter's Shooting"

"Teen-Age Gunslinging Is On the Rise, in Search of Protection and Profit"

"15-Year-Old Sentenced in a Family Murder Plot"

"A Series of Killings. . . Raising Fears That Another Serial Killer at Work"

"Despite Gang Truce, L.A. 'A War Zone' "

"Man Dies After Fight Over Bowling Ball"

"Threat of Crime Rises on the Main Highways"

"Capital Is Capital of Gunfire Deaths"

"For Kids, Nowhere to Hide: Gunfire Part of Life in Chicago Projects"

"Grisly Case of Serial Killer Grips Russia"

"In L.A., 3d Day of School Racial Brawls"

"Florida Guard to Patrol Road to Halt Attacks"

"Two Held in Grisly Texas Killings"

" 'Preppie' Killer Up for Parole"

"Day Care Owner Is Convicted of Child Molesting"

" 'Grandma' Death Plot Widens"

"Mom Dies in Latest Carjacking"

"Carjacking: Motorists 'Frightened to the Bone' "

"Arson Spree Has Seattle on Edge"

"A Student in Minneapolis is Called Notorious 'Bordertown Bandit' "

Nothing much has changed since then. Toward the end of 1995, a *Minneapolis StarTribune* headline blared: "Deadly Business: Drugs, Gangs, and Cash Made 1995 Minneapolis' Most Homicidal Year." Most of you can find similar headlines, if you glance through your local papers or watch your local television news. On the same day as that dire *Minneapolis Star Tribune* headline, the FBI reported that homicide rates nationally were the lowest in several decades, including in major cities. The *real* news about the lower homicide rates according to nearly all reports, was a collective, "Yes, the rates have gone down, BUT. . . ." Then followed a chorus of commentary that crime rates are going *up* in rural areas and that homicide rates are only in a temporary lull, soon to be broken by a "bloodbath" created by the growing crop of violent teenagers.[1]

Is there an epidemic of violence, as these headlines suggest? Is serial killing on the rise? Are youths more violent than ever? Has the desire for thrills, money, cars, and other trappings of the "fast life" put the public in ever-greater danger from crime? Is the drop in urban homicide rates only a lull before a bloodbath? Criminal justice students need to know the answers to these and other questions to fully understand the policies and day-to-day operations of police departments, courts, and corrections agencies.

This chapter answers the following questions on the basis of information that helps put the operation of criminal justice within the context of statistics and theories about crime, criminals, and victims.

1. What kinds of crime are there? How is the amount of crime distributed among violent, property, and other types of crime?

2. How is crime distributed across time and space? Does it affect cities, suburbs, towns, and rural areas equally? Does it vary according to time of day, week, or year?

3. How does crime affect men and women, social classes, age groups, racial groups, and ethnic groups?

4. How do we measure crime and its effects?

5. What are the trends in crime in the United States? Is the amount of various kinds of crime increasing, decreasing, or remaining steady?

6. What explains criminal behavior? Do people choose to commit crimes using rational decision making and free will? Or are such decisions determined by forces largely beyond the will of individuals, such as biology, psychology, social structure, social process, and social conflict?

7. What about the victims of crime? Who are they? What are the effects of victimization? Why do victims report—or *fail* to report—crimes to the police? How important are victims to the criminal justice system?

Crime and Criminals

The prolific dean of sixteenth-century English justices of the peace, William Lambarde, organized his widely used handbook according to a classification of crimes that was already old. Lambarde named the following categories of crimes, listed from most to least serious:

1. *Crimes against the state,* namely, treason and sedition.

2. *Crimes against persons,* mainly the violent crimes of homicide, rape, and assault.

3. *Crimes against habitation,* namely, arson and burglary.

4. *Crimes against both persons and property,* specifically, robbery, a violent crime to obtain property.

5. *Crimes against property,* including the various forms of theft.

6. *Crimes against the family,* such as bigamy and adultery.

7. *Crimes against public administration,* mainly bribery and obstruction of justice.

8. *Crimes against public order and decency,* such as vagrancy, drunk and disorderly conduct, disturbing the peace, and prostitution.

With remarkably few modifications, these classifications are still used. This section divides crime into fewer categories than did Lambarde, but it maintains the distinctions among crimes against the state, crimes against persons, crimes against habitation, crimes against property, crimes against acquaintances, and crimes against public order and decency. It also adds a section on crimes involving occupations.

Measuring Crime

Measuring crime in the United States is based on three standard sources:

1. Police reports. Crime information collected by local police departments.

2. Victim surveys. Information from victims of crime collected by the U.S. Bureau of the Census.

3. Offender surveys. Information gathered from individuals asking them about the crimes they have committed.

All these sources are useful, but none either fully or accurately measures crime. This is because so much crime goes either unreported, unrecorded, or both.

Reasons for Measuring Crime For centuries, societies have kept track of crimes, although the reasons have varied over time. The first crime statistics were intended to measure the "moral health" of society. Crime statistics, called *"statistique morale"* or *"moralstatistik"* by nineteenth-century statisticians, supposedly revealed how "bad" a society was. The idea persists in the popular belief that rising crime rates indicate a breakdown in moral values and social civility.[2]

Another intended use of crime statistics is to assess the effectiveness of criminal justice agencies. Jeremy Bentham, the great eighteenth-century criminal law reformer, noted that accurate crime figures are a "political barometer, by which the effects of every legislative operation relative to [crime and punishment] may be indicated." Today, police departments, courts, and prison officials study crime rates to measure how effectively they are enforcing the law. The public tends to hold police, judges, corrections officers, and lawyers responsible for rising crime rates; however, these same agents seldom receive credit if crime rates fall.[3]

As emphasis has shifted from criminals to victims, researchers and public policymakers have turned to crime statistics as a way to measure victimization. The National Crime Victim Survey (NCVS), for example, concentrates on a range of variables related to victimization. The Bureau of Justice Statistics has even devised a **"crime risk index"** that measures the risk of becoming the victim of a crime.[4]

Finally, measuring crime can help to develop and test criminal justice theory. For example, the kinds, amounts, and trends of crime may shed light on the various explanations of crime. In this sense, crime statistics reveal more about criminal justice administration—the decisions, practices, and policies of police, prosecutors, judges, and corrections officers—than they do about the actual amount and nature of crime.[5]

Uniform Crime Reports (UCR)

The **Uniform Crime Reports (UCR)** is the oldest continuing series of national crime statistics. It began in 1930 when the International Association of Chiefs of Police (IACP), an association of reform-minded police chiefs, culminated nearly a decade of effort to promote national crime statistics. The UCR reports both raw numbers of crimes and the rates of crime per 100,000 people. The two main sources of these numbers are:

1. Crimes reported to the police by victims, other witnesses, or the police themselves.
2. Persons arrested by the police.

Therefore, the UCR is primarily derived from records produced by law enforcement agencies. Hence, agencies are both the primary and the largest *official* source of information about the kinds, amounts, and trends of crime. The UCR is also the source for the most widely reported crime statistics. It is the *only* basis for most television, radio, and newspaper commentary on crime in the United States. Of course, specific instances of murder, rape, and drug crimes provide the daily fare of crime news served to television viewers, radio listeners, and newspaper readers. Criminal justice policymakers, legislators, sociologists, and politicians also rely heavily on the statistics that the UCR publishes.[6]

The UCR was based on the idea that **crimes known to the police** were the best measure of crimes actually committed. The program depended—and still depends—on the voluntary participation of local law enforcement agencies. They collect and report the information from their jurisdictions. After a few years during which the IACP ran the program, local agencies began sending their data to the FBI. The FBI compiles the data and reports it annually in the publication *Crime in the United States.*[7] Crimes known to the police became the basis for the **Crime Index,** or **Part I offenses,** a list of first seven and, since 1979, eight offenses. (See Table 2.1.) The Crime Index is supposed to show the movement, fluctuations, and trends of the total U.S.

Table 2.1
Crime Index Offenses

1. Murder and non-negligent manslaughter.
2. Forcible rape.
3. Robbery.
4. Aggravated assault.
5. Larceny-theft.
6. Burglary.
7. Motor vehicle theft.
8. Arson (mandated by Congress in 1979).[8]

Part II offenses *raw numbers of all offenses not reported in the Crime Index.*
dark figure in crime *offenses not reported or recorded.*

crime rate. It is the most widely reported crime statistic, reporting both the raw numbers and the rate of offenses for every 100,000 people in the population.

Part II offenses are reported only in raw numbers of arrests. (See Table 2.2.)

Approximately 16,000 police departments, covering about 95 percent of the nation's population, collect numbers on all of the following subjects:

1. Offenses known to the police.
2. Index Crimes cleared by arrest.
3. Persons arrested (See Table 2.2).
4. Homicide patterns.
5. Law enforcement personnel.

Useful as it is as a long-standing, continuing series of official police reports on crime, law enforcement, and law enforcement personnel, the UCR has its limits. First, the UCR cannot overcome the inherent limitation in all the official numbers regarding crime—it can only report and record crimes that the police know about. The number of crimes not reported and recorded are called the **dark figure in crime.** Crimes that the police do not know about are only part of this "dark figure." At each successive stage in the criminal process, the number of actual crimes excluded from the official statistics grows. That is to say, there are fewer arrests than reported crimes, fewer indictments than arrests, fewer convictions than indictments, and fewer sentences to prison than convictions.

The police discover a few crimes on their own, but they know about the vast majority of crimes because the public—victims, their relatives, neighbors, and bystanders—reports them. Of course, just as the police can only

Table 2.2
Part II Offenses

Simple assault
Forgery and counterfeiting
Fraud
Embezzlement
Stolen property (buying, receiving, possessing)
Vandalism
Weapons (carrying, possessing, etc.)
Prostitution and commercialized vice
Sex offenses (except forcible rape and prostitution)
Drug abuse violations
Gambling
Offenses against family and children
Driving under the influence
Liquor laws
Drunkenness
Disorderly conduct
Vagrancy
All other offenses

record crimes they know about, others can only report crimes they know have taken place. Some businesses, for example, only discover shoplifting and employee theft when they discover shrinkages in their inventories. Another problem that we will discuss in the section on victims also affects the numbers of crimes coming to police attention: even when people know about crimes, they do not always report them to the police.[9]

Second, not all crimes reported to the police get recorded by the police. According to Victoria W. Schneider and Brian Wiersema, informal policies within police departments dictate that officers overlook some crimes. For example, police may overlook minor drug offenses to avoid scaring away bigger dealers.[10]

Also, police officers, like the rest of us, "loathe" filing crime reports, according to criminologist Wesley G. Skogan. Moreover, criminologist Marvin Wolfgang found that the police failed to report from 20 to 90 percent of criminal events (depending on the crime) in New York City because "commanders were pressured to reduce crime, and did so by down-grading offenses." Sociologist Donald Black, in a sample of 554 cases recorded in Boston, Chicago, and Washington, D.C., found that when victims are related to suspects, officers are unlikely to file reports.[11]

Even when crimes are reported and recorded, the UCR distorts the true picture of crime. The Crime Index, for example, excludes white-collar crimes. Hence, the Index counts a street thief who steals $250, but not a bank executive who embezzles $75,000, because the white-collar crime of embezzlement is not an Index crime.

Furthermore, the UCR *over*represents *serious* crimes and *under*represents *minor* crimes. The Crime Index, for example, includes both attempted and completed crimes, so that attempted murders, rapes, robberies, burglaries, and thefts are counted as if they were actually completed. In addition, people tend to report only the most serious crimes to the police, and the police tend to record only the most serious crimes reported to them. In fact, the UCR reporting procedures permit departments to record only the most serious Index crime if several crimes occurred during one event. For example, consider a victim who reports that during a burglary, the burglar took $3,000 in cash and several diamond rings, raped an occupant, and drove off in the family car. The victim has reported five Index crimes—one burglary, two larcenies, one rape, and one auto theft. The department records only one crime, rape, because the UCR rates it the most serious of the five Index crimes.[12]

Another problem arises from the discretionary decision making allowed local law enforcement agencies in recording crimes. Although the FBI supplies departments with a handbook of guidelines for recording the data, jurisdictions define crimes differently and not always according to the UCR definition. Furthermore, police do not apply uniform definitions when they record crimes. For example, robbery, burglary, and larceny all involve taking property, yet they differ significantly. Robbery involves force or threatened force; home burglary invades privacy; larceny, a pure property offense, includes neither force nor invasion of privacy. However, local police often record robbery, larceny, and burglary interchangeably. According to one estimate, data errors are in the 40 percent range.[13]

Inaccuracies also occur in the persons-arrested category. The UCR guidelines provide police departments with a definition of arrest, but departments do not always subscribe to it. When asked, many local reporting agents cannot even recall what the UCR definition of arrest is. When asked how they defined arrest for reporting purposes, 16 percent said that they recorded any restraint at all imposed on citizens; 11 percent said they recorded driving a suspect to the station; 29 percent said more than four hours of detention constituted arrest; 58 percent listed telling suspects, "You're under arrest"; and 100 percent counted charging and booking.[14]

Bureau of Justice Statistics (BJS) *federal agency responsible for reporting to the public criminal justice statistics and research, and for sponsoring criminal justice research.*

Furthermore, although FBI guidelines require that every person arrested count as a separate arrest, 11 percent of agencies admit they count only every arrest that results in a formal *charge.* Finally, although FBI rules call for counting summonses and citations as arrests, many police departments do not include them. The police record only about one-third of the crimes reported to them, and unrecorded crimes do not become part of the UCR.[15]

Various conditions determine whether reported crime translates into recorded crime. For example, law enforcement agencies officially recognize crimes within families less frequently than crimes between strangers. Furthermore, the preferences of complainants also influence police recording decisions. Officers rarely record a crime against the wishes of reporting victims. Subjective reactions based on face-to-face encounters with victims or witnesses also influence an officer's decision to record a crime. The social status of a complainant affects police decisions. White-collar complainants are more likely to get official recognition, particularly if the suspects are of "lower" status than the complainants. The behavior of complainants toward police officers influences recording decisions. If victims defer politely, they probably will get their desired disposition. Disrespectful or abrasive complainants are less likely to receive official recognition; police officers often disregard complaints if citizens do not display "proper respect toward police." The gap between FBI guidelines and actual practice is an excellent example of discretionary adaptation of rules to societal and other influences.[16]

Two researchers, David Seidman and Michael Couzens, illustrate this discretion in reporting the following incident:

> One police report contains the account of a man who was robbed as he got out of a cab. The report says he was not injured and labels the case a simple larceny. In fact, according to the victim he was slugged repeatedly in the face by the robber. The police officer who compiled the report interviewed the sixty-one-year-old man while he still wore a blood-stained bandage wrapped around his injured neck.[17]

Reporting aggregate crime rates, meaning crimes per 100,000 in the general population, introduces another shortcoming. Aggregates derive from figures based on the total reporting population, often combining populations that should remain distinct. For example, knowing how many 18-year-old men or women commit larceny compared to other 18-year-old men and women reveals more than knowing how many larcenies are committed per 100,000 people in the general population. In fact, aggregate data obscure the influence of age on crime. What looked like a general reduction in crime during part of the 1980s turned out to be more a decrease in the population of adolescents and young adults, who commit disproportionate numbers of crimes. Criticism notwithstanding, because of their immediacy to the event, crimes known to the police are still the best available crime statistics. More than a generation ago, the distinguished criminologist Thorsten Sellin noted that "the value of criminal statistics decreases as the procedures take us farther away from the offense itself."[18]

The **Bureau of Justice Statistics (BJS)**—the agency responsible for funding many criminal justice information projects—in connection with the FBI and the general law enforcement community, has begun to implement major reforms in the UCR. The reformed UCR includes two redesigned Index and arrest categories, Group A and Group B offenses. Group A includes the original eight Index crimes known to the police, with some changes in definition, and adds 14 additional offenses, including drug offenses, fraud, embezzlement, pornography, statutory rape and incest, and weapons law violations. The UCR reports arrests for 11 Group B offenses, including such crimes as bad checks, loitering, driving while intoxicated, nonviolent family offenses, Peeping Toms, and a catchall known as "all other crimes."

incident-based reporting
reporting by local police
departments to the FBI of both
summaries of crime figures and
details of each criminal event.
**National Crime Victimization
Survey (NCVS)** national survey of
crime victims conducted by the U.S.
Census Bureau.

The UCR has also begun a shift to **incident-based reporting,** meaning that local agencies will not simply submit summaries of crime figures, but will also include the details of each criminal event. The new reporting system will also include new categories of information related to the offense, offender, and victim. Offense data will separate attempts from completed crimes and will include information such as suspected use of alcohol, narcotics, or other drugs, or the use of a weapon in committing the crime. Offender data will include age, gender, and race. Victim data will include age, gender, race, ethnic origin, whether resident or nonresident, type of injury sustained, and relationship of victim to offender. These changes will undoubtedly produce a marked improvement in the quality, breadth, and depth of official statistics of crime. However, they cannot eliminate, or even reduce by themselves, the dark figure in crime.[19]

National Crime Victimization Survey (NCVS)

The **National Crime Victimization Survey (NCVS)** is based on the idea that if you want to shed light on the dark figure in crime, you should talk to the victims of crime. Therefore, the NCVS focuses on victim surveys, not official crime statistics. (Table 2.3 compares the NCVS with the UCR.) The NCVS, conducted by the U.S. Bureau of the Census, is the only national crime statistic that includes crimes the police do not know about. Furthermore, it is the only national data

Table 2.3
Uniform Crime Reports and the National Crime Victimization Survey

	Uniform Crime Reports	National Crime Survey
Crimes measured:	(1) Homicide (2) Rape (3) Robbery (personal and commercial) (4) Assault (aggravated) (5) Burglary (residential and commercial) (6) Larceny (commercial and household) (7) Motor vehicle theft (8) Arson	(1) Rape (2) Robbery (personal) (3) Assault (aggravated and simple) (4) Household burglary (5) Larceny (personal and household) (6) Motor vehicle theft
Scope:	Crimes reported to the police; considerable flexibility in developing small-area data	Crimes both reported and not reported to the police; all data available for a few large geographic areas
Collection method:	Police departments report to FBI or to centralized state agencies who report to FBI	Survey interviews;' periodically measures the total number of crimes committed by asking a national sample of 49,000 households that include 101,000 persons age 12 or older about their experiences as victims during specific time periods
Information:	(1) Offense counts (2) Crimes cleared by arrest (3) Persons arrested (4) Persons charged with crimes (5) Law enforcement officers killed and assaulted (6) Characteristics of homicide victims	(1) Victim age, sex, race, education, and income (2) Victim-offender relationship (3) Crime details, such as time and place, whether reported to police, use of weapons, physical injury, and economic loss
Sponsor:	Department of Justice Federal Bureau of Investigation (FBI)	Department of Justice research arm, the Bureau of Justice Statistics (BJS)

Figure 2.1

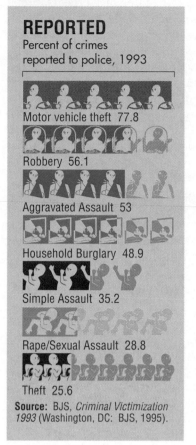

REPORTED
Percent of crimes
reported to police, 1993

Motor vehicle theft 77.8

Robbery 56.1

Aggravated Assault 53

Household Burglary 48.9

Simple Assault 35.2

Rape/Sexual Assault 28.8

Theft 25.6

Source: BJS, *Criminal Victimization
1993* (Washington, DC: BJS, 1995).

base that, in the words of James Garofalo, who has used the NCVS extensively in his own research, "allows case-level analyses of victims and their victimization." According to Garofalo, "These two characteristics make the NC[V]S a potential information gold mine for researchers interested in the causes, trends, processes, and outcomes of crimes." Victims directly provide details of crimes. At six-month intervals, interviewers from the Census survey about 100,000 individuals aged 12 or over in a sample of 50,000 households. They interview a sixth of the sample monthly on a rotating schedule, gathering information regarding the previous six months.[20]

The NCVS measures levels of criminal victimization of both individuals and households. The survey includes crimes not reported to the police such as rape, robbery, assault, burglary, motor vehicle theft, and larceny. Criminal homicide is not included because, obviously, the victim is dead. The interviewers ask if any member of the household 12 years or older was a crime victim within the past six months. The questionnaire asks about the victim's age, race, sex, educational level, and income. It also elicits information about the crime, including location, amount of personal injury, and economic loss. The survey also determines facts about the perpetrator, such as relationship to victim, gender, age, and race. Finally, the interviewer asks victims if they reported crimes to the police, and the reasons why they did or did not do so.[21]

Annually, the BJS, administrator of the NCVS, issues a general report, *Criminal Victimization in the United States,* summarizing NCVS findings. The BJS also publishes special bulletins and reports stemming from its surveys, such as *Violent Crime by Strangers, Households Touched by Crime,* and *Elderly Victims.*[22]

Perhaps the most significant contribution of the NCVS is to clearly demonstrate what researchers and policymakers have long suspected: official crime statistics of the UCR considerably underreport the actual amount of crime. The NCVS has found that citizens report only about 38 percent of all NCVS offenses. Moreover, victims report violent crimes more often than property crimes, and completed crimes more than attempts. Figure 2.1 shows the percent of crimes reported to the police in 1993.

Another major purpose of NCVS is to ask citizens why they do and do not report crimes to the police. The most frequent reasons have to do with the seriousness of the crime. The most common reason victims give for reporting violent crimes is to prevent further crimes against them by the same offender (20 percent); for property crimes, so that the victim could recover property. Common reasons for not reporting a violent crime are that it was a private matter (20 percent), or the crime was not successful (17 percent). The most common reason for not reporting property crimes is that the victim had gotten back the property. Responses vary little according to race, ethnicity, gender, or class, and few victims decide to report or not to report because of their lack of confidence in, or distrust of, the police.[23]

The NCVS sheds some light on the dark figure in crime, but like the UCR it still underreports the total number of crimes. Just as people do not report all crimes they know about to the police, victims do not report all crimes committed against them to the interviewers. They do not report crimes for a number of reasons, including:

1. They are embarrassed or ashamed, fearing ridicule and contempt.
2. They distrust interviewers and so cover up the crime.
3. They are acquainted with, or are related to, offenders.
4. They do not know they are concealing crimes.
5. They are apathetic.

Most of the failure to report, however, stems from simple forgetfulness. Six months can be too long to remember crimes, especially minor ones. One check showed that recall during the first three months is 70 percent; from three to six months it is only 50 percent. Another showed a decrease of 61 percent in reporting crimes from the first to the last month of the survey.[24]

The federal government sponsored a study that dramatically demonstrates the underreporting of rape in the United States. For the National Women's Study, researchers conducted telephone interviews with a sample of more than 4,000 women designed to represent a cross section of all adult women in the United States. Women were asked about rapes occurring in the last year and about sexual assaults throughout their lifetimes. Based on the sample responses, the study estimated that 683,000 adult women were raped in 1990—more than five times the number reported to the NCVS for the same period! "These data show us what experts have been saying for a while," said Professor Mary Koss, who did her own study of rape among college women in 1987. "There is a lot more rape than has been reflected in the Federal statistics."[25]

The Bureau of Justice Statistics has redesigned its survey to produce more accurate reporting of rape, other sexual assaults, and all violent crimes. Questions now ask victims specifically if attacks included "any rape, attempted rape, or other type of sexual assault." Also, the new survey replaces technical terms with words that describe violent crimes by the behavior involved. Respondents are also encouraged to talk about violent incidents even if they do not believe they are crimes. The redesign has increased the amount of reported violent crime victimization. For example, from 1987 to 1991, when the old system was still in effect, the average annual rate of violent victimization per 1,000 persons was 5.4 women; the rate for 1992-1993, after the redesign went into operation, rose steeply to 9.4. BJS staff attribute this dramatic increase to the redesign that uncovers more crimes.[26]

While the NCVS, like the UCR, underestimates the total amount of crime, it probably overrepresents trivial crimes. According to Wesley Skogan, "most victimizations are not notable events. The majority are property crimes in which the perpetrator is never detected. The financial stakes are small, and the costs of calling the police greatly outweigh the benefits."[27]

Sampling issues also distort the figures in the NCVS. Like all household surveys, whether conducted by the Census Bureau or others, the NCVS underrepresents some parts of the population. Young black males and illegal aliens are consistently underrepresented; so are people with particular lifestyles, such as drifters, street hustlers, and the homeless. Furthermore, the NCVS does not survey prisons, jails, and juvenile corrections facilities. Prisoners surely have higher victimization rates than does the general population. Wealthy people, too, may escape the survey because they tend to insulate themselves from all kinds of interviews.[28]

Another sampling problem arises because some of the most serious crimes in the survey—rape, robbery, and aggravated assault—are extremely low in numbers. Between 1973 and 1992 the number of rapes reported by the 160,000 households was well under 200 annually, the number of robberies a little over 1,000, and the number of aggravated assaults between about 1,500 and 1,800. National estimates based on these low base numbers subject the NCVS to a considerable amount of sampling error.[29]

The NCVS redesign is broader than the revised questions. Following a thorough review of its methods, the NCVS has attempted to improve and expand its reporting generally. Interviewers ask about victimizations that occurred in various "domains," such as work and leisure, attempting to provide cues to help trigger memory of incidents. The BJS has also added new independent variables to the NCVS. Interviewers ask about interaction between victim and offender, including detailed questions about what victims did about the incident when it occurred. Interviewers also ask lifestyle questions, such as whether victimization occurred while shopping, during an evening away from home, or on public transportation. They also inquire about perceived offender substance abuse and the means offenders used to cause victim injury. They also ask about the race, ethnicity, and gender of offenders. These changes cannot overcome the sampling problems mentioned before, nor can they eliminate the problems created by the memory lapses and fears of victims. Nevertheless, they have definitely made the picture of crime presented in the NCVS more accurate and more complete than it was before.[30]

Self-Reports **Self-reports** originated from the hypothesis that asking people about their criminal behavior was the best way to measure crime. James F. Short and F. Ivan Nye, in one early survey, asked juveniles about their delinquent acts. Nearly a third admitted to such officially unreported acts. College students admitted to similar unreported acts. Moreover, 60 percent of a sample of adult men between the ages of 20 and 30 admitted to driving while intoxicated, 44 percent to shoplifting, and 13 percent to breaking and entering. Sixty-nine percent of those who reported public drunkenness or driving while intoxicated were not arrested, and 33 percent of the shoplifters escaped without arrest.[31]

The early self-report surveys focused on less serious crimes. The Short and Nye scale lists the following offenses: driving a car without a license; skipping school; defying parental authority; taking trifles worth less than two dollars; buying and drinking beer, wine, or liquor illegally; vandalism; and sexual relations with the opposite sex. Recently, self-reporting has turned to asking felons about their criminal behavior, although serious obstacles stand in the way. First, it is difficult to find substantial samples of offenders, unless researchers are unusually well connected to criminals; they have to rely on the criminal justice system for study subjects. When a sample of convicted offenders is found, it may not represent all criminals, or even all *convicted* criminals. The sample may well overrepresent multiple offenders or "unsuccessful" criminals—the assumption being that successful criminals do not get caught or at least avoid imprisonment. Furthermore, even a representative sample does not guarantee accuracy concerning events that occurred on impulse, about which offenders may well not tell the truth. Offenders may exaggerate the professionalism of their actions and minimize the hurt they inflicted on their victims. They may not trust the researchers. Whatever assurances they are given about confidentiality, prisoners may remain convinced that what they say will affect their chances for release. They will paint the best possible pictures of themselves, or they may simply want to play games.[32]

Despite these shortcomings, researchers have conducted a number of surveys of convicted felons. Mark A. Peterson and Harriet B. Barker, for example, surveyed 624 incarcerated male felons in five California state prisons. In the survey, respondents reported on the type of crimes they had committed during a three-year period. The survey targeted violent crimes, such as armed robbery, use of a weapon, aggravated beating, and attempted murder. For all offenses except rape and murder, respondents admitted to committing crimes other than, and in addition to, those they were convicted for.[33]

The felons also reported on their prior criminal records, reasons for committing crimes, and perceptions of the payoffs and penalties. Highly active criminals tend to think of themselves as a particular type, such as a burglar, a thief, or a robber. About a fourth considered themselves "straight." Those who considered themselves criminals reported the highest number of crimes; those who called themselves straight reported the least. Nearly half reported that economic hardship led them to commit crimes, about a third blamed a desire for high living and high times, and about a sixth cited temper. Those who reported high living as their motivation committed the most crimes; offenders who reported economic need reported less violent crimes. Finally, respondents who perceived the greatest payoffs in crime over a straight life committed more crimes.[34]

In *The Armed Criminal in America,* James D. Wright surveyed more than 1,800 convicted adult male felons incarcerated in 10 states. The survey asked

Figure 2.2

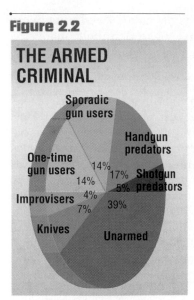

**THE ARMED
CRIMINAL**

these men how and why they obtain, carry, and use firearms, especially in committing crimes. Wright found a typology of criminals based on their use of weapons. The largest group (39 percent), unarmed criminals, had never committed any crime while armed. The "knife criminals" and "improvisers," armed with a variety of ready-to-hand weapons, constituted about 11 percent. Roughly the other half of the sample was made up of "gun criminals," more than half of whom used a gun only once or sporadically, the rest (22 percent) consisting of "handgun" and "shotgun predators." These last committed nearly half of all the crimes reported (Figure 2.2).[35]

The gun criminals reported that guns made many crimes easier to commit and that they had lived around guns all their lives. Furthermore, the majority reported that they kept their guns loaded at all times and that they fired them regularly, often at other people. Half reported firing a gun at someone; half also reported someone had fired on them. Many reported that a "man" armed with a gun is "prepared for anything that might happen." When asked how they would respond to a ban on small, cheap handguns, they responded that they would carry bigger, more expensive handguns. Asked about their response to a total ban on handguns, a majority of gun criminals— and more than three-quarters of the "predators"—responded that they would carry sawed-off shoulder weapons.[36]

Like the UCR and NCVS, self-reports do not produce wholly accurate and complete crime statistics. Some offenders, like some victims, forget and deceive. Furthermore, to date, self-reports do not represent national samples. They survey particular groups, such as juveniles, college students, and felons, from specific regions or states. Criminologist Gwynn Nettler, after reviewing self-surveys, concluded:

> Asking people questions about their behavior is a poor way of observing it. . . . It is particularly ticklish to ask people to recall their "bad" behavior. Confessional data are at least as weak as the official statistics they were supposed to improve upon.[37]

Measuring Occupational Crime Measuring occupational crime presents the greatest challenges to those who gather crime statistics. The UCR does not include occupational crimes, which citizens rarely report. The NCVS does not ask questions about occupational crime. Attempts to measure white-collar crime through victim surveys face several difficulties. There is often no identifiable, single victim. In many cases, individual victims do not feel a significant loss. Measuring organizational crime by extracting data from official records of formal proceedings in white-collar crime cases has all the shortcomings of the UCR, plus one more. Isolated court cases do not reveal the widespread harm commonly suffered by many individuals affected by corporate crime.[38]

Official records of formal proceedings against corporations, including criminal prosecutions and violations of the regulations of federal agencies such as the Securities and Exchange Commission and the Environmental Protection Agency, have produced some significant findings. Edwin Sutherland's pioneering study of the nation's largest corporations, *White Collar Crime,* and Marshall Clinard and Peter Yaeger's more recent survey of giant corporations, *Corporate Crime,* represent two notable examples.[39]

The most promising measures of blue-collar crime stem from self-surveys of employees. These concentrate on employee theft or other property misappropriation. In addition to interviews and questionnaires, blue-collar crime reporting relies on informants, that is, researchers who work in particular business places and report what they observe. Richard Hollinger and John P. Clark, for example, combined anonymous questionnaires and face-to-face interviews with both executives and employees in several industries and communities. To study employees "cheating" at work, Gerald Mars

treason *crime against the state of levying war against the U.S., joining with enemies of the U.S., or giving aid and comfort to the enemies of the U.S.*
sedition *crime against the state of stirring up treason or rebellion by means of communication or agreement.*
domestic terrorism *difficult-to-define crime of U.S. citizens attacking institutions and officials of the U.S.*
index crimes *eight serious crimes that act as a barometer of the general trends and patterns of crime.*
violent crimes *least numerous but most disturbing crimes that threaten, injure, or kill individuals.*

interviewed more than 100 informants selected simply because they were available, not according to any rational selection basis.[40]

Crimes Against the State

The two main crimes that threatened the existence of the sixteenth-century English state—treason and sedition—remain crimes today, albeit rare. **Treason** is the crime of levying war against the United States, joining with the enemies of the United States, or giving aid and comfort to the enemies of the United States. **Sedition** is the crime of stirring up treason or rebellion by means of communication or agreement. The United States have added a third crime that can overlap with treason and sedition—domestic terrorism.

Domestic terrorism, although rare, raises great public fear and anxiety, just as its perpetrators intend. Domestic terrorism is difficult to define. According to researchers at the Rand Corporation, terrorism

> has become almost a "fad" word, indiscriminately applied to a range of acts and motivations often beyond the political character essential in distinguishing terrorism from other acts of criminal, but non-politically motivated, violence. Non-terrorist criminals use terror to achieve immediate goals, such as pulling a knife on a mugging victim to get money or other valuables, or overpowering a rape victim to get immediate sexual or other psychological gratification. What distinguishes domestic terrorists from other violent criminals is that domestic terrorists use violence in the name of long-term political goals, such as reducing the power of the federal government. Acts of terroristic violence are intended to "terrify" the government into submitting to those goals. Perhaps nothing more clearly demonstrates the nature of domestic terrorism than the bombing of the federal office building in Oklahoma City that killed more than 100 men, women, and children for the purpose, claim the perpetrators, of warning the federal government to stop exercising what they perceive as unconstitutional power against citizens.[41]

Serious Crimes

The FBI, in its annual survey of crimes that have officially come to the attention of the police, singles out eight crimes against persons and property considered serious enough that people are most likely to report them. The FBI calls these **index crimes,** a sort of barometer of general patterns and trends in crime. (See Table 2.4, which lists and defines these eight crimes.)

Violent Crimes Lambarde's crimes against persons—commonly called **violent crimes** today—were of great concern in the sixteenth century; they remain of at least equal concern at the end of the twentieth century. Murder, rape, assault, and robbery generate fear, can cause serious physical and emotional injury, and in the case of robbery, harms both persons *and* their property. (See Table 2.4.) Violent crimes against persons receive a great deal of attention from the public, news media, politicians, and criminal justice professionals. Such crimes even attract a large share of television and movie productions. Even the casual observer notices the time that the news media, particularly local news, devotes to violent crime. I have informally noted that local television news in Minneapolis and St. Paul sometimes devote up to one-third of news time to murders, rapes, and robberies. These stories are usually first to appear on the screen. Furthermore, rarely a day goes by without the reporting of some violent crime. Whenever available, bloody pictures accompany these stories.

Table 2.4
Index Crimes

Index Crimes	Definition
1. Murder and Non-negligent Homicide	Willful killing of one person by another.
2. Forcible Rape	Carnal knowledge of a female forcibly and against her will. Assaults or attempts to commit rape are also included, but statutory rape without force and other sex offenses are not included.
3. Robbery	Taking or attempting to take anything of value from the care, custody, or control of a person by force, threat of force, or violence, and/or by putting the victim in fear.
4. Aggravated Assault	Unlawful attack by one person of another for the purpose of inflicting severe or aggravated bodily injury. This type of assault is usually accompanied by the use of a weapon likely to inflict death or great bodily harm. Attempts are included, since the use of a gun, knife, or other weapon would probably result in injury or death if the crime were completed.
5. Burglary	Unlawful entry of a structure to commit a felony or theft. The use of force is not required. Burglary is divided into three categories: forcible entry, unlawful entry without force, and attempted forcible entry.
6. Larceny-Theft	Unlawful taking, carrying, leading, or riding away of property from someone else's possession. It includes shoplifting, picking pockets, purse snatching, thefts from vehicles, and other thefts in which no force, violence, or fraud occurs. It does not include embezzlement, "con" games, bad checks, or forgery, or motor vehicle theft.
7. Motor Vehicle Theft	Theft or attempted theft of motor vehicles, including cars, trucks, buses, motorcycles, motorscooters, and snowmobiles. It does not include taking motor vehicles for temporary use by those having lawful access to the vehicle taken.
8. Arson	Any willful or malicious burning or attempt to burn, with or without the intent to defraud, a dwelling house, public building, motor vehicle or aircraft, or personal property of another. Only fires determined through investigation to have been willfully or maliciously set are included. Fires of suspicious or unknown origins are excluded.

The attention that violent crimes receive is understandable, even though their number is far less than the numbers of serious property offenses. (See Figure 2.3, showing the combined serious property and violent crime rates from 1993.) The attention persists even though the most commonly reported violent crime, aggravated assault, occurs about one-third less than does the least common serious property crime, motor vehicle theft. (See Figure 2.4.) The attention persists despite the shrewd observation of criminologist Marcus Felson in his interesting and provocative book *Crime in Everyday Life* that

> Most of the . . . homicides in the United States in 1990 would not interest Sherlock Holmes: Only 312 were by strangulation, 36 by drowning, 14 by explosives, and 11 by poison. Only 65 of these homicides were killings of law enforcement officers: only one-third of 1%. . . . Only 2% of the 1990 homicides involved romantic triangles, and only 6.5% involved narcotics felons. And not all of these offenses are very interesting.[42]

Professor Felson, to be fair, does not "deny the significance of these deaths, but [the numbers] [do] point out that interesting homicides are such a small share of total homicides and an even tinier share of major crimes." Violent crime is obviously a serious matter, despite its low rates relative to serious property offenses, because violent crime can cause emotional and physical injury, even death.[43]

Crimes Against Homes and Other Structures

Intrusions into homes in the form of burglary and destruction by arson were regarded as serious crimes in the sixteenth century, and they retain special significance today beyond their purely property nature. Both burglary and arson threaten the security that we associate with the ancient idea that a person's home is a "castle," the last haven of refuge against a hostile world. Few question that the image of a burglar entering private homes, particularly at night, raises fears that stretch far beyond property loss. Since the sixteenth century, even the government must have special authority—search warrants—to enter homes. (See Chapter 6.) The "pure" property crimes, mainly stealing other people's property, far outnumber crimes against the state, persons, and homes combined.

Property Crimes

Property crimes make up the largest portion of the index of serious crimes. Larceny-theft makes up more than half of the

Figure 2.3

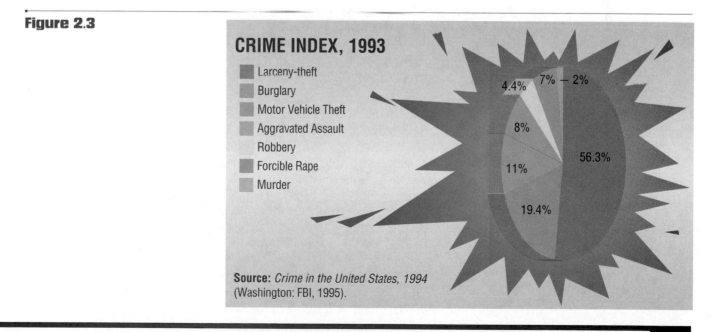

CRIME INDEX, 1993

- Larceny-theft
- Burglary
- Motor Vehicle Theft
- Aggravated Assault
- Robbery
- Forcible Rape
- Murder

4.4%   7% — 2%

8%

56.3%

11%

19.4%

Source: *Crime in the United States, 1994* (Washington: FBI, 1995).

Figure 2.4

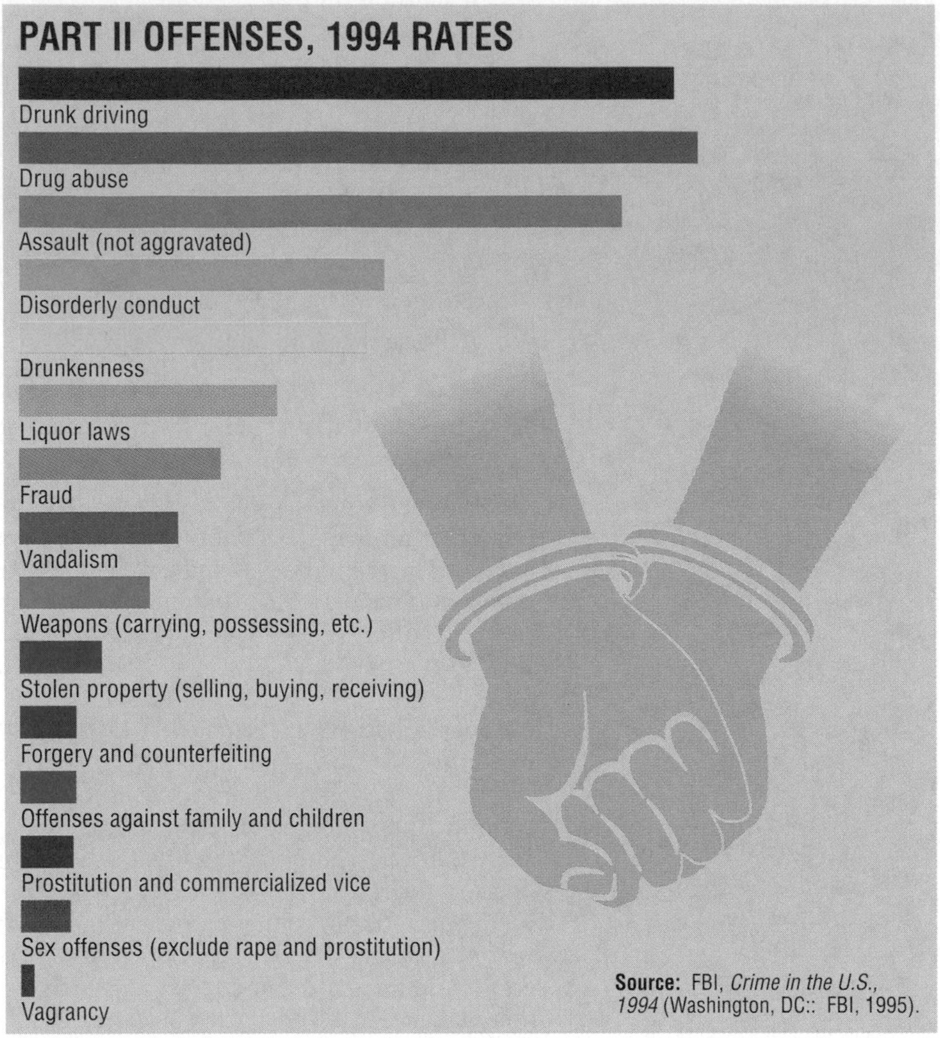

PART II OFFENSES, 1994 RATES

Drunk driving

Drug abuse

Assault (not aggravated)

Disorderly conduct

Drunkenness

Liquor laws

Fraud

Vandalism

Weapons (carrying, possessing, etc.)

Stolen property (selling, buying, receiving)

Forgery and counterfeiting

Offenses against family and children

Prostitution and commercialized vice

Sex offenses (exclude rape and prostitution)

Vagrancy

Source: FBI, *Crime in the U.S., 1994* (Washington, DC:: FBI, 1995).

property crime index. The FBI counts burglary, arson, and robbery as property crimes. Burglary and arson may generate, in victims and potential victims, more than simply a fear of losing property or having it damaged or destroyed. Robbery surely generates fear in its victims. Nonetheless, the FBI counts them as property crimes because the motivation for committing all three is mainly to get money or property of value. (See Figure 2.3 depicting the combined rate of larceny-theft, burglary, robbery, and motor vehicle theft.)

Other Offenses

The combined index offenses pale in raw numbers when compared to what the FBI calls "Part II offenses," or all other crimes. The combined rate for offenses other than the index crimes is almost ten times greater than the rate for index offenses. For example, in 1994, the combined total of Part I, or Index offenses, was 2,384,244 at a rate of 1,148.4 per 100,000 people; the combined total of Part II, or all other offenses, was 11,865,793 at a rate of 4,566 per 100,000 people. Figure 2.4 shows the Part II offenses at their 1994 rates.

This distribution of crimes—few violent crimes, many more property crimes, and then a vast number of other offenses—has led Marcus Felson to write that all of the major crime data "lead to the conclusion that most crime is very ordinary."[44]

Property offenses far outnumber violent crimes.

Crimes Against Public Decency Public decency offenses include, among others, illicit sexual conduct, gambling, and drug offenses. Critics argue that sinister motives lie behind criminalizing morals offenses. For example, they maintain that drug offenses originate as much in racial and ethnic prejudices as in health and safety concerns. Public drunkenness laws were enforced more vigorously when German and Irish immigrants were not yet accepted into the American mainstream. Opium-related criminal law reflected discrimination against Chinese immigrants. Laws against marijuana were enacted as a means of discriminating against Mexicans. Heroin-related behavior became criminal only when African Americans were noticed using it. Cocaine was widely used without legal consequences throughout the twentieth century. Even now, critics say, politicians and the news media talk as if "crack," "ice," and other inexpensive cocaine derivatives constitute the real "scourge."[45]

Controversy has surrounded morals offenses since at least the early 1900s, when reformers began recommending that such offenses be removed from the criminal law and left to religious institutions, social condemnation, and individual conscience. Opponents to the public morals offenses argue that in modern society, morals and crime are not equivalent. Morals are a private matter and, as the sociologist Gilbert Geis put it, "not the law's business." According to critics, morals offenses are "victimless crimes." For example, they maintain that adults who choose to engage in sex for money with other adults do not hurt anyone. Opponents of victimless crimes also contend that the government cannot enforce morals offenses. People will seek out sexual pleasure, find places to gamble, and learn about drugs to buy, use, manufacture, or grow, no matter what the law says. Futile efforts to enforce criminal laws against prostitution, gambling, and drug abuse waste valuable time and scarce money. In addition, attempting to enforce public morals laws creates an irresistible profit incentive not only for citizens but also for the police.[46]

Supporters maintain that morals offenses *do* have victims. The families of gamblers suffer when gamblers lose money. The customers of prostitutes are exposed to diseases. Drug abusers do not just destroy themselves; they also prey on innocent people. In a larger sense, supporters say, morals offenders victimize the whole society because their own moral decline leads to social disintegration. Morals act as the glue that holds society together. By upholding morals, the criminal law helps preserve society.

Morals offenses pose difficult criminal justice policy questions: questions about how to serve the basic purposes of criminal justice, how to distribute scarce resources, and how to achieve effective law enforcement. Legislatures, police departments, prosecutors' offices, courts, jails, prisons, and other corrections agencies must decide how much time and effort to devote to morals offenses, particularly when major crimes that kill, injure, and otherwise harm people compete for scarce public funds and personnel.

Drug Offenses The debate over the decriminalization of public morals offenses has taken on added urgency with regard to drug offenses. A former prosecutor, now a U.S. district court judge, calls the latest war on illicit drugs "bankrupt." According to him, in his nearly 12 years of dealing with drug law offenses on the bench proved the futility of sentencing drug law offenders, and "seeing our criminal justice system overwhelmed by a social phenomenon" frustrated him. Supporters not only of continued criminalization but also of more aggressive enforcement respond that decriminalization would be an "unqualified national disaster." Conservative pundit and one-time federal drug czar William Bennett predicts that decriminalization would lead to increases in the deaths and suffering of hundreds of thousands of "crack" babies, children, and other innocent people. Supporters of continued criminalization of heroin, cocaine, marijuana, and other drugs point to the increase in alcohol abuse and its social costs following the end of Prohibition in the 1930s.

The drug problem has risen nearly to the top of the public agenda, and few are arguing for decriminalizing. Quite the opposite, as the numbers of drug offenses clearly demonstrate. Legislatures have expanded the definitions of a range of drug-related offenses connected with the use, transport, purchase, and sale of drugs. Police, prosecutors, and judges have joined in the stricter enforcement of these laws. Jails and prisons are crowded with drug offenders.

Accumulating research supports the conclusion that drug abuse, particularly the use of and trafficking in crack cocaine, is not without victims. A major survey sponsored by the National Institute of Justice has shown that the sale and use of crack is hastening an already serious decay of life in the inner cities. The trade in crack has helped the criminal underclass subculture to flourish. The values of this class include:

- Illegal means are better than legal means to earn money.
- Other people's money is for the benefit of the offender.
- Violence is an effective and prestigious means to gain criminal returns and reputation.
- Illicit money should buy luxury items, drugs, and entertainment, not the necessities of life.
- Participants should remain unknown to the police, tax, and other officials.[47]

The expansion of the crack trade and the criminal underclass associated with it diminish the attractiveness of legitimate work for some inner-city observers, particularly young people. Understandably, the opportunity to make a lot more money, acquire prestige, and work many fewer hours than low-paying legitimate jobs can possibly provide has a strong appeal. Never mind the reality that most drug traffickers make little money, run risks of getting hurt or killed, and eventually get caught. The *chance* for success and excitement in the business of illegal drugs lures some people more than the *reality* of a low-paying, dreary job without a future and without security or fringe benefits. Most people who wash dishes or cars do not have paid holidays, vacation time, health care, sick days, or pensions.

The use of and trade in crack and other illegal drugs hurts law-abiding residents in the inner city, the vast majority of whom, it needs emphasizing, neither use nor trade in crack or any other illegal drug. The level of violence increases, making it risky even to go to school or work. Drug abuse also drains public resources that could support other social services. Life in the inner city is difficult enough; the small minority of the criminal underclass makes life even harder.[48]

One widely held belief is that in order to support their drug habits, drug abusers commit other crimes. The empirical research on the link between drugs and crime, however, is mixed. Dana Hunt, senior analyst at Abt Associates in Cambridge, Massachusetts, conducted an ethnographic study (an intensive field observation and interviews to gather data) of prostitutes and drug use. Among heavy drug users, particularly among those who have limited means of support, Hunt found that prostitution is a common practice at some point in the drug user's career. The serious drug abuser is also likely to commit a range of other crimes, including dealing drugs, shoplifting, burglary, and con games. However, drug abuse did not lead directly to prostitution. In most cases, heavy drug users were committing other crimes before they turned to prostitution. In other words, drug use does not lead to initial involvement in consensual crimes, but it plays a role in the continuation of criminality, according to Hunt's research.[49]

Researchers and many policymakers used to assume there was a simple causal connection between drugs and predatory crime. That is, they assumed people committed drug crimes purely for material gain, to support their habits. They included theft, burglary, and robbery in their assumption as long as the primary motive for the commission of those crimes was getting money. According to these researchers, drug use compelled the commission of predatory crimes in order to support the addiction. They concluded that this is especially true of minority men.

Researchers Jan Chaiken and Marcia Chaiken, relying on self-reports of criminality, found that the relationship between drugs and predatory crime is considerably more complex than earlier research indicated. (See the section on self-reports, earlier in this chapter.) Their subjects included schoolchildren, addicts in treatment centers, inmates of jails and prisons, defendants in criminal cases, and some inner-city youth, probationers, and adult street populations. The Chaikens found no simple general relationship between high rates of drug use and high rates of predatory crime:

> There are a few severely addicted people who commit no crimes apart from illegal possession; and there are criminals who commit numerous serious crimes but are not involved in drug use. Moreover, for most people, changes over time of individuals' use or nonuse of drugs are not systematically related to their participation or nonparticipation in criminal activity.[50]

The Chaikens noted two exceptions to these conclusions. First, among high-rate offenders who used heroin, the number of crimes committed was directly related to the degree of drug use. When heroin use was high, so was criminality; when heroin use declined, so did criminality. Second, predatory criminals who used large amounts of many different drugs committed more crimes for longer periods of time than did other drug users.[51]

The Chaikens concluded that most drug users who commit predatory crime do so because of irregular employment or weak attachments to parents. These criminogenic forces are obviously beyond the control of criminal justice. They also concluded that the lack of a strong general relationship between drug use and crime means that even large-scale reductions in drug use would probably not significantly reduce the amount of predatory crime. Despite these findings, they nevertheless reached the cautious conclusion that criminal justice programs that focus on high-rate predatory offenders who use high levels of many different drugs, and programs concentrating on high-rate predatory criminals who use heroin, *may* reduce the amount of predatory crime.[52]

Geography and Demography of Crime

The crime statistics in the preceding sections are misleading because they are aggregated figures. This means they are totals for the entire country, without taking into account geography and demography. In fact, crime is unevenly distributed geographically, and according to age, gender, class, race, ethnicity, and occupation.

Geography of Crime   Crime rates vary from one region of the country to another, from state to state, from city to city, and among metropolitan areas, cities outside metropolitan areas, and rural areas. Figure 2.5 shows the significant variation in violent crime rates among metropolitan areas, cities outside metropolitan areas, and rural areas. Even this does not tell the whole story. We are all familiar with the phrase "high-crime area." Our knowledge of the distribution of crime demonstrates that crime varies even within neighborhoods within cities. Nearly all the increases in homicides in recent decades have taken place in the lowest-income neighborhoods. What this tells us emphatically is that changes in criminal behavior affect areas and groups within areas differently.[53]

Figure 2.5

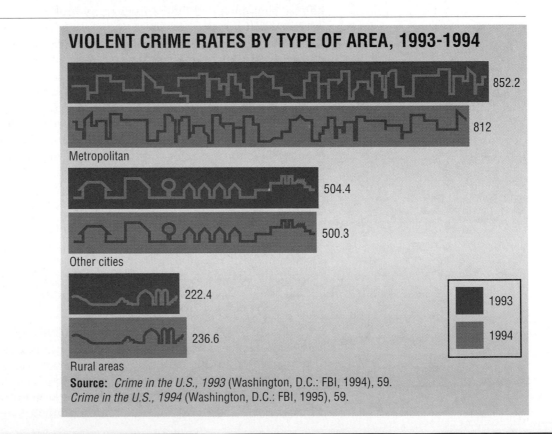

VIOLENT CRIME RATES BY TYPE OF AREA, 1993-1994

852.2

812

Metropolitan

504.4

500.3

Other cities

222.4

236.6

Rural areas

1993

1994

Source: *Crime in the U.S., 1993* (Washington, D.C.: FBI, 1994), 59.
Crime in the U.S., 1994 (Washington, D.C.: FBI, 1995), 59.

Offender-Victim Relationship Crime is also distributed unevenly between strangers and acquaintances. The rate of crime between offenders and victims varies depending on their relationship. Therefore, it is important to distinguish the following types of relationships:

1. Intimates (spouses, ex-spouses, boyfriends, girlfriends).
2. Relatives (parents, children, siblings, grandparents, in-laws, cousins).
3. Acquaintances.
4. Strangers.

Crimes involving intimates, relatives, and acquaintances range across a wide spectrum of behavior, from the violent crimes of murder, rape, robbery, and assaults to petty thefts. Most people fear victimization by strangers when, tragically, the people they know are more likely to kill, rape, assault, and otherwise prey on them.[54]

The Vera Institute of Justice, which analyzed a random sample of New York City court records and interviewed police officers, prosecutors, defense attorneys, and judges,

> found an obvious but often overlooked reality: criminal conduct is often the explosive spillover from ruptured personal relations among neighbors, friends and former spouses. Cases in which the victim and defendant were known to each other constituted 83 percent of rape arrests, 69 percent of assault arrests, 36 percent of robbery arrests, and 39 percent of burglary arrests.[55]

Acquaintance crimes, particularly crimes involving intimates and relatives, are difficult to measure because they usually take place in private and because victims hesitate to report them. For these reasons, crimes within families frequently do not enter the criminal justice system. According to one nationwide survey of crime victims, 48 percent of domestic violence incidents were not brought to police attention, mostly because the victims believed that violence within families is a private matter (49 percent), but also because the victims feared reprisal (12 percent). Even though such acts clearly violate the criminal law, victims rarely report crimes if they know their perpetrators.

According to the FBI's *Crime in the United States,* about 47 percent of the murders known to police were committed by intimates, relatives, and acquaintances. (See Figure 2.6 for a breakdown of these acquaintance homicides.) According to the NCVS, intimates commit over 13 percent of rapes, robberies, or assaults. (See Figure 2.7.) According to Murray A. Strauss and others who interviewed more than 2,000 husbands, wives, children, brothers, and sisters, from 50 to 60 percent of all husbands assault their wives at least once during marriage. Although women are much less likely than men to be victims of violent crimes in general, they are much more likely than men to be victimized by their intimates, that is, their husbands and boyfriends. Women represent 70 percent of intimate homicide victims. Intimate victims represent more than 90 percent of non-fatal violence victims. (See Figure 2.8.)

In addition to violent crimes against intimates, some estimate that, every year, parents physically assault as many as 100,000 to 200,000 children, sexually abuse 60,000 to 100,000, and kill 5,000! Abuse varies according to social class. Stephen Brown used an anonymous questionnaire to survey 110 high school freshmen concerning parental abuse. The survey revealed that lower-class parents more frequently abused their children physically, while middle-class parents more commonly abused their children emotionally, for example, by making them feel guilty. Furthermore, although less frequent than parent-child crimes, crimes between siblings also occur.[56]

Sometimes, children commit crimes against their parents. Most often, it is middle-aged children who commit crimes against their aging parents. In

Figure 2.6

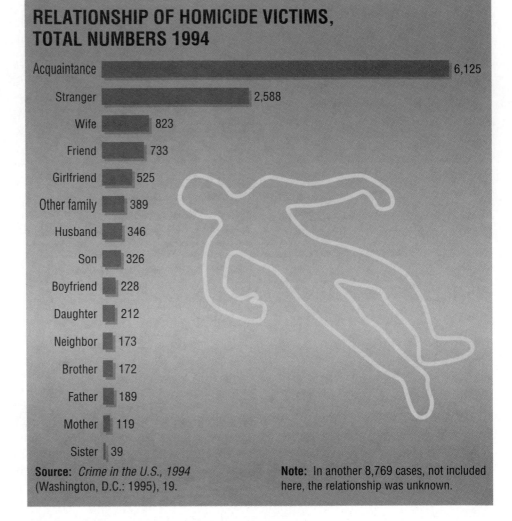

RELATIONSHIP OF HOMICIDE VICTIMS, TOTAL NUMBERS 1994

Acquaintance	6,125
Stranger	2,588
Wife	823
Friend	733
Girlfriend	525
Other family	389
Husband	346
Son	326
Boyfriend	228
Daughter	212
Neighbor	173
Brother	172
Father	189
Mother	119
Sister	39

Source: *Crime in the U.S., 1994* (Washington, D.C.: 1995), 19.

Note: In another 8,769 cases, not included here, the relationship was unknown.

Figure 2.7

RELATIONSHIP OF INTIMATE VICTIMS OF VIOLENT CRIMES

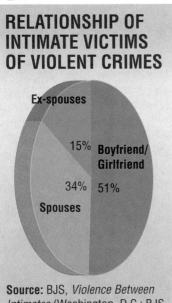

Ex-spouses

15% Boyfriend/Girlfriend

34% 51%

Spouses

Source: BJS, *Violence Between Intimates* (Washington, D.C.: BJS, November 1994).

one case, the state of Oregon charged Sue Gifford, 41, with kidnapping her 83-year-old father, a victim of Alzheimer's disease, from a nursing home and abandoning him at an Idaho racetrack. Oregon also charged her with perjury on a petition for guardianship of her father, and with 20 counts of theft and welfare fraud. The state sought the money for the nursing home that cared for Gifford's father.[57]

Family violence receives most of the attention, but property crimes also occur within families. In a pilot study, Alan J. Lincoln and Murray A. Strauss administered a voluntary and anonymous questionnaire to 450 randomly distributed New England college students. The questionnaire asked about property crimes committed within their families against other family members. Among these college students, property crimes—including forgery, fraud, vandalism, and extortion by one family member against another—had occurred in 73 percent of the families.[58]

Female Criminality Many more men enter the criminal justice system than women do. Figure 2.9 graphically illustrates the wide gap between men and women arrested for violent and property crimes. Early criminologists, criminal justice officials, and public policymakers believed that women committed crimes mainly having to do with sex. In the mid-1950s, for example, one criminologist wrote that girls were beyond the scope of his theory of juvenile delinquency because boys committed a variety of delinquent acts while girls were overwhelmingly sexually delinquent. In the past, criminologists also applied different theories to explain female and male

Figure 2.8

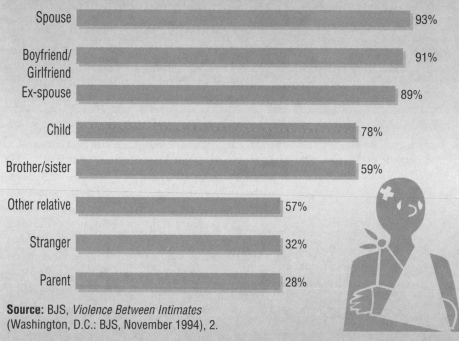

VICTIMS OF NON-FATAL VIOLENT CRIME

Spouse	93%
Boyfriend/ Girlfriend	91%
Ex-spouse	89%
Child	78%
Brother/sister	59%
Other relative	57%
Stranger	32%
Parent	28%

Source: BJS, *Violence Between Intimates*
(Washington, D.C.: BJS, November 1994), 2.

Figure 2.9

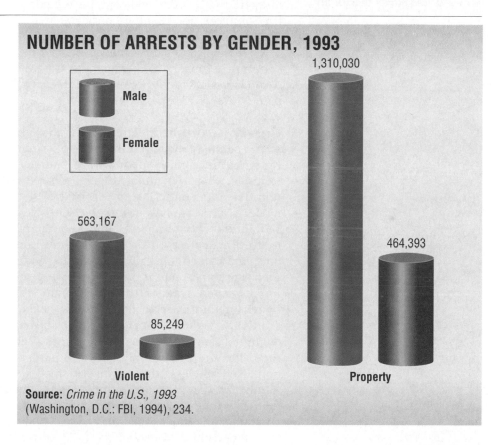

NUMBER OF ARRESTS BY GENDER, 1993

Male
Female

1,310,030

563,167

464,393

85,249

Violent   Property

Source: *Crime in the U.S., 1993*
(Washington, D.C.: FBI, 1994), 234.

criminality. Women committed crimes because of individual pathology; men committed crimes due to social forces.

The government has enforced the criminal law against women mainly for crimes against public order (prostitution) and nonviolent crimes, predominantly shoplifting and petty theft. According to some writers, this practice has changed dramatically. Some attribute the change to the women's movement and increased female emancipation. Freda Adler, in a widely cited book, *Sisters in Crime,* reported that in increasing numbers "women are using guns, knives, and wits to establish themselves as full human beings, as capable of violence and aggression as any man."[59]

Darrell Steffensmeier challenged Adler's "new female crime type" thesis. Surveying the Uniform Crime Reports from 1965 to 1980, Steffensmeier found that female crime had not changed in nature during those years, at least not according to official statistics. Although the police arrested women more frequently in 1980 than in 1965, petty theft almost exclusively accounted for the increase, with a slight increase in forgery, embezzlement, and fraud. Roy Austin also used the Uniform Crime Reports, but divided the period into shorter segments. He found that from 1968 to 1972, women committed more traditionally "female" crimes, as well as more robberies, burglaries, and auto thefts. Austin concluded that these were the years of women's "liberation," using divorce and female employment rates as a measure of liberation.[60]

Self-report data show that women and men commit the same types of crimes, even if they do so at different rates. According to criminologists Stephen E. Brown, Finn-Aage Esbensen, and Gilbert Geis, in summarizing a group of self-report data, "female offending appears to be very similar to male criminality, except that the former occurs at a less frequent rate."[61]

In the aggregate, it may be true that men commit crimes at higher rates than women do. It is surely true that most assessments of female crime depend on the aggregate data in the national reports of crime in the United States. But the picture gets considerably more complex when researchers disaggregate the data by geography, gender, and race. Deborah R. Baskin and Ira Sommers, for example, disaggregated arrests for violent crimes in New York City. They found "tremendous similarity in violent offending between black females and white males." In fact, they found that black women actually committed robbery and aggravated assault at *higher* rates than white men. Also, across all violent crimes, the rates for black women surpassed those for both white and Hispanic women.[62]

Career Criminals

Literature and folklore have long recognized that some people devote their lives to crime and become career criminals. Empirical research supports these literary impressions. We now know, for example, that a criminal underworld existed in London from at least the mid-sixteenth century. Members of this "society" were the predecessors of the modern professional criminal—pickpockets, confidence game offenders, shoplifters, counterfeiters, fences, burglars, arsonists, and hired killers. Career criminals regard themselves as criminals, associate largely with criminals, and make their living by criminal activity. In general, they take pride in their work and respect others who are professional criminals.[63]

A second type of career criminal, the **violent predator,** has drawn increasing attention in the past few years. Unlike the original professional criminals, violent predators do not specialize in one type of crime. They commit a range of serious street crimes—robbery, burglary, theft, assault, and rape. They represent only about 25 percent of the general criminal population. Nevertheless, this relatively small group commits a disproportionate number of street crimes. Chronic repeat offenders (that is, those arrested more than five times for something more serious than traffic offenses) commit 61 percent of all crimes. According to one study, career violent predators committed 61 percent of the homicides, 76 percent of the rapes, 73 percent of the robberies, and 65 percent of the aggravated assaults in Philadelphia.[64]

The Rand Corporation surveyed prison inmates in California, Texas, and Michigan and asked about their criminal careers. Researchers found that violent predators frequently rob and assault other people to get money, by force if necessary. Violent predators also actively pursue such crimes as burglary, theft, credit card forgery, and fraud. The most active 10 percent commit 135 robberies, more than 500 burglaries, 500 thefts, and 4,000 drug deals every year! These findings, and similar studies elsewhere, have generated great interest in career criminals, especially violent predators. Police, prosecutors, judges, and prisons focus on them, and criminal justice policies and practices are being changed as a result.[65]

The Rand researchers found the following characteristics of violent predators:

1. They are under 23 years of age.
2. They have committed serious crimes for more than six years.
3. They begin to commit crimes well before they are 16.
4. They are likely to commit violent and property crimes by the time they are 18.
5. They have spent considerable time in juvenile institutions.
6. They have weak, if any, family ties.
7. They are unemployed or have difficulty keeping jobs.
8. They began to use "hard" drugs as juveniles and they continue to use them.[66]

It is important to note that *identifying* these characteristics does not automatically translate into useful criminal justice policy and practice. The Rand researchers conducted their research in prisons, so their subjects were already identified and convicted. Furthermore, the felons reported information about crimes they had committed but that had not been discovered, information on their juvenile records, and employment and other personal data not readily accessible to either researchers or decision makers. In practice, therefore, criminal justice practitioners cannot obtain such information when they most need it—*before* offenders commit crimes. Obviously, potential offenders are not going to reveal information that might lead to increased surveillance, arrest, prosecution, conviction, and, ultimately, punishment.

Singling out violent predators also raises questions of fairness and constitutional protections afforded all people before conviction. Police investigation and arrest methods may punish individuals before conviction, violating the presumption of innocence. Furthermore, singling out violent predators punishes individuals for their characteristics or character, not their behavior. This violates the law's requirement that guilt must be based on offenders' behavior or actions, not on their status or condition. (See Chapter 3.) Moreover, the evidence suggests that practitioners cannot accurately predict who will commit predatory crimes in the future. This inaccuracy renders unfair the designation of certain people as targets for intense police investigation and arrest efforts, more vigorous prosecution, and harsher penalties. Only a very few young men with long juvenile records, heavy drug habits, irregular employment, and weak family ties are violent predators. Finally, Alfred Blumstein and Jacqueline Cohen, who studied arrest records in Washington, D.C., and Detroit, estimated far fewer average robberies and burglaries than indicated by the Rand study. This and other studies revealing the inconclusive state of our knowledge about career criminals led Michael Gottfredson and Travis Hirschi to conclude that criminal justice practitioners and academics should spend only "a small portion of . . . time and effort" on the career criminal.[67]

On the other hand, some believe that finding violent predators who commit two or three robberies and two burglaries a week and make 10 drug deals a day is worth some infringement on freedom. Police, prosecutors, and judges who devote particular efforts toward young, unemployed, unattached, known offenders with drug problems do inconvenience, even occasionally harass, innocent young people. Nevertheless, supporters maintain, the use of profiles will lead to the early apprehension, prosecution, and conviction of some violent predators and so to a safer society.

historical note

One thing stands out with startling clearness in the picture of the criminal as we know him in the police stations—his youth. . . . During 1934 the New York City police arrested 4,894 persons under sixteen years of age and 3,539 between the ages of sixteen and twenty.

Austin MacCormick, 1935

Research findings regarding the violent predator compel us to ask the public policy question: How many innocent, non-dangerous people in the general population are we willing to subject to intense criminal justice attention in order to identify a few highly dangerous, violent predators? One example of the effort to prevent crime by incarcerating "career criminals" is a statute in the state of Washington. The Washington "sexual predator" law authorizes the state to indefinitely lock up anyone who has committed at least one violent crime, if they have a criminal history of sexual misconduct.

Occupational Crime   In 1939, Edwin H. Sutherland, then president of the American Sociological Association, coined the phrase **"white-collar" crime.** By white-collar crime, Professor Sutherland meant crimes committed by "respectable" people, "or at least respected business and professional men." Sutherland was not the first sociologist to study crimes of the "respectable" classes. The famous French sociologist, Émile Durkheim, in 1902 noticed that the most "blameworthy acts are so often absolved by success" that business people could escape liability for the harms they cause. A few years later, in 1907, the American sociologist Edward A. Ross complained that members of a new criminal class, which he called "criminaloid," used their prominent business positions to exploit consumers but escaped criminal liability because they did not fit the accepted definitions of criminals. Since their motive was profit, not injuring others, neither they nor the public considered their actions to be crimes.[68]

Today, sociologists use the broader term, **occupational crime,** to include not simply white-collar crime, but more generally the use of employment, occupation, or professional position to commit crimes. Crimes committed by middle- and upper-class individuals, professionals, politicians, white-collar and blue-collar workers, corporations and other business enterprises, labor unions, and even government employees who illegally use their positions to secure gain, power, or advantage all fall into this category.

Some occupational crimes are committed for private, personal gain. Others, organization crimes, are committed to enhance illegally the power, prestige, and profits of organizations. A bank clerk who takes money from the bank in order to make payments on an expensive home has taken advantage of employment for purely private gain. Corporate executives who fix prices or mastermind illegal takeovers in order to enhance the power of their companies and raise their profits have committed organization crimes.[69]

Property crimes, what one expert calls "clever theft," are the most publicized occupation-related offenses. According to the criminologist and white-collar expert Marshall Clinard and his colleagues:

> White-collar crime is stealing—but not so plain and not so simple. It is clever theft, like that committed by a pickpocket, but is far more clever—because it operates in a manner which throws a smoke screen over the crime, either to hide the fact that there has been a crime at all, or to delay its discovery, or to insulate the receiver of the loot. And because the stealing is artful, proving criminal intent is usually made difficult by greater confusions than where a common thief is apprehended. The tools of crime are paper, pens, printing presses, advertising, glib talk, and even exploitations of government programs intended to protect the public from deception.[70]

Occupational and organization crimes also cause physical harm. Even if perpetrators do not intend physical harm in unlawfully pursuing profit and power, such crimes can make people ill or injure and even kill them. Traditionally, if the actions of corporations injured or killed people, victims sought redress either in tort actions or through government administrative agencies. On the rare occasions when the government filed criminal complaints, it virtually always charged corporations with misdemeanors, not felonies. As a result, corporations have escaped assault and criminal homicide charges, being cited instead for violating safety and health codes.[71]

It is difficult to prosecute corporate crime, because the criminal law requires identifying specific wrongdoers and proving that they intended to hurt or kill their victims. Identifying individual wrongdoers in complex organizational structures is often impossible. Even if identified, most corporate wrongdoers did not intend to hurt or kill anyone. They sought only personal gain, organizational advantage, or both. In this respect, corporate and other organization crime differs from street and relational crime, in which the principles of criminal law and specific legal definitions of crime clearly apply: identifiable perpetrators definitely intend to cause harm to their victims. In corporate crime, on the other hand, identifying perpetrators, proving criminal acts and criminal intent, and linking them through the causation requirement of the criminal law are frequently impossible. In the few instances where the government has prosecuted and obtained convictions, the punishment of corporations and their executives appeared mild in comparison to the harms suffered.

The following *You Decide*, "Did the Owner 'Kill' and 'Injure' His Employees?" illustrates how difficult it is to get convictions against organizations.

You Decide — Did the Owner "Kill" and "Injure" His Employees?

On 3 September 1991, fire burst out in the Imperial Food Products chicken processing plant in Hamlet, North Carolina, when a ruptured hydraulic line resulted in fluid spraying over a gas-fired chicken fryer. A fireball filled the plant with toxic smoke, killing 25, injuring 56, and leaving 150 others without jobs when the plant closed. The plant, the leading employer in the community, had no fire alarm or sprinkler system, its exits were not marked, and the doors were locked when the fire occurred. Many of the dead were found at the plant exits, stuck in poses of escape. Some bodies were found in a freezer where, the fire chief said, workers had apparently fled to avoid the fire. Employees complained that there were too few exits, and that others were blocked and locked. "They were screaming, 'Let me out!'" said Sam Breeden, who was passing by the plant when fire broke out. "They were banging on the door." Blackened footprints were left on one door, where workers tried to kick their way out to escape the fire. One of the firefighters discovered his own father among the dead.

Charles Jeffres, North Carolina assistant labor commissioner, said the state had never received a complaint about the plant. State officials said a shortage of inspectors and lack of resources had prevented the state from inspecting the plant during the eleven years the company operated. "I'm sure that there are many others [that have not been inspected]," Jeffres said. "The high-hazard plants do have a higher probability of being inspected but even so, we can't get to all of them," he added. The state has fewer than twenty health and safety inspectors, about half

of them in training. Labor Commissioner John Brooks said that was enough for a county, "but hardly supportive" for the state.

The state charged the owner of Imperial Food Products, Inc., Emmett Roe, and two plant managers—John Hair and Brad Roe, Emmett Roe's son—with twenty-five counts of involuntary manslaughter. About a year after the fire, the state dropped the charges against managers John Hair and Brad Roe in exchange for a guilty plea by Emmett Roe. The judge sentenced Emmett Roe to twenty years in prison. Roe had faced a maximum of ten years on each of the twenty-five counts. Under parole guidelines, he could serve less than three years. "I'm confident that the person who's responsible for that locked door policy is in prison," said David Graham, the assistant district attorney.[72]

Questions

Did Emmett Roe intend to burn his employees to death? What exactly did he do wrong? Should he go to prison for it? If so, for how long? Did the managers commit a crime? Did the state officials who failed to inspect the plant? What about the legislators who did not appropriate enough money for inspectors? What about the voters who are responsible for the government? Did the employees assume the risk when they worked in an unsafe plant? How do you decide who is responsible here? Does responsibility mean criminal responsibility? Emmett Roe faces at least 19 lawsuits filed by relatives of the dead workers. Is this more appropriate than a prison term?

Employee theft is the most prevalent blue-collar crime. A survey of employees at 583 supermarkets revealed that 62 percent admitted to stealing cash or property. The average employee admitted to stealing $143 a year. Annual losses due to employee theft at these supermarkets was about $3,500,000. Employees also engaged in more indirect theft. Sixty-two percent admitted to some form of "time theft," such as sick-day abuse; and 87 percent admitted to some form of general counterproductivity, including wasting materials and supplies, arguing with customers, and working under the influence of drugs and alcohol. According to the Food Marketing Institute, "The typical employee thief worked the evening or night shift, was male, aged 16 to 20, reported having significantly more employers during the last year, and endorsed a set of attitudes that tended to rationalize and justify the legitimacy of employee theft."[73]

Richard Hollinger, Karen Slora, and William Terris tested the proposition that employee theft occurs more frequently in occupational settings that rely on "marginal" workers, especially those who are young with little tenure, who believe that their employers treat them unfairly. Hollinger and his associates collected questionnaire data from 341 employees in fast-food corporations. Sixty percent admitted to some theft of company property in the past six months. Over one-third admitted to "altruistic" stealing, such as using employee discounts for friends. Eighty percent engaged in counterproductive activities, such as coming late to work and calling in sick when they were not sick. Hollinger and his associates found that employee theft was principally due to a combination of age (most altruistic thieves were under 21), perceived employer unfairness, and tenure. Counterproductive activities were due mainly to perceived employer unfairness, regardless of age or tenure.[74]

John Clark and Richard Hollinger found that employees steal in a variety of ways. Some "borrow money" from a cash register; others take merchandise home in handbags or briefcases, sell goods to friends for a kickback, or damage products in order to buy them at a discount. Employees who misappropriate their employers' property do not consider themselves criminals, nor do they call their misappropriation stealing.[75]

Crime Trends

The two major crime statistics, the UCR's crime index, and the NCVS's criminal victimization, give different answers to questions about trends in crime. The UCR reports a steady increase in the number and rates of index crimes (Figure 2.10). The NCVS, on the other hand, shows a relatively steady amount of crime reported by victims in its surveys (Figure 2.11). What are we to make of these mixed conclusions? The NCVS measures actual crime more accurately because it measures crimes that victims report as having actually happened; the UCR index measures only crimes that victims or others have reported to the police and which police have officially recorded and sent to the FBI. The rise in UCR index crime rates represents higher reporting and recording rates more than higher actual crime rates. In other words, the amount of crime reported by victims to the Census Bureau interviewers has remained fairly steady, while the number of crimes entering the criminal justice system has increased markedly.[76]

Explanations of Criminal Behavior

For a man, pimping is a good way of making money, but the fastest way is narcotics, and the safest and best way of all is numbers. Even though my whores were making a lot of money, I just didn't like pimping that much. It ain't my style. . . . I missed stickup quite a bit. . . .

Figure 2.10

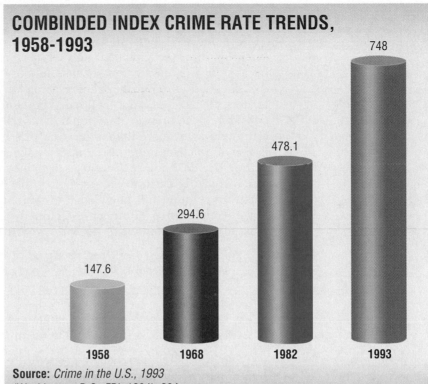

COMBINDED INDEX CRIME RATE TRENDS, 1958-1993

Source: *Crime in the U.S., 1993* (Washington, D.C.: FBI, 1994), 234.

Figure 2.11

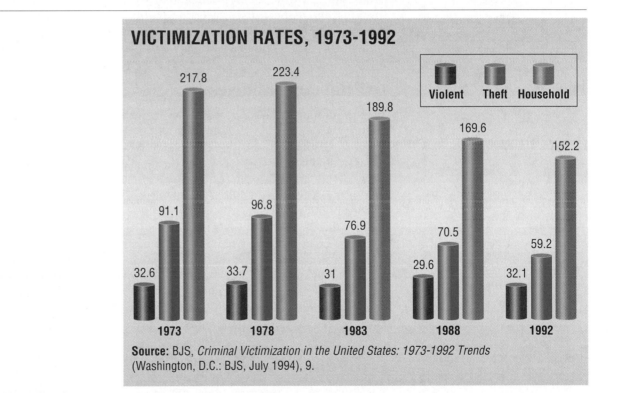

VICTIMIZATION RATES, 1973-1992

Source: BJS, *Criminal Victimization in the United States: 1973-1992 Trends* (Washington, D.C.: BJS, July 1994), 9.

What I really missed was the excitement of sticking up and the planning and getting away with it. . . . [As for numbers] I didn't really get into it, just like I didn't like pimping—there wasn't enough excitement in it. . . . [When I was a drug dealer] I was doing something like a grand worth of heroin a day. . . . I was rolling in drugs and rolling good. I'm well off. I'm dressing nice and keeping a knot in my pocket. I've got a nice ride. I've got me a stable of broads, so I'm cool.[77]

This is the way John Allen, a career robber from a poor neighborhood in Washington, D.C., explained why he preferred robbing to other crimes—not because of the money, but because robbery was more exciting.

The causes of crime have fascinated and puzzled moralists, political leaders, legislators, and policymakers for centuries. Criminologists have considered the origins of criminal behavior fundamental to the discipline of criminology for more than a hundred years, but knowing the causes of crime is also of practical importance. Policymakers cannot control and reduce crime if they do not know what causes it. Unfortunately, criminologists have not discovered the definitive causes of crime; hence, policymakers must make decisions without full knowledge of the consequences. Criminologists have, however, identified a number of factors that correlate with criminal behavior. Most of these explanations fall into two broad categories:

1. Explanations based on the *free choice* of individuals.
2. Explanations based on influences that *determine* behavior.

The deterministic explanations, in turn, fall into two subcategories:

1. Explanations based on individual determinants.
2. Explanations based on societal determinants.

The first explanations for crime were religious. An ancient and long-standing theory held that criminals were possessed by demons, and that their behavior reflected this demonic possession. Some authorities believed the individual chose to admit the demons; others contended that the individual could not control the demonic possession. So, even the early history of thinking about the causes of crime highlights a tension between two philosophical positions much broader than criminology, but relevant to criminal behavior theories—the tension between free will and determinism.

Utilitarian Theories

The demonic possession theory began to lose its credibility during the eighteenth-century "Age of Reason," or Enlightenment, when a new theory arose to displace it. The great English philosopher Jeremy Bentham, with considerable assistance from the ideas of Italian criminologist Cesare Beccaria, developed the utilitarian theory of crime causation. Bentham believed that individuals could choose between criminal and lawful behavior. He further believed in the principle of utility: human beings seek pleasure and avoid pain. They choose crime because the pleasures of crime outweigh the potential pain of getting caught and punished. Although his rational theory made common sense, Bentham did not test his theory with scientific observations. Nevertheless, it had—and still has—an enormous impact on formal criminal law. The assumptions of free will and responsibility lie at the heart of the general principles of criminal law. (See Chapter 3.) Free will also influences a number of current explanations of criminal behavior.

Economic Theories

The theories and research of economists have led to a resurgence of the idea of free will as a central element in the explanation of criminal behavior. Since the late 1960s, several studies by economists have prompted criminologists to study a theory that many criminal justice personnel and the general public have subscribed to since at least the eighteenth century: the theory that people are rational and make decisions according to what they *perceive* is their self-interest. Some economists have taken these basic assumptions and

historical note

We are by no means near the time when any man can fix, with mathematical accuracy, the exact weight and force of each causal factor which pushes or pulls toward antisocial actions.

Charles R. Henderson, 1908

refined them into highly sophisticated "econometric models" represented by complicated equations.

These models, far more comprehensive than anything social scientists had heretofore designed, share several basic propositions, including:

1. Individuals are rational.

2. Individuals are free to choose among a range of alternative courses of action.

3. Individuals are motivated by gain, both monetary and psychic.

4. Individuals will choose the course of conduct that produces the most gain (or, alternatively, results in the least loss).

5. Where illegal conduct produces more gain than legal conduct, illegal conduct will dominate.[78]

The economic being weighs the gains from illegal conduct against the risks of detection, arrest, conviction, and punishment. A rational person motivated by gain, therefore, will not commit a crime if the threat, or at least the *perceived* threat, of criminal justice action is great enough. The deterrent power of this action is not limited to actual punishment; it also includes the possibility of being convicted—presumably without actually suffering imprisonment—being arrested without prosecution, or even being discovered or detected without further action.[79]

Economic theorists do not restrict economic causation theories to property crimes. They claim that their theories have general application. In perhaps the most controversial application, the economist Isaac Ehrlich contends that the propositions outlined above apply to crimes against persons, and even to murder. Professor Ehrlich maintains that despite the

> abhorrent, cruel, and occasionally pathological nature of murder, there is no reason to expect that persons who hate or love others are less responsive to changes in costs and gains associated with activities they may wish to pursue than persons indifferent toward the well-being of others.[80]

If this explanation is true, then it has significant implications for criminal justice policy. Professor Ehrlich addresses one implication by applying economic theory to the deterrent effect of the death penalty. He asserts that for every person executed for committing murder between 1933 and 1967, eight innocent lives may have been saved! If Professor Ehrlich is right, criminal justice policymakers should pay close attention to the economic explanation for criminal behavior and the free will, rationalist, self-interest assumptions underlying it.[81]

The economic theory of criminal behavior can lead to two different approaches to reducing crime. One is to raise the cost of illegal behavior to make crime less "profitable," that is, make more arrests and convictions and levy stiffer punishments. This course has been followed in the past and is most widely recommended today. It also enjoys wide public support, as the perennial promises by politicians to "get tough on criminals" amply demonstrate. The second approach, to increase the gains from lawful behavior, has not enjoyed a great deal of support. It requires significant alterations—some even say unwarranted intrusions—into areas traditionally not matters for public regulation. For example, higher wages and better working conditions might make crime less attractive by making life less frustrating. If higher wages, better job security, and more chances for advancement make washing cars attractive enough, individuals will prefer washing cars—at least temporarily—to stealing them. But government interference to the degree required to bring about such changes are not acceptable in our free-market economy.

Critics have found many faults with the economic theory of crime causation. Their objections cover a broad spectrum. Some have challenged the free will and rationalist assumptions on which the theory rests. Michael

Gottfredson and Travis Hirschi maintain that one of the most serious failings of the economic analysis is that it treats criminal behavior as a job—the "illegitimate equivalent of labor-force participation." They contend that the decision to commit crimes, unlike the decision to go to work, does not have career characteristics such as specialization; it is not a source of lasting income; its pursuit is not compatible with legitimate activities; and criminals do not "respond to fluctuations in risk created by crime-control bureaucrats." Moreover, Gottfredson and Hirschi say that the data on property crime simply do not support the "view of crime derived from economic models of work." As an example, Gottfredson and Hirschi point out that data on burglars refutes the economic theory:

> The model age for burglars is about seventeen, and the rate of burglary declines rapidly with age. The most likely "pecuniary" outcome for a burglar is *no* gain, and his next offense is likely to be something else than burglary. Shoplifting of something he does not need and cannot use is high on the list of probabilities, or an offense likely to terminate his legitimate and illegitimate careers—such as rape, assault, or homicide—for (again) no pecuniary gain is also highly probable. In the unlikely event that he is legitimately employed, his most likely victim will be his employer, an act difficult to reconcile with maximization of long-term utility or the equation of legitimate work with risk avoidance. Because research shows that offenders are versatile, our portrait of the burglar applies equally well to the white-collar offender, the organized-crime offender, the dope dealer, and the assaulter; they are, after all, the *same* people.[82]

According to criminologists Ronald V. Clarke and Marcus Felson, "the economist's image of the self-maximizing decision maker, carefully calculating his or her advantage, did not fit the opportunistic, ill-considered, and even reckless nature of most crime."[83]

Others have criticized the economic model because self-interest is not the only motive for human behavior. According to Amitai Etzioni, "Individuals are simultaneously under the influence of two major sets of factors—their pleasure, and their moral duty. . . ." Robert H. Frank, in a collection of essays entitled *Beyond Self-Interest,* argues that we often ignore our self-interest when we

> trudge through snowstorms to cast our ballots, even when we are certain they will make no difference. We leave tips for waitresses in restaurants in distant cities we will never visit again. We make anonymous contributions to private charities. We often refrain from cheating even when we are sure we would not be caught. We sometimes walk away from profitable transactions whose terms we believe to be "unfair." We battle endless red tape to get a $10 refund on a defective product. And so on.[84]

Others have attacked the highly sophisticated equations that are an essential element in econometric models, claiming that they are too mechanistic, too cold, calculated, and unemotional to reflect what most people are really like. Clarke and Felson maintain that "the formal mathematical modeling of criminal choices by economists often demanded data that was unavailable or could not be pressed into service without making unrealistic assumptions about what they represented." Still other critics find that even if these highly refined equations can accurately explain human behavior, they require much more sophisticated data than their creators have used up to this point. Professor Ehrlich's startlingly specific findings about the deterrent effect of the death penalty on individuals relied on aggregate national statistics of reported murders. His opponents say conclusions assessing the highly complex psychology behind why murderers kill require more than a correlation between fancy equations and crude reported crime rates.[85]

Despite these criticisms, the economic explanation of crime has forced criminologists to rethink basic questions about both the causes of crime and criminal justice policies based on those causes. It has, moreover, probably motivated other social scientists to design their research projects more carefully. Finally, the economic explanation of criminal behavior stemmed the tide of a century of "positivist" research that attacked both rationalist, free-will assumptions and the policies of deterrence and retribution that had dominated social science research and criminal justice rhetoric, if not actual practice, since the eighteenth century.

Rational Choice Perspective

The decision to commit a crime affects all the decisions in criminal justice. The decisions of police, prosecutors, judges, juries, and corrections depend on the decisions of offenders—decisions about which crime to commit, the target of the crime, the method and moment. More knowledge of offender decisions has direct relevance to crime control policies. For example, two major justifications for criminal punishment—deterrence and retribution—depend on whether criminals freely choose to commit their crimes (see Chapter 11).

Drawing on the theory and empirical findings of a number of disciplines, including economics, political science, sociology, criminology, and law, the **rational choice perspective** assumes that criminal behavior is essentially rational, that is, the product of reason. This behavior, though, is only *roughly* rational; the rational choice perspective allows for both irrational and pathological components in criminal behavior.[86]

The interest in decision making and its relevance to criminal justice policy has spurred considerable research on the rational choice perspective to explain criminal behavior. Instead of emphasizing the differences between criminals and "the rest of us," rational choice stresses some of the similarities. The rational choice perspective includes three major elements:

1. A reasoning criminal
2. A crime-specific focus
3. Separate analyses for criminal involvement and criminal events.

The reasoning criminal perspective assumes that people commit crimes for a purpose, and that they make decisions to commit crimes on the basis of information. In the words of two scholars of rational choice, Ronald V. Clarke and Marcus Felson,

> crime is purposive behavior designed to meet the offender's commonplace needs for such things as money, status, sex, and excitement, . . . meeting these needs involves the making of (sometimes quite rudimentary) decisions and choices, constrained as these are by limits of time and ability and the availability of relevant information.[87]

The perspective begins with the assumption that offenders seek to benefit themselves by committing crimes. Obtaining benefits requires rational decision making, however rough and affected by irrationality and pathology that decision making may be. Rational decision making means criminals have specific goals, alternative means of obtaining them, and at least some information for choosing the best alternative to obtain their goals.

In addition, the rational choice perspective adopts a crime-specific focus. The **crime-specific focus** recognizes that decision making differs according to the crime being contemplated and committed. Crime-specific focus requires more refined definitions than do other crime theories. Burglary, for example, requires a different analysis than does robbery, and even burglary and robbery may require further definition. The decision to rob a

criminal involvement *process of choosing initially to get involved, to continue being involved, and to stop being involved, in crime.*
criminal event *refers to the specific crimes that offenders decide to commit.*

convenience store, rob a bank, or "mug" a person on the street each requires its own special process of decision making. The decision to commit a commercial burglary is not the same as the decision to commit a residential burglary. Furthermore, the decisions about where to commit burglaries differ. Empirical research indicates that burglars of people in public housing, in middle-class neighborhoods, and in wealthy enclaves vary considerably in kinds of individuals, motivations, and methods. Similarly, bank robbers differ from street muggers, and car thieves from shoplifters (see Figure 2.12).

Finally, the rational choice approach requires making a distinction between criminal involvement and criminal events. **Criminal involvement** refers to the process of choosing to get involved in crime, continuing to be involved, and stopping one's involvement. The **criminal event** refers to the decision to commit specific crimes. The criminal event depends on a number of factors, including:

- General needs and desires for money, sex, friendship, status, and excitement.
- Previous experience in committing specific crimes.
- Opportunities to commit a specific crime at a particular time and place (see Figure 2.13).

Empirical research into a variety of crimes, including shoplifting, burglary, robbery, and illegal drug use, has demonstrated some support for all three elements in the rational choice perspective—the reasoning criminal, a crime-specific focus, and separate analyses for criminal involvement and crimi-

Figure 2.12

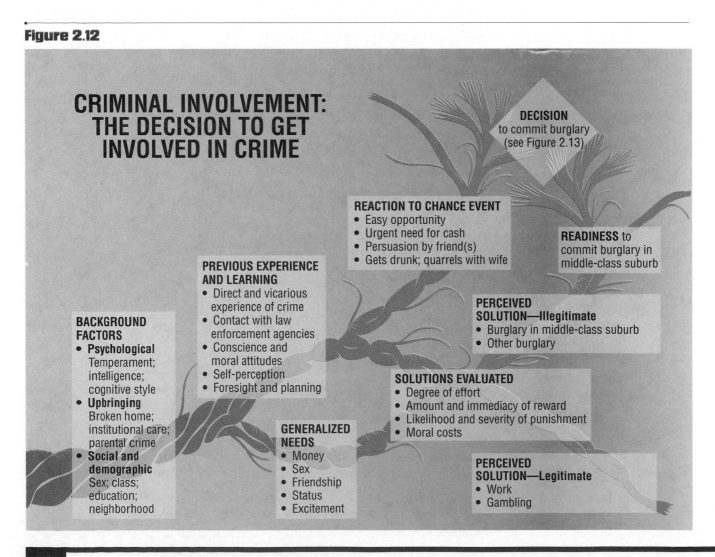

CRIMINAL INVOLVEMENT: THE DECISION TO GET INVOLVED IN CRIME

DECISION to commit burglary (see Figure 2.13)

READINESS to commit burglary in middle-class suburb

REACTION TO CHANCE EVENT
- Easy opportunity
- Urgent need for cash
- Persuasion by friend(s)
- Gets drunk; quarrels with wife

PREVIOUS EXPERIENCE AND LEARNING
- Direct and vicarious experience of crime
- Contact with law enforcement agencies
- Conscience and moral attitudes
- Self-perception
- Foresight and planning

PERCEIVED SOLUTION—Illegitimate
- Burglary in middle-class suburb
- Other burglary

BACKGROUND FACTORS
- **Psychological** Temperament; intelligence; cognitive style
- **Upbringing** Broken home; institutional care; parental crime
- **Social and demographic** Sex; class; education; neighborhood

GENERALIZED NEEDS
- Money
- Sex
- Friendship
- Status
- Excitement

SOLUTIONS EVALUATED
- Degree of effort
- Amount and immediacy of reward
- Likelihood and severity of punishment
- Moral costs

PERCEIVED SOLUTION—Legitimate
- Work
- Gambling

Figure 2.13

THE CRIMINAL EVENT: The Decision to Commit a Specific Burglary

DECISION to commit burglary (see Figure 2.12)

REJECTED MIDDLE-CLASS AREA
• Unfamiliar
• Distant
• Neighborhood watch
• No public transport

SELECTED MIDDLE-CLASS AREA
• Easily accessible
• Few police patrols
• Low-security housing
• Larger gardens

HOME NOT BURGLED
• Nosy neighbors
• Burglar alarm
• No rear access
• Visible from street
• Window locks
• Dog

BURGLED HOME
• No one at home
• Especially affluent
• Detached
• Patio doors
• Bushes and other cover
• Corner site

nal events. The research demonstrates a weak form of rationality. Criminals may not gather all possible information and use it to the greatest benefit, but they do consider risks and payoffs. According to one experienced safecracker:

> Usually, the assessment of economic value precedes the assessment of risk. A safecracker may, while on legitimate business, spot a particularly "easy" safe. He may then assess the probable economic value of the safe's contents. Whether the value is high or low, if the risks are low, he may "make" the safe. On the other hand, if both are high, he may also attempt the job.[88]

Richard T. Wright and Scott H. Decker studied burglars in St. Louis. Their sample of 105 residential burglars demonstrated that burglars have rational motives for committing burglaries. Wright and Decker concluded that both their sample and those of other researchers showed that

> In the overwhelming majority of cases, the decision to commit a residential burglary arises in the face of what offenders perceive to be a pressing need of cash. Previous research consistently has shown this to be so and the results of the present study bear out this point. More than nine out of ten of the offenders in our sample—95 out of 105—reported that they broke into dwellings primarily when they needed money.[89]

Typical of this type of residential burglar was Larry William, who told the interviewers,

> Usually when I get in my car and drive around I'm thinking, I don't have any money, so what is my means for gettin' money? All of a sudden I'll just take a glance and say, "There it is! There's the house." . . . Then I get this feelin', that right moment, I'm movin' then.[90]

Wright and Decker found that burglars in their sample were not motivated "by a desire for money for its own sake." Rather, they wanted the money to "solve an immediate problem." Burglary for them was a "matter of day-to-day survival." According to two burglars in the sample:

> Usually what I'll do is a burglary, maybe two or three if I have to, and then this will help me get over the rough spot until I can get my shit

Professional burglars carefully choose their targets and methods.

straightened out. Once I get it straightened out, I just go with the flow until I hit that rough spot where I need money again. And then I hit it . . . the only time I would go and commit a burglary is if I needed it in that point in time. That would be strictly to pay light bill, gas bill, rent. (Dan Whiting)

You know how to stretch a dollar? I'll stretch it from here to the parking lot. But I can only stretch it so far and then it breaks. Then I say, "Well, I guess I got to go put on my black clothes. Go on out there like a thief in the night." (Ralph Jones)[91]

Of course, the need for cash is not always to meet basic needs such as paying the rent and light bill and buying food. Sometimes it is to "keep the party going." When Wright and Decker asked the burglars in their sample what they spent the money for, almost 75 percent said for "high living." Most commonly, "high living" meant buying drugs. As Janet Wilson, one of the burglars put it, "Long as I got some money, I'm cool. If I ain't got no money and I want to get high, then I go for it." A substantial number of burglars "needed" money for "keeping up appearances" by buying status items, particularly brand-name clothes and high-status cars.[92]

Rational choice applies not only to the decision to *commit* a crime. It also applies to *target selection*, meaning the person to rob or place to burglarize. Although in many cases, burglars do not indulge in high-level reasoning in planning their burglaries, a number of investigators have "shown that target decisions approximate simple common-sense conceptions of rational behavior." Wright and Decker found that among their sample of St. Louis burglars

[A] majority of the offenders typically had a potential residential burglary target already lined up. This involved not merely having a specific dwelling in mind, but also possessing reliable information about such things as the routine of its occupants. In most cases, the target initially had been located during the course of the offender's daily activities and then casually kept under surveillance for a period of time. Sometimes, though, the target was selected because the offender either knew the occupants personally or else had received a tip from someone with inside knowledge of the place.[93]

Rational choice applies, finally, to assessing the risk of getting caught. Some researchers have concluded that burglars think little, if at all, of getting caught when they decide to commit burglary. Neal Shover and David Honaker, for example, interviewed a sample of Tennessee state prisoners who were repeat property offenders nearing the end of their prison terms. Most of the prisoners (62 percent) said they did not consider the risk of getting arrested; the remaining 38 percent said they gave some thought to arrest but easily dismissed the idea and got on with their planned burglaries. The following exchange took place between the interviewer and one of the burglars who never thought about getting caught:

> Q: Did you think about . . . getting caught?
> A: No.
> Q: [H]ow did you manage to put that out of your mind?
> A: [It] never did come into it.
> Q: Never did come into it?
> A: Never did, you know. It didn't bother me.

And the following exchange took place with one of the burglars who considered getting caught but easily dismissed the notion:

> Q: Did you worry much about getting caught? On a scale of one to ten, how would you rank your degree of worry . . . ?
> A: [T]he worry was probably a one. You know what I mean? The worry was probably one. I didn't think about the consequences, you know. I know it's stupidity, but it didn't—that [I] might go to jail, I mean—it crossed my mind but it didn't make much difference.[94]

Shover and Honaker concluded that their study of burglars and various other studies of property offenders demonstrate that "many serious property offenders seem to be remarkably casual in weighing the formal risks of criminal participation." They quote one of their subjects as summing up this conclusion: "you think about going to prison about like you think of dying. . . ."[95]

Kenneth Tunnell also questions the rationality of career property offenders. Tunnell maintains that rational decisions require the weighing of both the *benefits* and the *risks* of committing crimes. Tunnell interviewed 60 repeat property offenders in a Tennessee prison. Their crimes included everything from armed robbery to petty theft. The interviews showed that these offenders considered only the *benefits,* not the *risks,* of committing property crimes. They believed not only that they would not get caught, but also that if they *did* get caught they would receive only short prison sentences. They also believed that prison was not a threatening environment. According to Tunnell,

> the rationality of the respondents' decisions is debatable because they could not have considered realistically the possible outcomes of their actions. They were predisposed to calculate erroneously because they assessed the degree of punishment unrealistically.[96]

Julie Horney and Ineke Haen Marshall, on the other hand, found that property offenders do consider and accurately perceive the risk of getting caught and punished for committing a wide range of crimes. They interviewed more than 1,000 convicted men sentenced to the Nebraska Department of Corrections. They asked them what they perceived to be the chances of getting arrested for a range of property crimes. Horney and Marshall found that experienced criminals have an accurate perception of the risk of getting punished for most crimes. They have learned through experience that "what actually happens when rules are violated is often nothing." They take this into account in their decision to commit crimes. This weighing of the chances of getting caught supports the rational choice perspective.[97]

A sample of Washington, D.C., drug dealers may add further support to rational choice theory. Rand Corporation researchers selected a sample of persons charged with drug offenses in the District of Columbia between 1985 and 1987. They found that drug dealing was profitable, if not at the level that makes great fortunes. It does, however, pay a lot more than the legitimate work available to most urban youths with poor education and job skills. The Rand researchers estimated that drug dealers make an average of $30 an hour, including free drugs. The risks, of course, are also high. Drug dealers face an annual risk of a little more than 1 in 100 chance of getting killed, a 7 percent chance of serious injury, and a 22 percent chance of going to prison. The real risks of death, injury, and imprisonment did not deter these Washington, D.C., residents from dealing drugs.[98]

This choice in favor of the profits from dealing drugs, against the known risks of death, injury, and imprisonment, may support rational choice theory, but it presents major problems for law enforcement agencies. "Drug selling is an important career choice and a major economic activity for many black males living in poverty," according to the Rand study. Improving employment prospects would probably do little to reduce drug selling, because many dealers have developed expensive drug habits. Raising legitimate wages by 50 percent, to about $10.50 an hour, is unrealistic in view of the low education and job skill level of most dealers. Besides, even $10.50 an hour falls far short of the $30 an hour they can make dealing drugs. According to researchers, society must teach young people to avoid the lure of short-term gains. The realities of frequent imprisonment and expensive drug dependency are not worth it.[99]

The benefits of committing crimes include a range of gains, not all of them related to money. Floyd Feeney examined the reasons why robbers committed crimes. He found that robbers decided to rob for various motivations (see Table 2.4).

Definite goals are a critical element of rational decision making. Another critical element is the availability of alternatives to crime to achieve goals. Kenneth Tunnell, in his interviews with career robbery and burglary prison inmates referred to earlier, found that these offenders did not perceive any real alternative to committing crimes. Forty-two out of 60 believed they had no alternatives to committing robbery or burglary. Approximately equal numbers of the remaining inmates said that to avoid robbery and burglary, they had tried another crime, tried to borrow money, tried to find a job, or rejected the work ethic.[100]

Rationality, of course, does not apply to all crimes, nor in equal measure. Crimes of passion do occur, and some criminals are psychotic or suffering from biological defects affecting behavior. Furthermore, rationality seems more prominent in experienced criminals than in amateurs. Finally, criminals committing the same type of crime act with varying degrees of rationality. Contrast the following statements by robbers to Floyd Feeney as to why they committed a particular robbery:

[Robber 1:] There wasn't no food in the house, you know. Scrounging. And I'm forced into having to do something like this. I know I was desperate. Besides, I was going out stealing anything I could get a hold of, get a little money to get some food.

Table 2.5
Motivation for
Committing Robbery

Motivation	Percent
Money	(57)
For drugs	17
For food and shelter	8
For other specific items	16
General desire for money	16
Other than Money	(24)
Excitement	6
Anger	6
Impress friends	6
Not sure; drunk or on drugs	6
Not Really a Robber	(19)
Recover money owed	5
Interrupted burglary	4
Fight turned into a robbery	4
Partner started robbery	6

foreground forces in crime
immediate motivations that lie behind the decision to commit crimes.

[Robber 2:] I have no idea why I did this. Well, guess it was for some money, but I didn't have no problem, really, then. You know, everybody got a little money problem, but not big enough to go and rob somebody. I just can't get off into it. I don't really know why I did it.[101]

Empirical studies also support the crime-specific element of the rational choice perspective. For example, while commercial burglars and robbers both planned their crimes, robbers were more determined to carry out their crime, and many more robbers were drunk or under the influence of some other drug at the time of the crime. Support for the crime-specific focus also appears within crime categories. Commercial robberies are more often planned than street muggings. Finally, the research supports the importance of distinguishing between involvement in crime generally and the decision to commit a specific offense.[102]

The rational choice perspective creates some methodological problems. To understand the choices criminals make requires getting information from "real" criminals. Most real criminals likely to be interviewed are in prisons and jails, and so are not necessarily a representative sample. For instance, they may not tell the truth because of the implications on either the conditions or length of their imprisonment. Perhaps even more important, incarcerated offenders tend to be older, serious, and persistent criminals, which slants the data toward experience and planning. Attempting to interview ex-offenders or those not incarcerated adds the difficulty of identifying and contacting individuals. Gathering information about criminals also raises the issue of privacy. Finally, as with all interviews, researchers face the problem of accuracy.[103]

The "Seduction" of Crime

Like the rational choice researchers, Jack Katz, in his intriguing *Seductions of Crime,* concentrates on the decision to commit crimes. Katz explores what he calls the **foreground forces in crime,** "the positive, often wonderful attractions within the lived experience of criminality." This foreground perspective elaborates on the rational choice theory by delving into the motivations for committing crimes. The foreground perspective allows for crime's economic motives, but as does the reasoning criminal, Katz explores other motivations, particularly the thrill of committing crimes. Finally, the foreground perspective does not reject the background forces of traditional sociological theory. It is an effort to add to them as explanations of criminal behavior.

Traditional criminologists have neglected these foreground forces, Katz laments, in favor of the **background forces** elaborated in sociological theories of crime:

> The social science literature contains only scattered evidence of what it means, feels, sounds, tastes, or looks like to commit a particular crime. Readers of research on homicide and assault do not hear the slaps and curses, see the pushes and shoves, or feel the humiliation and rage that may build toward the attack, sometimes persisting after the victim's death. How adolescents manage to make shoplifting or vandalism of cheap and commonplace things a thrilling experience has not been intriguing to many students of delinquency. Researchers of adolescent gangs have never grasped why their subjects so often stubbornly refuse to accept the outsider's insistence that they wear the "gang" label. The description of "cold-blooded senseless murder" has been left to writers outside the social sciences. Neither academic methods nor academic theories seem to be able to grasp why such killers may have been courteous to their victims just moments before the killing, why they often wait until they have dominated victims in sealed-off environments before coldly executing them, or how it makes sense to kill them when only petty cash is at stake. Sociological and psychological studies of robbery rarely focus on the distinctive attractions of robbery, even though research has now clearly documented that alternative forms of criminality are available and familiar to many career robbers. In sum, only rarely have sociologists taken up the challenge of explaining the qualities of deviant experience.[104]

The "thrill" of crime is a form of seduction for some people.

Katz maintains that the study of foreground forces may clear up some major deficiencies in existing theories of criminal behavior. Many, perhaps most, brain-damaged and psychotic people do not commit crimes. Many, probably most, who have suffered from the criminogenic forces created by the social structure and social processes of modern America do not commit crimes. At the same time, many who commit crimes have no physiological or psychic defects. Many criminals have escaped the criminogenic forces identified by theories of social structure, process, and control. Finally, many who fit the causal profiles of the biological, psychoanalytic, and sociological theories "go for long stretches without committing the crime to which theory directs them." "Why," asks Katz, "are some people who were not determined to commit a crime one moment determined to do so the next?"[105]

The answer to his question, Katz maintains, lies in the "seduction," the "thrill" of crime. Katz maintains that the foreground perspective explains not only crimes such as stickups or robbery, but also cold-blooded and passionate murder, theft, and probably most other crimes. The foreground approach requires finding out what, at the moment the person committed the crime, was the distinctive restraint or seductive appeal that the criminal's social, biological, and psychological background cannot explain.

According to Katz, at the moment of crime the criminal feels seduced, drawn to, compelled to commit the crime. Such feelings are not morally special—everyone feels them. What is unique is the seduction to commit a crime. Furthermore, feeling compelled does not mean that the crime was beyond the person's control; it was still a choice. At the moment of the crime, says Katz, there is a transition from subjective choice to act to objective, determined seduction or compulsion, but the criminal controls the transition.

Situation Theories

Situation theories of crime reject, or at least minimize, the motivation of offenders as an explanation for criminal behavior. Situation theories have their intellectual roots not in the eighteenth-century Enlightenment, but in the twentieth-century human ecology perspective that focused on plotting the distribution of crime geographically among neighborhoods and temporally according to time of day, day of the week, and month of the year. **Situation theories** study the "location of targets and the movement of offenders and victims in time and space." Central to situation explanations of crime are opportunity and temptation. Situation theories assume that offenders are goal oriented, but their decisions are "not calculated to maximize success, but rather to meet their needs with a minimum of effort." This explanation assumes that most criminals, like most other people, are "middling in morality, in self-control, in careful effort, in pursuing advantage." Therefore, criminal behavior depends on the situation—specifically, on time and space, opportunity, and temptation. Situation explanations look at the *modus operandi* of offenders "not merely as interesting material for undergraduate classes, but rather as central information for professional criminologists."[106]

In 1979, Lawrence E. Cohen and Marcus Felson introduced one of the best known of the situation explanations of crime, the **routine activities theory.** Routine activity theory focuses on the importance of time and space in the explanation of criminal behavior. According to Cohen and Felson,

> No matter at what level data were measured or analyzed, that approach kept returning . . . to specific points in time and space . . . and to changes from moment to moment and hour to hour in where people are, what they are doing, and what happens to them as a result.[107]

While routine activity theory brings time and space into the foreground, it pushes into the background both the individual motivation of criminals and the agencies of criminal justice. Whether money, power, status, sex, or thrills motivate offenders to commit crimes is not the significant inquiry; any motivation will do. According to Cohen and Felson, people are

> treated virtually as objects and their motivations scrupulously avoided as a topic of discussion, in stark contrast to the heavy motivational emphasis of virtually all contemporary criminology at that time. . . . Thus, at the outset the approach distinguished clearly between criminal inclinations and criminal events and made that distinction a centerpiece rather than a footnote.[108]

All that is needed to explain crime, according to Cohen and Felson, is the convergence of three elements:

1. A motivated offender (never mind what that motivation is).
2. A suitable target.
3. The absence of a capable guardian.

A likely offender is "anybody who for any reason might commit a crime." A suitable target of crime is "any person or object likely to be taken or attacked by the offender." In a sense, this means anyone or any property in the right place at the right time. The capable guardian is not usually a police officer or a security guard. Cohen and Felson offer this explanation for omitting the police as capable guardians:

> This was the result of a conscious effort to distance routine activity theory from the rest of criminology, which is far too wedded to the criminal justice system as central to crime explanation. . . . [W]idespread media linkage of the police and courts to crime . . . [is incorrect]. [I]n fact most crime involves neither agency. Indeed, the most likely persons to prevent a crime are not policemen (who seldom are around to discover crimes in the act) but rather friends, relatives, bystanders, or the owner of the property targeted.[109]

Biological Theories

As discussed earlier, the theory of the rational criminal who has the capacity to decide whether to commit crimes grew out of the eighteenth-century Enlightenment and its emphasis on free will and rationalism. Situation theories stemmed from human ecology theories of the first half of the twentieth century. Biological theories of crime arose out of the nineteenth-century reaction to calling reason and free will the basis of human behavior. According to these theories, forces outside the control of individuals determine how people behave, hence the term **determinist theories of crime.** Criminals are born, not made, according to biological theories. Crime originates in the genes of criminals, not in their free choice.

Cesare Lombroso, a famous Italian psychiatrist turned criminologist, designed a crime causation theory based on skull shapes. As a young doctor at an asylum in Pavia, he performed an autopsy on an Italian version of Jack the Ripper. In the course of his examination, he detected an abnormality in the dead man's skull. Lombroso describes his discovery, which formed the core of what would later be called his "criminal anthropology":

> At the sight of that skull, I seemed to see all at once, standing out clearly illumined as in a vast plain under a flaming sky, the problem of the nature of the criminal, who reproduces in civilised times characteristics, not only of primitive savages, but of still lower types as far back as the carnivora.[110]

According to Lombroso, criminals have little or no control over their actions. They are atavistic, or "throwbacks" to lower-order creatures. Lombroso also believed it possible to measure criminality scientifically by the physical characteristics, particularly skull and body shapes, of known criminals. Although criminologists have discarded these crude associations as an explanation of crime, and despite great controversy, efforts continue to establish an association between body types and delinquent behavior.[111]

Perhaps the most sensationalized modern physiological theory of crime causation is that violent behavior is linked to abnormal chromosomes. Until 1960, it was widely accepted that males have two sex-linked chromosomes, one X and one Y. Using sophisticated methods, biologists discovered that some men have two or sometimes even three Y chromosomes. Then, in 1965, Scottish researchers reported an astonishing correlation. A high proportion of tall, violent, male mental patients had an extra Y chromosome! In a subsequent wave of studies in mental hospitals and prisons, researchers attempted to discover whether violence could be traced to these newly identified "supermales" with "chromosomes of criminality."[112]

This plethora of studies yielded mixed results. Some research corroborated the chromosome-violence link; other studies contradicted it. A Danish study indicated that large men with extra Y chromosomes showed no special proclivity toward violence. However, it did show that in a large group of Danish men (more than 30,000), those with extra Y chromosomes committed more crimes than did men with normal chromosome configurations. Such findings, however, do not prove that abnormal chromosomes cause violent behavior; correlation is not causation. Causation means that one thing produces a result; in this case, that the XYY chromosome produces violent behavior. Correlation means only that two things are associated. An association of YY or YYY chromosomes with violence does not prove that YY or YYY chromosomes cause violence. Furthermore, important noninherited variables not measured in the study might also be associated with crime. The configuration of chromosomes may be only one, and not necessarily an important, explanation of criminal behavior. Other significant variables might include anything from nutrition to neighborhoods and family relationships.[113]

Twin studies are less dramatic than the XYY-chromosome theory, but they illustrate another attempt to link biology to crime. In one well-known study, Karl Otto Christiansen investigated all twins born in a particular part of Denmark between 1881 and 1910. He found that if one fraternal twin was a criminal, there was approximately a 12 percent chance that the other twin would be one, too. In identical twins, the chance jumps to about 35 percent. Although these links are weak, the study establishes a definite correlation between twins and the incidence of criminal behavior.[114]

Modern discoveries in brain research have also led to biological theories that link violent behavior to brain dysfunction. Research has placed the centers for rage and aggression in the limbic system. Theorists postulate that chemical imbalance in the limbic system, or damage to the limbic tissue itself—it is not clear which—results in violent behavior. According to the findings of brain researchers, many individuals who act violently have brain diseases that can be described, diagnosed, treated, and controlled—which is to say that violence is related to brain malfunction. Researchers also maintain that individuals who lose control of their anger, repeatedly attacking or injuring others and themselves, want and need medical help but are not getting it. In one study of 150 such people seen for treatment, nearly half had been driven to attempted suicide by their despair at what they had done. All of them felt anguish from the social and personal consequences of their acts; all had gone to doctors many times before for advice and aid. Most physicians are not aware of how often a brain abnormality may underlie violent behavior, and they are not accustomed to considering violence a medical problem. Consequently, they reject violent people as patients, dismissing them as incurable sociopaths or psychopaths when, say brain researchers, they should instead be looking for evidence of brain dysfunction.[115]

Despite the research of neurologists, psychiatrists, and biologists, criminologists are extremely wary of biological theories of crime. Physiological theories discount sociological variables that might explain criminal behavior. Furthermore, physiological research does not explain—or even report on—the people in the population who have such dysfunctions but are not violent or do not commit crimes.

Some criminologists are now engaged in research that they hope can discover and establish links between biology and crime. The results of this research have led to a variety of interesting but inconclusive links:

Biological Theories

- Jail inmates who consumed high levels of caffeine and sugar engaged in more antisocial conduct than those in a control group who did not consume these high levels.[116]
- Hypoglycemia (low blood sugar levels) may contribute to violent behavior.[117]
- Abnormal quantities of copper, zinc, chromium, and manganese have been found in violent offenders.[118]
- Minimal brain dysfunctions due to as yet unestablished causes appear in some people subject to explosive rage.[119]

Premenstrual syndrome (PMS), caused by a deficiency of the hormone progesterone, has drawn attention in the past five years as a possible cause of women's criminal behavior. One case involved Sandie Craddock, a 29-year-old London barmaid, who attacked and killed a co-worker. "While she was in prison awaiting trial," her physician recalls, "she was a good prisoner for twenty-eight days each month, and on the twenty-ninth day she would engage in what the prison psychiatrist called 'attention-getting behavior.' She tried to slash her wrists, she tried to strangle herself, she tried to set herself on fire." Craddock had an extensive arrest record that corresponded to a twenty-nine-day cycle.[120]

In women who are physiologically normal, progesterone imbalance does not cause severe distress. However, for those (like Sandie Craddock) who suffer other chemical imbalances, the problem can be severe, particularly if an endorphin imbalance in the brain results. Endorphins, the "natural tranquilizers," affect the function of the pituitary gland, which in turn influences mood, behavior, and premenstrual dysfunctions such as fluid retention and digestive problems. An endorphin imbalance can produce severe and dangerous mental disturbances—such as suicidal and murderous impulses, the two most relevant to criminal justice.

The prestigious National Research Council, research arm of the National Academy of Sciences, has given new credibility to the biological origins of crime. Its report, published as *Understanding and Preventing Violence,* was compiled by 19 prominent scholars and scientists from a range of disciplines. The report calls for the consideration of biological and genetic factors, as well as the criminogenic forces in society, in the search for the causes of violence. A detailed survey of the present state of knowledge in sociology, psychology, psychiatry, law, genetics, and biology, the report recognizes the complexity of the causes of crime. According to the report, "research strongly suggests that violence arises from interactions among individuals' psychosocial development, their neurological and hormonal differences, and social processes. Consequently, we have no basis for considering any of these 'levels of explanation' any more fundamental than the others."[121]

Mark Moore, professor of criminal justice policy at Harvard University, offered this bleak assessment of the report: "You come to the important point of view that the causes of violence are complex and therefore elusive. The hope that we might be able to base policy on definite knowledge of the causes of violence is receding." The report, like all biological theories of crime, also faces criticism by some that it reflects racism. Just a month before the council announced its report, the federal government, under pressure from protesters, withdrew financial support for a conference on the possible genetic causes of crime.[122]

Psychoanalytic Theories

Psychoanalytic psychology as another theory of criminal behavior arose out of the nineteenth-century determinist intellectual tradition. Under the influence of Freud, psychoanalytic psychology became a significant force in the 1920s. It reached its high point during the 1950s and 1960s, after which it came under increasing attack from people who saw the theory as an excuse for brutalizing and reducing the dignity of individuals. During the 1980s, critics from all over the political spectrum joined in the assault on psychoanalytic psychology. Conservative critics saw the theory as responsible for a soft and permissive attitude toward crime, providing an unacceptable excuse for antisocial behavior.

Freud himself rarely addressed the topic of crime, but his followers believed that the following elements of psychoanalytic theory can be applied to criminal behavior:

1. The notion that aggression and sex are powerful drives that must be expressed.
2. The idea that the unconscious plays at least as important a role as the conscious in governing behavior.
3. The linchpin of the theory, the concept of psychic determinism—that all human behavior is determined, not chosen, by the unconscious forces of sex and aggression.

If individuals do not develop "healthy" ways to express sex and aggression, an "illness," known as neurosis (less serious) or psychosis (serious), results. These illnesses can lead to aberrant violent and sexual behavior, much of which violates the criminal law. Aberrant behaviors arise due to faulty early childhood development. According to Freudians, the most important formation period occurs in very early childhood, particularly in the first five years. Hence, according to psychoanalytic theory, illness, not "badness," determines (or causes) crime. In its most extreme form, this theory takes the position that "all criminals are sick." One practical consequence of such determinist thinking is that we cannot blame or punish sick people for the behavioral consequences (crimes) of their illness.

Sociological Theories

Renewed interest in the rational choice perspective and the biological origins of crime, and some remaining commitment to psychoanalytic explanations have influenced criminology. However, sociological or background explanations of crime clearly dominate criminological research and writing. Neighborhoods, social status, race, gender, age, education, and values loom much larger than mental illness, brain damage, and chemical imbalance as subjects for research into criminal behavior. The major sociological theories that link crime to conditions in society relate to the connection between crime and

● Social structure.
● Social process.
● Social control.
● Time and space.

All these sociological theories explain crime as the product of social structure and processes, unlike biological and psychoanalytic theories which trace the origins of crime to individual differences. Biosocial theories, however, as their name implies, do take social influences into account.

strain theory *social structure explanation of criminal behavior that focuses on the effects of frustration experienced by those who work hard yet fail to attain the American dream.*

Social Structure Theories Social structure theory links individual criminal behavior to poverty, unemployment, poor education, and other criminogenic forces in the structure of society. According to social structure theorists, crime is located mainly in the lower classes because flaws in the social structure increase the odds that individuals in that part of society will commit crimes. Social structure theories dominated during the 1950s and 1960s, in part because of the reformist ideas prevalent at the time. If crime was a product of poverty, unemployment, and poor education, then the reduction of poverty, higher employment, and better education could remove the "root causes" of crime. Although it is common during the 1990s to refer to these same social factors as related to criminal behavior, the emphasis has shifted to social control theories.

The great nineteenth-century sociologist Émile Durkheim originated the "strain" theory of crime. At the time Durkheim formulated his theory of anomie, the weakening of social norms, France was in a period of transition from monarchy to democracy and from an agricultural rural society to an industrialized nation. A society in transition, said Durkheim, weakens the bonds that ordinarily govern behavior. Social norms also weaken, and Durkheim believed this anomie contributes to criminal behavior.

Strain Theory In 1938, the American sociologist Robert K. Merton, borrowing from Durkheim, announced his own version of anomie in a paper entitled "Social Structure and Anomie." Gilbert Geis, the sociologist, has called Merton's paper "the single most influential formulation in the sociology of deviance, and . . . possibly the most quoted paper in modern sociology." According to Merton, society establishes goals toward which all strive, but at the same time the social structure makes it difficult or impossible for everyone to achieve these goals. In America, according to Merton, the goals are wealth, power, and prestige based on hard work. Strain theory applies to those who work hard yet fail to attain the American dream. The success story in America is that of rags to riches. You may be a Burger King employee today, but if you work hard and stick to it, you will soon manage a Burger King, and eventually start your own chain of fast food restaurants. The trouble is, many people work hard and play by the rules, but obtain neither wealth, nor power, nor prestige. According to Merton, society only praises success. Winning, not fair play, is the goal.[123]

Not everyone who fails to attain the American dream turns to crime, and Merton accounts for this. People respond to strain in five ways, according to Merton—by conforming, ritualizing, retreating, innovating, or rebelling. Conformists continue to follow the rules even if they fail. Ritualists continue to go through the motions of following the rules, but they have given up; they no longer pursue the goals. Conformists and ritualists pose no problem for criminal justice. The others do. Retreatists drop out of society, neither aspiring to the goals nor following the rules. They become transients, homeless, and/or drug addicts. Although they commit few if any crimes against others, they do violate the laws of loitering, public drunkenness, and disorderly conduct. Moreover, they flout the work ethic so central to American values.

Innovators aspire to the legitimate goals of wealth, power, and prestige, but they are willing to use illegitimate means to obtain their goals. Savings-and-loan executives who risked others' savings for their own personal gain, burglars who steal VCRs, and students who cheat on tests all have acceptable goals, but they have chosen improper and illegal ways to reach them. **Strain theory,** as Merton stated it, explains the criminal behavior of innovators mainly at the lower end of the social structure, because the lack of legitimate means to success occurs more often there. Rebels reject both the goals and the means of society. Rebels replace acceptable goals with others. Street gangs, for example, might seek more members as an important goal and use violence and intimidation as the means of getting them.

Some theorists have extended strain theory to organization crime. Relative deprivation, that is, feeling deprived when compared to others around you who are doing better, causes strain for people in organizations who are not as successful as others. They may be doing exceptionally well by the standards of people below them, but they do not look down; they hunger for the position, salary, and prestige of those above them. This "anomie of affluence" leads some to put rules aside in order to reduce their deprivation (lack of success). Hence, the same strain that produces street crime in lower-income individuals leads to organizational crime in the middle and upper income individuals. Their motivations are similar, even though manifestations differ.[124]

Opportunity Theory

In 1960, Richard Cloward and Lloyd Ohlin introduced an expansion of strain theory called **opportunity theory.** Although they agreed with much of strain theory, they maintained that Merton overlooked illegitimate opportunity structure. Just as the availability of legitimate opportunities varies according to location in the social structure, so does access to illegitimate opportunities. Cloward and Ohlin concluded that criminal behavior depends on the criminal opportunities available.[125]

The delinquent youth Stanley, in Clifford Shaw's classic *The Jack-Roller*, describes a community with criminal opportunities:

> Stealing in the neighborhood was a common practice among the children and approved by the parents. Whenever the boys got together they talked about robbing and made more plans for stealing. I hardly knew any boys who did not go robbing. The little fellows went in for petty stealing, breaking into freight cars, and stealing junk. The older guys did big jobs like stick-up, burglary, and stealing autos. The little fellows admired the "big shots" and longed for the day when they could get into the big racket.[126]

Social Process Theories

Social structure theory cannot explain all crime. After all, crime occurs in all social classes, and most people in the lower classes do not commit crimes. Other forces must operate to explain criminal behavior. **Social process theories** examine the experiences of individuals in families, peer groups, schools, and other social institutions responsible for establishing values and behavior. Abundant research establishes an association between the quality of one's experience with these institutions and criminal behavior. For example, most prison inmates come from single-parent homes, have relatives and friends who have served time in prison, are school dropouts or education underachievers, and have poor work skills and employment records (see Chapter 13). Social process theorists agree that criminogenic forces in society affect behavior, but they disagree over how. Social learning theorists maintain that individuals at birth are blank slates and can learn any values and behavior. Social control theorists believe that everybody is born with the desire to break the rules. Social conflict theorists maintain that the rich and powerful define criminal law and administer criminal justice in order to protect their property, safety, and values from less powerful groups in society.

Social Learning Theory

When I was a boy, a neighbor told her son to stay away from that Joel Samaha because, she warned, I would "put bad bugs in his head." The commonsense notion that people learn criminal behavior from others underlies **social learning theory.** This notion in turn depends on the assumption that at birth we are blank slates upon which our parents, friends, teachers, religious leaders, government, and other representatives of social institutions write the attitudes, beliefs, and values that determine our behavior.

Edwin Sutherland, a distinguished criminologist mentioned earlier in this chapter, formulated the most prominent social learning theory—**differential association.** According to Sutherland, criminal behavior—like behavior in general—depends on the associations people have. If an individual has more associations with breaking the law than with obeying it, criminal behavior follows. All associations do not have equal influence. The most frequent and longest-lasting associations, such as with family and friends, are most important, and the most intense associations teach the most enduring lessons about how to behave. People in low-income neighborhoods who associate with "street criminals" learn to act like street criminals, not because people who live in poor neighborhoods are "bad" or by nature different from others, but because that is the way social beings behave. By the same reasoning, corporate criminals learn criminal behavior called white-collar crime.[127]

The following *You Decide,* "Do Abused Children Become Adult Violent Criminals?" examines the cycle-of-violence hypothesis: that a childhood history of physical abuse, neglect, or both predisposes the survivor to later violence.

You Decide — Do Abused Children Become Adult Violent Criminals?

The National Institute of Justice (NIJ) sponsored the most detailed study to date on the relationship between childhood abuse and adult criminal behavior. The study found that childhood abuse increased the odds of future delinquency and adult criminality by 40 percent.

Study design

The study followed 1,575 cases from childhood through young adulthood, comparing two groups:

1. A study group of 908 officially recorded cases of childhood abuse or neglect.
2. A comparison group of 667 not officially recorded as abused or neglected, matched to the study group according to sex, age, race, and approximate socioeconomic status.

The study design used the following definitions:

● *Physical abuse*—injuries including bruises, welts, abrasions, lacerations, wounds, cuts, and bone and skull fractures.
● *Sexual abuse*—assault and battery with the intent to satisfy sexual desires; fondling or touching in an obscene manner; rape; sodomy; and incest.
● *Neglect*—extreme failure to provide adequate food, clothing, shelter, and medical attention.

Juvenile court records and probation records, and arrest data from federal, state, and local law enforcement records provided the information for abuse, neglect, and criminal records.

Study findings

The study findings are as follows:

● *Juvenile record*—Abused or neglected persons faced a higher risk of beginning a life of crime at an earlier

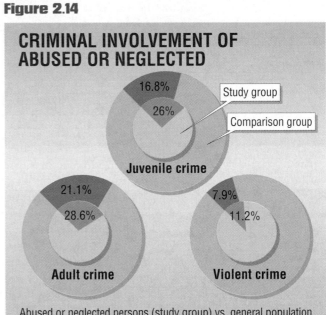

Figure 2.14

CRIMINAL INVOLVEMENT OF ABUSED OR NEGLECTED

16.8% — Study group
26% — Comparison group
Juvenile crime

21.1%
28.6%
Adult crime

7.9%
11.2%
Violent crime

Abused or neglected persons (study group) vs. general population (comparison group) who became involved in crime.

age, with more significant and repeated criminal involvement (see Figure 2.14).

● *Adult record*—Abused and neglected persons were no more likely to continue a life of crime than other children. Both the study and the comparison groups had roughly the same arrests as adults for both violent and nonviolent crimes.

In short, childhood abuse and neglect had no apparent effect on the movement of juvenile offenders toward adult criminal behavior. Distinguishing what promotes the onset of criminal behavior from what promotes its continuation into adulthood is an important topic for future research.

Does only violence beget violence?

By examining violent behavior in relation to physical and sexual abuse, neglect, and a combination of them in the study group, and violent crime in the comparison group, researchers tested the notion that childhood victims of violence resort to violence themselves as they grow up. Physically abused children were more likely to face later arrest for violent crimes than children experiencing other forms of abuse or neglect. However, the neglected group followed close behind. Figure 2.15 illustrates the study results.

According to the NIJ, this finding offers persuasive evidence for the need to take concerted preventive action against child abuse and neglect. Nationwide, the incidence of neglect is almost three times that of physical abuse. Neglect is also potentially more damaging to the development of a child than abuse (provided the abuse involves no neurological impairment). In one study of the influence of early malnutrition on subsequent behavior, previously malnourished children had attention deficits, reduced social skills, and poorer emotional stability than a comparison group. The present study suggests that

Figure 2.15

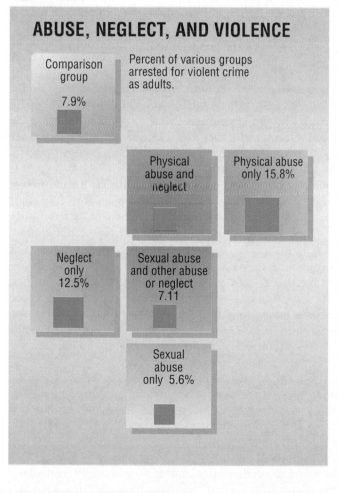

ABUSE, NEGLECT, AND VIOLENCE

Percent of various groups arrested for violent crime as adults.

Comparison group 7.9%

Physical abuse and neglect

Physical abuse only 15.8%

Neglect only 12.5%

Sexual abuse and other abuse or neglect 7.11

Sexual abuse only 5.6%

those differences include a greater risk of later criminal violence.

Policy recommendations

The NIJ recommends the following actions:

1. *Improved identification procedures.* It is imperative to improve the procedures for identifying child abuse and neglect, such as those for police response and follow-up.

2. *Outside-the-home placement.* Placement outside the home—including foster homes, guardianships, and special homes and schools—is one possible buffer for children. Although scholars and practitioners criticize these placements, the NIJ surveyed other research that showed no negative effects from removing abused and neglected children from their homes. The survey of this research, according to the NIJ, challenges the assumption that it is necessarily unwise to remove children from negative family situations. The instability caused by removal, especially if children move from one placement to another, is important but did not lead to a higher likelihood of arrest or violent criminal behavior.

3. *Follow-up and in-person interviews.* The present study demonstrates that abuse and neglect create an increased risk of juvenile delinquency, adult criminal behavior, and violent behavior. However, a large number of abused and neglected children did not have later official arrest records. Furthermore, the majority of abused and neglected children did not become delinquents, adult criminals, or violent offenders.

The NIJ has conducted a follow-up study. The interviews explore recollections of early childhood experiences, schooling, adolescence, undetected alcohol and drug problems, undetected delinquency and criminality, and important life experiences. Preliminary findings of the follow-up suggest that many study subjects experienced:

● Delinquency and criminality.
● Depression and suicide attempts.
● Alcohol and drug problems.
● Unemployment, or employment in low level service jobs.

Questions

1. Do you think the evidence shows that abuse and neglect cause delinquency, adult crime, and violent crime?
2. Does the study prove the sociological theory of differential association in particular and social learning theory in general?
3. What does it have to say about social control theory?
4. On the basis of this study, what policy decisions do you recommend?
5. Would you recommend completion of the follow-up study first?
6. Would you recommend early intervention in neglect and abuse cases?
7. What intervention? Out-of-home placement? Criminal prosecution of the abusers? Counseling? Anything else?

subculture theories *social process explanation that stresses the importance of the values of groups in determining behavior.*

social control theory *social process explanation that assumes people are rule breakers by nature and need controls to inhibit them from committing crimes.*

Subculture Theories The ideas of association and culture combine in the development of **subculture theories.** These theories vary greatly, but two exemplify their basic ideas. Albert Cohen, who studied under both Sutherland and Merton, has applied and expanded their theories to explain juvenile delinquency. In American society, Cohen argues, the same pressures to succeed are placed on "lower-class boys" as on others, but these youths lack adequate legitimate avenues to that success. In association with others in their predicament, the boys band together and make their own rules for success that allow them to win within their own subculture.[128]

Marvin Wolfgang and Franco Ferracuti have identified another subculture, the subculture of violence. As its name implies, this offshoot of Sutherland's and Merton's theories hypothesizes a subculture that glorifies violence. According to Merton, recourse to violence is acceptable to certain groups—particularly Southerners, blacks, and lower-class males—when courage, manhood, or honor are challenged by insults, threats, or weapons.[129]

Corporations produce a subculture of competition in which the goal is success, measured in money, power, and prestige. Although there are broader, countervailing cultural values such as fairness, democracy, and so on, the premium is on success. This leads some members to break the law to achieve success, a decision the subculture tacitly approves, encourages, and—some say—even demands.[130]

Social Control Theory Social structure and social process theories treat crime as a morally neutral concept. Children are clean slates at birth, born without any predisposition to commit crimes. Bad environment both creates the motivation and provides the opportunity to commit crimes. **Social control theory** rejects these ideas. It assumes that people are rule breakers by nature. As Travis Hirschi, the leading proponent of social control theory, put it:

> control theory [is] a theory in which deviation is not problematic. The question "Why did they do it?" is simply not the question the theory is designed to answer. The question is, "Why don't we do it?" There is much evidence that we would, if we dared.[131]

People obey rules because of their ties to established institutions of social control. Families, peer groups, churches, and schools keep in check the natural desire to break rules and satisfy selfish interests. When ties to these institutions weaken, deviation and crime increase. Social bonds do not reduce the motivation to get what you want; they reduce the chance that you will give in to the motivation.[132]

Hirschi identified four elements in the social bond that curb the natural desire to break rules. First, attachment to others makes us sensitive to their opinions. Attachment to those whose opinions we respect, particularly parents, teachers, coaches, neighbors, and peers, according to control theorists, is the best predictor of conformity to rules. The second element in the social bond is commitment to the conventional order. The greater the desire to get a job, take advantage of educational opportunities, and keep a good reputation, the greater the chances of conformity to rules. Involvement, the third element, means that the busier you are with conventional activities, the less time you have to get into trouble. According to the old adage, "idle hands tempt the devil." Finally, the stronger an individual's belief in the conventional order, the less likely he or she is to break the rules.

Hirschi reports the results of testing his theory in *Causes of Delinquency.* Data obtained from police reports, self-reports, and schools for more than 3,000 boys in a California youth project supported Hirschi's version of social control theory. A number of criminologists have come to similar results on the basis of further empirical studies.[133]

Control theory explains both street crime and organization crime. Organizations do not provide controls on deviance. Rules do not apply, especially

labeling theory *explanation of criminal behavior that asserts that the criminal justice system creates criminals by defining people as criminals.*

social conflict theories *explanations of criminal behavior that emphasize the power structure and control of society and its institutions by the rich and powerful.*

historical note

[By bringing] young people who have committed misdemeanors of minor importance into the criminal justice system we are bringing up professional criminals.

William Bonger, 1905

at the very top. The ends justify the means. According to control theory, the rules are obstacles to a greater goal. Hence, organizational criminals are freed from the bonds that lead to compliance with rules.[134]

Labeling Theory In his now classic *Outsiders*, Howard Becker developed the influential **labeling theory.** According to Becker, individuals do not commit crimes because they cannot manage the stresses in society. Nor do they commit crimes because they associate with other criminals and learn crime from them. Rather, transitory deviant episodes are turned into criminal careers because outsiders—moral entrepreneurs—notably police, courts, and corrections officers, attempt to suppress such behavior. In other words, the criminal justice system creates criminals. More broadly, society's response to crime defines some people as criminals and, by so doing, causes crime. Whether these people have broken the criminal law is immaterial. What is critical is that once this formal process has defined them as criminals, they start to act like criminals. Society's actions shape their self-image.[135]

Labeling theory endeavors to shift the emphasis from the behavior of the criminal to the behavior of those who operate the criminal justice system. It focuses on the actions, processes, and structures within criminal justice that cause, or at least contribute to, lawbreaking. Labeling theory has drawn attention to the harmful effects of contacts with criminal justice agencies, particularly the police and corrections officials. The theory had a direct influence on public policy during the 1960s and 1970s in programs that diverted people out of the criminal justice system into alternative social programs (see Chapter 13).[136]

Social Conflict Theories

Another product of the 1960s was a group of **social conflict theories** that rejected the established rational choice, biological, psychoanalytic, and sociological explanations of crime. In Chapter 3, you will explore the social conflict perspective as it applies to criminal law. Here, it is enough to note that social conflict theories place the responsibility for criminal behavior on the power structure and on the control of society and its institutions by the rich and powerful. The rich and powerful define crime to protect their property interests, their safety, and their values. They use the power of government to preserve the status quo. Their influence over the definition of and responses to crime, whether consciously intended or not, has the effect of criminalizing the behavior of the poor, the weak, and the "different." According to social conflict theory, the causes of crime lie not in individual defects or in rational choice, but in the social structure and process that unevenly distributes the power to decide both what is criminal and how to respond to criminal behavior.

Explanations of Criminal Behavior and Criminal Justice Policy

Theories of crime have important implications for criminal justice policy. This is because the response to crime depends upon the explanation of why the criminal behavior occurred. The criminal law, for instance, rejects sociological determinism, resting its principles—and to a very large extent its practices—on eighteenth-century concepts of individualism and free will and their modern counterparts. Also, the legal definitions of crime show a definite bias against crimes committed by the "lower classes." After the adversary process has run its course, sociological theories may play some part in sentencing and in correctional programs, although these biases are not usually articulated.

To some, especially during the 1960s, sociological crime theories suggest that neither formal nor informal criminal justice offers the best response to the crime problem. The best response is to remove the "root" causes of crime, causes deeply embedded in the social structure and processes of modern America. According to this view, the best response of society to crime might be to ameliorate those conditions and processes that cause crime. To some, this means altering the entire social structure of capitalism. Others believe it entails adjusting capitalism to allow for more equal distribution of wealth and opportunity. For others, the best societal response to crime involves changing the values that lead to unacceptably high levels of self-interest and pursuit of individual success. Whatever their particular program, all sociological theories commonly emphasize working to change society, on the grounds that criminogenic conditions in society cause crime.[137]

Unfortunately, society's criminogenic conditions stubbornly resist change. Furthermore, even if we knew how to alter families, peer groups, and other intimate groups, the mere attempt to do so would offend some of our most dearly held values and beliefs about freedom, privacy, and independence. Assuming that all these obstacles could be overcome, the results, although they might be enduring, would be a very long time in coming. Enormous practical hurdles may lie behind sociologists' eagerness to pursue the worthwhile and respectable goal of explaining why crime occurs, rather than to propose specific public policy recommendations to solve the crime problem.[138]

Practically speaking, most criminal justice policies and practices stem from theories based on individual explanations of crime, not on curing criminogenic conditions in society. Those who subscribe to the view that individuals choose to commit crimes believe that the way to reduce crime is to make the punishments for crime painful enough to deter its commission. Biological and psychoanalytic determinists who focus on the physiological and psychiatric defects in individuals maintain that criminals should not be blamed or punished, but treated and "cured"; or if it is impossible to cure them, to provide long-term care.[139]

Crime Victims

In colonial times, crime victims played a central part in criminal justice. They conducted their own investigations, secured warrants, paid witnesses, and hired private attorneys to prosecute their cases. Colonial law allowed victims to collect damages from offenders; it even authorized binding offenders in servitude to victims. Wealthy victims paid the government to incarcerate criminals. In other words, criminal justice was victim-centered and relied heavily on victims in its administration. By the early twentieth century, criminal justice had become society-centered. Punishment was calculated by the harm done to society, not to the individual victim. Victims lost most of their role in criminal justice, and offenders lost most of their responsibility to victims.[140]

In 1993, the NCS reported 43.6 million victimizations among residents in households who were aged 12 or older. Victims sustain physical injury in rapes, robberies, and assaults. They suffer financial losses from stolen, damaged, or destroyed property, lost income, medical expenses, and the cost of protection against crime. Victims' emotional distress ranges from fear and helplessness to anger and the desire for revenge. A husband and wife whose house was burglarized said:

> [Wife:] That made me angry inside, that someone would do that and upset my children. . . . It was somewhat revenge . . . anger toward that person and feeling like they had no business in my home. . . . The more I thought about it . . . the more revenge I felt.

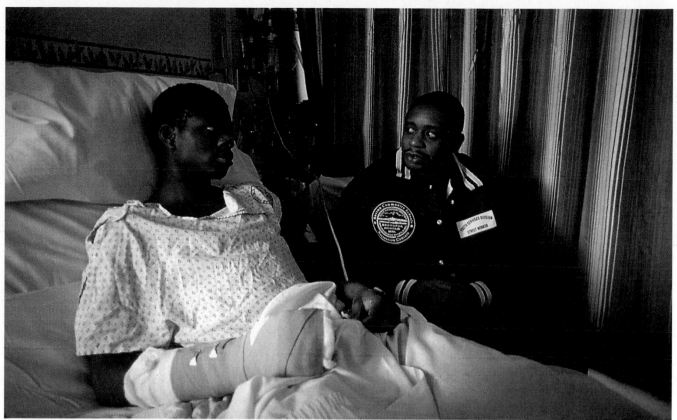
Young African American men are at high risk of criminal victimization.

[Husband:] It's unfair that you work for something, like this lawn mower was nothing of value really, but you work hard for it and somebody takes it away from you when you're about to enjoy it or continue to enjoy it.

Another victim went even further:

Six young men rob a teenager of his gold jewelry while he waits for a subway train. The next night the victim chances upon the offenders at the same station. He comes up to them and simply utters, "Remember me?" Although they don't recognize him and look puzzled he takes out a pistol and shoots three of them before fleeing.[141]

Crime victims may suffer not only from the actions of criminals but also from the reactions of employers. A bank teller found this out when she handed over money to a robber. The robber handed her a note that read, "This is a stickup. Put all the money in a bag and no one will get hurt." She was too panicky to slip in a specially treated bundle of bills that would trigger an electronic beam at the entrance to the bank. The beam would have set off shots of red dye and tear gas at the robber when he tried to escape. The next morning her boss told her either to take a demotion and pay reduction or an unpaid indefinite leave of absence. She quit, saying, "I did what any normal person would do—I gave the man the money. For three years I've been a loyal employee and this is what I get."[142]

Crime victims may also suffer from the interventions of the criminal justice system. Police, prosecutors, and judges, although perhaps unintentionally, can treat victims as if they are at fault. Police officers may ask embarrassing questions. Prosecutors and court personnel do not always keep victims informed about the progress of their cases. Police and prosecutors withhold victims' property as evidence. Victims lose time from work and family to cooperate with police and prosecutors. Often not prepared to testify in court, victims may experience apprehension, fear, and other discomfort. Victims may also fear retaliation from those they testify against.[143]

Types of Victims

Victimization does not fall randomly over the general population. Most people never experience it, or do so only once; a minority experience frequent victimization. Research dispels the common perception that elderly and other vulnerable citizens suffer disproportionately from crime. In fact, for people aged 65 or over, violent crime claims victims five times less often; stolen car crimes, four times less often; and home burglaries, half as often. This, of course, does not mean that the elderly do not suffer from crime. Victimization, and fear of victimization, may well traumatize the elderly more than it does younger victims. This fear erodes the quality of life for elderly citizens, forcing them to stay at home, too fearful to venture outside.[144]

Most street and family crime victims resemble their perpetrators: young, poor, male, urban, and nonwhite. Victimization also strongly correlates with lifestyle. Criminologists have developed theories built around this correlation. The earliest of these theorists faced strong opposition on ideological grounds. During the 1970s, feminists and victims' advocates complained that such theories blamed the victims. Despite opposition, one of these theories, the **lifestyle-exposure theory,** has received considerable acceptance among criminologists.[145]

According to the basic premise of the lifestyle-exposure theory, introduced by Michael S. Hindaling, Michael Gottfredson, and James Garofalo, differences in the lifestyles of victims account for the demographic differences in criminal victimization. Variations in lifestyles are important because they reflect differences in exposure to the places, times, and activities associated with crime. Gender, race, and income relate strongly to personal lifestyles and therefore to crime. According to the theory, crimes will take place disproportionately against young, single, low-income African-American men because this group spends more time outside the home at night, taking part in activities during which crimes often occur. Figure 2.16 shows the different rates of homicide in 1994 committed against nonwhite and white males.[146]

Lawrence W. Sherman, Patrick R. Gartin, and Michael E. Buerger identified the locations where most crimes take place, called **"hot spots,"** by analyzing more than 300,000 emergency calls for one year in Minneapolis. They found that these hot spots produce most calls to police and most calls reporting predatory crimes, such as robberies, rapes, and thefts. Because older people, married couples, and others with steady employment appear infrequently in these hot spots, particularly at night, they less often become victims.[147] (See Chapter 5.)

Victim-proneness occurs in rape, purse snatching, pocket picking, ordinary theft, burglary, and automobile theft; but not in robbery and assault, with one notable exception. Marvin E. Wolfgang, Terence P. Thornberry, and Robert M. Figlio, in a follow-up to a famous self-report survey, asked birth cohorts questions not only about their crimes but also their victimizations between ages 12 to 18, and 18 to 26. The responses showed that a lifestyle within a subculture of crime involves becoming both a predator and a victim in personal, but not property, crimes.[148]

Occupation also has an effect on victimization. More than one million people are the victims of violent crime on the job. Every year, someone steals personal belongings from more than two million workers while they work, and the cars of another 200,000. These victimizations cost an average of about 3.5 days of work per person every year. Among those victimized while working, men are more likely to be the victims of violent crime, but women are just as likely to be the victims of theft. Race is also related to victimization. The National Institute for Occupational Health and Safety (OSHA) has found that the rate of work-related homicides for African-Americans was nearly twice that of white workers during the 1980s.

Figure 2.16

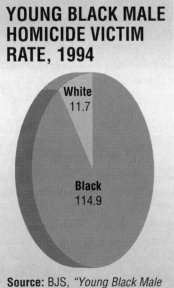

YOUNG BLACK MALE HOMICIDE VICTIM RATE, 1994

White
11.7

Black
114.9

Source: BJS, *"Young Black Male Victims"* (December 1994).

Figure 2.17

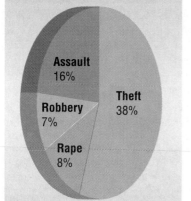

VICTIMIZATION AT WORK, 1987-1992

Assault
16%

Theft
38%

Robbery
7%

Rape
8%

Note: The percent is the percent of the total of these crimes that occur while at work

Source: BJS, *Violence and Theft in the Workplace, 1987-1992* (Washington, D.C.: BJS, July 1994).

African-American taxi drivers and gas station attendants have especially high homicide rates. Experts at OSHA speculate that the reason for the higher rates is that more African Americans work in dangerous neighborhoods than do white Americans. Figure 2.17 depicts a sample of crimes occurring while people work.[149]

Improving the Treatment of Victims

In the past 20 years, interest in victims has reemerged. However, Americans hold ambivalent attitudes toward victimization, as our literature reveals. Some writers focus on victims' helplessness against outside forces. Saul Bellow says that literature "pits any ordinary individual against the external world and the external world conquers him, of course."[150]

Much literature pushes victims into the background, focusing attention on—and frequently engendering sympathy for—criminals. Truman Capote said of his *In Cold Blood*, which recounted a brutal Kansas murder:

> It's what I really think about America. Desperate, savage, violent
> America in collision with safe, insular, even smug America—people
> who have every chance against people who have none.

In the British film "A Clockwork Orange," young thugs terrorize law-abiding people, but the real sympathy lies with Alex, one of the thugs, who becomes the "victim" of modern penological methods. Some literature blames the victims. In *The Murdered One Is Guilty*, for example, the victim precipitated the crime. Many television crime dramas focus on "cops and robbers," pitting enforcement against thugs, rapists, and drug dealers with no mention of the victims. Law enforcement, of course, always triumphs.[151]

Story lines that sympathize with victims sometimes go to the other extreme. Wronged individuals take the law into their own hands and wreak terrible revenge on their attackers, as in the film "Next of Kin," which reenacts a blood feud between residents of Appalachia and an Italian family responsible for a young man's death. The audience cheers as the avengers beat, stab, torture, torment, and kill the Italians in a virtual blood bath at the end of the film.

Ambivalence aside, the government relies heavily on victims in identifying, apprehending, prosecuting, and convicting criminals. Said political scientist James Q. Wilson, "The most important person in the criminal justice system may not be the judge, police officer, or prosecutor—it may be the victim." In appreciation of the victims' critical function in law enforcement, both federal and state governments have taken actions to improve treatment of victims.[152]

The federal Victim and Witness Protection Act of 1982 protects and assists victims in federal crimes by

1. Making it a felony to threaten victims and witnesses.
2. Providing for the inclusion of victim impact statements in pre-sentence reports.
3. Giving trial judges authority to order offenders to make restitution to their victims.
4. Requiring judges who do not order restitution to give written explanations of why they did not.[153]

The U.S. attorney general ordered all U.S. attorneys' offices and the FBI to establish victim-witness coordinators to ensure that victims and witnesses receive services, such as providing witnesses with waiting areas separate from defendants and defense witnesses before they testify, giving them instructions about what happens in court, and providing victims the opportunity to address the court at sentencing.

In 1984, Congress enacted the Victims of Crime Act, which created a $100 million crime victims' fund derived from criminal fines in federal offenses. The fund provides money for state victim-compensation programs and other programs that assist crime victims. States have also adopted legislation to assist crime victims. The most common statutes assisting victims of violent crime make citizens who report crimes and cooperate with investigation and prosecution eligible to receive from $10,000 to $15,000 for medical expenses, funeral expenses, lost wages, and the support of deceased victims' dependents. This low monetary cap, however, severely restricts the real help victims receive. Furthermore, most legislation does not allot money for psychotherapy or compensation for property loss.

Some states have established victim-witness assistance programs, most frequently under the auspices of prosecutors. These programs provide such services as:

- *Personal advocacy*—helping victims receive all the services they are entitled to in both social service and criminal justice agencies.
- *Referral*—recommending or obtaining assistance other than that given by the assistance programs.
- *Restitution assistance*—urging judges to order (or probation authorities to collect) restitution, and helping violent-crime victims fill out the proper papers necessary to receive compensation.
- *Court orientation*—helping victims and witnesses understand the criminal justice system and their participation in it.
- *Transportation*—taking victims and witnesses to and from court, to social service agencies, and, if necessary, to shelters.
- *Escort services*—escorting witnesses to court and staying with them during proceedings.
- *Emotional support*—giving victims support during their ordeals with crime and with the criminal justice proceedings following it.[154]

Thirteen states have victim's rights provisions in their constitutions. Typical provisions require that the criminal justice system

- Treat victims with compassion and respect.
- Inform victims of critical stages in the trial process.
- Invite victims to attend and comment on trial proceedings.

"I feel as if our movement is picking up the steam that it needs to carry through all 50 states," said Linda Lowrance, chairwoman of the Victims' Constitutional Amendment Network. Criminal defense lawyers, however, complain that victim's rights provisions violate the presumption of innocence. According to Nancy Hollander, president of the National Association of Criminal Defense Lawyers, "By calling someone a victim of a crime, you're assuming guilt." No one has comprehensively evaluated the effectiveness of these provisions, according to John Stein, deputy director of the National Organization for Victim Assistance. However, specific studies have shown that victim impact statements make people "feel better" about the criminal justice system, even though the statements have little or no effect on sentencing or punishment of convicted offenders. Roberta Roper, whose daughter was raped and murdered, could not attend the trial of her daughter's murderers because Maryland has no victims' rights law. Forced to watch the trial by pressing her nose against the small pane of glass in a wooden courtroom door, Roper felt she had let her daughter down by not being in court. "By being a presence at the trial, we could as a family bear witness to the fact that Stephanie lived, and she mattered. We were denied that."[155]

At the time of the crime, however, victims must rely heavily on self-protection. According to the NCS, three-quarters of victims reported taking self-protective measures against offenders, including resisting, trying to

Figure 2.18

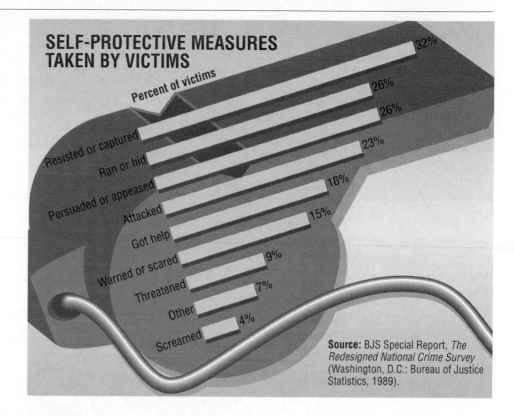

SELF-PROTECTIVE MEASURES TAKEN BY VICTIMS

Percent of victims

Resisted or captured	32%
Ran or hid	26%
Persuaded or appeased	26%
Attacked	23%
Got help	18%
Warned or scared	15%
Threatened	9%
Other	7%
Screamed	4%

Source: BJS Special Report, *The Redesigned National Crime Survey* (Washington, D.C.: Bureau of Justice Statistics, 1989).

capture, persuading, and running away. More than half of those who took self-protective measures reported that their actions had a positive effect. About 7 percent reported that the measures made the situation worse, while 6 percent reported that both positive and negative effects resulted.[156] Figure 2.18 depicts the main ways in which crime victims protect themselves.

The Decision to Report a Crime

Discretionary decision making is the essence of informal criminal justice. Of all the decision makers, crime victims may be the most important. They are the gatekeepers of the criminal justice system. If victims do not report violent crimes and crimes against property to the police, then those crimes do not receive official notice or response. Victims report crimes for a variety of reasons, as was discussed in the section on the National Crime Victim Survey. Whatever the reason, reporting means getting involved in the criminal process. This means spending time, perhaps losing work, and risking retaliation. After the time is spent the results may be frustrating, because the police could not apprehend the perpetrator, the penalty did not satisfy the victim, or the property was not recovered.

The decision to report a crime also affects the criminal justice system. Without the report of the victim, the police do not know about—and cannot apprehend and arrest—suspects in most property and violent crimes. If the police cannot arrest suspects, prosecutors cannot charge them with crimes, courts cannot convict them, and correctional facilities cannot punish them. On the other hand, if victims report all crimes, then the criminal justice system, already overloaded, may be asked to deal with many more crimes than it can manage.

The decision to report—or not to report—a crime also affects society. Will the highly discretionary, low-visibility decisions of victims satisfy a society that demands retribution and believes that more apprehensions and more criminals punished will reduce crime? Furthermore, is it fair and just to allow victims to decide who enters the criminal justice system? Will they select only members of certain groups in society, or choose to report only some kinds of crime? Does society want victims to determine whether criminal justice officials devote scarce resources to the kinds of crimes victims report, or does society want money and time for other types of crimes (like organizational crime, family crimes, and drug offenses) that victims rarely report?

Summary

In order to understand decision making in the day-to-day operations of police departments, courts, and corrections agencies, it is necessary to know something about the subject matter of the work of these agencies—crime, criminals, and victims. The term 'crime' covers a broad spectrum of behavior, including crimes against the state, crimes against persons, crimes against homes, crimes against property, crimes against public order and decency, and occupational crimes. Our knowledge about the kinds and amounts of crime and the trends in crime comes from three main sources: official reports, victimization surveys, and self-reports. For nearly two centuries, statisticians have measured crime for a number of reasons: to assess the moral strength of society; to determine the effectiveness of crime control policies and practices; to measure the extent of victimization; and to evaluate the validity of criminal justice policies.

The Uniform Crime Reports (UCR), the major official source of crime statistics, collects information that local police departments report to the FBI. In Part I, the UCR publishes the numbers and rates of the eight index crimes of murder, forcible rape, aggravated assault, robbery, burglary, larceny-theft, vehicle theft, and arson. These are crimes believed serious enough that people will report them; therefore, they represent an index of serious crime in the United States. Law enforcement agencies include numbers of both completed and attempted crimes reported to them. In Part II, the UCR reports the numbers and rates of arrests for a large number of less serious offenses.

The National Criminal Victimization Survey (NCVS), the major source of information about victims, collects information about crimes that the victims are willing to report to interviewers from the U.S. Census Bureau. NCVS asks every member 12 and older in a sample of households whether they have been the victim of either completed or attempted personal crimes (rape, robbery, and assault) and property crimes (burglary, motor vehicle theft, and theft).

Self-report surveys ask specific groups of people in the population whether they have committed crimes. Up to this point, most self-reports have surveyed convicted felons and young people. Self-reports are based on the idea that if you want to know about crimes, ask the people who commit them.

All three major statistical sources suffer from the "dark figure in crime"— the number of crimes committed but not known, reported, or recorded. More crimes are committed than victims either know about or report to the police. Police departments can only report the crimes that come to their attention. Victims fail to report crimes not only to the police but also to the interviewers from the U.S. Census Bureau. They fail to report for reasons ranging from fear of retaliation to apathy. Offenders do not always reveal the true nature and extent of their criminal behavior for several reasons, including fear of discovery and failure to remember.

Despite the "dark figure in crime," statistics tell us some important things about crime and criminals in the United States. Violent crimes occur much less frequently than "ordinary" crimes against property, public order, and decency. The UCR records a steady increase in the amount of crime over the past several decades. The NCVS shows that the number of victimizations is substantially higher than the number of crimes reported to the police, especially the number of property offenses. On the other hand, the NCVS reports that the amount of criminal victimization has remained fairly steady over the past two decades.

General figures mask the important reality that crime is unevenly distributed according to geography, age, gender, social class, ethnicity, relationship, and occupation. Crime varies from one region to another, from urban to rural areas, from large cities to suburbs and towns, and from one neighborhood to another. Men commit more crimes than women. Career criminals commit a disproportionate number of crimes. Different occupational groups commit different types of crimes. Crimes also vary according to whether victims and offenders are intimates or relatives, acquaintances, or strangers.

Explanations for criminal behavior fall into two broad categories: those based on free will and those based on determinism. Free will explanations, including utilitarianism, economic theories, rational choice, and the "seduction" of crime, are based on the idea that individuals choose to commit crimes. Determinist explanations are based on the idea that forces beyond the control of individual choice determine criminal behavior. These forces may be individual pathology or located outside the individual in the structure, processes, and conflicts of society. Whatever the explanations for criminal behavior, they influence criminal justice policies and day-to-day decision making in agencies. This is because the response to criminal behavior depends, at least in part, on the explanation for criminal behavior.

Crime victims have played an increasingly minor role in criminal justice administration. During colonial times, victims were an integral part of detection, apprehension, prosecution, and punishment of criminals. Despite recent efforts to enhance their role, today's victims play only a minor role in criminal justice, except for their vital importance in bringing crimes to the attention of the police. Crime victims suffer not only from those who committed crimes against them but from what they perceive as negative experiences with the criminal justice system. Contrary to common belief, the age, gender, social class, race, and ethnicity of the victims of crime strongly resemble that of criminal offenders.

Review Questions

1. Identify and briefly describe the three major sources for measuring crime.

2. List the four major reasons for measuring crime.

3. Identify the major parts of the UCR, the way in which the UCR obtains its information, the strengths and weaknesses of the UCR, and the changes made to improve the UCR.

4. Identify the major parts of the NCVS, the way in which the NCVS obtains its information, the strengths and weaknesses of the NCVS, and the changes made to improve the NCVS.

5. Describe the nature of, the strengths of, and the weaknesses of self-reports as a source of information about crime.

6. What are the major difficulties in measuring occupational crime?

7. Identify and briefly define all the major kinds of crimes.

8. According to available research, what do we know about the relationship between drugs and crime?

9. Explain the relationship between geography and crime.

10. Explain how crime varies according to the major relationships of victims to offenders.

11. Compare male and female criminality.

12. What is a career criminal? Explain the problems with using the concept of the career criminal to make criminal justice policy.

13. Define the kinds of occupational crime and explain its special difficulties for criminal justice.

14. According to the UCR and NCVS, what can we say about the trends in crime over the last few decades?

15. Identify and define the two major categories of explanations of crime.

16. Identify all the major explanations of crime and briefly describe the major elements of each.

17. Explain the importance of explanations of criminal behavior to criminal justice policy and practice.

18. Identify the major types of crime victims and compare the demographic characteristics of victims with those of offenders.

19. Describe the changing role of victims since colonial times.

20. Explain the importance of victims in criminal justice today.

Notes

1. Front page headline, *Minneapolis StarTribune*, 17 December, 1995.

2. Richard Sparks, "Criminal Opportunities and Crime Rates," in *Indicators of Crime and Criminal Justice: Quantitative Studies*, Stephen E. Feinberg and Albert J. Reiss, Jr., eds. (Washington, D.C., June 1980), 18.

3. Ibid.

4. Patrick A. Langan and Christopher A. Innes, *The Risk of Violent Crime* (Washington, D.C.: Bureau of Justice Statistics, May 1985), 1.

5. Donald Black, "Production of Crime Rates," in *The Manners and Customs of the Police* (New York: Academic Press, 1980), 65–67; Richard F. Sparks, "A Critique of Marxist Criminology," in *Crime and Justice: An Annual Review of Research*, Norval Morris and Michael Tonry, eds. (Chicago: University of Chicago Press, 1980), 2:159–210.

6. For a criticism of the law enforcement bias in crime news, see Kenneth B. Nunn, "The Trial as Text: Allegory, Myth and Symbol in the Adversarial Criminal Process," *American Criminal Law Review* 32 (1995).

7. Yoshio Akiyama and Harvey M. Rosenthal, "The Future of the Uniform Crime Reporting Program: Its Scope and Promise," in Doris Layton MacKenzie, Phyllis Jo Baunach, and Roy R. Roberg, eds., *Measuring Crime: Large Scale, Long Range Efforts* (Albany: State University of New York Press, 1990), 49–50; Eugene C. Poggio et al., *Blueprint for the Future of the Uniform Crime Reporting Program, Final Report of the UCR Study* (Washington, D.C.: Bureau of Justice Statistics, May 1985), 1.

8. *Crime in the United States, 1993* (Washington, D.C.: Federal Bureau of Investigation, 1994); Victoria W. Schneider and Brian Wiersema, "Limits and Use of the Uniform Crime Reports," in *Measuring Crime*, 21–27.

9. Schneider and Wiersema, "Limits and Use," in *Measuring Crime*, 25.

10. Ibid., 26.

11. Ibid., 26.

12. Darrell Steffensmeier and Miles D. Harar, "Did Crime Rise or Fall During the Reagan Presidency? The Effects of an 'Aging' Population on the Nation's Crime Rate," *Journal of Research in Crime and Delinquency* 28 (1991): 333–35.

13. *Criminal Justice Newsletter*, July 15, 1987, 7; Poggio et al., *Blueprint for the Future*.

14. Lawrence W. Sherman, *The Quality of Police Arrest Statistics* (Washington, D.C.: The Police Foundation, August 1984).

15. Ibid.

16. "Production of Crimes Rates," ibid., 69–80; Walter Gove et al., "Are Uniform Crime Reports a Valid Indicator of the Index Crimes? An Affirmative Answer with Minor Qualification," ibid., 451–501; Vera Institute of Justice, *Felony Arrests: Their Prosecution and Disposition in New York City's Courts* (New York: The Vera Institute of Justice, 1977).

17. Seidman and Couzens, "Getting the Crime Rate Down," 465.

18. Thorsten Sellin, "The Significance of Records of Crime," *Law Quarterly Review* 67 (1951): 489–504; Steffensmeier and Harar, 343.

19. "Structure and Implementation Plan for the Enhanced UCR Program," mimeograph (Washington, D.C.: Federal Bureau of Investigation, November 1988).

20. BJS, *The National Crime Survey: Working Papers* 1 (1981): 1; James Garofalo, "The National Crime Survey, 1973–1986: Strengths and Limitations of a Very Large Data Set," in *Measuring Crime*, 75; BJS, *Rape and Other Sexual Assaults Against Women*, (Washington, D.C.: BJS, August 1995).

21. BJS, *Criminal Victimization in the United States, 1987* (Washington, D.C.: Bureau of Justice Statistics, October 1988).

22. Ibid.

23. BJS, *Criminal Victimization in the United States, 1990* (Washington, D.C.: Bureau of Justice Statistics, 1992), 100.

24. Wesley G. Skogan, "Poll Review: National Crime Survey Redesign," *Public Opinion Quarterly* 54 (1990): 256–272.

25. David Johnston, "Survey Shows Number of Rapes Far Higher than Official Figures," *New York Times*, April 23, 1992.

26. Ronet Bachman and Linda Salzman, *Violence Against Women: Estimates from the Redesigned Survey* (Washington, D.C.: Bureau of Justice Statistics, August 1995).

27. Richard F. Sparks, "Surveys of Victimization—An Optimistic Assessment," *Crime and Justice* 3 (1981): 1–60; Wesley Skogan, *Victimization Surveys and Criminal Justice Planning* (Washington, D.C.: National Institute of Law Enforcement and Criminal Justice, 1978), 14.

28. Garofalo, "The National Crime Survey," 81–82.

29. Ibid., 82; Bureau of Justice Statistics, *Sourcebook of Criminal Justice Statistics–1993* (Washington, D.C.: Bureau of Justice Statistics, 1994), Table 3.2.

30. Technical Report, *New Directions for the National Crime Survey* (Washington, D.C.: Bureau of Justice Statistics, March 1989).

31. James F. Short and F. Ivan Nye, "Reported Behavior as a Criterion of Deviant Behavior," *Social Problems* 5 (1957–58): 207–213; John A. O'Donnell et al., *Young Men and Drugs—A Nationwide Survey*, monograph no. 5 (Washington, D.C.: National Institute on Drug Abuse, 1976).

32. Mike Hough, "Offenders' Choice of Target: Findings from Victim Surveys," *Journal of Quantitative Criminology* 3 (1987): 356; Richard T. Wright and Scott H. Decker, *Burglars on the Job: Streetlife and Residential Break-ins* (Boston: Northeastern University Press, 1994), 5–6.

33. Mark A. Peterson and Harriet B. Barker, *Who Commits Crimes: A Survey of Prison Inmates* (Cambridge, Mass.: Oelgeschlager, Gunn and Hain, 1981), xix–xxi.

34. Ibid., xxv.

35. James D. Wright, *The Armed Criminal in America* (Washington, D.C.: Bureau of Justice Statistics, November 1986).

36. Ibid.

37. Quoted in John Braithwaite, *Inequality, Crime, and Public Policy* (London: Routledge and Kegan Paul, 1979), 21.

38. Richard Sparks, *Testimony to House Subcommittee on Crime, Committee of the Judiciary, White Collar Crime,* Second Session, 95th Congress, June 21, July 12 and 19th, and December 1, 1978, 163–64.

39. Sutherland, *White Collar Crime;* and Marshall B. Clinard and Peter C. Yaeger, *Corporate Crime* (New York: Free Press, 1980) . Albert J. Reiss and Albert D. Biderman survey the value of these sources in *Data Sources on White Collar Crime* (Washington, D.C.: National Institute of Justice, 1980).

40. Richard Hollinger and John P. Clark, *Theft by Employees* (Lexington, Mass.: Lexington Books, 1983); Gerald Mars, *Cheats at Work* (London: Allen and Unwin, 1982).

41. Kevin Jack Riley and Bruce Hoffman, *Domestic Terrorism: A National Assessment of State and Local Preparedness* (Santa Monica: Rand, 1995), 2–3.

42. Marcus Felson, *Crime in Everyday Life* (Thousand Oaks, California: Pine Forge Press, 1994), 3.

43. Ibid.

44. Felson, *Crime in Everyday Life,* 3.

45. Richard J. Bonnie and Charles H. Whitebread II, "The Forbidden Fruit and Tree of Knowledge: An Inquiry into the Legal History of Marijuana Prohibition," *Virginia Law Review* 56 (1971): 1010–16; for an opposite view, see Stephen Steinberg, *The Ethnic Myth* (New York: Atheneum, 1981).

46. Gilbert Geis, *Not the Law's Business: An Examination of Homosexuality, Abortion, Prostitution, Narcotics, and Gambling in the United States* (New York: Shocken Books, 1979); Piers Bourne, "Empiricism and the Critique of Marxism on Law and Crime," *Social Problems* 26 (1979): 373–85; William J. Chambliss and Robert Seidman, *Law, Order, and Power,* 2d ed. (Reading, Mass.: Addison-Wesley Publishing Company, 1982), chap. 7.

47. Bruce Johnson, Terry Williams, Kojo A. Dei, and Harry Sanabria, "Drug Abuse in the Inner City: Impact on Hard-Drug Users and the Community," in Michael Tonry and James Q. Wilson, eds., *Drugs and Crime* (Chicago: University of Chicago Press, 1990), 10–11.

48. Ibid., 30–31.

49. Dana E. Hunt, "Drugs and Consensual Crimes," in *Drugs and Crime.*

50. Jan M. Chaiken and Marcia R. Chaiken, "Drugs and Predatory Crime," in *Drugs and Crime,* 203–39.

51. Ibid., 212.

52. Ibid., 234–35.

53. Samuel Walker, *Sense and Nonsense About Crime and Drugs,* 3rd edition (Belmont, Calif.: Wadsworth Publishing Company, 1994), 6.

54. BJS, *Violence Between Intimates* (Washington, D.C.: BJS, November 1994), 1; David Finkelhor et al., *The Dark Side of Families: Current Family Violence Research* (Beverly Hills: Sage Publications, 1983); Patrick A. Langan and Christopher Innes, *Preventing Domestic Violence Against Women* (Ann Arbor, Mich.: The Criminal Justice Archive and Information Network, Fall 1986); Walter Gove et al., "Are Uniform Crime Reports a Valid Indicator of the Index Crimes? An Affirmative Answer with Minor Qualifications," *Criminology* 23 (1986): 464–65.

55. Vera Institute of Justice, *Felony Arrests,* rev. ed. (New York: Longman, 1981).

56. Cited in Murray Strauss, Richard Gelles, and Suzanne Steinmetz, *Behind Closed Doors: Violence in the American Family* (New York: Doubleday, 1980), 49; Stephen E. Brown, "Social Class, Child Maltreatment, and Delinquent Behavior," *Criminology* 22 (1984): 259–78.

57. Deeann Glamser, "Daughter on Trial in Abandonment Case," *USA Today,* November 17, 1992.

58. Alan J. Lincoln and Murray A. Strauss, *Crime and the Family* (Springfield, Ill.: Charles C. Thomas, 1985), 71–87.

59. Barbara Raffel Price and Natalie J. Sokoloff, eds., *The Criminal Justice System and Women* (New York: Clark Boardman, 1982), 121–28; James A. Inciardi and Harvey A. Siegel, *Crime: Emerging Issues* (New York: Praeger, 1977), 138.

60. Darrell Steffensmeier, "Trends in Female Crime," *The Criminal Justice System and Women,* 117–129; Roy L. Austin, "Women's Liberation and Increases in Minor, Major, and Occupational Offenses," *Criminology* 20 (1982): 407–30.

61. Stephen E. Brown, Finn-Aage Esbensen, and Gilbert Geis, *Criminology: Explaining Crime and Its Content* (Cincinnati: Anderson Publishing Co., 1991).

62. Deborah R. Baskin and Ira Sommers, "Females' Initiation into Violent Street Crime," *Justice Quarterly* 10 (1993): 560.

63. John L. Macmullen, *The Canting Crew: London's Criminal Underworld, 1550-1700* (New Brunswick, N.J.: Rutgers University Press, 1984).

64. Alfred Blumstein et al., *Criminal Careers and "Career Criminals,"* Volume I (Washington, D.C.: National Academy Press, 1986), 1; Marvin Wolfgang, Robert Figlio, and Thorsten Sellin, *Delinquency in a Birth Cohort* (Chicago: University of Chicago Press, 1972); Paul E. Tracy, Marvin Wolfgang, and Robert Figlio, *Delinquency in Two Birth Cohorts* (Chicago: University of Chicago Press, 1985).

65. Jan M. Chaiken and Marcia R. Chaiken, *Varieties of Criminal Behavior: Summary and Implications* (Santa Monica: Rand Corporation, August 1982), 14.

66. Ibid., 18–19.

67. Samuel Walker, *Sense and Nonsense About Crime,* 2d ed. (Pacific Grove, Calif.: Brooks/Cole Publishing Company, 1989), 59; Alfred Blumstein and Jacqueline Cohen, "Estimating Individual Crime Rates from Arrest Records," *Journal of Criminal Law and Criminology* 70 (1979): 561–85; Michael Gottfredson and Travis Hirschi, "The Value of Lambda Would Appear to Be Zero: An Essay on Criminals, Criminal Careers, Selective Incapacitation, Cohort Studies, and Related Topics," *Criminology* 24 (1986): 213–34.

68. Edwin H. Sutherland, "White-Collar Criminality," *American Sociological Review* 5 (1940): 1; Émile Durkheim, *The Division of Labor in Society* (New York: Free Press, 1964), 2; Edward A. Ross, "The Criminaloid," the *Atlantic Monthly,* April 1907.

69. Albert J. Reiss and Albert D. Biderman, *Data Sources on White-Collar Crime* (Washington, D.C.: National Institute of Justice, 1980); Herbert Edelhertz, *The Nature, Impact and Prosecution of White Collar Crime* (Washington, D.C.: National Institute of Justice, 1970); Herbert

Edelhertz et al., *A Manual for Law Enforcement Agencies* (Washington, D.C.: National Institute of Justice, 1977).

70. Marshall B. Clinard et al., *Illegal Corporate Behavior* (Washington, D.C.: National Institute of Law Enforcement and Criminal Justice, 1979).

71. Reiss and Biderman, *Data Sources,* 11–12; Richard Rashke, *The Killing of Karen Silkwood* (New York: Penguin Books, 1981).

72. Donald Smothers, "25 Die, Many Reported Trapped, As Blaze Engulfs Carolina Plant," *New York Times,* September 4, 1991; "Factory Owner Is Given Prison for Fatal Blaze," *New York Times,* November 15, 1992.

73. Food Marketing Institute, "Picking Out the Bad Tomatoes," *Security Management* 36 (1992): 6–7.

74. Richard Hollinger, Karen Slora, and William Terris, "Deviance in the Fast-Food Restaurant," *Deviant Behavior* 13 (1992): 155–84.

75. Hollinger and Clark, *Theft by Employees;* Mars, *Cheats at Work.*

76. BJS, *Criminal Victimization in the United States, 1990* (Washington, D.C.: Bureau of Justice Statistics, 1992), 8.

77. Jack Katz, *Seductions of Crime: Moral and Sensual Attractions in Doing Evil* (New York: Basic Books, 1988), 166.

78. Gary Becker, "Crime and Punishment: An Economic Approach," *Journal of Political Economy* 76 (1968): 169–217; Ann Dryden Witte, "Estimating the Economic Model of Crime with Individual Data," *Quarterly Journal of Economics* 91 (1980): 57–84.

79. Ann Dryden Witte, "Crime Causation: Economic Theories," *Encyclopedia of Crime and Justice* 319.

80. Isaac Ehrlich, "The Deterrent Effect of Capital Punishment: A Question of Life and Death," *American Economic Review* 65 (1975): 397–417.

81. Ibid., 398.

82. Michael Gottfredson and Travis Hirschi, *A General Theory of Crime* (Stanford: Stanford University Press, 1990), 74.

83. Ronald V. Clarke and Marcus Felson, eds., *Routine Activity and Rational Choice* (New Brunswick: Transaction Publishers, 1993), 5.

84. Both Etzioni and Frank are quoted in Brian Forst, ed., *The Socio-Economics of Crime and Justice* (Armonk, N.Y.: M. E. Sharpe, 1993), 5–6.

85. Clarke and Felson, *Routine Activity and Rational Choice,* 5.

86. This section relies heavily on Derek B. Cornish and Ronald V. Clarke, eds., *The Reasoning Criminal: Rational Choice Perspectives on Offending* (New York: Springer-Verlag, 1986).

87. Clarke and Felson, *Routine Activity and Rational Choice,* 6.

88. P. Letkemann, *Crime as Work* (Englewood Cliffs, N.J.: Prentice-Hall, 1973), 151.

89. Wright and Decker, *Burglars On the Job,* 36.

90. Ibid.

91. Ibid., 37.

92. Ibid., 37–38.

93. Ibid., 101.

94. Neal Shover and David Honaker, "The Socially Bounded Decision Making of Persistent Property Offenders," *Howard Journal of Criminal Justice* 31 (1992): 279.

95. Ibid., 281.

96. Kenneth D. Tunnell, "Choosing Crime: Close Your Eyes and Take Your Chances," *Justice Quarterly* 7 (1990): 673–90.

97. Julie Horney and Ineke Haen Marshall, "Risk Perceptions Among Serious Offenders: The Role of Crime and Punishment," *Criminology* 30 (1992): 575–92.

98. Peter Reuter, Robert MacCoun, and Patrick Murphy, *Money from Crime* (Santa Monica: The Rand Corporation, 1990), viii–xix.

99. Ibid., xiv.

100. Kenneth D. Tunnell, "Property Criminals as the Lumpenproletariat: A Serendipitous Finding," *Nature, Society, and Thought* 3 (1990): 45.

101. Quoted in Floyd Feeney, "Robbers as Decision-Makers," in Cornish and Clarke, *The Reasoning Criminal,* 57; For similar findings, see Thomas Gabor et al., *Armed Robbery: Cops, Robbers, and Victims* (Springfield, Ill.: Charles C. Thomas Publisher, 1987), 62–69.

102. Cornish and Clarke, *The Reasoning Criminal,* 8.

103. Richard Wright, Scott Decker, Allison Redfern, and Dietrich Smith, "A Snowball's Chance in Hell: Doing Fieldwork with Active Residential Burglars," *Journal of Research in Crime and Delinquency* 29 (1992): 148–61.

104. Katz, *Seductions of Crime,* 3.

105. Ibid., 4.

106. Clarke and Felson, *Routine Activity and Rational Choice,* 10–11.

107. Ibid., 3.

108. Lawrence E. Cohen and Marcus Felson, "Social Change and Crime Rate Trends: A Routine Activity Approach," *American Sociological Review* 44 (1979): 588–608; Ronald V. Clarke and Marcus Felson, eds., *Routine Activity and Rational Choice,* (New Brunswick, N.J.: Transaction Publishers, 1993), 1–14; Marcus Felson, *Crime in Everyday Life* (Thousand Oaks, California: Pine Forge Press, 1994), 2.

109. Clarke and Felson, *Routine Activity and Rational Choice,* 2–3.

110. Gina Lombroso-Ferrero, *Criminal Man,* rpt. (Montclair, N.J.: Patterson Smith, 1972), 6–7.

111. Juan B. Cortes with Florence M. Gatti, *Delinquency and Crime: A Biopsychological Approach* (New York: Seminar Press, 1972).

112. Ysabel Rennie, *The Search for Criminal Man* (Lexington, Mass.: Lexington Books, 1978), 224.

113. Sarnoff A. Mednick and Jan Volavka, "Biology and Crime," in *Crime and Justice: An Annual Review of Research* (Chicago: University of Chicago Press, 1980), 2:92–94; Vicki Pollock et al., "Crime Causation: Biological Theories," in *Encyclopedia of Crime and Justice,* Sanford Kadish, ed. (New York: Free Press, 1983), 310–11.

114. "A Review of Studies of Criminality Among Twins," and "A Preliminary Study of Criminality in Twins," in *Biosocial Bases of Criminality,* Sarnoff Mednick and Karl Otto Christiansen, eds. (New York: Gardner Press, 1977).

115. Vernon H. Mark and Frank R. Ervin, *Violence and the Brain* (New York: Harper & Row, 1970), 5.

116. B. D'Asario et al., "Polyamine Levels in Jail Inmates," *Journal of Orthomolecular Psychiatry* 4 (1975): 149–52.

117. J. A. Yaryura-Tobias and F. Neziroglu, "Violent Behavior, Brain Dysrythmia and Glucose Dysfunction, A New Syndrome," *Journal of Orthopsychiatry* 4 (1975): 182–88.

118. Paul Cromwell et al., "Hair Mineral Analysis: Biochemical Imbalances and Violent Criminal Behavior," *Psychological Reports* 64 (1989): 259–66; Louis Gottchalk et al., "Abnormalities in Hair Trace Elements as Indicators of Aberrant Behavior," *Comprehensive Psychiatry* 32 (1991), 229–37.

119. R. R. Monroe, *Brain Dysfunction in Aggressive Criminals* (Lexington, Mass.: D. C. Heath, 1978).

120. Robin Marantz Henig, "Dispelling Menstrual Myths," *New York Times Magazine,* March 7, 1982.

121. Albert J. Reiss, Jr. and Jeffrey A. Roth, eds., *Understanding and Preventing Violence* (Washington, D.C.: National Academy Press, 1993), 102.

122. [77]Fox Butterfield, "Study Cites Biology's Role in Violent Behavior," *New York Times,* 1992.

123. Émile Durkheim, *Suicide: A Study in Sociology* (New York: Free Press, 1951); Robert K. Merton, "Social Structure and Anomie," in *Social Theory and Social Structure,* enlarged ed. (New York: Free Press, 1968), 185–214; quote from Marshall Clinard in Brown, Esbensen, and Geis, *Criminology: Explaining Crime and Its Content,* 305.

124. William Simon and John H. Gagnon, "The Anomie of Affluence: A Post-Mertonian Conception," *American Journal of Sociology* 82 (1976): 356–78; Alex Thio, "A Critical Look at Merton's Anomie Theory," *Pacific Sociological Review* 18 (1975): 139–58.

125. Richard Cloward and Lloyd Ohlin, *Delinquency and Opportunity: A Theory of Delinquent Gangs* (New York: Free Press, 1960).

126. Clifford Shaw, *The Jack-Roller* (Chicago: University of Chicago Press, 1966), 54.

127. Edwin H. Sutherland and Donald R. Cressey, *Criminology,* 10th ed. (Philadelphia: J. Lippincott Co., 1978), 83–97; Sutherland, *White Collar Crime.*

128. Albert K. Cohen, *Delinquent Boys: The Culture of the Gang* (New York: Free Press, 1955); Albert K. Cohen, "Crime Causation: Sociological Theories," *Encyclopedia of Crime and Justice,* 1:346.

129. Marvin Wolfgang and Franco Ferracuti, *The Subculture of Violence* (London: Tavistock, 1967).

130. James W. Coleman, *The Criminal Elite* (New York: St. Martin's Press, 1985), 202–204.

131. Travis Hirschi, *Causes of Delinquency* (Berkeley: University of California Press, 1969), 34.

132. Francis T. Cullen, *Rethinking Crime and Deviance Theory* (Totowa, N.J.: Rowman and Allenheld, 1983), 137–42.

133. This summary is based on Brown et al., *Criminology: Explaining Crime and Its Content,* 373.

134. Ezra Stotland, "White Collar Criminals," *Journal of Social Issues* 33 (1977): 179–96.

135. Cullen, *Rethinking Crime and Deviance Theory,* 123; Howard Becker, *Outsiders* (New York: Free Press, 1973).

136. Cullen, *Rethinking Crime and Deviance Theory,* 125–28.

137. The President's Commission on Crime, Law Enforcement and the Administration of Justice, *The Challenge of Crime in a Free Society* (Washington, D.C.: U.S. Government Printing Office, 1967); Jeffrey Reiman, *The Rich Get Richer and the Poor Get Prison,* 2d ed. (New York: John Wiley and Sons, 1984); Currie, *Confronting Crime;* Wilson and Herrnstein, *Crime and Human Nature;* and Wright, *Great American Crime Myth,* all discuss these broad issues in some detail.

138. James Q. Wilson, *Thinking About Crime,* rev. ed. (New York: Basic Books, 1983), especially chap. 3; Lloyd Ohlin, "The President's Commission on Law Enforcement and the Administration of Justice," in Mirra Komarovsky, ed., *Sociology and Public Policy,* (New York: Elsevier, 1975), 93–115.

139. David Rothman, *Conscience and Convenience: The Asylum and Its Alternative in Progressive America* (Boston: Little, Brown and Company, 1980).

140. Robert Elias, *The Politics of Victimization* (New York: Oxford University Press, 1986), 11–12.

141. Martin S. Greenberg and R. Barry Ruback, *Social Psychology and the Criminal Justice System* (Dubuque, Iowa: Kendall/Hunt Publishing Company, 1991); first victim response quoted in Martin S. Greenberg, R. Barry Ruback, and David R. Westcott, "Seeking Help from the Police: The Victim's Perspective," in Arie Nadler, Jeffrey D. Fisher, and Bella M. DePaulo, eds., *New Directions in Helping,* vol. 3 (New York: Academic Press, 1983), 81; second quote from Andrew Karmen, *Crime Victims,* 2d ed. (Pacific Grove, Calif.: Brooks/Cole Publishing Company, 1990), 2.

142. Karmen, *Crime Victims,* 2.

143. James Q. Wilson, moderator, *Crime File: Victims* (Washington, D.C.: Bureau of Justice Statistics, 1985).

144. Terance D. Miethe and Robert F. Meier, *Crime and Its Social Context: Toward an Integrated Theory of Offenders, Victims, and Situations* (Albany: State University of New York Press, 1994), 2; Fay Lomax Cook, "Crime Among the Elderly: The Emergence of a Policy Issue," in *Reactions to Crime,* Dan E. Lewis, ed. (Beverly Hills, Calif.: Wadsworth, 1979), 123; Raymond A. Eve and Susan Brown Eve, "The Effects of Powerlessness, Fear of Social Change and Social Integration on Fear of Crime Among the Elderly," *Victimology* 9 (1984): 290; U.S. Congress, House of Representatives Select Committee on Aging, *In Search of Security: A National Perspective on Elderly Crime Victimization* (Washington, D.C.: U.S. Government Printing Office, 1977).

145. Miethe and Meier, *Crime and Its Social Context,* 2.

146. Robert F. Meier and Terance D. Miehe, "Understanding Theories of Criminal Victimization," in Michael Tonry, ed., *Crime and Justice: A Review of Research,* vol. 17, (Chicago: University of Chicago Press, 1993), 459–465; Michael S. Hindaling, Michael Gottfredson, and James Garofalo, *Victims of Personal Crime* (Cambridge, Mass.: Ballinger Press, 1978).

147. Eduard Ziegenhagen, *Victims, Crime and Control* (New York: Praeger, 1977), 5; Kevin Wright, *The Great American Crime Myth* (Westport, Conn.: Greenwood Press, 1985), 57–62; Lawrence E. Cohen and Marcus Felson, "Social Change and Crime Rate Trends: A Routine Activity Approach," *American Sociological Review* 44 (1979): 588–608; Lawrence W. Sherman, Patrick R. Gartin, and Michael E. Buerger, "Hot Spots of Predatory Crime: Routine Activities and the Criminology of Place," *Criminology* 27 (1989): 27–55.

148. Albert J. Reiss, Jr., "Victim Proneness in Repeat Victimization by Time of Crime," in *Indicators of Crime and Criminal Justice: Quantitative Studies*, Steven E. Feinberg and Albert J. Reiss, Jr., eds. (Washington, D.C.: Bureau of Justice Statistics, 1980), 47–57; Marvin E. Wolfgang, Terence P. Thornberry, and Robert M. Figlio, *From Boy to Man, From Delinquency to Crime* (Chicago: University of Chicago Press, 1987), chap. 13.

149. BJS. *Violence and Theft in the Workplace, 1987-1992* (Washington, D.C.: BJS, July 1994); "Death at Work," *The Wall Street Journal,* 22 March 1994.

150. Elias, *The Politics of Victimization,* 14.

151. Ibid., 15.

152. Wilson, *Crime File: Victims.*

153. *Public Law* 97–291.

154. *National Law Journal,* December 25, 1989-January 1, 1990, 12.

155. "Victims' Rights Amendments Pass in 5 States," *New York Times,* November 8, 1992.

156. BJS, *The Redesigned National Crime Survey: Selected New Data,* spcl. rpt. (Washington, D.C.: Bureau of Justice Statistics, January 1989).

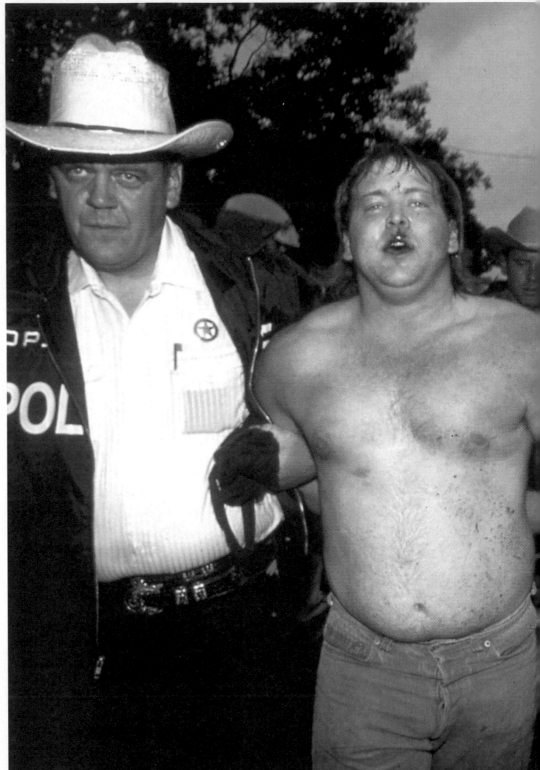

d the Law

CHAPTER MAIN POINTS

1. *Criminal law defines criminal behavior and harms, and prescribes punishments for violations.*
2. *The law of criminal procedure prescribes the rules that the government must follow in the enforcement of the criminal law.*
3. *To qualify as crimes, conduct and/or harm must violate a specific law that prescribes a specific penalty conforming to the general principles of criminal law, and that the government enforces according to established procedures.*
4. *All crimes consist of at least two elements, the* actus reus *and the* mens rea. *Some crimes, such as murder, have the additional element of causing a specific harmful result.*

5. *Defenses to criminal liability are either justifications or excuses.*
6. *Due process limits both the criminal law and the enforcement of the criminal law.*
7. *The Fifth Amendment due process clause prohibits the federal government from denying any person life, liberty, or property unless the agencies follow specific procedures.*
8. *The Fourteenth Amendment requires state and local governments to extend to state proceedings most of the rights guaranteed in the Bill of Rights to the United States Constitution.*
9. *Societal influences create demands to write societal values into criminal law and its enforcement.*
10. *Both consensus and conflict in our pluralistic society have shaped the content of criminal law and procedure.*

N o crime without law" and "No punishment without law," proclaim two ancient maxims. These maxims stand for the proposition that crime control in a democracy must operate within the framework—and only under the authority—of law. None of the behavior discussed in Chapter 2 can be criminal without a specific law defining it as a crime and prescribing a punishment for it. No action taken or decision made by any police officer, prosecutor, defense attorney, judge, jury, probation officer, corrections officer, or parole officer (to be discussed in the remaining chapters of this book) is allowed except by the authority of law. The sources of this authority are the national and state constitutions, federal and state statutes, and court decisions interpreting these constitutions and statutes.

Informally, the legal framework and authority is broad and flexible enough to allow ample room for discretionary decision making. Legal terms, like all other words, are at best imperfect symbols for what they represent. No written rule defining criminal behavior can precisely describe all the behavior it is intended to prohibit. No provision defining the power of criminal justice agencies can fully account for all the actions that power allows. No rule can cover all contingencies that may arise after the rule is written.

Finally, no rule, however clear and predictive, can—or should—eliminate the influences of ideology, economics, social structure and processes, and individual personality. In short, the tension between formal rules and informal, discretionary decision making—between formal and informal criminal justice—also applies to criminal law and criminal procedure.

This chapter examines the constitutional and legal framework within which day-to-day criminal justice operations take place. Both criminal law and the law of criminal procedure affect these operations. The **criminal law** tells private individuals what behavior the law prohibits and prescribes the punishment for criminal behavior. In short, criminal law is the formal definition of crime and punishment, the primary source of the actions of criminal justice agencies. The **law of criminal procedure** tells public officials what actions they are allowed to take to control crime. It also prescribes the consequences for official actions that the law does not allow. In other words, the law of criminal procedure defines the extent and limits of government power to enforce the criminal law in our constitutional democracy.

Criminal Law

Much reprehensible behavior, some of which causes considerable harm, occurs in every society. No society defines all this behavior and its consequences as criminal. The criminal law distinguishes—sensibly—unethical, immoral conduct and injury from criminal conduct and criminal harm. For example, it is wrong to cheat on your girl or boy friend or to lie to your friends, but neither is a crime. It may even be illegal to cheat in business but yet not a crime to do so. Criminal law is, at least in theory, society's last resort against reprehensible behavior, because it is expensive, cumbersome, and intrudes deeply into privacy and liberty, often with only limited effect. Therefore, society relies on other social control mechanisms, such as the disapproval of friends, internal agency sanctions, and private lawsuits, to discourage harmful conduct.

To qualify as crimes, conduct or harm must satisfy the following requirements:

1. A specific law gives clear and prior warning as to what conduct the law prohibits.
2. The law prescribes a specific penalty for the prohibited conduct.
3. The particular law conforms to the general purposes and principles of criminal law.
4. The punishment prescribed and actually administered accords with the Constitution's prohibition against cruel and unusual punishment.

The Principles of Criminal Law

In Chapter 2, we discussed the wide range of behavior included within the scope of criminal law, noting that it includes everything from brutal murders, to household burglaries, to eating in buses and spitting on the street. Legally, all this behavior has one common element: it must comply with the general principles of criminal law. The main sources of these principles are:

1. The national and state constitutions.
2. The general principles of criminal liability.
3. The principles of justification and excuse.

The Constitution and Criminal Law

The U.S. Constitution commands that the government can punish citizens only when specific laws warn them in advance that their behavior or the harm their behavior causes will result in a specific punishment. Three provisions in the

ex post facto law *a law that criminalizes behavior that occurred before the law was passed.*

due process clauses *parts of the 5th and 14th amendments to the U.S. Constitution that guarantee fair procedures in denying people life, liberty, and property.*

federalism *the division of political power between federal and state governments.*

substantive due process *the meaning of life, liberty, and property as it applies to the definition of crimes and punishments.*

procedural due process *laws that govern the actions of police, courts, and corrections in enforcing the criminal law.*

void-for-vagueness *rule that laws are invalid unless they define clearly what the law prohibits.*

equal protection of the laws *rule that prohibits separating persons by unacceptable criteria, such as gender, race, religion, and ethnicity.*

Constitution concern advance warning. First, Article I, Section 9 includes the requirement that "No ... *ex post facto* law shall be passed." An ex post facto law is a retroactive law. That is, it criminalizes conduct that was not criminal before the passage of a statute. For example, if a state passes a statute on January 5, 1997, that raises the drinking age from 18 to 21, it cannot prosecute a 19-year-old who bought a beer on New Year's Eve, 1996. In other words, people must know *before* they act that what they do is criminal.

The two other provisions concerning advance warning are the **due process clauses** of the Fifth and Fourteenth Amendments. The Fifth Amendment clause provides that "No person shall be ... deprived of life, liberty, or property without due process of law. ..." This clause prohibits the *federal government* from denying citizens life, liberty, or property without due process of law. The Fourteenth Amendment due process clause provides that "No state shall ... deny any person life, liberty, or property without due process of law." This imposes a due process requirement on the *states*.

The matter of due process gets complicated, requiring an understanding of **federalism:** the division of political power between federal and state governments. Each has its own legislatures, courts, and executive branches. The Fifth Amendment due process clause, and all the other rights (See Chapter 6 for a discussion of the application of this principle to local police, Chapters 9 and 10 to courts, and Chapter 14 to corrections) in the first 10 amendments to the U.S. Constitution, applies directly only to the federal government. The Fourteenth Amendment due process clause applies to state executives, legislatures, and courts.

Due process is further complicated because it comprises two types of protections. **Substantive due process,** or the meaning of life, liberty, and property, applies mainly to criminal law, that is, to the definition of crimes and punishments. **Procedural due process** refers to criminal justice administration, or laws that governs the actions of police, courts, and corrections in enforcing the criminal law. One major aspect of substantive due process is that statutes must define crimes precisely, or the courts will declare them **void-for-vagueness.** The Supreme Court has rules that a statute

> which either forbids or requires the doing of an act in terms so vague that men [and women] of common intelligence must necessarily guess at its meaning and differ as to its application, violates the first essential of due process of law.[1]

The Nebraska Supreme Court applied the void-for-vagueness rule to a Lincoln, Nebraska, city ordinance which prohibited "any indecent, immodest, or filthy act in the presence of any person." The court overturned the conviction of a man whom a passerby saw standing naked in front of his window eating a bowl of cereal for breakfast. The court ruled that the ordinance was too vague:

> We know of no way in which the standards required of a criminal act can be met in those broad, general terms. There may be those few who believe persons of opposite sex holding hands in public are immodest, and certainly more who might believe kissing in public is immodest.[2]

The Fourteenth Amendment also prohibits states from denying citizens the **equal protection of the laws.** The U.S. Supreme Court has interpreted this clause as prohibiting *unreasonable* classifications, but not all distinctions. According to the Court, the equal protection clause prohibits government from separating persons by unacceptable criteria, such as gender, race, religion, ethnic background, and, in some instances, age. For example, a statute that made it a crime for women to smoke in public, but not men, violated the equal protection clause. On the other hand, the Supreme Court ruled that California's statutory rape law, which defined the crime as sexual intercourse with a *female* under 18, did not violate the equal protection clause

"Drunk and disorderly conduct" is an offense that is difficult to define.

because of the state's compelling interest in reducing "the tragic human costs of illegitimate teenage pregnancies." The Court argued that

> because the Equal Protection Clause does not "demand that things which are different in fact . . . to be treated in law as though they were the same," this Court has consistently upheld statutes where the gender classification is not invidious, but rather realistically reflects the fact that the sexes are not similarly situated in similar circumstances.[3]

The due process clause also protects the controversial right of privacy. The right to privacy, not specifically mentioned in the U.S. Constitution, embodies the idea that a free society ought to maximize human autonomy, that government should leave citizens alone in the privacy of their homes. The Constitution contains no mention of a right to privacy. Nevertheless, the Supreme Court, in the important case of *Griswold v. Connecticut,* struck down a statute making it a crime for married couples to use contraceptives. Justice Douglas wrote that the Constitution creates a "zone of privacy" around the "intimate relation of husband and wife," and that the statute had a "destructive impact upon the relationship."[4]

The Supreme Court has construed the right of privacy narrowly; in fact, some justices have consistently maintained that the Constitution implies no right of privacy at all. In 1986, for example, the Court upheld a Georgia sodomy law against a challenge that the right to privacy protected sexual acts in private between consenting adult homosexuals. In the case, police officers followed a man and his companion to the man's home. The men went into the bedroom and closed the door. The police officer knocked on the door and awakened a house guest sleeping on a couch in the living room. The guest allowed the officer to enter the house. The officer surprised the two men in

actus reus *element of criminal liability referring to the criminal act or physical element in crime.*

concurrence *element of criminal liability referring to the joining of the* actus reus *and the* mens rea.

mens rea *element of criminal liability referring to the criminal state of mind or the mental element in crime.*

causing a particular result *element of criminal liability referring to the* actus reus *resulting in a specific harm.*

proof beyond a reasonable doubt *enough evidence legally obtained and properly presented that will convince an ordinary, reasonable person that a defendant in a criminal trial is guilty.*

attempt *the incomplete crime of taking substantial steps beyond mere preparation toward committing a crime.*

conspiracy *the incomplete crime of agreeing to commit a crime or to do a legal act by illegal means.*

solicitation *the incomplete crime of encouraging another person to commit a crime.*

bed having sex. The Court ruled that the right to privacy does not protect the homosexual lifestyle.[5]

Unlike the United States Constitution, several state constitutions have specifically provided for a right to privacy. The Alaska constitution, for example, provides that "the right of the people to privacy is recognized and shall not be infringed." The Alaska criminal code made possession of marijuana a criminal offense. A man was convicted for possessing a small amount of marijuana for his personal use in his home. The Alaska Supreme Court overturned the conviction. According to the court:

> The privacy amendment . . . was intended to give recognition and protection to the home. Such a reading is consonant with the character of life in Alaska. Our . . . state has traditionally been the home of people who prize their individuality and who have chosen to settle or to continue living here in order to achieve a measure of control over their own lifestyles which is now virtually unattainable in many of our sister states.[6]

The Principles of Criminal Liability

All crimes consist of at least three elements:

1. A criminal act, called the physical element or ***actus reus,***
2. concurring with, called the element of ***concurrence,***
3. a criminal intent, called the mental element or ***mens rea.***

Crimes including only these three elements, the vast majority of all crimes, consist of criminal conduct itself. A few crimes require that the criminal conduct cause a particular result. Such crimes, mainly criminal homicide, include in addition to the three elements of criminal conduct the element of **causing a particular result.** Murder committed with a firearm, for example, consists not only of the act of shooting joined with the intent to kill, but also requires that the shooting cause the death of the victim. To convict a person of a crime, the prosecution has to prove all these elements beyond a reasonable doubt. **Proof beyond a reasonable doubt** means enough evidence legally obtained and properly presented that will convince an ordinary, reasonable person that the defendant is guilty.

Actus Reus   The principle of *actus reus* reflects the basic commitment to the idea that crime requires action. The principle of *actus reus* excludes from criminal liability the mere intent to act or to cause harm. The requirement of action also excludes status from the scope of criminal liability. In other words, the criminal law does not punish people for who they are, what they think or wish, or what they merely *intend* to do. It punishes completed action and harm.

There are some exceptions to the strict requirement of completed action. Taking substantial steps toward completing a crime is called **attempt,** and is exemplified by the man who chased his wife with a gun he had forgotten to load. He caught up with her, pointed the gun at her head, and pulled the trigger several times. "It won't shoot! It won't shoot!" he shouted. He was convicted of attempted murder. He intended to kill his wife; he took substantial steps toward turning his intention into action. The law of attempt is based on the idea that persons determined to commit crimes and whose actions go a substantial way toward completing the crimes should not escape criminal liability by a stroke of luck.

Other forms of uncompleted crimes also meet the *actus reus* requirement. Agreeing to rob a bank is the crime of **conspiracy** to commit robbery. Even asking another to commit a crime, such as a man who offered his friend $3,000 to kill his wife, is the crime of **solicitation** to commit

general intent *intent to commit the actus reus of a crime.*
specific intent *intent to do something in addition to the* actus reus.
transferred intent *intent to harm one person but instead harming another.*
constructive intent *cases in which actors did not intend harm, but their actions caused a result that the criminal law prohibits.*
criminal recklessness *conscious creation of a high risk of causing harm.*
tort *liability in personal injury and product liability lawsuits between private parties, the non criminal but still wrongful injury for which the injured party can recover damages in court.*
criminal negligence *unconscious creation of a high risk of causing harm.*

murder. Furthermore, possession of a wide range of items and substances, such as some kinds of weapons and drugs, is a crime in most jurisdictions. Despite the failure to complete the crime, all the crimes described above require at least some action—*pulling* the trigger, *agreeing* to commit murder, *asking* another to commit a crime, and *acquiring* possession. The law takes the position that we need not await actual harm in order to impose criminal liability. Action sufficient to demonstrate dangerousness—that is, the determination to complete the crime—satisfies the *actus reus* requirement.[7]

Mens Rea *Mens rea,* or "guilty mind," really refers to four kinds of criminal intent:

1. General intent.
2. Specific intent.
3. Transferred intent.
4. Constructive intent.

General intent has various meanings. Sometimes it refers to doing something at an undetermined time or an intent directed at an unspecified object, such as firing a gun into a crowd, intending to kill whomever the bullet strikes. It also means an intent to commit the *actus reus.* In larceny, for example, taking and carrying away another's property constitutes the *actus reus.* The intent to take and carry away constitutes the general intent in larceny. **Specific intent** requires an intent to do something in addition to the *actus reus.* Larceny, for example, requires not only the general intent to commit the *actus reus* but also the specific intent to deprive the owner permanently of possession of the property. Criminal homicide, for another example, requires not only the general intent to shoot a gun but also the specific intent to cause the death of another person. **Transferred intent** refers to cases in which the actor intends to harm one victim but instead harms another. For example, if you aim and fire your gun at Dominique as she walks down the street with Scottie, and the bullet hits and kills Scottie, the law transfers your intent to kill Dominique to the intent to kill Scottie. Some refer to transferred intent as "bad aim" cases. However, transferred intent also refers to any similar crime, such as intending to burn down one house but instead burning another.

In general, specific, and transferred intent, the actors intend either to act, cause a particular result, or both. **Constructive intent** extends criminal liability to cases in which actors did not intend harm, but their actions caused a result the criminal law prohibits. Constructive intent runs roughly parallel to what some prefer to call reckless and negligent wrongdoing. **Criminal recklessness** means to create high risks of harm purposely or consciously. Reckless wrongdoers may not intend to hurt anyone—in fact, they probably hope their recklessness hurts no one—but they risk causing harm anyway. If you purposely or knowingly leave a loaded gun lying within a 2-year-old boy's reach, and he, much to your later horror, picks it up, pulls the trigger, and kills himself while you are out of the room, you are reckless. You did not mean to kill him. Indeed, the last thing you wanted was even to hurt him; but your recklessness led to his death.

Negligence means unconsciously creating a high risk of serious harm, usually death or serious bodily harm. Negligent wrongdoers *unconsciously* create risks. The mental state of criminal negligence differs from the negligence required for **tort,** or liability in personal injury and product liability lawsuits between private parties. **Criminal negligence** requires a *high* risk, one that involves "a *gross* deviation from the standard of care that a reasonable person would observe." Negligence in tort liability means simply the lack of ordinary care that a reasonable person would exercise. Of course, the meanings of deviation, reasonable person, high risk, ordinary risk, and gross deviation all leave wide room for interpretation.[8]

Strict liability offenses constitute an exception to the *mens rea* requirement. **Strict liability** imposes liability without fault. The government need only prove that defendants either engaged in prohibited conduct or caused a prohibited result. In strict liability, whether the defendants caused harm intentionally, recklessly, or negligently is irrelevant. The criminal law did not recognize strict liability until the transformations brought about by the Industrial Revolution. Public transportation, factories, and large-scale consumer purchasing created high risks to health and safety and made the requirement of personal and individual culpability meaningless. Large size and diffused managerial responsibility characterized these new enterprises. They created risks to victims whom they did not personally know, and whom they did not intend to injure. Nevertheless, the principle of *mens rea* excluded acts of exposing the public to serious injuries, incurable diseases, or deaths from criminal liability.

Legislatures responded with a wide range of strict liability offenses, justified on two grounds. The statutes were aimed at conduct that created high risks of serious harm to large numbers of people who needed the services and employment associated with the high-risk behavior, and from whom the providers derived labor and profit. Furthermore, strict liability never results in incarceration; fines constitute the primary penalty.

Concurrence It is not enough that someone intends to commit a crime and takes actions that appear consistent with the intent. The intention must set the actions in motion. In other words, the bad state of mind must come before the bad action. For example, Lucy buys a VCR from Damien without knowing it is stolen. The next time he sees her, Damien tells Lucy that he stole the VCR from Lucy's enemy Catherine. Lucy is so delighted that Catherine suffered the loss that she decides to keep the VCR. She has not committed the crime of receiving stolen property because the intent to steal did not generate her action in buying the VCR in the first place. However, it is possible to have actions follow a bad state of mind and still not have concurrence. For example, Gretchen hates Lorraine. She plans to kill her, but she changes her mind because she does not want to go to prison. As luck would have it, two months after she abandons her plan to kill Lorraine, Gretchen accidentally runs her down with her car. Gretchen is delighted and rejoices in Lorraine's death, but she is not guilty of murder because her intent to kill did not spur the action of running Lorraine down.[9]

Causing a Harmful Result In crimes that require not only criminal conduct but also a specific result, the conduct must *cause* the result. The element of causation consists of two kinds of cause: cause in fact and legal cause. Cause in fact means that "but for" the acts of the defendant, the result would not have taken place. That is to say, the result would not have taken place in the absence of the actions. For example, Kibbe and his companion robbed Stafford and left him on a country road. Blake, a college student returning to school, accidentally ran Stafford down and killed him. "But for" Kibbe and his companion leaving Stafford on the road, Blake would not have run Stafford down and killed him. In other words, the actions of Kibbe and his companion set in motion a chain of events that in fact led eventually to Stafford's death. Kibbe and his companion, therefore, were the cause in fact of Stafford's death.

Cause in fact is necessary but not sufficient to prove the element of causation. Causation requires not only factual but legal cause. Legal cause becomes a problem mainly in cases where the result is greater than the actor intended or expected. So, even though the result would not have occurred if

Conviction for murder requires not only proving that this victim was "beaten," "tortured," and "shot multiple times" but also that these acts caused the victim's death.

the defendant had not acted, the laws still may not hold the defendant accountable for the result. In the end, legal causation is more a question of policy than of science. Legal causation asks the question: Is it fair to hold the defendant accountable for the result of the actions he or she set in motion? Usually, the answer is no, if the result is either remote from the initial action or the actions of someone or something else intervenes and causes the result. For example, Pat stabbed Sam in a rage. Sam refuses either to take care of the wound or go to the doctor because he does not want to spend the money. Finally, after nearly a day, he is so weak from loss of blood that he goes to an emergency room where he receives a transfusion. He develops an infection from an old needle that was accidentally used and died three weeks later. Fairness may lead to the conclusion that the intervening actions—Sam's voluntary refusal to bind the wound and go to the doctor, and the actions of the hospital staff in using the dirty needle were the *legal* cause of his death. In other words, it does not seem fair to hold Pat accountable for Sam's death, even though in fact Sam would not have died if Pat had not stabbed him.

General Principles and Specific Crimes

Actus reus, mens rea, concurrence, causation, and resulting harm are general principles; they do not define specific crimes. For example, they do not define the particular act in burglary (breaking and entering), or the *mens rea* in first-degree murder (purposely and with premeditation). According to legal theorists, specific crimes apply general principles to particular conduct and harm.[10]

The most serious crimes—criminal homicide, rape, aggravated assault, robbery, arson, burglary, and theft—contain highly refined definitions of all the material elements. In the lesser offenses, particularly crimes against public order and morals, the definitions are broader—some would say vaguer— and adherence to the general principles relaxes. For example, statutes defining vagrancy, disturbing the peace, and loitering rarely refer to the acts, mental states, and resulting harms that constitute the offenses.

Mens Rea in Japanese Criminal Law

The Japanese penal code recognizes the importance of the mental element in criminal liability. Specific intent and negligence are two basic forms of *mens rea* in the code. An act committed without intent is not criminal except as specifically provided for in the law. In other words, there are no strict liability crimes in Japan. Japanese criminal law, therefore, has incorporated the principle of no crime, no punishment without *mens rea*. However, the code has introduced some exceptions to the rule. Some special administrative-type laws provide for punishment of negligent crimes even though no specific provision in the code makes such conduct crimes.

alibi *a defense to criminal liability that places the defendant at a different location than the crime scene when the crime occurred.*

defenses of justification *defenses to criminal liability based on the assertion that defendants were responsible for what they did but that under the circumstances it was right for them to do it.*

defenses of excuse *defenses to criminal liability based on the assertion that what defendants did was wrong but that under the circumstances they were not responsible for what they did.*

affirmative defense *requirement that defendants must prove the elements of the defense.*

Defenses to Liability

The defenses permit defendants either to avoid criminal liability totally, as in acquittal, or to receive an alternative to conviction, such as commitment to a mental hospital in the defense of insanity. Defenses arise in three ways. In **alibi,** defendants could not have committed the crime because, for example, they were in another state when it occurred. Other defenses arise because of the lack of a material element, such as in rape where the victim consented to sexual penetration. Finally, some defenses arise out of the principles of justification (self-defense being the best known) and excuse (insanity being the best known). This section focuses on these third kinds of defenses.

In **defenses of justification,** defendants admit that they committed the crime but contend that under the circumstances what they did was right, or justified. Hence, in self-defense, technically speaking, defendants argue: "I killed my victim intentionally, but because he or she was about to kill me. Under the circumstances, it was right for me to kill." Notice that the justification focuses on the defendant's *actions,* that is, the rightness of conduct. In **defenses of excuse,** defendants admit that what they did was wrong, but contend that under the circumstances they were not responsible. Hence, in the insanity defense, again speaking technically, defendants argue that they were wrong to commit their crimes, but because they suffered from mental diseases or defects that impaired their ability to know or control what they were doing, they are not legally responsible. Notice that the excuse focuses on *actors,* that is, the lack of responsibility of individuals.[11]

Defenses of Justification

The justifications for crimes include a cluster of defenses related to actions taken to protect people, homes, and property, and to carry out public duties. This chapter focuses on self-defense and the defense of homes and property. The defense of execution of public duties we save for chapters including examples of criminal justice officers acting in the course of their professional responsibilities. We usually think of killing in self-defense; however, the defense applies to any justified force. Self-defense includes self-protection; it excludes preemptive strikes and retaliatory attacks. The *defendant* must prove self-defense, unlike the case against defendants that the government must prove beyond a reasonable doubt. The law designates this requirement that the defendant prove the elements of the defense an **affirmative defense.**

Self-Defense The right of self-defense justifies the use of force against attackers only in the following circumstances:

1. The defendant did not provoke the attack.
2. The use of force was a last resort.
3. The attack was imminent.
4. The defendant used only the amount of force required to repel the attack.
5. The defendant intended only to defend against an imminent attack, not to prevent a future attack or to retaliate for a past attack.

Self-defense is not limited to the defense of oneself. Historically, it included repelling attacks against members of one's immediate family. Several states still require a special relationship between the defender and the person attacked. Other states have abandoned this requirement, permitting the defense of any other person.

Two recent kinds of cases have raised questions about the application of the defense of self-defense. The first concerns battered women. Some of these women respond to long-term battering by eventually killing their batterers. When charged with criminal homicide, they may claim they were acting in self-defense. In a New Mexico case, George Gallegos was a heavy drinker. Over the years, whenever he drank, he was likely to beat his wife. During one of the beatings when she was pregnant, he had thrown her against a wall, causing the premature birth of one of her children. Gallegos had frequently put a gun to his wife's head, threatening to kill her; had put a knife on her breasts, threatening to cut them off if they grew larger; and on the day of the killing had sodomized her against her will.

On that day, Mrs. Gallegos told her husband that she was tired of being hurt. When she threatened to leave, he pulled his gun and told her he would kill her if she tried. That evening, when he called her into the bedroom, Mrs. Gallegos testified that she was afraid, that she did not know whether her husband intended to kill, rape, or beat her. She picked up his loaded shotgun in the living room. While he was lying on the bed, she cocked the rifle and shot him, then stabbed him numerous times. The trial court refused Mrs. Gallegos's request to introduce evidence of self-defense to the jury, who convicted her of voluntary manslaughter. The appeals court reversed the decision, ordering a new trial so that she could introduce evidence of self-defense.[12]

A second problem of self-defense concerns people who, particularly if they live in large cities become frightened by the brutal attacks they read about and take measures to defend themselves. The *You Decide* in this section relates the case of Bernhard Goetz, who generated national attention when he shot four youths in a New York City subway. The case demonstrates some of the complexities of applying the law of self-defense, and of balancing the law against the jury's discretion to act according to powerful influences outside the letter of the law.

You Decide

Can You Shoot Muggers When They Approach?

People v. Goetz, 68 N.Y.2d 96, 506 N.Y.S.2d 18, 497 N.E.2d 41 (1986) Chief Justice Watchler delivered the following opinion:

A Grand Jury has indicted defendant on attempted murder, assault, and other charges for having shot and wounded four youths on a New York City subway train after one or two of the youths approached him and asked for $5. The lower courts, concluding that the prosecutor's charge to the Grand Jury on the defense of justification was erroneous, have dismissed the attempted murder, assault, and weapons possession charges. We now reverse and reinstate all counts of the indictment.

Facts

On Saturday afternoon, December 22, 1984, Troy Canty, Darryl Cabey, James Ramseur, and Barry Allen boarded an IRT express subway train in The Bronx and headed south toward lower Manhattan. The four youths rode together in the rear portion of the seventh car of the train. Two of the four, Ramseur and Cabey, had screwdrivers inside their coats, which they said were to be used to break into the coin boxes of video machines. Defendant Bernhard Goetz boarded this subway train at 14th Street in Manhattan and sat down on a bench towards the rear section of the same car occupied by the four youths. Goetz was carrying an unlicensed .38-caliber pistol loaded with five rounds of ammunition in a waistband holster. The train left the 14th Street station and headed towards Chambers Street.

It appears from the evidence before the Grand Jury that Canty approached Goetz, possibly with Allen beside him, and stated "Give me five dollars." Neither Canty nor any of the other youths displayed a weapon. Goetz responded by standing up, pulling out his handgun and firing four shots in rapid succession. The first shot hit Canty in the chest; the second struck Allen in the back; the third went through Ramseur's arm and into his left side; the fourth was fired at Cabey, who apparently was then standing in the corner of the car, but missed, deflecting instead off a wall of the conductor's cab. After Goetz briefly surveyed the scene around him, he fired another shot at Cabey, who then was sitting on the end bench of the car. The bullet entered the rear of Cabey's side and severed his spinal cord.

All but two of the passengers fled the car when, or immediately after, the shots were fired. The conductor, who had been in the next car, heard the shots and instructed the motorman to radio for emergency assistance. The conductor then went into the car where the shooting occurred and saw Goetz sitting on a bench, the injured youths lying on the floor or slumped against a seat, and two women who had apparently taken cover also lying on the floor. Goetz told the conductor that the four youths had tried to rob him.

While the conductor was aiding the youths, Goetz headed towards the front of the car. The train had stopped just before the Chambers Street station and Goetz went between two of the cars, jumped onto the tracks, and fled. Police and ambulance crews arrived at the scene shortly thereafter. Ramseur and Canty, initially listed in critical condition, have fully recovered. Cabey remains paralyzed, and has suffered some degree of brain damage.

On December 31, 1984, Goetz surrendered to police in Concord, New Hampshire. . . . Later that day, after receiving Miranda warnings, he made two lengthy statements, both of which were tape recorded with his permission. In his statements, which are substantially similar, Goetz admitted that he had been illegally carrying a handgun in New York City for three years. He stated that he had first purchased a gun in 1981 after he had been injured in a mugging. Goetz also revealed that twice between 1981 and 1984 he had successfully warded off assailants simply by displaying the pistol.

According to Goetz's statement, the first contact he had with the four youths came when Canty, sitting or lying on the bench across from him, asked "How are you?" to which he replied "Fine." Shortly thereafter, Canty, followed by one of the other youths, walked over to the defendant and stood to his left, while the other two youths remained to his right, in the corner of the subway car. Canty then said "Give me five dollars." Goetz stated that he knew from the smile on Canty's face that they wanted to "play with me." Although he was certain that none of the youths had a gun, he had a fear, based on prior experiences, of being "maimed."

Goetz then established "a pattern of fire," deciding specifically to fire from left to right. His stated intention at that point was to "murder [the four youths], to hurt them, to make them suffer as much as possible." When Canty again requested money, Goetz stood up, drew his weapon, and began firing, aiming for the center of the body of each of the four. Goetz recalled that the first two he shot "tried to run through the crowd [but] they had nowhere to run." Goetz then turned to his right to "go after the other two." One of these two "tried to run through the wall of the train, but . . . he had nowhere to go." The other youth (Cabey) "tried pretending that he wasn't with [the others]" by standing still, holding on to one of the subway hand straps, and not looking at Goetz. Goetz nonetheless fired his fourth shot at him. He then ran back to the first two youths to make sure they had been "taken care of." Seeing that they had both been shot, he spun back to check on the other two. Goetz noticed that the youth who had been standing still was now sitting on a bench and seemed unhurt. As Goetz told the police, "I said '[Y]ou seem to be all right, here's another,' " and he fired the shot which severed Cabey's spinal cord. Goetz added that "if I was a little more under self-control . . . I would have put the barrel against his forehead and fired." He also admitted that "if I had had more [bullets], I would have shot them again, and again, and again."

After waiving extradition, Goetz was brought back to New York and arraigned on a felony complaint charging him with attempted murder and criminal possession of a weapon. The matter was presented to a Grand Jury in January 1985, with the prosecutor seeking an indictment for attempted murder, assault, reckless endangerment, and criminal possession of a weapon. . . . [T]he Grand Jury indicted defendant on one count of criminal possession of a weapon in the third degree for possessing the gun used in the subway shootings, and two counts of criminal possession of a weapon in the fourth degree. . . . It dismissed, however, the attempted murder and other charges stemming from the shootings themselves.

Several weeks after the Grand Jury's action, the People, asserting that they had newly available evidence, moved for an order authorizing them to resubmit the dismissed charges to a second Grand Jury. . . . [T]he second Grand Jury filed a 10-count indictment, containing four charges of attempted murder, four charges of assault in the first degree, one charge of reckless endangerment in the first degree, and one charge of criminal possession of a weapon in the second degree. . . . On October 14, 1985, Goetz moved to dismiss the charges contained in the second indictment alleging, among other things, that the evidence before the second Grand Jury was not legally sufficient to establish the offenses charged and that the prosecutor's instructions to that Grand Jury on the defense of justification were erroneous and prejudicial to the defendant so as to render its proceedings defective.

On November 25, 1985, while the motion to dismiss was pending before Criminal Term, a column appeared in the *New York Daily News* containing an interview which the columnist had conducted with Darryl Cabey the previous day in Cabey's hospital room. Cabey told the columnist in this interview that the other three youths had all approached Goetz with the intention of robbing him. . . . The court, after inspection of the Grand Jury minutes . . . held . . . that the prosecutor, in a supplemental charge elaborating upon the justification defense, had erroneously introduced an objective element into this defense by instructing the grand jurors to consider whether Goetz's conduct was that of a "reasonable man in [Goetz's] situation." The court . . . concluded that the statutory test for whether the use of deadly force is justified to protect a person should be wholly subjective, focusing entirely on the defendant's state of mind when he used such force. It concluded that dismissal was required for this error because the justification issue was at the heart of the case. . . . On appeal by the People, a divided Appellate Division affirmed Criminal Term's dismissal of the charges. . . .

Justice Asch, in a dissenting opinion in which Justice Wallach concurred, disagreed with both bases for dismissal relied upon by Criminal Term. On the justification question, he opined that the statute requires consideration of both the defendant's subjective beliefs and whether a reasonable person in defendant's situation would have had such beliefs. . . . Justice Wallach stressed that the plurality's adoption of a purely subjective test effectively eliminated any reasonableness requirement contained in the statute. Justice Asch granted the People leave to appeal to this court. We agree with the dissenters.

Opinion

Penal Law article 35 recognizes the defense of justification, which "permits the use of force under certain circumstances." Penal Law § 35.15 (1) sets forth the general principles governing all such uses of force: "[a] person may . . . use physical force upon another person when and to the extent he reasonably believes such to be necessary to defend himself or a third person from what he reasonably believes to be the use or imminent use of unlawful physical force by such other person." Section 35.15 (2) provides: "A person may not use deadly force upon another person under circumstances specified in subdivision one unless (a) He reasonably believes that such other person is using or about to use deadly physical force . . . or (b) He reasonably believes that such other person is committing or attempting to commit a kidnapping, forcible rape, forcible sodomy or robbery."

Thus, consistent with most justification provisions, Penal Law § 35.15 permits the use of deadly physical force only where requirements as to triggering conditions and the necessity of a particular response are met. As to the triggering of conditions, the statute requires that the actor "reasonably believes" that another person either is using or about to use deadly physical force or is committing or attempting to commit one of certain enumerated felonies, including robbery. As to the need for the use of deadly physical force as a response, the statute requires that the actor "reasonably believes" that such force is necessary to avert the perceived threat.

Because the evidence before the second Grand Jury included statements by Goetz that he acted to protect himself from being maimed or to avert robbery, the prosecutor correctly chose to charge the justification defense. . . . The prosecutor properly instructed the grand jurors to consider whether the use of deadly physical force was justified to prevent either serious physical injury or a robbery, and, in doing so, to separately analyze the defense with respect to each of the charges. . . .

When the prosecutor had completed his charge, one of the grand jurors asked for clarification of the term "reasonably believes." The prosecutor responded by instructing the grand jurors that they were to consider the circumstances of the incident and determine "whether the defendant's conduct was that of a reasonable man in the defendant's situation." It is this response by the prosecutor—and specifically his use of "a reasonable man"—which is the basis for the dismissal of the charges by the lower courts. As expressed repeatedly in the Appellate Division's plurality opinion, because section 35.15 uses the term "he reasonably believes," the appropriate test, according to that court, is whether a defendant's beliefs and reactions were "reasonable to him." Under that reading of the statute, a jury which believed a defendant's testimony that he felt that his own actions were warranted and were reasonable would have to acquit him, regardless of what anyone else in defendant's situation might have concluded. Such an interpretation defies the ordinary meaning and significance of the term "reasonably" in a statute, and misconstrues the clear intent of the Legislature, in enacting section 35.15, to retain an objective element as part of any provision authorizing the use of deadly physical force. . . .

We cannot lightly impute to the Legislature an intent to fundamentally alter the principles of justification to allow the perpetrator of a serious crime to go free simply because that person believed his actions were reasonable and necessary to prevent some perceived harm. To completely exonerate such an individual, no matter how aberrational or bizarre his thought patterns, would allow citizens to set their own standards for the permissible use of force. It would also allow a legally competent defendant suffering from delusions to kill or perform acts of violence with impunity, contrary to fundamental principles of justice and criminal law. We can only conclude that the Legislature retained a reasonableness requirement to avoid giving a license for such actions. The plurality's interpretation, as the dissenters . . . recognized, excises the impact of the word "reasonably."

Accordingly, the order of the Appellate Division should be reversed, and the dismissed counts of the indictment reinstated.

Questions

New York tried Goetz for attempted murder and assault. The jury acquitted him of both charges. The jury said Goetz "was justified in shooting the four men with a silver-plated .38-caliber revolver he purchased in Florida." They did convict him of illegal possession of a firearm, for which the court sentenced Goetz to one year in jail. Following the sentencing, Goetz told the court that this case is really more about the deterioration of society than it is about me. . . . Well, I don't believe that's the case. . . . I believe society needs to be protected from criminals.[13]

Criminal law professor George Fletcher followed the trial closely. After the jury acquitted Goetz, Professor Fletcher noted that

> the facts of the Goetz case were relatively clear, but the primary fight was over the moral interpretation of the facts. . . .
>
> I am not in the slightest bit convinced that the four young men were about to mug Goetz. If he had said, "Listen, buddy,

I wish I had $5, but I don't," and walked to the other side of the car, the chances are 60-40 nothing would have happened. Street-wise kids like that are more attuned to the costs of their behavior than Goetz was.[14]

Do you agree with Professor Fletcher? Or do you agree with what Bernhard Goetz did? Did the jury apply the law of self-defense correctly, according to the standards set out in the text? What influences outside the law influenced the jury's verdict of acquittal? Should the fear of city dwellers take precedence over narrow legal definitions? Explain.

---

common law *translation of the traditions, customs, and values of the English community into legal rules.*

Defense of Home and Property

From the earliest days of the **common law,** when the traditions, customs, and values of the English community were translated into legal rules, killing a person who attempted to break into one's house at night was justifiable homicide. Modern law follows the common-law rule in granting owners the right to use force to defend their homes. Colorado has enacted a "make-my-day law" to protect occupants of homes who use force against intruders. The law grants immunity from legal action, including criminal prosecution, to occupants of homes who use force, including deadly force, against "one who has made an unlawful entry into the dwelling."[15]

The make-my-day law generated controversy when David Guenther—who later killed his own wife—shot at his neighbors and killed one of them. David Guenther was unpopular in the neighborhood. He constantly got into altercations with neighbors, abused his wife in the sight and hearing of neighbors, and generally annoyed them. One evening during a party, some neighbors decided to harass David Guenther. They banged on his car, shouted obscenities, and challenged Guenther to come out of his house. They left when Pam Guenther, David's wife, threatened to call the police. Later, when the party goers heard a loud noise at the front door, one of them ran to the door, saw no one, proceeded to the Guenthers, and knocked.

The evidence conflicted at this point, but shortly after the neighbor knocked on the door, David Guenther appeared, and from the doorway fired four shots from a Smith and Wesson .357 Magnum six-inch revolver. One shot wounded the person who had knocked, a second wounded another who was walking across the Guenthers' front yard to help, and a third killed Josslyn Volosin, who was trying to break up the fight. Colorado charged Guenther with second-degree murder and first-degree assault. The trial court dismissed the charges, ruling that the make-my-day law immunized Guenther from prosecution. The Colorado Supreme Court overruled the trial court, holding that the make-my-day law protects only against those who actually *enter* houses.[16]

Most states also permit the use of force to protect property other than homes. Texas, for example, authorizes the use of deadly force to "protect land or tangible property, and movable property . . . when and to the degree [they] reasonably believe the deadly force is immediately necessary . . ." to prevent the commission of serious felonies, such as robbery and arson, if they "reasonably believe" they cannot protect their property "by any other means," or if "the failure to use deadly force" would expose them or others to a "substantial risk of death or serious bodily injury."[17]

Defenses of Excuse

The criminal law recognizes a substantial list of defenses that focus on individual characteristics or conditions that excuse criminal liability. The defenses of excuse include

- Mistake of law and fact.
- Age.

● Duress.
● Entrapment.
● Intoxication.
● Insanity.
● Diminished capacity.
● Mental and biological syndromes.

Mistake   The law distinguishes between two kinds of mistakes, mistake of law and mistake of fact. **Mistake of law** means that a person did not know, or misunderstood, a law. **Mistake of fact** means that defendants did not know a fact at all, or if they did know the fact, they misinterpreted it. Mistake of law is not a defense to criminal liability in most instances. Everyone has heard the saying "Ignorance of the law is no excuse." Suppose you find a $100 bill lying in the street. You take the money and spend it, believing in the old adage, "Finders keepers, losers weepers." Later, someone discovers your find and reports it to the police, who arrest you. You are charged and convicted of theft. You are guilty because the law does not authorize finders to keep lost property. Your ignorance of the law, despite your honest belief that the money you found belonged to you, is not a defense.

Sometimes mistake of law does excuse criminal liability, such as ignorance of the law following reasonable efforts to learn what the law is. For example, Harold Ostrovsky was convicted of fishing without a valid permit. He challenged the constitutionality of the statute requiring permits to fish. The trial judge ruled the statute unconstitutional. Ostrovsky then proceeded to fish again. The Alaska Supreme Court later reversed the trial judge's decision, ruling instead that the statute was constitutional. Alaska prosecuted Ostrovsky for violations of the statute occurring after the trial judge's ruling, but prior to the supreme court's reversal. Ostrovsky argued that the defense of mistake excused him because he had honestly and reasonably relied on the trial judge's ruling that the statute was unconstitutional. The court accepted his defense of mistake of law.

Mistake of fact, on the other hand, has always been a defense to criminal liability. The rationale is that due to a mistake of fact there is no *mens rea* that set the criminal acts in motion. For example, suppose you go to the coat room where you left your coat, pick up one identical to yours, put it on, and go home. In *fact,* the coat belongs to another person. You have satisfied all the requirements for the *actus reus* of larceny—taking and carrying away someone else's property. However, your state of mind does not satisfy the larceny *mens rea*—intending to deprive the owner permanently of possession. Your mistake of fact as to the ownership of the coat excuses your action.

Age   Since the earliest days of the English common law, immaturity has excused criminal liability. The common law recognized three categories of maturity:

1. Individuals too young under all circumstances to be criminally responsible.
2. Individuals mature to the extent that they may or may not be criminally responsible.
3. Individuals mature enough to be criminally responsible in nearly all circumstances.

Modern law still recognizes these categories, but states vary as to the exact age they attach to them. Most states are increasingly integrating the categories to coincide with the jurisdiction of the juvenile court. The modern age categories generally give juvenile courts exclusive jurisdiction up to age 15 or 16. Between 16 and 18, juveniles can be certified; that is, authority to hear their cases can be transferred to adult criminal courts. Usually, this occurs when juveniles are accused of murder, rape, aggravated assault, robbery, and, increasingly, drug-related offenses.

This young man's actions may cause loss and damage to property but his age may "excuse" his criminal responsibility.

duress *defense that a third person forced the defendant to commit the crime.*

As more people live longer, old age has occasionally provided an excuse to criminal liability. In one case, a husband asked his wife of 50 years to get him some bagels. She forgot. According to the prosecutor, "the guy goes berserk and he axes his wife; he kills the poor woman with a Boy Scout-type ax!" The prosecutor did not charge the old man, saying: "What do we do now? Set high bail? Prosecute? Get a conviction and send the fellow to prison? You tell me! We did nothing. The media dropped it quickly and, I hope, that's it." Incidentally, this case provides another excellent example of discretion adapting law to social reality. The law did not provide this man with an excuse of age. The prosecutor did not follow the law automatically; he exercised his independent judgment as to what constituted justice in this individual case, and how best to allocate scarce resources and balance the law and broad community values.[18]

Duress Defendants forced by others to commit crimes have the excuse of **duress.** States vary as to the circumstances that duress comprises. The circumstances relate to:

1. The crimes to which the defense applies.
2. The definition of duress.
3. The connection between the coercion and the completion of the crime.
4. The belief of the defendant regarding the coercion.

In some states, duress is a defense to all crimes except murder; in others, it excuses only minor crimes. States also differ as to the definition of duress. Some recognize only threats to kill unless the defendant commits a crime; others accept threats to do serious bodily harm. Threats to harm others, to damage reputation, or to destroy property do not qualify. Most states require that defendants face immediate harm unless they commit the crime. The degrees of immediacy, however, vary from state to state. Some require the threat of "instant death"; others accept imminent threats.

Entrapment Law enforcement officers who entrap citizens into committing crimes create the excuse of **entrapment.** American law rejected the entrapment defense until the twentieth century because, as one court put it:

> We are asked to protect the defendant, not because he is innocent, but because a zealous public officer exceeded his powers and held out a bait. The courts do not look to see who held out the bait, but to see who took it.[19]

In the course of the twentieth century, attitudes have evolved from indifference to government inducements to commit crime to a limited sympathy toward entrapped defendants. In addition, the law of entrapment reflects a growing intolerance of government pressures on law-abiding citizens to commit crimes. Present entrapment law attempts to catch habitual criminals, but not at the expense of innocent citizens.[20]

The entrapment defense arises because police find it difficult to detect consensual crimes or crimes without complaining witnesses, such as prostitution, gambling, pornography, official wrongdoing, and illicit drug offenses. The cases of John DeLorean, the former General Motors executive convicted for cocaine trafficking; the "Greylord" investigation that exposed bribery among older judges and court personnel in Chicago; and "Abscam," the exchange of money and other valuables for favorable legislation from members of the U.S. Congress, are all instances in which suspects required government encouragement to commit convictable acts. From Henry VIII to Hitler and Stalin, most police states have used government agents to repress political opponents. Furthermore, government enticement flouts the wise admonition of the great English prime minister William Gladstone that government should make it *easy* to do right and *difficult* to do wrong, and the Lord's prayer entreaty to "*lead* us not into temptation, but *deliver* us from evil."[21]

The law does not prevent police encouragement. Encouragement includes law enforcers who

- Act as victims, intending by their actions to encourage suspects to commit crimes.
- Communicate their encouragement to suspects.
- Have some influence on the commission of a crime.

Agencies adopt various techniques to enforce the laws against unsuspecting participants, including making requests to commit crimes, forming personal relationships with suspects, appealing to personal considerations, promising benefits as a result of committing crimes, and supplying and helping to obtain contraband.[22]

Entrapment occurs when law enforcement crosses the line between encouragement and unacceptable inducement. Courts measure when officers cross the line by two tests. The majority adopts the **predisposition test,** which focuses on defendants' intent. According to this view, entrapment occurs only when the government induces defendants who were not predisposed—that is, had no desire—to commit crimes. The crucial question in the predisposition test is: Where did criminal intent originate? If it originated with the defendant, then the government did not entrap the defendant.

Sherman v. United States illustrates the predisposition test. In this case, a government undercover agent, Kalchinian, met Sherman in a drug treatment center, struck up a friendship with him, and eventually asked Sherman to get him some heroin. Sherman, an addict in treatment to control his addiction, at first refused. After several weeks of Kalchinian's pleading, Sherman broke down and obtained the requested heroin. The Supreme Court ruled that Kalchinian entrapped Sherman, because Sherman's reluctance and his being in treatment hardly predisposed him to commit the crime.[23]

A minority of courts adopts the **inducement test.** This test measures which government actions constitute reasonable encouragement, as opposed to improper inducement. According to the inducement test, if the government engages in conduct that would induce an ordinary, law-abiding citizen to commit the crime, the court should dismiss the case. The inducement test aims at deterring "unsavory police methods." Ordinarily, entrapment is not a constitutional question. It focuses on either *mens rea,* as in the predisposition test; or, as in the inducement test, on the public policy question of proper law enforcement conduct. In some cases, however, government conduct may be so outrageous that it violates due process of law. According to retired Supreme Court Justice Lewis Powell, due process of law might "reverse the conviction of a predisposed defendant," depending on "the outrageousness of police behavior."[24]

The *You Decide,* "Was the Defendant Entrapped?" illustrates one tactic government agents use to encourage habitual criminals to commit crimes, and also how difficult it might be to draw the line between acceptable encouragement and prohibited entrapment.

You Decide | "Was the Defendant Entrapped?"

An undercover FBI agent developed a sexual relationship with a target. After a period of sexual intimacy, she asked the target to sell illegal drugs to some "friends" who, unknown to the target, were FBI agents. The Ninth Circuit Court of Appeals said that it saw "no principled way to identify a fixed point along the continuum from casual physical contact to intense physical bonding beyond which the relationship becomes a violation of due process." The court rejected the claim that the FBI agent's sexual intimacy violated the due process clause.[25]

Do you agree? Can the law answer such questions? Or does the answer depend more on using discretion to reflect the values lying behind the law and enforcement practices in question?

Intoxication The law distinguishes between voluntary and involuntary intoxication. Voluntary intoxication never excuses criminal liability. It may, however, negate *mens rea.* For example, a heavily intoxicated person may not have the mental capacity to premeditate a killing; premeditation is a material element in first-degree murder. Involuntary intoxication sometimes excuses criminal liability. Involuntary intoxication includes cases in which defendants do not know they are taking intoxicants, or know it but do so under duress. In a case in which a man took cocaine tablets that his friend told him were "breath perfumer" pills, the court allowed the defense of involuntary intoxication.[26]

Taking intoxicants knowingly qualifies as the defense of involuntary intoxication only under extreme duress. One such case involved an 18-year-old youth traveling with an older man across the desert. The man insisted that the youth drink some whiskey. When the youth declined, the man became abusive. The youth, afraid the man would abandon him in the middle of the desert, drank the whiskey, got drunk, and killed the older man. The court rejected the involuntary intoxication defense, holding that the older man had not compelled the youth to drink against his will.[27]

Insanity The insanity defense commands great public, philosophical, religious, and scholarly attention. However, it plays only a small part in the day-to-day operations of criminal justice. Defendants rarely plead insanity, and rarely succeed if they do. The few defendants who plead insanity successfully do not automatically go free. The defense of insanity requires that defendants were insane at the time they committed the crime, because that is when they must have had the *mens rea* required to impose criminal liability. Special proceedings follow virtually all successful insanity pleas to determine whether the defendants are still insane. This determination is necessary because otherwise such defendants would go free. Only if courts find defendants mentally ill and dangerous can they detain them. Courts invariably find defendants mentally ill and dangerous and order them detained in maximum security hospitals that resemble prisons. They remain in these hospitals until they regain their sanity, which usually takes a long time and may not happen at all. John Hinckley, the attempted assassin of President Reagan in the early 1980s, is typical. He is still detained in a maximum security hospital where he will probably remain for the rest of his life.

Insanity is a legal, not a medical, term. Hence, mental illness and insanity are not synonymous; only some mental illnesses constitute insanity. Furthermore, insanity includes not only mental illness but also mental deficiencies. Specifically, only mental illnesses and deficiencies that sufficiently impair either reason or will (or both) constitute insanity. Mental illness or deficiency constitutes a necessary, but not sufficient, component of insanity. Three tests determine insanity:

1. The right-wrong test or *M'Naughten* rule.
2. The right-wrong test supplemented by the irresistible impulse test.
3. The substantial capacity or American Law Institute test.

The **right-wrong test** focuses on mental diseases and defects that impair the capacity to reason. The test, frequently called the *M'Naughten* rule, had its origins deep in history, but its present form derives from a famous English case during the reign of Queen Victoria. In 1843, Daniel M'Naughten had the paranoid delusion that the prime minister, Sir Robert Peel, had masterminded a conspiracy to kill him. M'Naughten shot at Peel in delusional self-defense, but mistakenly killed Peel's personal secretary. The jury acquitted M'Naughten. On appeal, the House of Lords—England's highest court of appeals—formulated the right-wrong test. The test consists of five elements: That defendants

1. at the time of the crime
2. suffered from a mental disease or defect
3. that so impaired their capacity to reason
4. that either they did not know what they were doing, that is, they did not understand the nature and quality of their actions,
5. or, if they knew what they were doing, they did not know it was wrong to do it.[28]

Several jurisdictions have supplemented the right-wrong test with the **irresistible impulse test.** The irresistible impulse test focuses on mental diseases and defects that affect defendants' willpower, or the ability to control their actions, at the time of the crime. The irresistible impulse test requires that the defendant

1. at the time of the crime
2. suffered from a mental disease or defect
3. that caused the loss of power to choose between right and wrong.

In other words, defendants know right from wrong, but their mental disease or defect so affects their willpower that it has created the irresistible impulse to commit the crime.

The right-wrong test, supplemented in some states by irresistible impulse, remained the law in most states until the 1960s. At that time, the **substantial capacity test,** often called the ALI (American Law Institute) test, came into prominence. The substantial capacity test focuses on both reason and will. Formulated by the American Law Institute, the substantial capacity test requires that defendants

1. at the time of the crime
2. as a result of mental disease or defect
3. lacked substantial capacity
4. to appreciate the wrongfulness (criminality) of their conduct
5. or to conform their conduct to the requirements of the law.

Significantly, the test focuses on *substantial* capacity. In other words, the mental disease or defect need not have totally destroyed reason or will. It is enough that it substantially impairs reason or will.

John Hinckley's assassination attempt on former President Reagan, graphically captured and replayed hundreds of times on television, horrified the nation. In his trial, Hinckley pleaded insanity, claiming he shot at the president to gain actress Jodie Foster's attention. The jury acquitted Hinckley on a verdict of not guilty by reason of insanity. Despite Hinckley's confinement to a maximum security hospital, where he remains, a public outcry resulted from the belief that he had somehow "gotten away with" trying to kill a popular president. Criminal law professor Charles Nesson, for example, wrote:

> To many Mr. Hinckley seems like a kid who had a rough life and who lacked the moral fiber to deal with it. [But] lots of people have tough lives, many tougher than Mr. Hinckley's, and manage to cope. The Hinckley verdict let those people down. For anyone who experiences life as a struggle to act responsibly in the face of various temptations to let go, the Hinckley verdict is demoralizing, an example of someone who let himself go and who has been exonerated because of it.[29]

The Hinckley case produced a powerful reaction and a flurry of legislation regarding the insanity defense. Some jurisdictions shifted the burden of proving insanity from government to defendant, and raised the standard of proof, sometimes to proof beyond a reasonable doubt. Others, intending to ensure that defendants are labeled "guilty" and spend time incarcerated, revised the verdict from not guilty by reason of insanity to guilty but insane. Others returned to a strict right-wrong test of insanity. The irresistible impulse test had always generated criticism, never empirically demonstrated but powerfully felt, that it somehow contributed to weakening willpower.

California, for example, in a referendum overwhelmingly approved by the voters, returned to a pre-M'Naughten insanity definition, the "wild-beast" test. According to the wild-beast test, defendants must demonstrate the reasoning and willpower of wild beasts, that is, a mental disease or defect that has totally destroyed their capacity both to know right from wrong and to exercise any willpower to control their actions. The California Supreme Court later rejected that formulation, interpreting the referendum to mean a return to right-wrong from the substantial capacity test that was in effect at the time the referendum passed.[30]

Diminished Capacity
Some defendants suffer from mental diseases or deficiencies that do not impair their reason and will sufficiently to satisfy the insanity tests. **Diminished capacity** provides a defense in some jurisdictions if the impairment affects the defendant's capacity to form *mens rea*. Many states reject this defense, maintaining that there is no middle ground: a person is either sane or insane. At the other extreme, the American Law Institute Model Penal Code recommends that evidence of diminished capacity should always be admissible to negate *mens rea*. The few jurisdictions that permit evidence of diminished capacity restrict its use to specific intent crimes of more than one degree—usually murder. Ordinarily, this means that defendants can show diminished capacity to premeditate a murder, thereby reducing charges from first- to second-degree murder.

This conduct may be criminal but is it *malum in se*?

Syndrome Defenses Various syndromes affecting mental states have led to novel defenses in criminal law. We have already discussed one of these syndrome defenses—that of the battered woman—in the section on self-defense. A New York case introduced the possibility of another syndrome defense, the premenstrual syndrome (PMS) defense. A medical team in a hospital emergency room diagnosed welts on a young girl's legs and blood in her urine as the result of child abuse. At a preliminary hearing, her mother admitted to beating her child but argued that she blacked out due to PMS and, hence, could not have formed the intent to hurt her daughter. The prosecutor dropped the felony charges, so the PMS defense never reached court.[31]

The aftermath of the Vietnam War gave rise to yet another syndrome defense. As is widely demonstrated, the war took a heavy emotional toll on combat soldiers. The effects have created what some call a "mental health crisis which has had a dramatic impact on the incidence of major crime." Medical research has demonstrated a correlation between the stress of guerrilla-type warfare and later antisocial conduct, called the posttraumatic stress syndrome. Lawyers have begun using this syndrome to formulate a "Vietnam War vet" defense.[32]

Classifications of Criminal Law

Criminal law classifies crimes according to various criteria, including the

- Type and duration of punishment.
- "Evil" of the crime committed.
- Social harm inflicted.

Felony, Misdemeanor, and Violation Crimes classified according to the type and duration of penalties are felonies, misdemeanors, and violations. These are ancient classifications, demonstrating how the past influences present criminal law. The great legal historian Frederic William Maitland

capital felonies *felonies punishable by death or life imprisonment.*

misdemeanors *crimes punishable either by fines or up to one year in jail.*

gross misdemeanors *offenses punishable by jail terms from 30 days to one year.*

petty misdemeanors *offenses punishable by fines or up to 30 days in jail.*

violation *petty offenses punishable by fines and not part of a criminal record.*

mala in se *offenses that are inherently "evil."*

mala prohibita *offenses that are illegal only because a law defines them as crimes.*

maintained that the reasons for old classifications may have long since died, but their ghosts rule us from the grave. He meant that even when classifications have outlived their usefulness, they influence present practice. Dividing crimes into felonies and misdemeanors is one example. Historically, felonies were crimes punishable by death. Present law divides felonies into **capital felonies,** punishable by death or life imprisonment, and ordinary felonies, punishable by one year or more in prison. Therefore, the category includes both serial killers such as Ted Bundy at one extreme and individuals who steal $500 at the other. The breadth of its scope makes the classification largely meaningless in any sociological sense. It serves mainly as an administrative device to determine who gets the death penalty, life imprisonment, or incarceration in a state prison.[33]

Misdemeanors include crimes punishable either by fines or up to one year in jail. Common misdemeanors include simple assaults and battery, prostitution, and disorderly conduct. Most jurisdictions divide misdemeanors into **gross misdemeanors,** punishable by jail terms from 30 days to one year, and **petty misdemeanors,** punishable by fines or up to 30 days in jail. A third category of crime, **violation,** is punishable by a small fine and does not count as part of a criminal record. Traffic offenses fall into this group.

Mala in Se and Mala Prohibita

Another legal classification sorts crimes according to their perceived "evil." This old arrangement overlaps the felony, misdemeanor, and violation categories and defines some crimes as inherently bad (the Latin *mala in se*). Crimes such as murder and rape fall into this category. Other behavior constitutes a crime only because the law says so (the Latin *mala prohibita*). Parking in a no-parking zone is *malum prohibitum*.

This classification reflects the roots of American criminal law in the religious and moral codes of England and colonial America. Although morality was frequently viewed as a preoccupation of the New England Puritans, the Anglicans of Virginia, Pennsylvania Quakers, and Maryland Catholics also infused criminal law with a moral component. The major felonies and the "morals" offenses—fornication, prostitution, sodomy, gambling, and public drunkenness—descend from this religious and moral heritage.[34]

In practice, no clear line separates *mala in se* and *mala prohibita* offenses. In fact, research demonstrates that despite legal theories that cling to the distinction, and notwithstanding talk of an ethical core in the criminal law, perpetrators consider "justifiable" many crimes formally classified *mala in se*. That is, perpetrators consider their "criminal" actions as informal means to put right a keenly felt wrong. They may concede that their conduct "technically" violates criminal law, but they believe that what they did definitely was not *evil*. The sociologist Donald Black has written:

> There is a sense in which conduct regarded as criminal is often quite the opposite. Far from being an intentional violation of a prohibition, much crime is moralistic and involves the pursuit of justice. It is a mode of conflict management, possibly a form of punishment, even capital punishment. Viewed in relation to law it is self-help. To the degree that it defines or responds to the conduct of someone else—the victim—as deviant, crime is social control.[35]

Despite these findings, legal theorists maintain that some crimes *are* inherently evil. The *You Decide,* "Are Some Crimes Inherently Evil" asks you to consider the usefulness of the distinction.[36]

The notion of inherently evil crimes suggests a consensus as to what constitutes serious crime. Research does not confirm this conclusion. Not everyone agrees that activities such as drug use, gambling, and consensual adult sexual conduct are inherently evil, even if they are crimes. What about the following findings?

● More than one-third of all college men would rape if they thought they could get away with it.[37]

● Most murders are committed by people who think they are righting some wrong done to them. According to Donald Black, "most intentional homicide in modern life is a response to conduct that the killer regards as deviant. Homicide is often a response to . . . matters relating to sex, love, or loyalty, to disputes about domestic matters (financial affairs, drinking, housekeeping) or affronts to honor, to conflicts regarding debts, property, and to child custody, and to other questions of right and wrong." For example, one youth killed his brother during an argument about the brother's sexual advances toward their younger sisters.[38]

● The vast majority of assaults occur between people who know each other. In most cases, assailants believe they are redressing grievances. They, in fact, take the law into their own hands in order to punish a wrongdoer. They do not believe they were wrong in what they did, even though they may agree it was against the law to do so. For example, some brothers attacked and beat their sister's boyfriend because he turned her into a drug addict. In another case, a gang member shot his gang leader for taking "more than his proper share of the proceeds from a burglary. Years later, the same individual shot someone who had been terrorizing young women—including the avenger's girlfriend—in his neighborhood. Though he pleaded guilty to 'assault with a deadly weapon' and was committed to a reformatory, not surprisingly he described himself as 'completely right' and his victim as 'completely wrong.' "[39]

● Many property offenders know their victims. They have taken or destroyed their victims' property because they believe their victims deserved it. For instance, a man broke into his ex-wife's apartment to take back property he believed was rightfully his.[40]

● A former burglar noted, "We always tried to get the dude that the neighbors didn't like too much or the guy that was hard on the people who lived in the neighborhood. I like to think that all the places we robbed, that we broke into, was kind of like the bad guys."[41]

● In many cases vandalism turns out to be not wanton violence, but an effort to punish what the vandals consider to be wrongdoing. One young man found that someone had broken the radio antenna on his automobile. When he found out who did it, he slashed the culprit's tires in retaliation.[42]

All these examples are crimes, according to the criminal codes of virtually all jurisdictions. Yet none of the perpetrators considered what they did to be evil. Quite the contrary; although "criminals" according to the law, they believed that they were exercising justified social control over "wrongdoers." Ironically, the criminals considered themselves victims; they believed that they had to commit crimes in order to rectify wrongs against them.[43]

---

damages money awarded to plaintiffs in non-criminal lawsuits to recover for injuries they suffered from the actions of defendants.

Crimes and Torts   Some harms can lead to legal actions even though they are not crimes. These private legal wrongs are called torts. Torts provide the grounds on which individuals sue each other, or engage in private litigation. They differ from criminal actions, at least formally, in several respects. In criminal cases, the government and the defendant are the parties to the case; hence, the title of the criminal case is *State* (or *United States,* or sometimes *Commonwealth) v. Simmons* (defendant). In private civil actions, on the other hand, injured persons (plaintiffs) sue individuals who have harmed them (defendants); hence, *Chan v. Gonzalez.* Criminal cases rest on the notion that crime harms society generally, leaving individual injuries to tort actions. Plaintiffs in tort actions seek money, called **damages,** to recoup for injuries. Almost all crimes against persons and property also constitute torts. A burglary, for instance, consists of the tort of trespass; a criminal assault is the tort by the same name.

Criminal prosecutions and tort actions may arise out of the same event, but criminal and tort proceedings are not mutually exclusive. Victims can sue for, and the government can prosecute, injuries arising out of the same conduct. For example, a burglary victim can sue the burglar for trespass and, at least theoretically, collect damages. The government can prosecute the burglar and, if it obtains a conviction, impose punishment.

The criminal law defines what is a crime. The law of criminal procedure governs the enforcement of the criminal law once the criminal law is defined. The law of criminal procedure is the formal side of decision making in law enforcement agencies. It prescribes rules for decisions made at each step in the criminal process, from detecting crime to punishing offenders. These rules derive from several sources, including federal and state constitutions, statutes, court decisions, and the rules and regulations of criminal justice agencies. (See Chapter 1 for fuller discussion of these sources.)

Throughout the book, we will examine the law of criminal procedure as it specifically affects police, courts, and corrections. In this chapter, we focus on overarching principles. Table 3.1 contains a list of the specific provisions in the Bill of Rights and the stages of the criminal process to which they relate.

Due Process of Law

The fundamental constitutional principle of the law of criminal procedure is "due process of law," guaranteed by the due process clauses of the Fifth and Fourteenth Amendments. As defined earlier in this chapter, the due process clauses provide that neither the federal government nor the states "shall deprive any person of life, liberty, or property without due process of law."

We have already discussed substantive due process in connection with the criminal law. We need only mention here that in enforcing the criminal law, as in defining it, the government cannot make decisions or take actions that deprive any person of life, liberty, or property without following proper procedures. Furthermore, the same principles of federalism apply to the law of criminal procedure as apply to criminal law. As early as 1833, the Chief Justice of the U.S. Supreme Court, John Marshall, expressed the view that criminal procedure is a state and local matter. When Congress proposed the Bill of Rights, he wrote, if Congress had meant to take the extraordinary step of "improving the constitutions of the several states . . . they would have declared this purpose in plain . . . language." Therefore, Marshall concluded, the question of whether the Bill of Rights applied to state and local procedure is "of great importance, but not of much difficulty." He meant that the federal Bill of Rights did *not* apply to the states.[44]

Table 3.1
The Bill of Rights and Criminal Justice

The Police
Fourth Amendment
(1) Guarantee against unreasonable search and seizure.

Fifth Amendment
(2) Right to a grand jury indictment.
(3) Right against double jeopardy.
(4) Right to due process.
(5) Right against self-incrimination.

The Courts
Sixth Amendment
(6) Right to a speedy and public trial.
(7) Right to an impartial jury.
(8) Right to notice of charges.
(9) Right to confront witnesses.
(10) Right to a lawyer.

Courts and Corrections
Eight Amendment
(11) Prohibition against excessive bail.
(12) Prohibition against cruel and unusual punishments.

Following the Civil War, the country adopted a number of amendments to the Constitution. The original purpose of these was to bring former slaves into full citizenship, particularly in the former Confederate states. Insofar as criminal justice is concerned, the due process clause of the Fourteenth Amendment is the most important of these "Civil War Amendments." The Fourteenth Amendment, among other things, specifically prohibits the states from depriving citizens of life, liberty, or property without due process of law. Despite this specific prohibition, courts did not apply the due process clause to the states until the 1930s.

It is probably not simply a coincidence that just as Hitler rose to power in Germany, the U.S. Supreme Court decided the landmark Scottsboro case, *Powell v. Alabama*. Both the German war machine during World War I and the rise of fascism had revived fears of arbitrary government. This led to rethinking the application of the Bill of Rights to state and local criminal procedure. The Scottsboro case involved seven black male teenagers traveling on a train from Tennessee through Alabama. The seven youths got into a fight with seven white male teenagers. The black youths threw the white youths off the train, leaving behind two young white women. The women later accused the black youths of gang raping them. Before the train reached Scottsboro, Alabama, a sheriff's posse seized the black youths and took them and the young women to Scottsboro. A hostile mob met them in Scottsboro. The sheriff called up the militia, which guarded the prisoners, courthouse, and courthouse grounds from that point through the arraignment, trial, conviction, and sentencing. In fact, "the proceedings, from beginning to end, took place in an atmosphere of tense, hostile and excited public sentiment."[45]

The black youths were all young, illiterate, and far from home with no friends, relatives, or acquaintances nearby. They were confined under close guard without a lawyer during the few days following the incident until they were found guilty. The court did not appoint a lawyer for them until the morning of the trial. Within minutes, the jury found all seven defendants guilty and the court sentenced them all to death. The U.S. Supreme Court decided—at least in these circumstances—that the Fourteenth Amendment due process clause applied to the states. For the Court, Justice Sutherland wrote:

> It has never been doubted by this court . . . that notice and hearing are preliminary steps essential to the passing of an enforceable judgment, and that they, together with a legally competent tribunal having jurisdiction of the case, constitute the basic elements of the constitutional requirement of due process of law. The words of [the great lawyer, Daniel] Webster . . . that by "the law of the land" is intended "a law which hears before it condemns" have been repeated . . . in a multitude of decisions. . . . [T]he necessity of due notice and an opportunity of being heard is . . . among the "immutable principles of justice which inhere the very idea of free government which no member of the Union may disregard."[46]

The Fundamental Fairness Doctrine

The U.S. Supreme Court has formulated two constitutional doctrines by which to apply the provisions of the Bill of Rights to the states. *Powell v. Alabama* represents the application of the **fundamental fairness doctrine,** or substantive due process doctrine. The fundamental fairness doctrine focuses on the *substance* of fairness, rather than on the *form* of procedure. According to fundamental fairness, due process might include the protections of the Bill of Rights, but it is not equivalent to the Fourth, Fifth, Sixth, and Eighth Amendments. In other words, due process derives its meaning independent of the Bill of Rights. Supreme Court Justice Felix Frankfurter, the doctrine's major proponent, said that fundamental fairness means "those

incorporation doctrine *rule that prescribes that the due process clause of the 14th Amendment includes the procedures guaranteed in the Bill of Rights.*

selective incorporation doctrine *rule that prescribes that the due process clause of the 14th Amendment incorporates only some of the rights guaranteed in the Bill of Rights.*

canons of decency and fairness which express the notions of justice of English-speaking peoples even toward those charged with the most heinous offenses."[47]

To determine fundamental fairness, the Court decided on a case-by-case method what offended those "notions of justice." For example, in *Rochin v. California,* police officers unlawfully entered Rochin's house and forced open his bedroom door. Inside, they found Rochin partially dressed, sitting on the bed with his wife. The officers noticed two capsules on the nightstand. When they asked, "Whose stuff is this?" Rochin grabbed the capsules and put them in his mouth. The officers "jumped upon him" and tried to pull the capsules out of his mouth, but he swallowed them. The police took him to a hospital and forced him to submit to stomach pumping. The vomiting produced by the stomach pumping produced the two capsules, which contained morphine. In reversing Rochin's conviction, the Supreme Court wrote:

> The proceedings by which this conviction was obtained do more than offend some fastidious squeamishness or private sentimentalism about combating crime too energetically. This is conduct that shocks the conscience. Illegally breaking into the privacy of the petitioner, the struggle to open his mouth and remove what was there, the forcible extraction of his stomach's contents . . . are methods too close to the rack and screw.[48]

The Incorporation Doctrine

According to the **incorporation doctrine,** the due process clause guarantees procedural regularity in all cases. Procedural regularity means the procedures specifically spelled out in the Bill of Rights. Therefore, the due process clause of the Fourteenth Amendment *incorporated* the safeguards in the Fourth, Fifth, Sixth, and Eighth Amendments, requiring state proceedings to adhere to them. Some jurists, such as Supreme Court Justice Hugo Black, maintained that the due process clause incorporated all of the Bill of Rights, but the Court never accepted this reading. Instead, during the 1960s, the Court opted for a **selective incorporation doctrine.** The selective incorporation doctrine looked at whether the particular provision in the Bill of Rights was *fundamental* to fair procedure. As of this writing, the Court has incorporated the rights against unreasonable seizures, against self-incrimination, to assistance of counsel, to confront opposing witnesses, to compulsory process to obtain witnesses, and to the prohibition against cruel and unusual punishment. It has *suggested,* but has not specifically ruled, that public trial, notice of charges, and prohibition of excessive bail are also incorporated. It has ruled that due process does *not* require indictment by a grand jury. Once a right is incorporated, it applies in the entirety of its meaning to state proceedings. As one of the doctrine's critics, Associate Supreme Court Justice John Harlan, Jr., put it, the incorporated right applies to the state, "jot for jot and case for case."[49]

Virtually every state has a bill of rights in its constitution that parallels, if not specifically duplicates, the federal Bill of Rights. States cannot *reduce* the state standards below those guaranteed in the federal Bill of Rights; the federal standard represents a constitutional minimum. However, states can *raise* the state standard above the federal standard, and occasionally they have done so. For example, in one leading case, the Michigan Supreme Court differed with the U.S. Supreme Court on whether the Fourth Amendment search and seizure clause permits states to conduct DWI checkpoints at which all motorists are stopped and checked for signs of intoxication. Although upheld by the U.S. Supreme Court, these "seizures" are not supported by probable cause or reasonable suspicion, which the Fourth Amendment ordinarily requires. (See Chapter 6 on police and the law.)

A motorist challenged Michigan's DWI checkpoint law on the grounds that it violated both the unreasonable search and seizure clause in the Fourth Amendment and the parallel clause in the Michigan constitution. The Supreme Court held that the stops were reasonable Fourth Amendment seizures, even though they were not backed up by any facts suggesting that the stopped motorists were intoxicated. The Michigan Supreme Court ruled, however, that stops without reasonable suspicion of intoxication were unreasonable seizures under the Michigan constitution. In raising the minimum standard, Michigan in effect expanded the right against unreasonable searches and seizures for people in Michigan beyond their rights under the United States Constitution. According to the Michigan court,

> [O]ur courts are not obligated to accept what we deem to be a major contraction of citizen protections under our constitution simply because the United States Supreme Court has chosen to do so. . . . This court has never recognized the right of the state, without any level of suspicion whatsoever, to detain members of the population at large for criminal investigatory purposes. . . . In these circumstances, the Michigan Constitution offers more protection than the United States Supreme Court's interpretation of the Fourth Amendment.[50]

Social Theories of Criminal Law and Procedure

Criminal law and procedure do not exist in a value-neutral state outside society. They are living institutions that respond to political and ideological influences. Stating the principles of criminal law and procedure does not explain how and why they originated. Analyzing the words of statutes, court decisions, and legal principles does not explain why legislatures enact particular criminal codes, does not reveal the reasons for courts' interpretations of these codes, and does not account for why the criminal law excludes many social harms from its scope. Social scientists do not accept the proposition that specific statutes simply apply neutral principles of criminal law. They search instead for the influences that create society's demands to write its wishes into criminal law.[51]

Furthermore, examining formal criminal law does not reveal how the criminal law operates in practice; it does not explain discretion. Nonlegal interests influence which crimes citizens decide to report to the police; who the police select for arrest, prosecutors choose for prosecution, juries decide to convict, or judges proceed to sentence; who gets incarcerated; and what decisions are made in corrections agencies. Law reflects the societal values and interests that determine these choices. Law upholds these values and interests, prohibits conduct that threatens them, and authorizes punishment for those who violate them. In other words, law is not a set of moral absolutes; it is a social institution, shaped by time, place, and circumstance.[52]

Consensus and Conflict Perspectives

Our pluralistic society has greatly influenced both the creation of criminal law and the administration of criminal justice. The diverse values of racial, ethnic, and cultural groups make it impossible to explain criminal law and its enforcement without accounting for the influence of pluralism. This requires an exploration of the connection between society and criminal law and procedure.

Throughout history, two contrasting views of the nature of society and social change have prevailed among social theorists. According to the **consensus perspective,** a general agreement regarding values exists in society. The state protects these common values. To the extent that conflict exists, the state mediates among groups with competing values. According to the consensus theory, the state represents the values and interests of the whole society, not those of any particular group or groups. According to the **conflict perspective,** conflict—not consensus—is normal. Conflict is not always violent and out of control. Revolution and civil war only rarely resolve conflict; more frequently, debate and consultation do. Society is composed of groups with conflicting values and interests. The dominant group usually wins the revolutions, civil wars, debates, and consultations. The state represents the values and interests of the group or groups with enough power to control social institutions.[53]

Consensus Theory Consensus theory has an ancient heritage, going back at least to Plato and Aristotle. Its modern version owes much to Émile Durkheim, the great nineteenth-century French sociologist whose ideas have influenced the sociology of law and have contributed to criminal justice theory. Durkheim enunciated two fundamental propositions relevant to understanding the sociology of criminal law:

1. Crime is conduct "universally disapproved of by members of each society. Crimes shock sentiments which, for a given social system, are found in all healthy consciences."
2. "An act is criminal when it offends strong and defined states of the collective conscience."[54]

Based on these ideas, Durkheim suggested two broad hypotheses of the consensus theory:

1. Criminal law is a synthesis of a society's essential morality, based on values that are shared by all "healthy consciences."
2. Society creates crime in order to establish moral boundaries that, if violated, threaten society's basic existence. In other words, the definition of behavior as criminal notifies ordinary people how far they can go without undoing social order.[55]

Sociologist Kai Erikson's classic study, *Wayward Puritans,* tested Durkheim's boundary hypothesis. Erikson studied witchcraft among seventeenth-century New England Puritans. He analyzed evidence about creating, prosecuting, and punishing witchcraft, concluding that the community created "crime waves" to solidify moral boundaries in order to keep the community from disintegrating. Puritans needed witchcraft to keep society from wandering outside settled behavioral boundaries.[56]

Empirical evidence from modern times also supports Durkheim's synthesis hypothesis. Blacks and whites, men and women, rich and poor, young and old, well-educated and poorly educated people agree about what constitutes serious crime. In 1983, researchers asked a selected sample to rank the seriousness of various crimes. The answers displayed broad consensus on the following: Violent crimes were considered most serious, property crimes less serious, and public-order crimes least serious. This compares favorably with rankings in most criminal codes. Table 3.2 contains the results of this comprehensive survey of American opinion concerning the seriousness of offenses. Do your own rankings agree with these findings?[57]

Conflict Theory Consensus theory dominated mainstream criminology in the 1940s and 1950s. Then, in the late 1950s, social conflict theories reemerged. The conflict theorists challenged the notion that consensus is the "normal" state of society. Instead, conflict theory—which enjoys a history in social thought as old as consensus theory—assumes that conflict is the normal state of society. It assumes further that social control requires active constraint, sometimes in the form of coercion. Common values and interests do not produce social control, because they do not exist in real societies. Society is divided into competing classes and interest groups, the most powerful of

Table 3.2

Consensus on the Seriousness of Crimes

Severity Score	Offense—10 Most Serious
72.1	Planting a bomb in a public building (the bomb kills 20 people)
52.8	Forcibly raping a woman, who dies from the injuries
43.2	Robbing a victim at gunpoint, who dies from the robber's shots when the victim struggles
39.2	Husband stabbing a wife to death
35.7	Stabbing a victim to death
35.6	Intentionally injuring a victim, who dies as a result
33.8	Running a drug ring
27.9	Wife stabbing her husband to death
26.3	Skyjacking a plane
25.9	Forcibly raping a woman with no *physical* injury resulting
Severity Score	**Offense—10 Least Serious**
1.1	Disturbing the neighborhood with noisy behavior
1.1	Taking bets on the numbers
1.1	Group hanging around a street corner after police tell them to move on
0.9	Running away from home when under 16
0.8	Being drunk in public
0.7	Breaking the curfew law when under 16
0.6	Trespassing in the back yard of a private home
0.3	Being a vagrant
0.2	Playing hooky from school when under 16[58]

which dominate social institutions, including legislatures, criminal justice agencies, and their processes. The dominant group writes criminal laws that attempt to further their interests and impose their values on the whole society. These laws then become an instrument enabling the dominant classes and interest groups to retain their dominance, and to prevent conflict.[59]

Conflict theory has many variants, but all shift the emphasis from law *breaking* to law *making* and law *enforcing.* Until modern conflict theory reemerged in the late 1950s, most criminologists began their study with criminal law already in place. They considered *criminals,* not criminal *law,* to be the social problem. Conflict theory changed all that. The emphasis on law making and law enforcing led to an examination of criminal law and its enforcement in a new and different light. Conflict theory maintains that criminal law does not reflect absolute, agreed-on principles or universal moral values. Instead, criminal law defines, and criminal justice agencies preserve and protect, the interests and values of the dominant social groups. Criminal law and procedure are means of preserving the dominant group or groups' definition of social order.[60]

Radical Theory Dissatisfaction with both consensus and conflict theory, and with mainstream criminology and criminal justice in general, contributed to the creation of a "new," or radical criminology in the 1960s. It was not, however, exactly new. It drew on the long tradition of social conflict theory discussed in the last section and on Marxist theory. Radical criminology maintains that mainstream criminologists and criminal justice professionals are apologists, if not lackeys, for a capitalist ruling class that dominates the state. Radicals disagree over whether the dominant class consciously exploits the working class, or whether the structure of capitalist society inevitably determines their exploitative actions. Instrumentalists contend that the ruling class consciously decides to exploit. Structuralists maintain that capitalists do not exploit by conscious design, but rather because capitalism by its nature requires exploitative class relationships and class conflict. They believe that the capitalist social and economic structure requires exploitation to operate; criminal law forms but an instrument of that structure. Although the rhetoric often ran high in the 1960s and 1970s, radical criminologists developed a criminal justice theory based on the following propositions:

1. The state's primary purpose is to protect the dominant class in society.
2. This requires controlling the lower classes.
3. The ruling class exploits the working class by wringing profit from overworked laborers.
4. Criminal law controls workers so capitalists can get richer and secure protection for their accumulated riches.
5. Brute force is not always necessary to protect these interests and control the workers. Myths—that laws protect everybody, that everyone has rights against state abuse of power, that everyone can succeed if they will only follow the rules—are important. Sometimes laws that benefit workers are passed, mainly to give substance to the myths. Capitalists do not always get their way; they sometimes lose a battle here and there, but basically criminal law is an instrument to control lower classes.
6. Capitalists sometimes have to commit crimes to maintain the existing power arrangements. Thus, police violate citizens' rights, government abuses its authority, corporations fix prices, and so on. They try not to do this too often because it threatens the myth that law is neutral, just, and evenhanded.
7. Workers commit crimes mainly out of necessity. They prey on other workers, and sometimes capitalists, in order to survive: They steal what they cannot earn. Or, out of frustration with existing unjust arrangements, they erupt in violence against others. Occasionally, they commit "heroic crimes," like attacking the power structure. Their crimes are not bad or evil; they are utilitarian actions necessary to survive in capitalist society.[61]

These brief descriptions oversimplify the consensus, conflict, and radical social theories. Consensus theorists do not maintain that harmony and negotiation always prevail in politics and society; nor do they claim that their theories explain everything in criminal justice. Conflict theorists do not demand an interpretation of social interaction that totally excludes agreement and social cohesion. Radical criminologists do not contend that class determines all laws, that capitalists always win and workers always lose. Consensus, conflict, and radical theorists do maintain that criminal law reflects their theoretical view of social reality.

The Politics of Criminal Law and Procedure

The consensus, conflict, and radical theories suggest but do not elaborate on the political process involved in legislating criminal law and criminal procedure. The decisions to define certain behavior as a crime and to establish rules of criminal procedure depend not only on the ideological approaches to law. They also depend on the interaction of individuals, public and private interest groups, and criminal justice professionals. Scholars have long ago revised the theory that laws reflect the unaltered will of the majority. Sometimes public outrage does get translated relatively unaltered into criminal law. During the 1940s, outrage over a few heinous sex crimes led to the enactment of sexual psychopath laws. More recently, a spate of carjackings spurred Congress and the president into rare quick action when they passed specific federal legislation dealing with taking cars by violence.

An interest group theory has replaced the pure democracy explanation of criminal law and procedure enactments. According to this theory, public and private groups, led by moral entrepreneurs, or reformers, put pressure on legislators by a variety of means to purify society. Prohibition and anti-prostitution crusades are two examples of how the theory can explain the politics of criminal law. However, neither public outrage nor moral crusades explain the enactment of the bulk of criminal law or the law of criminal procedure. Recent research shows that criminal justice professionals decide the content of run-of-the-mill legislation, that is, the majority of criminal law and criminal procedure. This happened in the revision of most states' and the federal government's criminal procedure codes that took place during the 1960s and 1970s. Barton Ingraham, in an analysis of the enactments of these revisions, concluded:

> Legislative reform of criminal procedure . . . is usually initiated by some agency or official of the state with law-making or law-enforcing authority. The job of drafting the new code is then placed in the hands of a group consisting mostly of lawyers, judges, and law professors.[62]

Timothy Lenz reached a similar conclusion in a detailed analysis of sentencing reform in Indiana, Minnesota, and Mississippi. He found that although conditions might bring legislation into public view and generate heated opposition, the public "is not constantly watching over" the legislative process. As a result, "policy is usually the domain of a narrow set of political and professional interests." Richard Hollinger and Lonn Lanza-Kaduce examined the enactment of computer crime legislation that rapidly spread throughout the country during the 1970s. They found that, except for one organization linked to the private security industry and the American Bar Association, few interest groups influenced this legislation. They concluded that neither interest groups nor moral entrepreneurs were responsible for most computer crime legislation. Instead, computer crime experts and legislators wrote most of the laws.[63]

Summary

Substantive criminal law defines what behavior and harms are criminal. The law of criminal procedure prescribes the rules governing how the government enforces the criminal law once behavior and harms are defined as crimes. Only behavior defined according to the principle of legality, the principles of criminal liability, and the principles of justification and excuse can be criminal in our constitutional democracy. In substantive criminal law, the principle of legality, as it is expressed in due process, requires that criminal statutes specifically define the behavior and harm that the criminal law prohibits and punishes. The principles of criminal liability, also known as the material elements in crime, include the requirements of a *mens rea* that generates an *actus reus*. In crimes that require causing a harmful result, the criminal act and state of mind must concur to produce the harmful result.

The defenses to criminal liability include alibi, negation of a material element, and the justifications and excuses. The justifications focus on *action*, justifying it by claiming that under the circumstances it was right for the person to act. Self-defense, the defense of others, and the defenses of home and property are the principal justifications. The excuses focus on *actors*, excusing them if they were not responsible, even if their actions were wrong. The major excuses include insanity, immaturity and advanced age, duress, involuntary intoxication, and entrapment.

Understanding the law of criminal procedure requires keeping in mind the federal nature of American government. That is, we have federal, state, and local criminal procedure. Most criminal justice administration, and hence, most criminal procedure is state and local. Due process is the overarching principle that governs the law of criminal procedure. Both the Fifth and the Fourteenth Amendments impose the requirement of due process on the law of criminal procedure. The due process clause of the Fifth

Amendment prohibits the federal government from denying any person life, liberty, or property without due process of law. The Fourteenth Amendment due process clause imposes the same prohibition on the states. By means of the Fourteenth Amendment due process clause, the Supreme Court has interpreted due process to require that the states guarantee to criminal suspects and defendants most of the protections in the Bill of Rights to the United States Constitution.

The substantive criminal law and the law of criminal procedure comprise more than the principles of legality, criminal liability, justification, and excuse. Societal influences create demands to write societal interests into law. The definitions of crimes and the enforcement of law respond to these demands. Social scientists focus on understanding the interests that determine a range of decisions, including which crimes citizens report to the police; who the police select for arrest, prosecutors choose for prosecution, juries decide to convict, and judges proceed to sentence; and what decisions corrections agencies make.

The pluralistic society of the United States has greatly influenced criminal law and procedure. The diverse values stemming from culture surrounding race, ethnicity, gender, and social status have all contributed both to the substantive and procedural criminal law as they operate day to day. Consensus theory posits that criminal law codifies the law, and criminal justice agencies administer it, according to agreed-on basic values and interests. Conflict theory perceives society as divided into competing classes and interest groups, the most powerful of which dominate criminal law creation and administration.

Review Questions

1. Define and identify the differences between criminal law and criminal procedure.

2. What are the requirements for qualifying conduct and/or harm as a crime?

3. Identify the main sources of criminal law.

4. Define and explain due process as it relates to criminal law.

5. Explain the void-for-vagueness doctrine.

6. Identify and define the material elements in criminal liability.

7. List and define the four kinds of *mens rea.*

8. Compare and contrast the general principles of justification and excuse.

9. Identify and define the main defenses of justification and excuse.

10. List and describe the main legal classifications of crimes.

11. Describe the relationship of the Bill of Rights in the United States Constitution to state and local criminal procedure.

12. Describe the informal influences on the formation and enforcement of criminal law.

13. Compare and contrast consensus, conflict, and radical theories as they relate to criminal law and procedure.

14. Explain the politics of enacting criminal law and criminal procedure.

Notes

1. *Lanzetta v. New Jersey,* 306 U.S. 451, 453 (1939).

2. *State v. Metzger,* 319 N.W.2d 459 (Neb. 1982).

3. *Michael M. v. Superior Court of Sonoma County,* 450 U.S. 464 (1981).

4. *Griswold v. Connecticut,* 381 U.S. 479 (1965).

5. *Bowers v. Hardwicke,* 478 U.S. 186 (1986).

6. *Ravin v. State,* 537 P.2d 494 (Alaska 1975).

7. *State v. Damms,* 100 N.W.2d 592 (Wis. 1960) (attempted murder); *State v. Furr,* 235 S.E.2d 193 (N.C. 1977) (solicitation to commit murder).

8. American Law Institute, *Model Penal Code,* Section 2.02(2)(d).

9. See Wayne R. LaFave and Austin W. Scott, Jr., *Criminal Law,* 2d ed. (St. Paul: West Publishing Co., 1986), 267–277.

10. Jerome Hall, *General Principles of Criminal Law,* 2d ed. (Indianapolis: Bobbs-Merrill, 1960), 1–26.

11. Douglas N. Husak, "Justifications and Accessories," *Journal of Criminal Law and Criminology* 80 (1989): 496–497; George Fletcher, *Rethinking Criminal Law* (Boston: Little, Brown, 1978), 759.

12. *State v. Gallegos,* 719 P.2d 1268 (App. 1986).

13. *New York Times,* 14 January 1989.

14. Quoted in *New York Times,* 23 January 1989; see also George Fletcher's interesting book on the Goetz trial, *A*

Crime of Self-Defense: Bernhard Goetz and the Law on Trial (New York: Free Press, 1988).

15. *Colorado Statutes,* Section 18-1-704.5, 8b, C.R.S. (1986).

16. *People v. Guenther,* 740 P.2d 971 (Colo. 1987).

17. *Texas Criminal Code,* Section 9.42.

18. Fred Cohen discusses the case in *Criminal Law Bulletin* 21 (1985): 9.

19. *People v. Mills,* 70 N.E. 786, 791 (N.Y. 1904).

20. Paul Marcus, "The Development of Entrapment Law," *Wayne Law Review* 33 (1986): 5.

21. James Tuohy and Rob Warden, *Greylord: Justice Chicago Style* (New York: Putnam Press, 1989); Jonathan C. Carlson, "The Act Requirement and the Foundations of the Entrapment Defense," *Virginia Law Review* 73 (1987): 1011.

22. Lawrence P. Tiffany et al., *Detection of Crime* (Boston: Little, Brown, 1967).

23. *Sherman v. United States,* 356 U.S. 369 (1958).

24. Concurring in *Hampton v. United States,* 425 U.S. 484 (1976).

25. *United States v. Simpson,* 813 Fd.2d 1462 (9th Cir. 1987).

26. *People v. Penman,* 110 N.E. 894 (Ill. 1915).

27. *Burrows v. State,* 297 P. 1029 (Ariz. 1931).

28. *M'Naughten's Case,* 8 Eng. Rep. 718 (1843).

29. "A Needed Verdict: Guilty but Insane," *New York Times,* 1 July 1982, 29.

30. *People v. Skinner,* 704 P.2d 752 (Cal. 1985).

31. "Not Guilty Because of PMS?" *Newsweek,* 8 November 1982, 111.

32. John R. Ford, "In Defense of the Defenders: The Vietnam Vet Syndrome," *Criminal Law Bulletin* 19 (1983): 434–43.

33. Stephen E. Brown, "Involuntary Smoking: A Case of Victims Without Crime," 1984 Meeting of Mid-South Sociological Association; Thomas Simmons, "Should the Library Throw the Book at 'Em?" *New York Times,* 23 February 1985.

34. David Flaherty, "Law and the Enforcement of Morals in Early America," in *Law in American History,* Donald Fleming and Bernard Bailyn, eds. (Boston: Little, Brown, 1971), 203–53.

35. Donald Black, "Crime as Social Control," *American Sociological Review* 48 (1983): 34–45.

36. Rollin M. Perkins and Ronald Boyce, *Criminal Law,* 3d ed. (Mineola, N.Y.: Foundation Press, 1982), 88.

37. Neil A. Malamouth, "Rape Proclivity Among Males," *Journal of Social Issues* 57, no. 4 (1981): 140.

38. Donald Black, "Crime as Social Control," 34–36.

39. Ibid., 36.

40. Ibid., 37.

41. Ibid.

42. Ibid.

43. Peter Rossi et al., "The Seriousness of Crimes: Normative Structure and Individual Differences," *American Sociological Review* 39 (1974): 224–237.

44. *Barron v. Baltimore,* 32 U.S. 7 Pet. 243, 250 (1833).

45. Francis A. Allen, "The Law as a Path to the World," *Michigan Law Review* 77 (1978): 157–58.

46. *Powell v. Alabama,* 287 U.S. 45 (1932).

47. *Rochin v. California,* 342 U.S. 165 (1952).

48. Ibid.

49. Jerold H. Israel, "Selective Incorporation Revisited," *Georgetown Law Journal* 71 (1982): 274; Justice Harlan concurring in *Duncan v. Louisiana,* 391 U.S. 145 (1968).

50. *Michigan v. Sitz,* 496 U.S. 444 (1990); *Sitz v. Department of State Police,* 506 N.W.2d 209 (Mich. App. 1993), 218.

51. Lawrence Friedman, *A History of American Law,* 2d ed. (New York: Simon and Schuster, 1985).

52. For a good introduction to the enormous body of literature on the relation of law to society, see Friedman, *A History of American Law,* 36–56.

53. Ralf Dahrendorf, "Out of Utopia: Toward a Reorientation of Sociological Analysis," *American Journal of Sociology* 64 (1958): 126; Thomas J. Bernard, *The Consensus-Conflict Debate: Form and Content in Social Theories* (New York: Columbia University Press, 1983); William J. Chambliss, *Criminal Law in Action* (Santa Barbara: Hamilton Publishing Company, 1975), vii; Douglas Hay, "Crime and Justice in Eighteenth- and Nineteenth-Century England," in *Crime and Justice: An Annual Review of Research,* Norval Morris and Michael Tonry, eds., 2 (1980): 45–84.

54. Émile Durkheim, *The Division of Labor in Society* (New York: Free Press, 1933), 73–80.

55. William Chambliss and Robert Seidman discuss this in *Law, Order, and Power,* 2d ed. (Reading, Mass.: Addison-Wesley Publishing Co., 1982), 171–206.

56. Kai T. Erikson, *Wayward Puritans: A Study in the Sociology of Deviance* (New York: John Wiley and Sons, 1966).

57. Rossi, "The Seriousness of Crimes," 227–37.

58. *The Severity of Crime* (Washington, D.C.: Bureau of Justice Statistics, January 1984).

59. William J. Chambliss, *Criminal Law in Action,* 2d ed. (New York: Macmillan Publishing Company, 1984), 16–31.

60. David Greenberg, ed., *Crime and Capitalism: Readings in Marxist Criminology* (Palo Alto: Mayfield Publishing Co., 1981), 1–26, 190–94.

61. Richard Quinney, *Class, State, and Crime: On the Theory and Practice of Criminal Justice* (New York: David McKay Co., 1977).

62. Barton L. Ingraham, "Reforming Criminal Procedure," in Alvin W. Cohn and Benjamin Ward, eds., *Improving Management in Criminal Justice* (Beverly Hills: Sage Publications, 1980), 28.

63. Timothy Lenz, "Group Participation in the Politics of Sentencing Reform" (University of Minnesota, Ph.D. dissertation, 1986), 282; Richard C. Hollinger and Lonn Lanza-Kaduce, "The Process of Criminalization: The Case of Computer Crime Laws," *Criminology* 26 (1988): 101.

PART TWO

Police

oles of the Police

CHAPTER MAIN POINTS

1. American policing originated in the medieval notion of community responsibility for law enforcement.

2. Fundamental social changes in the 1800s led to the creation of public police departments with paid police officers.

3. Twentieth-century reform movements have aimed to create a professional police.

4. In the past 20 years, American policing has markedly improved.

5. American law enforcement reflects our federal system and the separation of powers.

6. Despite local variations, police departments share the fundamental characteristics of bureaucratic organizations performing similar functions.

7. Police departments vary in administrative style depending on the community they serve, the goals their chiefs set, and the values and ambitions of individual officers.

8. More people now work in private security than in public policing.

9. Police departments provide the only around-the-clock public service.

10. Police perform three main functions: law enforcement, order maintenance, and community service.

11. Formally, the law requires the police to enforce all laws, all the time; informally, discretion permits the police to perform their functions according to community, administrative, and personal priorities.

12. Police spend the least amount of their time enforcing the criminal law.

13. Police functions overlap and reinforce each other.

Every profession has a mission. Armies have the mission to win wars; doctors to cure the sick; teachers to educate the young. To fulfill these missions, professionals play particular roles, become part of organizations, and engage in a range of strategies. Of course, the mission and, therefore, the roles and strategies of professions is not so clear and focused as these statements suggest. Armies are sometimes dispatched to keep the peace, and soldiers play the role of "peacekeepers." Doctors may pursue the mission of ending suffering, playing the role of "ministers of mercy" by allowing or even helping terminally ill patients to die. Teachers sometimes go beyond their traditional mission, helping students through crises by assuming the role of counselor. All these added missions, roles, and strategies can be sources of controversy.

Perhaps no profession has more complex and varied missions than policing. Perhaps none has faced more controversy both from within and outside as to what police missions, roles, and strategies ought to be. Police expert and criminologist Carl B. Klockars asked the students in his introductory course on American police to write down a definition of 'police.' These are some of those definitions. Which do you think is correct? When you have finished the chapter, reconsider these definitions and your own.

1. The police are a body of handsome young men and women . . . who bravely fight the forces of evil to make the world safe for decent people. [This definition was offered by a handsome and humorous young man who worked for the campus police.]

2. The police are a bunch of hot shots who get their kicks from hassling blacks, students, and most other people who are trying to have a good time. [This definition was the effort of a tall, thin, hairy fellow with a widely advertised appetite for controlled substances.]

3. The police are an agency of government which enforces the law and keeps the peace. [This one came from a very serious young woman who always sat in the front row. She remembered it from another class.]

4. The police are a weapon the state uses to oppress the working classes, the poor, and minorities. [The author of this definition was an intense young Marxist.]

5. The police are the people who come into my father's restaurant to get free food. [This from a second-generation Eastern European student.]

6. The police are the people who drive police cars. [The effort of one of the brightest students I have ever taught. She went on to become a lawyer.][1]

To the public, to politicians, in most of the news media, and on television and movie dramas, the police mission is to enforce the laws against serious crimes, such as murder, rape, robbery, aggravated assault, and, increasingly, drug law violations. To fulfill this mission, the police mainly play the role of crime fighters. In reality, the police mission and roles are much more complex. This chapter explores the major missions and roles of the police. Chapter 5 examines the strategies police use to accomplish their missions.

Formal and Informal Sides of the Police Mission

"The police in modern society . . . have an 'impossible' task," wrote police expert Peter K. Manning twenty years ago.

To much of the public [Manning continues] the police are seen as alertly ready to respond to citizen demands, as crime-fighters, as an efficient, bureaucratic, highly organized force that keeps society from falling into chaos. The policeman himself considers the essence of his role to be the dangerous and heroic enterprise of crook-catching and the watchful prevention of crimes. . . . They do engage in chases, in gunfights, in careful sleuthing. But these are rare events.[2]

This "rare" side of police work that looms so large in the public mind and on television is the formal side. Here, particularly with serious crimes, laws and other formal rules substantially affect day-to-day actions and decision making in the form of arrests, searches, interrogation, and identification procedures. (See Chapter 6.) Police officers spend far more time and their departments expend far more resources on the other side of police work—maintaining order and providing other services to communities. For this much larger side of police work, informal, discretionary decision making is most common. Both in defining disorder and in responding to it, police officers are granted wide discretion, which they are called on frequently to exercise. Police departments are the only public service agency on call 24 hours a day, 365 days a year. People call the police to solve all kinds of problems, from fights, drunkenness, rowdy youths, prostitutes, and panhandlers on the street, to domestic disturbances, noisy parties, lost children, and animals in distress, to directions to the nearest hospital, post office, or school. With the exception of schools, police departments touch the lives of

Figure 4.1

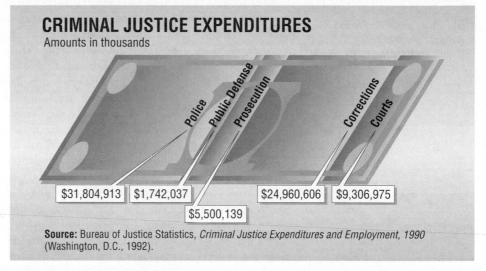

CRIMINAL JUSTICE EXPENDITURES
Amounts in thousands

Police | Public Defense | Prosecution | Corrections | Courts

$31,804,913 | $1,742,037 | | $24,960,606 | $9,306,975

$5,500,139

Source: Bureau of Justice Statistics, *Criminal Justice Expenditures and Employment, 1990* (Washington, D.C., 1992).

more citizens in more ways than any other public agency. The police also consume the largest share of criminal justice expenditures (see Figure 4.1). About 17,000 independent police agencies employ more than a half million people.

In maintaining order, the police, like most other "street-level bureaucracies," balance conflicting interests in enforcing vaguely defined standards. They use their judgment to "do the right thing," without clear guidelines and with little consensus. However, whether in maintaining order, providing services, or enforcing criminal law, one distinctive feature more than any other defines the role of the police—they have the power to back up their decisions with force.[3]

According to Jerome H. Skolnick, sociologist of the police, and James J. Fyfe, former New York City police officer and now professor of criminal justice,

> Statistics suggest that the risk of physical injury is greater in many lines of industrial work than in policing, but cops are the ones to whom society accords the right to use, or to threaten to use, force. This assignment and the capacity to carry it out are said to be the central feature of the role of police in society.[4]

History of Police

The earliest organized police forces were those of ancient Egypt and Mesopotamia. Sometime around 1500 B.C., these societies established police forces that were recognized as efficient and effective, although they had reputations for torturing suspects to obtain confessions and mistreating prisoners. The testimony of police in court was considered accurate and trustworthy. The Roman Empire also had an organized police force. In 27 B.C., Emperor Augustus appointed an urban officer with power to maintain public order. In 6 A.D., the Roman *vigiles,* a large police force that patrolled the streets of Rome day and night, was created.[5]

English Origins

About 900 A.D. in England, law enforcement became the responsibility of local inhabitants. After the Norman Conquest in 1066, King William instituted true community policing. The "frankpledge" required every male over 12 years of age to form a group of 10 members, called a tithing. All swore to apprehend, hold, bring to court, and testify against members of their tithing who committed crimes, or to report rumors and information that raised suspicions about members' behavior. The law imposed heavy fines for breaches of frankpledge. Ten tithings constituted a hundred, over which a constable appointed by a local noble had charge. Hundreds were in turn grouped into shires (counties), supervised by shire reeves (sheriffs).[6]

The frankpledge system never worked effectively. People had enough to do merely to survive. Furthermore, sheriffs could not supervise constables who were widely scattered, linked if at all by poor, dangerous, and frequently impassable roads. In 1285, the Statute of Westminster remodeled frankpledge into the parish constable-watch system. Every parish, the smallest unit of government in medieval England, appointed two constables, either by lot or by some form of election by freeholders. Constables, who served without pay for one year, selected watchmen to aid them in their three primary duties. First, they maintained order, patrolling town and village streets from dusk until dawn, ensuring that all local people were indoors and quiet, that no strangers were wandering about, and that generally "all's well." Second, they performed services, such as lighting street lamps, clearing garbage from streets, and dousing fires. Third, they enforced the criminal law. Supposedly, they engaged in both proactive and reactive policing. **Proactive policing** means that the police themselves initiate action to control crime, hence the term *proactive*. **Reactive policing** means that the police respond to calls from victims and witnesses, hence the term *reactive*. As proactive police, their mere presence was supposed to deter crime, and by patrolling streets, lanes, and alleys they were supposed to search aggressively for wrongdoing. Reactively, they raised and administered the hue and cry, whereby they and those they ordered to help pursued suspects caught red-handed (literally, with blood on their hands) to the parish border.

Colonial America

The American colonies adopted the watch system with few, if any, modifications. As with the English police, American police mainly reacted to calls for help, seldom adopting a proactive posture. Although they were frequently admonished to take such initiative, stories abound about their failings in that regard. In fact, the evidence shows that only considerable pressure could rouse them to do anything. Their unwillingness to act comports with their position as unpaid amateurs compelled to perform a thankless task after hours (they served only during the night). Criminal investigation was a private matter. Colonial America had no counterparts to the modern detective; victims built their own cases. Constables' crime-fighting responsibilities ended with the hue and cry.[7]

The Nineteenth Century

The local parish constable-watch system endured both in England and the United States until the mid-1800s, when rapid population increases, crowded cities, and industrialization produced fundamental and rapid social change and dislocations. Riot, general disorder, and increased crime, particularly property offenses, rendered the watch system virtually unworkable. Calls to replace it with various substitutes began as early as the mid-1700s. Sir John Fielding and Henry Fielding (author of the classic British novel *Tom Jones*), two London magistrates, Patrick Colquhoun, magistrate and law reformer, and Jeremy Bentham, the great philosopher and law reformer, called for a proactive police. Henry Fielding, when he became chief magistrate in Bow Street, appointed about a half dozen "thief takers." Known as the "Bow Street Runners," they consisted of a roving band of former London constables who pursued lawbreakers, broke up criminal gangs, and arrested suspects.[8]

In the end, England modified the constable-watch system into a strengthened and centralized constabulary. In 1829, under Prime Minister Sir Robert Peel's leadership, Parliament mandated publicly funded police forces (ever since called "Bobbies") throughout England. Like the old constabulary, the Bobbies were reactive police forces. They maintained order, provided services (the street lights still needed lighting!), and responded to calls regarding crime. But they were organized into "chains of command," capable of deployment in large and small groups. They were also better trained, better paid, and considerably more numerous.

In 1845, New York organized a police force modeled on the British constabulary. Philadelphia and Boston quickly followed suit. By 1855, cities as far inland as Milwaukee had adopted English-style police departments. Their principal organization consisted of a chief, assisted by a deputy, who headed citywide departments, subdivided into precincts, patrolled by paid officers. Officers eventually wore uniforms and carried guns as well as "nightsticks," or batons as they were called then. Police work ceased to be a duty; it became a job.[9]

The "new" police strongly resembled the old in several respects. Despite encompassing more territory, police localism persisted, reflected in intradepartmental controversy, rivalry, and friction between divisions and precincts. Nineteenth-century police continued to perform the traditional multiple functions of their colonial forebears. The Boston police chief, for instance, supervised fire fighting and street cleaning as well as peacekeeping and crime fighting. No one questioned this four-pronged responsibility, or found it odd. In fact, the word 'police'—from the word 'polity'—meant broad, general governmental responsibility for public good, not the narrower crime fighting that modern usage prescribes.[10]

Detective work remained private. Police departments did not add special detective units until the late 1800s. No amount of change in police structure and personnel could possibly prevent the upheaval that immigration, urbanization, and industrialism caused in a formerly rural, Protestant, Anglo-Saxon America. However, social turmoil did provoke calls for police reform, primarily for better officers not only to staff the new units, but also to patrol the streets.[11]

The Progressive Era

As the twentieth century opened, the typical urban police officer in the United States was a poorly paid, low status white male, a recent immigrant with little or no education, appointed by a local politician and expected to enforce the law according to the ward's wishes. According to Richard A. Staufenberger,

> They knew who put them in office and whose support they needed to stay there. Their job was to manage their beat; often they became completely enmeshed in the crime they were expected to suppress. Corruption, brutality, and racial discrimination, although not universal, were characteristic of most big city departments.[12]

Throughout the twentieth century, improving the police has meant creating a "professional" police force. A professional police force consists of the following elements:

- Expert officers, formally educated and trained.
- Autonomous departments, free of external political influence.
- Department-formulated and -implemented rules.
- Administrative efficiency.
- Impartial, uniform enforcement of the criminal law.[13]

Professionalization has sometimes been imposed on police departments from the outside in the form of statutes and judicial decisions. Some have

Police in the Progressive Era were intimately involved with the community they served.

professionalized their departments from within, in a process called administrative rule making. No matter what the source, not everyone agrees that a professional police force should include all the characteristics in the bulleted list. Some observers have rediscovered what they perceive to have been the advantages of the more personalized police departments of the nineteenth century.[14]

Two great reform waves during the twentieth century catalyzed the police reform movement. In the Progressive Era, from about 1900 to 1914, sweeping reforms were instituted throughout criminal justice. Progressive Era reforms included three major proposals intended to make police departments more professional and subject to rules, less personal and subject to discretionary judgments:

1. Centralize by concentrating most authority in an autonomous chief.
2. Upgrade personnel by means of selection, training, and discipline.
3. Restrict the police role to enforcing the criminal law.

These reforms originated outside police departments, were urged by middle-class, civic-minded reformers, and largely failed.[15]

From 1920 to 1960

From the 1920s through the 1950s, reforms inspired by innovative chiefs enjoyed greater success. Richard Sylvester, chief of the Washington, D.C., Police Department, during his tenure as president of the reformist International Association of Chiefs of Police, preached reforms to police chiefs around the nation. He stressed technological innovations, concentration on crime control, and police professionalism.[16]

August Vollmer, chief of the Berkeley, California, Police Department, pioneered many police reforms during this era. He introduced intelligence tests, psychiatric tests, and neurological tests to aid in the selection of police recruits. He became the first chief to call for college education for police and to hire college students as police officers. Furthermore, Vollmer established close links with the University of California at Berkeley. He also initiated scientific crime detection and crime-solving methods. Furthermore, the Berkeley Police Department became the first to use automobile patrol.

Another reformist chief, O. W. Wilson, one of Vollmer's students, advocated bureaucratic efficiency as a critical element in police reform. As chief of the Wichita, Kansas, Police Department, Wilson conducted the first systematic study of the effectiveness of one-officer squad cars. Wilson's study found that single officer squads were efficient, effective, and economical. Wilson implemented single officer patrol, despite vigorous complaints from officers about the risk to their safety.[17]

Technological advances during the first decades of the twentieth century also contributed to police professionalism. The patrol car made it possible to cover large areas in shorter periods of time. The two-way radio improved supervision and enhanced the power of the police to communicate with each other. The telephone created a link between citizens and the police. Technology and professionalism had their disadvantages, however. They raised public expectations about, and demands for, police service. Moreover, technology and professionalism diminished—and sometimes removed entirely—the personal relationships police had with the communities they served.

The 1960s

The second great reform movement took place during the 1960s. Self-styled liberal reformers called for formalizing the criminal process, particularly the whole range of police-citizen encounters, from street contacts to interrogation and other procedures in police departments. The cataclysmic transformation to modern America that began in the years after the Civil War and then accelerated bore some bitter fruit by the 1960s. A predominantly urban, industrial, pluralist America challenged rural, agricultural America, dominated by white Anglo-Saxon Protestant men and their values. The challengers demanded to share the promises of American life—abundance, freedom, and justice. Their hopes were raised and quickly dashed. The belief that a "quick fix" could assure everybody an opportunity to share the good life evaporated. Understanding the police in the 1960s requires appreciating the false hopes and the resulting frustration, anger, destruction, and, ultimately, realistic goals that resulted from this turmoil.[18]

Liberals called for "professional police" while riots raged and reports of street crime rates soared, especially in the nation's largest cities. It was becoming increasingly difficult to deny that poverty, race, and gender created a chasm between the promise and reality of American life. The disorder and destruction created by riots and the fear and frustration brought on by street crime in major cities focused attention on the police, who bore the major responsibility for dealing with both problems. Big city police became convenient scapegoats for upheaval, crime, and disorder. But to any thoughtful observer, it was clear that the police could not allay or alter the fundamental causes of disorder that lay beneath the social and economic realities in American life, brought into such sharp and painful focus during those troubled days.

"Law and order" was a major theme of the 1964 presidential election campaign. The significance of the Republican nominee Barry Goldwater's appeals for law and order were not lost on Lyndon Johnson, despite his landslide victory. In the aftermath of the election, Johnson created the President's Commission on Law Enforcement and the Administration of Justice. The Crime Commission, as it was called, gave serious attention to:

● The complex police role in American society.
● The fragmented nature of law enforcement.
● The poor training and minimal education of police officers.
● Police corruption, brutality, and prejudice.
● The separation of police from the communities they serve.
● The consequent diminution in the public support on which effective policing ultimately depends.[19]

Intense and often sharply critical public attention catapulted the police unionization movement into prominence. By the late 1960s, police officers were frustrated, angry, and fed up with poor pay, unrelenting criticism, dictatorial chiefs, urban riots, unrealistic demands that they solve the nation's social problems, and Supreme Court opinions that "handcuffed the police instead of the criminal." Regardless of whether this "handcuffed police" perspective was accurate or whether unions were the answer, almost all large-city departments, except those in the South, became unionized.

Unionization had a major impact on police administration. It wrought a revolution in police management by reducing the power of management. Police chiefs now had to share their power by negotiating with unions over many issues. Furthermore, according to historian of the police Samuel Walker, the union movement "won dramatic improvement in salaries and benefits for officers along with grievance procedures that protected the rights of officers in disciplinary hearings." Not everyone favored unionization—and it still has its share of critics. Some reformers believed unions "resisted innovation and were particularly hostile to attempts to improve police community relations." Nevertheless, the union movement represents a major concrete result of the troubled 1960s.[20]

The Legacy of Twentieth-Century Reform

Historically, achievement falls short of promise in reform movements, and this was true of both great twentieth-century police reform movements. A new federal agency, the Law Enforcement Assistance Agency (later, Administration), or LEAA, was created to accelerate reform in criminal justice. However, controversy surrounded the LEAA from its inception because the agency symbolized a basic ideological conflict. Liberals who wanted more expenditures for reform, training, and innovative programs criticized the LEAA as a repressive component in the Nixon administration's law-and-order campaign. They claimed the LEAA's sole aim was to supply police with sophisticated weaponry to suppress legitimate grievances. Conservatives defended the expenditures and the policies behind them as necessary to preserve order in a rapidly disintegrating society. Still others, mainly social scientists, challenged the agency's effectiveness in reducing crime or preserving order and criticized its failure to concentrate on evaluating existing, and creating experimental, programs. Congress gradually reduced its funding until the LEAA dissolved in 1980.[21]

In the 30-plus years since the President's Commission issued its report, we have witnessed considerable progress, despite problems that have plagued American policing since colonial times. The government awarded early grants to local police departments to improve police-community relations and to upgrade hardware, such as radios and other equipment. In 1969, the Nixon administration launched a major effort to aid departments engaged in programs to reduce specific crimes, such as robbery and burglary. Education and training have increased. Police have formulated and adopted more and better-articulated policies, and they have developed rules governing police practices. Finally, we have enormously advanced our knowledge of policing. More than courts and corrections have, police departments have willingly participated in evaluations of their work, even when research has found police practices deficient. They have also established experiments that have led to changes in policies and practices. These advances demonstrate that the legacy of the 1960s includes more than riot, disorder, and dislocation.[22]

The Structure of Law Enforcement

As a law enforcement agency, American police reflect our federal system, operating at federal, state, county, and municipal levels. Unlike most other countries, the United States has no national police force. Law enforcement agencies operate within the executive branch of federal, state, county, and municipal government, varying in size, operation, and style. All law enforcement agencies enjoy virtual autonomy. However, they have in common a bureaucratic structure that formally operates according to a hierarchical chain of command. Local law enforcement agencies, the primary concern of this book, all operate under similar, if not identical, legal codes. Still, despite the formal structure, police officers exercise wide discretion in performing most functions. In addition to public police, private security forces have also played their part in American law enforcement; today, they constitute a significant part of the police structure.

Federal Law Enforcement Agencies

The executive branch of government, and nominally the president, controls federal law enforcement. In fact, a large number of independent federal agencies perform a variety of law enforcement functions. The opposition to centralized police, particularly a national police force, led to the piecemeal creation of federal agencies to enforce specific federal laws. The major federal law enforcement agencies include:

- *U.S. Marshal's Service.* The Marshal's Service is a separate agency within the Department of Justice. The marshals protect the federal courts, judges, and jurors; guard federal prisoners from arrest to conviction; investigate violations of federal fugitive laws; serve summonses; and control custody of money and property seized under federal law.
- *The U.S. Customs Service.* Customs inspectors examine all cargo and baggage entering the country. Special agents investigate smuggling, currency violations, criminal fraud, and major cargo frauds. Special customs patrol officers concentrate on contraband, such as drugs and weapons, at official border crossings, seaports, and airports.
- *The Bureau of Alcohol, Tobacco, and Firearms (ATF).* ATF deals with the criminal use of explosives and with arson. Working with state and local police, it investigates arson cases. ATF has also pursued motorcycle gangs, such as the Hell's Angels, who violate federal firearms and explosives laws, for drug trafficking.
- *Immigration and Naturalization Service (INS).* INS administers immigration and naturalization laws. Border patrol agents patrol more than 8,000 miles of land and coastal boundaries to the United States. INS takes into custody and arranges for the deportation of illegal aliens entering or residing in the country.
- *Drug Enforcement Administration (DEA).* DEA enforces all federal narcotics and dangerous drug legislation.

● *Federal Bureau of Investigation (FBI).* The FBI investigates more than 200 federal crimes. In addition to law enforcement, the FBI assists other federal, state, and local agencies, through its extensive fingerprint files and other records. The FBI National Academy provides aid for some enforcement agencies throughout the country.

Federal law enforcement agencies receive a lot of public attention, far in excess of their actual presence and effect. This is particularly true in the wake of some horrible tragedy following the politically controversial use by the government of deadly force against families and organizations. Two such tragedies occurred in the early 1990s, and they prompted widespread criticism and calls for not only restrictions on the use of deadly force but also a major cutback in federal law enforcement in local areas. In August 1992, Randy Weaver, a self-proclaimed white separatist, was a fugitive from justice for failing to appear at his trial on charges that he sold illegal weapons. Weaver, his family, and federal officers engaged in a shootout in Ruby Ridge, Idaho, during an attempt by federal agents to apprehend Weaver. When Deputy United States Marshal William Degan approached Weaver's cabin, the shootout began. Both Degan and Weaver's son Samuel were killed. In another shootout the following night, Weaver's wife and another son, 14 years old, were also killed. More than 100 federal, state, and local officers then surrounded the cabin where Weaver and his three daughters, ages 16 years, 10 years, and 10 months, remained.[23]

In February 1993, 100 ATF agents moved in on a compound where David Koresh and dozens of his Branch Davidian followers were living near Waco, Texas. In a 45-minute gun battle between the Davidians and the ATF, four agents were killed, several other agents were wounded, and an unknown number of Davidians were killed and wounded. The compound remained

Federal law enforcement generated controversy for its use of force against David Koresh and his followers in Waco, Texas.

surrounded while negotiations continued, the object of which was to get the Davidians to leave the compound, where it was believed they were stashing firearms. In April, FBI agents, having lost patience with the negotiations, attacked the compound with a tank and tear gas. A fire broke out, burning the compound to the ground and killing everyone inside.[24]

State Law Enforcement Agencies

Some states have true state police agencies with statewide authority. These state police forces originated with the Texas Rangers, who in the early 1800s patrolled the Texas settlements. Following the Civil War, Massachusetts and Connecticut created state police agencies to combat vice. In the wake of labor-management strife as a consequence of rapid industrialization, Pennsylvania adopted a state police agency to quell industrial violence. These states overcame resistance generated by a fear that centralized state police agencies threatened both civil liberties and local autonomy.

In the years following 1910, when the number of motor vehicles proliferated, the need for highway traffic control generated new calls for state police. States such as Texas, Pennsylvania, Connecticut, and Massachusetts added a state trooper division to their existing organization. Most states never overcame the opposition to a centralized state police agency, but they did adopt special state highway patrol agencies with authority limited to traffic law enforcement. State highway patrol officers have only limited authority to perform general law enforcement duties, such as investigating crimes occurring in a state trooper's presence or on or near state highways.

Governors appoint the directors of state police or state highway patrols. Advanced technology in traffic devices, alcohol testing, and communications systems all require officers to have greater ability and more training. Increasing numbers of states are setting statewide entry requirements and training standards for police officers, either through agency-established academies or in conjunction with institutions of higher learning. Following training, line officers advance in rank through either civil service or merit plans. In addition to enforcement agencies and training institutions, most states maintain "crime lab" or "criminalistics" services; some support investigative units.

County Law Enforcement Agencies

Sheriffs' departments enforce the criminal law in most rural and unincorporated portions of the more than 3,000 counties in America. In most instances, sheriffs do not interfere in municipal law enforcement because most incorporated towns and cities have their own police forces. In addition to county law enforcement, sheriffs' departments have two other major duties. They maintain the county jails, which hold pretrial detainees and to which courts sentence most misdemeanants. Finally, the sheriff is an officer of the county court. The sheriff's office supplies bailiffs to provide security and management of detainees on trial, transport prisoners to and from court, and serve a range of court papers, such as summonses, forfeiture and eviction notices, and court judgments.

Municipal Police Departments

Local police departments make up the great bulk of law enforcement agencies in America. Police departments differ widely in size. The "Big Six" departments, including New York City, Los Angeles, Chicago, Houston, Philadelphia, and Detroit, face the most serious violent crime. Together, they are responsible for 7 percent of the nation's population, but 23 percent of its violent crime, including 22 percent of the murders and 34 percent of the robberies. The Big Six also face most of the problems of poverty and race relations. They and the departments of other large cities receive most of the public attention. Their shootings, scandals, and corruption always make the national news. Big-city police departments also receive most of the attention of researchers. It is big-city police departments to which this book most often is referring when the general term "police" or "police department" appears.[25]

The New York City Police Department employs more than 30,000 officers, but most police departments employ only a few people. Ten thousand of the nation's departments employ fewer than 10 sworn officers. Many, such as the one in Empire, California, employ a single officer. In most of these small towns, crime is not a major problem. The majority of calls to the police involve traffic violations and minor disturbances. Although most of our attention is drawn to the operation, decision making, and problems of big-city police departments, we should not lose sight of all the law enforcement that takes place in thousands of small-town police departments around the country.[26]

Private Police

The first private security officer, Allan Pinkerton, worked mainly for railroads and factory owners, providing security and combating industrial violence during strikes. Modern private security has also grown mainly in response to business needs. However, residents in large-city apartment complexes and condominiums have also stepped up their use of private security guards. Private security is a for-profit industry. It provides personnel, such as guards, investigators, couriers, and bodyguards. It also supplies equipment, including safes, locks, alarm systems, and closed-circuit television. In addition, it furnishes services, including monitoring, employee background checks, polygraphs, and drug testing. Businesses or others can either hire private security directly or contract for specific services and equipment.[27]

Many states grant private security personnel the authority to make felony arrests. Unlike sworn police officers, private police need not give arrestees the Miranda warnings. Private security guards cannot detain suspects or conduct searches without suspects' consent. Some states have special legislation authorizing private security to act as "special police" within a specific jurisdiction such as a plant, store, or university campus.[28]

Some jurisdictions require private security firms to secure licenses, either state, local, or both. Sworn police officers may "moonlight" for private security firms during their off-duty hours; most police departments permit moonlighting. Some departments contract with private concerns to provide personnel and use the revenue for department needs. For example, Miami and St. Petersburg, Florida, allow off-duty police officers to work armed and in uniform; the departments even arrange jobs for their officers.[29]

New York City lets companies form "business districts" that pay special taxes for private security. A number of private security forces patrol various parts of the city to augment public police. For example, 29 uniformed but unarmed security guards patrol a 50-block section of Manhattan. A former police borough commander directs the force, and a surtax imposed by property owners on themselves pays for it. Security guards start at about 10 dollars an hour, take a special 35-hour training course at John Jay College of Criminal Justice, and spend two more weeks training on the street. Squads patrol from 8 A.M. to midnight. Similar private security forces patrol other areas: A 285-member unit patrols Rockefeller Center; a 49-member unit patrols South Street Seaport; Roosevelt Island has an unarmed 46-member force commanded by a former police official. New York City police officers may moonlight, but only out of uniform.[30]

Figure 4.2

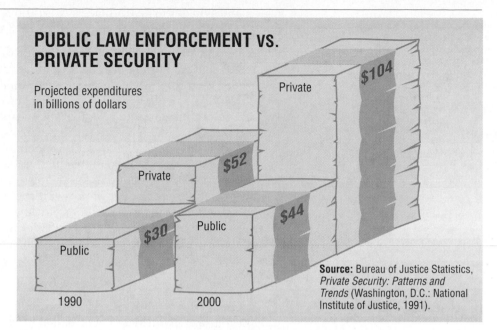

PUBLIC LAW ENFORCEMENT vs. PRIVATE SECURITY

Projected expenditures in billions of dollars

Private $104

Private $52

Public $30

Public $44

Private

Public

1990

2000

Source: Bureau of Justice Statistics, *Private Security: Patterns and Trends* (Washington, D.C.: National Institute of Justice, 1991).

quasi-military organizations
formation of police agencies into formal bureaucracies with highly developed divisions of labor and a hierarchical authority structure.

While public police protection, which grew rapidly during the 1960s and 1970s, stabilized during the 1980s, private security continued to grow. By 1990, private security had become the "nation's primary protective force," outspending public law enforcement by 73 percent and employing two and a half times the workforce. Spending for private security in 1990 reached $52 billion; private security agencies employed 1.5 million people. Public law enforcement spent $30 billion and employed 600,000. It is expected that public expenditures for law enforcement will reach $44 billion by the year 2000; private security expenditures will dwarf them at $104 billion. The annual rate of expenditure of private security will double that of expenditures for public law enforcement (see Figure 4.2).[31]

In some precincts, more off-duty police are performing police functions than are officers on duty. Because these officers wear uniforms, off-duty employment swells both the availability and visibility of police officers. On the other hand, off-duty employment raises concerns about conflict of interest in serving private interests, fears of corruption, and possible lawsuits for alleged misconduct. To reduce the risk of these problems, department orders and regulations frequently limit the kinds of employment officers can accept.[32]

Police Organization

Most police departments are **quasi-military organizations,** that is, they are formal bureaucracies with highly developed divisions of labor and a hierarchical authority structure. This quasi-military nature is apparent in several familiar characteristics. Police officers wear uniforms that resemble military uniforms. Police officers are divided into a hierarchy of ranks with names that sound military—patrol officer, sergeant, lieutenant, and captain. Unlike every other domestic agency (but like the military), the police can lawfully use force as an instrument to carry out policy. Police officers can detain, strike, shoot, and even kill in the lawful performance of their duties. The police operate according to a military command structure. The chief issues orders from the top, which subordinates must obey. Insubordination leads to disciplinary action. Borrowing also from the military, the police frequently refer to law enforcement as a "war" on crime, and criminals as the "enemy."

One U.S. attorney general closely followed the military model in opening a "crime summit" in 1991. He urged law enforcement officials to attack street crime and "violent drug traffickers" with the same "vigor and valor shown by our troops" in the then-recent Persian Gulf war:

> [L]et us turn once again to the example of Desert Storm and the great might that was brought to bear upon a threatening and violent enemy. Under the brilliantly coordinated "command and control," the Gulf coalition forces made the best use of firepower guided by great ingenuity and relentless certainty. We had the weapons to do the job: "smart" weapons that worked with deadly effect against an enemy finally reduced to desperate encounter, ineffectual response, and abject retreat.
>
> Here at home in the fight against violent crime we should employ, to be sure, the same command and control, the same ingenuity and certainty. Only here we battle not with the weapons of the military, but with the far stronger weapon of our laws. We need to make sure our laws are just as smart—just as efficient and effective against criminals— as those weapons that turned back the ruthless and violent intrusion by Saddam Hussein's forces.[33]

This description of the New York City Police Academy captures the same quasi-military view of police:

> "Attention," the drill sergeant yelled at 200 men and women. One man slouched. Another saluted with his left hand. "About face." A few turned the wrong way. A few more stumbled. The sergeant was not amused. "This is unbelievable!" the sergeant bellowed at a new crop of police recruits on their first day of gym class at the Police Academy. "Look straight ahead when you're at attention. Do things in unison." "You're not civilians anymore," he told them. "You're in a semimilitary outfit."[34]

The bureaucratic side of police department structure requires considerable routine and conformity to prescribed procedures, sometimes frustrating police officers and leading some experts to conclude that bureaucracy turns the police officer from self-directed professional to "hourly worker." Officers work fixed shifts, punch in and out, and pay careful attention to exactly how many hours they work. Jerome H. Skolnick and David H. Bayley refer to this bureaucratic dimension of police work and the frustration it causes some officers in *The New Blue Line:*

> They discuss endlessly among themselves their accumulated sick days, the amount of overtime worked, and vacation rotations. They live in a tightly supervised, formalistic environment, constantly checking what they do against set rules. Perhaps the most telling item of equipment patrol officers carry is a small bottle of "white-out," . . . used for correcting errors in the reports they write, fitting them exactly to the form demanded by the department. "Who's got the white-out?" is heard more often in patrol circles than "Let's be careful out there."[35]

The military model of policing describes the formal, outward appearance of police organization, not the informal reality of day-to-day operations. Soldiers wait for orders from officers before they take action, and most of the time they follow the orders closely. Police officers, on the other hand, have wide discretion and are left largely on their own to make decisions. They can decide whether or not to issue traffic tickets, arrest disorderly citizens, stop suspicious persons, or help lost people. Soldiers cannot and do not decide whether to move into an area, shoot at the enemy, or take other actions.

Another problem with the military model is that it creates problems for the police. If they are akin to the military and are engaged in a "war" against crime and drugs, then they have an enemy. Since "all's fair in war," some police officers might use excessive force or otherwise illegally invade the privacy and liberty of anyone they consider the "enemy." The "enemy"—in this case, people in the community—may follow the same maxim, putting the police in danger. According to Skolnick and Fyfe, referring to the attorney general's call to arms like that in Desert Storm,

> However stirring this call, it relies upon an inexact analogy and is far more likely to produce unnecessary violence and antagonism than to result in effective policing. The lines between friend and foe were clear in the Arabian desert, but police officers on American streets too often rely on ambiguous cues and stereotypes in trying to identify the enemies in their war. When officers act upon such signals and roust people who turn out to be guilty of no more than being in what officers view as the wrong place at the wrong time—young black men on inner-city streets at night, for example—the police may create enemies where none previously existed.[36]

Police Management Styles

The quasi-military bureaucratic structure of most police departments does not signify that they operate according to uniform practices. Departments vary in management style according to

- The community they serve.
- The goals their chiefs set.
- The values and ambitions their individual officers hold.

In other words, the formal structure of police departments adapts to serve the professional, ideological, political, and societal needs of its personnel and the community. Police chiefs definitely feel the pressure from political sources, according to research findings. A survey of Kentucky police chiefs showed that 56 percent felt political pressure from mayors, city managers, city council members, and business leaders. This pressure is related to a broad range of decisions, including the hiring of officers, the promotion and demotion of officers, the arrest of offenders, the enforcement of specific laws, and the provision of special services to specific groups in the community.[37]

James Q. Wilson's landmark *Varieties of Police Behavior* emphasized the political dimensions to police organization. Wilson identified three basic styles in police departments—the watchman, the legalistic, and the service styles. The one chosen depends on the political culture of the community.[38]

The **watchman style of policing** originated in immigrant communities. Watchman-style officers are decidedly nonbureaucratic. They focus on caretaking and maintaining order. In watchman-style departments, the police commonly ignore minor violations, exercising discretion to determine not what behavior violates the criminal law, but what may threaten order in the community. Watchmen-style officers avoid formal arrest; they settle disputes informally according to "street justice."

The **legalistic style of policing** predominated in Yankee-Protestant, or "good government" communities. Legalistic departments emphasize criminal law enforcement. Uniform, impartial arrests for all violations of law characterize the legalistic style. This style places a premium on the formal side of criminal justice; it concentrates on reducing discretion to an absolute minimum.

Wilson found that the third major management style, the **service style of policing,** also originated in "good government" communities. Service-style departments, like legalistic-style departments, rely on a bureaucratic formalism. They take all requests for service seriously, regardless of whether they stem from criminal law violations, maintaining order, or simply providing information. Officers often intervene but rarely arrest, particularly for minor violations. Instead, they counsel, issue written warnings, or make referrals to social service agencies.

Which style is best? That depends on the goals of the department. If the goal is to enforce the criminal law and serve the will of the community, then the legalistic style that minimizes discretion and emphasizes formal rules is best. If the goals are service and order maintenance, then the police are expected to rely on their professional judgment, not on prescribed rules for every situation. These goals require an emphasis on informal discretion, not formal rules.[39]

The Roles of the Police

Americans place enormous demands on their local police. Historically, local police departments have provided the only around-the-clock, 365-days-a-year public service with the authority to compel obedience. Society expects the police to solve most problems and to solve them *now*. This unreasonable expectation is not new. Brand Whitlock, the reform mayor of Toledo, Ohio, recognized it in 1910. He complained that when anything, however minor, "bothered" people, their first reaction is, "It's time to call the police."[40]

Today, as throughout our history, the demands for a police response to problems fall into three main categories:

1. Enforcing the criminal law, sometimes called crime fighting.
2. Maintaining public order, sometimes called peace keeping.
3. Providing emergency, informational, and other community services.

The response to these demands ranges across a broad spectrum of policies and operations. The following *You Decide* introduces you to the nature and complexity of police functions, and the range of responses police utilize to perform them.

You Decide   What Do Police Do? How Do They Do It?

After receiving routine instructions at the roll call held at the precinct station, Officers Garcia and Ranello started out for the area in which they would spend their tour of duty. The officers soon received instructions from the dispatcher to handle a fight in an alley. Upon arrival, they found a group of young men surrounded by their parents, wives, and children.

One of the young men, A, had a couple of knives in his hand. While the knives were within legal limits, Officer Garcia took them (and later disposed of them in a trash can). Another of the young men, B, stood by his mother. The third, C, stood by A, from whom the knives had been taken.

The mother of B was the complainant. She claimed that C had attacked her son with a knife, and she demanded that C be arrested and jailed. C readily admitted he had been fighting with B, but he claimed that he had just tried to protect A. C had been drinking and was belligerent. He indicated a readiness to take on anyone and everyone, including the police. He kept shouting and was obviously antagonizing the officers.

A attempted to explain the situation. He stated that he had been the one originally fighting B, and that C had merely come to his aid. B concurred in this account of

what had taken place, though he did not reflect much concern as the supposed victim of the attack.

A's mother-in-law interrupted at this time to claim that A was innocent; that the fight was B's fault. B's mother did not stand for this accusation and entered the fray.

The confusion spread. Other police officers, in the meantime, had arrived at the scene, and the number of observers had grown. Officers Garcia and Ranello decided to take the participants to the precinct station, where conditions would make it possible to conduct a more orderly inquiry.

At the station, the families and participants were separated and talked with individually. The mother of B insisted on signing a complaint against C and A, but finally relented toward A when he promised not to allow C to come to his apartment.

C was then formally arrested and charged with disorderly conduct. A and B were sent home with their wives and mothers. By charging C with disorderly conduct rather than a more serious crime, the officers observed that they were saving themselves some paperwork. They felt that their action in letting the mother sign a complaint against the "loudmouthed" C had served to pacify her.

records (arrests and convictions) and interviews with victims demonstrated that arrested individuals were about half as likely to repeat their violence as those who were not arrested—18 percent of all offenders repeated their violence, while only 10 percent of the arrested offenders repeated theirs.[58]

The Minneapolis Domestic Violence Study changed both the law and police policy throughout the country regarding domestic cases, dramatically demonstrating the effect that experimental research can have on criminal justice policy. The U.S. attorney general's Task Force on Family Violence endorsed the Minneapolis findings and recommended that state and local agencies adopt a policy of arrest in domestic violence cases. Fifteen states and the District of Columbia enacted mandatory arrest laws in misdemeanor domestic violence cases. By 1988, 90 percent of police agencies either "encouraged" or "required" arrest in minor domestic assault cases. Arrests for minor assaults increased a dramatic 70 percent between 1984 and 1989.[59]

The Minneapolis experiment was not the only reason for this dramatic change in policy. The highly publicized case of Tracey Thurman probably also contributed to the change. Thurman received a $2.5 million damage award in a lawsuit she won against the Torrington, Connecticut, Police Department. Police officers ignored months of complaints by Tracey Thurman against her husband, Charles Thurman. Responding to her final call, several officers stood by while Charles Thurman beat and kicked Tracey Thurman while holding the bloody knife he had already used to stab her in the chest, neck, and throat. Only when he approached her while medics were carrying her away on a stretcher did the police finally arrest Charles Thurman, who turned out to be a short-order cook at a café frequented by the police.[60]

The concern over police liability highlighted by the Thurman case was not the only other influence that explains the popularity of the Minneapolis experiment. The widespread adoption of the policy of arresting suspects in minor domestic assault cases took place in the favorable social context provided by the 1980s. That social context included an increasingly "get tough on crime" attitude, a disillusionment with rehabilitation of criminals, a heightened awareness of domestic violence, the victims' rights movement, and the vehemence of advocacy groups. James Meeker and Arnold Binder suggested that this context was more important than the Minneapolis experiment in changing police policy in domestic assault cases. They asked a regionally balanced sample of rural and urban police departments to rank eight separate influences on changes in domestic violence policy. The respondents (54 percent of the total) ranked the Minneapolis experiment last.[61]

Police officers strongly support the arrest policy in domestic violence cases, according to one survey of a midwestern community of about 60,000 that adopted a spouse arrest policy. A survey of 115 patrol officers and command officers, conducted by Paul Friday, Scott Metzger, and David Walters, found that officers supported the policy because it gave them more power, even though they were uncertain of the effect of the policy. Arrest data for the two years following the first arrest showed that initial arrest had little effect on subsequent calls.[62]

The popularity of the policy to arrest for minor domestic assault was probably premature. Only half the victims responded to follow-up efforts to determine whether violence was repeated. The follow-up continued only for six months, researchers had difficulty contacting many of the victims, and no data exist for recurrence of violence after this period. Moreover, after the initial crackdown, Minneapolis police officers backed off from complying with the policy. University of Nebraska researchers surveyed 100 Minneapolis police officers after the new policy was adopted. Ninety-nine of the 100 said that they "should make their own decisions about problems that arise on duty," 77 officers responded that they "usually do what they think necessary even if their supervisors disagree," and 43 said that they "should use their own standards of police work even when department procedures prohibit them from doing so."[63]

Crime Control Institute criminologist Michael Buerger described one of these deliberate refusals to follow the policy of arrest:

> Two officers responded to a "heavy domestic" call, and were met in the hall by the victim. She had sustained obvious injuries; one description was that "the side of her face was like hamburger." Her assailant was still at the scene when the officers arrived. Instead of arresting the suspect, the officers yelled at the woman (some alleged that derogatory remarks were made to her), and told her not to waste their time by calling again. The officer told the male assailant to go back into the apartment, take a shower, and cool off. Then the officers left, clearing the call as "GOA," which ordinarily means that they had no contact with the offender because he was gone before the squad [car] arrived.[64]

Furthermore, according to Sherman, "What the Minneapolis experiment did *not* prove . . . was that arrest would work best in every community, or for all kinds of people." Replications of the experiment in Omaha, Charlotte (North Carolina), Milwaukee, Miami, and Colorado Springs challenge the initial conclusion drawn from Minneapolis that arrest works best. In three cities, according to Sherman, arrest "backfired," that is, it actually increased incidents of future domestic violence! The major conclusions drawn from a survey of the experiments in these six cities include:

- Arrest increases domestic violence in those who have nothing to lose, especially the unemployed.
- Arrest deters domestic violence in cities with higher white and Hispanic populations.
- Arrest deters domestic violence in the short run (30 days), but escalates violence later in cities with higher proportions of unemployed black suspects.
- A small but chronic group of violent couples produces most of the domestic violence.
- Offenders in Omaha who flee the police are deterred by arrest.[65]

The debate over whether arrest is the most effective policy in domestic violence cases is far from over. Just as the replications called the policy into question, some researchers are now challenging the replications. Joel Garner, Jeffrey Fagan, and Christopher Maxwell have concluded that these were not true replications but only studies that resembled the Minneapolis research. They concluded that "the available findings do not offer a single replication of the measures and analysis used in the Minneapolis study." For example, the Minneapolis experiment included "threats of violence and property damage as failures equivalent to actual violence. . . . None of the . . . [replications] uses these outcome criteria. . . ."[66]

Garner and his associates not only challenge whether the studies are replications, but they also criticize the characterizations of the studies by other researchers:

> Once made public, the findings from the SARP [Spousal Abuse Replication Programs] experiments have been interpreted in ways that on occasion conflict with the original authors. For instance, Sherman summarizes SARP findings in the following manner:
>> The best way to compare the findings across experiments is still to focus on the effects of arrest compared to nonarrest, the central policy issue for state legislatures and police agencies. The most important finding for them is that arrest increased domestic violence in Omaha, Charlotte, and Milwaukee.

He also reports

> There is evidence that arrest had a deterrent effect in Minneapolis, Colorado Springs, and Metro-Dade but the cumulative evidence is somewhat mixed.

> Notably, these statements about an escalation effect in Omaha and Charlotte are not the conclusions of the original authors of the Omaha and Charlotte experiments. . . . This fact warrants emphasis since the Sherman interpretation has become a commonly accepted representation of the published results.[67]

Due both to empirical research and to changing attitudes toward family violence in general, the criminal justice system no longer treats battering wives as solely a "family matter." In fact, the New York Police Department was sued for failing to arrest wife beaters whose assaults were serious enough to qualify as felonies. The department settled the suit, agreeing to arrest all husbands if "there is reasonable cause to believe that a husband has committed a felony against his wife." Most jurisdictions do not yet treat spouse battering entirely as a criminal justice matter. The policy in most, if not all, jurisdictions is to stop the criminal process at arrest. In fact, the domestic violence research has focused on the deterrent effects of arrest, not on prosecution and conviction. Failure to carry domestic violence cases beyond arrest raises a constitutional question: Is arrest in domestic assault cases criminal punishment? If so, then police departments are acting like courts, violating the principle of separation of powers.[68]

You Decide | Is Arrest the Best Policy for All People?

Consider the case of Chuck Switzer, a white, middle-aged resident of a Minneapolis suburb and a long-term wife beater. He was raised in a Great Plains farmhouse, where his father's brutal physical discipline included killing Switzer's dog and sticking Switzer's fingers in an electrical socket. Switzer began to beat his wife on their wedding night, because Mrs. Switzer failed to have an orgasm. His subsequent beatings were prompted by such failures as dinner not being ready on time, children making too much noise, or other disruptions of normal routine. His wife finally sought relief from police, and Mr. Switzer was arrested. His reaction was to thank her for helping him to confront his problems, for which he went on to receive counseling. By both their accounts, the arrest broke the pattern of repetitive violence. Switzer's arrest shamed him, but his middle-class life and employment helped to reintegrate him into that world as a repentant and recovering abuser.[69]

Consider the composite case of "William Smith," a white, unemployed, 24-year-old in Milwaukee. Like Chuck Switzer, Smith was abused as a child and beat his first lover. Unlike Switzer, Smith had both a juvenile and adult arrest record, for nondomestic crimes. He also had no steady job and no home, living with women supported by Aid to Dependent Children. He beat at least three different women over a three-year period in which Milwaukee police kept records on domestic violence. After he was arrested for beating one woman, he reacted with anger

and a desire to "get even." He beat her twice as often in the next six months as he had in the preceding six months. He then beat other women, with a total frequency of domestic violence that was higher than police had detected before the first arrest. Being arrested created no shame in him—only rage. It sent no message from people he cared about that his conduct was an important failure to achieve self-control. Rather, Smith lived in a world where self-control was not expected, and arrest was no different from any other challenge to his "toughness."[70]

Stake in conformity theory

Rutgers University sociologist Jackson Toby explained the delinquent behavior of "hoodlums" according to a theory he called the stake in conformity theory. Toby wrote, "For those with social honor, disgrace is a powerful sanction. For a boy disapproved of already, there is less incentive to resist the temptation to do what he wants when he wants to do it." Toby applied his stake in society theory to places as well as people. According to Toby, "communities differ in the proportion of defeated people. A community with a high concentration of them has an even higher crime rate than would be expected by adding up the predispositions of its individual members." According to police expert Lawrence S. Sherman, who applied Toby's stake in society theory to domestic violence cases, "individuals with a higher stake in conformity would fear arrest more than those with a lower stake, regardless of the neighborhood they live in. Yet the disgrace of arrest is likely to be lower in neighborhoods with a lower average stake in conformity— or *higher* where, as in Minneapolis, the average stake in the community is quite high."[71]

Social control theory

According to social control theory, everyone has a natural tendency to commit crimes. Only strong bonds to conventional society keep people from committing crimes. Failure to develop these strong bonds at an early age causes crime, according to this theory. In other words, the greater their bonds to conventional society, the greater people's resistance to committing crimes. People with strong ties to or involvement in family, churches, schools, and jobs demonstrate this bonding that inhibits their desire to commit crimes. Sherman noted a

> conflict between the implications of the [social control] theory and standard police and public conceptions of justice. *Those with the most conventional lifestyles would be most deterred by arrest; those with the least attachment to convention would be least deterred or worse.* (Emphasis added.) . . . If the control theory of crime is correct, and if it interacts with sanctions so that more socially bonded people are more deterrable, then the unfairness [of arrest based on deterrability] will seem great indeed. Those who would be *most* highly recommended for arrest would be those most involved with the church, family, community organizations, and the labor force. Those *least* likely to be recommended for arrest would be the marginal characters of low "moral worth" that police love to punish: the unemployed, unmarried, nonchurchgoing riffraff.[72]

Shame theory

The Australian sociologist John Braithwaite devised a theory that puts shame at the center of causing and preventing crime. Braithwaite argues that communitarian societies such as Japan have low crime rates because of the powerful influence of shaming in the prevention of socially unacceptable behavior. Western societies, on the other hand, have separated criminal punishment from public shaming. He argues that this separation has contributed to the increase of crime in Western societies. A survey that Kirk R. Williams and Richard Hawkins conducted of predominantly white, employed males in a national sample seems to lend support for the theory as an explanation for domestic violence. Their data showed that humiliation was the most highly rated consequence of arrest for wife assault, *not* losing jobs or going to jail. In other words, arrest deters wife beating because of the fear of shame, not the fear of going to jail.[73]

Too much shame, according to Braithwaite, will have a similar effect to not enough shame—it can cause crime. Lawrence S. Sherman has applied Braithwaite's theory and Williams's and Hawkins's survey results to domestic violence. According to Sherman,

The dilemma shaming theory raises is that the effectiveness of legal sanctions may depend on a foundation of informal social control. If formal sanctions can only deter socially interdependent people, what do we do about people who are not well bonded to others? If exercise can only strengthen a well-fed body, more exercise would be a foolish prescription for a starving body. Yet that may be just what punishment does to people who are not enmeshed in a stable social network committed to conventional social institutions. More legal sanctions may simply push them beyond Braithwaite's tipping point of "too much" stigma, causing them to commit more crime than they would if left unpunished. Yet these are usually the same people who commit the most crimes and most "deserve" punishment as a matter of justice or fairness.[74]

Ghetto poverty theory

The Harvard sociologist Lee Rainwater, in his classic study of the Pruitt-Igoe housing project in St. Louis, concluded that shame was used too much. According to Rainwater,

> Children are shamed for not doing the right thing, but they are also shamed by parents and peers for not being tough enough to cope with their problems. . . . As the child grows up he increasingly acquires an awareness that nothing he can do will protect him from danger or attack, whether from his parents for failure to meet their standards, or from his caretakers (e.g. school teachers and police) who always seem to want something from him other than what he is doing.[75]

Applying Rainwater's findings to domestic violence, Sherman suggests that this much shame is "well past the hope of using shame to mold behavior to comply with social norms." Pride becomes the adaptive strategy, which in the case of arrest for domestic assault can lead to more, not less, violence. "If someone is shamed when a lover or spouse has him arrested, the pride response may require retaliation against that lover, or more violence against other lovers in the future." Therefore, arrest of a person overdosed on shame may create a strategy of "*defiance* for avoiding the shame of arrest by a proudly assertive posture of 'knowing no shame.' "[76]

Questions

Considering the theories outlined above, is arrest the best policy in domestic violence cases? Assume you are a police administrator: Would you adopt a policy of arresting all people where there is probable cause to believe they had committed a minor assault? Or would you adopt a policy of arresting respectable, employed people but not those who are unemployed and not respectable? Or would you leave arrest to the discretion of individual police officers, after explaining to them the results of the research on the theories outlined below? Explain your decision.

---

community service *police mission focusing on providing information and physically assisting people in need.*

Community Service

Community service consists of both providing information and physically assisting people in need. Citizens routinely call the police for information: Where is the football stadium? How do I find the nearest hospital? Why are the sirens blaring? They also call on the police to help them, for example, find lost children and pets or rescue a drowning person. The police have cared for the "down and out," particularly people who were intoxicated, poor, and mentally ill, throughout police history. Until the 1920s, jails offered temporary lodging for intoxicated, destitute, and roaming mentally ill people police brought to them. This service died out after the 1920s, and some jurisdictions decriminalized public drunkenness. Reformers hoped that decriminalization would shift the responsibility for public drunkenness to public service agencies, freeing the police to devote time to "real crimes." Decriminalization did not, however, produce the hoped-for results. Since the police cannot allow intoxicated individuals to lie in the street, instead of taking them to jail the police now transport such persons to detoxification centers for sobering up and treatment. Due to cumbersome entry procedures, commitment for treatment may take more time than an arrest.[77]

Patrol officers have conflicting attitudes toward intoxicated individuals. Some act with considerable compassion, making arrests to protect them from muggers or from freezing on winter nights. Other officers harass intoxicated people, particularly if they are annoying "respectable citizens," driving them away from businesses or middle-class shoppers. The varied police response to public drunkenness demonstrates how the police can use the legal power to arrest as a tool to perform community service functions. They take drunk people to jail both to protect them and to keep the streets clear and orderly. In settling problems, the police do not sort criminal law enforcement, order maintenance, and public service into neat categories. They draw on whatever means they consider appropriate at the time.[78]

The police also combine community service with peacekeeping and criminal law enforcement when they deal with mentally ill people. Most

Helping people—a major but often overlooked police mission.

The Role and Function of the Police in Germany

The German police do not perform functions of "general service to the public," according to Dilip K. Das, who worked for the Indian Police Service in the 1960s and based his conclusion on research on police in six countries: India, Australia, New Zealand, Canada, Germany, and Finland. Professor Das lists the following functions of the police in Germany:

1. Controlling crime.
2. Preserving public safety.
3. Guaranteeing the orderly flow of traffic.
4. Maintaining internal security at mass meetings, catastrophes, and riots.
5. Fighting threats to liberal democracy.

Helmut Kohl, as leader of the Christian Democratic Union and the Christian Social Union opposition parties, called for the expansion of police power to maintain order. Franz Josef Strauss of the Christian Social Union ridiculed the "concept of the police as social referee or social engineer." He called the concept "mere fancy." According to Strauss, the police should devote all their time to the following pursuits:

1. "Ruthless implementation of the law."
2. "Prevention of crime."
3. "Execution of state authority."
4. "Elimination of ideas giving rise to terrorism."

Source: Dilip K. Das, *Policing in Six Countries Around the World* (Chicago: Office of International Criminal Justice, 1993), 152–53.

states have statutes authorizing the police to manage mentally ill persons, even when they have not broken the law. Two alternative procedures call this service into operation. One results from court orders directing the police to find particular mentally ill individuals and take them to a hospital. The other grants the police emergency power to initiate steps to confine a person who officers believe is "mentally ill and because of his illness is likely to injure himself or others if not immediately hospitalized."[79]

The police spend as much time serving the mentally ill as arresting major felony suspects. Mental health reforms favoring community treatment place a heavy burden on the police. Community treatment often means putting mentally ill people "on the streets," where police must deal with problems arising from their outpatient status. The police exercise broad discretion in their response to emergency mental health service. Their responses range, at one extreme, from taking people to psychiatric hospitals under civil (noncriminal) statutes or arresting them for some criminal offense, to neither arresting nor committing them at the other extreme. Although statutes strictly govern both arrest and emergency mental illness apprehension, the law does not control the initial decision not to arrest or apprehend.[80]

Sometimes, the police do not select a caretaker; they administer "psychiatric first aid" instead. For example, one agitated mentally ill woman told officers that neighbors were pursuing her, attempting to attack her with an imaginary weapon. Her highly vocal distress not only disturbed her, but also had potential for causing considerable turmoil in the neighborhood. Police listened patiently to her story, never questioning its veracity. After an hour spent searching her house for the evidence they knew they would never find, they kindly advised her how to call the police if she had any more trouble and further convinced her not to question the suspected neighbors. She was calm and satisfied when they left. They had "handled the problem" and restored peace to the area.[81]

Police refer some people to psychiatric emergency service. According to a survey of referrals to the emergency psychiatric service in the Cincinnati Hospital, police referrals account for 22 percent of the total. People referred by police were among the most likely to be diagnosed by professionals as a danger to themselves or others. More than half required restraints, and one-quarter required medication; half of those requiring medication were diagnosed as psychotic. Therapists, according to the survey, believed that police make more appropriate referrals than others who refer persons to psychiatric emergency service.[82]

Reality and Myth About the Roles of the Police

Anyone who watches television "cop" shows, or who reads newspapers or watches the news on television, "knows" that the police spend their time fighting crime. The reality of police work, however, is a complex mix of enforcing the criminal law, maintaining order, and performing public services. Many police administrators do not challenge the crime-fighter image. Police department annual reports commonly present elaborate detail about formal street crime enforcement, while perhaps a brief and passing reference to "other" work covers the enormously important and time-consuming informal order maintenance and service functions. Some patrol officers also consider criminal law enforcement their primary responsibility; they treat order maintenance and service as annoying, unimportant, and distracting interruptions.

Police officers who rescue citizens from drowning or other life-threatening emergencies probably dismiss these heroic deeds as mere interruptions, while extolling even their failed efforts to catch robbers in hot pursuit. One television reporter interviewed a patrol officer who received a "cop of the year" award. The officer commented that what made his job worthwhile was chasing and, with luck, catching felons! He spoke as if he spent most of his time doing just that. Studies completed from the late 1960s to the middle of the 1980s showed that the police spend less than 25 percent of their time enforcing the criminal law, although a more recent study casts some doubt on this percentage. Carl B. Klockars and Stephen D. Mastrofski studied the ways Wilmington, Delaware, police spent their time. At first, by merely replicating earlier studies, they found about the same distribution of effort among law enforcement, order maintenance, and public service. However, when they removed officer free time (the time officers spend on patrol between calls) and added police-initiated actions, they concluded that the police spend almost half their time fighting crime. Still, this falls far short of the crime-fighting image so prominently displayed on television and in the newspapers, and encouraged in the public mind.[83]

Crime Fighting and Community Service

Some evidence suggests that the crime-fighting myth may be losing its supremacy. Professor James Q. Wilson notes that at least some police administrators are aware of, and willing to talk openly about, the precedence of maintaining order and providing services over law enforcement. A study based on observing three California departments reports that patrol officers willingly, even eagerly, nurture their community service functions, from which they derive considerable satisfaction. Some departments issue clear policy statements regarding the importance of order maintenance and service.[84]

A Minneapolis Police Department Annual Report stated:

> City policing entails much more than law enforcement and control of crime. Police are called upon to resolve family problems, deal with various other citizen conflicts, and to respond to a miscellany of non-criminal emergencies, many of which pose a serious threat to persons and property.[85]

The foreword to the same annual report states that if this and other parts of the department's statistical profile are disseminated among "those with strong interests in policing," they can be "an instrument for police improvement."

In June 1992, the New York City Police Department honored 83 officers for superior police work. The work was not catching robbers or drug dealers. Instead, it included painting over graffiti on buildings, escorting old people to places where they could shop, and encouraging prostitutes to get drug treatment. One officer commented that transporting clowns and jugglers to the children of Bedford-Stuyvesant was not exactly what he had in mind when he became a New York City police officer. "I had in mind to protect life and property. But I get a good sense of accomplishment and fulfillment out of bringing joy and a little bit of happiness to youngsters in the neighborhood I patrol."

Officer Francis Badillo and his partner, Officer Myron Leary, created a shuttle-van service to take elderly people to the bank and shopping. This helped them see the "positive side of their tough South Bronx beat." The police commissioner told the honored officers that they were all success stories who epitomized the "cop who is concerned with his neighborhood."[86]

Twenty years ago, police expert George Kelling offered the following excellent summary of the complex police function, a summary that still holds true and probably will continue to well into the twenty-first century:

> Although the crime-related functions of the police were historically important and continue to be so, it is insufficient to define the police either predominantly or exclusively on the basis of those functions. Their functions are far broader, and consist of peace-keeping and management functions essential to urban life. Taking this point of view the police are not just a part of the criminal justice system, but also are a key element of urban government. They are the primary contact citizens have with government. . . . [P]olice services constitute more than 30% of the cost of city government. The police are available 24 hours a day. They resolve conflicts between families, groups, interests and individuals. All police rhetoric about crime fighting aside, it is clear, from observing the needs of citizens and what the police actually do, that the order and service functions are the functional heart of policing.[87]

The American Bar Foundation maintains that all 11 of the following are "objectives and priorities for police service . . . by design or default":

1. To identify criminal offenders and criminal activity and, where appropriate, to apprehend offenders and participate in subsequent court proceedings.
2. To reduce opportunities for commission of some crime through preventive patrol and other measures.
3. To aid individuals who are in danger of physical harm.
4. To protect constitutional guarantees.
5. To facilitate movement of people and vehicles.
6. To assist those who cannot care for themselves.
7. To resolve conflicts.

8. To identify problems that are potentially serious for law enforcement or government.

9. To create and maintain a feeling of security in the community.

10. To promote and preserve civil order.

11. To provide other services on an emergency basis.

Not everyone agrees that the police should perform such a wide variety of services. Some recommend, instead, that the police narrow their focus to concentrate on serious crime. Professors Gordon Hawkins and Norval Morris maintain that

> the immense range of police obligations and duties must be drastically reduced. A variety of means are suggested here [transferring traffic control, most misdemeanors, and minor violations to other agencies] for both diminishing the range of their responsibilities and enabling the more effective use of their resources in the prevention and control of serious crime [murder, rape, robbery, and burglary in particular].[88]

Overlap of Functions

Police functions do not fall easily into separate compartments. As demonstrated by problems of public drunkenness, mental outpatients, and domestic disputes, police functions overlap and blend to a considerable degree. Perhaps more important, they reinforce each other. As James Q. Wilson observes:

> Though the law enforcement, order maintenance, and service provision aspects can be analytically distinguished, concretely they are thoroughly intermixed. Even in a routine law enforcement situation (for example, arresting a fleeing purse snatcher), how the officer deals with the victim and the onlookers at the scene is often as important as how he handles the suspect. The victim and onlookers, after all, are potential witnesses who have to testify in court; assuring their cooperation is as necessary as catching the person against whom they will testify. The argument about whether "cops" should be turned into "social workers" is a false one, for it implies that society can exercise some meaningful choice over the role the officer should play. Except at the margin, it cannot.[89]

Some have also suggested that the crime-fighter image lends effectiveness to the peacekeeping and community service work. For example, police effectiveness depends on respect for police authority, in particular the ultimate police authority to use force. A wife beater less willingly obeys an unpleasant order given by a service-oriented police officer than one issued by a crime fighter who shows a willingness to arrest and put him in jail. So, too, individuals "needing help" listen more to a crime fighter's orders than to those of a community service agent.[90]

According to police expert Herman Goldstein:

> We've learned that what the police do in their "order maintenance" function may have a very important bearing on their capacity to deal with crime; that citizen attitudes and cooperation are heavily influenced by the effectiveness of the police in providing the wide range of services that the public has come to expect from them.[91]

The Police Roles and Drug Laws

Traditionally, police departments employed two basic enforcement strategies in drug cases. Retrospective techniques were aimed at major dealers and distributors. Investigators interviewed witnesses and examined physical evidence in order to build a case against suspects. Prospective techniques were directed at small-time dealers. They involved undercover and "buy-and-bust" operations. Most drug dealing occurred in private. During the mid 1980s, the drug problem changed. The wide availability and low price of crack cocaine greatly increased the number of sellers and buyers on the street. Stranger-to-stranger sales took place at busy intersections, or "open-air markets." A new system of drug dealing involved a complicated network of sentries, bag people to hold the drugs, an actual drug seller, and a nearby cache. "Drug entrepreneuring, replete with business equipment such as cellular telephones and remote beepers, reached new heights."[92]

Along with the now-visible and highly volatile market—the city streets—came increases in violence, in other crimes, and in youth involvement. With these problems came demands for a police solution. Police sweeps, asset forfeiture, and reverse sting operations—where officers pose as sellers instead of buyers—became more prominent. The evidence is mixed as to the effectiveness of these techniques, but the dissatisfaction with the visible illegal drug trade and its associated evils has remained high enough to cause some to look beyond law enforcement alone for answers.

Recent police efforts against drug offenses provide a dramatic example of combining law enforcement and public service roles. Police administrators and officers have become increasingly convinced that law enforcement alone cannot solve the drug problem. Drug law enforcement has strained personnel and budgets to the maximum. Arrests for drug law violations have soared. Police overtime budgets have also risen. Patrick V. Murphy, former New York police commissioner and now director of police policy for the U.S. Conference of Mayors, said, "You hear police chiefs saying things like, 'Do I want to

DARE is a popular police anti-drug effort that has received mixed empirical reviews about its effectiveness.

lose a cop in a raid on a crack house when there are 100 other crack houses in my city? Let's talk about alternatives.' " President of the International Association of Police Chiefs, and chief of police in Shrevesport, Louisiana, Charles A. Gruber said in Congressional testimony: "For all our policing, we understand that law enforcement is not the solution to the problem of drugs in our society." Los Angeles Sheriff Sherman Block, in discussing the new police role of reducing the demand for drugs, added: "We have come to the conclusion while many responsibilities belong to other disciplines, if they are not being adequately carried out, at some point we'll have to deal with the failure."[93]

Police departments provide a variety of drug use prevention services, especially in schools. Officers and sheriffs go to elementary schools in many cities to teach assertiveness, stress management, and skills needed to resist the lure of drugs. The Shrevesport, Louisiana, Police Department has set up seven centers to help young people find prenatal care, jobs, and education. The most widely used program, Drug Abuse Resistance Education (DARE), originated in Los Angeles in 1983 as a joint venture between the Los Angeles Police Department and the Los Angeles United School District. Specially trained uniformed police officers go to fifth- and sixth-grade classrooms to give 17 highly structured lessons intended to help children learn how to resist drugs (see Table 4.1). Police officers who participate in the program receive instruction in changing their "hardened street ways" into "caring teaching skills." Officer Harreld D. Webster, a DARE mentor, said, "We assist them to remove the macho image and become teachers." Webster noted that DARE, once dismissed by officers as "kiddie cops," has gained respect.[94]

DARE has become the most popular drug education program in the country. First offered in about 50 Los Angeles elementary schools, DARE spread by 1994 to 4,700 communities in every state, and even six foreign countries. Evaluations of the effectiveness of DARE have shown mixed results. The University of Illinois surveyed 1,800 sixth and seventh graders. DARE graduates tended to view drugs more negatively and the police more positively than those who did not participate in DARE. On the other hand, a study of 3,000 students in Kentucky found "no really compelling evidence" that DARE works. Use of marijuana, alcohol, and tobacco among DARE graduates was about the same as among other students.[95]

Dennis P. Rosenbaum and his colleagues conducted the most extensive, thorough, and methodologically sound study of DARE. They established and carried out a longitudinal, randomized experiment to estimate the effects of DARE on the attitudes, beliefs, and drug use of students in the year following exposure to the program. They found no statistically significant overall effect on drug use, and few effects on attitudes or beliefs about drugs. However, they did find that

> females exposed to DARE were twice as likely as females without DARE to cease their use of alcohol. Males exposed to DARE, however, were less likely than males without DARE to quit using alcohol. Thus, relative to the control condition, DARE appears to encourage females to quit using alcohol but to have the opposite effect for males.[96]

One aspect of DARE, encouraging participants to report their parents to the police, has created a debate over privacy and individual liberties, and over the proper role of the police. As teachers, police officers gain the trust of students and become their confidantes. Then, as law enforcement officers, some police use the information students give them to arrest parents. The *You Decide,* "Should Kids Report Their Parents to the Police?" examines this issue.

Table 4.1
DARE Lessons

Topic	Description
1. First Visit/Personal Safety	Introduction of DARE and law enforcement officer safety practices; discussion of personal rights.
2. Drug Use and Misuse	Harmful effects of misusing drugs.
3. Consequences	Consequences of using and choosing not to use drugs.
4. Resisting Pressure	Sources and types of pressures to use drugs.
5. Resistance Techniques	Strategies for resisting peer pressure.
6. Building Self-Esteem	Identifying positive qualities, the importance of self-image, giving and receiving compliments.
7. Assertiveness	Personal rights and responsibilities; situations that require assertiveness skills.
8. Managing Stress Without Drugs	Identifying sources of stress; when stress can help and hurt; how to manage stress; deep breathing exercise.
9. Media Influences	How the media influences behavior; advertising techniques.
10. Decision Making and Risk Taking	Risk-taking behavior; reasonable and harmful risks; influences on decisions; consequences of choices.
11. Drug Use Alternatives	Reasons for using drugs; alternative activities.
12. Role Modeling	Meet older student leaders who do not use drugs.
13. Forming Support Systems	Types of support groups; barriers to friendships; suggestions for overcoming barriers to making friends.
14. Ways to Deal with Gang Pressures	Types of gang pressure; differences between gangs and groups; consequences of gang behavior.
15. DARE Summary	Review of DARE.
16. Taking a Stand	Taking the appropriate stand when pressured to use drugs.
17. DARE Culmination	Award assembly; recognition of DARE participants.

You Decide   "Should Kids Report Their Parents to the Police?"

Police chief James Gilway teaches a DARE class at Searsport Elementary School in Maine. One day, he asked the 11-year-olds if they knew anyone who used drugs. A few of the students raised their hands, but Crystal Grendell did not. Gilway did not ask for the names, and the discussion turned to handling the pressure to experiment with drugs at parties. He did encourage students to talk to him privately outside class about anything that was bothering them. A few days later, Crystal went to the police station. She eventually told Chief Gilway that her parents kept marijuana plants and smoked marijuana.

According to Gilway, Crystal volunteered the information. "This is a good little girl just thinking of her family." He denied that the conversation had anything to do with

DARE. Crystal claimed she wanted her parents to stop smoking marijuana, although she did not tell them that. She also said that Chief Gilway pressed her for details and promised her "nothing would happen to my parents." Gilway disputes this.

The next day, Chief Gilway and two state drug agents interviewed Crystal for about an hour at school. That afternoon, two Searsport police officers and four drug agents converged on the Grendell home. The police took Crystal's 8-year-old sister, who was alone in the house, to the neighbors. A few minutes later, a police car took Crystal to another town, where she was hidden by the police. Gilway says the police were only babysitting Crystal to prevent possible abuse. Inside the house, police confiscated the marijuana plants. If allowed to grow to their full height, the plants could have produced one ounce of smokeable marijuana. The police arrested Crystal's parents for growing 49 marijuana plants in their bedroom. Mrs. Grendell was fired from her job, although the charges against her were dropped. Mr. Grendell pleaded guilty to growing marijuana, but was not fired.

A year later, Crystal, still troubled by the incident, says, "I would never tell again. Never. Never." Mr. and Mrs. Grendell say they hold no grudge against Crystal. "I can't blame Crystal for what she did. She told the truth when asked questions by authorities. That's what I've always told her to do," said her mother. The Grendells blame themselves for Crystal's troubles. "This would never have happened if we hadn't smoked," said Mrs. Grendell. Both parents say they never smoked in front of their children and never went to work high. They used marijuana like other people "having a few beers." Nevertheless, both vow they will never smoke marijuana again.

"This is the stuff of Orwellian fiction," said Gary Peterson, head of Parents Against DARE. "This is Big Brother putting spies in our homes." Parents Against DARE, consisting of about 20 families, questions whether the police can teach objectively about drugs. While the parents oppose drug use by their children, some of them smoke marijuana. The parents wonder if DARE is turning their children against them.

Law enforcement officers say that students rarely tell on their parents. "There are skeptics out there who think this is a program to spy on families. That's simply not true. The main purpose is to curb drug use," said Captain Patrick Froehle, commanding officer for the Los Angeles Police Department DARE division. Furthermore, police insist they would be wrong not to act on the information. If they did not act, children may continue to live with parents who might be neglecting or abusing them. According to Captain Froehle:

> In such environments, there are usually no morals, values or training for the child. My personal opinion is that an arrest is the best thing that could ever happen to that parent. Marijuana could lead to harder drugs, which, in turn, could ultimately lead to death. What may turn out to be negative for the parent is positive for society.[97]

Also, students are not permitted to mention names in DARE classes. What happens after the class between the officer and the students is no different from what happens in cases involving other crimes, according to the police. Some police officers, however, have qualms about using the information. "You're damned if you do and damned if you don't. Sometimes, I almost feel like a traitor," says Officer Anne Corcoran, a DARE teacher for the Boston Police Department. "I look into the children's eyes and I see them saying, 'How dare you? I confided in you and you let me down.' "

No one knows how many students tell on their parents. The police do not compile statistics, and they do not volunteer to give out what information they have. Parents who are charged usually want to avoid publicity. In one case, a DARE student turned in her stepfather, a professor at a small college in Iowa, for smoking marijuana. After the police arrested him, the professor had to leave the state to find work. The professor told the judge, "As a result of . . . turning us in to the police an emotional door was closed and she felt virtually alienated from her mother and has gone to live with her father."[98]

The question has become a matter of public debate in Maine, where Crystal Grendell turned in her parents. In a column in the local newspaper, eight residents were asked whether children should report their parents for smoking marijuana. One answered, "If the children are affected by it, yes, they should turn them in." Two had mixed feelings. Five said no. Speaking for those opposed, Roxanne Morse, a high school teacher, said, "It reminds me of the Soviet Union when people who weren't good Communists were at risk of being turned in by their children."

Summary

Public policing has an ancient heritage. The Roman emperors hired police forces to patrol the streets of Rome. American policing originated in the medieval community requirement that everyone over 12 years old belong to a tithing that made each member responsible for the crimes of others. The constable-watch system required residents to patrol the streets as a public duty. When the Industrial Revolution, urbanization, and population increase led to disorder and crime in most European and American cities during the 1800s, the constable-watch system gave way to organized police departments and paid police officers. Professionalism has been the main theme in most twentieth-century police reform, characterized by departments free from political influence, centralized authority in the chief, trained police officers, the latest technology, and control of police discretion. During the last 20 years, American policing has advanced on all these fronts.

American law enforcement consists of largely autonomous federal, state, county, and municipal agencies, reflecting our federal system and the separation of powers. These agencies fall, at least nominally, under the executive branch of government's jurisdictions. Despite local variations, police departments share fundamental characteristics. Highly formalized quasi-military bureaucracies, they perform similar functions and enforce similar laws. Police departments vary in administrative style depending on the community they serve, the goals their chiefs set, and the values and ambitions of individual officers. Watchman-style departments concentrate on maintaining public order; legalistic departments make criminal law enforcement the highest priority; service departments target answering calls from the public for service, whatever they may concern. Although private policing has always existed alongside public police, private security forces have grown rapidly during the past 20 years. Private security now outnumbers public police in numbers of persons employed.

Police departments provide the only around-the-clock emergency public service. Citizens call the police to solve virtually any problem they believe they cannot solve by themselves. The public demand for police service goes far beyond enforcement of the criminal law. Calls for service fall into three main categories: criminal law enforcement, order maintenance, and public information and assistance. Formally, the law requires the police to enforce all laws all the time; informally, discretion permits the police to perform their functions according to community, administrative, and personal priorities.

The use and amount of discretion depends on the situation and the officer's rank. The police rely more on formal law and rules, less on discretionary judgment, in the enforcement of laws against serious crimes, such as murder, rape, and robbery. They rely increasingly more on discretion in the enforcement of misdemeanors such as public drunkenness, and in other order-maintenance situations. Discretion in police departments also increases as authority moves down the police hierarchy. Police officers need to rely on discretion most in the most difficult situations: how to settle disputes and maintain order, what laws to enforce, and how to interpret vague descriptions such as "disorderly conduct." Domestic assaults and dealing with intoxicated and mentally ill persons require great skill and judgment. With respect to domestic assaults, police departments have recently begun reducing police discretion by requiring officers to arrest instead of choosing alternatives such as counseling and separating the parties.

The police spend the least amount of their time enforcing the criminal law, which has led to calls to reduce police time for public service and order maintenance. However, police functions do not fall neatly into categories; they overlap. More important, according to some experts, they reinforce each other. Good community service leads to greater public confidence; greater public confidence leads to more reports of crimes and, hence, improved law enforcement. Good public order, according to some, leads to more obedience to rules in general and, again, better law enforcement. Recently, in response to the strain on police resources in enforcing drug-related offenses, police departments have enlarged their public service role by sponsoring prevention programs in schools and communities. These programs aim to reduce the demand for drugs, thereby eliminating the need for a later criminal justice response.

Review Questions

1. Describe the major stages in police history.
2. What are the main elements in police professionalism?
3. Describe the basic features in the structure of American law enforcement.
4. What are the major federal agencies and their functions?
5. Distinguish between state police and state highway patrol.

6. What are the major functions of sheriffs' offices?

7. What characteristics do municipal police departments share?

8. List and describe the three principal police administrative styles.

9. What is the function and significance of private security forces?

10. Describe the three major police functions. How do the police allocate their time among the three?

11. Explain the formal and informal dimensions of the three major police functions.

12. What are the arguments for and against concentrating on law enforcement and reducing other services by the police?

Notes

1. Carl B. Klockars, *The Idea of Police* (Beverly Hills: Sage Publications, 1986), 7–8.

2. Peter K. Manning, "The Police: Mandate, Strategies, and Appearances," reprinted in Victor E. Kappeler, *The Police and Society: Touchstone Readings* (Prospect Heights, Ill.: Waveland Press, Inc., 1995), 103.

3. Egon Bittner, *The Functions of the Police in Modern Society* (1970), 36–47; James Q. Wilson, *Varieties of Police Behavior* (Cambridge, Mass.: Delgeschlager, Gunn and Hain: Harvard University Press, 1968), 4–5.

4. Jerome H. Skolnick and James J. Fyfe, *Above the Law: Police and the Excessive Use of Force* (New York: Free Press, 1993), 94.

5. Patrick B. Adamson, "Some Comments on the Origin of the Police," *Police Studies* 14 (1991): 1–2.

6. This section rests on my own research into English law enforcement, some of which appears in Joel Samaha, *Law and Order in Historical Perspective* (New York: Academic Press, 1974), and then draws on all of the following: David H. Bayley, "Police: History," in *Encyclopedia of Crime and Justice,* Sanford H. Kadish, ed., Vol. 3 (New York: Free Press, 1983), 1120–25; Thomas A. Critchley, *A History of Police in England and Wales, 900–1966* (London: Constable, 1967); Roger Lane, *Policing the City* (New York: Atheneum, 1975); Sidney L. Harring, *Policing a Class Society: The Experience of American Cities, 1865–1915* (New Brunswick, N.J.: Rutgers University Press, 1983); Robert Fogelson, *Big-City Police* (Cambridge, Mass.: Harvard University Press, 1977); James F. Richardson, *The New York Police: Colonial Times to 1901* (New York: Oxford University Press, 1970); Eric Monkkonen, *Police in Urban America, 1860–1920* (Cambridge: Cambridge University Press, 1981); and Samuel Walker, *A Critical History of Police Reform: The Emergence of Professionalism* (Lexington, Mass.: D.C. Heath and Company, 1977).

7. Evelyn Parks, "From Constabulary to Police Society," in *Criminal Law in Action,* William Chambliss, ed., 2d ed. (New York: Macmillan, 1984), 209–22; Roger Lane, "Urban Crime and Police in Nineteenth-Century America," in *Crime and Justice: An Annual Review of Research,* Norval Morris and Michael Tonry, eds., Vol. 2 (Chicago: University of Chicago Press, 1980), 1–45; Mark H. Moore and George L. Kelling, "Learning from Police History," *The Public Interest* (Spring, 1983): 51.

8. Thomas Critchley, *The Conquest of Violence: Order and Liberty in England* (London: Constable and Company, 1970), 69.

9. Lane, *Policing the City,* contains an excellent history of Boston's police.

10. Ibid.

11. Harring, *Policing a Class Society;* Parks, "From Constabulary to Police Society."

12. Richard A. Staufenberger, *Progress in Policing: Essays on Change* (Cambridge, Mass.: Ballinger Publishing Company, 1980), 8–9.

13. Staufenberger, "Personnel Upgrading," in *Progress in Policing.*

14. Wilson, *Varieties of Police Behavior;* Herman Goldstein, *Policing a Free Society* (Cambridge, Mass.: Ballinger Publishing Company, 1977); Michael K. Brown, *Working the Street: Police Discretion and the Dilemmas of Reform* (New York: Russell Sage Foundation, 1981), Chapter 2.

15. Craig D. Uchida, "The Development of the American Police," in *Critical Issues in Policing,* Roger Dunham and Geoffrey P. Alpert, eds. (Prospect Heights, Ill.: Waveland Press, 1989), 24.

16. Ibid., 25.

17. Nathan Douthit, "August Vollmer: Berkeley's First Chief of Police and the Emergence of Police Professionalism," *California Historical Quarterly* 54 (1975): 101–24.

18. We are deluged with writings about the 1960s. Two excellent places to start are the good general summary of the political tensions and turmoil of the period in Allen J. Matusow's, *The Unraveling of America: A History of Liberalism in the 1960s* (New York: Harper & Row, 1984), and the thorough examination of the liberal and conservative criminal justice response in Thomas E. Cronin et al., *U.S. vs. Crime in the Streets* (Bloomington: Indiana University Press, 1981).

19. Crime Commission Report, *The Police* (Washington, D.C.: Government Printing Office, 1967); Staufenberger, "The Role of the Police," in *Progress in Policing,* 13–18.

20. Samuel Walker, *The Police in America,* 2d ed. (New York: McGraw-Hill, 1992), 27–28.

21. Malcolm M. Feeley and Austin D. Sarat, *The Policy Dilemma: Federal Crime Policy and Enforcement, 1968–1978* (Minneapolis: University of Minnesota Press, 1980); Staufenberger, *Progress in Policing.*

22. Ibid.

23. *Chicago Tribune,* 25 and 31 August 1992.

24. *Chicago Tribune,* 20 April 1993.

25. The Police Foundation, *Annual Report, 1989* (Washington, D.C.: The Police Foundation, 1989), 3–4, cited in Walker, *The Police in America,* 42.

26. FBI, *Crime in the United States 1994* (Washington, D.C.: Federal Bureau of Investigation, 1995).

27. BJS, *Report to the Nation on Crime and Justice,* 2d ed. (Washington, D.C.: Bureau of Justice Statistics, 1988), 66.

28. Ibid.

29. Ibid.

30. "Security Guards Are Hired Increasingly to Fight Crime on the Streets," *Wall Street Journal,* 22 March, 1994; Ralph Blumenthal, *New York Times,* 22 August 1989.

31. William C. Cunningham, John J. Strauchs, and Clifford W. Van Meter, *Private Security: Patterns and Trends* (Washington, D.C.: National Institute of Justice, 1991).

32. Albert Reiss, Jr., *Public Employment of Private Police* (Washington, D.C.: Bureau of Justice Statistics, 1988).

33. Quoted in Skolnick and Fyfe, *Above the Law,* 114.

34. "Police Academy Adapts to Changing New York," *New York Times,* 6 February 1987.

35. Jerome H. Skolnick and David H. Bayley, *The New Blue Line* (New York: Free Press, 1986), 125.

36. Skolnick and Fyfe, *Above the Law,* 114.

37. Kenneth Tunnel and Larry K. Gaines, "Political Pressures and Influences on Police Executives: A Descriptive Analysis," *American Journal of Police* 11 (1992): 10.

38. Wilson, *Varieties of Police Behavior.*

39. Robert H. Langworthy, "Organizational Structure," in *What Works in Policing,* Gary W. Cordner and Donna C. Hale, eds. (Cincinnati: Anderson Publishing, 1992), 103.

40. Brand Whitlock, *Forty Years of It* (New York: D. Appleton and Company, 1914), 239.

41. Adapted with modifications from the President's Commission on Law Enforcement and the Administration of Justice, Task Force Report: *The Police* (Washington, D.C.: U.S. Government Printing Office, 1967), 15–16.

42. Brian Forst et al., *What Happens After Arrest?* (Washington, D.C.: National Institute of Law Enforcement and Criminal Justice, 1977), 17; BJS, *Report to the Nation,* 62 (victimization reports for aggravated assault).

43. Goldstein, *Policing a Free Society,* Chap(ter)s 3 and 4.

44. Floyd Feeney and Adrienne Weir, eds., *The Prevention and Control of Robbery* (Davis, Calif.: University of California, Davis, 1974), summary volume; Floyd Feeney, "Robbers as Decision-Makers," in Derek B. Cornish and Ronald V. Clarke, *The Reasoning Criminal: Rational Choice Perspectives on Offending* (New York: Springer-Verlag, 1986), 61–65.

45. Most of these examples were taken from Kenneth Culp Davis, *Police Discretion* (St. Paul: West Publishing Company, 1975), 3–7.

46. Ibid.

47. Joseph Wambaugh, *The Blue Knight* (Boston: Little, Brown, 1972); Jonathan Rubenstein, *City Police* (New York: Farrar, Straus, and Giraux, 1973); Wilson, *Varieties of Police Behavior,* Chapter 2.

48. Wilson, *Varieties of Police Behavior,* Chapter 3; Rubenstein, *City Police.*

49. Joyce Purnick, *New York Times,* 4 July 1984.

50. Brown, *Working the Street,* Chapter 8; Mike Weiss, *Double Play* (Reading, Mass.: Addison-Wesley, 1984), 80–81.

51. Rubenstein, *City Police,* 53.

52. Brown, *Working the Street,* Chapter 6.

53. Donald Black, *The Manners and Customs of the Police* (New York: Academic Press, 1980), 146; Brown, *Working the Street,* 289.

54. Joel Garner and Elizabeth Clemmer, *Danger to Police in Domestic Disturbances—A New Look* (Washington, D.C.: Bureau of Justice Statistics, November 1986); Mary Rose Stanford and Bonney Lee Mowry, "Domestic Disturbance Danger Rate," *Journal of Police Science and Administration* 17 (1990): 244–49.

55. Lawrence W. Sherman, *Policing Domestic Violence: Experiments and Dilemmas* (New York: Free Press, 1992), 31.

56. Vera Institute of Justice, *Felony Arrests* (New York: Longman, 1981); BJS, *Intimate Victims: A Study of Violence Among Friends and Relatives* (Washington, D.C.: Bureau of Justice Statistics, January 1980); Walker, *The Police in America,* 130.

57. Joel Garner, Jeffrey Fagan, and Christopher Maxwell, "Published Findings from the Spouse Assault Replication Program: A Critical Review," *Journal of Quantitative Criminology* 11 (1995): 4.

58. Lawrence W. Sherman and Richard A. Berk, *The Minneapolis Domestic Violence Experiment* (Washington, D.C.: The Police Foundation, 1984); "The Specific Effects of Arrest for Domestic Assault," *American Sociological Review* 50 (1985): 262–63; Lawrence S. Sherman and Ellen G. Cohn, "The Impact of Research on Legal Policy: The Minneapolis Violence Experiment," *Law and Society Review* 23 (1989): 117–44.

59. *Police Report on Domestic Violence: A National Survey* (Washington, D.C.: Crime Control Institute, 1986); Sherman, *Policing Domestic Violence,* 1–2, 14, 104.

60. *Thurman v. City of Torrington,* 595 F.Supp. 1521 (D. Conn. 1984).

61. James Meeker and Arnold Binder, "Reforms as Experiments: The Impact of the 'Minneapolis Experiment' on Police Policy," *Journal of Police Science and Administration* 17 (1990): 147–53.

62. Paul C. Friday, Scott Metzger, and David Walters, "Policing Domestic Violence: Perceptions, Experience, and Reality," *Criminal Justice Review* 16 (1991): 198–213.

63. Michael Steinman, "Anticipating Rank and File Police Reactions to Arrest Policies Regarding Spouse Abuse," *Criminal Justice Research Bulletin* 4 (1988): 1–5, as summarized in Sherman, *Policing Domestic Violence,* 113.

64. Michael E. Buerger, ed., *The Crime Prevention Casebook: Securing High Crime Locations* (Washington, D.C.: Crime Control Institute, 1992), 231, as quoted in Sherman, *Policing Domestic Violence,* 114.

65. Sherman, *Policing Domestic Violence,* 2–5.

66. Garner et al., "Published Findings from the Spouse Assault Replication Program," 9, 24–25.

67. Ibid., 7.

68. *Bruno v. Codd,* 396 N.Y.S.2d 974 (1977), and consent decree; *Bruno v. McGuire,* New York State Supreme Court, index #21946/76, quoted in Goldstein, *Policing a Free Society,* 247.

69. Sherman, *Policing Domestic Violence,* 162.

70. Ibid., 163.

71. Ibid., 159–60.

72. Ibid., 161.

73. Kirk R. Williams and Richard Hawkins, "Perceptual Research on General Deterrence: A Critical Review," *Law and Society Review* 20 (1986): 545–72.

74. Sherman, *Policing Domestic Violence,* 161–3.

75. Lee Rainwater, *Behind Ghetto Walls: Black Families in a Federal Slum* (Chicago: Aldine Publishing Co., 1970), 229, as quoted by Sherman, *Policing Domestic Violence,* 164.

76. Sherman, *Policing Domestic Violence,* 164–5, 170.

77. Raymond Nimmer, *Two Million Unnecessary Arrests: Removing a Social Service Concern from the Criminal Justice System* (Chicago: American Bar Foundation, 1971); Edwin M. Schur and Hugo Adam Bedau, *Victimless Crimes: Two Sides of a Controversy* (Englewood Cliffs, N.J.: Prentice-Hall, 1974); Charles W. Weis, *Diversion of the Public Inebriate from the Criminal Justice System* (Washington, D.C.: National Institute of Law Enforcement and Criminal Justice, 1973).

78. Donald J. Black, *The Manners and Customs of the Police* (New York: Academic Press, 1980), 29–32.

79. Egon Bittner, "Police Discretion in Emergency Apprehension of Mentally Ill Persons," *Social Problems* 14 (1967): 279.

80. Herman Goldstein, "Improving Policing: A Problem-Oriented Approach," *Crime and Delinquency* (April 1979): 254.

81. Bittner, "Police Discretion," 286, 288.

82. Gary N. Sales, "A Comparison of Referrals by Police and Other Sources to a Psychiatric Emergency Service," *Hospital and Community Psychiatry* 42 (1991): 950–51.

83. Egon Bittner, "Florence Nightingale in Pursuit of Willie Sutton: A Theory of the Police," *The Potential for Reform in Criminal Justice,* Herbert Jacob, ed. (Beverly Hills: Sage Publications, 1974), 27–31; John A. Webster, "Police Task and Time Study," *The Journal of Criminal Law, Criminology, and Police Science* 61 (1970): 94–100; Black, *Manners and Customs of the Police;* Eric J. Scott, *Calls for Service: Citizen Demand and Initial Police Response* (Washington, D.C.: National Institute of Justice, July 1981); Jack R. Greene and Carl B. Klockars, "What Do Police Do?" in Carl B. Klockars and Stephen D. Mastrofski, eds., *Thinking About Police,* 2d ed. (New York: MacGraw-Hill, 1991), 281.

84. Wilson, *Varieties of Police Behavior,* ix-x; Brown, *Working the Street,* 236.

85. Minneapolis Police Department, *Annual Report 1983,* 1, 16.

86. George James, "Police Heroics, Minus the Car Chases," *New York Times,* 9 June 1992.

87. The Police Foundation, *The Newark Foot Patrol Experiment* (Washington, D.C.: Police Foundation, 1981), 112.

88. Norval Morris and Gordon Hawkins, *The Honest Politician's Guide to Crime Control* (Chicago: University of Chicago Press, 1967), 9.

89. James Q. Wilson, *Thinking About Crime,* rev. ed. (New York: Basic Books, 1983), 111–12.

90. Elaine Cumming et al., "Policeman as Philosopher, Guide and Friend," *Social Problems* 12 (1965): 285.

91. William O. Douglas Institute, *The Future of Policing* (Seattle: William O. Douglas Institute, 1984), 11.

92. David Hayselip, Jr. and Deborah Weisel, "Local Level Drug Enforcement," in *What Works in Policing?* (Cincinnati: Anderson Publishing, 1992), 36–37.

93. Robert Rheinhold, "Police, Hard Pressed in Drug War, Are Turning to Preventive Measures," *New York Times,* 28 December 1989.

94. Ibid.

95. Joseph Pereira, "In a Drug Program, Some Kids Turn In Their Own Parents," *Wall Street Journal,* 20 April 1992; Lewis Donohew, Howard Sypher, and William Bukoski, eds., *Persuasive Communication and Drug Abuse Education* (Hillsdale, N.J.: Erlbaum Associates, 1991).

96. Dennis P. Rosenbaum et al., "Cops in the Classroom: A Longitudinal Evaluation of Drug Abuse Resistance Education (DARE)," *Journal of Research in Crime and Delinquency* 31 (1994): 1–31.

97. Quoted in Periera, "In a Drug Program."

98. Ibid.

5 Police Strategies

CHAPTER MAIN POINTS

1. *Police strategies in the form of police operations are adopted in order to carry out the police missions discussed in Chapter 4.*

2. *Police strategies have always been, and still are, either reactive or proactive.*

3. *Patrol is the major police strategy.*

4. *The mobilization of patrol is stimulated mainly by citizen calls and much less often by the police themselves.*

5. *Preventive patrol in motor vehicles has dominated police strategies for most of the 20th century.*

6. *Empirical research suggesting the shortcomings in the effectiveness of preventive patrol stimulated the return to foot patrol, as well as a range of other proactive strategies.*

7. *Differential response time experiments show positive results in saving police resources and allowing officers to respond to more calls.*

8. *Foot patrol experiments demonstrate that while foot patrol does not reduce crime, it does reduce fear and improve people's attitude toward the police.*

9. *Single-officer patrol is as effective as, but less expensive than, traditional two-officer patrol.*

10. *Proactive, or "crime-attack," police strategies have increased due to research demonstrating the shortcomings in preventive patrol, police concern over career criminals, and public anger and fear over violence and illegal drugs.*

11. *"Hot spots" patrol is based on the idea that some addresses at certain times need more police response than others.*

12. *In aggressive field investigation, the police themselves initiate actions to check out suspicious circumstances, places, and people; they do not wait for people to call them into action.*

13. *Undercover police operations enjoy a long history, but they arouse controversy and the results of their effectiveness are mixed.*

14. *Crackdowns have produced mixed results, showing short-term reductions in some crimes in some places, but not in others.*

15. *Good preliminary investigations by patrol officers can significantly enhance the chances of successful prosecution and conviction, as well as the release of innocent people.*

16. *The significance and success of follow-up investigations by detectives show mixed results in the research.*

17. *Community policing enjoys increasing popularity because of the demonstrated and perceived failures of other strategies to reduce crime and control disorder.*

18. *Community policing involves residents, businesses, and organizations in the whole community in both the definition and solution to problems.*

19. *Community policing shifts authority from chiefs and the centralized bureaucracy of police departments to patrol officers in neighborhoods.*

20. *Like all police strategies, community policing is not a panacea, and it is too early to state its effectiveness because the research shows mixed results.*

All public and private professional organizations adopt strategies to carry out their missions. Police are no different in this respect. They, too, rely on a range of strategies intended to fulfill their missions to maintain order, enforce the criminal law, and perform social services. From at least the sixteenth century, English and American police have both initiated action and responded to calls from others to achieve their missions. In other words, they have relied on both proactive and reactive strategies. All modern police operations derive from three ancient strategies that were intended to both proactively and reactively achieve police missions. These strategies were walling, wariness, and watching.

Walling consisted of building walls surrounding entire towns to control entry. Today, locks, barred windows, alarms, fences, and other individual security devices have replaced city walls. However, in some places, walling in the old sense seems to have returned. Whitley Heights in Los Angeles is where famous movie stars like Marlene Dietrich, Rudolph Valentino, and Judy Garland lived. Just two blocks away is the high-crime Hollywood Boulevard. In 1992, residents of Whitley Heights each contributed $3,000 to erect electronic gates to the streets leading into the neighborhood. "There have been rapes, robberies, muggings, even murders. We just feel like we're under siege." Opposing this modern walling of Whitley Heights, Jon Jay argues, "Los Angeles could become a gated city."

Until the 1800s, wariness consisted of curfews to keep people home at night and out of trouble, and to relieve the suspiciousness of strangers. Today, staying home at night, exercising care around strangers, and avoiding "dangerous" places represent wariness. Walling and wariness are mainly individual and private responsibilities, although police departments and private security forces increasingly support these private efforts.[1]

Historically, watching was a joint effort between civilians and police officers. Residents spent most of their time at or near home; hence, they were more likely to notice suspicious people and circumstances. With the advent of the automobile, two-income families, single-adult households, and heavily populated cities and suburbs, however, residents spend less time at home and know few, if any, neighbors. They do not know who "belongs" in the neighborhood and who does not.[2]

From the early 1800s until the 1980s, two new strategies dominated policing: preventive patrol and criminal investigation. Uniformed police patrolled the streets to prevent and interrupt crime and to apprehend suspects. Whatever crimes uniformed officers did not prevent from occurring in the first place, detectives followed up by questioning victims, witnesses, and suspects. The police applied preventive patrol and follow-up investigation to all problems, whatever their nature. Research since the 1960s has demonstrated the limits of both traditional patrol and follow-up investigation in controlling crime.[3]

Limits demonstrated by research, growing public frustration and anger over illegal drugs and violence, fear of crime, and impatient demands to "do something" to control crime led to insistence that the police adopt more aggressive proactive strategies to "attack" crime. The police responded with various crime-attack strategies, including aggressive field investigation, de-

reactive police patrol *strategy that mobilizes the police when citizens call them to request service.*

coys, undercover operations, roadblocks, drug raids, and saturation patrol. Crime-attack strategies raise empirical questions regarding their effectiveness. They also raise ethical questions about the kind of police appropriate to a constitutional democracy that values privacy and liberty. Despite such questions, crime-attack strategies are major police strategies in the late twentieth century.

Patrol Strategies

Despite the publicity surrounding and popularity of new police strategies such as community-oriented policing, patrol is still the "backbone" of American police operations. Patrol consumes most of the resources of police departments; in some small departments, patrol is usually the total operation. The medieval word "patrol" meant "to walk or paddle in mud or dirty water." Today, patrol officers move through the streets, sometimes on foot, but usually in vehicles. Patrol is the most visible police activity; most people ordinarily notice no other. Patrol cars, aptly named prowlers, either move slowly (prowling) to survey the beat, or speed through the streets, sirens screaming and red lights flashing, pursuing suspected lawbreakers. These familiar sights illustrate the main purposes of patrol. The slow prowler suggests the watching or surveillance function of patrol; the high-speed chase demonstrates its criminal apprehension function.

Patrol Mobilization

Two major sources stimulate police responses in most instances:

1. Individuals call the police to report crimes.
2. Police officers discover crimes while they patrol, or actively seek out crime in crime-attack operations.

Calls from private individuals account for up to 90 percent of all police responses. Discovery of this large percent shattered a firmly entrenched myth that police discover most crimes; in fact, private individuals determine criminal law enforcement in most cases. If victims or witnesses do not call, the police can do little or nothing. In the remaining 10 percent of cases, the police discover crimes either while cruising or walking a beat or by aggressively searching for crime. When police respond to calls, private individuals decide the target of police mobilization. When police seek out criminal or other suspicious behavior, the police choose the target of mobilization. Although the vast majority of policing remains reactive, evidence suggests an increase in police-initiated operations, fueled by public outrage and fear of violence and drugs.[4]

Most patrol is, therefore, **reactive police patrol,** that is, the police mobilize when private individuals call them to request service. Citizen calls mobilize police patrol in several steps; discretion significantly affects each. In the first step, victims and witnesses call the police. However, many never make those calls. See Chapter 2 for a discussion of the reasons people decide not to call the police. Second, police telephone operators, usually untrained civilians, answer all citizen calls. These "street-level bureaucrats" possess enormous discretionary power either to cut off or confer police services. Private individuals always encounter police operators first; nearly half the callers will never have any direct contact with the police. Police telephone operators promise police action in only 47 percent of the calls they receive. Although some departments permit supervisors to monitor these calls, most go unreviewed. The "unit promised" category means the operator responded with the assurance, "We'll send a car right away." Sometimes, when operators are busy or irritated, they answer callers abruptly and rudely. Instead of a

preventive patrol *strategy in which police cars cruise randomly through the streets.*

reassurance that a car will soon be there, distraught people receive only a hurried "Okay" or "Yup." In general, the more serious the problem, the more likely a car is promised—80 percent for violent crimes, but 69 percent for nonviolent crimes, for example. (Figure 5.1)[5]

Operators do not send patrol cars directly. They fill out cards manually or punch a computer keyboard, forwarding the calls to dispatchers. Dispatchers, the third step in police response, ultimately decide whether patrol officers get citizen calls. Dispatchers have wide discretion in handling calls. They might not assign cars to calls at all, simply letting them drop. Or, if dispatchers pass calls to patrol officers, they classify them as violent crime, domestic, or others. Patrol officers, of course, cannot act unless they receive calls from dispatchers. The responses of patrol officers to the calls of dispatchers are the last step in the citizen-initiated mobilization process. Patrol officers, like operators and dispatchers, have wide discretion in responding to citizen calls. They drop some calls, hurry to the scene in others, or proceed with no particular urgency, depending on their reading of the situation.

Types of Patrol

Motor patrol, which was introduced just after World War I, had largely replaced foot patrol by the 1940s. Administrators considered it superior to foot patrol. According to the respected police administrator and reformer Orlando Wilson, motor patrol has several advantages over foot patrol. Motor patrol obviously has the advantage in speed over foot patrol. Moreover, motor patrol, unpredictable and irregular, introduces an element of chance into crime control. In addition, cars provide more efficient service than foot patrol: they operate in all weather conditions; they facilitate transporting prisoners, stolen goods, weapons, and equipment. Wilson believed that **preventive patrol,** police cars cruising randomly through the streets, created the feeling that police were everywhere, and hence might appear any time. A sense of police presence and power was supposed to deter would-be criminals

Figure 5.1

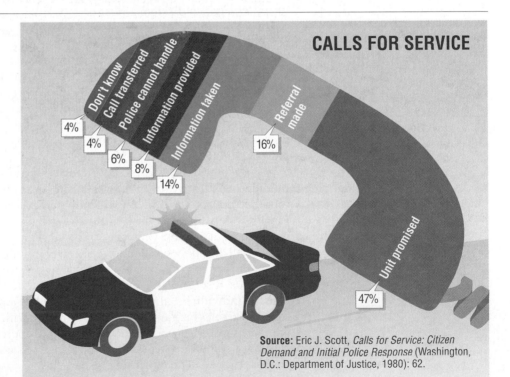

CALLS FOR SERVICE

Don't know 4%
Call transferred 4%
Police cannot handle 6%
Information provided 8%
Information taken 14%
Referral made 16%
Unit promised 47%

Source: Eric J. Scott, *Calls for Service: Citizen Demand and Initial Police Response* (Washington, D.C.: Department of Justice, 1980): 62.

and reassure law-abiding people. According to police experts Jerome Skolnick and James Fyfe, preventive patrol

> is based on the premise that the presence of uniformed cops and marked police cars will send would-be criminals elsewhere, will keep jaywalkers on the sidewalk, and will cause motorists to check their speedometers.[6]

Officers patrol when they are not answering calls for service or performing other assigned duties. On average, officers spend about half their time patrolling. What do they actually do on patrol? Patrolling activity varies by "jurisdiction, by beat, by time of day and individual," according to Gary Cordner and Robert Trojanowicz:

> Patrolling can be stationary or mobile; slow-, medium-, or high-speed; and oriented toward residential, commercial, recreational or other kinds of areas. Some patrol officers intervene frequently in people's lives by stopping cars and checking out suspicious circumstances; other officers seem more interested in . . . parked cars and the security of closed businesses; still other officers rarely interrupt their continuous patrolling. Some officers devote all of their uncommitted time to loafing or personal affairs.[7]

According to Wilson and other early supporters, preventive patrol had several presumed advantages (presumed because never empirically evaluated):

- Prevented crime from occurring.
- Intercepted crimes in progress.
- Prevented traffic accidents.
- Intercepted dangerous drivers.
- Contributed to making law-abiding people feel safe and secure.[8]

 *positive*

Motor patrol, telephones, and finally the two-way radio added to the mobility of the police and the speed with which they could respond to citizen calls. But these technologies also changed the fundamental nature of policing from a personal operation of individuals with intimate knowledge of and contact with community people, to a bureaucratic, mechanical, centralized operation. Technological advances that far outstripped anything in place when Chief Wilson extolled motor patrol have further isolated, mechanized, and bureaucratized preventive patrol. Computers can schedule cars to follow patterns structured according to complex mathematical formulae, pinpointing the exact location of patrol cars at all times. Computer terminals—now commonplace in patrol cars—provide rapid access to information.

negative

Technological dominance has also contributed to poor police-community relations, especially in high-crime areas where the public sees the police as a hostile occupational force that dominates the poor, weak, young, and others on the fringes of "respectable" society. Isolated in their temperature controlled "rolling fortresses," with windows rolled up to protect them from the smells and dangers of the areas they patrol, the police "seem unable to communicate with the people they presumably serve." In the angry words of the novelist James Baldwin,

> The only way to police a ghetto is to be oppressive. None of the Police Commissioner's men, even with the best will in the world, have any way of understanding the lives led by the people they swagger about in twos and threes controlling. Their very presence is an insult, and it would be, even if they spent their entire day feeding gumdrops to children. . . . He moves through Harlem, therefore, like an occupying soldier in a bitterly hostile country; which is precisely what, and where he is, and is the reason he walks in twos and threes.[9]

These police officers can establish close contact with the community even while their position on horses helps them to retain their authority.

The eminent sociologist of the police, Professor Albert J. Reiss, Jr., concluded that this

> insulation of the police came at a high price. The patrol officer in his air-conditioned and heated car no longer got out of the police vehicle to do preventive patrol or to learn more about the community being policed. The insulation of the police from the public to control corruption and to respond rapidly to their calls had served primarily to insulate the police from the public they were to serve. No longer did the public have confidence that the police were handling, or could handle their problems, and many, particularly minority groups, felt alienated from the police.[10]

Despite criticisms, many police administrators continued to believe that the benefits of preventive motor patrol exceeded its detriments. They were convinced that motor patrol reduced crime and citizen fear, increased citizen satisfaction, and led to arrests. Those sympathetic to the police, wanting to alleviate the growing problem of police-citizen alienation, proposed public service officers and community relations programs as solutions.[11]

Beginning in the 1970s, a series of empirical evaluations uncovered several deficiencies in preventive patrol. For example, prisoners admitted to interviewers that they were neither frightened nor deterred by police presence. Attempts to increase perceived police presence by permitting officers to use squad cars for their personal use had little, if any, deterrent effect. Moreover, patrol does not affect crimes committed indoors. Even when preventive patrol is effective, it concentrates on main streets, leaving side and back streets, alleys, and even the rears of buildings on main streets largely unattended.[12]

These evaluations also indicate that crimes of passion are largely beyond the reach of preventive patrol. Enraged or demented individuals, hardly aware of anyone's presence when they give vent to explosive impulses, do not consider whether patrol officers will observe or catch them. In addition, skilled criminals quickly discover where the police concentrate their efforts; they avoid those places, or at least wait until a squad car passes before they make their moves.[13]

Andrew Halper and Richard Ku report that, according to one police administrator:

> Patrolmen in uniform are expected to be highly visible and thus deter crime by their conspicuous presence. But given the cost of personnel and the resources available to the city, it is inconceivable that enough uniformed patrolmen could be employed to completely cover the city in this way. Indeed, if the entire municipal budget were directed for this purpose it would still be inadequate. In any event, a patrolman in uniform, while a reassuring sight to many, is not the deterrent to crime that many people assume him to be. In a sense he performs the functions of a scarecrow, which is to say that he can only be effective within the short range of his ability to effectively observe and respond to criminal activity. In this respect his presence can be as reassuring to criminals as to the law-abiding. The potential felon, knowing where a policeman is, can safely deduce where he is not, and guide himself accordingly.[14]

The Kansas City Preventive Patrol Experiment

The most famous and perhaps the most influential study of preventive patrol, the **Kansas City Preventive Patrol Experiment,** tested the effectiveness of preventive patrol under carefully controlled conditions. Researchers divided 15 beats into three groups matched for similar crime rates and demographic characteristics. For one year, the police applied three distinct patrol strategies to each group. In the control group, they applied traditional preventive patrol; one car drove through the streets whenever it was not answering calls. In group two, proactive patrol, they greatly increased patrol activity; cars drove through the beats two to three times more often than in the control group. In group three, designated reactive patrol, they eliminated preventive patrol entirely; a patrol car entered the streets only in response to calls.

Before, and again following the experiment, interviewers asked business people and neighborhood residents if they had been crime victims, their opinion about the quality of law enforcement, and about their fear of crime. To the surprise of many, the experiment revealed that "the three experimental patrol conditions appeared not to affect crime, service delivery and citizen feelings of security in ways the public and the police often assume they do." The experimental conditions did not significantly *decrease*

- Crime rates.
- Rates of reporting crime to the police.
- People's fear of crime.
- Opinion about effectiveness of police services.
- Police **response time.**

At the same time, they *increased*

- Respect for the police in the *control* beats.
- Citizen fear in the proactive beats.[15]

Does the Kansas City Preventive Patrol Experiment prove that preventive motor patrol wastes police time and taxpayers' money? Some have rushed to that conclusion. However, Cordner and Trojanowicz caution that the Kansas City study merely "demonstrated that varying the level of motorized patrol between zero cars per beat and 2-3 cars per beat, for one year in one city, had no effect." James Q. Wilson, author of the influential *Varieties of Police Behavior,* warns that the experiment did not prove that adding police presence of all kinds is useless in controlling crime. It only showed that random, preventive motor patrol in marked cars did little good, regardless of whether it was proactive, reactive, or a little of both. Results might have differed substantially had officers responded to calls more quickly, in unmarked cars or on foot. Reported crime declined in Flint, Michigan, for example, when the Flint Police Department adopted foot patrols.[16]

The Kansas City Preventive Patrol Experiment had several definitely positive effects. It demonstrated the willingness of police departments to engage in research to evaluate the effectiveness of their programs. According to police expert Herman Goldstein, the experiment also "demonstrated that the police can undertake complex experiments that require altering routine operations with results that are beneficial to the agency . . . and to the entire police field." The experiment also opened up the possibility of freeing expensive patrol resources for other police activities; administrators might divert as much as 60 percent to investigation, surveillance, and community service without diminishing the effectiveness of patrol. Finally, by challenging traditional practices, according to J. L. Ray LeGrande of the Miami Beach Police Department, "It was a breakthrough in research—as important as using the police radio for the first time."[17]

Improving Response Time

Two major assumptions underlie preventive patrol:

1. It improves response time; that is, it permits the police to respond to trouble more quickly.
2. Rapid response time increases the number of crimes solved and suspects arrested.

The National Advisory Commission on Criminal Justice Standards and Goals, for example, concluded that if police can get to a crime scene within two minutes, "it can have dramatic effects on crime." Many departments—without the benefit of data establishing an empirical relationship between rapid response and arrest, witness availability, and conviction—bought faster cars, hired more patrol officers, and purchased high-tech communications systems.

Two tactics specifically related to reducing response time are

● The emergency 911 telephone number.
● Computer-assisted automobile vehicle monitoring (AVM) system.

Dialing 911 permits people to contact the police quickly; AVM facilitates rapid police response to these calls.[18]

Evaluation research shows that neither tactic by itself reduces crime. Researchers discovered that the time it takes a citizen to report a crime, not the speed with which the police respond, determines whether the police make an arrest and locate witnesses necessary to prosecution and conviction. People rarely call the police immediately. Too upset to call anyone at first, they wait up to an hour after the event to make any calls. When they do call, it is usually their family and friends first, and then the police. Furthermore, response time has no effect on apprehension, charge, and conviction rates. Just because police officers arrive on the crime scene does not mean that they get either the information they need to apprehend suspects or the evidence required to charge and convict them. Finally, the level of citizen satisfaction with the police does not depend on response time. These negative assessments obviously disappoint administrators who have devoted energy and resources to improving response times.[19]

Differential Police Response

Response time studies led police departments to consider the possibility of responding to calls differentially. Police departments in Wilmington, Delaware, and Birmingham, Alabama, participated in a **differential response** study to determine the number of noncritical calls and to discover if people were willing to accept delayed responses to such calls. About 15 percent of the calls were critical, 55 percent routine; the police could handle another 30 percent by other means. People who called the police said that alternative responses to a patrol car coming to the scene would have satisfied them. Therefore, 85 percent of all calls to the police involved noncritical issues that did not require a squad car arrival to satisfy people.[20]

The National Institute of Justice (NIJ) funded a test of the Wilmington, Delaware, **Management-of-Demand (MOD) System.** According to MOD, the police handled noncritical calls with alternatives to a patrol car on the scene. The alternatives included 30-minute delays to on-the-scene responses, telephone reporting, walk-in reporting, and scheduled appointments. Michael F. Cahn and James Tien assessed crime rates and victim satisfaction before and after MOD went into effect. They found that crime rates did not increase under MOD, that citizen satisfaction with the police continued, and that MOD freed resources for other police activities.[21]

The Police Executive Research Forum (PERF) designed a model response system. In this model, civilian complaint-takers answer all citizen calls, classify them as critical or noncritical, and transfer the critical calls to dispatchers for immediate response. Complaint-takers stack the noncritical calls, asking callers to file reports later. The Wilmington, Delaware, Police Department implemented the model, and the Police Executive Research Forum evaluated it. The evaluation reported positive results. The system saved police resources and allowed the department to handle more calls without increasing the number of police officers.[22]

Evaluation of a refined version of the model response system (tested in Toledo, Ohio, Greensboro, North Carolina, and Garden Grove, California) established several significant conclusions regarding response time:

- Fast police response accounted for less than 5 percent of arrests for serious crimes.
- Most service calls do not require fast response by patrol units.
- Different responses do not alienate people if they know in advance how the police will handle their calls.
- Differential response saved the Garden Grove Police Department 8,000 person hours, or more than $223,000 during the first year.[23]

Foot Patrol

Foot patrol has returned to police operations as a way to bring the police and private individuals closer together. The increased contact enables officers to see, appreciate, and intervene in minor disturbances and to enhance people's sense of security in their neighborhoods. According to Stephen Mastrofski,

> Imbued with a proprietary interest in the neighborhood's well-being and armed with a rich knowledge of its people and places, the officer is expected to enlist citizens' assistance and thus reinforce the informal social control mechanisms of the community. Ultimately these efforts are expected to contribute to more positive police-community relations, less fear of crime and disorder, and an actual reduction in crime and disorder.[24]

Evaluations showing the benefits of foot patrol have encouraged a number of police departments to adopt foot patrol as part of their operations.

The oldest form of patrol, foot patrol has returned to popularity in several U.S. cities.

Some, such as Boston, Massachusetts, Flint, Michigan, and Newark, New Jersey, have shifted substantially toward foot patrol. The evaluation in Flint showed that foot patrol reduced both the fear of crime and actual crime rates. Foot patrol in Flint was so popular that despite severe financial problems, the city voted three times for special tax increases to maintain and expand the program. The Newark Foot Patrol Experiment, the other major evaluation, produced mixed results. It showed reduced fear of crime but no decrease in the amount of crime.[25]

Single-Officer Patrol

Patrol is labor-intensive, that is, it relies heavily on people, not labor- and cost-saving equipment. Salaries take up 80 percent of police budgets. Therefore, patrol is the most expensive police operation, particularly the two-officer patrol that prevailed in American policing until the 1980s. Faced with declining budgets, the cost effectiveness of one-officer patrol appealed to budget-conscious administrators. Many officers, however, strongly opposed it. Administrators saw the chance to reduce the cost of patrol officers by half by moving from the traditional two-officer patrol to one. Patrol officers, on the other hand , believed that partners who backed each other up in dangerous situations enhanced their safety. PERF evaluated one-officer patrol in San Diego in the late 1970s. Several of its findings supported the use of one-officer over two-officer patrol units. According to the study, the San Diego one-officer patrol units:

- Were more cost effective.
- Were less often involved in resisting arrest situations.
- Resulted in fewer assaults against officers.
- Resulted in fewer injuries of officers.
- Generated fewer citizen complaints.
- Showed similar levels of proactivity as two-officer units, including traffic warnings, field interrogation, business checks, arrests, and crime report filing.[26]

Other studies have supported most of these findings, although one study suggests that one-officer units are less likely to make arrests and file serious

proactive police operations
tactic that focuses on the concentration of crime problems in small proportions of offenders, places, and victims.

charges. According to Mastrofski, who conducted a major survey of police operations:

> It seems reasonable to postulate that the greater efficiency of one-officer units creates a facilitative environment for higher "productivity" policing in the areas that departments typically monitor (arrests, citations and field interrogations), but how that available time is actually used will be heavily influenced by departmental policies that affect officers' incentives to conform their actions to departmental priorities.[27]

These findings and their appealing budgetary implications have led to increased one-officer patrol use, despite rank-and-file officer and police union opposition to it. One-officer patrol are now common in many departments. Nearly a third of departments surveyed by PERF use one-officer patrol on the evening shift. However, some of the largest departments do not use it. Chicago assigns all officers in the evening shift to two-officer cars; New York City assigns 98 percent and Cleveland 93 percent to them. After a fight with the police union, New York City did set up one-officer patrol, but they are deployed in only 14 of its total of 123 precincts, and only in low-crime areas, during daylight hours, and when the single officer is armed with shotguns "which fire a blast of pellets that knock down targets."[28]

Proactive Policing

Research demonstrating the shortcomings in preventive patrol, police concern over career criminals who return to the streets to frighten residents, public anger and fear over violence and illegal drugs, and the recognition that the reduction of fear is a legitimate police objective have led police departments to turn to new tactics and strategies. In several of these, the police do not wait for calls for service; they initiate action. One survey indicates that nearly half the departments surveyed had instituted some form of police-initiated mobilization, or proactive police operations. **Proactive police operations,** usually in the form of special crime-attack units, focuses on the concentration of crime problems in small proportions of offenders, places, and victims. Crime-attack operations include using decoys, undercover patrol, saturation patrol, raids, roadblocks, informants, and field interrogation; targeting repeat offenders; policing repeat-complaint addresses; and policing to maintain order. Crime-attack units focus on two kinds of targets:

1. *Trouble spots,* sometimes called "hot spots," such as restaurants where "known suspects hang out," neighborhoods with particularly high burglary rates, bars where disturbances are common, or addresses from which a large number of calls come.

2. *Troublemakers,* such as known criminals or repeat offenders.[29]

Criminal justice researchers have demonstrated that a few people account for the lion's share of people arrested for crimes. In Kansas City, Missouri, for example, 2.7 percent of the 500,000 persons arrested two or more times in 1990 accounted for 60 percent of all arrests. Similarly, a few addresses account for most calls for police service. A major study of these hot spots in Minneapolis showed that 5 percent of the 115,000 street addresses and intersections accounted for 100 percent of the calls to police to report criminal sexual conduct, robbery, and auto theft.[30]

Crime-attack operations generate controversy, much of it based on ideology. Opponents contend that proactive policing of all kinds threatens individual rights in a free society; some even contend that it makes America a police state. These critics maintain that responses to citizen calls most befit life in a democracy. On the other hand, many individuals and groups—especially those who believe crime-attack strategies might reduce violence, illegal drugs, and the number of chronic offenders in the community—strongly favor aggressive tactics. Liberty and privacy cannot exist, supporters of crime-attack operations maintain, in communities ravaged by violence, drugs, and career criminals. Supporters also believe that court restrictions on law enforcement practices have forced the police to rely on decoys, informants, and other crime-attack tactics.[31]

"Hot Spots" Patrol

"Hot spot" patrol distinguishes police response by location. Crime is not evenly distributed throughout an area, particularly if that area is a city. Over half the crimes in a city come from *three* percent of the addresses. Furthermore, crime in these "hot spots" is further concentrated into "hot" days of the week and times of the day. Therefore, says Lawrence W. Sherman, expert on police strategies, "most addresses, and even most blocks, in any city go for years without any crime—even in high-crime neighborhoods."[33]

Hot spot response is based on the idea that some addresses at certain times need more police response than others. The traditional strategy of even distribution of patrol, giving every resident an equal share of patrol whether they need it or not, is not the best use of police resources. Evaluations of experiments in which police have concentrated patrol visibility on high crime times and places are modest, but positive. Hot spot patrol can reduce—or at least displace—identified crime problems. In the major experiment, the Minneapolis Hot Spots Patrol Experiment, "three hours a day of intermittent, unpredictable police presence was applied to" a random selection of the "worst" hot spot intersections in the city. Robbery fell 20 percent, and crimes overall fell 13 percent in these intersections. The number of fights and disturbances was cut in half in the experimental areas. The success of hot spot patrol may depend on what the police do when they get to the hot spots. The Minneapolis police officers did little except drive around. They rarely got out of their cars to talk to people or to interrogate suspects. According to Sherman, who conducted the experiment, "More aggressive efforts may have reduced crime even further—or made it worse."[34]

Aggressive Field Investigation

Aggressive field investigation means that the police themselves decide to check out suspicious circumstances, places, and people; they do not wait for people to call them. Police action can take various forms, including checking locks on buildings; shining spotlights through windows; watching, following, stopping, questioning, and sometimes frisking suspicious persons for weapons, stolen property, or contraband. Suspicious people might be in cars, standing in a public place, walking down the street, or just "hanging around." Aggressive field investigation, however, rarely extends to entering homes.[35]

Numerous circumstances prompt field investigations. People out too late at night arouse police suspicions, although what constitutes "too late" differs from place to place. In small towns, it might mean after 10:00 P.M.; in cities, it could be an hour after the bars close. Location is also important. Three men in their twenties who are huddled near a jewelry store's side entrance at 1:30 A.M. certainly make a seasoned officer wary. A shiny, clean car displaying old, dirty license plates suggests a stolen car with switched plates. Six suspicious-looking young people of mixed races parked in a car near a recently robbed store, or two young men pacing up and down in front of a clothing store in a high-crime area suggest that delinquents are "casing the joint." Hence, a variety of circumstances might lead officers to believe that places or people do not "look right." Crime attack calls for officers to probe these suspicious circumstances.[36]

Proactive Policing in Germany

According to Dilip K. Das, former police administrator from India and student of international policing:

> In spite of their marked identity with the state, their strong organizational hierarchy, and their conscious social control role, the police [in Germany] complain of their powerlessness. They perceive that society, politicians, courts, and academics are unsympathetic. In Frankfurt the local police were engaged in an anti-drug experiment called "Argos." They sought to induce drug dealers and users to move to more observable locations to prevent the increasing expansion of drug trading. The police were not, however, optimistic about achieving success, because they seemed convinced that they were alone and powerless in the battle against drugs, prostitution, and violence.
>
> Those who were engaged in "Argos" felt that the laws concerning drugs and prostitution were very liberal, because liberalism was a political ploy. If the police knew that a prostitute was suffering from AIDS, they had no way to stop her from practicing her trade. According to the police, many local politicians, particularly those belonging to the Green Party, were interested in presenting a liberal image.
>
> As a result, lax legal provisions dealt with prostitutes, drug dealers, demonstrators, and others. Thomaneck refers to the "police as the whipping boys of the nation" and to their "frustration and aggression," because the press has written about "neofascist tendencies in the police force," "gruesome police misconduct," and other reactionary trends.
>
> Police pointed to a steep rise in crime in Frankfurt and attributed it to liberal policies and restraints on the police. The courts, the prosecutors, the legislators, and other public agencies were not, the police complained, reinforcing the laws against drugs, prostitution, and other activities that generated crime. In one case, the police received a call from the manager of a restaurant who said a customer had locked himself in the restaurant restroom. The police came, broke down the restroom door, and discovered a man under the influence of drugs. However, they brought no charges. The police said
>
>> they were reluctant to bring charges against drug users, because stringent proofs were reportedly demanded in the courts. Possession of drugs, the police complained, was difficult to prove, because contraband was secretly delivered at predetermined locations. Most police undercover agents were known to drug traffickers who would hide when the police appeared. . . . Perhaps the German courts lack confidence in police fairness and integrity.[32]

Undercover Police Work

undercover police operations
proactive police tactic of using disguises in sting and reverse sting operations to identify criminal activity while it is occurring.

Covert, meaning **undercover, police operations** are not unique to late twentieth-century enforcement of illicit drug laws. Henry VIII used them during the 1520s to enforce the English Reformation. Since about 1900, the police have used such tactics extensively to fight vice and political crime. But since the 1970s, undercover police activity has expanded and changed its form. According to criminologist Gary T. Marx, undercover work

> is now invoked to attack street crimes and even to go after white collar crime and official corruption. All this is very controversial, at least among some groups, but the latter two seem to inspire particularly pronounced rancor. Undercover police tactics such as Operation Greylord uncovered corruption among Chicago judges, the ABSCAM Operation discovered bribe taking by members of Congress, and the sting operation against the mayor of Washington, D.C., showed that the mayor used illegal drugs. Police have used these same tactics to uncover other white-collar and organization crimes.[37]

The Street Crimes Unit (SCU) of the New York City Police Department uses undercover officers in a crime-attack unit that focuses on street mugging. Carefully selected and specially trained officers and supervisors use both plainclothes surveillance and decoy tactics to apprehend street muggers in the act of committing their crimes. Decoy police officers, disguised as potential crime victims, walk the streets. A backup team stationed nearby and dressed to blend into the area comes to the decoys' aid and arrests muggers. SCU focuses on making quality arrests, those that will hold up in court without subjecting officers or private individuals to increased danger. SCU officers constitute an elite corps of individuals who look for more than "ordinary" police work and eagerly seek to fight crime. They want to advance their careers, secure monetary advantages, avoid quasi-military chains of command, express their individuality, and feel pride and self-esteem in being part of such an elite organization. For these reasons, their extremely high morale motivates them to do the best job possible.[38]

SCU officers devote a great deal of time developing decoy and surveillance abilities to maximum levels. Officers spend hours—often on their own time—learning disguises that help them blend into a neighborhood without being recognized. They learn what makes a "good pinch," an arrest that will stand up in court. They enhance their skills in minimizing injury to themselves and innocent people while maximizing their effectiveness in high-crime areas. The unit's supporters believe that decoy operations and plainclothes surveillance outwit street criminals at their own game. Critics of the unit maintain that this work necessitates unwarranted and destructive deception of the public by government officials.[39]

The New York City Police Department reported that the 5 percent of its officers assigned to SCU accounted for more than 18 percent of all felony arrests, more than 50 percent of robbery arrests, and 40 percent of burglary and auto-theft arrests. Because the department did not design SCU as an experiment, the figures do not explain whether SCU alone accounted for the arrests. Furthermore, some evidence suggests that decoys actually encourage crime and increase its commission. One survey showed that a special unit made 216 robbery arrests in 16 weeks, a most impressive achievement until it also pointed out that more than half those arrested would not have committed the robberies if the police had not put the temptation there in the first place.[40]

 **You Decide**   ## "When Is Undercover Police Work Ethical?"

Gary T. Marx, who has written extensively on undercover police, tells of the following real incidents involving ethical issues raised by undercover police work. Assume that you are an officer. How would you resolve the questions Marx raises? Would your answers be different if you were the friend, loved one, or relative of the suspects turned up by the undercover work? What ethical standards would you set to?

[1.] The case of a San Francisco police officer and 16 of his fellow officers raises the issue of "[t]he conflict of goals between preventing crime and encouraging it in order to apprehend criminals." [The 17 officers] patrolled the streets in plainclothes looking for parking violators and meter jammers. The officer reported that his unit was effective because "if you have a uniformed officer there, no one is going to wipe off their tires." To which the skeptic might respond, "Isn't that what we want uniformed officers for—to prevent violations? Do we really want to encourage people to break the rules because we want them to think no one is there?" Underlying the officer's remark is the need to write citations in order to meet productivity goals. The unstated assumption here is, "We want to create a situation in which, because they never know whether or not a police officer is watching, persons won't wipe off their tires." This "myth of surveillance" comes with other costs, but it is believed to be more efficient than obtaining that result only when a uniformed officer is actually present. From the standpoint of empirical impact, we don't know if it is a myth.

[2.] The issue of the sometimes conflicting goals of preventing crimes and making arrests can also be seen in the case of Malcolm X's daughter, Quiblah Shabazz, who was accused of hiring a pretend hit man to avenge her father's death. When the informant was asked why he didn't try to discourage the plot, he said, "I'm supposed to sound like a murderer, remember? A hit man wouldn't agree to kill someone and then say it's wrong." When a suspect is hesitant (e.g., Shabazz indicated that she was leery, wanted to put the plot on hold, and missed a planned meeting), should the informant respect this apparent withdrawal or ambivalent intent, or persist? In this case, 38 of 40 phone calls were initiated by the informant, and he appears to have done most of the talking on the tapes.

[3.] The issue of when undercover police should intervene to prevent a crime has continued to raise moral and practical questions. Thus, in Dallas an undercover officer watched a woman being raped by a group he had infiltrated. He pretended to be sick to avoid participating. He stated, "You don't want to ruin your credibility." Would he feel the same way if his wife, sister, or mother had been the victim?

[4.] In New York, police had prior information that a drug dealer planned to rob an undercover agent. They did not intervene to stop this and the agent was shot. Some critics within the department claimed the operation should have been aborted. Dangers such as this are reflected in agent folktales. Question: What does an undercover agent do? Answer: He's like the kid they use down in Louisiana for alligator bait. They tie him to the end of a rope and he walks out into the swamp. All the kid can do is hope they jerk the rope back in time.

[5.] Police in a Long Island sting were criticized for permitting the illegal dumping of toxic waste to continue for what critics saw as an inordinate amount of time. Pollution was created in order to fight it. In a nonenforcement example in Boston, a drug informant was permitted to run an after-hours club in exchange for his cooperation. This led to neighborhood complaints about noise, disorder, and increased crime, and to beliefs about the "police corruption" that permitted the place to flourish.

[6.] An inquiry in Los Angeles found that a 19-member special surveillance unit had often failed to prevent those it was watching from attacking people in armed robberies and burglaries. While in many cases suspects could have been arrested beforehand for lesser offenses or on existing arrest warrants, detectives waited for a violent felony to occur because that would make for a stronger case and a longer sentence. The department has now implemented a policy instructing officers to protect potential crime victims even if this jeopardizes an undercover investigation. The policy reads, "Reverence for human life must always be the first priority when considering the extent to which a criminal incident is allowed to progress or deteriorate . . . during a stakeout or the surveillance of known criminals."

[7.] The unit has also been accused of dispensing punishment before trial. In a successful civil trial, a federal jury found the Los Angeles chief of police and nine officers in the surveillance unit liable for the death of three robbers and the wounding of a fourth. The suit accused the unit of being a "death squad" prone to shooting suspects instead of arresting them. In this case, police had tracked the robbers for weeks. As the robbers entered their getaway car after holding up a restaurant, the officers opened fire, later claiming the suspects had pointed guns at them. The weapons turned out to be unloaded pellet guns.

[8.] The issue of intervention, as well as an example of unintended consequences from covert surveillance, can be seen in a St. Louis case. The FBI, hoping to record evidence of terrorist activities, planted listening devices in the apartment of a Palestinian-American. Instead, it recorded the suspect's murder of his teenage daughter. An incriminating conversation("Do you know that you are going to die tonight?") and the girl's screams as she begged her parents not to kill her were captured by an automated listening device. The FBI surveillance unit was not staffed the night of the murder. It is not clear whether authorities could have intervened in time to prevent the murder even if they had been listening. However, there were earlier recordings of phone conversations in which the accused discussed various methods of getting rid of the daughter.[41] Reprinted with permission from: Blomberg, Thomas G. and Cohen, Stanley (ed.). *Punishment and Social Control: Essays is Honor of Sheldon L. Messinger.* (New York: Aldine de Gruyter) Copyright © 1995 Walter de Gruyter, Inc., New York, pp. 101–102.

Police Crackdowns

Police crackdowns is a proactive strategy in which a sharp increase in police activity is supposed to dramatically raise the real, or at least the perceived, threat of getting caught for committing crimes. Crackdowns are an old police practice that have produced mixed results. In some research, crackdowns have produced at least *short-term* reductions in a wide range of crimes, including drunk driving, robbery, drug dealing, and prostitution. It is not clear whether the reduced criminal activity in one place merely moved to other places, called **displacement.** However, Lawrence W. Sherman, who has studied police crackdowns, says that a

> review of eighteen police crackdowns around the United States and in five other countries shows that fifteen were successful, with little clear evidence of displacement. The London prostitution crackdown, for example, found no indication that the prostitutes pushed from one area had been arrested in any other area of London.[42]

In fact, argues Sherman, quite the opposite of displacement occurs as a result of crackdowns. "Rather than displacing crime to surrounding areas, crime prevention measures reduce crime in nearby areas where they had not been implemented." According to Sherman's research,

> the key to making crackdowns work is to keep them short and unpredictable. Long-term police crackdowns all show a "decay" in their deterrent effects over time. Short-term crackdowns, in contrast, show a free

bonus of "residual deterrence" after the crackdown stops, while potential offenders slowly figure out that the cops are gone. Random rotation of high police visibility across different short-term targets can accumulate free crime prevention bonuses and get the most out of police visibility. Even if displacement to other spots occurs, the unpredictable increases in police presence at any hot spot may create generally higher deterrent effects from the same number of police officers.[43]

Crackdowns, while apparently modestly successful in some places, raise questions about the proper balance between crime control and due process in a constitutional democracy (see Chapter 2). Crackdowns bring the police into much greater contact with people's lives. As a result, crackdowns limit the privacy and liberty of all people where they occur, not just of the individuals who commit crimes or "cause trouble." Some residents protest that while crackdowns may reduce crime, they also turn their neighborhoods into "police states." Young African American men, particularly, complain that the police "hassle" them simply because they are young, African American, and in the neighborhood. Inevitably, crackdowns will involve innocent people who have no intention to commit crimes or cause trouble.[44]

Police crackdowns on drug dealing have produced mixed results. Heightened fear of drug offenses and frustration over the seeming lack of success in reducing their numbers have led to an increase in the use of crackdowns. The theory of drug crackdowns is that a steep increase in police presence will enhance at least the perceived risk of getting caught buying or selling drugs. Robert E. Worden, Timothy S. Bynum, and James Frank evaluated the costs and benefits of drug crackdowns. Table 5.1 lists their findings.[45]

Worden and his colleagues also surveyed the research on the effectiveness of a number of crackdowns. The results were inconsistent. Some, such as a crackdown on street-level heroin dealing in Lynn, Massachusetts, produced all the benefits listed in Table 5.1. Interviews with residents and merchants indicated a substantial reduction in the visibility of heroin dealing. Interviews with treatment workers and addicts indicated that it was riskier to buy and sell heroin. Furthermore, treatment demand increased 85 percent following the crackdown. Burglaries fell 38 percent, robberies fell 18.5 percent, and all other crimes against persons fell 66 percent in the year

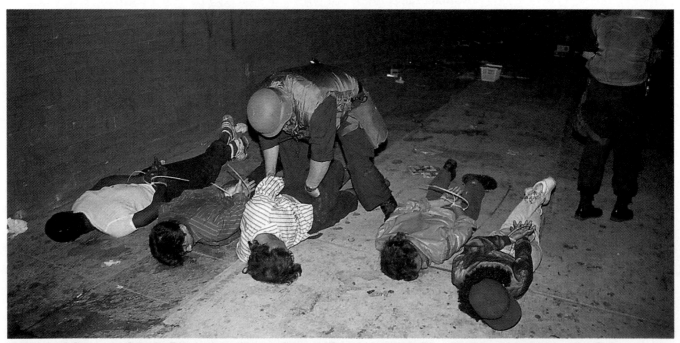

Police crackdowns on drug dealing, such as this one, have produced mixed results, according to empirical evaluations.

Table 5.1
Drug Crackdowns

Benefits	Costs
Reduction in the visibility of drug dealing	Increased numbers of officers
Reduction in the amount of drug using	More equipment
Reduction in the number of drug users	Loss of success in activities elsewhere
Reduction in the number of street crimes associated with drug use and trafficking	Increases in other crime
Improvement in the quality of life in the neighborhoods where crackdowns occur	Increase in police abuse of power
Improvement in residents' attitudes toward police	Increased subversion by police of their power
	Erosion of residents' respect for police authority
	Reduction in residents' willingness to cooperate with police

following the crackdown. However, there was no control group, so it is impossible to tell if these benefits accrued from the crackdown or from something else. A later, similar crackdown in Lawrence, Massachusetts, failed to produce the same results. Interviews with addicts indicated only a slight reduction in the availability of heroin. The numbers of crimes against persons fell 28 percent in the 28 months following the crackdown, but the numbers of burglaries, robberies, and thefts *increased.* Clearly, drug crackdowns produce definitely mixed results.[46]

Assessing Crime-Attack Strategies

Crime-attack operations raise questions about the kind of police responses that are proper in a constitutional democracy. Should the police mobilize their power only when either private individuals specifically request them to do so or when officers discover crimes in progress during routine patrol? Should the police limit their response strictly to law enforcement according to citizen demand? Or does the control of illegal drugs, violence, and predatory criminals, and the fear they cause among law-abiding people, demand that the police take aggressive action? In these circumstances, should the police passively wait for crimes to take place and merely react? Or should the police take immediate action to prevent or at least reduce the amount of crime? The answers to these questions go to the fundamental issue of the balance between social order and individual liberty and privacy. Obviously, the values of liberty and privacy cannot thrive in a society destroyed by crime. On the other hand, order without liberty and privacy would destroy what makes life worth living in a free society. Research on the effectiveness of proactive policing in controlling crime and apprehending criminals, as we have noted, is decidedly mixed.

Despite debate, the police have continued to expand their crime control operations. In addition to crime-attack strategies, the police—with the help of police researchers—have begun to introduce a whole new philosophy of policing. Community-oriented policing and its relative, problem-oriented policing, change the focus of policing. From the centralized, bureaucratic police department where administrators define policies and adopt strategies, the focus shifts to neighborhoods where administrators rely upon both patrol officers and the community both to identify problems and to set the police agenda for responding to them. Unlike traditional patrol and investigation, which consist of strategies looking for problems, community-oriented policing analyzes problems and selects from a range of responses to solve them.[47]

Some experts question the short-term results obtained by crime-attack strategies. They argue that special units are effective partly, if not entirely, because they are experimental or pilot projects. In maintaining that "all pilot projects are successful," one police chief applied the **Hawthorne principle,** whereby merely creating a new and closely watched project has at least a temporary positive influence. "No one has followed up on most special units to see how they did over time, as opposed to the short period when all eyes, so to speak, focused on them and most observers hoped for the best."[48]

Supporters respond that anticrime units enhance the public's image of the police department. Most people are both intrigued and impressed with the "clever, seductive character" of the projects, especially "widely publicized demonstrations of the make-up artists' abilities to disguise burly officers." They give officers assigned to them an important boost in morale, to say nothing of the satisfaction officers derive from doing what most went into police work to do—fight crime. Furthermore, supporters maintain, quality arrests are the norm in special crime-attack units. Unlike ordinary arrests, which lead to conviction in only a minority of cases, these quality arrests produce high conviction rates. The usual witness and victim problems do not jeopardize the prosecution's case. Since special crime unit officers have caught the perpetrators in the act, officers are themselves eyewitnesses to crime and can so testify to what they saw first-hand, which is the best type of evidence.[49]

Criminal Investigation

Crime stories, whether on television or in novels, provide excitement, drama, suspense, and mystery. From Sherlock Holmes in the 1800s to *NYPD Blue* in the 1990s, detectives sleuth out clues in dangerous, unsavory places, subject their clues to laboratory analysis and brilliant intuition, and, practically without fail, catch the bad guy. To many people, police work means criminal investigation by detectives. However, according to John Eck, research during the 1960s and 1970s "showed that detective work is often boring, usually requires only normal decision-making powers, and seldom leads to solutions. The reason is that most crimes betray scant leads." Research conducted during the 1980s and 1990s indicates that criminal investigation is neither as exciting as the public believes nor as ineffective as the research of the 1960s and 1970s suggested.[50]

Most departments divide criminal investigation into preliminary investigation conducted by patrol officers and follow-up investigation conducted by detectives.

Preliminary Investigation

The role of patrol officers in criminal investigation is to conduct **preliminary investigations,** that is, to collect information at crime scenes and to write reports of what they learned. These reports, called **incident reports,** contain basic facts about the crime, the identity and description of victims and potential witnesses, the whereabouts of suspects (if known), the description of the crime scene, and other pertinent information, such as the statements of witnesses. Police departments and prosecutors rely heavily on incident reports in deciding whether to continue the criminal process. Incident reports that contain "good" information, such as the names and addresses of

follow-up investigation

investigations conducted by detectives following reports from the initial investigation by patrol officers.

several witnesses, the names and addresses of suspects—or at least good descriptions of them—and accurate, detailed stolen property descriptions raise the chances of successful prosecution and conviction. Furthermore, good preliminary investigation also reduces the chance of involving innocent people as suspects. Police incident reports containing the names of two witnesses instead of one raises convictions by 60 percent![51]

Criminal investigation research has revealed that patrol officers make most arrests. They either arrest suspects at the scene of the crime, or they obtain identifications from victims or witnesses that lead to arrests. Only a small percentage of index crime arrests results from detective investigations. In addition, detective investigations rarely result in identifying *unknown* criminals. As a result of these findings, police departments have begun to train patrol officers to conduct more extensive investigations, which they have started to do. Some departments now provide patrol officers with feedback from prosecutors' offices regarding the final outcome of cases that officers have investigated.[52]

Follow-Up Investigation

Television and film dramas portray brilliant detectives who solve virtually any crimes they investigate. Researchers who have studied detectives in real life have challenged this picture of ingenious crime-solving sleuths. However, the empirical research has produced inconclusive and even contradictory results. Peter Greenwood, Jan Chaiken, and Joan Petersilia of the Rand Corporation examined cleared cases of homicide, aggravated assault, felony morals, robbery, burglary, theft, auto theft, forgery, and fraud in Berkeley, Long Beach, Los Angeles, Miami, and Washington, D.C. They concluded that the great majority of cases were not solved by detective **follow-up investigation.** Instead, they were solved either because the police already knew the identity of the suspect by the time the case reached the detective or because patrol officers had already arrested the suspect.[53]

John Eck collected data from three police departments: De Kalb, Illinois, County, Georgia, St. Petersburg, Florida, and Wichita, Kansas. Eck examined the activities of both patrol officers and detectives in gathering information about suspects. He concluded that cases fell into three categories. Two groups—weak cases where there is little evidence, and strong cases with a lot of evidence—require little effort by either patrol officers or detectives. In these groups, therefore, cases are solved or not solved because of existing circumstances, not the efforts of police. However, in the third group, cases where there is moderate evidence, effort does make a difference. The more time spent on the case, the greater the chance of an arrest. In these cases, the work of detectives "is extremely important with respect to the subsequent making of follow-up arrests."[54]

Steven G. Brandl and James Frank reviewed both initial and follow-up investigation reports of burglary and robbery cases in a midwestern municipal police department that employed 245 sworn officers, 30 of whom were assigned to the detective division. They concluded that time spent on cases with moderate information about suspects *does* increase the likelihood of arrests. According to Brandl and Frank, perhaps the reason detectives spend more time on cases with a moderate amount of information about suspects is

> because of the detectives' reasonable expectation that with just a little more information these cases could conclude with an arrest. The analyses also show that, overall, significantly more time was spent on burglary and robbery cases that were solved than on cases that were not solved. This directly contradicts the conclusion of Greenwood et al. that "the cases that get solved are primarily the easy ones to solve."[55]

Time spent by detectives in follow-up investigation, like gathering fingerprints, sometimes increases the likelihood of arrests.

The National Institute of Justice (NIJ) sponsored research during the 1970s that demonstrated that no amount of investigation will solve many serious crimes. As a result, detectives can screen out cases they cannot solve, leaving time and resources for other activities. Many departments now follow up only cases with sufficient solvability factors. Research indicated, for example, that departments could predict with 80 percent accuracy whether they could solve burglary cases on the following solvability factors: time when the burglary took place, whether a witness reported it, whether an on-view report existed, whether the police had usable fingerprints, and whether they had a suspect either named or described.[56]

Several studies underscore the crucial role of private individuals in effective criminal law enforcement. Information provided by private individuals to the police leads to the solution of far more crimes and to the apprehension of many more perpetrators than elaborate police detective work. The awareness of private individuals and their prompt, complete, and accurate reports to the police, not magical police genius and super weapons, are instrumental in apprehending and convicting suspects. According to police experts Jerome H. Skolnick and David H. Bayley:

> Crimes are not solved—in the sense of offenders arrested and prosecuted—through criminal investigations conducted by police departments. Generally, crimes are solved because offenders are immediately apprehended or someone identifies them specifically—a name, an address, a license plate number. If neither of these things happens, the studies show, the chances that any crime will be solved fall to less than one in ten. Despite what television has led us to think, detectives do not work from clues to criminals; they work from known suspects to corroborating evidence. Detectives are important for the prosecution of identified perpetrators and not for finding unknown offenders.[57]

Solving crimes is the most visible and, perhaps to some, the most important part of the work of detectives. However, in real life, detectives perform a variety of other important, if not so dramatic, functions. On a typical day, completing routine paperwork, reviewing new cases, processing prisoners in custody since the night before, and making required court appearances take up much of the morning. Dealing with suspects consumes considerable time, especially when it offers the opportunity to clear additional crimes. Eager to solve as many crimes as possible, detectives try to connect suspects to more than the case at hand. Linking crimes requires looking through arrest records, talking to suspects, and perhaps arranging lineups. That leaves the detectives' afternoons free for follow-up investigations to interview witnesses, check leads, and search for evidence.

However contradictory and inconclusive the research concerning follow-up investigation by detectives, one thing is certain: private individuals, patrol officers, *and* detectives play critical and complementary roles in criminal investigation. This research has led to specialization. Patrol officers assume more responsibility for cases on their beats; investigative specialists assist them; and departments retain centralized investigative units for major crimes against persons.[58]

Community Policing

In the last twenty years, a growing dissatisfaction with patrol and criminal investigation has led to the adoption of two new strategies of policing—community-oriented policing and problem-oriented policing. The main thrust of these new strategies is to broaden input into police decision making. **Problem-oriented policing** draws upon this broadened input to expand the approach to policing so that police are solving problems instead of simply responding to specific incidents. According to Skolnick and Fyfe, these strategies have become "widespread, prevalent, and fashionable not because . . . [they have] been proved to work but because the alternatives . . . have been proved to fail." As we have seen in past sections, during the 1970s and 1980s, police researchers and managers discovered the limits of traditional police strategies in controlling crime. According to Skolnick and Fyfe,

> [P]olice managers, informed by criminal justice researchers, have learned that hiring more police does not necessarily result in less crime or increase the proportion of crimes solved. The same can be said for enlarging police budgets or licensing police to be *aggressive* in their prevention efforts. The most that can be warranted is that, if cops were to disappear entirely, there would be more crime. But once a certain threshold of police department size has been reached—long ago in most major cities—neither more police nor more money helps much. Variations in crime, clearance rates, and public disorder are related to such stubbornly intractable factors as income, levels of employment, education, and population heterogeneity. Throwing money at law enforcement offers no solutions to these larger persistent social factors that are so highly correlated with crime. Besides, in the declining budget climate of the 1990s, there isn't much money to throw at either police or social problems. Hence, the search for a new approach to policing.[59]

Communication and cooperation between police and the communities they serve did not begin with community- and problem-oriented policing. For a long time, police departments have taught the general public and children about traffic safety. Recently, the police have applied the same educational techniques used in their efforts to reduce traffic accidents to crime prevention and criminal law enforcement. In some communities, police distribute brochures telling people how to protect themselves from victimization. In others, service-oriented "officer friendlies" meet with community organizations to instruct residents in crime prevention. Special sessions might be held to tell business people how to protect themselves against certain crimes, to help homeowners safeguard their homes from burglary, and to aid senior citizens in staving off street muggers.

Police departments have also begun to participate in citizen walling and wariness efforts. They urge people to secure their property and advise them about the best ways of doing it. In some cities, such as Detroit, helping people protect themselves against crime is a central police department policy. When faced with severe budget cuts that reduced law enforcement personnel from 5,800 to less than 4,000, the Detroit Police Department created a new Crime Prevention Section to achieve "intensive community mobilization for self-defense." As one sergeant said, "When manpower is cut, crime prevention becomes more important." Said another, "Crime prevention is not a frill. It is crucial when manpower for traditional services has been cut back." Police inspected apartment buildings, commercial establishments, and private residences, telling residents how to improve security. Sometimes the officers installed dead-bolt locks and other hardware at public expense.[60]

An increasing number of private detectives and companies provide surveillance over businesses and homes. Voluntary citizen watch groups organize to patrol their neighborhoods. Thousands of towns and cities have Neighborhood Watch programs, often encouraged by police departments. The Detroit Police Department's Crime Prevention Section mobilized people to join Neighborhood Watch for residences, Apartment Watch for high-rise apartments, Business Watch for commercial establishments, and Vertical Watch for office buildings.[61]

In addition to Neighborhood Watch, two other programs hope to promote citizen vigilance. "Storefront" programs bring local police facilities to locations that are more inviting to people. The informal settings encourage people to

Community oriented policing relies on residents like these to help the police identify and solve community problems.

come in and talk to police about crime and other problems. In citizen patrol, residents walk around their neighborhood to check for problems and report them to the police. The Guardian Angels are the most widely known citizen patrol, but there are many others that focus on city blocks or other neighborhood areas. The Minneapolis Police Department sums up the importance of citizen participation in crime prevention:

> It is clear that a neighborhood's freedom from criminality rests considerably upon the efforts of citizens themselves to be watchful of suspicious individuals or circumstances, to be prudent in safeguarding their persons or their property, and to be ready and willing to cooperate with their police. There is strong evidence to indicate that such citizen activity, particularly when organized and coordinated, is quite effective in preventing a substantial amount of crime.[62]

Community-Oriented Policing

Like the traditional community education programs and the various self-help programs, both **community-oriented policing** and problem-oriented policing involve residents. However, community- and problem-oriented policing do so to a more significant degree. They emphasize the importance of residents and other private individuals in actually defining and solving problems. Community- and problem-oriented policing shift the focus from police dominance to police-citizen cooperation, a shift that fits naturally with the knowledge that people make powerful contributions to criminal law enforcement and to solving other community problems. Table 5.2 sets out the differences between traditional and community-oriented policing.

Community-oriented policing although it varies greatly from department to department, emphasizes a number of elements, including:

- Improving and increasing contacts between police and members of the community.
- Expanding the definition of police work to include a broad range of community problems, not just criminal law enforcement.
- Decentralizing the police bureaucracy.

Table 5.2
Community-Oriented and Traditional Policing

Community-Oriented Approach	Traditional Approach
Private individuals are partners in crime control and order maintenance.	Police officers are responsible for crime control and order maintenance; private individuals are victims, witnesses, and offenders, not partners.
Authority is decentralized and organization is more flexible, allowing officers to respond individually to specific problems in specific neighborhoods.	Authority is centralized in a bureaucratic organization that focuses on applying the same responses throughout the city or town.
Officers typically are out of squad cars solving problems or building bridges with the community and helping to organize it.	Officers are typically in squad cars driving around to prevent crime and investigate suspicious circumstances and people.
Advocates are usually academics and police reformers.	Advocates are usually police executives.[3]

- Emphasizing proactive community problem solving that relies on a broad range of public and private agencies, individuals, and citizen groups.[64]

Community-oriented policing is more than a proactive operation. It is a broad strategy that draws upon patrol, criminal investigation, education, and also non-police community resources to solve a broad range of problems, including crime, drug abuse, disorder, and poor quality of life. In other words, community-oriented policing looks beyond the narrow view of police working alone to enforce the criminal law. Instead, its ambitious goal is to forge an alliance among private individuals, the police, business, and public and private agencies to identify and solve not just crime problems, but also problems related to the quality of life.

Community-oriented policing emphasizes that people themselves are the first line of defense against crime. To get the most benefit from private individuals, community-oriented policing adopts the technique of allowing people to nominate the problems they want the police to work on. This opens up the police to goals they may not have considered. People often express their *fear* of crime as much or more than they mention actual victimization. What triggers their fears may not be serious crime, but signs of disorder and deterioration in their neighborhoods, such as abandoned buildings, littered streets, and groups of youths hanging around the streets. Community-oriented policing changes not only the means of policing but also its ends—to reduce both crime and the fear of crime. The way to reduce crime and the fear of it, according to community-oriented policing, is by focusing on quality of life issues in the community.[65]

Advocates have identified the following advantages of community-oriented policing:

- Moving police officers from the anonymity of patrol cars to direct engagement with the community gives officers more information about problems unique to the neighborhood and insights into solving these problems.
- Freeing officers from reacting to crimes already committed permits them to spend more time on active crime prevention.
- Making police operations more visible to the public increases police accountability to the public.
- Decentralizing operations allows officers to develop a better understanding of how neighborhoods work, what their problems are, and how to respond to them.
- Encouraging officers to view private individuals as partners improves relations between the police and the public.
- Moving discretionary decision making downward from police administrators to patrol officers puts more authority in the hands of those who know best the problems and expectations of the community.
- Developing a relationship between the police and the public encourages people to take more initiative in preventing and solving crimes, drug abuse, disorder, and other community problems.[66]

Community-oriented policing does not mean that police submit entirely to the community's wishes. For example, community-oriented policing requires that in the face of demands for vengeance by an angry community, the police must treat suspects fairly and humanely, and protect their constitutional rights. They must also allocate resources to the whole community, not to either the neighborhoods with the most power or the residents with the loudest voices. In other words, community-oriented policing calls for police departments to be more responsive and accountable to the people, not that the police become the mere servants of the people.[67]

Problem-Oriented Policing

Community-oriented policing has taken many forms around the country, so it is difficult to generalize about what it typically consists of. Problem-oriented policing, perhaps the best known form of community policing, has drawn considerable attention. Problem-oriented policing includes three major themes:

- Increasing effectiveness by attacking underlying problems that give rise to incidents consuming police and detective time.
- Relying on the expertise and creativity of line officers to study problems and develop innovative solutions.
- Becoming more involved with the public to make sure the police are addressing the needs of people.

Problem-oriented policing focuses on groups of events instead of isolated incidents; in short, it shifts from incident-driven strategies to problem-solving techniques. This shift has altered two traditional emphases:

- From police department autonomy to other agencies and the public.
- From a narrow concentration on the criminal law response of arrest to a broader aim of solving underlying problems that lead to crime.

Instead of treating calls for help and service as separate, individual events and responding only by arrest, problem-oriented policing emphasizes analyzing incidents and deriving solutions that draw on a wide variety of public and private resources.[68]

The strategy consists of four parts:

- *Scanning.* Instead of relying on criminal law concepts such as robbery and burglary, groups of officers related incidents to problems and defined these problems in more precise and useful terms. For example, a single robbery might be part of a pattern of prostitution-related robberies committed by transvestites in center-city hotels.
- *Analysis.* After defining the problem, officers collect information from a variety of public and private sources, not just police data. They use the information to discover the underlying nature of the problem, its causes, and options for solutions.
- *Response.* Working with private individuals, businesses, and public and private agencies, officers tailor a program of action suitable to the characteristics of the particular problem. Solutions may include arrest, but they frequently involve other community agencies and organizations.
- *Assessment.* Finally, officers evaluate the effectiveness of their response to determine if they actually solved or alleviated the problem.[69]

The National Institute of Justice tested problem-oriented policing in Newport News, Virginia, with the cooperation of then Chief of Police Darrel Stephens. The department created a task force, made up of 12 members from all ranks and units, to design the process. The task force focused on several persistent problems. For example, tired of dealing with prostitute-related robberies, midnight-watch patrol officers and their sergeant decided to apply the problem-oriented approach. First, Officer James Boswell interviewed prostitutes who worked the downtown area to learn how they solicit, what happens when they get caught, and why they continue engaging in prostitution. Prostitutes told Boswell that they worked the downtown bars because they found customers easily and could avoid police observation, and that arrests were merely annoyances. Judges routinely sentenced them to probation; probation officers did not enforce the conditions of probation.[70]

Based on what he learned from the interviews, Boswell devised a response. He worked with the Alcoholic Beverage Control Board and local bar owners to move prostitutes out onto the streets. At police request, the Commonwealth's attorney asked judges to put stiffer penalties on prostitution: Prostitutes had to stay out of the downtown area or go to jail for three months. Boswell worked with the vice unit to make sure officers arrested prostitutes and that officers also knew the names of prostitutes on probation. They sent prostitutes on probation to jail. Within weeks, all but a few prostitutes had left downtown. Then Boswell talked to prostitutes' customers, telling them that most prostitutes working the streets were men posing as women. He also personally intervened in street transactions, introducing customers to their male "dates." The Navy arranged for Boswell to talk to incoming sailors about transvestite prostitutes and the dangers of prostitution-related robberies by them. In three months, the number of prostitutes working downtown dropped from 28 to 6; robbery rates fell in half. After a year and a half, neither prostitution nor robbery had returned to their earlier levels.[71]

Assessment of Community Policing

Community policing has drawn wide attention and considerable support from some criminal justice reformers. Many police departments have adopted it at least on a small scale. Federal and state funding have encouraged it. It is, however, not a panacea, any more than earlier strategies have been. It is too early to tell just how effective community policing is in reducing crime and the fear of crime, and in preserving the quality of life in communities that practice it. Existing research is incomplete, tentative, and mixed. Some kinds of community policing work in some places under some conditions at least for a time, as the examples in the *You Decide* and the preceding text suggest. But researchers have also revealed difficulties in community policing.

In a major review of community policing, Professors Dennis P. Rosenbaum and Arthur J. Lurigio point to other obstacles—both inside and outside police departments—to the evaluation of community policing. These obstacles have had the effect of limiting the implementation of community policing to specialized units within police departments or to specific districts within the jurisdiction of police departments. No large department has implemented community policing throughout the entire organization. Inside police departments, entrenched bureaucratic procedures and the fear of change among rank-and-file police officers create major obstacles to implementing community policing. Outside obstacles may be even greater. According to Rosenbaum and Lurigio:

> police agencies often assume that after community residents and groups are invited to participate in community policing, everyone will come forth and get involved. This assumption is generally false and is especially fallacious when applied to inner-city minority neighborhoods, where participation levels are historically low and where police-community relations are poor at best. Police departments are again discovering that public awareness and education are indispensable first steps on the road to successful implementation.[72]

Rosenbaum's and Lurigio's survey of research indicated that both the fear of retaliation from drug dealers and gang members and distrust of the police and other public agencies accounted for the low participation.[73]

In addition to the difficulties in implementing community policing programs, most of the evaluations have not involved experimental designs that can measure the effects of programs. The major study paid for by the Bureau of Justice Statistics to evaluate eight community policing programs, for example, relied solely on qualitative data because the programs differed greatly. Furthermore, the programs were in effect prior to the evaluation and continued after its termination, thus making it impossible to conduct a before-and-after comparison to determine their effects.[74]

Rosenbaum and Lurigio do report that their survey of research suggests the tentative answer that community policing "can have some positive effects on the community's perceptions and feelings about crime, disorder, and the police." Wesley G. Skogan, for example, reported that 9 of 14 targeted areas in 6 cities showed positive changes in the attitudes of residents toward the police, 7 showed less fear of crime, 6 showed declines in perceived disorder, and 3 showed reductions in victimization. Lurigio and Rosenbaum, in a review of 12 studies on the impact of community policing on police personnel, reported positive effects in the following areas:

● Enhanced job satisfaction.
● Satisfaction with a perceived broadening of the police role.
● Improved relations with private individuals and co-workers.
● Greater expectations for community involvement in crime prevention.[75]

Nevertheless, Rosenbaum and Lurigio conclude that, overall,

[a]lthough problem solving has since emerged as the dominant strategy for operationalizing community policing concepts, a paucity of rigorous evaluations have been designed to estimate the effects of these programs on either community residents or the police. In addition, few process studies have focused on the types of methods employed during problem-solving activities or the outcomes associated with those efforts.[76]

But they find an encouraging trend in the increase of case study methodology to analyze and describe problem-solving strategies. This approach, say Rosenbaum and Lurigio, "should eventually lead to the accumulation of trustworthy knowledge about the individual, social, and organizational factors that either facilitate or impede problem-solving and community-engagement activities."[77]

You Decide   ## "Is Problem-Oriented Policing Good Policy?"

Police expert Lawrence Sherman devised, and the Minneapolis Police Department inaugurated, a problem-oriented police program called the Repeat Call Address Policing (RECAP) Experiment. In the experiment, a small team of officers was supposed to develop problem-solving techniques that could be used throughout the department. Four hand-picked patrol officers and one sergeant were moved from 911 response to work at reducing the number of calls that came from addresses making the most 911 calls. According to Michael E. Buerger, a participant observer of the RECAP experiment, the officers were supposed to "devise and implement strategies to resolve the underlying problems that produced repeat calls for police service at their addresses." The police chief granted the team wide latitude to "do anything they wanted to solve the problems at their addresses, as long as it was legal, Constitutional, and ethical."[78]

The addresses were selected by an objective measure of problem seriousness. Any address that "generated a

high level of police responses was deemed to be a 'problem' for the purposes of the experiment. . . . Excessive demand for police resources at a single address, rather than public perceptions of crime or deteriorating civility, became the standard by which 'problems' were measured." The addresses were divided into two groups, the top 250 commercial and residential addresses. Then the addresses in each group were randomly assigned either to the experimental unit or to a control group. The addresses in the experimental group were divided among the four officers in the RECAP unit. "The program sought to identify as many types of problems, and generate as many innovative police responses to them, as possible."[79]

The basis for the RECAP strategy is the routine activities theory discussed in Chapter 2, the theory that crime results from the intersection in time and space of (1) motivated offenders, (2) suitable targets (victims), and (3) absent or inadequate guardians.[80]

Consider the following two problems drawn from the many encountered by the RECAP unit. The officers in RECAP describe the problems, their responses to them, and their assessment of the success or failure of their efforts. Were they successes or failures? How would you evaluate the decisions made and the problems faced? Put yourself in the place of the officers. What decisions would you have made? Defend your decisions.

Problem 1
Residential address
1986 calls: 40
1987 calls: 39
Result: down 1 call, 3% reduction

Premises
This is a two-story wood frame single residence home that has been converted to a duplex. The house has two entrances, front and back. The building is in somewhat run-down condition. The back yard has a six-foot board fence around it. The owner does not live on the premises, and there is no designated caretaker or property manager. The residents who have lived here generally have been single-parent minority families on welfare.

Environment
This is a low- to middle-class residential neighborhood. The people in the neighborhood are mainly black minorities. There is a mixture of working class and welfare people, with about a 50-50 mixture of owned and rented homes.

Diagnosis
A single woman and her three small children lived here. She moved here from Gary, Indiana, and had left most of her family behind. The police began to be called as soon as the woman moved onto the property.

The only adult male she knew in this area was an ex-boyfriend (the father of her children), who was the primary problem at this address. The ex-boyfriend was a drug addict, constantly in need of money. He always showed up at the residence on the first of the month to get part of the woman's welfare money. She would resist, and he would assault her.

The ex-boyfriend really had no permanent address during this time. He apparently had many "girlfriends" that he lived with, and he was just using the victim for his financial security. I suspect that he was using his other girlfriends in a similar way, though I have no reliable source of information to substantiate my suspicions. The victim was reluctant to do anything about prosecuting the suspect because she still cared about him, and because she was afraid of him.

Ideal action plan
Since almost all the calls centered on the destructive personal relationship between the resident and her former boyfriend, my action plan focused on both sides of that relationship. The short-term need was to keep the ex-boyfriend from preying on the woman. The long-term solution was to change the victim's attitude towards the relationship, and empower her to make positive changes in her lifestyle that would free her from the influence of men like her tormentor.

Obstacles to implementation
The victim's character and/or life skills presented one obstacle. She never really was aware of her rights, or knew and didn't want to do anything about it. She adopted a passive response to my initial suggestions, agreed to adhere to my recommendations, but rarely followed through. I could tell that she was a desperately lonely individual, but I could not tell whether she was really interested in making a change in her situation.

Finding the suspect, in order to bring enforcement action against him, was very difficult. He was very elusive, had no fixed address, and used three aliases. Several other agencies were also looking for him, without success.

The police response was a barrier to short-term control of the offender's behavior. Patrol units that responded to calls at this address did not follow department policy by arresting the suspect according to State Statutes (when he was there), or by making adequate reports for follow-up when he had fled the scene.

Overcoming the obstacles
When I first established contact with the woman, I explained her legal rights to her, and the procedures she would need to go through to keep her ex-boyfriend away from the premises. I explained to her about calling the police, about having him arrested for trespass or domestic abuse (whichever was appropriate in any given case), and about obtaining a restraining order to bar him from the premises. I explained that once a restraining order was issued, he could be arrested for being on the property even when he hadn't assaulted her.

She listened to the explanations, nodded, and agreed to do all of these things, but did nothing at all once I left. The calls kept piling up, the same thing over and over again: domestics and assaults. I could not tell whether she just didn't understand that she had to have an active role in things, or didn't want anything substantial done, or lacked the capacity to follow through with the necessary steps. Finally, I found an ally in the property owner.

Involving the landlord
The owner became concerned about the situation after the woman first moved in and the suspect began to damage his building. The ex-boyfriend kicked in the front door, damaging the whole wall and causing $800 damage. The precinct's property crimes investigators did not follow up on the preliminary report until I brought it to their attention and explained all the problems associated with what must have appeared to be a routine Damage To Property report. As a result of my intervention, a warrant was issued for the suspect's arrest.

The owner of the building became more cooperative after that, apparently convinced that I was serious about helping. He valued the woman as a decent person who was in most ways a good renter, but he told her that he could not tolerate the repeated destruction of his property when the ex-boyfriend came looking for money. The landlord told her that she would be evicted if she didn't get a restraining order to keep the suspect away. When it became apparent that she could not easily get to the Hennepin County Government Center (in downtown Minneapolis) to obtain a restraining order, the owner drove her there in his car.

The patrol force's role

We encountered two separate problems in the course of this case. The police response was routinely poor, with patrol units apparently exercising little or no effort to apprehend the suspect. To them, the situation was "just another domestic," with "just another so-called victim" who really didn't want the police to do anything, and who wouldn't do anything to help herself. (There were times when I felt the same way, but I didn't have the luxury of just blowing her off that way.)

This address became part of RECAP's Domestics Tracking Project, where we assessed the patrol force's response to Domestic calls at selected addresses. The police did not make a report after the first violation of the restraining order, so I made one when I learned of it (several days later, in following up from the weekly call sheets). As a result, and again with the landlord's help, the woman signed a complaint against her ex-boyfriend for violation of the order, and another warrant for his arrest was issued. Shortly after that, a two-officer car was called to the address when the ex-boyfriend broke in, assaulted the woman, and then fell asleep on the bed. One officer went in to wake him, while the second officer talked with the complainant in the hallway. The suspect jumped up, ran past the officer in the bedroom, past the other officer in the hall, and out the front door. Neither officer pursued him, and the squad cleared the call GOA (Gone On Arrival).

In another incident, an officer working alone responded to the woman's report that the ex-boyfriend was in the house. When the woman told the officer she had a restraining order, the officer returned to the squad car to radio in for verification that the order had been served on the suspect. While the officer was at the car, the suspect fled the house and avoided apprehension.

When I learned (through the call sheets) of the two incidents above, I checked with the woman for the details, and then looked for the Reports. Finding that none had been made, I wrote a report for each incident. I then drove the woman to the City Attorney's Office and walked her through the process of signing a Complaint for violation of the restraining order, and obtained a Warrant for the ex-boyfriend's arrest.

Problems enforcing the orders for protection

During this process, I learned that just because a report of a violation of a restraining order is made, it does not mean that a warrant will be issued automatically. The truth was that the victim had to go to the investigative unit to obtain a copy of the police report, then hand-carry the Report to the City Attorney's office. An interview with an Assistant City Attorney was required before a Complaint could be signed, and an arrest warrant signed by a Judge. I had never gone through this particular process before, and I was amazed and appalled at the number of barriers the procedure placed in front of the victim.

This finding led to a meeting with the City Attorney's Office, the commander of the Assault Unit, and the commander of the RECAP Unit, trying to hammer out a procedure for police officers to sign the Complaint instead of the victim. This in turn led to RECAP's involvement with the Criminal Justice Coordinating Committee's Task Force on Domestic Violence, described in a separate chapter.

Conclusion

The ex-boyfriend was eventually arrested on the damage to property and violation of restraining order warrants, tried, and convicted. He served 21 days in the workhouse, but upon his release, he returned to his former ways. He started appearing at the house again, assaulting the woman and causing more damage to the property. This time the landlord moved his tenant to another building that he owned, hoping that the ex-boyfriend would not be able to track her down.

The move backfired. The woman began bringing in other men, encountering similar problems of assault and property damage (I lost track of the case once the woman moved, since her new residence was not a RECAP address: I do not know if the ex-boyfriend was one of the actors at the new place or not). Her landlord lost patience with her, and ultimately evicted her outright.

Problem 2

Residential address
1986 calls: 101
1987 calls: 42
Result: down 59 calls, a 58% reduction

Premises

This address is a three-story, 12-unit apartment building that occupies one corner of the block. Attached to it are half a dozen 2-story townhouse residences (each with its own individual street address) which stretch to the next corner. The front of the building faces Plymouth Avenue; the rear exits onto the parking lot and alleyway.

This address is one of six identical or mirror-image complexes which fill five consecutive blocks along Plymouth Avenue. It is managed by the Plymouth Townhouse Association, an independent entity owned by the same Philadelphia-based ownership group that runs the nearby Parkview Apartments (two of which were in the RECAP group, and two in the Control).

Environment

The property is located in the high crime area of the northside. The area is the number one location for residential burglaries. There is also a high incidence of personal crimes such as assaults, street robberies, and auto thefts. The working poor comprise the bulk of the residents of the neighborhood, but the chronically unemployed are a common sight.

The whole area is still under the stigma of the racial riots in the early 1960s. There has been a reluctance to invest any money in the area, and consequently the neighborhood is in a depressed state, economically and culturally. The only new construction in the area has been the townhouse complexes and the new Fourth Precinct police station.

I knew two of my RECAP addresses—1515 Plymouth, another of the same Plymouth Townhouse complexes, and the McDonald's at Plymouth and Penn—were located on this strip. After the experiment ended, I learned that all of the other Plymouth Townhouse complexes were in the Control group; so were a nearby MCDA high-rise and a store in the shopping complex between the townhouses and the McDonald's. All of these addresses were subject to the common problems of the area, including gang activities which centered on the retaining wall between the McDonald's and the shopping mall.

The high unemployment and increasing use of drugs had spawned a proliferation of new gang activity. Gangs were in evidence in the past, but the new migration of poor and uneducated blue collar workers from Chicago and Detroit, and economically depressed areas such as Kansas City and Gary, Indiana, intensified the problem of the gangs.

Diagnosis

The main problem was the domestic problems in three apartments. The tenants of these apartments accounted for 70% of the total calls to the building. One apartment accounted for 25% of the total. The manager confirmed the diagnosis of the trouble apartments. He was starting the eviction process for those tenants when I made contact with him.

A second problem, which was not as evident from the call sheets, was the prevalence of drug dealing in the area. The manager was aware of the drug dealing in the neighborhood, but had found no evidence of dealing in the building. He knew as I did that the dealers had a habit of parking their vehicles on the side of the building, and then selling their drugs from their "pride ride." As the customers were well known to the dealers, it was extremely hard for the police to make an undercover buy to substantiate an arrest.

Ideal action plan

There turned out to be no need to develop an action plan. It was quite apparent from my first meeting with the manager of the building that he wanted the building cleaned up, and was willing to do anything he had to do to accomplish that. I asked about the three apartments that were prominent in the data sheets and what he felt I could hope to do by working with these people. He was aware that there was a problem, but not to that extent. He said I shouldn't waste my time: they were all being evicted, and wouldn't be allowed into the rental units he controlled. I provided him with a copy of the data sheets and made the offer to provide any data in the future.

What you can do with a can of yellow paint

The manager went to the alderman in the area and demanded the street be made a no-parking area. Normally, the alderman would want a petition for such a move. Due to the enormous drug problems in the area, and the fact that it was an election year, the street was "yellowed" (painted yellow to indicate "no parking") within two weeks. Surprisingly, this simple move eliminated the drug dealing as well as the illegal gambling from the side of his building. I thought that the dealers would relocate in an area close to this site, but to date, nothing like that has occurred. I expect that the dealers are selling their wares in another location, but they are not in the immediate vicinity.

Follow-up

There was little follow-up done at this building. The manager took such a dominant role in the everyday management of the property that I had little to do. The calls had dropped from 101 in the previous year to just 42 in the current year. I think this is an indication of the benefits of a tough management policy, and of following up on any problems that arise in the day-to-day management.

Conclusion

The basic premise of working with the address was to reduce police calls. I think that was accomplished. The manager was willing to do some proactive "policing" on his own, hopefully a sign of the coming times. If we can show the future managers and building owners that working proactively will reduce the problems at an address, the whole experiment will have been a success.

The RECAP final report announced, among others, the following findings:

- "the residential locations, relative to the control group, showed a 21 percent reduction in assault, a 12 percent reduction in disturbances, and a 15 percent reduction in calls related to drunkenness";
- "commercial targets showed a 9 percent reduction in theft calls; and a 21 percent reduction in shoplifting calls at seven stores participating in a special program";
- residential burglaries were up 27 percent compared to controls;
- calls for commercial predatory crime (criminal sexual conduct, robbery and kidnapping combined) were up 28 percent at the experimental addresses relative to controls."[81] Reprinted with permission from: Buerger, Michael E., ed., *The Crime Prevention Casebook: Securing High Crime Locations* (Washington, D.C.: Crime Control Institute, 1992) © 1992

Questions

Do these findings indicate that problem-oriented policing is good policy? Explain your answer. How do you define "good" policy? Some experts argue that the goals set for problem-oriented policing are too high. According to the experimenters, these

> mixed results . . . suggest that merely focusing police attention on chronic problems cannot guarantee their solution . . . the results of a test with objective target selection seem far more modest than results of quasi-experiments using subjective target selection. When the most troublesome addresses in a city are intentionally selected as targets, perhaps a more appropriate goal would be "managing" rather than "solving" problems.[82]

Do you agree? Defend your answer.

Participant observer Michael Buerger concluded that the experiment may be more useful than it might appear at first glance. He listed the following reasons:

1. Every new program is successful when measured in the short term. Then, due to declining officer and citizen satisfaction, displacement of problems, or return of problems to the "reclaimed" area, the success wears off. RECAP measured calls and results for a full year, longer than the few months or weeks of most "successful" programs.
2. As police departments "open up more of their prioritization to citizen input, they may well end up with problem addresses similar to those worked on by RECAP."
3. The rhetoric of problem solving frequently oversells the possibility of its success. "Possible outcomes are promoted as if they were automatic, painless, and inevitable, when in fact they are not."

4. Unrealistic rhetoric leads to unrealistic expectations. When these expectations are not fulfilled, they "can lead to burnout and bail-out of formerly committed officers whose enthusiasm is a critical element of the successes, small or otherwise."

5. "The prime benefit to others of the RECAP experience may well be to make the exercise of problem solving more real, and to more fully engage the participation of police officers who are grounded in what *is*, not what ought to be."[83]

Summary

The police adopt strategies in order to fulfill their missions of controlling crime, maintaining order, and performing other public services. Modern policing derives from three ancient practices: walling and wariness, both of which relied heavily on individuals, and watching, for which police departments eventually assumed responsibility. From the nineteenth century through the 1980s, preventive patrol and criminal investigation were the major police operations. Officers on foot or in vehicles cruised randomly through the streets in the belief that a powerful police presence would deter potential criminals and reassure law-abiding people. Preventive patrol rests on the assumptions that it permits police to respond more quickly to trouble, and that rapid response controls crime. Research has challenged these assumptions, causing police departments to reassess and redeploy resources from patrol to other police activities.

Citizen calls account for up to 90 percent of all police responses. Citizen calls mobilize the police response in several steps, all of which allow for broad discretion. Research demonstrating preventive patrol's shortcomings and increasing concern about crime have led to more aggressive police activities. Nearly half the departments in one survey said they had adopted proactive tactics, or police-initiated responses to crime. These crime-attack operations—"hot spots" patrol, aggressive field investigation, undercover police work, and police crackdowns—have both strong advocates and active critics. Supporters tout the need for strong strategies to deal with drugs, violence, and quality of life crimes. Critics warn that proactive police strategies threaten the values of a constitutional democracy, and they argue that they raise ethical questions.

Most police departments have separate investigative units, composed of detectives who conduct follow-up investigations to crimes for which patrol officers have filed incident reports. Follow-up investigations aim to identify and apprehend suspects, convict defendants, and satisfy victims. Traditionally, departments assumed that they could solve all the most serious cases, and that specially trained detectives could even solve most cases involving unknown criminals. Research in the past 20 years has demonstrated that many serious crimes go unsolved no matter how thoroughly detectives investigate them. Furthermore, most arrests depend on patrol officers, not detectives. However, detectives can contribute to cases that are not yet solved but which with some more effort can be solved. Detectives, moreover, play a major role in getting evidence that prosecutors can use to convict offenders once patrol officers have arrested them. These findings have led to case screening on the basis of solvability factors, to increased participation by patrol officers in investigations, and to concentrating detectives' efforts on the period following arrest.

The knowledge that private individuals play a crucial role in criminal law enforcement has led to major police efforts to educate the public about what they can do to aid in crime control. Education programs stress crime prevention and law enforcement. The police hope to educate the public enough to encourage an interest in police work, but not so much as to stimulate direct citizen action. Police departments have organized neighborhood watch programs, taught people how to secure their homes and protect themselves, and aided senior citizens in preventing street muggings.

Public dissatisfaction with the limits of traditional patrol and criminal investigation in controlling crime, and research that has demonstrated these limits, have led to the development of new strategies, including community-oriented policing and problem-oriented policing. These strategies shift the emphasis from responding to single incidents to drawing on public and private agencies and services, as well as on line officers' expertise, to solve the underlying problems that lead to specific crimes. Community-oriented policing allows people to establish priorities for police operations and focuses on community cooperation as an important goal. Problem-oriented policing involves scanning, analysis, response, and assessment to solve community problems. Evaluations of community-oriented and problem-oriented policing have shown mixed results.

Review Questions

1. Identify and describe the three major ancient operations from which most modern police strategies derive. Give some modern examples of these ancient operations.

2. Identify and describe the two strategies that have dominated policing since the 19th century.

3. Identify the reasons why police turned to more proactive strategies since the 1960s.

4. What strategy is called the "backbone" of U.S. policing? Why?

5. Identify the two major sources that stimulate the mobilization of patrol. Which source is responsible for most patrol mobilization?

6. Identify the stages in which patrol is mobilized and explain the role of discretion in both of these stages.

7. Define and list the advantages of preventive patrol.

8. Explain the positive and the negative effects of technology on police patrol.

9. List and describe the major deficiencies in patrol that researchers have uncovered since the 1960s.

10. Describe fully the Kansas City Preventive Patrol Experiment and accurately state the results and the implications of that experiment.

11. Identify the two major assumptions regarding patrol and response time. What has research demonstrated about the validity of these assumptions?

12. Define differential police response and explain the results of research regarding its effectiveness.

13. Why has foot patrol returned as a kind of patrol strategy? Fully describe the Newark Foot Patrol Experiment. State the results of the experiment on crime, fear of crime, and attitudes toward the police.

14. Why have departments shifted from two- to one-officer patrol? What are the effects of the shift?

15. Identify the two kinds of targets on which proactive policing focuses.

16. What has research demonstrated about the people and places responsible for crime?

17. Summarize the ideological conflict over proactive policing.

18. Define and describe the results of research regarding the effectiveness of "hot spots" patrol.

19. Define aggressive field investigation, and identify the circumstances that prompt it.

20. What are the major issues in undercover police work?

21. What is the theory underlying police crackdowns? What has research demonstrated about the effectiveness of crackdowns?

22. Why is the "Hawthorne principle" important regarding the assessment of crime-attack strategies?

23. What is preliminary criminal investigation, who conducts it, and what has research demonstrated about its importance and effectiveness?

24. What is follow-up investigation, who conducts it, and what has research demonstrated about its importance and effectiveness?

25. What are the major elements in community-oriented policing? How does community policing contrast with traditional police strategies? What has research demonstrated about the effectiveness of community-oriented policing?

26. What is problem-oriented policing, how does it relate to community-oriented policing, and what has research demonstrated about its effectiveness?

Notes

1. Sally Ann Stewart, "L.A. Residents Seek Security in Gates," *USA Today,* 23 December 1992.

2. Lawrence W. Sherman, "Patrol Strategies for the Police," in *Crime and Public Policy,* James Q. Wilson, ed. (New Brunswick, N.J.: Transaction Books, 1983). 163.

3. Lawrence W. Sherman, "Police in the Laboratory of Criminal Justice," in *Critical Issues in Policing,* Roger G. Dunham and Geoffrey P. Alpert, eds. (Prospect Heights, Ill.: Waveland Press, 1989), 48.

4. Lawrence W. Sherman, "Attacking Crime: Police and Crime Control," in *Modern Policing,* Michael Tonry and Norval Morris, eds. (Chicago: University of Chicago Press, 1992), 172.

5. Eric J. Scott, *Calls for Service: Citizen Demand and Initial Police Response* (Washington, D.C.: U.S. Department of Justice, 1980), 59-67.

6. Jerome H. Skolnick and James J. Fyfe, *Above the Law: Police and the Excessive Use of Force* (New York: The Free Press, 1993), 251-252.

7. Gary W. Cordner and Robert C. Trojanowicz, "Patrol," in *What Works in Policing?* Gary W. Cordner and Donna C. Hale, eds. (Cincinnati: Anderson Publishing Co., 1992), 5.

8. Ibid., 5-6.

9. Police Foundation, *Newark Foot Patrol Experiment,* 11; James Baldwin, *Nobody Knows My Name* (New York: Dell, 1962), 66-67, quoted in Skolnick and Fyfe, *Above the Law* (New York: Free Press, 1993), 240.

10. Albert J. Reiss, Jr., "Police Organization," in *Modern Policing,* 53.

11. *Newark Foot Patrol Experiment,* 11.

12. George L. Kelling et al., *The Kansas City Preventive Patrol Experiment: A Summary Report* (Washington, D.C.: The Police Foundation, 1974), 9-10; Herman Goldstein, *Policing a Free Society* (Cambridge, Mass.: Ballinger Publishing Company, 1977), 49-54.

13. Ibid.

14. Andrew Halper and Richard Ku, *An Exemplary Project: New York City Police Department Street Crimes Unit* (Washington, D.C.: U.S. Government Printing Office, 1975), 1-2.

15. Kelling, *Kansas City Preventive Patrol Experiment.*

16. James Q. Wilson, *Thinking About Crime,* rev. ed. (New York: Basic Books, 1983), 65-66; Flint study cited in Sherman, "Patrol Strategies for the Police," 153-54.

17. Goldstein, *Policing a Free Society,* 52; Joan Petersilia, "Influence of Research on Policing," in *Critical Issues in Policing,* 232.

18. The National Advisory Committee on Criminal Justice Standards and Goals, *Police* (Washington, D.C.: U.S. Government Printing Office, 1973), 193.

19. U.S. Department of Justice, *Response Time Analysis: Executive Summary* (Washington, D.C.: U.S. Government Printing Office, 1978); Brian Forst et al., *What Happens After Arrest* (Washington, D.C.: National Institute of Law Enforcement and Criminal Justice, 1977), chaps. 3, 5; George L. Kelling and David Fogel, "Police Patrol—Some Future Directions," in *The Future of Policing,* Alvin W. Cohn, ed. (Beverly Hills, Calif.: Sage, 1978), 166-67; Brian Forst et al., *Arrest Convictability as a Measure of Police Performance* (Washington, D.C.: National Institute of Justice, 1982); Sherman, "Patrol Strategies for the Police," 153; Petersilia, "Influence of Research on Policing," 233.

20. Petersilia, "Influence of Research on Policing," 234.

21. Michael F. Cahn and James Tien, *An Alternative Approach in Police Response: Wilmington Management of Demand Program* (Washington, D.C.: National Institute of Justice, 1981).

22. Ibid.

23. Reported in Petersilia, "Influence of Research on Policing," 235.

24. Stephen D. Mastrofski, "The Prospects for Change in Police Patrol: A Decade of Review," *The American Journal of Police* 9 (1990): 37.

25. Cordner and Trojanawicz, "Patrol," 10.

26. Mastrofski, "Prospects for Change in Police Patrol," 31.

27. Ibid.

28. Lee A. Daniels, "How Many Does It Take to Staff a Squad Car," *New York Times,* 6 December 1991; Walker, *Police in America,* 89.

29. Wilson, *Thinking About Crime,* 68-74; Susan E. Martin and Lawrence W. Sherman, "Selective Apprehension: A Police Strategy for Repeat Offenders," *Criminology* 24 (1986): 155-73.

30. Lawrence W. Sherman, Dennis Rogan, and Robert Velke, "The Menagerie of Crime: Targets for Police Crime Control Strategies," Unpublished manuscript (Washington, D.C.: Crime Control Institute, 1991); Sherman, "Attacking Crime: Police and Crime Control," *Modern Policing,* 178.

31. Richard Staufenberger, ed., *Progress in Policing* (Cambridge, Mass.: Ballinger Publishing Company, 1980), 69.

32. Dilip K. Das, *Policing in Six Countries Around the World* (Chicago: Office of International Criminal Justice, 1993), 157-59.

33. Lawrence W. Sherman, "The Police," in *Crime,* James Q. Wilson and Joan Petersilia, eds. (San Francisco: Institute for Contemporary Studies, 1995), 331.

34. Ibid., 333-334.

35. Goldstein, *Policing a Free Society,* 49-54.

36. Jonathan Rubenstein, *City Police* (New York: Farrar, Straus and Giroux, 1973), chap. 6.

37. Geoffrey R. Elton, *Tudor Policy and Police* (Cambridge, England: Cambridge University Press, 1973); Gary T. Marx, "Who Really Gets Stung? Some Issues Raised by the New Police Undercover Work," *Crime and Delinquency* (April 1982): 165; Gary T. Marx, *Undercover: Police Surveillance in America* (Berkeley: University of California Press, 1988); Gerald M. Caplan, ed., *ABSCAM Ethics: Moral Issues and Deception in Law Enforcement* (Washington, D.C.: The Police Foundation, 1983).

38. Halper and Ku, *An Exemplary Project,* 2.

39. Ibid.

40. Wilson, *Thinking About Crime,* 69-70; Goldstein, "Improving Policing," 237.

41. Gary T. Marx, "Recent Developments in Undercover Policing," in *Punishment and Social Control: Essays in Honor of Sheldon Messinger,* Thomas G. Blomberg and Stanley Cohen, eds.(New York: Aldine De Gruyer, 1995), 101-102.

42. Sherman, "The Police," in *Crime,* 332.

43. Ibid.

44. Lawrence W. Sherman, "Police Crackdowns," *NIJ Reports* (March/April 1990), 2-6.

45. Robert E. Worden, Timothy S. Bynum, and James Frank, "Police Crackdowns on Drug Abuse and Trafficking," in *Drugs and Crime,* Doris Layton MacKenzie and Craig D. Uchida, eds. (Thousand Oaks, Calif.: Sage Publications, 1994), 95-97.

46. Ibid., 101-103.

47. William Spelman and John E. Eck, *Problem-Oriented Policing* (Washington, D.C.: Bureau of Justice Statistics, January 1987); George L. Kelling and Mark H. Moore, *The Evolving Strategy of Policing* (Washington, D.C.: Bureau of Justice Statistics, November 1988); John J. Broderick, "Review Essay: Community Policing and Problem-Oriented Policing," *American Journal of Police* 10 (1991): 135.

48. Quoted in Staufenberger, *Progress in Policing,* 80.

49. Ibid.

50. John E. Eck, "Criminal Investigation," in *What Works in Policing?*, 19; Steven G. Brandl and James Frank, "The Relationship Between Evidence, Detective Effort, and the Disposition of Burglary and Robbery Investigations," *American Journal of Police* XIII (1994): 149-168.

51. Forst et al., *What Happens After Arrest*, 24-32; Forst et al., *Arrest Convictability*.

52. See Peter W. Greenwood and Joan Petersilia, *The Criminal Investigation Process*, Vols. I-III (Santa Monica, Calif.: The Rand Corporation, 1975); Peter Greenwood, Jan Chaiken, and Joan Petersilia, *The Criminal Investigation Process* (Lexington, Mass.: D.C. Heath, 1977); John E. Eck, *Solving Crimes: The Investigation of Burglary and Robbery* (Washington, D.C.: Police Executive Research Forum, 1983); and Brandl and Frank, "Relationship Between Evidence."

53. Greenwood, Chaiken, and Petersilia, *Criminal Investigation Process*.

54. John E. Eck, *Solving Crimes*, quoted in Brandl and Frank, "Relationship Between Evidence," 149.

55. Brandl and Frank, "Relationship Between Evidence," 163-164.

56. Petersilia, "Influence of Research on Policing," 240.

57. Jerome H. Skolnick and David H. Bayley, *The New Blue Line* (New York: Free Press, 1986), 5.

58. Richard A. Myren and Carol Henderson Garcia, *Investigation for Determination of Fact: A Primer on Proof* (Pacific Grove, Calif.: Brooks/Cole Publishing Co., 1989), 104-106.

59. Skolnick and Fyfe, *Above the Law*, 251.

60. Skolnick and Bayley, *New Blue Line*, 53-55.

61. Robert Yin et al., *Patrolling the Neighborhood Beat: Residents and Residential Security* (Santa Monica, Calif.: Rand Corporation, 1976); Sherman, "Patrol Strategies for the Police," 145.

62. Minneapolis Police Department, *Annual Report*, 1984.

63. This table is based on Craig D. Uchida and Brian Forst, "Controlling Street-Level Drug Trafficking: Professional and Community Policing Approaches," in *Drugs and Crime: Evaluating Public Policy Initiatives*, Doris Layton MacKenzie and Craig D. Uchida, eds. (Thousand Oaks, Calif.: Sage Publications, 1994), 78-81.

64. Dennis P. Rosenbaum and Arthur J. Lurigio, "An Inside Look at Community Policing: Definitions, Organizational Changes, and Evaluation Findings," *Crime and Delinquency* 40 (1994): 301.

65. Mark H. Moore, "Problem-Solving and Community Policing," in *Modern Policing*, 123.

66. "Community Policing in the 1990s," *National Institute of Justice Journal* (August 1992): 3-4.

67. Ibid.

68. Kelling and Moore, *Evolving Strategy of Policing*, 2.

69. Spelman and Eck, *Problem-Oriented Policing*, 2.

70. Ibid., 2.

71. Ibid.

72. Dennis P. Rosenbaum and Arthur J. Lurigio, "An Inside Look at Community Policing Reform: Definitions, Organizational Changes, and Evaluation Findings," *Crime and Delinquency* 40 (1994): 304.

73. Ibid.

74. Randolph M. Grinc, "Angels in Marble," 439.

75. Wesley G. Skogan, "The Impact of Community Policing on Neighborhood Residents: A Cross Site Analysis," in *The Challenge of Community Policing: Testing the Promises*, Dennis P. Rosenbaum, ed. (Thousand Oaks, Calif.: Sage Publications, 1994), 167-181; Rosenbaum and Lurigio, "An Inside Look," 310.

76. Ibid.

77. Ibid.

78. Michael E. Buerger, "The Problems of Problem-Solving: Resistance, Interdependencies, and Conflicting Interests," *American Journal of Police* XIII (1994): 2.

79. Ibid., 4.

80. Ibid., 3.

81. Ibid., 5-6.

82. Spelman and Eck, *Problem-Oriented Policing*.

83. Buerger, "Problems of Problem-Solving," 28-29.

6 Police and the Law

CHAPTER MAIN POINTS

1. *Police take a wide range of actions to carry out their mission to enforce the criminal law.*

2. *Most criminal law enforcement requires the gathering of information to back up the actions police take, and to support the proof required to prosecute and convict the guilty and to free the innocent.*

3. *The objective basis requirement limits, but does not eliminate, police discretionary judgments.*

4. *Many times police decide not to arrest suspects when they have the objective basis to do so.*

5. *The Constitution balances the needs of government in criminal law enforcement and the privacy and liberty rights of innocent, suspected, and guilty individuals.*

6. *Courts are mainly responsible for determining the meaning of the words in the Constitution, but police officers determine the day to day application of these provisions.*

7. *The duration, intensity, and location of contacts between police officers and individuals determine whether the contacts are arrests.*

8. *The reasonableness of an arrest depends on whether probable cause backs it up and whether the arrest was carried out in a reasonable manner.*

9. *Except in emergencies, police officers cannot enter homes without warrants in order to arrest people.*

10. *The use of deadly force is a Fourth Amendment seizure.*

11. *Far more frequent than deadly force, but less visible, is the use of less-than-deadly force in law enforcement.*

12. *Both the right against unreasonable searches and the exercise of the power to search have long histories.*

13. *The purpose of the Fourth Amendment "unreasonable searches" clause is to make sure that the government gathers the information it needs to control crime without conducting "unreasonable" searches.*

14. *The Supreme Court has expressed a definite preference for searches based on warrants; however, most searches are not based on warrants.*

15. *The reasonableness of searches with warrants depends on probable cause and particularity.*

16. *The reasonableness of searches without warrants depends on the government interest in law enforcement outweighing the privacy interests of individuals.*

17. *Until 1968, stops and frisks were left to the discretionary judgment of individual officers.*

18. *The Fifth Amendment prohibits compelled self-incrimination.*

19. *The Miranda warnings are required only prior to custodial interrogation.*

20. *Most suspects waive their right to remain silent in custodial interrogation.*

21. *The voluntariness of confessions depends on whether the totality of circumstances shows an absence of coercion.*

22. *It is easier to show that a crime was committed than to identify the perpetrator.*

23. *The Supreme Court has applied both the Sixth Amendment right to counsel clause and the due process clauses of the Fifth and Fourteenth amendments to insure the reliability of identification procedures.*

24. *The initial enthusiasm for DNA profiles as an identification procedure has dissipated in the face of evidence of misuse of the profiles.*

25. *The exclusionary rule prohibits the use of good proof because of bad methods.*

26. *Empirical research shows that the exclusionary rule affects only a small percent of cases and suggests that the rule deters police violations of the Constitution.*

To fulfill their missions of enforcing the criminal law, maintaining order, and providing other services, the police take a wide range of actions. These actions include everything from verbally giving directions to out-of-town visitors and warnings to people who are attending a loud party, to forcibly detaining and even shooting suspected felons. Most of these actions, particularly those associated with services not related to criminal law enforcement and many that involve order maintenance, involve minimal interference with individuals. As a result, these mainly discretionary judgments in the area of non-law enforcement services produce few complaints and, for the most part, no comment.

Police actions taken to enforce the criminal law, and sometimes those taken to maintain order, are quite a different matter. Scrutiny, complaints, and review of police decisions arise when the police deprive people of what they consider their freedom of movement; intrude upon what they believe is their "own business"; and use physical force to coerce them into doing what they do not want to do. These actions are reminders, not only to the people involved but also to the rest of us, that we have fallen short, sometimes far short, of our ideals of living peacefully and according to the law. Because we have fallen short, we need someone—namely, the police—to coerce us into peaceful, orderly, and lawful behavior. This coercion, when it takes the form of police surveillance; arrests, searches, and other seizures; police interrogation; police identification procedures, such as lineups; and police use of force, including deadly force, is the subject of this chapter.

Two contradictory myths have prevailed about the police and criminal law enforcement. According to one myth, the **ministerial myth,** the police act purely mechanically, that is, they make decisions strictly according to prescribed rules, without any room for discretionary judgment. The other myth maintains that the police act without restraint, according to their racist, sexist, class prejudices, and in their personal interest. In reality, just as in other instances when police exercise their ultimate power—the power to coerce—they are neither wholly free to enforce the criminal law as they please nor fully bound to enforce all the laws without discretion.[1]

Most criminal law enforcement requires the gathering of information to back up police actions and to support the proof required to prosecute and convict the guilty and to free the innocent. So if the aim of the police is to get cases into court, they must gather information that prosecutors and courts will accept. This information is called **admissible evidence.** It is admissible only if the police gathered it according to the requirements of the Constitution. According to police expert Carl B. Klockars,

> What the courts offer to police is the opportunity, if they wish to take advantage of it, to seek the state's capacity to punish. In effect, the courts say to the police that if they wish to make use of that capacity, they must demonstrate to the courts that they have followed certain procedures in order to do so. . . . Only on those occasions that the police wish to employ the state's capacity to punish do the two institutions [courts and police] have any relationship of any kind. Despite the enormous growth in police law in the past quarter century, the courts

have no more "control" over the police than local supermarkets have over the diets of those who shop there.[2]

In the day-to-day reality of police work, the police often do not take advantage of the opportunity to bring cases to prosecutors and courts. Critical to understanding the role of the law in police work is that the law plays a much less significant part than might appear from the attention it receives in courts, on television, and in the news. W. F. Walsh, for example, demonstrated that police officers arrest only a few people for felonies, even where felony offense rates are high. Forty percent of the officers assigned to a high-crime area in New York City did not make a single felony arrest in an entire year; 68 percent of the officers in the area made only three arrests in the same year. Furthermore, according to another empirical investigation by the sociologist Donald J. Black, frequently the police do not arrest even when they have a legal right to do so and plenty of information to back up the arrest. Black found that the police decided to arrest in only 27 percent of the cases of violent felonies where they had ample evidence to do so. These and other studies demonstrate that the police exercise wide discretionary judgment as to whether cases, even felonies, go to prosecutors and the courts. In other words, they do not always decide to take criminal cases to court.[3]

This surprising finding must be seen in context. A number of constraints operate to explain it. A fragmented criminal justice system, scarce resources, community norms, and other order maintenance and public service responsibilities all contribute to police decision making (see Chapter 4). In many instances, bringing cases into the criminal justice system is *not* the object of police actions, even in what might appear to be clear cases of criminal law violations. Whatever the reasons for not bringing cases into the criminal justice system, it is important to keep in mind that large amounts of police action are not a matter of law.

Practically speaking, the constitutional rights and other rules that are the subject of this chapter are only relevant if and when police officers and departments want criminal suspects charged with crimes. In these cases, the police face numerous formal limits. First are the general principles embodied in the rule of law, separation of powers, and federalism, discussed in Chapter 3. In addition, specific provisions in the U.S. Constitution, state constitutions,

Police officers exercise wide discretion in bringing cases into the criminal justice system, even when individuals provide them with plenty of information to make arrests.

federal and state statutes, court decisions, and administrative rules all prescribe guidelines for gathering evidence and dealing with suspects. However, even this seemingly formidable barricade of federalism, separation of powers, rights, and rules allows considerable room for informal police discretionary decision making.

According to the courts, the balance between public interest in criminal law enforcement and in individual privacy and liberty does not require—in fact, we cannot realistically expect—mechanical submission to rules. Individual police officers and their departments must have room to make discretionary judgments. However, just as private citizens must face punishment if convicted of crimes, sanctions follow from police violations of constitutional commands stemming from the abuse of their discretion. Courts might exclude evidence illegally obtained. Individuals can sue police officers, chiefs, departments, or other governmental agencies for the violation of constitutional rights. Police departments may discipline offending officers, even removing them from the force in serious cases.

Law Enforcement and the Constitution

To enforce the criminal law, the police need information, which they obtain by a variety of operations—surveillance, stop and frisk, arrest, searches, and identification procedures. All coercive government actions against the lives, property, liberty, and privacy of individuals require an **objective basis,** that is, facts to back them up. Hunch, whim, or mere suspicion will not do; only facts suffice. Coercive action covers a wide spectrum, ranging from brief stops on the street entailing slight loss of liberty to capital punishment, the ultimate deprivation of life itself. The requirement of facts differs only in degree. A few facts are enough to back up a street stop; capital punishment demands proof beyond a reasonable doubt (see Chapter 10).

The objective basis requirement controls police discretion in criminal law enforcement. Prosecutors rely mainly on the police to gather the facts necessary to prove guilt beyond a reasonable doubt. However, police cannot obtain the facts to prove guilt without first having enough facts to back up the searches, interrogations, identification procedures, and so on that they need to obtain that proof. Information, therefore, largely determines the formal criminal process. Naturally, the police would like the freedom to obtain and control this information. Suspects and defendants, of course, would like to keep this information from police. And innocent people, understandably, want the assurance that the police will not coercively interfere with their liberty, privacy, and property unless they have enough information to back up their actions.

The Constitution balances, in general terms, the interests of government in criminal law enforcement with the privacy and liberty rights of innocent, suspected, and guilty individuals; the Supreme Court arbitrates any conflict that arises over this general balance. Four provisions apply specifically to balancing police power and the rights of individuals—the Fourth, Fifth, Sixth, and Fourteenth Amendments to the U.S. Constitution:

> *Amendment IV*—The right of the people to be secure in their persons, houses, papers and effects, against unreasonable searches and seizures, shall not be violated, and no warrants shall issue, but upon probable cause, supported by oath or affirmation, and particularly describing the place to be searched, and the persons or things to be seized.
>
> *Amendment V*—No person shall be compelled in any criminal case to be a witness against himself, nor be deprived of life, liberty or property without due process of law.
>
> *Amendment VI*—In all criminal prosecutions, the accused shall enjoy the right . . . to be confronted with the witnesses against him . . . and to have the Assistance of Counsel for his defence.

Amendment XIV—No state shall make or enforce any law which shall abridge the privileges and immunities of citizens of the United States; nor shall any state deprive any person of life, liberty or property without the due process of law; nor deny to any person within its jurisdiction the equal protection of the laws.

Key words and phrases in these provisions require interpretation. We have discussed the meaning of the due process clause and the Supreme Court's interpretation of it in Chapter 3. The following examples illustrate terms in the Fourth, Fifth, and Sixth Amendments:

1. Police officers pat down the outer clothing of a citizen whom they think might have a weapon and drugs. Have the police searched the person? If so, was the search "unreasonable?"

2. Police approach a citizen on the street and ask, "What are you doing here?" Have they "seized" the citizen? If so, was the seizure "unreasonable"?

3. Police officers receive an anonymous tip that a black man wearing a red cap has just carried a concealed weapon into Jean's bar. Do the police need "probable cause" to search a man who fits the description? Do they have probable cause?

4. Police officers tell a suspect that if he does not confess to a murder, they will arrest his mother as an accomplice. The suspect confesses. Have the police "compelled" the suspect to be a witness against himself?

5. Is a traffic ticket a criminal "case" or criminal "prosecution"?

6. Is an arrest for rape a criminal case or "prosecution"?

7. Are lineups and show-ups "confrontations" between witnesses and the accused?

Who interprets these terms? Sometimes, legislatures enact laws to define them. More frequently, courts define their meaning. Most important, courts, especially the U.S. Supreme Court, decide whether to leave the interpretation to the discretionary judgment of individual police officers; whether the police must receive prior judicial approval for proposed actions; or whether police officers can take initial action subject to later review by the courts. Regardless of who interprets them, the Fourth and Fifth Amendments require balancing society's interests in criminal law enforcement against its interest in individual autonomy, liberty, and privacy. Furthermore, it is police officers who determine the application of provisions to day-to-day actions on the street and at the police station.

One way to view the history of criminal procedure as a whole is as the gradual **formalization** of—application of legal and administrative rules to—government actions. At first, formal rules controlled only the procedures during a criminal trial. Since the 1600s, developments have diminished discretion and have subjected proceedings both before and after a criminal trial to formal rules. We save discussion of the formalization of proceedings during and following trial for later. In examining the formalization of police procedures, we must distinguish between procedures that take place on the street before the police formally invoke the criminal process by arrest, and actions that take place in the police station following arrest.

During the 1960s, the Supreme Court, led by a former California prosecutor, Chief Justice Earl Warren, began to curtail police discretion in law enforcement. First, the Court restrained police actions in the station regarding suspects in custody. Then it applied the Fourth and Fifth Amendments to police–citizen encounters on the street and in other public places outside the police station. All these extensions of constitutional rights and their consequent restraints on police discretion generated heated controversy. Many police, lawyers, and members of the public believed that legal restraints on police discretionary decision making prevented effective crime control. At the same time, others hailed the restraints as a bulwark against police abuse and a step toward guaranteeing individual liberty and privacy in an increasingly authoritarian world.

During the 1970s under Chief Justice Warren Burger, and then during the 1980s under Chief Justice William Rehnquist, the Supreme Court returned some of the discretion lost to the police during the 1960s. However, the Supreme Court has remained committed to the principle of applying the Constitution to both police-citizen contacts outside, and police practices inside the police station. In the first half of the 1990s, the Supreme Court continued to balance the need for government power to enforce the criminal law against the societal interest in restraining the government from subjecting citizens to unwarranted intrusions and deprivations.[4] (See Chapter 3.)

Arrest

The Fourth Amendment requires the answer to three questions regarding arrest:

1. When is an official interference with a citizen's freedom of movement a "seizure" within the meaning of the Fourth Amendment? In other words, what is the constitutional definition of an arrest?

2. If the arrest is a seizure, when is an arrest an "unreasonable" seizure?

3. If the arrest is an unreasonable seizure, what are the remedies for violations of constitutional rights?

The Definition of Arrest

Police actions affecting the freedom of movement of individuals range from voluntary encounters to forced seizures. Police officers who approach people to ask them questions have not seized citizens. Police officers who stop people against their will and question them have seized, but have not necessarily arrested, them. Whether police officers **arrest** the people they have detained depends on three qualities of the detention:

1. The *intensity* of the detention (how much it invades liberty and privacy).

2. The *duration* of the detention (how long it lasts).

3. The *location* of the detention (was the individual involuntarily moved from the place of detention?).

Clearly, police officers have arrested people when they say, "You're under arrest," transport them to the police station, book them, and then detain them overnight. Most cases, however, do not satisfy the requirements of intensity, duration, and location so clearly. Applying the criteria becomes more difficult if, for example, officers do not take suspects to the police station, release them after 15 minutes, and spend that 15 minutes in friendly questioning. The opinions in *Florida v. Royer,* decided by the United States Supreme Court and excerpted in the *You Decide* that follows, introduce you to the difficulties that can arise in determining when a contact between police officers and individuals is a "seizure," and if it is, when the seizure is an arrest.

You Decide — "When Did the Police Arrest Royer?"

The following has been extracted from the decision handed down by the Supreme Court in *Florida v. Royer,* 460 U.S. 491 (1983).

Facts

Detectives Johnson and Magdalena, plainclothes narcotics detectives, observed Royer at Miami International Airport.

They believed that Royer's mannerisms, luggage, and actions fit the "drug courier profile." The detectives approached Royer on the concourse, identified themselves, and asked if Royer had a "moment" to talk to them; Royer answered, "Yes." On request, but without saying he consented, Royer produced his airline ticket and driver's license. When asked why his driver's license bore the name Royer and his ticket and luggage, Holt, Royer said a friend bought the ticket. The detectives then told Royer they were narcotics investigators and that they suspected him of transporting narcotics. The detectives did not return Royer's ticket and identification, but asked Royer to accompany them to a room, approximately 40 feet away. Royer said nothing but accompanied the officers to the room. Detective Johnson described the room as a "large storage closet," containing a desk and two chairs. Fifteen minutes later, after obtaining Royer's luggage, opening it with a key Royer supplied, and finding marijuana in it, the officers told Royer he was "under arrest."

Opinion

Law enforcement officers do not violate the Fourth Amendment by merely approaching an individual on the street or in another public place, by asking him if he is willing to answer some questions, by putting questions to him if the person is willing to listen.... Nor would the fact that the officer identifies himself as a police officer, without more, convert the encounter to a seizure.... Asking for and examining Royer's ticket and his driver's license were no doubt permissible in themselves, but when the officers identified themselves as narcotics agents, told Royer that he was suspected of transporting narcotics, and asked him to accompany them to the police room, while retaining his ticket and driver's license and without indicating in any way that he was free to depart, Royer was effectively seized for the purposes of the Fourth Amendment. These circumstances surely amount to a show of official authority such that a reasonable person would not have believed he was free to leave....

At the time Royer produced the key to his suitcase, the detention to which he was then subjected was a more serious intrusion on his personal liberty than is allowable on mere suspicion. By the time Royer was informed that the officers wished to examine his luggage, he had identified himself when approached by the officers and had attempted to explain the discrepancy between the name shown on his identification and the name under which he had purchased his ticket and identified his luggage. The officers were not satisfied, for they informed him they were narcotics agents and had reason to believe that he was carrying illegal drugs. They requested him to accompany them to a police room. Royer went with them. He found himself in a small room—a large closet—equipped with a desk and two chairs. He was alone with two police officers who again told him that they thought he was carrying narcotics. He also found that the officers, without his consent, had retrieved his checked luggage from the airlines. What had begun as a consensual inquiry in a public place had escalated into an investigatory procedure in a police interrogation room, where the police, unsatisfied with previous explanations, sought to confirm their

suspicions. The officers had Royer's ticket, they had his identification, and they had seized his luggage. Royer was never informed that he was free to board his plane if he so chose, and he reasonably believed that he was being detained. At least as of that moment, any consensual aspects of the encounter had evaporated.... As a practical matter Royer was under arrest.

Dissent

The public has a compelling interest in detecting those who would traffic in deadly drugs for personal profit.... In my view, the police conduct in this case was minimally intrusive. Given the strength of society's interest in overcoming the extraordinary obstacles to the detection of drug traffickers, such conduct should not be subjected to the requirement of probable cause.... The key principle in the Fourth Amendment is reasonableness—the balancing of competing interests.... On the one hand, any formal arrest, and any seizure having the essential attributes of a formal arrest, is unreasonable unless it is supported by probable cause.... In my view, it cannot fairly be said that, prior to the formal arrest, the functional equivalent of an arrest had taken place.... Royer was not taken from a private residence, where reasonable expectations of privacy perhaps are at their greatest. Instead, he was approached in a major international airport where, due in part to extensive antihijacking surveillance and equipment, reasonable privacy expectations are of significantly lesser magnitude.... Royer was not subjected to custodial interrogation.... Instead, the officers first sought Royer's consent to move the detention forty feet to the police room.... The question is whether the move was voluntary.... Royer consented voluntarily to this change of locale.... Certainly, the intrusion on Royer's privacy was not so extreme as to make the countervailing public interest in greater flexibility.... I do not understand why the [Court] fails to balance the character of the detention and the degree to which it intruded upon Royer's privacy against its justification as measured by ... the law enforcement interest.... The intrusion was short-lived and minimal. Only fifteen minutes transpired from the initial approach to the opening of the suitcases. The officers were polite, and sought and immediately obtained Royer's consent at each significant step of the process....

The [Court] concludes that somewhere between the beginning of the forty-foot journey and the resumption of the conversation in the room the investigation became so intrusive that Royer's consent evaporated, leaving him as a practical matter under arrest. But if Royer was legally approached in the first instance and consented to accompany the detectives to the room, it does not follow that his consent went up in smoke and he was arrested upon entering the room.... Other than the size of the room ... there is nothing ... which would indicate that Royer's resistance was overborne by anything about the room. Royer, who was in his fourth year of study at Ithaca College ... simply continued to cooperate with the detectives as he had from the beginning of the encounter. Absent any evidence of ... coercion ... the size of the room does not transform a voluntary consent into a coerced consent.

Consider the duration, intensity, and location of the police contact with Royer. At what point, if at all, did the police arrest Royer? What specific facts support your conclusion? If you had this encounter, at what point would you "not feel free to leave?" Do you think the answer to these questions depends on your perspective? For example, would police officers and defense attorneys answer these questions differently? Should the answers to these constitutional questions depend on the biases created by these "perspectives"? Explain your answer.

probable cause to arrest *amount of facts required to lead an officer to believe that a crime was committed, is being committed, or is about to be committed, and that the person arrested is responsible.* **articulable facts and circumstances** *precise and specific basis for government action sufficient for a judge to weigh their contents and make an independent judgment.*

The "Reasonableness" Requirement

The reasonableness of an arrest depends on two factors:

1. The *objective basis* for it (that is, the number of facts and circumstances that back it up).
2. The *manner of execution* (that is, how the officer made the arrest).

Objective Basis—The Requirement of Probable Cause According to the Fourth Amendment, probable cause is the objective basis required to back up an arrest. **Probable cause to arrest** requires that the police base arrests on facts and circumstances that would lead a reasonable officer to believe the person arrested has committed, is committing, or is about to commit a crime. These facts or circumstances must be **articulable facts and circumstances,** that is, they must be precise and specific enough for a judge to weigh their contents and make an independent judgment as to whether they add up to probable cause. Probable cause denotes quantity. It stands somewhere between zero facts and all the facts. More technically, probable cause stands between a hunch, whim, or mere suspicion that someone has committed a crime, and absolute proof that a person has committed a crime. According to the prestigious American Law Institute's *Model Code of Pre-*

Rarely do the police come upon such clear direct evidence of criminal activity as the illegal purchase of this gun.

Arraignment Procedure, drawn up by lawyers, police administrators, judges, scholars, and other criminal justice experts:

> In determining . . . [probable cause] to justify an arrest . . . a law enforcement officer may take into account all information that a prudent officer would judge relevant to the likelihood that a crime has been committed and that a person to be arrested has committed it, including information derived from any expert knowledge which the officer in fact possesses and information received from an informant whom it is reasonable under the circumstances to credit, whether or not at the time of making the arrest the officer knows the informant's identity.[5]

Direct information, hearsay, or a combination of both can satisfy the probable cause requirement. **Direct information** consists of first-hand information, that is, facts and circumstances personally known to the officers. It is information that officers see, hear, touch, or even smell themselves. For example, an officer who sees a suspect pace up and down and peer in a window has direct information. **Hearsay** is second-hand information. That is, it is facts or circumstances that officers learn from someone else. The "someone else" is ordinarily a victim, witness, other police officer, or an informant. For example, a witness who calls a police officer and says, "I saw a man walking up and down peering in a jewelry store window" provides the officer with hearsay information.

Although probable cause requires more than mere suspicion or hunches, it does not mean legal guilt (proof beyond a reasonable doubt is discussed in Chapter 10), or even that suspects are more guilty than not. The police might have probable cause to arrest, but not proof beyond a reasonable doubt to convict. They can still arrest, and probably should. Arrest, in the legal sense, allows the police to detain suspects or "freeze" a situation long enough for prosecutors to decide whether they have enough evidence to charge suspects. Juries, or in some cases judges, decide if the government has proof of guilt beyond a reasonable doubt. This distinction between probable cause and proof beyond a reasonable doubt, not "technicalities" or judges "soft on crime," explains—at least, in the formal legal sense—why nearly half the arrests police officers make do not result in convictions.[6]

Reasonableness also includes the manner of arrest, that is, the way police officers execute the arrest. The Fourth Amendment refers to warrants, which require the approval of a magistrate. Ideally, police officers should obtain warrants *before* they make arrests. Practically, however, virtually all arrests are made without warrants, and police do not violate the reasonableness requirement by doing so. In most instances, officers do not have probable cause to arrest until immediately prior to the arrest. The Supreme Court has held that reasonableness does not require officers to delay an arrest in such cases simply because the police do not have a warrant. If police officers enter homes to make arrests, then the Supreme Court has ruled that the Fourth Amendment requires them to obtain a warrant unless they are acting in an emergency, such as when they are in "hot pursuit" of a fleeing suspect.[7]

You Decide   "Did the Officers Have Probable Cause to Arrest?"

In *People v. Washington,* the defendant, Michael Washington, appealed the judgment entered in the Superior Court of the City and County of San Francisco revoking his probation and sentencing him to three years in prison. The revocation of probation and the sentence were based on the finding that Washington possessed cocaine. On appeal, Washington argued that the cocaine used against him at the probation revocation hearing was the product of an illegal arrest because the officers did not have probable cause to arrest him. The following is taken from the court's opinion:

> Officers Lewis and Griffin were in the vicinity of 1232 Buchanan Street. They observed defendant along with four other individuals in a courtyard area between 1133 Laguna and 1232 Buchanan. Defendant and the others were observed talking in a "huddle" formation with "a lot of hand movement" inside the huddle, but the officers could not see what was in the hands of any member of the group. The officers then walked toward the group, at which point everyone looked in the officers['] direction, whispered, and quickly dispersed. When defendant saw the officers, he immediately turned around and started walking at a fast pace through the lobby of 1232 Buchanan. The officers followed him for a quarter of a block when Officer Griffin called out to defendant. Defendant replied, "Who me?" Officer Griffin answered, "Yes," and defendant immediately ran away. The officers gave chase. Two minutes later, while still chasing defendant, Officer Lewis saw defendant discard a plastic bag containing five white bundles. Officer Lewis scooped up the bag as he continued to give chase. Shortly thereafter, the officers apprehended defendant.

> During the probation revocation hearing, Officer Lewis testified that during the four years he had been a patrolman he had made at least 100 arrests concerning cocaine in the area frequented by defendant that night. On cross-examination, Officer Lewis answered in the affirmative when asked if most of the black men he saw in the area usually had something to hide if they ran from police. The officer stated that prior to the chase he saw no contraband, nor was anything about the group's dispersal significant. Nor did the officer explain why they singled out defendant to follow. The trial court denied defendant's motion to suppress and revoked the defendant's probation.

Did officers Lewis and Griffin have probable cause to arrest Washington? The court held that they did not:

> Prior to defendant's abandonment of the cocaine, the police lacked the "articulable suspicion that a person has committed or is about to commit a crime." The officers spotted the group of men in an open courtyard at 6:15 P.M.; the men made no attempt to conceal themselves and did not exhibit any furtive behavior. The hand gestures were, on the police officer's own testimony, inconclusive and unrevealing. Furthermore, the time at which the detention occurred is not the "late or unusual hour . . . from which any inference of criminality may be drawn." The fact that defendant was seen in what was a high crime area also does not elevate the facts into a reasonable suspicion of criminality. Courts have been "reluctant to conclude that a location's crime rate transforms otherwise innocent-appearing circumstances into circumstances justifying the seizure of an individual."

> Once the officers made their approach visible, they gave no justification for their decision to follow defendant apart from the others in the group. Neither officer knew defendant or knew of defendant's past criminal record, nor did Officer Lewis testify that defendant appeared to be a principal or a leader in the group. Further, the defendant had the right to walk away from the officers. He had no legal duty to submit to the attention of the officers; he had the freedom to "go on his way," free of stopping even momentarily for the officers. By walking at a brisk rate away from the officers, defendant could have been exercising his right to avoid the officers or avoid any other person, or could have simply walked rapidly through sheer nervousness at the sight of a police officer.

> We see no change in the analysis when defendant decided to run from the officers. Flight alone does not trigger an investigative detention; rather, it must be combined with other objective factors that give use to an articulable suspicion of criminal activity. No such factors existed, nor does Officer Lewis's assertion that the "black men [they] see in the project usually have something to hide when they run" justify a detention. "[M]ere subjective speculation as to the [person's] purported motives . . . carries no weight." Thus, prior to defendant's abandonment of the contraband, the circumstances of defendant's actions were not reasonably consistent with criminal activity. . . .

> . . . [T]he officers conceded they had no objective factors upon which to base any suspicions that the group was involved in illegal activity, and the officers offered no explanation why they singled out defendant to follow. Indeed, the only justification for engaging in pursuit was that defendant was a black male, and that it was the officer's subjective belief that black men run from police when they have something to hide. Thus, a single factor—the defendant's race—triggered the detention.[8]

Questions

What were the facts on which Officers Lewis and Griffin based their arrest? Assume you are the prosecutor in the case. How would you try to convince the judge that the arrest was legal? Now assume you are the defense counsel. How would you argue that the arrest was illegal? Now you are the judge. How would you decide the case? Write an opinion explaining your decision.

The Manner of Arrest—Entering Homes and Using Force The reasonableness of an arrest depends upon not only its objective basis, probable cause, but also on the manner in which the police execute the arrest. The reasonableness of the manner of arrest arises primarily in two situations:

1. When the police enter private homes in order to make arrests.
2. When the police use force to make arrests.

The law is clear about entering homes to make arrests: except in emergencies, such as where police officers are in "hot pursuit" of a fleeing suspect, the Fourth Amendment requires officers to get a warrant before they enter private homes to arrest suspects. Furthermore, officers must announce their presence before they enter, and they must give those inside at least a brief time to get to the door. They need not wait for long, however, because the suspect may flee out the back door, or may destroy evidence or

It is not an "unreasonable seizure" to handcuff an arrested suspect, if handcuffing will prevent escape and protect officers.

fleeing felon doctrine *common law doctrine that law enforcement officers could, if necessary, use deadly force to apprehend any fleeing felony suspect.*

contraband before the police enter. So police officers have not unreasonably seized a suspect if they obtain a warrant, knock on the door saying, "Open up, police," wait for a brief period, and when no one answers or opens the door, knock down the door, enter, and arrest the suspect named in the warrant.

The use of force to make arrests, and in fact the use of force by police officers in general, is an uncertain, controversial, and difficult subject. We leave the problem of police use of force generally to Chapter 7. Here, we discuss only the relationship between the Fourth Amendment "unreasonable seizure" clause and the police use of deadly force. That is, when is the use of deadly force a seizure, and, if it is, when is it an unreasonable seizure? If it is an unreasonable seizure, what are the remedies for it? The Supreme Court has interpreted the Fourth Amendment to require that police officers can use only reasonable force before, during, and after arrests. Historically, the **fleeing felon doctrine** governed the use of force. Under that doctrine, law enforcement officers could, if necessary, use deadly force to apprehend any fleeing felony suspect. The fleeing felon doctrine made sense in medieval England where there were few felonies, all of them capital; guns were rare; and lack of technology made it difficult to apprehend criminals. In the centuries that followed, a long list of noncapital, nonviolent felonies was enacted, applying the doctrine to many more crimes. Also, police forces armed with guns were created, making the chance of killing fleeing suspects more likely. Finally, advances in communications technology increased the tools police could use to apprehend escaped felony suspects. Despite these fundamental changes, most American states retained the fleeing felon doctrine until the 1960s.

The civil rights movement, the corresponding heightened concern for the rights of criminal defendants, and the loss of life during the urban riots of the 1960s coalesced to cause a reevaluation of the fleeing felon doctrine. Changes in the doctrine occurred formally by means of statutes, administrative rules, and court decisions. Most statutes limited the doctrine to "forcible felonies." By 1985, about half the states had adopted statutes limiting the use of deadly force.

In 1985 the Supreme Court, in the landmark case of *Tennessee v. Garner*, ruled that the fleeing felon doctrine is unconstitutional. Because half the states had already outlawed its use and most urban departments had already restricted the doctrine, the decision affected primarily medium-sized and small towns and rural areas. The following *You Decide*, "Can the Police Shoot to Kill a Fleeing Burglar?" examines the Supreme Court's reasons for striking down the fleeing felon doctrine.

You Decide — "Can the Police Shoot to Kill a Fleeing Burglar?"

The following is an edited version of the Supreme Court opinion in *Tennessee v. Garner*, 471 U.S. 1 (1985), that ruled Tennessee's fleeing felon statute violated the Fourth Amendment to the U.S. Constitution. This was a case in which a police officer shot and killed 15-year-old Edward Garner. Garner's father sued the police department for the wrongful death of his son. The police department argued that the officer was only following the state of Tennessee's fleeing felon statute. Garner's lawyers argued that the statute violated the Fourth Amendment because shooting fleeing felons under all circumstances is an "unreasonable seizure."

Facts

At about 10:45 p.m. on October 3, 1974, Memphis police officers Elton Hymon and Leslie Wright were dispatched to answer a "prowler inside call." On arriving at the scene they saw a woman standing on her porch and gesturing toward the adjacent house. She told them she had heard glass breaking and that "they" or "someone" was breaking in next door. While Wright radioed the dispatcher to say that they were on the scene, Hymon went behind the house. He heard a door slam and saw someone run across the back yard. The fleeing suspect, Edward Garner, stopped at a six-foot-high chain link fence at the edge of the yard. With the aid of a flashlight, Hymon was able to see Garner's face and hands. He saw no sign of a weapon and, though not certain, was "reasonably sure" and "figured" that Garner was unarmed. He thought Garner was 17 or 18 years old and about 5'5" or 5'7" tall. [In fact, Garner was a fifteen-year-old eighth grader, 5'4" tall, weighing somewhere around 100 or 110 pounds.] While Garner was crouched at the base of the fence, Hymon called out "Police! Halt!" and took a few steps toward him. Garner then began to climb over the fence. Convinced that if Garner made it over the fence he would elude capture, Hymon shot him. When asked at trial why he fired, Hymon stated:

> Well, first of all it was apparent to me from the little bit that I knew about the area at the time that he was going to get away because, number 1, I couldn't get to him. My partner then couldn't find where he was because, you know, he was late

coming around. He didn't know where I was talking about. I couldn't get to him because of the fence here, I couldn't have jumped this fence and come up, consequently jumped this fence and caught him before he got away because he was already up on the fence, just one leap and he was already over the fence, and so there is no way I could have caught him.

Hymon also stated that the area beyond the fence was dark, that he could not have gotten over the fence easily because he was carrying a lot of equipment and wearing heavy boots, and that Garner, being younger and more energetic, could have outrun him. The bullet hit Garner in the back of the head. Garner was taken by ambulance to a hospital, where he died on the operating table. Ten dollars and a purse taken from the house were found on his body.

In using deadly force to prevent the escape, Hymon was acting under the authority of a Tennessee statute and pursuant to police department policy. The statute provides that "[i]f, after notice of the intention to arrest the defendant, he either flees or forcibly resists, the officer may use all the necessary means to effect the arrest." The department policy was slightly more restrictive than the statute, but still allowed the use of deadly force in cases of burglary. The incident was reviewed by the Memphis Police Firearm's Review Board and presented to a grand jury. Neither took any action.

Opinion

The use of deadly force to prevent the escape of all felony suspects, whatever the circumstances, is constitutionally unreasonable. It is not better that all felony suspects die than that they escape. Where the suspect poses no immediate threat to the officer and no threat to others, the harm resulting from failing to apprehend him does not justify the use of deadly force to do so. It is no doubt unfortunate when a suspect who is in sight escapes, but the fact that the police arrive a little late or are a little slower afoot does not always justify killing the suspect. A police officer may not seize an unarmed, nondangerous suspect by shooting him dead. The Tennessee statute is unconstitutional insofar as it authorizes the use of deadly force against such fleeing suspects.

Although the circumstances of this case are unquestionably tragic and unfortunate, our constitutional holdings must be sensitive both to the history of the Fourth Amendment and to the general implications of the Court's reasoning. By disregarding the serious and dangerous nature of residential burglaries and the longstanding practice of many states, the Court effectively creates a Fourth Amendment right allowing a burglary suspect to flee unimpeded from a police officer who has probable cause to arrest, who has ordered the suspect to halt, and who has no means short of firing his weapon to prevent escape. I do not believe that the Fourth Amendment supports such a right, and I accordingly dissent.

Questions

Do you agree with the majority or the dissent in the case? What arguments persuaded you? In an investigation of the impact of the decision, Abraham N. Tennenbaum found

> a significant reduction (approximately sixteen percent) between the number of homicides committed before and after the decision. This reduction was more significant in states which declared their laws regarding police use of deadly force to be unconstitutional after the *Garner* decision. Evidence suggests that the reduction is due not only to a general reduction in shooting fleeing felons, but also to a general reduction in police shooting.[9]

What impact, if any, do the findings of Tennenbaum have on your position? Explain.

> **searches** *power of the government to examine the homes, property, papers, effects, and person of individuals for evidence of crime, weapons, and contraband.*

Shooting draws the most public attention, but other means to arrest occur more frequently. Some of these have caused considerable debate. The Supreme Court has not decided whether the use of choke holds, Mace, and other mechanisms to subdue suspects during and following arrest constitutes Fourth Amendment "seizures." Some lower courts have held that they do not constitute seizures. In determining their reasonableness, the courts examine whether the police have applied excessive force, in which case such methods do constitute unreasonable seizures. Using this test, a federal appeals court found the use of Mace reasonable to subdue an intoxicated suspect who refused to remain in a small room near the booking area in a police station.[10]

Searches

The right against unreasonable **searches** is ancient. The Babylonian Talmud of the Jews recognized the need to be left alone by prohibiting putting up buildings where they could allow looking into dwellings. Cicero in 57 B.C. spoke of citizens' homes as "sacred . . . hedged about by every kind of sanctity." Under the Code of the Byzantine Emperor Justinian in 533 A.D., a "freeman could not be summoned from his house" because it is "everyone's safest place, his refuge and his shelter." The roots of the right against government searches run deep in British history and in the history of the United States. In 1505, John Fineux, Chief Justice of the Court of King's Bench in England, held that "the house of a man is for him his castle and his defence."[11]

Despite the long tradition lauding the *right* to be free from unreasonable searches, the exercise of the *power* to search has also had a long history. In England, searches were used extensively. One major area of controversy began with the invention of the printing press. The fear of the vicious verbal attacks in the form of seditious libels against English monarchs led to the use of the power to search in order to stamp out this type of objectionable speech. By the 1700s, seditious libels increased with the low respect the English had for their imported German kings, the four Georges of the House of Hanover. General warrants, or writs of assistance, gave a range of officials blanket authority to break into shops and homes to look for seditious libels. These warrants were valid for the life of the monarch, so a person holding one could enter any house at any time for years on end. The practice was to issue the writs at the beginning of a new monarch's reign; they were valid until the reigning monarch died.

General warrants were also used in combating smuggling to evade customs duties on a growing list of goods imported into England from its rapidly expanding empire. Writs of assistance to search houses and shops for smuggled goods were common in the American colonies, but they generated considerable controversy both here and in Britain. In England, William Pitt, the Earl of Chatham, spoke the most famous words ever uttered against the power of government to search in a speech to the House of Commons (see Historical Note in margin).

In America, the young lawyer and future president John Adams watched the great colonial trial lawyer James Otis argue a widely publicized writs of assistance case in Boston. Otis argued that writs of assistance were illegal, maintaining that only searches with specific dates, naming the places or persons to be searched and seized, and based on probable cause were lawful where free people lived. The arguments of Otis moved Adams to write years later: "There was the Child Independence born." Despite the great oratory hurled against writs of assistance, however, both the Crown in the mother country and the colonial governors continued to use them widely. But the writers of the Bill of Rights did not forget the hostility to general warrants, and they wrote their opposition to them into the prohibition against "unreasonable searches."

The purpose of the Fourth Amendment "unreasonable searches" clause is to make sure the government gathers the information it needs to control crime without conducting "unreasonable searches." But it leaves the government with considerable power to conduct searches.

According to former prosecutor John Wesley Hall, Jr.:

The raw power held by a police officer conducting a search is enormous. An officer wielding a search warrant has the authority of the law to forcibly enter one's home and search for evidence. The officer can enter at night and wake you from your sleep, roust you from bed, rummage in your drawers and papers and upend your entire home. Even though the particularity clause of the warrant defines the scope of the search, the search, as a practical matter, will be as intense as the officer conducting a stop or warrantless search chooses to make it. The power of an officer conducting a stop or warrantless search is also quite intense. Nothing can be more intimidating or frightening to a citizen than being stopped by the police and being asked or told to submit to a search.[12]

You Decide   "Was the Search 'Reasonable?'"

Drug officers got a tip from an informant that retirees Marian and William Hauselmann were operating a methamphetamine lab. A SWAT team in ski masks went to the Hauselmanns' home, kicked in the door, and held the Hauselmanns at gunpoint for 45 minutes while they searched for evidence. "They put a pillowcase on my head and handcuffed me and forced me to stay on the floor," said Mrs. Hauselmann. "My husband and I tried to speak and they screamed to shut up. It was the worst thing that ever happened to us." William Hauselmann, 64, who suffers from a heart condition, said the officers stepped on his back and cut his face while wrestling him to the floor.

The officers found nothing. The Hauselmanns say the worst vice they have is eating too much bratwurst. They live on 20 acres for their cows and enjoy their eight grandchildren. Mrs. Hauselmann complains of sore wrists from the heavy plastic handcuffs. "Funny thing is, after

they realized their mistake, they had to ask us for something to cut them off with," she said. The Hauselmanns say they can't sleep and are tense. "But we're not going to a shrink. I think we'll be O.K. It's those police who need psychiatrists." The officers apologized to the Hauselmanns and offered to pay for the doors they kicked in. "We all feel very badly," said Sheriff's Lieutenant Richard McFarren.[13]

Questions

Was the search reasonable? That is, was the informant's tip probable cause? Was kicking in the door reasonable? Was the action once inside reasonable? How do you decide what is reasonable? Should the officers have gotten a warrant? Does knowing that the police made a mistake affect your answer? Legally, only what officers know *before* they search can be taken into account in determining probable cause. Defend your answer.

Searches with Warrants

According to the Supreme Court, the Fourth Amendment includes two types of searches: searches with warrants and searches without warrants. The Court has ruled that the Fourth Amendment states a clear preference for searches based on warrants. Only searches that fall within a list of well-defined exceptions are reasonable without warrants, according to the Court.

The reasonableness of a search based on a warrant depends on:

1. The **particularity of the warrant**, that is, on how adequately the warrant describes the places and persons to be searched, and things or persons to be seized.

2. **Probable cause to search** that backs up the warrant, that is, an accompanying **affidavit** (sworn statement) must state facts and circumstances that would lead a reasonable officer to believe that the places or persons searched will yield the items or persons named in the search warrant.

The attitudes of police officers toward the warrant requirement varies. L. Paul Sutton found that:

> a few [officers] acknowledged that the warrant requirement is appropriate for everyone's protection. Many seem to accept the requirement as a necessary part of law enforcement. Some are begrudgingly resigned to it as a reality that has to be dealt with. Others appear to regard the requirement as one of a long series of unnecessary intrusions of the court into what they consider to be the exclusive province of law enforcement; to these officers, the requirement is largely something to be gotten around.[14]

These attitudes, Sutton found, stem from a variety of origins. According to a veteran officer, the search warrant is another "game" the courts have created. He assured researchers that the game was easy for the officers to win. "One way or another . . . cops would get what they wanted." Others complain about the frustration and delay in getting warrants. It takes several hours between the time officers decide they need a warrant and when they actually have one in hand. According to one deputy sheriff narcotics detective:

> We will go out to a yard and see marijuana plants growing in the back of the yard. Then what we have to do is go get a judge to sign a warrant stating that you have seen the marijuana plants there, which all seems a waste of time since they always sign the warrant if we have seen the marijuana plant, and since we know that they are going to sign the warrant. We still have to go through the rigmarole.[15]

Officers also complain about the inconsistencies of the judges who issue the warrants. One detective said:

> You get a lot of different rulings from different judges; judges don't all see the law exactly the same. . . . One judge might make a ruling . . . and one judge might throw it out.

Another expressed exasperation this way:

> We went through everything—search warrants, etc.—all the way down the line. We got to the [misdemeanor] court, and [his/her] royal highness thought [he/she] knew more than the U.S. Supreme Court who ruled on a case identical to [ours] and [the misdemeanor court judge] said [what we had done] wasn't good enough.[16]

Underlying the officers' frustration over delay and inconsistency is a conflict between the values of due process and law enforcement. Police officers see their job as enforcing the criminal law and controlling crime; they want to do so with the least amount of hassle and the greatest degree of efficiency. Judges stress the need for due process, the legal procedures whereby officers collect the evidence for criminal prosecutions.

Searches Without Warrants

Searches based on proper warrants are reasonable. But most searches, like most arrests, are made without warrants. The Supreme Court has created a number of exceptions to the warrant requirement. The major exceptions include

- Searches accompanying arrests
- Searches of vehicles
- Plain-view searches
- Consent searches
- Stops and frisks

The vast majority of searches in day-to-day law enforcement fall within one of these exceptions. Such searches are reasonable if the facts of each case pass the **balancing test of reasonableness** established by the Court. According to this test, courts look at the facts of each case in order to balance the following interests:

1. The interests of the government in enforcing the criminal law; and
2. The right of individuals to be left alone by the government. This is often called a form of the right to privacy.

In balancing the needs of government to enforce the criminal law and the right of individuals to their privacy, courts evaluate the facts of each case to determine whether the government need to invade the privacy of individuals and their homes outweighs the degree of invasion of privacy against individuals.

Searches Accompanying Arrest In day-to-day criminal law enforcement, the most common searches are those that accompany arrest. Searches accompanying arrests, known as **searches incident to arrests,** are made without warrants at the time of lawful arrests. Such searches are reasonable if they meet three requirements:

1. Officers had probable cause to arrest the suspect.
2. The purpose of the search was either to search for weapons to protect officers from armed suspects or to preserve evidence from destruction.
3. The invasion of the person of the arrested suspect was no greater than was necessary to discover and seize either weapons or evidence.

The Supreme Court applied the balancing test of reasonableness to warrantless searches incident to arrests in the landmark case *Chimel v. California.* The police arrived at Chimel's house with an arrest warrant, but not a search warrant. They asked permission to "look around," which Chimel denied them. The police searched the house anyway. In a bedroom dresser drawer, they found coins Chimel stole during a burglary of a coin shop. Chimel challenged the search's reasonableness, but the trial court and two California appeals courts upheld his conviction. When Chimel appealed to the Supreme Court, the Court balanced the invasion of Chimel's home against the government interest in catching a burglar. To do this, the Court had to decide how extensively the police could reasonably search accompanying (or "incident to") Chimel's lawful arrest. The Supreme Court decided that the search was "unreasonable." The Court wrote:

> When an arrest is made, it is reasonable for the arresting officer to search the person arrested in order to remove any weapons that the latter might seek to use in order to resist arrest or effect his escape.

These photos demonstrate clearly the difference between a search (going over the man on the left) and a seizure (taking the knife on the right).

consent search search made without either warrants or probable cause that is agreed to by the person being searched.

Otherwise, the officer's safety might well be endangered, and the arrest itself frustrated. In addition, it is entirely reasonable for the arresting officer to search for and seize any evidence on the arrestee's person in order to prevent its concealment or destruction. And the area into which an arrestee might reach in order to grab a weapon or evidentiary items must, of course, be governed by a like rule. A gun on a table or in a drawer in front of one who is arrested can be as dangerous to the arresting officer as one concealed in the clothing of the person arrested. There is ample justification, therefore, for a search of the arrestee's person and the area "within his immediate control"— construing that phrase to mean the area from within which he might gain possession of a weapon or destructible evidence. . . .

The search here went far beyond the petitioner's person and the area from within which he might have obtained either a weapon or something that could have been used as evidence against him. . . . The scope of the search was, therefore, "unreasonable" under the Fourth and Fourteenth amendments, and the petitioner's conviction cannot stand.[17]

Consent Searches The second most common kind of search without warrant is the **consent search,** that is, one in which individuals agree to allow the police to conduct searches of their persons, homes, and personal effects. People can give up their right against unreasonable searches and seizures. If they do, the searches and seizures are reasonable without either warrants or probable cause. But the consent must be *voluntary*. In *Schneckcloth v. Bustamonte,* the leading Supreme Court case on consent searches, police officers asked the driver of a car if it was "okay to look in the trunk of the car." The driver replied, "Sure, go ahead." According to the Supreme Court, the police legally seized stolen checks they found in the trunk because the driver voluntarily consented to the search.[18]

Critics maintain that most people believe they are obliged to comply with the requests of police officers. In other words, ordinary people treat the requests of police officers as implied commands. Therefore, consent to police requests is not truly voluntary. To meet this objection, some say the Fourth Amendment requires that before officers can search without warrants or probable cause, they must not only obtain voluntary consent but also a specific waiver of the right against unreasonable searches, similar to the situation involving confessions. (See the following section on interrogation.) According to this position, police officers have to advise people that they do not have to consent to the request to search. If people do consent, the officers can seize any incriminating evidence they find and use it against the person consenting or others.

Arrest in Japan

The Japanese Code of Criminal Procedure authorizes the police to make emergency arrests. The police can make an emergency arrest without a warrant if the officer reasonably believes a suspect has committed a crime punishable by at least three years imprisonment, when there is an urgent need to arrest and there is no time to apply for a warrant. The police have to apply for a warrant immediately after the arrest, and if the judge refuses, the police must release the suspect immediately. In practice, most Japanese courts grant the police at least two or three hours to get judicial approval for an emergency arrest. Setsuo Miyazawa, a Japanese sociologist, reports the following emergency arrest from his observations of Japanese police.

At the Kikusui police box, at 11:15 P.M. on February 23, the squad leader brings in the suspect driver of a truck overloaded with steel bars. The squad leader is tense, his face flushed. The man has not been arrested yet; questions at this stage are merely to identify him, and he needs not be told of his right to remain silent.

Squad leader: Where do you live, mister? Where's your house?

Man: Toyohira town.

Squad leader: Your birth date? Speak up. You know what I am saying. Where did you have your job, mister? A construction company, I guess.

The squad leader decides to make an emergency arrest on the basis of the vehicle. His desire to uncover the existence of prior offenses is clear:

Squad leader: How many previous offenses? Ah, theft, is it? I'll arrest you. Put out your hand.

At 11:23 P.M., after putting handcuffs on the suspect, the leader conducted a body frisk.

Squad leader: How did you open up the car?

Man: Pliers.

Squad leader: Where did you get them?

Man: They were right there.

The leader immediately called the Eastern Police Station and inquired into previous offenses.

Squad leader: Where were you caught? How long did you go up for?

Man: At the Sapporo Prison. A year and a half.

Squad leader (to the police box staffer): Let's make this an emergency arrest for theft of a vehicle, with the steel bars to be added later.

The suspect is finally informed of his rights, and at 11:27 P.M., the leader requests a car from the station to transport the suspect. His concern that he meet the deadline for securing an arrest warrant after an emergency arrest becomes apparent.

Squad leader: (on the phone) It won't make an arrest of a flagrant offender. I'm making an emergency arrest. It's an emergency arrest, so we won't have time—please hurry. I can't base the emergency arrest on the steel bars, either. That would be putting arrest before investigation. (To police box staffer) We could add driving without a license, couldn't we? He ran away, so I scolded him, "Why did you run?" He said, "Because I don't have a license." When I went to check out that yakuza [organized crime member] that came into the police box a while ago, a car was cruising around. We will seize the truck, and return it to the victim. Cokes and the water heater in the truck were his. The man sniffles, speaks in a tearful voice.

Patrolman Abe: Did you buy Cokes?

Suspect: 960 yen [approximately $3.20].

Patrolman Baba: Where? Today? When? (To another staffer) Will you call the victim company and tell them about the steel rods?

At 11:42 P.M., a car arrives with detectives.

Detective Ando (to the suspect): Did you stack it yourself? Took a long time, I'll bet. Where did you carry it from? Ah, and this? You used this to open it with, eh? How did you do that?

Continued

The police box officers must immediately hand over the case to the detectives. The detectives decide to take statements at the station, but the patrol officers want to retain their control of the case.

Deputy squad leader (to Detective Abe): What if we hauled the steel bars out, and dragged this guy to the scene for a look? (To the man) Where did you plan to sell the steel?

At 11:50 P.M., the suspect is taken to the station. At midnight, the victim of theft of the vehicle, a company president, arrives at the police box. The officers there decide to send him to the station and have him identify the vehicle. The deputy squad leader of the police box contrasts the skill of this squad leader with the ability of ordinary patrol officers, and expresses discontent that for patrol officers, cases must be sent on to the specialists for more investigation and final disposition. He also says that detectives are not mainly concerned about the offense for which the suspect was arrested, but about the possibility of clearing as many separate offenses as possible by attributing them to this suspect:

Deputy squad leader: Looks like an emergency arrest, a good case. Our squad leader came from the detectives, so he has a good sixth sense. The detectives want separate offenses, so they took the guy to the station. They are in competition with the Patrol. In the Patrol, we can't get separate offenses, you know. But they didn't arrest him themselves, and that doesn't set too well. Sweating away writing up papers for someone else's case, I don't know what to say.

At 2:00 A.M., the investigation at the police box is concluded. The squad leader does not hide his elation at the opportunity to effect an arrest, which suggests that such opportunities are scarce indeed.

Squad leader: Professor, you brought a case with you. (Referring to the luck brought by my being there.) The arrest warrant for the truck was accepted over the phone. We'll use the theft of the steel bars as grounds for detention. Today is our day, eh? I'll take care of the paperwork afterwards.

Detectives have been investigating this suspect since then, and on March 14th, at 1:00 P.M., a detective explains to me what has been going on at the station. He hopes to learn of any separate offenses and will use the detention at the station detention cell to investigate this possibility.

Detective Ando: In the end, he was sent to the prosecutor as a single offender with no accomplice. He's been in three times in ten years, so we decided to charge him as a habitual offender. He's in the station detention cell now because there should be separate offenses.

Detective Ando again informs me of developments on March 20. The suspect is still in the station detention cell and remains there even after he is indicted for the initial charge, although he is now a defendant in the court.

Detective Ando: Emergency arrest was on the 23rd of February, at 11:20 P.M. Suspect was put into detention by the judge at the station detention cell, and indicted on the 6th of this month. Suspect was charged with habitual theft, including the truck, steel rods, and Cokes. A theft from a warehouse.

It is April 4 now, but the suspect is still in the station detention cell. At 4:10 P.M., the squad leader, now transferred to the First Detective Department, reviews questionable aspects of the case at the station. This implies that the police officers have engaged in questionable behavior while they were clearly aware of its nature.

Squad leader: The steel rods would not justify an emergency arrest. There was no report from the victim. The vehicle itself is doubtful, too. It happened between 5 and 9 o'clock, the report came in at 10, and he was spotted at 11, which means that it's too spread out both in time and in distance.

Finally on April 11, at 1:00 P.M., more than one-and-a-half months after the emergency arrest, an order comes from the prosecutor to transfer the suspect to the outside detention center. It seems that this is to be done because the defendant-suspect has nothing more to offer to detectives about other offences.[35]

Reprinted from *Policing in Japan: A Study on Making Crime,* Translated by Frank G. Bennett, Jr., with John O. Haley, by Setsuo Miyazawa, pp. 44–46, by permission of the State University of New York Press. © 1992, State University of New York.

The Supreme Court specifically rejected this call for a waiver test in *Schneckcloth v. Bustamonte.* Instead, the Court held that the law assumes people know they have rights. To claim their rights, people have to assert them. Assertion carries its risks, however, because officers might read a refusal to consent to request to "look around" as evidence of guilt, perhaps even sufficient to establish probable cause to search. The courts have not solved this "damned if you do, damned if you don't" problem. However, the Supreme Court has held that mere refusal to cooperate with police officers is not enough to add up to probable cause.

Searches of Vehicles

The reasonableness of warrantless vehicle searches also depends on balancing the government interest in law enforcement and the privacy interest of individuals. The capacity to move vehicles easily facilitates escape and the destruction of evidence. Requiring a warrant to search the vehicle, therefore, places too heavy a burden on law enforcement. By the time officers obtain the warrant, the vehicle has gone. Furthermore, the Supreme Court has held that people have a reduced privacy interest in their vehicles, compared to the privacy interest they have in their homes. For these reasons, searches of vehicles are reasonable without warrants, if they are based on probable cause. According to the Supreme Court, the danger to the public of using vehicles as instruments of crime, the reduced privacy interest of individuals in their vehicles, and the probable cause to support them justify searches of vehicles without warrants. Not everyone agrees that less privacy surrounds vehicles than homes. Also, despite the use of mobile homes and some vans as temporary or even permanent residences, the Supreme Court has held that the government interest in law enforcement outweighs the individual privacy interest in these "hybrid" vehicles.[19]

Plain-View Searches

According to the law of **plain-view searches,** law enforcement officers can lawfully seize weapons, contraband, stolen property, or evidence that are in plain view. Plain view is really an incorrect term, since the rule applies to discoveries by any of the ordinary senses—sight, smell, hearing, and touch. Plain view, plain smell, plain hearing, and plain touch searches are reasonable under the following conditions:

1. The discoveries of evidence, weapons, contraband, or persons are made by the *ordinary* senses.
2. Officers discover the objects of persons *unintentionally.*
3. Officers, when they make the discoveries, are where they have a *legal right* to be.

Consider this example: Officers stop a car for running a red light. They see a plastic bag full of marijuana lying on the front seat. They have used their ordinary sense of sight to make the discovery. They have unintentionally discovered the marijuana by virtue of their being in a position to see it without any further action on their part. They have a legal right to stand outside the car on a public road where they have lawfully stopped a driver for a traffic violation. On the other hand, officers who use high-powered telescopes to see into the apartment of a suspect hundreds of feet away are not using their *ordinary* senses. Officers who see a television set they suspect is stolen do not *unintentionally* discover evidence if they turn the set upside down in order to get its serial number, check out the serial number to find out it is stolen, and the check reveals that it is stolen. Officers are not *legally* where they have a right to be if they break into a house and, while they are standing in the living room, discover cocaine lying on a table in plain view.[20]

stop and frisk *Fourth Amendment seizure and search that is less invasive than full-blown search and seizure.*

reasonable suspicion *objective basis for stops and frisks that requires enough facts or circumstances to suspect an individual may be committing, may be about to commit, or may have committed a crime, or that the suspect may be armed.*

Legally speaking, unintentional plain-view discoveries (and discoveries by means of the other senses) made without technological enhancements are not Fourth Amendment searches at all. As a result, they require neither warrants nor probable cause to back them up. Limiting the police to "looking around" in places where they have a right to be, seizing only items they can see without the enhancement of technological devices, serves both the public interest in controlling crime and the protection of individual privacy—even if they are not protected by the Fourth Amendment. Therefore, the seizure of items in plain view, or discovered by the other ordinary senses of touch, smell, and hearing, are not unreasonable seizures.

Stop and Frisk

In the course of normal duty, patrol officers encounter large numbers of people. Citizens frequently initiate these contacts because they want information or help, or because they want to report crimes. Less frequently, patrol officers themselves witness criminal activity, and they initiate contact with the suspects to arrest people or issue them citations. These kinds of contacts rarely arouse controversy. However, patrol officers also initiate a third kind of contact, field investigation, also called **stop and frisk,** that is not so widely accepted (see Chapter 5). The objective basis for stops and frisks is **reasonable suspicion.** In stop and frisk, officers stop, question, and sometimes pat down individuals because they reasonably *suspect* that these individuals *may* be committing, *may* be about to commit, or *may* have committed a crime. (Compare this definition with probable cause in which officers reasonably *believe* that a suspect *is* committing, *is* about to commit, or *has* committed a crime.) "Suspect" is not so strong a conclusion as "belief," and, of course, "may" is not so certain as "is." Police can also lawfully frisk a suspect they have lawfully stopped if they reasonably suspect that the suspect is armed.

Stopping suspicious persons and demanding to know who they are and why they are out and about is an old practice. Ancient statutes and court decisions empowered English constables to detain "suspicious nightwalkers" and hold them until morning in order to investigate their suspicious behavior. Until the mid-1960s, police-initiated contacts with people on the street and in other public places did not arouse controversy. These encounters were left to the discretion of individual officers. During the 1960s, the police discretionary power to stop and frisk became a matter of public concern.[21]

The due process revolution discussed in Chapter 3 led reformers to call for extending constitutional protections to all contacts between officers and individuals, and to subjecting those encounters to review by the courts. This resulted in a formalization of the period of criminal investigation occurring before the arrest of suspects. This formalization caused—and still causes—bitter controversy. The police and their supporters argue that police expertise and professional independence require that discretion, not formal rules, govern street encounters prior to arrest. Civil libertarians, on the other hand, maintain that citizens, especially those on the "fringes of society," need—and a free society requires—the Constitution to follow them wherever they go.

For complex reasons not yet sorted out, the courts, led by the Supreme Court, formalized stop and frisk during the 1960s. Despite strong opposition at the time, and some modification over the years since then, this formalization has remained intact. Furthermore, what happens in the police station—which was until the 1960s another sanctuary from formal judicial interference—has also come under constitutional protection.

Patrol officers regularly confront suspicious circumstances that call for further information from someone seen on the street or in a car, persons unknown to the officers and whom they will probably never see again. To enforce the criminal law effectively, officers need the discretion to "freeze the situation" briefly to check out suspicious circumstances and people. These suspicions frequently do not amount to probable cause. Also, if officers approach citizens and detain them, the citizens may endanger officers. If they suspect persons may be carrying a weapon, they pat them down for weapons. Courts and legislatures, neither experts nor present during these contacts, rarely second-guess the decisions of officers on the street to stop and frisk citizens. In most cases, officers decide quickly whether they have probable cause to arrest; if not, they release the detained person.

Encounters between individuals and police officers occur far more often on the street or in cars than inside police stations. In San Diego, for example, during one six-month period, the police recorded more than 21,000 stops on the street. They arrested only 392, or less than 2 percent, of the citizens they stopped. Since police do not record stops if they absolve citizens immediately, virtually no stops result in arrests.[22]

The 1960s reform wave focused attention on street encounters between citizens and the police. Some legislatures, such as in New York, passed stop-and-frisk laws specifically authorizing the police to approach citizens, detain them briefly to check out suspicions, and frisk them for weapons if necessary. In 1968, the Supreme Court took the opportunity to decide whether stops were arrests and frisks were seizures. The landmark case *Terry v. Ohio* balanced the interests of law enforcement and the rights of individuals to go about without interference from the government.

Terry and a companion walked up and down a Cleveland street, peering into a men's clothing store. Officer McFadden, a 37-year veteran of the Cleveland Police Department, observed them from across the street. He suspected that they were "casing" the store in preparation for a robbery, but he lacked probable cause to arrest them. So he approached them, asking their names and the reason they were there. When Terry mumbled in response, McFadden spun him around and ran his hands quickly over Terry's outer clothing. Feeling something hard in Terry's overcoat pocket, McFadden reached inside the coat and removed a gun. The Supreme Court had to decide whether police officers can stop citizens on the street and pat them down without probable cause to arrest them. The Court had three choices:

1. Stops are not seizures, and frisks are not searches; therefore, they fall within the realm of informal police discretion and decision making.
2. Stops are arrests, and frisks are full body searches; therefore, they must satisfy the formal constitutional requirement of probable cause and other aspects of reasonable search and seizures.
3. Stops are seizures but lesser ones than full arrests, frisks are searches, but lesser ones than full body searches; therefore, they require only reasonable suspicion, not full probable cause, to back them up.[23]

The Court chose the third option; it brought stop and frisk within the formal law of search and seizure, but relaxed the probable cause standard. The Court acknowledged that good police work requires officers to stop citizens on the street to investigate suspicious circumstances and prevent crime. If Officer McFadden had not checked out Terry and his companion, they might have robbed the clothing store. To protect citizens from unwarranted stops, the Court extended the Fourth Amendment's protection to both stops and frisks. The justices refused to engage in a semantics battle—they simply agreed that stops constitute seizures, and frisks searches, within the meaning of the Fourth Amendment. Since stops are lesser deprivations than full-blown arrests, and frisks less intrusive than full-body searches, they require fewer facts than probable cause. Instead, they require reasonable suspicion, facts that lead officers to suspect that crimes may be afoot and that suspects may be armed.

Stop and frisk has strong critics, who claim that it arouses hostility and therefore harms good police relations with the community. They argue that the price paid in hostility is not worth the benefit derived from crimes the practice might prevent or criminals it might lead to apprehending. Some research challenges these conclusions. In a study sponsored by the respected Police Foundation, John E. Boydstun evaluated stop and frisk in San Diego. The city was divided into three areas. In the control area, stops and frisks were conducted without any changes in police activities. In the Special Field Interrogation Area, only officers trained to reduce potential friction between subjects and officers conducted stops and frisks. In the No Field Interrogation Area, stops and frisks were suspended for the nine-month experimental period. The results of the experiment showed that San Diego's aggressive field interrogations had at least some deterrent effect without raising much community hostility.[24]

You Decide   "Are Police Sweeps Good Policy?"

Consider the following articles. The first describes a proposal by the Republican governor of Minnesota to introduce police sweeps in Minneapolis. The second describes the elements of the Minnesota Senate Democrats' anticrime proposals. The third describes the police stop practices in Beverly Hills. The final two selections comment on the outcome of police sweeps in public housing units in Chicago.

"Governor Proposes $20 Million Anticrime Program"

by Conrad deFiebre, Minneapolis Star Tribune, 29 December 1995

A tough-talking Gov. Arne Carlson announced a $20 million proposal Thursday to fight crime in the Twin Cities, including state funding to extend a controversial Minneapolis police tactic of street sweeps to much of the metro area. Carlson said increased stop-and-frisk efforts modeled after Minneapolis' Operation Safe Streets will hit hard at criminals coming to Minnesota "from Illinois or elsewhere. . . . We're going to harass them out of here, and I mean it."

Under the governor's plan, which requires approval from the Legislature, up to $5 million in state money would pay overtime to officers from the State Patrol and 11 metro jurisdictions. The officers would "sweep neighborhoods of any kind of illegality, period," Carlson said. Carlson also urged using $15 million in state bonding money to buy sophisticated equipment to link fragmented metro police radio communications across city and county lines.

The centerpiece of his proposal, however, is an apparently unprecedented level of state involvement in local law enforcement in Minnesota—and specifically in support of police tactics that some have called unfair and indiscriminate. In the police sweeps envisioned by Carlson, officers would saturate targeted high-crime neighborhoods, making arrests for traffic and curfew violations,

loitering, truancy and other minor offenses in an effort to find and seize guns and drugs.

"It's zero tolerance," said Don Davis, former Brooklyn Park police chief who is now Carlson's deputy commissioner of public safety. "It's a very, very drastic step. I'm apologizing in advance to the good citizens who might get caught in this, but it's a technique that has to be used."

Minneapolis police say their efforts last summer led to the seizure of more than 160 guns and a marked reduction in reports of shots fired, although the city's number of homicides has already set a record. Some black men have complained of being repeatedly stopped simply because of their skin color. But the state must step in now with money and police for "a very serious crackdown," Carlson said, because crime has become a major concern to all Minnesotans.

"The bulk of Minnesota citizens no longer feel safe, no matter where they live," the governor said. "That's a first and a serious red flag. . . . When safety is placed in jeopardy, everything else is in jeopardy." Fear of crime is even impeding efforts to improve the state's economic climate, transportation and education, he said.

Carlson announced his initiative at the Minneapolis police precinct station on Plymouth Av. with dozens of officers lined up behind him. Officials from several agencies that would benefit from the plan voiced enthusiastic support for it. With the state money, said Minneapolis Police Chief Robert Olson, "we hope we'll be able to double our efforts." Richard Eckwall, St. Paul deputy chief, said his department intends to apply for the state money, even though its crime-fighting efforts differ from those in Minneapolis.

Meanwhile, a group of St. Paul and Minneapolis DFL [Democrat Farmer Labor party] legislators plan to announce today another set of crime-fighting ideas, including state matching funds to help cities pay for so-called "Clinton cops"—new officers hired with federal assistance. But Sen. Allan Spear, DFL-Minneapolis, chairman of the state Senate Crime Prevention Committee, said he also expects to back Carlson's plan. "If this involves putting more law enforcement officers on the streets, that's a concept I support," Spear said.

In addition to Minneapolis and St. Paul, Carlson's program would include officers from Bloomington, Brooklyn Center, Brooklyn Park, Burnsville, Columbia Heights, Maplewood, St. Louis Park and Hennepin and Ramsey counties. State troopers may participate under provisions allowing them to do local police work at the request of local authorities, said State Patrol Chief Col. Mike Chabries.

"Anybody who violates the law, we're going to harass," Carlson said. "I don't want one single criminal to feel comfortable in the state of Minnesota." Reprinted with permission of Minneapolis StarTribune, Copyright 1995

* * *

"Senate DFL Presents Anticrime Package"

by Conrad deFiebre, **Minneapolis Star Tribune,**
30 December 1995

DFL legislators presented their prescription for Minnesota's burgeoning crime problems Friday, urging equal parts of stepped-up law enforcement and help for kids before they can become hardened criminals. A day after Republican Gov. Arne Carlson proposed a tough state-backed crackdown on crime in the Twin Cities, the DFLers said his ideas would complement their own. But they also criticized Carlson's plan as one-dimensional and too meddlesome in local affairs.

"We should not be planning police strategy at the Capitol," said Sen. Allan Spear, DFL-Minneapolis. "The governor is a latecomer to the crime issue. We're glad he's now on board, but there's a sense of a quick fix in his proposal. There just is no quick fix for problems like the homicide rate in Minneapolis." That comment set off a round of sniping between Republican and DFL leaders, an indication that crime may be one of the most volatile issues of the 1996 political season.

State Republican Chairman Chris Georgacas blamed Spear and other Minneapolis DFL officials for allowing the city's crime to flourish. Rep. Wes Skoglund, DFL-Minneapolis, then scolded Carlson for advocating reduced sentences for some drug and property offenders.

The DFL plan includes these proposals:

● A $2.5 million state appropriation to provide local matching funds for 100 federally subsidized "Clinton cops," new officers who would concentrate community policing efforts in high-crime areas. (Carlson's plan calls for $5 million to pay overtime to existing officers for neighborhood sweeps and expanded block club programs.)

● About $1 million for 11 new early childhood programs intended to break cycles of family violence that can lead to later crime. Included are home visits by nurses to newborns and their parents, crisis nurseries and youth programs.

● All-day kindergartens at elementary schools in impoverished neighborhoods. Proponents cited research showing that graduates of high-quality preschool programs are at least four times less likely to become repeat criminals.

● Intensive supervision and support for juvenile offenders after their release from detention centers, using college interns as in a successful Missouri program.

Cost estimates were not available for the last two components, but Sen. Randy Kelly, DFL-St. Paul, said the entire proposal would require $6 million to $8 million. The DFLers proposed footing the bill with up to $5 million a year in savings in the state prison system. They said that could be done by sending 200 inmates to the low-cost city-run Prairie Correctional Facility in Appleton, Minn., doubling the number of inmates eligible for shortened "boot camp" sentences and making prison industries more profitable.

Corrections officials say these notions are already being studied or implemented, and Georgacas accused the DFLers of expropriating Republican ideas of prison industry privatization. But that was just the warmup for Georgacas' broadside. "Minneapolis probably would not have a record homicide rate if Spear had not fought Republican ideas like 'three strikes, you're out' . . . if DFLers had not made welfare eligibility requirements and benefits levels so attractive for non-Minnesotans, and if [DFL] Hennepin County Attorney Mike Freeman had not made plea-bargaining an all-too-common practice," he said.

Spear, however, said the DFL plan is a more comprehensive and tight-budgeted approach to fighting crime. Noting that the state is planning a $100 million prison in Rush City, he said: "We need to prevent the need for another prison after that. Building prison after prison is a budget-buster. . . . We know there's a significant correlation between the well-being of kids and the crime rate. If we can help at-risk kids, these are the things we need to do now to help keep ourselves safe in the future." Reprinted with permission of Minneapolis StarTribune, Copyright 1995

* * *

"Stops Prompt Suit Blacks: Cops Target Us in Beverly Hills"

by Sally Ann Stewart, **USA Today,** *11 November 1995*
BEVERLY HILLS—People who know Pat Earthly can't understand why he has been repeatedly stopped and interrogated by Beverly Hills police officers. "Anyone who meets Pat would be impressed with what an even-headed and bright individual he is," says Sharon Davis, a foundation executive who's married to the lieutenant governor. Earthly, 29, sexton at All Saints' Episcopal Church in this glittery city of palm trees, pricey designer boutiques and luxury cars, is certain he knows why he's been stopped: He's black.

Today, Earthly joins five teen-age boys—including four Beverly Hills High School football players—in filing a federal lawsuit against the city and police department, saying their civil rights were violated. Earthly, who says he has been illegally stopped or searched four times, and the others are seeking money and an end to what they say is police harassment of young black men. "I want to see a change and have some type of justice for people who look like myself," says Earthly, an aspiring singer-songwriter-pianist. "I don't think police should be able to stop people just because we're black."

They don't, says Frank Salcido, spokesman for the 126-officer force in the town of 31,971. "Our practice is to treat everyone with respect and to meticulously respect the rights of individuals." Earthly doesn't buy that. He recalled once being forced by police officers to lie on the ground in handcuffs in front of his church colleagues. His offense: Police say Earthly's car was missing a brakelight.

Ralph and Cheryl Jones understand. They say that in January their 15-year-old son, Moacir, was walking with three other boys to a video store near the family's apartment. En route, a police officer stopped and ordered the boys to place their hands against a wall. At least five other police cars and a motorcycle officer also responded. The boys were handcuffed and interrogated about where they were going and where they lived. And when Moacir slumped his shoulders, Ralph Jones says, one police officer became so enraged that he threw Moacir against a storefront wall. Eventually, the boys were released— without being charged with anything. "They not only didn't apologize, but they really were very arrogant about the whole thing," says Ralph Jones, a church choir director and a Santa Monica-Malibu School District music teacher. "One officer even said to me, 'You're lucky this is all that happened.' "

Civil rights lawyer Leo Terrell, who's not involved in the case, says he expected such a federal suit. Police mistreatment of black men, he says, "has been whispered about for years. Young black men know that if they are in Beverly Hills, they're going to be followed. The only unique thing about this case is that 99% of the time the police get away with it." Lawyer Robert Tannenbaum, a former Beverly Hills mayor, says he expects the trial to begin by spring. "When I was mayor, if I'd ever known anything like this was going on, I would have put a stop to it. It's critical that people in this community clean their house." Although City Manager Mark Scott made a personal, verbal apology to Earthly in April, All Saints parish administrator Sam Williamson says, "We see no change in their policy."

* * *

Chicago introduced "Operation Clean Sweep," a program of police sweeps into the Cabrini Green public housing units, in 1989. They conducted house-to-house searches and required residents to show their identification in order to enter the projects. Responding to complaints that their actions were illegal searches, the chairman of the Chicago Public Housing Authority responded, "We are not infringing on rights. We are restoring our citizens' rights to a safe and decent environment."[25] Copyright 1995, USA Today. Reprinted with permission.

"Judge to Rule on Chicago Gunsweeps"

by Robert Davis, USA Today, *4 April 1994*
A federal judge is expected to decide this week whether Chicago police may search public housing projects for guns without a warrant. Critics say the searches infringe on residents' rights, and U.S. District Judge Wayne Andersen put a temporary end to the practice in February, calling it "a greater evil than the danger of criminal activity."

But then came more gunfire, death and rhetoric. Mayor Richard Daley fought for the sweeps, arguing that "public housing is owned by the people," and the people "do not want guns, gangbangers and drugs in their building." Harvey Grossman of the American Civil Liberties Union, which opposes the sweeps, says: "You simply cannot toss out the Constitution."

As the city and the ACLU fight in public and in the court, gunfire continues to crack. During the last weekend of March, for example, police were called for 300 reports of shots fired at Robert Taylor Homes, a 6-story public housing project on the South Side. "It was like Vietnam," says Tammera Evans, 48, who has lived there since 1983. "It was H-E-L-L with a gun. You couldn't go in front of a window or take the garbage out." Now the city, which broke a record for killings in March with 88 dead, wants to again sweep apartments for guns. Police began searching homes without warning or warrants after a 7-year-old boy was killed by a sniper in 1992. The ACLU, which sued to stop the searches, now wants a permanent ban. But many scared residents want police to continue.

"The people I represent want security," says Thomas Sullivan, a former U.S. attorney who is fighting the ACLU on behalf of some complex residents. "They are sick and tired of the kind of violence they are subjected to. These are fine people who are just being terrorized." The fear has left many residents willing to give up some of their constitutional rights. "Go ahead, invade my privacy. I give you permission. Hurry up," says Evans. "The way it is now, I can't go out to the store; the mailman doesn't want to come in here. It's like I'm in a prison." Police can "look in my drawers, under my sink, wherever they want to look" to get the guns out of her building, the violence out of her face, says Evans. "I want my safety."

Sullivan, who is representing project residents for free, says "reams of rhetoric" over the gun sweep have "missed the point" of the problem. Lousy security means "anybody can just walk right into those buildings." He wants security changed the way the Secret Service recommended to the Housing and Urban Development Department last year, including simple tasks like building a sturdy fence. "The sweeps are really just a . . . fix that doesn't get down to the real problems," says Sullivan. "These tenants don't want gangs in their building."

In court last week, Andersen said the problem ultimately may be up to politicians to fix. "There are no magically right answers," he said. "Everything is imperfect." Copyright 1994, USA Today. Reprinted with permission.

* * *

"Residents' Hopes Rise as Murders Decline in CHA [Chicago Housing Authority] Sites"

by Flynn McRoberts, Chicago Tribune, *7 January 1995*
The death of Eric Morse last October refocused attention on Chicago Housing Authority developments as places of great peril for children. To make matters worse, there was this inescapable irony: CHA preventive programs are headquartered in the Ida B. Wells high-rise from which Eric was dropped to his death, allegedly because he wouldn't steal candy for two 10- and 11-year-old boys. Yet 1994 was a substantially safer year for most CHA children, at least judging from statistics that show four of them, including Eric, under age 15 were murdered last year. The year before, that figure was 10, and in 1992 it was 14 out of the nearly 35,000 kids in that age group living in CHA housing.

No one knows exactly why the number is declining, or if it is just a statistical anomaly. But there are those who live in and work in or for CHA who believe it is more than that; for them it's a glimmer of hope after years of bad news. Residents, police and authority personnel point to a range of factors that might help explain the lower death toll.

Those include better cooperation between police and residents and an emerging number of resident leaders who have helped push some criminal activity to other neighborhoods—good news for them, if not for the city as a whole, which recorded 930 homicides in 1994, the third-highest total in its history. People like Melanie Thomas, grandmother of 18 and a 17-year resident of CHA's Washington Park development, say they can't help but notice a difference. "It used to look like an Easter parade of people wanting to buy drugs," said Thomas, the captain of the tenant patrol for her South Side building. Now, there are just "a few teenagers who wanna be" dealing, she said.

Brenda Stephenson, a member of the West Side Rockwell Gardens' resident council, said the gunplay has "decreased drastically over here" in the last year and a half. One reason, she said: Gang members "are not hanging out as much as they used to. So that gives other gang members fewer targets to shoot at." In addition, she said, the Nation of Islam affiliate that is helping to privately manage the development has "sort of talked the gangs into putting the guns down and fistfighting when they get into discrepancies. So that's a plus, at least over here in Rockwell."

Though the crime statistics show a gradual, albeit small, decrease in crime throughout CHA developments, neighborhoods without large CHA developments, such as Englewood, have suffered more violence in the last year or two. But in areas where young children have not been killed by gunfire or abuse, the murder statistics don't necessarily give the whole picture. For example, things appear to be safer now than they were last spring when a flurry of gang-related shootings tore through the Robert Taylor Homes, said Kweli Kwaza, a program supervisor for CHA's preventive programs. But he said, "Sometimes when crime is high, people keep their kids inside."

While pinpointing reasons for the statistical decline in crime isn't easy, police attribute some of it to the cooperation of residents and a law enforcement mix of security sweeps and community policing. The greater presence of city and CHA police walking the buildings "seems to have shifted a lot of this crime out of the developments," said Robert Guthrie, commander of the Chicago police public housing division. "They're all walking and talking in the halls and stairwells. And it's been a deterrent to some of the crime we've had in public housing." Guthrie said the sniper death of 7-year-old Dantrell Davis in October 1992 at the Cabrini-Green complex caused more CHA residents to unite with police in crime-fighting efforts. "They started working with the police," he said. "They had had enough." He dismisses the belief of many residents that gang truces are responsible for much of the drop in shootings. "If there's a gang truce, how come there are so many murders in South Chicago and South Shore? The same gangs are there that are in the developments. . . . It

seems like these gang truces coincide with law enforcement efforts."

The impact of other possible factors on the decline of deaths among the young is difficult to quantify. For instance, no figures are available on the number of children in CHA developments who have been taken into protective custody by state authorities. But anecdotal evidence suggests that number might be declining because of new intensive family preservation programs such as those funded through the Illinois Department of Children and Family Services.

Barbara Reynolds, supervisor of such a program run by the Children Home and Aid Society, said that of the 32 cases it has handled since January 1994, children have gone into protective custody in only two instances. DCFS is monitoring the other 30, but the children are still with their families. The program is a "last-chance effort to preserve the family unit," Reynolds explained, in which therapists with just two cases apiece provide a minimum of 10 to 20 hours a week of basic parenting instruction and other services. The society's 28-day program, which gets 95 percent of its cases from CHA, expects to save the state money by "reducing the number of children who are being placed in foster care or group homes," she said.

For their part, CHA administrators and resident leaders say the decline in the number of murdered children shows that efforts to get tenants to work together are finally starting to pay off. Bernita Lucas, the authority's acting director of preventive programs, said she hopes the new Republican-controlled Congress keeps that in mind. "I hope they take great caution and care in what social programs they may slash or cut out," she said, "because these programs raise social consciousness both outside and inside the fishbowl" that is public housing. "These programs are about helping people become self-sufficient," Lucas said, pointing out that some members of the CHA's 600-member tenant patrol no longer participate because they have gotten jobs and moved out of public housing.

Similarly, the CHA's resident management program—aimed at eventually turning over buildings to tenants—has helped create a growing number of people with "a heightened sense of value in their community," according to Lucas. "It's not luck," she said of the declining numbers of child homicides in CHA developments. "It happens because people in the community are committed to a change." That means people like Thomas, who said the visibility of CHA tenant patrols, with their trademark navy blue jackets and yellow lettering, has discouraged some of the drug dealing in her building. "Just putting on your jacket and doing those walk-downs, that is what has stopped (much) of the crime that was going on."

Also gone are the days when she simply remained quiet, figuring "if you keep to yourself, you stay out of trouble." Or, as Lucas put it, now there are "folks who can never go back home and just stay inside." Copyright 1995, Chicago Tribune. Reprinted with permission.

Questions

What are the advantages Governor Carlson sees in his proposed police sweep policy for Minneapolis? Why did the governor propose the policy? Is what happened in

Beverly Hills the implementation of a policy? Is it the effect of deliberate race discrimination? Was what happened a mistake? What are the reasons for the decline in the murders of children in the Chicago Public Housing units, according to the article? How important are the complaints that Operation Clean Sweep violates people's rights? In what ways, if any, does police sweep policy in Minneapolis relate to the Beverly Hills stop practices and the actions of the Chicago Housing Authority? Suppose you are a criminal justice policy advisor to Governor Carlson. What policy would you recommend, having read about Beverly Hills and Chicago?

Interrogation

Miranda warnings *requirement that before officers can conduct custodial interrogations they must inform suspects of their right to remain silent and to have a lawyer.*

The Fifth Amendment provides, among other things, that "no person shall be compelled to be a witness against himself in any criminal case." Several empirical questions involving police interrogation and confessions have never been answered, although police investigators, legal commentators, and partisans regularly express strong feelings about them. Many police interrogators, prosecutors, and judges believe that interrogation is a crucial—indeed, indispensable—part of criminal investigation. Many cases would go unsolved if officers could not interrogate suspects. Others maintain that police interrogation goes against the values of a free society and that the government should not convict people from evidence out of their own mouths. Police interrogators maintain that interrogation not only helps to convict the guilty but also aids in freeing the innocent. Critics argue that the police use unethical tactics, including lying, deceit, and tricks to get confessions.[26]

No one knows what goes on in interrogation rooms because they are secret, except to the two interested parties—the interrogating officers and the interrogated suspects. Neither of these parties can give a trustworthy and unbiased account of what happens during interrogation. As to the need for interrogation, we do not know how many unsolved cases could have been solved with the help of interrogation, nor how many solved cases required interrogation and confession.[27]

Police interrogation and the confessions of suspects raise not only empirical questions but also controversial constitutional and ethical issues:

1. When do suspects acquire their right against self-incrimination?
2. What does interrogation mean?
3. How do citizens waive their right against self-incrimination?
4. When may officers question citizens without warning them of their right against self-incrimination?
5. What is a voluntary confession?

Miranda v. Arizona

In 1966, the U.S. Supreme Court tried to answer these questions in perhaps the most controversial and famous case ever decided involving the police and criminal law enforcement, *Miranda v. Arizona.* The Court ruled that the Fifth Amendment protects suspects against coercive custodial police interrogation. The Court said that confessions extracted by "third-degree" (physical brutality) were not the only form of involuntary incrimination. According to a majority of the Court, simply being in a police station was sufficiently intimidating to call for Fifth Amendment protection. To secure that protection, the Court devised rules to cover custodial interrogation, meaning interrogation while a suspect is in custody "at the station or otherwise deprived of his freedom of action in any significant way."[28]

Before interrogation, the police must give the **Miranda warnings,** an action that has come to be called "reading suspects their rights." According to the Court, officers who interrogate suspects in custody must do all of the following, in order to assure the voluntariness of incriminating statements obtained during the custodial interrogation:

1. *Warn* suspects in clear and certain terms that they have the right to remain silent.
2. *Explain* to suspects that the government can and will use anything said against suspects.
3. *Inform* suspects that they have the right to consult with a lawyer during interrogation.
4. *Assure* suspects that the government will appoint a lawyer if suspects cannot afford counsel.

In addition, although they are not part of the warnings specifically read to suspects, the Court ruled that:

1. If at any time during interrogation, suspects express a desire to remain silent, the interrogation must cease immediately.
2. If no lawyer is present, a heavy burden rests on the prosecution to prove suspects waived their rights voluntarily.
3. No evidence obtained in violation of these rules is admissible in court.
4. No suspect may be penalized for asserting the right to remain silent. Therefore, the prosecution may not use silence at trial to show suspects had something to hide.[29]

Court decisions since *Miranda* have clarified points left vague in the original decision. When or where does the suspect have the right to warnings? What if police interrogate a suspect at home, in the presence of family and friends? The courts have decided the warnings do not have to be given in this case, because such familiar surroundings are not likely to intimidate the suspect. On the other hand, simply because questioning takes place in the station does not automatically require the police to warn suspects. What if a suspect comes to the station in response to a police officer's note saying "I want to discuss something with you" left at the suspect's apartment? The Supreme Court ruled that the questioning that followed at the station did not require *Miranda* warnings because the suspect was "invited," not "taken," to the station. According to the Supreme Court, not all police questioning requires warning. Police who stop and briefly question citizens on the street during field investigation do not have to give the warnings. Nor does *Miranda* protect against routine questions asked at booking, such as "What is your name?" "Where do you live?" and "Are you married?"[30]

The *Miranda* decision stirred a bitter debate about the balance between police power and the rights of suspects. Those who opposed *Miranda* claimed it handcuffed the police in their fight against crime. Some extremists even blamed the decision for the rapidly rising crime rates of the 1960s. Others defended the decision as a major stride toward true liberty. *Miranda* became a pawn in the political issue of law and order. Congress joined the fray and in 1968 attempted to repeal the decision in the Safe Streets Act that President Nixon signed into law.[31]

Research strongly suggests that neither the fears nor the hopes that *Miranda* spawned were justified. Suspects who are warned seldom ask for a lawyer; the police have recorded about as many confessions since the decision as before; and the decision has had little or no apparent effect on clearance and conviction rates. The decision has had a weak impact on police practice because of the following reasons:

1. The warnings are not given in a way that truly denotes their meaning and significance.

2. Many suspects cannot grasp their meaning and really do not understand that the police are collecting evidence to be used against them.

3. Many suspects who do talk really want to tell their story to the police.

4. Suspects who grasp the meaning of the *Miranda* warnings probably already know their rights and will assert them whether the police give them the warnings or not.[32]

Voluntariness of Confessions

Police officers who interrogate suspects and obtain confessions or other incriminating statements may not have satisfied the requirements of the Constitution even if they have properly warned suspects and secured a knowing and voluntary waiver of their right to remain silent. The Fifth Amendment prohibits the police from *compelling* suspects to confess. Therefore, all admissions and confessions obtained during interrogation must be voluntary. Voluntariness, according to the Supreme Court, is a legal question that depends on the totality of the circumstances of each individual case. A confession is compelled under the voluntariness test if all of the circumstances in the case demonstrate:

1. Coercive actions by police officers or others who conduct the interrogation.

2. A causal link between the coercive actions and the incriminating admissions and confessions.

According to Chief Justice Rehnquist, writing for a majority of the Supreme Court in the confession case of *Colorado v. Connelly*:

> [T]he cases considered by this Court over . . . 50 years . . . have focused on the crucial element of police overreaching. While each confession case has turned on its own set of factors justifying the conclusion that police conduct was oppressive, all have contained a substantial element of coercive police conduct. Absent police conduct causally related to the confession, there is simply no basis for concluding that any state actor has deprived a criminal defendant of due process of law. . . . [A]s interrogators have turned to more subtle forms of psychological persuasion, courts have found the mental condition of the defendant a more significant factor in the "voluntariness" calculus. But this fact does not justify a conclusion that a defendant's mental condition, by itself apart from its relation to official coercion, should ever dispose of the inquiry into constitutional "voluntariness."[33]

The most common circumstances that courts consider in determining whether coercive action has caused people to confess include:

- Number of interrogators.
- Length of the questioning.
- Place of questioning.
- Denial of food, water, and toilet facilities.
- Threats, promises, lies, and tricks.
- Denial of access to a lawyer.
- Characteristics of the suspect, such as age, gender, race, physical and mental condition, education, and experience with the criminal justice system.

The *You Decide,* "Was the Confession Voluntary?" includes an excerpt from the confession case of *Colorado v. Connelly,* from which the preceding quote by Chief Justice Rehnquist is taken.

"Was the Confession Voluntary?"

Facts

Francis Connelly approached a uniformed Denver police officer and began confessing to a murder. Taken aback by these statements, the officer asked Connelly if he had ever undergone therapy for a mental disorder. Connelly responded that he had. The officer gave Connelly the *Miranda* warnings, after which Connelly continued to give details of the murder. After Connelly offered to show the police where the murder took place, the Denver police held him overnight. The next morning Connelly became visibly disoriented and spoke of voices that ordered him to come to Denver to confess to the murder. At the trial, a state hospital psychiatrist testified that Connelly had been in a psychotic state the day before he confessed and suffered from chronic schizophrenia. Connelly had told the psychiatrist that the "voice of God" told him he had either to confess or to commit suicide.

Questions

Was the confession voluntary? Both the trial court and the Colorado Supreme Court said no. In *Colorado v. Connelly,* the United States Supreme Court ruled that the confes-

sion was admissible. For the Court majority, Chief Justice William Rehnquist held that some form of police coercion is absolutely essential to violate due process on the grounds of an involuntary confession. In other words, although the totality of circumstances surrounding confessions is relevant to determine voluntariness, police coercion stands as a necessary circumstance in a finding of involuntariness. Justice Brennan dissented, writing:

> Today the Court denies Mr. Connelly his fundamental right to make a vital choice with a sane mind, involving a determination that could allow the State to deprive him of liberty or even life. . . . Surely in the present stage of our civilization a most basic sense of justice is affronted by the spectacle of incarcerating a human being upon the basis of a statement he made while insane. Because I believe that the use of a mentally ill person's involuntary confession is antithetical to the notion of fundamental fairness embodied in the due process clause, I dissent.

Do you agree with Rehnquist or Brennan? Was the confession voluntary because it was without coercion? Was it involuntary because Connelly was insane? Explain your reasons.

Voluntary does not mean totally free of influence. The *Miranda* warnings were intended to remove coercion from police custodial interrogation. They were not meant to eliminate all pressure on criminal suspects. According to one commentator:

> At trial, after establishing probable cause of guilt and when the defendant enjoys the protection of a neutral bench, a personal advocate, and public scrutiny, the government may not so much as put a polite question to the defendant. But, between arrest and commitment, the police may badger, trick, and manipulate the suspect in an environment solely within their control and to which no other witness is admitted. With respect to confessions, society insists on enjoying "at one and the same time the pleasures of indulgence and the dignity of disapproval."[34]

Identification Procedures

Proving that a crime was committed and showing how it was committed is easier than identifying the perpetrator. In some cases, of course, identification is not a major problem. Some suspects are caught red-handed; victims and witnesses personally know other suspects; others confess. Technological advances have led to the increasing use of novel scientific evidence to identify criminals. Bite-mark evidence helped to convict the notorious serial rapist and murderer Ted Bundy. Fiber evidence helped to convict Wayne Williams of the murder of two out of 30 murdered young African Americans in Atlanta. This chapter will examine the best-known "novel scientific evidence": DNA (deoxyribonucleic acid) testing. DNA testing lifts samples of body fluid from the victim, much like lifting fingerprints, and then matches these samples with the body fluids of the suspect. Heralded as the "single greatest advance in the 'search for truth' . . . since . . . cross-examination," many courts have found DNA evidence admissible. Problems have come to light, however, in the use of DNA, and now some courts are rethinking their initial enthusiasm for it.

The Dangers of Mistaken Identifications

The most common—and probably most problematic—cases are those relying on the eyewitness identification of strangers. (Obviously, eyewitness identification is not a problem where witnesses know the suspect.) The police rely on three major procedures to help eyewitnesses identify suspects. In **lineups,** witnesses try to identify a suspect standing in a line with other individuals. In **show-ups,** witnesses attempt to identify suspects without other possible suspects present. This may be in the police station or elsewhere. Police officers may take witnesses to observe suspects at work or in other places. In both lineups and show-ups, a confrontation, that is, an encounter, occurs between suspects and the witnesses who may incriminate them. Suspects may not actually see witnesses, but witnesses look directly at suspects, perhaps through a one-way mirror. In **photo identification,** witnesses look at a picture or pictures—"mug shots"—in order to identify suspects. Identification procedures are critical in many cases; in some, they are the only evidence available. The procedures are also fraught with the danger of identifying the wrong person.

Witness identification of strangers is notoriously low in reliability, even in ideal settings. The most common identification procedures—lineups and photographic identification—are not ideal and, hence, render eyewitness identification still less reliable. According to one expert, faulty identifications present the "greatest single threat to the achievement of our ideal that no innocent man shall be punished." Best guesses (reliable exact figures are not available) are that about half of all wrongful convictions are due to eyewitness error. To take but one example, seven eyewitnesses swore that Bernard Pagano, a Roman Catholic priest, robbed them with a small, chrome-plated pistol. In the middle of Pagano's trial, Ronald Clouser admitted that he, not Father Pagano, had committed the robberies.[36]

Misidentification occurs because of three normal mental processes taking place at three points in time:

1. *Perception*—the information taken in by the brain at the time of the original event.
2. *Memory*—the information retained from the original event in the interval between the event and the lineup, show-up, or photographic array.
3. *Recall*—the information retrieved at the time of the lineup, show-up, or photographic array.

Improper suggestive measures used by law enforcement probably account for some errors in identification. However, according to the widely accepted findings of psychologists who have studied perception, memory, and recall, the great majority probably are attributable both to the inherent unreliability of human perception and memory, and to human susceptibility to unintentional, and often quite subtle, suggestive influences.[37]

As for the witnessing of the original event, the brain does not record exactly what the eye sees. For about a century, psychologists have demonstrated that the eye is not a camera that records exact images on the brain. Cameras have no expectations; expectations and higher thought processes influence people's perceptions. Like beauty, the physical characteristics of perpetrators of crimes are in the eye of the beholder. The brain cannot process all that the eye sees because of natural limits on perception. Furthermore, even trained observers pay selective attention to the events they experience. They notice only certain features, leaving later gaps in memory. The accuracy of initial impressions depends on a variety of circumstances, including the

1. length of time the witness observed the stranger;
2. distractions during the observation;
3. focus of the observation;
4. stress to the witness during the observation;
5. race of the witness and the stranger.[38]

The longer the witness observes the stranger, the more reliable the perception. Distractions such as other activity during the observation, however, reduce reliability. Witnesses who gain a general impression, such as a whole face, are more reliable than those who focus on a single characteristic, such as a scar. But many witnesses focus on other details, such as what experts call "weapon focus," where they may remember a gun but not the person who carried it. The perceptions of highly stressed witnesses are less reliable than those of witnesses under low stress. Distractions and stress play a particularly large role in criminal events, that is, in the events where accuracy is most important. According to C. Ronald Huff, an identification expert who conducted one study:

> Many of the cases we have identified involve errors by victims of robbery and rape, where the victim was close enough to the offender to get a look at him—but under conditions of extreme stress. . . . Such stress can significantly affect perception and memory and should give us cause to question the reliability of such eyewitness testimony.[39]

Identifying a stranger of the same race is more reliable than identifying someone of a different race. In one famous experiment, researchers showed observers a photo of a white man brandishing a razor blade in an altercation with an African American man on a subway. When asked immediately afterward to describe what they saw, over half the observers reported that the African American man was carrying the weapon.

> [C]onsiderable evidence indicates that people are poorer at identifying members of another race than of their own. Some studies have found that, in the United States at least, whites have greater difficulty recognizing blacks than vice versa. Moreover, counterintuitively, the ability to perceive the physical characteristics of a person from another racial group apparently does not improve significantly upon increased contact with other members of that race. Because many crimes are cross-racial, these factors may play an important part in reducing the accuracy of eyewitness perception.[40]

The problem of cross-race identifications is aggravated by findings that African American identify whites better than whites identify African American and other racial groups. That is, whites are most susceptible to the "they all look alike" phenomenon. Curiously, accuracy does not improve with increased contact with members of the other race.[41]

Memory fades over time. It fades most during the first few hours following the identification of a stranger, then remains stable for several months. What happens during the lapse of time, however, can dramatically affect the reliability of memory. Curiously, witnesses' confidence about their recall grows as time passes, while, in fact, actual memory is fading. The confidence of witnesses is highly unreliable, despite the heavy weight accorded this confidence by judges and juries. The dangers of suggestion are high following an event. The mind combines everything about the event, whether the witness learned it at the time or later, and stores all the information in a single "bin." According to psychologist and respected eyewitness research expert Elizabeth Loftus, witnesses added to their stories depending on how she described an incident. Later, they drew this information out of the "bin" during the identification process.[42]

Steven Penrod, identification researcher at the University of Wisconsin, says this embellishment is natural to all of us. "A witness tells his story to the police, to the family, then to friends, then to the prosecutor." As the story gets retold, it becomes less reality and more legend. "[Witnesses] feel very confident about what they now think happened and that confidence is communicated to the jury."[43]

Outside influence and witness self-confidence affect the accuracy of identification in lineups, show-ups, and photographic displays. Witnesses tend to treat these situations as multiple-choice tests without a "none of the above" choice. They feel they have to choose the "best" likeness. Witnesses are afraid they might look foolish if they "don't know the answer," or they respond easily to suggestion, particularly in uncomfortable or threatening situations. Suggestions—mostly not intended, it should be stressed—by authority figures, such as the police, aggravate these tendencies. For example, witnesses will feel pressure simply because the police have arranged an identification procedure. Witnesses believe the police must have found the culprit—why else would they have arranged the identification event? So, the witnesses believe that the culprit must be among the people in the lineup or photo array.

Once witnesses identify a stranger, it is difficult to shake their conclusion, even if it is wrong. This fact is extremely important for at least three reasons. First, a convincing amount of research runs counter to the commonsense idea that confidence bespeaks accuracy. Quite the contrary, according to the research; confidence says little if anything about accuracy. It might even show less accuracy. Second, the confidence of a witness identification plays a major role in the decisions of jurors. Most jurors believe a confident identification and readily dismiss other evidence in the face of it. Thus, the confident, but wrong, identification of a suspect is particularly damning.[44]

Finally, despite the dangers of faulty identification, the courts rarely reject eyewitness identification testimony. For example, during trials, prosecutors often ask victims or other witnesses if they see the person who committed the crime in the courtroom. If witnesses answer yes, which they invariably do, then prosecutors ask them to point to that person, which they also invariably do. Courts also regularly admit evidence of prior identifications, such as those made during lineups. One court said,

> We think it is evident that an identification of an accused by a witness for the first time in the courtroom may often be of little testimonial force, as the witness may have had opportunities to see the accused and to have heard him referred to by a certain name; whereas a prior identification, considered in connection with the circumstances surrounding it, serves to aid the court in determining the trustworthiness of the identification made in the courtroom.[45]

The possibility of misidentification has led to efforts to reduce its likelihood, although rules and procedures can do nothing to improve the inherent human limits on perception and memory. The only part of the identification process that law enforcement agencies and courts can affect is the recall of information during identification procedures. These efforts may take the form of police department rules regarding the number of persons required to participate in lineups and the number of photographs required in arrays; the kinds of people who participate in lineups and the characteristics and quality of photographs in arrays; and the conditions under which witnesses participate in lineups, show-ups, and photographic arrays. Sometimes the effort involves the testimony of expert witnesses or the instructions of judges to juries during trial regarding the problems of reliability in identification procedures.

Identification Procedures and the Constitution

The Supreme Court relies on the Sixth Amendment right to counsel and the due process clauses of the Fifth and Fourteenth Amendments in deciding identification procedure cases. A minority of the Supreme Court at one time argued that the right to counsel and due process promoted process interests, such as controlling police misconduct during identification procedures. The present Court, however, solidly supports the view that the constitutional requirements governing identification procedures promote only the interest in accurate fact-finding in particular cases—to convict the guilty and to free the innocent. According to the Court, the government violates the right to counsel and due process only if police misconduct in identification procedures leads to an incorrect result.

Identification procedures take place three times:

1. Prior to formal charges.
2. Between the initiation of formal adversary proceedings and the trial.
3. At the trial.

The right to counsel attaches only after adversary proceedings against the accused begin (see Chapter 10), and applies only to identification procedures involving a *confrontation* between the accused and witnesses. Witnesses face accused people in lineups and show-ups, but not in photographic displays. The due process clause, on the other hand, applies to all identification procedures—lineups, show-ups, and photographic displays—whenever they occur. The right to counsel cannot, of course, improve at all the witness's perception and memory of the original event. Furthermore, it is doubtful that the presence of a lawyer can detect most of the unintentional suggestive influences of lineups and show-ups, such as the atmosphere of multiple-choice test without a "none of the above" choice. In other words, a lawyer can guard against the idea that the eyewitness has come to identify the "best choice," not the "right person."

Lineups and show-ups after the initiation of formal proceedings represent the smallest number of identification cases. Most take place before prosecutors decide to charge suspects with crimes; these make up the next largest number of identification cases. The most frequent identification procedure is photographic identification where no right to counsel exists at all because photographic displays are not confrontations, according to the Supreme Court's interpretation of the confrontation clause in the Sixth Amendment. The right to counsel, therefore, applies to the fewest number of cases. In lineups and show-ups before formal proceedings begin and in all photographic displays whenever they take place, the police can proceed without the presence of a defense attorney.

The due process clauses of the Fifth and Fourteenth Amendments provide the basis for insuring correct identification at lineups and show-ups before trial, and photographic identification whenever it occurs. In early decisions, the Supreme Court seemed to indicate that the focus of the due process protection was on deterring police from misconduct in the administration of lineups, show-ups, and photographic arrays. But, by the 1970s, the Court had made it clear that the primary purpose of the due process clauses is to protect against the denial of life, liberty, or property based on evidence of unreliable identification. The Supreme Court has established a two-stage inquiry to determine whether identification procedures violate the due process rights of defendants:[46]

1. Due process requires that courts determine if a procedure was impermissibly or unnecessarily suggestive.
2. Due process requires that, if the procedure was suggestive, the totality of the circumstances show that the suggestive procedure was "so corrupting as to lead to a very substantial likelihood of . . . misidentification."

Hence, if the totality of circumstances indicates that the identification was reliable, it is admissible as evidence, despite its unnecessary or impermissible suggestiveness.[47]

Lineups

Lineups, generally more reliable than either show-ups or photographic displays, depend for their reliability on making sure that enough individuals participate in them and that the participants share similar characteristics. The International Association of Chiefs of Police (IACP) recommends the following standards for establishing lineups that will produce accurate identification:

1. Include five or six participants.
2. Participants ought to be the same gender, the same race, and nearly the same age.
3. Participants should have about the same height, weight, skin and hair color, and body build.
4. All participants should wear similar clothing.

Despite these recommendations, accepted as suitable by most commentators, lineups consist mainly of police officers and inmates of the local jail. Suspects often stand out from the others. This is not usually because of intended suggestiveness by the police, but rather because police officers and jail inmates are ordinarily the only people available. Courts rarely exclude evidence based on lineups that do not meet the requirements of the IACP.

Show-Ups

Show-ups, or identifications of a single person, are considerably more suggestive and substantially less reliable than lineups. The main reason for their unreliability is the suggestiveness of presenting a single person to identify. Despite this, courts usually admit testimony derived from show-ups in several circumstances. For example, if show-ups take place within a few hours of a crime, two reasons justify admitting identifications from them: (1) the need for quickly solving the crime and (2) the desirability of eyewitnesses' fresh, accurate identifications. Furthermore, when witnesses accidentally confront suspects, as in courthouse corridors, courts admit identification based on those meetings. Other cases in which courts have admitted show-up identifications include when they occur in emergencies, such as when witnesses are hospitalized; when suspects are at large, such as when police cruise crime scenes with witnesses; and when external circumstances "prove" the identification accurate, such as when the witness already knows the suspect.[48]

Photographic Identification

The least reliable form of identification is a photograph. A photograph is only two-dimensional, hence, not entirely true to life. The fewer photos used, the less reliable the identifications. Furthermore, photographs in which the suspect stands out are highly suggestive. In addition, police can make remarks—such as, "Is this the one?" or "The suspect is in this group of photos"—that lead to particular conclusions. Despite their recognized unreliability and despite the urging of commentators that courts should exclude them if lineups and show-ups can be substituted, photographs are the most widely used means of identification. Courts accept photographic identification regularly. They have the approval of the United States Supreme Court, which said, "[T]his procedure has been used widely and effectively in criminal law enforcement." Courts generally have rejected defendants' claims of the unreliability of photographic identification, even the least accurate of all—the single-photograph identification.[49]

DNA Testing

DNA (deoxyribonucleic acid) testing can potentially identify or exclude suspects in cases either where suspects have left DNA at the scene of a crime or where victims have left DNA on items traceable to perpetrators. This capacity to use DNA to identify criminal suspects has come about because of rapid advances in molecular biology in the past 15 years. DNA is a long, double-stranded molecule found in everyone's chromosomes. Chromosomes are carried in the nucleus of body cells that have nuclei, including white blood cells, sperm cells, cells surrounding the hair roots, and saliva cells. DNA testing involves comparing the DNA samples in the nuclei of cells found at crime scenes with either similar DNA samples taken from the nuclei of cells of suspects, or DNA samples left by victims on items traceable to perpetrators. The most widely used test is called DNA fingerprinting, or DNA profiling. In this test, long sections of DNA are broken into fragments. Fragments that tend to vary from person to person are measured. If samples from crime scenes have different lengths from those of the suspect, that excludes the suspect. If the sample at the scene and that of the suspect have the same lengths, the samples might have a common source. However, they might also match by chance. To reduce the element of chance, laboratories measure six or more distinct fragments. Two commercial laboratories, Cellmark Diagnostics Corporation and Lifecodes Corporation, and the FBI are the major sites for DNA testing in the United States.[50]

DNA testing quickly entered the legal system, heralded by one court as "the greatest advance in crime fighting technology since fingerprinting." Then a serious scientific controversy broke out over DNA testing. Some challenged the theory of DNA itself. Others challenged the testing methods. Most, however, accepted the soundness of the theory and the testing technology, but attacked the admission of the tests. According to Professor Edward Imwinkelried of the University of California Davis Law School:

> My reading of the proficiency studies of forensic DNA testing laboratories is that the most common cause of error is not the inherent limitations of the technique, but the way in which the specific test was conducted. What the courts don't understand is that no matter how impressive studies are of the validity of a scientific technique, they are worthless as a guarantee of reliability unless you replicate the variables of the experiment.[51]

In 1989, knowledgeable defense counsel obtained the aid of disinterested scientists in order to successfully challenge DNA evidence in *People v. Castro.* Lifecodes, the laboratory that did the testing, violated its own rules and was charged with scientific fraud. In the face of unanimous scientific opinion, including experts hired by the prosecution, Lifecodes admitted that the testing did not amount to a match. The wide coverage the case received in both the popular and scientific press led to a full-scale debate. So heated did the controversy become, according to John Hicks, head of the FBI Laboratory Division, that "[t]his is no longer a search for the truth, it is a war."[52]

The correct identification of criminal suspects by means of DNA testing depends on the answers to the following three questions, and the inferences jurors or other fact finders make about them:

1. Is a reported match between the sample at the scene of the crime and the sample from the suspect a true match?
2. Is the suspect the source of the trace of DNA left at the scene of the crime?
3. Is the suspect the perpetrator of the crime?

A reported match strongly suggests a true match. However, mistakes in DNA processing do occur. Technical errors, such as enzyme failures, salt concentrations, and dirt spots, can produce misleading patterns. Human errors, including contaminations, mislabelings, misrecordings, misrepresentations, case mix-ups, and errors of interpretation also occur. Assuming the match is true, it strongly suggests that the suspect is the source of the trace of DNA left at the scene of the crime. However, the match might be coincidental. The coincidence depends on the frequency of matching traits among the population, usually the ethnic group of the suspect. However, the validity of this reference population depends on the correct ethnic group identification. Source probability errors also occur.

Prosecutors, experts, and jurors often exaggerate the weight given to the match between the trace and the suspect by speaking in terms of odds. According to one trial transcript, for example, after testifying that the blood of a victim matched a sample from a blanket, the following exchange took place:

Q: [Prosecutor]: And in your profession and in the scientific field, when you say match what do you mean?

A: [Expert]: They are identical.

Q: [Prosecutor]: So the blood on the blanket . . . Can you say it came from [the victim]?

A: [Expert]: With great certainty I can say that those two DNA samples match and they are identical. And with population statistics we can derive a probability of it being anyone other than the victim.

Q: [Prosecutor]: What is the probability in this case?

A: [Expert]: In this case that probability is that it is a one in 7 million chance that it could be anyone other than that victim.

According to Professor Jonathan Koehler at the University of Texas at Austin, the expert's claim that population statistics can determine the probability that the victim was not the source is false.[53]

Finally, evidence that the suspect is the source of the trace is also evidence that the suspect committed the crime. But not necessarily; the suspect could have left the trace innocently, either before or after the commission of the crime. The use of the match to prove guilt depends on an inference, perhaps a fair inference but not automatic or always correct. Whatever the problems and criticisms of the use of DNA testing to identify suspects and link them to crimes, the impact of DNA (and other scientific evidence, too, for that matter) is substantial. According to one researcher, about 25 percent of jurors said they would have voted not guilty if it were not for the introduction of scientific evidence. In another survey, 75 percent of judges and lawyers throughout the United States said they believed judges accorded scientific evidence more credibility than other kinds of evidence, and 70 percent said they believed jurors did the same.[54]

The Exclusionary Rule

Everyone knows what happens, or is *supposed* to happen, when private persons break the law: they are punished—or, at least, they *should* be punished. Most people are not so clear about what happens, or should happen, when government officials break the law. Mechanisms to enforce the constitutional standards and values that underpin the law of criminal procedure range across a broad spectrum. They include three types of actions:

1. *Legal and administrative actions against individual officers,* including criminal prosecution, civil lawsuits, and disciplinary action within the officer's agency or department. (See Chapter 7.)

2. *Civil actions against the heads of criminal justice agencies, the agencies themselves, or the government units responsible for the agencies,* including suits for damages and court orders (injunctions) prohibiting specific conduct. (See Chapter 7.)

3. *Process remedies that affect the outcome of criminal cases,* including dismissing cases, reversing convictions, and excluding or suppressing evidence.[55]

Chapter 7 examines the remedies of criminal prosecution and suing the police. This chapter examines the major process remedy: excluding illegally obtained evidence from judicial proceedings. For now, it is enough to note that these three types of remedies are not mutually exclusive; injured parties need not choose among them. At least in theory, they are all available in the same case. For example, the state might prosecute a police officer for breaking and entering to illegally search a house. The individual whose house the officer illegally entered can sue the officer for the damages incurred in the illegal breaking and entering. The officer's department can suspend the officer for the wrongful act. Finally, a court trying the defendant whose house was the object of the illegal entry may apply the **exclusionary rule** that excludes the evidence obtained from the illegal search and, in some instances, may dismiss the case against the victim of government lawbreaking—even if the defendant is clearly guilty! This rarely happens in practice, but it could; the law does not require that injured parties choose one action above others.

Throwing out "good" evidence that might convict "bad" criminals is a highly controversial consequence of illegal government action. But that is what the exclusionary rule does: It forbids the government to use confessions obtained in violation of the right against self-incrimination guaranteed by the Fifth Amendment, and it prohibits the use of physical evidence gathered through unreasonable searches and seizures prohibited by the Fourth Amendment. The rule also excludes evidence obtained in violation of the Sixth Amendment right to counsel, and eyewitness identifications obtained by procedures so suggestive that their unreliability violates the due process clauses of the Fifth and Fourteenth Amendments. Occasionally, the Supreme Court has also extended the rule to include stationary violations, such as those involving federal wiretapping legislation.[56]

The exclusionary rule excludes *good evidence* because of *bad practices.* It puts the search for truth second to the means police use to obtain the truth. In other words, the exclusionary rule stands for the proposition that the ends (finding the truth) do not justify the means (constitutional procedures) in criminal law enforcement. In our constitutional democracy we support criminal law enforcement, but not at any price. Violating proper procedures is simply too high a price to pay for obtaining convictions. If the government does not obey the law, the public loses confidence in the law. That lost confidence, in turn, breeds contempt for and hostility to the law. In the end, both law and order suffer.[57]

In *Olmstead v. United States,* Justice Oliver Wendell Holmes, recognizing the dilemma of having to exclude reliable evidence that could convict guilty defendants, wrote the following defense of the exclusionary rule:

> [W]e must consider two objects of desire, both of which we cannot have, and make up our minds which to choose. It is desirable that criminals should be detected, and to that end that all available evidence should be used. It also is desirable that the Government should not itself foster and pay for other crimes, when they are the means by which the evidence is to be obtained. . . . For my part, I think it is less evil that some criminals should escape than that the Government should play an ignoble part.[58]

Social Costs and Deterrent Effects

By the 1980s, a majority of the Supreme Court applied a deterrence rationale for exclusion of evidence. The Court weighed the social cost of letting criminals go free by excluding evidence of guilt against the possible deterrent effect such exclusion has on law enforcement officers. The deterrence rationale definitely limited the number of cases in which evidence was excluded. If the social costs outweighed the deterrent effect (which in virtually every case the Court found that it did), then the evidence was admissible.[59]

The questions of the social cost incurred by lost convictions and of the effectiveness of the exclusionary rule in deterring unconstitutional police behavior have generated heated debate among scholars. A majority of the Supreme Court since the 1970s has routinely concluded that the social cost outweighs the deterrent effect of the rule. However, empirical research does not support that conclusion. Even the early research was not conclusive, some of it not even valid.

In an extensive study of the exclusionary rule among Chicago narcotics officers, Myron W. Orfield, Jr., reported several important findings. Chicago narcotics officers are *always* in court when judges suppress the evidence they have obtained. They *always* understand why the court excluded the evidence. This experience has led them to seek search warrants more often and to be more careful when they search for and seize evidence without warrants. Prior to the decision in *Mapp v. Ohio* (which applied the exclusionary rule to state and local law enforcement), police officers rarely obtained warrants. By 1987, in the narcotics division of the Chicago Police Department at least, "virtually all preplanned searches that are not 'buy busts' or airport-related searches occur with warrants."[60]

Orfield's study also demonstrated that the exclusionary rule "punishes" officers. The Chicago Police Department initiated an officer rating system in response to the exclusionary rule making the loss of evidence due to exclusion a personal liability to police officers. Suppression of evidence can negatively affect both assignments and promotions. Orfield also found that some police officers still lie in court to avoid the suppression of illegally seized evidence. This in-court police perjury limits the effectiveness of the exclusionary rule. However, strong responses to police perjury by both the police department and the courts have reduced the impact of perjury on the practical application of the exclusionary rule. Finally, Orfield reported that every officer believed the courts should retain the rule. They all saw the rule as a positive development with just about the right amount of a deterrent element, although they would like a "good faith" exception to warrantless searches. They believed that a tort remedy (discussed in Chapter 7) would "overdeter" the police in their search for and seizure of evidence.[61]

The social costs of letting guilty criminals go free by excluding credible evidence that would convict them are not nearly so high as is commonly thought. Researchers have found that the exclusionary rule affects only a minuscule number of cases in an extremely narrow range of crimes. The rule does not affect prosecutions of murder, rape, robbery, and assault; primarily, illegal drug dealing, gambling, and pornography prosecutions suffer from it. In California, for example, the rule is overwhelmingly connected to drug offenses, not violent felonies. How many cases do courts dismiss because of the exclusionary rule? Available evidence suggests only a few. In California, illegally seized evidence led to dismissals in a mere 0.8 percent of all criminal cases and only 4.8 percent of felonies. Less than one-tenth of one percent of all criminal cases will be dismissed because the police seized evidence illegally. The rule leaves violent crimes and serious property offenses virtually unaffected.[62]

The American Bar Association gathered information from police officers, prosecutors, defense attorneys, and judges in representative urban and geographically distributed locations regarding problems they face in their work. They also conducted a telephone survey of 800 police administrators, prosecutors, judges, and defense attorneys based on a stratified random

Figure 6.1

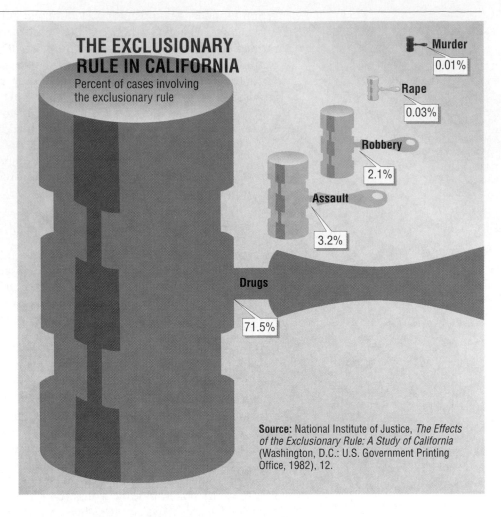

THE EXCLUSIONARY RULE IN CALIFORNIA
Percent of cases involving the exclusionary rule

Murder 0.01%

Rape 0.03%

Robbery 2.1%

Assault 3.2%

Drugs 71.5%

Source: National Institute of Justice, *The Effects of the Exclusionary Rule: A Study of California* (Washington, D.C.: U.S. Government Printing Office, 1982), 12.

selection technique to obtain a representative group of small to large cities and counties. The results showed:

> Although the prosecutors and police . . . interviewed believe that a few Fourth Amendment restrictions are ambiguous or complex, and thus, present training and field application problems, they do not believe that Fourth Amendment rights or their protection via the exclusionary rule are a significant impediment to crime control. . . . A number of . . . police officials also report that the demands of the exclusionary rule and resulting police training on Fourth Amendment requirements have promoted professionalism in police departments across the country. Thus, the exclusionary rule appears to be providing a significant safeguard of Fourth Amendment protections for individuals at modest cost in terms of either crime control or effective prosecution. This "cost," for the most part, reflects the values expressed in the Fourth Amendment itself, for the Amendment manifests a preference for privacy and freedom over that level of law enforcement efficiency which could be achieved if police were permitted to arrest and search without probable cause or judicial authorization.[63]

According to Thomas Y. Davies, who studied the exclusionary rule in California, prosecutors practically never reject cases involving *violent* crimes because of the exclusionary rule. He found that prosecutors rejected for prosecution 0.06 percent of homicide, 0.09 percent of forcible rape, and 0.13 percent of assault cases because of illegal searches and seizures. They rejected less than one-half of one percent of theft cases and only 0.19 percent of burglary cases. The largest number of cases rejected for prosecution due to illegal searches and seizures involved the possession of small amounts of drugs. (see Figure 6.1) Other studies reached similar results, that is, that the exclusionary rule affects only a small portion of cases, and of that small number, most are not crimes against persons. Furthermore, all cases rejected or lost because of illegally obtained evidence are not lost because of the exclusionary rule. Peter F. Nardulli, for example, found that in some cases of drug possession, the police were not interested in successful prosecution but rather in getting contraband off the street.[64]

The Exclusionary Rule on Balance

In view of its limited application, restrictions on the exclusionary rule hardly seem adequate cause either for critics to rejoice or supporters to lament. Perhaps its strongest claim as a policy instrument is that it helps to ensure judicial integrity. Courts, by excluding illegally obtained evidence, keep the criminal justice system pure. The exclusionary rule exacts the price of setting a few criminals free in order to maintain the rule of law. It sacrifices the correct result in an individual case for the general interest in constitutional government.[65]

Summary

The police take a variety of actions to fulfill their missions of providing services, maintaining order, and enforcing the criminal law. Rarely do most of these, particularly actions taken to provide services and many to maintain order, evoke comment. However, when the police initiate certain actions mainly to enforce the criminal law but sometimes to maintain order, it is quite a different story. These frequently unwanted invasions of liberty and privacy provoke controversy. Most actions taken to enforce the criminal law arise out of the need for information. These information-seeking actions— including surveillance, stop and frisk, arrest, searches, interrogation, and identification procedures—require an objective basis in fact. Mere suspicion will not suffice. The greater the government invasion, the more facts the law requires to back it up. The objective basis requirement limits, but does not remove, police discretion in enforcing the criminal law.

The Constitution balances the government need for enough power to enforce the law with the privacy and liberty of innocent, suspected, and guilty individuals. These limits fall mainly under the Fourth, Fifth, Sixth, and Fourteenth amendments to the U.S. Constitution and similar provisions in state constitutions. The key terms in understanding the Fourth Amendment are "unreasonable," "searches," and "seizures"; to understanding the Fifth Amendment, "compelled," "criminal," and "case"; to understanding the Sixth Amendment, "confronted with witnesses," and "criminal prosecution"; to understanding the Fourteenth Amendment, "state" and "deprivations of life, liberty, and property." The history of the law of criminal procedure shows the gradual application of formal rules to the discretionary judgments of officials in proceedings before and after criminal trials. During the 1960s, the Supreme Court tried to balance discretionary judgments with formal rules in the day-to-day contacts between police officers and individuals both in police stations and on the street.

The Fourth Amendment prohibits only "unreasonable seizures." Whether a contact between an individual and a police officer is a Fourth Amendment seizure depends on its intensity, duration, and location. Whether an arrest is reasonable depends on both the objective basis to back it up, namely, probable cause, and the manner in which the police execute the arrest. Executing arrests raises problems mainly in entering homes and in the use of force before, during, and following arrests. The Supreme Court has held that officers must have arrest warrants in order to enter private homes to arrest suspects. Before, during, and after arrests, the Supreme Court has ruled that officers may use only reasonable force when they deal with suspects. According to the Court, deadly force is a Fourth Amendment seizure, and it has decided that police pursuits, under some circumstances, are also seizures. Researchers have demonstrated that departments with effective deadly force rules experience sharp decreases in citizen and officer deaths. High-speed chases endanger, injure, and kill police officers, fleeing motorists, and innocent citizens. Research findings have led some policymakers to recommend continued use of pursuits, and others to recommend restrictions on their use.

Searches fall within two broad categories: searches with warrants and searches without warrants. The Supreme Court has expressed a strong preference for searches based on warrants. In order to obtain a search warrant, officers must demonstrate to a judicial officer both that they have probable cause and that they can specifically identify the persons and places they want to search and the persons and things they want to seize. In practice, most searches fall within a substantial list of exceptions to the warrant requirement. The major exceptions include searches incident to lawful arrests, consent searches, vehicle searches, and plain-view searches. The Supreme Court has adopted a balancing test to determine whether searches without warrants are reasonable. This approach to reasonableness balances the needs of the government to enforce the criminal law with the liberty and privacy interests of individuals. To balance these needs, courts look at the degree of intrusion, the need for the intrusion, the facts supporting it, and the privacy of individuals subjected to the search. If the government need outweighs the invasion against individuals, the search is reasonable.

Criminal investigations can require police interrogation of suspects. Although no empirical studies have demonstrated the need for interrogation, the belief in the need for them is strong. According to the Fifth Amendment, the government cannot compel a person to confess or otherwise make incriminating statements. The principal constitutional questions surrounding police interrogation include: When does the right go into effect? What is the meaning of interrogation? How can the right be waived? When may officers question citizens without warning them of their right against self-incrimination? The famous case of *Miranda v. Arizona* prohibits custodial interrogation until police officers warn suspects of their right to remain silent. Police need not warn citizens they stop on the street and question briefly, nor those who voluntarily come to the police station. Furthermore, when public safety demands it, police need not warn citizens before questioning them.

The practice of stopping and questioning suspicious people on the streets and in other public places is ancient. Until the 1960s, this practice was left wholly to police discretion. In 1968, in the leading case of *Terry v. Ohio*, the Supreme Court held that the Fourth Amendment protects people on the street from unreasonable stops and frisks, holding that stops are Fourth Amendment seizures and frisks are Fourth Amendment searches. Applying the formal requirements of the Fourth Amendment to these contacts between the police and individuals, however, still allowed the police considerable leeway to exercise discretionary judgment. The Court ruled that since stops and frisks entail less invasions against individual liberty and property than full-blown arrests and full-body searches, officers may briefly detain people, and when necessary pat them down for weapons, with fewer facts than the probable cause required for full searches and arrests.

It is much easier to determine that a crime has been committed than it is to identify the perpetrator. This is especially true when the perpetrator is a stranger to the victim or to other witnesses. Eyewitness identification is notoriously unreliable. In order to reduce the chances of misidentification, the Supreme Court has imposed some restrictions on the use of eyewitness identification. The Court has ruled that after indictment, suspects have a right to a lawyer at any identification procedure in which the defendant faces a witness, such as in lineups and show-ups. Furthermore, the Court has also ruled that identification procedures that raise a substantial likelihood of misidentification violate due process. DNA testing—the use of genetic tracing—was hailed as an effective scientific means of identification that could overcome the shortcomings of traditional lineups, show-ups, and photo arrays. However, the limits of the accuracy and predictability of DNA testing has caused some retreat from the initial enthusiasm for it.

Both direct and indirect remedies exist to enforce constitutional standards of law enforcement. The government can prosecute police officers who commit crimes in order to enforce the criminal law. Individuals can sue officers, their departments, municipalities, or other governmental units for violations of constitutional rights. Police departments can discipline officers by warnings, transfers of duty, fines, and suspensions. The exclusionary rule prohibits the use of evidence in judicial proceedings, however reliable it is, if police officers violated the Constitution to obtain the evidence. These violations occur when officers obtain evidence by means of either illegal searches and seizures or coerced confessions. The exclusionary rule, despite the publicity attending it, does not carry the high social costs usually attributed to it. The rule rarely affects the outcome of most cases, especially murder, rape, robbery, burglary, and other felonies. Furthermore, some evidence suggests that the rule deters police misconduct.

Review Questions

1. Identify the range of activities that police use to accomplish their missions. Explain why some of these actions arouse little controversy and others arouse a great deal.

2. Identify and explain the two myths concerning the police and criminal law enforcement. What is the reality?

3. What is the importance of information in criminal law enforcement?

4. What is the day-to-day reality of the police bringing criminal cases to prosecutors and the courts? What explains this reality?

5. Practically speaking, when are the constitutional rights of suspects important in police work?

6. Explain the importance of discretion in criminal law enforcement.

7. Define and explain the importance of the objective basis requirement in criminal law enforcement.

8. Identify the four main constitutional provisions governing criminal law enforcement, the key words and phrases that require interpretation, and who interprets these terms.

9. Explain the importance of formalization in the history of criminal procedure. Describe effects this history has had on police discretion in criminal law enforcement.

10. To what three questions does the Fourth Amendment require answers?

11. Identify and explain the three elements that determine whether a police encounter with an individual is a Fourth Amendment arrest.

12. Identify and explain the two elements that determine the reasonableness of a Fourth Amendment arrest.

13. Identify, define, and describe the types of information that determine the objective basis for arrest.

14. What are the conditions under which police officers can enter homes to arrest suspects without violating the Fourth Amendment?

15. When can the police use deadly force without violating the Fourth Amendment?

16. Briefly describe the history of the right against unreasonable searches and the exercise of the power to search.

17. Under what circumstances are searches with warrants reasonable Fourth Amendment searches?

18. What is the general test that the Supreme Court has adopted to determine the reasonableness of searches without warrants?

19. What kinds of searches are the most common? *after arrest*

20. Identify the major types of searches without warrants and the purpose of these searches. Explain under what circumstances each is reasonable.

21. Define stops and frisks, briefly describe their history, and explain their purpose in relationship to the Fourth Amendment.

22. Describe the empirical, constitutional, and ethical issues in police interrogation.

23. State the *Miranda* warnings and the circumstances under which they are required.

24. In addition to the warnings requirement, what other important rulings did the Supreme Court make in *Miranda v. Arizona?*

25. Practically speaking, what effect did the *Miranda* decision have on the number of confessions?

26. Explain the test of the voluntariness of confessions.

27. Identify and briefly describe the major circumstances courts consider in determining the voluntariness of confessions.

28. Which is easier, proving that a crime was committed or proving who committed it? Explain your answer.

29. Explain the dangers of misidentification.

30. Identify and define the three principal eyewitness identification procedures. Rank them from most to least reliable and from most to least widely used.

31. How has the Supreme Court sought to insure the reliability of eyewitness testimony?

32. What is a DNA profile? Why did courts initially adopt DNA testing with enthusiasm? What has cooled their enthusiasm?

33. What three types of actions are available to remedy constitutional violations by the police?

34. Describe the controversial consequence of the exclusionary rule.

35. Explain how the exclusionary rule stands for the proposition that the ends do not justify the means in criminal law enforcement.

36. How did Justice Holmes explain how to resolve the dilemma of having to exclude reliable evidence that could convict guilty defendants?

37. What is the rationale that the Supreme Court has adopted to justify the exclusionary rule?

38. What have empirical studies revealed about the social costs and the deterrent effects of the exclusionary rule?

Notes

1. Lawrence Sherman, "Legal Issues in Law Enforcement," in *The Future of Policing*, Alvin W. Cohn, ed. (Beverly Hills, Calif.: Sage, 1978), 119–49.

2. This is Carl B. Klockars's paraphrase of Bittner's position in "The Rhetoric of Community Policing," *Thinking About Police*, 2d ed., Carl B. Klockars and Stephen D. Mastrofski, eds. (New York: McGraw-Hill, 1991), 532.

3. W. F. Walsh, "Patrol Officer Arrest Rates: A Study of the Social Organization of Police Work," *Justice Quarterly* 2 (1986) :271–290; Donald J. Black, *Manners and Customs of Police* (New York: Academic Press, 1980); both cited in Klockars, "The Rhetoric of Community Policing," 532.

4. Herbert Packer, *The Limits of the Criminal Sanction* (Palo Alto: Stanford University Press, 1968), chaps. 8–12.

5. American Law Institute, *A Model Code of Pre-Arraignment Procedure, Proposed Official Draft, Complete Text and Commentary* (Philadelphia: American Law Institute, 1975), 13–14.

6. Floyd Feeney et al., *Arrests Without Conviction: How Often They Occur and Why* (Washington, D.C.: National Institute of Justice, 1983); Brian Forst et al., "Prosecution and Sentencing," in *Crime and Public Policy*, James Q. Wilson, ed. (New Brunswick, N.J.: Transaction Books, 1983), 165–68; Vera Institute of Justice, *Felony Arrests* (New York: Longman, 1981); Donald J. Black, *The Manners and Customs of the Police* (New York: Academic Press, 1980), chap. 4; *The Prosecution of Felony Arrests 1980* (Washington, D.C.: Bureau of Justice Statistics, 1985), 7–17.

7. *United States v. Watson*, 423 U.S. 411 (1976); *Payton v. New York*, 445 U.S. 573 (1980).

8. *People v. Washington*, 236 Cal.Rptr. 840 (1987).

9. Abraham N. Tennenbaum, "The Influence of the *Garner* Decision on Police Use of Deadly Force," *Journal of Criminal Law and Criminology* 85 (1994): 241.

10. *Justice v. Dennis*, 834 F.2d 380 (4th Cir. 1987).

11. William J. Cuddihy, "The Fourth Amendment: Origins and Original Meaning, 602–1791" (unpublished dissertation, Claremont Graduate School, 1990), xc–xcvi.

12. John Wesley Hall, Jr., *Search and Seizure*, 2d ed. (Deerfield, Ill.: Clark, Boardman, 1991), ix.

13. Maria Goodavage, "But '180 Degrees' Wrong," *USA Today*, 1 December 1992.

14. "Getting Around the Fourth Amendment," *Thinking About Police*, 434–35.

15. Quoted in "Getting Around the Fourth Amendment," 436.

16. Quoted in "Getting Around the Fourth Amendment."

17. *Chimel v. California*, 395 U.S. 752 (1969).

18. *Schneckcloth v. Bustamonte*, 412 U.S. 218 (1973).

19. *California v. Carney*, 471 U.S. 386 (1985).

20. Joel Samaha, *Criminal Procedure*, 3d ed. (St. Paul: West Publishing Company, 1996), 75–78 and cases cited therein.

21. Loren G. Stern, "Stop and Frisk: An Historical Answer to a Modern Problem," *Journal of Criminal Law, Criminology, and Police Science* 58 (1967): 532; Frank Remington, "The Law Relating to 'On the Street' Detention, Questioning, and Frisking of Suspected Persons and Police Arrest Privileges in General," *Journal of Criminal Law, Criminology, and Police Science* 50 (1960): 390.

22. John E. Boydstun, *San Diego Field Interrogations: Final Report* (Washington, D.C.: Police Foundation, 1975), 45; *Terry v. Ohio*, 392 U.S. 1 (1967).

23. *Terry v. Ohio*, 392 U.S. 1 (1967).

24. American Law Institute, *Model Code of Pre-Arraignment Procedure*, 273–76; Boydstun, *San Diego Field Interrogations*, 40–64.

25. *New York Times*, 16 October 1989.

26. Samaha, *Criminal Procedure*, 293–296.

27. Ibid.

28. *Miranda v. Arizona*, 384 U.S. 436 (1966).

29. Ibid.

30. *State v. Anderson*, 332 So.2d 452 (La.1976); *Oregon v. Mathiason*, 429 U.S. 492 (1977); *United States ex rel Hines v. LaVallee*, 521 F.2d 1109 (2d.Cir. 1975).

31. United States Senate, Committee on the Judiciary, Subcommittee on Criminal Laws and Procedures, *Hearings, Controlling Crime Through More Effective Law Enforcement* (Washington, D.C.: U.S. Government Printing Office, 1967).

32. Wayne R. LaFave and Jerold Israel, *Criminal Procedure*, vol. 1 (St. Paul: West Publishing Company, 1984), 484.

33. *Colorado v. Connelly*, 479 U.S. 157 (1986).

34. Donald A. Dripps, "Foreword: Against Police Interrogation—And the Privilege Against Self-Incrimination," *Journal of Criminal Law and Criminology* 78 (1988): 701.

35. Setsuo Miyazawa, *Policing in Japan: A Study on Making Crime* (Albany: State University of Albany, 1992), 44–46.

36. "Pagano Case Points Finger at Lineups," *National Law Journal* (September 10, 1979): 1.

37. "Notes: Did Your Eyes Deceive You? Expert Psychological Testimony on the Unreliability of Eyewitness Identification," *Stanford Law Review* 29 (1977): 970.

38. Gary L. Wells, "Eyewitness Behavior," *Law and Human Behavior* 4 (1980): 238.

39. Quoted in Martin Yant, *Presumed Guilty: When Innocent People Are Wrongly Convicted* (Buffalo: Prometheus Books, 1991), 99.

40. Samuel R. Gross, "Loss of Innocence: Eyewitness Identification and Proof of Guilt," *Journal of Legal Studies* 16 (1987): 398–99; "Notes: Did Your Eyes Deceive You?" 982–83.

41. "Notes: Did Your Eyes Deceive You?" 982.

42. Cited in Yant, *Presumed Guilty,* 100.

43. Quoted in Yant, *Presumed Guilty.*

44. "Notes: Did Your Eyes Deceive You?": 969; David Bazelon, "Eyewitness News," *Psychology Today* (March 1980): 102–4; LaFave and Israel, *Criminal Procedure,* 1:551–53; Gross, "Loss of Innocence," 401.

45. *Basoff v. State,* 208 Md. 643, 119 A.2d 917 (1956).

46. *Manson v. Braithwaite,* 432 U.S. 98, 97 S.Ct. 2243, 53 L.Ed.2d 140 (1977).

47. *Rodriguez v. Young,* 906 F.2d 1153 (7th Cir.1990).

48. LaFave and Israel, *Criminal Procedure,* 590–91.

49. Ibid., 588–60.

50. Kenneth R. Kreiling, "DNA Technology in Forensic Science," *Jurimetrics Journal* 33 (1993): 449; William C. Thompson, "Evaluating the Admissibility of New Genetic Identification Tests: Lessons from the 'DNA War,' " *Journal of Criminal Law and Criminology* 84 (1993): 26–27.

51. Quoted in Stephanie Goldberg, "A New Day for DNA?" *American Bar Association Journal* 78 (April 1992): 85.

52. *People v. Wesley,* 140 Misc.2d 306, 533 N.Y.S.2d 643 (Cty.Ct.1988), affirmed 183 A.D.2d 75, 589 N.Y.S.2d 197 (1992) ("greatest advance" and "war" quoted in Thompson, "Evaluating the Admissibility," 23; *People v. Castro,* 144 Misc.2d 956, 545 N.Y.S.2d 985 (Bronx Cty. 1989); Kreiling, "DNA Technology in Forensic Science," 449.

53. Quoted in Jonathan J. Koehler, "Error and Exaggeration in the Presentation of DNA Evidence at Trial," *Jurimetrics Journal* 34 (1994): 21.

54. Koehler, "Error and Exaggeration"; surveys of jurors, judges, and lawyers reported in Paul C. Giannelli, "Criminal Discovery, Scientific Evidence, and DNA," *Vanderbilt Law Review* 44 (1991): 794.

55. Jon O. Newman, "Suing the Lawbreakers: Proposals to Strengthen the Section 1983 Damage Remedy for Law Enforcers' Misconduct," *Yale Law Journal* 87 (1978): 447–67.

56. *Mapp v. Ohio,* 367 U.S. 643, 81 S.Ct. 1684, 6 L.Ed.2d 1081 (1961); *Miranda v. Arizona,* 384 U.S. 436, 86 S.Ct. 1602, 16 L.Ed.2d 694 (1966); *United States v. Wade,* 388 U.S. 218, 87 S.Ct. 1926, 18 L.Ed.2d 1149 (1967); *Gelbard v. United States,* 408 U.S. 41, 92 S.Ct. 2357, 33 L.Ed.2d 179 (1972); *United States v. Caceres,* 440 U.S. 741, 99 S.Ct. 1465, 59 L.Ed.2d 733 (1979).

57. William A. Schroeder, "Deterring Fourth Amendment Violations," *Georgetown Law Journal* 69 (1981): 1361, 1378–86.

58. 277 U.S. 438, 470, 48 S.Ct. 564, 575, 72 L.Ed.2d 944 (1928).

59. Schroeder, "Deterring Fourth Amendment Violations."

60. Myron W. Orfield, Jr., "The Exclusionary Rule and Deterrence: An Empirical Study of Chicago Narcotics Officers," *University of Chicago Law Review* 54 (1987): 1017–18, 1029.

61. Ibid., 1027–28.

62. National Institute of Justice, *The Effects of the Exclusionary Rule: A Study of California* (Washington, D.C.: U.S. Government Printing Office, 1982), 12.

63. American Bar Association, *Criminal Justice in Crisis* (Chicago: American Bar Association, 1988), 11.

64. Thomas Y. Davies, "A Hard Look at What We Know (and Still Need to Learn) About the 'Social Costs' of the Exclusionary Rule: The NIJ Study and Other Studies of 'Lost' Arrests," *American Bar Foundation Research Journal* (1983): 640; Peter F. Nardulli, "The Societal Costs of the Exclusionary Rule Revisited," *University of Illinois Law Review* (1987): 235.

65. Yale Kamisar, "Does (Did) (Should) the Exclusionary Rule Rest on a 'Principled Basis' Rather Than on 'Empirical Propositions?' " *Creighton Law Review* 16 (1983): 565.

Issues in Police and

Policing

CHAPTER MAIN POINTS

1. A change in police culture has focused on the use and control of force.

2. The police are one of the strongest vocational subcultures in United States society.

3. Coercion and its discretionary use are fundamental to the police.

4. Since the 1960s, efforts have increased to recruit police officers who demographically reflect the people in the communities they represent.

5. Recognition of the complexity of the police mission and the difficulties of discretionary decision making led to dissatisfaction with the traditional requirements of physical strength and the "manly virtues" as sufficient qualifications for police officers.

6. Emphasis has been placed on the importance of education in making good police officers, but the empirical research has produced mixed results as to the effectiveness of education.

7. The transition from civilian to police officer is lengthy, stressful, and fundamental.

8. Recruits learn many formal rules and the principle of obedience to superiors, as well as the informal reality of how to get around both, in the police academy.

9. In traditional field training, rookies learn from older officers "to forget everything they learned in the academy."

10. Some departments go beyond traditional training to broaden the perspectives of rookies.

11. The barriers of gender, ethnic origin, and race have weakened somewhat in the recruitment of police officers.

12. Empirical research has demonstrated that women police officers perform about the same as men and that their attitudes do not differ substantially from those of male officers.

13. Police stress affects not only job performance but also family life and physical and mental health outside of work.

14. Police misconduct covers a broad spectrum of behavior.

15. Explanations for police misconduct range from inherently bad individuals to the effects of socialization as police officers.

16. The fundamental problem of the abuse of force arises out of the defining characteristic of police work—the need for the legitimate use of force.

17. Force, particularly deadly force, is infrequently used in practice.

18. The effectiveness of rules in reducing the abuse of force depends not only on their content but also on the commitment of police management to enforcing the rules.

19. High-speed chases, a form of deadly force, endanger not only officers and the people they chase but also innocent bystanders.

20. Research has revealed racial and class disparities in the use of force.

21. Police corruption ranges across a wide spectrum of behavior.

22. Criminal prosecutions for police misconduct are rare.

23. Civil lawsuits for police misconduct receive a lot of attention, but in fact represent a small number of instances of misbehavior.

24. Internal review procedures are by far the most common mechanism for holding police officers accountable for their misconduct.

25. External review of police misconduct by civilians is common in the largest cities in the country.

26. The effectiveness of external and internal review is difficult to measure, but both sustain about the same small proportion of complaints filed against police officers.

27. Police chiefs have the sole authority to discipline police officers under both internal and external review procedures.

W e did things differently then. Things that we've outgrown," said a Savannah, Georgia, police sergeant, explaining why police officers no longer shoot people as often as they did in the 1970s. "Back then, we used to routinely point our guns at unarmed people." By the early 1980s, such practices were almost unheard of in his department, the sergeant said. According to police researcher Lawrence W. Sherman, this sergeant's remark captures a fundamental shift in policing in the United States:

> This change in police culture is nothing short of extraordinary. For generations big-city police departments maintained a culture of policing that placed little restriction on firearms use. The long-term persistence of that pattern is not surprising, since corporate cultures are easier to maintain than to change. Some academic critics in the 1970's announced what they concluded was the failure of a broad social movement for police reform over a half century. To the contrary . . . the essence of policing, the distribution of coercion in the community, [has changed dramatically].[1]

This shift stems from a variety of causes. Some of it has to do with the discovery by criminal justice researchers that police work is not formal and legalistic but informal and discretionary, that it involves maintaining order and providing service more than enforcing the criminal law. Some of the change is the legacy of research showing the limits of first preventive police operations and then of the more aggressive crime-attack strategies. A great deal has to do with the attraction to problem-oriented and community policing, and the hope that these approaches can not only help the police keep pace with a rapidly increasing technocratic society, but also stem the tide of violence, drugs, and other problems of the 1990s and beyond.

The change in police culture that Sherman notes, and the success in meeting the challenges of policing in the future, also depend on the recruitment, training, and socialization of police officers, the subjects of this chapter. Successful recruitment, training, and socialization all add to the effectiveness and appropriateness of police strategies (Chapter 5) to carry out police missions (Chapter 4), and improve the chances that the police will act according to the law (Chapter 6). Moreover, they can reduce the chances of police misconduct associated with abuse of power.

No form of recruitment, no amount of training, and no promotion policies can entirely eliminate police misconduct. Therefore, review of the policies and practices discussed in this chapter is essential. This review may occur inside law enforcement agencies or outside. Outside review may occur in the courts or by specially created review boards. Review can also consist of some mixture of external and internal review. Creating and operating review mechanisms that are both fair to and enjoy the confidence of everyone concerned is difficult, if not impossible. That is because "everyone concerned" includes individual police officers, people who believe they are the objects of police misconduct, police unions, police management, and all the racial, ethnic, and other groups that make up the communities the police serve. All these groups hold strong, often highly emotional and opposing views about not only the definition of police misconduct but also who should define misconduct, what the consequences of misconduct should be, and who should impose these consequences.

Police Working Personality

Every social group develops customs, rules, and interpretations of the world around them. Some of these rules are written, but most are not. Unwritten rules or customs govern much of what any group says, does, or thinks about its work and the rest of members' lives. Where is it written, for example, that you don't walk up to strangers and ask how much money they make or how their sex life is going? Nowhere, of course. But most people living in "respectable" American society, a group of sorts, know they should not ask strangers either question. Members of occupations, like all groups, develop their own special set of informal rules. The police are no different in this respect. According to James Ahern, the late police chief of New Haven, Connecticut:

> The day the new recruit walks through the doors of the police academy he leaves society behind to enter a profession that does more than give him a job, it defines who he is. For all the years he remains, he will always be a cop.[2]

The police are "one of the strongest vocational subcultures" in America, a subculture pervaded by norms of unity, loyalty, perceptions of danger, and suspicion. Observation of this subculture has led to a consensus among social scientists that there is a distinct **police working personality**. Early studies found the police to be authoritarian, suspicious, racist, hostile, insecure, conservative, and cynical. Later research has found the subject more complex. Not all officers have the same style. William Muir, in his *Streetcorner Politicians*, applied the famous sociologist Max Weber's attributes of *passion* and *perspective* to the working personality of police officers. Passion is the capacity to recognize the need to use force and the willingness to use it. Police officers with passion can deal with situations in which they must coerce others in order to achieve just ends. Perspective is the capacity of officers to understand human suffering and the limits on dealing with that suffering. These officers have the "tragic perspective." They know that issues are not either absolutely right or wrong, or good or bad; life is more complex to them.[3]

In cross-tabulating the attitudes of 28 patrol officers in a California city, Muir found four ideal types of the police working personality:

1. *Professionals* possess both passion and perspective. They use force when necessary, but they also understand the suffering of others. They are the "good cops" who know they cannot solve all the problems they encounter, but they try to provide fair, humane law enforcement.
2. *Enforcers* have passion, that is, they have no reservation about using force. But they lack perspective; they do not understand the complexity of human nature. They like to lock people up. They are the cynical, authoritarian type that early research stressed.
3. *Reciprocators* have perspective, but they hesitate or cannot use force when necessary. They are lenient; they want to help, not hurt. They are social workers.
4. *Avoiders* lack perspective and passion. They suffer from low skills and low self-esteem. They avoid the responsibility of providing quality service of any kind.[4]

John Broderick, after conducting his own survey of police attitudes and surveying all the major research concluded that, although they vary in detail,

These officers are part of "one of the strongest vocational subcultures" in the United States.

most studies of the working personality of the police agree with Muir's findings, no matter what size department or in what part of the country the department operates.[5]

J. Snipes and Stephen Mastrofski found the police working personality still more complex. It does not depend solely on attitudes of individual police officers, but upon the situations in which they find themselves. For example, a police officer may readily use force in a robbery, but not in a shoplifting case. Officers in crime-attack situations may rely on force, but not when answering a call about a loud party. Police officers may rely on force in some neighborhoods and not in others, or with some kinds of people and not others. In other words, police style is not wholly a matter of personality; it depends on the type, manner, and circumstances of encounters between officers and private individuals. Stephen M. Cox and James Frank distributed hypothetical situations to patrol officers. One proactive and one reactive scenario took place in a high-crime area of an inner city, followed by one proactive and one reactive situation in a suburban "yuppie" neighborhood. The researchers found that officers changed their style depending on the type of intervention and, to a lesser extent, on the neighborhood.[6]

Social scientists have disagreed over whether the police working personality derives from innate character traits, or from the socialization process of training, street experience, and the police subculture. At first, researchers concluded that the police personality was inherently different from other groups. The majority of later studies found that to the extent the police possess a working personality, it derives from socialization through the police academy, field training, and patrol experience.[8]

Recruitment, Training, and Promotion

Two major influences have brought about changes in the selection, training, and promotion of police officers. Until these changes, most police officers were white men from blue-collar backgrounds. Most police departments, at least publicly, focused on their law enforcement mission. In 1967 the first major influence, President Johnson's Crime Commission, documented widespread police corruption, discrimination, and failure to respond to the needs and demands of communities. The commission challenged the assumptions that the "manly virtues" and the capacity to obey orders—the qualities sought

Comparative Criminal Justice

According to police experts Jerome Skolnick, author of the classic *Justice Without Trial*, a study of police work, and James Fyfe, a former New York City police officer, now a professor of criminal justice:

> Social scientists have studied police in every part of the United States, in Europe and in Asia. The fundamental culture of policing is everywhere similar, which is understandable since the same features of the police role—danger, authority, and the mandate to use coercive force—are everywhere present. This combination generates and supports norms of internal solidarity, or brotherhood. Most police feel comfortable, and socialize mainly, with other cops, a feature of police culture noted by observers of police from the 1960s to the 1990s. Every cop has a story about a social occasion where an inebriated guest would make a joking or half-joking remark that deprecated police or set them apart. Most cops prefer to attend parties with other police, where drinking and carousing can occur without fear of civilian affront or knowledge. Cops don't trust other people—which is practically everybody who is not a cop. . . . Different philosophies and styles can be introduced into policing. . . . Yet cops on patrol in New York, Philadelphia, Los Angeles, London, and Stockholm—with whom we and others have ridden and observed—are remarkably comparable, with kindred occupational perspectives and working personalities.[7]

in traditional police forces—were the qualities most needed to make a "good" police officer. The commission rejected the prevailing requirements of height, financial credit history, and the absence of *any* criminal record that were supposed to screen for competent officers. Instead, the commission argued, those requirements effectively, if not consciously, excluded large segments of society from police work. As a result, the most visible form of law enforcement did not represent women or African, Native, Latin, and Asian Americans. The commission recommended the adoption of screening devices that eliminate arbitrary and exclusionary effects.

The second major influence was the application of federal civil rights legislation to local police departments. In 1972, federal legislation extended the 1964 Civil Rights Act to prohibit race, gender, religious, and national origin discrimination in public employment.[9]

Disagreement over the definition of "good" police officers added to the challenges of the Crime Commission and civil rights legislation. To some segments of society, good police officers maintain the status quo; to others, they change it. To some segments, good police officers aggressively fight crime; to others, they help people in trouble. To some, good officers follow the letter of the law; to others, they bend the rules to get results.

Despite such disagreements, no one denied that personality, recruitment, training, and advancement affect both the effectiveness of police operations and the degree of police deviance, such as corruption and brutality. Robert D. Meier and Richard E. Maxwell reported a growing consensus that psychological testing can determine the emotional and psychological fitness of recruits. Over half the nation's police departments now use some form of psychological testing. Unfortunately, psychologists and psychiatrists disagree as to what makes a good police officer and, therefore, do not agree on what they are looking for and how to find it in the tests. Furthermore, a growing body of empirical research casts doubt on the accuracy of predictions of future officer performance based on psychological testing. Benjamin Wright, William Doerner, and John Speier analyzed data from the Tallahassee Police Department to test the relationship between pre-employment psychological test results and performance of recruits during their initial field training. The results showed no relationship between the results of the Minnesota Multiphasic Personality Inventory and California Personality Inventory and field performance. The researchers concluded that the results suggest a need to reshape the police selection process. [10]

Traditional selection procedures and training methods, and socialization into the police subculture following training, favored the creation of a homogeneous conservative, authoritarian, punitive, and cynical police working personality. Most traditional departments maintained various physical, mental, and character requirements. The minimum 5'8" height and 150-pound weight requirements made it difficult for women to enter police work. Traditional civil service examinations favored whites. Physical agility tests—timed runs, carrying weights, and repeat trigger-pulling—favored men. Character investigations that eliminated potential recruits with even the most minor criminal records favored whites. Oral interviews allowed gender and race to affect judgments. Traditional screening produced a homogeneous group of recruits: young, white men with blue-collar backgrounds and high school diplomas who entered police work because it promised job security. Furthermore, recruits did not reveal authoritarian, punitive, or cynical personalities *before* becoming officers. Instead, the working personality developed from the teaching in the police academy, field training, and street experience *after* entering police work.[11]

A 1990 survey of police departments throughout the country found that 75 percent still used a physical performance test in recruiting officers; 20 percent used it in selecting graduates from basic training. Seventy-one percent screened for substance abuse in recruiting officers; 20 percent used the screen in selecting graduates. Most used written tests that the departments evaluated for validity. Somewhat less than 40 percent failed basic training.[12]

The recognition of the complexity of our pluralistic society; demands for equal opportunity by women and by ethnic and racial minorities; recognition of the multiple missions of police; the large part discretion plays in performing those missions; the limits of preventive patrol and other traditional police operations in reducing violence, illegal drugs, and other problems; and the popularity of community and problem-oriented policing all put pressure on traditional ideas about the "right" police personality. The "manly virtues" and obeying the orders of police managers were no longer considered enough to meet the challenges of policing.

For example, community policing and problem-oriented policing require great skills in recognizing, selecting, and solving community problems; in drawing on a wide array of resources in the community; and in working with residents and groups in the community. (See Chapter 5.) This kind of work requires officers who are sensitive to neighborhoods, aware of the varying interests within neighborhoods—or even in buildings within neighborhoods—with the skills to communicate, the capacity to seek solutions, and the knowledge of where to look. In short, this work requires the exercise of good judgment. It calls for the development and exercise of discretion.

Police expert Egon Bittner, in discussing the qualities of problem-oriented police officers, writes:

> The question that would . . . be asked of a performance is not if it complied with rules and regulations, but whether it showed adequacy of skill, knowledge, judgment, efficiency and other relevant criteria of good work. Moreover, such judgment would not be passed by one's administrative superiors, although their judgment need not be ruled out entirely, but by one's professional colleagues.[13]

Education

The demands for police officers who possessed more than physical strength and the capacity to obey orders did not begin with the recognition of the complexity of society and the police mission, nor with the growing popularity of community and problem-oriented policing. August Vollmer, the famous reform police chief of Berkeley, California, recommended higher education for police officers as early as 1920. Little movement in that direction occurred until the 1960s, however, when training and education became the foremost measures to "upgrade" the police. In 1959, California created a Commission on Peace Officer Standards and Training. By 1977, 45 states had similar commissions. In 1967, only 15 percent of the departments surveyed required training of any sort. By 1977, 90 percent of departments did. In 1967, police officers received 279 training hours; by 1977, the number had risen to 471 hours. The advance in educational level was almost as dramatic. In Dallas in 1968, for example, only 11 officers had college degrees; by 1975, 625 had bachelor's degrees, 21 had masters', and 450 were studying for degrees. In Florida, only 6 percent of police officers had attended college in 1960; by 1975, 23 percent had done so.[14]

In 1989 the Police Executive Research Forum reviewed research, surveyed 502 departments, and visited seven departments to determine the present state of police officer education in the United States. They reported that the national average educational level had risen from 12.4 years in 1967 to 13.6 years in 1989. Seventy-two percent of African Americans and 73 percent of Hispanic Americans employed had attended college. Nearly two-thirds of departments had a formal policy in favor of higher education.[15]

A number of police chiefs in the 1990s have commented on the importance of police education. Neil Behan, chief of Baltimore County police, said, "When I was a rookie 43 years ago, we knew where we stood as officers. In those days, you spent an entire career in the same department with that department's same mind-set. It took a very special person to break away." Now Behan tells his 1,545-member department that he will promote no one to senior management without a college degree "or the imminent prospect of one." Charlie Johnson, chief of police in the Denver suburb of Lakewood, said: "I want disciplined, dedicated, tolerant people who understand how society works and want to solve problems, not just answer distress calls." Allen H. Andrews, Jr., chief of police in Peoria, Illinois, maintained that "society is more complicated now. Society and I expect officers not just to be law enforcers but to be the grease on the wheels of solving social conflicts." Andrews sends all recruits to special courses on courtesy and body language so they can read people's movements and focus on their own attitudes and intentions.[16]

According to the Police Executive Research Forum, research suggests that higher education can benefit police officers in many ways:

- Develops a broader base of information for decision making.
- Provides additional years and experience for increasing maturity.
- Inculcates responsibility through course requirements and achievement.
- Teaches the history of the country, the democratic process, individual rights, and the values of a free society.
- Engenders the ability to handle difficult and ambiguous situations with creativity and innovation.
- Teaches the "big picture" of the criminal justice system and a fuller understanding and appreciation of prosecution, courts, and corrections.
- Develops a greater empathy for minorities and discrimination.

- Encourages tolerance and understanding of differing life-styles and ideologies.
- Helps officers communicate with and respond to people and their problems in a competent, civil, and humane manner.
- Develops officers who can deal innovatively and flexibly with problem-oriented and community policing.
- Helps officers develop better communications and community relations skills.
- Engenders more "professional" demeanor and performance.
- Enables officers to cope with stress.
- Makes officers less authoritarian and cynical.
- Prepares officers to accept and adapt to change.
- Helps reduce the number of lawsuits against police departments, because college-educated officers know the law better.[17]

An increase in the numbers of college-educated officers does not automatically translate into improved quality and effectiveness. Despite a growing nationwide emphasis on training, and with some departments and even state laws requiring higher education, a growing body of research supports the conclusion of one researcher that "there is growing doubt that training in its present form achieves the objectives its proponents hold out for it." Robert Worden measured the attitudes and performance of officers who obtained bachelor's degrees before entering police work, officers who became police officers before obtaining a degree, and officers without college degrees. He surveyed both officers and private individuals in 24 police departments in three metropolitan areas: St. Louis, Rochester, and Tampa-St. Petersburg. He found only marginal differences in both attitudes and performance among the three groups:

> Although college-educated officers may be superior from the perspectives of supervisors, who find that such officers are more reliable employees and better report writers, they are not superior from the perspective of police clientele, who are concerned principally with effective and courteous contacts with police. Therefore this analysis suggests that patrol officers' performance and morale will be affected neither by policies that encourage in-service education nor by entry requirements that include college education.[18]

In another study, Worden relied on data collected from observations of over 5,000 police-citizen encounters. He looked at a number of officer characteristics and their relationship to the use of force, finding that officers who earned bachelor's degrees were more likely to use force generally. However, Wordon also found that officers with bachelor's degrees were *less* likely to use *excessive* force.[19]

Victor Kappeler, Allen Sapp, and David Carter, in an analysis of citizen complaints against officers in a medium-sized department, found that officers with college degrees had fewer citizen-generated complaints for rudeness than officers without college degrees. However, they had more department-generated complaints of rules violations. The results of these and other studies do not necessarily prove that college education has no positive effect on police attitudes and performance. They do suggest the need for more research. In a major review of the research on the increase in the numbers of college-educated police officers, Stephen Mastrofski concluded that whether the increase has significantly affected police practice "remains mostly unanswered." He called for more data that demonstrate the relationship between the personal characteristics of officers, the kind of education received, and the willingness of departments to encourage and facilitate the skills and lessons of college education. Despite increased education, Mastrofski wonders, "Can one teach old cops new tricks, or is there an experiential threshold beyond which few officers respond to new approaches?"[20]

Complicating the answer to the question of whether education and training "work," administrators and researchers do not agree as to what training and education police officers *should* receive. Should instructors teach by lecturing, the most efficient, economical educational method? Or, since discretion requires judgment, should teachers utilize discussion and problem-solving methods to encourage recruits to think critically? Should police officers have a college or university degree? Should it be a liberal arts degree or a specialized criminal justice major? In regard to training, how many hours does adequate training require? Is vicarious classroom learning enough, or should recruits have field training as well? What priority should training receive in the whole police operation? Most important, what purpose does training serve, and does training accomplish that purpose?[21]

Clearly defined training goals cannot be established unless departments have defined police missions. However, not everyone agrees what those missions should be. Some take a broad view of training and advanced education, even going so far as to claim as a goal that they will bolster the general social status of police officers as educated professionals in the community. Others take a much narrower view. They believe that training should stick to preparing police officers to carry out the mission of effective and fair criminal law enforcement. Still others view training as an opportunity to reform police administration, such as reducing the emphasis on law enforcement and enhancing order maintenance and public service functions. Others hope that training will develop in officers a better capacity to make judgments and solve problems that will enhance the strategies of community and problem-oriented policing.[22]

The Police Academy

Whatever the nature of the police working personality, however it comes to be, and no matter what the effects of education, researchers have consistently found that "the transition from civilian to police officer is a long and complicated series of stages, inviting much upheaval and self doubt." For most officers, this transition begins in the **police academy**, where recruits are socialized by means of learning the formal rules of the academy; the laws of search, seizure, interrogation, and identification; technical skills, including crime scene preservation, pursuit driving, weapons use, self-defense, and report writing; and the informal, unwritten rules of how to behave and react in the academy. Rules govern virtually everything in police academies, and military-like officers attempt to enforce them. Rules focus on punctuality, neatness, order, attentiveness, and obedience to authority.[23]

The many rules and the quasi-military nature that characterize most academies generate a strong sense of group solidarity among recruits, foster an attitude that rules are something to "get around," and lead recruits to view administrators as punishers. Neither the rules of the traditional academy nor the formal laws of criminal procedure answer recruits' most pressing questions: "What is it really like out there on the streets? How do I arrest someone who doesn't want to be arrested? Exactly when do I use my nightstick and how do I do it? What do the other patrol officers think of me?" Recruits learn some of the answers to these questions from instructors or other experienced officers in the form of **police "war stories."** Most of these stories, such as the following one related by Jonathan Rubenstein and drawn from the Philadelphia Police Department's academy, stress two themes, **police defensiveness** and **police depersonalization.**[24]

> A jack is a beautiful weapon, but it is very dangerous, fellas. I remember once we were looking for a guy who had beaten up a policeman and escaped from a wagon. I found him hiding under a car. To this day

I don't know if he was coming out to surrender or to attack me, but he was just coming out before I told him to move. He was a real big guy and I didn't wait. I had my jack ready, and as he came up I hit him as hard as I could. I thought I killed him. He was O.K., but since then I haven't carried a jack unless I was going on some dangerous job. I don't want to beat someone to death, and with a jack you can never be sure. You should get yourself a convoy and use it in your fist. If you punch for a guy's heart, the whipping action of the spring will snap it forward and break his collarbone. Then you've got him.[25]

This war story portrays both themes. Officers learn they not only need to defend themselves but also to develop defensiveness. They learn not to trust "outsiders." According to Richard Harris, a journalist who attended a police academy in New York City, instructors told recruits that politicians do not know what they are doing, African Americans and other minority individuals are criminal threats who deny the work ethic, reporters will distort all police stories, women cause special problems by false accusations of sexual assault, and, in general, "anyone who was not a law enforcement officer was not to be trusted."[26]

The story of using the blackjack also illustrates how the traditional academy encourages recruits to depersonalize individuals, as this instructor did by describing the use of force in such a cold, matter-of-fact manner. The themes of defensiveness and depersonalization stem in large part from the perceived danger of police work. In fact, other occupations carry greater risk of death and injury than police work does. (See Figure 7.1.) Police deaths and injuries, however, usually arise from willful, deliberate attacks. Furthermore, as respected police experts David H. Bayley and Egon Bittner note:

> Police continually deal with situations in which physical constraint may have to be applied against people who are willing to fight, struggle, hit, stab, spit, bite, tear, hurl, hide, and run. People continually use their bodies against the police, forcing the police to deal with them in a physical way. While police seem to be preoccupied with deadly force, the more common reality in their lives is the possibility of a broken nose, lost teeth, black eyes, broken ribs, and twisted arms. Few officers are ever shot or even shot at, but all except the rawest rookie can show scars on their bodies from continual encounters with low-level violence.[27]

Figure 7.1

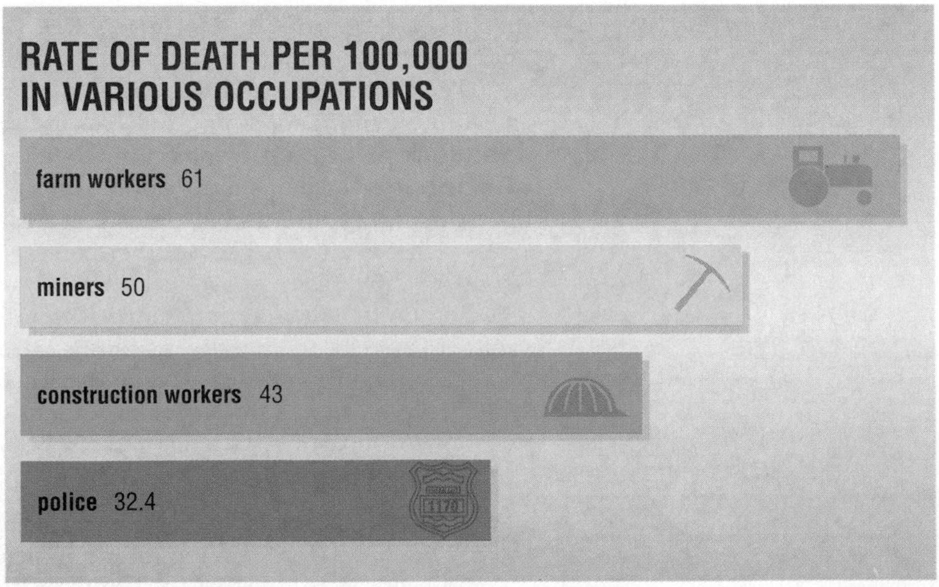

RATE OF DEATH PER 100,000
IN VARIOUS OCCUPATIONS

farm workers 61

miners 50

construction workers 43

police 32.4

Field Training

New police officers finish their academy training insecure about whether what they have learned will help them on the street. Departments usually require **field training** that places rookies in the hands of older officers who are supposed to help them break with the academy and teach them the craft of policing. But training involves more than learning skills and techniques. According to James Fyfe,

> *Everything* that supervisors do or tolerate, every interpretation of broad departmental philosophy, every application of specific rules and policies is a training lesson that has at least as much impact on officers' performance as what they may have learned in their rookie days.[28]

Field training officers are fabled to tell rookies, "Forget what they told you in the police academy, kid, you'll learn how to do it on the street." When they do that, says Fyfe,

> formal training is instantly and irreparably devalued. Worse, when officers actually see firsthand that the behavioral strictures in which they are schooled are routinely ignored in practice, formal training is neutralized and the definitions of appropriate behavior are instead made in the secrecy of officers' locker rooms.[29]

In teaching rookies the craft of policing, experienced officers emphasize that "real" policing involves "heavy" calls, such as "man with gun," "shots fired," and "officer needs assistance." The true test of a good officer, according to the traditional standards, is the ability and willingness to risk injury in these situations.[30]

Some older officers are experienced in field training, and some departments establish structured field training and evaluation. In other departments, the officers have had little or no training in evaluating rookies. William G. Doerner and E. Britt Patterson describe field training in Tallahassee, Florida, before a court case prompted the department to improve its field training:

> post-academy training consisted of a thirty-day observation period with a senior patrol officer. The veteran officer imparted words of wisdom as needed and answered any questions that the rookie had. At the end of the assignment, the senior officer would submit a recommendation. . . . [T]here were no . . . standardized training modules. A sound performance rating system, particularly one anchored in actual job tasks, was absent. What this practice amounted to was an indefensible extension of the antiquated "good old boy" system. . . .[21]

Innovations in Education and Training

Some departments provide broader educational experience than the traditional academy and field training. Some accept courses that are supposed to improve critical thinking because administrators believe such courses improve the capacity of police officers to make sound discretionary judgments. Some departments accept liberal arts courses, and even degrees, as satisfying both entry and advancement criteria. Instructors in some law enforcement courses have adopted problem-solving approaches, the case method, and discussion to enhance prospective officers' ability to make judgments. Experienced officers sometimes act as guest lecturers, interacting with students who hope to become officers and with other students. The interaction can prove enriching to students, instructors, and officers.

Field experiences that broaden the perspectives of new officers are supposed to improve their understanding and effectiveness. Community service internships offer recruits the opportunity to gain a broader perspective on crime and criminal law enforcement. To improve understanding of the criminal justice system beyond the police department, some officers spend time in prosecutors' offices to appreciate the complexities of charging suspects; in public defenders' offices getting the defense point of view; and in judges' chambers learning about the difficulties of sentencing. Some departments give officers the opportunity to learn more about the cultural diversity in their district by assigning them to hospital emergency rooms, alcoholic detoxification clinics, psychiatric wards, welfare offices, and schools.[32]

The San Diego Police Department introduced an innovative field experience aimed at sensitizing police officers to the authority they wield by subjecting them to it. Trainees and their supervisors traveled to San Jose, California, for the field training phase. In a stimulating and educational session, officers were placed in situations designed to attract the attention of the local police. The exercise attempted to give officers first-hand experience of police interrogation from a non-police perspective. Some officers felt they were harassed; others felt they were subjected to unnecessary physical handling or illegal arrest. However, not all the contact experiences were negative; some very good interrogations were conducted. The San Diego officers in training had to think about what they had done to attract the attention of the local police. This led the trainees to examine their own motives for selecting particular individuals for field interrogations.[33]

Training in improving discretionary decision making, whether by means of courses in critical thinking or field experiences, works best when departments recruit applicants adaptable to these innovations. Almost everyone agrees that police work requires officers intelligent enough to grasp difficult problems and to decide quickly on a response. Beyond that, controversy lies. Some want to improve the effectiveness of discretionary decision making generally, because it plays such a large role in all police missions—maintaining order, enforcing the criminal law, and providing other services. Others want to focus strictly on producing more effective crime fighters. John E. Boydstun, who studied field interrogation in San Diego, expresses the broad view of training:

> [R]ecruits should be able to understand the cosmopolitan nature of an urban area and appreciate differences between cultures. They must learn to tolerate unconventional behavior and respect divergent lifestyles. They must be able to appreciate the meaning of freedom and be sensitive to the awesome consequences stemming from the unbridled use of authority. They must take on the commitment to protect constitutional guarantees. They must subscribe to the value our society attaches to limiting the use of force, and they must learn to appreciate the controls exercised over the use of police powers and the role of the community in directing and reviewing police conduct.[34]

Women and Minority Officers

Adequate training and intelligent recruits do not by themselves produce "good" police officers and effective policing. Police departments perform best when they secure strong public support. Competent personnel who reflect the cultural diversity and gender division of the community as a whole is one way to assure public support. Calls for closer connections between the police and the community, the law requiring affirmative action and equal employment opportunity, and the values of an open and diverse society all encourage hiring and advancing women and minorities in policing. Recruitment of minorities and women has challenged police administrators for decades. Empirical and impressionistic evidence suggest a weakening, but by no means a removal, of barriers based on race, ethnic origin, and gender.[35]

Women Officers

The image of the police as crime fighters and the importance of coercion as the underlying reality of all police work resulted in "policing being one of the most resistant occupations to accepting women employees." Until 1972, female police officers were extremely rare. Those few were limited to working with "women, children and typewriters." Women were considered simply unsuited for "real" police work. Under the 1972 amendments to the Civil Rights Act of 1964, women acquired the legal right to equal opportunity in law enforcement. After 1972, police departments removed many discriminatory hiring and deployment practices. James Fyfe claims that the resulting increase in women officers is so great that "the traditional view of policing as a nearly exclusive white male occupation is quickly becoming outmoded . . . in virtually every population category and geographic region."[36]

Susan E. Martin of the Police Foundation, however, maintains that the available evidence on women in policing presents a "mixed picture." A 1973 survey of cities serving populations of 250,000 or more found that women comprised 2 percent of sworn law enforcement personnel; nearly all departments excluded these women from patrol duties. By 1979, 87 percent of departments serving more than 50,000 assigned women to patrol; women comprised 3.38 percent of the sworn officers in those cities. Very few women, however, had risen above the entry rank of patrol officer. Some experts maintained that limited seniority accounted for the failure of women to advance during the 1970s.[37]

During the 1980s, the percent of sworn women officers continued to rise; by 1985 it reached 7.5 percent of sworn officers in departments serving more

According to empirical research the odds are that this woman is as effective an officer as the men in her department.

gender model of police attitudes *model of women police that predicts differences in attitude between women and men police officers because of their different early socialization into gender roles.*

job model of police attitude *model of women police that predicts no differences in attitude between women and men police officers because socialization to work overrides prior socialization into gender roles.*

than 50,000, and 8.6 percent in departments serving more than 250,000; and in suburban departments it reached 10 percent. In 1989, Susan E. Martin, who conducted the survey that reported these results, wrote that the bad news is that women officers, despite these gains, comprise "only a token proportion of all police personnel." The FBI reported that by October of 1994, sworn women officers had risen to 11.85 percent of total sworn officers in departments serving more than 50,000 people. In cities serving more than 250,000 people, the percent reached 14.2. The trend is definitely up, but the proportion of women sworn police officers is far below the percentage of women in the total population.[38]

The skepticism among traditional police departments and officers, and among the public, about women police officers generated considerable research about their effectiveness. Nine surveys representing a broad cross-section of the country's police departments demonstrated that women patrol officers perform as well as men patrol officers. For example, performance ratings of women after their first year in the Washington, D.C., Police Department were similar to those of men in their first year of service. Women stood up to difficult circumstances as well as men. They resigned or were terminated at about the same rate as men. According to former Police Chief Cullinane of Washington, D.C., "It's an accomplished fact. Some cities are still in court, saying women can't do the job—that you can't put women on patrol. Well, you can go out on the streets of the District of Columbia any time, day or night, and watch women do the job."[39]

The empirical research regarding the *performance* of women police officers led to questions and research about their *attitudes*. One theory explaining the attitudes of women police officers is the **gender model of police attitudes**. The gender model predicts differences in attitude between women and men police officers because of their different early socialization into gender roles. According to Carol Gilligan, women develop a "morality of care" which depicts "society as an interdependent and interconnected web of personal relationships." The theory predicts that the morality of care leads women to take a broad view of the police mission, that is, to provide service. Men, on the other hand, the theory predicts, develop a "morality of justice," which concentrates on law enforcement, hierarchy, rules, and discipline.[40]

A second theory, the **job model of police attitude**, predicts that women and men do not differ in their attitudes toward police work because socialization to work overrides prior socialization into gender roles. In other words, women may come into police work with different attitudes than men but after attending the academy, going through field training, and especially after working as police officers for a period of time, the attitudes of men and women converge into a similar police officer attitude. Alissa Pollitz Worden tested these theories by measuring attitudes in a large data set that surveyed 1,435 police officers in 24 police departments. She found that women and men officers had similar attitudes on a range of subjects concerning policing. Both favored uniform over selective law enforcement; women did not define the police mission in broader terms than men; the longer women worked, the more their views of people converged with the views of men; the views of women and men also converged over time with respect to their willingness to accept legal restrictions on their work. According to Worden,

> The most striking finding in this study is the failure of gender to explain much or any variation in the array of attitudes examined, even when potentially confounding variables are controlled. Overall, female as well as male police officers were predictably ambivalent about restrictions on their autonomy and the definition of their role, only mildly positive about their public clientele, complimentary of their colleagues, and unenthusiastic about working conditions and supervisors. What should one conclude from this about theories of gender differ-

ences and their applicability to policing? . . . [T]aken as a whole, these findings offer little support for the thesis that female officers define their role or see their clientele differently than do males, and one must therefore remain skeptical . . . about claims that women bring to their beats a distinctive perspective on policing.[41]

Minority Officers

Dr. Elysee Scott, executive director of the National Organization of Black Law Enforcement Executives (NOBLE), remembers that as she was growing up in a small Louisiana town in the 1950s, African-American police officers rode around in police cars marked "Colored Only." African-American officers could arrest only "colored" people; if a white person committed a crime in an African-American neighborhood, African-American officers had to call for a white officer to make the arrest. Beginning in the 1960s, following brutality by white officers against African Americans, civil rights legislation, lawsuits brought by African Americans, and demands for minority hiring, the position of African American and other minority officers changed from what Dr. Scott remembers from the 1950s.[42]

Beginning in the 1960s, the number of African-American police officers has grown. (See Figure 7.2.) However, these aggregates are misleading because some departments reflect the racial makeup of their communities better than others. In 1992 in New York City, for example, African Americans made up 11.4 percent of the police force but 28.7 percent of the population. In Los Angeles in 1992, on the other hand, the percent of African-American police officers and the African-American population of the city were identical—14 percent. In that same year, Rodney King was beaten and the Christopher Commission documented a racist climate in the Los Angeles department. Obviously, merely employing minority police officers is not enough to eliminate problems.[43]

Samuel Walker surveyed police departments in the nation's 50 largest cities. He found that between 1983 and 1988, those departments "made uneven progress in the employment of African American and Hispanic officers." While nearly half the big-city departments made significant progress in employing African-American officers, 17 percent reported declines in the

Figure 7.2

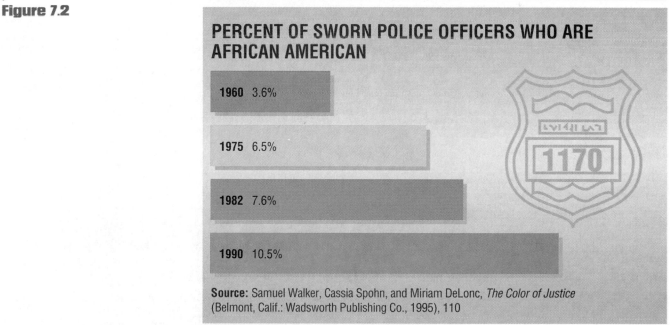

PERCENT OF SWORN POLICE OFFICERS WHO ARE AFRICAN AMERICAN

1960 3.6%

1975 6.5%

1982 7.6%

1990 10.5%

Source: Samuel Walker, Cassia Spohn, and Miriam DeLonc, *The Color of Justice* (Belmont, Calif.: Wadsworth Publishing Co., 1995), 110

percent of African-American officers. Similarly, 42 percent of the departments hired more Hispanics; 11 percent reported declines. Affirmative action plans play a significant role in police employment trends, according to Walker. Nearly two-thirds of the departments reported operating under such plans. Twenty-three of the plans were court ordered, seven voluntary. Despite the unevenness of the progress in hiring African-American and Hispanic officers, a survey of all police departments in the country revealed that the numbers of African-American and Hispanic police officers roughly compared to their representation in the general population (see Figure 7.3.)[44]

A *New York Times* survey showed that despite efforts by the New York Police Department to recruit more women and minorities, most NYPD officers are white males who grew up in the suburbs or in low-crime neighborhoods in the city. Seventy-five percent of the men are Roman Catholics. Most of them followed friends or relatives into the department. The survey, along with interviews with graduates of the department's police academy, "suggests that a resilient network of whites, born of the Irish, Italian, and German immigrant streams of a much older New York, has built an enduring cultural pipeline into the department."

> Vincent Gerard, 21, is a product of the pipeline. He grew up in Whitestone, Queens, went to Holy Cross High School in Bayside and earned a two-year associate's degree in criminal justice at St. John's University. He is Sicilian-Irish, he said, and his mother's father was a police officer who died in a fire in the line of duty.
>
> "I took the test when I was a junior in high school," he said. "My mother saw the announcement in the newspaper. I also took the housing police test, the transit police test and the fireman's test. My next-door neighbor is a housing detective. He would tell me stories about cops."[45]

African-American police chiefs have increased significantly in numbers since the 1960s. In 1976, Hubert Williams, chief of the Newark, New Jersey, Police Department, was the only African-American police chief in the country. By 1990, African Americans headed one-quarter of the 50 largest city police departments, including New York, Chicago, Philadelphia, Baltimore, Detroit, Washington, and Miami.[46]

The *You Decide* on race, ethnic, and gender hiring asks you to assess the value of quotas to establish more racially balanced police departments.

Figure 7.3

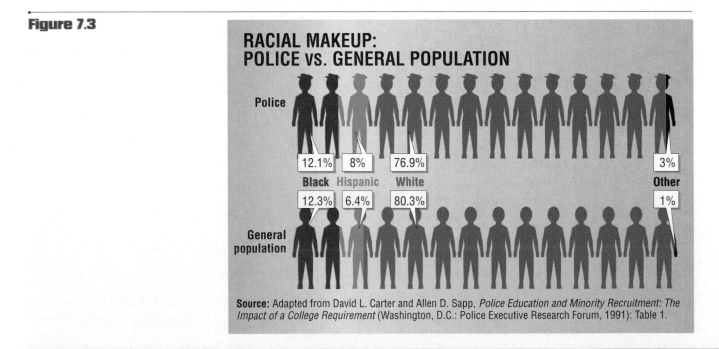

RACIAL MAKEUP: POLICE vs. GENERAL POPULATION

Police: Black 12.1%, Hispanic 8%, White 76.9%, Other 3%

General population: Black 12.3%, Hispanic 6.4%, White 80.3%, Other 1%

Source: Adapted from David L. Carter and Allen D. Sapp, *Police Education and Minority Recruitment: The Impact of a College Requirement* (Washington, D.C.: Police Executive Research Forum, 1991): Table 1.

Should Courts Establish Hiring Quotas?

In a long-drawn-out court battle that dates back to 1973 and that the parties finally settled in 1989, Chief Judge Curtin found the hiring practices of the Buffalo, New York, Police Department discriminatory. He fashioned a remedy based on quotas of women, Hispanics, and African Americans. This case resembles many that courts have already decided, and numerous others still in progress. Do you agree with Judge Curtin's orders? Why? How would you alter them?

The following is extracted from the court opinion in *United States of America v. City of Buffalo*, 633 F.2d 643 (2d Cir. 1988).

CURTIN, Chief Judge

The United States government challenged the employment practices of the Buffalo Police Department in a lawsuit originally filed in August 1973. The action sought to enforce Title VII of the Civil Rights Act of 1964, as amended by the Equal Employment Opportunity Act of 1972. Section 703(a) of Title VII, 42 U.S.C. §2000e-2(a) states the central premise of the Act:

> It shall be an unlawful employment practice for an employer (1) to fail or refuse to hire or to discharge any individual, or otherwise to discriminate against any individual with respect to his compensation, terms, conditions, or privileges of employment, because of such individual's race, color, religion, sex, or national origin. . . .

The act proscribes not only overt discrimination but also practices that are fair in form, but discriminatory in operation. The touchstone is business necessity. If an employment practice which operates to exclude Negroes cannot be shown to be related to job performance, the practice is prohibited.

I. General population statistics

Census figures show that the population of the City of Buffalo is 20.4 percent Black and between 3.2 percent to 3.9 percent Spanish-surname Americans (hereinafter "SSA"). In addition, the labor force in the City is 17.5 percent Black and 40.6 percent Female. In 1973, the police department employed 1,395 uniformed personnel of whom 36 (2.6 percent) were black males, 2 (0.1 percent) were black females, 3 (0.2 percent) were SSA males, and 16 (1.1 percent) were white females. As of the same date the department employed 911 patrolmen of whom 24 (2.6 percent) were black males and 3 (0.3 percent) were SSA males. No women were employed in the patrolman position. Meanwhile, of the 42 police cadets employed by the Department at that time, 3 (7.1 percent) were black males.

At that time the Police Department also employed 95 full-time nonuniformed personnel (clerks, typists, cleaners, etc.). Of these, 45 (47.4 percent) were white females, 2 (2.1 percent) were black males, and 5 (5.2 percent) were black females. Of the 7 blacks employed, 5 were cleaners or charwomen.

Here the evidence indicates a substantial disparity between the general black, SSA, and female population in the City of Buffalo and the representation of those groups in the work force of the Police Department.

II. Written examinations

The Government argues that the Police Department uses written examinations in their job selection process that have a discriminatory impact upon black and SSA candidates for positions.

A. Disproportionate impact

Of the 621 people taking the February 1973 written patrolman examination, 86.6 percent were white, 11.7 percent were black, and 1.6 percent were SSAs. The New York State Department of Civil Service designated 70 percent as a passing grade. The examination results showed that 43.4 percent of the whites received at least a 70 percent grade while only 8.2 percent of the blacks and 10 percent of the SSAs achieved a passing score. The significant disparity between the passing grades of whites and both black and SSA candidates establishes a case of discrimination in the Police Department testing programs.

B. Relation to job performance

Such tests are impermissible unless "predictive of or significantly correlated with important elements of work behavior which comprise or are relevant to the job or jobs for which candidates are being evaluated." Although the examiner admits that numerous critical areas of work behavior are involved in the patrolman job, only three areas were tested: good judgment, preparation of written material, and the understanding and interpretation of reading material. The court finds that the defendants have failed to show the validity of the 1973 written patrolman examination. As such, it stands in violation of Title VII.

III. Height requirements

Prior to and including the last competition for patrolman in 1973, persons applying for appointment were required to be at least 5'9" in height. During the last competition for police cadet, applicants were required to be at least 5'7" in height; prior to that they were required to be at least 5'9" in height. Applicants meeting these minimum physical requirements were then permitted to take written and physical agility examinations.

A. Minimum height standards

The government has introduced statistical findings to show a case of discrimination against both women and SSA individuals through the use of the absolute height requirements of 5'9" for police patrolman and of 5'7" for police cadet. According to a U.S. Department of Health, Education, and Welfare publication, males between the ages of eighteen and twenty-four average 68.7" (5'8.7") in height, while females in the same age group average only 63.8" (5'3.8") in height. This necessarily eliminates the vast majority of American women from job selection as a patrolman and has a disproportionate effect on them. Furthermore, statistics for the New York and New Jersey geographical area introduced by the government show that the 5′9″ standard eliminates 80.6 percent of SSA males aged seventeen to twenty-six as compared to only 48.5 percent of non-SSA males. The 5′7″ standard eliminates 54.7 percent of SSA males aged seventeen to twenty-six, but only 21.3 percent of non-SSA males. These disparities certainly establish a case of discrimination through use of absolute height requirements.

The burden now falls to the defendants to justify the absolute height requirements as job related. They have introduced the testimony of Police Commissioner Blair as to the importance of height in successful job performance by police officers. He stated that the average height of males eighteen to thirty-four in the northeast United States is 5′10″ and that approximately 60 percent of the male arrestees in the City of Buffalo are 5′9″ or taller. Furthermore, it was his opinion that the height of police officers serves as a deterrent to the need for use of force by the police since it will keep people from engaging in antisocial acts and will enable the police to obtain submission with minimum use of force. Although the opinions of the commissioner are to be accorded substantial weight due to his experience in the field of crime control, standing alone they do not provide sufficient justification to uphold minimum height requirements.

IV. High school diploma requirement

In addition to the age, height, weight, and vision requirements, an applicant for either the police or fire departments must possess a high school diploma or equivalency diploma. The government challenges this requirement as another violation of Title VII . . . I find that a high school education is a bare minimum requirement for successful performance of the policeman's responsibilities. This reasoning has been followed by several courts to uphold the high school requirement.

V. Sex discrimination

At completion of trial, there had never been a single woman patrolman [or] cadet. Furthermore, not a single woman was on the eligibility lists for any of these positions. No attempt had ever been made to recruit women for these positions. Under Title VII the purpose of the sex discrimination provisions is to eliminate disparate treatment of female employees and to provide equal access to the job market for both men and women. The act rejects the notion of "romantic paternalism" toward women and seeks to put them on an equal footing with men. . . . In order to discriminate lawfully on the basis of sex, an employer must show that sex is a bona fide occupational qualification (bfoq) reasonably necessary to the operation of that employer's business.

Looking to the evidence presented in this case, we find not only a case of sex discrimination but an absolute bar to the hiring of women for the positions in the Buffalo Police Department. Defendants present no evidence to establish a bfoq that would justify this absolute bar. Plaintiff, on the other hand, has provided the court with sub-

stantial evidentiary materials in the form of statistical studies and job evaluations that demonstrate the ability of women to act as patrolmen, as well as their current active status in these positions in other police and fire departments throughout the United States. Furthermore, they demonstrate the existence of a large, qualified pool of women in the Buffalo area who have shown an interest in this field of work. This court finds that the Police Department has failed to show the necessary bfoq to justify its total failure to hire women for the position of patrol officer.

VI. Relief

1. The city shall seek to achieve the long-term goal of reaching a minority composition in the ranks of uniformed personnel within the Police Department comparable to that of the work force within the city as a whole, according to the most recent census.
2. The city shall adopt and seek to achieve the interim goal of making 50 percent of all entry-level and/or police officer appointments from among qualified black and SSA applicants.
3. The city shall adopt and seek to achieve an interim goal of making 50 percent of all police officer appointments from among qualified black and SSA applicants.
4. In addition, the defendants shall take affirmative steps to recruit and hire women in numbers commensurate with their interest and with their ability to qualify on the basis of performance-related criteria for positions as police officers. Within eighteen months following December 11, 1978, the court shall, upon motion of plaintiff and after evidentiary hearing, consider the entry of specific long-term and interim hiring goals for women in this position.
5. No long-term goal for hiring females in the police department shall be set at this time. However, the defendants shall adopt and seek to achieve an interim goal of making 25 percent of all entry-level and/or police officer appointments from among qualified women applicants. A minority woman shall count toward both interim goals.
6. The interim hiring goal for minorities shall remain in effect until the minority composition of the uniformed personnel of the police department and fire department is at least equal to the percentage of minorities in the labor force of the City of Buffalo according to the most recent census, or until this court has found, after a hearing, that all proposed selection procedures for entry-level and/or police officer positions have been validated in accordance with the Uniform Guidelines on Employee Selection Procedures, and that no further interim goals are appropriate.

Questions

What precisely were the prejudicial practices? What arguments did the court give for their unfairness? Do you agree? Give the arguments for and against quotas. Would you impose hiring quotas on police departments? Defend your answer.

Court decisions such as *U.S. v. City of Buffalo*, instigated by minorities and women demanding equal hiring practices, provide an impetus to reform. Women and minorities, however, have not acted alone. Reform-minded administrators believe in more representative departments as a matter of fairness; pragmatists support it on the grounds that minority officers can effectively deal with minority members of the community and lessen tensions between police and the nonwhite community.[47]

Police Stress

Stress plays a part in the lives of everyone. Some stress is not only inevitable, it can be good. For example, the physical stress of "working out" improves your cardiovascular system, and feeling pressure that causes you to study harder for an exam can improve your score. **Police stress**, however, refers to the *negative* pressures related to police work. Police officers are not superhumans. According to Gail Goolkasian and others, research shows that

> they are affected by their daily exposure to human indecency and pain; that dealing with a suspicious and sometimes hostile public takes its toll on them; and that the shift changes, the long periods of boredom, and the ever-present danger that are part of police work do cause serious job stress.[48]

Dr. Hans Selye's classic *The Stress of Life* describes the effect of long-term environmental threats he calls "stressors." Dr. Selye maintains that the unrelieved effort to cope with stressors can lead to heart disease, high blood pressure, ulcers, digestive disorders, and headaches. Stressors in police work fall into four categories:

- Stresses inherent in police work.
- Stresses arising internally from police department practices and policies.
- External stresses stemming from the criminal justice system and the society at-large.
- Internal stresses confronting individual officers.[49]

Police stress arises from several features of police work. Alterations in body rhythms from monthly shift rotation, for example, reduce productivity. The change from day to a swing, or graveyard, shift not only requires biological adjustment, but also complicates officers' personal lives. Role conflicts between the job—serving the public and enforcing the law and ethical standards—and personal responsibilities as spouse, parent, and friend act as stressors. Other stressors in police work include:

- Threats to officers' health and safety (see Figures 7.4 and 7.5).
- Boredom, alternating with the need for sudden alertness and mobilized energy.
- Responsibility for protecting the lives of others.
- Continual exposure to people in pain or distress.
- The need to control emotions even when provoked.
- The presence of a gun, even during off-duty hours.
- The fragmented nature of police work, with only rare opportunities to follow cases to conclusion or even to obtain feedback or follow-up information.[50]

Administrative policies and procedures, which officers rarely participate in formulating, can add to stress. One-officer patrol cars create anxiety and a reduced sense of safety. Internal investigation practices create the feeling of being watched and not trusted, even during off-duty hours. Officers sometimes feel they have fewer rights than the criminals they apprehend. Lack of

Figure 7.4

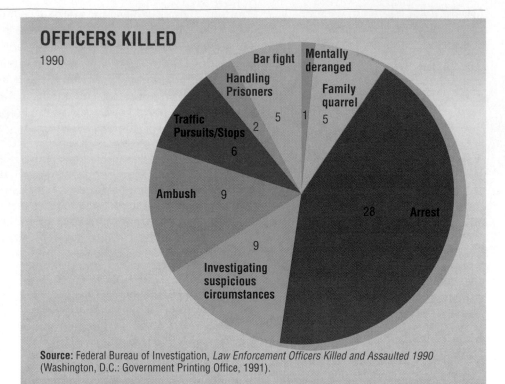

OFFICERS KILLED

1990

- Bar fight
- Mentally deranged
- Handling Prisoners 5
- Family quarrel 5
- Traffic Pursuits/Stops 6
- 2
- 1
- Ambush 9
- 28 Arrest
- 9 Investigating suspicious circumstances

Source: Federal Bureau of Investigation, *Law Enforcement Officers Killed and Assaulted 1990* (Washington, D.C.: Government Printing Office, 1991).

Figure 7.5

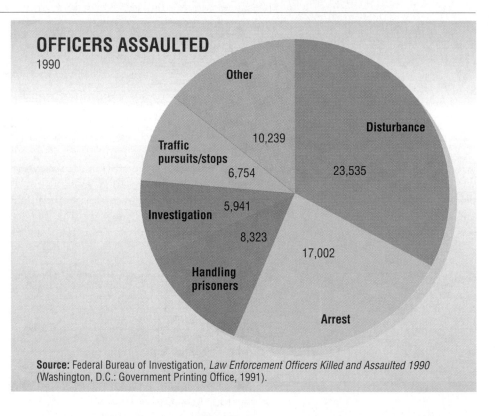

OFFICERS ASSAULTED

1990

- Other 10,239
- Disturbance 23,535
- Traffic pursuits/stops 6,754
- Investigation 5,941
- 8,323
- 17,002
- Handling prisoners
- Arrest

Source: Federal Bureau of Investigation, *Law Enforcement Officers Killed and Assaulted 1990* (Washington, D.C.: Government Printing Office, 1991).

rewards for good job performance, insufficient training, and excessive paperwork can also contribute to police stress.[51]

The criminal justice system creates additional stress. Court appearances interfere with police officers' work assignments, personal time, and even sleeping schedules. Turf battles among agencies, court decisions curtailing discretion, perceived leniency of the courts, and release of offenders on bail, probation, or parole also lead to stress. Further stress arises from perceived lack of support and negative attitudes toward police from the larger society. (Most public opinion surveys, however, show strong support for and positive attitudes toward police.) Stress also stems from distorted and/or unfavorable news accounts of incidents involving police, and the inaccessibility and perceived ineffectiveness of social service and rehabilitation agencies to whom officers refer individuals.[52]

Women and minority officers face additional stressors. They are more likely to face disapproval from fellow officers and from family and friends for entering police work. Supervisors, peers, and the public question women officers' ability to handle the emotional and physical rigors of the job, even though research indicates women can do so. The need to "prove themselves" to male officers and to the public constitutes a major stressor for women officers.

Stress contributes not only to the physical disorders mentioned earlier, but also to emotional problems. Some research suggests that police officers commit suicide at a higher rate than other groups. Most investigators report unusually high rates of divorce among police. Although some maintain that researchers have exaggerated the divorce rate among police, interview surveys demonstrate that police stress reduces the quality of family life. A majority of officers interviewed reported that police work inhibits non-police friendships, interferes with scheduling family social events, and generates a negative public image. Furthermore, they take job pressures home, and spouses worry about officers' safety. Systematic studies do not confirm the widely held belief that police suffer from unusually high rates of alcoholism, although indirect research has established a relationship between high job stress and excessive drinking. Finally, officers interviewed cited guilt, anxiety, fear, nightmares, and insomnia following involvement in shooting incidents.[53]

In the past, departments either ignored officers with problems or dealt with them informally by assigning them to desk jobs. During the 1950s, some departments began to formalize their responses, usually by incorporating officer-initiated Alcoholics Anonymous groups made up exclusively of alcoholic officers. In the 1970s, departments instituted "employee assistance" programs to deal with problem officers, particularly those suffering from alcoholism. These programs have expanded into a broad range of responses to police stress. Some programs focus on physical fitness, diet, relaxation, and biofeedback to cope with stress. Others emphasize family counseling to involve spouses in reducing police stress, such as Kansas City's Marriage Partner Program, or Minnesota's Couple Communications Program.

Police Misconduct

Police misconduct covers a broad range of behavior, so it means little without definition. It can mean something as minor as accepting a free cup of coffee in a local restaurant, or as serious as trafficking in drugs and intentionally beating up and killing people. In this section, the major forms of **police misconduct** include:

- Abuse of force.
- Discrimination.
- Corruption.

Explanations of Police Misconduct

Police misconduct may represent the shortcomings of individual officers. This **"rotten apple" theory of police misconduct** is based on the hypothesis that recruitment and training inevitably fail to screen out a few bad officers. These "rotten apples" have deep-seated characteristics that they brought with them to police work; they may be sadists, racists, sexists, or any number of things peculiar to them as individuals.

Misconduct might also arise out of the shortcomings of training and police work itself. "Bad" officers might start out as idealists but become "bad" due to the failures of administrative rules, leadership, and the socialization processes of education, training, and field experiences. In some instances, police training and socialization might contain the message that the police cannot do their job by following the book. In order to serve what they and much of the public call "justice," these officers resort to "dirty means." They fabricate evidence, intimidate, and sometimes even torture suspects because they believe they have to in order to get around such obstacles to justice as the exclusionary rule. This is the only way, they believe, that they can prove someone the officers "know" is guilty has committed a crime. Professor Carl Klockars calls this the **Dirty Harry problem**, derived from the Clint Eastwood *Dirty Harry* movie in which Harry Callahan, the tough detective, tortures a clearly guilty suspect because he will not tell where he has buried alive a young rape-kidnapping victim. In such cases, officers achieve what they consider a good end by illegal means. Responsibility for police misconduct, if it is even considered misconduct, lies with the institution, not the individual.[54]

Abuse of Force

In a perfect world there would be no need for police. There would be no conflict and everyone would obey the law. In a second-best world, people who broke the law would voluntarily comply with police requests. However, in the real world both obedience to the law and voluntary compliance with police are far from complete. Therefore, police must use force to do their job; hence, the defining characteristic of police is the **legitimate use of force**. According to Egon Bittner, "the capacity to use coercive force lends thematic unity to all police activity in the same sense in which . . . the capacity to cure illness lends unity to everything that is ordinarily done in the field of medical practice."[55]

Uneasiness about the police use of force has an ancient history. The Romans asked, "Sed quis costodiet ipsos custodes?" (Who will watch the watchmen?) As we saw in the history of police in Chapter 4, the establishment of professional police forces faced stiff opposition. Once established, the English "bobbies" were allowed to carry only truncheons, and those they had to keep concealed except to defend themselves against physical assault. In America, departments acquiesced in but did not openly approve the use of weapons until some years after the establishment of public police departments. But the use of force was common, even necessary, because of the difficulty in arresting suspects. Officers faced a generally disrespectful public and other difficulties as well. Most arrests were for drunkenness and public disorder, which required that officers use physical force to subdue the people they arrested. Once officers subdued arrested people, they faced the difficulty of transporting them, on foot, back to the stationhouse. In the twentieth century, at least the *perception* if not the *reality* of the **abuse of force** has contributed to some of the worst riots in American history—Harlem in 1935, Watts in 1965, Miami in 1980, and Los Angeles in 1992. These riots were not just about police use of force generally, but about the perceived or real use of excessive force against African Americans specifically. The question of race is inescapably connected to the problem of police use of excessive force.[56]

After the riots in Los Angeles sparked by the acquittal in 1992 of the police officers accused of beating Rodney King, the ambivalence about the use of force came into bold relief. By chance, a young man trying out his newly acquired camcorder recorded Los Angeles police officers beating King following a high-speed chase in which King tried to elude capture. The sight

This Nigerian police officer exercises his legal authority to use both his gun and his whip to order this accused thief to roll in mud and garbage.

of many officers using clubs, boots, and other means to keep King down was etched into the public mind by repeated showings of the tape on television, night after night. There followed a great debate over the use of force by the police. The beating, the acquittal, and the death and destruction that followed revealed three critical points:

1. The defining characteristic of police work—the *legitimate* use of coercive force—is critical to effective police work.
2. The need for *legitimate* use of force creates the central problem of police misconduct—the *excessive* use of coercive force.[57]
3. Much of the perception, if not the reality, of the excessive use of force is held by members of racial minority groups.

Bringing these points out into the open produced a rich discussion and generated considerable research that tried to tell us what we know—and don't know—about the kinds and amounts of police use of force; about policies and practices regarding the use of force; and about the effectiveness of these policies and practices. The debate over police use of force hardly began with Rodney King. New York journalist Lincoln Steffens opened the twentieth century with a series of articles reporting the wanton brutality of Patrolman "Clubber Williams" of the New York Police Department. The Wickersham Commission lamented the abuse of force by police officers in 1930. The President's Commission on Law Enforcement repeated the lament in 1967. The debate provoked by the beating of Rodney King, the initial acquittal of the officers, the ensuing riots, the later conviction of the officers, and their ultimate release promises to continue until at least the year 2000 much as Steffens started it in 1900.

Types and Amounts of Force

> Simply put, . . . no one knows what excessive force is. . . . [I]t follows that all the talk of wanting to reduce or eliminate it is largely meaningless. . . . Needless to say, if no one knows what excessive force is, it also follows that empirical research that accurately measures it or its reduction is non-existent.[58]

These words of police expert Carl B. Klockars were written to underscore the difficulties in defining, measuring, and responding to the abuse of force by police officers. Although the line between legitimate and excessive force is difficult to draw, experts have classified police force in several ways:

- non-deadly and deadly
- violent and nonviolent
- reasonable and excessive
- necessary and unnecessary

The distinction between non-deadly and deadly force is that deadly force can cause serious bodily injury or death. Shooting at suspects, even if they do not die or even if the shots miss them, is an exercise of deadly force. Violent force means the use of physical force; nonviolent means verbal coercion such as orders, advice, warnings, and persuasion. Reasonable and excessive are legal terms. Reasonable means the amount of force necessary to accomplish compliance with legitimate police authority; excessive means more force than is required to accomplish the legitimate purpose. Reasonable force is lawful; excessive is illegal.

Necessary and unnecessary force is an expansion of the other classifications. These categories were created by James Fyfe, who explains that both necessary and unnecessary force are lawful. Unnecessary violence occurs when "police officers who know better cause bloodshed in situations that might have been resolved peaceably and bloodlessly by more capable officers." Fyfe warns that "unnecessary force is far more likely than brutality to generate either widespread resentment of the police or civil liability for the police."[59]

For 30 years, observers have reported that the police use force infrequently. Estimates cover a broad range. Robert E. Wordon reported that the police used force in only 60 out of 5,688 (1.05 percent) police-citizen encounters. Ross Lundstrom and Cynthia Mullen, on the other hand, reported that the police used force in 1,750 out of 11,989 (14.6 percent) of incidents where officers used force to arrest and transport people to detox centers and mental hospitals. Of course, situations vary from place to place, situation to situation, and probably by race. Angus Campbell and Howard Schuman asked people in 15 cities about their negative experiences with the police. Two percent of a sample of whites said that police had "roughed them up;" seven percent of the African Americans said the police had "roughed them up."[60]

The Police Foundation, a Washington-based research organization devoted to police reform and improved policing, with the support of the National Institute of Justice, conducted the most thorough and detailed study yet of the kinds and amounts of police use of force. Researchers surveyed a sample of state, county, and municipal law enforcement agencies in order to determine the types and amounts of force used by law enforcement officers. Figure 7.6 reports the results of this survey.[61]

How often do police abuse the use of force? Little is known on this point. One reason is that it is difficult to measure. Most studies suffer validity and reliability problems. Observational studies usually generate too little data for generalizing, and they suffer from officers being influenced by having someone watching them work. Surveys and interviews of civilians measure

Figure 7.6

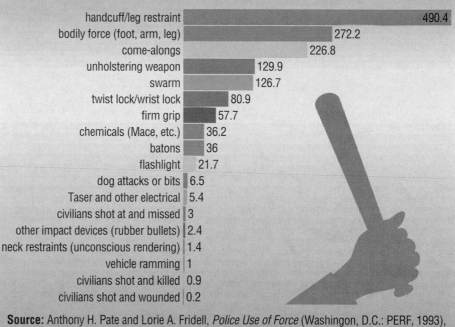

USE OF FORCE BY CITY POLICE, RATE PER 1,000 OFFICERS, 1991

handcuff/leg restraint	490.4
bodily force (foot, arm, leg)	272.2
come-alongs	226.8
unholstering weapon	129.9
swarm	126.7
twist lock/wrist lock	80.9
firm grip	57.7
chemicals (Mace, etc.)	36.2
batons	36
flashlight	21.7
dog attacks or bits	6.5
Taser and other electrical	5.4
civilians shot at and missed	3
other impact devices (rubber bullets)	2.4
neck restraints (unconscious rendering)	1.4
vehicle ramming	1
civilians shot and killed	0.9
civilians shot and wounded	0.2

Source: Anthony H. Pate and Lorie A. Fridell, *Police Use of Force* (Washingon, D.C.: PERF, 1993), based on Table 6.1

perceptions of excessive force that may differ substantially from reality. Surveys and interviews of police officers also suffer from perception problems, and police officers may give socially desirable responses. Data from agency records reflect more the perspectives of the agency than actual behavior. Furthermore, departments willing to allow researchers access are probably the most progressive. Official agency records measure excessive force indirectly, since they contain information only about complaints that civilians bring to them, not all the incidents of force and excessive force.[62]

Deadly Force It has always been unlawful for police officers to use unnecessary force in their work. The courts, statutes, and police department rules have always limited the use of force to that which is reasonable under the circumstances. This vague directive does not give much guidance to police officers. During the 1970s, as a result of a number of influences, law enforcement agencies, particularly urban departments, began to draft administrative rules outlining policies and practices regarding the use of force. Most of these rules were limited to the use of deadly force. Some were directed at the use of deadly force to apprehend violent felony suspects. Others restricted the use of deadly force to suspects whom officers believed would endanger community safety unless they were apprehended immediately. A few forbade the use of deadly force except in the defense of the life of officers or other innocent people. Most departments that adopted rules restricting deadly force were urban departments.[63]

The Police Foundation studied the deadly force rules of police departments in Birmingham, Alabama; Detroit, Michigan; Indianapolis, Indiana; Kansas City, Missouri; Oakland, California; Portland, Oregon; and Washington, D.C. The authors of the study recommended the following policy changes:

1. Departments should develop rules governing the use of deadly force. Police administrators and other public officials, private individuals, and especially police line officers (patrol officers) who actually use guns should formulate the rules.

2. Officers should shoot only to defend themselves or others, and to apprehend suspects in deadly or potentially deadly felonies. Departments should list the felonies included, such as assault with a deadly weapon and armed robbery.[64]

Formulating, implementing, and enforcing deadly force rules pose challenges to police administrators. Line officers suspect proposed changes, and police unions oppose them. Administrators hesitate to put firearms policies in writing because courts might later permit people who are suing the police to use the rules in court. Some courts have held departments legally liable for violating their own rules. The California Supreme Court, for example, permitted the written firearms policy of the Los Angeles Police Department to be used as evidence in a wrongful death action involving an officer who deviated from the rules.[65]

In 1990, the Commission on Accreditation for Law Enforcement Agencies adopted the following standard for the use of deadly force:

> Standard 1.3.2 . . . an officer may use deadly force only when the officer reasonably believes that the action is in defense of human life, including the officer's own life, or in defense of any person in immediate danger of serious injury.
> Standard 1.3.3 . . . the use of deadly force against a "fleeing felon" must meet the conditions required in 1.3.2.[66]

Compelling reasons lie behind the adoption of rules that tighten firearms use. Researchers estimate that police kill about 600 people every year, shoot and wound another 1,200, and fire at, but miss, another 1,800. The numbers vary from city to city. For example, from 1974 to 1978, Chicago and Los Angeles police fatally shot about the same number of people: Chicago, 132, and Los Angeles, 139. However, Chicago police wounded 386 people while Los Angeles police wounded only 238. Chicago police fired on 2,876; Los Angeles, only on 611. Furthermore, the incidence of police shootings varies from neighborhood to neighborhood within cities. Chicago's Near West Side, for example, is 27 times more likely than the Near North Side to experience a police shooting in an average year. Rates also vary from city to city. New Orleans police are 10 times more likely to kill people than are Newark police.[67]

Deadly force not only kills suspects; officers die as well. In 1995, 162 police officers died while on duty. Contrary to public perceptions, it is not always suspects who kill officers. In a substantial number of fatalities, officers accidentally shoot other officers. Departments with effective deadly force rules show sharp decreases not only in citizen deaths, but also in officer deaths. In Kansas City, Missouri, for example, after the department adopted a rule that prohibited police from shooting juveniles except in self-defense, the numbers of youths under 18 shot by the police dropped dramatically. James Fyfe showed that not only did police shootings drop sharply following New York City Police Department adoption of a strict deadly force rule, but the numbers of police officers shot at also dropped. Hence, deadly force rules appear to reduce not only citizen but also police fatalities and woundings.[68]

According to researchers, the following techniques to control shooting show promise:

- Policies narrowing officer shooting discretion.
- Violence-reduction training to help officers abide by a "shoot only as a last resort" policy.
- Use of modern communications equipment and interagency cooperative arrangements that enable officers to summon whatever assistance they need.
- Protective equipment, such as lightweight soft-body armor suitable for routine wear by officers, and "less lethal weapons," including

Figure 7.7

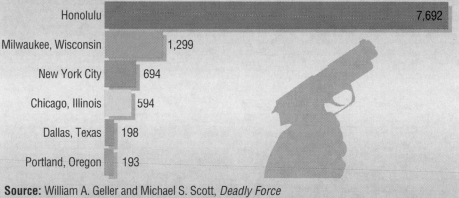

NUMBER OF YEARS STATISTICALLY FOR OFFICER TO KILL A SUSPECT

Honolulu	7,692
Milwaukee, Wisconsin	1,299
New York City	694
Chicago, Illinois	594
Dallas, Texas	198
Portland, Oregon	193

Source: William A. Geller and Michael S. Scott, *Deadly Force* (Washington, D.C.: Police Executive Research Forum, 1992), 60.

TASERs (electronic dart guns), stun guns (compact cattle prods), rubber bullets, and other similar devices.

● Strong personnel policies, increased supervision of line officers, and fair but firm accountability up the chain of command for inappropriate officer aggressiveness and for deficient firearms training, procedures, and practices.

● Counseling for officers who desire help in dealing with job and other stresses and with post-shooting trauma.

● "Cultural awareness" training to sensitize officers to ethnic, religious, or other group traits that might have a bearing on an officer's appraisal of a suspect's dangerousness and on an officer's ability to reduce it.

● Departmental reward systems that honor equally both an officer's decisiveness in using deadly force when necessary and his or her ability to resolve situations by less violent means when that option is available.[69]

How many shootings is too many? Compared with the total number of contacts police have with individuals, shootings are rare. Figure 7.7 depicts the number of years an average police officer would have to work, statistically, in order to kill a suspect. A study of New York City patrol officers found that officers used force of any sort in less than one tenth of one percent of all encounters with private individuals. They shot at civilians five times out of 1,762 times that observers saw officers use any physical force.[70]

Who do the police shoot? According to a survey of all studies on deadly force over the past 30 years, William A. Geller and Michael S. Scott describe the typical shooting:

> The most common type of incident in which police and civilians shoot one another in urban America involves an on-duty, uniformed, white, male officer and an armed, black, male civilian between the ages of 17 and 30 and occurs at night, in a public location in a high-crime precinct, in connection with a suspected armed robbery or a "man with a gun" call.[71]

Nearly all the studies report that the police shoot at more African Americans than whites (see Figure 7.8). Here is a sample of the findings:

● Chicago police officers shot at African Americans 3.8 times more than at whites during the 1970s.

Figure 7.8

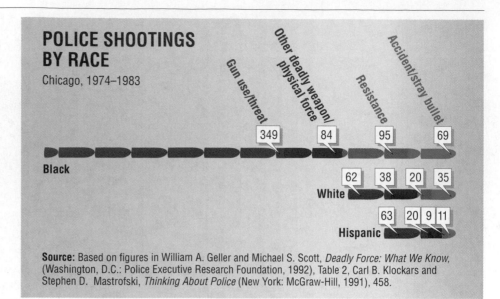

POLICE SHOOTINGS BY RACE

Chicago, 1974–1983

Gun use/threat

Other deadly weapon/ physical force

Resistance

Accident/stray bullet

Black: 349 | 84 | 95 | 69

White: 62 | 38 | 20 | 35

Hispanic: 63 | 20 | 9 | 11

Source: Based on figures in William A. Geller and Michael S. Scott, *Deadly Force: What We Know,* (Washington, D.C.: Police Executive Research Foundation, 1992), Table 2, Carl B. Klockars and Stephen D. Mastrofski, *Thinking About Police* (New York: McGraw-Hill, 1991), 458.

- New York City police officers shot at African Americans 6 times more than they shot at whites during the 1970s.
- Dallas police officers shot at African Americans 4.5 times more than at whites during the 1970s and 1980s.
- St. Louis police officers shot at African Americans 7.7 times more than they shot at whites during 1987-1991.
- Memphis police officers fatally shot at African Americans 5.1 more times than they shot at whites from 1969 to 1974; 2.6 times more from 1980 to 1984; and 1.6 times more from 1985 to 1989. Considering only property crime suspects, Memphis police officers were 9.4 times more likely to shoot at blacks than at whites from 1969 to 1974; 13 times more from 1980 to 1984; and blacks were the only property crime suspects shot at from 1985 to 1989.[72]

The shooting of *fewer* African Americans by the police has accounted almost exclusively for a reduction in shootings over the past few decades. A survey of 57 cities showed that the ratio of African American to white killings fell from 7 to 1 in 1971 to 2.8 to 1 in 1979. Do the racial disparities in shooting indicate racism among the police? Researchers have theorized that the difference may lie in other factors, such as poverty and violent crime. The Dallas Police Department, in a report on the disproportionate number of African and Hispanic Americans shot at, ruled out racism as the cause for the disparity:

> This is not to say that Blacks and Hispanics are more likely to attack the police officers or are more criminally inclined because of race or heritage. On the contrary, violent crime is well recognized as being a lower socio-economic class phenomenon. Blacks and Hispanics comprise a large majority of this lower socio-economic group because of discrimination in education and employment in previous decades. Typically, in large cities, the majority of individuals in these lower socio-economic classes are Black or Hispanic. (In the city of Dallas, the percent of families below the poverty level is 5.2% for Whites, 17.7% for Hispanics, and 21.7% for Blacks.[73]

Lawrence Sherman, who has conducted major research on all aspects of the police, disagrees:

> In the absence of more conclusive evidence, the demonstrably higher rates of police homicide for blacks strongly suggests racial discrimina-

tion on a national basis. Although such patterns are quite likely to vary from one city to the next, such a variation would support the argument that present procedures allow police homicide to be administered in a discriminatory fashion.[74]

Some research suggests that most police officers shoot for reasons other than race. Figure 7.9 depicts the distribution of reasons for why officers use deadly force. However, most existing research suffers from methodological problems. Often, the only information available on police shootings is the written report of the officer who fired the shots. According to Michael E. Donahue of the Savannah, Georgia, Police Department and Frank S. Horvath of Michigan State University:

> It is naive to believe that such written reports always reflect exactly what took place during such an incident. That is not to say, however, that either police officers or other witnesses deliberately lie about such events—even though it is likely that some do—but that these events usually occur quite quickly, and that even the best recollection of what was observed may not always square with the facts.[75]

One study by James Fyfe shows racial discrimination in some types of shootings. Fyfe studied shootings by the Memphis Police Department (the department involved in the case excerpted in the Chapter 6 *You Decide*, "Can Police Shoot to Kill a Fleeing Burglar?"). He reviewed the data for six years, 1969 to 1974, and concluded that

> the data strongly support the assertion that police [in Memphis] did differentiate racially with their trigger fingers, by shooting blacks in circumstances less threatening than those in which they shot whites. . . . [The] black death rate from police shootings while unarmed and non-assaultive (5.4 per 100,000) . . . is 18 times higher than the comparable white rate (0.3).[76]

Following the shooting of 13-year-old Edward Garner (described in Chapter 6), Memphis adopted a more restrictive shooting policy to allow the use of deadly force only to prevent the commission of "dangerous felonies." Following the Supreme Court decision in *Tennessee v. Garner*, Memphis restricted its shooting policy still further. According to the new policy, shooting was justified only if the suspect had committed a "violent felony" and posed "a threat of serious physical harm to the officer or to others unless he is immediately apprehended." Jerry R. Sparger and David J. Giacopassi reviewed records of police shootings in Memphis during each succeeding

Figure 7.9

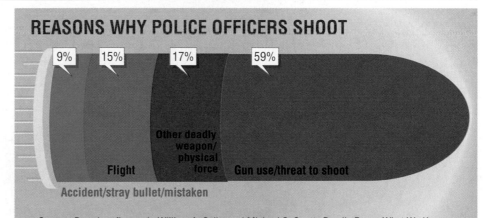

REASONS WHY POLICE OFFICERS SHOOT

9% Accident/stray bullet/mistaken
15% Flight
17% Other deadly weapon/physical force
59% Gun use/threat to shoot

Source: Based on figures in William A. Geller and Michael S. Scott, *Deadly Force: What We Know*, (Washington, D.C.: Police Executive Research Foundation, 1992), Table 2, Carl B. Klockars and Stephen D. Mastrofski, *Thinking About Police* (New York: McGraw-Hill, 1991), 458.

shooting policy. Following each restriction on the fleeing felon doctrine, a review of incidents showed a marked reduction in the total number of police shootings. Furthermore, "the apparently discriminatory shooting practices which occurred under the prior deadly force policies have been eliminated almost entirely." Moreover, the number of African-American deaths resulting from shooting has steadily declined (see Figure 7.10). However, despite the apparent end of discriminatory shooting *practices*, and the reduction in the numbers of fatalities, Sparger and Giacopassi report that the *rate* of African-American deaths from police shooting remains 56.5 percent higher than the rate of white deaths.[77]

Despite the mixed results of studies of disparities in the shooting of nonwhites by the police, few deny that race influences some shootings. According to an African American police officer who testified to the Independent Commission on the Los Angeles Police Department in the course of investigating police use of force in the Rodney King case:

> There are many fine white officers who are doing their job and do not harbor racist sentiments. However, there is still a significant group of individuals whose old line, deep-seated biases continually manifest themselves on the job.[78]

High-Speed Chases Shooting suspects is not the only form of police use of force—in fact, despite its high visibility, it is the rarest. High-speed chases, a controversial means to apprehend suspects, are more common than shootings and are also a form of deadly force. Police pursuits have attracted considerable attention from both courts and researchers. Jerome Skolnick and James Fyfe explain why some officers initiate high-speed chases:

> During our years in police cars, we have been at the cop's end of more than thirty high-speed chases. Younger cops, hotshot cops, aggressive cops, relish the exhilaration of these pursuits. People who haven't ridden in patrol cars for a full shift cannot appreciate how tedious policing

Figure 7.10

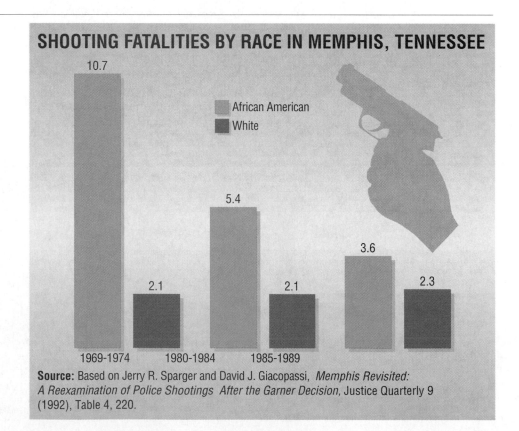

SHOOTING FATALITIES BY RACE IN MEMPHIS, TENNESSEE

African American
White

10.7

5.4

3.6

2.1   2.1   2.3

1969-1974   1980-1984   1985-1989

Source: Based on Jerry R. Sparger and David J. Giacopassi, *Memphis Revisited: A Reexamination of Police Shootings After the Garner Decision, Justice Quarterly 9* (1992), Table 4, 220.

can be even in the world's most crime-ridden cities. Patrol policing, like military combat and the lives of cowboys, consists mostly of periods of boredom, broken up by interludes of excitement and even of terror. For police, a chase is among the most exciting of all work experiences: the sudden start of a chase is a jolt not unlike that experienced by the dozing fisherman who finds suddenly that he has a big and dangerous fish on the other end of his line.[79]

Pursuits endanger, and sometimes injure or even kill, police officers, suspects, and innocent people in the path of the chase. In one two-week period, eight pursuits in southern California killed ten people, three of them within a five-hour period. All but two of the ten people killed were bystanders. Police managers and officers disagree over high-speed chases. Some criticize the practice, particularly when it involves property crimes. "In one precinct . . . I had 10 officers out injured and five vehicles totaled," said William R. Celester, chief of police in Newark, New Jersey. "It's not worth it to take a life, like my son's life, for a bad license plate or a stolen car," said Una Corley Groves, whose son was killed by a Federal Parks cruiser as it sped through a red light in pursuit of a driver who had just run the light. Public anger flared when a car being chased by the U.S. Border Patrol in southern California crashed a school crossing, killing six people, including four teenage students, and leading to demands that the police curtail their chases.[80]

The commissioner of the California Highway Patrol responds that letting fleeing suspects or anyone else simply drive away invites anarchy:

> It's no different than waging a war. There are some inherent risks. There are going to be losses, unfortunately. This is a battle where we are trying to bring crime to a halt. . . . The number of deaths and injuries attributable to police pursuits is minuscule compared to the overall deaths that would result if you did not allow the police to engage in pursuits.[81]

Captain Thomas Shook, commander of the Richmond Police Department, complains of an unhealthy trend in the country of blaming the police for the tough tactics they use. "We in society are losing the battle between anarchy and civilization."[82]

High speed chases may reduce crimes, such as car thefts, but they can also result in accidents that injure and kill people.

Mayor Dick Greco, of Tampa, Florida, won election running on a campaign to relax Tampa's recently enacted high-speed chase policy. Tampa had restricted high-speed chases to violent felonies, such as murder, kidnapping, and robbery. Soon after Greco's election, the city relaxed the policy to allow chases of suspected car thieves. Tampa had one of the highest car theft rates in the nation. In the year following the reintroduction of high-speed chases, police statistics showed a 50 percent reduction in car thefts, from 5,699 to 2,788. However, a number of accidents occurred during these chases. In one, officers knocked a house off its foundation. In another, two German tourists were killed. Police Chief Bonnie Holder stood by the policy, despite the casualties. After the deaths, Deputy Chief Kenneth H. Taylor said, "The policy doesn't say go out and have an accident. We didn't kill anybody. Some felons who decided to buck the law endangered everybody. I totally reject the idea that the police caused any of this."[83]

Geoffrey P. Alpert and Roger G. Dunham studied police pursuits based on pursuit-reporting forms and supporting documents by officers in Florida's Metro-Dade County Police Department. He found that 54 percent of pursuits were initiated for traffic infractions; 32 percent for suspected felony stops; 12 percent because of calls "to be on the lookout for" a specific offender; and 2 percent to make stops for reckless driving while intoxicated (DWI). Figure 7.11 depicts the results of these pursuits. Accidents occurred in more than half the pursuits in which officers arrested suspects. At the same time, failure to chase might permit a suspect to escape apprehension. Alpert found that many traffic pursuits resulted in arrests for serious felonies not related to the traffic offense.[84]

Publicity over accidents, injuries, and deaths from high-speed chases has brought pursuit driving under scrutiny. Pursuit driving demands the exercise of discretion; the law guides police discretion to engage in high-speed chases. Researchers have drawn contradictory policy implications from recent studies of police pursuits. The California Highway Patrol, following a pursuit study, represents one point of view:

> Attempted apprehension of motorists in violation of what appear to be minor traffic infractions is necessary for the preservation of order on the highways of California. If approximately 700 people will attempt to flee from officers who participated in this six-month study, knowing full well that the officers will give chase, one can imagine what would happen if the police suddenly banned pursuits. Undoubtedly, innocent people may be injured or killed because an officer chooses to pursue a suspect, but this risk is necessary to avoid the even greater loss that would occur if law enforcement agencies were not allowed to aggressively pursue violators.[85]

On the other hand, Stone and DeLuca, authors of a police administration textbook, maintain that

> one of the major areas of controversy . . . is the practice of pursuing fugitives at high speed. High-speed pursuit is an exceedingly dangerous kind of police operation. It is dangerous not only for the police officer and the fugitive, but equally so for innocent citizens who happen to be in their path. . . . More often than not, a high-speed pursuit ends only when either the fugitive or the officer is involved in a collision, often a fatal one.[86]

High-speed police pursuits raise several policy issues. One is the analogy between deadly force and police pursuits. According to police specialist Gordon E. Misner, "If the circumstances don't reasonably permit the use of deadly force, they also do not warrant engaging in a high-speed chase!" Most police departments, according to a survey Misner conducted, did not generally equate deadly force and police pursuits. However, several did use the

Figure 7.11

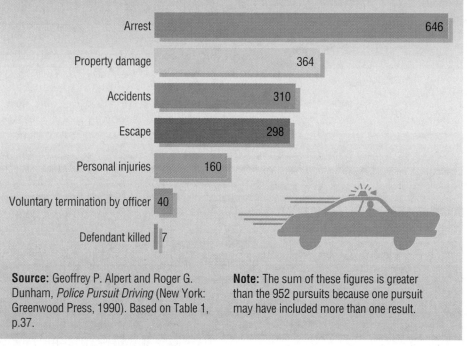

RESULTS OF POLICE PURSUITS, METRO-DADE COUNTY POLICE DEPARTMENT, 1985-1987

Arrest	646
Property damage	364
Accidents	310
Escape	298
Personal injuries	160
Voluntary termination by officer	40
Defendant killed	7

Source: Geoffrey P. Alpert and Roger G. Dunham, *Police Pursuit Driving* (New York: Greenwood Press, 1990). Based on Table 1, p.37.

Note: The sum of these figures is greater than the 952 pursuits because one pursuit may have included more than one result.

deadly force analogy in cases of "ramming," or deliberately touching a pursued vehicle to "alert the driver that the pursuing officer is serious about stopping!"[87]

Pursuits also raise issues of peer group pressure, the idea that chases put the machismo of pursuing officers on the line. Lee P. Brown, when he was chief of the Houston Police Department, in a cover message to a new pursuit policy, wrote:

> Remember the criminals will continue to be out there in the future and they can be found and arrested by other means. So if you decide not to chase based on the risks involved, you will not be subject to criticism. However, if you decide that you should chase, we will support you and offer acceptable standard operating procedures to assist you. The safety and well-being of our officers and the public we serve is the first and foremost priority in our minds, and we will continue to work toward that end with you.[88]

A Houston officer referred to the importance of altering organizational culture from "Chase them until the wheels fall off" to "Why risk your life to chase some traffic violator?"[89]

The Louisiana State Police caution their officers as follows regarding chases:

> When the violator begins to seriously endanger the lives of innocent persons upon the highway, by passing on curves or in the face of on-coming traffic, the trooper should discontinue the pursuit except as follows:
>
> a. The violator is a felon who has committed a crime which endangered life; or
>
> b. The actions of the violator are such that the trooper reasonably believes that his continued freedom would seriously jeopardize the lives of others.[90]

Policies and Practices Regarding Force Researchers who have evaluated police use of force policies have emphasized that the mere making of rules—however good the content—is not enough to change what happens in day-to-day police decision making on the street. Jerome H. Skolnick and James J. Fyfe surveyed several cities where unwritten rules "overwhelmed" written rules governing shooting. Lawrence W. Sherman argues that reductions in shootings following the adoption of rules do not mean that rules alone can reduce the use of deadly force. In all the cities he studied, Sherman said, the rules were accompanied by "intense public criticism of the police and an increasingly severe administrative and disciplinary posture toward shooting." Fyfe maintains that the adoption of a new Firearms Discharge Review Board to enforce a new shooting policy was instrumental in the reduction of shootings in New York City. Following the Rodney King incident, the Independent Commission of the Los Angeles Police Department said, "The problem of excessive force in the LAPD is fundamentally a problem of supervision, management, and leadership." William B. Waegel examined shootings in Philadelphia to assess the effectiveness of a statute that changed the old law giving police officers the right to shoot *any* fleeing felony suspect, to the more restrictive rule authorizing officers to shoot only fleeing *forcible* felony suspects. The number of unlawful shootings remained high after the change in the law. Waegel concluded that changes in laws may not be enough. Reductions in unlawful shootings require changes in police behavior. Changes in police behavior will not take place unless police leadership insist, and by their example demonstrate, that they demand compliance with the rules.[91]

Two projects dramatically illustrate the importance of training in the reduction of force. Psychologist Hans Toch and two colleagues, J. Douglas Grant and Ray Galvin, assembled a group of officers, some of whom had histories of violent encounters and some whom their supervisors identified as "good" officers. The group was allowed to define the problem of police-citizen violence, identify its causes, develop a strategy for dealing with it, and put the strategy into operation. The officers started by creating a Violence Prevention Unit. The unit reviewed the files of officers whose records indicated frequent incidents of violence. The unit then conducted an investigation, collecting information about the officers with violence problems from supervisors and fellow officers. A study group reviewed the information and developed questions to ask at a meeting with violence-prone officers. The meeting explored the key incidents of violence, allowed the subject to summarize the incidents, and then discussed how the pattern of incidents led to violence. Alternatives that might avoid violence were then discussed. Before participation in the discussions, the most violence-prone officers engaged in conflicts four times more often than other officers. Following participation, the incidents were cut in half.[92]

A scandal arising out of an incident resembling in some ways the Rodney King case prompted a violence-reduction training program in the Metro-Dade County Police Department. Several police officers beat an African-American insurance agent into a coma following a chase for a traffic violation. To make the injuries look like they were caused by a traffic spill (the man was on a motorcycle), the officers drove their squad car over the motorcycle. The man died four days later. When the officers' cover-up was discovered, they were tried for manslaughter. A jury acquitted them, and a riot followed the acquittal. But out of the tragedy came a success story: the Metro-Dade Police/Citizen Violence Reduction Project. The project was designed to defuse potentially violent situations between police and private individuals. A task force of police officers, investigators, supervisors, and trainers analyzed reports of 100 encounters between private individuals and police that culminated in the use of force, injuries to officers, or complaints against officers. From their analyses, the task force drew up detailed lists of "Dos and Don'ts" for the four most frequent potentially violent encounters: traffic stops, stops of suspicious vehicles, responses to reported crimes, and disputes. The lists were built into a training program. In the year and a half following completion of the training program, the use of force by officers, injuries to officers, and complaints against officers all dropped by between 30 and 50 percent.[93]

Police Corruption

When police engage in conduct they are sworn to prevent, it corrodes public confidence and breeds resentment. Police officials who preach obedience to law and then proceed to break it themselves can hardly rely on citizen cooperation in maintaining an orderly society. Indeed, such behavior invites people to become lawbreakers. Police corruption impairs effective policing from within the police department itself. Officers who are "on the take" have less time to spend on police duties. In fact, they frequently resent having to perform their police responsibilities, particularly when these interfere with their pursuit of private gain. Corrupt sergeants, captains, inspectors, and other supervisors weaken administrative control over patrol officers. A commander taking payoffs is not an effective supervisor. Weak supervision also leads officers "typically [to] respond more slowly to calls for assistance, avoid assigned duties, sleep on the job, and perform poorly in situations requiring discipline."[94]

Police corruption is a form of occupational crime: misusing police authority for private gain. (See Chapter 2.) Corruption varies from department to department. It might affect only one or two officers or pervade a whole department. The definition of corruption also varies. It can include everything from a top official regularly extorting thousands of dollars a month from vice operations, to a patrol officer accepting a free cup of coffee from a neighborhood restaurant. According to former New York Police Commissioner Patrick Murphy, "Except for your paycheck, there is no such thing as a clean buck."[95]

The most common corrupt practices include:

1. *Mooching*—free meals, liquor, groceries, or other items.
2. *Chiseling*—demands for free admission to entertainment.
3. *Favoritism*—gaining immunity from traffic violations.
4. *Prejudice*—giving nonwhites less than impartial treatment.
5. *Shopping*—picking up small items from stores left unlocked after business hours.
6. *Extortion*—demanding money in exchange for not filing traffic tickets.
7. *Bribery*—receiving payments of cash or "gifts" for past or future assistance in avoiding arrest, or in falsifying or withholding evidence.
8. *Shakedown*—appropriating expensive items for personal use and attributing their loss to criminal activity when investigating a break-in or burglary.
9. *Perjury*—lying to provide an alibi for fellow officers apprehended in illegal activity.
10. *Premeditated theft*—executing a planned burglary to gain forced entry in order to acquire unlawful goods.[96]

The causes of corruption run deep, beyond simple human greed—a quality by no means restricted to police officers. Police in their everyday work deal with the worst side of humanity: "prostitutes, junkies, bums, petty thieves, and burglars." Such contacts lead many officers to conclude that society is generally "on the take." Also, police officers often view the criminal process, especially lower criminal court proceedings, as an exercise in futility. They watch masses of offenders pass haphazardly through undignified lower courts; they see prosecutors, defense attorneys, and judges get their share of dirty money. Officers bitterly recognize that the corruption of prosecutors

This officer boasted to a screen writer that he purposely beat people up because they were African Americans.

and judges is largely immune from scandalous exposure. From this arises the belief that everybody is on the take, but only the police are scandalized. In the end, this steady diet of ineffectiveness and wrongdoing leads some police officers to conclude that their own corruption is no worse than, perhaps not even as bad as, that of others. Furthermore, they come to believe it really makes no difference anyway, considering the inability of the criminal process to reform what, to the police, is largely a corrupt society.[97]

Police discretion also permits the decisions of officers *not* to enforce laws to stand without review in most instances. Furthermore, corruption is addictive. Officers frequently spend graft-augmented income on large new purchases, such as homes and cars. To keep up the payments, the increased income becomes a necessity that leads to dependence on money acquired by corrupt practices.

Exposing and correcting corruption are difficult. According to the Knapp Commission, a group that investigated police corruption in the New York City Police Department in the 1970s,

> a code of silence brands anyone who exposes corruption a traitor. At the time our investigation began, any policeman violating the code did so at his peril. The result [is]: "The rookie who comes into the department is faced with the situation where it is easier for him to become corrupt than to remain honest." Two principal characteristics emerge from this group loyalty: suspicion and hostility directed at any outside interference with the department, and an intense desire to be proud of the department.
>
> . . . The interaction of stubbornness, hostility and pride has given rise to the so-called "rotten-apple" theory. According to this theory . . . any policeman found to be corrupt must promptly be denounced as a rotten apple in an otherwise clean barrel. It must never be admitted that his individual corruption may be symptomatic of underlying disease. . . . The doctrine made impossible the use of one of the most effective techniques for dealing with any entrenched criminal activity, namely, persuading a participant to help provide evidence against his partners in

crime. If a corrupt policeman is merely an isolated rotten apple, no reason can be given for not exposing him the minute he is discovered. If, on the other hand, it is acknowledged that a corrupt officer is only one part of an apparatus of corruption, common sense dictates that every effort should be made to enlist the offender's aid in providing the evidence to destroy the apparatus.[98]

Accountability for Misconduct

We all know what happens—or should happen—when ordinary people break the law. They are supposed to be held accountable for their lawbreaking by criminal prosecution and punishment, or at least by paying damages for the injuries they have caused other people. Similarly, police officers who break the law, depending on the kind and degree of their wrongdoing, must be held accountable. Until the 1960s, the police responded to complaints about misconduct informally. According to Professor Douglas W. Perez, former deputy sheriff of Contra Costa County, California,

> The local precinct captain, lieutenant, or sergeant would attempt to pacify indignant citizens and investigate misconduct if time permitted. . . . In departments with no systematized complaint reception and adjudication procedure, citizens were influenced, cajoled, and even threatened out of making complaints against the police. Such practices, while commonplace, did not become the subject of controversy until the 1960s.[99]

In that decade, the public watched on television some highly publicized (probably *over*-publicized) scenes of urban riots, anti-war demonstrations, and the use of police force to quell riots and control protests. Some academics and politicians began to blame the disorder on police racism and abuse of force. Commissions investigating the causes of the riots and protests seemed to agree. They, together with a growing number of civic groups and even some reformers from within the police ranks, called for various mechanisms to control police misconduct. Some of the mechanisms, such as criminal prosecution and suing the police, were ancient. Others were new to the twentieth century, such as the creation of special units inside police departments controlled by police themselves, and review procedures outside police departments that relied on citizen participation.

Criminal Prosecution

Most police abuse of force is not only a violation of police rules, it is also a crime. For example, a police officer who *illegally* shoots a person and the person dies has committed some form of criminal homicide, depending on the intent and surrounding circumstances. Suppose the worst kind of case: a police officer abuses her authority to use deadly force and intentionally but unnecessarily shoots and kills a man because she is prejudiced against African-American men. This is murder. Suppose the stories were true that Detective Mark Fuhrman (a prosecution witness in the O. J. Simpson case) told an aspiring screenplay writer, on tape, about purposely beating up people because they were African American? Such incidents comprise the felony of aggravated assault, the most serious possible crimes that police officers might commit. Much more common, however, are the illegal searches and arrests that may be burglaries, criminal trespasses, false imprisonment, and perhaps even kidnapping.

How likely is it that police officers whose misconduct is criminal behavior will be charged with crimes, convicted, and punished? Not very. (See Figure 7.12.) In the first place, the invasions of life, liberty, and property that result from police misconduct are often not accompanied by the criminal intent required as a material element in the crime. Furthermore, it is difficult to

Figure 7.12

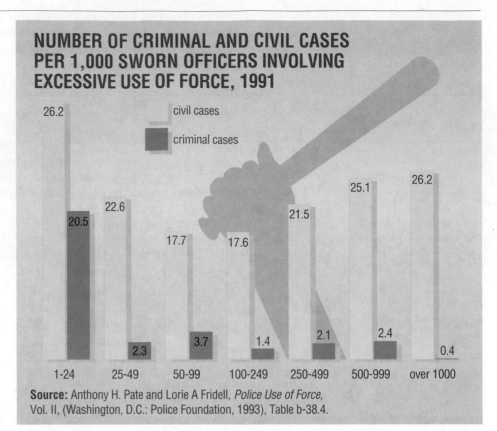

NUMBER OF CRIMINAL AND CIVIL CASES PER 1,000 SWORN OFFICERS INVOLVING EXCESSIVE USE OF FORCE, 1991

civil cases
criminal cases

	1-24	25-49	50-99	100-249	250-499	500-999	over 1000
civil cases	26.2	22.6	17.7	17.6	21.5	25.1	26.2
criminal cases	20.5	2.3	3.7	1.4	2.1	2.4	0.4

Source: Anthony H. Pate and Lorie A Fridell, *Police Use of Force,* Vol. II, (Washington, D.C.: Police Foundation, 1993), Table b-38.4.

plaintiffs *individuals who sue the police in civil lawsuits.*
damages *money awarded to plaintiffs in civil lawsuits.*
injunctions *court actions in civil lawsuits that order defendants either to do or to refrain from doing something.*
torts *actions by police that violate duties imposed on all people.*

prove guilt beyond a reasonable doubt, even though officers may have in fact committed the crime. Witnesses may not exist, or if they do, they are not credible. Even if they are credible, they may not be sympathetic. After all, many people who are subjects of police misconduct are themselves "marginal," that is, not the most "respectable" members of society. They themselves may have criminal histories. Rarely will a prosecutor or a jury (or, for that matter, the public) side with a "real" criminal over police officers who, after all, are "only trying to do their job."

★ Civil Lawsuits

Individuals who sue the police, called **plaintiffs**, usually seek one of two legal remedies: **damages**, that is, money compensation, or **injunctions**, that is, court orders requiring individual police officers and departments to do or stop doing something plaintiffs claim violates their rights. Lawsuits brought by private plaintiffs against individual officers and their departments arise from both federal and state sources. Most illegal actions by police officers are state **torts**, that is, they violate duties imposed on all people. State law provides that injured parties can sue and obtain money from the party who injures them. Many torts are civil versions of the crimes mentioned in the last section. For example, illegal searches and seizures may include all of the following state torts for which plaintiffs can sue for damages: wrongful death, assault, battery, false arrest, false imprisonment, trespass, and breaking and entering. The difference between torts and crimes is that the standard of proof for crimes is "beyond a reasonable doubt," as opposed to the preponderance of evidence required to win a tort case. (See Chapter 10.) The result in a criminal case is that convicted defendants either pay a fine, go to jail or prison, or get probation; defendants in tort cases pay damages to plaintiffs out of their own pockets.

The **doctrine of official immunity** limits the liability of police officers for their torts. According to the doctrine, police officers cannot be legally liable for exercising their discretion unless they engage in intentional and malicious wrongdoing. According to the Minnesota Supreme Court, for example, "[t]o encourage responsible law enforcement . . . police are afforded a wide degree of discretion precisely because a more stringent standard could inhibit action." Therefore, according to the court, a police officer was not liable for the death of a small boy killed during a high-speed chase in which the officer was attempting to apprehend a fleeing shoplifter. Official immunity protected the officer; otherwise, the court maintained, officers in the future might hold back in their vigorous enforcement of the law. The **doctrine of *respondeat superior*** imposes liability on state and local governments and their agencies for the torts of individual police officers. That is, individuals can sue the departments or local governments responsible for the police.[100]

In addition to state tort law, federal law enforcement officers who violate the constitutional rights of individuals violate the federal *Civil Rights Act of 1871*, also known as the Ku Klux Klan Act, passed following the Civil War. This act allows individuals to sue state and local governments, their agencies, and their agents for violations of rights guaranteed by the United States Constitution. Suits under the Civil Rights Act are commonly called **Section 1983 actions**, because these actions arise under Chapter 42, §1983 of the United States Code. Section 1983 provides:

> Every person who, under color of any statute, ordinance, regulation, custom, or usage, of any State or Territory, subjects, or causes to be subjected, any citizen of the United States or other person within the jurisdiction thereof to the deprivation of any rights, privileges, or immunities secured by the Constitution and laws, shall be liable to the party injured in an action at law, suit in equity, or other proper proceeding for redress.[101]

State and local officers and agencies are not always liable any time they violate the federal constitutional rights of individuals. The Supreme Court has created a **defense of qualified immunity** for officers whose actions are "objectively reasonable." Qualified immunity shields officers from "liability for civil damages insofar as their conduct does not violate clearly established statutory or constitutional rights of which a reasonable person would have known." Qualified immunity, according to the Court, strikes a balance "between the interests in vindication of people's constitutional rights and in public officials' effective performance of their duties." The leading qualified immunity case is *Anderson v. Creighton*, in which FBI agents searched the Creightons' home without a warrant and without probable cause, looking for one of the Creightons' relatives. Justice Antonin Scalia, speaking for the Court, said the test of "objective reasonableness" strikes the proper balance by granting qualified immunity if "a reasonable officer could have believed" the action was lawful. The Court conceded that FBI Agent Anderson violated the Fourth Amendment prohibition against unreasonable searches and seizures when he entered and searched the Creightons' house. But an unreasonable search does not automatically translate into civil liability under §1983. If Anderson could have believed his unreasonable search was reasonable, it was nevertheless objectively reasonable for purposes of suing a government agent. Therefore, the Creightons cannot prevail in suing Anderson under §1983. This leads to the tongue-twisting and almost comical-sounding result that an unreasonable search is not objectively unreasonable for the purposes of §1983 if an officer could have believed the search was reasonable.[102]

The United States Supreme Court is the *final* interpreter of §1983. However, most cases are actually decided without appeal by the lower federal courts, or sometimes in state courts, in actions that join both individual officers and departments, and §1983 and state law tort claims. Most plaintiffs do not prevail in their suits against either units of government or individual officers.

Bringing and winning a §1983 action against a police department head, the department itself, or the municipality in charge of the department is more complicated than suing individual police officers who commit the torts. In *Monell v. New York City*, the Supreme Court concluded that the Civil Rights Act applies to municipalities and other local government units. The Court established the following guidelines for suing local governing bodies for damages or injunctions. People can sue local government units for:

1. Unconstitutional actions that "implement or execute a policy statement, ordinance, regulation, or decision officially adopted and promulgated by that body's officers."

2. Unconstitutional actions taken pursuant to "custom, even though such a custom has not received formal approval through the body's decisionmaking channels."

Government units are liable only if:

3. Their unconstitutional actions under 1 or 2 "caused a constitutional tort."[103]

The *You Decide*, "Is the City Liable?" examines some of the difficulties in suing a city for the torts of its police officers.

You Decide   "Is the City Liable?"

Thurman v. City of Torrington, 595 F.Supp. 1521 (D.Conn.1984)

The federal district court for the district of Connecticut dealt with the question of whether the failure of police officers to prevent injuries in a domestic violence case was caused by a policy of treating domestic assault cases different from stranger assaults, thus violating the equal protection clause of the Fourteenth Amendment.

Facts

In October 1982, Charles Thurman attacked plaintiff Tracey Thurman at the home of Judy Bentley and Richard St. Hilaire in the City of Torrington. Mr. St. Hilaire and Ms. Bentley made a formal complaint of the attack to one of the unnamed defendant police officers and requested efforts to keep the plaintiff's husband, Charles Thurman, off their property. On or about November 5, 1982, Charles Thurman returned to the St. Hilaire-Bentley residence and using physical force took Charles J. Thurman, Jr. [their child] from said residence. Plaintiff Tracey Thurman and Mr. St. Hilaire went to Torrington police headquarters to make a formal complaint. At that point, unnamed defendant police officers of the City of Torrington refused to accept a complaint from Mr. St. Hilaire even as to trespassing.

On or about November 9, 1982, Charles Thurman screamed threats to Tracey Thurman while she was sitting in her car. Defendant police officer Neil Gemelli

stood on the street watching Charles Thurman scream threats at Tracey Thurman until Charles Thurman broke the windshield of plaintiff Tracey Thurman's car while she was inside the vehicle. Charles Thurman was arrested after he broke the windshield, and on the next day, November 10, 1982, he was convicted of breach of peace. He received a suspended sentence of six months and a two-year "conditional discharge," during which he was ordered to stay completely away from the plaintiff Tracey Thurman and the Bentley-St. Hilaire residence and to commit no further crimes. The court imposing probation informed the defendant of this sentence.

On December 31, 1982, while plaintiff Tracey Thurman was at the Bentley-St. Hilaire residence, Charles Thurman returned to said residence and once again threatened her. She called the Torrington Police Department. One of the unnamed police officer defendants took the call, and, although informed of the violation of the conditional discharge, made no attempt to ascertain Charles Thurman's whereabouts or to arrest him.

Between January 1, 1983, and May 4, l983, numerous telephone complaints to the Torrington Police Department were taken by various unnamed police officers, in which repeated threats of violence to the plaintiff by Charles Thurman were reported and his arrest on account of the threats and violation of the terms of his probation was requested.

On May 4 and 5, l983, the plaintiff Tracey Thurman and Ms. Bentley reported to the Torrington Police Department that Charles Thurman had said that he would shoot the plaintiff. Defendant police officer Storrs took the written complaint of plaintiff Tracey Thurman, who was seeking an arrest warrant for her husband because of his death threat and violation of his "conditional discharge." Defendant Storrs refused to take the complaint of Ms. Bentley. Plaintiff Tracey Thurman was told to return three weeks later on June 1, 1983, when defendant Storrs or some other person connected with the police department of the defendant City would seek a warrant for the arrest of her husband.

On May 6, 1983, Tracey Thurman filed an application for a restraining order against Charles Thurman in the Litchfield Superior Court. That day, the court issued an *ex parte* restraining order forbidding Charles Thurman from assaulting, threatening, and harassing Tracey Thurman. The defendant City was informed of this order. On May 27, 1983, Tracey Thurman requested police protection to get to the Torrington Police Department, and she requested a warrant for her husband's arrest upon her arrival at headquarters after being taken there by one of the unnamed defendant police officers. She was told that she would have to wait until after the Memorial Day holiday weekend and was advised to call on Tuesday, May 31, to pursue the warrant request.

On May 31, 1983, Tracey Thurman appeared once again at the Torrington Police Department to pursue the warrant request. She was then advised by one of the unnamed defendant police officers that defendant Schapp was the only policeman who could help her and that he was on vacation. She was told that she would have to wait until he returned. That same day, Tracey's brother-in-law, Joseph Kocsis, called the Torrington Police Department to protest the lack of action taken on Tracey's complaint. Although Mr. Kocsis was advised that Charles Thurman would be arrested on June 8, 1983, no such arrest took place.

On June 10, 1983, Charles Thurman appeared at the Bentley-St. Hilaire residence in the early afternoon and demanded to speak to Tracey Thurman. Tracey, remaining indoors, called the defendant police department asking that Charles be picked up for violation of his probation. After about 15 minutes, Tracey went outside to speak to her husband in an effort to persuade him not to take or hurt [their child] Charles Jr. Soon thereafter, Charles began to stab Tracey repeatedly in the chest, neck, and throat.

Approximately 25 minutes after Tracey's call to the Torrington Police Department and after her stabbing, a single police officer, the defendant Petrovits, arrived on the scene. Upon the arrival of Officer Petrovits at the scene of the stabbing, Charles Thurman was holding a bloody knife. Charles then dropped the knife and, in the presence of Petrovits, kicked the plaintiff Tracey Thurman in the head and ran into the Bentley-St. Hilaire residence. Charles returned from within the residence holding the plaintiff Charles Thurman, Jr. and dropped the child on his wounded mother. Charles then kicked Tracey in the head a second time. Soon thereafter, defendants DeAngelo, Nukirk, and Columbia arrived on the scene but still permitted Charles Thurman to wander about the crowd and continue to threaten Tracey. Finally, upon approaching Tracey once again, this time while she was lying on a stretcher, Charles Thurman was arrested and taken into custody.

It is also alleged that at all times mentioned above, except for approximately two weeks following his conviction and sentencing on November 10, 1982, Charles Thurman resided in Torrington and worked there as a counterman and short order cook at Skie's Diner. There he served many members of the Torrington Police Department, including some of the named and unnamed defendants in this case. In the course of his employment Charles Thurman boasted to the defendant police officer patrons that he intended to "get" his wife and that he intended to kill her.

Opinion

The defendant City now brings a motion to dismiss the claims against it. The City first argues that the plaintiff's complaint should be dismissed for failure to allege the deprivation of a constitutional right. Though the complaint alleges that the action of the defendants deprived the plaintiff Tracey Thurman of her constitutional right to equal protection of the laws, the defendant City argues that the equal protection clause of the Fourteenth Amendment "does not guarantee equal application of social services." Rather, the defendant City argues that the equal protection clause "only prohibits intentional discrimination that is racially motivated."

The defendant City's argument is clearly a misstatement of the law. The application of the equal protection clause is not limited to racial classifications or racially motivated discrimination. The equal protection clause will be applied to invalidate state laws which classify on the basis of alienage for the purpose of the distribution of economic benefits unless that law is necessary to promote a compelling or overriding state interest. The equal protection clause will be applied to strike down classifications based on legitimacy at birth if they are not related to an important governmental objective. And lastly, the equal protection clause will be applied to a legitimate state interest. Classifications on the basis of gender will be held invalid under the equal protection clause unless they are substantially related to strike down classifications which are not rationally related to a legitimate governmental purpose.

In the instant case, the plaintiffs allege that the defendants use an administrative classification that manifests itself in discriminatory treatment violative of the equal protection clause. Police protection in the City of Torrington, they argue, is fully provided to persons abused by someone with whom the victim has no domestic relationship. But the Torrington police have consistently afforded lesser protection, plaintiffs allege, when the victim is (1) a woman abused or assaulted by a spouse or boyfriend, or (2) a child abused by a father or stepfather. The issue to be decided, then, is whether the plaintiffs have properly alleged a violation of the equal protection clause of the Fourteenth Amendment.

Police action is subject to the equal protection clause and section 1983 whether in the form of commission of violative acts or omission to perform required acts pursuant to the police officer's duty to protect. City officials and police officers are under an affirmative duty to preserve law and order, and to protect the personal safety of persons in the community. This duty applies equally to women whose personal safety is threatened by individuals with whom they have or have had a domestic relationship as well as to all other persons whose personal safety is threatened, including women not involved in domestic relationships. If officials have notice of the possibility of attacks on women in domestic relationships or other persons, they are under an affirmative duty to take reasonable measures to protect the personal safety of such persons in the community. Failure to perform this duty would constitute a denial of equal protection of the laws.

Although the plaintiffs point to no law which on its face discriminates against victims abused by someone with whom they have a domestic relationship, the plaintiffs have alleged that there is an administrative classification used to implement the law in a discriminatory fashion. It is well settled that the equal protection clause is applicable not only to discriminatory legislative action, but also to discriminatory governmental action in administration and enforcement of the law. Here the plaintiffs were threatened with assault in violation of Connecticut law. Over the course of eight months the police failed to afford the plaintiffs protection against such assaults, and failed to take action to arrest the perpetrator of these assaults. The plaintiffs have alleged that this failure to act was pursuant to a pattern or practice of affording inadequate protection, or no protection at all, to women who have complained of having been abused by their husbands or others with whom they have had close relations. Such a practice is tantamount to an administrative classification used to implement the law in a discriminatory fashion.

If the City wishes to discriminate against women who are the victims of domestic violence, it must articulate an important governmental interest for doing so. In its memorandum and at oral argument the City has failed to put forward any justification for its disparate treatment of women. . . . Such a practice was at one time sanctioned by law:

> English common law during the eighteenth century recognized the right of husbands to physically discipline their wives. Subsequently, American common law in the early nineteenth century permitted a man to chastise his wife "without subjecting himself to vexatious prosecutions for assault and battery, resulting in the discredit and shame of all parties concerned." Some restrictions on the right of chastisement evolved through cases which defined the type, severity, and timing of permissible wife-beating. . . . In our own country a husband was permitted to beat his wife so long as he didn't use a switch any bigger around than his thumb. . . .

Today, however, any notion of a husband's prerogative to physically discipline his wife is an "increasingly outdated misconception." A man is not allowed to physically abuse or endanger a woman merely because he is her husband. Concomitantly, a police officer may not knowingly refrain from interference in such violence, and may not "automatically decline to make an arrest simply because the assaulter and his victim are married to each other." Such inaction on the part of the officer is a denial of the equal protection of the laws.

In addition, any notion that defendants' practice can be justified as a means of promoting domestic harmony by refraining from interference in marital disputes has no place in the case at hand. Rather than evidencing a desire to work out her problems with her husband privately, Tracey Thurman pleaded with the police to offer her at least some measure of protection. Further, she sought and received a restraining order to keep her husband at a distance. . . . Accordingly, the defendant City of Torrington's motion to dismiss the plaintiff Tracey Thurman's complaint on the basis of failure to allege violation of a constitutional right is denied.

The plaintiffs have alleged in paragraph 13 of their complaint as follows:

> During the period of time described herein, and for a long time prior thereto, the defendant City of Torrington, acting through its Police Department, condoned a pattern or practice of affording inadequate protection, or no protection at all, to women who have complained of having been abused by their husbands or others with whom they have had close relations. Said pattern, custody or policy, well known to the individual defendants, was the basis on which they ignored said numerous complaints and reports of threats to the plaintiffs with impunity.

While a municipality is not liable for the constitutional torts of its employees on a *respondeat superior* theory, a municipality may be sued for damages under section 1983 when "the action that is alleged to be unconstitutional implements or executes a policy statement, ordinance, regulation, or decision officially adopted and promulgated by the body's officers" or is "visited pursuant to governmental 'custom' even though such a custom has not received formal approval through the body's official decision-making channels." *Monell v. New York City Department of Social Services,* 436 U.S. 658, 690, 98 S.Ct. 2018, 2035, 56 L.Ed.2d 611 (1978).

Some degree of specificity is required in the pleading of a custom or policy on the part of a municipality. Mere conclusory allegations devoid of factual content will not suffice. As this court has pointed out, a plaintiff must typically point to the facts outside his own case to support his allegation of a policy on the part of a municipality.

In the instant case, however, the plaintiff Tracey Thurman has specifically alleged in her statement of facts a series of acts and omissions on the part of the defendant police officers and police department that took place over the course of eight months. From this particularized pleading a pattern emerges that evidences deliberate indifference on the part of the police department to the complaints of the plaintiff Tracey Thurman and to its duty to protect her. Such an ongoing pattern of deliberate indifference raises an inference of "custom" or "policy" on the part of the municipality. Furthermore, this pattern of inaction climaxed on June 10, 1983 in an incident so brutal that under the law of the Second Circuit that "single brutal incident may be sufficient to suggest a link between a violation of constitutional rights and a pattern of police misconduct." Finally, a complaint of this sort will survive dismissal if it alleges a policy or custom of condoning police misconduct that violates constitutional rights and alleges "that the City's pattern of inaction caused the plaintiffs any compensable injury." Accordingly, defendant City of Torrington's motion to dismiss the plaintiffs' claims against it, on the ground that the plaintiffs failed to properly allege a custom or policy on the part of the municipality, is denied. . . .

For the reasons stated above, the City's motion to dismiss the complaint for failure to allege the deprivation of a constitutional right is denied; the City's motion to dismiss the claims of Charles Thurman, Jr. is granted; the City's motion to dismiss claims against it for failure to properly allege a "custom" or "policy" on the part of the City is denied. . . .
SO ORDERED.

Questions

What constitutional rights did the city allegedly violate? What facts did the plaintiff allege to demonstrate the un-constitutional acts? What facts demonstrate a "custom" or "policy"? Did these facts cause injury to Tracy Thurman? Explain. Why did the court grant the motion to dismiss the complaint alleging violations of Charles Thurman, Jr.'s constitutional rights? Was he not injured? Explain. Wayne LaFave, an expert on criminal procedure and the author of many leading works on the subject, has commented that the rule that requires courts to determine whether an unconstitutional action was caused by the "execution of a government's policy or custom" raises difficult questions. Is a directive in a police department manual official policy? Is the lack of sufficient police training ever official policy? Is a pattern of non-discipline for the actions of officers official policy?[104]

---

internal affairs units (IAU)
special units within police departments to investigate police misconduct.

Internal Review

Criminal cases against the police are rare, curtailed by the discretionary judgments of prosecutors that prosecuting police officers is difficult and unwise. Civil suits against the police are also difficult to bring, and they are sporadic as well because they depend on the resources and the will of complainants. By far the most pervasive and systematic review of police misconduct is internal review. Most large and mid-sized departments have **internal affairs units (IAU)**, special units within the police department, usually attached to the office of chief.[105]

According to Professor Douglas W. Perez, a former deputy sheriff, "most cops do not like internal affairs." They view IAU skeptically, at best. Some even consider IAU investigators traitors. Nevertheless, most officers believe that IAU operations are necessary. In some measure, internal review is a defense against external review, which police officers believe threatens police control of their own profession and operations. The famed Chicago chief of police, O. W. Wilson, said, "It is clearly apparent that if the police do not take a vigorous stand on the matter of internal investigation, outside groups—such as review boards consisting of laymen and other persons outside the police service—will step into the void."[106]

Internal affairs operations consist of four stages:

1. Intake.
2. Investigation.
3. Deliberation.
4. Disposition.

The Internal Affairs Section of the Oakland, California, Police Department is considered an excellent unit; we will use it as an example of how internal review should proceed through these four stages. The unit is housed in the department building. The department intake policy is that "anyone anywhere should accept a complaint if a citizen wishes it taken." Oakland takes most complaints at the department, but it also accepts telephone and anonymous complaints. All complaints alleging excessive force, police corruption, and racial discrimination are followed up. Supervisors have the discretion not to follow up anonymous complaints believed to be hoaxes. Furthermore, the unit has the discretion not to follow up on complaints of "such a minor nature that the unit or person first contacted can dispose of the incident *to the satisfaction of the complainant* without the necessity of a formal investigation." Seventy-eight percent of internal review units surveyed encourage the handling of complaints informally.[107]

Someone other than the intake officer is assigned to investigate the complaint. The investigator gathers documentary evidence and interviews witnesses, usually interviewing the officer against whom the complaint is filed last. If officers refuse to respond, they are subject to discipline, which might include dismissal for refusing a direct order of the chief.

The completed investigation then goes to the supervisor of the Internal Affairs Section. If the supervisor is satisfied, it goes to the decision-making or deliberation stage. The case usually goes up the chain of command, first in line being the immediate supervisor of the officer complained against. The supervisor discusses the case with the officer and gives one of four possible dispositions:

1. *Unfounded*—The investigation proved that the act did not take place.
2. *Exonerated*—The acts took place, but the investigation proved that they were justified, lawful, and proper.
3. *Not sustained*—The investigation failed to gather enough evidence to clearly prove the allegations in the complaint.
4. *Sustained*—The investigation disclosed enough evidence to clearly prove the allegations in the complaint.[108]

If the disposition is unfounded, exonerated, or not sustained, the case is closed. If it is sustained, the supervisor makes a disciplinary recommendation. (See Figure 7.13 for a survey of the dispositions of internal review cases concerning excessive force.) These recommended disciplinary actions can include:

● Reprimand.
● Written reprimand.
● Transfer.
● Retraining.
● Counseling.
● Suspension.
● Demotion.
● Fine.
● Dismissal.

After the initial disposition, the case goes up the chain of command for review until it finally reaches the chief. In about half the cases, there is a discrepancy between the chief's recommendations and those of the immediate supervisor. These discrepancies are important because the immediate supervisor, usually a sergeant of patrol, works on the street with other patrol officers. The supervisors of sergeants usually go along with the recommen-

Figure 7.13

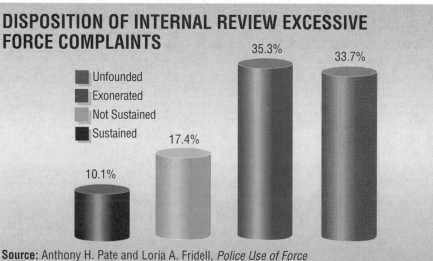

DISPOSITION OF INTERNAL REVIEW EXCESSIVE FORCE COMPLAINTS

- Unfounded
- Exonerated
- Not Sustained
- Sustained

10.1% 17.4% 35.3% 33.7%

Source: Anthony H. Pate and Loria A. Fridell, *Police Use of Force* Vol. I, (Washington, D.C.: Police Foundation, 1993), 116.

dations of sergeants. Chiefs of police, on the other hand, are removed from the day-to-day street operations of patrol officers and their immediate supervisors. They have department-wide perspectives and are responsible to "local political elites" for their department's performance. So chiefs may find the disciplinary penalty too light and make it heavier. According to Perez, "Oakland chiefs are often seen from below as abusive of police officers, always increasing punishments, never going along with the lighter recommendations." Oakland, however, may not be typical in this respect. (Figure 7.14 depicts the disciplinary measures taken in a national sample of city police departments.)[109]

External Review

The fundamental objection to internal review is that the police cannot police themselves. In other words, to the question, "Who will watch the watchmen?" the answer is, "Not the watchmen!" Hence, the growth of external review procedures. **External review of police misconduct (civilian review)** is a procedure in which individuals or others who are not sworn police officers participate in the review of complaints against the police. Usually called civilian review, it has generated controversy for nearly half a century. The central issue in external review is whether civilians should participate in the complaint process of police misconduct. The police have opposed external review because it invades their professional autonomy; because they have no confidence in outsiders knowing enough about police work to review it; and because they know that outside scrutiny would pierce the "blue curtain" that hides their "real" work from public view. Strong police unions, chiefs who opposed external review, and the creation of internal review procedures discussed in the last section successfully prevented external review during the 1960s, when it became a popular proposal of some liberal reformers and citizen groups.[110]

Since the 1960s, however, external review has grown rapidly, at least in the largest cities; by 1994, 72 percent of the 50 largest cities had created civilian review procedures of some sort. The growth of civilian review became possible, in part, because the opposition of police unions and chiefs either lessened or was overcome, and because internal review did not change public *perceptions*, especially among African Americans in large cities, that police misconduct, particularly the use of excessive force, was still a major

Figure 7.14

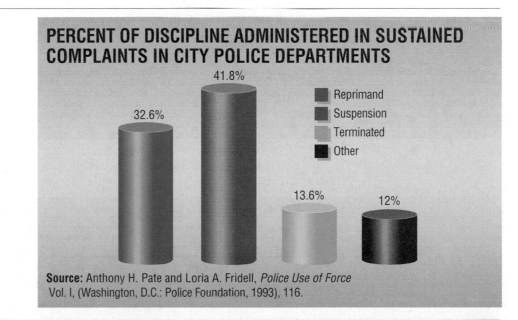

PERCENT OF DISCIPLINE ADMINISTERED IN SUSTAINED COMPLAINTS IN CITY POLICE DEPARTMENTS

41.8%
32.6%
13.6%
12%

- Reprimand
- Suspension
- Terminated
- Other

Source: Anthony H. Pate and Loria A. Fridell, *Police Use of Force* Vol. I, (Washington, D.C.: Police Foundation, 1993), 116.

problem. Furthermore, the beating of Rodney King added momentum to the movement to create civilian review procedures.[111]

Types The differences among civilian review procedures all turn on the degree of participation in the decision-making process by people who are not sworn police officers. "Degree of participation" means the point in the process when unsworn officers take part in the review procedures. These points are:

1. The initial investigation to collect the facts.
2. The review of the investigation reports.
3. The recommendation for disposition to the chief.
4. The review of decisions made by the chief.

A survey of the civilian procedures of the 50 largest U.S. cities, conducted by Samuel Walker and Vic W. Bumphus in 1991, identified three major types of review procedures, based on the four points in the decision-making process:

- *Class I systems.* Individuals who are not sworn police officers conduct the initial fact-finding investigation. Their reports go to a person or panel, also not sworn officers, who recommend action to the chief.
- *Class II systems.* Sworn officers conduct the fact-finding investigation. Civilians recommend action to the chief.
- *Class III systems.* Sworn officers conduct the initial fact-finding investigation. Sworn officers also recommend action to the chief. If complainants are not satisfied with the disposition of the complaint, they can appeal the decision to a panel of civilians.[112]

Despite differences, all three systems share three important characteristics. First, none of them can discipline police officers. The most they can do is *recommend* disciplinary action to police chiefs. Under civil service laws, only police chiefs can actually decide on disciplinary action against police officers. Second, all existing review procedures were established either by municipal ordinance or state statute. Therefore, they are all on a solid legal footing that makes it more difficult to alter or abolish them. Third, and reflected not only in the legislative authority given to them but also in public opinion surveys, civilian review procedures enjoy broad public support. A Louis Harris poll reported that 80 percent of adults favored review by a mixture of civilians and sworn police officers. Only 15 percent favored review by civilians alone, and a mere 4 percent supported review by sworn officers alone.[113]

Effectiveness The growing number of civilian review procedures prompts the natural question, "Does civilian review work?" The answer depends both on the definition of effectiveness and the measures of effectiveness. Effectiveness can mean at least four things, all of which are important in determining the value of civilian review procedures:

1. Maintaining effective control of police misconduct.
2. Providing resolutions to complaints that satisfy individual complainants.
3. Preserving public confidence in the police.
4. Influencing police management by providing "feedback from consumers."[114]

It is difficult to measure the effectiveness of civilian review because the official data are ambiguous. Take the number of complaints, for example. A large number of complaints might mean a large volume of police misconduct. But it can also indicate confidence in the review procedures. Following the Rodney King incident in Los Angeles, observers noted that San Francisco, a

knock-down force *enough police force to cause a suspect to fall to the ground.*

city known for its strong review procedures, received more complaints than the much larger city of Los Angeles. The Independent Commission heard a number of citizen complaints that the LAPD created "significant hurdles" to filing complaints, that they were afraid of the process, and that the complaint process was "unnecessarily difficult or impossible." The ACLU collected evidence suggesting that the LAPD "actively discouraged the filing of complaints." The beating of Rodney King, in fact, would never have come to public attention without the video, according to the Independent Commission. This is because, according to the Commission, the efforts of Rodney King's brother Paul to file a complaint following the beating were "frustrated" by the LAPD.[115]

The numbers and rates of complaints are also difficult to assess because we do not know the numbers of incidents about which people do not file complaints. In one national survey, of all the people who said that the police mistreated them, only 30 percent said they had filed complaints. One thing, however, seems clear. Misconduct is not distributed evenly among individuals and neighborhoods. In one survey, only 40 percent of the addresses in one city had any contact with the police in a year. Most contacts between private individuals and the police occur in neighborhoods in which poor people live. In New York City, the rate of complaints ranges from 1 to 5 for every 10,000 people, depending on the neighborhood. According to Walker and Bumphus,

> Official data has consistently indicated that racial minority males are disproportionately represented among complainants. Thus, the perception of a pattern of police harassment is a major factor in conflict between the police and racial minority communities.[116]

Whatever the ambiguity of numbers and rates in the official statistics, observers have noted that civilian review procedures sustain complaints against police officers at a low rate. Furthermore, the rates of complaints that are sustained in civilian review do not substantially differ from the rates of sustained complaints by internal affairs units. These similar rates suggest that police fears that civilian review will be a "kangaroo court" were unfounded. Minority groups and civil rights advocates, on the other hand, ought to take comfort in knowing that review by civilians produces similar results to review by sworn police officers.[117]

Other Responses to Misconduct

A more positive method of dealing with police misconduct relies on training and other socialization measures to improve police-community relations. For example, advocates for the positive approach argue the effectiveness of convincing officers to use unflappable responses to unpleasant behavior. Taking an insult without reaction wins more respect and obedience than responding emotionally to insults. James Q. Wilson, a supporter of the positive approach, recommends that recruitment, training, and the police subculture should aim at producing police officers

> who can handle calmly challenges to their self-respect and manhood, are able to tolerate ambiguous situations, have the physical capacity to subdue persons, are able to accept responsibility for the consequences of their own actions, can understand and apply legal concepts in concrete situations, and are honest.[118]

The *You Decide* "What Is Police Brutality?" examines the complexities in judging what police officers *should* do, whether they could have acted differently in specific situations, and how to affect police actions.

What Is Police Brutality? What Is the Correct Remedy for It?

At about 10:30 p.m. on Thursday, November 5, 1992, Malice Green, a 35-year-old African-American man, picked up a friend, Ralph Fletcher, in front of a suspected crack house on Detroit's west side. The house was at 23rd Street and Warren Avenue, in (according to the police) a neighborhood "riddled with drugs and prostitution." According to plainclothes officers Larry "Starsky" Nevers, 52 (a 24-year veteran) and his partner Walter "Hutch" Budzyn, 47 (a 19-year veteran), they had been watching Mr. Green for some time outside the crack house. (They acquired the nicknames of Starsky and Hutch, according to a police official, from the popular TV show about two tough cops who sometimes broke the rules to do "justice." The official said that both officers had a history of brutality complaints. But, he added, none of the complaints were ever sustained, and Nevers was the highest-decorated officer in his precinct.)[119]

Green at one point drove off, returning with a group of people whom he dropped off at the crack house. When he drove off again, the two officers followed him, pulling him over a short distance away. As they passed Green's car, Nevers and Budzyn flashed a light at Green. Then they backed up toward Green's car. Green got out of his car. The officers asked for Green's driver's license and his car registration. Green got back in his car, opened the glove compartment, reached into it, and then appeared to hold something in his hand. The officers radioed for backup help. One of them ordered Green to drop whatever he had in his hand. When Green did not drop it, the officers began pounding first Green's hand and then his head with their three-pound flashlights, a police official said. Green still refused to open his fist. The two officers said Green resisted them violently, but Ralph Fletcher, Green's friend, contradicted them. Fletcher said Green "wouldn't open his hands, so they beat him up. It's just that simple. They beat him up. They had flashlights and sticks." Some other residents also said that Green did not resist the officers.

The struggle quickly escalated. The officers flagged down two ambulances that happened to be nearby. The four emergency workers saw pools of blood in the street and noticed some officers wiping blood off their hands and off Green's car. Four more police cars sped to the scene, including that of an African-American supervising sergeant, Freddie Douglas. "We stood here for five minutes while they beat him. We begged them to stop," said Green's friend Fletcher. Sergeant Douglas reportedly did not stop the beating, but he made sure the traffic kept moving. According to one police official who requested anonymity, Douglas said, " 'Take it easy,' but that's it." Police Chief Stanley Knox said that the officers used force in Green's car, outside, while he was handcuffed and after the paramedics arrived.

According to several witnesses, a white officer got out of his patrol car, pulled Green off his seat, and started beating him with his fist in the face, chest, and stomach. One officer stood on Green's neck as the other officers handcuffed him. At least two other officers also hit Green. Near the end of the encounter, an emergency worker sent this computer message to his supervisor: "What should I do if I witness police brutality . . . murder?" Malice Green was dead on arrival at a Detroit hospital.

It was not clear what Mr. Green had in his hand. Later, one of the officers turned in four pieces of crack cocaine that they said Green was holding. An autopsy later revealed that Malice Green had small amounts of alcohol in his urine and cocaine in his blood. Joann Watson, of the NAACP, said Green "was minding his own business, talking to some friends. The two white policemen who inflicted the blows have a tremendous reputation for roughing up African-American males. This time the abuse reached a deadly level." Others praised Starsky and Hutch as "courageous cops on mean streets."

Two days following the incident, Officer Nevers said, "I must've done something wrong. A guy died. If I can ever sleep again I'm going to wake up and say this is a dream, it didn't happen, it didn't happen." But he added, "Nobody knows what it's like out there."

Malice Green had spent most of his life in Detroit. He had no police record there. At the time of his death he was unemployed, but he had worked at a steel mill in Gary, Indiana. At the time of his death, according to his sister, Green was planning to move to North Carolina where his wife lives. His mother said that Malice was a "gentle man" who loved basketball and baseball. The African-American mayor of Detroit, Coleman Young, was swept into office in 1972 on a campaign against police brutality. Despite his crusade, however, a study by the Detroit Free Press found that the city lost $12 million on police assault suits in 1990, compared to $9 million in Los Angeles, the site of the widely publicized Rodney King case. Los Angeles has twice as many police officers as Detroit and three times as many people. Nevertheless, Mayor Young says he is satisfied that Detroit does not have a "Rodney King police department," and Arthur Johnson, president of the local NAACP, says that is why Detroit did not avenge Green's death with violence as Los Angeles did in the case of Rodney King. "People have seen the serious efforts Mayor Young has made to give this department a new face and to raise its sense of community respect." Detroit has an African-American chief of police and a substantial number of African-American officers, although the police department racially and ethnically still does not "look like" its general population (see Figure 7.15).

Following the death of Malice Green, these actions were taken:

November 6, 1992—Police Chief Stanley Knox suspended seven officers without pay, including the supervising sergeant, Douglas, who Knox said failed to stop the attack.

Figure 7.15

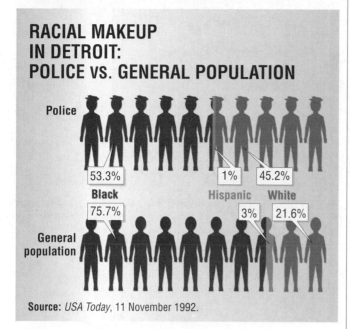

RACIAL MAKEUP IN DETROIT: POLICE VS. GENERAL POPULATION

Police

53.3% — Black

1% — Hispanic

45.2% — White

General population

75.7% — Black

3% — Hispanic

21.6% — White

Source: *USA Today*, 11 November 1992.

November 6, 1992—Mayor Young held a news conference in which he said, "I am shocked and sickened. Every officer found to be guilty of any misconduct in connection with this tragic incident will be dealt with in the harshest manner possible." Chief Knox, who attended, said, "This incident is disgraceful and a total embarrassment. To receive a blow like this actually brought tears to my eyes. We believe in taking action and taking action immediately. This type of thing will not be tolerated." He said the department would seek criminal charges against the officers by the county prosecutor's office. When asked if he saw a parallel to the Rodney King case and the riots that followed acquittal of the officers charged with the use of excessive force, Chief Knox responded, "I think we all do."

November 8, 1992—Jesse Green, Jr., Malice's father, urged calm. "Whatever they do ain't going to bring him back. I've told all his friends not to do anything about it. Just let it be. Let the lawyers take care of it. They made a mistake, let them pay for it."

November 11, 1992—Jesse Green, Jr. vowed, "I'm going to get justice." Mayor Young announced, "From what I've heard . . . I think it was murder. I have worked too long and too hard . . . to have something like this happen."

November 16, 1992—Prosecutors charged Walter Budzyn and Larry Nevers with second-degree murder (up to life imprisonment), supervising sergeant Freddie Douglas with involuntary manslaughter (up to 15 years imprisonment), and Robert Lessnau with assault with intent to do great bodily harm (up to 10 years imprisonment).

Professor Samuel Walker, police expert, said he knew of no case in which police officers had ever been charged with murder due to the use of excessive force. The county prosecutor said he would resist any attempt to move the trial out of Detroit. A police officer told the Detroit *Free Press*, "Nobody likes a dirty or brutal cop, but the chief has already convicted some men before there's been an investigation." Tom Schneider, president of the

Detroit Police Officers' Association, said, "We are concerned that the officers charged may not be able to receive a fair trial in Wayne County in light of the prejudicial statements by the Mayor, the Chief of Police, and others since the incident occurred."

November 16, 1992—The four officers pleaded not guilty. Officers Nevers and Budzyn were released on $100,000 bond. Sergeant Douglas was released on $25,000 bond. Officer Lessnau was released on $10,000 bond. The judge scheduled a preliminary hearing for 14 December 1992 to determine whether the prosecutor had enough evidence to go to trial.

December 14, 1992—At the preliminary hearing, a pathologist testified that Malice Green died from at least 14 blows to the head that bruised his brain and tore off part of his scalp. A witness testified that he saw Officer Nevers joke with bystanders as Malice Green lay motionless in a pool of blood. While Officer Budzyn beat Green, according to the witness, Nevers continually offered Green crack. The witness also said that Nevers reached into his police car, pulled out a toy gun, and tossed it to a bystander. Later, Nevers asked for it back "because it's his evidence." Lawyers for the officer called the testimony "unbelievable."

December 14, 1992—Following a closed-door hearing without the officers present, Chief Knox fired the four men charged with crimes. Officer Nevers's lawyer said, "It would have been fair to the officers at least if he had waited until the preliminary examination before any departmental proceedings continued." Jose DeSosa, president of the California state chapter of the NAACP, said, "Just the mere firing is not sufficient. . . . There needs to be a trial and they need to be held accountable."

December 24, 1992—A judge ordered Officers Budzyn, Nevers, and Lessnau to stand trial; he dismissed the charges against Sergeant Douglas because, according to the judge, the prosecution had not shown that Douglas's failure to intervene "caused" Green's death.

The basic idea of the use of force is to bring resisting suspects under control as quickly as possible, with the minimum of force necessary and with the minimum amount of injury to both suspects and officers. Officers are trained to use an escalating level of responses to accomplish this. The Los Angeles Police Department uses the following range of tactics to bring suspects under control:

- Firm grip (tightly grabbing a suspect's arm).
- Compliance holds (applying bending and twisting pressure to sensitive tendon and joint areas of the hands and arms).
- Batons or nightsticks (or flashlights as substitutes).
- Pushing and shoving.
- Karate kicks and punches.
- A swarm (organized tackle by several officers).
- Spraying with chemical irritants (tear gas).
- TASER (stun gun).
- Choke holds (upper body control holds).
- Shooting.[120]

Every time a Los Angeles police officer uses non-deadly force, the department requires the officer to document the incident on a Use of Force Report. In an extensive survey of these reports, Greg Meyer, a police tactics consultant and member of the Los Angeles Police Department, found that the Los Angeles police used less-than-deadly force in about one out of every 89 arrests, meaning that approximately 10 times a day, Los Angeles police officers used force. About seven times a day, the police used enough force to "cause the suspect to fall to the ground," called **knock-down force**.[121]

In a comparison of various knock-down tactics, Meyer's data showed that the TASER, an electronic immobilization device, was as (or more) effective than most traditional knock-down tactics. More important, it was much safer. Meyer's data showed that TASERS and tear gas produced no injuries to either suspects or police officers (Figure 7.16). On the basis of his analysis, Meyer concludes:

> Expanded use of nonlethal weapons and the development of the next generation of such devices ["Star-Trek-style ray guns"] would lead to fewer and less severe injuries to suspects and officers, reduced civil liability claims and payments, and an improved public image for law enforcement.[122]

Others agree. James K. Stewart, former director of the National Institute of Justice, noted that:

> Law enforcement officials have long recognized that a wide and dangerous gap exists in the range of tools that are available to them. The most common law enforcement tools, the nightstick and the gun, may be either too weak or too strong a response to many police situations. In violent confrontations, officers may be obliged to choose an unnecessarily strong response for lack of an effective alternative weapon.[123]

According to unpublished work by the Police Foundation, the benefits of more weapons like TASERs, stun guns, and tear gas sprays include "fewer citizen injuries and deaths, fewer officer injuries and deaths, improved police-community relations, reduced exposure to departmental liability for wrongful police actions, and improved police morale."[124]

Questions

According to the facts set out here, did "Starsky" and "Hutch" engage in police brutality? What should happen to officers who do not actually strike blows, but are present during an incident of police brutality? What should happen to supervisory officers who are present? How would you define police brutality? Which of the steps taken following the incident do you think were proper? Would any of Greg

Figure 7.16

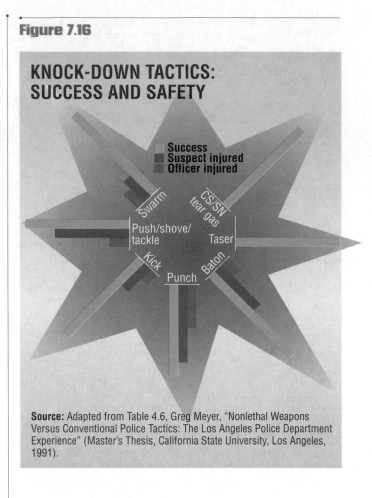

KNOCK-DOWN TACTICS: SUCCESS AND SAFETY

□ Success
■ Suspect injured
■ Officer injured

Swarm / CS/SN tear gas / Push/shove/tackle / Taser / Kick / Baton / Punch

Source: Adapted from Table 4.6, Greg Meyer, "Nonlethal Weapons Versus Conventional Police Tactics: The Los Angeles Police Department Experience" (Master's Thesis, California State University, Los Angeles, 1991).

Meyer's findings and recommendations help to prevent future incidents such as the case of Malice Green? Do you think Malice Green's father should succeed in his lawsuit if the police are found to have acted brutally? How much should he receive? Defend your answer. Consider the preceding sections of the chapter on police accountability. Which of the actions do you recommend: Criminal prosecution? Civil suit? Internal review? External review? Training to improve police-community relations? Defend your answer. Do you think your answer depends on your own experience and background? Explain.

Summary

The complex missions of the police, the strategies they undertake to fulfill those missions, and the law and discretionary judgment through which these missions are fulfilled and strategies carried out give rise to a number of issues. First is the type of people who want to become police officers. Early research found that the police had a distinct working personality. They are authoritarian, suspicious, racist, hostile, insecure, conservative, and cynical. Later research has found the subject more complex. The police personality stems not only from the attitudes of officers but also from the situations in which they find themselves. Researchers have disagreed over whether the working personality arises from innate character traits or from the socialization of police through training and work experience.

Second, issues arise regarding the recruitment, training, and promotion of police officers. The old standards of "manly virtues" and willingness to obey orders are no longer acceptable for a number of reasons. Our pluralistic society, equal opportunity, the multiple missions of the police, the major role of discretion in police decision making, the limits of the effectiveness of traditional police strategies, and the popularity of community policing contributed to the demands for police forces more representative of the communities they serve and more capable of sound decision making. Some believe that better (and higher) education will produce better discretionary decision makers, but research on the effectiveness of education is mixed. Most recruits go through stages in their training. The police academy teaches many formal rules, but it also socializes recruits to the informal norms of police work. Following the academy, rookies are ordinarily assigned to an older, experienced officer who routinely tells them to forget about what they learned in the academy—now, they are going to learn "real" police work. Some departments add instruction in critical thinking and internships in other criminal justice and community agencies in order to improve police decision making.

To fulfill equal opportunity demands and improve policing by making officers more representative of their communities, departments throughout the country have made efforts to hire more women and minority officers. The results of the efforts are mixed. While more women and minority officers now work in departments, increase in numbers is not evenly distributed, and the proportion of women and minority officers is still below their membership in the communities they serve. Whatever their distribution, empirical research has dispelled fears about the inability of women officers to do "real" police work. Both their performance and their attitudes are similar to that of men officers. It is not clear whether the reasons for the similarity of attitude lie in the character of women who enter police work or in the socialization of the academy, field training, and actual work experience.

The demands of their complex missions and the judgment required to carry out these missions cause stress among police officers. This stress is not limited to their work. It creates both physical and emotional problems outside work and within families.

The defining character of police work is the need to use legitimate force to fulfill missions and carry out strategies. This defining character, however, gives rise to the fundamental problem of police misconduct—abuse of force. An uneasiness about police use of force has run throughout Western history. Experts have classified police force in a number of ways, including non-deadly and deadly, violent and nonviolent, reasonable and excessive, necessary and unnecessary. Most research has demonstrated that the police use force rarely, and deadly force even more rarely than non-deadly force. However, what force they use is used more against African Americans than whites. It is difficult to measure, though, how often the police *abuse* the use of force. High-speed chases, a form of deadly force, threaten and sometimes injure and kill not only police officers and the people they are chasing, but also innocent bystanders.

Most of the empirical research available has demonstrated that rules can definitely reduce both the use of force and the number of injuries and deaths. Furthermore, rules can accomplish these reductions without endangering public safety. However, researchers have also demonstrated that neither the mere adoption of rules nor the content of the rules is enough by itself to change police behavior. To change behavior, police management has to demonstrate leadership by making it clear to rank-and-file officers that management is serious about the rules and prepared to enforce them. Some research has also demonstrated the effectiveness of training in reducing the use and abuse of force.

Corruption is a form of occupational crime: using police authority for private gain. Depending on who defines it, corruption can include everything from accepting free cups of coffee to receiving thousands of dollars of extortion money from vice operations. The causes of corruption include

15. What has empirical research revealed about the performance and attitudes of women police officers?

16. Define police stress. List its causes and describe some of its effects.

17. List and explain the major possible causes of police misconduct.

18. What is the defining characteristic of the police? How does it relate to the fundamental problem of police misconduct?

19. Explain the nature and history of "uneasiness" about police use of force.

20. List the major types and amounts of force used by police.

21. How often do police use and abuse force?

22. List the two recommendations of the Police Foundation following its study of the use of deadly force.

23. Summarize the extent of the use of deadly force by police officers.

24. Identify the promising techniques revealed by researchers in controlling the use of deadly force.

25. How many police shootings is too many? Who do the police shoot? Describe the race distribution in police shootings. What is the explanation for the distribution?

26. Why are high-speed chases considered deadly force? Who do high-speed chases endanger? Who do the police chase? What is the outcome of their chases?

27. What are the principal findings of researchers about the effectiveness of policies and practices regarding the use of force by police?

28. Describe the main elements of the Oakland and Metro-Dade County training programs regarding the use of force. Why are these programs important?

29. Define police corruption, identify its causes, and discuss ways to deal with it.

30. Identify and define the major ways of holding the police accountable for misconduct.

31. Explain the rationale for criminal prosecution for police misconduct. How often is it used? What are the reasons for its shortcomings?

32. How are civil suits for police misconduct different from criminal prosecutions? What are the major remedies in civil lawsuits? How often are lawsuits against the police successful?

33. Define and explain the significance of official immunity and *respondeat superior* in lawsuits against the police.

34. What is a "Section 1983 action"? What is the significance of qualified immunity in these actions?

35. Why is it harder to sue a department or city than an individual police officer?

36. Define internal review of police. Why do police officers accept but dislike it?

37. Identify and explain the four major stages in the process of internal review. Explain how the Oakland Police Department internal affairs unit operates through these four stages.

38. Identify and explain the four possible dispositions of complaints against the police.

39. Identify the possible disciplinary actions in complaints that are sustained. Who is responsible for deciding the disciplinary action? How do the recommendations of sergeants and the disciplinary actions of chiefs differ?

40. Define external review. What is the fundamental objection to it? Why do the police object to it? How extensive is external review?

41. Identify the four main points in the process of external review when unsworn officers might participate in review of police misconduct.

42. Describe the main elements in Class I, II, and III systems of external review. What major characteristics do all three have in common?

43. Identify the four major definitions of effectiveness regarding external review.

44. Explain why it is difficult to measure the effectiveness of external review.

45. Identify some alternatives to criminal prosecution, civil lawsuits, and internal or external review in dealing with police misconduct.

Notes

1. Lawrence W. Sherman et al., "Citizens Killed by Big City Police, 1970-1984" (Washington, D.C.: Crime Control Institute, 1986), 15.

2. Quoted in Jerome H. Skolnick and James J. Fyfe, *Above the Law: Police and the Excessive Use of Force* (New York: Free Press, 1993), 91.

3. William K. Muir, *Streetcorner Politicians* (Chicago: University of Chicago Press, 1977).

4. Summarized from John J. Broderick, *Police in a Time of Change*, 2d ed. (Prospect Heights, Ill.: Waveland Press), 10–11.

5. Ibid.

6. J. Snipes and Stephen Mastrofski, "An Empirical Test of Muir's Typology of Police Officers," *American Journal of Criminal Justice* 16 (1990): 268–96; Stephen M. Cox and James Frank, "The Influence of Neighborhood Context and Method of Entry on Individual Styles of Policing," *American Journal of Police* 11 (1992): 1–23.

7. Skolnick and Fyfe, *Above the Law*, 92.

8. Edward A. Thibault, Lawrence M. Lynch, and R. Bruce McBride, *Proactive Police Management* (Englewood Cliffs, N.J.: Prentice-Hall, Inc., 1985), 21; Richard J. Lundman, *Police and Policing* (New York: Holt, Rinehart and Winston, 1980), 73; Milton Rokeach et al., "The Value Gap Between Police and Policed," *Journal of Social Issues* 27, no. 2 (1971): 155–71; Bruce N. Carpenter and Susan M. Raza, "Personality Characteristics of Police Applicants: Comparisons Across Subgroups and with Other Populations," *Journal of Police Science and Administration* 15 (1987): 10–17.

9. President's Commission on Law Enforcement and the Administration of Justice, *The Challenge of Crime in a Free Society* (Washington, D.C.: U.S. Government Printing Office, 1967); Egon Bittner, "Some Reflections on Staffing Problem-Oriented Policing," *American Journal of Police* 9 (1990): 189–95.

10. Robert D. Meier and Richard E. Maxwell, "Psychological Screening of Police Candidates: Current Perspectives," *Journal of Police Science and Administration* 15 (1987): 210–15; Alan W. Benner, "Psychological Screening of Police Applicants," in *Critical Issues in Policing,* Roger C. Dunham and Geoffrey P. Alpert, eds. (Prospect Heights, Ill.: Waveland Press, 1989), 73; Geoffrey P. Alpert, "Hiring and Promoting Police Officers in Small Departments—The Role of Psychological Testing," *Criminal Law Bulletin* 27 (1991): 261–69; Benjamin S. Wright, William G. Doerner, and John C. Speier, "Pre-employment Psychological Testing as a Predictor of Police Performance During an FTO Program," *American Journal of Police* 9 (1990): 65–84.

11. Lundman, *Police and Policing,* 75–76.

12. International City/County Management Association, *Police Personnel Recruitment.*

13. Bittner, "Some Reflections on Staffing," 195.

14. Richard A. Staufenberger, "Personnel Upgrading," *Progress in Policing* (Cambridge, Mass.: Ballinger Publishing Company, 1980), 43, 55–57.

15. David L. Carter, Allen D. Sapp, and Darrel W. Stephens, *The State of Police Education: Policy Direction for the 21st Century* (Washington, D.C.: Police Executive Research Forum, 1989).

16. All quoted in *New York Times,* 23 April 1990.

17. David L. Carter and Allen D. Sapp, *Police Education and Minority Recruitment: The Impact of a College Requirement* (Washington, D.C.: Police Executive Research Forum, 1991), 2–4; David L. Carter and Allen D. Sapp, "Higher Education as a Policy Alternative to Reduce Police Liability," *Police Liability Review* 2 (1990): 1–3.

18. Lawrence W. Sherman et al., *The Quality of Police Education* (San Francisco: Jossey-Bass, 1978); Robert E. Worden, "A Badge and a Baccalaureate: Policies, Hypotheses, and Further Evidence," *Justice Quarterly* 7 (1990): 565, 588–90.

19. Robert E. Worden, "The 'Causes' of Police Brutality," in *And Justice For All: Understanding and Controlling Police Use of Force* by William A. Geller and Hans Toch, eds. (Washington: Police Executive Research Forum, 1995), 45.

20. Victor E. Kappeler, Allen D. Sapp, and David L. Carter, "Police Officer Higher Education: Citizen Complaints and Rule Violations," *American Journal of Police* 11 (1992): 37–54.

21. Herman Goldstein, *Policing a Free Society* (Cambridge, Mass.: Ballinger Publishing Company, 1977), 272.

22. Richard N. Harris, "The Police Academy and Professional Self-Image," in *Policing: A View from the Street,* Peter K. Manning and John Van Maanen, eds. (Santa Monica: Goodyear Press, 1978), 273–91; Lieutenant Gene Berry, "The Uniformed Crime Investigator," *Law Enforcement Bulletin* (March 1984): 1.

23. William G. Doerner and E. Britt Patterson, "The Influence of Race and Gender upon Rookie Evaluations of their Field Training Officers," *American Journal of Police* XI (1992): 31; Lundman, *Police and Policing,* 78–80.

24. Lundman, *Police and Policing,* 81–82.

25. Jonathan Rubenstein, *City Police* (New York: Farrar, Straus, and Giroux, 1973), 282.

26. Richard Harris, *The Police Academy: An Inside Story* (New York: John Wiley and Sons, 1973), 53.

27. David H. Bayley and Egon Bittner, "Learning the Skills of Policing," in *Critical Issues in Policing,* 93.

28. James J. Fyfe, "Training to Reduce Police-Civilian Violence," in *And Justice For All,* 164.

29. Ibid.

30. Ibid.

31. Doerner and Patterson, "Influence of Race and Gender," 25.

32. Michael S. McCampbell, *Field Training for Police Officers: State of the Art* (Washington, D.C.: National Institute of Justice, 1986).

33. John E. Boydstun, *San Diego Field Interrogation: Final Report* (Washington, D.C.: U.S. Government Printing Office, 1975), 11.

34. Boydstun, *San Diego Field Interrogation,* 263.

35. *Critical Issues in Policing,* 311.

36. Alissa Pollitz Worden, "The Attitudes of Women and Men in Policing: Testing Conventional Wisdom and Contemporary Wisdom," *Criminology* 31 (1993): 203–204; Joanne Belknap and Jill Kastens Shelley, "The New Lone Ranger: Policewomen on Patrol," *American Journal of Police* XII (1993): 47; James Fyfe quoted in "Female Officers on the Move? A Status Report on Women in Policing" by Susan E. Martin, in *Critical Issues in Policing,* 312.

37. Martin, "Female Officers," 313.

38. Susan E. Martin, *Women on the Move? A Report of the Status of Women in Policing* (Washington, D.C.: Police Foundation, May 1989); U.S. Department of Justice, *Crime in the United States 1994* (Washington, D.C.: U.S. Government Printing Office, November 19, 1995), Table 74, p. 294.

39. Martin, "Female Officers," 316; The Police Foundation, *Policewomen on Patrol: Final Report* (Washington, D.C.: The Police Foundation, 1974); Catherine H. Milton, "The Future of Women in Policing," in *The Future of Policing,* Alvin W. Cohn, ed. (Beverly Hills, Calif.: Sage Publications, 1978), 196.

40. Alissa Pollitz Worden, "The Attitudes of Women and Men in Policing," 205–206.

41. Ibid., 228–229.

42. Peggy S. Sullivan, "Minority Officers: Current Issues," in *Critical Issues in Policing,* 331.

43. Samuel Walker, Cassia Spohn, and Miriam DeLonc, *The Color of Justice: Race, Ethnicity, and Crime in America* (Belmont, Calif.: Wadsworth Publishing Company, 1996), 110.

44. Samuel Walker, "Employment of Black and Hispanic Police Officers, 1983–1988: A Follow-up Study" (Omaha: University of Nebraska, Center for Applied Urban Research, February 1989).

45. *New York Times,* 10 September 1994.

46. Arlene Williams, National Organization of Black Law Enforcement Executives, *New York Times,* 23 April 1990.

47. Goldstein, *Policing a Free Society,* 269–70.

48. Gail A. Goolkasian et al., *Coping with Police Stress* (Washington, D.C.: National Institute of Justice, 1985), 1.

49. Hans Selye, *The Stress of Life* (New York: McGraw-Hill, 1976).

50. Goolkasian, *Coping with Police Stress*.

51. Harold E. Russell and Alan Biegel, *Understanding Human Behavior for Effective Police Work*, 2d ed. (New York: Basic Books, 1982), 280–98.

52. Goolkasian, *Coping with Police Stress*.

53. Cited in Goolkasian, *Coping with Police Stress*.

54. James J. Fyfe, "The Split-Second Syndrome and Other Determinants of Police Violence," in *Critical Issues in Policing*, 465–79; Carl B. Klockars, "The Dirty Harry Problem," in *Thinking About Police*, 2d ed., Carl B. Klockars and Stephen D. Mastrofski, eds. (New York: McGraw-Hill, 1991), 413–23.

55. Anthony M. Pate and Lorie A. Fridell, *Police Use of Force: Official Reports, Citizen Complaints, and Legal Consequences*, Vol. I (Washington, D.C.: PERF, 1993), 5; Bittner quote on page 17.

56. Ibid., "Foreword," by Hubert Williams, 6–7.

57. Wayne A. Kerstetter, "Who Disciplines the Police? Who Should?" in *Police Leadership in America: Crisis and Opportunity*, William A. Geller, ed. (New York: Praeger, 1985), 149–182.

58. Carl B. Klockars, "A Theory of Excessive Force and Its Control," in *And Justice for All*, 11–12.

59. James J. Fyfe, "Training to Reduce Police-Citizen Violence," in *And Justice For All*, 165.

60. Robert E. Worden, "The Causes of Police Brutality: Theory and Evidence," in *And Justice For All*, 31–60; Ross Lundstrom and Cynthia Mullen, "The Use of Force: One Department's Experience," *FBI Law Enforcement Bulletin* (January 1987): 6–9; Angus Campbell and Howard Schuman, "Racial Attitudes in Fourteen American Cities," *Supplemental Studies for the National Advisory Committee on Civil Disorders* (Washington, D.C.: U.S. Government Printing Office, 1969).

61. Anthony M. Pate and Lorie A. Fridell, *Police Use of Force: Official Reports, Citizen Complaints, and Legal Consequences* (Washington, D.C.: Police Foundation, 1993), 21–25, 73–78.

62. Pate and Fridell, *Police Use of Force*, 24.

63. Mark Blumburg, "Controlling Police Use of Deadly Force: Assessing Two Decades of Progress, " in *Critical Issues in Policing*, 443–44.

64. Ibid.

65. *Grudt v. Los Angeles*, 2 Cal.3d 575 (1970).

66. William A. Geller and Michael S. Scott, *Deadly Force: What We Know* (Washington, D.C.: Police Executive Research Foundation, 1992), 476.

67. Lawrence O'Donnell, *Deadly Force* (New York: William Morrow Co., 1983), 14; Geller and Scott, *Deadly Force*, 59–60.

68. O'Donnell, *Deadly Force*, 14; William A. Geller, *Crime File: Deadly Force* (Washington, D.C.: National Institute of Justice, 1985); Milton, *Police Use of Deadly Force*, 10; James Fyfe quoted in O'Donnell, *Deadly Force*, 14; *Criminal Justice Newsletter*, 15 February 1996, 5.

69. Geller, *Crime File: Deadly Force*.

70. Geller and Scott, *Deadly Force*, 60; New York State Commission on Criminal Justice and the Use of Force, "Report to the Governor," Vol. I, (1987), reported in Geller and Scott.

71. Geller and Scott, *Deadly Force*, 143.

72. Ibid, 147–48.

73. Quoted in Geller and Scott, 152–53.

74. Quoted in Geller and Scott, 155.

75. Michael E. Donahue and Frank S. Horvath, "Police Shooting Outcomes: Suspect Criminal History and Incident Behaviors," *American Journal of Police* 10 (1991): 21.

76. James J. Fyfe, "Blind Justice: Police Shootings in Memphis," *Journal of Criminal Law and Criminology* 73 (1982).

77. Jerry R. Sparger and David J. Giacopassi, "Memphis Revisited: A Reexamination of Police Shootings After the *Garner* Decision," *Justice Quarterly* 9 (1992): 211–25.

78. Independent Commission on the Los Angeles Police Department ("Christopher Commission"), *Report of the Independent Commission on the Los Angeles Police Department* (Los Angeles: Independent Commission on the Los Angeles Police Department, 1991), 80.

79. Skolnick and Fyfe, *Above the Law*, 11.

80. Seth Mydans, "Alarmed by Deaths in Car Chases, Police Curb High-Speed Chases," *New York Times*, 26 December 1992.

81. Quoted in Mydans, "Alarmed by Deaths."

82. Quoted in Mydans, "Alarmed by Deaths."

83. *New York Times*, December 17, 1995.

84. Geoffrey P. Alpert and Roger G. Dunham, *Police Pursuit Driving: Controlling Responses to Emergency Situations* (New York: Greenwood Press, 1990), 38; Geoffrey P. Alpert, "Questioning Police Pursuits in Urban Areas," *Journal of Police Science and Administration* 15 (1987): 298–306.

85. Geoffrey P. Alpert, "Police Pursuits—Linking Data to Decisions," *Criminal Law Bulletin* 24 (1988): 453.

86. Quoted in Alpert, "Police Pursuits," 453–54.

87. Gordon E. Misner, "High-Speed Pursuits: Police Perspectives," *Criminal Justice, the Americas* (December-January 1990): 15.

88. Quoted in Misner, "High-Speed Pursuits."

89. Quoted in Misner, "High-Speed Pursuits."

90. Quoted in Misner, "High-Speed Pursuits," 17.

91. Skolnick and Fyfe, *Above the Law*; Lawrence W. Sherman, "Reducing Police Gun Use: Critical Events, Administrative Policy and Organizational Change," in *The Management and Control of Police Organizations*, Maurice Punch, ed. (Cambridge: M.I.T. Press, 1983), 98–125; *Report of the Independent Commission of the Los Angeles Police Department* (1991); William B. Waegel, "The Use of Lethal Force by Police: The Effect of Statutory Change," *Crime and Delinquency* 31 (1984): 121–140; all cited and discussed in Pate and Fridell, *Police Use of Force*, 26–27.

92. Hans Toch and J. Douglas Grant, *Police as Problem Solvers* (New York: Plenum Press, 1991), 214.

93. Discussed in Skolnick and Fyfe, *Above the Law*, 181–184.

94. Goldstein, *Policing a Free Society*, chap. 2, 190–92.

95. Lawrence W. Sherman, *Scandal and Reform* (Berkeley: University of California Press, 1978), 30–31; Murphy quoted in Goldstein, *Policing a Free Society*, 201.

96. Ellwyn R. Stoddard, "Blue Coat Crime," in *Thinking About Police*, 340–41.

97. Goldstein, *Policing a Free Society*, 197–99; Rubenstein, *City Police*, 382–83; Commission to Investigate Allegations of Police Corruption and the City's Anti-Corruptional Procedures, *Commission Report* (New York: Braziller, 1972), 5–6.

98. Commission to Investigate Allegations of Police Corruption.

99. Douglas W. Perez, *Common Sense About Police Review* (Philadelphia: Temple University Press, 1994), 87.

100. *Susla v. State*, 311 Minn. 166, 247 N.W.2d 907, 912 (1976); *Pletan v. Gaines et al.*, 494 N.W.2d 38, 40 (Minn. 1992).

101. 42 U.S.C.A. §1983 (1976).

102. 483 U.S. 635, 107 S.Ct. 3034, 97 L.Ed.2d 523 (1987).

103. *Monell v. New York City Department of Social Services*, 436 U.S. 658, 98 S.Ct. 2018, 56 L.Ed.2d 611 (1978).

104. Wayne R. LaFave, *Search and Seizure*, 2d ed. (St. Paul: West Publishing Company, 1987), 1:248–49.

105. David B. Griswold, "Complaints Against the Police: Predicting Dispositions," *Journal of Criminal Justice* 22 (1994): 215–221; Kerstetter, "Who Disciplines the Police?" in *Police Leadership in America: Crisis and Opportunity*, 149–182; Douglas W. Perez, *Common Sense About Police Review* (Philadelphia: Temple University Press, 1994), 87–88.

106. Perez, *Common Sense About Police Review*, 88–89.

107. Perez, 92–93.

108. Perez, 96.

109. Perez, 96–97.

110. Samuel Walker and Vic W. Bumphus, "The Effectiveness of Civilian Review: Observations on Recent Trends and New Issues Regarding the Civilian Review of the Police," *American Journal of Police* XI (1992): 1.

111. Ibid., 5–7; Samuel Walker and Betsy Wright, *Citizen Review of the Police, 1994: A National Survey* (Washington, D.C.: Police Executive Research Forum, 1995), 1–2.

112. Walker and Bumphus, "The Effectiveness of Civilian Review," 3–4.

113. Ibid., 4.

114. Ibid., 8.

115. Pate and Fridell, *Police Use of Force*, 39.

116. Walker and Bumphus, "The Effectiveness of Civilian Review," 10.

117. Ibid., 16–17.

118. James Q. Wilson, *Thinking About Crime*, rev. ed. (New York: Basic Books, 1983), 112.

119. This *You Decide* is based on the following sources: Jim Schaefer and Roger Chesley, "Detroit Driver Beaten to Death by Police After Drug Stop," *St. Paul Pioneer Press*, 7 November 1992; Don Terry, "Death After Police Beating Inspires Fear in Detroit," *New York Times*, 8 November 1992; Doron P. Levin, "Detroit Punishes Officers in Man's Death," *New York Times*, 7 November 1992; Robert Davis, "Detroit Quiet After Beating; Arrests Due," *USA Today*, 9 November 1992; Patricia Edmonds, "No Violence, But Detroit Bitter," *USA Today*, 11 November 1992; Doron Levin, "4 Detroit Officers Charged in Death," *New York Times*, 17 November 1992; "Autopsy in Beating Finds Drugs," *New York Times*, 19 November 1992; Sandra Sanchez, "Hearings Held on Charges," *USA Today*, 17 November 1992; Steve Marshall and Maryann Struman, "Detroit Officers Arraigned," *USA Today*, 17 November 1992; "Detroit Dismisses 4 Police Officers in Fatal Beating," *New York Times*, 18 November 1992.

120. *Los Angeles Police Department, Training Bulletin* (September 1986).

121. Ibid., 5–6.

122. Greg Meyer, "Nonlethal Weapons Versus Conventional Police Tactics: The Los Angeles Police Department Experience" (Master's Thesis, California State University, Los Angeles, 1991), 59.

123. Quoted in Meyer, "Nonlethal Weapons," 20.

124. Quoted in Meyer, "Nonlethal Weapons."

PART THREE

Courts

8

Courts and Courtro

om Work Groups

CHAPTER MAIN POINTS

1. *Formality increases from proceedings in the lower criminal courts, to the trial courts, to the appellate courts.*

2. *Criminal courts balance the rule of law and informal demands created by professional, organizational, political, and societal interests.*

3. *Efficient, economical, and speedy disposition of cases is the major organizational goal of the criminal courts.*

4. *Case disposition takes place within a close personal and working relationship among judges, prosecutors, and defense attorneys.*

5. *Criminal courts act not only as legal institutions but also as social service agencies, seeking what is "best" for victims and offenders who come before them.*

6. *Prosecutors perform a range of formal and informal functions, with wide discretion to decide whether to prosecute suspects and, if they do, what charges to bring against them.*

7. *Defense attorneys perform the formal duties of defending clients and ensuring the government prosecutes according to the rule of law; informally, they are part of the courthouse work group seeking to get along and negotiate settlements.*

Following arrest, suspects become defendants, and decision making shifts from the police station to the criminal courts. Prosecutors, defense attorneys, and judges play the leading roles and make most of the decisions in court proceedings. In the formal sense, courts are legal institutions. Courthouses are "palaces of justice." In the courtrooms of these justice palaces, aggressive prosecution and vigorous defense, umpired by judges applying the rule of law, are supposed to ensure that truth and justice will win out. In reality, decisions take place not only openly in formal court proceedings according to the rule of law, they also occur less visibly in the corridors.[1]

Informally, courts are both political and social institutions. Courts, like legislatures and the offices of mayor, governor, and president, are aware of and respond to the wants and demands of the public, interest groups, and individuals. Witness the enormous increase in drug offense cases that reach the criminal courts, due in large part to public demands to "crack down on drug dealers." Hence, lawyers, probation officers, clerks, and bail bondsmen exercise considerable discretion that results in decisions balancing both legal rules and extralegal professional, organizational, political, and societal goals. This discretionary decision making influences and often circumvents formal decision making. Court proceedings in many cases, therefore, merely ratify what lawyers and other criminal justice personnel have already decided informally. The visible, open, publicized formal court proceedings governed by the rule of law mask the great importance of this discretionary decision making outside the courtroom. Most decisions following arrest, as well as those preceding it, reflect professional, organizational, political, and societal interests in addition to constitutional, legal, and judicial principles, doctrines, and rules.[2]

Criminal Courts

The criminal courts control several decision points that either move defendants further into the criminal process, divert them into social service agencies, or remove them from the criminal process. (See inside front cover and Chapter 1.) Before trial, criminal courts arraign defendants (command them to come to court to hear and answer charges against them; assign lawyers to indigent defendants (defendants too poor to afford lawyers); set, review, alter, or deny bail; and conduct pretrial hearings. They also dispose of criminal cases. Most publicized but fewest in number, these courts dispose of cases by formal trial proceedings presided over by judges. More numerous are less formal proceedings in which magistrates dispose of cases in pretrial hearings and perfunctory lower criminal court proceedings that mix formal rules and informal discretionary judgments. In the vast majority of cases, however, dispositions—all convictions, of course—follow pleas of guilty resulting either from informal plea bargaining or from simple pleas of guilty without any negotiation. Courts also review criminal cases following conviction either by appeal or by other post-conviction proceedings.[3]

Criminal courts are arranged into three tiers (see Figure 8.1):

- **Lower Criminal Courts**— courts of limited authority to hear and determine minor cases and to conduct pretrial proceedings.

- **Trial Courts**— courts of general authority to conduct pretrial and trial proceedings.

- **Appellate Courts**— courts with the authority to hear and decide appeals and other proceedings following conviction.

Lower Criminal Courts

Lower criminal courts are called by various names around the country, such as superior, municipal, county, justice of the peace, or magistrate's courts. They are known as courts of **limited jurisdiction,** meaning that their authority is limited to trying minor criminal cases and to conducting preliminary proceedings in felony cases. Legally, defendants in lower criminal courts have the same rights as defendants in trial courts. In practice, however, judges try most cases less formally than in trial courts, and they try them without juries. Lower criminal courts are not **courts of record,** that is, they do not keep written records of proceedings unless defendants pay for them. Lower criminal court decisions are not as final as those of trial courts. Trial courts can retry cases heard in lower criminal courts in proceedings known as trials *de novo.*

The lower courts decide the great bulk of criminal cases—traffic offenses, drunk and disorderly conduct, shoplifting, and prostitution. Hence, they are the first and, in most instances, the only contact most people ever have with the criminal courts. Defendants appear in trial courts only for criminal trials (about two out of 100 cases), or rarer still, in appellate courts on criminal appeals. Adding to their importance, the lower criminal courts decide bail, assign lawyers to indigent defendants, and conduct other pretrial proceedings, such as preliminary hearings to test the government's case against defendants, and hearings to decide the legality of confessions, searches, and seizures.

Figure 8.1

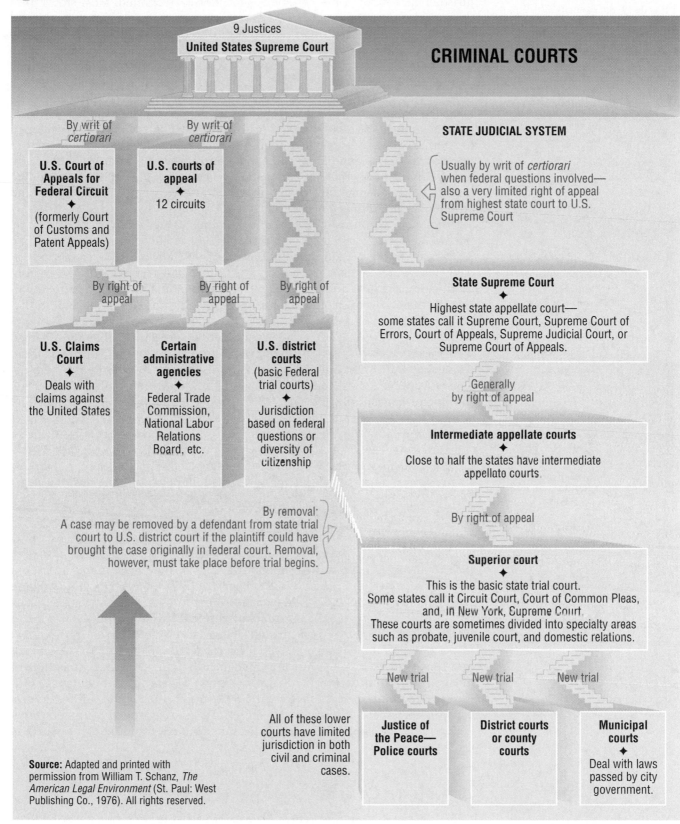

9 Justices
United States Supreme Court

CRIMINAL COURTS

By writ of *certiorari*

By writ of *certiorari*

STATE JUDICIAL SYSTEM

U.S. Court of Appeals for Federal Circuit
◆
(formerly Court of Customs and Patent Appeals)

U.S. courts of appeal
◆
12 circuits

Usually by writ of *certiorari* when federal questions involved— also a very limited right of appeal from highest state court to U.S. Supreme Court

By right of appeal

By right of appeal

By right of appeal

State Supreme Court
◆
Highest state appellate court— some states call it Supreme Court, Supreme Court of Errors, Court of Appeals, Supreme Judicial Court, or Supreme Court of Appeals.

U.S. Claims Court
◆
Deals with claims against the United States

Certain administrative agencies
◆
Federal Trade Commission, National Labor Relations Board, etc.

U.S. district courts
(basic Federal trial courts)
◆
Jurisdiction based on federal questions or diversity of citizenship

Generally by right of appeal

Intermediate appellate courts
◆
Close to half the states have intermediate appellate courts.

By removal:
A case may be removed by a defendant from state trial court to U.S. district court if the plaintiff could have brought the case originally in federal court. Removal, however, must take place before trial begins.

By right of appeal

Superior court
◆
This is the basic state trial court.
Some states call it Circuit Court, Court of Common Pleas, and, in New York, Supreme Court.
These courts are sometimes divided into specialty areas such as probate, juvenile court, and domestic relations.

New trial

New trial

New trial

All of these lower courts have limited jurisdiction in both civil and criminal cases.

Justice of the Peace— Police courts

District courts or county courts

Municipal courts
◆
Deal with laws passed by city government.

Lower criminal courts vary greatly across the country and even within jurisdictions. Some of the variation is formally determined. Most states limit the jurisdiction of lower courts to misdemeanors with a maximum one-year penalty. Some states restrict their authority to deciding minor offenses with three-month maximum jail sentences, while others extend their authority to crimes carrying punishments of up to seven-year's imprisonment. Forty-two percent of lower criminal courts can impose a maximum $500 fine; 39 percent can set fines in excess of $500; 19 percent can levy only up to $100. Informal influences also lead to differences. Community standards, local politics, and city size create differences in proceedings from one jurisdiction to another, from one court to another in the same jurisdiction, and even from one courtroom to another in the same courthouse. Disorderly conduct and drunk driving may predominate in some courts; prostitution may take up the time of others. Some courtrooms may conduct only first appearances, and others only preliminary hearings.[4]

In about two-thirds of lower court systems, judges are not required to be members of the bar. Some states require these judges to attend training courses or pass an examination. However, the judges in lower courts will have less training than the least experienced lawyers who appear before them. Some states require only a high school diploma to qualify for membership on the bench of the lower courts. The Constitution does not require that lower criminal court judges have legal training. In *North v. Russell,* the Supreme Court held that trials before non-lawyer judges do not deny defendants charged with misdemeanors due process of law. In that case, Lonnie North was tried, convicted, and sentenced to a term of imprisonment in a Kentucky criminal trial presided over by Judge C. B. Russell, "a coal miner without any legal training or education whatever," who testified that he had only a high school education, was not familiar with the Kentucky rules of criminal procedure, and did not know the rights guaranteed to criminal defendants by the U.S. Constitution. Nevertheless, the Supreme Court ruled that the proceeding did not deny North his right to due process of law. According to David A. Harriss, "many lower court judges are marginally qualified to rule on complex legal issues, decide guilt or innocence, and pass sentence."[5]

Trial Courts

Of all court proceedings, the criminal trial receives the most public attention, even though it is the rarest of all judicial events. (Chapter 10 discusses the criminal trial.) These trials take place in courts known variously as district or circuit courts. Trial courts are **courts of general jurisdiction,** meaning that they have the authority to hear and decide all criminal cases from capital felonies to petty misdemeanors. Trial courts decide felony cases, over which they have both exclusive and original jurisdiction. **Original jurisdiction** means that **adjudication** (court proceedings) begins in trial courts. **Exclusive jurisdiction** means that only the trial courts can adjudicate these cases. Trial courts adhere to formal rules more than lower criminal courts do. They permit only members of the bar to preside as judges, and they are courts of record.

Appellate Courts

Appellate courts hear and decide appeals of trial court decisions. Proceedings in the appellate court are the most formal of all three levels of courts. The federal judiciary and 39 states have a two-tiered appellate structure. Intermediate appellate courts hear most appeals initially; mainly, they review cases to determine whether the government has carried its burden of proving all material elements of crimes beyond a reasonable doubt, and whether defendants have carried their burden in establishing their defenses. Supreme courts, or courts of last resort, review intermediate appellate court decisions, complicated questions of law, and the constitutional rights of criminal defendants.

All jurisdictions grant defendants the right to review lower and trial court decisions. Many states provide for automatic appeal of death sentences. Defendants base most review on irregular proceedings in the lower and trial courts. The reversal of a conviction on appeal only sets aside the prior conviction; the government can retry defendants. State appellate courts decide about 80 percent of all appeals. The U.S. Supreme Court decides about 150 cases a year with full opinion; 200 to 300 cases decided with opinion is the norm for state supreme courts. The principal mechanism for review in federal cases is by writs of *habeas corpus* and *certiorari*. The petition for a writ of *habeas corpus,* meaning, literally, "you have the body," asks for review on the grounds that a detention facility has unlawfully detained a prisoner. These reviews rarely succeed. In the petition for a writ of *certiorari,* literally, "to certify the record" of a lower court, defendants ask appellate courts to review proceedings of lower courts.[6]

Functions of the Criminal Courts

Criminal courts perform several functions, and their leading figures—judges, prosecutors, and defense attorneys—play different roles in their operation. Perhaps most familiar is the formal role of criminal courts, in which they administer justice according to due process of law, requiring that all proceedings comply with constitutional and legal safeguards. It is up to the courts, as "palaces of justice," to assure compliance with the rule of law. They are supposed to guarantee impartial, evenhanded, and public application of the law in all cases.[7]

Society demands much of its criminal courts. They are to balance the demands for justice according to the rule of law and the demands of professional, organizational, political, and societal interests. The formal demands include the expectation that the criminal court will, according to the great, early twentieth-century jurist Roscoe Pound,

> meet society's demand that serious offenders be convicted and punished, and at the same time it is expected to insure that the innocent and the unfortunate are not oppressed. It is expected to control the application of force against the individual by the state, and it is expected to find which of two conflicting versions of events is the truth. And so the court is not merely an operating agency, but one that has a vital educational and symbolic significance. It is expected to articulate the community's most deeply held, most cherished views about the relationship of the individual and society. The formality of the trial and the honor accorded the robed judge bespeak the symbolic importance of the court and its work.[8]

In most criminal courts, the informal professional, organizational, and societal goals receive higher priority than the formal goals outlined in the quote from Roscoe Pound. Ever since the middle of the nineteenth century, observers have noted that the lower criminal courts in particular fail to live up to their high formal responsibilities. In the courts of large cities, cramped, noisy, and undignified courtrooms hurry defendants through important decisions in the most perfunctory manner.[9]

In the 1950s, Professor Caleb Foote observed one Philadelphia magistrate who decided 55 cases in 15 minutes. Four defendants were tried, convicted, and sentenced in 17 seconds! The magistrate accomplished this by merely reading off the defendant's name, taking one look at him, and saying, "Three months." In the 1970s, in another city, magistrates decided 72 percent of the cases before them in less than a minute each, according to a sociologist who systematically observed the court's proceedings for three months. Most reports indicate that things have not changed much since these observations.[10]

According to Professor Harry I. Subin, the New York criminal court in 1993 was

> overwhelmed by a flood of cases . . . [and, therefore] accomplishes very little. It does not dispense justice. It simply disposes of each day's business in any way it can, so it can be ready to dispose of the next day's business. And because substantive action would slow things down, the court very rarely conducts legal proceedings or imposes punishment on the guilty.[11]

The Manhattan lower criminal court in the 1990s disposes of most cases in less than four minutes.[12]

Observers express conflicting views regarding this emphasis on informality and speed. According to one experienced trial judge, "For many years I have been dismayed by the fact that [most criminal] cases were allocated only fifteen to twenty minutes." The emphasis on speed, according to critics, has produced "assembly-line justice," not the deliberation that justice requires. But Stephen J. Schulhofer, who observed lower criminal courts in Philadelphia for several months, reached a different conclusion. After allowing for individual differences in judges, prosecutors, and defense attorneys, he found that magistrates conduct misdemeanor trials according to genuine adversarial proceedings. Even though it took only 25 minutes on the average, and often less than 10 minutes, to decide these cases, Schulhofer concluded that they received all the time needed to decide them fairly and accurately. Judges listened carefully to witnesses, often taking notes.[13]

Judges and attorneys, according to Schulhofer, took the rules of evidence seriously. Attorneys raised objections, and

> judges often sustained them [objections] at the price of slowing down the trial. In a simple assault case, Judge KA sustained several defense objections to the form of the prosecutor's direct examination. At the end of the trial, KA made much of the prosecutor's ineptitude and said he found it "hard to believe that this case went on for half an hour or an hour." (In fact, the trial had consumed 22 minutes.)[14]

Thomas W. Church, Jr., observed four criminal courts in the Bronx, Detroit, Miami, and Pittsburgh. He found the adversary system alive and well in the local legal culture of those courts

> by observing the obvious distaste many lawyers working in a prosecuting attorney's office seem to have for the defense side in general, a feeling often reciprocated by defense attorneys. (Possibly the most graphic evidence of this antipathy came during the summer I was conducting interviews in Miami when the annual prosecutor-public defender softball game degenerated into a fist fight.) After years of scholars' debunking the "adversary myth," it may be that the adversary system is in need of . . . bunking."[15]

Mass justice predominates in some courts, adversary proceedings in others, and both exist to some extent in all, making it impossible to generalize about criminal courts. The degree to which each of these systems controls practice depends on local legal culture, the values and customs that make up the environment of particular courtrooms.

Due Process Functions

The formal side to the modern U.S. court system has historical roots in the reaction to eighteenth-century English abuses of power. Originally intended to serve a predominantly rural society with a small, relatively homogeneous population, courts were supposed to protect individuals against excessive government power, a revolutionary concept that placed individuals at center stage and armed them with court-protected rights against the government. Criminal court procedures developed out of a highly suspicious attitude toward government power. This judicial system was based on the idea that the government and citizens accused of crime are in a contest, or adversary proceeding. To be fair, the contesting parties must enjoy a roughly equal chance to prevail. Adhering to prescribed rules best secures fairness and equality. Due process of law, that government can proceed against citizens only according to rules, embodies this concept. The old saying, "It is better that ten guilty persons go free than to punish one innocent person," expresses the idea in popular terms.[16]

In the **adversary system,** sometimes called the "sporting theory of justice," prosecutors represent the government and defense attorneys represent the accused. Both fight vigorously for the victory of their sides. As adversaries on opposite sides of a case, each presents only his or her side. However, they cannot win at any cost; they must fight according to the rules of the laws and constitutions of the state and federal governments. In this struggle or, more politely, contest or game, judges preside as umpires, impartially enforcing the rules. Juries, armed with the instructions in the law as explained by judges and their own common sense, sort out facts from fiction and discover the "true" facts. This image reflects the highest ideals of American justice—an open, fair, impartial, dignified conflict that sorts out the guilty from the innocent, punishing one and vindicating the other.[17]

The adversary process assumes that through free and open competition over the facts, the truth will triumph. However, these time-consuming legal functions cannot easily take place in the face of pressures to achieve countervailing informal goals. The adversary system never operated fully according to its ideals. Its emphasis on individual rights and limited government power secured by judicial proceedings not only differed from eighteenth-century practices, but was also cumbersome, inefficient, and slow. Formal judicial proceedings were rigid and, ironically, did not allow for individual differences. Even in rural, sparsely populated, homogenous eighteenth-century America, the adversary system presented major drawbacks. The problems worsened when society became predominantly urban and industrial, when immigrants of many different ethnic origins crowded into cities and factories, and when values shifted from extolling individual rights to meeting the demand for order. The state was no longer an object of suspicion, but instead became an instrument for social order and the "reform" of individuals. Courts that convicted innocent people were no longer the problem, critics warned; rather, the problem was a legal system that set criminals free because of individual rights that made it virtually impossible to convict them.[18]

By the early twentieth century, the due process functions of the criminal courts faced increasing challenges from societal demands for order, the growing need for efficient, economical administration, and the expanding requirements of a complex, modern criminal court bureaucracy. As a result, informal action more consistent with achieving crime control, efficiency, economy, and internal organizational goals began to supplant formal due process goals in criminal courts.[19]

historical note

In America we take it as a matter of course that a judge should be a mere umpire, to pass upon objections and hold counsel to the rules of the game, and that the parties should fight out their own game in their own way without judicial interference .... [This] leads counsel ... to deal with rules of law and procedure exactly as the professional football coach with the rules of the sport.

Roscoe Pound, 1906

Crime Control Function

Due process emphasizes individuals over society. Crime control, on the other hand, gives primacy to society's interest in order. (See Chapter 2.) Formal legal rules may well place limits on the crime control function of courts, but they by no means eliminate it. Thus, friction between formal due process and informal crime control often arises. Crime control bears a harsher image than due process. The "nasty, brutish" side of life gets portrayed in criminal courts. Courts are supposed to punish thieves, muggers, rapists, and burglars because of the pain and suffering they have already wrought in the lives of their victims and the fears they have spawned in those who might be next. One typical judge said, "There's no use kidding yourself. We have a particular type of clientele in this court: The criminal court is a cesspool of poverty." The public expects criminal justice to punish these "bad" people. Prosecutors are supposed to be ruthless, defense lawyers should not be allowed to "get their clients off on technicalities," and judges should not be "soft on criminals" or "handcuff the police" in their fight against crime.[20]

Organizational Function

Neither the due process nor the crime control image completely describes the reality of criminal courts. Criminal courts are complex organizations in which neither due process nor crime control triumphs as the ultimate goal. Due process and the whole rubric of formal rules and procedures cannot work precisely as legal theorists say. Justice is a vague goal, subject to widely differing interpretations. The due process goals that favor criminal defendants often conflict with the crime control goals that call for enforcing the law and protecting society. Moreover, no agreed-on method can achieve all these goals, even if their definitions were clear and not in conflict. No one really knows for sure what "works" to control crime, protect society, and restrain individuals all at the same time.

In addition, the courts operate within a constantly shifting and uncertain environment not entirely under the control of judges, prosecutors, or defense counsel. The public changes its mind about what it wants from courts; budgets shrink and expand unpredictably; and, most of all, different types of people come before the courts. In such vaguely defined circumstances, with multiple and conflicting goals, unproved and uncertain methods, and a shifting and unpredictable environment, making decisions according to uniform rules and procedures is virtually impossible. Informality permits necessary flexibility to make discretionary judgments in these fluid situations.[21]

Bureaucratic Function

Courts are bureaucratic organizations. Bureaucracies place high premiums on administrative values, especially efficiency, economy, and speed. The pride some judges take in managing case dispositions well reflects this high regard for bureaucratic values. A New York State chief judge's summary of his achievements shows his pride and satisfaction:

> New York has become one of the few states where the courts are disposing of more cases than they are taking on. We've made the courts more manageable. The courts are working much better than they did, they're producing much more, and they're more nearly up to date than they were six years ago.[22]

Social Service Function

In addition to their legal and organizational functions, courts also act as social service agencies. In this capacity, they seek what is "best" for the victims and offenders who appear in court. As one Pittsburgh judge put it, "We don't sentence the crime, we sentence the offender; so you have to consider the

historical note

If some degree of education in criminal investigation, in psychology and kindred sciences of human behavior, and in psychiatry and sciences which deal with mental and moral diseases would come to be recognized as part of the requisite training of the criminal lawyer, the criminal field of law practice would gain a prestige which it does not now possess; not to speak of the greater competence which this special knowledge would bring.

Roscoe Pound and Felix Frankfurter, 1922

person first." Another said, "You have to consider what type of person [the defendant] is. I try to glean from the background, the kind of woman he is married to, from the nature of his offense, from his relationship to his children and from his associations." Adopting this approach, one judge granted probation to an armed robber because he learned that the victim provoked the defendant. Furthermore, he was also favorably impressed because the defendant's wife was a "neatly dressed woman in her twenties who appeared mature and seemed to have a settling effect on the defendant."[23]

Using this **substantial justice approach,** judges look at each case individually in order to award "meaningful justice." The substantial justice approach emphasizes informal criminal justice. According to the approach, formal rules can actually impede doing substantial justice; individual cases do not always fit the prescribed rules of criminal law and criminal procedure. Extenuating and aggravating circumstances and differing individual needs call for different procedures and results, so the substantial justice approach relies heavily on discretion.[24]

Sometimes, the social service and legal functions of courts are integrated. The tension between law and discretion usually prevents bringing these functions into the open. However, the extraordinary growth in the case load of drug cases led Dade County, Florida, to establish a special Drug Court. The Miami Drug Court Model is a hybrid that combines "elements of both criminal justice and drug treatment." According to John S. Goldkamp and Doris Weiland, guiding the creation of the drug court was the "notion that an effective and flexible program of court-supervised drug treatment could reduce demand for illicit drugs and hence involvement in crime and reinvolvement in the court system."[25]

The Miami Drug Court accepts only defendants without prior convictions who are charged with third degree felony drug possession. Goldkamp and Weiland examined a sample cohort of defendants for a period of 18 months. Their research produced a number of positive findings, including:

- Far fewer Drug Court defendants than other felony drug and non-drug defendants were sentenced to incarceration for longer than one year.
- Drug Court defendants generated far fewer rearrest rates than other felony drug defendants.
- When Drug Court defendants were rearrested, the length of time to their first rearrest averaged from two to three times longer than that of comparison groups.
- Drug Court defendants had a higher rate of failure to appear for court appearances, but this was due to the far higher number of times that the court required Drug Court defendants to appear.[26]

Courthouse Work Groups

Criminal courts have as their major organizational goal the efficient, economic, and quick disposition of cases. Harmony within the court organization is also a goal. Discretion and negotiation, not the adversary process according to written rules, are the means to achieve these goals. Prosecutors, judges, and defense attorneys form a **courthouse work group,** or "courtroom elite," whose primary mission is the disposition of criminal cases. The large number of cases in most criminal courts makes this goal difficult to achieve, particularly in cumbersome formal adversary proceedings. Legally prescribed "speedy trial" requirements aggravate the pressures created by heavy caseloads.[27]

Case disposition takes place within a close working and personal environment. Judges, prosecutors, and defense attorneys see each other regularly, have similar backgrounds, and many have similar career aspirations. They have much more in common than the adversary process suggests. According to Peter F. Nardulli, who has extensively studied the courtroom work group:

> In many [Chicago] courtrooms daily sessions were frequently preceded (as well as followed) by "coffee klatches" held in the judge's chambers. The coffee klatches were usually attended by the judge, public defender, the two assistant attorneys and a handful of private defense attorneys, who may or may not have had a case in that courtroom on the day in question. Conversations ranged from the fate of the Blackhawks or Bulls the night before, the potential impact of some changes in criminal law or procedure, the cases scheduled for that day, to what happened in the annual football game between the state's attorney's office and the public defender's office. "War stories" concerning unusual criminal cases in which the various participants had been involved were also related frequently, and occasionally some political gossip was exchanged. Oftentimes these klatches evolved into plea bargaining sessions involving concerned participants, with opinions and comments by bystanders freely registered. In short, these sessions were not unlike those that might take place in any office or shop.[28]

After interviewing more than 500 judges, prosecutors, and defense attorneys in major cities throughout the country, Paul B. Wice concluded:

> Despite their locations in a hectic urban setting, the criminal courts which I visited seemed like traditional villages. The high level of intimacy and frequency of interaction between nearly all of the courtroom work group made many defendants and outsiders unfamiliar with the court's inner workings incredulous as to the possible existence of adversary proceeding. Although the "kibitzing" is curtailed during the time when court is in session, it is never completely absent. In the hallways, around the snackbars, in the courtrooms during recesses, and before and after the day's business, the friendly joshing never seems to end. Whether this exaggerated conviviality serves as a type of necessary social lubricant to disguise actual tensions, or is an accurate measure of their camaraderie, is difficult to discern. Whichever purpose it serves, it is an omnipresent style of interaction that typified almost every city visited.[29]

Amid the relationships of the courtroom work group, defendants are alien even to their lawyers who, like the judges and prosecutors, rarely question their clients' guilt. Particularly if cases have gone beyond charging, judges, prosecutors, and defense lawyers usually agree that defendants have committed some offense; they need only agree on a punishment. The courtroom work group's strong desire to dispose of cases has several sources. They carry a large volume of cases, all with deadlines. Since they agree on guilt, they consider most cases routine. The courtroom elite want to get along with each other; hence, they prefer amicable negotiation and settlement to haggling and dispute. The courtroom elite have other business. They are professionals who do not get paid overtime. Once they move through the day's docket, they want to get on to other matters. In view of these common work group goals, due process and crime control share in the priorities of the elite. The common goal to dispose of cases and the desire and need to maintain a continuing positive work group relationship softens formal role conflicts among prosecutors, defense counsel, and judges.[30]

Herbert Jacob and James Eisenstein describe the desire for "group cohesion" and some of its consequences:

> Pervasive conflict is not only unpleasant; it also makes work more difficult. Cohesion produces a sense of belonging and identification that sat-

The courtroom work group dominates informal discretionary decision making in the criminal courts.

isfies human needs. It is maintained in several ways. Courtroom work groups shun outsiders because of their potential threat to group cohesion. The work group possesses a variety of adaptive techniques to minimize the effect of abrasive participants. For instance, the occasional defense attorney who violates routine cooperative norms may be punished by having to wait until the end of the day to argue his motion; he may be given less time than he wishes for a lunch break in the middle of a trial; he may be kept beyond usual court hours for bench conferences. Likewise, unusually adversarial defense or prosecuting attorneys are likely to smooth over their formal conflicts with informal cordiality. Tigers at the bench, they become tame kittens in chambers and in the hallways, exchanging pleasantries and exuding sociability.[31]

The "justice" negotiated behind the scenes in the courthouse corridors, judges' chambers, or even the restrooms overshadows the criminal trial that looms so large on television and movie screens. "Justice by consent"—so important to a smooth-functioning organization—dominates the criminal courts, not the much-touted criminal trial. This informal reality, in which crime control and due process share the work group's own agenda and relationships, confuses citizens, often to the point of resentment and bitterness. "Deals" that prosecutors and defense attorneys make and that judges approve are inconsistent, or so they appear to be, with both due process and crime control.[32]

As parts of an organization, judges, prosecutors, and defense attorneys do not oppose each other in competition for the truth. They are a team, negotiating the best settlement possible with minimal dispute and maximum harmony within the courtroom work group. They have the largely thankless task of doing what they can to balance an array of competing, often irreconcilable, demands and values. Such balancing rarely satisfies anyone because no one gets everything he or she wants—that is the meaning of settlement, as opposed to victory. In the adversary system, the goal is victory, and there is always a winner, or at least it seems that way from the outside. In the negotiation process, the goal is settlement, and the result is always at best "only half a loaf." Negotiation and settlement should not suggest injustice. They can represent the best resolution to a complex problem.[33]

"The decision as to who will make the decisions affects what decisions will be made," Jack Peltason, scholar of federal courts, wrote more than 40 years ago. The statement is still true. Even though we pride ourselves on being a "government of laws" and not individuals, judges play a major policy-making role in American criminal justice. Therefore, since the personal characteristics of judges affect decision making, it is important to know something about these characteristics.[34]

The personal characteristics of judges vary significantly. In a major study of urban criminal court judges, Martin A. Levin compared judges in Minneapolis and Pittsburgh. In Minneapolis, middle-class, Protestant men, who before becoming judges had practiced law in firms representing business and corporate interests, dominate the bench. They have had little or no outside experience with the clients who dominate the criminal courts. They are deeply committed to uniform, predictable rules and procedures. Most Pittsburgh judges, on the other hand, have mainly working-class, ethnic backgrounds. They have had direct life contact with the typical court client. Pittsburgh judges favor informal justice that tailors decisions to the needs of individual defendants. Judges in Pittsburgh tailor justice to societal interests, and interpret legal rules to do so. Despite these differences, most judges are upper middle-class, white, male Protestants with a better than average education.[35]

Jurisdictions select judges by three methods: popular election, appointment, and the merit plan. Thirty-two states elect judges, some in partisan, others in nonpartisan elections. Thirty-seven states and the federal government appoint judges; the president nominates and the Senate approves federal judges; governors appoint state judges. Twenty-two states select judges according to the merit system or the Missouri Bar Plan. (Missouri created the merit plan idea in 1940 to overcome the widespread use of political patronage in judicial selection.) In the merit system, lawyers, citizens, and an incumbent judge make up a commission that draws up the list of nominees. From this list, governors appoint judges to their brief initial term. After that, judges must face the electorate. The ballot asks simply whether to retain sitting judges. If approved, judges serve until the next election.[36]

Minneapolis typifies the merit system, Pittsburgh the election system. Minneapolis judges appear on the ballot, but they do not campaign. The governor appoints them to an interim term; the voters approve their appointment at the next election. Governors may appoint judges from their own party, but they generally choose nominal Democrats or Republicans who do not actively participate in party activities. Campaign literature never mentions judges' party affiliations. Pittsburgh judges run for office in the traditional way. Billboards advertise their candidacy; they openly and vocally run as Democrats or Republicans.[37]

Controversy over the merit and election systems can run high. For example, Chief Justice John Hill of the Texas Supreme Court proposed a merit system for Texas in 1987. Pressures from the development of a two-party system, the increasing specialization of the bar, and the growth of urban counties spurred the chief justice to act. The proposal failed. Some attorneys, politicians, minority and women's groups, and the populist tradition of electing most state officials blocked the plan.[38]

Supporters of the merit system argue that selection based on party loyalty precludes impartial judging. Competence in the law and the ability to judge according to it comprise the only acceptable criteria for judgeships. Supporters of the elective system promote its democracy. Elected judges are responsive and responsible to the community they serve. If they fail to meet community needs and standards, the voters will remove them. Judicial decisions ought to reflect politically sensitive judgments about community values.[39]

Figure 8.2

AFRICAN-AMERICAN STATE COURT JUDGES

- African Americans
- Other

— 293

8,139

Major Courts

Source: Derived from B. L. Graham, "Judicial Recruitment and Racial Diversity on State Courts", in *Courts and Justice,* G. Larry Mays and Peter R. Gregware, eds. (Prospect Heights, Ill.: WavelandPress, 1995), 219.

Minority and Women Judges

A variety of interest groups—political parties, bar associations, businesses, police unions, civil rights organizations—debate and try to influence the selection of judges, because of the power of judges to shape criminal justice policy. These groups want that policy shaped to benefit their particular interests. Members of women's and minority groups, like other interest groups, seek the appointment of women and minority judges who will represent their interests. Minority groups especially feel the need for representation on state courts because they are most likely to come in contact with state criminal justice. Barbara Luck Graham analyzed data derived from a list of African-American judges compiled by the Joint Study for Political Studies and the Judicial Council of the National Bar Association, and from information provided by the clerks and administrators of state courts of general and limited jurisdiction. She found that African-American judges are underrepresented on state courts, making up about 3.6 percent of all seats. (See Figure 8.2.) She also found that most African-American judges either serve on the lower criminal courts or are quasi-judicial officials. (See Figure 8.3) However, she also found that the rate of appointment for African-American judges is improving. (See Figure 8.4.) It is not clear whether the explanation for the underrepresentation of African Americans on state courts is due to structural or other reasons. Some research suggests that judicial selection procedures favor the selection of white judges. Other research suggests that the relatively small number of African-American attorneys explains the small number of African-American judges. Whatever the reason, despite the significant gains that African-American attorneys have made in securing selection to state courts, they are still significantly underrepresented.[40]

Women have served as lower court judges since 1870. The first woman was elected to a trial court in 1921. By 1940, 21 states had women judges; by 1950, the number had risen to 29. The best estimates indicate that by 1991, about 8 percent of state and 9 percent of federal judges were women. By the year 2000, estimates are that women will make up nearly 50 percent of all lawyers and that the number of women judges will also increase. Little empirical research, however, indicates what effect gender has on judicial decision making. The only available research suggests that male judges

Figure 8.3

PERCENT OF AFRICAN-AMERICAN JUDGES ON TRIAL AND LOWER COURTS

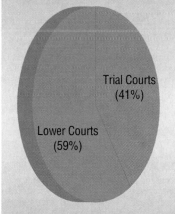

Trial Courts (41%)

Lower Courts (59%)

Source: Derived from B. L. Graham, "Judicial Recruitment and Racial Diversity on State Courts", in *Courts and Justice,* G. Larry Mays and Peter R. Gregware, eds. (Prospect Heights, Ill.: WavelandPress, 1995), 220.

Figure 8.4

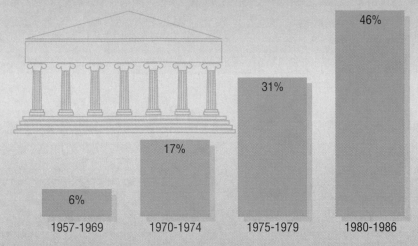

YEAR WHEN AFRICAN-AMERICAN STATE COURT JUDGES RECIEVED JUDGESHIP

6% — 1957-1969

17% — 1970-1974

31% — 1975-1979

46% — 1980-1986

Source: Derived from B. L. Graham, "Judicial Recruitment and Racial Diversity on State Courts", in *Courts and Justice*, G. Larry Mays and Peter R. Gregware, eds. (Prospect Heights, Ill.: WavelandPress, 1995), 221.

Women have served as lower court judges since 1870.

sentence women defendants more leniently than they do men. One study found that while women were more "liberal" in sex discrimination cases, their decisions in criminal cases differed little from the decisions of men.[41]

Prosecutors

Prosecutors provide a vital link between police and courts, and courts and corrections. Police in nearly every jurisdiction in the country bring arrests to prosecutors' offices, not to courts. Prosecutors, not judges, decide whether these cases ever get to court. Enormous power results from this nexus. Prosecutors can bring police work to a halt and render courts and corrections powerless by failing to charge. Even when they charge, they shape the course of events by what specific offenses they choose to prosecute, by what arrangements they make with defense attorneys, and by what sentences they recommend to judges.[42]

American prosecutors are unique in that they are wholly public officials. In most countries, prosecution is traditionally a private matter. Called variously county, district, or city attorneys, about 2,300 chief prosecutors employ about 21,000 assistant prosecutors for the prosecution of criminal cases in state courts. Except for 94 U.S. attorneys and the prosecutors appointed in five states, prosecutors are elected officers. Since the prosecutor's office is often considered a stepping stone to higher office—many prosecutors go on to become senators, governors, and even presidential candidates—prosecutors are highly political creatures. They regularly face the electorate, and if they want to move up the political ladder they must pay attention to public opinion and party power distribution. This is not to say they are corrupt; all available evidence suggests they are not. But it does make clear how prosecutors as political figures must respond to local partisan and community pressures.[43]

Prosecutors perform multiple functions and attempt to satisfy conflicting goals. Their formal roles include being both the chief law enforcement officer and guardian officer of justice in the criminal courts. More than 60 years ago, United States Supreme Court Justice Sutherland described these two functions in a classic statement. The function of the prosecutor

> is not that he shall win a case, but that justice shall be done. As such, he is in a peculiar and very definite sense the servant of the law, the twofold aim of which is that guilt shall not escape or innocence suffer. He may prosecute with earnestness and vigor—indeed, he should do so. But, while he may strike hard blows, he is not at liberty to strike foul ones.[44]

Prosecutors act not only as formal legal officers, but as office administrators, forming policy, managing cases and their office staff. Prosecutors are also careerists. As such, they prepare to run for higher public office, enter lucrative and prestigious private practice, or simply maintain comfortable working conditions until they retire. These formal legal goals and informal organizational and personal goals are not always in harmony. They require prosecutors to perform multiple functions, as well as to relate to various other criminal justice agencies, each of which has different goals and priorities.

The informal functions of prosecutors revolve around their role as head of an independent criminal justice agency, the prosecutor's office, or variously the county, district, and city attorneys' offices. Heads of prosecutors' offices hold exclusive power to charge arrested suspects with crimes, to divert them into some social service agency such as drug or alcohol counseling, or to drop the matter altogether, thus effectively terminating the criminal justice process. We discuss these largely discretionary decisions in Chapter 9. The formal role of prosecutors centers on their position as officers of the court, bound by the rules governing adjudication. To understand prosecutors fully, remember that they act as administrative heads of organizations with broad discretion, and as officers of the court subject to judicial supervision following charges.[45]

Law Enforcement Function

Prosecutors choose what crimes and suspects to prosecute, and they decide how to measure successful prosecution. For example, they may decide that welfare fraud deserves high priority and measure their success in dealing with it by either the number of convictions, the ratio of convictions to acquittals, or the types and lengths of sentences they achieve. Whatever crimes they choose to prosecute most vigorously, and however they measure their law enforcement success, prosecutors are influenced by public opinion. As elected officials, some respond to community pressure more readily than others. If prosecutors see themselves as the people's representatives, they take their cues from public opinion on particular crimes and punishments, "try[ing] primarily to reflect community opinion." Hence, if welfare recipients who are "ripping off the taxpayers" bother the public, prosecutors will fight welfare-related offenses. If the community believes drunk drivers are "getting off too easy," the representative-of-the-people-type prosecutors will seek a high conviction rate and harsh sentences for drunk drivers. The heightened prosecution of drug offenses is the most dramatic current example of the exercise of prosecutorial discretion in response to public pressure.[46]

Other prosecutors believe their law enforcement role requires that they not only satisfy public wishes but also effectively control crime. Such prosecutors see themselves more as experts elected by the public to use their best professional judgment to decide which crimes to prosecute, what sentences to request, and how to measure success. As public interest lawyers they work for the community's best interest, not simply to satisfy the public's desires. When asked how he views the public, one prosecutor who considers himself a trustee of the public's best interest replied, "with a jaundiced eye."[47]

Prosecutors do not always enjoy harmonious relationships with police. Sixty years ago, the National Commission on Law Observance and Enforcement found "frequent and characteristic want of cooperation between investigating and prosecuting agencies in the same locality." Both police and prosecutors are law enforcement officers on the same side in controlling street crime. Nevertheless, they have frequently clashed. Prosecutors and police generally come from different backgrounds. Prosecutors have advanced training in law that most police officers lack. Furthermore, prosecutors have assimilated values from law school and the courts that can lead them to overemphasize their importance to the criminal justice system.[48]

Prosecutors work in different surroundings from the police. The police work on the streets. Prosecutors work in and around the criminal courts with other lawyers. Prosecutors focus on legal guilt, that is, getting sufficient constitutionally admissible evidence to win cases. Traditional police officers

Most prosecutors do not get the public attention that Marcia Clark received during the murder trial of O. J. Simpson.

act on factual guilt, that is, on individuals, they "know" are guilty. Police can view legal rules and the legal subculture prosecutors live in not only as a personal rebuke to police work, but also as a system that compromises the interests of victims, police, and the public by making "deals" that lead to reduced charges, diversions, and light sentences. For prosecutors, whose work world is the courts, *conviction for a crime less than factual guilt suggests may suffice.* Police who work the streets do not consider convictions for crimes less serious than factual guilt an appropriate end to criminal justice. They believe the government should prosecute, convict, and punish street criminals for the crimes they actually commit, not for some lesser offense.[49]

In some places, police-prosecutor teams have overcome some of the problems arising out of their different interests. The teams, consisting of police investigators and prosecutors, work closely from the early stages of investigation all the way to conviction in order to establish legal guilt. In 1987, Maine created an entirely new agency, the Bureau of Intergovernmental Drug Enforcement. In unprecedented language, the statute charged the agency with the responsibility for "the integration and coordination of investigative and prosecutorial functions in the State with respect to drug law enforcement." For the first time, state law "mandates that prosecutors and investigators team up to create a more efficient and effective drug law enforcement strategy." "It's not an investigation and then a trial; it's a unitary process, a case throughout," according to Assistant U.S. Attorney for Maine, John Gleason.[50]

The agency has reduced basic misunderstandings arising out of the different vantage points of police and prosecutors. Bureau supervisor Dan Ross said,

> We have had to change some of our ideas because the attorney's perspective is that of the courtroom. Officers may not be concerned with how things appear in court because they tend to concentrate on just the facts. But the attorney has to care because appearances are so important in getting a conviction.[51]

For example, to obtain evidence, investigators frequently rely on informants. Prosecutors hesitate to call informants as witnesses. Despite their persuasiveness to police investigators, prosecutors know that such witnesses negatively impress jurors. Investigators now realize this and gather additional evidence. Prosecutors also benefit from the teamwork because, as one prosecutor observed, "The insights I have gained into case investigation translate into better courtroom performance." As prosecutors work closely with investigators, they learn that officers must make quick decisions to search based on limited information. Knowing this, prosecutors can make more effective arguments for the good faith exception to the search warrant requirement, an area, according to one prosecutor in Maine, "where prosecutors are sometimes weak."[52]

Laconia, New Hampshire, has adopted police-prosecutor cooperation to test its effectiveness in misdemeanors, order maintenance problems that rarely receive publicity but account for the largest expenditures of police resources. In Laconia, a prosecutor with an office in the police department prosecutes all misdemeanor arrests. Officers consult with the prosecutor about filing criteria and investigative practices, and the prosecutor provides timely information on case dispositions. This information leads to police decisions that close legal loopholes in cases of driving while intoxicated (DWI), disorderly conduct, theft, and assault. According to the chief of police in Laconia, the close contact between police and prosecutors has also reduced the number of lawsuits against the police. The chief says, "A higher degree of legal awareness has developed and it is reflected in the officers' actions on the street."[53]

A New York program adopted to decrease felony case attrition by improving the coordination between police and prosecutors in preparing cases produced mixed results. James Garofolo examined felony arrests and interviewed prosecutors and liaison officers in a sample of six county prosecutor's offices and the New York State Police. Four of the counties instituted the liaison program and two did not. The liaison program had little effect on felony case attrition; liaison officers had little effect on whether cases resulted in conviction. However, liaison officers did affect the amount of case "slippage," that is, a conviction for an offense less than the charge, such as from a Class E felony to a Class A misdemeanor. It also simplified the communication channels between prosecutors and arresting officers.[54]

Officers of the Court

In addition to enforcement officers who control crime, as officers of the court the law requires prosecutors to seek justice according to law. They are supposed to uphold and protect defendants' constitutional rights even as they prosecute them for crimes. Prosecutors are expected to tailor the law to meet individual needs as well as apply the law evenhandedly. These are difficult functions to perform because so little is known about exactly what individuals "need" and what punishment satisfies the purposes of criminal law. Further, no one agrees about the purposes of punishment: about whether it should merely punish, deter others from committing crimes, or rehabilitate offenders. In addition, as officers of the court with responsibility for protecting the constitutional rights of defendants, prosecutors are legally bound to enforce laws and other rules controlling police conduct. This either brings them into direct conflict with police or forces them to balance their formal public duty and their informal relationships with police.[55]

Administrative Officers

Prosecutors are also administrators of organizations in which goals often unrelated to law enforcement or court proceedings are paramount. Prosecution offices, especially large ones, have basic organizational goals: efficiency, economy, and smooth-working relations among staff and between staff and outside agencies, such as police, public defenders, and courts. As administrators, prosecutors strive to further the organization's effective, efficient, economical, and speedy dispatch of business, often by using limited public resources in the most cost-effective manner. Accordingly, prosecutors may put a premium on cases and crimes that produce the greatest impact for the quickest and most economical processing. Prosecutors as administrators also favor rules that foster routine, regular, predictable results. Here, prosecutors may emphasize the uniformity of cases, rather than the uniqueness of individuals.[56]

Careerists

Finally, prosecutors are careerists. They seek to advance in the legal profession, not necessarily as prosecutors or even judges, but as private practitioners. If they want to be career prosecutors, they build amicable relationships with their superiors and with members of related agencies, mainly the police, public defenders, and judges. If they aspire to higher public office, local political interests influence their actions. If private practice appeals to them, they seek the goodwill of members of private law firms.[57]

Not all prosecutors perform their various functions with equal vigor. They develop prosecutorial styles, much as the police develop policing styles. Some prosecutors favor their role as chief law enforcer and, as a result, stress conviction rates. Others lean toward the role of court officer, emphasizing the need to prosecute only according to rules that do not violate defendants' rights. Still others are concerned mainly with running efficient, economical organizations where cases are processed rapidly with minimal obstruction or difficulty. Some treat prosecution as only a stepping stone to a higher political office or more lucrative law practice, or as "just a job" in which hassles are to be minimized and material benefits gained. Others are career prosecutors who work to establish good working relationships with the other criminal justice agencies, particularly courts, police, and defense counsel.[58]

Structure and Management

Prosecution management varies greatly according to jurisdiction size, geography, resources, and technology. Every jurisdiction has a chief prosecutor, an elected officer, usually with a four-year term. In small jurisdictions, prosecutors work alone or with a few assistants who know each other personally and who work together closely. Such prosecutors often have private practices also. In large jurisdictions, prosecutors' offices are large agencies with many assistants whom chief prosecutors rarely see, or may not even know. Chief prosecutors—usually called district attorneys in states, and U.S. attorneys in federal jurisdictions—rarely appear in court. They set general office policy, deal with the public, and manage relations with other criminal justice agencies. Some chief prosecutors are career prosecutors, but most eventually enter private practice, become judges, or run for higher political office.[59]

Assistant prosecutors are young attorneys, frequently recent law school graduates. They are appointed to office on the basis of not only their professional credentials but also their political connections. Democrats usually appoint Democratic assistant prosecutors; Republicans appoint Republicans. Assistant prosecutors do not often make prosecution a career. Most stay fewer than five years and then enter private practice. According to one New York City assistant prosecutor, "You're not supposed to stay too long. Sixty percent leave after three years. The longer you stay the less career value is the ADA [assistant district attorney] experience."[60]

Former assistant prosecutors rarely enter prestigious corporate law firms. They usually remain in low-status criminal law practice, often becoming defense attorneys. A few become judges, but former assistant prosecutors rarely run for political office. Rising salaries for assistant prosecutors and shrinking opportunities in private practice have reduced high prosecutor turnover.[61]

Assistant prosecutors work according to two basic modes. Under the zone system, or horizontal case assignment, assistants manage different phases of the criminal process. Some assistants draft complaints, others go to court for arraignment, others to try cases, and still others to argue cases on appeal. The case system, or vertical case management, links assistants to particular cases; assistants manage individual cases from arraignment through trial. Zone system assistants become experts in criminal procedure (arraignment, preliminary hearing, pretrial motions, and trial); case system assistants become experts in criminal law (homicide, rape, burglary). The most prominent current use of the case system is in career-criminal units. To target repeat offenders, assistant prosecutors in a specialized career-criminal unit have adopted police-prosecutor teams, such as those discussed in the section on the law enforcement function of prosecutors. If the police arrest career criminal suspects, assistants in the career unit prosecute the cases.[62]

Chief prosecutors in large urban areas cannot know the individual cases on their dockets. They deal with several judges with different ideologies. Assistants do not know in detail the office's policies and, by the time they do, have probably entered private practice. Therefore, effective management of large prosecutors' offices demands that chief prosecutors set clear goals and establish statistical and accounting mechanisms for measuring whether policy goals are met and for determining whether to alter current policies. Prosecutors resist quantifying their work, displaying an occupational antipathy for statistics, efficiency, or accounting. Typical of many prosecutors, one told William F. McDonald in his study of prosecutors, "I'm a lawyer. I don't have to be quantified. I make my judgment, exercise my discretion in accordance with what my perception of the public needs are and whether I think they should be satisfied. My assistants are professionals."[63]

This approach leads to perceptions inconsistent with reality for individual assistant prosecutors with varying degrees of insight, experience, and maturity. In the words of one former chief prosecutor:

> Such an office, characterized by unchecked exercise of discretion directed toward no discernible goal, leads to knee-jerk reactions to daily problems, the solution of which is never predictable. This type of office can best be characterized as exemplifying management by crisis. In this office there exists very little paperwork; and what little there is, when it depends on a lawyer to complete it, is very nearly never done.[64]

Information management technology has altered management in the offices of some prosecutors. PROMIS (Prosecutors' Management Information Service) was developed by the Institute for Law and Social Research (INSLAW), a nonprofit research and development corporation in Washington, D.C. It comprises the "richest source of criminal justice facts ever gathered." Its data base includes 150 facts about "street crime" cases and defendants that allow prosecutors to track cases from arrest to conviction.[65]

PROMIS data have led to a number of significant findings:

- Most arrests for serious crimes terminate in outright dismissal.
- Police officers poorly trained in collecting and preserving evidence, not constitutional restrictions, account for most dismissals.
- A few police officers account for most arrests resulting in conviction.
- A small subset of defendants, career criminals, commits many robberies and burglaries.
- Cases against career criminals are just as likely to result in dismissal as cases against other defendants.
- Many dismissals result from witnesses' failure to appear in court to testify.[66]

PROMIS research projects have led to changes in prosecution policies and practices in some jurisdictions. Many prosecutors' offices now have career offender programs that use PROMIS data to prosecute offenders responsible for large numbers of street crimes and to seek maximum sentences for those they convict. In other offices, victim witness programs notify witnesses about court appearances, assure that they appear for them, and counsel witnesses on courtroom procedure. PROMIS has also affected the creation and effectiveness of police-prosecutor teams.[67]

Defense Counsel

Criminal defense attorneys, like all other criminal justice professionals, perform both formal and informal functions. The best known and most public is the formal function of defending the rights of the accused. Perhaps more in line with the reality of day-to-day defense operation is the informal decision making regarding guilty pleas and getting along with the courtroom work group.

Formal Functions

Formally, criminal defense attorneys are advocates who zealously represent their clients. As champions of the accused, their role in the adversary system is to challenge the government at every point in its effort to convict defendants. Defense counsel has the formal responsibility to see to it that the government proves every element of the case beyond a reasonable doubt and only by means of evidence legally obtained and presented in court.

Criminal defense lawyers, therefore, according to Rodney J. Uphoff, who has both practiced and studied criminal defense, "may actually frustrate the search for truth. Indeed, defense counsel may be ethically required to do so." This responsibility to zealously defend their clients exists even when counsel knows that the defendants they represent are guilty. The *You Decide,* "Should 'Guilty' Defendants Have a Lawyer?" deals with this frequently misunderstood and criticized responsibility to defend the guilty.[68]

You Decide   Should "Guilty" Clients Have a Lawyer?

Alan Dershowitz, the famous defense attorney and Harvard law professor, in his popular book *The Best Defense,* makes the following strong argument for why lawyers should defend guilty defendants:

> The zealous defense attorney is the last bastion of liberty—the final barrier between an overreaching government and its citizens. The job of the defense attorney is to challenge the government; to make those in power justify their conduct in relation to the powerless; to articulate and defend the right of those who lack the ability or resources to defend themselves. (Even the rich are relatively powerless—less so, of course, than the poor—when confronting the resources of a government prosecutor.)
>
> One of the truest tests of a free country is how it treats those whose job it is to defend the guilty and the despised. In most repressive countries there is no independent defense bar. Indeed, a sure sign that repression is on the way is when the government goes after the defense attorneys. Shakespeare said, "The first thing we do, let's kill all the lawyers." Hitler, Stalin, the Greek colonels, and the Chinese Cultural Revolutionaries may not have killed all the lawyers first, but they surely placed defense attorneys—especially vigorous and independent ones—high on their hit lists.
>
> One of the surest ways of undercutting the independence of defense attorneys is to question the propriety of their representing the guilty. Those who argue that defense attorneys should limit their representation to the innocent, or indeed to any specific group or category, open the door to a system where the government decides who is, and who is not, entitled to a defense. Granting the power to the government, to the bar, or to any establishment, marks the beginning of the end of an independent defense bar—and the beginning of the end of liberty.
>
> The role of the defense attorney who defends guilty clients is the hardest role in the criminal justice system to explain to the public. In 1980 I traveled to China to advise the People's Republic on its criminal justice system. Most Chinese lawyers seemed to understand the need for free and independent judges and prosecutors. But hardly anyone—even those lawyers who had suffered most under the Cultural Revolution—

> seemed willing to justify the actions of a defense attorney representing a client whom he knew to be guilty and "counterrevolutionary." (Every society has its own favorite epithets for those it most despises.) "Why should our government pay someone to stand in the way of socialist justice?" was the question I was most often asked. I tried to explain that justice—whether socialist, capitalist, or anything else—is a process, not only an end; and that for the process to operate fairly, all persons charged with crime must have the right to a defense. Since not all defendants are created equal in their ability to speak effectively, think logically, and argue forcefully, the role of a defense attorney—trained in these and other skills—is to perform those functions for the defendant. The process of determining whether a defendant should be deemed guilty and punished requires that the government be put to its proof and that the accused have a fair opportunity to defend.
>
> I also tried to explain to the Chinese lawyers that laws that are today directed against counterrevolutionaries may tomorrow be directed at them. As H. L. Mencken once put it: "The trouble about fighting for human freedom is that you have to spend much of your life defending sons of bitches, for oppressive laws are always aimed at them originally, and oppression must be stopped in the beginning if it is to be stopped at all."
>
> To me the most persuasive argument for defending the guilty and the despised is to consider the alternative. Those governments that forbid or discourage such representation have little to teach us about justice. Their systems are far more corrupt, less fair, and generally even less efficient than ours. What Winston Churchill once said about democracy can probably also be said about the adversary system of criminal justice: It may well be the worst system of justice, "except [for] all the other [systems] that have been tried from time to time."
>
> Attorneys who defend the guilty and the despised will never have a secure or comfortable place in any society. Their motives will be misunderstood; they will be suspected of placing loyalty to clients above loyalty to society; and they will be associated in the public mind with the misdeeds of their clients. They will be seen as troublemakers and gadflies. The best of them will always be on the firing line, with their licenses exposed to attack.

There will never be a Nobel Prize for defense attorneys who succeed in freeing the guilty. Indeed there are few prizes or honors ever bestowed on defense lawyers for their zealousness. The ranks of defense attorneys are filled with a mixed assortment of human beings from the most noble and dedicated to the most sleazy and corrupt. It is a profession that seems to attract extremes. The public sometimes has difficulty distinguishing between the noble and the sleazy; the very fact that a defense lawyer represents a guilty client leads some to conclude that the lawyer must be sleazy. Being so regarded is an occupational hazard of all zealous defense attorneys.

The late Supreme Court Justice Felix Frankfurter once commented that he knew of no title "more honorable than that of Professor of the Harvard Law School." I know of none more honorable than defense attorney.[69]

The Best Defense, by Alan Dershowitz. Copyright 1982. Reprinted with permission of Random House, Inc.

Questions

What reasons does Dershowitz give for being a defense attorney? Do you agree? A common question people ask defense attorneys is, "How can you defend these people?" Does Dershowitz answer the question? Would you defend a guilty person? Why? Why not? Defend your answer.

Informal Functions

Experts disagree as to whether the reality of day-to-day practice conforms to the formal functions of criminal defense lawyers. In the 1960s, Abraham Blumberg called the practice of criminal defense law "a confidence game." According to Blumberg, organizational pressures generated by the courtroom work group lead criminal defense lawyers to abandon the role of zealous advocate for the accused. Instead, they "help the accused redefine his situation and restructure his perceptions concomitant with a plea of guilty." Relationships with judges and prosecutors, according to Blumberg, outweigh the needs of clients. In order to maintain good relations, judges, prosecutors, and defense lawyers join together in an "organized system of complicity."[70] Blumberg describes the relationship this way:

> Accused persons come and go in the court system schema, but the structure and its occupational occupants remain to carry on their respective career, occupational and organizational enterprises. The individual stridencies, tensions, and conflicts a given accused person's case may present to all the participants are overcome because the formal and informal relations of all the groups in the court setting require it. The probability of continued future relations and interaction must be preserved at all cost.[71]

Most defense attorneys can only dream of the fame and money received by lawyers like Gerry Spence who defend clients like Emelda Marcos.

Criminal defense lawyers vary greatly individually, but the criminal defense bar can be divided into three general types:

1. Elite defense attorneys.
2. Private defense counsel.
3. Public defenders.

Elite, private defense lawyers such as Johnny Cochran, Gerry Spence, and F. Lee Bailey have highly lucrative criminal law practices that bring them great wealth, fame, and prestige. Few criminal defense lawyers, however, fall into this elite category. Most private defense attorneys have little prestige or glory; instead, they eke out a barely adequate living by "haunting the courts in hope of picking up crumbs from the judicial table." These lawyers have given rise to the unflattering terms "shyster" and "ambulance chaser." Much of their business arises from walking the halls of jails and lower courts, where they find their clients—suspects or defendants who need lawyers immediately. The largest group of criminal defense attorneys are public defenders, funded by the government and working in established public defender's offices. In 1993, public defenders represented 80 percent of all criminal defendants.[72]

Defense counsel, like all criminal justice professionals, play a number of roles. Some adhere to their formal role as guardian of their clients' rights and their formal duty to defend vigorously their clients' interests. According to one defense lawyer in Arthur Lewis Wood's classic study of the defense bar:

> It's a criminal lawyer's function to get a criminal off or help him get a lighter sentence. He's helping him preserve his freedom. Whether it's good for society to have a criminal loose is another question. It may not be good for society, but that is the lawyer's job. It's his duty to the client; everybody knows it. His job is to preserve his client's freedom.[73]

Other criminal defense lawyers enjoy the conflict that criminal trial work provides. These competitors' commitment to the constitutional principles underlying criminal defense work takes second place to the satisfaction they derive from courtroom drama and fighting for the underdog. Another lawyer in Arthur Wood's study noted that "Criminal law offers a wonderful chance to fight injustice and to help people." The competitor role does not necessarily conflict with the defender role, particularly when lawyers who love to compete also believe deeply in the rights of defendants. The elite, private criminal defense lawyers most readily fall into this category.[74]

Criminal defense lawyers, particularly public defenders, play informal roles that do give rise to potential conflict with their formal defender role. Public defenders, and to a lesser extent other lawyers for the poor, are not only lawyers, but constitute an integral part of the courthouse work group. They know, work with, need to get along with, and socialize with prosecutors and judges on a continuing basis. As such, attorneys for the indigent act not only as their clients' lawyers, but also as agents of the government, "surrogates of the prosecutor, a member of their 'little syndicate.' " Since the government pays public defenders, some people, not surprisingly, view them as agents of the government—a suspicion apparently widely held among indigent defendants. The "friendly adversary" relationship between defense counsel and prosecutors, their supposed opponents, feeds this suspicion. Opponents are not supposed to be friends.[75]

According to David W. Neubauer, who has studied day-to-day decision making in criminal justice systems in "middle America,"

> If they are friendly adversaries, then we begin to suspect something is amiss. For example, if you visit most courtrooms, you will see the prosecution and defense exchange pleasantries before, after, and during the court appearances. You may even see two lawyers strenuously arguing

historical note

Public defense would almost entirely eliminate the disreputable lawyers who are so frequently to be found in criminal practice. The existence of these lawyers is favored on the one hand by the professional criminals who need the services of unscrupulous counsel and on the other hand by the poor and ignorant defendants whose precarious situation makes them the easy prey of such lawyers.

Maurice Parmelee, 1911

their case in court, and then having lunch together. Some commentators interpret such actions to mean that the defense has closer ties to the prosecution than to the client, and the client suffers.[76]

Can lawyers vigorously defend clients whom they have never seen before and probably will never see again, especially when it may antagonize professional peers with whom defense attorneys have ongoing relationships? Recent empirical evidence suggests that defense attorneys wage a hard fight in the adversary system, drive a hard bargain in plea-negotiating sessions, and still maintain close professional, peer, and personal relationships with prosecutors and judges. In other words, defense lawyers do not take personally either the fights over defending clients in court or the arguments for clients out of court. They treat them as simply part of their job of defending clients.[77]

Law practice involves unwritten norms of conduct. In a profession based on conflict in court, rules have developed to keep the conflict confined to court. There is enough disagreement without adding bad personal relations among the attorneys. For this reason, lawyers are expected to confine their disputes to the courtroom. As one judge commented, "Yesterday two lawyers started arguing about their case in the corridor after the hearing. That just shouldn't happen. Lawyers have to know how to channel disagreement." Thus, if defense and prosecution are on good terms, this does not mean that the adversary process has broken down. It may be only a reflection of the normal rules of conduct expected of lawyers. The "cooperation" of defense and prosecution is a product of these general expectations about how lawyers should conduct themselves. We should not equate effective advocacy with hostility.[78]

Some criminal defense lawyers primarily commit themselves neither to their formal role of upholding constitutional rights nor to their informal role of maintaining good working relationships with prosecutors and judges. They merely try to make a living. In fact, according to one study, most criminal defense lawyers practice criminal law as the only way they can get by financially. Not at the top of their law school classes, they could not command top jobs in large law firms or in corporations. They entered general practice and let minor criminal work help pay their bills. This is especially true of the majority of private criminal defense attorneys referred to earlier. These lawyers form an outer ring, beyond the elite corporate lawyers and the less

This defense counsel has to balance her formal role of vigorously defending her client and her participation in the informal courtroom work group.

elite but still middle-status lawyers such as personal injury and labor lawyers who oppose corporations.[79]

Generally, these lawyers neither like their work nor believe it accomplishes anything noble for anybody. One of them said:

> It's not a very acceptable way of earning a living—at least according to many other lawyers. You are always dealing with shady characters. I take criminal cases but I would just as soon get away from it.[80]

Others view defense work, particularly the trial experience gained as a public defender, as a good credential to obtain positions in prestigious corporate law firms. In a sense, these lawyers treat criminal defense work as an apprenticeship for private law practice. In fact, except in high-paying public defender's offices like the one in Los Angeles, where some attorneys earn close to $100,000 a year, most public defenders leave public defense work after a few years and go on to private practice. The same pattern exists for prosecutors, many of whom go on to the same private law firms that defenders enter. This trial work apprenticeship and their later close association in private practice draw defense lawyers and prosecutors closer together than their formal adversary relationship indicates. The pull of the work group and the apprenticeship is considerably stronger than the formal roles of prosecutor and defense counsel.[81]

Summary

The criminal courts are institutions central to the American criminal justice system. Criminal courts follow the dual system of justice: there are both federal and state court systems. Criminal courts, whether federal or state, are divided into three tiers: courts of limited jurisdiction, courts of general jurisdiction, and courts of appellate jurisdiction. Proceedings are relatively informal in lower criminal courts; they are highly formal in trial and appellate courts. Criminal courts are complex institutions required to perform several functions, both formal and informal, that often lead to conflicting goals. Formally, they strive to administer justice according to law. Informally, they are expected to control crime by punishing criminals, and to settle and reconcile the demands of society, the law, defendants, and victims. They are supposed to do all of this efficiently, economically, and with dispatch.

The criminal courts have several leading participants, all with formal and informal roles, and all influenced by the courts' various functions. Judges, ranging widely in background and philosophy, and selected in a variety of ways throughout the country, preside over criminal courts. Prosecutors decide whom to prosecute and what charges to file, and they present the state's case in criminal proceedings. In this capacity, prosecutors are independent criminal justice professionals with wide discretion and few formal controls. Prosecutors are also officers of the court who have a duty to see that justice is done. That is, they are obliged to vindicate the innocent and to find the "right" or "just" disposition for the guilty. At the same time, they are expected to protect society and individual victims. In addition to their formal roles, prosecutors are also administrators and career lawyers. These various roles and their relationship with police, judges, and defense attorneys make prosecution a complex function.

The Constitution guarantees the right to counsel in criminal cases. The formal defense counsel role is to secure clients a vigorous defense against state charges. The criminal defense bar consists of three types of lawyers: elite, highly paid private attorneys; much less prestigious, lower-paid private lawyers; and public defenders. Only a few people can afford the famous criminal defense attorneys. People of moderate means hire the less prestigious private attorneys. Most defendants cannot afford lawyers. For them, attorneys are assigned either from a list of volunteers or from a public defender's office. Formally, defense lawyers derive their roles and functions from the constitutional right to counsel. They are obligated both by the Constitution and professional standards to zealously defend their clients and make sure that the government proves its case beyond a reasonable doubt by means of evidence obtained according to the law. Informally, defense lawyers are members of a courthouse work group in which relationships with prosecutors and judges can conflict with their formal responsibility to defend clients.

Courts, prosecution, and defense counsel, therefore, fill formal roles and functions that emphasize criminal law and procedure. At the same time, they play informal roles that are not always in harmony with their formal legal responsibilities. The courts, prosecution, and defense are social institutions called on to respond to community demands regarding crime control and law enforcement. In addition, they are bureaucracies in which economy, efficiency, and order are highly prized.

Judges, prosecutors, and defense attorneys form a work group that, like other organizations, has its own agenda of internal goals. The criminal courts balance the informal interests of harmonious work relationships and case disposition against the formal adversary rules of criminal procedure and societal demands for punishment. Finally, courts provide apprenticeships for future private attorneys. Some defense counsel and prosecutors regard their tenure as a method of gaining trial experience that will aid them later when they seek positions in prestigious law firms. These informal roles, functions, and relationships all shape the decisions made during formal court proceedings.

Review Questions

1. List the functions of the criminal courts.
2. Define and distinguish among the three principal levels of criminal courts.
3. What are the major formal and informal interests that the criminal courts balance?
4. Describe the origins of the formal side of the modern court system.
5. Describe the adversary process.
6. Define and explain the interests that due process emphasizes.
7. How do criminal courts balance due process and crime control?
8. What are the major organizational goals of the criminal courts?
9. Describe and explain the significance of the courtroom work group.
10. Describe the social service function of the criminal courts.

11. Describe the personal characteristics of judges and the principal judicial selection methods.
12. Describe the extent of minority representation on the criminal courts, the distribution of minority judges among the types of criminal courts, and the trends in minority representation.
13. Describe the representation of women on criminal courts and summarize the empirical research on the influence of gender on the decision making of judges.
14. Describe the formal and informal functions of prosecutors.
15. Describe the formal and informal functions of defense attorneys.
16. How do defense counsel balance their formal and informal functions?

Notes

1. Arthur Rosett and Donald R. Cressey, *Justice by Consent: Plea Bargains in the American Courts* (Philadelphia: J. Lippincott, 1976), 1; Peter F. Nardulli, James Eisenstein, and Roy B. Flemming, *The Tenor of Justice* (Urbana: University of Illinois Press, 1988), 211–14.

2. Frances Kahn Zemans, "In the Eye of the Beholder: The Relationship Between the Public and the Courts," in *Courts and Justice,* G. Larry Mays and Peter R. Gregware, eds. (Prospect Heights, Ill.: Waveland Press, 1995), 7–8.

3. Herbert Jacob, *Crime and Justice in Urban America* (Englewood Cliffs, N.J.: Prentice-Hall, 1980), 80–88.

4. James J. Alfini, *Misdemeanor Courts* (Washington, D.C.: U.S. Department of Justice, 1981), 13.

5. Doris M. Provine, *Judging Credentials: Nonlawyer Judges and the Politics of Professionalism* (Chicago: University of Chicago Press, 1986), xi; *North v. Russell,* 427 U.S. 328 (1976); David A. Harriss, "Justice Rationed in the Pursuit of Efficiency," in *Courts and Justice,* 72.

6. BJS, *Report to the Nation on Crime and Justice: The Data* (Washington, D.C.: Bureau of Justice Statistics, October 1983).

7. Rosett and Cressey, *Justice by Consent,* 1; James Eisenstein, Roy B. Flemming, and Peter F. Nardulli, *The Contours of Justice: Communities and Their Courts* (Boston: Little, Brown and Company, 1988), 3–7.

8. Roscoe Pound, "The Administration of Justice in American Cities," *Harvard Law Review* 12 (1912).

9. Alfini, *Misdemeanor Courts,* 14.

10. Caleb Foote, "Vagrancy-Type Law and Its Administration," *University of Pennsylvania Law Review* 104 (1956): 605; Maureen Mileski, "Courtroom Encounters: An Observation Study of a Lower Criminal Court," *Law and Society Review* (May 1971): 479; Lois Forer, *Money and Justice* (New York: W. W. Norton, 1984), 3; President's Commission on Law Enforcement and the Administration of Justice, *The Challenge of Crime in a Free Society* (Washington, D.C.: U.S. Government Printing Office, 1967), 128.

11. Harry I. Subin, "230,000 Cases, Zero Justice," *New York Times,* 19 December 1991.

12. "Rising Caseload in Manhattan Courts," *New York Times,* 16 February 1987; Barbara Boland and Brian Forst, "Prosecutors Don't Always Aim to Pleas," *Federal Probation* 49 (1985): 11; Elliot Spitzer, "Faster Justice in New York," *New York Times,* 1 March 1993; Paul B. Wice, *Chaos in the Courthouse: The Inner Workings of the Urban Criminal Courts* (New York: Praeger, 1985), 18.

13. Stephen J. Schulhofer, "Justice Without Bargaining in Lower Criminal Courts," *American Bar Foundation Research Journal* (1985): 562.

14. Ibid.

15. Thomas W. Church, Jr., "Examining Local Legal Culture," *American Bar Foundation Research Journal* (1985): 453.

16. Eisenstein, Flemming, and Nardulli, *The Contours of Justice,* 5.

17. Pound, "The Administration of Justice," 302–328.

18. Everett P. Wheeler, "Reform in Criminal Procedure, " *Annals of the American Academy of Political and Social Science* (1910): 185–89.

19. Sheldon Glueck, ed., *Roscoe Pound and Criminal Justice* (Dobbs-Ferry, N.Y.: Oceana Publications, 1965): Rosett and Cressey, *Justice by Consent,* 53–55.

20. Martin A. Levin, *Urban Politics and the Criminal Courts* (Chicago: University of Chicago Press, 1977), 60.

21. Amitai Etzioni, *Modern Organizations* (Englewood Cliffs, N.J.: Prentice-Hall, Inc., 1964); James D. Thompson, *Organizations in Action* (New York: McGraw-Hill, 1967); Charles Perrow, *Complex Organizations: A Critical Essay,* 2d ed. (Glenview, Ill.: Scott, Foresman and Company, 1979).

22. *New York Times,* 30 December 1984.

23. Levin, *Urban Politics and the Criminal Courts,* 129–30.

24. Levin, *Urban Politics and the Criminal Courts;* John F. Padgett, "The Emergent Organization of Plea Bargaining," *American Journal of Sociology* 90 (1985): 753–800.

25. John S. Goldkamp and Doris Weiland, *Assessing the Impact of Dade County's Felony Drug Court: Final Report* (Philadelphia: Crime and Justice Research Institute, 1993).

26. Ibid.

27. Peter F. Nardulli, *The Courtroom Elite* (Cambridge, Mass.: Ballinger Publishing Company, 1978).

28. Ibid., 179.

29. Wice, *Chaos in the Courthouse,* 48.

30. Ibid., 110–13, 152; see also Peter F. Nardulli, "Organizational Analyses of Criminal Courts: An Overview and Some Speculation," in *The Study of Criminal Courts: Political Perspectives,* Peter F. Nardulli, ed. (Cambridge, Mass.: Ballinger Publishing Company, 1979); James Eisenstein and Herbert Jacob, *Felony Justice* (Boston: Little, Brown and Company, 1977), 27.

31. Eisenstein and Jacob, *Felony Justice,* 24–25.

32. Levin, *Urban Politics and the Criminal Courts,* 3; Rosett and Cressey, *Justice by Consent,* 2.

33. Nardulli, Eisenstein, and Flemming, *Tenor of Justice,* 373–74.

34. Peltason quoted in Elliot E. Slotnik, "Review Essay on Judicial Recruitment and Selection," in *Courts and Justice,* 200.

35. Levin, *Urban Politics and the Criminal Courts;* David W. Neubauer, *America's Courts and the Criminal Justice System,* 3d ed. (Pacific Grove, Calif.: Brooks/Cole Publishing Company, 1988), 170.

36. BJS, *Report to the Nation,* 64.

37. Levin, *Urban Politics and the Criminal Courts.*

38. Anthony Champagne, "Judicial Reform in Texas," *Judicature* 72 (1988): 146–59.

39. Stuart S. Nagel, *Improving the Legal Process* (Lexington, Mass.: Lexington Books, 1975), 31–32; William Hall and Larry Aspin, "What Twenty Years of Judicial Retention Elections Have Told Us," *Judicature* 70 (1987): 340; John M. Scheb II, "State Appellate Judges' Attitudes Toward Judicial Merit Selection and Retention: Results of a National Survey," *Judicature* 72 (1988): 170–74.

40. Barbara Luck Graham, "Judicial Recruitment and Racial Diversity on State Courts," in *Courts and Justice,* 216.

41. Edited transcript of American Judicature Society Annual Meeting, August 4, 1990, "Different Voices, Different Choices?" in *Courts and Justice,* 230–232.

42. Peter W. Greenwood et al., *Prosecution of Adult Felony Defendants in Los Angeles County: A Policy Perspective* (Santa Monica: Rand Corporation, March 1973); Joan Jacoby, *The American Prosecutor: A Search for Identity* (Lexington, Mass.: D. C. Heath, 1980); John Buchanan, "Police-Prosecutor Teams: Innovations in Several Jurisdictions," *National Institute of Justice Reports* (May/June 1989): 2–8.

43. BJS, *Report to the Nation,* sec. 3; BJS, *Prosecutors in State Courts, 1992* (Washington, D.C.: Bureau of Justice Statistics, 1993); American Bar Association, *Standards Relating to the Prosecution Function and the Defense Function* (New York: American Bar Association, 1971), 16-22; Malcolm Feeley, *The Process Is the Punishment* (New York: Russell Sage Foundation, 1979).

44. *Berger v. United States,* 195 U.S. 78 (1935).

45. David W. Neubauer, *Criminal Justice in Middle America* (Morristown, N.J.: General Learning Press, 1974), chap. 3; Lief H. Carter, *The Limits of Order* (Lexington, Mass.: Lexington Books, 1974).

46. Neubauer, *Criminal Justice in Middle America,* 45; Leonard Mellon, Joan Jacoby, and Marion Brewer, "The Prosecutor Constrained by His Environment: A New Look at Discretionary Justice in the United States," *Journal of Criminal Law and Criminology* 72 (1981): 52.

47. Mellon, Jacoby, Brewer, "The Prosecutor Constrained."

48. *Prosecution* (Washington, D.C.: U.S. Government Printing Office, 1931), 17; Brian Forst, *Improving Police-Prosecutor Coordination* (Washington, D.C.: Institute for Law and Social Research, 1981), 1–3.

49. Malcolm M. Feeley and Mark H. Lazerson, "Police-Prosecutor Relationships: An Interorganizational Perspective," in *Empirical Theories About Courts,* Keith O. Boyum and Lynn Mather, eds. (New York: Longman, Inc., 1983), 229–32; Floyd Feeney, *Case Processing and Police-Prosecutor Coordination* (Davis, Calif.: University of California, Davis, Center on Administration of Criminal Justice, 1981), 4–6.

50. Buchanan, "Police-Prosecutor Teams," 2–3.

51. Ibid.

52. Ibid., 4.

53. Ibid., 7.

54. James Garofolo, "Police, Prosecutors, and Felony Case Attrition," *Journal of Criminal Justice* 19 (1991): 439–49.

55. Wayne R. LaFave, *Arrest: The Decision to Take a Suspect into Custody* (Boston: Little, Brown and Company, 1965), 515.

56. *The Study of Criminal Courts,* 108–111.

57. Carter, *The Limits of Order,* 71–74.

58. Ibid., 62–75; Neubauer, *Criminal Justice in Middle America,* chap. 3.

59. BJS, *Prosecutors in State Courts, 1990* (Washington, D.C.: Bureau of Justice Statistics, 1992), 1.

60. Jacob, *Crime and Justice in Urban America,* 76–77; Feeley, *The Process Is the Punishment,* 70–71; William F. McDonald, ed., *The Prosecutor* (Beverly Hills, Calif.: Sage Publications, 1979), 251.

61. *The Prosecutor,* chap. 9; Wice, *Chaos in the Courthouse,* 63.

62. Jacob, *Crime and Justice in Urban America,* 78–79; BJS, *Prosecutors in State Courts,* 3.

63. *The Prosecutor,* 138.

64. Ibid., 139.

65. Brian Forst et al., *What Happens After Arrest* (Washington, D.C.: National Institute of Law Enforcement and Criminal Justice, 1977), v.

66. *The Prosecutor,* 127.

67. Ibid., 127–34.

68. Rodney J. Uphoff, "The Criminal Defense Lawyer: Zealous Advocate, Double Agent, or Beleaguered Dealer?" in *Courts and Justice,* 16.

69. Alan Dershowitz, *The Best Defense* (New York: Random House, Inc., 1982).

70. Abraham Blumberg, "The Practice of Law as Confidence Game: Organizational Co-Optation of a Profession," *Law and Society Review* 1 (1967): 20, 22.

71. Ibid., 20.

72. Jack Ladinsky, "The Impact of Social Backgrounds of Lawyers on Law Practice and the Law," *Journal of Legal Education* 16 (1963): 128; Wice, *Chaos in the Courthouse,* 63–64; Andy Court, "Is There a Crisis?" *The American Lawyer* (January/February 1993), 46.

73. Quoted in Arthur Lewis Wood, *Criminal Lawyer* (New Haven, Conn.: College and University Press, 1967), 67; Lynn M. Mather, "The Outsider in the Courtroom: An Alternative Role for Defense," in *The Potential for Reform in Criminal Justice,* Herbert Jacob, ed. (Beverly Hills, Calif.: Sage Publications, 1974), 263–89, makes a good case for the importance of this role and its existence, despite pressures to adopt the informal roles; William F. McDonald, *The Defense Counsel* (Beverly Hills, Calif.: Sage Publications, 1983).

74. Wood, *Criminal Lawyer.*

75. Jonathan D. Casper, *American Criminal Justice* (Englewood Cliffs, N.J.: Prentice-Hall, 1972), 107, 110–11.

76. Neubauer, *Criminal Justice in Middle America,* 78.

77. McIntyre, *The Public Defender,* 148 ff.

78. Ibid.

79. Ladinsky, "The Impact of Social Backgrounds of Lawyers," 128.

80. Ibid., 64.

81. Anthony Platt and Randi Pollock, "Channeling Lawyers: The Careers of Public Defenders," in *The Potential for Reform in Criminal Justice;* Emily Barker, "Paying for Quality," *The American Lawyer* (January/February 1993), 83.

9 Proceedings Before

Trial

CHAPTER MAIN POINTS

1. *The decision to file charges marks the formal entrance into the criminal justice system, when suspects become defendants.*
2. *Prosecutors enjoy broad discretion in charging suspects with crimes.*
3. *The major reason that prosecutors decide not to charge suspects with crimes is the lack of enough evidence to convict defendants.*
4. *Few suspects go free because of constitutional limits on police power.*
5. *At the first appearance, charges are read against defendants, they are assigned an attorney, and bail decisions are made.*
6. *All criminal defendants who are charged with crimes involving the penalty of incar-ceration have a right to a lawyer, even if they are unable to afford a lawyer.*
7. *Most poor defendants are represented by public defenders.*
8. *The decision to bail or detain defendants balances crime control, public safety, and economy against formal constitutional rights of citizens.*
9. *Most defendants on bail appear in court and do not get arrested for or convicted of other serious crimes while on pretrial release.*
10. *The decision to proceed to trial is made by judges in preliminary hearings, by community representatives in grand jury indictment, and by prosecutors in informa-tion.*

very year, the police arrest about ten people for felonies for every one convicted felon who goes to prison (see Figure 9.1). In this and the following chapters, we explain what happens to the 10 percent of arrested persons who do go to prison and how the remaining 90 percent are disposed of. Both the law and discretion account for the reduction of cases between arrest and incarceration. (See Chapter 1 for an explanation of the funnel effect in general.) Table 9.1 depicts the major decisions and decision makers determining whether arrested persons go free or are subjected to further processing, and describes the nature and consequences of that processing.

Figure 9.1

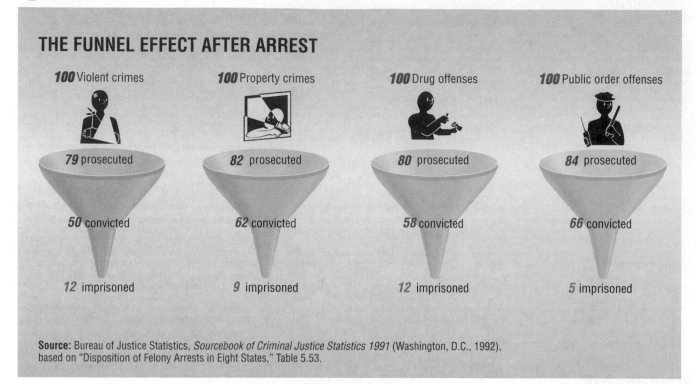

THE FUNNEL EFFECT AFTER ARREST

100 Violent crimes

79 prosecuted

50 convicted

12 imprisoned

100 Property crimes

82 prosecuted

62 convicted

9 imprisoned

100 Drug offenses

80 prosecuted

58 convicted

12 imprisoned

100 Public order offenses

84 prosecuted

66 convicted

5 imprisoned

Source: Bureau of Justice Statistics, *Sourcebook of Criminal Justice Statistics 1991* (Washington, D.C., 1992), based on "Disposition of Felony Arrests in Eight States," Table 5.53.

Table 9.1
Decisions and Decision Makers from Arrest to Prison

Decision Makers	Decisions
Prosecuter	▲ Charge with a crime
	▲ Divert to social service agency
	▲ Dismiss case
	▲ Test case by grand jury or judge
	▲ Plea-bargain
	▲ Try case
	▲ Recommend sentence
Judge	▲ Set bail
	▲ Assign counsel
	▲ Bind defendant over for trial
	▲ Rule on motions and objections before, during, and after trial
	▲ Sentence defendants
Bail bondsman	▲ Put up money bail
	▲ Pursue defendants who fail to appear
Grand jury	▲ Indict
	▲ "No bill" or dismiss charge
Defense counsel	▲ Advise defendant how to plead
	▲ Plea-bargain with prosecutor
	▲ Develop strategy to defend client's interest
Defendant	▲ Plead guilty or not guilty
	▲ Accept plea bargain
Court personnel	▲ Conduct bail investigation
	▲ Conduct pre-sentence investigation and report
Trial jury	▲ Convict
	▲ Acquit

The Decision to Charge

decision to charge *power of prosecutors to initiate formal proceedings against suspects and to decide what crimes to charge them with.*

initial case screening *preliminary decision of prosecutors to charge based on the results of police investigations.*

charge *initiation of formal proceedings against criminal suspects.*

diversion *redirection of suspects into some alternative to criminal proceedings.*

adjudication *formal proceedings that take place in court.*

Successful prosecutor and late Supreme Court Justice Robert Jackson noted that the power of prosecutors to charge people with crime bestows on them "more control over life, liberty, and reputation than any other person in America." The converse and virtually nonreviewable power *not* to charge may confer even greater power on the prosecutor. Despite this power, prosecutors share the **decision to charge**—or not to charge—suspects with crimes with other decision makers, including:

- Citizens who complain to the police.
- Patrol officers who respond to the complaints.
- Detectives who investigate complaints in order to gather evidence and witnesses.
- Victims and other witnesses who provide testimony and other information.
- Judges who conduct the first appearance and other preliminary proceedings.
- Grand jurors who hand up indictments.
- Defendants who agree to plead guilty, or refuse to plead guilty, to a specific crime.[1]

The point when prosecutors first encounter criminal cases varies considerably among jurisdictions. In a few jurisdictions, police screen arrests first, dropping some cases before contacting prosecutors. Los Angeles police drop or refer to social service agencies nearly half the arrests; prosecutors never see these cases. Police in a few other cities file cases directly with criminal courts; prosecutors receive these cases after preliminary court proceedings. In most jurisdictions, however, the police take cases directly to prosecutors shortly after arrest. Whenever the exact point they become involved in criminal cases, court decisions since 1883 have granted prosecutors "unfettered discretion" in making three vital decisions:

1. Whether to charge suspects with crimes.
2. What crime or crimes to charge suspects with.
3. Whether to discontinue prosecution after filing charges (*nolle prosequi*).[2]

Prosecutors base their initial decision to charge on the incident reports, or "rap sheets" (lists of prior offenses), and any other information or physical evidence police investigations have produced. This **initial case screening** provides prosecutors with three alternatives:

- **Charge,** or initiate formal proceedings.
- Divert suspects into some alternative to criminal proceedings, such as drug or alcohol treatment (**diversion**).
- Drop cases outright, which releases suspects without conditions.

If prosecutors decide to charge, then they must also decide precisely what charges to file. Prosecutors make these decisions before judicial proceedings begin, that is, before judges or defense lawyers ever see them. Prosecutors can also divert suspects out of the criminal justice system and into some other social service agency, usually alcohol or other drug treatment, but occasionally into restitution programs.[3]

As soon as prosecutors file charges, formal court proceedings (**adjudication**) begin. Although prosecutors share decision making with judges, defense lawyers, and court services personnel, they remain leading figures from arrest through sentencing. Prosecutors participate in pretrial release and detention decisions with judges, defense lawyers, and, usually, pretrial release agencies. They appear at all preliminary hearings, preside over grand jury proceedings, and present the government's case against defendants at trials. Prosecutors also participate in plea bargaining and sentencing. In 1967, President Lyndon Johnson's Crime Commission called prosecutors the "key administrative officer[s] in the processing of cases." They still are.[4]

nolle prosequi *action to discontinue prosecution after filing charges.*

Consequences of the Decision to Charge

The charging decision holds far-reaching consequences, both for criminal law enforcement and for individual suspects. The decision to file cases marks the formal entry of suspects into the judicial system. At this point, criminal suspects become criminal defendants. Although legally, filing turns suspects only into defendants, not into convicted criminals, penalties accompany even criminal charges that do not result in conviction. Defendants may lose their jobs or, at least, miss work. They may lose their freedom if denied bail. In addition, defendants can suffer damage to their reputations. Criminal charges also affect defendants' families and the community, perhaps in unemployment compensation, the expense of treatment programs, and eventually welfare payments.[5]

Becoming a criminal defendant is a form of "degradation ceremony," to borrow Erving Goffman's phrase. According to Abraham S. Blumberg:

> The accused is confronted by definitions of himself which reflect the various worlds of the agent-mediators—yet are consistent for the most part in their negative evaluation of him. The agent-mediators have seized upon a wholly unflattering aspect of his biography to reinterpret his entire personality and justify their present attitude and conduct toward him. Even an individual with considerable personal and economic resources has great difficulty resisting pressures to redefine himself under these circumstances. For the ordinary accused of modest personal, economic and social resources, the group pressures and definitions of himself are simply too much to bear. He willingly complies with the demands of agent-mediators, who in turn will help "cool him out."[6]

The decisions not to charge or to drop charges already filed (called ***nolle prosequi***) effectively terminate criminal cases. Sometimes, dropping cases frees suspects completely, with no strings attached. Prosecutors terminate other cases conditionally by "diverting" them into noncriminal channels. They may bring civil rather than criminal actions against defendants. They may agree not to charge if suspects agree to participate in social service programs, such as chemical or other treatment and psychological counseling. They may withdraw some charges in return for defendants' acting as informants in prosecuting other cases. "It's simple," said one prosecutor, "It's when you use one crook to catch a crook." In short, prosecutors hold the power to charge suspects with crimes or to set them absolutely or conditionally free.[7]

Prosecutors also determine what charges to file. For example, in homicide cases they might charge first-degree murder, second-degree murder, voluntary manslaughter, or involuntary manslaughter. In bodily injury cases, they may charge aggravated assault, attempted murder, or simple assault and battery. In thefts from persons, they may charge armed robbery, simple robbery, larceny from the person, or simply larceny. Because the penalties vary for each of the specific crimes, prosecutors in effect set the upper limits of criminal punishment.

Influences on the Decision to Charge

The charging decision is an excellent example of how law and sociology influence decisions in criminal justice. "Let the punishment fit the crime," the eighteenth-century Italian criminal reformer Caesere Beccaria and his followers argued. According to that maxim, criminal justice ought to focus on the legal elements in the crimes committed and let the punishment follow from the crimes committed. Modern prosecutors, however, have turned the eighteenth-century call around and let the crime fit the punishment. In practice, prosecutors decide how much punishment the "badness" of the act and the "sinisterness" of the suspect deserve, and then look for a crime to fit the punishment. They cannot prosecute unless they can meet two legal requirements:

1. The presence of the material elements of the crime in the facts surrounding the case.
2. The availability of enough admissible and reliable evidence to prove the elements of the crime beyond a reasonable doubt.

Legal Influences Using a combination of interviews with prosecutors and the data base PROMIS (Prosecutors' Management Information Service) that tracks defendant movement through the criminal process, Barbara Boland, Paul Mahanna, and Ronald Sones have uncovered several legal factors that explain why prosecutors drop cases. Most frequently, prosecutors drop cases because of "case weakness," or insufficient proof to convict. Case weaknesses arise primarily out of witness and physical evidence problems. Some witnesses fail to appear, are reluctant, or refuse to testify. Others lack credibility due to drug or alcohol abuse or involvement in crime. Some cases lack more than one credible witness; conviction frequently requires two or more. Physical evidence problems include missing or questionable fingerprints; no stolen property or weapons recovered; and the failure to obtain medical evidence.[8]

In less than one tenth of one percent of all cases, prosecutors decide not to charge because police violated the constitutional rights of suspects. This small number contradicts the widely held belief that constitutional safeguards against unreasonable searches and seizures present a major stumbling block to prosecution. This is not to say that even 1 percent of cases is acceptable; surely the public does not think so. All available evidence suggests, however, that failure to collect enough high-quality evidence to assure conviction, not obtaining it illegally, accounts for most of the decisions not to charge suspects with crimes. For every case dropped because of the violation of constitutional rights, 20 are dropped because the police failed to obtain sufficient evidence to charge and convict.[9]

These findings dispel the myth that suspects go free because the Constitution affords too many rights to criminals. In addition, the findings suggest that legal problems—inadequate or untrustworthy testimony and missing physical evidence—account for most case attrition. In other words, incomplete police work, not illegal police tactics, leads prosecutors to drop most cases. Research also suggests that the law of evidence does not wholly dominate charging decisions; informal influences also affect the decision to charge. Prosecutors may not weigh evidence objectively, that is, according to legal standards. Cases appear strong or weak according to prosecutors' personal values, the local legal culture, and other environmental factors.[10]

According to Brian Forst, who has studied the decision to charge for two decades, concluding a survey of prosecution:

> In short, whether an arrest ends in conviction depends in the first place on factors over which the prosecutor has no control: the strength of the evidence as presented to the police officer, the effectiveness of the officer in bringing the best available evidence (both tangible and testimonial) to the prosecutor, and the seriousness of the offense. Nonetheless, prosecution resources and practices—and the exercise of discretion—do play a significant role in determining whether arrests lead to conviction.[11]

Extralegal Influences The legal requirements are necessary, but not sufficient, to explain the charging decision. Extralegal sociological considerations also affect the decisions. Sociologist Donald Black calls them the

social structure of the case. According to Black, "the strength of the case is a sociological as well as a legal question." Therefore, prosecutors must ask:

> Who allegedly killed whom? That is, what were the characteristics of the alleged victim and the accused? Was this an upward or a downward murder (was the social status of the accused below or above the social status of the victim)? Or was it a lateral murder (between equals)? If lateral, at what status level were the principals: low, intermediate, or high? And what was the relational structure of the crime? Were the victim and the accused acquainted? If so, how well? Who are the witnesses for each side? . . . Anyone who ventures into the legal world without knowing how to assess the sociological strengths and weaknesses of a case has a disadvantage. Any law school that does not offer a course on this subject is denying its students valuable knowledge about how the law actually works.[12]

The major sociological influences on the decision to charge include

- Seriousness of the offense.
- Sinisterness of the offender.
- Organizational pressure on prosecutors to "win" cases.

The reality of criminal justice justifies the wide discretion of prosecutors to charge. Most statutes cannot account for variations in individual cases. Legislatures pass many criminal laws, making a crime out of virtually everything particular groups in society disapprove, without regard to enforceability. Some prosecutors believe that criminal codes constitute "society's trash bin"; the charging process gives prosecutors an efficient way to scour it. In addition, prosecutors have to "individualize justice" according to the circumstances of individual cases. Possessing one marijuana cigarette is not the same as possessing 150. Prosecutors do, and probably should, respect the wishes of victims who want to forgive their attackers. Burglars who break into stores to steal compact disk players have not caused the same harm as those who break into homes in the dead of night, terrorizing occupants in their beds.

Sometimes, *not* prosecuting suspects serves justice better than criminal prosecution. A minor property offender willing to return a stolen television

The "social structure" of the Unabomber case included both a serious offense and a sinister offender.

sinister defendants *defendants charged with crimes who instill fear for extralegal reasons.*

set and pay for the inconvenience to the victim probably fares better if not prosecuted. Scarce resources demand that prosecutors set priorities because they cannot prosecute all cases. Accordingly, they prosecute the most serious crimes and, among the most serious crimes, pick the most "dangerous" offenders.

Celesta A. Albonetti examined the decision to charge in 400 robbery and burglary cases by interviewing prosecutors in the Jacksonville, Florida, state's attorney's office. She found that a number of sociological variables influenced charging decisions. Prosecutors are less likely to reduce charges against **sinister defendants,** those who instill fear for extralegal reasons, when they are

- Habitual offenders.
- Between the ages of 18 and 23.
- Strangers to their victims.

Albonetti also found that prosecutors are less likely to reduce charges when they regard the crime as serious. Prosecutors regard robbery as a more serious crime than burglary, because robbery is more likely to cause physical harm to victims. They also regard crimes in which defendants carry weapons as serious enough not to reduce charges. She found that race and gender had no effect on the decision to reduce charges. She found that legal variables, particularly the number of witnesses and the amount of physical evidence, and problems of admissibility of evidence were not significant in the decision to reduce charges. This finding conflicts with other studies that have found these legal variables significant. Albonetti does not reject the importance of legal variables. In burglary and robbery cases, recovery of stolen property in the possession of the suspect is more important than witnesses in proving the legal elements in the case.[13]

Lisa Frohman observed the screening process in more than 300 sexual assault cases in two branch offices of a West Coast metropolitan district attorney's office. One office served a white middle- to upper-class community, the other an African American and Latino lower-class community. Frohman found that the organizational pressure to win cases influenced the screening process. The promotion policy in the prosecutor's office encourages prosecutors to accept only "strong" or "winnable" cases. Promotions are based on conviction rates, and the office gives more credit to convictions than to guilty pleas. The stronger the case, the better the chance for a guilty verdict, the better the "stats" for promotion. The office discourages taking risks on weaker cases. It treats high ratios of not guilty verdicts as an indicator of incompetence. On the other hand, it gives credit to prosecutors for the number of cases they reject, because the rejections reduce the caseload of an overworked court.[14]

Frohman found that prosecutors reject cases if they can discredit the allegations of sexual assault. They attempt to discredit the allegations of sexual assault in order to further their careers and support the organizational goal of reducing the caseload. Prosecutors rely on two techniques in discrediting the allegations of sexual assault:

1. Finding discrepancies in the accounts of victims.
2. Looking for ulterior motives for the victim alleging sexual assault.

Typical of the discrepancy technique is that used by Tamara Jacobs, a prosecutor who rejected one case because

> in the police report [the victim] . . . said all three men were kissing the victim. Later in the interview she said that was wrong. It seems strange because there are things wrong on major events like oral copulation and intercourse . . . for example, whether she had John's penis in her mouth. Another thing wrong is whether he forced her into the bedroom

immediately after they got to his room or, as the police report said, they all sat on the couch and watched TV. This is something a cop isn't going to get wrong.[15]

Frohman reports the following comment by another prosecutor, Sabrina Johnson, as typical of the technique of finding an ulterior motive to justify rejecting a case for prosecution:

> She doesn't tell anyone after the rape. Soon after this happened she met him in a public place to talk business. Her car doesn't start, he drives her home and starts to attack her. She jumps from the car and runs home. Again she doesn't tell anyone. She said she didn't tell anyone because she didn't want to lose her business. Then the check bounced, and she ends up with VD. She has to tell her fiancé so he can be treated. He insists she tell the police. It is three weeks after the incident. I have to look at what the defense would say about the cases. Looks like she consented, and told only when she had to because of the infection and because he made a fool out of her by having the check bounce.[16]

The *You Decide*, "When Should Prosecutors Charge?" asks you to weigh the legal and sociological factors prosecutors consider important in charging rape and fraud.

You Decide   When Should Prosecutors Charge?

Charging Factors in Rape

Professor Susan Estrich of the Harvard Law School relates the following incident in *Real Rape*, her study of sexual assault and the legal system:

> The man telling me this . . . story is an assistant district attorney in a large Western city. He is in his thirties, an Ivy League law school graduate, a liberal, married to a feminist. He's about as good as you're going to get making decisions like this. This is a case he did not prosecute. He considers it rape—but only "technically." This is why.
>
> The victim came to his office for the meeting dressed in a pair of tight jeans. Very tight. With a see-through blouse on top. Very revealing. That's how she was dressed. It was, he tells me, really something. Something else. Did it matter? Are you kidding!
>
> The man involved was her ex-boyfriend. And lover; well, ex-lover. They ran into each other on the street. He asked her to come up and see *Splash* on his new VCR. She did. It was not the Disney version—of *Splash*, that is. It was porno. They sat in the living room watching. Like they used to. He said, "Let's go into the bedroom where we'll be more comfortable." He moved the VCR. They watched from the bed. Like they used to. He began rubbing her foot. Like he used to. Then he kissed her. She said no, she didn't want this, and got up to leave. He pulled her back on the bed and forced himself on her. He did not beat her. She had no bruises. Afterward she ran out. The first thing she did was flag a police car. That, the prosecutor tells us, was the first smart thing she did.
>
> The prosecutor pointed out to her that she was not hurt, that she had no bruises, that she did not fight. She pointed out to the prosecutor that her ex-boyfriend was a weight lifter. He

told her it would be nearly impossible to get a conviction. She could accept that, she said; even if he didn't get convicted, at least he should be forced to go through the time and expense of defending himself. That clinched it, said the D.A. She was just trying to use the system to harass her ex-boyfriend. He had no criminal record. He was not a "bad guy." No charges were filed.

> Someone walked over and asked what we were talking about. About rape, I replied; no, actually about cases that aren't really rape. The D.A. looked puzzled. That was rape, he said. Technically. She was forced to have sex without consent. It just wasn't a case you prosecute.[17]

Table 9.2 shows the rank order of factors that prosecutors interviewed by researchers at the Battelle Law and Justice Study Center considered most important in deciding whether to charge suspects with rape or a lesser charge.

Notice that over half the prosecutors considered important the use of force, proof of penetration, promptness of reporting, extend of suspect identification, injury to victim, circumstances of initial contact, relationship of victim and accused, use of a weapon, and resistance by the victim. Four of these factors relate to resistance to force. Prosecutors weighed factors related to consent as less important. They considered least important personal characteristics of victim and offender, such as age, race, occupation, and criminal record.

Reprinted by permission of the publisher from *Real Rape* by Susan Estrich, Cambridge, Mass.: Harvard University Press, Copyright © 1987 by the President of the Fellows of Harvard College.

Questions

Do you agree with the rankings in Table 9.2? Do they indicate that prosecutors take mainly formal or informal legal factors into account when charging rape? Do you agree with the prosecutor's decision in the case Professor Estrich relates? Consider the factors prosecutors take into account in charging rape. Which of these factors do you consider important? Legally, rape requires the intent to penetrate sexually against the will and without the consent of the victim. Does the charging decision in rape indicate that prosecutors follow the law, or do organizational, community, professional, and other informal interests mainly influence their decisions? What factors should prosecutors consider? In what order of importance? Defend your answer.[18]

Table 9.2
Factors in Filing Rape Charges

Rank	Factor	Percent Choosing
1	Use of physical force	82.0
2	Proof of penetration	78.0
3	Promptness of reporting	71.3
4	Extent of suspect I.D.	67.3
5	Injury to victim	63.3
6	Circumstances of initial contact	61.3
7	Relationship of victim and accused	60.7
8	Use of weapon	58.0
9	Resistance by victim	54.0
10	Witnesses	36.0
11	Suspect's previous record	31.3
12	Age of victim or suspect	24.7
13	Alcohol or drug involvement	12.7
14	Victim's previous arrest record	10.7
15	Sexual acts other than intercourse	9.3
16	Location of offense	4.0
17	Accomplices	3.4
18	Race of victim and suspect	0.7
19	Occupation of suspect	0.7

Identified violent crime suspects frequently know their victims; they are their victims' spouses, lovers, friends, or casual acquaintances. Prosecutors, even in serious bodily injury felonies, consider relational crimes unattractive. Victims either reluctantly cooperate or, worse, decide after charging that they do not want prosecution to continue. In stranger assault, New Orleans prosecutors, for example, charge within a day or two of arrest. If victims know their attackers, prosecutors routinely delay the charging decision for a week because so many victims change their minds after a suspect's arrest. Prosecutors reject assault charges between family members at the rate of 40 percent, three times greater than the rate at which they reject stranger assault cases. The following *You Decide*, "Should Relationship Influence the Decision to Charge?" considers some of the issues involved in the decision to charge in crimes involving offenders and victims who have some kind of relationship.[19]

You Decide   Should Relationship Influence the Decision to Charge?

In a sample drawn from New York City, more than half of the cases of assault in which the offenders and victims had some prior relationship (24 of 46) were dismissed; in 22 (92 percent) of these dismissals, the primary reason given in interviews was the victim's refusal to cooperate with the prosecution. An assistant district attorney described one of them:

> This woman was charged on the complaint of her common-law husband. She then filed a complaint against him for

assault. I don't know which of them called the police first. The charge against her was reduced in the Complaint Room to assault in the third degree [a misdemeanor]. Because they were both complainants in court, I was able to speak to them both. They told me they did not wish to continue prosecution. They told me that they were both drinking and apparently they both started to insult each other. It wasn't clear who struck first, but the common-law husband struck his wife with a shovel, hitting her in the eye, and she struck him in the arm with an exacto knife, causing injury. Neither said they were injured seriously, though the arresting police officer had written up her assault against her husband as assault in the second degree, while his assault against her was a third-degree assault. She was also charged with possession of a weapon as a misdeameanor, which was also dropped because the husband refused to testify as to how the knife was used. The knife was not classified as a dangerous instrument *per se.*

When I had satisfied myself that neither had been injured seriously, I looked at their past records. He had one previous arrest ten years ago, I don't recall for what, and she had no prior arrests. I felt that since there had not been problems with the law, and neither one had any sort of record, there was no reason to keep this case in court.

This case is typical of prior relationship assaults in a number of ways: first, the victim was not interested in pressing for a conviction and was reconciled with the assailant after the arrest had been made; second, the victim was not entirely innocent; and third, the passion of the relationship led to infliction of injuries in the attack, but the injuries were not so obviously serious that the attack fit the definition of assault in the second degree, thus justifying a felony charge.[20]

© 1977 The Vera Institute of Justice. *Felony Arrests: Their Prosecution and Disposition in New York City's Courts,* 1977. Reprinted with permission.

Questions

If you were an assistant prosecutor working in the screening room in New York City, would you file charges in this case?

---

first appearance proceeding where charges are read to defendants, lawyers are assigned, and bail decided.

Prosecutors also refuse to charge trivial cases, those not worth spending time and resources to prosecute. Instead of charging, prosecutors recommend diversion into counseling or restitution. They might also decide not to charge for practical reasons. For example, more than 90 percent of prosecutors surveyed by Michael Benson and his associates agreed that the primary reason they did not prosecute more business and environmental crimes was not political, but practical: the level of available resources.[21]

Research indicates that race and gender insignificantly affect the decision to charge. Celesta A. Albonetti found no effect of race or gender in the decision to reduce burglary and robbery charges. Barbara Boland and others reported mainly legal considerations in the decision to charge in the jurisdictions they surveyed. W. Boyd Littrell found little evidence of race or gender influencing the decision to charge in the New Jersey jurisdictions he examined.[22]

The First Appearance

After arrest and charge, defendants appear in lower criminal courts for their **first appearance**. For defendants detained following arrest, the first appearance usually takes place the next day or, if the defendant is arrested on a weekend, within two days. Most jurisdictions have rules that require bringing detained suspects before a magistrate promptly. Bailiffs escort the detained defendants into court in groups from small holding cells behind or beside the courtroom. In most urban courts, these defendants are poor. Judges perform three functions at the first appearance:

1. Read the charges against defendants and inform them of their rights.
2. Appoint lawyers for indigent defendants.
3. Decide whether to bail or detain defendants prior to trial, and set the initial terms for bail or detention.

Reading the charges and informing defendants of their rights are done in a straightforward, short statement by the judge with few implications, however this function is performed. The appointment of counsel for the defendant and the decisions regarding bail carry greater consequences.

At the first appearance, judges appoint attorneys for poor defendants and decide whether to release defendants on bail.

Appointment of Defense Counsel

pro bono *assistance*
appointment of counsel who voluntarily assist defendants without monetary compensation.

The Constitution guarantees the right to a lawyer, but this right governs only the formal side of the appointment of counsel for the defense. The formal, constitutional side of the appointment of defense counsel says little, if anything, about the informal operation of counsel for criminal defendants.

The Right to Counsel

The Sixth Amendment to the U.S. Constitution provides that "in all criminal prosecutions, the accused shall enjoy the right to have the Assistance of Counsel for his defense." The right to counsel provision raises several questions that the Amendment does not answer:

1. At what point in the criminal proceedings does the right to counsel take effect?
2. Do poor people have a right to free counsel?
3. How poor is poor?
4. Do defendants have the right to a lawyer in all crimes, no matter how petty?

Originally, courts interpreted the Sixth Amendment right to counsel to mean that defendants could have lawyers if they could afford to hire them or were fortunate enough to obtain counsel who voluntarily assisted them without pay (***pro bono*** **assistance**). The lawyer's code of professional ethics has traditionally required lawyers to represent the poor without fees, on the theory that lawyers are not only champions of their clients but also officers of the court, bound to see that justice is done. Voluntary *pro bono* assistance still provides legal assistance to some indigent criminal defendants. Does the Sixth Amendment require free legal counsel to indigent criminal defendants? If so, who should assign or appoint counsel for the indigent? In 1942, the U.S. Supreme Court ruled in *Betts v. Brady* that indigent criminal defendants in federal courts have a right to free counsel. The states, however, were left to fashion their own rules.[23]

In 1963, the Supreme Court, in the landmark case *Gideon v. Wainwright*, extended the right to free counsel to indigent defendants in state cases. The case arose in Florida, where only indigent defendants charged with capital offenses had the right to assigned counsel. Florida prosecuted Gideon with breaking and entering a poolroom "with intent to commit a misdemeanor," a felony in Florida at the time. Appearing in court without funds and without a lawyer, Gideon asked the court to appoint or assign counsel to represent him. This exchange followed:

> The Court: Mr. Gideon, I am sorry, but I cannot appoint Counsel to represent you in this case. Under the laws of the State of Florida, the only time the court can appoint Counsel to represent a defendant is when that person is charged with a capital offense. I am sorry, but I will have to deny your request to appoint Counsel to defend you in this case.
>
> The Defendant: The United States Supreme Court says I am entitled to be represented by Counsel.[24]

In a jury trial, Gideon conducted his own defense as well as could be expected from a layman. He made an opening statement to the jury, cross-examined the state's witnesses, presented witnesses in his own defense, declined to testify himself, and made a short argument "emphasizing his innocence to the charge contained in the information filed in this case."[25]

The jury returned a verdict of guilty, and the court sentenced Gideon to five years in the state prison. Gideon filed a *habeas corpus* petition in the Florida Supreme Court attacking his conviction and sentence on the grounds that the trial court's refusal to appoint counsel for him denied him rights "guaranteed by the Constitution and the Bill of Rights by the U.S. Government." The Florida Supreme Court, without an opinion, denied all relief. Gideon then appealed to the U.S. Supreme Court.[26]

The Supreme Court reasoned that failure to afford legal assistance to all defendants rendered equal justice before the law impossible. The government has prosecutors to present its case to the best advantage. To decide cases fairly, lawyers must also present defendants' sides of the story. According to the Court, "the right to be heard would be, in many cases, of little avail if it did not comprehend the right to be heard by counsel."[27]

The Supreme Court in *Gideon v. Wainwright* did not clarify what offenses the right to assigned counsel included. In 1972, in *Argersinger v. Hamlin*, the Court extended the right to counsel to misdemeanants who faced jail sentences. According to the Court, the framers of the Constitution intended to include all criminal defendants who actually faced incarceration, not just defendants charged with felonies. Furthermore, the Court ruled that justice requires that defendants must have counsel *before* they plead guilty, the prevailing form of disposition in modern criminal courts. The Court reasoned that the enormous pressure in modern courts to decide misdemeanor cases rapidly makes counsel necessary to ensure fairness. This is especially true, said the Court, because defendants with lawyers fare much better in court than those without lawyers.[28]

Argersinger left an important question unanswered. Does the right to counsel extend to indigent defendants in petty misdemeanor cases that do not require jail sentences as penalties? The Supreme Court answered that question in 1979, in *Scott v. Illinois*. The Court ruled that the right to counsel applies only to cases in which defendants are subject to an actual jail term. According to the Court, requiring appointed counsel in all criminal cases "would create confusion and impose unpredictable, but necessarily substantial, costs on fifty quite diverse states." In a strong dissent, Justice Brennan argued that the Sixth Amendment covers all criminal cases. Furthermore, he maintained that the government cannot sacrifice constitutional rights to administrative convenience and budgetary considerations. According to Justice Brennan, "This Court's role in enforcing constitutional guarantees for

public defenders *defense attorneys who work full time in public defender offices to represent indigent defendants.*

assigned counsel *lawyers in private practice whom judges select to represent indigent defendants on a case-by-case basis.*

contract attorneys *private attorneys who operate under contracts with local jurisdictions to represent indigent defendants for a fee.*

criminal defendants cannot be made dependent on the budgetary concerns of state governments."[29]

The constitutional right to a lawyer for defendants who cannot afford a lawyer—the great bulk of criminal defendants (see Figure 9.2)—is carried out in three ways:

1. Public defenders, either elected or appointed, work full time in public defender offices to represent indigent defendants.

2. Assigned counsel, lawyers in private practice, are on lists from which judges select individual lawyers on a rotating basis to represent indigent defendants on a case-by-case basis, either for a fee or *pro bono.*

3. Contract attorneys, private attorneys operating under contracts with local jurisdictions, represent indigent defendants for an agreed-on fee.

About 75 percent of all state prison inmates and 80 percent of all defendants charged with felonies in the nation's largest counties relied on either a public defender or on assigned counsel for legal representation. Standards for determining indigence vary among the states. About half of all felony defendants qualify as indigent. Fewer misdemeanor defendants qualify, because most states impose higher standards for defendants charged with minor crimes.[31]

Criminal Defense in Practice

In practice, criminal justice rarely provides in full the constitutionally mandated right to counsel. To be sure, defendants with sufficient means to hire top criminal defense lawyers obtain effective representation. These defendants demand and make the proverbial "phone call" to summon their lawyers to police stations to protect their rights. Private attorneys stay through every step in the criminal process, fighting for their clients and watchdogging every prosecutorial move to assure that the government remains within constitutional bounds. Defendants with adequate resources rarely suffer abuse in police, prosecutorial, or judicial actions.

One-third of all indigents rely on assigned, unpaid counsel, and only half the public defender systems in existence are well-staffed offices. Lack of money and

Figure 9.2

TYPE OF COUNSEL FOR FELONY DEFENDANTS IN THE NATION'S 75 LARGEST COUNTIES, 1992

59%

22%

18%

10%

Public Defender
Assigned Counsel
Hired
Pro So

Source: BJS, *Indigent Defendants,* (Washington, D.C.: BJS, February 1996).

Prosecution and Defense Counsel in the Former Soviet Union

In the former Soviet Union—and the republics that have succeeded it—the court is the main participant in the trial of criminal defendants. The primary duty of the court is to establish the truth. Factual guilt is the only ground for conviction. Investigators from the Ministry of Interior investigate all cases. The Procurator's Office supervises the investigation. It is the duty of the procurator to ensure that the investigation proceeds according to the law. Procurators can vacate unlawful decisions made by investigators, discharge investigators, give investigators binding orders, and dismiss cases.

The procurator represents the government. However, if investigations do not demonstrate guilt in fact, the procurator must withdraw accusations against defendants. Procurators have the burden of appealing every unlawful or unproved judgment to a higher court. Procurators have no authoritative or directive power vis-a-vis the court. Procurators must obey all the rulings of the court, saving all objections for review by the higher court.

As soon as investigators complete the preliminary investigation, investigators or procurators must notify the employer either orally or in writing that their employee has committed a crime. Such information is usually made public at a general meeting of the workers. People discuss the event and may decide to authorize one of their members to represent them in court.

Defendants enjoy the presumption of innocence and the several rights of the accused that follow from the presumption:

- To know the charges against them.
- To present evidence.
- To enter petitions.
- To file complaints over the actions and decisions of officials.
- To file challenges.
- To have access to all the results of investigations.
- To have a lawyer.

Lawyers for the defense participate in criminal cases from the time the preliminary investigation ends and the accused receives a record of the proceedings. From the time of appointment, defense counsel has the right to meet with the accused without any limits on the number or length of the meetings. Defense counsel also has a right to have access to all the material in the case and to conduct certain investigations. Defense counsel also has the right to file complaints against the actions of the investigator, procurator, and the court. Defense counsel cannot abandon the defense of the accused once they accept the case. Defendants, however, can dismiss their counsel on their own initiative at any stage of the investigation or trial.[30]

personnel make it virtually impossible to carry out the constitutional right to counsel. Only 5 percent of all indigent defendants see a lawyer prior to their first appearance before a magistrate. Thus, defendants' encounters with the police are effectively without counsel. Furthermore, most public defenders are inexperienced and receive no special training. Less than 2 percent of assigned counsel have had any training whatsoever beyond a law degree. Thus, the most inexperienced and least-trained lawyers defend indigent clients.[32]

Bill Kennedy heads one of the best public defender's offices in the country. He testified to the House Judiciary Committee Finance Division of the Minnesota legislature in its 1993 session that the number of serious felonies handled by the public defender in Hennepin County has mushroomed in the past five years. The number of appeals the office handles has increased 60 percent, with only a single half-time position added to cover the burden. Kennedy said, in part:

> We are really at the last crisis point in our public defense system. Other lawyers won't say it but I'm going to say it: We are all walking violations of the state and federal constitutions in terms of the service we give our clients. [Without new resources, the whole system] is going to come apart.[33]

According to Lawrence Hammerling, deputy in the Minnesota State Public Defender's Office, "We simply do not have the time to provide the quality of representation to which [our clients] are legally entitled. It's alarming, demoralizing and, ultimately, not legal."[34]

Despite these apparently discouraging conclusions, considerable empirical evidence suggests that public defenders do as well for their clients as private defense counsel do for theirs. Sociologist Lisa J. McIntyre concluded that "numerous empirical studies have failed to find any evidence that clients of public defenders fare worse (at least in terms of case outcomes) than defendants who are represented by private lawyers."[35]

Roger A. Hanson, Brian J. Ostrom, William E. Hewitt, and others analyzed a random sample of 4,000 felony cases from nine courts and interviewed 125 defense attorneys. They found that public defenders

- Disposed of their cases as fast as did privately retained lawyers.
- Were as successful as privately retained counsel at obtaining favorable outcomes for their clients.
- Were compensated, trained, and received about the same level of support as prosecutors in the same jurisdictions.[36]

Robert Spangenberg, who has conducted major studies of criminal defense, challenges the validity of Hanson and his colleagues' study, labeling it "a sloppy piece of research." And, Spangenberg says, the study suffers from a selective hypothesis fallacy. According to Spangenberg, Hanson "went to the jurisdictions in the country that were among the best-funded public defense systems . . . and he's drawing conclusions based on those sites."[37]

David Lynch, former public defender, after studying defense lawyers in two counties, reports that the courtroom work group and the collusion that occurs within it corrupts the relationship between public defenders and their clients:

> I have witnessed countless criminal defendants who claimed they were being "sold out" by their lawyers. Many asked the court, almost always unsuccessfully, to appoint new counsel. Some later filed collateral attacks, alleging coercion, to the entry of their guilty pleas. These allegations were almost always found to be unsubstantiated. Like mental institution inmates yelling "conspiracy," prison inmates yelling "conspiracy" were never taken credibly, even though the similarities of their tales of woe should have made people wonder.[38]

New York City, in connection with the Vera Institute of Justice, designed a five-year experiment to improve the effectiveness of defense counsel and at the same time reduce costs and enhance the working of the criminal justice

Figure 9.3

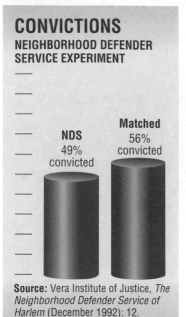

CONVICTIONS
NEIGHBORHOOD DEFENDER
SERVICE EXPERIMENT

NDS
49%
convicted

Matched
56%
convicted

Source: Vera Institute of Justice, *The Neighborhood Defender Service of Harlem* (December 1992): 12.

Figure 9.4

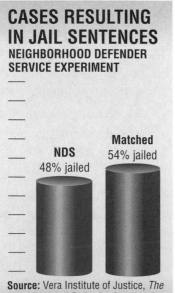

CASES RESULTING IN JAIL SENTENCES
NEIGHBORHOOD DEFENDER
SERVICE EXPERIMENT

NDS
48% jailed

Matched
54% jailed

Source: Vera Institute of Justice, *The Neighborhood Defender Service of Harlem* (December 1992): 12.

system. The Neighborhood Defender Service of Harlem began operations in December 1990, based on three principles:

- *Early intervention.* Instead of waiting for a court to assign counsel, NDS begins its work as soon as an indigent person accused of a crime asks for assistance. Public defenders interview many clients at the police station immediately after arrest. Some contact defenders even earlier, if relatives or friends tell clients the police are looking for them.
- *Team defense.* Small teams of lawyers, community workers, and an administrative assistant work together, instead of assigning lawyers to handle cases on their own. A senior attorney heads each team. The team is designed to make someone available to clients at all times, to include both legal and other representatives in the preparation of cases, and to provide emotional support and professional training for staff.
- *Client-centered representation.* Representation is designed around all the legal consequences of the accusation of a crime, not simply the resolution of a particular case. These other consequences include forfeiture of cars, cash, and leaseholds, eviction, termination of parental rights and welfare benefits, and deportation.[39]

The Neighborhood Defender Service has put these features at the core of its experiment. Its office is located in a building in central Harlem, nowhere near a courthouse. Posters on the street and in subways advertise the availability of its services, "telling Harlem residents how to handle themselves if arrested and to call NDS [Neighborhood Defender Service] immediately if they cannot afford a private lawyer." The office itself is also unusual. It contains "teams of lawyers and nonlawyers working together in an open-space plan." The large percentage of nonlawyers reflects the priority given to investigation and social services. Most of the nonlawyers—administrative assistants, interns, and community workers—work in teams alongside the lawyers. The community workers (mostly young college graduates) handle most of the investigation—not retired police officers, who are usually found in charge of investigation in the offices of public defenders. The NDS attorneys represent their clients in many courthouses in all stages of the criminal process and even in civil cases, particularly in the growing instances of forfeitures in drug cases.[40]

The principles of early intervention, increased investigation, and total representation seem to work, according to an interim evaluation. At the end of the first year, the Vera Institute of Justice evaluated the experiment. Vera matched clients in NDS with similar clients defended by the regular public defender's office in Manhattan. (See Figures 9.3, 9.4, and 9.5.)[41]

According to the Vera researchers:

The results in the NDS cases are striking when compared to those in the matched cases handled by traditional defenders. Despite the fact that the arrest, charges, prior records, and personal characteristics of the defendants were similar, the NDS cases resulted in less pretrial detention, fewer convictions, fewer sentences of incarceration, and shorter sentences when incarceration was imposed.

These outcomes, moreover, were the results of decisions made by the same prosecutors and judges applying the same laws and policies to both samples of cases. None of the cases in the NDS sample, and only three of the matched cases, resulted in trial, so juries were almost irrelevant to these results.

By representing clients in their new way, the NDS teams were able to persuade prosecutors and judges that the decisions they made in these cases should be different, and significantly less severe and costly, than the decisions they made in similar cases handled by traditional defenders.[42]

Bail and Detention

bail *release of defendants pending the final disposition of their cases.*
commercial bail *practice of bail bonding as a private business.*

historical note

Criminal procedure of the Americans has only two means of action—committal and bail. ... It is evidence that a legislation of this kind is hostile to the poor man, and favorable only to the rich. The poor man has not always a security to produce ... and if he is obliged to wait for justice in prison, he is speedily reduced to distress.

Alexis de Tocqueville, 1832

Figure 9.5

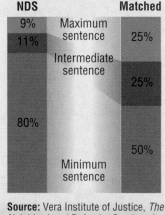

LENGTH OF PRISON SENTENCES
NEIGHBORHOOD DEFENDER SERVICE EXPERIMENT

NDS		Matched
9%	Maximum sentence	25%
11%		
	Intermediate sentence	25%
80%		
		50%
	Minimum sentence	

Source: Vera Institute of Justice, *The Neighborhood Defender Service of Harlem* (December 1992): 14.

Virtually all misdemeanor defendants and nearly two-thirds of all felony defendants are released prior to conviction. **Bail,** the release of defendants pending the final disposition of their cases, is an ancient practice. More than two thousand years ago, the Greek philosopher Plato wrote that prosecutors must

> demand bail from the defendant [who] shall provide three substantial securities who guarantee to produce him at the trial, and if a man be unable or unwilling to provide these securities, the court must take, bind and keep him, and produce him at the trial of the case.[43]

The practice Plato described prevailed until about a hundred years ago. Then personal sureties or guarantors all but disappeared; financial surety replaced them. At first, defendants had to deposit whatever amount judges deemed necessary to secure their appearance at trial. If defendants appeared as scheduled, the court returned their money. Commercial bail, or the bail bond system, has replaced direct financial surety. During the 1960s, many jurisdictions established pretrial release programs that relied on nonfinancial release conditions. Fears about rising crime rates and consequent concern for public safety have led to a return to greater reliance on pretrial detention, instead of release pending the determination of guilt. However, the number of defendants, including felony defendants, released before their cases are decided remains large (see Figure 9.6).[44]

The Constitution, statutes, and judicial decisions formally govern the decision to detain or release defendants. The law of bail, however, does not fully explain the system of bail and its practices as they operate day to day. Bail bondsmen (men own and operate most bail bond offices) and pretrial release agencies determine the actual operation of bail in most cases. The Constitution, laws, and judicial decisions limit, but do not control, decision making by bondsmen and pretrial release agencies.

Commercial Bail

From the nineteenth century until the 1960s, most jurisdictions in the United States required money bail. Although pretrial release programs, pretrial detention, and preventive detention supplement it, **commercial bail,** or bail bonding as a private business, still plays a major role in pretrial release. Judges set the bail amount. Defendants pay a fee to the bondsmen, usually 10 percent of the bail amount. Bondsmen guarantee to pay forfeitures—the face amount of the bail bond—if defendants do not appear. Fees are bondsmen's livelihood. Suppose a court sets bail at $1,000. If a defendant secures a bail bond for a 10 percent fee, the bondsman retains the $100 (10 percent of the bail amount). If, on the other hand, a defendant has the money to deposit the $1,000 with the court, the court returns the full amount when the defendant appears.

Commercial bail has drawn sharp criticisms since at least the 1920s. Andy Hall, in his survey of pretrial release programs, listed the following objections:

- Commercial bail discriminates against poor defendants.
- It is impossible to translate the risk of flight and/or danger into money values.
- The premise that money will secure appearance is questionable because bondsmen keep the money paid.
- Judges may set bail high in order to punish defendants prior to conviction.
- Commercial bail transfers the release decision from judges to bail bondsmen.

Figure 9.6

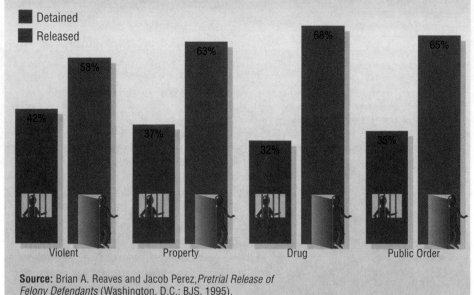

PERCENT OF FELONY DEFENDANTS RELEASED AND DETAINED IN 75 MOST POPULOUS COUNTIES, 1992

■ Detained
■ Released

Violent: 42% / 58%
Property: 37% / 63%
Drug: 32% / 68%
Public Order: 35% / 65%

Source: Brian A. Reaves and Jacob Perez, *Pretrial Release of Felony Defendants* (Washington, D.C.: BJS, 1995).

- It provides for little or no supervision of defendants.
- It fosters corrupt and abusive practices.
- Pretrial detention informally punishes poor defendants prior to legal proof of guilt.[45]
- Commercial bail discriminates, either directly or indirectly, against racial minorities.[46]

Some states have abolished the private bail bond system. In these states, defendants generally pay their 10 percent directly to the court. If they appear, the court returns their deposits. Defendants who fail to appear forfeit their deposits; they also remain legally liable for the full remaining amount of bail.

Technically, when defendants fail to appear on private bail bonds, courts can collect the full amount from the bondsmen; bondsmen can recoup the amount paid from defaulting defendants. In practice, this rarely happens. Elaborate and entrenched informal rules assure that bondsmen will not forfeit the amount of bail bonds. Bondsmen in Connecticut, for example, avoid forfeiture in several ways. They can compromise or come to an agreement with the court to reduce the forfeited amount. They can secure continuances from the court for a period during which they look for defendants. Finally, they can attempt to find and bring their customers to court. From his observations in a Connecticut lower court, Malcolm M. Feeley concluded that bondsmen lost only about 3 percent of the face amount of bond forfeitures.[47]

Competing Bail Policies

Bail raises fundamental and conflicting public policy questions. Society has an interest in crime control; freeing defendants until trial may endanger public safety. Bailed defendants might escape prosecution; if they committed the crimes with which they are charged, criminals have escaped. Furthermore, while free, they may commit more crimes. In addition, bailed defendants can injure, threaten, and intimidate victims and witnesses.[48]

The public interest also requires protecting innocent people from unwarranted government intrusions and deprivations. Detaining legally innocent defendants encroaches on their liberty. Pretrial detention disrupts defendants' family lives and interrupts, sometimes terminates, employment. Furthermore, it impairs the capacity of accused persons to aid in their own defense; they have difficulty contacting witnesses and talking with their lawyers. Detention also lessens the bargaining power of defendants, either when pleading or at sentencing. More seriously, pretrial detention amounts to incarceration before trial. Legally, defendants are innocent until prosecutors prove them guilty beyond a reasonable doubt. Poor jail conditions exacerbate the punitive aspects of pretrial detention.

Pretrial detention is also expensive. The direct economic costs of detaining suspects in jail, paying welfare benefits to dependents, and providing public defense counsel, along with the loss of tax revenue from the wages of defendants, "are enormous," says Steven R. Schlesinger, former director of the Bureau of Justice Statistics. According to Schlesinger, "A defendant who is detained on a petty theft involving a few dollars may cost the government thousands of dollars."[49]

The decision to release or detain criminal defendants balances these competing policy goals. The social interest in crime control and public safety necessarily conflicts with deprivation of pretrial liberty and economy in government. Balancing crime control, individual rights, and economy satisfies no one fully. The prospect of bailed defendants free to do possible further harm until the government proves them guilty beyond a reasonable doubt disturbs those committed to crime control. Incarcerating legally innocent defendants troubles civil libertarians. Fiscal conservatives demand that taxpayers get the most for their tax dollars and object to spending money not demonstrably effective in controlling crime.

The Law of Bail

The Eighth Amendment to the United States Constitution commands: "Excessive bail shall not be required." Notice that the Eighth Amendment does not guarantee the right to be free before trial; it prohibits the imposition of *excessive* bail. In the landmark bail case, *Stack v. Boyle,* the U.S. Supreme Court considered just what the phrase "excessive bail" means. Twelve people were charged with conspiring to advocate overthrowing the government by force, a federal crime. The trial court set bail at $50,000 for each defendant. The defendants protested that the amount was excessive and submitted evidence that their financial resources, family relationships, health, prior criminal records, and other information all indicated that less money would assure their appearance. The trial court ignored this information, accepting instead a government statement that four other defendants in similar circumstances had fled the jurisdiction of the court. The Supreme Court ruled that bail had "not been fixed by proper methods."[50]

Sometimes, no amount of money can secure a defendant's appearance. In *United States v. Abrahams,* Abrahams was arrested for defrauding the federal government, a felony punishable by up to five years' imprisonment. A federal magistrate set bail at $100,000. Abrahams posted the bail, was released, and jumped bail by failing to appear for a hearing to remove the case to another jurisdiction. When Abrahams was charged before a U.S. district court, the government prosecutor took the position that he should be held without bail, for the following reasons:

- Abrahams had three previous convictions in both federal and state courts.
- He was an escaped state prisoner from New Jersey.
- He had given false information at the previous bail hearing.

- He had failed to appear on 18 January 1978, as ordered by Magistrate Pierce.
- Using the name Layne, he had failed to appear in a California case and was a fugitive from the courts of that state.
- He had used several aliases in the past.
- He had transferred 1.5 million dollars to Bermuda in 1976 and 1977.[51]

The prosecutor in the case argued:

> The record before us depicts a man who has lived a life of subterfuge, deceit and cunning. He is an escaped felon. He did not hesitate to flee to Florida and forfeit $100,000 to avoid the removal hearing. There is nothing in the record that suggests that bail will result in his appearance at trial. Every indication is to the contrary. This is the rare case of extreme and unusual circumstances that justifies pretrial detention without bail.[52]

Abrahams presents one extreme of money bail—where no amount can secure a defendant's appearance. At the other extreme, indigent defendants cannot pay even $50 to secure their release. The U.S. Supreme Court has never squarely decided that money bail amounts to excessive bail for indigents. However, a federal appeals court reviewed Florida's bail procedure as it applies to indigents. A group of indigent defendants brought an action challenging Florida's bail practices. They argued that money bail was unconstitutional for indigents, who were jailed to await their cases' outcomes simply because they were poor.[53]

In the midst of the lawsuit, Florida adopted new rules that provided alternatives to money bail for those released prior to disposition. These nonmonetary alternatives are almost identical to the ones in effect under the federal Bail Reform Act. However, unlike federal law, Florida law neither established priorities among the alternatives nor indicated any presumption favoring nonmonetary conditions over money bail. The same indigents challenged the new Florida rules on grounds similar to their reasons for challenging the old Florida pure money bail practice. The court said:

> At the outset we accept the principle that imprisonment solely because of indigent status is invidious discrimination and not constitutionally permissible. The punitive and heavily burdensome nature of pretrial confinement has been the subject of convincing commentary.[54]

The court went on to hold, however, that indigence did not require Florida either to establish a presumption in favor of nonmonetary bail for indigents or to create priorities among various bail conditions. The court said each case must be decided individually, leaving it to the discretion of magistrates as to what condition or combination of conditions best serves the interests of society and poor defendants. In short, indigent defendants do not have a constitutional right to nonmonetary bail and are not unconstitutionally discriminated against simply because they are required to advance money bail.[55]

Pretrial detention makes it difficult for defendants to help their lawyers build the strongest defense against the government's case. Jailed defendants pose serious obstacles for defense counsel. They cannot help locate witnesses or evidence. Attempting to confer in crowded jails with restricted hours impedes the development and implementation of an effective defense strategy. Time spent in jail often adversely affects defendants' demeanor and appearance in court. Their complexion looks pallid, their clothing rumpled, and they exhibit a "jailed look." If convicted, a detained defendant who has lost a job and been separated from family and other relationships has a much poorer chance for probation than one "who has earned money, kept his job, and maintained strong family ties."

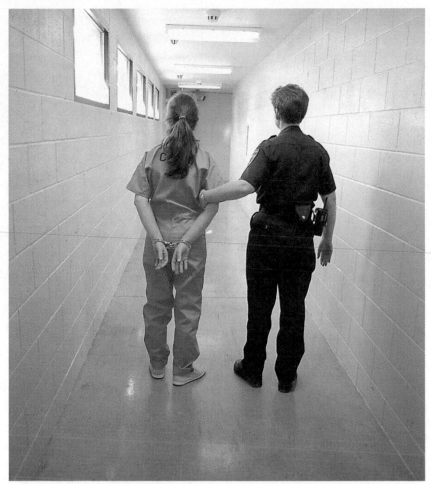

Pallid complexion and jail uniforms gives a "jailed look" to defendants who are denied bail.

release on recognizance release of defendants solely on their promise to appear at trial.
conditional release release of defendants subject to a range of nonmonetary conditions.

The Federal Bail Reform Act   Ever since the Judiciary Act passed in 1789, defendants in federal courts have possessed a statutory right to bail. According to that statute, defendants in federal courts *shall* be bailed, except in capital cases. The Bail Reform Act of 1966 favored nonmonetary release if it assured the appearance of defendants. The most common nonmonetary kind of release is ROR (or simply OR)—**release on recognizance**—which releases defendants solely on their promise to appear at trial. A second form of nonmonetary release is conditional release. In **conditional release,** judges can impose a range of nonmonetary conditions, including maintaining regular contact, either by telephone or in person, with a pretrial program; reporting for regular drug monitoring or treatment; and being placed in the custody of a third party. Release on unsecured bonds does not require putting up any money, but it results in a bail forfeiture if defendants fail to appear. (See Figure 9.7.)[56]

Despite the emphasis on nonmonetary release, bonds requiring at least some cash advances are common (see Figure 9.7). All monetary releases are based on bonds of various types. In full cash bonds, defendants have to put up the entire amount either in cash or in collateral equal to the full amount. In the deposit bond, defendants usually put up 10 percent of the cash amount. In the surety bond, bail bondsmen put up 10 percent of the cash amount of bail.

The 1966 Bail Reform Act also specifies what information the court may use to determine the conditions of release, including:

- Nature of the offense charged.
- Amount of evidence against the defendant.
- Past criminal record of the defendant.

Figure 9.7

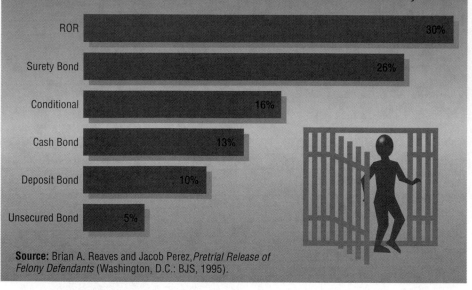

TYPES OF RELEASE IN 75 LARGEST COUNTIES IN U.S., 1992

- ROR — 30%
- Surety Bond — 26%
- Conditional — 16%
- Cash Bond — 13%
- Deposit Bond — 10%
- Unsecured Bond — 5%

Source: Brian A. Reaves and Jacob Perez, *Pretrial Release of Felony Defendants* (Washington, D.C.: BJS, 1995).

- Ties of the defendant to the community, such as family, property owned, and job.
- Mental condition of the defendant.
- Length of residence of the defendant in the community.
- Failure of the defendant to appear at required court proceedings.[57]

Defendants denied release can demand that judges promptly reconsider the conditions. If judges reaffirm their initial decisions not to release defendants, they must provide written reasons for the conditions imposed. The Act prescribes potentially severe penalties for defendants who fail to appear. Bail jumpers forfeit any security pledged and are subject to as much as a $5,000 fine or a maximum of five years in prison. In short, the courts can release defendants on liberal conditions but reserve the right to punish them severely for failure to appear.[58]

State Bail Statutes State bail statutes vary widely, but since the 1970s they have reflected a shift from emphasizing defendants' rights and the securing of their appearance in court to concentrating on crime control and community safety. A Florida law, for example, states clearly that "it is the intent of the legislature that the primary consideration be the protection of the community from risk of physical harm to persons." Ten state statutes briefly list gross criteria, leaving the bail decision to judges as "a matter of sound discretion." Others resemble the federal act and list release conditions in detail.[59]

Whether or not statutes formally prescribe procedures in detail, most judges act similarly in practice. Judges base bail decisions primarily on the seriousness of charges against defendants, a clear and easily applied standard. The strength of the prosecution's case against defendants also carries weight, as does the prior criminal history, or "rap sheet," of defendants. In most localities, judges give little or no weight to community ties or defendants' background and character.[60]

Preventive Detention

The preference for nonmonetary bail arose in the 1960s heyday of criminal justice reform, when activists favored individual rights. During the 1970s the pendulum swung in the other direction, and concern for public safety came to the fore. After long debate and wrangling, Congress enacted the Bail Reform Act of 1984. One provision added a broader **preventive detention** provision to federal law. Preventive detention allows courts to order detention of defendants who endanger either public safety in general or specific individuals, such as victims and other witnesses. The Act lists various "dangerous" indicators, including arrests for violent crimes; arrests during probation, parole, or while on bail; and multiple arrests for repeat offenders. Before detaining defendants for public safety, the Act entitles them to a hearing to determine whether their release endangers the community or individuals.[61]

Civil libertarians objected to the constitutionality of the preventive detention provision, on the grounds that it constitutes cruel and unusual punishment, violates the presumption of innocence, and deprives citizens of liberty without due process of law. Some social scientists objected to preventive detention because of empirical research demonstrating the difficulty of predicting future behavior, particularly dangerous behavior. Social scientists also maintain that preventive detention incarcerates people unnecessarily because those called on to predict dangerousness overpredict it. They do not wish to hazard freeing someone who may conceivably cause harm. Judges overpredict defendants' potential dangerousness, despite consistent evidence indicating that a minority of defendants released on bail commit crimes while they are free. One survey found that 16 percent of freed defendants were arrested for some offense during pretrial release; only 5.1 percent of those arrested were convicted.[62]

The Supreme Court rejected these arguments, upholding the Act's preventive detention provisions in *United States v. Salerno*. The government charged Salerno with 29 counts of racketeering and conspiracy to commit murder. At his arraignment, the government asked the judge to detain Salerno because no release condition could assure community safety. At a detention hearing, the government presented evidence that Salerno was the "boss" of the Genovese organized crime family. Wiretaps showed that Salerno had participated in conspiracies to commit murder. Witnesses corroborated the wiretap evidence. Salerno provided character witnesses, presented evidence of a heart condition, and challenged the government's evidence, but the trial judge allowed the detention. The Supreme Court ruled that preventive detention does not constitute punishment; it amounts to a regulatory device to assure public safety. The Constitution allows for balancing individual liberty and community safety; in this case, according to the Court, the need for public safety outweighed Salerno's right to freedom pending legal determination of his guilt.[63]

In a strong dissent, Justice Marshall wrote:

> It is a fair summary of history to say that the safeguards of liberty have frequently been forged in controversies involving not very nice people. Honoring the presumption of innocence is often difficult; sometimes we must pay substantial social costs as a result of our commitment to the values we espouse. But at the end of the day the presumption of innocence protects the innocent; the shortcuts we take with those whom we believe to be guilty injure only those wrongfully accused and, ultimately, ourselves.
>
> Throughout the world today there are men, women, and children interned indefinitely, awaiting trials which may never come or which may be a mockery of the word, because their governments believe them to be "dangerous." Our Constitution, whose construction began two centuries ago, can shelter us forever from the evils of such unchecked power. Over 200 years it has slowly, through our efforts, grown more durable, more expansive, and more just. But it cannot protect us

if we lack the courage and the self-restraint to protect ourselves. Today, a majority of the Court applies itself to an ominous exercise in demolition.[64]

Bail Reform

Whatever the formal law of bail, critics have historically called bail a major social problem. The thrust of all bail reform stems from three basic complaints:

1. Bail decision making is corrupt.
2. Bail decision making is unfair.
3. Bail decision making is ineffective.

Charles Dickens complained about corrupt bail bondsmen in the nineteenth century; Felix Frankfurter, later a Supreme Court justice, and Roscoe Pound, reformist dean of the Harvard Law School, reported serious shortcomings in bail administration in Cleveland in 1920. In 1954, law professor Caleb Foote empirically demonstrated that, in Philadelphia, defendants who cannot afford bail are much more likely to be convicted and serve longer sentences than defendants free on bail. In other words, poor people not only lose their freedom before conviction but also receive more severe punishment after conviction. According to considerable historical evidence, then, social class influences bail. Well-to-do defendants go free, and the poor go to jail. More recent findings corroborate these historical studies regarding the class distinctions between bailed and detained defendants. John S. Goldkamp studied bail in Philadelphia. In a regression analysis that controlled for other factors, he found that pretrial detention did not *per se* affect the determination of innocence or guilt, but did influence the length of prison sentences imposed.[65]

Following Professor Foote's study, bail reform became a serious pursuit. Reformers established an agenda that, unlike prior efforts, has endured. The bail reform agenda from about 1960 until 1980 contained several items aimed at reducing all of the following:

- Class bias in bail that favors the well-to-do over the poor.
- Harsh treatment experienced by detained defendants.
- Long delays in securing release.
- Cost of bail.
- Corruption, such as kickbacks from jailers who recommend particular bondsmen and avoidance of forfeiture fees.
- Failure-to-appear rates.

Peter R. Jones and John S. Goldkamp added to this list of complaints about corruption and unfairness another reason for dissatisfaction with bail decision making—the ineffectiveness of judges in deciding who to detain and who to release. According to Jones and Goldkamp, the furor raised over bail in the 1970s and 1980s boiled down to frustration over

> two sides of the same coin—a widespread public policy concern that bail/pretrial release decisionmaking by the judiciary was ineffective. On the one hand, the jails were being needlessly filled with defendants before trial; on the other, too many "dangerous" defendants were being released to prey once again on the public.[66]

Bail reform has significantly advanced from the agenda set in the 1960s. Significantly, courts have not spearheaded bail reform. Instead, administrative agencies have altered what many believed was a major social problem. Informal administration has produced more reform than the constitutional, legal, and judicial efforts.[67]

In 1960, two New Yorkers, one an elderly philanthropist and the other a young social worker, were so shocked by jail conditions that they agreed to set up a pretrial release agency to help arrested suspects obtain release on their own recognizance. The two reformers convinced city officials to let them establish an experimental pretrial release agency. Known as the Manhattan Bail Project, the experiment was underway by the fall of 1961. Law students interviewed defendants as soon after arrest as possible in order to find out if they had close community, family, and employment ties in New York City. If such ties were verified, the law students went to the arraignment and argued for the release of defendants on their own recognizance.[68]

After a year, the project evaluated itself by comparing a control group of arrestees who were not released with those who were recommended for release and freed. Despite the fears of officials that enormous numbers would fail to appear (FTA), the evaluation revealed "overwhelming and persuasive evidence" that the project was viable. Those released on their own recognizance had lower FTA rates than those in the control group who posted bond. In fact, the project reported that only three ROR defendants failed to appear in court, a dramatically successful rate.[69]

The Manhattan Bail Project won high acclaim and soon became widely emulated. Robert F. Kennedy, then U.S. attorney general, ordered U.S. attorneys to release as many defendants as possible on their own recognizance. As discussed, the 1966 Bail Reform Act made ROR the primary bail condition. The Ford Foundation supported further bail projects that sprang up in Des Moines, San Francisco, and several other cities. Enthusiasm for the program continued to grow and spread. In 1968, 61 new projects were established; by 1969 there were 89; and in 1973 the number had grown to 112. In 1982, it was estimated that more than 200 pretrial release projects were in operation.[70]

In a survey of bail reform written in 1986, Steven R. Schlesinger noted that ROR does not discriminate against the poor, does not expose defendants to the "legal, social, and economic hardships of jail," and has outperformed the traditional bond system, since only 11 percent of ROR defendants were arrested compared to 25 percent who raised money bail.[71]

Two other reforms were introduced in addition to ROR. First, the **ten percent bond program** permits defendants to pay 10 percent of the bail amount to the court, not to bondsmen. If defendants appear, all or most of the money advanced is returned, unlike the typical bond that is considered a bondsman's fee for guaranteeing the appearance of defendants. Second, police **summonses** and **citations** are replacing arrests and bonds to appear in court. These practices, closely akin to "getting a traffic ticket," are increasingly being implemented in minor criminal offenses.[72]

Predicting Misconduct on Bail

Two reports assessed bail reform from after the formation of the Manhattan Bail Project until 1980. Both showed that pretrial release grew in most cities. Between 1962 and 1971, felony releases increased from 48 to 67 percent and misdemeanor releases from 60 to 72 percent. By 1980, release rates had risen to 80 percent in many jurisdictions, and the average dollar amount of bail had declined. These two developments allowed the release of large numbers of defendants who would previously have been denied bail.[73]

Researchers also found that "only a few bail violators become real fugitives from justice; most eventually return." More than 87 percent of all released defendants appeared for every scheduled appearance. In addition, most defendants who failed to appear were not fugitives from justice. Their failure to appear was inadvertent. They forgot a date, got confused about where they should go, or missed the scheduled time. Sometimes they were given the wrong time, date, or courtroom. All these registered as failures, but they differ from defendants who intentionally stayed away to avoid judicial proceedings. All but about 2 percent who did not appear for their first appearance eventually did show up in court.[74]

Beginning in the 1980s, bail reform has shifted its focus from favoring release to demanding restrictions on pretrial release and adding preventive detention as a justification for pretrial detention. Criminal justice personnel regularly call for "tightening" bail practices. The growing numbers of pretrial detainees in the nation's jails clearly indicate the increased use of pretrial detention. Furthermore, detainees continue to be "disproportionately young, male, low income or unemployed, and black."[75]

Originally, evaluators believed that careful screening for defendants with the closest community ties produced these impressive results. The Manhattan Bail Project used an objective release system based on an elaborate **bail point system** that determined community ties by assigning points for employment, residence, family, and other relationships with the community. Most other bail projects around the country adopted similar point scales.[76]

Some research suggests that neither community ties nor elaborate scales to weigh them affect appearance rates. The intensive follow-up procedures used in the Manhattan Bail Project actually accounted for the high appearance rates. Law students personally contacted released defendants so they knew exactly when to appear in court; then the students took measures to assure that released defendants actually appeared. Follow-up is simpler, less costly, and serves greater numbers of bailed defendants than the point system.[77]

John S. Goldkamp evaluated the point system in Philadelphia. He concluded, in an elaborate regression analysis, that

> no decision criteria—including community ties, charging seriousness, or any others promulgated . . . have been found to do what presumably they are employed to do; that is, they cannot predict risk of flight or pretrial dangerousness.[78]

The prediction of pretrial misconduct in the form of either committing crimes while on bail or of jumping bail has not succeeded when using community ties, demographic, and legal-criminal history factors as predictors. According to Chester L. Britt III, Michael R. Gottfredson, and John S. Goldkamp, "Virtually every prediction model of pretrial failure over-predicts the number of defendants who are likely to fail to appear at trial or to be rearrested."

Drug Testing to Reduce Pretrial Misconduct

Britt, Gottfredson, and Goldkamp studied the value of monitoring the use of drugs by defendants on bail as a means to reduce not only their use of drugs but also their pretrial misconduct. They relied on a computerized case-tracking system in Pima and Miracopa Counties in Arizona to select a control group and experimental group of similar defendants on bail. The computerized system included information about prior record, court appearance history, offense, living arrangements, bail decision, failure to appear, and criminal behavior while on bail. The control group received normal supervision; the experimental group received drug monitoring during pretrial release.[79]

No significant differences in failure to appear or rearrest rates between the two groups occurred in Pima County, except that members of the monitored group were slightly less likely to get rearrested for the possession of drugs. In Miracopa County, arrests and failure to appear rates were *higher* in the monitored group than in the control group. On the basis of their findings, the authors concluded that

> systematic drug testing and monitoring in the pretrial setting . . . is not likely to achieve significant or major reductions in pretrial misconduct.

Figure 9.8

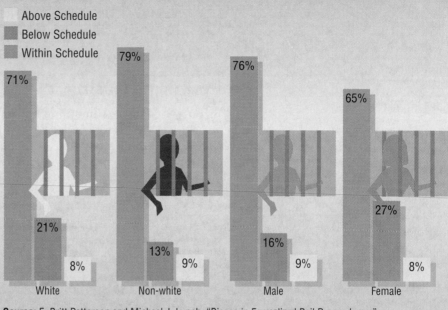

RACE AND GENDER DIFFERENCES IN BAIL SCHEDULE

□ Above Schedule
■ Below Schedule
■ Within Schedule

White: 71%, 21%, 8%
Non-white: 79%, 13%, 9%
Male: 76%, 16%, 9%
Female: 65%, 27%, 8%

Source: E. Britt Patterson and Michael J. Lynch, "Biases in Formalized Bail Proceedures," *Race and Criminal Justice,* Michael J. Lynch and E. Britt Patterson, eds. (New York: Harrow and Heston, 1991).

At the same time that these programs fail to achieve their stated goal of reducing rates of pretrial misconduct, they carry a heavy price tag. In both Pima County and Miracopa County the cost of drug testing programs averaged from $400,000 to $500,000 per year. Given the high financial costs of these programs, including the testing and staffing required to accomplish them, it seems reasonable to question the effectiveness and cost-effectiveness of drug testing the released pretrial population.[80]

Race and Gender Bias in Bail Decisions

Some research has suggested that bail decisions suffer from race and gender discrimination. E. Britt Patterson and Michael J. Lynch examined the compliance of judges with the bail schedule of a large western city. They found that the schedule did not remove race and gender disparities in bail decisions. Whites, particularly white women, were more likely to receive bail below the schedule than nonwhites. When they controlled for other variables that might affect the outcome of the bail decision, such as the seriousness of the offense and the dangerousness of the defendant, they found that nonwhites and men were no more likely than whites and women to receive bail in *excess* of the schedule. However, whites and women were significantly more likely than nonwhites to receive bail *below* the schedule. (See Figure 9.8.) Patterson and Lynch concluded that "although minorities were not treated more harshly than whites, they were discriminated against because they were not given the same benefit of the doubt as were whites."[81]

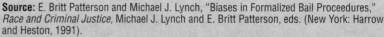

Testing the Government's Case

A variety of court proceedings take place following the initial appearance but before the final disposition of cases either by trial or guilty plea. The preliminary hearing and the grand jury review test the strength of the government's case by formal review of the evidence against defendants. Hearings on pretrial motions determine the constitutionality of confessions and searches and seizures, decide whether the trial should move to another location, and provide for the discovery of evidence and witnesses the prosecution and defense intend to use at trial. The *voir dire* proceeding selects the trial jury.

Preliminary Hearing

Preliminary hearings, sometimes called **probable cause hearings** because they test the objective basis of the government's case against defendants, take place after the first appearance, the appointment of counsel, and the determination of bail. The length of time between first appearance and preliminary hearing varies from a few days in some jurisdictions to a number of weeks in others. The primary formal function of the preliminary hearing is to test the government's case against defendants. It offers the first opportunity for *judicial* screening of cases, cases that up to this point only police and prosecutors have reviewed. At preliminary hearings, judges review prosecutors' charging decisions to determine whether sufficient evidence, or probable cause, exists to warrant further proceedings. If judges decide that cases deserve further action, they **bind over defendants;** that is, they order them to trial on the charges against them. If judges determine that the prosecution's case lacks probable cause, they dismiss charges. Although prosecutors *can* recharge in the future, as a practical matter prosecutors rarely reopen cases dismissed at preliminary hearings.[82]

Indictment and Information

The government can also initiate criminal proceedings and test probable cause by **indictment,** a formal written accusation by the grand jury, an ancient practice originating in medieval England. Grand jury proceedings can be held in place of preliminary hearings, or they can follow preliminary hearings as a second screening device. Dismissals at preliminary hearings do not prevent grand juries from reconsidering probable cause to send a case to trial. In other words, if magistrates dismiss cases, prosecutors can bring them to grand juries for another try, in the hope of winning a more favorable outcome. On the other hand, if judges bind cases over, grand juries can decide not to indict. **Grand juries** are composed of private citizens chosen to serve from one to several months. Traditionally, 23 people sat on a grand jury; today, as few as six make up grand juries, with 12 to 16 most common. Compared to the unanimous verdict usually required to convict, it takes a simple majority of grand jurors to indict.

Indicting by grand jury screening and binding over in preliminary hearings both rest on the same objective foundation, or quantum of proof: probable cause. However, major differences separate preliminary hearings from grand jury proceedings. Grand jury hearings are not adversary proceedings; only the government presents evidence. Defendants can neither offer evidence nor appear before grand juries. Furthermore, grand jury proceedings are secret and closed; preliminary hearings are open and public. Grand jurors or others who "leak" any information presented to grand juries face severe penalties. Finally, magistrates preside in preliminary hearings; prosecutors oversee grand jury proceedings.[83]

Prosecutors can bypass the grand jury and initiate proceedings following their own review of probable cause in an instrument called an **information.** Most states using the information procedure require that a preliminary hearing follow the filing of an information. The preliminary hearing prevents

Some critics call preliminary hearings "mini trials" that waste valuable time.

a criminal prosecution from proceeding solely on the prosecutor's probable cause determination. In other words, the preliminary hearing in information jurisdictions screens what a grand jury review screens in indictment jurisdictions.

The adoption of the information process followed long-standing criticisms of grand jury review. In the eighteenth century, the famous English law reformer Jeremy Bentham attacked the process, and objections to it have continued since. Some reformers demand its outright abolition; others call for severe restrictions on its power. Abolitionists consider grand jury review "essentially worthless." They agree with the former prosecutor who said he could "indict anybody, at any time, for almost anything before a grand jury."[84]

This criticism depicts grand juries as rubber stamps for prosecutors. Statistics indicate that grand juries rarely disagree with prosecutors. Between January 1, 1974, and June 30, 1977, 235 cases were presented to the San Francisco grand jury, and indictments were returned in all 235. The ratio has not changed significantly since then. Also, according to critics the grand jury "is costly in terms of space, manpower and money," and it delays case processing because grand juries are not as accessible as magistrates.[85]

Despite criticism, supporters of grand jury review claim several advantages. They maintain that grand juries effectively screen criminal cases. According to supporters—who count prosecutors among their numbers— grand jurors do have minds of their own. The low rate of refusals to indict has little or nothing to do with prosecutors dominating the grand jury room; instead, the many indictments result from careful preliminary screening. Prosecutors bring only strong cases that persuade the grand jury to indict. In fact, prosecutors say they present cases for which they have not only probable cause but also proof beyond a reasonable doubt. The high ratio of indictments to convictions—more than 98 percent result in conviction— supports this conclusion.

The preliminary hearing, indictment, and information represent different ways to test the government's case against defendants before trial. The preliminary hearing places the decision in the magistrate's or judge's hands; the information, in the prosecutor's; and the indictment, in the community's representatives—the grand jurors. Each has a check on its authority to

arraignment *bringing of defendants to open court in order to read the charges against them and to require them to plead to the charges.*

nolo contendere *unusual plea of "no contest" to criminal charges.*

discovery *proceeding asking for the other side to produce evidence.*

initiate the criminal process. The grand jury can review and reverse a preliminary hearing bind over or an information; and magistrates can review grand jury indictments. Despite its tenacious and occasionally truculent critics, grand jury remains an alternative to information and preliminary hearing in serious and sensitive cases. In these cases, prosecutors can receive support and share the responsibility with the grand jury, a body that represents the community.

Arraignment and Pretrial Motions

Following preliminary hearing, the decision to bind over, grand jury indictments, or prosecutorial informations, the criminal court has the authority to dispose of cases by trial or by defendants' plea of guilty. The court obtains the authority to dispose of cases by arraigning defendants. **Arraignment** consists of bringing defendants to open court, reading the charges against them, and demanding that they plead either not guilty, guilty, or *nolo contendere* (no contest) to the charges. The arraignment and plea to charges formally set the stage for the criminal trial. Informally, they provide the opportunity either to start, continue, or ratify a plea agreement.

During the period between arraignment and trial, prosecution and defense can file pretrial motions that lead to pretrial hearings. Most states require the defense *before* trial to make objections to the indictment or information, to request the prosecution's evidence (known as **discovery**), and to object to the government's evidence (fruits of illegal searches and seizures). The government can also request discovery in the form of a pretrial motion. Pretrial motions and hearings occur in only 10 percent of all felony cases and in less than 1 percent of misdemeanor prosecutions. Courts dismiss practically no misdemeanor cases and only about 5 percent of felony cases in pretrial hearings arising out of objections in pretrial motions. Pretrial motions, in the rare instances when they take place, occur mainly in cases involving non-complaining victims, such as drug-related felonies. Politicians and the press greatly exaggerate the numbers of violent—or even nonviolent—criminals set free by pretrial motions to exclude evidence illegally obtained under the search and seizure clause (See Chapter 6.)[86]

Summary

Following arrest, the police role in criminal justice diminishes; the lawyers take over. When police take cases to prosecutors' offices, the decisions to terminate criminal proceedings or continue them become prosecutors' responsibilities. During initial screening, prosecutors exercise wide discretion to charge, divert, or drop cases altogether. Prosecutors also determine the specific charges to file against suspects (who become defendants once prosecutors file charges). Several influences, both formal and informal, affect prosecutors' decisions. The main formal influence, the strength of the case against defendants, or legal guilt, hinges on how much confidence prosecutors have in witnesses and physical evidence of guilt. Contrary to public belief, weak—not illegally obtained—evidence stands in the way of charging and convicting defendants.

Informal influences also affect prosecutors' charging decisions. Prosecutors refuse to charge because they believe cases are trivial, take up more time than they are "worth," delay more important cases, may not make a good impression in the community, and may disrupt good working relationships with judges and defense lawyers. Hence, bureaucratic, work group, and career concerns materially affect prosecutors' charging decisions.

The "right" to counsel does not mean that everyone can have a lawyer for all cases. A means test determines the poverty of a defendant, and defendants in minor offenses are not covered by the constitutional guarantee. Many defendants go unrepresented in criminal cases, especially in the early stages from arrest to first appearance in court.

The U.S. Constitution, most state constitutions, many statutes, and court opinions guarantee some pretrial release. Therefore, bail is an established, formal legal phenomenon. In practice, criminal defendants can be divided into two classes: bailed and jailed. One purpose of bail is to secure defendants' appearances in court. Historically, money bail was the predominant means to secure this appearance. Since the 1960s, alternatives to money bail have become common, especially ROR, which places defendants in the custody of reliable persons, and conditional release. The courts have not led the attempts to reform the bail system. Instead, administrative agencies have spearheaded the move away from money bail and the presumption in favor of release instead of detention.

The second purpose of bail is to assure the safety of the community through preventive detention. Preventive detention generates considerable controversy. Civil libertarians argue that it violates citizens' constitutional rights; social scientists maintain that predicting dangerousness eludes empirical forecasting. Despite objections, the U.S. Supreme Court has upheld preventive detention as a constitutionally permissible mechanism to regulate pretrial criminal process.

Pretrial release, particularly ROR, increased from 1960 until 1980. Overwhelming numbers of released defendants appear for all their scheduled court appearances. The few who do not appear are not fugitives from justice; their failure to appear is accidental, and all but 2 percent eventually appear. Most defendants do not commit crimes while bailed. Since 1980, pretrial detention has increased with a shift in emphasis from the rights of defendants to the need for public safety. Whatever the ideological forces underlying bail, its use has great consequences for defendants. On bail, defendants are not only free, but they also can help prepare their defense, stay off welfare, prove to courts they are responsible, and provide for their families. Defendants detained during adjudication temporarily lose their freedom and are also more likely to be convicted, to be sentenced to prison, and to serve longer terms. Despite programs such as the Manhattan Bail Project, aimed at developing and implementing nonmonetary bail systems, most jurisdictions continue to rely on monetary bail and pretrial detention. Since most detained defendants are poor, the use of a monetary bail system represents a class phenomenon in America.

A number of court proceedings follow the first appearance. The grand jury and preliminary hearing test the government's case against defendants. The prosecutor presides over the grand jury, a body composed of citizens. It meets secretly without the presence of a judge, defense counsel, or defendant. It hears only the prosecution's evidence. Grand juries ordinarily follow the recommendation of prosecutors as to whether to indict suspects. Preliminary hearings are public, adversary proceedings, presided over by judges. Both prosecution and defense participate in preliminary hearings, presenting at least some of their cases against and for defendants. Judges determine whether to bind defendants over for trial or dismiss the case against them.

Pretrial motions deal with a number of issues regarding the admissibility of evidence, particularly whether the police obtained it by coerced confession or unreasonable search and seizure. Despite popular opinion, defendants file only a few motions to suppress evidence, and they lose most of them. Pretrial motions also decide whether to change the location of the trial and order the discovery of evidence. Following the pretrial motions, if defendants have not already pleaded guilty, the criminal process moves to the next stage—the most visible and popular event—the criminal trial.

Review Questions

1. What is the difference between a suspect and a defendant?

2. How do prosecutors obtain criminal cases?

3. Why is the prosecutor said to be the most important official in criminal justice?

4. What alternatives do prosecutors have when they receive criminal cases?

5. Compare prosecutorial and police discretion.

6. What is the significance of filing charges?

7. Explain the importance of the decision not to charge.

8. Identify the major legal and extralegal influences on the decision to charge.

9. What is the significance of evidence of guilt in the decision to charge?

10. What is the significance of the exclusionary rule on the decision of prosecutors to charge?

11. What decisions are made at the first appearance?

12. Explain the major elements in the constitutional right to counsel.

13. Identify and describe the three major types of criminal defense for the poor.

14. What are the results of empirical studies on the effectiveness of defense of the poor?

15. Describe and explain the significance of the Neighborhood Defender Service.

16. What formal and informal interests does the bail decision balance?

17. Explain the elements of the constitutional right to bail.

18. List the major criticisms of commercial bail.

19. What are the competing policies that underlie bail?

20. Identify and explain the major elements of the Federal Bail Reform Act of 1966.

21. What are the major elements of state bail statutes?

22. Explain preventive detention and discuss its constitutionality.

23. Why is bail decision making regarded as a major social problem?

24. List the major items in the agenda of bail reform from the 1960s to the 1980s.

25. Explain the significance of the Manhattan Bail Project.

26. What are the best predictors of bail misconduct?

27. Explain the point system for pretrial release and assess its effectiveness.

28. Compare and contrast the preliminary hearing and grand jury review.

29. What are the formal and informal functions of grand jury review and preliminary hearings?

30. Describe the major pretrial motions and state their importance.

Notes

1. *Journal of the American Judicature Society* 34 (1940): 18–19; W. Boyd Littrell, *Bureaucratic Justice: Police, Prosecutors, and Plea Bargaining* (Beverly Hills: Sage Publications, 1979), 32–33.

2. Barbara Boland et al., *The Prosecution of Felony Arrests, 1986* (Washington, D.C.: Bureau of Justice Statistics, June 1989); *People v. Wabash, St. Louis and Pacific Railway,* 12 Ill. App. 263 (1883); Celesta A. Albonetti, "Criminality, Prosecutorial Screening, and Uncertainty: Toward a Theory of Discretionary Decision Making in Felony Case Processings," *Criminology* 24 (1986): 624.

3. William F. McDonald, *Plea Bargaining: Critical Issues and Common Practices* (Washington, D.C.: National Institute of Justice, July 1985), 11–15.

4. President's Commission on Law Enforcement and Administration of Justice, *The Challenge of Crime in a Free Society* (Washington, D.C.: U.S. Government Printing Office, 1967), 10; McDonald, *Plea Bargaining,* 26ff.

5. Boland et al., *Prosecution of Felony Arrests;* U.S. Department of Justice, *Principles of Federal Prosecution* (Washington, D.C.: U.S. Department of Justice, 1980), i.

6. Abraham S. Blumberg, *Criminal Justice* (Chicago: Quadrangle Books, 1970), 69.

7. Candace McCoy, "The Types, Rationales, and Effects of Inducing Defendant Cooperation in Federal Prosecutions," unpublished paper, The American Society of Criminology, annual meeting, 1989, 8.

8. BJS *The Prosecution of Felony Arrests, 1988* (Washington, D.C.: Bureau of Justice Statistics, 1992); Brian Forst, "Prosecution and Sentencing," in *Crime,* James Q. Wilson and Joan Petersilia, eds. San Francisco: (Institute for Contemporary Studies Press, 1995), 366.

9. Forst, "Prosecution and Sentencing," 367, note 17, p. 588.

10. Peter F. Nardulli, James Eisenstein, and Roy B. Flemming, *The Tenor of Justice* (Urbana: University of Illinois Press, 1988), chap. 7; Forst, "Prosecution and Sentencing," 367.

11. Forst, "Prosecution and Sentencing," 367–368.

12. Donald Black, *Sociological Justice* (New York: Oxford University Press, 1989), 24.

13. Celesta A. Albonetti, "Charge Reduction: An Analysis of Prosecutorial Discretion in Burglary and Robbery Cases," *Journal of Quantitative Criminology* 8 (1992): 317–33.

14. Lisa Frohman, "Discrediting Victims' Allegations of Sexual Assault: Prosecutorial Accounts of Case Rejections," *Social Problems* 38 (1991): 213–26.

15. Quoted in Frohman, 216.

16. Quoted in Frohman, 220.

17. Susan Estrich, *Real Rape* (Cambridge: Harvard University Press, 1987), 8–9.

18. Battelle Law and Justice Study Center, *Forcible Rape: A National Survey of the Response by Prosecutors,* vol. 3 (Washington, D.C.: National Institute of Law Enforcement and Criminal Justice, 1977), 18–19.

19. Boland et al., *Prosecution of Felony Arrests;* Brian Forst, "Prosecution and Sentencing," in *Crime and Public Policy,*

James Q. Wilson, ed. (New Brunswick, N.J.: Transaction Books, 1983), 168–169.

20. Vera Institute of Justice, *Felony Arrests: Their Prosecution and Disposition in New York City's Courts* (New York: Vera Institute of Justice, 1977), 31–32.

21. Michael Benson et al., "District Attorneys and Corporate Crime: Surveying the Prosecutorial Gatekeepers," *Criminology* 26 (1988): 505–518.

22. Celesta A. Albonetti, "Criminality, Prosecutorial Screening, and Uncertainty: Toward a Theory of Discretionary Decision Making in Felony Case Processings," *Criminology* 24 (1986): 623–644.

23. *Betts v. Brady,* 316 U.S. 455 (1942).

24. *Gideon v. Wainwright,* 372 U.S. 335 (1963).

25. Ibid.

26. Ibid.

27. Ibid.

28. *Argersinger v. Hamlin,* 407 U.S. 25 (1972).

29. *Scott v. Illinois,* 440 U.S. 367 (1979).

30. Valery M. Savitsky and Victor M. Kogan, "Socialist Law Systems," in *Major Criminal Justice Systems,* 2d ed., George F. Cole, Stanislaw J. Frankowski, and Marc G. Gertz, eds. (Newbury Park, Calif.: Sage Publications, 1987), 205–211.

31. BJS, *Indigent Defendants* (Washington, D.C.: Bureau of Justice Statistics, February 1996).

32. Andy Court, "Is There a Crisis?" *The American Lawyer* (January/February, 1993).

33. "Defenders Make Their Case," *Sessions Weekly,* 11.

34. Ibid.

35. Lisa J. McIntyre, *The Public Defender: The Practice of Law in the Shadows of Repute* (Chicago: University of Chicago Press, 1987), 3.

36. Roger A. Hanson et al., *Indigent Defenders Get the Job Done and Done Well* (Williamsburg, Va.: National Center for State Courts, 1992).

37. Court, "Is There a Crisis?" 46.

38. David Lynch, "The Impropriety of Plea Bargaining," *Law and Social Inquiry* 19 (1994): 124.

39. Court, "Is There a Crisis?" 3.

40. Ibid.

41. Ibid., 11–14.

42. Vera Institute of Justice, *The Neighborhood Defender Service of Harlem: Research Results from the First Year* (New York: Vera Institute of Justice, December 1992).

43. Brian A. Reaves and Jacob Perez, *Pretrial Release of Felony Defendants, 1992* (Washington, D.C.: Bureau of Justice Statistics, 1995), 1; Plato, *Laws* (Cambridge, Mass.: Harvard University Press, 1926), 2:261.

44. John S. Goldkamp, "Danger and Detention: A Second Generation of Bail Reform," *Journal of Criminal Law and Criminology* 76 (1985): 1–75.

45. Andy Hall et al., *Pretrial Release Program Options* (Washington, D.C.: National Institute of Justice, June 1984).

46. Samuel Walker, Cassia Spohn, and Miriam DeLonc, *The Color of Justice: Race, Ethnicity, and Crime in America* (Belmont, Calif.: Wadsworth Publishing Company, 1996), 128.

47. Malcolm M. Feeley, *The Process Is the Punishment* (New York: Russell Sage, 1979), 96–111; see also Steven R. Schlesinger, "Bail Reform: Protecting the Community and the Accused," *Harvard Journal of Law and Public Policy* 9 (1986): 182.

48. Schlesinger, "Bail Reform," 173–202.

49. Ibid., 178–79.

50. *Stack v. Boyle,* 342 U.S. 1 (1951).

51. *United States v. Abrahams,* 575 F.2d 3 (1st Cir. 1978).

52. Ibid.

53. *Pugh v. Rainwater,* 557 F.2d 1189 (5th Cir. 1977).

54. *Pugh v. Rainwater,* on rehearing, 572 F.2d 1053 (5th Cir. 1978).

55. Ibid.

56. 18 United States Code Ann., §§ 3146-3151; Reaves and Perez, *Pretrial Release of Felony Defendants, 1992.*

57. 18 U.S. Code Ann., § 3146.

58. Ibid., §§ 3146, 3150.

59. Fla. Stat. Ann. § 907.041(1) (St. Paul: West Publishing Company, 1985); Ga. Code Ann. § 27-901(a) (1983 & Supp. 1985).

60. Paul Wice, *Freedom for Sale* (Lexington, Mass.: Lexington Books, 1974); Wayne R. LaFave and Jerold H. Israel, *Criminal Procedure* (St. Paul: West Publishing Company, 1984), 2:114; Goldkamp, "Danger and Detention," 8–9.

61. BJS, *Pretrial Release and Detention: The Bail Reform of 1984* (Washington, D.C.: Bureau of Justice Statistics, February 1988).

62. John Monahan, *The Clinical Prediction of Dangerousness* (Rockville, Md.: U.S. Department of Health and Human Services, Public Health Service, Alcohol, Drug Abuse, and Mental Health Administration, National Institute of Mental Health, 1981); Henry J. Steadman and Joseph J. Cocozza, *Careers of the Criminally Insane: Excessive Social Control of Deviance* (Lexington, Mass.: Heath, Lexington Books, 1974); David J. Rabinowitz, "Preventive Detention and *United States v. Edwards:* Burdening the Innocent," *The American University Law Review* 32 (1982): 201.

63. *United States v. Salerno,* 481 U.S. 739 (1987).

64. Ibid.

65. *Criminal Justice in Cleveland* (Cleveland: The Cleveland Foundation, 1923), 290–92; "Compelling Appearance in Court: Administration of Bail in Philadelphia," *University of Pennsylvania Law Review* 102 (1954): 1031–1079; Malcolm M. Feeley, *Court Reform on Trial* (New York: Basic Books, 1983), 40–44; John S. Goldkamp, *Two Classes of Accused* (Lexington, Mass.: Ballinger Publishing Company, 1979), 209–211.

66. Peter R. Jones and John S. Goldkamp, "The Bail Guidelines Experiment in Dade County, Miami: A Case Study in the Development and Implementation of a Policy Innovation," in Mays and Gregware, *Courts and Justice,* 390.

67. Ibid., 44.

68. Feeley, *Court Reform on Trial,* 44–45.

69. Vera Institute of Justice, *Programs in Criminal Justice Reform, Ten-Year Report, 1961-1971* (New York: Vera Institute of Justice, 1972), 31.

70. Feeley, *Court Reform on Trial,* 46–47.

71. Schlesinger, "Bail Reform," 182–83.

72. Floyd Feeney, *The Police and Pretrial Release* (Lexington, Mass.: Heath, Lexington Books, 1982).

73. Wayne H. Thomas, *Bail Reform in America* (Berkeley: University of California, 1976); Mary A. Toborg, *Pretrial Release: A National Evaluation of Practices and Outcomes* (Washington, D.C.: National Institute of Justice, 1981).

74. Mary A. Toberg, *Pretrial Release: A National Evaluation of Practices and Outcomes* (Washington, D.C.: National Institute of Justice, 1981).

75. BJS, *Pretrial Release and Detention;* Goldkamp, *Two Classes of Accused,* 221.

76. Goldkamp, *Two Classes of Accused,* 53–59; Goldkamp, "Danger and Detention," 10–14; Schlesinger, "Bail Reform," 180–185; Hall, *Pretrial Release Program Options.*

77. Vera Institute of Justice, *Programs in Criminal Justice Reform,* 53–59.

78. Goldkamp, *Two Classes of Accused,* 221.

79. Chester L. Britt III, Michael R. Gottfredson, and John S. Goldkamp, "Drug Testing and Pretrial Misconduct: An Experiment on the Specific Deterrent Effects of Drug Monitoring Defendants on Pretrial Release," *Journal of Research on Crime and Delinquency* 29 (1992): 62–78.

80. Ibid., 77.

81. E. Britt Patterson and Michael J. Lynch, "Biases in Formalized Bail Procedures," in *Race and Criminal Justice,* Michael J. Lynch and E. Britt Patterson, eds. (New York: Harrow and Heston, 1991); discussed in Walker, Spohn, and DeLonc, *The Color of Justice,* 129.

82. Kathleen B. Brosi, *A Cross-City Comparison of Felony Case Processing* (Washington, D.C.: Law Enforcement Assistance Administration, 1979); LaFave and Israel, *Criminal Procedure,* 2:253–54.

83. *Hawkins v. Superior Court,* 22 Cal.3d 584 (1978).

84. Ibid.

85. Ibid.; LaFave and Israel, *Criminal Procedure,* 2:283.

86. LaFave and Israel, *Criminal Procedure,* 1:27.

Trial and Guilty Ple

as

CHAPTER MAIN POINTS

1. *Few defendants go to trial; most case dispositions occur by guilty plea or informal decisions.*

2. *Criminal trials are elaborate fact-finding proceedings that determine legal guilt, act as symbols of justice, and influence informal decision making.*

3. *The Sixth Amendment to the U.S. Constitution guarantees defendants the right to a "speedy" trial and the right to a jury trial in all criminal prosecutions, with jurors who represent a fair cross section of the community.*

4. *Fair trial requires an atmosphere that does not prejudice defendants.*

5. *Opening statements provide attorneys with the opportunity to present their respective overviews of the case.*

6. *Direct examination prohibits asking leading questions; it requires narrative answers.*

7. *Cross-examination permits leading questions; it extracts yes or no answers.*

8. *Judges determine the admissibility of evidence, according to whether it is relevant, material, nonprejudicial, and legally obtained.*

9. *Closing arguments allow the prosecution and defense their last opportunity to address juries directly and convince juries of their cases.*

10. *Judges instruct the jurors in the law; juries decide the truth and degree of proof in the facts.*

11. *The guilty plea illustrates the informal side to the determination of guilt.*

12. *Guilty pleas are either straight or result from plea bargaining.*

13. *Local legal culture accounts for variations in plea bargaining among jurisdictions.*

14. *Plea negotiations may relate to charge, sentence, or facts at trial.*

15. *Strength of the government's case is the major element in prosecutorial plea bargaining.*

16. *Prosecutors make "sweet deals," rather than taking a chance on obtaining a conviction for a more serious charge at trial.*

17. *The consequences of a trial and the attitude of defense counsel toward defendants favor informal plea negotiation over formal adjudication.*

18. *Judges supervise, and in a few cases participate in, plea negotiations.*

19. *The Constitution authorizes voluntary, knowing pleas of guilty.*

20. *Defendants who plead guilty waive the right to remain silent, the right to a jury trial, and due process of law.*

21. *Plea bargaining generates controversy and demands for either its abolition or reform.*

The criminal trial is the high point in formal criminal justice. Highly visible and public, it attracts attention by its high drama and sometimes gory details about the many horrors people can inflict on each other. Criminal trials dispose of only a few cases in practice. Informal, low-visibility, private negotiations between prosecutors for the government and defense counsel for the defendant determine the outcome in most criminal cases. The proceedings in court merely ratify formally and publicly what the parties have already decided informally outside the courtroom.

You have already read about the formal-informal relationship in police actions on the street and in police departments, in prosecutors' offices prior to filing charges, and during the first appearance. You will read about it following conviction at sentencing and in correctional administration in later chapters. Adjudication reveals the formal-informal dichotomy in its boldest relief. Formal proceedings set standards, publicize norms, and underscore procedures that affect informal decisions. Accommodation through negotiation—balancing formal requirements and informal needs—permits discretionary judgments to facilitate sound, economical, decisions acceptable to the government, the accused, and—perhaps not emphasized as much as it deserves—the public.

Disposition by Trial

Fewer than three out of 100 felony arrests ever reach trial. Practically no misdemeanor arrests do so. Before trial, courts have dismissed charges, or defendants have pleaded guilty (see Chapter 9, Figure 9.1). Nevertheless, just as courts represent the formal centerpiece of criminal justice institutions, trials are the high point of the formal criminal process. Legally, every action from arrest through pretrial motion aims at trial; from it flows all consequences of adjudication. The criminal trial exerts a total effect greater than the sum of its parts. It influences cases that never reach trial; it affects informal decisions of police, prosecutors, defense attorneys, and corrections officers and administrators. All look to trial outcomes as defining boundaries within which informal criminal justice operates; formal rules limit informal discretion, even if they do not wholly control it.

The criminal trial serves several formal purposes. It is a symbol of justice. If all goes as it should, a criminal trial shows that crime does not pay, that the innocent receive vindication, and that the criminal justice system effectively distributes justice. Unpopular trial outcomes can teach the opposite. The trial then becomes a negative symbol, proof that the wicked prevail, that crime pays, and that power, privilege, and clever lawyers can determine who gets convicted and who goes free. Such unfavorable lessons lead to contempt for criminal justice institutions and processes. For good or ill, the trial teaches a public, visible, and potent lesson about the integrity, fairness, and effectiveness of the criminal justice process.

Criminal trials are elaborate fact-finding proceedings. According to strict rules, they ferret out the facts that prove legal guilt. **Legal guilt** means guilt that the government has proved beyond a reasonable doubt by evidence admissible according to the Constitution (see Chapter 6). Although police investigation and plea negotiations informally establish **factual guilt,** that is, that the defendant has committed a crime, and the predominance of guilty pleas removes the need for trials in most cases, the criminal trial remains the most visible means to prove legal guilt. Criminal trials assure that fact finding proceeds fairly and according to due process of law. Rules governing changes of venue, jury selection, obtaining and presenting evidence, speedy trial, and proof beyond a reasonable doubt attempt to assure accurate fact finding regarding legal guilt.

Trials influence actions in the vast majority of cases that never reach the trial stage. Expectations about what a judge and jury might do shape police decisions to arrest, prosecutorial decisions to charge, defense counsel willingness to negotiate, and defendants' decisions to plead guilty. These agents base their expectations and predictions on what judges and juries have done in cases that have gone to trial. Police, prosecutors, and judges are all aware that "juries do not merely determine the outcome of the cases they hear; their decisions profoundly influence the 90 to 95 percent of cases that are settled through informal means." Juries can become popular representatives in the "halls of justice," guarding against undue, improper, and vindictive government action. Leading jury experts have called this the "halo effect."[1]

Jury Trial

The **jury trial** is an ancient proceeding. In the Magna Carta of 1215, King John promised that "no free man shall be taken or imprisoned or in any way destroyed except by the lawful judgment of his peers." The Sixth Amendment to the United States Constitution provides that defendants "in all criminal prosecutions" have the right to trial "by an impartial jury of the State and district" where the crime was committed. In *Duncan v. Louisiana,* the U.S. Supreme Court ruled that the due process clause of the Fourteenth Amendment requires the states to provide a jury trial in criminal prosecutions.[2]

Trials decide two major types of questions:

- Questions of law.
- Questions of fact.

According to the law, juries decide the facts and judges decide the law in jury trials. The questions of fact, mainly including the testimony of witnesses and physical evidence, all have to do with proof of guilt beyond a reasonable doubt. It is the duty of the jury to decide whether the government has proved its case by weighing both the quantity and the truth of the testimony and other evidence presented. Judges decide the legal questions, including the rules of evidence, the rules of procedure, and the definition of crimes. Not all criminal trials are jury trials. **Bench trials** are trials without juries in which judges decide both the legal and the fact questions.

The right to a jury trial does not guarantee the right to a jury of 12 members. In *Williams v. Florida,* the Supreme Court held that six-member juries did not violate the Sixth Amendment. According to the Court, the Sixth Amendment aims to assure accurate, independent fact finding by preventing government oppression. Six-member juries, the Court concluded, do not materially impair jury effectiveness. Not everyone agrees. Studies have shown that six-member juries are less reliable, do not save time, and are less likely to represent a cross section of the community.[3]

The Supreme Court has also declared that the right to jury trial does not include the right to a unanimous verdict. The Court has decided, for example, that neither 11-to-1 nor 10-to-2 votes to convict in felony cases violate the Sixth Amendment. The reason, according to the Court in *Apodaca v. Oregon:* the commonsense judgment of peers does not depend on whether all jurors agree to convict. The jury has served its purpose in guarding against unfair government prosecution even in less-than-unanimous votes:

> [The court could] perceive no difference between juries required to act unanimously and those permitted to convict by votes of 10-to-2 or 11-to-1. [In] either case, the interest of the defendant in having the judgment of his peers interposed between himself and the officers of the state who prosecute and judge him is equally well served.[4]

In a companion case, *Johnson v. Louisiana,* the Court rejected the argument that proof beyond a reasonable doubt required a unanimous verdict; it decided that a 9-to-3 guilty verdict in a robbery case complied with the right to an impartial jury:

> Nine jurors—a substantial majority of the jury—were convinced by the evidence. Disagreement of the three jurors does not alone establish reasonable doubt, particularly when such a heavy majority of the jury, after having considered the dissenters' views, remains convinced of guilt.[5]

Critics of the *Apodaca* and *Johnson* decisions argue that unanimity instills confidence in the system, assures participants' careful deliberation, and guarantees the hearing of minority viewpoints. Furthermore, unanimity prevents government oppression and supports the established legal preference for freeing 100 guilty persons rather than convicting one innocent individual. Finally, unanimity comports better with the requirement that criminal conviction rest on proof beyond a reasonable doubt.[6]

The Political Nature of Juries

The law and constitutional framework of the jury do not explain how the jury actually operates. The nineteenth-century French commentator on American government, Alexis de Tocqueville, wrote that "the jury is, above all, a political institution, and it must be regarded in this light in order to be understood." De Tocqueville's observation is no less true today than it was more than 150 years ago. Jurors try hard to make their decisions based entirely on the facts and their rational assessment of them. In clear-cut cases where the evidence and arguments of lawyers lead only to one result—either guilty or not guilty—this is probably what they do. But in cases that can go either way, extralegal influences enter the jury room and impinge on jurors' deliberations and decisions.[7]

Research has shown that jurors try hard to get at the truth. "I just stuck to the facts," most say when asked how they decided. And they are not lying. Their reliance on extralegal considerations is subconscious. Jurors operate according to a **liberation hypothesis,** say Harry Kalven and Hans Zeisel in their classic study of the jury. According to Kalven and Zeisel, determining the truth and making value judgments are intertwined. In close cases, the jurors' value judgments unconsciously affect their finding of the facts. In all cases, but particularly in close cases, the facts are ambiguous, lending themselves to a number of interpretations. The trial process heightens the possibility of reading the facts in at least two starkly contrasting ways. The prosecution argues forcefully for the interpretation that supports conviction; defense counsel argues equally strongly for that which supports acquittal. The ambiguities in the evidence, the adversary process, and the closeness of the case "liberate" jurors to decide cases according to their own values. They resolve doubts in favor of their sentiments.[8]

Personal prejudice may determine the sentiments of jurors. But most frequently their sentiments reflect the values of their community, which they represent in the jury room. These values range across a broad spectrum, including

- Conservative and liberal views concerning the crime problem and the value of punishment.
- Values and positions regarding gender, race, and ethnicity.
- Conflicts in moral standards.
- Beliefs about law and social problems such as self-defense, euthanasia, police power, drug use, the homeless, and the environment.[9]

The verdicts in cases involving the use of force by the police reflect the influence of community values. In communities with strong sentiments about law and order, jurors rarely convict the police on charges of police brutality. The Southern California community of Simi Valley, where police officers were tried for using force against Rodney King, is one of these. The jury, despite what looked like a clear case of excessive force to some who watched the videotape of the incident, acquitted the officers. They accepted the argument that the police are a "thin blue line" between respectable citizens and violence and disorder. Unpleasant as the use of force was, the police were using it to protect law-abiding citizens from criminals.

In other communities, the use of force by police looks different. In the Bronx, where juries are more than 80 percent African American and Hispanic, juries acquit African-American defendants 47.6 percent of the time, nearly three times the national rate of acquittal. This is true even though most crime victims are also African American and Hispanic. In one case, Larry Davis, alleged major drug dealer and multiple murderer, was acquitted twice during a time when he was the most wanted fugitive in New York City. Davis's case and others like it led a Bronx prosecutor to comment, "It's bizarre. Everything here is truly stood on its head. The jurors are overwhelmingly suspicious of cops. If you have a case involving cops, you are almost certain to lose." The case produced an article entitled, "Bronx Juries: A Defense Dream, a Prosecutor's Nightmare."[10]

The acquittal of O. J. Simpson raised a spate of commentary about race influencing the decisions of juries. Commentators argue that the evidence, far more than race, determines verdicts. Jury watchers say otherwise. According to Benjamin A. Holden, Laurie P. Cohen, and Eleena de Lisser, "race plays a far more significant role in jury verdicts than many people involved in the justice system prefer to acknowledge." Race-based verdicts, of course, are not by any means limited to African-American juries deciding in favor of African-American defendants. All-white juries in the South for centuries convicted African Americans accused of committing crimes against whites no matter what the evidence, while whites who raped and killed African Americans were acquitted. In death penalty cases, whites acquit white defendants accused of killing African Americans more often than they acquit African Americans accused of killing whites.[11] (See Chapter 11.)

Jury nullification, the power of juries to ignore the formal law and decide cases according to informal extralegal considerations, "fits neatly into a tradition of political activism by U.S. juries," and enjoys a long heritage in both English and United States history. William Penn benefitted from nullification in 1670 when an English jury acquitted him for following his conscience in practicing his Quaker beliefs, a crime under English law. During colonial times, John Peter Zenger also violated the law by publishing material that criticized the British government. Zenger's lawyer told the jury they had the right "beyond all dispute to determine the law and the fact[s]." The jury followed his suggestion and acquitted Zenger.[12] Paul Butler, a professor of criminal law who is studying jury activism among African Americans, maintains that African-American jurors should "presume in favor of nullification." According to Professor Butler:

> Jury nullification is power that black people have right now and not something that Congress has to give them. Black people have a community that needs building, and children who need rescuing, and as long as a person will not hurt anyone, the community needs him there to help.[13]

Critics maintain that juries disregarding the law by acquitting defendants guilty beyond a reasonable doubt sets a bad example; it breeds lawlessness in society generally. Ahmet Hisim, an assistant state's attorney in Baltimore says, "It's terrible and sad that juries will base their opinions on race bias rather than facts. . . ." Nevertheless, the courts have sustained jury nullification, upholding acquittals in criminal cases against all attack. Juries have an absolute right to acquit; neither the government nor defendants can appeal against it. Evidence suggests that juries exercise this power, particularly if they know about and understand it. Irwin Horowitz studied the effects of juror knowledge of nullification on 144 prospective jurors. He found that when juries received full nullification information from a judge or defense attorney, they were more likely to acquit a sympathetic defendant; when they did not receive the information, they were likely to judge a dangerous defendant more harshly. Knowledge of nullification definitely reduced the value of formally presented evidence and increased the discretionary power of juries.[14]

Jury Selection

The extent to which juries represent community values and sentiments depends on the selection process. The Sixth Amendment guarantees trial by an impartial jury. The Federal Jury Selection and Service Act of 1968 requires that jurors be selected at random, from a "fair cross section of the community," and from the district where the court convenes. It also prohibits exclusion from jury service based on race, color, religion, sex, national origin, or economic status. Most states have followed this general outline in assuring an impartial criminal trial jury.[15]

Implementing jury selection requirements varies from jurisdiction to jurisdiction. To fulfill the random selection requirement, jurisdictions can compile a master roll of names using voter registration lists, actual voter lists, tax rolls, telephone directories, or even lists of driver's license registrations. Lists made up from these sources disqualify minors, people unable to speak or write English, convicted felons, and recent residents. Poor health, old age, hardship, and distance also excuse citizens from jury duty. Members of some occupations, such as doctors, government workers, and members of the armed forces, do not appear on jury lists; the law in most jurisdictions exempts them from jury duty.[16]

Martin A. Levin has argued that jurors cannot represent a cross section of the community because they are drawn from unrepresentative lists, and because attorneys can remove prospective jurors by peremptory challenge. Multiple prospect lists, including voters, public utility customers, driver's licenses, telephone directories, and tax rolls, would produce more representative jurors.[17]

The jury panel, the names left after removing those excused and exempted, provides the basis for the **voir dire** (examination of prospective jurors by judge and lawyers) and subsequent selection of the actual jury. The *voir dire* gives prosecutors and defense counsel the means to impanel jurors whom they find suitable and to exclude those whom they consider undesirable. They can remove jurors either by challenge for cause or peremptory challenge. In the **challenge for cause,** both prosecution and defense can object to as many prospective jurors as they like, as long as they can demonstrate

Jurors are supposed to represent a "cross section of the community."

prejudice to the judge's satisfaction, such as women in rape cases, bar owners in drunk-driving cases, and white men in a black gang-rape case. Prosecution and defense also have a specified number of **peremptory challenges,** in which they may remove prospective jurors without cause or explanation. Peremptory challenge is an old practice; even in Elizabethan England, at one time defendants could peremptorily remove 35 prospective jurors.[18]

The jury selection process has given rise to a great deal of litigation. Two questions dominate this litigation:

1. Is the jury a randomly selected, fair cross section of the community?
2. Alternatively, have particular groups been systematically or intentionally excluded from jury panels and juries?

The Supreme Court has ruled that "selection of a petit jury from a representative cross section of the community is an essential component of the Sixth Amendment right to a jury trial." However, the Court also made clear that impartiality does not require that juries "mirror the community and reflect the various distinct groups in the population." For example, a jury need not contain 8 percent Hispanics simply because the community has an 8 percent Hispanic population. The Constitution, according to the Court, bars the intentional or systematic exclusion of recognized racial groups or genders from a chance to participate; it does not require that they actually sit on juries. Defendants have no constitutional right to have poor people, rich people, African Americans, Caucasians, young people, baby-boomers, or old people represented on the jury.[19]

Fair Trial

Fair trials require an atmosphere that does not prejudice the jury against defendants. In a notorious case, the State of Ohio tried Dr. Sam Sheppard for brutally murdering his socialite wife. The newspapers were filled with "evidence" (actually rumors) about Sheppard's "guilt," nearly all editorials were against him, and reporters even disrupted the trial proceedings in their efforts to scoop "sensational" stories. Although the jury convicted him, the U.S. Supreme Court ruled that Sheppard could not receive a fair trial in such a "carnival atmosphere."[20]

Trial judges bear the primary responsibility for assuring defendants fair trials. They may grant motions for **change of venue,** the transfer of a trial to a new location. Judges can also **sequester the jury** to ensure fairness. When judges order sequestration, they isolate jurors from the public so that they cannot receive news about the trial from outside the courtroom. Generally, juries are sequestered in hotels where they cannot read newspapers, watch television, or otherwise receive news about the trial. Sequestration occurs only in sensational trials that receive a lot of public attention and reporting in newspapers and on television and radio.[21]

Trial judges can also restrict trial publicity by curtailing news reports, limiting what lawyers can say to the press, and barring reporters from the courtroom. These restrictions on publicity all raise questions concerning the First Amendment guarantee of free press. Most press restrictions are permissible only when trial publicity seriously jeopardizes chances for a fair trial.

Finally, judges have wide discretion to control courtroom behavior. They can remove "unruly" spectators and "troublesome" members of the press if their behavior interferes with the decorum of the courtroom. Judges have less freedom to deal with disruptive defendants, because the Sixth Amendment guarantees defendants the right to be present at their own trials. Nevertheless, judges can remove defendants who make it impossible to proceed. Short of removal, judges have ordered bailiffs to gag and bind unruly defendants in order to assure orderly proceedings.[22]

Proving Guilt

The criminal trial constitutes a highly formal mechanism to determine guilt. The prosecution follows a set procedure to present physical evidence, such as murder weapons and blood-stained clothing; to examine and cross-examine witnesses; to argue cases to the jury (or judge in a bench trial, a trial without a jury); and to rebut the opposition's arguments. The formal purpose of this highly popularized sparring is to determine the legal guilt of the accused according to a long-entrenched standard, **proof beyond a reasonable doubt.** In criminal cases, prosecutors must prove guilt to the degree that it is completely consistent with the guilt of the defendant and inconsistent with any other plausible conclusion. All evidence the state presents serves that purpose, or at least formally is supposed to serve it. The state must find, arrange, present, and support the case against defendants. The defense has no obligation to aid the state in its case. Defendants, in other words, do not need to prove their innocence. They are, to use the well-worn phrase, innocent until proven guilty. Therefore, the defense role in criminal trials is essentially negative: to cast doubt on the prosecution's case, not to create a case on its own.[23]

According to the Supreme Court in the landmark case *In re Winship,* the Constitution requires the reasonable doubt standard. The standard's role in "the American scheme of criminal procedure" is "vital" because it reduces the risk of mistakenly convicting innocent people. The Court decided that criminal defendants have at risk such vital interests—loss of property, liberty, and sometimes life, as well as the stigma attached to conviction—that reasonable doubt about guilt should prevent such consequences from befalling a citizen in a free society. Placing a heavy burden on the prosecution, it is believed, reduces the margin of error in criminal convictions. The reasonable doubt standard also "command[s] the respect and confidence of the community in applications of the criminal law." A lesser standard of proof reduces the law's moral force and leaves citizens uncertain about the capacity of courts to condemn guilty and vindicate innocent people.[24]

In trying to help jurors come to a decision, courts have struggled to define proof beyond a reasonable doubt. Here are some common definitions, extracted from the cases:

- A doubt of about 7 1/2 on a scale of 10.
- A doubt that would cause prudent persons to hesitate before acting in a matter of importance to themselves.
- A doubt based on reason and common sense.
- Not frivolous or fanciful doubt.
- Substantial doubt.
- Persuasion to a moral certainty.[25]

The *You Decide* "Was There Reasonable Doubt" applies the reasonable doubt standard to a case of possession of cocaine with the intent to distribute.

You Decide   Was There Reasonable Doubt?

State v. Dewitt, 611 A.2D 926 (1993)
A Connecticut statute provides that:

. . . [A]ny person who manufactures, distributes, sells, prescribes, dispenses, compounds, transports with the intent to sell or dispense, possesses with the intent to sell or dispense, offers, gives or administers to another person any controlled substance which is a hallucinogenic substance other than marihuana, or a narcotic substance, except as authorized in this chapter, for a first offense, shall be imprisoned not more than fifteen years and may be fined not more than fifty thousand dollars or be both fined and imprisoned; and for a second offense shall be imprisoned not more than thirty years and may be fined not more than one hundred thousand dollars, or be both fined and imprisoned; and for each subsequent offense, shall be imprisoned not more than thirty years and may be fined not more than two hundred fifty thousand dollars, or be both fined and imprisoned. . . .

The following has been extracted from the opinion and decision of the court in *State v. DeWitt*.

Facts

On September 13, 1988, at about 8:45 P.M., Officers Nicholas Ortiz and John Losak of the Bridgeport Police Department were assigned to conduct a narcotics investigation at Father Panik Village, building 13. They drove into the courtyard between buildings 9 and 13 in an unmarked police car and parked near a dumpster. The well-lighted area was known for high narcotics trafficking, especially cocaine and crack. The officers observed the defendant standing about four feet from them in the courtyard between concrete traffic barriers and the dumpster. There were other individuals in the area who left when the uniformed officers exited the car. The defendant had not been observed approaching anyone or conducting any transactions.

The defendant saw the officers and placed a clear plastic bag containing several red objects in his mouth. Ortiz testified that narcotics are often placed in plastic sandwich bags and that street level dealers place the bags in their mouths hoping that the police will not see the drugs. The defendant turned his back on the officers just before he was seized. They removed the bag from his mouth and found it to contain forty-four plastic vials with red caps. A field test indicated that a white substance in the vials was cocaine. No significant amount of money was seized from the defendant.

Ortiz indicated that each of the vials of cocaine would be worth $5 and would allow a user to be high for fifteen to twenty minutes. Ortiz testified that a typical buyer would purchase between one and five vials at a time. Losak testified that buyers typically purchased one or two vials at a time, but he had arrested buyers who had purchased five to ten vials at once. A state toxicologist testified that each vial tested contained between 42.9 and 58.6 milligrams of cocaine that was 82.2 to 86.9 percent pure. This, he said, was typical of crack cocaine seized in the Bridgeport area. The defendant testified that the forty four vials of cocaine were for his and a friend's use and that he had no intention of selling them.

Opinion

The defendant claims that the evidence presented by the state prior to his motion for a judgment of acquittal was insufficient to sustain a conviction on the charge of possession with intent to sell narcotics because the state failed to prove his intent to sell. The defendant's argument is that the forty-four vials found in his possession do not allow an inference of his intent to sell, but rather would allow an inference that he intended the vials for

personal use. He argues, therefore, that the trial court should have granted his motion for acquittal. We disagree.

We ascertain whether a jury could REASONABLY have concluded that the cumulative effect of the established evidence, and the inferences REASONABLY drawn from those evidentiary FACTS, established guilt BEYOND a REASONABLE DOUBT. Where a group of FACTS are relied upon for PROOF of an element of the crime it is their cumulative impact that is to be weighed in deciding whether the standard of PROOF BEYOND a REASONABLE DOUBT has been met and each individual FACT need not be proved in accordance with that standard. Thus, each essential element of the crime must be proven beyond a reasonable doubt; and a jury may not speculate or resort to conjecture but may draw only reasonable, logical inferences from the proven facts.

This case is similar to *State v. Napoleon*, 530 A.2d 634, 532 A.2d 78 (1987). In *Napoleon*, the defendant was standing with a group of men rolling a marihuana cigarette when police officers approached. He threw a bag into a nearby automobile and attempted to leave. The bag was found to contain four manila envelopes of marihuana and four glassine bags of cocaine. The defendant had fifteen foil packets and four more glassine bags containing cocaine and heroin on his person. This court upheld the conviction of possession of narcotics with intent to sell, stating that evidence of the location of the defendant in an area known for drug trafficking, the packaging of the narcotics in a manner commonly used for retail sale, and the quantity of the narcotics was sufficient to support the verdict.

In this case, Ortiz and Losak testified that the defendant was standing in an area known for high narcotics trafficking, that he was in possession of a large quantity of narcotics packaged in a manner used by street dealers, and that, when police officers approached, he hid the narcotics in his mouth in a manner used by street level dealers. On the basis of the officers' testimony about quantities purchased by typical buyers, the jury could have concluded reasonably that the amount possessed by the defendant was not intended for his personal use. A trier of fact could have concluded reasonably at the close of the state's case, without any consideration of the defendant's evidence, that the state had proven beyond a reasonable doubt that the defendant possessed narcotics with an intent to sell them. The trial court, therefore, properly denied the defendant's motion for a judgment of acquittal.

The judgment is affirmed.

Questions

Suppose you are on the jury in this case. Did the prosecution prove its case "beyond a reasonable doubt"? If so, define proof beyond a reasonable doubt and list the facts in this case proving that the defendant possessed cocaine with the intent to sell it. If not, explain what a reasonable doubt is, and explain why you have a reasonable doubt that DeWitt possessed the cocaine with the intent to sell it.

Opening Statements

Opening statements allow both prosecution and defense to present juries with their respective overviews of the case. The lawyers make their opening

In the opening statements, lawyers for both prosecution and defense lay out their theories of the case.

subpoena *order of a court commanding that witnesses appear in court to present relevant testimony.*

direct examination *first examination of a witness conducted by the side on whose behalf the witness was called.*

cross-examination *examination of a witness by the party opposed to the one who called the witness.*

statements after jury selection but before presenting any evidence. Although prosecutors present no evidence at this point, opening statements can impress juries with the nature and gravity of the charges against defendants. In introducing their case, prosecutors can enlighten juries about how the prosecution intends to develop its case. This helps juries to make more sense of testimony and physical evidence that do not always appear in logical order. Juries also have less tendency to become bored, frustrated, and irritated if they can follow the case. Finally, opening statements allow prosecutors to persuade juries. Lawyers have only two opportunities to address the jury directly without interruption: during the opening statements and closing arguments.

Calling and Examining Witnesses

In the adversary system, lawyers determine which witnesses to call. Both defense and prosecution have broad powers to **subpoena,** meaning to command witnesses by court order to appear in court to present relevant testimony. Ordinary witnesses receive travel money and a small daily fee that, incidentally, rarely compensates them for time lost from work. Expert witnesses, such as fingerprint specialists and psychiatrists, receive full compensation for their court time. Although broad, the subpoena power cannot violate either the Fifth Amendment protection against self-incrimination or a range of privileged relationships, such as lawyer-client, doctor-patient, and sometimes husband-wife.

The prosecution calls government witnesses first. After the prosecution has completed its case, the defense calls its witnesses. First, the side who called the witness conducts the **direct examination.** Following the direct examination, the lawyer on the other side conducts the **cross-examination** of the witness. Occasionally, re-direct and re-cross-examination follow. The manner of questioning differs in direct and cross-examination. A proper direct examination question is, "Where were you on October 8 at about 8:00 P.M.?" In direct examination, lawyers cannot ask leading questions, questions that steer witnesses to desired answers. For example, they cannot ask the defendant, "You were at the victim's house on October 8, at about 8:00 P.M., weren't you?" **Leading questions,** that is, questions that essentially tell the witness how to answer, are proper and typical in cross-examination. Witness answers in direct examination require narration, sometimes in considerable length. Yes or no answers typically suffice in cross-examination.

Direct and cross-examination questioning differ for two main reasons. First, unless they are **hostile witnesses** (defense witnesses favorable to the prosecution and prosecution witnesses favorable to the defense), witnesses favor the side that called them. Witnesses usually give answers damaging to the other side, and opposition lawyers have not had the opportunity to learn what these witnesses will say. Second, direct witnesses have discussed what they know with the lawyer who calls them to testify.

George P. Fletcher, professor of criminal law at Columbia University and a respected writer on criminal law, attended the trial of Bernhard Goetz, who pleaded self-defense to a charge of attempted murder for shooting four youths in a New York subway (see *You Decide* in Chapter 3). In his book about the Goetz trial, Fletcher observes that

> lawyers at trial are directors as well as performers in presenting their client's version of the truth. They make theatrical decisions about the order in which to present their witnesses, they coach them like directors in rehearsal, and they lead their witnesses gently through their parts. Their presentation of the truth reflects art and rhetoric as well as rational argument.
>
> Their role [in direct examination] stops short of prompting their witnesses when they do not perform as expected. Prompting falls under the ban against asking "leading questions." A lawyer disappointed in his witness may not try to put words in his mouth. He cannot ask (assuming that the witness would be prepared to answer "yes"), "Isn't it true that you saw the gunman smiling as he was shooting?" He must try to elicit this testimony without giving away the script.
>
> But when they turn into critics on cross-examination, lawyers can ask all the leading questions they want and insist, often contemptuously, that the witness answer "yes" or "no."[26]

Fletcher describes defense attorney Barry Slotnick's skill in leading witnesses in cross-examination. Slotnick wanted to establish that Goetz fired the shots against the youths in rapid succession, not pausing between shots:

> The tactic became clear on the cross-examination of. . . Victor Flores, who claimed actually to have seen Goetz fire at two of the youths as they were running toward him and away from Goetz. He heard four shots "one after another."
>
> On cross-examination, Slotnick took advantage of his legal option to restate Flores's testimony in his own language and ask Flores to answer "yes" or "no" whether that was his view of what happened. Thus he reformulated Flores's first statement about the pattern and rapidity of the shots by asking, "And the three shots or the four shots. . . that you hear in rapid succession after the first shot, were all going in your area, is that correct?" Having gained Flores's assent to the phrase "rapid succession," Slotnick began using the label over and over again in cross-examination. The jury heard Flores say "yes" to this description so often—five more times—that the words came to seem like his own.[27]

The case that Slotnick was eliciting on cross-examination became clear in a question that he put solely for the jury's benefit:

> So it is fair to say that as far as your witnessing what occurred, the fact that he might have walked over to a rear seat and shot somebody and said something to them, like "you don't look bad, here's another," something like that, that really never happened?[28]

Admission of Evidence

Evidence is either physical evidence, such as weapons, stolen property, and fingerprints, or testimonial, the words of witnesses. Admissible evidence must be:

- Relevant.
- Material.
- Nonprejudicial.
- Reliable.
- Legally obtained (see Chapter 6 on illegally obtained evidence).

Relevant evidence is evidence that relates to the elements of the crime. In robbery, for example, relevant evidence is evidence proving that the defendant, by force or the threat of force, took something of value from the victim. Relevant evidence that can prove these material elements is **material evidence** (sometimes called **probative evidence**). The court excludes evidence, even if relevant and material, if it unfairly prejudices defendants. For example, evidence that a defendant on trial for murder has committed previous assaults and other violent crimes, although clearly relevant and material because it shows the defendant is capable of committing violent crimes, can also lead the jury to conclude, perhaps erroneously, that the defendant has actually committed this murder simply because the defendant committed other violent crimes. The prejudice to the defendant outweighs the probative value of the evidence.

Courts also exclude **hearsay evidence,** information not directly known by the witness that is offered for its truth at trial, even if relevant, material, and not prejudicial to defendants. For example, a police officer who did not see a robbery gives hearsay evidence when she testifies that a bank teller told her the defendant entered the bank with a gun and ordered the teller to turn over all the money. Only the bank teller saw the robbery first-hand, and only the teller can testify in court. Juries cannot weigh hearsay as first-hand, and lawyers cannot cross-examine eyewitnesses; therein lies the unreliability of hearsay and the reason for its exclusion.

It is the responsibility of judges to determine the relevance, materiality, prejudice, and reliability of evidence, and they nearly always decide outside the hearing of the jury. Sometimes prosecutors, defense counsel, and judges meet in the judge's chambers to decide admissibility, but often they huddle around the bench, speaking in hushed voices so they cannot be heard discussing problematic physical evidence (such as pictures of mutilated murder victims or possibly illegally seized drugs) or lines of questioning (such as prior convictions).

Closing Arguments

The experienced prosecutor Steven Phillips explains the importance of the closing argument:

> It is one of the few arts left in which time is of no consequence. Standing before twelve people, a lawyer can be brief or lengthy—the choice is his own; there are no interruptions, and a captive audience. All that matters are those twelve people; they must be persuaded, or everything that has gone before is in vain. Summation is the one place where lawyers do make a difference; if an attorney can be said to "win" or "lose" a case, the chances are that he did so in his closing argument to the jury.[29]

Charging the Jury

Following the closing arguments, judges instruct, or "charge," the jury. **Jury instructions** explain to the jury the law governing the case. Judges begin by explaining the jury's role in the case: the court decides the law; the jury decides the facts. For example, in a murder trial, the judge explains the legal meaning of premeditation required for a first-degree murder conviction. The jury decides whether the facts prove beyond a reasonable doubt that the defendant premeditated the killing. Hence, the judge may instruct the jury that premeditation in this state means any lapse of time, however brief, between the intention to kill and the act of killing. Therefore, if you the jury find that the defendant killed the deceased even instantaneously following her intention to kill him, you may find the defendant guilty of premeditated murder.

The long, complex, and technical legal definitions and requirements found in judge's instructions often demand a great deal from juries:

> A judge's charge to the jury is an amazing exercise in optimism. For two or three hours he reads to twelve laymen enough law to keep a law student busy for a semester. Twelve individuals, selected more or less at random, sit there, unable to take notes or ask questions. Somehow, just by listening, it is presumed everything spoken by the judge will take root in their collective intelligence.[30]

Following the charge, the jury retires to a designated place to deliberate. They may ask for clarification in the instructions, further review of the evidence, and sometimes just rereading of some of the testimony. When they have reached their decision, all parties return to the courtroom for the familiar scene endlessly depicted on television and movie screens and described in written works. After the jury verdict, the most formal public event in criminal justice ends. Adjudication sometimes continues in criminal appeals, but the high drama of adjudication effectively ends with the jury verdict.

Summary of Disposition by Trial

Adjudication, formal judicial decision making, covers the period following defendants' first appearance to conviction or acquittal by jury or judge. Preliminary hearings, grand jury review, prosecutorial informations, or some combination of them test the government's case against defendants in order to determine whether to proceed to trial. Preliminary hearings screen by means of open, adversary proceedings with judges presiding. Grand jury review proceeds in secret, non-adversary proceedings in which the jury hears only the government's case and over which prosecutors preside. Prosecutors alone initially file informations, subject to later review by preliminary hearing. Grand jury review, the most ancient of the testing mechanisms, has declined in use; the preliminary hearing and information have become more common. Whatever the mechanism, the government must present probable cause, not proof beyond a reasonable doubt, of guilt; in other words, sufficient evidence to justify having a trial.

Cases passing this initial testing proceed to arraignment, in which defendants appear in open court to hear and plead to charges. Arraignment sets the stage for the most public formal criminal justice proceeding—the criminal trial. The criminal trial represents the symbolic high point of adjudication. Due process and adversary system values receive great attention in the trial. Criminal trials determine legal guilt. Trials proceed according to highly formalized rules. Prosecutors manage the government's case and must prove defendants guilty beyond a reasonable doubt. Defendants, shielded by the safeguards of the Constitution, need not do anything to help the government prove its case. Judges preside over trials, much as umpires oversee baseball games, making calls on the rules and warning against their violation. After prosecution and defense present their cases, juries (or judges where there is no jury) decide whether prosecutors have borne their heavy burden of proving defendants guilty beyond a reasonable doubt. The jury acquittal, even when proof beyond a reasonable doubt exists, stands against all challenges, ensuring that community values ultimately prevail in the determination of legal guilt.

Adjudication, with trial as its culminating high point, represents formal decision making. Few defendants, however, go to trial because many plead guilty or are dismissed. These pleas and dismissals represent outward formalities behind which lies informal, and until recently largely invisible, discretionary decision making, such as that discussed in the next section on plea bargaining. Formal and informal decision making sometimes conflict, but more often interact. Adjudication defines the boundaries of informal decisions made behind the scenes; informal negotiations determine the actual content of most dispositions in criminal cases.

Disposition by Guilty Plea

To the superficial observer, a courtroom is a dignified place for the solemn proceedings of public trials. The elevated bench for the judge, and the witness and jury boxes, dominate the room. Wood paneling, high ceilings, and the railing separating participants from spectators further bespeak decorum and formality. The trial of criminal defendants, however, is not what actually takes place in most courtrooms most of the time. First appearances of defendants, pretrial hearings, and conferences among judges, prosecutors, and defense attorneys—not trials—are the most common activities in criminal courtrooms. "First-appearance court" or "guilty-plea court" are more accurate descriptions than trial courts. For all their dramatic symbolism and despite their indirect influence on the decisions of police, defense, and prosecutors, criminal trials are rare events. A tiny minority of persons, charged mainly with murder, rape, and armed robbery, go to trial. The vast majority of defendants plead guilty before trial. The numbers of guilty pleas, or informal dispositions, as with most other decisions in criminal justice, vary from a minority of dispositions in some jurisdictions to virtually all in others. For example, in New York City, 97.5 percent of felony defendants plead guilty, while in Philadelphia, only 26 percent do so. Even more misdemeanor defendants plead guilty. In New Haven, Connecticut, not one trial took place out of 1,640 cases filed in the lower criminal courts![31]

Scholars have known for a long time that only a few criminal trials take place and that informal guilty pleas dispose of most criminal cases. As early as the sixteenth century, criminal court records in England show that an overwhelming number of criminal defendants pleaded guilty. In more modern times, a survey of the criminal process in early twentieth-century Cleveland, Ohio, showed that guilty pleas disposed of half the felony cases scheduled for criminal court. It was not until the 1960s, however, that the guilty plea acquired widespread attention and became subject to careful scrutiny and considerable criticism.[32]

Why do so many defendants plead guilty? Some claim that the plethora of rights given criminal defendants and the adversary system that places a premium on argument and procedure cannot deal with the great numbers of criminal cases. Others point to the lack of resources to hire judges and other staff to manage criminal trials. Others focus on rising crime rates that have placed too heavy a burden on criminal courts. Some researchers of formal organizations and many judges and lawyers argue that efficiency and economy demand disposition by guilty plea. Others interpret guilty pleas as the inevitable outcome of the courtroom work group's desire for harmony and the natural human desire for predictability. Some maintain that the costs of pleading not guilty are too high in time, money, and the risk of longer sentences or higher fines. Others maintain that guilty pleas, especially in large urban areas, are part of a system of imposing discipline on "dangerous"

historical note

The records of this office show that in the representation of clients, a greater percentage of pleas of "Guilty" are entered than those of "Not Guilty."

Ernest R. Orfila, 1928

straight pleas *pleas of guilty without negotiation.*

negotiated pleas *guilty pleas in exchange for concessions from the government.*

dead-bang cases *cases in which a guilty verdict is virtually certain.*

lower-class people. Some combination of all these reasons explains the prevalence of the guilty plea. Whatever the reasons, the guilty plea emphasizes the significance of informal decision making in the disposition of criminal cases.[33]

Straight Pleas

Guilty pleas are not all alike. Some guilty pleas, called **straight pleas,** do not result from negotiations. Some defendants want to plead guilty, or at least their lawyers want them to do so. **Negotiated pleas,** or the "copped" pleas of ill repute, do involve bargaining and trade-offs. Research has not yet revealed how many defendants enter straight guilty pleas, although available information suggests large numbers. According to Michael L. Rubenstein, Steven Clarke, and Theresa Wright, who analyzed court documents and interviewed judges, prosecutors, and defense attorneys in Alaska, "most defendants ple[a]d guilty even when the state offer[s] them nothing in exchange for their cooperation." After examining several jurisdictions, political scientist Milton Heumann concluded, "Most court personnel (regardless of ideological persuasion) will readily admit that in many cases there are simply no contestable factual or legal issues." Barbara Boland and Brian Forst estimate that "the majority of pleas in the United States may involve no negotiation at all." Perhaps defendants plead guilty because they know they are guilty, or because they believe that a trial would be hopeless or, worse, might lead to harsher punishment. (See the *You Decide* entitled "Can an Innocent Defendant Plead Guilty?" later in this chapter.)[34]

Rubenstein, Clarke, and Wright obtained data from police, jail, and court records. They interviewed every judge, prosecutor, and criminal defense attorney in Anchorage, Fairbanks, and Juneau to determine the effects of a ban on plea bargaining in Alaska. They asked why defendants give up their right to jury trial without getting concessions in return. The quotes in this and other sections draw on their study typify the group interviewed. One experienced defense lawyer gave the following representative answer:

> Well, where you've got a nineteen-year-old kid who's ripped off somebody else's stereo and he confessed to it, what do you gain from going to trial? You can go to jury trial and your client gets on the stand and says, "I didn't do it," and you say, "Well, you confessed to it, and we found the stereo in your house." You know what's going to happen then? I mean, your client is either going to have to perjure himself, or he's not going to take the stand. And, if he doesn't take the stand, and if it takes you four days to try the case, you have nothing to argue at the end. The judge is going to say, "What happened here? Why did you waste thousands of dollars putting us all through this?" You know, they're going to pay a price for this—it's only natural.[35]

Dead-bang cases, cases of virtually certain conviction, most often lead to straight pleas, but so do cases involving particularly gory evidence or sympathetic victims. Defendants fare worse in trials where judges and juries listen and see the evidence and witnesses for several hours or days. Some defendants plead guilty without a bargain because their lawyers believe putting up a fight will ruin a "previous posture of compliance and cooperation."[36]

> Now if the guy is a "boy scout" [said one defense lawyer] I might advise him to enter a guilty plea. Keep the image consistent that way. Take this guy charged with a first-offense burglary in a dwelling. He confessed when he was arrested and he helped the cops retrieve the property. He had no real defenses. If he had exercised all his constitutional rights it would have hurt him. He'd have gone to jail. I could advise him that if he continued in the cooperative mode in which he had already begun

when I started representing him he'd have the best chances of probation. He got straight probation and a suspended imposition of sentence. He could never have gotten that disposition if he had exercised his constitutional rights.[37]

Straight pleas do not always originate for such noble reasons. Defense attorneys admit that occasionally the advantages from guilty pleas accrue not to their clients, but to themselves. Some guilty pleas help lawyers "avoid the three or four grueling courtroom days usually required for a felony trial, not to mention more time spent in pretrial preparation." As one assistant public defender put it:

> You really have to watch yourself if you have three or four trials scheduled over the next month, and you are picking up new cases. If a case looks bad you may automatically say, "Well, that person is going to plead guilty." There is only so much you can take. As a defense attorney you have a wide range of rationalizations for not going to trial. The defense attorney does not misrepresent, so much as he comes up with rationalizations why clients shouldn't go to trial. And it isn't difficult to do this in any given case.[38]

Sometimes a lawyer will advise a client to plead guilty because of the only too human reluctance to appear foolish in public:

> Fear of embarrassment was one of the big things that I have had to get over as a trial attorney [one defense lawyer admitted candidly]. Some cases are just embarrassing.[39]

Another lawyer said:

> You know, that's got to be the toughest thing, when you just don't have very much to argue at all, and you're sitting through a trial just searching for something to say at the end of the case. There are a lot of attorneys that wouldn't subject themselves to that, who would rationalize that their clients would gain something by entering their pleas.[40]

Defense attorneys also believe—and empirical findings support their belief—that insisting on a trial results in harsher penalties. In the words of one assistant public defender:

> In violent crimes the judge sees the victim and hears the whole ugly story. Naturally he's going to give a tougher sentence. In fraud cases the judge has a chance to sit and think, "Boy, this guy really premeditated this fraud; he's too slick to trust."[41]

One judge bluntly and without apology revealed:

> The defendant played the odds; they went against him. He played and he declined to plead. He put the state to the burden of proof, and the state won. There is nothing wrong with [giving him a harsher sentence for losing the gamble].[42]

Finally, going to trial is expensive. Those who can afford a lawyer can measure that cost in dollars. According to one defense attorney, private lawyers "simply have to inform their client how much it will cost them to pursue their claim of innocence at trial. This causes a lot of defendants to sober up." Not even indigent defendants wish to draw out their cases for months. They want to get the case over with as soon as possible for the perfectly understandable reason that it makes life easier.[43]

Negotiated Pleas

In negotiated pleas, defendants plead guilty in exchange for concessions from the government. Straight pleas and plea bargains stem from similar self-serving motives. Defendants plead guilty because they—or their lawyers—want to save time, money, hassle, embarrassment, defeat, and harsher penalties. Plea bargaining describes a variety of actions. Broadly defined, it comprises "every form of discussion between the prosecution and defense" that might lead to disposition without a trial. These discussions might take place as early as arrest or as late as sentencing. According to this definition, prosecutors engage in plea bargaining when they grant immunity to defendants in order to secure testimony against accomplices. Such offers might well result from negotiation, but they are not *plea* bargaining. Defendants granted immunity before being charged haven't really plea bargained, because without a charge there is no plea over which to bargain.[44]

More accurately, plea bargaining refers only to guilty pleas in exchange for concessions made by the government. In **express bargaining,** prosecutors, defendants, defense lawyers, and sometimes trial judges meet face-to-face to work out specific concessions. Express or explicit bargaining prevails in most jurisdictions. Implicit bargaining involves no direct meetings. Instead, local practice, sometimes called the **going rate for guilty pleas,** determines concessions. According to Milton Heumann, the going rates vary from one community to another, and are

> products of the individual courthouse and community, and are not primarily shaped by state or national considerations. In one jurisdiction an armed robber may receive eight years after a trial and five years if he pleads; in another, the comparable figures may be seven and four, or ten and eight, and so on.[45]

In **implicit bargaining,** defense attorneys can fairly assume that if their clients plead guilty to "normal" crimes, they will receive concessions in line with the going rate. According to one Detroit judge familiar with the practice, "The system operates in terms of defense attorney and defendants' expectations—what is widely known as a rate. It's an expectation model."[46]

Implicit bargaining should not mean unclear consequences. The consequences are, says Heumann,

> usually made very explicit! That is, defendants are told clearly by someone—usually their lawyers, but sometimes by judges, prosecutors, police officers, or others—that they had better plead guilty or they will be punished more severely if they go to trial.[47]

Concessions in negotiations usually take three forms. In **charge bargaining,** prosecutors drop some charges and/or file charges less serious than the facts justify in exchange for defendants' guilty pleas. For example, a defendant who has committed a first-degree murder carrying a mandatory life term might plead guilty to second-degree murder with a term of 20 years to life. The plea to second-degree murder gives the judge discretion to sentence the defendant to less than life imprisonment. In **sentence bargaining,** pleading guilty "on the nose," defendants plead guilty to charges actually warranted by the facts in the case, but with the understanding that the judge will grant, or at least the prosecutor will request, a lenient sentence, such as probation. In **slow pleas,** defendants go to trial, but the trial is short and superficial. The government and defense agree to set aside the rules of evidence, and they stipulate, or agree, not to argue over guilt; conviction becomes a foregone conclusion.[48]

Plea bargaining varies from community to community. **Local legal culture** (attitudes, values, and expectations regarding law and the legal system) determines whether charge bargaining, sentence bargaining, or slow pleas predominate. History and tradition contribute to that culture. In Detroit, for example, sentence bargaining rarely takes place; charge bargaining predominates because the courts historically have prohibited prosecutors from participating in sentencing. In Washington, D.C., sentence bargaining predominates. There, the prosecution historically has had to address the court in order to make a "pitch" for a particular sentence. In Los Angeles, slow pleas have enjoyed a long tradition.[49]

Public opinion also shapes local legal culture. Plea bargaining disposes of run-of-the-mill cases, cases that do not attract public attention. In highly visible, sensational cases generating great public interest, trials occur more frequently. Research suggests that public opinion favors trial over bargaining in such spectacular cases, and that prosecutors and courts follow that opinion. The distinguished former U.S. Attorney General Edward Levi recommended the following to U.S. attorneys:

> [Consider] what the public attitude is toward prosecution under the circumstances of the case. There may be situations where the public interest might be better served by having the case tried rather than by being disposed of by means of a guilty plea—including situations in which it is particularly important to permit a clear public understanding that "justice is done" or in which a plea agreement might be misconstrued to the detriment of public confidence in the criminal justice system. For this reason, the prosecutor should be careful not to place undue emphasis on factors which favor disposition of a case pursuant to a plea agreement.[50]

According to James Eisenstein and Herbert Jacob, the courtroom work group also contributes to the local legal culture's influence on plea bargaining. They found that defense attorneys, prosecutors, and judges have established practices, values, and norms concerning not only the "going rates" for crimes but also the "way things are done." The work group rarely acts outside this social organization context. If they do, they proceed with considerable discomfort.[51]

The Prosecutor and Plea Bargaining

Plea bargaining varies according to the roles its key participants—prosecutors, defense counsel, and judges—play. Prosecutors' discretion in charging

Plea bargaining is one of the best known but little understood aspect of informal discretionary decision making in criminal justice.

and sentencing decisions conditions their role in plea bargaining. Discretion not only affects decisions in individual cases, but also orders general charging policies in prosecutors' offices. In small or rural jurisdictions, individual case discretion, not general charging policies, constitutes the norm. In large, urban jurisdictions, however, general charging policy includes plea bargaining.

Urban and rural policy differences have historical roots. As jurisdictions grow and become more complex, a transformation occurs; plea bargaining changes with it. Delaware County, Pennsylvania, for example, grew from a small, rural jurisdiction to a large, suburban one in about 20 years. Plea bargaining changed too, from implicit bargaining with heavy judicial participation in the 1950s to explicit bargaining between prosecutors and defense counsel with little or no judicial participation by the 1970s.[52]

The Prosecutor's Decision to Negotiate Beginning in the 1920s, researchers have studied the prevalence of guilty-pleas. In the past decade, they have turned from the question of the prevalence of guilty pleas to the question of why prosecutors negotiate pleas. Early impressionistic and anecdotal evidence and recent quantitative analyses have shown broad agreement on the five major influences on prosecutors' decisions to negotiate pleas:

- Seriousness of the offense.
- Criminal history of the defendants.
- Strength of the government's case.
- Reputation of defense counsel.
- Heavy caseloads.[53]

The weight given to each of these reasons varies. Herbert S. Miller, William McDonald, and James Cramer, in a random 10 percent sample of all jurisdictions with populations of more than 100,000, extensively interviewed judges, prosecutors, public defenders, private defense attorneys, clerks, probation officers, and police officers. Several of the quotes from individuals in this section represent typical answers to questions in their survey. Miller and his associates asked prosecutors what most influenced their decisions to prosecute. Figure 10.1 depicts the reasons for negotiating and the percent of each reason.[54]

In determining the strength of their case, prosecutors examine both the source and the quality of information available to them. As a primary source of that available information, the police investigation significantly influences plea bargaining. A senior prosecutor in Delaware County, Pennsylvania, said that prosecutors ask the arresting officer who brings them the case jacket "whether [or not] this guy is [in] trouble." Sometimes the officer "[will] tell you that although he looks like trouble, [he really is not a bad guy or vice versa.] Sometimes [the police can] tell you [that] he is a known troublemaker [in their jurisdiction.]"[55]

Prosecutors do not always take police officers at their word or automatically accept their recommendations. A senior prosecutor from Dade County, Florida, explained:

> If the policeman says I don't like this guy and want to bust his ass and doesn't explain himself any further, I am not satisfied that he really tried to make the case. But on the other hand if the policeman reports that this guy is only the wheel man and won't give us the names of the two robbers who pulled the job, then I am willing to go along with a request for a tougher deal. Or if they say, the defendant told one story to the policeman at the crime scene and is now telling a different story, then I'll take this information into account as a legitimate concern of the police.[56]

Figure 10.1

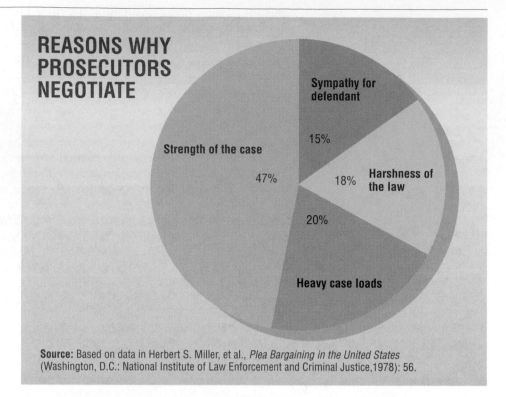

REASONS WHY PROSECUTORS NEGOTIATE

Sympathy for defendant 15%

Harshness of the law 18%

Strength of the case 47%

20%

Heavy case loads

Source: Based on data in Herbert S. Miller, et al., *Plea Bargaining in the United States* (Washington, D.C.: National Institute of Law Enforcement and Criminal Justice,1978): 56.

Victims also supply information to prosecutors. What victims say affects prosecutors' assessments of offense seriousness and/or the dangerousness of defendants. Again, as the Dade County chief prosecutor explains:

> If an employee stabs his employer in the back or brings his employer close to bankruptcy as a result of embezzlement or other violations of trust, then I feel that the victim's request for a tough sentence should be respected. Also, if a victim tells me that he has been calling the police about this defendant for two years and the police have never arrested him before and that during that time this guy has been making a lot of trouble, then that would count heavily with me. I would go along with his request for a tough plea deal.[57]

The "Right" Bargain   How do prosecutors know what charges to press and what sentences to recommend? What is a "good deal" from prosecutors' perspectives? How do they know they are not "giving away the store" or, conversely, demanding too much? The answer begins with the "going rates" or local "market values" for particular crimes. Market values rarely mirror statutory penalty prescriptions, and they vary from court to court within particular jurisdictions. For example, in Pennsylvania, first-degree burglary, a felony carrying prison time, informally has a going rate of much less. In Montgomery County it receives only a few days in jail, while in neighboring Philadelphia it gets automatic probation. In addition to market value, a "good bargain" also considers seriousness of the offense, defendant dangerousness, and the strength of the government's case.[58]

Learning the market values and how to integrate them with offense seriousness, offender dangerousness, and case strength in order to arrive at the "right" bargain is difficult but critical for prosecutors who hope to survive and do well. Values not only vary across jurisdictions, but they also differ within specific jurisdictions according to particular judges' ideas about the seriousness of individual crimes and the dangerousness of individual criminals. To deal with these particular variations, new prosecutors learn to incorporate into their decisions those informal, but nonetheless powerful, work-group standards in effect at the local courthouse. Senior staff rarely aid junior prosecutors in this respect. In Delaware, Pennsylvania, the senior prosecutor instructed new prosecutors only to:

> Protect yourself. You're a lawyer first and a prosecutor second. Check with somebody. Don't be Mr. Nice-Guy. Don't make a fool of yourself or a reputation of poor judgment. Don't bring stuff into a judge and have it rejected.[59]

Prosecutors like neither surprises nor losses. They can avoid both if they refrain from striking bargains for less than the going rates. Young prosecutors learn quickly that they cannot automatically bargain outside the going rates. Pressures from defense counsel, judges, and even other prosecutors urge the newcomer to be "reasonable." One new prosecutor learned this the hard way. In his first bargained case, he asked for the maximum sentence. Amid laughter, a senior prosecutor stepped up, took the file from the novice's hand, and made clear to the judge that the state wanted considerably less (in other words, the going rate, not the maximum penalty).[60]

Strength of the Government's Case

In most jurisdictions, prosecutors consider case strength the single most important ingredient in plea bargaining. Miller and his associates report that "virtually all prosecutors regard weak cases as prime targets for plea negotiations." Plea-bargaining guidelines in one jurisdiction permit negotiated pleas "when the state has a weak case and the odds of conviction are not great." William F. McDonald, who interviewed prosecutors in 31 jurisdictions, found only one exception to this view. In Kalamazoo, Michigan, prosecutors adopted a policy of "plead the gold and take the dogs to trial."[61]

What makes a strong case is a complicated matter. A defendant might have committed the crime, but the government may not have sufficient or solid enough evidence to assure conviction. In other words, the government can establish factual guilt outside court, but not legal guilt in court. A St. Louis prosecutor had charged a defendant with murder on no more evidence than a photograph a pawnbroker took of the suspect pawning the victim's television set the day after her apartment was burglarized and she was murdered. When asked if he was worried that the defendant might be innocent, he replied he knew the defendant was guilty because:

> I sent two of my best investigators who are black and competent men out on the street to check out the case. They went down to the section of town where this guy hangs out and they talked to the people down there about his involvement in this crime. They found out that the street talk says he's guilty. The guys down there on wise-guy alley say he did it, so I know he is guilty.[62]

Prosecutors may speak confidently about their ability to determine the strength of a case, sometimes coming up with as much as a 50 percent probability of conviction, but their confidence does not always reflect empirically sound judgments. The Institute for Law and Social Research (INSLAW) studied the Superior Court in the District of Columbia. It concluded that prosecutors—at least inexperienced ones—made unreliable estimates about a defendant's chances for conviction. Presumably, inexperienced prosecutors "guesstimate" or use "common sense," not empirical data, to draw conclusions about criminal cases.[63]

Four conditions weaken the government's case against criminal defendants:

- Only shaky evidence connects defendants to crimes.
- Defendants have committed criminal acts but lacked requisite intent. Absent *mens rea,* a material element in most serious crimes, defendants cannot be convicted.

- Defendants have committed acts with requisite intent, but other legal flaws mar the case. For example, police illegally seized evidence needed to convict; the government cannot use it to prove guilt.
- Evidence available at charging has disappeared or weakened. Witnesses die or leave town; victims lose resolve, forget, or decide after all they do not want the defendant to suffer.[64]

If any one or a combination of the preceding conditions weakens cases, many prosecutors make "**sweet deals**," sometimes called settling for half a loaf. Those who justify this practice claim it is better to get convictions on lesser charges without trials than to go to trial on the "right" charge and risk losing totally by acquittal. "Hard-liners" do not agree. One prosecutor argued that the law should protect only factually innocent defendants; if defendants committed crimes, prosecution should follow, and "legal technicalities should not stand in the way."[65]

Offense and Offender Seriousness In determining offense seriousness, prosecutors go beyond the crude outlines of the technical crime charged and consider defendants' actual behavior. For example, burglary includes a wide range of actions, from something as serious as breaking into a sleeping woman's bedroom at night with the intent of raping her to the more minor crime of entering a locked office with the intent of stealing a typewriter. Some embezzlements are worse than others; for example, consider an embezzler who takes an employer's money wrongfully, but does not threaten the business's very existence. One prosecutor remembered a case he had overestimated. He charged a man with attempted murder for breaking into his ex-girlfriend's apartment and shooting up the place with a shotgun. If the prosecutor had a similar case today, he would be more flexible. He would not look at the case as one of attempted murder; instead, he would call it some domestic disturbance offense because the man never pointed the gun at his ex-girlfriend.[66]

Prosecutors cite defendants' prior criminal record as the most frequently used determinant of offender seriousness. Defendants' "bad records," however, matter less in measuring their seriousness as offenders than whether they are "bad persons."[67]

Herbert S. Miller quotes an experienced prosecutor on the point:

> I've got the police department record. I can see where the kid lives, what kind of neighborhood it is. I find out the place where the guy is hanging around and whether there are other scum in the area. I've got his prior arrests and their dispositions. Plus I have all the information from the policeman who made the arrest or brought the defendant's records over to the DA. You can always ask the police officer whether this guy is trouble. Sometimes the police tell you that although he looks like trouble, he's really not a bad guy, or vice versa. Sometimes they tell you he is a known troublemaker.[68]

Prosecutors do not look at case strength and at offense and offender seriousness in isolation. In weak cases involving serious offenses and "bad news" offenders, prosecutors will probably seek a bargain for some conviction, even if it is only half a loaf. In Miller and his associates' national survey of plea bargaining, one prosecutor reflected this attitude in the admission that he would not dismiss murder, drug, and robbery cases, even lacking evidence to convict, because of their seriousness. According to sociologist Howard Daudistel, in practice prosecutors blur the distinction between case strength and offender seriousness. Weighing evidence, a highly subjective exercise, permits offender seriousness to determine case strength inappropriately, Daudistel found. Prosecutors' character evaluations often influence the way they evaluate the evidence against defendants; they sometimes associate either bad character with strong cases or "good citizens" with weak cases. In other words, personal character colors the evidence; prosecutors do not weigh it independently.[69]

The Prosecutor's Influence on Plea Bargaining

Prosecutors play four principal roles in plea bargaining, each with different and sometimes conflicting goals:

- Administrator.
- Advocate.
- Judge.
- Legislator.

Each role affects plea bargaining differently. As administrators, prosecutors primarily manage caseloads, which most consider too heavy. Prosecutors seek the administrative goal of rapid, efficient, and smooth case disposition. "We are running a machine here. We know we have to grind them out fast," said one Los Angeles trial assistant. A Manhattan prosecutor observed, "Our office keeps eight courtrooms extremely busy trying 5 percent of the cases. If even 10 percent of the cases ended in a trial, the system would break down. We can't afford to think very much about anything else." Administrative concerns have varying effects on plea bargains, depending on the actual or perceived pressure of case backlogs. A Los Angeles prosecutor who had earlier refused to bargain approached defense counsel the day before the case was scheduled for trial and said, "Look, I'm awfully tired, and I have a bad calendar for tomorrow. Do you still want that deal you suggested?"[70]

Although prosecutors contend, and no doubt believe, that heavy caseloads force them to plea bargain, empirical research casts doubt on their contention. No simple relationship exists between caseload pressure and guilty pleas. Comparing trial rates in districts with extremely high volume and those with minimal caseload pressures showed no significant differences in the percentage of cases disposed of by trial and those disposed of by guilty plea. In Connecticut, where court caseloads were cut in half with no corresponding reduction in personnel, numbers of guilty pleas did not decline at all.[71]

Not all prosecutors emphasize administrative considerations most. In fact, an overwhelming number consider their advocate role most important; as advocates, they fight crime by convicting criminals. In the broadest sense, the prosecutor represents the general public. However, victims, their families, and the entire law enforcement community look toward prosecutors in particular as their advocates in criminal justice. As advocates, prosecutors seek the maximum number of convictions; case strength weighs most heavily in plea bargaining. "Half a loaf is better than none" expresses the advocate's philosophy. A Chicago prosecutor said, "When we have a weak case for any reason, we'll reduce to almost anything rather than lose."[72]

Advocacy can lead to disparate treatment for similar defendants. One defense lawyer in Chicago said that

> when a prosecutor has a dead-bang case he is likely to come up with an impossible offer like thirty to fifty years. When the case has a hole in it, however, the prosecutor may scale the offer all the way down to probation. The prosecutor's goal is to get something for every defendant, and the correctional treatment the defendant may require is the last thing on their minds.[73]

Informally, prosecutors can act as judge and legislator. According to the doctrine of separation of powers, they cannot legally judge or legislate; so they become quasi judges, or quasi legislators. As informal judges, prosecutors

Prosecutors contend that heavy caseloads force them to plea bargain, but empirical evidence casts doubt on this contention.

seek to do the right thing for defendants. If defendants plead guilty to a charge, prosecutors let their particular circumstances and need for proper correctional treatment take priority, so the state can provide the "right" treatment. As legislators, prosecutors may grant concessions because they consider the law too harsh according to current public opinion. Conversely, prosecutors in their formal advocate role seek the maximum penalty, or even refuse a "deal" if they believe the public demands severe punishment for certain crimes, such as welfare fraud, child sexual abuse, and, currently, drug-law violations. As quasi legislators, prosecutors place heavy emphasis on going rates and current market values in making plea bargains.

Defense Counsel and Guilty Pleas

From the perspective of defense counsel, the most important decision in criminal cases is whether to plead guilty or to go to trial. Formally, the law requires defendants to make that decision for themselves: it is unconstitutional for defense lawyers to plead for clients against their will. However, in practice, criminal defense lawyers play a crucial role in straight and negotiated guilty pleas as well as in not-guilty pleas.[74]

A manual for defense lawyers says that they

> may and must give the client the benefit of counsel's professional advice on this crucial decision; and often counsel can protect the client from disaster only by using a considerable amount of persuasion to convince the client that a plea which the client instinctively disfavors is in fact in his or her best interests. This persuasion is most often needed to convince the client that s/he should plead guilty in a case in which a not-guilty plea would be totally destructive.[75]

Defense Counsel and Straight Guilty Pleas

Defense attorneys consider circumstances similar to the ones prosecutors deem important when advising clients to plead guilty. First, if the prosecution has a strong case and there is no good defense against it, defense counsel is likely to recommend that their clients plead guilty. Second, circumstances that will prejudice the trier of fact (jury, or judge in bench trials) can lead defense counsel to recommend a straight plea. These circumstances may include violent sex crimes, especially brutal crimes even in the absence of sexual assaults, crimes against children, and, currently, virtually all drug-law violations. Defense counsel usually favor guilty pleas when confronted with abrasive defendants; sympathetic defendants, on the other hand, recommend themselves for not-guilty pleas. Also, the criminal records of defendants, especially if long and offensive, will prejudice juries against defendants. Finally, unfavorable, heavy news coverage will lead defense counsel to avoid trial.

Some circumstances might make a trial disadvantageous for the accused at sentencing. Defendants who plead guilty generally receive lighter sentences for their cooperation. Defense counsel have an obligation to apprise defendants of both the possibility and consequences of conviction, including the maximum penalties for the offense charged; mandatory minimum sentences for the offense charged; rules regarding probation and parole, particularly actual prison or jail time; forfeiture statutes that permit confiscation of cars and other paraphernalia used to commit liquor, gambling, and narcotics offenses; civil rights restrictions imposed on convicted felons; and privately imposed sanctions, such as higher insurance rates and restrictions on employment, admission to professions, and admission to educational institutions. Defendants weigh these factors in deciding whether to plead guilty immediately, enter into plea bargaining, or plead not guilty and go to trial.

Defense Counsel and Negotiated Pleas

The severe consequences that may befall convicted defendants heavily influence the plea-bargaining decisions of defense counsel. Thus, most defense lawyers view plea bargaining as integral to serving their clients well. As one expert put it:

> Experienced criminal lawyers know that one of defense counsel's most important functions, perhaps the most important, is working out with the prosecutor the best possible disposition of a client's case in situations in which there is no realistic prospect of acquittal. The lawyer not only may properly do this, but s/he violates the obligation to represent the client adequately if s/he does not.[76]

Such weighty matters require lengthy deliberations. Defendants who can afford private attorneys generally receive the time and attention they deserve. The great bulk of criminal defendants who rely on public defenders spend little, if any, time working out the proper plea with the lawyers. According to one survey, defendants spend "a total of five to ten minutes conferring" with their public defender lawyers, "usually in rapid, hushed conversations in the courthouse."[77]

Not only do time pressures cause difficulties, but defense counsel also play conflicting roles in criminal justice. Their most widely known and accepted formal role involves a vigorous defense of their clients' interests, but defense counsel also have informal obligations to the courthouse work group. As such, they want to dispose of cases with minimum friction and disruption. Like prosecutors and judges, they do not like surprises or losses, and negotiated pleas minimize both. Nor do they, or any other members of the courtroom elite, want bad relations with colleagues they encounter daily. Defendants are in adjudication only once and will then probably never return, at least not to the same work group's bailiwick. Prosecutors, defense attorneys, and judges, on the other hand, stay in the work group long after defendants leave. David Lynch, who worked both as a prosecutor and a public defender, in his description of "workgroup pathologies," reveals how much closer to the work group public defenders feel than they do to most of their clients.

> Part of "doing time" was having to put up with the constant stress and abuse heaped on us by ill-tempered and antisocial clients, whose sole audience for their angry outbursts against "the system" was their public defenders, whom they often considered to be incompetent, hired cronies of the state. . . . This was the sort of individual we public defenders were expected to represent to the best of our abilities. This was the sort of individual who caused us to become cynical about our role as "liberty's last champion" (the logo on our office's baseball team shirts) and who tended to alienate us from our work. This was the sort of individual who made us love plea bargaining. Plea bargaining unfortunately plays right into the hands of alienated public defenders. . . . It makes cases "go away," taking with them some of the stress, work, combat, and (very important) the client—whose "companionship" one often wishes to minimize and whose guilt one often believes (correctly or incorrectly) to be so obvious.[78]

Defense Counsel and Their Clients The pressure to plea bargain arises not only from the work-group relationship and the urge to "go along in order to get along." Attitudes toward defendants also favor negotiation over adjudication. In particular, defense lawyers usually believe that their clients are guilty of something; otherwise, the police would not have arrested them in the first place, nor would prosecutors have charged them with crimes after reviewing the arrest. Such an attitude directly contradicts the formal "presumption of innocence" that supposedly enshrouds every criminal defendant in the system prior to conviction. It replaces the formal presumption with its informal opposite, "the presumption of guilt," which far more often affects defense counsel's decisions. "The public defender learns to view most of his clients as wrongdoers who should be convicted of some crime and punished, rather than as presumably innocent men who should be defended."[79]

Defense lawyers who operate on such a belief may "lean on" their clients to plead guilty to ensure a more lenient sentence. Even when lawyers believe their clients are innocent, they may pressure them to plead guilty because they think it is better to accept a lenient sentence than to risk conviction at trial and harsher punishment. Leaning on defendants may arise from a combination of the belief in clients' guilt, the belief that defendants can get a better deal by pleading guilty, and from the desire to comply with the norms of the courtroom work group. Former public defender and prosecutor David Lynch who later wrote of his experiences, reveals this combination of motives in his description of the process of "client control."

> Defense attorneys knew all too well that if they brought too many cases to trial, they would be seen as either unreasonable and worthy of professional ostracism or as a fool who was too weak to achieve "client control." Many attorneys I knew became masters of the fine art of "chair therapy," in which a client who insists on a trial is made to sit in the hall of the courthouse (or in the courthouse lockup) for days on end during the courthouse trial terms, waiting for his day in court, until he accepts a deal. Some (usually unintentionally) resorted to "good cop/bad cop" routines, in which a resistant defendant is subjected to the screams of his or her attorney, followed by the lawyer's associate, who tries to calmly help the accused see the light. Usually, however, defense attorneys, aware that incredible trial penalties were attached to the "right" to a jury trial, only needed to tell a defendant of the unconscionable sentences that had been meeted out to others who dared to create work for a judge.[80]

Ironically, defendants in plea-bargaining jurisdictions may do better without lawyers, for several reasons. Asking for a lawyer might send out a signal that defendants are "troublemakers." Judges may rule more leniently when defendants are not represented by counsel. In weak cases, prosecutors are more likely to charge defendants represented by counsel during screening. One prosecutor admitted that "if defense counsel were present when certain weak cases were about to be screened out, the prosecutor might first offer a plea deal to the attorney." In other words, the presence of a defense attorney led the prosecutor to charge a defendant in a weak case that otherwise would have been screened out.[81]

Judges and Plea Bargaining

Judges enter into plea bargaining in one of two ways. They may either participate during the negotiations or supervise after lawyers have struck bargains. Sometimes they do both. About one in four judges participates in plea bargaining in felony cases, and one in five participates in misdemeanor plea bargaining. Judges play a supervisory role that is widely accepted as proper; but strong controversy exists over whether judges ought to participate in plea bargaining.[82]

Judicial participation in plea bargaining varies according to individual judges' styles and from jurisdiction to jurisdiction. Researchers have identified six participation types. By observing, interviewing, and surveying judges in several jurisdictions, Miller and his associates found that:

- Some judges never participate in any way in plea bargaining. They neither explicitly nor implicitly enter plea negotiations, nor do they "lean on" participants.
- Some avoid explicitly participating, but gently "lean on" participants, or facilitate the bargaining process.
- Others bargain implicitly only.
- Some active judges bargain implicitly and heavily pressure participants to "force" guilty pleas.
- Some judges participate still more actively, bargaining explicitly and offering general sentence recommendations.
- A final group, the most active participant judges, not only bargain explicitly but also make specific sentence recommendations.[83]

Judges who refuse to participate at all oversee what prosecutors, defense counsel, and defendants have already decided. These judges believe they cannot effectively and impartially supervise a process in which they participate. In these "pure" jurisdictions, judges seldom second-guess the actual arrived-at bargain. They accept the prosecutor's dominant role in recommending sentence. In fact, in most cases prosecutors and judges agreed on sentencing 100 percent of the time and never less than 95 percent of the time, leading some to conclude that judges have relinquished their sentencing powers. One judge admitted he had never changed a prosecutor's recommendation. If he did not like the recommendation, he might tell the prosecutor that the sentence was not in line with current rates, so the prosecutor would think about it for future cases, but the judge would not change the recommendation in the current case.[84]

Judges who avoid both explicit and implicit participation do not pressure defendants indirectly by punishing them more severely if they go to trial. These "pure" judges who remain aloof from the bargaining process preside, almost without exception, in felony courts. In misdemeanor courts, judges feel that the sheer number of cases demands that they "encourage" defendants to plead guilty.[85]

Judges who lean on participants try to keep the flow of cases moving as smoothly and swiftly as possible. They stress administrative-bureaucratic values, believing, as one Oregon judge put it, that they have "to keep the pleas coming in." One Alaska judge said some cases should never go to trial. For instance, cases in which defendants have no legal defense and where there are no real questions of factual or legal guilt waste the time and money of prosecutors, defendants, and defense lawyers and squander badly needed court dates as well. Therefore, according to Miller and his associates, judges "facilitate" guilty pleas

> by speaking with defense attorneys or prosecutors regarding the case. If a particular prosecutor insisted on trying such cases the judge would in various informal ways indicate displeasure and would even go so far as to question why the case was in trial at all.[86]

These judges encourage bargaining in dead-bang cases (those where guilt appears obvious) in order to preserve court time for complicated cases. A judge in Colorado Springs said that if he had several hard cases and several easy ones, "he felt obligated to make time for the troublesome cases by clearing out those where there was little question as to guilt."[87]

Few judges exert harsh pressure to force bargaining toward guilty pleas; most merely lean on prosecutors and defense counsel. These judges cite heavy caseloads as the single most important reason for pressuring prosecution and defense. According to one observer, judges in this category made sure "no stone was left unturned to arrive at a plea of guilty. This included arm twisting, forcing, jerking the defense attorney around, and coming down on the defendant."[88]

A judge presiding over a burglary case in New York City's criminal courts provides an excellent example of arm twisting. When the case was called, one of the two defendants did not have a lawyer. Rather than continue the case, the judge appointed an attorney from among those present in the courtroom. The district attorney immediately offered a two- to four-year sentence in return for a guilty plea. The judge said, "After today, it's 3 to 6, after that it's 4 to 8. If they're ever going to plead, today is the time to do it." When the defendant rejected the bargain (the judge had appointed the lawyer only moments before), the judge said, "We'll make it very easy. It's 4 to 8 after today. Let's play hardball."[89]

These pressures included assigning defense attorneys to tough judges, denying continuances, overruling motions, and using other judicial techniques to force prosecutors and defense counsel to bargain. No judges in this group said they punished defendants for going to trial, but they did point out that going to trial created the risk that information adverse to defense and prosecution might surface and influence their sentencing decisions.[90]

Judges bargain implicitly when they systematically impose heavier sentences on convicted defendants who demand a trial. Such judges justify differential sentencing on several grounds. Defendants who admit their guilt show remorse and have, therefore, taken the first step toward rehabilitation; they deserve a lesser penalty. Other judges abide by the slogan, "if you want to win big, you'd better be prepared to lose big," meaning that defendants who put the state to the burden of a trial will pay a price if the state wins. One Chicago judge feels that defendants who "waste" taxpayers' money and the court's time "deserve more time in jail for the problems [they] create." Judges who sentence publicly after a trial often apply differential sentencing because they are under considerably more pressure to sentence harshly than are judges who do so in the obscurity of the plea-bargaining process.[91]

Judges who bargain explicitly and make general sentence recommendations enjoy considerable flexibility. In general, they specify only that they will give prison time as opposed to probation, or the upper instead of lower range of time incarcerated. Judges who bargain explicitly and indicate general sentences do so because they consider predictability critical to the criminal justice system: defendants should have a good idea of what will happen to them if they plead guilty, and lawyers ought to have indications of what will result from their work. At the same time, these judges show concern about retaining judicial independence. If they promise an exact sentence, they feel they have abdicated their primacy in sentencing.[92]

The most active judges not only bargain explicitly concerning pleas but also commit themselves to specific sentences following the negotiation process. Explicit bargaining might take place in formal pretrial negotiating conferences such as those in Alameda County, California, and Cook County, Illinois. It might be done informally in judges' chambers, or even in court with defense counsel and prosecutor huddling with the judge at the bench. Such informal bargaining sessions are common in Dade County, Florida, and El Paso County, Colorado.[93]

Judges specify caseload pressure as their single most frequent reason for participating in plea negotiations. When judges feel great pressure from heavy caseloads, they say they have to "keep things from getting bogged down." One Hartford, Connecticut, judge admitted that

> he became in fact a prosecutor when 835 cases were backlogged. He reduced the backlog to 299 cases by ordering the prosecuting attorney to select his two best assistants and setting up conferences at five-minute intervals day and night for six days. He enforced attendance of the prosecutor and defense attorney under threat of an arrest warrant. Under these conditions defense attorneys went to prosecutors and disposed of easy cases. The judge then ordered them into his chambers to discuss "sticky cases" and make a plea recommendation. They then marched back into court to recite the recommended disposition onto the record. He observed, somewhat ironically, that this practice "stinks" because a judge becomes a prosecutor. He did, however, indicate pleasure with the results.[94]

According to the American Bar Association Committee on Professional Ethics, judges "should not be a party to advance arrangements for the determination of sentence whether as a result of a guilty plea or a finding of

Judges are required to make sure that defendants understand what pleading guilty means and to determine that the plea is voluntarily made.

guilty based on proof." The American Bar Association Standards asserted that the "trial judge should not participate in plea discussions."[95]

Some jurisdictions prohibit judicial participation by statute or court rule. Under the Federal Rules of Criminal Procedure, for example, the "court shall not participate in any such discussions." One court interpreted this rule to mean that

> the sentencing judge should take no part whatever in any discussion or communication regarding the sentence to be imposed prior to the entry of a plea of guilty, conviction, or submission to him of a plea agreement.[96]

Only some states follow the federal practice. In Pennsylvania, for example, if judges participate at all, guilty pleas are invalid. In Wisconsin, on the other hand, judicial participation does not invalidate guilty pleas. Sometimes, different rules apply to charge and sentence bargaining. Some courts say judges ought not to participate in charge bargaining, but can and should play a major role in sentence bargaining.[97]

Guilty Pleas and the Constitution

Judicial *supervision* of plea bargaining does not vary nearly as much as *participation* in it, a difference due largely to formal constraints placed on supervision. Three constitutional provisions require judges to supervise the process: the Fifth Amendment protection against self-incrimination, the Sixth Amendment guarantee of a jury trial, and the Fourteenth Amendment requirement that no state deprive a citizen of life, liberty, or property without due process of law. In general, these provisions demand that judges make sure defendants plead guilty *knowingly* and voluntarily. According to these criteria:

> A plea of guilty entered by one fully aware of the direct consequences, including the actual value of any commitments made to him by the court, prosecutor or his own counsel, must stand unless induced by threats (or promises to discontinue improper harassment), misrepresentation (including unfulfilled or unfulfillable promises), or perhaps by promises that are by their nature improper as having no proper relationship to the prosecutor's business (e.g., "bribes").[98]

To satisfy the "knowingly" requirement, judges need to assure that defendants:

- Understand the charges against them, meaning the material elements of the crime charged.
- Fully appreciate that pleading guilty waives their rights against self-incrimination and to a jury trial.
- Appreciate the consequences of pleading guilty—that they know the maximum and minimum sentences awarded the crime.

Judges formally determine that defendants voluntarily and knowingly plead by a formal discussion with them called the colloquy. In federal courts, the colloquy consists, in part, of the following: Judges ask defendants if bargaining produced their guilty pleas. If so, they must reveal the terms of the agreement to the judge. Then judges advise defendants of the possible consequences of their guilty pleas. The *You Decide,* "Can an Innocent Defendant Plead Guilty?" allows you to analyze a leading Supreme Court decision on the voluntariness requirement of a guilty plea.[99]

Can an Innocent Defendant Plead Guilty?

North Carolina v. Alford, 400 U.S. 25 (1970)

On December 2, 1963, Alford was indicted for first-degree murder, a capital offense under North Carolina law, punished with death unless the jury recommends that the punishment shall be life imprisonment. The following has been extracted from the Court's opinion.

A murder which shall be perpetrated by means of poison, lying in wait, imprisonment, starving, torture, or by any other kind of willful, deliberate and premeditated killing, or which shall be committed in the perpetration or attempt to perpetrate any arson, rape, robbery, burglary or other felony, shall be deemed to be murder in the first degree and shall be punished with death: Provided, if at the time of rendering its verdict in open court, the jury shall so recommend, the punishment shall be imprisonment for life in the state's prison, and the court shall so instruct the jury. All other kinds of murder shall be deemed murder in the second degree, and shall be punished with imprisonment of not less than two nor more than thirty years in the state's prison.

The court appointed an attorney to represent [Alford], and this attorney questioned all but one of the various witnesses who appellee said would substantiate his claim of innocence. The witnesses, however, did not support Alford's story but gave statements that strongly indicated his guilt. Faced with strong evidence of guilt and no substantial evidentiary support for the claim of innocence, Alford's attorney recommended that he plead guilty, but left the ultimate decision to Alford himself. The prosecutor agreed to accept a plea of guilty to a charge of second-degree murder, and on December 10, 1963, Alford pleaded guilty to the reduced charge.

Before the plea was finally accepted by the trial court, the court heard the sworn testimony of a police officer who summarized the state's case. Two other witnesses besides Alford were also heard. Although there was no eyewitness to the crime, the testimony indicated that shortly before the killing, Alford took his gun from his house, stated his intention to kill the victim, and returned home with the declaration that he had carried out the killing. After the summary presentation of the state's case, Alford took the stand and testified that he had not committed the murder but that he was pleading guilty because he faced the threat of the death penalty if he did not do so.

After giving his version of the events of the night of the murder, Alford stated:

> I pleaded guilty on second degree murder because they said there is too much evidence, but I ain't shot no man, but I take the fault for the other man. We never had an argument in our life and I just pleaded guilty because they said if I didn't they would gas me for it, and that is all.

In response to questions from his attorney, Alford affirmed that he had consulted several times with his attorney and with members of his family and had been informed of his rights if he chose to plead not guilty. Alford then reaffirmed his decision to plead guilty to second-degree murder:

> Q [by Alford's attorney]. And you authorized me to tender a plea of guilty to second-degree murder before the court?
> A. Yes, sir.
> Q. And in doing that, that you have again affirmed your decision on that point?
> A. Well, I'm still pleading that you all got me to plead guilty. I plead the other way, circumstantial evidence; that the jury will prosecute me on—on the second. You told me to plead guilty, right. I don't—I'm not guilty but I plead guilty.

In response to the questions of his counsel, he acknowledged that his counsel had informed him of the difference between second- and first-degree murder and of his rights in case he chose to go to trial. The trial court then asked appellee if, in light of his denial of guilt, he still desired to plead guilty to second-degree murder and appellee answered, "Yes, sir. I plead guilty on—from the circumstances that he [Alford's attorney] told me." After eliciting information about Alford's prior criminal record, which was a long one, the trial court sentenced him to thirty years' imprisonment, the maximum penalty for second-degree murder.

Ordinarily, a judgment of conviction resting on a plea of guilty is justified by the defendant's admission that he committed the crime charged against him and his consent that judgment be entered without a trial of any kind. The plea usually subsumes both elements, and justifiably so, even though there is no separate, express admission by the defendant that he committed the particular acts claimed to constitute the crime charged in the indictment. Here Alford entered his plea but accompanied it with the statement that he had not shot the victim.

If Alford's statements were to be credited as sincere assertions of his innocence, there obviously existed a factual and legal dispute between him and the State. Without more, it might be argued that the conviction entered on his guilty plea was invalid, since his assertion of innocence negatived any admission of guilt, which, as we observed last Term in [Betts v.] Brady, is normally "[c]entral to the plea and the foundation for entering judgment against the defendant."

In addition to Alford's statement, however, the court had heard an account of the events on the night of the murder, including information from Alford's acquaintances that he had departed from his home with his gun stating his intention to kill and that he had later declared that he had carried out his intention. Nor had Alford wavered in his desire to have the trial court determine his guilt without a jury trial. Although denying the charge against him, he nevertheless preferred the dispute between him and the State to be settled by the judge in the context of a guilty plea proceeding rather than by a formal trial. Thereupon, with the State's telling evidence and Alford's denial before it, the trial court proceeded to convict and sentence Alford for second-degree murder.

State and lower federal courts are divided upon whether a guilty plea can be accepted when it is accompanied by protestations of innocence and hence contains only a waiver of trial but no admission of guilt. Some courts, giving expression to the principle that "[o]ur law only authorizes a conviction where guilt is shown," require that trial judges reject such pleas. But others have concluded that they should not "force any defense on a defendant in a criminal case," particularly when advancement of the defense might "end in disaster." They have argued that, since "guilt, or the degree of guilt, is at times uncertain and elusive. . . [a]n accused, though believing in or entertaining doubts respecting his innocence, might reasonably conclude a jury would be convinced of his guilt and that he would fare better in the sentence by pleading guilty." As one state court observed nearly a century ago, "[r]easons other than the fact that he is guilty may induce a defendant to so plead, [and] [h]e must be permitted to judge for himself in this respect." An individual accused of crime may voluntarily, knowingly, and understandingly consent to the imposition of a prison sentence even if he is unwilling or unable to admit his participation in the acts constituting the crime.

Nor can we perceive any material difference between a plea that refuses to admit commission of the criminal act and a plea containing a protestation of innocence when, as in the instance case, a defendant intelligently concludes that his interests require entry of a guilty plea and the record before the judge contains strong evidence of actual guilt. Here the state had a strong case of first-degree murder against Alford. Whether he realized or disbelieved his guilt, he insisted on his plea because in his view he had absolutely nothing to gain by a trial and much to gain by pleading. Because of the overwhelming evidence against him, a trial was precisely what neither Alford nor his attorney desired. Confronted with the choice between a trial for first-degree murder, on the one hand, and a plea of guilty to second-degree murder, on the other, Alford quite reasonably chose the latter and thereby limited the maximum penalty to a thirty-year term. When his plea is viewed in light of the evidence against him, which substantially negated his claim of innocence and which further provided a means by which the judge could test whether the plea was being intelligently entered, its validity cannot be seriously questioned. In view of the strong factual basis for the plea demonstrated by the state and Alford's clearly expressed desire to enter it despite his professed belief in his innocence, we hold that the trial judge did not commit constitutional error in accepting it.

Alford now argues in effect that the state should not have allowed him this choice but should have insisted on proving him guilty of murder in the first degree. The states in their wisdom may take this course by statute or otherwise and may prohibit the practice of accepting pleas to lesser included offenses under any circumstances. But this is not the mandate of the Fourteenth Amendment and the Bill of Rights. The prohibitions against involuntary or unintelligent pleas should not be relaxed, but neither should an exercise in arid logic render those constitutional guarantees counterproductive and put in jeopardy the very human values they were meant to preserve.

At the time Alford pleaded guilty, North Carolina law provided that if a guilty plea to a charge of first-degree murder was accepted by the prosecution and the court, the penalty would be life imprisonment rather than death. The provision permitting guilty pleas in capital cases was repealed in 1969. Though under present North Carolina law it is not possible for a defendant to plead guilty to a capital charge, it seemingly remains possible for a person charged with a capital offense to plead guilty to a lesser charge.

Questions
The *Alford* case raises an important question regarding guilty pleas. Alford agreed to the plea bargain because he thought he would lose at trial, even though he insisted he was innocent. In other words, if he was telling the truth, he was innocent even if the evidence against him was overwhelming. The Supreme Court decided his plea was still voluntary because Alford, with the help of competent counsel, made a judgment based on reality. The plea was not coerced; it only took into account the legal proof against him. In the Court's opinion, he decided voluntarily not to take the chance he would be convicted in a trial and sentenced to death. Do you agree that this is a voluntary and intelligent plea? Is this rule better than the rules applied in the jurisdictions to which the Court refers that do not accept pleas accompanied by protestations of innocence?

Judges also determine whether sufficient facts support guilty pleas. The Federal Rules of Criminal Procedure, for example, provide that judges cannot "enter a judgment upon such a plea without a factual basis for the plea." Generally, judges question prosecutors and defendants and examine presentence reports to make sure guilty pleas rest on sufficient evidence of guilt. They ask, how much evidence has never been specified?[100]

Inquiring into factual bases of guilty pleas has several functions. It protects defendants against pleading guilty to crimes the facts do not fit. For example, one defendant pleaded guilty to four counts of interstate transportation of stolen money orders when he had crossed state lines only once. The judge's failure to inquire into the factual basis of the plea led to conviction on four crimes when, on the basis of the facts, the defendant had committed only one. Inquiring into the evidence also helps judges determine defendants' willingness to plead guilty and their understanding of the charges against them. It generates a fuller and more adequate record, making later review more accurate and successful challenges to the agreed-on plea bargain less likely.[101]

Plea Bargaining Reform

Despite its widespread practice, plea bargaining has generated great controversy. It has both many supporters and many critics. Those who favor it point to the benefits it confers on the whole criminal justice system, on taxpayers, and on defendants. These benefits include:

- Plea bargaining promotes administrative efficiency by controlling court calendars and moving cases swiftly through the criminal process after arrest.
- Plea bargaining saves tax dollars since negotiating costs less than trying cases, especially with a jury.
- Plea bargaining insures prompt correctional measures for defendants.
- Plea bargaining, by requiring the admission of guilt, promotes rehabilitation of defendants.
- Plea bargaining reduces the humiliation and misery to defendants that can accompany a public trial.
- Plea bargaining results in lesser punishment.

Opponents point to reasons why plea bargaining should be either totally abolished or at least substantially curtailed. They maintain that informal discretionary bargaining is inherently wrong in our adversary system. Furthermore, plea bargaining corrodes public confidence in criminal justice because it smacks of corruption, "deals," and evading punishment for crime. According to criminal law professor George P. Fletcher, in his interesting book *With Justice for Some:*

> Though roughly 90% of all cases are disposed of consensually without trial, there is something unseemly about the prosecution's trading a lower charge in return for the defendant's cooperating and waiving his right to trial. The very idea that the authorities cut special deals with particular defendants offends the rule of law. Many legal systems on the Continent, Germany most strongly, have long rejected this kind of discretionary justice. . . . Germans refer to American-style discretionary justice as the. . . principle of expediency as opposed to the. . . principle of legality, which demands prosecution according to the extent of the perceived legal violation. Even-handed justice under the law should mean that everyone receives the same treatment: no leniency for those who promise something in return.[102]

Whether or not these claims are in fact true, the public believes them. Critics also point to the unfairness of plea bargaining. Guilty defendants escape the full consequences of their wrongdoing by pleading guilty to crimes less serious than those they have actually committed. Innocent defendants, on the other hand, feel compelled to plead guilty when they have committed no crime at all. For example:

> San Francisco defense attorney Benjamin Davis. . . represented a man charged with kidnapping and forcible rape. The defendant was innocent, Davis says, and after investigating the case Davis was confident of an acquittal. The prosecutor, who seems to have shared the defense attorney's opinion on this point, offered to permit a guilty plea to simple battery. Conviction on this charge would not have led to a greater sentence than thirty days' imprisonment, and there was every likelihood that the defendant would be granted probation. When Davis informed his client of this offer, he emphasized that conviction at trial

seemed highly improbable. The defendant's reply was simple: "I can't take that chance."[103]

Critics of plea bargaining consider such a situation repugnant to the very notion of justice. Bargaining, according to critics, also distributes lenient sentences unevenly and unfairly. It reduces the law's deterrent effect because it results in lower sentences for guilty defendants. It impairs correctional measures because it curtails judges' sentencing discretion. It punishes defendants who go to trial: considerable research demonstrates that defendants who insist on trial are punished more harshly if they are convicted than if they had pleaded guilty to the same charge.[104]

Despite criticism, calls for change and plea-bargaining research did not begin in earnest until the 1960s. Lyndon Johnson's Crime Commission took a harsh view of plea-bargaining practices. Furthermore, although the Supreme Court approved plea bargaining as a "necessity" in 1971, in 1973 the prestigious National Advisory Commission on Criminal Justice Standards and Goals, appointed by Richard Nixon, recommended:

> As soon as possible, but in no event later than 1978, negotiations between prosecutors and defendants—either personally or through their attorneys—concerning concessions to be made in return for guilty pleas should be prohibited.[105]

In the midst of this increased awareness of, and growing debate over, plea bargaining, the most famous plea bargain in history was struck. The vice president of the United States and the U.S. attorney general made a deal over the vice president's alleged criminal conduct. This highly publicized "deal" provided further impetus for debate and generated a large amount of fruitful research. Both have contributed to persistent calls for plea-bargaining reform. As a result, several jurisdictions have abolished plea bargaining. Others, such as the federal judiciary, have attempted to regulate plea bargaining by bringing it out into the open and subjecting it to rules and regulations. Some have restructured plea bargaining by, for example, eliminating judicial participation and adding victim participation in negotiations.

Abolishing Plea Bargaining

In 1975, Alaska Attorney General Avrum Gross surprised criminal justice practitioners in his own state and aroused the interest of professionals and scholars nationwide when he banned plea bargaining in Alaska. A follow-up study to determine the ban's effects revealed several startling conclusions.[106]

Courts in Alaska did not collapse under a crush of criminal trials; defendants continued to plead guilty at about the same rate, for the reasons already reviewed. The ban did not affect sentences for violent crimes (murder, rape, robbery, and felonious assault). On the other hand, "clean kids," young defendants with no criminal record, convicted of the least serious property felonies—burglary, larceny, or receiving stolen property—received longer sentences. Plea bargaining no longer provided an opportunity for first-time property offenders to receive probation or lighter prison sentences.[107]

Attorney General Gross's ban also returned sentencing to trial judges where, formally, it has always been. Prior to the ban, judges routinely accepted the recommendations of prosecutors, meaning that informally prosecutors sentenced convicted offenders. Without plea bargaining, routine cases were disposed of more rapidly. Time spent bargaining over the sentences of nonviolent criminals prior to the ban was no longer necessary; they continued to plead guilty without negotiation. "In short, prosecutors learned that they could achieve the same results under the attorney general's new system, but with less time spent on routine cases."[108]

Alaska's plea ban has had mixed results. It has destroyed some well-entrenched myths concerning plea bargains, showing that drastically reduc-

case-load hypothesis *assumption that pressure to dispose of large numbers of criminal cases requires plea bargaining to keep the courts working at a reasonable, efficient, economical pace.*

pretrial settlement conferences *meeting of judges, defendants, victims, and police officers to conduct plea negotiations.*

ing plea bargaining does not break down the criminal justice system. On the contrary, the ban actually hastened case dispositions, at least in routine, nonviolent felonies. It gave prosecutors and defense attorneys more, not less, time to try cases. Banning plea bargaining, however, was not a panacea: Evils once attributed to plea bargaining continued unabated following the plea ban. Defendants' incomes still affected the quality of pretrial dispositions and trials. Defendants who went to trial still received harsher sentences than those who pleaded guilty. Race, income, and employment status remained telling determinants on sentences. Furthermore, according to law professors Franklin Zimring and Richard Frase, the ban sometimes caused undue rigidity, particularly for first-time, nonviolent property offenses.

> A shaky prosecution witness, a faulty police investigation, or an attractive defendant may provide irresistible inducements to bargain, and make negotiated settlement[s] seem by far the most sensible recourse.[109]

The finding that the abolition of plea bargaining did not break down the criminal justice system by overburdening the courts with trials supports the case-load hypothesis. According to the **case-load hypothesis**—widely held by criminal justice practitioners but disputed by a number of empirical studies—the pressure to dispose of large numbers of criminal cases requires plea bargaining to keep the courts working at a reasonable, efficient, economical pace. Some research, however, supports the case-load hypothesis. Malcolm D. Holmes, Howard C. Daudistel, and William A. Taggart reviewed the ban on plea bargaining in El Paso, Texas, using data published by the Texas Judicial Council Annual Reports. These data include annual numbers of felony cases pending at the beginning of each year; the number of cases added each year; jury trial dispositions each year; and convictions each year. Holmes and his associates found that following the ban on plea bargaining in El Paso

- The majority of defendants still pleaded guilty.
- The number of jury trials increased.
- The rate of dispositions fell.
- The number of convictions remained mostly unchanged.

Using a quasi-experimental time-series design, the researchers concluded that the case-load pressure hypothesis has some validity; following the ban on plea bargaining, even a small increase in adversariness increased the time it took to dispose of cases. In other words, going to trial in place of plea bargaining definitely slows up the disposition rate. The El Paso study indicates an important truth about criminal justice research: What may be true for one place and time may not be true for another. The differences between the circumstances in El Paso, Texas, and Alaska may explain the difference in outcome. It may also, however, point to another truth: The methodology followed in the El Paso study (a time-series analysis) contrasted to a single point in time—once before and once after the ban in Alaska—may explain the difference in support for the case-load pressure hypothesis.[110]

Pretrial Settlement Conferences Plea bargaining excludes some people with a vital interest in the case—victims, defendants, police officers, and judges. To meet this deficiency, researchers conducted a field experiment in Dade County, Florida. They established **pretrial settlement conferences** to restructure plea bargaining. In these conferences, all negotiations took place before judges, and defendants, victims, and police officers were invited to attend.[111]

The experiment tested several hypotheses about conferences:

- Increased participation by judges, victims, defendants, and police officers would make plea bargaining more "open and seemly."

Comparative Criminal Justice

Guilty Pleas in Germany

The German Code of Criminal Procedure, in effect for more than a century, mandates a celebrated rule of compulsory prosecution. In all cases of "serious crimes," the German prosecutor must prosecute "all prosecutable offenses, to the extent that there is a factual basis." Prosecutors do not have discretion to charge in misdemeanor cases, but only if the defendant's guilt is "minor" and "there is no public interest in prosecuting." Therefore, except on grounds of pettiness in misdemeanor cases, the law requires German prosecutors to prosecute all cases in which the evidence permits.

According to Professor John Langbein, who has studied German criminal procedure extensively, strong incentives encourage the rule of compulsory prosecution. If prosecutors decide not to prosecute either because of lack of evidence or insufficiency at law, victims or relatives of the victim can obtain a review of the decision. If the prosecutor's superiors uphold the decision of the prosecutor, citizens can appeal to the courts in a proceeding to compel prosecution. Prosecutors are members of a career service, in which promotions depend strictly on merit. Prosecutors avoid blotting their records with citizen complaints. To avoid complaints, especially successful ones, prosecutors resolve doubts in favor of prosecution.

Furthermore, according to Langbein, charge bargaining has no counterpart in Germany. Prosecutors, duty bound to prosecute all cases, have no authority to reduce a charge in return for a plea of guilty. The rule of compulsory prosecution requires prosecutors to take all cases to trial in the strongest form that the evidence allows.

The German rule of compulsory prosecution is not a fluke, says Langbein. The rule is intended to achieve goals important to German criminal justice:

- Treating similar cases alike.
- Following legislative definitions of crime.
- Preventing political interference in prosecutions.

According to Professor Langbein,

> German law forbids plea bargaining, and German legal professionals of all sorts—judges, prosecutors, academics, and (most importantly) defense counsel—consistently maintain that the law is obeyed. The disdain that American plea bargaining evokes in Germany is not confined to legal circles. Even in the ordinary press, American plea bargaining is regarded with astonishment bordering on incredulity.

Source: John Langbein, "Land Without Plea Bargaining: How the Germans Do It," *Michigan Law Review* 78 (1978): 204–25.

- Increased citizen participation would enhance citizen satisfaction with plea bargaining.
- Police satisfaction with case dispositions would improve by making the police knowledgeable participants in the plea-bargaining process.
- Police presence would increase police understanding of the process and lead to greater support for case dispositions that the police might otherwise have criticized as too lenient.
- Judicial participation would protect the public interest in criminal case disposition instead of putting most control in the hands of prosecutors and defense lawyers.
- The participation of victims would focus attention on their legitimate concerns about the criminal status of the offender and their claims to compensation for injury or damage.

- Victims have both a moral right and a psychological need to participate in criminal case dispositions that involve them.
- Defendants have a right to have their interests protected at sentencing.

As to the rights and needs of victims, the criminologist Norval Morris wrote in another connection:

> At present, victims of crimes are treated very shabbily by our criminal justice system. The system appears to serve its functionaries more than the public. Victims are repeatedly interrogated; they make too many trips to pretrial and trial hearings, at most of which they sit and do nothing, unable to hear the proceedings, forbidden to talk or read, bewildered as to what is going on, wondering if they are the wrongdoers or not, and reflecting on their lost wages and other costs. If the criminal process is the taking over by the state of the vengeful instincts of the injured person—buttressed by the recognition that harm to the victim is also harm to the state—then it would seem, at first blush, that the victim at least has a right to be informed of, and where appropriate involved in, the processes that have led to whatever is the state settlement of the harm that has been done to him. . . . [I]t is a matter of courtesy and respect for the individual victim.[112]

All in all, the field experiment was designed to test whether, and to what extent, changing the structure of plea bargaining would have positive results.

The Dade County pretrial settlement conferences took place in judges' chambers. Judges wore business suits instead of the forbidding black robes. Participants sat around the room or gathered about a table in an atmosphere more like a conference than a court proceeding. Generally, conference sessions were brief, averaging about 10 minutes, with some lasting 25 minutes. Conference topics most often included the facts of the case, recommendations, and defendants' prior records. The personal backgrounds and circumstances of victims and defendants became subjects of discussion somewhat less frequently. Since most conferences generally lasted about 10 minutes, they covered matters only superficially.

Judges were the most active participants in the proceedings and made the most frequent contributions to every topic. In 40 percent of the cases, prosecutors said nothing about the facts of the case, and in over half the cases, prosecutors said nothing about defendants' prior records. Defense attorneys discussed defendants' prior records—usually to clear up misunderstandings—and defendants' personal characteristics in more than a third of the cases. Police officers contributed facts relating to the crime in about 70 percent of the cases; they added to information about defendants' backgrounds in more than half the cases.

Victims were passive in the conferences they attended. Occasionally, they commented on the facts but practically never expressed views about disposition, except occasionally to approve what judges and lawyers recommended. The often-expressed fear that victims would demand maximum sentences simply did not materialize. In fact, victims and defendants played a minor role in the deliberations overall. Furthermore, victim attendance was disappointing: only 32 percent of invited victims ever came to the conferences. Defendants attended pretrial conferences at a higher rate—66 percent—but only minimally participated in them. If they commented at all, they usually contributed information about either the facts of the case or their background. They rarely said anything about disposition or recommended sentences.

Conferences did not noticeably affect case dispositions. Cases went to trial at similar rates, sentences remained comparable, and the time and expense involved in processing cases stayed about the same. However, the conferences did modify victims' and police attitudes toward plea bargaining and the criminal justice system. Slightly more than half the victims and police expressed greater approval and understanding of plea bargaining and the criminal process after the experiment. The Dade County efforts to restructure plea bargaining, therefore, only slightly altered the results of plea bargaining. The pretrial settlement conference did enhance, if only marginally, victims' and police confidence in plea bargaining; it was not a panacea.

Administrative Rule Making Some experts have recommended reforming plea bargaining by subjecting it to written guidelines established by those who participate in it. Although not a widespread practice, formal administrative rules are increasingly used as a device to control discretion in the bargaining process. The American Bar Association's Standards Relating to Pleas of Guilty include rules for prosecutors, defense attorneys, and judges. The standards permit prosecutors to bargain over charges and sentence recommendations. They require defendants' approval to all plea bargains, and demand that defense counsel clearly outline to defendants all the alternatives available in the case. Although they prohibit judges from participating in plea bargaining, they allow prosecutors and defense counsel to submit written agreements to judges prior to guilty pleas. If judges initially accept agreements but later reject them, defendants can change their pleas.[113]

Summary of Disposition by Guilty Plea

Informally arrived at, low-visibility guilty pleas—not public criminal trials in an adversary setting—determine the outcome of the vast majority of criminal cases. Not all guilty pleas result from plea bargaining; many defendants enter straight guilty pleas, for which the government concedes nothing in return. Defendants might negotiate pleas either explicitly or implicitly in return for some concession from the state. The government and defense can negotiate the charge or the sentence. In charge bargaining, defendants plead guilty in exchange for a charge less than the crime committed. In sentence bargaining, defendants plead guilty in exchange for a reduced sentence.

Plea bargaining occurs for several reasons. Administratively, plea bargains permit quick, efficient, economical processing. Philosophically, they facilitate early rehabilitation; defendants show public remorse in the plea, and the government can devote time saved from trial to treatment. From social organizational and social psychological perspectives, negotiation suits the courtroom work group's interest in harmony and predictability.

By pleading guilty, defendants waive their rights to trial by jury and against self-incrimination. The U.S. Supreme Court has upheld the constitutionality of guilty pleas resulting from negotiations, as long as defendants understand the consequences of their plea and plead voluntarily. Despite its legality, plea bargaining has strong and persistent critics. Some call it an immoral violation of the adversary system, an unfair practice that hurts the innocent and favors the guilty; an unsavory method of secret dealing between lawyers; and a callous disregard of victims and defendants. Efforts to meet these criticisms range from the extreme of abolishing plea bargaining to the milder reform of writing rules to guide participants in their negotiations. Nothing has been a panacea, but each reform has shed light on, and sometimes improved, attitudes toward this pervasive practice of deciding criminal cases.

Review Questions

1. What is the significance of adjudication in the formal-informal dichotomy in criminal justice?

2. How are most criminal cases disposed of?

3. Explain the significance of the criminal trial.

4. What specific rights do defendants have regarding jury trials?

5. What does fair trial mean?

6. Describe and explain the functions and significance of the steps in criminal trial, from opening statements through verdict.

7. Contrast direct and cross-examination.

8. How do judges determine the admissibility of evidence?

9. What is the significance of guilty pleas in the criminal justice system?

10. Compare and contrast straight and negotiated pleas.

11. Explain the significance of local legal culture in plea bargaining.

12. Explain the differences among the principal types of plea negotiations.

13. Why is the strength of the government's case the major element in prosecutorial plea bargaining?

14. Describe the various roles prosecutors play in plea negotiations.

15. Explain defense counsel's role in plea-bargaining decisions.

16. How does defense counsel's attitude affect plea bargaining?

17. What is the role of judges in plea negotiations?

18. Why do judges participate in plea negotiations?

19. What is the constitutional significance of guilty pleas?

20. List the major arguments in favor of, and against, plea bargaining.

21. Contrast and explain the effects of the ban on plea bargaining in Alaska and El Paso, Texas.

22. Describe pretrial settlement conferences and their results.

23. What role has administrative rule making played in plea bargaining?

Notes

1. Harry Kalven, Jr. and Hans Zeisel, *The American Jury* (Chicago: The University of Chicago Press, 1966), 31–32; Charles Silberman, *Criminal Violence, Criminal Justice* (New York: Random House, 1978), 283.

2. *Duncan v. Louisiana,* 391 U.S. 145 (1968); James J. Gobert, "In Search of the Impartial Jury," *Journal of Criminal Law and Criminology* 25 (1988): 669–742.

3. Wayne R. LaFave and Jerold H. Israel, *Criminal Procedure* (St. Paul: West Publishing Company, 1984), 2: 695–96.

4. *Apodaca v. Oregon,* 406 U.S. 404 (1972).

5. *Johnson v. Louisiana,* 406 U.S. 356 (1972).

6. LaFave and Israel, *Criminal Procedure,* 2: 698.

7. De Toqueville quote from James P. Levine's excellent book *Juries and Politics* (Pacific Grove, Calif.: Brooks/Cole, 1992), 14.

8. Kalven and Zeisel, *The American Jury,* 163–67.

9. Levine, *Juries and Politics,* 16.

10. Levine, *Juries and Politics,* 128; Benjamin A. Holden, Laurie P. Cohen, and Eleena de Lisser, "Color Blinded? Race Seems to Play an Increasing Role in Many Jury Verdicts," *The Wall Street Journal,* 4 October 1995; John Kifner, "Bronx Jurors: A Defense Dream, A Prosecutor's Nightmare," *New York Times,* 5 December 1988.

11. Holden, Cohen, and de Lisser, "Color Blinded?"

12. Quoted in Holden, Cohen, and de Lisser, "Color Blinded?"

13. LaFave and Israel, *Criminal Procedure,* 2: 700.

14. Hisim quoted in Holden, Cohen, and de Lisser, "Color Blinded?"; Irwin A. Horowitz, "Jury Nullification: The Impact of Judicial Instructions, Arguments, and Challenges on Jury Decision Making," *Law and Human Behavior* 12 (1988): 439–53.

15. 28 U.S.C.A., §§ 1861–69.

16. LaFave and Israel, *Criminal Procedure,* 2: 708.

17. Martin A. Levin, "The American Judicial System: Should It, Does It, and Can It Provide an Impartial Jury to Criminal Defendants?" *Criminal Justice Journal* 11 (1988): 89–124.

18. William Lambarde, *Eirenarcha* (London: n.p., 1581).

19. *Taylor v. Louisiana,* 419 U.S. 522 (1975); *Holland v. Illinois,* 493 U.S. 474 (1990).

20. *Sheppard v. Maxwell,* 384 U.S. 333 (1966).

21. Steven Phillips, *No Heroes, No Villains: The Story of a Murder Trial* (New York: Random House, 1977), 218.

22. *Illinois v. Allen,* 397 U.S. 337 (1970).

23. Henry Campbell Black, *Black's Law Dictionary,* 5th abridged edition (St. Paul: West Publishing Company, 1983), 635; *In re Winship,* 397 U.S. 358 (1970).

24. Ibid. *In re Winship.*

25. Joel Samaha, *Criminal Procedure* (St. Paul: West Publishing Company, 1990), 540.

26. George P. Fletcher, *A Crime of Self-Defense: Bernhard Goetz and the Law on Trial* (New York: Free Press, 1988), 116, 231.

27. Ibid., 121–122.

28. Ibid.

29. Phillips, *No Heroes, No Villains,* 196–97.

30. Ibid., 213.

31. Stephen J. Schulhofer, "Is Plea Bargaining Inevitable?" *Harvard Law Review* 97 (1984): 1061–62; BJS, *Report to the Nation on Crime and Justice* (Washington, D.C.: Bureau of Justice Statistics, 1988), 83; Malcolm Feeley, *The Process Is the Punishment* (New York: Russell Sage, 1979), 310.

32. Joel Samaha, *Law and Order in Historical Perspective* (New York: Academic Press, 1974); Roscoe Pound and Felix Frankfurter, eds., *Criminal Justice in Cleveland* (Cleveland: The Cleveland Foundation, 1922), 93; Arthur Rosett and Donald R. Cressey, *Justice by Consent* (New York: Harper & Row, Publishers, 1976); Albert W. Alschuler, "Plea Bargaining and Its History," *Law and Society Review* 13 (1979): 211; Joseph Sanborn, "A Historical Sketch of Plea Bargaining," *Justice Quarterly* 3 (1986): 111.

33. Peter F. Nardulli, James Eisenstein, and Roy B. Flemming, *The Tenor of Justice: Criminal Courts and the Guilty Plea* (Urbana, Ill.: University of Illinois Press, 1988); Mike McConville and Chester Mirsky, "Guilty Plea Courts: A

Social Disciplinary Model of Criminal Justice," *Social Problems* 42 (1995): 216–234.

34. Michael L. Rubenstein, Steven Clarke, and Theresa Wright, *Alaska Bans Plea Bargaining* (Washington, D.C.: U.S. Government Printing Office, 1980), 81; Milton Heumann, "Author's Reply," *Law and Society Review* 13 (1979): 651; Barbara Boland and Brian Forst, "Prosecutors Don't Always Aim to Pleas," *Federal Probation* 49 (1985): 10–15. For contrasting views see Schulhofer, "Is Plea Bargaining Inevitable?" 1044, and Feeley, *The Process Is the Punishment*, 168–75.

35. Rubenstein, Clarke, and Wright, *Alaska Bans Plea Bargaining*, 81.

36. Ibid., 82.

37. Ibid., 85.

38. Ibid., 86.

39. Ibid., 87.

40. Ibid., 88.

41. Ibid., 91.

42. Ibid., 92.

43. Defense attorney quoted in Feeley, *The Process Is the Punishment*, 186.

44. William F. McDonald, "From Plea Negotiation to Coercive Justice: Notes on the Respectification of a Concept," *Law and Society Review* 13 (1979): 385–92.

45. Milton Heumann, "Thinking About Plea Bargaining," in *The Study of Criminal Courts*, Peter F. Nardulli, ed. (Cambridge, Mass.: Ballinger Publishing Company, 1979), 208, 210.

46. Ibid., 9.

47. Ibid., 7.

48. Lynn M. Mather, "Some Determinants of the Method of Case Disposition: Decision-Making by Public Defenders in Los Angeles," *Law and Society Review* 8 (1974): 187.

49. Lawrence M. Friedman, *American Law* (New York: W. W. Norton, 1984), 6; Heumann, "Thinking About Plea Bargaining," 211–12; Thomas W. Church, Jr., "Examining Local Legal Culture," *American Bar Foundation Research Journal* 3 (1985): 449–518.

50. Heumann, "Thinking About Plea Bargaining," 213–14.

51. James Eisenstein and Herbert Jacob, *Felony Justice* (Boston: Little, Brown, 1977), 286. See also Nardulli, Eisenstein, and Flemming, *The Tenor of Justice*, for more recent assessments to similar effect.

52. Herbert S. Miller et al., *Plea Bargaining in the United States* (Washington, D.C.: National Institute of Law Enforcement and Criminal Justice, 1978), 56; and, more recently, Nardulli, Eisenstein, and Flemming, *The Tenor of Justice*.

53. Albert W. Alschuler, "The Prosecutor's Role in Plea Bargaining," *University of Chicago Law Review* 36 (1968): 50; Miller et al., *Plea Bargaining in the United States*, 60–61; Lynn Mather, *Plea Bargaining or Trial? The Process of Criminal Case Disposition* (Lexington, Mass.: Lexington Books, 1979); Celesta A. Albonetti, "Race and the Probability of Pleading Guilty," *Journal of Quantitative Criminology* 6 (1990): 316–18; Dean J. Champion, "Private Counsels and Public Defenders: A Look at Weak Cases, Prior Records, and Leniency in Plea Bargaining," *Journal of*

Criminal Justice 17 (1989): 253–63; Brian Forst, "Prosecution and Sentencing," in *Crime*, James Q. Wilson and Joan Petersilia, eds., (San Francisco: Institute for Contemporary Studies Press, 1995), 366–368.

54. Miller et al., *Plea Bargaining in the United States*, 62.

55. Ibid., 67–68.

56. Ibid.

57. Ibid., 71–72.

58. Ibid., 80.

59. Ibid., 82.

60. Ibid., 83.

61. Ibid., 101–102; William F. McDonald, *Plea Bargaining: Critical Issues and Common Practices* (Washington, D.C.: National Institute of Justice, 1985), 65.

62. Quoted in Miller et al., *Plea Bargaining in the United States*, 93.

63. Cited in Miller et al., 103.

64. Ibid., 106–107.

65. Ibid., 108.

66. Ibid., 117–118.

67. Institute for Law and Social Research (INSLAW), *Curbing the Repeat Offender* (Washington: INSLAW, 1977).

68. Miller et al., *Plea Bargaining in the United States*, 119.

69. Howard Daudistel, "Deciding What the Law Means: An Examination of Police Prosecutor Discretion," Ph.D. dissertation, University of California, Santa Barbara, 1976, 162–64.

70. Quoted in Franklin E. Zimring and Richard S. Frase, *The Criminal Justice System* (Boston: Little, Brown, 1980), 506–507.

71. Milton Heumann, *Plea Bargaining: The Experience of Prosecutors, Judges and Defense Attorneys* (Chicago: University of Chicago Press, 1978), 29–31.

72. Ibid., 507.

73. Ibid., 508.

74. *Jones v. Barnes*, 51 U.S.L.W. 5151 (July 5, 1983). 463 U.S. 745.

75. Anthony Amsterdam, *Trial Manual for the Defense of Criminal Cases* (Philadelphia: American Law Institute, 1984), 1: 229.

76. Ibid., 235.

77. Jonathan D. Casper, *American Criminal Justice* (Englewood Cliffs, N.J.: Prentice-Hall, 1972), 10.

78. David Lynch, "The Impropriety of Plea Agreements," *Law and Social Inquiry* 19 (1994): 121–122.

79. Miller et al., *Plea Bargaining in the United States*, 168.

80. Lynch, "The Impropriety of Plea Agreements," 123.

81. Ibid., 185–86.

82. LaFave and Israel, *Criminal Procedure*, 2: 627.

83. Miller et al., *Plea Bargaining in the United States*, 230–31, 243–44.

84. Ibid., 244–45.

85. Ibid., 246.

86. Ibid., 246–48.

87. Ibid., 248.

88. Ibid., 249.

89. Quoted in Stephen J. Schulhofer, "No Job Too Small: Justice Without Bargaining in the Lower Criminal Courts," *American Bar Foundation Research Journal* 3, (1985): 585, note 234.

90. Miller et al., *Plea Bargaining in the United States,* 249–50.

91. Ibid., 263–64.

92. Ibid., 260.

93. Ibid., 250.

94. Ibid., 252.

95. LaFave and Israel, *Criminal Procedure,* 2: 626.

96. *United States v. Werker,* 535 F.2d 198 (2d Cir. 1976), *certiorari* denied 429 U.S. 926.

97. *Commonwealth v. Evans,* 252 A.2d 689 (Pa. 1969); *State v. Wolfe,* 175 N.W. 2d 216 (Wis. 1970); LaFave and Israel, *Criminal Procedure,* 2:632–34.

98. *Brady v. United States,* 397 U.S. 742 (1970); *Shelton v. United States,* 246 F.2d 571 (5th Cir. 1957); *Federal Rules of Criminal Procedure,* Rule 11.

99. *Federal Rules of Criminal Procedure,* Rule 11.

100. LaFave and Israel, *Criminal Procedure,* 2: 652–53.

101. *Gilbert v. United States,* 466 F.2d 533 (5th Cir. 1972); LaFave and Israel, *Criminal Procedure,* 2: 652–53.

102. George P., Fletcher, *With Justice for Some: Victims' Rights in Criminal Trials* (Reading, Mass.: Addison-Wesley, 1995), 191.

103. Zimring and Frase, *The Criminal Justice System,* 523.

104. Ibid., 542–63.

105. National Advisory Commission on Criminal Justice Standards and Goals, *Courts* (Washington, D.C.: U.S. Government Printing Office, 1973), standard 3.1, 46.

106. The material on the Alaska ban on plea bargaining is derived from Rubenstein, Clarke, and Wright, *Alaska Bans Plea Bargaining,* 219–43.

107. Michael L. Rubenstein and Teresa J. White, "Alaska's Ban on Plea Bargaining," *Law and Society Review* 13 (1979): 374–77.

108. Ibid.

109. Zimring and Frase, *The Criminal Justice System,* 684.

110. Malcolm D. Holmes, Howard C. Daudistel, and William A. Taggart, "Plea Bargaining Policy and State District Court Loads: An Interrupted Time Series Analysis," *Law and Society Review* 26 (1992): 139–53.

111. This section relies on Wayne A. Kerstetter and Anne M. Heinz, *Pretrial Settlement Conference: An Evaluation* (Washington, D.C.: U.S. Department of Justice, 1979).

112. Norval Morris, *The Future of Imprisonment* (Chicago: University of Chicago Press, 1974), 55–56.

113. American Bar Association, *Standards Relating to Pleas of Guilty* (Chicago: American Bar Association, 1968).

11 Sentencing

CHAPTER MAIN POINTS

1. *Determinate sentencing characterized the early history of American criminal justice; indeterminate sentencing dominated until the 1970s; and since then determinate sentencing has again held sway.*

2. *Legislatures, courts, and administrative agencies share sentencing authority.*

3. *Most sentencing reform focuses on discrimination, disparity, and discretion.*

4. *Most sentencing reforms have shifted the balance from informal to formal determinants of sentencing.*

5. *Convicted defendants enjoy fewer formal protections at sentencing than during trial.*

6. *The public supports the threat of death more than it supports actual capital punishment, and support for the death penalty decreases as knowledge about its administration increases.*

7. *The Supreme Court has upheld the constitutionality of the death penalty.*

8. *Research has produced conflicting conclusions as to the deterrent effect of capital punishment.*

9. *Controversy surrounds both the degree and tolerance of error in administering the death penalty.*

10. *Research shows that the death penalty as currently administered discriminates against those who kill whites, particularly blacks who kill whites.*

Twice a year in eighteenth-century England, the scarlet-robed royal judges of Assize put on their "black caps of death" and rode circuit throughout all the county towns in the kingdom. They displayed their power surrounded by pomp and ceremony, and wielded their authority by means of speeches, rulings, grand jury charges, and other pronouncements. And they did it all in public, accompanied by the local gentry in the midst of large crowds of ordinary people gathered to witness the spectacle. Nowhere was the royal judicial power more evident than in the public pronouncement of the court's judgment of punishment—the sentence. Judges literally held the power of life and death over convicted felons, since all felonies from murder to larceny were punishable by death. The royal judges did not always sentence felons to hang. They possessed the discretion to stay the executions of sufficiently repentant wrongdoers. The power over life and death made their sentencing power all the more awesome. They took full advantage of the public proceedings to strike terror when they pronounced the death sentence, or to temper justice with mercy by sparing repentant convicts from the hangman's noose in a dramatic stay of execution.

> Methinks I see him [recalled one observer in 1785] with a countenance of solemn sorrow, adjusting the cap of judgment on his head. . . . He

**determinate or fixed
sentencing** *fixing of specific
penalties by legislatures according to
the seriousness of the offense.*
inderterminate sentencing
*determining of sentences by judges
and corrections authorities
according to individual offenders.*

addresses in the most pathetic terms, the consciences of the trembling criminals. . . shows them how just and necessary it is, that there should be laws to remove out of society, those, who instead of contributing their honest industry to the public good and welfare of society, have exerted every art that the blackest villainy can suggest, to destroy both. . . . He then vindicates both the *mercy,* as well as the *severity* of the law, in making such examples, as shall not only protect the innocent from outrage and violence, but also deter others from bringing themselves to the same ignominious end. He acquaints them with the certainty of speedy death and consequently with the necessity of speedy repentance. And on this theme he may so deliver himself, as not only to melt the wretches at the bar into contrition, but the whole auditory into the deepest concern. Tears express their feelings. . . . [M]any of the most thoughtless among them may. . . be preserved from thinking lightly of the first steps into vice. . . . The dreadful sentence is now pronounced. Every heart shakes with terror. . . .[1]

Modern judges do not hold the power of life and death solely in their own hands, nor do they possess unlimited discretion to sentence convicted offenders to prison or probation. The United States Constitution and most state constitutions prohibit "cruel and unusual punishments"; the denial of life, liberty, or property without due process of law; and the denial of the equal protection of the laws. Moreover, sentencing authority is distributed among legislatures, sentencing guidelines commissions, prosecutors' offices, judges, and corrections departments.

Furthermore, sentencing no longer culminates with the fanfare of public ceremonies conducted in the center of town with crowds gathered to watch and hear. Nevertheless, the judgment of punishment still fascinates—and concerns—the public. Sentencing also affects public policy makers, particularly during times of heightened concern about crime. Since about 1970, politicians, criminologists, reformers, and the public have subjected sentencing to searching criticisms. Along with these criticisms, public demands to "get tough" on violence, illicit drugs, and juvenile crime; rising violent crime rates; news accounts of gang activities; and increased knowledge about crime and criminal justice generated a ferment for sentencing reform. Virtually every legislature in the country has enacted some sentencing reform statute. Most of the reforms include

- Shifts in the philosophy of punishment from rehabilitation to retribution and incapacitation.
- Increases in the severity and to some extent the types of punishment.
- Transfers of sentencing authority from courts to legislatures and prosecutors.
- Restrictions and even abolition of discretionary indeterminate sentencing.
- Expansion of fixed sentencing based on written rules.

History of Sentencing

For more than a thousand years, policymakers have debated whether to fit sentences to the crime or to the criminal. In **determinate sentencing,** sometimes called **fixed sentencing,** legislatures "fix" or "determine" the specific penalty for crimes. Determinate sentencing attempts to fit the punishment to the crime. In **indeterminate sentencing,** legislatures set only the outer limits of possible penalties. The sentence and the actual time served depend upon the discretionary judgment of judges and correctional authorities as to the sentence that suits the particular offender. As early as 700 A.D., the Roman Catholic Church's penitential books revealed a tension between prescribing penance strictly according to the sin and tailoring it to suit individual sinners. The concern over judicial discretion in sentencing also has an ancient heritage. Arguments abound in the history of sentencing not only over *what* sentences to impose, but also over *who* should impose them. These early arguments regarding sinners and penance, judges and punishment, strikingly resemble current thought about the proper authority, aims, and types of criminal sentencing.[2]

In United States history, the debate over sentencing began during the 1630s in the colony of Massachusetts Bay. Political rivals of the great Puritan "father," John Winthrop, criticized him for exercising what they considered excessive discretion in sentencing criminals. Winthrop frequently tailored his penalties to suit the individual characters and conditions of defendants. Fair and just sentencing, he believed, required taking hardship, contrition, and other individual circumstances into account. The disparity and leniency in Winthrop's sentences disturbed his critics. Particularly offensive, they maintained, was the leniency based on personal circumstances that he sometimes extended to serious wrongdoers.

Winthrop responded that the law defined crimes only broadly; judges had to apply those broad definitions to particular cases. Each sentence, he said, depends on a combination of the facts of the case, the background and character of the defendant, and the general needs of the community. Hence, he argued, poor people should pay lighter fines than rich people, religious leaders should suffer harsher penalties for committing morals offenses than laypersons, and powerful colonists should receive more severe penalties for breaking the law than weak individuals. According to Winthrop, recruiting wise judges whose personal prejudices do not influence their sentencing provides the only remedy for the abuse of judicial discretion. Not convinced, the Massachusetts Bay Colony legislature enacted a determinate sentencing statute that prohibited judges from fitting sentences to individual offenders. Winthrop, who was the governor of the colony, had to accept the law, much to his distaste and displeasure.[3]

Fixed sentencing tailored to fit the crime prevailed more or less from the seventeenth until the latter part of the nineteenth century. Then began a shift toward indeterminate sentences tailored to fit individual criminals. However, neither fixed nor indeterminate sentences have ever totally dominated criminal sentencing. The tension between the needs for certainty and flexibility always present in law requires both a measure of predictability in punishment and a degree of flexibility toward individual needs in sentencing. Shifting ideological commitments, as well as other informal influences on sentencing, ensure that neither fixed nor indeterminate sentences will ever exclusively prevail.

Following the American Revolution, fixed but moderate penalties became the rule. States abolished the death penalty for many offenses. Rarity of use in practice rendered corporal punishment (whipping), mutilation (cutting off ears and slitting tongues), and shaming (the ducking stool) virtually obsolete. Imprisonment, up to that time used mainly to detain accused persons before trial, became the dominant form of criminal punishment by 1850. Statutes fixed prison terms for most felonies. In practice, liberal use of pardons, early release for "good time," and other devices permitted judges to use informal discretionary judgment in altering formally fixed sentences.[4]

The modern history of sentencing—with important echoes from the past—arose out of a growing dissatisfaction with legislatively fixed harsh prison sentences. Reformers complained that prisons were no more than warehouses for the poor, immigrants, and other "undesirables" at the lower end of society. Furthermore, prisons did not work. Crime continued at unacceptably high rates no matter how many offenders were locked up, and those who were released soon proved how futile imprisonment was by quickly returning to prison. Many public officials and concerned citizens

historical note

You have taken a perverse view of your rights, because you have not been sufficiently impressed with your duties, and now you are to be surrounded by special conditions which society has prepared for your benefit. You would not yield to social wisdom outside these walls; here you must yield.

Samuel George Smith, 1911

agreed. Particularly instrumental in demanding reform were prison administrators and other criminal justice officials.

The culmination of the dissatisfaction with the ineffectiveness of fixed prison sentences was an historic conference held in Cincinnati, Ohio, in 1870. This National Prison Congress called for a radical change in sentencing. Its "Declaration of Principles," based on the idea that sentencing should *reform* criminals, not simply *punish* them, called for the replacement of fixed with indeterminate sentences. "Mere lapse of time" to "pay" for past crimes, the transactions of the Congress proclaimed, should not determine sentence length. Rather, "satisfactory proof of reformation" ought to determine how long convicted criminals remain in prison.[5]

According to one conference leader, Zebulon Brockway,

> all persons in a state, who are convicted of crimes or offenses before a competent court, shall be deemed wards of the state and shall be committed to the custody of the board of guardians, until, in their judgment, they may be returned to society with ordinary safety and in accord with their own highest welfare.[6]

Even before the conference, Brockway, who was superintendent of the Detroit House of Correction, played an instrumental role in the enactment of the nation's first indeterminate sentencing law. A prototype statute appeared in Michigan in 1869. The statute empowered judges to sentence prostitutes to three years in houses of correction, but permitted inspectors to terminate such sentences if, in their discretion, a prostitute "reformed."[7]

New York enacted the first truly indeterminate sentencing law in 1878. The statute provided:

> Every sentence to the reformatory of a person convicted of a felony or other crime shall be a general sentence to imprisonment in the New York State reformatory at Elmira and the courts of this state imposing such sentence shall not fix or limit the duration thereof. The term of such imprisonment of any person so convicted and sentenced shall be terminated by the managers of the reformatory, as authorized by this act; but such imprisonment shall not exceed the maximum term provided by law for the crime for which the prisoner was convicted and sentenced.[8]

By 1922, all but four states had adopted some form of indeterminate sentencing law. The indeterminate sentence was born in the optimistic belief that under the direction of professionals, individuals could "reform" their lives of crime into lives of productive work. Proponents of the indeterminate sentence accepted the "findings" of contemporary social and physical scientists that both basic human "drives" and social "forces," mostly beyond the power of individuals, controlled human behavior. According to these "findings," individuals did not choose their actions freely; their heredity, physical characteristics, psyche, and environment thrust their behavior on them.

Proponents of the indeterminate sentence were not "bleeding hearts." Far from it. According to the rehabilitation experts, criminals were either corrigible or incorrigible. The corrigibles, usually under 30 years old, were pliable enough to respond to reformative measures. The incorrigibles, mainly over 30, were hardened criminals beyond hope of reformation. The corrigibles required stern measures to turn them into good citizens. Strict rules of conduct and highly programmed daily schedules of hard work, study, exercise, and healthy living habits were the order of the day. Harsh punishment, including solitary confinement on a diet of bread and water, paddling, and other forms of corporal punishment, were regularly administered to "reform" prisoners. This transformation from criminal to productive citizen usually required years of imprisonment followed by a long period of parole.

Corrigible prisoners had to prove that they had reformed by the outward display of following prison rules. Long periods of perfect behavior were often required before parole was granted. Parolees had to clinch the proof by keeping a job, living a clean life, and staying out of even minor trouble with the law. Prison officials, parole officers, and reformers believed that prisoners and parolees could easily fake reformation. Although they believed most prisoners were stupid, officials and reformers also had no doubt that prisoners were cunning.

The incorrigibles, on the other hand, could not reform, no matter how strong the efforts. The reformers, however, were not about to let the incorrigibles "get away" without working. They recommended that incorrigibles stay in prison for life, where they would be forced to work to support themselves since they could or would not voluntarily work for a living outside prison. If they could not be forced into earning their keep, then death was the only remaining option.[9]

According to reformers, judges trained in the narrow, rigid rules of law were not qualified to exercise the discretionary judgment required to decide either who was corrigible and incorrigible or when corrigibles could safely return to society. Only criminologists, physicians, psychiatrists, social workers, corrections officials, and other experts had the training to classify, treat, and proclaim the reformation of criminals.[10]

When the indeterminate sentence became the prevailing practice, administrative sentencing by parole boards and prison officials took precedence over legislative and judicial sentence fixing. At its extreme, judges set no time on sentencing, leaving it wholly to parole boards and corrections officials. More commonly, judges were free to grant probation, suspend sentences in favor of alternatives to incarceration such as community service, or pick confinement times within minimums and maximums prescribed by statutes. Parole boards and corrections officers determined the exact release time.

Indeterminate sentencing remained dominant until the 1970s, when several forces coalesced to oppose it. Prison uprisings, especially at Attica and the Tombs in New York in the late 1960s, dramatically portrayed rehabilitation as little more than rhetoric, and prisoners as deeply and dangerously discontented. Individual rights advocates challenged the widespread and unreviewable informal discretionary powers exercised by criminal justice officials in general and judges in particular. Demands for increased formal accountability spread throughout the criminal justice system. Courts required public officials to justify their decisions in writing and empowered defendants to dispute allegations against them at sentencing. Formalization even reached prisons in requirements that they publish their rules and grant prisoners the right to challenge rules they were accused of breaking (see Chapter 14).

Furthermore, widespread disillusionment with rehabilitation arose during the late 1960s, after it had dominated the rhetoric of penal policy for more than a half century. In addition, several statistical and experimental studies showed a pernicious discrimination in sentencing. In particular, some research strongly suggested that poor people and African Americans were sentenced more harshly than whites and more affluent Americans. Finally, official reports showed steeply rising rates of street crime. As a result of these developments, a distinguished panel of the National Research Council created to review sentencing practices concluded that by the early 1970s, a "remarkable consensus emerged among left and right, law enforcement officials and prisoners groups, reformers and bureaucrats that the indeterminate sentencing era was at its end."[11]

By the late 1970s, the emphasis in sentencing policy and practices shifted from fairness to crime prevention. Retribution, general deterrence, and incapacitation gained renewed popularity, while rehabilitation lost ground. Civil libertarians and conservatives agreed that the aim of sentencing practices

Figure 11.1

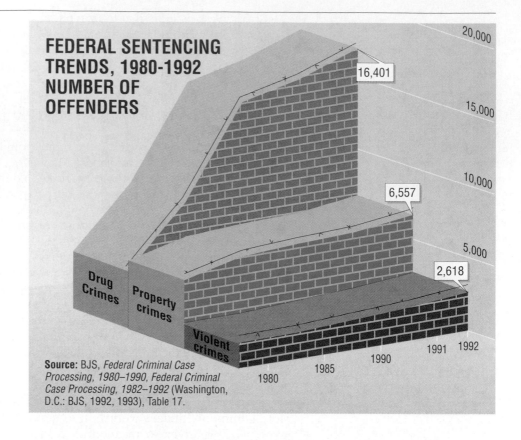

FEDERAL SENTENCING TRENDS, 1980-1992 NUMBER OF OFFENDERS

Drug Crimes

Property crimes

Violent crimes

16,401

6,557

2,618

20,000

15,000

10,000

5,000

1980 1985 1990 1991 1992

Source: BJS, *Federal Criminal Case Processing, 1980–1990, Federal Criminal Case Processing, 1982–1992* (Washington, D.C.: BJS, 1992, 1993), Table 17.

ought to be swift and certain punishment. They differed only on what the length of sentences should be. To civil libertarians, determinate sentencing meant *short,* fixed sentences; to conservatives, it meant *long,* fixed sentences. Three ideas came to dominate thinking about sentencing:

● Many offenders deserve severe punishment because they have committed serious crimes.
● Repeat career offenders require severe punishment to incapacitate them.
● All crimes deserve some punishment in order to retain the deterrent potency of the criminal law.

According to the National Council on Crime and Delinquency,

by 1990, the shift in goals of sentencing reform was complete. Virtually all new sentencing law was designed to increase the certainty and length of prison sentences to incapacitate the active criminal and deter the rest.[12]

Harsher penalties accompanied the shift in the philosophy of punishment. Public support for the death penalty grew, the Supreme Court ruled that it was not cruel and unusual punishment, courts sentenced more people to death, and states began to execute criminals. Judges sentenced more people to prison and sentenced them to longer prison terms, so that by 1996 the United States sentenced more people to prison for longer terms than almost any other country in the world. Figure 11.1 depicts the results of this shift in attitude and sentencing practice in state courts. Figure 11.2 shows the dramatic effects on sentencing of the hardening attitudes in federal courts toward drug offenses.

Sentencing Authority

In the popular image, sentencing involves a black-robed judge in a high-ceilinged courtroom, solemnly pronouncing the price that a convicted defendant must pay for committing a crime. In reality, several formal and informal

Figure 11.2

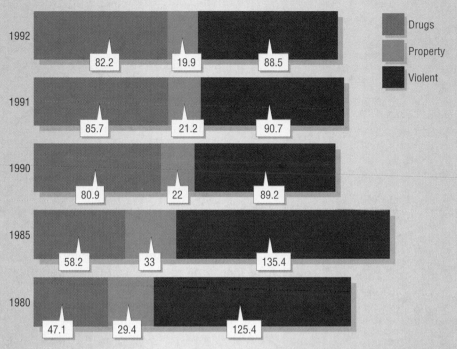

FEDERAL SENTENCING TRENDS, 1980-1992: AVERAGE MONTHS SERVED

	Drugs	Property	Violent
1992	82.2	19.9	88.5
1991	85.7	21.2	90.7
1990	80.9	22	89.2
1985	58.2	33	135.4
1980	47.1	29.4	125.4

Source: BJS, *Federal Criminal Case Processing, 1980-90, Federal Criminal Case Processing, 1982-92* (Washington, D.C.: BJS, 1992, 1993), Table 17.

restraints limit the power of judges to impose sentences. Formally, the law distributes the sentencing power among several public agencies. Legislatures enact statutes that prescribe penalties for crimes. However, these statutes typically grant judges at least some range within which they can choose the exact sentence. Statutes sometimes allow judges to choose between sentences of fines or jail terms, or within a range of years in prison. Occasionally, the law allows judges to sentence offenders to probation, restitution, or community service. Beginning in the 1970s, legislatures have increasingly restricted this judicial latitude, setting more fixed sentences, particularly, mandatory minimum sentences.[13]

Several informal influences also limit the sentencing power of judges. Most criminal conduct never comes to public attention unless victims and witnesses report it. Even if victims and witnesses do report crimes, unless they are willing, ready, and available to cooperate with police and prosecutors, defendants will not be convicted. The degree to which victims and witnesses provide adequate and convincing information affects not only conviction but also sentencing. Victims with the fortitude to carry through in a criminal prosecution and effectively describe their victimizations may influence judges to sentence more severely. Aggravating circumstances affect sentencing, and often only the testimony of victims and witnesses can prove them sufficiently.

The power to invoke the criminal process depends on police as well as victims. Their skill and success in investigating crimes bear directly on the strength of the case against defendants. The strength of government's case influences the sentencing decision. In short, judges cannot sentence offenders whom the police have not arrested, and judges depend heavily on the quality of police investigations in sentencing the defendants who actually

historical note

The so-called recidivists are not those who have been born to crime, but they are those who have been treated from the beginning by the retributive method of dealing with crime.

Samuel George Smith, 1911

appear before them. The prosecutors' charging power also affects sentencing. Defendants whom prosecutors do not charge, or whom they divert and dismiss later, obviously remain beyond the sentencing authority of judges. Prosecutors also influence sentencing by choosing the crime or crimes with which to charge defendants. The maximum and minimum penalties prescribed for these charges confine judges' sentences within these limits. Prosecutors also influence sentencing in guilty pleas, particularly negotiated pleas. Prosecutors often recommend, and in some jurisdictions promise, specific penalties. Judges rarely, if ever, reject penalties that prosecutors recommend.

Probation officers also affect sentencing. They conduct pre-sentence investigations on which many judges rely heavily in sentencing. Parole boards also play a major role in the sentencing process, particularly in **"bark-and-bite" sentencing.** The parole board's informal "bite" (the actual time served) reduces the judges' formal "bark" (the sentence pronounced in court). For most of this century, parole boards have released prisoners on an individual basis, depending on when they decided prisoners were "ready" to return to society. Until the 1970s, when some jurisdictions placed restrictions on their authority, parole boards had more power than judges in sentencing. They determined actual release dates, which were practically never challenged.

Prison officials also affect sentencing. They manage the prisons and can affect the length of time inmates remain in them. They advise parole boards concerning the release of prisoners; parole boards do not often ignore their advice. Corrections officials also control "good time," or the number of days deducted from sentences for good behavior. Because some jurisdictions award up to one day of reduced sentence for every day served without violating prison rules, and most grant at least one for every three, the power to determine rule violations can reduce sentences in most states by one-third, and in some by one-half. Judges wield no power over good time.

Governors and presidents also have the power to alter, even negate, the sentences of judges. **Executive clemency,** the power to **pardon** (forgive a criminal punishment) or **commute** (reduce a penalty, such as from execution to life imprisonment), provides yet another powerful limit to judicial sentencing authority.

This complex distribution of the sentencing authority reflects the structure, distribution, and operation of governmental power in general. The doctrines of separation of powers and of checks and balances render official decisions provisional: Prosecutors can overrule police decisions; judges can dismiss prosecutors' charges; parole boards, corrections officials, governors, and presidents can alter the sentences of judges. Because of this separation of authority, these same officials engage in frequent second-guessing among themselves. They attempt to anticipate and then counter the decisions of other officials. If prosecutors want defendants to serve no more than two years in prison and know that particular judges routinely sentence defendants in similar cases to five, prosecutors may well accept plea bargains carrying a maximum of two years in anticipation of such sentences. For example, to assure that convicted defendants actually serve three years, judges sentence them to nine years; they know that prisoners become eligible for release after serving one-third of their sentence. Parole boards, who know defendants plead guilty to offenses less serious than those they actually commit, base their release decisions on actual offense behavior to adjust for the bargain on the charge.[14]

Distributing sentencing authority does more than serve as a formal means of checks and balances and separation of powers. Informally, particularly in unpopular cases, the diffused responsibility for imposing sentence takes the onus off any one institution. For example, no one wants sole charge of sentencing—or releasing—a child abuser. Diffused decision making spreads sentencing responsibility among several officials, thereby permitting a practical solution to an unpleasant and difficult problem.[15]

Sentencing Models

legislative sentencing model
sentencing model in which legislatures prescribe specific penalties, which judges and parole boards cannot alter.

judicial sentencing model
sentencing model in which judges prescribe sentences within broad formal contours set by legislative penalties.

administrative sentencing model *sentencing model in which both legislatures and judges prescribe a wide range of allowable prison times for particular crimes.*

retribution *philosophy of punishment that looks backward in time to punish for crimes already committed.*

Throughout American history, three institutions have exercised sentencing power—legislatures, courts, and administrative agencies—in varying degrees of formality. In the **legislative sentencing model,** legislatures prescribe specific penalties, which judges and parole boards cannot alter. Of course, the police still have discretion to arrest, and prosecutors can tailor charges to suit particular circumstances, as we saw in Chapter 10. Offenders remain eligible for time off for good behavior—good time—as we will see in Chapter 13. Governors and presidents can freely commute or pardon accused and convicted offenders. The legislatively fixed model restricts discretion to alter penalties determined in advance of the crime and without regard to the person who committed it. In other words, punishment fits the crime, not the criminal. Therefore, removing discretion from judges and parole boards does not eliminate discretion from the entire system, but it does limit criminal lawmaking to legislatures.

In the **judicial sentencing model,** judges prescribe sentences within broad formal contours set by legislative penalties. Typically, a statute prescribes a range, such as one to ten years, zero to five years, twenty years to life. Judges then fix the exact time convicted criminals serve. In theory, once judges set a sentence, parole boards cannot alter it, nor does good time reduce it. Thus, on the day judges sentence them, defendants know exactly how long they will spend in prison. Neither prison officials nor parole boards have any discretion in sentencing under this model.

In the **administrative sentencing model,** both legislature and judge prescribe a wide range of allowable prison times for particular crimes. A burglar, for example, may receive a sentence to serve from one day to life. Administrative agencies, typically parole boards and prison administrators, determine the exact release date. Under this model, administrative agencies have broad discretion to determine how long prisoners serve and under what conditions they can be released.

These are, of course only models. As models, these sentencing schemes never operate in pure form. At all times in American history, all three sentencing institutions have overlapped considerably; all have exercised wide discretion. Plea bargaining, for example, has prevented fixing sentencing authority in any of these three. Charge bargaining circumvents legislatively fixed sentences, sentence bargaining avoids judicially fixed sentencing, and both provide means to alter administratively fixed sentences. In general, however, until recent sentencing reforms began to change policy and practice, legislatures set the general range of penalties, judges picked a specific penalty within that range, and parole boards released imprisoned offenders after some time in prison. According to this practice, judges, parole boards, and prison authorities possess considerable discretion in sentencing criminal defendants.

Determinants of Sentencing

The actual sentences judges select within the limits set by law depend on both formal and informal determinants. Formally, the norms expressed in the philosophies of punishment—retribution, rehabilitation, incapacitation, deterrence, and restitution—determine the sentence imposed. Informally, a range of personal, professional, organizational, political, and social influences affect the outcome of the case. Therefore, the sentence actually imposed depends on the legal, social, and even individual structure of particular cases.

Formal Determinants

Punishments, in the most general sense, rest on either retribution or utility. **Retribution** looks backward in time in an effort to punish for crimes already committed; **utilitarian punishment** looks forward in time to prevent future crimes. Hence, retribution focuses on the crime while utility emphasizes the offender. The ancient maxim "an eye for an eye" embodies the essence of retribution: criminals deserve punishment. Retribution assumes a natural human urge expressed in this simple example: If you bump your shin on the table leg, you want to kick the table. Punishment satisfies this assumed natural impulse toward revenge or, more politely, retribution. Retribution assumes free will, that is, it assumes that individuals can and do choose either to commit crimes or to refrain from doing so. If they choose to commit crimes, then they deserve punishment. In other words, retribution advocates the moral rightness of punishing wrongdoers.

Retribution does not look backward entirely; it also performs a utilitarian function. Nothing causes more public anger, breeds more resentment and contempt for law, and more deeply offends the sense of justice than when wrongdoers escape punishment. Retribution—in this sense, formalized vengeance—satisfies the demand for justice. It channels public outrage into the acceptable form of the criminal sentence. If criminal sentences do not satisfy this demand for justice, angry citizens may lose respect for law and even, on occasion, take it into their own hands.

During most of the world's history, retribution was considered a laudable sentencing objective. During the last century, however, retribution fell from favor among reformers devoted to reducing the number of capital offenses and ameliorating the cruel corporal punishments then still lawful, even though infrequently imposed. Some opponents called retribution barbaric, giving rise to the inaccurate belief that "punishment is obsolete." The opposition to retribution was short-lived relative to the whole of world history; it was mainly a Western European and United States phenomenon; and within those societies it affected mainly a small, elite group of academics and criminal justice reformers.

Retribution has returned as the dominant philosophy of punishment in the United States. Called **just deserts,** or the **justice model,** the idea that justice demands punishment has received increasing recognition since the 1970s. Andrew von Hirsch, in his influential *Doing Justice,* published in 1976, argued

> that we should punish criminals simply for the crime committed. We should not do it either to reform them, or to deter them, or to deter others. In other words, punishment should fit the crime already committed, not the criminal—nor the crimes either the criminal or others might commit in the future. The justice model responds to a general sense of justice but raises the difficult question: How much pain and in what form satisfies retribution? For example, how many years in prison is a rape worth?[16]

Political, social, and organizational influences hinder efforts to fix sentencing purely according to a model of justice. Joachim Savelsberg, in his analysis of the adoption and implementation of the Minnesota and federal sentencing guidelines, has demonstrated the effects of these informal influences on the formal structure and process of the justice model of sentencing. Savelsberg found that the same social, organizational, and political realities that led to the creation of the indeterminate sentence are today impeding the implementation of the determinate sentence.[17]

Crime prevention lies at the heart of utilitarian punishment. The three major utilitarian strategies to prevent crime include

- General deterrence.
- Incapacitation.
- Rehabilitation.

General deterrence focuses on those in the general population who are thinking about committing crimes. In theory, sentencing individuals who have already committed crimes "sends a message" to potential criminals, in effect threatening to punish them if they commit crimes. Deterrence, like retribution, assumes free choice. It assumes further that people seek pleasure and avoid pain. We cannot measure exactly the effectiveness of general deterrence, because we do not know how many people avoid committing crimes mainly because they fear punishment. Some researchers suggest that threats of punishment more effectively deter white-collar criminals than street criminals.[18]

Deterrence raises a question similar to the one asked about retribution: How much and what kind of pain will prevent potential offenders from committing crimes? In theory (from the time of Jeremy Bentham, the great English utilitarian philosopher who devised it), deterrence rested morally and practically on inflicting only the amount of pain necessary to affect behavior.

Early deterrence researchers focused on measuring deterrence by aggregate data, that is, by crime rates and conviction and imprisonment rates. More recently, researchers have turned their attention to individuals in the general population. For example, JoAnn L. Miller and Andy B. Anderson surveyed 751 individuals in Baltimore in the crime-prone group between ages 15 and 36. They distributed booklets containing 50 scenarios describing a potential crime opportunity, including an offense, possible economic gain from the crime, risk of getting caught, chance of getting convicted, and specific punishment imposed. They found that "men, especially white men, are more strongly influenced than black men or black women" by the certainty and severity of punishment.[19]

Incapacitation, also called **specific deterrence,** aims at preventing specific offenders from committing crimes. Its basic idea is simple: criminals removed from society cannot victimize innocent persons. Incapacitation can result from three methods:

- Capital punishment.
- Mutilation, such as castration and amputation.
- Incarceration.

Capital punishment, although on the increase since the late 1970s, is still an infrequent occurrence. Mutilation, virtually unheard of in modern America, has returned in a few jurisdictions, a sign of the tough attitude toward criminals. Incarceration, of course, does not prevent crimes against other prisoners, and it cannot incapacitate offenders beyond the term of their imprisonment.[20]

Rehabilitation, the third utilitarian strategy of crime prevention, also targets individual offenders. However, rehabilitation fashions penalties to suit criminals, not crimes. Rehabilitationists consider punishment distasteful, preferring instead to call the objective of criminal sentencing "treatment." The **medical model in criminal justice,** or treating instead of punishing criminals, stems from the idea that training, therapy, and teaching afford criminals the opportunity to change their lifestyles and become law-abiding citizens. Treatment, in the medical idiom, "cures" the "disease" of criminality. Hence, rehabilitating criminals prevents them from committing other crimes.[21]

Restitution obliges offenders to pay—literally—for their crimes. A sentence to restitution orders the convicted criminal to directly repay a victim, and frequently the state as well, for losses sustained from the crime. Although meant primarily to compensate victims, restitution has won support on the grounds that it rehabilitates criminals and prevents them from returning to lives of crime. What rehabilitative and deterrent success it might have depends on wrongdoers realizing, through direct compensation to victims, just how much suffering and loss their crimes have caused.[22]

These general philosophies of punishment affect sentences, but exactly how is difficult to assess because the philosophies are so varied and, in some cases, contradictory. For instance, sentencing highly intelligent muggers to learn legitimate ways to acquire money at Harvard Business School may satisfy the rehabilitative ends of punishment. However, most judges (and certainly the public) do not believe that attending college will satisfy the aims of retribution; imprisonment is more appropriate. Furthermore, judges rarely articulate their general philosophical aims in ways that social scientists can accurately measure. Judges may *say* the purpose of their sentence is to rehabilitate—and may *believe* what they say—when in fact they are incapacitating or punishing offenders. Figure 11.3 shows the results of one survey that asked 17 judges to give the purposes of their sentences of 982 adult offenders.[23]

Informal Determinants

Most informal, or functional, sentencing determinants arise out of the social structure of individual criminal cases. The particular facts surrounding cases and the characteristics of individual offenders influence the sentences judges impose. The legal definitions in criminal codes leave room for judicial discretion to take social characteristics into account in sentencing. Nevertheless, most research on sentencing confirms the pattern that we have noted with regard to other decisions in criminal justice: seriousness of the offense and dangerousness of the offender as reflected in criminal history weigh most heavily in determining the sentence imposed. Interviews with judges, for example, support the conclusion that judges consider offense seriousness the most important determinant in their sentencing, even though individual judges may define seriousness variously and imprecisely.[24]

Most judges surveyed say that past criminal record weighs second only to offense seriousness as the most important sentence determinant. However, the data rarely permit measuring what judges include as criminal records. Some count juvenile records. Others consider arrests part of a prior criminal record. Some judges count only prior convictions. Judges freely apply their own standards to the policy question: What *should* judges include? In this freedom, judicial discretion expresses informal determinants in sentencing.[25]

As in police decisions to stop and arrest, prosecutors' to charge, and the courtroom work group's to plea bargain, the social status of offenders and victims, their relationship to each other, and the specific characteristics of each affect judges' definitions of seriousness and, consequently, the sentences

Figure 11.3

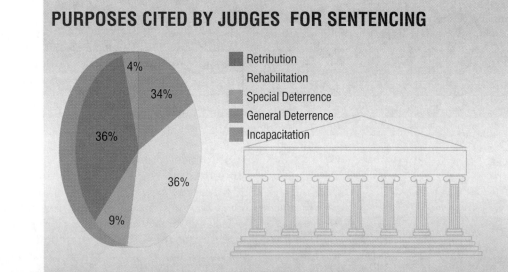

PURPOSES CITED BY JUDGES FOR SENTENCING

- Retribution
- Rehabilitation
- Special Deterrence
- General Deterrence
- Incapacitation

4%
34%
36%
36%
9%

Source: Gottfredsen and Gottfredsen, *Decision Making in Criminal Justice* (New York: Plenum, 1990), 146.

**pre-sentence investigation
(PSI)** *investigation of the prior
criminal record, the social history,
and sometimes a psychiatric
evaluation of defendants upon
which sentencing partially depends.*

they impose. Age, family relationships, employment status, and demeanor
affect sentencing. Judges do not give the same sentence to young first
offenders with families to support that they give to multiple offenders with no
family or employment ties. Offenders with well-established employment
records ordinarily do not receive sentences identical to those with little or no
work record. Judges treat guilty pleas more leniently than convictions at trial.
Status also affects sentencing. Low-status offenders who commit crimes
against high-status victims receive the harshest sentences. Low-status offenders who victimize low-status persons receive more lenient sentences than
high-status offenders who victimize high-status persons. High-status offenders
who victimize low-status individuals receive the most lenient sentences.
Similar outcomes may also characterize interracial and intraracial crimes,
and crimes involving gender differences.[26]

Organizational determinants also affect sentences. Heavy caseloads prevent giving careful individual attention to each case, and sentencing takes on
a routinized character to keep cases moving. Crowded prisons and jails lead
judges to sentence fewer offenders to incarceration and more to noninstitutional alternatives, such as probation, restitution, and community service.
Judges ordinarily sentence offenders in ways that do not unduly upset
courtroom work group relationships. Public opinion and political pressures
also influence sentencing. Famous defendants, prominent victims, or victims
who generate sympathy cause judges to tailor sentences to suit the facts of
the case. Heavy media attention also affects sentencing.

Personal and behavioral characteristics of individual victims and offenders also affect sentencing. Attractive female victims sometimes induce
harsher sentences. On the other hand, individual characteristics can soften a
penalty. In Wisconsin, a judge imposed no penalty on a convicted rapist
because "the victim's enticing dress and the general aura of permissiveness
provoked the offender." Victims who acted provocatively, used excessive
self-defense, consented, or were negligent can also reduce a judge's sentence.
Contrite, submissive, clearly remorseful offenders can reduce sentences.
Unrepentant ones can aggravate sentences. One judge ignored a defense
request for probation instead of prison time because a physician convicted of
involuntary manslaughter for recklessly providing a young patient with
barbiturates that killed her refused to accept responsibility for his actions.[27]

Despite these important individual, organizational, and social influences
on sentencing in particular cases, offense seriousness and offender dangerousness remain the dominant influences. After thoroughly reviewing all the
available research on sentencing, a distinguished panel of the National
Academy of Sciences concluded:

> Using a variety of different indicators, offense seriousness and offend-
> ers' prior record emerge consistently as the key determinants of sen-
> tencing. The more serious the offense and the worse the offender's
> prior record, the more severe the sentence. The strength of this conclu-
> sion persists despite the potentially severe problems of pervasive biases
> arising from the difficulty of measuring—or even precisely defining—
> either of these complex variables. This finding is supported by a wide
> variety of studies using data of varying quality in different jurisdictions
> and with a diversity of measures of offense seriousness and prior crimi-
> nal record.[28]

Pre-Sentence Investigation

Judges need adequate information in order to sentence defendants. The
pre-sentence investigation (PSI) and the pre-sentence report (PSR) based
on it provide this information. Pre-sentence investigation focuses on the prior
criminal record, the social history, and sometimes a psychiatric evaluation of

defendants. Most professional groups associated with sentencing have recommended mandatory PSIs. The federal government led the way in adopting the PSI, and most states have followed its lead.[29]

One major part of the PSR enumerates the facts of the case, drawn from the police report and the defendant's version of what happened. As might be expected, police and defendant versions often diverge widely. Judges usually accept the police version, which critics argue treats defendants unfairly. A second part of the PSI and PSR deals with the prior criminal record, that is, the **criminal history** of offenders. The criminal history naturally includes prior convictions. Most reports also contain records of arrests and dropped charges, even if they were not officially recorded. Controversy exists over whether criminal histories should count arrests, because arrests require only probable cause and convictions demand proof beyond a reasonable doubt.

Judges also consider the *social* history of defendants critical to their sentencing decisions. According to judges, social histories enable them both to determine defendants' potential for rehabilitation and to predict their future behavior. Social histories include such things as family history, employment record, and education of offenders. When available, psychiatric evaluations, although done infrequently, are also included.

The pre-sentence investigation and report cause some major problems. In the many cases involving guilty pleas, sentencing occurs *before* a PSI can affect the sentence. As a result, some judges withhold final acceptance of plea bargains until they have seen completed PSIs. If the PSI is completed in time, it may affect the plea negotiations themselves. Problems can also arise over the quality of information in the report. Overburdened probation officers, responsible for conducting most PSIs, must gather information while supervising convicted criminals on probation. Always pressed for time, probation officers cannot always verify information, and judges may unwittingly use this erroneous information to sentence defendants.

Moreover, changes in sentencing philosophy can make some information in PSIs irrelevant. For more than a century, pre-sentence information was tailored toward prediction and rehabilitation. In the shift toward retribution, deterrence, and incapacitation, information considered important for rehabilitation and prediction has little relevance. In addition, probation officers do not have as much influence on sentencing as their reported wide agreement with judges suggests. One study challenges the probation officer's central role

Sentences to "chain gangs" is an increasingly popular punishment.

in sentencing. Based on his 15 years of experience as a probation officer and on qualitative interviews with probation officers, Professor John Rosecrance concluded that probation officers write pre-sentence reports for three audiences: the court, the prosecutor, and the probation supervisor. They use the report to maintain their credibility, looking for cues from these audiences and providing them with recommendations that are "in the ballpark," that is, what judges, prosecutors, and supervisors want to hear. Probation officers make ballpark recommendations not to influence their audiences' perceptions of defendants, but to legitimate their own claim to being "reasonable."[30]

Types of Sentences

Judges can impose several types of sentences. Most dramatically, they can sentence convicted murderers to death or mutilation. They can also sentence convicted offenders to humiliating penalties. One judge ordered a shoplifter to walk through a shopping center with a sign reading, "I shoplifted from K-Mart." Another judge sentenced a drunk driver to put a sticker on his car notifying others of his conviction. An Indiana appeals court, however, ruled that a trial judge overstepped his bounds when he sentenced an unemployed father who failed to pay child support to stand on a courthouse lawn and hold a sign that read, "Need Job to Support Children."[31]

Judges can also sentence offenders to community service, such as working in hospitals, jails, or other public institutions, or to perform menial work such as cleaning streets or collecting trash. These punishments, although they attract attention, rarely occur in day-to-day criminal sentencing.

The most frequent sentence that judges impose is probation, followed in frequency by incarceration. Offenders convicted of less serious crimes, but not sentenced to probation, go to jail; convicted felons go to prison. In most jurisdictions, local jails house offenders with short sentences, usually less than one year, frequently for 30 days or less. Most convicted felons serve some time in prison, where sentences exceed one year. However, up to a quarter of felons receive probation in some jurisdictions, and about a fifth receive a split sentence, time in jail followed by release on probation for the remainder of the sentence. Judges also impose fines for many petty crimes.

You Decide   Are Castration and Electric Shock Appropriate Sentences?

Castration
While he was on probation for molesting a 7-year-old girl, Steven Allen Butler, a 28-year-old with a wife and child of his own, was convicted of aggravated sexual assault for repeatedly raping a 13-year-old girl. Butler, who shines shoes for a living, and who was in the Houston jail awaiting trial, asked the court to sentence him to castration instead of life imprisonment. At the sentencing hearing, Judge Michael McSpadden agreed to allow the castration in return for a plea of guilty to the charges of aggravated sexual assault. In return, Judge McSpadden said he would sentence Butler to 10 years probation, after which, if the probation was successfully completed, the conviction would be removed from his record. Butler's wife agreed to the castration. So did the parents of the victim.

Doctors who treat sex offenders, as well as advocates of victims' rights, criticize the castration of sex offenders.

They say castration is a "simplistic and questionable solution to a complex problem." "This is not the answer," says Cassandra Thomas, president of the National Coalition Against Sexual Assault. "It sounds good. It makes you feel good, but in the long haul it doesn't deal in any way with the basic issues of sexual assault." Surgical castration—the removal of the testicles—reduces the sex drive but does not necessarily eliminate the capacity to get an erection. Chemical castration—the use of drugs to suppress the sex drive—is less drastic.

Other countries offer castration as an alternative to prison. During the 1960s, Denmark castrated about 2,000 men, according to the distinguished criminologist Marvin Wolfgang. Wolfgang says, however, "I don't think castration is necessary. In Germany and Italy, they have used anti-androgens, which have been very effective in reducing the sex drive." Anti-androgens suppress the male hormones and are also used in the United States. Dr. John Money, who has worked with anti-androgens since 1966, says, "I know of several cases in which people chose to be treated with drugs, usually Depo-Provera, rather than go to jail. Usually it's a condition of probation. I know people call it chemical castration, but it's reversible, and it's not castration at all."

Judge McSpadden advocates castration because traditional punishment does not work. "We're all painfully aware," he says, "that present laws in Texas and elsewhere neither protect society nor effectively treat sex offenders. I've been on the bench 10 years, and I've seen over and over, the moment these people are released back into society, the violence begins again. Here in Harris County, we had 2,500 children raped last year, and these are just reported rapes. If we dare call ourselves a civilized society, we can't tolerate that and other daily violence we see."

But Cassandra Thomas argues that castration "buys into the myth that sexual assault is about sex. I think it ignores the issues of power, control, feelings of anger that are prime motivators." Dr. Michael Cox, director of the sexual abuse treatment center at Baylor College of Medicine in Houston, opposed the castration of Steven Allen Butler. "It's being held up as some sort of panacea that's somehow going to reverse the violent crime problem we have. I think it's a scary precedent. It purports to offer a simple and very primitive biological solution to a very complex social problem."

Legal experts say castration raises questions of coercion. "It's clear that mandatory castration, or any other corporal mutilation, would be cruel and unusual punishment," says Stephen Schulhofer, professor of criminal law at the University of Chicago. "So the question is, if the state can't directly take away your sexuality, should they be able to do it by the back door like this? But the other view is, if the defendant thinks it's a better choice, why should we take it away?"[32]

Copyright, 1992 by the New York Times Co. Reprinted with permission.

Questions

What are the arguments for and against castration? Do you favor compulsory surgical castration? Under what conditions? Why? Do you oppose castration of any kind? Defend your answer. Do you favor voluntary chemical castration? Defend your answer.

Electric Shock

The acute punishment of electric shock is easily demonstrated to be superior in every respect to our current punishment practices. Compare a typical occurrence in today's courtroom with what we would have in the future if only we could get it straight that it is pain, pure and simple, that is the essence of punishment.

The judge peers out over his glasses at the pathetic woman who sits across the courtroom. In a violent outburst she has just called him a heartless tyrant or something to that effect. The public defender and a courtroom guard restrain her.

"Mrs. Washington," says the judge. "This is your third shoplifting offense. You leave me no choice." He hesitates, expecting another outburst. Mrs. Washington's three-year-old daughter sits next to her, eyes wide and watery. The judge tries to avoid her gaze. "Mrs. Washington, it is the judgment of this court that you be sentenced to a minimum of six months in the penitentiary and a maximum of one year. Your daughter will be turned over to the care of the Department of Youth, since the presentence report indicates that you have no husband or relatives who could care adequately for her."

The mother is led, crying, out of the courtroom. The child pulls at her mother's skirt, crying "Mama! Mama!" But the hands of the court are upon her, and an innocent child is about to be punished for the crime of having a guilty mother.

Every day, all across America, many, many families and relatives of offenders suffer in this way. This means that literally thousands of people are punished for other people's crimes.

Now an example of what punishment of the future could be like. Twenty-year-old John Jefferson stands along with his lawyer, the public defender. "John Jefferson," says the judge, "the court has found you guilty of burglary in the first degree. Because this is your first offense, but the damage you did was considerable, I sentence you to. . . ." The judge pushes a few buttons at his computer console. The average sentence for similar cases to Jefferson's flashes on the display: five shock units. "You will be taken immediately to the punishment hall to receive five shock units. Court dismissed."

The victim of this crime is sitting at the back of the court. He approaches the court clerk, who directs him to the punishment hall where he will be able to watch the administration of the punishment. Jefferson's wife and child are ushered to the waiting room where they will await Jefferson's return after he has been punished. Meanwhile, in the punishment hall, Jefferson is seated in a specially designed chair. As part of the arrest procedure he has already received a medical examination to establish that he was fit to receive punishment.

In addition to the victim, a few members of the press are seated on the other side of the glass screen. The punishment technician, having settled the offender in the chair, returns to an adjoining room where he can observe the offender through a one-way screen. A medic is also present. The technician sets the machine at the appropriate pain level, turns the dial to 5, and presses the button. Jefferson receives five painful jolts of electricity to his buttocks. He screams loudly, and by the time the punishment is over, he is crying with pain. The technician returns and releases the offender. "Stand and talk a little," he says. Jefferson walks around, rubbing his buttocks. A shade drops over the spectators' screen.

"Do you still feel the pain?" asks the medic. "Goddam, I sure do! But it's getting better. Can I go now?" "Just sign here, and you've paid your dues." Jefferson sighs happily and asks, "Which way to the waiting room?" "Straight down the passage and second left." Jefferson enters the waiting room where his wife rushes into his arms, crying, "I'm so glad it's over! Thank goodness you weren't sent to prison."

We see in this example that only the guilty person is punished. The punishment administered is clean, simple, and, most importantly, convincingly painful. It is over in a brief time, and the offender is able to return to his family and his job. Punishment is confined only to the guilty. The side effects of punishment are minimized.[33]

Graeme Newman, *Just and Painful,* 2d edition, NY: Harrow and Heston Publishers, 1995. Reprinted with permission.

Questions

What arguments in favor of corporal punishment do you see in this excerpt? What arguments against it? What formal and informal purposes of punishment does it serve? Do you agree judges should use it? Why? Why not? Defend your answer.

Sentencing in Japan

The Japanese Criminal Code was enacted in 1908. Although the Justice Ministry, criminal law specialists, politicians, and practitioners recommended reforms following World War II, as of 1990 reforms were not yet implemented. Based on the German Criminal Code of 1871, the present Japanese Code retains the same sentencing alternatives as the German code, now nearly 125 years old. The principal sanctions include

● Death.
● Imprisonment with forced labor.
● Imprisonment without forced labor.
● Short-term imprisonment of up to thirty days.
● Fines.

Figure 11.4 depicts the distribution of these sentences in 1986.

Figure 11.4

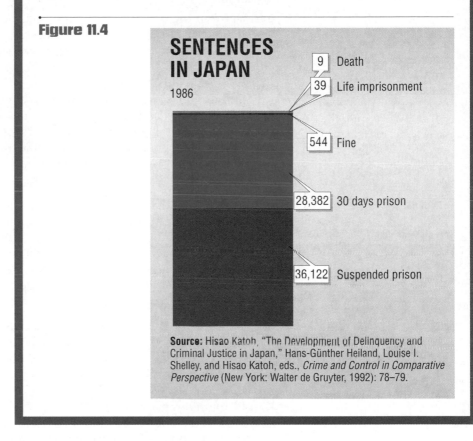

SENTENCES IN JAPAN
1986

9	Death
39	Life imprisonment
544	Fine
28,382	30 days prison
36,122	Suspended prison

Source: Hisao Katoh, "The Development of Delinquency and Criminal Justice in Japan," Hans-Günther Heiland, Louise I. Shelley, and Hisao Katoh, eds., *Crime and Control in Comparative Perspective* (New York: Walter de Gruyter, 1992): 78–79.

Disparity and Discrimination in Sentencing

sentencing discrimination *influence on sentencing of unacceptable criteria, such as race, ethnicity, and gender.*
sentencing disparity *the differences—not necessarily discriminatory—in sentences among individuals.*

Sentencing discrimination means the use of unacceptable criteria, such as race or gender, to determine what sentences to impose. **Sentencing disparity** means sentencing inequality of three different types:

1. *Different sentences imposed on similar offenders.* For example, two burglars the same age, with similar records, break into stores after hours and each takes $100 from the cash register. One burglar goes to prison, the other gets probation.
2. *Similar sentences imposed on different offenders.* For example, a five-time burglar gets the same sentence as a first-time burglar.

3. *Similar offenders receiving different sentences for unimportant differences.* For example, an armed robber who takes $1,000 receives a sentence twice as long as an armed robber who takes $750.[34]

Beginning with Lyndon Johnson's Crime Commission's report in 1967, a storm of popular criticism has blamed the indeterminate sentence for arbitrary and inconsistent penalties. One group of critics has focused on the amount of racial discrimination in sentencing. Researchers have tried to explain why in a general population of 11.5 percent adult African-American males in the United States, the sentenced population includes nearly 50 percent adult African-American males. As early as 1928, critics asserted that judges imposed more severe sentences on African Americans than on whites. Early critics also charged that women benefitted from reverse discrimination in sentencing. Women, it was reported, received probation and suspended sentences more frequently than did men.[35]

Later studies challenged these early findings. For example, according to some research, taking seriousness of offense and criminal records into account removed the disparity among minorities, women, and white adult men. Early research on the connection between race and sentencing suffered from two shortcomings. First, most sentencing research depended on **aggregate sentencing data;** that is, combined data from diverse localities. Aggregate data often obscure local differences. For instance, conclusions based on all sentences in a state might hide racially determined sentences in particular counties, or the use of aggregate data for one jurisdiction might obscure the racism of individual judges.[36]

A study in Georgia demonstrates the importance of disaggregating data. Martha A. Myers and Susette M. Talarico studied the impact of race on sentencing in a random sample of 16,798 Georgia felons. They compared these data with those from a comparable random sample of 1,685 Georgia felons from Fulton and Dekalb counties. They found little system-wide discrimination against African Americans.

> We expected that sanctions would be more severe in counties characterized by pronounced inequality, a sizeable percentage of black unemployed residents, and relatively high crime rates. In actuality, we found little evidence to support these expectations. . . . We found no consistent relationship with punitiveness in sentencing. Nor did the presence of large economically subordinate populations, whether black or unemployed, foster more severe sanctions.[37]

Second, when Myers and Talarico looked more closely at different communities, courts, and times, however, they found that "the absence of evidence of system-wide discrimination does not mean that all courts and judges are blind in the administration of criminal law. Interactive analysis revealed context-specific patterns of discrimination." As a result, they found significant differences in sentencing to prison, depending on the seriousness of the crime combined with the racial composition of the community. They also found that African Americans were incarcerated longer than whites on the average, no matter what the racial makeup of the community. Disparity could, however, result in leniency as well as severity:

> Importantly, however, there were many instances in which blacks receive disproportionately lenient punishment. Although this pattern may suggest a paternalism that is just as discriminating as disproportionate punitiveness, it nevertheless indicates that courts in Georgia do not have a heavy hand with black defendants in the general systemic sense or in every context where differential treatment is observed.[38]

Researchers clearly have not settled the problem of the degree and nature of racial discrimination and disparity in sentencing. The prestigious National

Academy of Sciences panel on sentencing research, after surveying all the research on discrimination in sentencing, concluded:

> Despite the number and diversity of factors investigated as determinants of adult sentences in different statistical studies, two-thirds or more of the variance in sentence outcomes remain unexplained. The literature indicates that offense seriousness and offender's prior record are the key determinants of sentences. Factors other than racial discrimination in sentencing account for most of the disproportionate representation of blacks in U.S. prisons, although racial discrimination in sentencing may play a more important role in some regions or jurisdictions, for some crime types, or in the decisions of individual participants. The evidence of discrimination on grounds of social and economic status is uncertain; the evidence on the role of sex in sentencing is only preliminary. The strongest and most persistently found effect of case processing variables is the role of guilty pleas in producing less severe sentences.[39]

Most research has not separated race from other characteristics such as gender, poverty, offense seriousness, and prior criminal record. Joan Petersilia of the Rand Institute in Santa Monica, California, studied convicted felons in California, Texas, and Michigan, hoping to sort out the important factors that influence sentencing. Controlling for these other influences, Petersilia found that more African Americans and Hispanics were sentenced more frequently to longer prison terms than were whites. In a replication relying on a larger data base, however, Petersilia, along with Stephen Klein and Susan Turner, found race not related to sentencing. Cassia Spohn and her associates, on the other hand, found that African-American males are sentenced to prison at a rate 20 percent higher than that for white males.[40]

According to Spohn and her colleagues:

> Judges in Metro City apparently do discriminate against black males in deciding between incarceration and lengthy probation. White males are more likely to receive probation, black males a short prison term.[41]

Furthermore, John H. Lindquist and his associates examined judicial processing of 2,859 men and women prostitutes in a southwestern Texas city, based on computerized judicial files in criminal district courts. They found that women, repeaters, and non-repeater minorities were more frequently convicted. Heterosexual offenders and minorities were more frequently jailed. Minorities were sentenced most harshly.[42]

Gary D. LaFree analyzed 755 defendants in Tucson and El Paso, whose most serious charge was robbery and burglary. He found major differences between the two cities. In Tucson, no significant differences appeared in the sentencing of Hispanics and non-Hispanics. In El Paso, on the other hand, Hispanics received longer sentences. Interviews with criminal justice officials suggested that the established Hispanic population in Tucson, versus the less-established Mexican American and Mexican national populations in El Paso, accounts for the difference in treatment. According to one El Paso prosecutor:

> We're sitting here on a border. Across the river from us, which is nothing more than an oversized mud puddle, is the city of Juarez, with over a million and a quarter residents. . . . Our police force is geared to the size of this city and what it can afford. El Paso does not have the economic base to support the city itself. In other words, we perceive El Paso as the city north of the Rio Grande, but bullshit, we're talking about another million and a quarter people that go back and forth like a tide.[43]

Another difference between the cities is the aggressive, adversarial stance toward prosecutors taken by Tucson public defenders, an attitude not found

Racial disparity clearly exists in the U.S. but it is not clear to what extent racial *discrimination* explains the disparity.

in other Arizona cities. In contrasting the public defenders of Tucson and Phoenix, for example, one Tucson public defender said of the relationship with prosecutors, "It's more of a combat mentality here." Another said that public defenders in Phoenix "are much more prone to plead a case out than we are." Texas, however, has no public defender system. Judges assign defenders from a list of private attorneys. As a result, indigent El Paso defendants get lawyers without trial experience.[44]

Finally, LaFree found significant differences in the language assistance provided by Tucson and El Paso. Both cities provide translators for defendants who cannot speak English. However, because of El Paso's high Hispanic population (over 60 percent, compared to 21 percent in Tucson) and the cost of providing translators (El Paso is a poorer community than Tucson), El Paso defendants suffer from inadequate translation, "a major block to equal treatment for southwestern Hispanics."[45]

The research in race, gender, and status discrimination in sentencing demonstrates that methodology and local variation account for much of the mixed results reported by researchers. Further research based on sophisticated methodology such as the sampling reviewed here, drawn from a greater variety of settings, should add to the incomplete state of our knowledge as of this writing. Research to date suggests disparities and discrimination in some places under some conditions. Answers to how extensive it is, how deliberate, and how linked to other factors await further research.

The broad range of sentencing options—such as one to five years, thirty years to life, or even one year to life—that is common under indeterminate sentencing statutes has also received major criticism. These sentences place no real limits on judicial discretion in sentencing; hence, the term **lawlessness in sentencing.** In a stinging rebuke to lawless sentencing, the distinguished federal judge Marvin E. Frankel, in his widely read and acclaimed *Criminal Sentences,* wrote:

> [T]he almost wholly unchecked and sweeping powers we give to judges in the fashioning of sentences are terrifying and intolerable for a society that professes devotion to the rule of law. Federal trial judges, answerable only to their varieties of consciences, may and do send people to prison for terms that may vary in any given case from none at all up to five, ten, thirty, or more years. This means in the great majority of federal criminal cases that a defendant who comes up for sentencing has no way of knowing or reliably predicting whether he will walk out of the courtroom on probation, or be locked up for a term of years that may consume the rest of his life, or something in between.[46]

Critics have also called indeterminate sentencing ineffective. Despite what they perceive as all-out efforts to treat and rehabilitate criminals, crime continues to increase. Political scientist James Q. Wilson, in his best-selling *Thinking About Crime,* reported that the public widely believed sentences were too lenient—that soft-hearted, weak-willed judges were "letting too many criminals off with a slap on the wrist." Hence, critics argued, swift, certain, and more severe penalties ought to replace existing open-ended sentences.[47]

Others argued that rehabilitation simply did not work, no matter how long prison sentences were. In the early 1970s, sociologist Robert Martinson headed a major study surveying rehabilitation programs in the United States. Martinson's study gained wide readership and characterized both pessimistic attitudes about reforming criminals and renewed confidence in retribution and incapacitation. Distorting Martinson's findings, critics concluded that "nothing works" when it comes to rehabilitation programs. As a result, these critics rejected the whole underlying rehabilitative premise on which indeterminate sentencing rested, leading one author to entitle an article "The Rehabilitation of Punishment" as an apt description of penal policy during the 1970s.[48]

A distinguished panel from the National Research Council of the National Academy of Sciences surveyed rehabilitation research and considerably softened Martinson's conclusions. The panel concluded that

> although there is little in the reported literature that demonstrably works, the conclusion that "nothing works" is not necessarily justified. It would be more accurate to say instead that nothing yet tried has been demonstrated to work. This is true because many plausible ideas have not been tried and because the research done so far, even when theoretically informed, has not been carried out satisfactorily. The research has been flawed by limitations in the evaluation of programs, the questionable degree to which treatments are actually implemented, and the narrow range of approaches actually attempted.[49]

Several researchers have concluded that ineffective programs, not rehabilitation itself, account for the failures of rehabilitation. Most programs lack adequate resources. Most adequately funded programs labeled "treatment" in fact rely on coercion and punishment. The few truly rehabilitative and adequately funded programs have registered promising results. These few successful programs suggest that some types of programs for some kinds of offenders show considerable promise.[50]

Two programs directed at helping ex-prisoners survive financially illustrate this point. Peter Rossi and others conducted an experiment with released felons in Texas and Georgia. The control group was released with no financial help. An experimental group was given up to six months of financial assistance, roughly equivalent to unemployment insurance. Called the Transitional Aid Research Project (TARP), the experiment showed that the prisoners who received financial assistance were arrested less frequently than those in the control group. Ann Dryden Witte found that North Carolina prisoners who were part of a work-release group in prison committed less serious offenses after they were freed than those who were not part of the work-release group.[51]

Despite criticism, rehabilitation still enjoys some support. Surveys indicate that although the public and some criminal justice professionals demand harsher punishment, most also want to rehabilitate offenders.[52]

Sentencing Reform

By the 1970s, attacks on rehabilitation and the indeterminate sentence created an active sentencing reform movement. A variety of reforms resulted, including bans on plea bargaining (see Chapter 10), determinate sentencing laws, sentencing guidelines, and mandatory minimum sentencing laws. All the reforms have focused on limiting or even eliminating discretion in sentencing. They all respond to demands for

- *Uniformity.* Similar offenses should receive similar punishment.
- *Certainty and Truth in Sentencing.* Convicted offenders, victims, and the public should know that the sentence imposed is similar to the sentence actually served.
- *Retribution, Deterrence, Incapacitation.* Rehabilitation of individual offenders is not the primary aim of punishment.

Determinate Sentencing Laws

Determinate sentencing laws limit judicial discretion by prescribing a narrow range of penalties from which judges can choose in sentencing offenders. In determinate sentencing, defendants know their release date at the time they are sentenced. California, a pioneer in indeterminate sentencing and rehabilitation, broke new ground in its 1976 determinate sentencing law. In an abrupt about-face, the state enacted the Uniform Determinate Sentencing Law, which proclaimed that "the purpose of imprisonment is punishment," not treatment or rehabilitation. The California law reflected widespread national dissatisfaction with the indeterminate sentencing system to rehabilitate offenders. In a pattern that was followed nationally, conservatives who believed indeterminate sentencing was too lenient made a formidable political alliance with liberals who believed indeterminate sentences were too severe and that they discriminated racially. The alliance successfully removed what both believed was a proven failure.[53]

The California law created four categories of offenders, each category including a small range of penalties:

- Category 1—sixteen months, two, and three years.
- Category 2—two, three, and four years.
- Category 3—three, four, and five years.
- Category 4—five, six, and seven years.

According to the law, "When a judgment of imprisonment is ordered, the court shall order the middle of the three possible prison terms, unless there are circumstances in mitigation or aggravation of the crime."[54]

Under the old indeterminate sentencing system, judges could impose high maximum penalties, but the parole board determined the actual time served, which was supposed to depend on the rehabilitation of individual offenders. Formally, the new law drastically reduced the authority of judges to impose sentences, and it removed the enormous power of the parole board

sentencing guidelines *method of sentencing that establish ranges of penalties within which judges can sentence offenders.*
presumptive sentencing guidelines *sentencing method in which either legislatures or special commissions set the types and ranges of sentences.*

to determine actual time served. In practice, the new system imposes sentences similar to those under the old laws. Presumptive sentences, or the discretion of judges to sentence within the narrow range, explain the limited effect of the statute. Based on the average time served under the old system, presumptive sentences allowed judges and others tied to the courtroom work group to continue practices in effect prior to the change and to reach similar results.[55]

The law may also have had some undesired results. It decreased, not increased, sentence uniformity. Under the old system, the parole board, called the Adult Authority, a centralized state agency, tended to decide like cases similarly, no matter what the law permitted. The new system placed most of the sentencing power in the hands of the prosecutor. Because the new law restricted the authority of judges to sentence and that of the Adult Authority to release, the charging discretion of the prosecutor and plea bargaining act as mechanisms that provide flexibility. Furthermore, although commitments to prison increased (in place of probation), length of time actually spent in prison decreased. In addition, substantial regional variations also resulted: "There was at least as much variation in the use of imprisonment, between counties, as there had been before the law came into effect—which is to say, quite a lot." These variations reflect an important dimension to all attempts to reform criminal justice by legislation—the "propensities of local officials" to serve their own interests and to reflect the "going rates" for criminal punishment as the "local legal culture" determines them.[56]

On the positive side, California's determinate sentencing law may have enhanced racial equity in sentencing. Stephen P. Klein, Susan Turner, and Joan Petersilia reviewed California sentencing based on official records of 11,553 persons convicted of assault, robbery, burglary, theft, forgery, and drug offenses. Using a combination of defendant and crime characteristics and criminal justice processing variables, they found no relation between race and sentence types, particularly prison or probation, or sentence length.[57]

California's experience with determinate sentencing contains an important lesson. Informal pressures, habits, and relationships among local work groups, along with formal objectives in criminal sentencing and punishment, create obstacles to changing long-established sentencing practices. Sentencing requires both enough certainty derived from formal controls to generate confidence in its fairness and sufficient flexibility to provide for individual differences. These differences arise from the facts and circumstances of each case; informal discretion furnishes that flexibility.

historical note

The indeterminate sentence rests fundamentally upon the theory that there is a difference in criminals that cannot be provided for by statute. The act does not always indicate the man, and a sudden access to temptation through the influence of association, through the lack of family influence, may cause him to commit an act which the statute declares a crime.

Minnesota State Parole Board, 1911-1912

Sentencing Guidelines

Seventeen states and the federal government have adopted some form of **sentencing guidelines** that establish ranges within which judges can sentence offenders. Most guidelines have at least four major purposes:

1. *Uniformity:* improving the chances that similar offenders who have committed similar offenses will receive similar penalties.
2. *Neutrality:* reducing the chances that race, gender, ethnicity, age, and class affect sentencing by restricting the type and length of sentence to the seriousness of the offense and the criminal history of the offender.
3. *Truth:* insuring that the type and length of sentences that offenders actually serve nearly equal the sentences judges impose. That is, "You do the crime, you do the time."
4. *Control:* preventing rapidly growing prison populations from overtaking prison space and state resources.

In **presumptive sentencing guidelines,** either legislatures or special commissions set the types and ranges of sentences. Judges *must* sentence within the prescribed ranges, unless they can justify in writing their departures from the guidelines according to criteria usually prescribed in a guidelines manual. **Voluntary sentencing guidelines** merely *suggest* possible sentences. Judges can, and often do, follow the suggested sentences, but they are not legally bound to do so. The specific types and exact ranges of sentences are either descriptive or prescriptive. In **descriptive sentencing guidelines,** the guidelines are based on what the sentencing practices within the state *actually are;* the guidelines merely put in writing what judges have actually been doing. **Prescriptive sentencing guidelines** develop new sentencing norms, based on what decision makers decide the type and range of penalties *should be.*

Minnesota, a pioneer guidelines state, adopted its guidelines in order to reduce judicial discretion and sentencing disparity without increasing prison populations. The Minnesota guidelines incorporate a "modified deserts sentencing model"; they base sentences on a combination of the severity of the convicted offense and the criminal history of the offender. The guidelines regulate both disposition, that is, the decision to impose a sentence of incarceration or probation, and the length of jail and prison terms. Figure 11.5 reproduces the Minnesota grid, or matrix as it is sometimes called, for determining sentences under the modified deserts model.

The rows on the grid contain offenses and the columns represent a score for criminal history. The bold line, called the disposition line, represents the boundary between presumptive stayed sentences, that is, those cases in which judges suspend prison sentences for the number of months specified in the grid. The numbers below the bold line are the presumptive executed sentences, that is, those cases in which judges sentence offenders to prison. The numbers in the cells present the range of months as guides to the sentence a judge may choose. For example, a first-time aggravated robbery conviction carries a recommended sentence of 48 months, but the judge can choose either 44 or 52 months without formally departing from the guidelines. Permitting judges to choose within a range without departing from the guidelines builds flexibility into the system, a flexibility that allows for differences in individual cases. Characteristics, such as the amount of money stolen, the extent of personal injury inflicted, and the criminal history of the offender can affect the sentence judges impose without undermining the basic goals of uniformity and equity.

According to the Minnesota Sentencing Guidelines Commission, judges can depart from the presumptive range when the "individual case involves substantial and compelling circumstances." The following are reasons for departing downward, that is, going below the presumptive range:

1. The victim was the aggressor in the crime.
2. The offender played a minor role in the crime.
3. The offender lacked the capacity of judgment due to physical or mental impairment.

Reasons for departing upward, that is, going above the presumptive range, include:

1. The victim was particularly vulnerable.
2. The victim was treated with particular cruelty.
3. The offense was a major drug offense.
4. The offender committed a crime against the person for hire.

If judges depart beyond the presumptive range, they must give written reasons for their departures. If judges depart *upward,* defendants can appeal the departure. If judges depart *downward,* the prosecution can appeal the departure.[58]

Terance D. Miethe and Charles A. Moore evaluated the impact of the Minnesota sentencing guidelines. They noted a shift in prison populations

Figure 11.5

Italicized numbers within the grid denote the range within which a judge may sentence without the sentence being deemed a departure. Offenders with nonimprisonment felony sentences are subject to jail time according to law.

Criminal History Score

Severity Level of Conviction Offense (Common offenses listed in italics)		0	1	2	3	4	5	6 or more
Sale of Simulated Controlled Substance	I	12[1]	12[1]	12[1]	13	15	17	19 *18-20*
Theft Related Crimes ($2500 or less) Check Forgery ($200-$2500)	II	12[1]	12[1]	13	15	17	19	21 *20-22*
Theft Crimes ($2500 or less)	III	12[1]	13	15	17	19 *18-20*	22 *21-23*	25 *24-26*
Nonresidential Burglary Theft Crimes (Over $2500)	IV	12[1]	15	18	21	25 *24-26*	32 *30-34*	41 *37-45*
Residential Burglary Simple Robbery	V	18	23	27	30 *29-31*	38 *36-40*	46 *43-49*	54 *50-58*
Criminal Sexual Conduct, 2nd Degree (a) & (b)	V	21	26	30	34 *33-35*	44 *42-46*	54 *50-58*	65 *60-70*
Aggravated Robbery	VI	48 *44-52*	58 *54-62*	68 *64-72*	78 *74-82*	88 *84-92*	98 *94-102*	108 *104-112*
Criminal Sexual Conduct, 1st Degree Assault, 1st Degree	VII	86 *81-91*	98 *93-103*	110 *105-115*	122 *117-127*	134 *129-139*	146 *141-151*	158 *153-163*
Murder, 3rd Degree Murder, 2nd Degree (felony Murder)	IX	150 *144-156*	165 *159-171*	180 *174-186*	195 *189-201*	210 *204-216*	225 *219-231*	240 *234-246*
Murder, 2nd Degree (with intent)	X	306 *299-313*	326 *319-333*	346 *339-353*	366 *359-373*	386 *379-393*	406 *399-413*	426 *419-433*

Presumptive stayed sentence; at the discretion of the judge, up to a year in jail and/or other non-jail sanctions can be imposed as conditions of probation. However, certain offenses in this section of the grid always carry a presumptive commitment to a state prison. These offenses include Criminal Vehicular Homicide, Third Degree Controlled Substance Crimes when the offender has a prior felony drug conviction, Burglary of an Occupied Dwelling when the offender has a prior felony burglary conviction, second and subsequent Criminal Sexual Conduct offenses and offenses carrying a mandatory minimum prison term due to the use of a dangerous weapon (e.g., Second Degree Assault). See sections **II.C Presumptive Sentence** and **II.E Mandatory Sentences.**

Presumptive commitment to state imprisonment. First Degree Murder is excluded from the guidelines by law and continues to have a mandatory life sentence. See section **II.E Mandatory Sentences** for policy regarding those sentences controlled by law.

from property offenders to violent criminals, an outcome consistent with the intent of the Minnesota legislature to move property offenders into community corrections. They also noted that, despite its rigorous and systematic construction, the system allows ample opportunity for sentencing disparity. Presumptive standards restrict the *direct* introduction of socioeconomic biases into sentencing decisions, but do not prevent their indirect entry. For example, since judges can depart from the ranges set in the guidelines, biases can remain hidden in these departures, despite the requirement that judges give written reasons for them. Also, the guidelines shift the more open form of discretion exercised by judges at sentencing to the less visible discretionary decision making of prosecutors in selecting charges and in plea bargaining. In summary, the guidelines cannot eliminate the influence of socioeconomic, gender, and racial biases from either judicial departures or prosecutorial discretion in charging and plea bargaining.[59]

Miethe and Moore compared dispositions before and after the guidelines were implemented. They found that offense severity, criminal history, weapon use, and personal crimes predicted both whether and how long judges sentenced convicted offenders to prison. In other words, the guidelines reduced the *direct* impact of social and class attributes. However, gender, marital status, and employment status continued to affect sentencing indirectly; they significantly relate to convicted severity and criminal history. Employment status continues to affect charging and plea-bargaining decisions.[60]

Joachim Savelsberg examined the changes effected by the implementation of the Minnesota sentencing guidelines. He noted that the Minnesota Sentencing Guidelines Commission tried to change the existing practice of sentencing property offenders to longer terms than violent offenders, as reflected in the grid shown in Figure 11.5. At first, Savelsberg discovered, the sentencing guidelines did change the practice. However, because prosecutors disagreed with the new policy, they tried to establish the old practice: harsher penalties for property offenders. They succeeded by "defining charges for property offenders in a more detailed way so that the criminal history score of property offenders added up faster." In other words, the guidelines merely shifted discretion and the influence of sociological factors from judges to the charging discretion of prosecutors. According to Savelsberg, the powerful, informal social, organizational, and ideological influences impeded, if they did not entirely defeat, the formal goal of sentencing according to the severity of the crime.[61]

The impact of sentencing guidelines on sentencing reform remains uncertain. Descriptive guidelines have little effect on judicial discretion. Voluntary guidelines depend on cooperation and support from all participants. Presumptive/prescriptive guidelines may have more effect, but sociological variables still affect the sentencing decision, as Savelsberg demonstrated in Minnesota. Political pressures also affect sentencing under guidelines. In Minnesota, for example, a combination of general demands for harsher punishment and a few highly publicized, gruesome rape-kidnapping-murders spurred the legislature to increase the severity levels of most crimes during the late 1980s and early 1990s. Sentencing guidelines, like all sentencing practices, must contend with contemporary political pressures, well-entrenched practices, and the need to balance certainty and predictability with flexibility and individual needs. They are, as they should be, a product of the society that creates them and in which they operate.[62]

You Decide   Were the Departures Justified?

United States v. Rivera, 994 F.2d 942 (1st Cir. 1993)

Facts
Each of these two appeals concerns the district court's power to impose a sentence that departs from the Sen-

tencing Guidelines. The first case involves Mirna Rivera, a single mother of three small children. Ms. Rivera was convicted of carrying about a pound of cocaine from New York to Providence. She appeals her 33-month sentence of imprisonment. She argues that the district court would have departed downward from the minimum 33-month Guidelines but for the court's view that it lacked the legal "authority" to depart. She says that this view is legally "incorrect" and she asks us to set aside her sentence.

The second case involves a union official, Robert Adamo, who embezzled about $100,000 from his union's Health and Welfare Fund. The district court departed downward from the 15- to 21-month prison term that the guidelines themselves would have required. Instead, the court imposed a term of probation without confinement. The court said that it was departing downward so that Mr. Adamo could continue to work and to make restitution to the fund. The government appeals. It argues that Adamo's circumstances are insufficiently unusual to warrant the departure.

We agree with the appellants in both cases. In our view, the district court sentencing Ms. Rivera held an unduly narrow view of its departure powers. The district court sentencing Mr. Adamo failed to analyze the need for departure in the way that the law requires. We consider both cases in this single opinion because doing so may help to illustrate an appropriate legal analysis for "departures." We shall first set forth our view of the portion of the law here applicable; and we shall then apply that law to the two appeals.

Opinion

The basic theory of the Sentencing Guidelines is a simple one. In order to lessen the degree to which different judges imposed different sentences in comparable cases, an expert Sentencing Commission would write Guidelines, applicable to most ordinary sentencing situations. In an ordinary situation, the statutes, and the Guidelines themselves, would require the judge to apply the appropriate guideline—a guideline that would normally cabin, within fairly narrow limits, the judge's power to choose the length of a prison term. Should the judge face a situation that was not ordinary, the judge could depart from the Guidelines sentence, provided that the judge then sets forth the reasons for departure. A court of appeals would review the departure for "reasonableness.". . .

The Sentencing Statute itself sets forth the basic law governing departures. It tells the sentencing court that it shall impose a sentence of the kind, and within the range. . . established for the applicable category of offense committed by the applicable category of defendant as set forth in the Guidelines. . . . The statute goes on immediately to create an exception for departures by adding that the sentencing court shall "impose" this Guidelines sentence unless the court finds that there exists an aggravating or mitigating circumstance of a kind, or to a degree, not adequately taken into consideration by the Sentencing Commission in formulating the Guidelines that should result in a sentence different from that described. . If the sentencing court makes this finding and sentences "outside the [Guidelines] range," it must state in open court. . . the specific reason for the imposition of a sentence different from that described [in the Guidelines]. The defendant may then appeal an upward departure, and the Government may appeal a downward departure. On appeal, if the court of appeals determines that the sentence. . . is unreasonable, . . . it shall state specific reasons for its conclusions and . . . set aside the sentence and remand the case for further sentencing proceedings with such instructions as the court considers appropriate. . . .

The Guidelines deal with departures in four basic ways.

1. *Cases Outside the "Heartland."* The [U.S. Sentencing] Commission intends the sentencing courts to treat each guideline as carving out a "heartland," a set of typical cases embodying the conduct that each guideline describes. The Introduction goes on to say that when a court finds an atypical case, one to which a particular guideline linguistically applies, but where conduct significantly differs from the norm, the court may consider whether a departure is warranted. . . .

. . . [A] case that falls outside the. . . guideline's "heartland" is a candidate for departure. It is, by definition, an "unusual case." And, the sentencing court may then go on to consider, in light of the sentencing system's purposes, whether or not the "unusual" features of the case justify departure. . . . Thus, (with a few exceptions) the law tells the judge, considering departure, to ask basically, "Does this case fall within the 'heartland,' or is it an 'unusual case?' "

2. *Encouraged Departures.* In certain circumstances, the Guidelines offer the district court. . . special assistance, by specifically encouraging departures. Part 5K [of the Guidelines] lists a host of considerations that may take a particular case outside the "heartland" of any individual guideline and, in doing so, may warrant a departure. The individual guidelines do not take account, for example, of an offender's "diminished capacity," which circumstance, in the Commission's view would normally warrant a downward departure. Nor do certain guidelines (say, immigration offense guidelines) take account of, say, use of a gun, which circumstance would remove the situation (the immigration offense) from that guideline's "heartland" and would normally warrant an upward departure. . . .

3. *Discouraged Departures.* The Guidelines sometimes discourage departures. Part 5H, for example, lists various "specific offender" characteristics, such as age, education, employment record, family ties and responsibilities, mental and physical conditions, and various good works. The Guidelines say that these features are "not ordinarily relevant" in determining departures. . . . At the same time, the Commission recognizes that such circumstances could remove a case from the heartland, but only if they are present in a manner that is unusual or special, rather than "ordinary." It may not be unusual, for example, to find that a convicted drug offender is a single mother with family responsibilities, but, at some point, the nature and magnitude of family responsibilities (many children? with handicaps? no money? no place for children to go?) may transform the "ordinary" case of such circumstances into a case that is not at all ordinary. Thus, a sentencing court, considering whether or not the presence of these "discouraged" factors warrants departure, must ask whether the factors themselves are present in unusual kind or degree. The Commission, in stating that those factors do not "ordinarily" take a case outside the heartland, discourages, but does not absolutely forbid, their use.

4. *Forbidden Departures.* The Commission has made several explicit exceptions to the basic principle that a

sentencing court can consider any "unusual case" (any case outside the heartland) as a candidate for departure. The Guidelines state that a sentencing court "cannot take into account as grounds for departure" race, sex, national origin, creed, religion, and socio-economic status. The Guidelines also state that "lack of guidance as a youth" cannot justify departure, that drug or alcohol abuse is not a reason for imposing a sentence below the Guidelines range, and that personal financial difficulties and economic pressure upon a trade or business do not warrant a decrease in sentence. Thus, even if these factors make a case "unusual," taking it outside an individual guideline's heartland, the sentencing court is not free to consider departing. But, with these. . . exceptions, the sentencing court is free to consider, in an "unusual case," whether or not the factors that make it unusual (which remove it from the heartland) are present in sufficient kind or degree to warrant a departure. The court retains this freedom to depart whether such departure is encouraged, discouraged, or unconsidered by the Guidelines. . . .

If the district court decides to depart, the defendant may appeal (an upward departure) or the Government may appeal (a downward departure). The statute then provides the appellate court with two important instructions. First, the court of appeals must decide if the resulting sentence is "unreasonable, having regard for" the sentencing court's reasons and the statute's general sentencing factors. Second, the court of appeals must (as it ordinarily does) give "specific reasons" for its decision. . . .

We now apply our "departure" analysis to the circumstances of the two cases before us, the appeal of Ms. Mirna Rivera, and that of Mr. Robert Adamo.

Mirna Rivera

For purposes of this appeal, we take Ms. Rivera to have transported about one pound of cocaine, from New York to Providence, with intent to distribute it, in violation of 21 U.S.C. § 841(a)(1), (b)(1)(B). The Guidelines provide a sentence of 33 to 41 months' imprisonment for a first time offender who has engaged in this conduct. See U.S.S.G. § 2D1.1(a)(3), (c)(10) (base offense level of 24); U.S.S.G. § 3B1.2(a) (reduction of 4 points for minimal participation); U.S.S.G. Ch. 5, Pt. A (sentencing table). Ms. Rivera argued to the district court that it should depart downward from this Guidelines sentence for the following reasons: (1) she has three small children, ages three, five, and six, who need a mother's care; (2) she lives solely on welfare, receiving no financial aid from her former husband; (3) she has virtually no contact with any other family member (except for a sister, with five children, also on welfare); (4) she has never before engaged in any criminal activity; and, (5) she committed this single offense because of an unwise wish to obtain money for Christmas presents for her children. The district court decided not to depart. Rivera claims that this decision reflects the court's incorrect belief that it lacked the legal authority to depart. And, she asks us to order a new proceeding.

After reviewing the record of the sentencing proceeding, we conclude that Rivera is correct. The district court's analysis of the nature of its power to depart is not consistent with the view of departures that we set forth in this opinion. We recognize a difference between "forbidden departures," and "discouraged departures." And, we believe that the district court did not realize that it had the legal power to consider departure, where departure is discouraged (but not forbidden), if it finds features of the case that show it is not ordinary.

At the sentencing hearing, the district court said:

> With respect to Defendant's argument that the Defendant's family situation, economic situation, warrants a departure, I must say that the guidelines are drawn to apply to everyone in exactly the same way, that it is clear from the guidelines that the economic situation and the family situation of the Defendant is not a consideration. There are those who certainly would disagree with that, but that is the principle that is embodied in the guidelines. They are age blind, they are sex blind, they are blind to family circumstances, and can result in their application in a certain amount of cruelty. But, that isn't a basis for making a departure. It's a situation where somebody tries to draw a straight line that applies to every situation that can possibly arise and this Court is without discretion to take what might well be thought by most people, at least, legitimate concerns into consideration. Simply put, I can't do that because the guidelines do not permit me to do that. So that Defendant's objection or request to make a downward departure is denied. . . . Your Counsel says that a court somewhere observed that these guidelines are not a straitjacket for a District Court. Well, I don't agree with that. Here is a circumstance where I'm satisfied that the reason you did this was to buy toys for your children at Christmas. It was a serious mistake. The pre-sentence report says this: There is no information suggesting that Ms. Rivera had any previous participation in a similar type criminal activity. The Defendant's lifestyle is not indicative of that of a drug dealer who has profited from ongoing criminal activity. Rather she appears destitute, relying on public assistance to support herself and her children. . . . If I had the authority to do it, I would not impose the sentence that I am about to impose. I would impose a lesser sentence because I think that these guidelines simply are unrealistic when applied to real-life situations like this. They may work in many circumstances, but they certainly don't work here.

In these statements, the court repeatedly said that it lacked the legal power to depart; it characterized the case before it as different from the "many circumstances" where the Guidelines might work; it added that it would depart if it could; it set forth several circumstances that might make the case a special one; and it described as identical ("sex blind" and "blind to family circumstances") guidelines that, in fact, differ significantly, the former involving a "forbidden" departure, and the latter a "discouraged" departure. Taken together, these features of the case warrant a new sentencing proceeding, conducted with the district court fully aware of its power to depart in "unusual cases" and where family circumstances are out of the "ordinary.". . . .

. . . The upshot is a difficult departure decision. On the one hand lie a host of quite special circumstances (though many are of the "discouraged" sort), and on the other hand lies the simple fact that Ms. Mirna Rivera did transport a pound of cocaine from New York to Providence. This is the kind of case in which, if the district court departs, its informed views as to why the case is special would seem especially useful and would warrant appellate court "respect."

We remand the case for further proceedings.

Robert Adamo

Mr. Adamo was convicted of embezzling about $100,000 belonging to the union Health and Welfare Fund of which he was a fiduciary, in violation of 18 U.S.C. § 664. He accepted responsibility for the crime, U.S.S.G. § 3E1.1. It was his first offense. The Guidelines provided a minimum prison term of fifteen months. See U.S.S.G. §§ 2E5.2, 2B1.1, 3B1.3 (base offense level of 4; increase of 8 points for amount of loss; 2 level enhancement for more than minimal planning; 2 level enhancement for fiduciary); U.S.S.G. Ch. 5, Pt. A (sentencing table). The district court, departing downward from the Guidelines, sentenced Mr. Adamo to probation alone, without any imprisonment.

The court gave the following reasons for its downward departure:

> When I look at these cases of sentencing, the first thing I ask myself is, "What sentence would I impose if there were no guidelines?" That's what I did for more than 20 years. And then I ask myself, "What's a just sentence in these circumstances? Am I going to be limited by these artificial guidelines made by people who have no idea of what kind of a case I'm going to have to decide?" No two cases are the same. . . . So that's where justice is in this case, having restitution made to this Health & Welfare Fund. If I send this defendant to prison I think it's foreordained that restitution will not be made. It may be made in some respect, but I'm sure the defendant would lose both his jobs and would find it very difficult to have employment which would allow him to make restitution. And a time in prison would serve no useful purpose in this case. The only factor in sentencing which would be accomplished is punishment, but the defendant has been punished just by being here—just being here and what's he's gone through in the last six months, and the notoriety of this. So, imprisonment serves no useful purpose in this case. It certainly isn't a matter of deterrence. I'm sure the defendant will never do anything like this again. Here is a man who has lived an exemplary life, he's worked two jobs to take care of his family. His wife has worked, and although they were making in the range of $70,000 a year, the problem of educating two children came up. It's a problem that everyone faces. This is where the error of judgment comes in. He took this money, not out of greed, not out of desire to own a fancy car or a palatial home and a boat, but to educate his children. He didn't think about the other alternatives. His daughter wanted to go to an expensive private school, instead of going to a local state school of some sort, and he thought that's what she should have. He didn't consider loans and other types of programs. This money was available, he took it—a terrible mistake. But that's the only mistake that he seems to have made, and I just don't think he should spend time in prison because of this one mistake. I want restitution made, so I'm going to exercise my best judgment in these circumstances. My best judgment is to have as long a term of probation as possible so that restitution can be made with the guidance of the probation office. So, I'm going to depart downward and impose a term of probation of five years. That's the maximum that I can impose. And one of the conditions of probation will be, and is, that the defendant shall pay restitution in the amount of $91,125.62 to the Health & Welfare Fund of the Building Service Employees International Union, AFL-CIO Local 334.

The court's explication of its reasons is useful, for it produces understanding and permits evaluation, both by appellate courts and by the Commission. We nonetheless believe the analysis does not permit the departure before us.

First, we believe. . . that the embezzlement guidelines encompass, within their "heartland," embezzlement accompanied by normal restitution needs and practicalities (i.e., the simple facts that restitution is desirable and that a prison term will make restitution harder to achieve). It would seem obvious, and no one denies, that the embezzlement guidelines are written for ordinary cases of embezzlement, that restitution is called for in many such cases, and that prison terms often make restitution somewhat more difficult to achieve. Moreover, the embezzlement guideline reflects the Commission's intent to equalize punishments for "white collar" and "blue collar" crime. Yet, as the Sixth Circuit has pointed out, a rule permitting greater leniency in sentencing in those cases in which restitution is at issue and is a meaningful possibility (i.e., generally white-collar crimes) would. . . nurture the unfortunate practice of disparate sentencing based on socioeconomic status, which the guidelines were intended to supplant. Further, the district court itself, stating that it did not wish "to be limited by these artificial guidelines," and that "no two cases are alike," seemed to disregard, rather than to deny, the scope of the embezzlement guideline. For these reasons, we join the Fourth and Sixth Circuits, in holding that ordinary restitution circumstances of this sort do not fall outside the embezzlement guideline's "heartland," and therefore do not warrant a downward departure.

Second, we recognize that a special need of a victim for restitution, and the surrounding practicalities, might, in an unusual case, justify a departure. But, we cannot review a district court determination to that effect here, for the district court made no such determination. . . . We mention this fact because the defendant has pointed to one unusual feature of the case. The record before us contains a suggestion that Mr. Adamo could keep his job (and therefore remain able to make restitution) were his prison term only one year, but he could not keep his job (and thus would lose his ability to make restitution) were he sentenced to the Guidelines prison term of one year and three months. We can imagine an argument for departure resting upon a strong need for restitution, an important practical advantage to the lesser sentence, and a departure limited to three months.

We are not arguing such a departure or saying that we would eventually find it lawful. We mention the special circumstance to underscore the need for reasoned departure analysis, sensitive to the way in which the Guidelines seek to structure departure decisions and to the role that such departures, and their accompanying reasons, can play in the continued development of the Sentencing Guidelines. . . . The district court, in Mr. Adamo's case, may wish to conduct such an analysis in light of the special features of the case to which the defendant has pointed. We therefore remand this case for new sentencing proceedings.

The sentences in both cases are vacated and the cases are remanded to the district court for resentencing.

So ordered.

What is the basic philosophy of the federal sentencing guidelines? Explain the difference between "heartland" and "unusual" cases and its effect on sentencing under the guidelines. What specific facts justify the departure in the case of Ms. Rivera? Would you allow the departure?

Argue the case for and against the departure, and then give your reasons for departing or not departing. What facts do not justify the departure in the case of Mr. Adamo? Would you disallow the departure? Give reasons why or why not.

mandatory minimum sentence laws *determinate sentencing laws that require offenders to serve at least some time in prison.*

Mandatory Minimum Sentencing Laws

The mandatory minimum sentence is one major response to complaints about indeterminate sentences and the concurrent public concern about crime. **Mandatory minimum sentence laws** require that offenders convicted under the laws serve at least some time—the "mandatory minimum"— in prison. Judges can neither suspend the mandated minimum sentence nor substitute probation for it. Prison and parole authorities cannot release offenders before the statutory minimum period has passed. Essentially, mandatory minimum sentence laws promise that "if you do the crime, you *will* do the time."

Mandatory penalties are very old. The Old Testament "eye for an eye" and "tooth for a tooth" are mandatory penalties. The Anglo-Saxon king Alfred prescribed a detailed mandatory penalty code, including such provisions as "If one knocks out another's eye, he shall pay 66 shillings, 6 1/3 pence. If the eye is still in the head, but the injured man can see nothing with it, one-third of the payment shall be withheld." As early as 1790, mandatory penalties were established for capital crimes. Throughout the nineteenth century, Congress enacted mandatory penalties—usually short prison sentences—for a long list of crimes, including refusal to testify before Congress, failure to report seaboard saloon purchases, or causing a ship to run aground by use of a false light.[63]

Until the 1950s, the use of mandatory minimum penalties was only an occasional occurrence in the twentieth century. Fear of crime and drugs in the 1950s, brought on in part, it was believed, by a Communist plot to get Americans "hooked" on especially potent "pure Communist heroin" from China, led Congress to enact the Narcotic Control Act of 1956. The Boggs Act, as it was called after its sponsor, signalled a shift to a heavier reliance on mandatory minimum sentences. The Senate Judiciary Committee explained why the Congress needed a mandatory minimum sentence drug law:

> [T]here is a need for the continuation of the policy of punishment of a severe character as a deterrent to narcotic law violations. [The Committee] therefore recommends an increase in maximum sentences for first as well as subsequent offenses. With respect to the mandatory minimum features of such penalties, and prohibition of suspended sentences or probation, the committee recognizes objections in principle. It feels, however, that, in order to define the gravity of this class of crime and the assured penalty to follow, these features of the law must be regarded as essential elements of the desired deterrents, although some differences of opinion still exist regarding their application to first offenses of certain types.[64]

The statute imposed stiff mandatory minimum sentences for narcotics offenses, requiring judges to pick within a range of penalties. Judges could not suspend sentences or put convicted offenders on probation. Offenders were not eligible for parole if they were convicted under the Act. For example, the Act punished the first conviction for selling heroin by a term of from 5 to 10 years of imprisonment. Judges had to sentence offenders to at least 5 years in prison; they could not suspend the sentence or put the offender on probation; offenders were not eligible for parole for at least the minimum period of the sentence. For second offenders, the mandatory minimum was raised to 10 years. The penalty for the sale of narcotics to persons under 18 years of age ranged from a mandatory minimum of 10 years to a maximum of life imprisonment or death.[65]

In 1970, Congress retreated from the mandatory minimum sentence approach. In the Comprehensive Drug Abuse Prevention and Control Act of 1970, Congress repealed virtually all the mandatory minimum provisions adopted in the 1956 Act, saying the increased sentence lengths "had not shown the expected overall reduction in drug law violations." Among the reasons for the repeal were that mandatory minimum penalties for drug law offenses

- alienated youth from the general society.
- hampered rehabilitation of drug offenders.
- infringed on judicial authority by drastically reducing judicial discretion in sentencing.
- reduced the deterrent effect of drug laws because even prosecutors thought the laws were too severe.

According to the House Committee considering the bill:

> The severity of existing penalties, involving in many instances minimum sentences, have led in many instances to reluctance on the part of prosecutors to prosecute some violations, where the penalties seem to be out of line with the seriousness of the offenses. In addition, severe penalties, which do not take into account individual circumstances, and which treat casual violators as severely as they treat hardened criminals, tend to make conviction more difficult to obtain.[66]

The retreat from mandatory minimum sentences was short-lived, as public concern about violence and drugs rose to the top of the national agenda. The public and legislatures blamed rising crime rates, in part at least, on the uncertainty and "leniency" of indeterminate sentences. Beginning in the early to mid-1970s, the states and federal government enacted more and longer mandatory minimum prison sentences. By 1991, 46 states and the federal government had enacted mandatory minimum sentencing laws. Although the list of such laws is long (the U.S. Criminal Code contains at least 100), the main targets of mandatory minimum sentences are drug offenses, violent crimes, and crimes committed with a weapon.[67]

Mandatory minimum sentences aim to satisfy basic aims of criminal punishment: retribution, incapacitation, and deterrence. They promise that serious crimes will receive severe punishment. Violent criminals, criminals who use weapons, and drug offenders cannot harm the public if they are in prison. The knowledge that committing mandatory minimum crimes will bring certain, severe punishment should deter other potential offenders.

Evaluations suggest that mandatory minimum penalties in practice do not always achieve the goals their proponents hoped they would. The National Institute of Justice assessed two mandatory minimum sentence laws, one in New York and one in Massachusetts. In 1973, the New York legislature enacted "the nation's toughest drug law." For example, the possession of two ounces of heroin or the sale of a single ounce carried a minimum 15 to 25 years in prison. A second conviction for the unlawful possession of any "stimulant, hallucinogen, hallucinogenic substance, or LSD," with intent to sell carried a minimum term of 1 to 813 years. Conviction for the possession of one ounce of marijuana carried a one-to five-year minimum prison sentence.

The results of the New York drug law were disappointing. Drug offense conviction rates dropped 30 percent. Heroin use following enactment was as widespread as before. Serious property crime—the kind generally believed to be linked to drug use—increased sharply, despite the tough legislation. The law probably did not deter convicted felons from committing further crimes.

A rigorous Department of Justice evaluation concluded that "the threat embodied in the words of the law proved to have teeth for relatively few offenders" because "mandatory sentencing laws directly affect only an end product of a long criminal justice process—the convicted offender." The statute also had some serious side effects. It slowed down the criminal process and worked a real hardship in some cases. One 38-year-old woman with no prior criminal record, for instance, was sentenced to life imprisonment for possessing one ounce of heroin.[68]

In 1974, Massachusetts enacted the Gun Control Act. The law imposed a mandatory minimum one-year sentence on anyone who failed to comply with the state's long-time requirement that handgun owners license their weapons. The law allowed no chance of reducing the minimum by probation, parole, or judicial manipulation. The National Institute of Justice evaluation showed more positive results from the Massachusetts gun control law than from the New York drug law. Despite widespread predictions that the law would not work, officials did not evade the law and more persons were imprisoned for violating it. Finally, fewer people carried firearms as a result of the stiff new penalties.[69]

Why these mixed results in Massachusetts and New York? First, the number of gun control cases was very small—the Massachusetts law increased the overall caseload by only about 70 cases a year, while the New York drug act covered thousands of cases. Second, the Massachusetts law enjoyed much more support than did the New York law. Mandatory minimum sentences, it seems from these results, depend for their effectiveness on the conditions in which they are implemented. Research regarding Michigan's Felony Firearm Statute further complicates matters. Michigan's gun law mandated an additional two-year minimum sentence for carrying a gun during the commission of a felony. A popular law because it distinguished between lawful and unlawful use of guns (which the Massachusetts law did not), the Michigan statute enjoyed wide support. The statute does not prohibit plea bargaining; nevertheless, the Wayne County prosecutor initiated a policy forbidding negotiations regarding the law. In a combined qualitative and quantitative analysis relying on interviews with judges, prosecutors, and defense attorneys, and on case dispositions in Detroit (Wayne County), Milton Heumann and Colin Loftin found that the law had little impact on the severity of sentences.[70]

In 1990, Congress ordered the United States Sentencing Commission to evaluate the rapidly increasing number of mandatory minimum sentencing in the federal system. The results of the Sentencing Commission's study provided little empirical support for the success of mandatory minimum sentencing laws. To determine the reasons for the support of mandatory minimum sentences, researchers first reviewed legislative history, statements by the executive branch, and views expressed in academic literature. The Commission also conducted and analyzed field interviews with judges, assistant U.S. attorneys, defense lawyers, and probation officers. They found, among others, the following reasons for supporting mandatory minimum sentences:

- *Equality.* Mandatory minimum penalties assure that the same offenses receive the same sentences.
- *Certainty.* Mandatory minimum penalties assure truth in sentencing because both the public and offenders know that offenders will really serve the minimum time in prison the sentence imposes.
- *Just Deserts.* Violent and drug offenders, habitual criminals, and criminals who use guns to commit crimes deserve mandatory long prison terms.
- *Deterrence.* Mandatory prison sentences deter crime by sending the strong message that those who commit mandatory minimum offenses *will* go to prison.

● *Incapacitation.* Mandatory prison terms protect public safety by locking up drug dealers and violent armed criminals.[71]

The Commission conducted an empirical study of federal mandatory minimum sentencing statutes. They used data from three major sources of pre-sentence reports prepared by probation officers; data derived from sentencing hearings, plea agreements, and sentencing guideline worksheets; and an in-depth analysis of a 12.5 percent random sample of drug and firearms cases. These were cases that extracted information about the amount of drugs by type and the facts regarding "using and carrying" firearms that triggered the mandatory minimum sentences.

Some of the findings were:

● Only a few of the mandatory minimum sentencing provisions are ever used. Nearly all those used relate to drug and weapons offenses.

● Only 41 percent of defendants whose characteristics and behavior qualify them for mandatory minimum sentences actually receive them.

● Mandatory minimum sentences actually introduce disparity in sentencing. For example, the Commission found that race influences disparity in a number of ways. Whites are less likely than Blacks and Hispanics to be indicted, or convicted at the mandatory minimum. Whites are also more likely than Blacks and Hispanics to receive reductions for "substantial assistance" in aiding in the prosecution of other offenders.

The mandatory minimum sentence laws allow an exception for offenders who provide "substantial assistance" in investigating other offenders, but only on the motion of prosecutors. Substantial assistance also leads to disparities quite apart from race. It tends to favor the very people the law was intended to reach—those higher up in the chain of drug dealing—because underlings can offer less assistance to the government. In one case, for example, Stanley Marshall, who sold less than one gram of LSD, got a 20-year mandatory prison sentence. Jose Cabrera, on the other hand, who the government estimated made more than $40,000,000 from importing cocaine and who would have qualified for life plus 200 years, received a prison term of 8 years for providing "substantial assistance" in the case of Manuel Noriega. According to Judge Terry J. Hatter, Jr., "The people at the very bottom who can't provide substantial assistance end up getting [punished] more severely than those at the top."[72]

● Mandatory minimum sentences do not eliminate discretion; they merely shift it from judges to prosecutors. Prosecutors can use their discretion in a number of ways, including manipulation of the "substantial assistance" exception and the decision not to charge defendants with crimes carrying mandatory minimum sentences, or to charge them with mandatory minimum crimes of lesser degree. New York prosecutors gave three reasons why they avoided mandatory minimum sentence laws: First, because of limited resources, charging every drug courier with a mandatory minimum crime would overwhelm the courts. Second, most couriers have limited culpability; therefore, they do not deserve mandatory prison sentences. Third, judges do not like sentencing low-level couriers to prison.[73]

The Commission recommended further study before drawing any final conclusions about the effectiveness of mandatory penalties. But their findings, along with other research, suggest that mandatory minimum penalties are not the easy answer to the crime problem that politicians promise and the public hopes.[74]

Was the Mandatory Minimum Sentence Appropriate?

Easterbrook, Circuit Judge United States v. Brigham, 977 F.2d 317 (7th Cir. 1992)

Facts

Steep penalties await those who deal in drugs. Buying or selling 10 kilograms of cocaine—even agreeing to do so, without carrying through—means a minimum penalty of 10 years' imprisonment, without possibility of parole. 21 U.S.C. §§ 841(b)(1)(A), 846. The "mandatory" minimum is mandatory only from the perspective of judges. To the parties, the sentence is negotiable. Did a marginal participant in a conspiracy really understand that a 10-kilo deal lay in store? A prosecutor may charge a lesser crime, if he offers something in return. Let's make a deal. Does the participant have valuable information; can he offer other assistance? Congress authorized prosecutors to pay for aid with sentences below the "floor." Let's make a deal.

Bold dealers may turn on their former comrades, setting up phony sales and testifying at the ensuing trials. Timorous dealers may provide information about their sources and customers. Drones of the organization—the runners, mules, drivers, and lookouts—have nothing comparable to offer. They lack the contacts and trust necessary to set up big deals, and they know little information of value. Whatever tales they have to tell, their bosses will have related. Defendants unlucky enough to be innocent have no information at all and are more likely to want vindication at trial, losing not only the opportunity to make a deal but also the two-level reduction the sentencing guidelines provide for accepting responsibility.

Mandatory minimum penalties, combined with a power to grant exceptions, create a prospect of inverted sentencing. The more serious the defendant's crimes, the lower the sentence—because the greater his wrongs, the more information and assistance he has to offer to a prosecutor. Discounts for the top dogs have the virtue of necessity, because rewards for assistance are essential to the business of detecting and punishing crime. But what makes the post-discount sentencing structure topsy-turvy is the mandatory minimum, binding only for the hangers on. What is to be said for such terms, which can visit draconian penalties on the small fry without increasing prosecutors' ability to wring information from their bosses?

Our case illustrates a sentencing inversion. Such an outcome is neither illegal nor unconstitutional, because offenders have no right to be sentenced in proportion to their wrongs. Chapman v. United States, _____U.S. _____, _____- _____, 111 S.Ct. 1919, 1928–29, 114 L.Ed.2d 524 (1991). Still, meting out the harshest penalties to those least culpable is troubling, because it accords with no one's theory of appropriate punishments.

Agents of the Drug Enforcement Agency learned from an informant that Craig Thompson was in the market to buy 10 kilograms of cocaine. The DEA's undercover agents feigned willingness to supply him. During negotiations, Thompson said that he had just sold 17 kilograms and needed 10 more that very day to tide his organization over until the arrival of a shipment that he was expecting. Thompson and the agents did not trust one another. Jeffrey Carter, one of Thompson's goons, searched an agent; the agent's gun, normal in the business, did not trouble Carter, but a transmitter or recorder would mean big trouble. Carter was not very good at his job; he didn't find the concealed recorder. Thompson ultimately agreed to pay $30,000 per kilogram, a premium price for quick service. After the agents let on that they didn't trust Thompson any more than Thompson trusted them, Thompson agreed to let the agents hold his Rolls Royce as collateral until payment. In the agents' presence, Thompson called Tyrone Amos and told him to pick up "ten of those things today" at a suburban motel. Thompson and Carter would hand over the Rolls in a different suburb.

At the appointed time, less than five hours after the agents first met Thompson, one team descended on a restaurant to receive the Rolls Royce and another decamped to the motel to "deliver" the cocaine. Amos arrived at the motel in a car driven by Anthony Brigham. Amos and the agents at the motel had a conversation; Brigham stayed in the car. Carter had not appeared at the restaurant with the Rolls Royce, so everyone settled down to wait. Brigham looked around the parking lot but scrunched down in his seat when the agents' Corvette drove slowly by. At the restaurant, Thompson and the agents discussed future deals of 50-100 kilograms per month. At the motel, Brigham paced nervously in the lobby. After touring the parking lot again, lingering over the Corvette, Brigham joined Amos at a nearby gas station, where Amos placed a phone call. The two had a conversation and returned to the motel, where Amos told the agents that Carter and the Rolls were still missing. While Amos and one agent were dining together some distance from the motel, Thompson paged Amos with news that the Rolls had arrived. Back at the motel, the agents went through the motions of delivering cocaine. As Amos headed for the agents' car to retrieve the drugs from the trunk, Brigham moved his car to a location from which he could keep the delivery in sight. But there was no cocaine. Before Amos could open the trunk other agents moved in, arresting Amos and Brigham, just as they pinched Thompson and Carter at the restaurant.

All but Brigham pleaded guilty and provided valuable assistance to prosecutors. All but Brigham were sentenced to less than the "mandatory" minimums. Thompson received 84 months' imprisonment and Amos 75 months, after the prosecutor made motions under § 3553(e). Carter, who was allowed to plead to a charge that did not carry a minimum term, received 4 years' probation, 4 months of which were to be in a work-release program run by the Salvation Army. That left Brigham, who went to trial, was convicted, and received the "mandatory" term of 120 months' imprisonment.

Opinion

Judge Easterbrook

Was the evidence sufficient? Appellate judges do not serve as additional jurors. After a jury convicts, the question becomes whether any sensible person could find, beyond a reasonable doubt, that the defendant committed the crime. That is a steep burden, for 12 persons, presumably sensible and having a more direct appreciation of the evidence than the written record affords to appellate judges, have unanimously found exactly that.

Brigham emphasizes that "mere" presence at a crime does not implicate the bystander in that offense. Conspiracy is agreement, and what proof of agreement did the prosecutor present? Brigham arrived with Amos, conferred with Amos, and was in position to watch an exchange occur. No one testified that Brigham had any role in the exchange or Thompson's organization. Although the prosecutor portrayed Brigham as a lookout, he asks: What kind of lookout would be unarmed, without radio, pager, cellular phone, or any other way to give or receive alerts? What countersurveillance operative would hunker down in the car rather than keep a hawk-eyed watch? Thompson, Carter, and Amos, who reaped rewards for their assistance, were conspicuously absent at Brigham's trial. Had they no evidence to offer against him?

No one questions the rule that "mere presence" at the scene of a crime does not prove conspiracy. "Mere" presence differs from, say, "revealing" presence. Like many a weasel word, "mere" summarizes a conclusion rather than assisting in analysis. When the evidence does not permit an inference that the defendant was part of the criminal organization, the court applies the label "mere presence." So we must examine the evidence, taking inferences in the light most favorable to the jury's verdict, rather than resting content with slogans.

Brigham shows up on short notice with Amos, who the jury could conclude was there to receive 10 kilograms of cocaine from strangers whom Thompson and Amos do not trust. Is Amos likely to come alone? Is a companion apt to be ignorant of the nature and risks of the transaction? For almost three hours Brigham remains at the motel, generally observant and generally nervous; he follows Amos to a pay phone where a telephone call and conversation ensue. Amos reveals the contents of this conversation to the agents; the jury could conclude that he revealed it to Brigham too. While Amos and an agent go to dinner, Brigham keeps watch. After Amos returns, eye contact and a nod from Amos lead Brigham to take up position where he can watch the trunk of the agents' car. Just what was Brigham doing for three hours in the lobby and parking lot of the motel, if not assisting Amos? He was not exactly passing through while a drug deal went down around him. Brigham did not testify, and his lawyer offered no hypothesis at trial. At oral argument of this appeal the best his counsel could do was to suggest that Brigham might have believed that Amos was picking up counterfeit money rather than drugs. Tell us another! The

jury was entitled to conclude that Brigham knew about, and joined, a conspiracy to distribute cocaine.

Thin the evidence was, but it was also sufficient. Evidence at sentencing shows that the jury drew the right inference. Amos related that he brought Brigham as a lookout. Brigham told the prosecutor that he was part of the organization and had been involved in some big-stakes transactions. But he was unable to provide enough information to induce the prosecutor to make the motion under § 3553(e) that unlocks the trap door in the sentencing "floor." Pleading guilty would have produced the 10-year minimum term, so Brigham went to trial; he had nothing to lose and some chance of being acquitted. The evidence at sentencing showed that Brigham knew that Thompson's organization dealt in multi-kilogram quantities, which supports the judge's conclusion that Brigham qualifies for the 10-year minimum. All that remains is Brigham's argument that the judge should have invoked U.S.S.G. § 5K2.0 to give him a break. Section 5K2.0 describes appropriate departures from the guidelines, but Brigham needed a departure from a minimum sentence prescribed by statute. That was available only on motion of the prosecutor under § 3553(e). Brigham does not contend that in declining to make the motion the prosecutor violated the Constitution. . . . Wise exercise of prosecutorial discretion can prevent egregious sentencing inversions. How that discretion is to be exercised is a subject for the political branches. Brigham joined the conspiracy and received a sentence authorized by Congress. His judicial remedies are at a close.

AFFIRMED.

Dissent

Judge Bauer

I respectfully dissent. Taking all the evidence as described in the majority opinion as absolutely true, and viewing it in the light most favorable to the government, I still do not find that any sensible juror could find Brigham guilty of the crime of conspiracy beyond a reasonable doubt. At oral argument, counsel for Brigham could only suggest, in answer to a question from the bench as to what explanation he could give for Brigham's actions on the day in question, "that Brigham might have believed that Amos was picking up counterfeit money rather than drugs." An unbelievable scenario. The fact is, no one testified as to what exactly Brigham was doing or why he was doing it; no one, in spite of the marvelous totally cooperating witnesses who, if the government's theory is correct, could have nailed Brigham's hide to the jailhouse wall. But they didn't. And it is not Brigham's missing explanation that is fatal; it is the government's inability to explain that creates the problem.

Tell us another, indeed, but only if it is the government tale; the accused has absolutely no burden to explain anything. The government accuses, the defendant says "prove it," and the government says the suspicious activity is enough to convince and convict. And so it proved.

I would have directed a verdict of "not guilty" had I been the trial judge and I construe my role in review to be the same. I do not believe the evidence sufficient to convince a sensible juror of proof beyond a reasonable doubt. The existence of cooperating witnesses who knew all and told nothing virtually implies the missing witness analysis: you had the control, you didn't produce, I infer the testimony would have been adverse to you.

I would reverse.

Questions

What exactly are Judge Easterbrook's objections to the mandatory minimum sentence he was obliged to impose in this case? Do you agree? Defend your answer.

"three-strikes-and-you're out" laws *mandatory minimum sentence in which three-time offenders are sentenced to mandatory life in prison.*
habitual felon laws *the earlier version of "three-strikes-and-you're-out" laws in which offenders who have multiple but not necessarily identical crimes are sentenced to mandatory life imprisonment.*

"Three Strikes and You're Out" Laws

Despite the shortcomings of mandatory minimum sentences, demonstrated by empirical evaluations, mandatory minimum sentencing continues to enjoy wide popularity. The form known as **"three-strikes-and-you're-out" laws** are especially popular. The basic thrust of these "three-strike" laws is to lock up for life dangerous offenders who habitually prey on innocent people. The catchy phrase may be new, but the idea of the three-strike laws is nearly 500 years old. In sixteenth-century England and in the American colonies, statutes imposed harsh penalties on criminals who committed identical crimes a particular number of times. By the late eighteenth century, these **habitual felon laws** were expanded in order to target repeat offenders of multiple but not identical crimes. New York, in 1797, enacted the first of these broader habitual offender laws. The New York law ordered a sentence of mandatory life imprisonment "at hard labor or in solitude, or both" for all offenders convicted of their second felony—no matter what that second felony was. Despite the move toward the indeterminate sentence in the period 1870–1970, habitual felon statutes flourished. By 1968, every state had some form of habitual felon statute.[75]

The three-strike laws are really no more than habitual felon laws with a new name and a *re*newed interest. By 1995, 37 states had proposed some form of three-strike legislation. Liberals and conservatives, Democrats and Republicans, the public and politicians all favor them. Michael G. Turner, Jody L. Sundt, Brandon Applegate, and Francis T. Cullen surveyed the enactment of

"Three-strikes-and-you're out" sounds good but researchers have not demonstrated that it reduces crime.

three-strike legislation. They found that conservatives were only slightly more enthusiastic about three-strike laws than were liberals, and that Republicans sponsored such laws only slightly more frequently than did Democrats in state legislatures. They speculate that the reason for the widespread popularity and consequent legislation is due to:

- General public dissatisfaction with the criminal justice system.
- The "panacea phenomenon"—the promise of a simple solution to a complex problem.
- The appeal of the catchy phrase—putting old habitual offender statute ideas into the language of modern baseball: "Three strikes and you're out."[76]

The effectiveness of three-strikes legislation in reducing crime is mixed, according to the small number of available empirical evaluations. Joan Petersilia, in a study of California's "get tough on crime" strategy, concluded that "the much higher imprisonment rates in California had no appreciable effect on violent crime, and only slight effects on property crime." According to a Rand Corporation study, three-strikes legislation in California *might* reduce "serious crime" by as much as 25 percent. However, the cost would be high: $5.5 billion, or $300 per taxpayer annually. According to a report issued by California's Center on Juvenile and Criminal Justice, during the first six months since the enactment of California's three-strikes law, the statute disproportionately affected African Americans. The report was based on an analysis by the Los Angeles Public Defender's Office, which looked at overall felony filings and three-strike felony filings against whites and African Americans. Using data from the California Department of Finance, the general population of African Americans and whites was compared to felony and three-strikes filings. Figures 11.6 and 11.7 depict the disparity.[77]

Figure 11.6

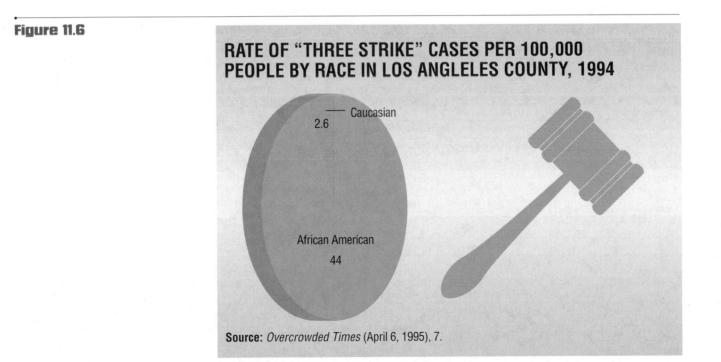

RATE OF "THREE STRIKE" CASES PER 100,000 PEOPLE BY RACE IN LOS ANGLELES COUNTY, 1994

Caucasian
2.6

African American
44

Source: *Overcrowded Times* (April 6, 1995), 7.

Figure 11.7

PERCENT DITRIBUTION OF "THREE STRIKE" CASES BY RACE IN LOS ANGELES, 1994

Caucasian
- 12.6 (Three Strike Cases)
- 19.7 (Felony Cases)
- 36.6 (General Population)

African American
- 57.3 (Three Strike Cases)
- 30.5 (Felony Cases)
- 10 (General Population)

Legend:
- Three Strike Cases
- Felony Cases
- General Population

Source: *Overcrowded Times* (April 6, 1995), 7.

Death Sentencing

guided discretion death penalty statutes *death penalty statutes that require juries in death penalty cases to consider specified mitigating and aggravating circumstances.*

bifurcated trials *two-stage trial in which the first stage determines guilt and the second stage decides death or life imprisonment.*

Perhaps no sentence has generated greater debate about its morality or more questions about its administration than the sentence of death. The United States Supreme Court has answered the fundamental legal question: Is the death penalty constitutional? In a series of decisions, the Court has ruled that the death penalty does not violate the cruel and unusual punishment clause of the Eighth Amendment, the due process clauses of the Fifth and Fourteenth Amendments, or the equal protection clause of the Fourteenth Amendment, under the following conditions:

- The sentence is for murder.
- Both mitigating and aggravating circumstances were considered before imposing the sentence of death.
- The sentence was not discriminatory according to race or other unacceptable criteria.

To meet these requirements, most states that authorize the death penalty have enacted **guided discretion death penalty statutes,** requiring juries to administer capital punishment according to statutory guidelines on mitigating and aggravating circumstances. Defendants charged with capital crimes under guided discretion statutes receive **bifurcated trials.** The first stage, the traditional trial, determines guilt. If the verdict is guilty, then the second stage, sentencing, takes place to decide death or life imprisonment. During this second stage, statutory guidelines listing aggravating and mitigating circumstances guide the jury's discretion. The principal aggravating circumstances include killing during the course of committing a felony such as armed robbery, previous convictions for homicide, killing strangers, and killing more than one victim. Mitigating circumstances include no prior criminal history, mental or emotional stress, victim participation in the crime, and playing only a minor part in the murder.

The debate over the constitutionality of the death penalty seems resolved: it is constitutional as long as it is administered according to guided discretion. Specifically, this means that courts must have full information about aggravating and mitigating circumstances involved in a particular case, that guidelines must be established for courts to follow in weighing these circumstances, and that full review of the death sentence must take place in the appeals courts.

The Supreme Court has also decided that the Constitution permits the execution of persons who murdered while they were juveniles, and of retarded persons who do not qualify for the insanity defense. When he was 15, William Wayne Thompson, with three older persons, shot his brother-in-law twice, cut his throat, chest, and abdomen, and broke his leg. The attackers then chained the body to a concrete block and threw it in a river. Thompson was convicted and sentenced to death. The Supreme Court ruled that the Constitution did not prevent his execution. Johnny Paul Penry raped, beat, and then stabbed Pamela Carpenter with a pair of scissors. She died a few days later. Dr. Jerome Brown testified that Penry was mentally retarded, probably due to brain damage at birth, that he had the mental age of a 6-1/2-year-old and the social maturity of a 9- or 10-year old. Penry was convicted and sentenced to death. The Supreme Court ruled that mental retardation did not prevent his execution.[78]

Facts about the Death Sentence

Although 36 states authorize the death penalty, and juries convict and courts sentence increasing numbers of murderers to death row, states execute practically none of them. This has led to an unprecedented number of death row inmates, but relatively few executions every year. In 1993, 38 prisoners were executed; 2,716 prisoners remained on death row. Since 1930, when the government began collecting statistics, the federal and state governments in the United States have executed 4,016 individuals, most of them prior to the 1950s. The numbers dwindled to zero from 1967 to 1977. Then, on January 17, 1977, a Utah firing squad executed Gary Gilmore. The execution was a media event, producing both a cover story in *Newsweek* and a Norman Mailer best-seller.[79]

On January 27, 1993, the state of Missouri executed Marsay Bolder by lethal injection, the 191st execution since Gary Gilmore's in 1977. The story was carried in a small article deep in the national news section of the *New York Times*. It took two unusually sensational back-to-back executions to bring capital punishment back onto the front pages of newspapers and the top of television news. On January 25, 1996, Utah child rapist-killer John Albert Taylor became the first prisoner to face the firing squad since Gary Gilmore. On January 26, Delaware double-murderer Billy Baily became the first person in that state to die by hanging since 1946. Both prisoners *chose* the old-fashioned firing squad and noose over lethal execution. Taylor said he wanted to put Utah to the greater expense and embarrassment of the firing squad. Baily said, "I was sentenced to hang. Asking a man to choose how to die is more barbaric than hanging." Figure 11.8 depicts executions and numbers on death row from 1987 to 1993.[80]

All death-row prisoners now awaiting death are convicted murderers. In 1991, two-thirds of the prisoners on death row had prior felony convictions; 8 percent had prior homicide convictions. The majority were white; 40 percent were African American, 173 were Hispanics, 23 were American Indians,

Figure 11.8

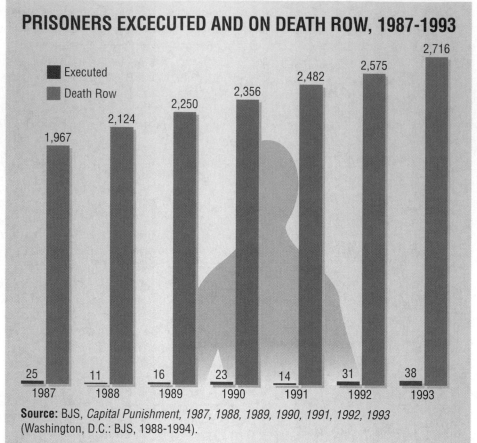

PRISONERS EXCECUTED AND ON DEATH ROW, 1987-1993

■ Executed
■ Death Row

1987: 25 executed, 1,967 Death Row
1988: 11 executed, 2,124 Death Row
1989: 16 executed, 2,250 Death Row
1990: 23 executed, 2,356 Death Row
1991: 14 executed, 2,482 Death Row
1992: 31 executed, 2,575 Death Row
1993: 38 executed, 2,716 Death Row

Source: BJS, *Capital Punishment, 1987, 1988, 1989, 1990, 1991, 1992, 1993* (Washington, D.C.: BJS, 1988-1994).

13 were Asian Americans, and 36 were women. Executed prisoners spend an average of seven years on death row. Most death-row inmates are undereducated and poor.[81]

Public Attitudes toward the Death Sentence

Support for the death sentence has risen steadily since the mid-1960s, when 42 percent of Americans polled favored capital punishment for murder. By 1980, two-thirds of those polled supported it; by 1995 the number reached 77 percent. Americans have not endorsed capital punishment this strongly since the 1930s, during the "wild forays of the Ma Barker Gang in the Midwest and the ruthless 'contract' slayings carried out in New York by Murder, Inc."[82]

The dramatic increase of support for capital punishment has several important dimensions. Public support has clear racial overtones. People surveyed support most strongly the execution of those they term "subnormal black" murderers. Capital punishment is most favored among people who do not know how it works in practice; they support capital punishment because of how they believe it *should* operate, not how it is in fact administered. When all the facts and circumstances about its actual operation become known, however, support weakens among most groups. Zeisel and Gallup, for example, found that 75 percent of those surveyed believe that the death penalty has a deterrent effect. However, if they were convinced that abolition of the death penalty would not increase the murder rate, support for the death penalty would drop from 70 to 55 percent. Furthermore, Bohm, Flanagan, and Harris studied public opinion in New York. They found that 72 percent of the respondents favored the death penalty but that 62 percent "would be willing to support a plan that sentenced a convicted murderer to prison for life, with no possibility of parole ever and have him work in a prison industry where his earnings would go to the victim's family." Peter R. Jones found that the way the surveys ask the question exaggerate support for the death penalty. Most surveys require an either/or response—Do you favor or do you oppose the death penalty? Allowing respondents to answer "no opinion" or "don't know" substantially reduces support.[83]

The public supports the *threat* of death more than it does actual execution. More than 80 percent favor the death penalty, but at the same time they hesitate to carry it out. According to criminologist Franklin Zimring,

> The death penalty is like the flag—a symbolic issue, powerful but not deep. [The majority's] enthusiasm for killing increases . . . with the distance from their [actual responsibility] for it. If our civilization had the stomach for this, we would have long since swept away the legal restrictions and gotten on with it. We want to have the death penalty as a statement, as the ultimate weapon like the missiles in the silo. But we really don't want to use it.[84]

According to Hugo Adam Bedau, a philosopher and death penalty opponent, the public is not really in favor of carrying out the threat of death in most cases:

> One might hazard the hypothesis that the average person seems convinced the death penalty is an important legal threat, abstractly desirable as part of society's permanent bulwark against crime, but that he or she is relatively indifferent to whether a given convict is executed on a given date as scheduled, or is indeed ever executed. To put it another way, there is no evidence that the two-to-one majority in favor of the death penalty for murder is also a two-to-one majority in favor of executing right now the hundreds of persons currently under death sentence.[85]

The Cost of the Death Sentence

A popular argument runs: "Kill them! Why spend the money on keeping killers alive in prison for life?" The reality is that the death sentence is extremely expensive. Texas leads the nation in both death-row population (almost 400) and executions (almost 20). It takes about seven-and-one-half years between the trial and the execution of a death-row prisoner, a cost to the taxpayers of about $2.3 million for every capital case. To imprison someone in a single cell at the highest security level in a Texas prison for 40 years costs $750,000.[86]

Dallas lawyer Vincent Perini, chairman of the Texas Bar Association's committee on representing death-row inmates, argues, "There's some things that a modern American city and state have got to have. You have got to have police and fire and public safety protection. You have to have a criminal justice system. You don't have to have a death penalty."[87]

Allen Hightower, however, chairman of the Texas House Corrections Committee, said that although life without parole would save millions of dollars, "From a correctional practice standpoint, if someone needs to go to prison for life, I'm for gassing them. The end result is that with no chance or hope of getting out, no matter how you behave . . . there's no reason not to stab a guard and no reason not to kill or rape another inmate." Hightower favored saving money by limiting appeals of death sentences. "Will we ever convict a person in the state that's not guilty? Sure. We've done it before, and we'll do it again. But our criminal justice system is the fairest system in the world." Texas Assistant Attorney General Bob Walt, who complained that defense tactics are the cause of the problem, also supports the death penalty despite its cost. "We have no shortage of violent characters in this state," he said. "The death penalty is something Texans want."[88]

Issues in Death Sentencing

The Supreme Court settled the legal argument over the death penalty, but it cannot settle the issues of morality, fairness, and efficacy surrounding the long, heated debate over the ancient punishment of death:

- The moral question: Is it right?
- The utilitarian question: Does it work?
- The fallibility question: Does it kill innocent people?
- The fairness question: Does it discriminate?

The Moral Question The debate over capital punishment remains, as it has historically, fundamentally a moral debate. Death penalty proponents point to two familiar Old Testament passages: one from Genesis, "Whoever sheds the blood of man, by man shall his blood be shed"; the other from Exodus, "Eye for eye, tooth for tooth, hand for hand, foot for foot, burn for burn, wound for wound, stripe for stripe." Opponents invoke the New Testament, alluding to the death of Christ to save sinners and his calls to forgive enemies and turn the other cheek. Jesus admonishes the crowd before the stoning of an adulteress: "He that is without sin among you, let him first cast a stone at her." Punishment will come after death, because God alone can punish. Even the Old Testament teaches, "Vengeance is *mine,* saith the Lord." Capital punishment is inconsistent with the merciful, redemptive aspect of both Judaism and Christianity, yet the Bible provides justification both to support and to condemn it. Amnesty International moves beyond scriptures to a more general moral condemnation: "The death penalty violates the right to life and the right not to be subjected to cruel, inhumane or degrading treatment."

Supporters of capital punishment also rely on general moral grounds to bolster their arguments. They maintain that it is right to hate criminals and to base punishment on our outrage at heinous crimes. It is as morally right to punish criminals for their wicked deeds as it is to praise heroes for their courageous deeds. If it is noble for soldiers in wartime to give their lives for their country, then it is morally right in a peaceable society to claim the lives of murderers for killing innocent people. According to Professor Ernest van den Haag:

> The life of each man should be sacred to each other man. . . . [I]t is not enough to proclaim the sacredness and inviolability of human life. It must be secured as well, by threatening with the loss of their own life those who violate what has been proclaimed as inviolable—the right of innocents to live.[89]

In the end, the moral debate over capital punishment is not a matter of science or logic; it is a question of values. Some people deeply believe that it is wrong for the state to kill anyone for any reason; others believe just as deeply that it is wrong not to execute heinous criminals.

The Deterrence Question A widespread popular belief has it that the harsher the punishment, the greater its general deterrent effect. Accordingly, the death penalty must have the greatest deterrent effect. Would-be murderers will hesitate if they believe execution awaits them. Criminal justice professionals, policymakers, and scholars, however, do not agree on the death penalty's deterrent effect. Indeed, nothing in recent years has generated more controversy concerning the death penalty than whether it prevents crime.

Since at least the sixteenth century, long before modern social science, observers have questioned the capacity of capital punishment to prevent crime. Lord Coke, the English judge never known for his compassion for criminals, said it made him "weep" that after sending 500 criminals to their deaths on the gallows in one year, no reduction in crime resulted. He lamented that crime actually increased. In the eighteenth century, both the Italian criminologist Cesare Beccarria and the American reformer Benjamin Rush argued that capital punishment did not reduce crime; in fact, the death penalty probably encouraged crime by its example.

Not until the past 30 years has social science developed research methods that could accurately measure the deterrent effect of the death penalty. The debate has shifted dramatically as a result of studies either conducted or inspired by criminologist Thorstin Sellin and economist Isaac Ehrlich. Sellin and his followers compared capital crime rates in states having the death penalty with the rate in neighboring, similar states that did not. In general, they found no significant difference in the capital crime rate between states that had the death penalty and those that did not. They concluded from this that the death penalty was not a significantly greater deterrent than life imprisonment. Of course, such a conclusion rests on the assumption—not proven—that other influences on the homicide rates did not account for the figures.[90]

These studies seemed to settle the empirical question until Isaac Ehrlich's provocative capital punishment study appeared in 1975. Ehrlich used a highly technical statistical device called regression analysis to measure the death penalty's deterrent effect. Regression analysis tests the relationship between the death penalty and the capital crime rate. It uses a complex mathematical formula to isolate the death penalty's effect on the capital crime rate from other influences, such as the age of the capital offenders. Regression analysis depends on including in the test all the many other influences on the rate, so that the influence of capital punishment will not be exaggerated. Ehrlich applied regression analysis to FBI homicide figures from 1934 to 1969. From that analysis, he concluded that "an additional execution per year" may have resulted in "seven or eight fewer murders" annually. During the 1980s, economists have made even bolder claims. Steven K. Layson, in another elaborate econometric analysis based on homicide data from 1936 to 1977, concluded that every execution prevents 18 murders.[91]

Ehrlich's study set off a firestorm. The U.S. Solicitor General used it to support the constitutionality of the death penalty. The Nixon administration hailed it as scientific proof that the death penalty did in fact deter capital crimes. Since Ehrlich's findings ran counter to prevailing evidence that the death penalty did not deter capital crimes, it generated a host of follow-up studies. These follow-up studies have uncovered serious flaws in the research. One criticism charged that Ehrlich's conclusions hold up only if the regression equation is in one of its more unusual forms, called logarithmic. If it is put in the more conventional linear regression, the deterrent effects of the death penalty disappear. Hence, using the more conventional regression formula, Ehrlich's findings did not hold up.[92]

The worst blow to Ehrlich's research came from a study of the use of the death penalty during the 1960s, omitting the years 1933 to 1960 that Ehrlich had included. Ehrlich had made much of the figures that showed that during the decade of the 1960s, while the death penalty was on hold, capital crime rates soared. The significant question is whether failure to execute capital criminals caused rising capital crime rates, or whether the relationship between them was coincidental. Brian Forst developed a rigorous test for Ehrlich's findings. Instead of aggregate data for the whole United States, Forst compared states having the death penalty to those that did not. He found that capital crime rates in all jurisdictions rose about the same amount, whether they had the death penalty or not. States that had never executed criminals and states that recently decided not to execute showed similar increases in capital crimes during the 1960s. On the basis of this comparative state analysis and some other more complicated matters, Forst concluded that capital punishment did not deter homicide. The debate continues without resolution into the 1990s.[93]

Some have argued that the death penalty *increases* homicides by example. William Bowers and Glenn Pierce examined the effects of executions on the homicide rates in New York State between 1907 and 1963. They reported that, on the average, there were two additional homicides in the month following executions for capital crimes. This led them to conclude that the death penalty has an effect just opposite to its intent. Instead of deterring capital crimes, particularly homicide, capital punishment encourages them. Bowers and Pierce say, "this suggests that the message of executions is one of 'lethal vengeance' more than deterrence." William C. Bailey, on the other hand, compared monthly homicide rates with the publicity executions received on television from 1976 through 1987. Bailey found support for neither the deterrence nor the brutalization thesis. Homicides were related neither to the amount nor to the type of publicity given to executions.[94]

Clearly, the death penalty incapacitates or specifically deters the executed person from killing again. Cases suggest the importance of this effect. In *Tison v. Arizona,* for example, the defendants aided their father, who was serving a life sentence for murdering a prison guard, in escaping from prison. He killed four more persons. Life without parole, an alternative to capital punishment receiving increasing attention, does not prevent killings in the prison environment.[95]

The Fallibility Question

According to critics, capital punishment's worst failing is that it operates imperfectly. The death penalty is fallible in at least three respects:

- Mistaken execution of the innocent.
- Discrimination against poor people and African Americans.
- Caprice in the selection.

The selection of so few to execute from so many the government could have convicted and from so many condemned to die, critics say, follows no rational pattern. As the experts put it, the choice is "freakish." Hotly debated is whether these imperfections fatally impair the death penalty as a creditable punishment.

Hugo Adam Bedau and Michael L. Radelet collected evidence of several thousand cases that might have resulted in the death penalty in the twentieth century. They concluded that 350 persons were mistakenly convicted, and 23 of these were executed. Mistakes stem from coerced confessions, suppression of evidence, perjury, and false identifications. Stephen J. Markman and Paul G. Cassell challenge Bedau and Radelet's methodology on the grounds that Bedau and Radelet subjectively evaluated the decisions in the capital cases they reviewed. Markman and Cassell copiously reassessed the evidence in the cases and concluded that proof of guilt beyond a reasonable doubt existed in all of them. Furthermore, they point out that nearly all the alleged errors occurred prior to *Furman v. Georgia.* Since then, the elaborate review of capital cases, they maintain, has not resulted in an unacceptable rate of errors. The debate continues. Bedau and Radelet replied to Markman and Cassell's challenge in a strong defense of their methodology and conclusions.[96]

The fallibility issue demands an answer to the question of how many mistakes are acceptable. Abolitionists say none, maintaining that the irrevocability of the death penalty puts innocent people at too high a risk. To proponents, the paucity of innocent people killed out of the thousands sentenced to death implies the death penalty is *almost* perfect. They claim further that the last innocent person was executed in the 1930s, demonstrating that even the few mistaken executions took place a long time ago. They say it cannot happen in modern times.

Abolitionists counter that the numbers cited are minimum figures and therefore represent the fewest innocent people executed. Some people executed may not deserve it even though they are technically guilty. Joey Kagebien, for instance, was sentenced to death for first-degree murder. He was one of several teenage boys who killed an Arkansas farmer, but he did not do the actual killing. Although that made no difference legally, it distinguished him from other first-degree murderers who receive death sentences. Therefore, Joey Kagebien does not appear among the innocent people sentenced to death; nor does Clifford Hallman, convicted of killing a woman in Tampa, Florida. After Hallman was on death row, authorities established that his victim died not from Hallman's attack, but from improper medical attention at Tampa General Hospital.

Cases do come to light periodically. The release of Randall Adams, who spent years on death row for a murder he did not commit (depicted in the docu-drama *The Thin Blue Line*), clearly demonstrates that human error occurs in death sentences. It seems to demonstrate also that errors come to light in the review process, even if it takes years for them to do so. No matter how few or many mistaken capital convictions and executions exist, cases like that of Wilber Lee and Freddie Pitts are important:

> After twelve years in jail for someone else's crime, Freddie Pitts and Wilber Lee walked out of prison here today, into the bright autumn sunshine and new lives as free men. The state, which twice convicted them of murder and kept them on death row for nine years after another man confessed to the crime, gave them an executive pardon and $100 and sent them on their way. They did not look back. "Is it over, Freddie?" Mr. Lee asked softly as the gates of the Florida State Prison hummed and buzzed and then opened electronically in front of them. "It's over, man," said Mr. Pitts as they strode through together. "It's really over."[97]

The Fairness Question Capital punishment falls most heavily on poor black men. Women are rarely sentenced to death, even though they commit almost 20 percent of all criminal homicides. Neither are middle-class people. Since John Webster, a famous professor of medicine at the Harvard Law School, was put to death in 1850, businesspeople, professors, lawyers, and doctors have escaped the ultimate penalty. Instead, as numerous studies have demonstrated, poor, undereducated, underemployed men face execution in America. According to Peter W. Lewis, all the death-row inmates in Florida are blue-collar workers—"truck drivers, laborers, carpenters, dishwashers, private security guards"—and other unskilled workers. According to Charles L. Black, "All or almost all . . . [death row inmates] are poor, at least in the frame of reference wherein the expenses of effective defense against crime are to be calculated."[98]

Adalberto Aguirre, Jr., and David V. Baker reviewed a wide range of empirical research on racial disparities in the death penalty. According to their research, the death penalty is imposed on African Americans in a "wanton" and "freakish" manner, despite the efforts of the Supreme Court in *Furman v. Georgia* and *Gregg v. Georgia* to eliminate racial discrimination in its use. The research surveyed by Aguirre and Baker also showed that "blacks who victimize whites consistently have the highest probability of receiving a capital sentence." This finding supports the claim that capital punishment "protects (through deterrence) that class of individuals (whites) who are least likely to be victimized."[99]

Discrimination in death sentences does not necessarily prove *intentional* or even *unconscious* racism. Racial discrimination patterns do suggest, however, that African Americans who kill Caucasians are considered worse criminals than Caucasians who kill Caucasians, worse than African Americans who kill African Americans, and worse than Caucasians who kill African Americans.[100]

Summary

The history of sentencing emphasizes the difficulty of resolving the tension between certainty, predictability, and equity in formal law and the need for discretion in accounting for differences among people and circumstances in particular cases. Sentencing also reflects the informal influences created by organizational goals and processes, ideology, public opinion, and other functional aims of criminal sentencing.

These formal and informal dimensions to sentencing revolve around three main issues: fixed versus indeterminate or open-ended sentences; judicial discretion; and legislative, judicial, and administrative dominance of the sentencing process. For most of the twentieth century, the indeterminate sentence as a means to reform criminals dominated. Under it, judges and administrative bodies exercised broad discretion in sentencing.

Since the early 1970s, disillusionment with the indeterminate sentence, discretion, and the rehabilitative ideal brought about demands for sentencing reform. Recent efforts have attempted to at least control, if not eradicate, discretion. Fixed sentences have returned to favor, and the retributive and incapacitative aims of punishment increasingly affect sentencing decisions. Extreme measures such as the mandatory minimum sentence and the determinate sentencing laws of some states lie at one end of the reform spectrum, while the various forms of sentencing guidelines lie at the other. Researchers report mixed results for these reforms; it is too early to tell just how much they bring discretion under control. Reform measures face obstacles arising from the need for flexibility demanded by both formal sentencing policies and informal functional realities.

Capital punishment has reemerged as an important criminal justice issue in the past decade. With the resurgence of the retributive notion of punishment and the Supreme Court's decisions upholding the constitutionality of the death penalty, death sentences and executions are increasing. Capital punishment is imposed in the United States only for murder, and only when safeguards such as careful review of death sentences are in place. With these restrictions, 37 states have capital punishment statutes.

The issues surrounding the death penalty have prompted heated debate and strong argument. The morality of the death penalty, debated for centuries, depends more on values than on logic or science. The Supreme Court has ruled that capital punishment is not cruel and unusual punishment if it is administered fairly and without discrimination. Empirical studies carried out in death penalty states, using highly sophisticated regression analyses, challenge whether these requirements are met. These studies conclude that race plays an important part in the capital punishment statistics, particularly when blacks kill whites.

The fallibility question, asking how many innocent people suffer the death penalty, emphasizes the imperfection of human action and the finality of capital punishment. Innocent people do get executed, or narrowly escape, sometimes after long years in prison. The deterrence question, asking whether the death penalty prevents murders, has generated enormous controversy. Economists have concluded that capital punishment does in fact prevent murders. Sociologists strongly disagree, and several have conducted empirical studies concluding that the death penalty does not deter murderers.

Review Questions

1. Describe the main points in the historical controversy involving sentencing.

2. Describe the main points in the development of sentencing types in American history.

3. List and explain the formal determinants in judges' sentencing power.

4. List and explain the role of the main sentencing models.

5. List and describe the informal determinants of sentencing.

6. What is the significance of the pre-sentence investigation?

7. List the major sentences judges can impose.

8. On what three problems does most sentencing reform focus?

9. What is the state of research concerning racial and gender discrimination and disparity in sentencing?

10. Describe the main elements in the sentencing reform movement of the 1970s.

11. What has been the consequence of most sentencing reforms?

12. What interests does sentencing balance?

13. Describe and explain the effects of mandatory sentencing.

14. Describe the main types of sentencing guidelines, and analyze their purposes and effects.

15. What has been the trend in public support for the death penalty? What explains the trend?

16. Does the public support the threat of death, or actual execution? Explain.

17. What is the relationship between support for the death penalty and knowledge about its actual administration? Explain.

18. List the moral arguments for and against the death penalty.

19. Under what circumstances is the death penalty constitutional?

20. Summarize the research surrounding the deterrent effect of capital punishment and the controversy surrounding it.

21. How many erroneous death sentences are there? How tolerable are mistakes? Explain the controversy surrounding the fallibility research.

22. Summarize the research regarding racial discrimination and the death penalty.

23. What nonracial factors affect death sentencing?

Notes

1. Quoted in Douglas Hay, "Property, Authority and the Criminal Law," in *Albion's Fatal Tree,* Douglas Hay et al., eds. (London: Allen Lane, 1975), 17–19.

2. Joel Samaha, "Discretion and Law in the Early Penitential Books," in *Social Psychology and Discretionary Law,* Richard Abt, ed. (New York: W. W. Norton, 1978).

3. Joel Samaha, "Fixed Sentences and Judicial Discretion in Historical Perspective," *William Mitchell Law Review* 15 (1989): 217–53.

4. David Rothman, *The Discovery of the Asylum* (Boston: Little, Brown, 1971).

5. *Transactions of the National Congress of Prisons and Reformatory Discipline* (Albany, N.Y.: American Correctional Association, 1971).

6. Zebulon Brockway, *Fifty Years of Prison Service* (New York: Charities Publication Committee, 1912), 401.

7. Twentieth Century Fund, *Fair and Certain Punishment* (New York: McGraw-Hill, 1976), 95.

8. Quoted in *Fair and Certain Punishment.*

9. This summary is based on a survey of reformatory and prison records of Stillwater State Prison and St. Cloud Reformatory in Minnesota during the period 1900–1920.

10. Edward Lindsey, "Historical Sketch of the Indeterminate Sentence and Parole Systems," *Journal of Criminal Law and Criminology* 16 (1925): 18, 96.

11. Alfred Blumstein et al., eds., *Research on Sentencing: The Search for Reform* (Washington, D.C.: National Academy Press, 1983), 48–52.

12. National Council on Crime and Delinquency, *Criminal Justice Sentencing Policy Statement* (San Francisco: NCCD, 1992), 6.

13. Michael H. Tonry, "Sentencing," *Encyclopedia of Crime and Justice,* Sanford Kadish, ed. (New York: Free Press, 1983), 4:1436.

14. Ibid.

15. Twentieth Century Fund, *Fair and Certain Punishment,* 117.

16. Andrew von Hirsch, *Doing Justice: The Choice of Punishments* (New York: Hill and Wang, 1976); Alexis Durham, "Crime Seriousness and Punitive Severity: An Assessment of Social Attitudes," *Justice Quarterly* 5 (1988): 131–53.

17. Joachim Savelsberg, "Laws That Do Not Fit Society: Sentencing Guidelines as a Neoclassical Reaction to the Dilemmas of Substantive Law," *American Journal of Sociology* 75 (1992): 1346–81.

18. Alfred Blumstein et al., eds., *Deterrence and Incapacitation: Estimating the Effects of Criminal Sanctions on Crime Rates* (Washington, D.C.: National Academy of Sciences, 1978).

19. JoAnn L. Miller and Andy B. Anderson, "Updating Deterrence Doctrine," *Journal of Criminal Law and Criminology* 77 (1986): 426–27, 437.

20. Blumstein et al., *Deterrence and Incapacitation.*

21. Susan E. Martin, Lee B. Sechrest, and Robin Redner, eds., *New Directions in the Rehabilitation of Criminal Offenders* (Washington, D.C.: National Academy Press, 1981).

22. Charles F. Abel and Frank H. Marsh, *Punishment and Restitution* (Westport, Conn.: Greenwood Press, 1984).

23. Blumstein et al., *Research on Sentencing,* chap. 2.

24. Ibid.

25. Ibid.

26. Donald Black, *Sociological Justice* (New York: Oxford University Press, 1989), chaps. 1 and 6.

27. Robert Elias, *The Politics of Victimization* (New York: Oxford University Press, 1986), 156–59; *Commonwealth v. Youngkin,* 427 A.2d 1356 (Pa. 1981).

28. Quoted in Michael R. Gottfredson and Don M. Gottfredson, *Decision Making in Criminal Justice: Toward a Rational Exercise of Discretion,* 2d. ed. (New York: Plenum Press, 1990), 153.

29. John Rosecrance, "The Probation Officers' Search for Credibility: Ball Park Recommendations," *Crime and Delinquency* 31 (1985): 539–554; Patrick D. McAnany, "Sentencing: Presentence Report," *Encyclopedia of Crime and Justice*, 4:1472–75.

30. Rosecrance, "Probation Officers' Search for Credibility"; John Rosecrance, "Maintaining the Myth of Individualized Justice: Probation Presentence Reports," *Justice Quarterly* 5 (1988): 236–56.

31. *New York Times*, 15 November 1992.

32. Tamar Lewin, "Texas Court Agrees to Castration for Rapist of 13-Year-Old Girl," *New York Times*, 7 March 1992.

33. Graeme R. Newman, *Just and Painful: A Case for the Corporal Punishment of Criminals* (New York: Free Press, 1983).

34. Vincent O'Leary, "Criminal Sentencing: Trends and Tribulations," *Criminal Law Bulletin* 20 (1984): 417–29; Barbara Boland et al., *Prosecution of Felony Arrests, 1980* (Washington, D.C.: Bureau of Justice Statistics, 1985), 28–29; Stephen J. Schulhofer, "Assessing the Federal Sentencing Process: The Problem Is Uniformity, Not Disparity," *American Criminal Law Review* 29 (1992): 835–836.

35. Thorsten Sellin, "Race Prejudice in the Administration of Justice," *American Journal of Sociology* 41 (1935): 212–17.

36. Stuart S. Nagel and Lenore J. Weitzman, "Women as Litigants," *Hastings Law Journal* 23 (1971): 171–98; "Alabama Law Review Summer Project 1975: A Study of Differential Treatment Accorded Female Defendants in Alabama Criminal Courts," *Alabama Law Review* 27 (1975): 676–746; Candace C. Kruttschnitt, "Sex and Criminal Court Dispositions: The Unresolved Controversy," *Journal of Research in Crime and Delinquency* 21 (1984): 213–32; Kathleen Daly, "Neither Conflict nor Labeling nor Paternalism Will Suffice: Intersections of Race, Ethnicity, Gender, and Family in Criminal Court Decisions," *Crime and Delinquency* 35 (1989): 136–68; Joan Petersilia, "Racial Disparities in the Criminal Justice System: A Summary," *Crime and Delinquency* 31 (1985): 15–35.

37. Martha A. Myers and Susette M. Talarico, *The Social Contexts of Criminal Sentencing* (New York: Springer-Verlag, 1987), 80–81.

38. Ibid., 170–71.

39. Blumstein et al., *Research on Sentencing.*

40. Joan Petersilia, "Racial Disparities," 21. For a general summary of the conflicting conclusions about race and sentencing, see Daniel Nagin and Luke-Jon Tierney, "Discrimination in the Criminal Justice System," in *Research on Sentencing*, Blumstein et al., eds.

41. Cassia Spohn et al., "The Effect of Race on Sentencing: A Re-Examination of an Unsettled Question," *Law and Society Review* 16 (1981-82): 86.

42. John H. Lindquist et al., "Judicial Processing of Males and Females Charged with Prostitution," *Journal of Criminal Justice* 17 (1989): 277–91.

43. Quoted in Gary D. LaFree, "Official Reactions to Hispanic Defendants in the Southwest," *Journal of Research in Crime and Delinquency* 22 (1985): 228.

44. Quotes are from LaFree, "Official Reactions," 229.

45. Ibid.

46. Marvin E. Frankel, *Criminal Sentences: Law Without Order* (New York: Hill and Wang, 1973), 5, 7.

47. James Q. Wilson, *Thinking About Crime*, 2d ed. (New York: Basic Books, 1983), chaps. 7–10.

48. Robert Martinson, "What Works?: Questions and Answers About Prison Reform," *The Public Interest*, no. 35 (1974): 22–54; Ted Palmer, "Martinson Revisited," in *Rehabilitation, Recidivism, and Research*, Robert Martinson et al., eds. (Hackensack, N.J.: National Council on Crime and Delinquency, 1976), 41–62; Marc F. Plattner, "The Rehabilitation of Punishment," *The Public Interest* (Summer 1976): 104–14.

49. Susan E. Martin, Lee B. Sechrest, and Robin Redner, eds., *New Directions in the Rehabilitation of Criminal Offenders* (Washington, D.C.: National Academy Press, 1981), 3.

50. Francis T. Cullen and Karen E. Gilbert, *Reaffirming Rehabilitation* (Cincinnati: Anderson Publishing Company, 1982); Donald R. Cressey, "Criminological Theory, Social Science, and the Repression of Crime," *Criminology* 16 (1978): 171–91; Seymour Halleck and Ann Witte, "Is Rehabilitation Dead?" *Crime and Delinquency* 23 (1977): 372–82; Elliott Currie, *Confronting Crime* (New York: Pantheon, 1985).

51. Peter Rossi et al., *Money, Work and Crime: Experimental Evidence* (New York: Academic Press, 1980); Ann Dryden Witte, *Work Release in North Carolina: An Evaluation of Its Post-Release Effects* (Chapel Hill, N.C.: Institute for Research in Social Science, University of North Carolina at Chapel Hill, 1975).

52. Cullen and Gilbert, *Reaffirming Rehabilitation*, 257–60.

53. *California Penal Code*, sec. 1170(a) (St. Paul: West Publishing Company, 1980).

54. *California Penal Code*, sec. 1170(b).

55. Jonathon D. Casper, David Brereton, and David Neal, *The Implementation of the California Determinate Sentence Law* (Washington, D.C.: National Institute of Justice, 1981); Pamela Utz, *Determinate Sentencing in Two California Courts* (Berkeley, Calif.: Center for the Study of Law and Society, 1981), 32–135; Sandra Shane-DuBow, Alice P. Brown, and Erik Olsen, *Sentencing Reform in the United States: History, Content and Effect* (Washington, D.C.: National Institute of Justice, 1985), 33–39.

56. Ibid.; Malcolm M. Feeley, *Court Reform on Trial*, (New York: Basic Books, 1983), 143–45; John Monahan and Laurens Walker, *Social Science in Law* (1985), 54–59, 80–81.

57. Stephen P. Klein, Susan Turner, and Joan Petersilia, *Racial Equity in Sentencing* (Santa Monica: Rand Corporation, 1988).

58. Minnesota Sentencing Guidelines Commission, *Minnesota Sentencing Guidelines and Commentary*, revised August 1995, 21–25.

59. Terance D. Miethe and Charles A. Moore, "Socioeconomic Disparities Under Determinate Sentencing Systems: A Comparison of Preguideline and Postguideline Practices in Minnesota," *Criminology* 23 (1985): 339.

60. Ibid., 357–61.

61. Savelsberg, "Laws That Do Not Fit Society," 1372.

62. See Richard Sparks, "The Construction of Sentencing Guidelines: A Methodological Critique," and Susan E. Mar-

tin, "The Politics of Sentencing Reform: Sentencing Guidelines in Pennsylvania and Minnesota," in *Research on Sentencing*, vol. 2, Alfred Blumstein et al., eds., for interesting and thorough discussions of sentencing guidelines; Richard Frase, "The Role of the Legislature, the Sentencing Commission, and Other Officials Under the Minnesota Sentencing Guidelines," *Wake Forest Law Review* 28 (1993): 345, 359–364.

63. Henry Scott Wallace, "Mandatory Minimums and the Betrayal of Sentencing Reform: A Legislative Dr. Jekyll and Mr. Hyde," *Federal Probation* (September 1993): 9.

64. United States Sentencing Commission, *Mandatory Minimum Penalties in the Federal Criminal Justice System* (Washington, D.C.: United States Sentencing Commission, August 1991), 5–7. For a discussion of the alleged Communist role in the perceived increased use of illicit drugs, see United States Congress, Senate, Committee on the Judiciary, *Hearing Before the Subcommitte to Investigate Juvenile Delinquency*, Miami, Florida, 83d Cong., 2d sess., 1954, 7.

65. U.S. Sentencing Commission, *Mandatory Minimum Penalties*, 6.

66. H. Rep. No. 1444, 91st Cong., 2d Sess. 11 (1970).

67. Judith A. Lachman, "Daring the Courts: Trial and Bargaining Consequences of Minimum Penalties," *Yale Law Journal* 90 (1981): 597–631.

68. National Institute of Justice, *Mandatory Sentencing: The Experience of Two States* (Washington, D.C.: National Institute of Justice, 1982); quotes from Samuel Walker, *Sense and Nonsense About Crime*, 2d ed. (Monterey, Calif.: Brooks/Cole, 1989), 89; Feeley, *Court Reform on Trial*, 118–28.

69. Wilson, *Thinking About Crime*, 135–36.

70. Feeley, *Court Reform on Trial*, 131; Milton Heumann and Colin Loftin, "Mandatory Sentencing and the Abolition of Plea Bargaining: The Michigan Firearm Statute," *Law and Society Review* 13 (1979): 393–430.

71. U.S. Sentencing Commission, *Mandatory Minimum Penalties*.

72. Wallace, "Mandatory Minimums," 11.

73. Ibid.; *Criminal Justice Newsletter*, November 15, 1993, 5.

74. Stephen J. Schulhofer, "Rethinking Mandatory Minimums," *Wake Forest Law Review*, 28 (1993): 199; Campaign for an Effective Crime Policy, "Evaluating Mandatory Minimum Sentences," (Washington, D.C.: Campaign for an Effective Crime Policy, unpublished manuscript, October 1993).

75. Michael G. Turner et al., " 'Three Strikes and You're Out' Legislation: A National Assessment," *Federal Probation* (September 1995): 16.

76. Ibid., 18, 32–33; Peter J. Benekos and Alida V. Merlo, "Three Strikes and You're Out!: The Political Sentencing Game," *Federal Probation* (March 1995): 3.

77. Benekos and Merlo, "Three Strikes," 7; "Three Strikes"—Serious Flaws and a Huge Price Tag," *Overcrowded Times* (October 1995): 3; Vincent Schiraldi, "Blacks Are Targets of 57 Percent of 'Three Strikes' Prosecution in Los Angeles," *Overcrowded Times* (April 1995): 7.

78. *Thompson v. Oklahoma*, 487 U.S. 815 (1988); *Penry v. Lynaugh*, U.S. (109 S.Ct 2934)(1989).

79. BJS, *Capital Punishment 1993* (Washington, D.C.: BJS, December 1994).

80. "Prisoner Is Executed After Supreme Court Won't Hold Hearing," *New York Times*, 28 January 1993; *USA Today*, 24 January 1996.

81. BJS, *Capital Punishment, 1991* (Washington, D.C.: Bureau of Justice Statistics, 1992).

82. *New York Times*, 10 September 1989; Hugo Adam Bedau, ed., *The Death Penalty in America*, 3d ed. (New York: Oxford University Press, 1982), 65; BJS, *Sourcebook of Criminal Justice Statistics, 1994* (Washington, D.C.: BJS, 1995), Table 2.57.

83. Peter R. Jones, "It's Not What You Ask, It's the Way You Ask It? Question Form and Public Opinion on the Death Penalty," *The Prison Journal* 74 (1994): 32–50; discussion of Zeisel and Gallup and of Bohm, Flanagan, and Harris taken from Jones's report of their results.

84. Franklin Zimring quoted in the *Washington Post: National Weekly Edition*, 13-19 November 1989.

85. Quoted in *New York Times*, 19 June 1989; Bedau, *Death Penalty in America*, 68.

86. "High Cost of Death Row," *Houston Chronicle*, 9 March 1992.

87. Quoted in "High Cost of Death Row."

88. Quoted in "High Cost of Death Row."

89. Amnesty International, *Proposal for a Presidential Commission on the Death Penalty in the United States of America* (London: Amnesty International Publications, 1980); Van den Haag quoted in Bedau, *Death Penalty in America*, 331.

90. Thorstin Sellin, *The Penalty of Death* (Beverly Hills, Calif.: Sage Publications, 1980).

91. Isaac Ehrlich, "The Deterrent Effect of Capital Punishment: A Question of Life and Death," *American Economic Review* 65 (1976): 397–417; Steven K. Layson, "Homicide and Deterrence: A Reexamination of the United States Time-Series Evidence," *Southern Economics Journal* 52 (1985): 68.

92. Bedau, *Death Penalty in America*, 95.

93. Brian Forst, "The Deterrent Effect of Capital Punishment: A Cross-State Analysis of the 1960s," reported in Bedau, *Death Penalty in America*, 131–32; Stephen J. Markman and Paul G. Cassell, "Protecting the Innocent: A Response to the Bedau-Radelet Study," *Stanford Law Review* 41 (1988): 121, 155; Hugo Adam Bedau and Michael L. Radelet, "The Myth of Infallibility: A Reply to Markman and Cassell," *Stanford Law Review* 41 (1988): 161, 168; Hans Zeisel, "The Deterrent Effect of the Death Penalty: Facts Versus Faith," in Bedau, *Death Penalty in America*, 132–33.

94. William J. Bowers and Glenn L. Pierce, "Deterrence or Brutalization: What Is the Effect of Executions?" *Crime and Delinquency* 26 (1980): 453; William C. Bailey, "Murder, Capital Punishment, and Television," *American Sociological Review* 55 (1990): 628–33.

95. William Weld and Paul Cassell, *Report to the Deputy Attorney General on Capital Punishment and the Sentencing Commission* 28 (February 13, 1987).

96. Hugo Adam Bedau and Michael L. Radelet, "Miscarriages of Justice in Potentially Capital Cases," *Stanford*

Law Review 40 (1987): 21–181; Markman and Cassell, "Protecting the Innocent."

97. *New York Times,* 20 September 1975.

98. Peter W. Lewis, "Killing the Killers: A Post-Furman Profile of Florida's Condemned," *Crime and Delinquency* 25 (1979): 203–204; Charles L. Black, Jr., *Capital Punishment: The Inevitability of Caprice and Mistake,* 2d ed. (New York: W. W. Norton, 1981), 94.

99. Adalberto Aguirre, Jr., and David V. Baker, "Empirical Research on Racial Discrimination in the Imposition of

the Death Penalty," *Criminal Justice Abstracts* 22 (1990): 147–48.

100. William J. Bowers and Glenn L. Pierce, "Arbitrariness and Discrimination under Post-Furman Capital Statutes," *Crime and Delinquency* 26 (1980): 630–31; Samuel R. Gross and Robert Mauro, "Patterns of Death: An Analysis of Racial Disparities in Capital Sentencing and Homicide Victimization," *Stanford Law Review* 37 (1984): 27–153; *McCleskey v. Zant,* 580 F.Supp. 338 (N.D. Ga. 1984), and *McCleskey v. Kemp,* 753 F.2d 877 (11th Cir. 1985).

PART FOUR

Corrections

and Intermediate Punishments

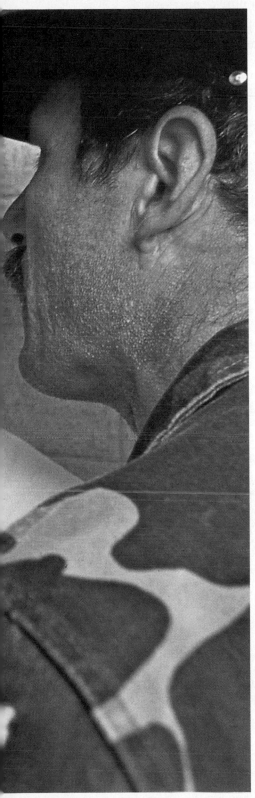

CHAPTER MAIN POINTS

1. *Criminal punishment takes place either in the community, in jails and prisons, or in a combination of community supervision and incarceration.*

2. *Most people under correctional supervision are in the community on ordinary probation.*

3. *Probation began as a sentence of leniency for first-time offenders, then became a means to rehabilitate offenders, and is now regarded as a way to punish offenders.*

4. *Probation officers play varied roles, including the sometimes-conflicting ones of law enforcement officer and counselor.*

5. *Probation is both an informal, discretionary decision-making process and a formal criminal sentence.*

6. *Probation is mainly intended for offenders who do not pose a risk to the community and who do not "deserve" harsher punishment.*

7. *Probationers are released only conditionally into the community, and probation can be revoked if probationers violate its conditions.*

8. *Probationers have fewer rights and are entitled to less due process than people who are not under correctional supervision.*

9. *Most probationers complete their probation successfully but success rates vary according to region of the country, age and past history of offenders, and time following the completion of probation.*

10. *The use of probation for felons is hotly debated, but the empirical evidence is mixed as to whether felony defendants are a major danger to the community.*

11. *Intermediate punishments provide a range of options between prison and ordinary probation.*

12. *There is great interest in and discussion of intermediate punishments, but they comprise only a small number of offenders under correctional supervision.*

13. *Intermediate punishments serve the purposes of both "just deserts" and the utilitarian aims of saving money and prison space.*

14. *Intensive supervised probation (ISP) is a tougher form of probation.*

15. *Empirical evaluations suggest that ISP is no more effective than ordinary probation in reducing recidivism but that it is more effective in administering "just deserts."*

16. *Home confinement, correctional boot camps, community service, fines, and day reporting centers provide judges with more options for "just deserts," but despite publicity they are not frequently used.*

17. *Little empirical evidence is available to measure the effectiveness of home confinement, correctional boot camps, community service, fines, and day reporting centers in reducing crime and saving money.*

After sentencing, convicted criminals move to the next stage of the criminal justice system—corrections. The term "corrections" derives from nineteenth- and early twentieth-century movements to "reform" or "correct" criminals. The missions of both community

corrections *most widely used label for the agencies and decision making related to the supervision of convicted criminals in custody.*

supervision and incarceration, however, go beyond "correcting" criminals— and did so even during the heyday of rehabilitation. Nevertheless, **corrections** remains the most widely used label for the agencies and decision making having to do with the supervision of convicted criminals while they are in state custody. The supervision of convicted offenders in state custody occurs in three ways:

1. In the community.
2. In jails and prisons.
3. In a combination of incarceration and community supervision.

Incarceration—particularly in prisons—receives an enormous amount of public and research attention. Most people convicted of crimes in the United States, however, are not in prison. About 60 percent of them are serving sentences in the community on probation, and the numbers are growing. Between 1980 and 1993, the probation population grew by more than 1.7 million people, more than the increase in either prison, jail, or parole populations. By the beginning of 1995, the number of adult probationers had climbed to nearly 3,000,000 people (see Figure 12.1). In addition to probation, some convicted criminals are sentenced to intermediate punishments, such as paying fines, performing community service, undergoing intensive probation, attending correctional boot camps, and wearing electronic monitors. This chapter discusses ordinary probation and intermediate punishments. The following chapters discuss incarceration in jails and prisons.[1]

Probation is often confused with parole, which in some ways it resembles. Both are forms of community supervision with somewhat similar aims and

Figure 12.1

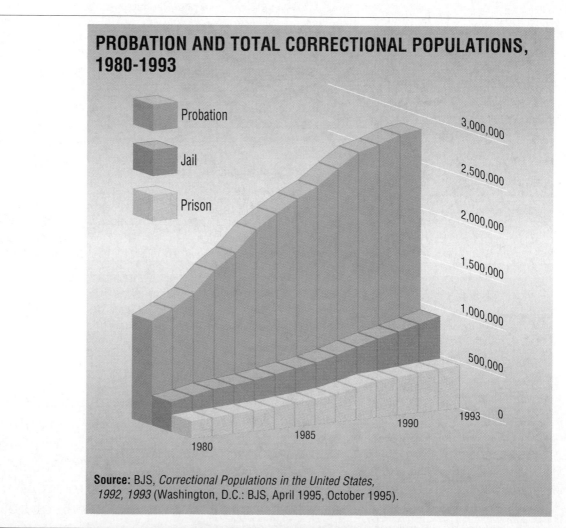

PROBATION AND TOTAL CORRECTIONAL POPULATIONS, 1980-1993

Source: BJS, *Correctional Populations in the United States, 1992, 1993* (Washington, D.C.: BJS, April 1995, October 1995).

operations. The principal difference is that probation *replaces* incarceration. Parole, on the other hand, *follows* incarceration. Also, counties usually administer probation, and states are responsible for the administration of parole. We save the discussion of parole for Chapter 15 as part of the subject of returning to society following imprisonment. Intermediate punishments "exist somewhere between incarceration and ordinary probation." Typically, intermediate punishments replace both incarceration and probation, with offenders remaining in the community under stricter supervision than ordinary probationers.

Traditionally, probation was aimed at rehabilitation and treatment of offenders. Intermediate punishments, on the other hand, focus on *punishment*. Although they have deeper roots, most intermediate punishments arose out of a combination of developments during the 1980s. These developments included rapidly expanding prison populations; shrinking government budgets; shifting penal policies from rehabilitation to retribution and incapacitation; and, among some academics and criminal justice professionals, a yearning for a middle ground between the two extreme options of prison and probation. Intermediate punishments were hailed during the 1980s as the latest corrections panacea. However, a growing body of empirical research points to the need for further experimentation and evaluation before pronouncing intermediate sanctions a success.[2]

Community corrections are expected to accomplish multiple, sometimes conflicting, missions, including:

● Punish offenders.
● Protect the community.
● Reduce crime.
● Save money.
● Prevent prison crowding.
● Rehabilitate offenders.
● Reintegrate offenders into the community.
● Provide humane treatment of offenders.

Considerable controversy surrounds both which of these missions ought to predominate and how effectively the substitutes for imprisonment reduce crime; punish, incapacitate, and rehabilitate offenders; and save tax dollars.

Probation

The basic idea of **probation**—substituting supervised release in the community for incarceration—is an ancient practice. Justices of the peace in sixteenth-century England commonly released minor offenders from custody if the offenders promised to "be of good behavior" and if they provided "sureties," that is, friends or family to secure their appearance at the next court session. If they broke their promise or did not appear in court at the scheduled time, they were put in jail. The "good behavior bond" continued as a common practice in colonial America and in the new United States. Also, until about 1800 in England, first-time nonviolent property offenders could plead "benefit of clergy." A successful plea of benefit of clergy meant that the offender could recite Psalm 51, beginning with the words "Have mercy on me . . . ." The plea of clergy was an instrument of leniency in a time of an extremely harsh criminal law. All felonies, including nonviolent property offenses, were punishable by death. The successful plea of benefit of clergy permitted first-time, nonviolent property offenders to escape not only the death penalty but also imprisonment. Benefit of clergy was not, in theory, available to repeat offenders, but was often allowed in practice.[3]

In the mid-1800s, a Boston shoemaker by the name of John Augustus earned the title of "first probation officer" in the United States by

historical note

[P]robation['s] ... fundamental object ... is the protection of society against crime. ... It is a more humane method of discipline than incarceration, justified only by the belief that it tends to control crime and protect the public as adequately as would a harsher punishment."

Charles E. Hughes, Jr., 1932

expanding on this old Elizabethan idea. In 1841, Augustus visited the Boston police court, where "a ragged and wretched looking man" charged with being a "common drunkard," begged Augustus to save him from the House of Correction. In return, the man promised Augustus, he would never drink again. Deeply moved by the episode, Augustus asked the magistrate to release the man into his custody for 30 days. During that time, Augustus fed the man and found him a job. The man stopped drinking and supported himself after that.[4]

Encouraged by his success, Augustus abandoned shoemaking and devoted the remainder of his life to "saving" Boston criminals. Over the years, magistrates released two thousand people into his custody, mainly drunks, prostitutes, juveniles, and gamblers. Augustus worked with them as he did with the first man, taking them into his home, finding them work, and encouraging them to lead "pure" lives. He claimed enormous success in reforming them, a success probably due to his devotion and to his selectivity. He gave all his energy to his newfound career. Equally important, he agreed to work only with "good risks," usually first-time, minor offenders who showed promise of success.[5]

Early in the twentieth century, probation became immensely popular. In the great Progressive reform wave of that time, probation became an integral part of American corrections. It was a favorite of reformers, and courts increasingly used it as an alternative to incarceration. By 1930, the federal government and 36 states had enacted probation legislation. By 1940, all but the most rural areas in the country had embraced probation.[6]

The Missions of Probation

Until the end of World War II, probation was clearly defined. Judges granted probation to first-time, minor offenders as an act of leniency. After the war, authorities began to doubt the wisdom and efficacy of prisons and other forms of incarceration as a means of "correcting" offenders. As a result, judges began to grant probation to repeat offenders, and even to some violent felons. They attached special conditions to the probation of these offenders, hoping that supervision in the community would more effectively reform them than would incarceration. Beginning in the 1970s, the enthusiasm for community corrections of all kinds, including probation, encountered a strong backlash. The demand for more punishment and for public safety worked against the presence of repeat felons "on the streets." Ironically, these demands ran counter to other public concerns—a rapidly growing prison population at great public expense. According to Todd R. Clear and Anthony A. Braga,

> Since the mid-1980s, disquiet about offenders under community supervision has maintained a collision course with an equivalent dismay over burgeoning prison populations. On the one hand, it has bothered policy makers that so many offenders, some of whom stand convicted of serious crimes, receive so little in the way of official control over traditional probation and parole methods. Yet the alternative, ever-expanding prison capacity, seems equally unpalatable in times of strained tax revenues.[7]

In spite of worries about probation, even though more people are being sent to prison, and although intermediate punishments are available in most jurisdictions, probation is still the punishment of choice. According to Joan Petersilia and her colleagues,

> When the prison population began to overwhelm existing facilities, probation and "split sentences" (a jail sentence followed by a term on probation) became the de facto disposition of all misdemeanors. As prison overcrowding becomes a national crisis, the courts are being forced to

Figure 12.2

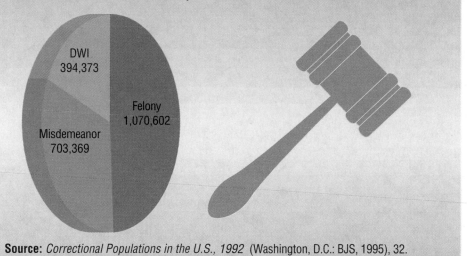

ADULTS ON PROBATION, BY TYPE OF OFFENSE 1992

DWI
394,373

Felony
1,070,602

Misdemeanor
703,369

Source: *Correctional Populations in the U.S., 1992* (Washington, D.C.: BJS, 1995), 32.

use probation even more frequently. Many felons without criminal records are now sentenced to probation . . . .[8] (See Figure 12.2.)

These conflicting goals of rehabilitation and leniency, punishment and controlling prison populations, have led to sometimes vaguely defined, frequently conflicting, and changing missions for probation over time. Edward J. Cosgrove, a federal probation officer, has nicely summarized these missions:

When Gannon and Friday were the role models for police officers, probation officers were an extension of the law. We kept "order" by seeing that people just did the right things. In the '70s, rehabilitation was the goal of supervision. The medical model taught us to diagnose a problem and then provide treatment. Help meant counseling; understanding the hardships of poverty illiteracy, and broken homes; rendering the necessary support to address these symptoms; and coping with the bad feelings and making changes.

As client needs seemed ever expanding, the '80s brought us the philosophy of reintegration. Probation officers could not expect to service all needs; so, the answer became brokering services: identify the problem and make the appropriate referral.

By the end of the '80s, the pendulum had swung from primary care to clients to listening to the needs of the community. Mercy was not to be forgotten, but disparity must be eliminated. Guidelines achieved this with a focus on retributive justice, with scant attention focused to rehabilitation of the individual. The offender will be held accountable. Society will be protected. The Probation Service responded with the development of Enhanced Supervision. The goals were ranked: enforce court orders, provide risk control, address the correctional treatment needs of the offender.

What does a probation officer do? To this day, I suffer a violent visceral pain whenever I hear some visiting academic discuss the "two hats" of the probation officer: cop or counselor. At last count, we wear at least 33 hats and the number is growing.[9]

Whether probation should punish offenders or rehabilitate them is a question never answered and, in fact, rarely addressed until the 1980s. Closely related questions include the following: Should the interest of society in crime control take precedence over the needs and rights of individual probationers? Should probation serve clients or society? Can it balance these functions and serve both?[10]

The tensions between control and service, between the interests of society and the needs and rights of probationers, and between punishment and rehabilitation have led social scientists to identify variations on several general roles that probation officers play:

● Law enforcement officer.
● Social worker.
● Bureaucrat.
● Social service broker.
● Bill collector.

The law enforcement role is played by **punitive probation officers** who consider themselves "guardians of middle-class morality." The punitive officer, according to Patrick D. McAnany and his colleagues,

> attempts to coerce the offender into conforming by means of threats and punishment, and emphasizes control, the protection of the community against the offender and the systematic suspicion of those under supervision.[11]

The social worker role is played by **welfare probation officers**. According to McAnany and his associates, the welfare officer

> has, as his ultimate goal, the improved welfare of the client, achieved by aiding him in his individual adjustment within limits imposed by the client's capacity. Such an officer believes that the only genuine guarantee of community protection lies in the client's personal adjustment since external conformity will only be temporary, and in the long run, may make a social adjustment more difficult. Emotional neutrality permeates his relationships. The diagnostic categories and treatment skills which he employs stem from an objective and theoretically based assessment of the client's needs and capacities.[12]

Protective probation officers combine the law enforcement and social worker roles by trying to balance the interests of clients and society. According to McAnany and his colleagues, protective officers

> vacillate literally between protecting the offender and protecting the community. His tools are direct assistance, lecturing, and alternately, praise and blame. He is perceived as ambivalent in his emotional involvement with the offender and others in the community as he shifts back and forth in taking sides with one against the other.[13]

Protective officers can act inconsistently, according to McAnany and his associates, "helping an offender find a job one day and issuing a technical violation the next. It is this officer who wraps his client in a warm hello hug, bruising him with his gun butt as he does so."[14]

Bureaucratic probation officers take their cues from the bureaucratic emphasis on efficiency, economy, and orderly procedure. Bureaucratic officers primarily stress following procedures, completing tasks, and making sure agencies run smoothly, efficiently, and economically, with minimal interruption or interference from either clients or outsiders. **Time-server probation officers** are, as their name implies, just putting in their time. They want to reduce the "hassle" from both clients and supervisors, collect their salary, and take advantage of their fringe benefits. Time-servers "don't make the rules; they just work here."[15]

Social service brokers reflect a shift in the mission of probation that arose during the late 1960s, when reintegrating offenders into the community

probation bill collector

probation officers who are in charge of seeing to it that probationers pay part of the cost of their probation.

became a popular probation policy goal. The mission of reintegration came about because of a shift in emphasis about the origins of crime from individual pathology to social problems like poverty, racism, unemployment, and lack of opportunity. This shift in emphasis affected probation. Social service brokers focused less on providing direct psychological counseling, and more on putting clients in touch with community social service agencies to help them become law-abiding, productive members of their communities.[16]

The 1990s witnessed the creation of yet another mission for probation—seeing to it that probationers pay at least part of the cost for the "privilege of being on probation." This mission is based on the idea that probation is a "break" for offenders, and so, they ought to pay for it. The **probation bill collector** has to collect these fees. Unfortunately, it is a lot easier to *charge* the fees than to *collect* them. Only about 40 percent of the fees are in fact collected. Furthermore, according to critics, probation officers pay more attention to collecting fees than they do to their clients. Nevertheless, probation fees bring in millions of dollars every year to support probation services.[17]

The multiple missions of probation and multiple roles for probation officers are all still present to some extent. However, as rehabilitation and the rights of offenders receded in the 1980s, retribution, public safety, and economy have become the dominant missions of probation. Hence, the law enforcement role for probation officers has overtaken the social worker and social service broker role.[18]

Retribution, public safety, and economy have become the dominant mission of probation officers in the 1990s.

suspended sentences
postponement of incarceration without either conditions or supervision, with judicial power to revoke the suspension at any time.
split-sentence probation
imposition of a sentence to a specific period of incarceration followed by a period of probation.
shock incarceration *imposition of a sentence to incarceration, after which offenders may petition the court to grant probation.*
intermittent incarceration
imposition of a sentence to incarceration with release for work, school, community service, and drug or other treatment during the day.

Nature and Types of Probation

Probation is not simply a combination of discretionary decision making related to leniency, treatment, reintegration, punishment, public safety, bill collection, control of prison populations, and saving of tax dollars. It is also a formal criminal sentence. Probationers are in state custody, legally accountable to the state, and subject to conditions that limit their freedom and privacy. The sentencing court retains the authority to change the conditions of probation and to revoke probation if probationers violate conditions. Probation is often confused with the suspended sentence. Unlike probation, **suspended sentences** do not impose conditions and do not require supervision. Judges can suspend sentences in two ways. They can sentence offenders to jail or prison and then suspend the execution of the sentence. They can also withhold both the imposition and the execution of the sentence. In both cases, offenders remain free, but they have incarceration "hanging over their heads." At any time, judges can revoke the suspension and impose and execute the sentence by sending them to jail or prison.[19]

Probation is predominantly, but not always, a form of correction that takes place outside prisons, jails, and other places of confinement. Sometimes, however, probation combines supervision in the community with incarceration. In **split-sentence probation,** judges sentence offenders to a specified time in jail or prison, followed by another period on probation. In **shock incarceration,** such as correctional "boot camps," judges sentence offenders to incarceration. Then, following a period of confinement, offenders may petition the court for probation. If they qualify, judges might let them serve the remainder of their sentences on probation. Shock incarceration intends to give offenders a "taste" of imprisonment, in the hope that it will "shock" them into staying out of trouble. Probation tests whether they have been sufficiently "shocked" to become people who work and play by the rules. In **intermittent incarceration,** probationers work, go to school, perform community service, and sometimes receive drug or other treatment during the day. They spend their nights and weekends in jails, workhouses, and, occasionally, in halfway houses.

Eligibility for Probation

Probation is not available to all convicted offenders. Virtually all offenders guilty of misdemeanors receive either probation or split-sentence probation. This eligibility is based on the assumptions that these offenders pose little threat to society and that a supervised life in the community will rehabilitate them. However, as Figure 12.2 indicates, significant numbers of felons are also on probation. Felony probationers are convicted of a range of felonies, as depicted in Figure 12.3. Probation was not intended for nor is it set up to deal with repeat felony offenders. According to Joan Petersilia and her colleagues who examined felony probation in California,

> . . .[C]an probation accommodate more serious offenders, supervise them appropriately, and prevent them from threatening public safety? The most vital and fundamental question is whether traditional probation—based principally on the treatment/service role—should even be considered a legitimate sentencing alternative for convicted felons.[20]

Probation is not distributed evenly among the general population of offenders. The majority of probationers are white men. (See Figure 12.4.)

Figure 12.3

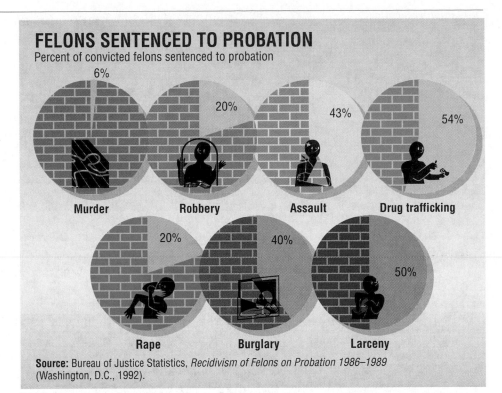

FELONS SENTENCED TO PROBATION
Percent of convicted felons sentenced to probation

6% Murder
20% Robbery
43% Assault
54% Drug trafficking
20% Rape
40% Burglary
50% Larceny

Source: Bureau of Justice Statistics, *Recidivism of Felons on Probation 1986–1989* (Washington, D.C., 1992).

Figure 12.4

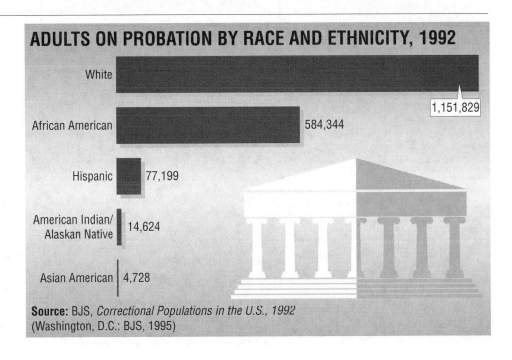

ADULTS ON PROBATION BY RACE AND ETHNICITY, 1992

White — 1,151,829
African American — 584,344
Hispanic — 77,199
American Indian/Alaskan Native — 14,624
Asian American — 4,728

Source: BJS, *Correctional Populations in the U.S., 1992* (Washington, D.C.: BJS, 1995)

Conditions of Probation

The conditions of probation can regulate most of the daily lives of probationers. Typical conditions of probation include

- Obey the law.
- Possess no weapons or explosives.
- Work, go to school, or get vocational training.
- Pay child support.

probation revocation
cancellation of probation for either technical violations or the commission of crimes.

technical probation violations
breaking of probation rules that do not amount to crimes.

- Obtain the written permission of the probation officer to change residence.
- Notify the probation officer of any arrests or criminal investigations.
- Make every effort to get a job and support dependents.
- Obtain written permission from the probation officer for all changes of employment.
- Refrain from traveling outside the community without written permission.
- Refrain from using or selling illegal drugs.
- Comply with any special conditions subsequently imposed by the probation officer or stipulated in the original sentence.[21]

In addition to these usual conditions, felony probationers usually have to fulfill special conditions. These include at least one of the following:

- Drug testing.
- Drug treatment.
- Alcohol treatment.
- Community service work.
- Mental health counseling.
- Residence in a community facility.
- Daytime reporting.
- House arrest.
- Paying probation fees to help pay the cost of probation.[22]

Figure 12.5 depicts the conditions of probation used by the U.S. District Courts for federal probationers.

Revocation of Probation

Probation ends either when probationers successfully complete the terms of their probation or when a court revokes (cancels) their probation. **Probation revocation** or cancellation occurs when probationers violate the terms of their probation. Revocation can result when probationers are either arrested for or convicted of a new crime (recidivism), or when they break probation rules that are not crimes (**technical probation violations**), such as failing to notify their probation officer of a change of address.

The most frequent reason for revocation of probation is committing a new crime. Technical violations are common—about half of all probationers commit technical violations. However, only about 20 percent of technical violations result in the revocation of probation. Some charge that the gap between violations and revocations erodes confidence in probation. According to Todd R. Clear and Anthony A. Braga,

> Critics portray an image of wanton disregard for program rules followed by little or no sanction from program managers. The result, it is sometimes argued, is a continuing breach of community safety.[23]

Clear and Braga conclude that despite the surface appeal of the critics' argument, the link between technical violations and public safety is not that simple. In the first place, the number of rules is growing and the surveillance capacity to enforce the rules is increasing, particularly by means of urine testing for drugs. Second, technical violations may point to a lack of discipline, but lack of discipline does not necessarily translate into threats to public safety. In other words, the failure of probationers to report an address change does not mean they are going to commit crimes.[24]

Revocation is not the only possible result of probation violations. A survey of violations in the Florida circuit courts showed that the courts revoked

Figure 12.5

PROB 7A
(Rev. 6/90)©

Conditions of Probation and Supervised Release

UNITED STATES DISTRICT COURT
FOR THE
_____

Name _____ Docket No. _____

Address _____

Under the terms of your sentence, you have been placed on probation/supervised release (strike one) by the Honorable _____, United States District Judge for the District of _____. Your term of supervision is for a period of _____, commencing_____.

While on probation/supervised release (strike one), you shall not commit another Federal, state, or local crime and shall not illegally possess a controlled substance. Revocation of probation and supervised release is mandatory for possession of a controlled substance.

CHECK IF APPROPRIATE:

☐ As a condition of supervision, you are instructed to pay a fine in the amount of _____; it shall be paid in the following manner _____.

☐ As a condition of supervision, you are instructed to pay restitution in the amount of _____ to _____; it shall be paid in the following manner _____.

☐ The defendant shall not possess a firearm or destructive device. Probation must be revoked for possession of a firearm.

☐ The defendant shall report in person to the probation office in the district to which the defendant is released within 72 hours of release from the custody of the Bureau of Prisons.

It is the order of the Court that you shall comply with the following standard conditions:

(1) You shall not leave the judicial district without permission of the court or probation officer;

(2) You shall report to the probation officer as directed by the court or probation officer, and shall submit a truthful and complete written report within the first five days of each month;

(3) You shall answer truthfully all inquiries by the probation officer and follow the instructions of the probation officer;

(4) You shall support your dependents and meet other family responsibilities;

(5) You shall work regularly at a lawful occupation unless excused by the probation officer for schooling, training, or other acceptable reasons:

(6) You shall notify the probation officer within seventy-two hours of any change in residence or employment;

(7) You shall refrain from excessive use of alcohol and shall not purchase, possess, use, distribute, or administer any narcotic or other controlled substance, or any paraphernalia related to such substances, except as prescribed by a physician;

(8) You shall not frequent places where controlled substances are illegally sold, used, distributed, or administered;

(9) You shall not associate with any persons engaged in criminal activity, and shall not associate with any person convicted of a felony unless granted permission to do so by the probation officer;

(10) You shall permit a probation officer to visit you at any time at home or elsewhere, and shall permit confiscation of any contraband observed in plain view by the probation officer;

(11) You shall notify the probation officer within seventy-two hours of being arrested or questioned by a law enforcement officer;

(12) You shall not enter into any agreement to act as an informer or a special agent of a law enforcement agency without the permission of the court;

(13) As directed by the probation officer, you shall notify third parties of risks that may be occasioned by your criminal record or personal history or characteristics, and shall permit the probation officer to make such notifications and to confirm your compliance with such notification requirement.

The special conditions ordered by the court are as follows:

Upon a finding of a violation of probation or supervised release, I understand that the Court may (1) revoke supervision or (2) extend the term of supervision and/or modify the conditions of supervision.

These conditions have been read to me. I fully understand the conditions, and have been provided a copy of them.

(Signed) _____ _____

     Defendant   Date

_____ _____

U.S. Probation Officer/Designated Witness   Date

---

probation and returned to prison only 17 percent of probation violators, and revoked probation and sent to county jails 11 percent. In the remainder of the cases, the courts did not revoke probation but instead modified the terms, sometimes by making the conditions stiffer, as in the 8 percent of probationers who were transferred from ordinary to intensive supervised probation, discussed later in this chapter.[25]

initial probable cause hearing
minimal inquiry to determine whether there is reasonable ground to believe that probationers have violated probation.

Probation and the Law

Probationers are convicted offenders. Therefore, they have fewer rights than people who are not in state custody because they have committed crimes. According to the Supreme Court, probationers "do not enjoy the absolute liberty to which every citizen is entitled, but only . . . conditional liberty properly dependent on observance of special restrictions." These restrictions are legal so long as they assure that "probation serves as a period of genuine rehabilitation and that the community is not harmed by the probationer's being at large." So, according to the Court, "supervision is a 'special need' of the State permitting a degree of impingement upon privacy that would not be constitutional if applied to the public at large."[26]

Probationers may have *fewer* rights than people who are not in state custody, but they are not totally devoid of rights. For instance, the Supreme Court has ruled in *Morrissey v. Brewer* and *Gagnon v. Scarpelli* that probationers are entitled to due process of law in the revocation of their probation. The due process clause provides that the state cannot take away persons' "life, liberty, or property" without "due process of law." According to the Court, "Revocation deprives an individual, not of absolute liberty to which every citizen is entitled, but only of the conditional liberty properly dependent on observance of special . . . [probation] conditions." In other words, probationers are entitled to the protection of the due process clause; however, since the liberty is conditional, they are not entitled to the same process to which fully free people are entitled.[27]

The lesser "process" that is "due" to probationers before the state can deprive them of the conditional liberty that revoking their probation demands "some orderly process, however informal." That orderly process must provide "an effective but informal hearing" to assure that "the finding of a . . . violation will be based on verified facts and that the exercise of discretion will be informed by an accurate knowledge of the . . . [probationer's] behavior." The hearing involves two stages:

1. Arrest and Preliminary Hearing.
According to the Supreme Court, due process requires an **initial probable cause hearing** that involves some

> minimal inquiry . . . at or reasonably near the place of the alleged . . . violation or arrest and as promptly as is convenient after arrest while information is fresh and sources are available. Such an inquiry should be seen as in the nature of a "preliminary hearing" to determine whether there is probable cause or reasonable ground to believe that the arrested person has committed acts that would constitute a violation of . . . [probation] conditions.[28]

"Disinterested persons" are to determine whether reasonable grounds exist to believe probationers have violated their probation and that probable cause exists to arrest them. Disinterested, however, does not mean that judges need to decide reasonableness and probable cause. Probation officers other than those who reported the violations are acceptable.[29]

In this stage, the state must notify probationers that the hearing will take place and that its purpose is to determine whether reasonable grounds exist to believe they have violated the conditions of their probation. The notice must list the specific alleged violations. Probationers can attend the hearing, tell their side of the story, and bring "letters, documents, or individuals" who can provide relevant information. Probationers can question individuals who have provided information upon which the alleged violations are based. Unless the hearing officer determines that "an informant would be subjected to risk of harm if his identity is disclosed, he need not be subjected to confrontation and cross-examination."[30]

Probationers do not have as many "rights" as people who have not been convicted of crimes.

final revocation hearing *the final evaluation of whether probatiioners have violated the conditions of their probation.*

Following the decision in *Morrissey v. Brewer,* the Supreme Court has ruled:

> The hearing officer shall have the duty of making a summary, or digest, of what occurs at the hearing. . . . Based on the information before him, the officer should determine whether there is probable cause to hold the . . . [probationer] for the final decision . . . on revocation.[31]

Decision makers should state the reasons and indicate the evidence for their decision. But, according to the Court, "it should be remembered that this is not a formal determination calling for 'formal findings of fact and conclusions of law.' "[32]

2. The Revocation Hearing. According to the Supreme Court, probationers have a right to a further hearing leading to more than the determination of probable cause. This **final revocation hearing** "must lead to a final evaluation of any contested relevant facts and consideration of whether the facts as determined warrant revocation." In the revocation, according to the Court, the probationer

> must have an opportunity to be heard and to show, if he can, that he did not violate the conditions, or, if he did, that circumstances in mitigation suggest that the violation does not warrant revocation. The revocation hearing must be tendered within a reasonable time after the . . . [probationer] is taken into custody.
>
> We cannot write a code of procedure; that is the responsibility of each State. . . . Our task is limited to deciding the minimum requirements of due process. They include (a) written notice of the claimed violations . . ; (b) disclosure . . . of the evidence against him; (c) opportunity to be heard in person and to present witnesses and documentary evidence; (d) the right to confront and cross-examine adverse witnesses (unless the hearing officer specifically finds good cause for not allowing confrontation); (e) a 'neutral and detached' hearing body . . . members of which need not be judicial officers or lawyers; and (f) a written statement by the factfinders as to the evidence relied on and reasons for revoking . . . [probation].[33]

Besides spelling out the constitutional rights of probationers regarding probation revocation, the Supreme Court has also decided some of the limits on other constitutional rights while a person is on probation. In the case of *Minnesota v. Murphy*, the Court ruled that probation officers do not need to give probationers the *Miranda* warnings when they question them about crimes they may have committed while on probation. The *You Decide*, "Are Probationer's Homes Their 'Castles?'" deals with the Court's definition of the rights of probationers against "unreasonable searches and seizures."

You Decide   "Are Probationers' Homes their 'Castles?'"

Griffin v. Wisconsin, 483 U.S. 868, 107 S.Ct. 3164, 107 S.Ct. 3164
97 L.Ed.2d 709, 55 USLW 5156 (1987)

Facts

On September 4, 1980, Griffin, who had previously been convicted of a felony, was convicted in Wisconsin state court of resisting arrest, disorderly conduct, and obstructing an officer. He was placed on probation. Wisconsin law puts probationers in the legal custody of the State Department of Health and Social Services and renders them "subject . . . to . . . conditions set by the court and rules and regulations established by the department." One of the Department's regulations permits any probation officer to search a probationer's home without a warrant as long as his supervisor approves and as long as there are "reasonable grounds" to believe the presence of contraband—including any item that the probationer cannot possess under the probation conditions. The rule provides that an officer should consider a variety of factors in determining whether "reasonable grounds" exist, among which are information provided by an informant, the reliability and specificity of that information, the reliability of the informant (including whether the informant has any incentive to supply inaccurate information), the officer's own experience with the probationer, and the "need to verify compliance with rules of supervision and state and federal law." Another regulation makes it a violation of the terms of probation to refuse to consent to a home search. Still another forbids a probationer to possess a firearm without advance approval from a probation officer.

On April 5, 1983, while Griffin was still on probation, Michael Lew, the supervisor of Griffin's probation officer, received information from a detective on the Beloit Police Department that there were or might be guns in Griffin's apartment. Unable to secure the assistance of Griffin's own probation officer, Lew, accompanied by another probation officer and three plainclothes policemen, went to the apartment. When Griffin answered the door, Lew told him who they were and informed him that they were going to search his home. During the subsequent search—carried out entirely by the probation officers under the authority of Wisconsin's probation regulation—they found a handgun.

Griffin was charged with possession of a firearm by a convicted felon, which is itself a felony. He moved to suppress the evidence seized during the search. The trial court denied the motion, concluding that no warrant was necessary and that the search was reasonable. A jury convicted Griffin of the firearms violation, and he was sentenced to two years' imprisonment. The conviction was affirmed by the Wisconsin Court of Appeals, 126 Wis.2d 183, 376 N.W.2d 62 (1985). On further appeal, the Wisconsin Supreme Court also affirmed. . . . 131 Wis.2d 41, 52–64, 388 N.W.2d 535, 539–544 (1986).

Opinion

We think the Wisconsin Supreme Court correctly concluded that this warrantless search did not violate the Fourth Amendment. . . . As his sentence for the commission of a crime, Griffin was committed to the legal custody of the Wisconsin State Department of Health and Social Services, and thereby made subject to that Department's rules and regulations. The search of Griffin's home satisfied the demands of the Fourth Amendment because it was carried out pursuant to a regulation that itself satisfies the Fourth Amendment's reasonableness requirement under well-established principles.

A probationer's home, like anyone else's, is protected by the Fourth Amendment's requirement that searches be "reasonable." Although we usually require that a search be undertaken only pursuant to a warrant (and thus supported by probable cause, as the Constitution says warrants must be), we have permitted exceptions when "special needs, beyond the normal need for law enforcement, make the warrant and probable-cause requirement impracticable." Thus, we have held that government employers and supervisors may conduct warrantless, work-related searches of employees' desks and offices without probable cause, and that school officials may conduct warrantless searches of some student property, also without probable cause. We have also held, for similar reasons, that in certain circumstances government investigators conducting searches pursuant to a regulatory scheme need not adhere to the usual warrant or probable-cause requirements as long as their searches meet "reasonable legislative or administrative standards."

A State's operation of a probation system, like its operation of a school, government office, or prison, or its supervision of a regulated industry, likewise presents "special needs" beyond normal law enforcement that may justify departures from the usual warrant and probable-cause requirements. Probation, like incarceration, is "a form of criminal sanction imposed by a court upon an offender after verdict, finding, or plea of guilty." Probation is simply one point (or, more accurately, one set of points) on a continuum of possible punishments ranging from solitary confinement in a maximum-security facility to a few hours of mandatory community service. A number of different options lie between those extremes, including confinement in a medium- or minimum-security facility, work-release programs, "halfway houses," and probation—which can itself be more or less confining depending upon the number and severity of restrictions imposed. . . . To a greater or lesser degree, it is always true of probationers (as we have said it to be true of parolees) that they do not enjoy "the absolute liberty to which every citizen is entitled, but only . . . conditional liberty properly dependent on observance of special . . . restrictions."

These restrictions are meant to assure that the probation serves as a period of genuine rehabilitation and that the community is not harmed by the probationer's being at large. These same goals require and justify the exercise of supervision to assure that the restrictions are in fact observed. Recent research suggests that more intensive supervision can reduce recidivism—see Petersilia, "Probation and Felony Offenders," 49 *Fed. Probation* 9 (June 1985)—and the importance of supervision has grown as probation has become an increasingly common sentence for those convicted of serious crimes. Supervision, then, is a "special need" of the State permitting a degree of impingement upon privacy that would not be constitutional if applied to the public at large. That permissible degree is not unlimited, however, so we next turn to whether it has been exceeded here.

In determining whether the "special needs" of its probation system justify Wisconsin's search regulation, we must take that regulation as it has been interpreted by state corrections officials and state courts. As already noted, the Wisconsin Supreme Court—the ultimate authority on issues of Wisconsin law—has held that a tip from a police detective that Griffin "had" or "may have had" an illegal weapon at his home constituted the requisite "reasonable grounds." Whether or not we would choose to interpret a similarly worded federal regulation in that fashion, we are bound by the state court's interpretation, which is relevant to our constitutional analysis only insofar as it fixes the meaning of the regulation. We think it clear that the special needs of Wisconsin's probation system make the warrant requirement impracticable and justify replacement of the standard of probable cause by "reasonable grounds," as defined by the Wisconsin Supreme Court.

A warrant requirement would interfere to an appreciable degree with the probation system, setting up a magistrate rather than the probation officer as the judge of how close a supervision the probationer requires. Moreover, the delay inherent in obtaining a warrant would make it more difficult for probation officials to respond quickly to evidence of misconduct—see *New Jersey v. T.L.O.*, 469 U.S., at 340, 105 S.Ct., at 743—and would reduce the deterrent effect that the possibility of expeditious searches would otherwise create. By way of analogy, one might contemplate how parental custodial authority would be impaired by requiring judicial approval for search of a minor child's room. And on the other side of the equation—the effect of dispensing with a warrant upon the probationer: Although a probation officer is not an impartial magistrate, neither is he the police officer who normally conducts searches against the ordinary citizen. He is an employee of the State Department of Health and Social Services who, while assuredly charged with protecting the public interest, is also supposed to have in mind the welfare of the probationer (who in the regulations is called a "client"). The applicable regulations require him, for example, to "[p]rovid[e] individualized counseling designed to foster growth and development of the client as necessary," and "[m]onito[r] the client's progress where services are provided by another agency and evaluat[e] the need for continuation of the services." In such a setting, we think it reasonable to dispense with the warrant requirement. . . .

We think that the probation regime would also be unduly disrupted by a requirement of probable cause. To take the facts of the present case, it is most unlikely that the unauthenticated tip of a police officer—bearing, as far as the record shows, no indication whether its basis was firsthand knowledge or, if not, whether the firsthand source was reliable, and merely stating that Griffin "had or might have" guns in his residence, not that he certainly had them—would meet the ordinary requirement of probable cause. But this is different from the ordinary case in two related respects: First, even more than the requirement of a warrant, a probable-cause requirement would reduce the deterrent effect of the supervisory arrangement. The probationer would be assured that so long as his illegal (and perhaps socially dangerous) activities were sufficiently concealed as to give rise to no more than reasonable suspicion, they would go undetected and uncorrected. The second difference is well reflected in the regulation specifying what is to be considered "[i]n deciding whether there are reasonable grounds to believe . . . a client's living quarters or property contain contraband." The factors include not only the usual elements that a police officer or magistrate would consider, such as the detail and consistency of the information suggesting the presence of contraband and the reliability and motivation to dissemble of the informant, but also "[i]nformation provided by the client which is relevant to whether the client possesses contraband," and "[t]he experience of a staff member with that client or in a similar circumstance." . . . We deal with a situation in which there is an ongoing supervisory relationship—and one that is not, or at least not entirely, adversarial—between the object of the search and the decisionmaker.

In such circumstances it is both unrealistic and destructive of the whole object of the continuing probation relationship to insist upon the same degree of demonstrable reliability of particular items of supporting data, and upon the same degree of certainty of violation, as is required in other contexts. In some cases—especially those involving drugs or illegal weapons—the probation agency must be able to act based upon a lesser degree of certainty than the Fourth Amendment would otherwise require in order to intervene before a probationer does damage to himself or society. The agency, moreover, must be able to proceed on the basis of its entire experience with the probationer, and to assess probabilities in the light of its knowledge of his life, character, and circumstances. . . .

The search of Griffin's residence was "reasonable" within the meaning of the Fourth Amendment because it was conducted pursuant to a valid regulation governing probationers. This conclusion makes it unnecessary to consider whether, as the court below held and the State urges, any search of a probationer's home by a probation officer is lawful when there are "reasonable grounds" to believe contraband is present. For the foregoing reasons, the judgment of the Wisconsin Supreme Court is Affirmed.

Dissent

Justice BLACKMUN, with whom Justice MARSHALL joins and as to Parts I-B and I-C, Justice BRENNAN joins and, as to Part I-C, Justice STEVENS joins, dissenting.

In ruling that the home of a probationer may be searched by a probation officer without a warrant, the Court today takes another step that diminishes the protection given by the Fourth Amendment to the "right of the people to be secure in their persons, houses, papers, and effects, against unreasonable searches and seizures." In my view, petitioner's probationary status provides no reason to abandon the warrant requirement. The probation system's special law enforcement needs may justify a search by a probation officer on the basis of "reasonable suspicion," but even that standard was not met in this case.

The need for supervision in probation presents one of the "exceptional circumstances in which special needs, beyond the normal need for law enforcement," . . . justify an application of the Court's balancing test and an examination of the practicality of the warrant and probable-cause requirements. The Court, however, fails to recognize that this is a threshold determination of special law enforcement needs. The warrant and probable-cause requirements provide the normal standard for "reasonable" searches. "[O]nly when the practical realities of a particular situation suggest that a government official cannot obtain a warrant based upon probable cause without sacrificing the ultimate goals to which a search would contribute, does the Court turn to a 'balancing' test to formulate a standard of reasonableness for this context." The presence of special law enforcement needs justifies resort to the balancing test, but it does not preordain the necessity of recognizing exceptions to the warrant and probable-cause requirements.

My application of the balancing test leads me to conclude that special law enforcement needs justify a search by a probation agent of the home of a probationer on the basis of a reduced level of suspicion. The acknowledged need for supervision, however, does not also justify an exception to the warrant requirement, and I would retain this means of protecting a probationer's privacy. Moreover, the necessity for the neutral check provided by the warrant requirement is demonstrated by this case, in which the search was conducted on the basis of information that did not begin to approach the level of "reasonable grounds." . . .

I do not think . . . that special law enforcement needs justify a modification of the protection afforded a probationer's privacy by the warrant requirement. The search in this case was conducted in petitioner's home, the place that traditionally has been regarded as the center of a person's private life, the bastion in which one has a legitimate expectation of privacy protected by the Fourth Amendment. . . . The Court consistently has held that warrantless searches and seizures in a home violate the Fourth Amendment absent consent or exigent circumstances. . . . " It is axiomatic that the 'physical entry of the home is the chief evil against which the wording of the Fourth Amendment is directed.' " And a principal protection against unnecessary intrusions into private dwellings is the warrant requirement imposed by the Fourth Amendment on agents of the government who seek to enter the home for purposes of search or arrest. It is not surprising, therefore, that the Court has recognized, as a "basic principle of Fourth Amendment law[,]" that searches and seizures inside a home without a warrant are presumptively unreasonable." . . .

A probationer usually lives at home, and often, as in this case, with a family. He retains a legitimate privacy interest in the home that must be respected to the degree that it is not incompatible with substantial governmental needs. The Court in *New Jersey v. T.L.O.* acknowledged that the Fourth Amendment issue needs to be resolved in such a way as to "ensure that the [privacy] interests of students will be invaded no more than is necessary to achieve the legitimate end of preserving order in the schools." The privacy interests of probationers should be protected by a similar standard, and invaded no more than is necessary to satisfy probation's dual goals of protecting the public safety and encouraging the rehabilitation of the probationer. . . .

There are many probationers in this country, and they have committed crimes that range widely in seriousness. The Court has determined that all of them may be subjected to such searches in the absence of a warrant. Moreover, in authorizing these searches on the basis of a reduced level of suspicion, the Court overlooks the feeble justification for the search in this case.

I respectfully dissent.

Justice STEVENS, with whom Justice MARSHALL joins, dissenting.

Mere speculation by a police officer that a probationer "may have had" contraband in his possession is not a constitutionally sufficient basis for a warrantless, nonconsensual search of a private home. I simply do not understand how five Members of this Court can reach a contrary conclusion. Accordingly, I respectfully dissent.

Questions

How did the Court reduce the rights of probationers when it comes to the right against "unreasonable searches" of homes? What reasons does the majority of the Court give for this reduction? Why does the dissent disagree with the majority decision? Which of the opinions—the majority or the dissent—do you agree with? Should probationers have any rights against searches by their probation officers? Defend your answer.

Effectiveness of Probation

Most probationers complete probation without violating the conditions of their sentence. On the average, about 80 percent of all probationers succeed—if success is measured by probationers not violating the conditions of probation, not getting arrested for crimes while on probation, and not absconding. Success rates, however, vary, from a high of 95 percent in Vermont to a low of 66 percent in Mississippi. Success is highest among young, new offenders and lowest among older, hardened offenders. Furthermore, arrest and conviction rise as time passes. So, although probationers might not fail while they are on probation, they may fail later. However, evidence suggests that close monitoring in the community, including surprise drug tests for addicts, reduces rearrest rates among advanced offenders. For low-risk offenders, the amount of supervision does not seem to affect failure rates.[34]

Some evidence suggests that probation might be more effective than imprisonment in preventing recidivism. Joan Petersilia and others studied 511 probationers and 511 offenders released from prison who matched each other closely in year they were sentenced, gender (male), county of conviction (Los Angeles or Alameda), conviction crime (assault, robbery, burglary, theft, or drug sale/possession), and a score reflecting factors associated with prison/probation decisions in California. Using other controls in analyzing the data, the study found associations, but not causal relations, among prison, probation, and recidivism. During the two-year period of the study, prisoners had higher recidivism rates than probationers. Seventy-two percent of the prisoners were rearrested, compared with 63 percent of probationers; 53 percent of the prisoners had new charges filed against them, compared with 38 percent of the probationers; and 47 percent of the prisoners were incarcerated, compared with 31 percent of the probationers. Prisoners' new offenses, however, were no more serious than probationers', even if there were more of them. Despite public apprehension and impatience, probation seems to work well on the whole. From all available evidence, probation is generally at least as effective as imprisonment, and possibly more so.[35]

The Bureau of Justice Statistics examined the results of felony probation by conducting the largest national follow-up survey of adult felony probationers ever. The survey used official records to track the progress of a sample of probationers (in 17 states) through their first three years on probation. Within three years of sentencing, 62 percent of the probationers in the sample were either arrested for a new felony or charged at a hearing with a violation of the conditions of their probation. Forty three percent were arrested for a felony within three years; 49 percent had a disciplinary hearing for a violation of probation. Figure 12.6 depicts the detailed progress of 100 felons based on the sample.[36]

The failure rates found in the BJS study, coupled with demands that we "get tough" on crime by putting more people in prison, have led to a heated policy debate about the use of probation, particularly for felons. This debate led Michael R. Geerken and Hennessey D. Hayes to examine the impact of probationer crime on the overall crime rates. They analyzed data on arrest, incarceration, and probation supervision for burglary and armed robbery in New Orleans. To determine probationers' impact, Geerken and Hayes "examined the percentage of all burglary and armed robbery arrests . . . that involved persons on probation. . . ." They found that probationers accounted for 8 percent of all adult arrests for burglary and armed robbery. According to Geerken and Hayes,

> These percentages are contrary to expectations and surprisingly low. They suggest that even the complete elimination of probation . . . would have a very negligible effect on the burglary and armed robbery

Figure 12.6

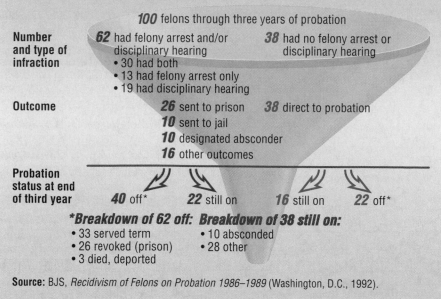

RECIDIVISM OF FELONS ON PROBATION

100 felons through three years of probation

| Number and type of infraction | *62* had felony arrest and/or disciplinary hearing | *38* had no felony arrest or disciplinary hearing |

• 30 had both
• 13 had felony arrest only
• 19 had disciplinary hearing

Outcome

26 sent to prison   *38* direct to probation
10 sent to jail
10 designated absconder
16 other outcomes

Probation status at end of third year

40 off*   *22* still on   *16* still on   *22* off*

Breakdown of 62 off: Breakdown of 38 still on:
• 33 served term   • 10 absconded
• 26 revoked (prison)   • 28 other
• 3 died, deported

Source: BJS, *Recidivism of Felons on Probation 1986–1989* (Washington, D.C., 1992).

---

either-or punishment practice
practice of either incarcerating offenders or placing them on ordinary probation.
intermediate sanctions
punishments that are less severe than incarceration but more severe than ordinary probation.

rates since more than 90 percent of all burglaries and armed robberies were committed by persons *not* on probation . . . at the time of the arrest. . . . We argue . . . that since a low percentage of all burglary and armed robbery arrests are of persons on probation . . . at the time, policy changes tightening or eliminating . . . [probation] can affect only a small percentage of these crimes.[37]

Intermediate Punishments

For most of the twentieth century, the United States followed an **either-or-punishment practice.** That is, convicted offenders were either incarcerated or put on ordinary probation. The wide range of actual criminal behavior, however, rarely falls neatly into the two extremes provided by either straight probation or incarceration. Punishment was often too harsh for offenders who did not deserve imprisonment, too lenient for offenders who were sentenced to probation. Justice demands a range of punishments that fit the range of actual criminal behavior. The demand for a more appropriate range of penalties—the application of the principle of just deserts to the punishment of offenders—is one reason for the rise of **intermediate sanctions.** Intermediate sanctions are punishments that are more severe than ordinary probation but not so harsh as confinement in jails and prisons.

The application of the principle of just deserts is not the only mission that intermediate sanctions are supposed to accomplish. Proponents of intermediate sanctions have "sold" them to legislators and the public on the claims that the sanctions can reduce prison crowding, protect the public, punish and rehabilitate offenders—and accomplish all of this while saving tax dollars. Of course, intermediate sanctions cannot completely accomplish all these far-reaching missions. They are not a panacea.[38]

The interest in intermediate punishments is not new. The ideas for intermediate punishments that have taken the public and politicians by storm, and criminal justice professionals with somewhat less force, have a long history. Home confinement is as old as recorded history. Henry VIII confined Catherine of Aragon for years in various palaces in England.

Intermediate Punishments in Nordic Countries

The amount of crime has increased significantly in the Nordic countries of Sweden, Finland, Norway, and Denmark since the 1950s. At the same time, however, the amount of imprisonment has steadily declined. Not only is imprisonment used less frequently, but the average length of sentences has also decreased. In Finland, for example, the median length of sentences declined from 7.6 months in 1950 to 3.3 months in 1985; the median length for property offenses fell from 9.8 months to 3.5 months.

Despite this decrease in imprisonment, Scandinavian countries have not replaced imprisonment with intermediate punishments such as those discussed in this chapter. The common alternatives to imprisonment are suspended sentences and fines, or, in Finland and Sweden, day-fines. Denmark and Norway are experimenting with community service, and perhaps Sweden and Finland may follow their lead.

Restitution is rarely used in Nordic countries, despite increased focus on the victim in Scandinavian criminal justice. However, the focus on victims has led to the greater use of mediation as an alternative to criminal justice. Norway has experimented with a network of "conflict councils," and other countries have adopted more limited mediation devices.

The penal policy of all the Nordic countries rests on general prevention; that is, that punishment reminds the public that society intends to enforce its norms. General prevention does not depend on deterrence by fear, but instead on deterrence through a combination of the high risk of detection and apprehension and the strengthening of internal norms. According to this view of prevention, a small fine for a traffic offense reinternalizes norms as effectively for traffic offenses as does imprisonment for robbery.[40]

Intensive supervised probation arose in the 1960s. The interest in principled grading of punishments arises out of a long-standing dissatisfaction with the either/or, in/out choice between incarceration and probation. A major shift from rehabilitation to retribution and community safety has generated demands for a richer variety of humane punishments that do not threaten community safety. Prison crowding and budgetary restraints increase the attractiveness of community alternatives that are more punitive and safer than ordinary probation.[39]

Local, state, and federal governments adopted a variety of programs in the 1980s and 1990s during the latest wave of popularity of intermediate sanctions. These include:

- Intensive Supervised Probation (ISP).
- Home confinement (often called house arrest or home detention).
- Shock incarceration (correctional boot camps).
- Fines.
- Community service.
- Day Reporting Centers.

Most states and the federal government have intermediate sanction programs.

Intensive Supervised Probation (ISP)

Crowded prisons, budget crunches, and the threat to public safety posed by felons on probation led to the adoption of intensive supervised probation

(ISP) in the 1980s. As its name implies, **intensive supervised probation** is a tougher form of probation. ISP probationers have more frequent contact with probation officers, are subject to more and stricter limits on their privacy and freedom, and are required to work, get treatment, or go to school. Close supervision of probationers dates back at least to the 1960s, when it was adopted as an experiment to determine the ideal caseload for probation officers. In one of the best-known and earliest (1967) evaluations of these early intensive supervision programs, federal probation authorities divided offenders into four levels of supervision: "intensive," which assigned only 20 offenders to each probation officer; "ideal," which assigned 50 offenders to each officer; "normal," which assigned 70 to 130 offenders to each officer; and "minimum," which assigned several hundred offenders to each officer. According to Arthur J. Lurigio and Joan Petersilia,

> After two years, it was shown that smaller caseloads did little except generate more technical violations. Crime rates were about the same for all categories of supervision . . . . As similar evidence accumulated, federal funding for criminal justice projects began to evaporate . . . . Under these circumstances, most of the earlier IPS projects were dismantled; they remained dormant until the early 1980s.[41]

Curiously, proponents of today's intensive supervised probation have largely ignored these findings. Intensive supervised probation is now the most popular and the most widely used intermediate punishment. Every state and the federal government has adopted some form of ISP (see Figure 12.7).[42]

Intensive supervised probation includes several ambitious aims:

● Reduce prison crowding.
● Increase community protection.
● Rehabilitate offenders.
● Prove that probation can work.
● Save money.

Figure 12.7

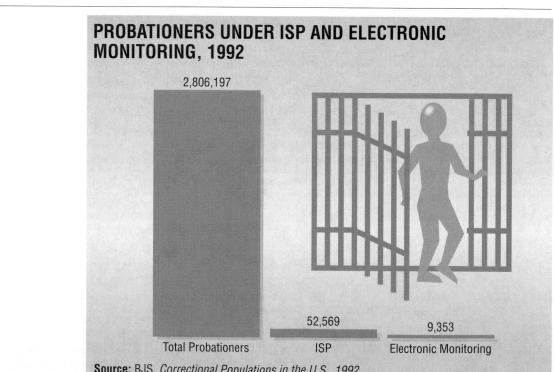

PROBATIONERS UNDER ISP AND ELECTRONIC MONITORING, 1992

2,806,197

52,569

9,353

Total Probationers   ISP   Electronic Monitoring

Source: BJS, *Correctional Populations in the U.S., 1992* (Washington, D.C.: 1995), Table 3.10

In addition to these widely publicized and widely accepted aims, intensive supervised probation serves a number of hidden missions:

- *The Institutional Mission.* Probation has an image problem; it is often regarded as a "slap on the wrist." ISP claims to be "tough" on criminals and promises to protect the community.
- *The Professional Mission.* ISP is supposed to generate more money for probation departments. Therefore, probation officers "get to do probation work the way it ought to be done" and they "work closely with just a few people so [they] can make a difference in their lives."
- *The Political Mission.* ISP allows probation departments to get in tune with the public "get tough on crime and criminals" attitude. This harmony with the public makes probation—and probation budgets—more saleable to the public.[43]

Supervision in most ISP programs includes frequent alcohol and other drug testing, unannounced visits by probation officers, intolerance of even minor violations of the conditions of probation, and regular—sometimes daily—contact with probation officers.[44]

ISP programs sometimes mix community supervision with incarceration. For example, New Jersey has an ISP program that includes an element of shock incarceration. Prisoners can apply for the ISP program only after serving a minimum of 60 days in prison. The median prison time served is about three-and-a-half months. New Jersey has accepted more than 1,460 offenders in its ISP program. Most offenders chosen are already sentenced to prison, represent an acceptable risk to the community, and have not committed a violent offense; a risk assessment instrument is used to screen them. While the majority of those selected fall into the category of nonviolent property offenders, a large number of alcohol and other drug related offenders are also included in the program. Some offenders have committed violent crimes.[45]

In the New Jersey program, probation officers carry a caseload of 16 probationers. Contacts average one daily, including twelve face-to-face meetings, seven curfew checks, and four urinalyses a month during the first six months in the program. Program rules include work requirements, curfew, abstinence from alcohol and other drugs, and payments of fines, restitution, and child support. Participants who violate even minor program rules return to prison. By 1989, of participants who entered New Jersey's program prior to December 31, 1985, 58 percent graduated from the program and 40 percent returned to prison because of violations. Urinalysis accounted for many returns to prison, misconduct that would remain undetected in ordinary supervision. Twelve percent of program participants were convicted of another offense at the end of two years, compared to 23 percent of a control group who served their normal prison terms.

In 1987, the Bureau of Justice Statistics provided funding for a rigorous experimental evaluation of intensive supervised probation. Seven jurisdictions in five states developed programs that were stricter than ordinary probation but less harsh than prison and jail. The programs identified serious repeat drug offenders on probation or parole, randomly assigning them to either the ISP or a control group. This assured that differences in outcome would not come from the participants but from the programs. The data indicated that both the experimental and control groups were similar in background and had committed similar offenses. Participants in the ISP group were tested more frequently for drug use, and they had more contacts with their probation officers than participants who were assigned to the control group. A 12-month follow-up study found

no significant variations . . . among the ISP and routine probationers . . . in terms of (a) the proportion rearrested, (b) the average number of arrests during the follow-up period, (c) the nature of the new offenses, or (d) the rate of arrests, controlling for street time (i.e., time not incarcerated.[46]

Despite these disappointing recidivism results, Joan Petersilia, Susan Turner, and Elizabeth Piper Deschennes concluded that the seven programs *did* accomplish another important mission of ISP—administer just deserts. According to the researchers,

> . . . [T]he programs were able to achieve another of their stated goals, that of imposing an intermediate punishment, for which the court-ordered sanctions were more credibly monitored and enforced than was possible with routine supervision. It appears that ISP, rather than rehabilitating the *offender,* rehabilitated the *system.* In the long run, such intermediate sanctions should escalate the cost of crime to the offender and help restore the principle of just deserts to the criminal justice system. And bridging the middle ground with intermediate sanctions should eventually enhance the deterrent effectiveness of the sentencing system as a whole.[47]

The *You Decide,* "Should Felons Serve Time in the Community," examines Georgia's intensive supervised probation program.[48]

You Decide — Should Felons Serve Time in the Community?

According to a Bureau of Justice Statistics assessment, Georgia's intensive supervised probation program, an alternative, intermediate form of punishment . . . changes the perception of probation as a "slap on the wrist" to that of a viable alternative to imprisonment. The core of such an alternative must be intensive surveillance, coupled with substantial community service and/or restitution. It must be structured to satisfy public demands that the punishment fit the crime, to show criminals that crime really doesn't pay, and to control potential recidivists.[49]

Georgia's . . . program, implemented in 1982, has stirred nationwide interest among criminal justice professionals because it seems to satisfy two goals that have long appeared mutually contradictory:

● Restraining the growth of prison populations and associated costs by controlling selected offenders in the community.
● At the same time, satisfying to some extent the demand that criminals be punished for their crimes.

The pivotal question is whether or not prison-bound offenders can be shifted into intensive probation supervision without threatening the public safety. A new research study, partially funded by the National Institute of Justice, suggests that intensive supervision provides greater controls than regular probation and costs far less than incarceration. The study was conducted by the Georgia Department of Corrections, Office of Evaluation and Statistics, and was assisted by an Advisory Board funded by the National Institute of Justice.

The Georgia Program

The IPS (Intensive Probation Supervision) program began in 1982 as a pilot in thirteen of Georgia's forty-five judicial sentencing circuits. By the end of 1985, it had expanded to thirty-three circuits and had supervised 2,322 probationers. While probation programs with varying degrees of supervision have been implemented throughout the country, Georgia's IPS is widely regarded as one of the most stringent in the nation. Standards include:

● Five face-to-face contacts per week.
● 132 hours of mandatory community service.
● Mandatory curfew.
● Mandatory employment.
● Weekly check of local arrest records.
● Automatic notification of arrest elsewhere in the state.
● Crime Information Network listing.
● Routine and unannounced alcohol and drug testing.

The supervision standards are enforced by a team consisting of a probation officer and a surveillance officer. The team supervises twenty-five probationers. In some jurisdictions, a team of one probation officer and two surveillance officers supervises forty probationers. The standards are designed to provide sufficient surveillance to control risk to the community and give a framework to treatment-oriented counseling. The counseling is designed to help the offender direct his energies toward productive activities, to assume responsibilities, and to become a law-abiding citizen.

Most offenders chosen for the IPS pilot program were already sentenced to prison, presented an acceptable risk to the community, and had not committed a violent offense. A risk assessment instrument was used to screen offenders. While the majority of those selected fell into the category of nonviolent property offenders, a large number of individuals convicted of drug- and alcohol-related offenses also were included as the program developed. Some of these offenses also involved personal violence.

Of the 2,322 people in the program between 1982 and 1985, 370 (or 16 percent) absconded or had their probation revoked. The remaining 1,952 were successfully diverted from prison; many are still under some form of probationary supervision. Some have successfully completed their sentence.

The Evaluation Findings

The evaluation evidence strongly suggests that the IPS program has played a significant role in reducing the flow of offenders to prison. The percentage of offenders sentenced to prison decreased and the number of probationers increased. The kinds of offenders diverted were more similar to prison inmates than to regular probationers, suggesting that the program selected the most suitable offenders. IPS probationers committed less serious crimes during their probation than comparable groups of regular probationers or probationers released from prison. The extensive supervision required seems to exert significant control and thus gives better results.

The cost of IPS, while much greater than regular probation, is considerably less than the cost of a prison stay, even when construction costs are not considered. In addition, society receives thousands of hours of community service from IPS offenders. Criminal justice practitioners seem to accept the program as suitable intermediate punishment. Judges particularly like it because it increases local control.[50]

Researchers express caution and the need for further experimentation before adopting intensive supervised probation in all jurisdictions. Some net widening occurs. [**Net widening** means that offenders who would be sentenced to ordinary probation if the only alternative to it is imprisonment, are instead sentenced to intermediate punishments when they are available.] For example, Georgia judges report "backdooring" by sentencing borderline offenders to prison while announcing they will "welcome an application for intensive supervision." Furthermore, intensive supervised probation does not necessarily reduce either prison population or costs. For example, one participant originally sentenced to one year in prison violated a rule on intensive supervised probation. They returned the offender to prison—for five years! Furthermore, intensive supervision can backfire. Some participants who could succeed with less supervision react negatively to intense supervision. Joan Petersilia cautions that what might work in Georgia, a state with a high incarceration rate that sends to prison offenders that other states may place on probation, may not work elsewhere.[51]

Questions

On the basis of the Bureau of Justice Statistics' description and assessment of Georgia's intensive probation supervision program, would you introduce a similar program in your community? What specific facts, findings, and arguments from the Georgia experience convince you—or do *not* convince you— to recommend an ISP program for your community? Explain.

Home Confinement—Electronic Monitoring

home confinement *sentencing of offenders to remain in their homes except for specific times and purposes.*

net widening *sentencing offenders to intermediate sanctions who would otherwise receive sentences of ordinary probation*

Home confinement—the sentencing of offenders to remain in their homes except for specific times and purposes—has a long history and a wide geography. Virtually since recorded history, in countries as widely scattered as Poland, India, South Africa, England, the Koreas, and the Soviet Union, it has existed, usually as a means to silence political dissent. However, home confinement did not become an alternative to incarceration on a broader scale until the early 1980s, when electronic surveillance, advanced community corrections ideas, serious jail overcrowding, the search for intermediate punishments, and budgetary restraints combined to make it a viable alternative. Home confinement, now used in more than 50 places, draws its participants mainly, but not exclusively, from misdemeanants, perhaps most frequently drunken drivers.[52]

The claimed benefits of home confinement include

- Reducing the stigma of incarceration while still punishing offenders.
- Maintaining family ties and occupational roles that improve chances for rehabilitation.
- Saving money from reduced jail and prison maintenance and construction costs, and from income from offenders.
- Protecting the public by keeping offenders "off the street."
- Meeting the demand for punishment.[53]

Constitutional objections—including the right to privacy and the rights against self-incrimination, search and seizure, and cruel and unusual punishment—are probably unfounded. The Supreme Court has tolerated electronic surveillance since the 1920s, has repeatedly accepted consent as a waiver to constitutional rights, and, perhaps most important, has recognized a doctrine of diminished constitutional rights for convicted criminals. Since participants in home confinement sign consent forms, these constitutional objections appear unlikely to succeed in eliminating programs.

Florida first adopted a statewide home confinement program in the 1980s. The program aimed at diverting nonviolent offenders from incarceration by providing round-the-clock surveillance. The Palm Beach Sheriff's Department operates one type of home confinement. A battery-powered, waterproof transmitter securely fastened by riveted straps to an offender's ankles emits a signal at regular intervals, with a maximum range of 100 feet, to a receiver/dialer at the offender's home telephone. The unit monitors the transmitter and automatically dials a host computer, describing the time offenders go beyond the range of the unit or tamper with, or remove, the transmitter. The host computer, a small PC at the sheriff's office, contains offenders' personal data, home address, telephone number, and weekly schedule, reflecting times offenders can leave home. The program prints a violation message for every unauthorized "left home," tampering, or removal.[54]

The program selects its participants from jail prisoners already in a work-release program. To qualify, prisoners must complete part of the work-release program in jail; they leave work during the day and return to the jail at night and on weekends. In addition to a good track record on work release, prisoners who volunteer must pass a further background check. Offenders' families must consent, offenders must reside in Palm Beach, and they must have a telephone. Offenders must return to jail every day, and the last day of every work week. At that time, they pay the program cost of nine dollars for each day in the program. At the same time, the sheriff's department checks the condition of the transmitter.[55]

More than 5,000 offenders have participated in Florida home confinement programs. The programs all emphasize work, confinement, payment for services, participation in community service, and heavy supervision. A surveillance team maintains a case load of 20. According to officers, team surveillance enables them to keep offenders "off guard," and provides personnel for night and weekend surveillance. Team surveillance illustrates the emphasis on the surveillance and supervision functions of probation officers.

Home confinement is not a cure-all but when used as a true alternative to incarceration it can save money, protect public safety, and punish offenders.

Responding to this emphasis, Florida trains home confinement officers in surveillance, self-defense, and search and seizure.[56]

Thomas G. Blomberg and Carol Bullock, in a statewide survey of officers, offenders, and offenders' families, found that officers indicated that most offenders either found employment or retained existing employment while on home confinement. Employers reported positive experience with offenders. Spouses reported that husbands were providing their families with full paychecks. All family members reported that participants showed more interest and involvement in their families and homes. Married and mature offenders did better than young offenders. Younger participants frequently failed to fulfill the home confinement program's requirements.[57]

Home confinement is not a panacea. It has not significantly reduced jail and prison populations. Net widening occurs and many offenders cannot qualify, particularly those without homes and telephones. Technology itself creates problems. Some telephone lines cannot transmit signals. Windstorms and thunderstorms can interrupt or send false signals. External radio signals can interfere with signals on transmitters. Iron and steel can block signals or create electromagnetic fields. When used as a true alternative to incarceration, however, home confinement costs less than jail, even when taking into account the costs of electronic surveillance devices. Moreover, it represents an intermediate punishment that allows for a principled approach to grading sanctions. It also provides for community safety while allowing offenders to maintain and perhaps strengthen family ties and employment.[58]

Shock Incarceration—Correctional Boot Camps

Correctional boot camps (also called **shock incarceration**), modeled on basic training in the military, focuses on young male offenders. Like other intermediate punishments, correctional boot camps are a response to prison crowding, the demand for more severe punishment, and budgetary restraints. Boot camps, also called shock incarceration, provide an alternative to prison for young, first-time, nonviolent offenders, particularly drug offenders. They are based on the assumption that they offer equal or greater deterrent and rehabilitative effects than traditional prisons. In 1994, 28 states were operating 43 boot camps; other states were planning to start them.

Correctional boot camps have received wide publicity. They are extremely popular with the public and, therefore, with state and national politicians. Even presidents have repeatedly advocated correctional boot camps as part of their crime control programs. One political candidate produced an effective commercial promising that young offenders who did not want to obey the law would "wind up breaking up rocks" in a correctional boot camp instead. Correctional boot camps stress a number of features in common with military boot camps:

- Strict discipline.
- Physical training.
- Drill and ceremony.
- Military bearing and courage.
- Physical labor.
- Summary punishment for minor misconduct.

According to a camp sergeant in a Georgia correctional boot camp, "Here being scared is the point. You have to hit a mule between the eyes with a two-by-four to get his attention . . . and that's exactly what we're doing with this program."[59]

The use of militarism, hard labor, and fear has a long history. In 1821, John Cray, deputy keeper of Auburn prison, turned away from solitary confinement because of the high rates of suicide and mental breakdowns. He replaced it with the requirement of downcast eyes, the lockstep, no talking, and long hours of hard work under close supervision. At Elmira Reformatory, Zebulon Brockway adopted Auburn's basic idea, with some "modern" twists, in the 1890s. Empirical evidence does not support the conclusion that more recent programs, such as "Scared Straight," deter offenders through fright. After surveying a considerable amount of the available research, Mary Morash and Lila Rucker concluded that

> the boot camp model is unlikely to provide a panacea for . . . the pressures arising from the problems of both prison overcrowding and public demands for severe punishment. Whether the point is to provide rehabilitation, to deter, or to divert people from prison, alternatives other than boot camp should be given careful consideration.[60]

The General Accounting Office, the National Institute of Justice, and several states have independently evaluated boot camps. After interviewing officials and reviewing NIJ data regarding boot camps in Florida and Georgia, the General Accounting Office concluded, somewhat more cautiously than Morash and Rucker, that

> available data are not sufficient to determine if boot camps reduce prison overcrowding, costs, or recidivism . . . . Boot camps may reduce prison overcrowding and prison costs if they involve offenders who would have otherwise been sent to prison, the offenders are incarcerated for a shorter time, and they are not readmitted to prison after their release at a greater rate than prisoners sentenced to regular prisons. However, the possibility that some offenders sent to boot camps would have been put on probation if they had not been sent to boot camps would affect any potential savings.[61]

Dale K. Sechrest reviewed shock incarceration reports based on National Institute of Justice research and gave boot camps the most negative assessment:

> Regardless of the media hype, there is no evidence that shock incarceration "works" for the offenders that need to be reached any more than scared straight or shock probation worked to any great degree. None. Yet these types of "quick-fix" solutions linger on. Shock programs like scared straight and boot camps appear to be "right" methods based on our middle-class understanding of how punishment works. The American Correctional Association [however] notes that "This deeply-rooted social problem cannot be eradicated by exposing [young criminals] to threats of force, intimidation, verbal abuse, or other practices that are meant to shock youths out of [undesired] behavior."[62]

> Doris Layton MacKenzie, Robert Brame, David McDowall, and Claire Souryal found mixed results at best when they compared boot camp graduates with comparison samples of prison parolees, probationers, and boot camp dropouts in eight states (Florida, Georgia, Illinois, Louisiana, New York, Oklahoma, South Carolina, and Texas). All the programs were chosen because they contained the core components of boot camps—military drill and ceremony, hard labor, physical training, strict rules and discipline. The programs, however, differed in other respects that can affect recidivism, including length of stay and the amount of time devoted each day to treatment. MacKenzie and her colleagues measured recidivism in a number of ways, including arrest, revocation for technical violations, and revocation for committing new crimes.[63]

Using regression analysis and other measures of the performance of boot camp graduates and comparison groups, MacKenzie and her colleagues concluded:

> If [the core] components [of boot camp] effectively reduce the recidivism of offenders, we would likely have observed a consistent pattern

The success of correctional boot camps, according to researchers, is decidedly mixed.

across states. That pattern would be one of lower recidivism rates for boot camp graduates in contrast to those of comparison groups. *This did not occur.* (Emphasis added) As a result, we conclude that these components in and of themselves do not reduce the recidivism of participating offenders.[64]

MacKenzie and her colleagues suggest why boot camp graduates of some programs do better than others. One possibility is the selection process. Boot camp identifies and selects

offenders who were at lower risk of recidivism in the first place. That is, boot camp completers may be at lower risk than the dropouts for some unanswered reason at the start of the program, and the boot camp program merely separates those who are low risks (the completers) from those who are higher risks (the dropouts).[65]

It may be that the key to boot camp success is not the military drill, strict discipline and rules, hard labor, and heavy physical exercise. Georgia, where boot camp graduates did *worse* than the comparison groups, had little treatment in the daily schedule. Louisiana boot camp graduates had the lowest arrest rate of all the programs in the study, fewer revocations than either parolees or dropouts, fewer crimes than parolees, and fewer technical violations than dropouts. One possible explanation is that the Louisiana program devoted three or more hours every day to treatment. The researchers call for more research on this aspect of boot camps and ask the critical question: Would programs that incorporate treatment *without the military atmosphere* do as well as those with the military atmosphere?[66]

In a related study of some of the boot camps just discussed, MacKenzie and Brame tried to answer that question. They compared a sample of those who completed boot camp and those who dropped out of boot camp with groups who were eligible for boot camp but did not attend. The researchers subjected the data collected from the samples to several statistical evaluations. They found "little conclusive evidence that" boot camps "had a positive effect on offender behavior." However, they did find that "supervision intensity plays an important role in shaping offenders' activities during community supervision." They conclude:

> The relatively weak association between shock incarceration [boot camp] and positive adjustment [meaning avoiding illegal activities, obtaining work and education, and meeting financial and family responsibility] should give policymakers reason for pause. While efforts to identify circumstances where shock incarceration is effective might be useful, it seems that the evidence weighs against concluding that shock incarceration programs are *broadly* effective at enhancing the ability of offenders to adjust more successfully in the community.[67]

Fines

The use of money as a punishment, that is, the use of **fines,** is an ancient practice, going back to the Old Testament notion of "an eye for an eye." Fines prevailed in England for much of the early part of the Middle Ages, when a price was put on all kinds of offenses, including maiming and murder. Fines have much to recommend them as appropriate criminal punishment. They are clearly aimed at both retribution and deterrence. They emphasize accountability by requiring offenders to pay their "debt to society" literally, in the form of money. All these aims are consistent with current sentencing policies. Fines also fulfill the aims of fairness and proportionality in punishment by allowing the size of the debt to society to be adjusted to the seriousness of offenses in our criminal law. The flexibility of monetary penalties also allows for the adjustment of the fine to the ability of the offenders to pay. Moreover, fines are already a current sentencing option in all American courts, whether large or small, urban or rural. Finally, and far from least important, fines generate revenue.[68]

In addition, fines fit in comfortably with basic American values. According to Michael Tonry and Kate Hamilton,

> It seems odd, in a country where economic incentives and rational calculation are so widely celebrated, that monetary penalties play so small a part in punishment of offenders. Although in practice fines are generally set in amounts too small to be commensurate to the seriousness of nontrivial crimes, in principle they can vary from small change to economic capital punishment. Although in practice fines are often collected haphazardly or not at all, in principle they can be collected with the same vigor and solicitude that characterize our friendly neighborhood finance companies. Although in practice increased use of fines seems to be unfair to the poor and unduly lenient to the rich, in principle amounts can be tailored to individuals' assets and incomes so as to constitute roughly comparable financial burdens.[69]

Why have fines not figured prominently in the repertoire of intermediate punishments? According to Sally T. Hillsman and Judith A. Greene,

> Among American criminal justice practitioners, there lingers a deep skepticism about the usefulness of fine sentences that focuses on the *absolute* size of the fine: Don't fines need to be large in order to be punitive and to deter? This emphasis on large fines leads to further issues about the fairness of fine sentences: If fines are large enough to punish and deter, how can they be collected from the majority of offenders who come before American courts? And if only those who can pay siz-

day fine *basing of the amount of a fine on the daily income of offenders.*

restitution *paying back of victims for the injuries and other losses caused by offenders.*

community service orders *sentences that order offenders to work without pay at projects that benefit either the public or public charities.*

able amounts are fined, are not these more affluent offenders buying their way out of the more punitive sentences to imprisonment?[70]

The answer to these questions, according to Hillsman, Greene, and a number of other proponents and researchers of fines as intermediate punishments, is a system that most European countries have put into effect—the **day fine.** Day fines base the amount of the fine on the daily income of offenders, hence the name *day* fine. In fact, the imposition of fines is based on a two-step process. In the first step, judges assign fine *units*. The more serious the offense, the more units are assessed for committing it. In the second stage, monetary amounts are attached to the units. The amount of money each unit costs offenders depends on their daily income. The higher their income, the greater the monetary value of each unit. The amount of the day fine is, therefore, directly dependent on the seriousness of the offense. However, the exact monetary *amount* varies widely so that it might impose an equivalent monetary *burden* on people of different economic worth.[71]

Lower criminal courts (see Chapter 8) have always been the primary users of fines. To determine the usefulness of day fines in the United States, an experiment was established in New York's Staten Island Criminal Court. The experiment was developed by a planning group comprising judges, prosecutors, public and private defense attorneys, court administrators, and planners from the Vera Institute of Justice. The planning group assigned fine units according to the seriousness of the offenses for which the court imposed sentences. They then created a method for attributing a monetary value to the fine units, basing the monetary value on a "fair share" of the daily, after-tax income of offenders. Fair share takes into account the offender's number of dependents and whether the offender's income is below the poverty line. According to Sally T. Hillsman,

> Using this method, the day-fine amounts in the Staten Island court could range from as low as $25 for a welfare recipient with three children who was convicted of the least serious offense in the court's jurisdiction, to $4,000 for a single offender with no dependents and a gross income of $35,000 who was sentenced for the most serious offense.[72]

The results of an interim evaluation of the experiment were promising. The court implemented day fines smoothly: virtually all fixed fines were replaced with day fines during the pilot year of the experiment. Revenue from fines rose 14 percent during the experiment because of the larger day fines imposed on affluent offenders. Despite the higher fines, collection rates did not decrease; they remained as good under the experiment with day fines as they were under the old fixed-fine system. The court enforced the sentences of 84 percent of day-fine offenders. Most offenders paid their fines, or a substantial part of them. Thirteen percent originally sentenced to day fines were returned to court for resentencing because they did not pay. These offenders were usually sentenced to community service or to jail.[73]

Community Service

Sentences that order offenders to work at projects for the benefit of the public hark back to two ancient practices. First is **restitution**—paying back victims for the injuries and other losses caused by offenders. The laws of the ancient Babylonians, Greeks, Romans, and Jews, and the laws of medieval Europe all provided for specific compensation that offenders had to pay their victims. When victims lost their central place in criminal justice (see Chapter 2), the use of restitution fell into disuse. Society as a whole took the place of individuals as the victim of crime. Community service orders took the place of restitution. **Community service orders** are sentences that order offenders "to work without pay at projects that . . . benefit the public or . . . public charities." Second, "offenders could avoid worse punishment if they performed hard manual labor on public projects (such as road building) or manned oars on galleys."[74]

Community service orders are most often used in lower criminal courts where the predominant business is traffic violations and other misdemeanors. Community service orders receive the most publicity in "celebrity cases." Michael Milkin, the notorious "junk bond" trader of the 1980s, was ordered to work in a charity full time for three years after his term in federal prison. Oliver North, who ran an illegal covert military operation out of the Reagan White House, and Zsa Zsa Gabor, the Hollywood celebrity who slapped a police officer when he stopped her for a traffic offense, also received community service sentences.[75]

Community service has several underlying purposes that have varied over time. During the 1970s, community service was acclaimed as a mechanism to serve a variety of utilitarian purposes. It was touted as a form of restitution; instead of paying back individual victims, however, community service paid back the entire community. Furthermore, community service was supposed to rehabilitate offenders. Reformers hoped that by working beside law-abiding people, offenders would develop a sense of responsibility. Judge Dennis Challeen, a booster of community service sentences, argued that

> they require offenders to make efforts toward self-improvement, thus removing them from their roles as losers and helping them to address their personal problems and character defects that alienate them from the mainstream of society.[76]

These utilitarian justifications for community service began to sound outdated in the atmosphere of tougher attitudes toward crime and criminals that began in the 1970s. The philosophy of "just deserts" replaced utilitarian aims such as rehabilitation. Community service came to be seen mainly as a way to punish criminals who deserve intermediate punishment. That is, they deserve to suffer more than ordinary probationers, but not so much as offenders in jails and prisons.[77]

Are community service sentences appropriate? This question boils down to both an empirical and a value assessment. Empirically, little evidence exists on the effectiveness of community service. The Vera Institute of Justice tried to estimate the crime control effects of community service sentences in its community service sentencing project. The project provided judges in the criminal courts of Manhattan, Brooklyn, and Queens the option of choosing between traditional short jail terms (90 days or less) and community service for chronic misdemeanor property offenders. Community service was not pleasant—and was not supposed to be. It was not intended to *humiliate* offenders, but it was definitely intended to *punish* them. Offenders worked 70 hours a week in crews, painting senior citizen centers and nursing homes, cleaning neighborhood lots, and renovating dwellings for low-cost housing.[78]

Six months later, between 39 and 51 percent of a sample of offenders sentenced to community service had been rearrested for some kind of property crime. This rearrest rate was identical to similar offenders who were sentenced to short jail terms. Hence, community service neither rehabilitated nor deterred property offenders in these New York City boroughs any more effectively than jail terms. Furthermore, since offenders cannot commit crimes in the community if they are in jail, those sentenced to community service may pose a greater risk to society. The project directors estimated that about 15 out of every 100 offenders sentenced to community service committed crimes because they were not in jail. However, community service did yield other benefits. The community received about 60,000 hours of useful work, some of which would probably not have been done at all if community service had not "donated" it.[79]

According to Douglas C. McDonald of the research team at the Vera Institute of Justice, the values reason is more compelling than the utilitarian reason for community service orders:

> My own view is that a more compelling reason for considering community service, as well as other intermediate sanctions, is that it provides a means of more finely matching deserved punishments with the severity of offenses. This suggests the importance of developing guidelines to determine how much unpaid labor, and of what sort, should be given for crimes of differing severity, although there may be compelling practical reasons for a fixed "dose" of hours or days to be served by all. . . .[80]

Day Reporting Centers

A handful of states have introduced day reporting centers, an intermediate punishment first used in Great Britain. **Day reporting centers** are mainly a way to reduce jail and prison crowding. They vary greatly, but all "combine high levels of surveillance and extensive services, treatments, or activities." Their clients include defendants denied bail before conviction; prisoners released conditionally from prison; and some offenders sentenced to day reporting as an intermediate punishment. Dale G. Parent gives one example: The Connecticut Prison Association reviewed "Frank's" case and recommended that the judge release him to Alternative Incarceration Center (AIC) in Hartford. The judge agreed.

> . . . [H]e ordered Frank to report to the AIC every morning and to file an itinerary showing where he would be, and how he could be contacted, for each hour of each day. The judge ordered Frank to look for a job (Frank used the association's employment project to find a job as a custodian in a local factory) and to attend drug-use counseling sessions at AIC. Finally, the judge ordered Frank to submit to random drug-use tests.[81]

As of the end of 1995, none of these day reporting center projects has been evaluated, so it is not possible to assess their effectiveness.[82]

The *You Decide,*, "Are Intermediate Sanctions Punitive Enough?" examines the attitudes of offenders toward community sanctions.

You Decide — Are Intermediate Sanctions Punitive Enough?

Joan Petersilia, director of the Criminal Justice Program at the Rand Corporation, suggests that we take seriously offenders' attitudes toward community punishments. Petersilia writes:

> Are community sanctions punitive enough to convince the public that the "punishment fit the crime?" Having studied the development of these intermediate sanctions, I have discovered that some serious offenders feel that ISPs are at least as punitive as imprisonment—if not more so. If this is true, then offenders' perceptions should be considered in structuring sanctions and in making sentencing decisions.
>
> Why is this issue worth studying? The most pragmatic reason is that ISPs offer some hope of relieving prison overcrowding—without draining the public purse. If it can be shown that other—less expensive—sanctions also have punitive qualities, then perhaps the public might accept that community-based sanctions are appropriate and quite consistent with their demand to "get tough" and hold criminals accountable for their crimes. If this link were made, the criminal justice system could save money and operate a system with more rehabilitation potential.
>
> More theoretical, but possibly more compelling, these hypotheses question some basic assumptions that underlie sentencing decisions, the structure of sanctions, and resource allocation in the criminal justice system. Consequently, those assumptions may be partly responsible for today's "crisis in corrections." It would probably have been salutary to question these assumptions long ago, but under present circumstances it is imperative to do so.

Punishment for Whom?

This country bases assumptions about "what punishes" on the norms and living standards of society at large. This practice overlooks two salient facts: First, most serious offenders neither accept nor abide by those norms—otherwise, they wouldn't be offenders. Second, most of the people who even "qualify" for imprisonment today come from communities where conditions fall far below the living standards most Americans would recognize. If their values and standards differ, why should their perceptions of punishment be the same? Nevertheless, criminal sanctions reflect society's values—negatively. The demand that serious criminals go to prison implies that prison imposes conditions that are intolerable and frightening to the law-abiding citizen. The belief that community sanctions are too lenient implies that no matter what conditions probation or parole impose, remaining in the community is categorically preferable to imprisonment.

When crime rates were lower and minor crimes could land a person in prison, many offenders might have shared these perceptions. Apparently, feelings are different among offenders who face prison sentences today. In several states, given the option of serving prison terms or participating in ISPs, many offenders have chosen prison. Pearson reports that about 15 percent of offenders who apply to New Jersey's ISP program retract their applications once they understand the conditions and requirements. Under the New Jersey structure, this means that they will remain in prison on their original sentences.

One of the more striking examples comes from Marion County, Oregon, which has been cooperating with researchers from the Rand Corporation in a randomized field experiment. Selected nonviolent offenders were given the choice of serving a prison term or returning to the community to participate in ISP. These offenders have been convicted, and the judge has formally imposed a prison term. After conviction, they were asked if they would agree to return to the community and participate in ISP, rather than go to prison. During the one-year study period, about a third of those eligible for the experiment have chosen prison instead of ISP.

What accounts for this seeming aberration? Why should anyone prefer imprisonment to remaining in the community—no matter what the conditions? Can we infer from this that prison conditions seem less "punishing" than ISP requirements to these offenders? To consider this possibility, we first need to understand why imprisonment may have lost some of its punitive sting.

Has the Punitive Power of Imprisonment Diminished?

Zimring and Hawkins note that sanctions are most likely to deter if they meet two conditions: "the social standing is injured by the punishment," and "the individual feels a danger of being excluded from the group." It is hard to imagine that prison terms have either of these attributes for repeat criminals. Possessing a prison record is not as stigmatizing as in the past, because so many of the offender's peers (and other family members) also have "done time." A recent survey shows that 40 percent of youths in state training schools have parents who have also been incarcerated. Further, about a quarter of all U.S. black males will be incarcerated during their lives, so the stigma attached to having a prison record is not as great as it was when it was relatively uncommon.

In fact, far from stigmatizing, imprisonment evidently confers status in some neighborhoods. Particularly for gang-affiliated and career criminals, a prison sentence enhances status when the offender returns to his neighborhood, especially in the inner cities. California's Task Force on Gangs and Drugs reported that during public testimony, gang members themselves "repeatedly stated that incarceration was not a threat because they knew their sentences would be minimal." Further, some gang members considered the short period of detention as a "badge of courage, something to brag about when they return to the streets." And according to the California Youth Authority, inmates steal state-issued prison clothing for the same reason. Wearing it when they return to the community lets everyone know they have "done hard time."

As for employment opportunities, imprisonment has had increasingly less effect for the people in question. As William Julius Wilson makes painfully clear in *The Truly Disadvantaged*, employment opportunities have been shrinking for people of lower economic status, especially in urban areas, so the effect of a prison record may not be as dramatic as it was when jobs were more plentiful.

Some have argued that for poor people, prison may be preferred, but few scholars take such discussions seriously. It is undoubtedly true, however, that the quality of a person's lifestyle when free certainly has some bearing on the extent to which imprisonment is considered undesirable. The grim fact—and national shame—is that for most people who go to prison, the conditions inside are not all that different from the conditions outside. The prison environment may be far below the ordinary standards of society, but so is the environment they come from. As the quality of life that people can expect when free declines, the relative deprivation suffered while in prison declines.

Social isolation is another presumably punitive aspect of imprisonment. Again, the values of society surface in the belief that when a person goes to prison he is "among aliens." In prison, he is isolated from the kinds of people he would customarily (and by preference) be among. For today's inmates, that is less likely to be true. The newly admitted inmate will probably find friends, if not family, already there.

The warden of Pontiac Penitentiary described it thus:
> When a new guy comes up here it's almost a homecoming—undoubtedly there are people from his neighborhood and people who know him. . . .

He goes on to recall how a ranking gang member, upon entry to prison, received a "letter from the ranking chief welcoming him into the family." As for real family, the warden in a Washington, DC., jail recently noted that his facility currently contained three generations of a particular family at once. He remarked that, "It was like a family reunion for these guys." Some even suggest that prison serves as a buffer for offenders who find the outside world particularly difficult. One man, just released from a Massachusetts prison, said:
> I have literally seen guys who have been released walk out the door and stand on the corner and not know which direction to go. And they eventually go back to prison. As horrible as it is, prison provides some sort of community.

And, finally, the length of time an offender can be expected to actually serve in prison has decreased—from eighteen months in 1984 to twelve months in 1987. But more to the point, for marginal offenders (those targeted for prison alternatives), the expected time served can be much less. In California, Texas, and Illinois, two- to three-year prison terms often translate into less than six months actually served. In Oregon, prison crowding has created a situation in which a five-year sentence can translate into three to four months of actual time served. Particularly when the prison system is the subject of a court order and offenders are released because of a "cap," prison terms can be quite short. Offenders on the street seem to be aware of this, even more so with the extensive media coverage such issues are receiving.

For the above reasons, then, it seems at least plausible that prison terms (on average) are not perceived as being as severe as they were historically. No one has ever surveyed prisoners or ex-convicts to find out how punitive they think imprisonment is. However, one could say their actions answer that question implicitly: More than 50 percent of today's prison inmates have served a prior prison term. Add prior jail sentences, and the percentage rises to 80 percent. Knowing what it's like, 80 percent of them evidently still think that the "benefits" of committing a new crime outweigh the "costs" of being in prison. This implies a lot about how punitive prison is for these offenders. However, it does not explain why they would choose imprisonment over intensive probation.

Why Would Offenders Choose Prison Over ISPs?

For many offenders, it may seem preferable to get that short stay in prison over rather than spend five times as long in an ISP. But what about the relative conditions? If the speculations above have any validity, better a short time in conditions that differ little from your accustomed life than a long time in conditions that are very different from the "ordinary standards" of your community.

Taking Marion County, Oregon, as an example, consider the alternatives facing convicted offenders:

IPS

The offender will serve two years under this sanction. During that time, the offender will be visited by a probation officer two or three times per week, who will phone on the other days. The offender will be subject to unannounced searches of his home for drugs and have his urine tested regularly for alcohol and drugs. He must strictly abide by other conditions set by the court—not carrying a weapon, not socializing with certain persons—and he will have to perform community service and be employed or participate in training or education. In addition, he will be strongly encouraged to attend counseling and/or other treatment, particularly if he is a drug offender.

Prison

A sentence of two to four years will require that the offender serve about three to six months. During his term, he is not required to work nor will he be required to participate in any training or treatment, but may do so if he wishes. Once released, he will be placed on two years routine parole supervision, where he sees his parole officer about once a month.

For these offenders, as for any of us, freedom is probably preferable to imprisonment. However, the ISP does not represent freedom. In fact, it may stress and isolate repeat offenders more than imprisonment does. It seems reasonable that when offenders return to their communities, they expect to return to their old lives. The ISP transforms those lives radically.

Their homes can be searched and they must submit regularly to urine testing. Offenders may well consider such invasions of their homes and lives more intrusive and unbearable than the lack of privacy in prisons—where it is an expected condition of life. The same is true of discipline and social isolation. By definition, imprisonment limits freedom of movement and activity, but once a person is in his own community, curfew and other restrictions may seem harder to take. Ironically, he may be less socially isolated from his peers in prison than in ISP.

Why Do Offenders' Perceptions Matter?

Having established the counter-intuitive fact that some serious offenders prefer imprisonment to ISPs, what are we to make of it? Whatever else, it does argue for reconsidering the range of sanctions this country has and the assumptions they reflect. The point is not to insist that on any absolute scale ISP is "worse" than prison. Rather, it is to suggest that the scale we currently use needs reexamining.

For the people who are likely to come under either sanction, how society at large views those sanctions is largely irrelevant. How offenders view punishment ought at least to be considered.[83]

Questions

Why should the views of offenders about punishment matter? What do offenders' attitudes suggest about the value of community punishments? What would you recommend as a result of Petersilia's arguments?

Summary

Following sentencing, convicted offenders are punished in the community, in jails and prisons, or in a combination of community supervision and incarceration. Only 25 percent of convicted offenders go to jail or prison. Probation, parole, and a range of community-based corrections and intermediate punishment account for the remaining 75 percent of correctional populations. More than 60 percent are on ordinary probation. Formally a legal sentence, probation is also an informal decision-making process. Probation has the varied missions of rehabilitating offenders, protecting society, relieving crowded prisons and jails, and saving taxpayers' money. Probationers remain free unless and until they either violate the technical conditions of their release or break the law. The roles of probation officers reflect the multiple purposes of probation: law enforcement, social work, social service brokers, bureaucrats, and bill collectors.

Throughout the twentieth century, judges followed an either-or sentencing policy. That is, they sentenced convicted offenders either to ordinary probation at one extreme or prison at the other extreme. A number of forces combined to create a dissatisfaction with either- or sentencing options. These forces included the failures of prison to reduce crime to levels satisfactory to professionals and the public, the "get tough" on crime and criminals attitude, overcrowded prisons, and the steeply rising cost of incarceration. Furthermore, there was a growing realization that the principle of "just deserts" required a broader range of punishments to punish fairly the great variety of crimes in our society. Intermediate punishments provided for a broader range of options between prison and ordinary probation.

Intermediate punishments aim to impose humane punishment at less cost while preserving community safety. These punishments range across a broad spectrum, including intensive supervised probation, home confinement, correctional boot camps, community service, fines, and day reporting centers. Although these intermediate punishments have received substantial publicity and have aroused great interest among criminal justice professionals, academics, and the public, they make up only a small portion of the numbers of offenders under correctional supervision. Most of these few are concentrated in intensive supervised probation (ISP) and home confinement.

Intermediate punishments are not panaceas. They will not suddenly solve the difficult problems of prison and jail crowding, community safety, and budgetary restraints. Researchers caution that the available empirical evaluations of the effectiveness of intermediate punishments are mixed. Nevertheless, intermediate punishments, particularly intensive supervised probation and home confinement, represent at least limited efforts to respond to the immediate problems of exploding prison and jail populations in a time of budgetary constraints and the long-term search for a set of principled sanctions for criminal behavior that can give offenders their "just deserts."

Review Questions

1. Explain the origin of the term "corrections."

2. Identify the three ways that offenders in state custody are supervised.

3. Identify the proportions of offenders under each of the three types of supervision.

4. Explain the difference between probation and parole.

5. Briefly recount the origins and the history of probation.

6. Identify and describe the traditional missions of probation. How have its missions changed since World War II?

7. Identify and describe the principal roles of probation officers.

8. Identify and describe the formal and informal dimensions of probation.

9. Identify and describe the major types of probation.

10. List the major criteria of eligibility for probation.

11. List the major usual and special conditions of probation.

12. Under what two circumstances does probation usually end?

13. What are the major reasons for the revocation of probation?

14. Explain the significance of the gap between probation violations and revocations.

15. Identify and describe the rights of probationers under the Constitution.

16. Identify and describe the two steps in the process of probation revocation.

17. Explain the controversy over granting felons probation.

18. According to empirical research, how effective is probation?

19. Describe the major reasons for the dissatisfaction with "either-or" sentencing.

20. Briefly describe the history of intermediate punishments.

21. List and describe the major intermediate punishments in use today.

22. Describe the major developments that led to the present interest in intermediate punishments.

23. How does intensive supervised probation (ISP) differ from ordinary probation? What are the major stated and hidden aims of ISP? According to the empirical evidence, has ISP achieved these aims? Explain your answer.

24. Explain the possible benefits of home confinement. How effective is home confinement, according to the empirical evidence available?

25. What are the major features of shock incarceration in correctional boot camps? According to the empirical evidence, how effective are correctional boot camps? Explain your answer.

26. List the major reasons that support fines as a form of criminal punishment. What is a "day fine?" According to the empirical evidence, how effective are fines? Explain your answer.

27. What are the principal justifications for community service as a form of intermediate punishment? Is community service an appropriate intermediate punishment? Explain your answer.

28. Explain what a day reporting center is. How effective is day reporting as a form of criminal punishment? Explain your answer.

Notes

1. BJS, *Probation and Parole, 1990* (Washington, D.C.: Bureau of Justice Statistics, 1992); "The Nation's Correctional Population Tops 5 Million," U.S. Department of Justice, press release, August 27, 1995.

2. Belinda R. McCarthy, ed., *Intermediate Punishments: Intensive Supervision, Home Confinement, and Electronic Surveillance* (Monsey, N.Y.: Willow Tree Press, 1987), 1; James M. Byrne, Arthur J. Lurigio, and Joan Petersilia, eds., *Smart Sentencing: The Emergence of Intermediate Sanctions* (Newbury Park, Calif.: Sage Publications, 1992); Norval Morris and Michael Tonry, *Between Prison and Probation: Intermediate Punishments in a Rational Sentencing System* (New York: Oxford University Press, 1990).

3. Joel Samaha, "The Recognizance in Elizabethan Law Enforcement," *American Journal of Legal History* 25 (1981): 189–204; Joel Samaha, *Law and Order in Historical Perspective* (New York: Academic Press, 1974).

4. Dean J. Champion, *Felony Probation: Problems and Prospects* (New York: Praeger, 1988), 1–3.

5. *John Augustus, First Probation Officer,* reprint (New York: National Probation Association, 1983).

6. David Rothman, *Conscience and Convenience* (Boston: Little, Brown, 1980), 82–83.

7. Todd R. Clear and Anthony A. Braga, "Community Corrections," in *Crime,* James Q. Wilson and Joan Petersilia, eds. (San Francisco: Institute for Contemporary Studies, 1995), 422.

8. Joan Petersilia et. al., *Granting Felons Probation* (Santa Monica: Rand Corporation, 1985), 1; Joan Petersilia, "A Crime Control Rationale for Reinvesting in Community Corrections," *The Prison Journal* 45 (1995): 479, 481.

9. Edward J. Cosgrove, "ROBO-PO: The Life and Times of a Federal Probation Officer," *Federal Probation* (September 1994): 29.

10. Patrick D. McAnany et al., *Probation and Justice: Reconsideration of Mission* (Cambridge, Mass.: Oelgeschlager, Gunn & Hain, 1984).

11. Ibid., 43.

12. Carlson and Parks, *Critical Issues in Adult Probation,* 43–44.

13. Ibid., 43.

14. McAnany et. al., *Probation and Justice,* 137.

15. Carlson and Parks, *Critical Issues in Adult Probation,* 46.

16. Todd R. Clear and George F. Cole, *American Corrections.* 3d. ed. (Belmont, Calif.: Wadsworth Publishing Company, 1994), 176.

17. Ibid., 176–177.

18. Vincent O'Leary, "Probation: A System in Change," *Federal Probation* 51 (1987): 8–11.

19. Harry E. Allen et al., *Probation and Parole in America* (New York: The Free Press, 1985), 81.

20. Petersilia et. al., *Granting Felons Probation,* 2.

21. Harry E. Allen and Clifford E. Simonson, *Corrections in America,* 4th ed. (New York: Macmillan, 1986), 154; Daniel Glaser, "Supervising Offenders Outside of Prison," in *Crime and Public Policy,* James Q. Wilson, ed. (New Brunswick, N.J.: Transaction Books, 1983), 213; Champion, *Felony Probation;* Fredrick A. Hussey and David E. Duffee, *Probation, Parole and Community Field Services: Policy, Structure and Process* (New York: Harper & Row, 1980), 10.

22. BJS, *Recidivism of Felons on Probation, 1986–1989* (Washington, D.C.: Bureau of Justice Statistics, 1992), 2–4.

23. Clear and Braga, "Community Corrections," 439.

24. Ibid.

25. Florida Department of Corrections, *Adult Probation and Parole Revocation Research Report* (Tallahassee, Fla., 1988).

26. *Griffin v. Wisconsin,* 483 U.S. 868 (1987). 874–875.

27. *Morrissey v. Brewer,* 408 U.S. 471 (1972), 480; *Gagnon v. Scarpelli,* 411 U.S. 778 (1973).

28. *Morrissey v. Brewer,* 485–486.

29. Ibid.

30. Ibid.

31. Ibid.

32. Ibid.

33. Ibid., 487–489.

34. BJS, *Correctional Populations in the United States, 1992* (Washington, D.C.: BJS, 1995), Table 3.6, 4; Glaser, "Supervising Offenders Outside of Prison," 225–27.

35. Joan Petersilia et al., *Prison versus Probation in California* (Santa Monica: Rand Corporation, 1986), vii.

36. Ibid., 5.

37. Michael R. Geerken and Hennessey D. Hayes, "Probation and Parole: Public Risk and the Future of Incarceration Alternatives," *Criminology* 31 (1993): 557.

38. Byrne, Lurigio, and Petersilia, *Smart Sentencing,* ix, xiii–xiv.

39. Norval Morris and Michael Tonry, "Between Prison and Probation-Intermediate Punishment in a Rational Sentencing System," *National Institute of Justice Reports* (January/February 1990): 8–10; *Crime and Delinquency, Special Issue: Intensive Probation Supervision* 36 (1990); McCarthy, *Intermediate Punishments.*

40. Matti Joutsen, "Developments in Delinquency and Criminal Justice: A Nordic Perspective," in *Crime and Control in Comparative Perspectives,* Hans-Gauunther Heiland, Lousc I. Shcllcy, and Hisao Katoh, eds. (Berlin: Walter deGruyter, 1992), 38–40.

41. Arthur J. Lurigio and Joan Petersilia, "The Emergence of Intensive Probation Supervision Programs in the United States," in *Smart Sentencing,* 7–8.

42. Todd R. Clear and Patricia Hardyman, "The New Intensive Supervision Movement," *Crime and Delinquency* 36 (1990): 43–45; Lurigio and Petersilia, "Emergence of IPS Programs," 5–6; Joan Petersilia, Susan Turner, and Elizabeth Piper Deschennes, "Intensive Supervision Programs for Drug Offenders," in *Smart Sentencing,* 18.

43. Lurigio and Petersilia, "Emergence of IPS," 11.

44. Michael Tonry, "Stated and Latent Functions of ISP," *Crime and Delinquency* 36 (1990): 175–76.

45. Frank S. Pearson and Alice Glasel Harper, "Contingent Intermediate Sentences," *Crime and Delinquency* 36 (1990): 75–86.

46. Petersilia, Turner, and Deschennes, "Intensive Supervision Programs for Drug Offenders," 19.

47. Ibid., 35.

48. Ibid.

49. Petersilia et al., *Granting Felons Probation,* 65.

50. Billie S. Erwin and Laurence A. Bennett, "New Dimensions in Probation: Georgia's Experience with Intensive Probation Supervision (IPS)," *National Institute of Justice, Research in Brief* (Washington, D.C.: Bureau of Justice Statistics, January 1985).

51. Tonry, "Stated and Latent Functions of ISP"; Clear and Hardyman, "The New Intensive Supervision Movement"; Joan Petersilia, "Georgia's Intensive Probation: Will the Model Work Elsewhere?"; McCarthy, *Intermediate Punishments,* 15–30.

52. Richard A. Ball, C. Ronald Huff, and J. Robert Lilly, *House Arrest and Correctional Policy: Doing Time at Home* (Beverly Hills: Sage Publications, 1988), 34, chap. 1.

53. Annesley K. Schmidt and Christine E. Curtis, "Electronic Monitoring," in McCarthy, *Intermediate Punishments,* 141–42.

54. Palm Beach Sheriff's Department, "Palm Beach County's In-House Arrest Work Release Program," in McCarthy, *Intermediate Punishments,* 182–83.

55. Ibid., 183–84.

56. Thomas G. Blomberg, Gordon P. Waldo, and Lisa C. Burcroff, "Home Confinement and Electronic Surveillance," in McCarthy, *Intermediate Punishments,* 173.

57. Reported in Blomberg, Waldo, and Burcroff, "Home Confinement," 173.

58. Schmidt and Curtis, "Electronic Monitoring," 148–49.

59. Ibid., 205.

60. Ibid., 218.

61. United States General Accounting Office, *Prison Boot Camps: Too Early to Measure Effectiveness* (Washington, D.C.: U.S. General Accounting Office, September 1988), 3; for a more recent mixed review, see also Doris Layton MacKenzie and Dale G. Parent, "Boot Camp Prisons for Young Offenders," in *Smart Sentencing,* 103–119.

62. Dale K. Sechrest, "Prison 'Boot Camps' Do Not Measure Up," *Federal Probation* (September 1989): 19.

63. Doris Layton MacKenzie, et al., "Boot Camp Prisons and Recidivism in Eight States," *Criminology* 33 (1995): 351.

64. Ibid.

65. Ibid., 353.

66. Ibid., 352–353.

67. Doris Layton MacKenzie and Robert Brame, "Shock Incarceration and Positive Adjustment During Community Supervision," *Journal of Quantitative Criminology* 11 (1995): 111–142, 138.

68. Sally T. Hillsman and Judith A. Greene, "The Use of Fines as an Intermediate Sanction," in *Smart Sentencing,* 124–125.

69. Michael Tonry and Kate Hamilton, eds., *Intermediate Sanctions in Overcrowded Times* (Boston: Northeastern University Press, 1995), 15.

70. Hillsman and Greene, "The Use of Fines," 125–126.

71. Ibid., 127–128.

72. Sally T. Hillsman, "Day Fines in New York," in *Intermediate Sanctions in Overcrowded Times,* 23.

73. Hillsman and Greene, "The Use of Fines," 133–134.

74. Douglas C. McDonald, "Unpaid Community Service as a Criminal Sentence," in *Smart Sentencing,* 183–184.

75. Ibid., 182.

76. Ibid., 187.

77. Ibid., 186.

78. Ibid., 189.

79. Ibid., 188–191.

80. Ibid., 191–192.

81. Dale G. Parent, "Day Reporting Centers," in *Intermediate Sanctions in Overcrowded Times,* 125.

82. Ibid., 127.

83. Joan Petersilia, "When Probation Becomes More Dreaded than Prison," *Federal Probation* 54 (1990): 23–27.

 # Prisons, Jails, and

Prisoners

CHAPTER MAIN POINTS

1. *The U.S. incarcerates a higher proportion of its population and incarcerates them longer than any other country except Russia.*

2. *About half of U.S. prisoners are convicted of violent offenses, the remainder for property, drug, and public-order offenses.*

3. *Prisons separate prisoners according to security risk and dangerousness into maximum, medium, and minimum security prisons.*

4. *Maximum and medium security prisons, which hold the majority of prisoners, focus on preventing prisoners from escaping and from injuring staff and each other.*

5. *Minimum security prisons focus on programs for rehabilitation of prisoners.*

6. *Most prisoners are young, nonwhite men who abuse alcohol and other drugs, and have prior criminal records.*

7. *Prisoners spend less time in prison than their sentences prescribe.*

8. *Jails hold pretrial detainees, convicted misdemeanants, and felons awaiting sentencing or space in prison.*

9. *New-generation jails and prisons are based on the philosophy of combining architecture and management to provide safe, humane confinement where convicted offenders are sent as punishment, not for punishment.*

10. *Women's prisons provide all security levels within the same facility.*

11. *Prison management depends both on architecture and management styles, which vary from place to place and from administrator to administrator.*

12. *Correctional officers are organized according to a quasi-military hierarchy of responsibility and their work conditions vary greatly from place to place, but they are everywhere responsible for supervising the daily life of prisoners.*

13. *Crowded facilities and public budgetary restraints have led to an increased number of private jails and prisons.*

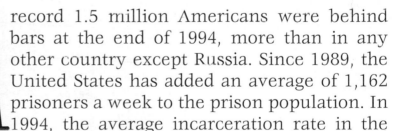

A record 1.5 million Americans were behind bars at the end of 1994, more than in any other country except Russia. Since 1989, the United States has added an average of 1,162 prisoners a week to the prison population. In 1994, the average incarceration rate in the United States was 386 per 100,000. Some individual states have much higher rates than that average. Georgia, for example, had an incarceration rate of 456 in 1994. The Georgia Department of Corrections boasts that this is more than "any other political entity in the world, higher even than in the Soviet Union or South Africa." Georgia, however, does not hold the record high incarceration rate in the United States. In 1994, the rate in Texas was 636. Some states are at the other extreme, incarcerating convicted people at a much lower rate. For example, in 1994 the incarceration rate in South Dakota was 78 and in Minnesota, 100. Nevertheless, since 1980, both the number of prisoners and the incarceration rate in the United States—even in states with lower

Figure 13.1

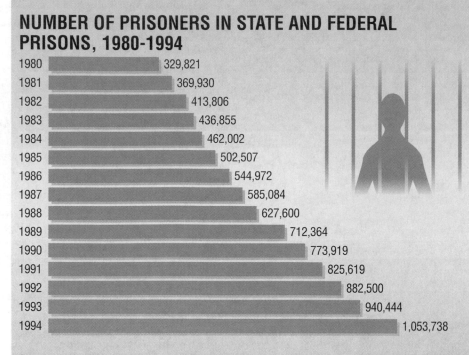

NUMBER OF PRISONERS IN STATE AND FEDERAL PRISONS, 1980-1994

Year	Number
1980	329,821
1981	369,930
1982	413,806
1983	436,855
1984	462,002
1985	502,507
1986	544,972
1987	585,084
1988	627,600
1989	712,364
1990	773,919
1991	825,619
1992	882,500
1993	940,444
1994	1,053,738

Source: BJS, *Prisoners in 1994* (Washington, D.C.: BJS, August 1995).

Figure 13.2

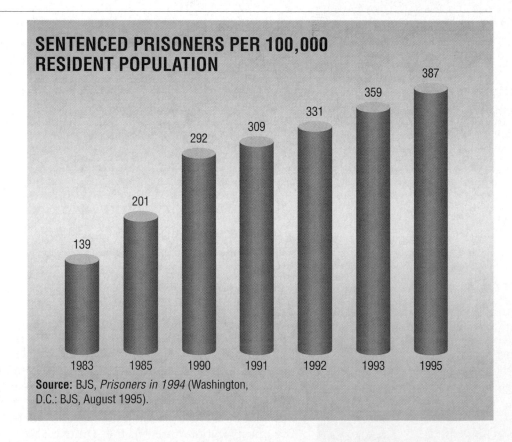

SENTENCED PRISONERS PER 100,000 RESIDENT POPULATION

Year	Number
1983	139
1985	201
1990	292
1991	309
1992	331
1993	359
1995	387

Source: BJS, *Prisoners in 1994* (Washington, D.C.: BJS, August 1995).

Comparative Criminal Justice

Comparative Criminal Justice

International Incarceration Rates 1993

Figure 13.3

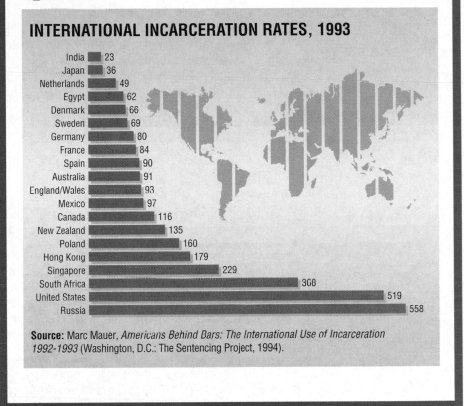

INTERNATIONAL INCARCERATION RATES, 1993

Country	Rate
India	23
Japan	36
Netherlands	49
Egypt	62
Denmark	66
Sweden	69
Germany	80
France	84
Spain	90
Australia	91
England/Wales	93
Mexico	97
Canada	116
New Zealand	135
Poland	160
Hong Kong	179
Singapore	229
South Africa	368
United States	519
Russia	558

Source: Marc Mauer, *Americans Behind Bars: The International Use of Incarceration 1992-1993* (Washington, D.C.: The Sentencing Project, 1994).

rates—have risen sharply. (See Figures 13.1 and 13.2.) In contrast, Western European rates are not only lower than in the United States, but they are declining. (See Comparative Criminal Justice, "Incarceration Rates for Selected Countries.")[1]

Incarceration in the United States is expensive. The cost of building, maintaining, and operating prisons was nearly $11.5 billion in 1990, a cost of $45.37 per U.S. resident. It cost an average of $15,513 to keep one prisoner confined for a year in state and federal prisons. (Some states spent much more than the average; Minnesota spent the most, $30,302. Others spent much less; Arkansas, for example, spent $7,557.) Federal and state governments are engaged in the biggest prison construction program in the history of American corrections. At present the U.S. has enough prison space to hold the city of Orlando, Florida. California spends as much on prisons as it does on higher education.[2]

Money spent on the steeply rising incarcerated population competes with dollars spent on other public services, such as education, health care, roads, and bridges. Why must we choose between spending money on public services for law-abiding people and spending it on convicted criminals? Why not allow taxpayers to keep more of their own money instead of spending it on building prisons and imprisoning offenders? The answer to these questions depends on the missions of prison. The missions of prison are similar to the purposes of sentencing discussed in Chapter 11: retribution, incapacitation, deterrence, and rehabilitation.

History of U.S. Prisons

Americans have always been schizophrenic about crime and punishment, and, therefore, about what to do with convicted offenders. According to sociologist and prison expert David A. Ward,

> The bureau [Federal Bureau of Prisons] has been criticized by conservative hardliners for running "country club" prisons and by liberals and prison reformers for operating a Devil's Island or a House of Pain. Some of the citizens and their elected officials want criminals to be executed or locked up until they die and others call for understanding, the repair of damages to personalities, and preparation for the offender to reenter the free world. Dealing with any group of lawbreakers is a complicated and difficult business with much diversity of opinion even among the experts. . . .[3]

The history of prisons is largely a history of the tensions inherent in the multiple missions of criminal punishment (see Chapter 11). This history is not known to many, but some knowledge of it is necessary to understand prisons in the United States. The tension between the missions of retribution and rehabilitation has been particularly strong. According to the criminologist and prison expert Norval Morris:

> The long, slow, painful dance of retribution and reform, first retribution leading, then reform, with rationalization for all the ornate steps in this dance being based on many unproved assumptions, is a performance that should be known to all who hope to understand contemporary punishments; but it is far from common knowledge.[4]

Punishment is as ancient as recorded history. One of the earliest known writings, the Code of Hammurabi, has, chipped in stone, a list of penalties strongly resembling the mandatory sentences of our own day. Prisons, too, are ancient, but their mission has changed. Until well into the 1700s, prisons were used to hold suspects and defendants to insure their appearance for trial, not to punish convicted offenders for their crimes. Punishment in colonial America took a number of forms, but prison was not one of them. Capital punishment was commonly prescribed, if not so frequently practiced. Occasionally, early American magistrates ordered corporal punishment, such as whipping or mutilation, including cropping ears and slitting nostrils. Public shaming—stocks, ducking stools, pillories, dunce caps, and signs such as "I am a fornicator"—also prevailed. Far more pervasive in practice than capital, corporal, and shaming punishments were fines and restitution.[5]

In 1785, Massachusetts designated Castle Island, a fortress guarding Boston Harbor, as the first statewide prison in the United States devoted solely to confining *convicted* offenders. At the same time, the Massachusetts legislature authorized judges to sentence offenders to long-term confinement as an alternative to the older public punishments, fines, and restitution. The statute authorizing the building of the prison provided that prisoners were expected to perform "hard labor." Another statute enacted the same year explained why: "Whereas idleness is often the parent of fraud and cheating . . . confinement to hard labour may be a means of reclaiming such offenders." Convicts served under military discipline, dietary and sanitary requirements were established, and a competent staff, including a physician and a chaplain, were provided. The basic idea was to remove offenders from a

penitentiary *early prisons in which prisoners had to remain silent to think about their crimes.*
Pennsylvania system *early prison system that required solitary confinement and silence.*
Auburn *or* **congregate system** *early prison system that imposed a rule of congregate work in absolute silence and solitary confinement at night.*

corrupting environment and to make them work. The isolation and the work was supposed to redeem their souls, reform their bodies, and instill in them the habits of law-abiding citizens ready, willing, and capable of doing the work of society.[6]

The "Solitary System"

The Quakers in Pennsylvania soon stole the limelight from Massachusetts as prison innovators. The Quakers considered physical pain inflicted purely for retribution barbaric and cruel. In an enlightened effort to reform "fallen" citizens, the Quakers designed the Walnut Street Jail in Philadelphia, built in 1790, followed by the Western Penitentiary in 1826 and the Eastern Penitentiary in 1830. The Walnut Street Jail represented the first use of segregated confinement in America. It provided adequate food, shelter, clothing, bedding, and medical care without fees—a major advance, since these necessities had always depended on prisoners' ability to pay for them. Prisoners made nails, cut stone, and did other work they could perform in their own cells. They had to remain silent at all times, supposedly meditating on their past wrongs and thinking about improving their lives in the future. Hence, the name **penitentiary.** The Eastern and Western penitentiaries had similar philosophies. Prisoners remained in solitary confinement performing tasks during the day—except Sunday—and meditating in silent isolation during their idle hours. This combination of solitary work and silent meditation came to be known as the **Pennsylvania system.**

The "Congregate System"

In 1817, New York built its own version of a new prison at Auburn, based entirely on solitary confinement in small cells and a strict rule of silence. Within a short time, however, so many prisoners committed suicide or had mental breakdowns, due to confinement in tiny cells with no exercise and no work, that authorities modified the system. The **Auburn** or **congregate system** imposed a rule of congregate work in absolute silence and solitary confinement at night. Keepers flogged on the spot anyone who broke the rules.

The Pennsylvania and Auburn systems had important common features. Prisons were huge, walled fortresses in which wardens had total control over their prisoners. Violating the rules of either silence or work resulted in swift, harsh punishment. Authorities considered both prison systems more humane methods of punishment than corporal and capital punishment and mutilation—and they may well have been, initially. Both intended to reform prisoners through the presumed salutary effects of silent meditation, hard work, healthy food, and religion. Under both systems it was assumed that following this regimen, prisoners would return to society as law-abiding, compliant citizens who worked for a living rather than preying on others.

Both systems were part of a much larger movement in nineteenth-century America: institutionalization. Historically, most life activities—work, play, education, and punishment—took place in or around individuals' homes. After about 1820, the center for these activities increasingly moved from the home to large, centralized buildings—factories, gymnasiums, hospitals, schools, "reformatories," and "penitentiaries."[7]

Most observers soon noted that penitentiaries did not reform their prisoners, and they discovered that the reformation of offenders was not their sole—perhaps not even their primary—purpose. Prisons were increasingly becoming custodial warehouses for criminals, and despite the reform efforts and humanitarian rhetoric, they could also be cruel. One prisoner from the

historical note

Anyone can see that the number of "criminals," as they are called, is never diminished, that no one is ever benefited by ... [prison]. They move in a constant circle, an endless procession, round and round ... criminal court, penitentiary, and criminal court again. ... And this goes on day after day, year after year. ... This process is called our "penal and correctional system."

Brand Whitlock, 1907

correctional institution *type of prison developed during the early 1900s that was based on the penal philosophy of rehabilitation.*
fortress prison *large, custody-oriented prison that began in the 1800s.*

Elmira Reformatory, an institution widely hailed for its reformatory ideals, reported the results of failing to complete a work assignment:

> I knew I was in for a beating and I had a terror of what was coming. I refused to leave my cell. They stuck into the cell an iron rod with a two-foot hook on the end, heated red hot, and poked me with it. I tried to defend myself, but my clothing took fire, and the iron burned my breast. I finally succumbed, was handcuffed and taken to the bathroom. I asked Brockway [the renowned, born-again Christian reformer] if I had not been punished enough. He laughed at me. I got half a dozen blows with the paddle right across the kidneys. The pain was so agonizing that I fainted. They revived me, and when I begged for mercy, Brockway struck me on the head with a strap, knocked me insensible. The next thing I knew I was lying on a cot in the dungeon, shackled to an iron bar. The next day I was again hoisted and beaten, returned to the dungeon, and after one day's rest, beaten again. Then I was put in the cell in Murder-er's Row, where I remained for twenty-one days on bread and water.[8]

The "Progressive" Reforms, 1890-1970

The Progressive reformers of the early twentieth century attacked the existing prisons as cruel and barbaric, just as the initiators of prisons had attacked capital, corporal, and mutilative punishments. These new reformers urged more effective means to "rehabilitate" offenders. Their methods combined humane treatment, counseling, vocational training, and discipline intended to make prisoners fit into society. The Progressives instituted many rehabilitative programs. They created the indeterminate sentence and parole boards, making imprisonment dependent on prisoners' gradual rehabilitation, not on their past crimes, and advocated separate facilities for men, women, and delinquent children.[9]

By the 1940s, the **correctional institution**—based on the penal philosophy of rehabilitation—emerged as the cruelty and harsh discipline in the custody-oriented **fortress prison** diminished. In principle and practice, correctional institutions were more humane and accommodating than "big houses," the name for old fortress prisons. They provided less intrusive discipline; more yard and recreational privileges; more liberal visitation and mail policies; more amenities, such as movies; and more rehabilitation programs, such as education, vocational training, and therapy.[10]

The Return to Punishment, 1970–Present

During the 1960s, reformers attacked these Progressive reforms. Liberals believed prisons were stripping away prisoners' rights in exchange for what prison administrators and treatment-oriented experts considered prisoners' "needs." From the conservative side came the attack that prisons did not punish prisoners sufficiently to prevent them from committing future crimes. Academics joined the chorus of criticism by claiming that rehabilitation did not work. All were convinced that the correctional institution was not working, as indicated by prison riots, rising crime rates, and recidivism. As a result, calls came for new goals for imprisonment; new kinds of prisons; different prison populations; revised prison conditions; a new breed of prison guard, called corrections officer, and a more modern administrative system within prisons; a heightened accountability to outside authorities; and even alternatives to incarceration for some types of prisoners.[11]

Nevertheless, according to prison scholar Robert Johnson:

> The benefits of correctional institutions are easily exaggerated. To my mind, the differences between the Big Houses and correctional institu-

violent prison *type of prison that started in the 1960s, housing younger, more violent prisoners who often exhibit racial and ethnic hatred.*

maximum security prisons *prisons that focus mainly on security because they house the most dangerous and escape-prone prisoners.*

tions are of degree rather than kind. Correctional institutions did not correct. Nor did they abolish the pains of imprisonment. They were, at bottom, simply more tolerable warehouses than the Big Houses they supplanted, less a departure than a toned-down imitation. Often, correctional institutions occupied the same physical plant as the Big Houses. Indeed, one might classify them as Big Houses gone soft.[12]

Today, we still call prisons correctional institutions. However, many criminologists maintain that since the middle of the 1960s a new type of prison has emerged to replace the correctional institution in everything but name. Criminologists call this new type of prison the **violent prison.** In Hans Toch's blunt language, the modern prison is a "human warehouse with a jungle-like underground." Extreme differences, distrust, and hatred divide prisoners. Nonwhites, particularly African Americans and Hispanics, now outnumber whites in many prisons, and racially constituted gangs and cliques often dominate. Identities based on "macho images" encourage violence. Links between gangs in the slums outside and prisoners from the gangs inside have altered the view that prisons are isolated from the surrounding community, particularly when they are located near large cities.[13]

Prison, in the eyes of many prisoners today, is the ultimate test of manhood. A man in prison is able to secure what he wants and protect what he has: "In here, a man gets what he can," and "nobody can force a man to do something he don't want to," are key elements of the belief system. Any prisoner who does not meet these standards is not a man, "has no respect for himself," and is therefore not entitled to respect from others. According to Professor Robert Blecker, who, with convicted armed robber John Allen, spent hundreds of hours observing life in Lorton Central Prison outside Washington, D.C.:

> Prisoners constantly confront life-threatening situations. If you let someone cut in line in front of you, others will take greater advantage. But if you confront him, you face possible lethal retaliation. Phone lines, canteen lines, chow lines, the gym—all are dangerous spots. A new prison ethos prevails among the younger generation: Smaller slights are taken as disrespect. Today's kids no longer settle "beefs" by fists; no longer is a fair fight one-on-one with equal weapons. Routinely, now, they wear masks and attack in groups.[14]

Maximum Security Prisons

Not all prisons are alike in the United States. Prisons are designed according to three security levels—maximum, medium, and minimum security. The design of prisons according to security level originated in the discovery in the 1800s that problems arose when hard-core criminals are confined in the same place with nondangerous, first-time offenders. Hence, the creation of separate prisons to confine different types of offenders. The "worst" offenders, including mainly violent and repeat offenders, are confined in **maximum security prisons**. Maximum security prisons hold about half of all prisoners in the United States. As the name implies, these prisons focus almost exclusively on security. Their main mission is to prevent prisoners from escaping or hurting themselves, each other, and prison staff. To prevent escape, high walls surround most maximum security prisons. Armed guards stand in observation towers watching the walls at all times, using searchlights and even electronic devices to prevent prisoner escapes. Inside maximum security prisons, supervision, surveillance, and control are extensive. Whenever prisoners move from one area of the prison to another, they do so only in groups and under close supervision by correctional officers.[15]

Traditional Maximum Security Prisons

In older maximum security prisons, large cell blocks arranged in tiers permit a single guard to observe hundreds of cells at one time. In cells, bars replace doors and windows. Television surveillance facilitates monitoring prisoners, not only in their cells but also in the shower, at meals, and even in the toilet. Prisoners may be strip-searched before and after visits—even visitors are subject to pat-downs. Officers take "head counts" throughout the day: anyone not accounted for prompts major efforts to locate the "missing" prisoner. Heavy metal furniture built into the walls and floors improves security, preventing the use of chairs and tables as obstacles or as weapons during disturbances. The large amount of metal creates high noise levels as it scrapes, clashes, and echoes—prisons are not quiet places. For security and other reasons, prisoners spend many hours in their cells with little or no activity.[16]

Most maximum security prisons are large and were built to last a long time. Most of them have. More than 40 percent were built before 1925; 11 percent were built before 1875! Eighty percent of all prisoners live in the oldest prisons, most of which hold more than 1,000 prisoners each. The largest prison in the United States is in Jackson, Michigan; it holds 5,000 prisoners! The oldest prisons are usually not only the largest but also have the largest populations. Maximum security prisoners are older and more violent than those incarcerated in other prisons.[17]

Super Maximum Security Prisons

The federal prison system has operated three **super maximum prisons**: the legendary Alcatraz from the 1930s until 1963; then, beginning in 1964, the federal penitentiary at Marion, Illinois; and, finally, since 1994, the Administrative Maximum (ADX) security penitentiary in Florence, Colorado. According to the Office of Public Affairs of the Federal Bureau of Prisons,

> Florence (ADX) has been designed to operate in a humane, safe manner that is in accord with all applicable legal standards and sound correctional practices. . . . Unusually high security prisons are necessary at institutions like Marion and Florence because they confine the most

Most maximum security prisons are old and surrounded by thick walls like this one.

serious escape and assault risks in the Bureau, as well as some equally dangerous inmates from a number of states. Most Marion inmates have demonstrated by highly assaultive, predatory, or serious escape-related behavior that they are in a stage of their institutional career where they cannot function in traditional, open population institutions of lower security. They are simply the most violent and dangerous inmates in the entire system, and most of them have proven it repeatedly.[18]

Therefore, according to the Bureau of Prisons,

> An unfortunate but real aspect of modern correctional administration in America is that many prison populations include growing numbers of extremely violent, predatory individuals. This, in part, is due to the emergence of prison gangs that seek to control internal drug trafficking and other illicit activity, and rely on threats, intimidation, assault, and murder to accomplish their objectives. Another threat to prison security comes from major offenders, who have immense outside assets, or lead sophisticated criminal organizations with resources that make violent, outside-assisted escapes a very real possibility. Furthermore, the lack of an enforceable Federal death penalty for murderous activity in prison means that, especially for inmates already serving life without parole, there is little effective deterrent to murder while incarcerated.[19]

Not all prisoners, of course, see the super maximum security prisons the same way as does the Federal Bureau of Prisons. One prisoner described life in super maximum security at Marion this way:

> Some men at Marion have grown up here in the harshest hole ever constructed. Deprived for so long of a normal existence, our measure of self-worth is gauged by our capacity to endure whatever physical or psychological torture is thrust upon us. Men along the tiers boast of surviving brutal riots, of running gauntlets of club-wielding guards, of being starved and beaten in places like San Quentin, Attica and Huntsville. It is both an indictment of society and a human tragedy that the state of imprisonment in America has been allowed to degenerate to this level.[20]

These relatively rare (but growing number of) super maximum security prisons fascinate and horrify (depending on your point of view) the press, public, and politicians. According to Professor David A. Ward, despite the small number of prisoners they have confined, Alcatraz (250 prisoners) and Marion (350 prisoners) "have been responsible for more newspaper and magazine articles, more movies and television spots, more hearings before congressional committees, and more debates among criminologists and penologists than have been produced by all other federal prisons combined." Alcatraz confined some of the great crime figures in our history—Al Capone, John Dillinger, Pretty Boy Floyd, and Baby Face Nelson. According to Professor Ward, "Marion contained a small, special unit to hold the country's high-visibility spies, an 'avowed racist' serial killer, and the country's most famous prison writer, Jack Abbott, author of *In the Belly of the Beast*." Marion is the "end of the line" for the "worst of the worst" prisoners. At Marion, prisoners are locked in their cells for 23 hours a day. Whenever convicts leave their cells, they are handcuffed, their legs are chained, and three guards armed with nightsticks surround them. (See Chapter 14 for a discussion of life at Marion.)[21]

New-Generation Maximum Security Prisons

Not all maximum security prisons fit the description of either the traditional or the super prisons. In recent years, a new idea for both building and managing maximum security prisons has arisen. **New-generation prisons** are based on the idea that offenders are sent to prison *as* punishment, not *for* punishment. These prisons are built so that both the architecture and the style of management contribute to a safe, humane confinement where the confinement itself is supposed to be the punishment. (See the following discussion on prison management styles.)

New-generation prisons usually contain six to eight physically separated units within a secure perimeter. Each unit contains 40 to 50 prisoners, with a cell for each inmate. Each also has dining rooms, a laundry, counseling offices, game rooms, and an enclosed outdoor recreation yard and work area. Because these units are only two levels high, continual surveillance from secure "bubbles" monitors all prisoners' interactions with each other and staff. These self-contained units make it possible to keep many prisoners secure within an overall large perimeter, while at the same time allowing for groups small enough to participate in congregate activities. The design also permits specialization. One unit focuses on drug dependency. Another houses prisoners attending school. A third concentrates on work projects. Another is reserved for disciplinary problems.[22]

Despite the pleasing architecture and variety of programs, new-generation prisons are still maximum security prisons. Most prisoners at Oak Park Heights, the new-generation prison in Minnesota, for example, are violent offenders. The prison houses not only the most dangerous prisoners in Minnesota, but also federal prisoners ranked in the highest-security category. Furthermore, prisoners have a choice of programs, but they cannot choose to do nothing. They can work, go to school, or obtain treatment; but they cannot sit in their cells. Furthermore, the security is the highest. Prisoners are under constant surveillance; they do not move about unattended. Table 13.1 reproduces the daily schedule and security counts at Oak Park Heights.

New generation prisons may look pleasing but they are still maximum security prisons that house the most dangerous prisoners under the strictest security.

Table 13.1
Daily Schedule and Counts

6:30	Wake-up
6:45–6:55	Live count—must show movement
7:00–7:20	Breakfast
7:35	Report to work
7:35–11:25	Work or program—receiving and orientation
11:25–11:40	Return to unit—stand-up count
11:40–12:15	Lunch
12:15	Return to work
12:15–3:25	Work or program—receiving and orientation
1:50–2:00	Education only—down to gym
2:00–3:30	Education only—mandatory gym
2:50–3:00	Verification count
3:25–3:35	Return to unit—verification count
3:35–4:50	Free time
4:50–5:00	Stand-up count
5:00–5:30	Dinner
5:30–8:30	Evening program
8:30–9:55	Evening program—free time
10:00	Stand-up count—inmates are locked
10:55–11:55	Shift change—live count
1:00	Live count
3:00	Live count
5:00	Live count

SOURCE: *Inmate Handbook,* Minnesota Correctional Facility, Oak Park Heights, Minnesota (courtesy of Dennis Benson, assistant warden).

Medium and Minimum Security Prisons

medium security prisons *the second most secure prisons that resemble maximum security prisons but with somewhat less constant supervision.*

minimum security prisons *the least secure prisons where rehabilitation is stressed and relatively more freedom and privacy are allowed than in maximum and medium security prisons.*

Medium security prisons confine about a third of all prisoners. **Medium security prisons** are generally enclosed by double fences topped with barbed wire. Outside cell blocks in units of 150 cells or fewer are common, as are dormitories and even cubicles in some facilities. Medium security prisons are not as old as maximum security prisons; more than 87 percent have been built since 1925. Although supposedly less focused on security, medium security prisons follow many practices common in maximum security prisons, such as head counts, electronic surveillance, and cell watching. Unlike maximum security prisoners, prisoners in medium security prisons work without constant supervision. The prison design, especially in newer medium security prisons, comes from campus or courtyard models.[23]

Minimum security prisons hold only 11 percent of all prisoners. **Minimum security prisons** are newer than both maximum and medium security prisons; most were built after 1950. Vocational training and treatment, not security, are the focus of minimum security prisons. Minimum security prisoners, mainly comprised of first-time, nonviolent, white-collar and younger offenders, are not considered dangerous or likely to escape.

The grounds of a minimum security prison resemble a college campus, with low buildings centered about a recreational area. (Critics call them resorts or, in the case of the federal minimum security prison camps, "Club Fed," because the media reported that during the 1970s and 1980s, Watergate conspirators and Wall Street inside traders spent their afternoons sunbathing and playing tennis.) Minimum security prisons emphasize trust and a more normal lifestyle. Prisoners eat in small groups, often at tables for four, instead of at long rows of tables that all face in one direction, a common feature of maximum and medium security prisons. Minimum security prisoners also have a modicum of privacy. Some even have private rooms with doors that prisoners may lock. Most minimum security prisons also provide a range of programs for prisoners, including vocational training, academic education, psychiatric treatment, and counseling. Some minimum security prisons supply family visiting facilities, where prisoners can stay with their families for up to three days at a time. A considerable number of prisoners work on the prison grounds or are released for the day on work-study programs that allow them to hold jobs or attend neighboring schools and colleges.[24]

Women's Prisons

In all societies, men convicts outnumber women convicts; hence, men's prisons also outnumber women's.

Women's prisons display little evidence of external security, probably because women's prisons provide for the full range of security levels— maximum, medium, and minimum—in the same location. Often a single cottage, dormitory, or wing makes up the maximum security area of a woman's prison. "Honor cottages" confine minimum security prisoners. Separate sections exist for prisoners of various ages, disciplinary statuses, programs, and sentence lengths. Their usually rural setting, absence of security apparatus, prevalence of private rooms, and typical cottage architecture make women's prisons relatively less gloomy than men's prisons. However, limited numbers usually mean limited educational opportunities and training. Most women's prisons focus on work that maintains the institution, such as cooking, cleaning, laundry, and sewing. Domestic work has characterized women's prisons since the separate women's prison movement in the late nineteenth and early twentieth centuries.[25]

Prison Administration

Research has revealed a variety of prison management styles. Dr. George Beto, former director of the Texas Department of Corrections, adopted a **control model of management,** a style that originated in the late nineteenth century at the famous Elmira reformatory and influenced many Progressive wardens and later prison administrators. The control model emphasized prisoner obedience, work, and education. Beto ran every prison in Texas as a maximum security prison. He believed that prisoners needed order, that only through order could they develop work and educational skills that would make their lives in prison more productive and also facilitate their later reintegration into the community. Formal, strict paramilitary lines from the warden and assistant wardens to the most junior correctional officer defined the duties within the prison. Official rules and regulations governed most actions of both staff and prisoners. Prisoners walked between painted lines in the corridors; loud talking constituted a punishable offense. In short, daily life inside the prisons was a busy but carefully orchestrated routine of numbering, counting, checking, locking, and monitoring inmate movement to and from work activities and treatment programs.[26]

Under the control model of management, political scientist John DiIulio, who studied prison management styles in Texas, Michigan, and California, found that

> officers had a sense of mission, an esprit de corps, and an amazing knowledge of the prison's history. Treatment and work opportunities were offered on a regular basis and well administered. . . . In short, life inside the Walls [the oldest prison in Texas] was in general safe, humane, productive, calm, stable, and predictable.[27]

Prisoners who violated the rules received the swift, certain punishment shifts of solitary confinement and extra work assignments. Prisoners who obeyed

building-tender system *prison management system that relies on prisoners to assist correctional officers in managing cell blocks.*
responsibility management approach *prison management model that stresses the responsibility of prisoners for their own actions, not administrative control to assure prescribed behavior.*

orders, worked, and "did their own time" received the carrot of the most liberal good time (time off for good behavior) provisions in American prisons—two days off for every productive, problem-free day served.[28]

The control model had its shortcomings. In Texas, it suffered from the **building-tender system,** which relied on prisoners to assist correctional officers in managing cell blocks. According to Dr. Beto:

> In any contemporary prison, there is bound to be some level of inmate organization, some manner of inmate society. . . . The question is this: who selects the leaders? Are the inmates to select them? Or is the administration to choose them or at least influence the choice? If the former, the extent of control over organized and semi-organized inmate life is lessened; if the latter, the measure of control is strengthened.[29]

The building-tender system led to a con-boss system in which prison gangs, organized along racial and ethnic lines, ran major parts of the Texas prison system. Violence, exploitation, fear, and disruption followed.[30]

The Michigan prison system exemplifies a **responsibility management approach.** This model stresses the responsibility of prisoners for their own actions, not administrative control to assure prescribed behavior. Michigan adopted not a single maximum security classification, but a number of security levels. Proper classification, according to the responsibility model, permits placing prisoners in the least restrictive prison consistent with security, safety, and humane confinement. Even prisoners in maximum security prisons should not live totally regimented lives. They should be given a significant degree of freedom and then held to account for their actions. According to one Michigan administrator:

> We go by the idea that prison should be as unrestrictive as possible. Don't misunderstand. Order comes first. You have to keep control. Security is number one through one thousand. But we don't have to smother people to keep things under control. We try to show inmates respect and expect it in return. We are more willing than Texas to give them air and then hold them accountable. . . . We attempt to operate safely in the least restrictive environment possible. . . . If Texas opts for the most restrictive, we opt for the least restrictive.[31]

The responsibility model creates a better prison milieu and focuses on the importance of prisoner responsibility. It also requires enormous paperwork. Furthermore, it has generated considerable opposition from some staff; among correctional officers, it has stimulated animosity toward the "brass" at headquarters in Lansing. One disgruntled officer complained:

> Lansing plays the spoiling grandparent. They come up with all sorts of goodies to spoil. They give the inmates their own way too much and then ask us to keep order and raise them properly. Bulls--t! They reap what they sow. We are made into scapegoats for their a------e schemes. We look like some kind of bartenders' union. We got rid of the symbols of authority. But we lost more than the symbols. Property control is a nightmare.[32]

According to one thirty-year veteran:

> I'd love to have a prison that could run the way the model says. But we've got a little problem: impulsive convicts and human nature. . . . This system deprives inmates of the right to safety in the name of giving them other rights. . . . A cellblock should be like a residential street. Would you want to live on a street where your neighbors were always shouting? Where most of what they shouted was vulgar and violent? Would you permit your neighbors to assault you and each other?[33]

Despite defects, Michigan prisons have provided more humane, safe, and secure confinement than many other state prisons. The control and responsibility systems do not exist in pure form in most prisons. Some states, such as California, balance elements of control and responsibility into what DiIulio calls **consensus prison management.**[34]

Prison management to a large extent reflects the personality and management style of prison wardens. Some believe it was the personality of George Beto that accounted for much of the success of the Texas prisons under the control model. Certainly, more than just the architecture of the new-generation prison at Oak Park Heights, Minnesota accounts for the virtual elimination of serious violent incidents, suicide, and drug use in that prison. The architecture has its counterpart in the new management philosophy that accompanies it. Warden Frank Wood (and his two successors) exemplifies this new management philosophy, which requires personal interaction among the warden, inmates, and staff. Wood spent more than 25 percent of his time, in his words, "eyeball to eyeball" with inmates and staff. He personally conducted the final prisoner orientation meeting that makes them "understand their responsibilities and the prison's responsibilities to them." Wood's philosophy also proposes that:

- "Staff should treat the inmates as we would want our sons, brothers, or fathers [and, presumably, in women's prisons our daughters, sisters, and mothers] treated."
- Inmates who do not work or go to school are not free to watch TV and "roam around their units" but are locked in their cells.
- The response to troublemaking is individual and not group punishment.
- Units are locked up on a random, regular basis for three to four days to "purge contraband."
- Every lock is tested every day.
- Inmates are kept very busy.
- The staff always promptly responds to inmate requests, however unimportant the requests may appear.
- Inmates are periodically rotated into the prison's mental health unit for observation and a change of environment, and for relief from nearby inmates and staff.[35]

The effects of this management philosophy, on the basis of existing research, appear positive. Oak Park Heights has virtually eliminated serious violence, both between prisoners and toward staff. Mark S. Fleisher, a cultural anthropologist, describes life in Lompoc, California, federal prison based on participant observation and open-ended interviews. Despite housing many violent prisoners, Lompoc has a relatively low rate of violence, due in part to management and prison culture that rewards peace and quiet.[36]

Prison administrators are often caught in a double bind because they serve competing formal and informal goals. Prisons are supposed to both punish and rehabilitate prisoners, as well as protect society and other inmates from assaultive, escape-prone prisoners. These conflicting goals lead to wardens' offending vocal interest groups. Measures taken to assure security or to punish prisoners inevitably generate criticism from counselors and others committed to rehabilitation. Actions taken to encourage prisoner rehabilitation anger line officers, who have the direct responsibility of maintaining prison security, and the large segment of the public that believes prisons exist to "punish" prisoners.[37]

Wardens work with increasingly tight budgets; crowded, frequently outdated, insecure buildings; and, in some locations, an untrained, uncommitted, highly mobile work force. Conflicting goals and limited resources are serious obstacles to effective prison administration. Increased court intervention into prison administration, the intrusion of gangs into prison society, rapid social change in the larger society, and racism have compounded the problems.[38]

Corrections Officers

The correctional officer, formerly called guard, is "the key figure in the penal equation, the man on whom the whole edifice of the penitentiary system depends." Work that is routine in most large, complex organizations becomes more so in prisons because of the closed and frequently monotonous nature of prison society. As the discussions of different prison architecture and management styles make clear, the work of correctional officers varies greatly depending on the kind of prison and administration. Advances have taken place during the last decade, and even since the first edition of this book appeared (1987), in both the quality of officers and the environment in which they work. Somewhat oversimplifying, we will distinguish between traditional prison guards who work in the old-style maximum security prisons and correctional officers who staff the growing numbers of new-generation prisons.[39]

According to Gordon Hawkins, guards in traditional maximum security prisons

> have nothing to do but stand guard; they do not use inmates productively any more than they themselves are used productively by prison managers. Guards manage and are managed in organizations where management is an end, not a means.[40]

In all prisons and under all management styles, officers perform several critical functions. They supervise living, work, dining, and recreation areas. In new-generation prisons these might be small units; in traditional prisons, large cell blocks and dining halls. Officers transfer prisoners to hospitals, courts, and even to community visits with their families. They take turns serving on disciplinary boards. They sit in towers and protect the gates that separate inside from outside and one area from another within the prison.[41]

Entry-level line officers do the major daily guard work in prisons. Some manage living areas: opening and closing gates; distributing medicine, mail, and laundry; and answering phones. The most important cell block duty is conducting the "count." Several times a day, officers account for every prisoner. Even one unaccounted-for prisoner leads to a halt in all operations and movement. Miscounting brings disciplinary action. In most large maximum security prisons, cell block duty is dangerous. Prisoners outnumber officers by as much as fifty to one, so officers depend more on communicating authority than on power. During cell duty, particularly in large cell blocks, chances increase that prisoners will assault, overwhelm, and take officers hostage. During riots, the situation worsens—prisoners may beat, rape, and sometimes kill officers.[42]

Other officers supervise the work areas, such as stores and factories, and watch the gates. Tower duty is the loneliest guard job because tower guards have no contact with anyone except by telephone or walkie-talkie. On tower duty, officers cannot read, listen to the radio, or watch television. In the past, tower duty was regarded as highly undesirable. In violent and insecure prisons, however, officers seek the relatively safer tower duty. Tower guards remind prisoners as no one or nothing else can of the true nature of their confinement. Consequently, tower guards and prisoners share an open animosity.[43]

Above line officers are sergeants, lieutenants, and captains. Sergeants supervise cell blocks, work units, kitchens, and hospitals. They check correctional officers' work, assign them to specific tasks, and even fill in for absentees. Lieutenants act as prison police officers who keep the peace by

Most officers in traditional prisons were white men.

stopping fights and other prison disturbances. They have to maintain order by "walking" prisoners to isolation or forcibly removing them from cells when necessary. When they are not settling disturbances, they go on preventive patrol, checking and "shaking down" prisoners for weapons and other contraband. Lieutenants police not only the prisoners, but also the line officers. They search lower-ranking officers for contraband and weapons, just as they do prisoners. The few captains manage the paperwork required by bureaucracy—personnel evaluations, budget preparations, and disciplinary committee reports. Records management is an onerous task, one that grows more ponderous as prisons turn to bureaucratic management and as courts and other outside agencies demand increasing accountability.

In traditional prisons, social distance separates line officers from lieutenants and captains. Since correctional officers are in a paramilitary organization, they receive orders from their superior officers, orders which lieutenants and captains expect the officers to carry out efficiently and effectively. In some prisons, lieutenants and captains scrutinize correctional officers as carefully as the officers in turn scrutinize the prisoners. Alleged drug trafficking results in both prisoner and line officer shakedowns. Lieutenants check on both prisoners and officers to make sure they are doing their jobs. Lieutenants write disciplinary reports, called "tickets," on officers, just as officers write them on prisoners.

Guard work and correctional officers differ greatly from region to region and from prison to prison. In some areas, correctional officer is not a highly sought-after career. A Harris poll showed that only 1 percent of teenagers interested in security work wanted to be correctional officers. Many officers took their positions only after long periods of unemployment or layoffs, or after accidents made it impossible for them to continue their prior line of work. One example shows the difficulty in recruiting correctional officers. Illinois faces chronic guard shortages despite low entry-level standards. The state poses no residency requirement, nor does it require a high-school diploma. It has lowered cutoff civil service examination scores for correctional officers, raised salaries for these positions, and accepts men between the ages of 18 and 55.[44]

The problems posed by understaffing are aggravated by the fact that most of the large institutions are located in rural areas. The guards, drawn largely from the local population, are practically all white and rural, in contrast to the predominantly African-American and urban inmate population they supervise.[45]

The "Other Prisoners"

Correctional officers are the "other prisoners," according to one expert. Their close contact with prisoners leaves them stigmatized. "Even close friends do not know what to make of the prevailing belief that correctional officers are sadistic, corrupt, stupid, and incompetent." Furthermore, officers, like prisoners, are often locked off from the outside world. Stateville, in Illinois, for example, supplies dormitories for guards living inside the prison, and trailer parks for married couples who live outside the prison walls. Officers frequently become the scapegoats for prison problems and failures. Higher-echelon administrators and treatment personnel can easily blame the officers for breaches of prison discipline and failures in prisoner rehabilitation.[46]

In some places, fear and uncertainty permeate the world of correctional officers. Correctional officers carry no weapons because prisoners might overpower them and use the seized weapons:

> I was back there on the job when it broke out. I think every officer out there was frightened because we had no weapons. The tower officers— they didn't know exactly what to do. They were firing warning shots. You couldn't see clearly what they were doing, so you didn't know whether to duck, run or stand still and then you look at the inmates and they are coming with sticks, baseball bats, iron bars and all this stuff. Any man who says he wasn't afraid, I'd have to call him a liar.[47]

Women and Minority Corrections Officers

Selection of correctional officers in many systems gives high priority to physical standards—height, weight, and general strength. Empirical data, however, do not indicate that guard work requires this premium on physical strength. According to Gordon Hawkins:

> One thing which is quite certain is that the almost universal insistence on certain physical standards which restrict the selection of potentially qualified employees is a mistake. The fact that a man weighs 145 pounds (the Attica requirement) is no index of character or ability or indeed of anything except the extent to which he can tip the scales. The officer's control over an inmate depends primarily on his skills of persuasion and leadership. Skill in interpersonal relations [is crucial].[48]

Prior to 1972, men exclusively guarded men. Due to the impetus of affirmative action lawsuits and federal and state legislation, that situation has begun to change. The number of women correctional officers varies from state to state. Nationwide, women constitute only about 6 percent of correctional officers. However, the number in some states is considerably higher. In

Louisiana, Wyoming, and Kentucky, more than 15 percent of correctional officers are women.[49]

Prison administrators have historically excluded women from guard work in men's prisons, primarily because of the general belief that women's physical weakness would allow male prisoners to overpower and assault them. Although few empirical studies have examined the point, informed opinion holds that in those prisons that employ women, women and men officers experience comparable assault rates. In Illinois, none of the 39 women officers and 28 women trainees serving in medium and maximum security men's prisons have been attacked by men prisoners. Corrections officials in New York regard gender integration a success, despite one knife attack on a woman officer in Attica.[50]

Women correctional officers encounter various reactions from prisoners and male staff, from total support to amusement to outright hostility. The warden of one maximum security prison for men reported:

> The presence of women is long overdue. We're glad to see women in our facility. It adds a new dimension to corrections. It's a little too soon to say, but I tend to think that women are more respected than male guards.[51]

A female correctional officer in San Quentin suggests that despite men's reluctance to have women colleagues, women have made male correctional officers less brutal.

> [Having women in the pen] brings about a calmer setting. It also forces male officers not to act as "big, bad and tough" because here they have this little 5′2″, 115 lb. woman standing beside them, putting a guy that is 6′4″, 230 lbs. in cuffs saying, "Come on now, act right," and not having any problem doing it. Whereas he might have to go in there with two or three other guys and tackle him down to cuff him. It also forces them to recognize that they can't go home and talk about how bad and

Empirical research suggests that the role officers play is more important than their gender or race in determining how they perform their work.

mean they are and what a tough day they have had because some little chickie can do the same thing he is doing.[52]

Some believe that adding nonwhite officers will improve guard work, but it is not clear whether this is true. Race conflicts in prisons affect officers as well as prisoners. In San Quentin, for example, although violence is missing from race relations among staff, racial conflicts and competition are still present. The Stanford Prison Experiment suggested that the role guards play is far more important than their sex or race in determining how they do their work. Students participated in an experiment in which some acted as officers and others as prisoners. Some officers enjoyed their dominant position and harassed prisoners:

> In less than a week the experience of imprisonment undid (temporarily) a lifetime of learning: human values were suspended, self-concepts were challenged and the ugliest, most base, pathological side of human nature surfaced. We were horrified because we saw some boys (guards) treat others as if they were despicable animals, taking pleasure in cruelty.

Craig Haney, Curtis Banks, and Philip Zimbardo found that:

> Although the black correction officers are younger, more urban, better educated, and more liberal than their white colleagues, there were no consistent differences in their attitudes toward prisoners, staff, correctional goals, or their occupation.[53]

Training

According to the Joint Commission on Correctional Manpower and Training: "Too often [officers] receive little useful direction from management or professionally trained staff, and they find themselves in something of a sink-or-swim situation." According to Gordon Hawkins, this is a situation not easily remedied because

> unfortunately, there is little scientific knowledge about handling offender populations, few principles for consistent practice, and almost no provision for assessing the value of particular measures in various situations. Custodial staff generally operate on the basis of lore which has made for continued improvements in practice in other fields and occupations. Very little has been written on group management practices with confined offenders. What there is has come mainly from social scientists and has little relevance for the line practitioner.[54]

Some regions, and some prisons, provide excellent training programs. The U.S. Bureau of Prisons conducts a prison officer training program that some state prisons have followed. The training covers conventional matters related to custodial care, disciplinary procedures, report writing, and other people-processing duties, but it does more. It offers a forty-hour introduction to interpersonal communications, with a twelve-hour segment devoted to improving staff relations. According to some experts, training also ought to include "a liberal component" to help officers "to be more tolerant, more capable of accepting difference, and generally more sympathetic (in the best sense) to the prisoner's position."[55]

The Future

The future for correctional officers looks brighter than the past. A growing number of officers are well paid and adequately trained, and they work under good conditions. Applicants eagerly seek positions in places such as

Minnesota's Oak Park Heights maximum security prison. In 1993, correctional counselors—as they are called there—started at about $23,615 a year with no experience. Sergeants earned up to $36,618, lieutenants up to $44,078, and captains up to $49,235. Minnesota has no problem recruiting; some correctional officers have moved from other parts of the country just to work at Oak Park Heights. Many have college degrees or have nearly completed them, although they are not required.[56]

Correctional officers at Oak Park Heights receive training not only in how to use force, but also in how to implement the institution's management philosophy, which stresses treating prisoners humanely and without violence. According to former warden Frank Wood, in his message to prisoners:

> You will be interacting with a well-trained staff of professional correctional practitioners who are among the finest in the field of corrections in this country. You will be treated with courtesy, respect and the personal dignity due any reasonable and rational person. In return, we expect that you display the same maturity in your interactions with staff. We have a very fundamental philosophy that is summed up in the statement: "AS STAFF, WE TREAT INMATES AS WE WOULD WANT TO BE TREATED IF WE WERE AN INMATE OR AS WE WOULD WANT OUR FATHER, BROTHER, OR SON TO BE TREATED IF THEY WERE AN INMATE."[57]

Promotion at Oak Park Heights is at least partly based on education: completing approved courses related to human relations helps correctional counselors advance from one level to another and to supervisory positions.

Working at Oak Park Heights is different from guarding at many prisons. Although it is a maximum security prison—it houses Minnesota's worst violent and repeat offenders and also some overflow of the most dangerous offenders from the federal prison system—no one has been murdered or seriously assaulted at Oak Park Heights since the prison opened. The *You Decide* on working at a new-generation prison examines the work at Oak Park Heights.[58]

You Decide — Would You Work in a New-Generation Prison?

The following was written by Dan Crutchfield, a correctional officer in Minnesota:

It's 6:30 in the morning, the beginning of another day as a correctional officer at Oak Park Heights (OPH). Arriving officers report to a designated area of the institution for their daily Watch Briefing and job assignments, which are given out by the Watch Lieutenant. The Watch Briefing consists of information from the previous shifts in the form of reports. These reports give detailed accounts of pertinent information regarding incidents that occur within the institution.

After the Watch Briefing officers then embark to their designated work areas throughout the institution. Unit officers report to their units where they are briefed by the officers they relieve. The officer just arriving for duty will go into the unit and take a count of all the inmates assigned to that particular unit (fifty-two maximum). A quick inventory is also taken on essential items officers are accountable for, such as keys and various security equipment. After the officers properly relieve the previous shift they must get ready for their watch. There are log books to fill out, paperwork to be completed, and daily activities to be scheduled. For the morning officers, the next main event will be getting the inmates "switched out" for breakfast.

Meals are served in each of the units at OPH. This is one of the security features of the institution. Instead of allowing inmates to travel through corridors in large crowds which are hard to monitor, a food cart is delivered to each unit. The food cart is prepared in the institution kitchen and is delivered to the units by inmate servers. Officers conduct a search of the food cart upon entering the units and the cart is checked for contraband, that is, anything that would be unauthorized.

When the meal is ready to be served by the inmate servers, two officers station themselves near the food cart. The officer in the security bubble (which operates all the doors electronically) will announce over a PA system that breakfast is served and announce which rooms will be switched out first. Officers by the food cart regulate the feeding, making sure there is an orderly procession through the food line and that inmates take the appropriate portions of food that is served. After everyone has gone through the food line there is a last call in which any inmates who wish to go through the line again may do so. After breakfast is served inmates sign up for sick call at the "bubble" and also for use of the phone later in the day after work.

The inmates work upstairs from where they reside. The officer in the security bubble makes an announcement over the PA system. This time the announcement is to report to work in five minutes. Inmates assigned to work in the shops upstairs gather around the flag area and proceed through various security doors. After the work switch out a verification check is made by the unit officers of the inmates upstairs, downstairs, or out of the unit for sick call. It is the correctional officer's duty to have an accurate accountability of all inmates assigned to his or her unit. Not only should the officer know how many inmates are assigned to the unit, but the officer should know their location out of the unit as well.

Unit officers stationed downstairs perform random security rounds and supervise unit workers, referred to as "swampers." The swampers are the custodians of the units. It is their job to keep the units clean. Inspections are made randomly by officers, to insure the job is done properly.

Room checks and shakedowns are also performed randomly, and in cases where they are necessary. Receipts are left in rooms where articles are removed with the officer's name on them, and description of each article removed along with the reason it was removed. At the end of the morning, the inmates working upstairs switch back downstairs into the unit. Once in the unit, the officer in the security unit bubble announces that inmates are to report to their rooms for count. The afternoon procedure is similar to the morning routine. Lunch is served in the same fashion. After lunch the inmates again switch back upstairs for work.

As an officer at OPH there are always new challenges in daily routines because of the diverse population incarcerated within the institution. Every day is different due to human nature, ultimately a tense situation is a learning experience. There is much personal satisfaction in de-escalating potential situations, the experience that is acquired while working in a correctional environment enables correctional officers to meet these challenges. It is not the old stereotype guard that is 6 foot 4 and 250 pounds who deals with a crisis situation by physical force in an intense situation that gets positive results. Rather, it is the officer who uses his skills in personal relationships, that knows how to deal with people in a positive manner that will be successful as a correctional officer.

Oak Park Heights is one of the world's most secure maximum security prisons. However, the usual tension and stress that is associated with a maximum security prison does not seem to exist at OPH. This is due to the chemistry of the Minnesota Department of Corrections. Officers are paid a lucrative salary that is competitive with other law enforcement agencies. Advancement is also available with the completion of college courses in the human relations field. There exists a positive atmosphere for correctional officers and inmates alike at OPH. This creates favorable working conditions that enable an officer to strive for a better working relationship with staff and inmates alike and not have to be preoccupied about survival. However, it should be understood that OPH is a maximum security prison and there are certain hazards that could surface due to the elements that exist in such a structural environment which houses individuals who are incarcerated due to their negative behaviors.

Questions

What are the strengths of Officer Crutchfield's job? Do you detect weaknesses? What are they? Would you want his job? Explain.

Source: Dan Crutchfield, Correctional Officer, Oak Park Heights Prison, Oak Park Heights, Minnesota. Reprinted by permission.

Jails

Jails, like prisons, are ancient institutions. The ancestors of American jails originated nearly five hundred years ago in England. The English jail, or "gaol" as the English spell it, held only criminal suspects who could not make bail. In the United States today, jail populations, like those of prisons, are rising sharply, more than doubling between 1983 and 1994 (see Figure 13.4). On June 30, 1994, the latest figures available when this book went to press showed that the jail population in the United States hit a record high of 490,442 persons, a 6.7 percent rise in one year. Between 1984 and 1993, the rate of jail inmates increased from 96 to 188 per 100,000 people. The increases are due to a number of reasons, including:

- An increase in the number of arrests.
- A growth in the number of people admitted to jails.
- An increase in the number of felons sentenced to local jails.
- An increase in the number of inmates charged with or convicted of drug offenses.
- More prisoners held in jails because of crowded state and federal prisons.[59]

Figure 13.4

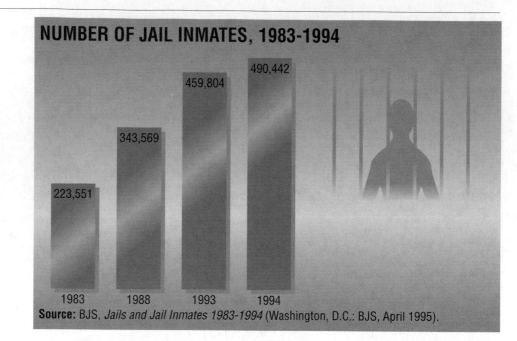

NUMBER OF JAIL INMATES, 1983-1994

223,551 — 1983
343,569 — 1988
459,804 — 1993
490,442 — 1994

Source: BJS, *Jails and Jail Inmates 1983-1994* (Washington, D.C.: BJS, April 1995).

Jail Inmates

Jails confine people both before and after conviction. Most inmates *sentenced* to jail are serving one year or less, but jails confine other people for varied time periods. These include:

- Defendants awaiting trial, conviction, and sentencing.
- Probation, parole, and bail-bond violators.
- Juveniles awaiting transfer to juvenile facilities.
- Mentally ill people awaiting transfer to mental health facilities.
- Individuals held for the military, for protective custody, for contempt, and as material witnesses.
- Inmates held for transfer to federal and state authorities.[60]

Jails hold people for short time periods—sometimes only a few hours, occasionally for more than a month or two, rarely more than a year. This causes a high turnover in jail populations, with many new persons replacing those who have just left. The average daily population of approximately 300,000 turns over so rapidly that it amounts to more than 20 million Americans spending some time in jail every year.[61]

Pretrial detainees make up about half the total jail population and spend an average of three months in jail. Most detainees are poor and African American, leading one expert to subtitle his book on jails the "ultimate ghetto" (see Figure 13.5). In fact, the incarceration rate for African-American males is six times that of white males. Many jails are not equipped and do not have the resources to provide special treatment for pretrial detainees. Therefore, and for the sake of security, legally innocent people live in the same conditions as, and follow identical routines of, convicted offenders.[62]

Jails are male-dominated institutions (90 percent of prisoners are men), but the number of women is increasing, almost tripling between 1983 and 1994, from 15,652 to 48,879. Almost half the increase was due to women held for drug offenses. Based on a survey of inmates in local jails, the Bureau of Justice Statistics found that about 40 percent of women arrested reported that they committed their offenses while under the influence of drugs.[63]

Figure 13.5

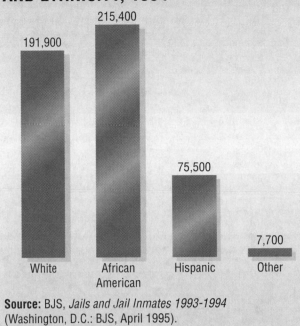

INCARCERATION IN JAILS BY RACE AND ETHNICITY, 1994

Source: BJS, *Jails and Jail Inmates 1993-1994* (Washington, D.C.: BJS, April 1995).

work release *practice that allows prisoners to leave jail for work and to return for evenings and weekends.*

institutional support *work program that provides for jail services by relying on the work of jail inmates.*

public works crews *jail work program in which inmates provide community services, such as street cleaning, storm cleanup, and park maintenance.*

According to the Advisory Commission on Jails, despite the increase in numbers of women in jail, they remain at a disadvantage:

> Women are frequently denied access to the cafeteria and recreational facilities and confined to a specific floor, wing, or cell for the duration of their confinement. By far the most common medical problems of incarcerated women are gynecological or obstetric. . . . Yet medical services of jails, when provided, are usually [by] physicians accustomed to and primarily concerned with men.[64]

Jail Programs

Residents in traditional jails get little recreation. On the average, they spend only two hours a day at indoor exercise and less than an hour at outdoor recreation. More than one thousand jails in the country provide no recreation at all for jail prisoners. Depriving prisoners of recreation can have harmful effects. Idleness, especially without radios and television sets to alleviate it, creates enhanced tension and violence, as well as mental and physical deterioration.[65]

Idleness stems not only from lack of recreation. Lack of work exacerbates it. Due to lack of resources, skepticism over the effectiveness of work programs, security reasons, and philosophical opposition to programs regarded as "coddling" criminals, only a few jails provide work programs for jail inmates. Three programs provide differing degrees of work. **Work release** allows prisoners to leave jail for work and to return for evenings and weekends. Work release alleviates boredom, provides meaningful activity, and defrays expenses incurred from keeping prisoners in programs. Participants frequently pay room and board from their earnings. **Institutional support** gives prisoners work in the jail itself, such as cleaning, cooking and serving food, and making repairs. Jail prisoners also form **public works crews** that provide various community services, such as street cleaning, storm cleanup, and park maintenance.

Jail Conditions

Jails and jail conditions vary greatly across the country. Some jails are modern, safe, clean, and efficiently and humanely administered. Others provide inadequate living conditions for prisoners and create security and control problems for jail managers. Ronald Goldfarb, leading jail expert, describes one type of jail:

> I can recall taking a three-day trip to see a sampling of correctional institutions in Georgia. I had seen eight different prison institutions in a state which was not famous for its progressive correctional institutions. Then I asked to see the Atlanta jail. I was shocked to discover conditions so horrible I could not believe them. The jail was far worse than the state prisons I had just seen. Inside a relatively modern exterior in a modest, busy part of town was a cramped, dark, dank interior. Large four-sided cages each held sixteen men, with disheveled beds and an open toilet. Inmates are kept inside these cages twenty-four hours a day throughout their often prolonged stays at the Atlanta jail. There is no privacy . . . and artificial air and light. A dismal atmosphere, a constant din, and a wretched stench pervaded the place.[66]

After four years spent traveling around the country studying jail conditions, Goldfarb concluded that such conditions were not peculiar to the Atlanta jail:

> One shocking paradox became apparent to me. Our prisons are used to incarcerate men convicted of serious crimes and our jails (while housing some convicted men) primarily hold people who are awaiting trial, who have been convicted of nothing; yet our jails are far worse than our prisons.[67]

Perhaps no single condition has done more to bring jails into national focus than crowding. Determining the amount of crowding creates problems due to at least four standards used to measure it. **Reported capacity** simply means whatever figure a particular jurisdiction designates as a jail's capacity. **Measured capacity** means one prisoner per cell. **Density** means the number of square feet of floor space per prisoner. **Occupancy** means the number of prisoners for each unit of confinement. The National Institute of Justice has put occupancy and density together and defines **crowded prisoners** as those who "live in a high density multiple occupancy confinement unit—i.e., a cell or dormitory shared with one or more inmates with less than sixty square feet of floor space per inmate." Using that measure, most large jails are overcrowded. In one survey, the National Sheriff's Association reported that 795 respondents listed overcrowding as the most serious problem in their jails.[68]

Many see buildings as the solution to jail problems—whether constructing new ones, renovating existing ones, or acquiring additional ones. The pro-builders consider more and improved buildings as absolutely essential to avert a crisis. Others contend that spending money on buildings foolishly wastes precious corrections dollars. Everyone agrees that buildings are expensive. New construction costs the most, averaging between $20,000 and $41,000 for every bed. Renovations are cheaper but still expensive, with estimates putting the amount at nearly $4,000 per bed. Maintaining jails is also expensive: taking care of one jail inmate costs more than $5,000 a year.

Building many more jails is unlikely—even if more jails could solve the problem of crowding—because of financial, political, and ideological reasons. Local governments, especially counties, face severe budget problems. When money is in short supply, roads and other services take priority over jails in the competition for funds. Politically, jails have no constituency—prisoners do not vote, and few voters support their cause. Ideologically, the "coddling criminals at the country club" idea hinders spending money on jails because people conclude that those who get in trouble, whether they are convicted or not, ought to be uncomfortable.

Taxpayers favor getting tough on criminals, but resist paying to do so. After the Lucas County Commissioners unveiled plans for a new jail, the *Toledo Blade* accused the commissioners of being

> undaunted, unhearing, and unswayed by common sense and moving into a position to cram down the public's craw an extravagant, overblown jail that will cost at least 11.4 million dollars. And that amount of money does not include the small fortune that will be spent on equipment and accessories to decorate the jail in the style and comfort its three hundred or so short-term inmates can be expected to enjoy.[69]

Jails and the Courts

Jails have increasingly come under the scrutiny and control of the federal government, which participates in local jail administration by providing direct financial aid, technical assistance, and training. But the courts, especially activist judges in the lower federal courts, have led the way in actively intervening in the administration of local jails. However, the Supreme Court has put limits on the degree to which courts may interfere. While accepting that jail inmates have rights, the Court, in the landmark case of *Bell v. Wolfish,* signaled a retreat from what activist judges in lower federal courts had been doing. (See Chapter 14 on prisoners and the law.)

New-Generation Jails

> The scene resembles a college dormitory with a student union lounge attached. At one end of a large, colorful room, a handful of young men are watching television; in another area, a second group watches a different set. Two inmates are playing ping-pong. A group of inmates goes up to the uniformed deputy, who is chatting amiably with someone, and asks him for the volleyball. He gives it to them, and they rush out the door to the recreation yard. Another man pads from the shower room to his private room, where he closes the door for privacy.
>
> The area is bright, sunny, and clean. The furniture—sofas and chairs—is comfortable and clean. The carpet on the floor is unstained. No one has scratched his initials in the paint or on the butcher-block tables and desks. Windows allow a view of the outside. Despite all the activity, the room is relatively quiet. The television volume is low, and no one is shouting.[70]

This describes the typical activity in a dozen or so **new-generation jails** in the United States. Endorsed by such prestigious bodies as the Advisory Board of the National Institute of Corrections, the American Jail Association, the American Institute of Architects' Committee on Architecture for Criminal Justice, and the American Correctional Association, new-generation jails combine architecture, management philosophy and operation, and staff training to produce a revolutionary change in jails and their administration. When the Federal Bureau of Prisons, traditionally an innovative force in American corrections, developed the new-generation jail concept, it followed the basic directive: "If you can't rehabilitate, at least do no harm." Three federal Metropolitan Correctional Centers (MCCs) were built in Chicago, New York, and San Diego to provide humane, secure detention.[71]

Inmates in new-generation jails resemble those in all jails, except for the 5 to 10 percent of mentally ill and especially violent prisoners whom new-generation jails screen out. Furthermore, these jails, like all jails, confine prisoners; prisoners cannot come and go as they please outside their own units. The differences between traditional jails and new-generation jails lie in architecture, management, and staff training. As to architecture, new-generation jails follow a **podular design.** Figure 13.6 illustrates the podular design of a living unit. In most traditional jails, a hallway or corridor lined with cells allows intermittent surveillance as officers periodically walk down the hallways (see Figure 13.7). Officers control only the area they can see; prisoners control the remainder. The podular design includes the following characteristics:

- Security concentration on outside perimeter—impregnable walls and windows.
- Restricted movement inside jail. (Unit officers do not have keys; officer in a control booth can allow movement in and out of the unit by closed-circuit television and intercom.)
- Free movement and as few barriers as possible inside living units.
- Living units with fewer than fifty prisoners to give officers an unobstructed view of the entire area.
- Private rooms for prisoners.
- Standard building materials for both cost and appearance.

Podular design allows officers to conduct constant surveillance. This surveillance might be remote, as it is in some new-generation jails in which physical barriers separate officers and prisoners. The other direct style, considered more desirable, puts officers in constant contact with prisoners to supervise their behavior. Officers do not have offices; they may have desks in the living unit.

Mixed reviews initially greeted new-generation jails. They were viewed as soft on criminals, providing them with a luxury motel at public expense. But they have achieved remarkable success. Violent incidents have diminished by as much as 90 percent. Homosexual rape has virtually disappeared. Private rooms allow prisoners to go to their own rooms to cool off instead of responding with violence. Vandalism and graffiti have nearly vanished. In the new jail at Pima, Arizona, for example, the number of damaged mattresses dropped from 150 a year to none; from two television sets needing repair per week to two in two years; from an average 99 sets of prisoners' clothes

Figure 13.6

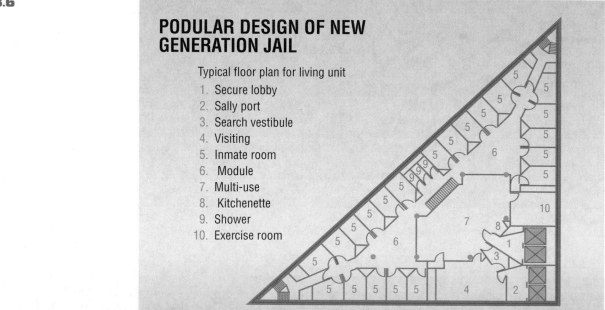

PODULAR DESIGN OF NEW GENERATION JAIL

Typical floor plan for living unit
1. Secure lobby
2. Sally port
3. Search vestibule
4. Visiting
5. Inmate room
6. Module
7. Multi-use
8. Kitchenette
9. Shower
10. Exercise room

Source: Supplied by Federal Bureau of Prisons, *Metropolitan Correctional Center* (Chicago, IL).

Figure 13.7

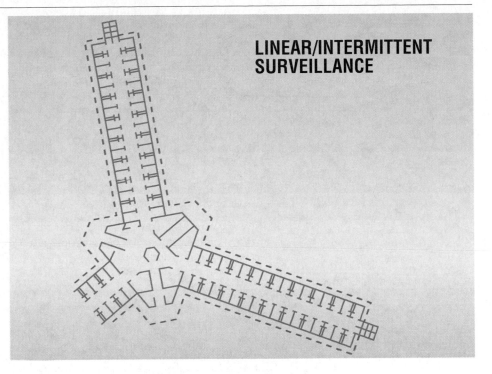

LINEAR/INTERMITTENT SURVEILLANCE

destroyed every week to 15 in two years. All this occurs in jails no more expensive, and perhaps cheaper to construct, than traditional jails. Vandal-proof materials cost much more than standard materials, such as porcelain plumbing. Operating costs drop as a result of the sharp reduction in staff absenteeism, by as much as 40 percent.[72]

Architecture alone does not account for the success of new-generation jails. "You can't run a new-generation jail with old-generation management," said the new commander of a major jail whose revamped podular design "had turned into a nightmare for staff and inmates." **Direct supervision** is indispensable to providing safe, secure, economical confinement. Direct supervision places officers in living units—not in control booths—and in constant contact with prisoners. Officers in constant contact get to know prisoners and can recognize and respond to trouble before it escalates into violence. Negotiation and verbal communication replace physical force. Strong evidence indicates that women officers do at least as well as men officers working in all-male units. Women make up as much as 40 percent of the officers in new-generation jails.[73]

New-generation jails have had positive effects not only on prisoners and budgets, but also on staff. Better surroundings benefit staff as much as, perhaps more than, prisoners, since in the long run staff spend more time in the jail than prisoners who face temporary confinement. According to Richard Weiner and his associates, jails that are clean, vandalism- and graffiti-free, carpeted, less noisy, safe, and peaceful also help staff morale:

> Officers and inmates [agree] that direct supervision works better than traditional approaches. Most of the officers acknowledged that what was good for the inmates helped them as well, by improving conditions and reducing tension.[74]

Stephen H. Gettinger reports:

> The relatively pleasant atmosphere of the new-generation jail is de-signed with the officer in mind even more than the inmate. Without fear of assault, officers can relax and pay attention to their jobs. They are encouraged to mix actively with the inmates and are given author-ity to solve problems on their own. Officers learn leadership skills that

will serve them well on the streets and equip them for management roles in the future. This job is more satisfying.[75]

New-generation jails are by no means panaceas. Women may not fare as well in them as men, according to Patrick G. Jackson and Cindy A. Stearns, who evaluated the new-generation jail in Sonoma County, California. Sonoma County built their jail after a federal court declared the conditions in the old jail unconstitutional. According to Jackson and Stearns,

> the cramped and poorly ventilated old jail was dirty, was loud, smelled, and, for most of the 225-or-so inmates and a much smaller staff, had all the negative trappings that go along with intermittent surveillance in linear facilities: a climate of fear, an absence of privacy, a lack of positive leadership, and so on.[76]

The new Sonoma County jail opened in 1991. A state-of-the art jail, it includes the two cornerstones of new-generation jails. First is podular architecture, including five two-tiered living quarters shaped in a semicircle facing an officers' station that is not enclosed by bars or glass barriers. Each "pod" contains a medical unit and a recreational area exposed to natural light, showers, carpeted floors, television, and telephones. Wall-to-wall carpet and acoustical ceilings reduce noise, pastel-painted walls improve appearance, and plenty of inexpensive wood and plastic furniture replaces the harsh metal of traditional jails. Second is direct supervision. Correctional officers are trained extensively in interpersonal communications. They manage problems proactively. Continuous, direct, and personal supervision is supposed to put control of the jail in the hands of the officers, not the inmates. Inmates are managed by positive reinforcement, not by "brute force or steel bars."[77]

Jackson and Stearns measured the attitudes, perceptions, and behaviors of inmates in the old jail before transfer, and in the new jail after transfer. They found that women experienced the conditions of confinement in the new-generation jail differently from men. Men's perceptions of jail improved while women experienced increased dissatisfaction. The researchers suspect that the reason for this difference lies in the new-generation jail philosophy that

> seeks to lessen the development, breadth, intensity, and/or continuity of interpersonal networks or peer groups that might be perceived as supportive of inmate control of an institution. It is precisely these kinds of relationships between inmates that past research suggests has been of differential importance to female and male inmates.[78]

In addition to the possible negative effects on women inmates, new-generation jails require more staff, an expense that taxpayers and administrators may feel they cannot afford in jails with fewer than 50 beds. Building traditional jails is also an easier sell in the political climate of "getting tough on criminals" in which new-generation jails can easily be portrayed as "coddling criminals." Administrators and managers also remain skeptical about direct supervision, although direct supervision has strong supporters across the political spectrum, including hard-line correctional officers and criminal justice professors, liberals and conservatives. These supporters advocate that we incarcerate people *as* punishment, not *for* punishment. They maintain that humane, safe, secure confinement is enough punishment without adding bad conditions. Besides, not only the inmates benefit from new-generation jail architecture and management; so do the people who work in the jails.[79]

Private Prisons and Jails

The administration of criminal justice in the United States has never been wholly public. Until 1850, police forces were private patrols, and privately hired detectives prevailed over public police forces. Until publicly funded prosecutors were established in the 1850s, victims were responsible for prosecuting their cases. Private defense attorneys are a major part of the criminal defense bar, although public defenders are common in large cities. Probation began as a private and often charitable operation in the middle of the nineteenth century. Juvenile corrections was largely a private operation as well during the nineteenth century, and about 40 percent of juvenile correctional facilities remain privately administered.

Private parties have also played their part in the history of adult corrections, although a lesser part than in other spheres of criminal justice. Until 1825, adult corrections was exclusively a public enterprise. In that year, the merchant Joel Scott offered to pay the state of Kentucky $1,000 to lease him all the prisoners in the inefficiently run and costly Frankfort prison. In return for the right to work the prisoners, Scott agreed to house, clothe, and feed them, and he promised further to pay the state half the profits made from the convict labor. This arrangement, which lasted until the 1880s, reported profits and no mistreatment of prisoners. Throughout the South and West, states followed Kentucky's example, contracting prisoners out to work in coal mines and factories and to build roads and railroads. Most states abandoned the contract labor system by 1900. Both organized labor and manufacturers who did not hire contract prison labor opposed the system because it competed unfavorably with free labor.[80]

Private business has also provided prison services, including food preparation and medical care, as well as education, training, and other programs. In addition, private organizations contracted to provide 70 percent of the Federal Bureau of Prisons' halfway houses. In 1986, the Corrections Corporation of America broke new ground in the history of adult corrections when it opened the first private state prison in the United States. The prison, located at Marion, Kentucky, is a 300-bed minimum security facility for "clients" within three years of parole. Great fanfare followed. Virtually all the news networks, print media, talk shows, and politicians talked again of an old device, **privatization,** private management of correctional facilities.[81]

Privatization has come to public attention as business takes advantage of the newest and perhaps largest "growth industry," and government seeks to cut public expenditures for the steep increase in the use of imprisonment. The demand for prison space to house the burgeoning prison population, the skyrocketing cost of building facilities, and the fiscal shortfalls in current public budgets have combined to generate the interest in private prisons. Both federal and state governments project large increases in demand for prison space.

The proposals for privatization have stimulated a lively debate. The National Sheriff's Association, at one end, expressed its disapproval of and opposition to private jails. At the other end, the executive director of the American Correctional Association suggested that "We ought to give business a try."

Available research provides at best mixed results to many questions surrounding private prisons and jails. Contracting out medical services and staff training to the private sector may be cost effective, according to some evidence. The National Institute of Justice found that private enterprise promises the most benefits in providing work programs, but saw little participation by businesses in such programs. Former Supreme Court Justice Warren Burger's hope for "factories with fences" instead of warehouses with walls has not come to pass. Private financing for prison construction holds some promise in easing the burden on general revenues and avoiding debt ceilings often placed on government unit bonding issues. Despite the publicity surrounding "prisons for profit," little change has occurred in the ownership and operation of state prisons. The Marion, Kentucky, prison (opened in 1986); a 200-bed, all-security-level women's prison in Grants, New Mexico (opened in 1989); and a 600-bed medium security prison in Winnfield,

Louisiana (opened in 1990) remain exceptions. Adult corrections are still overwhelmingly public, and promise to remain so.[82]

In a lengthy survey of private prisons, David Shichor found the following:

● There are no constitutional barriers to establishing private prisons.
● Available evidence does not strongly support the assumption that privatization is more cost-effective than public operation of prisons.
● Evaluations show that privately operated prisons and jails may provide higher-quality services for lower costs in some places under special circumstances.
● Negative consequences and hidden costs are potentially extensive.[83]

Prisoners

Most prisoners in the United States are nonwhite men under 30 years old who have not graduated from high school (see Figure 13.8). The numbers in Figure 13.8 represent only averages; as in all generalizations about criminal justice, national figures vary markedly according to region. To take but one example, consider the racial distribution of prisoners. Forty-five percent of the prisoners in state and federal prisons are African American. However, in Stateville, the Illinois maximum security prison near Chicago, 80 percent of the prisoners are African American. In Lorten Central, the prison outside Washington, D.C., 99 percent of the prisoners are African American. Furthermore, the racial and ethnic composition of prison populations is changing. The percent of nonwhite prisoners is rising; the rate of incarceration for African and Hispanic Americans has risen sharply since 1980 (see Figure 13.9). The number of older prisoners is also increasing. If the current practices of longer sentences and mandatory minimum sentences, particularly of the "three strikes and you're out" variety, continue (see Chapter 11), the graying of the prison population will continue to add to prison costs, particularly by contributing to a rise in geriatric costs.[84]

Most prisoners have grown up in single-parent homes, where they frequently endured sexual or physical abuse. Forty percent have immediate family members who have spent time in prison. Half have never married; 20 percent are divorced or separated. White prisoners have a much higher divorce and separation rate than African-American prisoners. Even though

Figure 13.8

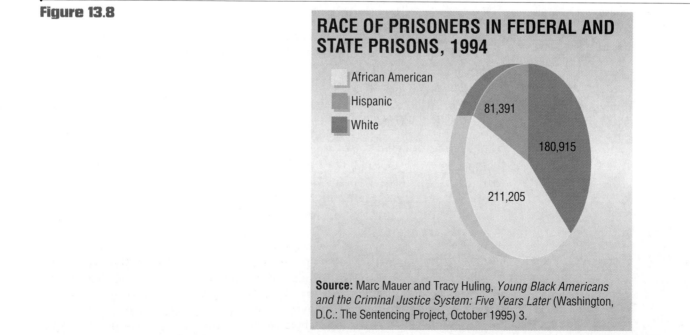

RACE OF PRISONERS IN FEDERAL AND STATE PRISONS, 1994

African American
Hispanic
White

81,391

180,915

211,205

Source: Marc Mauer and Tracy Huling, *Young Black Americans and the Criminal Justice System: Five Years Later* (Washington, D.C.: The Sentencing Project, October 1995) 3.

Figure 13.9

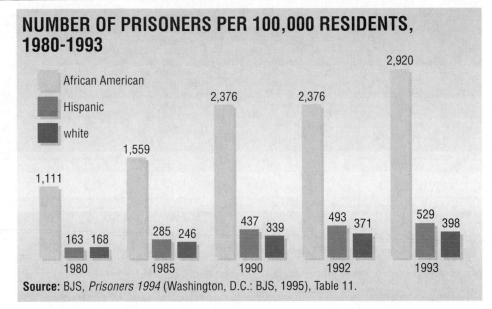

NUMBER OF PRISONERS PER 100,000 RESIDENTS, 1980-1993

African American

Hispanic

white

	1980	1985	1990	1992	1993
African American	1,111	1,559	2,376	2,376	2,920
Hispanic	163	285	437	493	529
white	168	246	339	371	398

Source: BJS, *Prisoners 1994* (Washington, D.C.: BJS, 1995), Table 11.

most prisoners are not married, more than half have children, and more than a third have three or more children, almost all under eighteen.[85]

The educational levels of prisoners fall far below the national average. In the general population, 85 percent of males between ages 20 and 29 have finished high school; only 40 percent of prisoners have done so. Prisoners have a school dropout rate three times greater than the general population. Six percent of all prisoners have had no schooling at all. Practically none have college degrees. Educational level is closely linked to conviction offense. White prisoners with more than a high-school education are more likely to commit drug offenses, fraud, embezzlement, and forgery. Public-order offenses are more common among prisoners with little education. Prisoners with some college education are less likely to either commit violent crimes or to have prior criminal records. Prisoners, on the whole, have poor work records. Most had little or no legal income before incarceration. Nearly 40 percent were unemployed. The incarceration rate for employed persons is 356 per 100,000. For the unemployed, it rises sharply to 933 per 100,000. Forty percent of prisoners have either never had legitimate jobs or worked only sporadically. Average income for half of all prisoners is at the poverty level.[86]

George Beto, former director of the Texas Department of Corrections—with his typical and welcome bluntness—depicted the character of most prisoners:

> Not only society but also governmental leaders need to remember the character of those who come to the doors and gates of America's prisons . . . they are the poor, the stupid, the inept, the flotsam and jetsam of society. Fifteen percent are illiterate; 90% are school dropouts; 65% come from broken homes; 40% had no sustained work experience prior to their incarceration; 20% are mentally retarded . . . they stumble from one mud puddle of life to another.[87]

Women Prisoners

Women comprise 6 percent of the prison population in the United States. The number of women incarcerated in the United States has tripled since 1980 (see Figure 13.10). The percent of women incarcerated in the United States is consistently higher than in most other countries. In Australia, for example, 2 percent of the prison population are women; Ethiopia, 1.9 percent; in Japan,

Figure 13.10

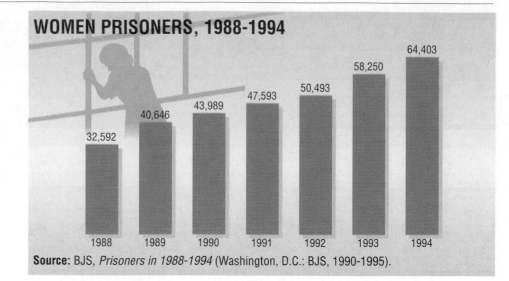

WOMEN PRISONERS, 1988-1994

						64,403

Source: BJS, *Prisoners in 1988-1994* (Washington, D.C.: BJS, 1990-1995).

2.2 percent; and in West Germany, 4 percent. According to a survey conducted by the American Correctional Association, women were first imprisoned for either theft or drug offenses. A considerable number of the women convicted of murder or manslaughter had killed husbands or boyfriends who had repeatedly and violently abused them. Women convicted of robbery were usually not the instigators of the crime. According to these findings, women prisoners are decidedly nonviolent. The traditional reasons given for the relatively small number of women prisoners compared to men have included the virtuous nature of women, their dependent status, and the code of chivalry. However, the reasons for the steep rise in the number of women prisoners since 1980 are *not* women's loss of virtue and dependence, nor the decline in chivalry, according to Barbara Owen and Barbara Bloom, who profiled women prisoners in California. It is mainly due to the growing numbers of women prosecuted and convicted of drug offenses, the increasingly harsh sentences for drug offenses, and the lack of both treatment and

The numbers of women prisoners is rising sharply, mainly because of the increasingly harsh penalties for drug offenses.

community sanctions for women drug offenders. In fact, Bloom and Owen argue that the "war on drugs" is really a war on women.[88]

The rise in the number of women prisoners has more to do with politics and policy than with an actual increase in the number of crimes women commit, according to Russ Immarigeon and Meda Chesney-Lind of the National Council on Crime and Delinquency:

> Women are arrested and imprisoned in greater numbers because of changes in legislative responses to the "war on drugs," law enforcement practices, and judicial decision-making rather than a shift in the nature of the crimes they commit. . . . [T]he drug war, in particular, with its emphasis on increasing the penalties for drug use and selling, may be having a significant effect on women's imprisonment. Simply put, the criminal justice system now seems more willing to incarcerate women.[89]

The National Council on Crime and Delinquency report, *Women's Prisons: Overcrowded and Overused,* recommended that correctional leaders avoid "build[ing] their way out of" the steep rise in the number of women convicted of crimes. As alternatives, the report recommends basing criminal sanctions on the "least restrictive alternative consistent with public safety." Women "overwhelmingly commit crimes that, while unacceptable, pose little threat to the physical safety of the community at large." Dennis Wagner observed women ex-convicts for two years after their release from Taycheedah women's prison in Wisconsin. He found that women were 44 percent less likely to commit further crimes than men. If they did recidivate, they were one-third less likely than men to commit serious crimes against persons. Joan McDermott surveyed female offenders in New York. She found that 16.9 percent of women released from prison returned, compared to 37.3 percent of men.[90]

Special Management Prisoners

Officially sanctioned segregation of prisoners occurs in the case of prisoners with special problems, for example, **protective custody units.** Prison administration developed protective custody as a method of providing around-the-clock protection for prisoners afraid to mingle with the general prison population. The special units devoted to protective custody increasingly house prisoners fearful of racial attacks.[91]

"You have three choices," one prison administrator answered regarding **special management inmates,** those in need of special care. "You can pitch your program to the majority of inmates, in which case the needs of special groups will not be met. You can tailor your efforts to the minority of special inmates, which means that the majority will suffer. Or you can run two separate programs."

Many prisons run two or more separate programs for special management inmates, who fall into three categories:

1. *The vulnerable*—that rapidly growing group of inmates requiring some form of protection in order to survive in the prison setting.
2. *The troublemaker*—those who must be subjected to additional restraints in order to protect other inmates, staff, or the security of the institution.
3. *The mentally abnormal*—those who, because of emotional or mental problems or retardation, cannot function in the general population without assistance or who need professional treatment and medication.

Special management inmates create problems for the prison administration. According to a report of the Bureau of Justice Statistics, "Prisons must handle large numbers of people in standardized ways if they are to stay within their budgets and if equity issues are not to be raised."[92]

Prisoner Illegal Drug Use

Virtually all available empirical research has attributed the steep increases in the numbers of prisoners generally, and particularly in the numbers of nonwhite and female prisoners, to the rise in arrest, prosecution, and sentencing of drug offenders. Moreover, most of the empirical research also demonstrates that a substantial number of prisoners are drug users. Seven out of every eight prisons test some prisoners for use of one or more illegal drugs. The methods used include questioning, pat-downs, clothing exchanges, and body cavity searches. Figure 13.11 depicts the results of drug testing in state prisons. In 1990, about 16 percent of prisoners in state prisons and a little over 3 percent of federal prisoners test positive for some drug. According to prisoner self-reports, more than one-third were under the influence of illicit drugs either when they committed their crimes or when they were admitted to prison. Nearly two-thirds of all prisoners say that they have used one or more illicit drugs at some time during their life. More than 40 percent used illicit drugs on a daily basis during the month before their commitment offense; 18 percent admitted to use of a major illicit drug on a daily basis during the month before their offense. Approximately 40 percent use amphetamines and barbiturates, nearly twice the rate for the general population. Rates of illicit drug use vary, but the largest number occurs in major cities. Even among cities, drug use varies greatly, from a high of 78 percent of men arrested in San Diego and 76 percent of women in Philadelphia, to a low of 30 percent of men arrested in Omaha and 39 percent of women arrested in Indianapolis.[93]

More than a third of prisoners drink heavily, meaning at any one drinking session they consume the equivalent of eight cans of beer, seven glasses of wine, or nine ounces of 82-proof liquor. During the year before they were arrested, two-thirds of all prisoners claimed, possibly as a rationalization, that they drank this heavily every day. For most prisoners under the influence of drugs at the time they committed their offenses, the drug was marijuana, usually combined with heroin. Women are more likely than men to use heroin; white prisoners drink more heavily than black prisoners. Finally, prisoners with long criminal records are more likely to drink right before committing crimes, drink more heavily, and get drunk more often than those with fewer prior convictions.[94]

Figure 13.11

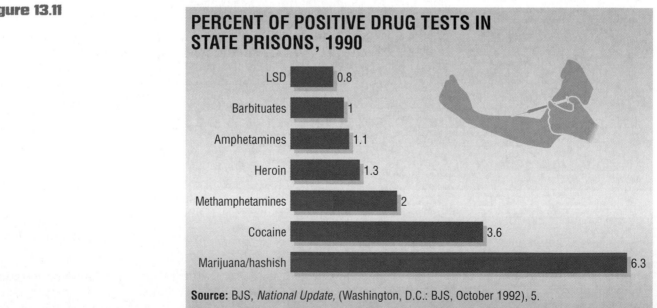

PERCENT OF POSITIVE DRUG TESTS IN STATE PRISONS, 1990

LSD	0.8
Barbituates	1
Amphetamines	1.1
Heroin	1.3
Methamphetamines	2
Cocaine	3.6
Marijuana/hashish	6.3

Source: BJS, *National Update,* (Washington, D.C.: BJS, October 1992), 5.

"Is There a 'Better Way' than Imprisoning Young African Americans?"

[In 1990, The Sentencing Project, a national nonprofit organization that promotes sentencing reform and conducts research on criminal justice issues, released a report documenting that 23 percent of African-American males between the ages of 20 and 29 were under some form of correctional supervision on any given day, either on probation or parole, or in jail or prison. In 1995, The Sentencing Project issued a follow-up report, entitled "Young Black Americans and the Criminal Justice System: Five Years Later." The new study reported that the situation had worsened considerably. The following excerpts are taken from the 1995 report.]

● Almost one in three (32.2%) young black men in the age group 20-29 is under criminal justice supervision on any given day—in prison or jail, on probation or parole.
● The cost of criminal justice control for these 827,440 young African American males is about $6 billion a year.
● In recent years, African American women have experienced the greatest increase in criminal justice supervision of all demographic groups, with their rate of criminal justice supervision rising by 78% from 1989-94.
● Drug policies constitute the single most significant factor contributing to the rise in criminal justice populations in recent years, with the number of incarcerated drug offenders having risen by 510% from 1983 to 1993. The number of Black (non-Hispanic) women incarcerated in state prisons for drug offenses increased more than eight-fold— 828%—from 1986 to 1991. . . .
● African Americans and Hispanics constitute almost 90% of offenders sentenced to state prison for drug possession. . . .

Criminal Justice Control Rates In the 1990s

Our 1990 report documented shockingly high rates of criminal justice control for young African American males in particular. We find that many of the contributing factors to these high rates endure or have worsened in the intervening years. As a result, they have failed to slow the increasing rate of criminal justice control for young black males and they have contributed to a dramatic rise in the number of black women in the criminal justice system. These factors include:

● The continuing overall growth of the criminal justice system;
● The continuing disproportionate impact of the "war on drugs" on minority populations;
● The new wave of "get tough" sentencing policies and their potential impact on criminal justice populations;
● The continuing difficult circumstances of life for many young people living in low-income urban areas in particular.

The Overrepresentation of Young Black Males in the Criminal Justice System

We have documented the dramatically high rates of criminal justice control for young black men. In many respects it would be quite surprising if these rates were not high, given the social and economic circumstances and crime rates in their communities. The growth of the criminal justice system in the past twenty years has coincided with a host of economic disruptions and changes in social policy that have had profound effects on income distribution, employment and family structure. Since the 1970s, many urban areas have witnessed the decline of manufacturing, the expansion of low-wage service industries and the loss of a significant part of the middle class tax base. Real wages have declined for most Americans during this period, with a widening of the gap between rich and poor beginning in the 1980s. For black male high school dropouts in their twenties, annual earnings fell by a full 50 percent from 1973 to 1989. Social service benefits such as mental health services and other supports have generally declined while the social problems that they address have been exacerbated.

The impact of these changes on the African American community has resulted from the intersection of race and class effects. Since African Americans are disproportionately represented in low-income urban communities, the effects of these social ills are intensified. As Douglas Massey and Nancy Denton have illustrated, the persistence of housing segregation exacerbates the difficult life circumstances of these communities, contributing to extremely high rates of unemployment, poor schooling, and high crime rates.

Over the years many researchers have examined the extent to which racial disparity within the criminal justice system can be explained by higher crime rates among blacks or other relevant factors. . . . While some studies have documented specific cases of racially unwarranted outcomes, much research has concluded that, with one significant exception, race plays a relatively minor role in sentencing and incarceration. Michael Tonry's review, for example, concludes that "for nearly a decade there has been a near consensus among scholars and policy analysts that most of the black punishment disproportions result not from racial bias or discrimination within the system but from patterns of black offending and of blacks' criminal records." Similarly, Alfred Blumstein's research has concluded that 76 percent of the racial disparity in prison populations is explained by higher rates of offending among blacks for serious offenses. But both authors find, as Tonry indicates, that drug law enforcement is the conspicuous exception. Blacks are arrested and confined in numbers grossly out of line with their use or sale of drugs. Blumstein concludes that for drug offenses, fully half of the racial disproportions in prison are not explained by higher arrest rates.

While scholars will continue to study the relative influence of race within the criminal justice system, several key issues should not go unaddressed in explaining these disparities. First, as noted above, it is difficult to isolate the relative influence of race and class in public policy and decision making. That is, to the extent that African Americans are overrepresented in the criminal justice system, to what degree is this a function of their being disproportionately low-income? . . .

Studies of sentencing practices reveal that the current offense and the offender's prior record are the most significant factors determining a prison sentence. But if low-income youth are more subject to police scrutiny and have fewer counseling and treatment resources available to them than middle class adolescents, their youthful criminal activities will more likely result in a criminal record that will affect their chances of going to prison later on. . . .

Impact of the "War on Drugs"

While debate will continue on the degree to which the criminal justice system overall contributes to racial disparities, there is increasing evidence that the set of policies and practices contained within the phrase "war on drugs" has been an unmitigated disaster for young blacks and other minorities. Whether or not these policies were consciously or unconsciously designed to incarcerate more minorities is a question that may be debated. In essence, though, what we have seen are policy choices that have not only failed to reduce the scale of the problem but have seriously eroded the life prospects of the primary targets of those policies. . . .

Looking at minorities overall, we find that African Americans and Hispanics represented almost 90% of all sentences to state prison for drug possession offenses in 1992, the most recent year for which data are available. While we have no available data regarding other factors which often correlate with a higher likelihood of incarceration, particularly prior criminal record, the findings displayed here are of such magnitude that they raise serious questions about the racial implications of current drug policies. In summing up the rationale and impact of prevailing drug policies, Professor Michael Tonry states:

> All that is left is politics. The War on Drugs and the set of harsh crime control policies in which it was enmeshed were undertaken to achieve political, not policy, objectives. It is the adoption for political purposes of policies with foreseeable disparate impacts, the use of disadvantaged black Americans as means to achieving politicians' electoral ends, that must in the end be justified. It cannot.

Impact of High Rates of Control on the African American Community

The high rate of incarceration of African American males raises concerns about its impact not only on the individuals who are incarcerated, but on their communities as well. As increasing numbers of young black men are arrested and incarcerated, their life prospects are seriously diminished. Their possibilities for gainful employment are reduced, thereby making them less attractive as marriage partners and unable to provide for children they father. This in turn contributes to the deepening of poverty in low-income communities.

The large scale rates of incarceration may contribute to the destruction of the community fabric in other ways as well. As prison becomes a common experience for young males, its stigmatizing effect is diminished. Further, gang or crime group affiliations on the outside may be reinforced within the prison only to emerge stronger as the individuals are released back to the community. With so few males in underclass communities having stable ties to the labor market, the ubiquitous ex-offenders and gang members may become the community's role models.

The cumulative impact of these high rates of incarceration has been to postpone the time at which large numbers of African American males start careers and families. While we should not ignore the fact that these men have committed crimes that led to their imprisonment, current crime control policies may actually be increasing the severity of the problem, particularly when other options for responding to crime exist.

Increasing Criminal Justice Control Rates for Women

While we have seen that criminal justice control rates for young black men are shockingly high and increasing, from 1989 to 1994 young African-American women experienced the greatest increase in criminal justice control of all demographic groups studied. The 78% increase in criminal justice control rates for black women was more than double the increase for black men and for white women, and more than nine times the increase for white men.

What is causing this dramatic increase in the numbers of young black women under criminal justice control? Although research on women of color in the criminal justice system is limited, existing data and research suggest it is the combination of race and sex effects that is at the root of the trends which appear in our data. For example, while the number of blacks and Hispanics in prison is growing at an alarming rate, the rate of increase for women is even greater. Between 1980 and 1992 the female prison population increased 276%, compared to 163% for men. Unlike men of color, women of color thus belong to two groups that are experiencing particularly dramatic growth in their contact with the criminal justice system. The key factor behind this explosion in the women's prison population is the war on drugs. We see this taking place at several levels. . . .

African American Women and The War on Drugs

Looking at the criminal justice data that are available by gender and race/ethnicity a picture emerges of individuals who are doubly disadvantaged. Nationally, between 1980 and 1992 the number of black females in state or federal prisons grew 278% while the numbers of black males grew 186%; overall the inmate population increased by 168% during this period.

An enormous increase in the numbers of black women incarcerated for drug offenses is the primary factor causing this trend. Our analysis of Justice Department data shows that between 1986 and 1991, the number of black non-Hispanic women in state prisons for drug offenses nationwide increased more than eight-fold in this five-year period, from 667 to 6,193. This 828% increase was nearly double the increase for black non-Hispanic males and more than triple the increase for white non-Hispanic females. . . .

Lack of Access to Treatment

Problems caused by the limited availability of drug treatment programs and facilities, particularly for low-income individuals, are also compounded for women. Overall, while women make up 33% of the addicted population, only 20.6% of treatment resources are used for women. A 1991 Bureau of Justice Assistance report indicates that women arrestees (interviewed at 4 DUF sites) have had limited treatment experience. Nearly three-fourths (71%) had never been in treatment for substance abuse, and only 4% were in treatment at the time of their arrest. . . .

Women, Children, and the Criminal Justice System: Is There a Better Way?

While more research is needed to determine how race and gender bias may have contributed to the rise in the number of women of color under criminal justice control, it seems clear that the war on drugs has succeeded only in criminalizing women already suffering under extreme socio- economic and psychological stress. The consequences of continuing on this path are dire not only for the women involved but for future generations. The multiple negative effects of parental arrest and incarceration on children, particularly if that parent is the primary caretaker, are well- documented, and include traumatic stress, loss of self-confidence, aggression, withdrawal, depression, gang activity, and interpersonal violence. As more and more inner-city children lose not only their fathers but their mothers, most often the primary caretakers, to the criminal justice system, their own risks for future involvement in crime and incarceration increase dramatically.

In recent testimony before the U.S. Senate Judiciary Committee, Elaine Lord, the warden of New York State's maximum security prison for women, suggests a very different course:

> We need to be more honest with ourselves that the vast majority of women receiving prison sentences are not the business operatives of the drug networks. The glass ceiling seems to operate for women whether we are talking about legitimate or illegitimate business. They [women] are very small cogs in a very large system, not the organizers or backers of illegal drug empires. This, coupled with a growing mood among the American public reportedly concerned about early intervention for troubled kids and more drug treatment in preference to more prisons, should give us the opening we need to look at better and more cost-effective ways of dealing with women offenders. . . .

Recommendations

. . . 1. Revise national spending priorities. Since the mid-1980s, both Republican and Democratic administrations have directed about two-thirds of federal drug funding toward law enforcement and only one-third toward prevention and treatment. The lack of available treatment has been documented by the Department of Health and Human Services which reports that of the 2.4 million drug users who could benefit from treatment, 1 million can not have access to treatment each year.

2. Expand drug treatment within the criminal justice system. Criminal justice personnel throughout the country uniformly cite the need for expanded treatment options. New programs such as drug courts and prosecutorial diversion to treatment have met with widespread professional and community support. With the exception of treatment in prison, efforts to expand funding for drug courts and other treatment options have been folded into block grant funding where they are not likely to receive a high level of support.

3. Provide treatment programs which address the multiple and specific needs of women. Despite the fact that women involved with the criminal justice system are more likely than men to use drugs, and use more serious drugs, existing treatment models have not always been designed to incorporate the particular circumstances and multiple needs of women. Programs that accommodate children and address the range of economic, social and psychological stressors that contribute to substance abuse and drug-related crime among women should be developed and made available to women.

4. Promote a renewed dialogue on drug policy. While drug policy discussions of the 1980s were often heated and contentious, they nonetheless served to explore the range of options available to respond to substance abuse. Little such discussion exists today, as seen by the low priority given by the Justice Department to its 1994 report on mandatory sentencing or the disciplining of former Surgeon General Joycelyn Elders for advocating a discussion of drug policy. It is unconscionable to inhibit a broad discussion of a range of policy alternatives, particularly as we continue to be confronted by the tragic consequences of current policies.

5. A long-term goal clearly should be to reduce crime and the numbers of people entering the criminal justice system. An intermediate strategy, though, could reduce the severity of criminal justice control without compromising public safety by creating a broader array of sentencing options for non-violent offenders who would otherwise be sentenced to prison.

6. A variety of sentencing policies adopted nationally since 1980 have exacerbated the problems faced by women and minorities in the criminal justice system. The injustices caused by mandatory sentencing and its failure to have an impact on crime have been well documented. Of particular concern here is the disparity in sentencing between crack cocaine and powder cocaine that is present in the federal courts and many states. In addition to the racial disparities that have been demonstrated, eliminating this disparity in the federal system would lead to a long-term reduction of about 15,000 person years in the federal prisons.

7. In recent years the federal government and some state legislatures have adopted policies requiring a fiscal impact statement prior to consideration of any sentencing legislation in an effort to help legislators assess the long-term costs of any changes.

8. Criminal justice policy is often short-sighted and formulated in response to emotional appeals. The political power of the crime issue, the media sensationalism around atypical crimes, and the persistence of high crime rates join to limit discussion and planning. Unfortunately, we have seen the consequences of more than two decades of heavy investment in the criminal justice system to the detriment of other social programs.

Those who suggest that high rates of crime and drug abuse demand immediate solutions need only look back a decade to the inception of the current "drug war." Despite an enormous increase in the number of drug offenders in prison since then, little progress can be claimed for the law enforcement approach. Had a different set of choices been made at that time, the country might have been the beneficiary of more humane and effective solutions.

Questions

Which, if any, of the recommendations would you adopt, if you were a criminal justice policymaker? Why? Does any of these policy recommendations point to a "better way" to deal with crime, drugs, and young African-American men and women? Explain your answer. If you believe that imprisonment is the "better way," how do you justify your response, in view of the report and the recommendations of the Sentencing Project?

Prisoner Crimes of Commitment

The popular conception is that prisons are full of violent criminals. Some may even think that the public outrage over violence and drugs, the growing number of mandatory minimum sentence laws, the longer sentences judges hand out, and the tougher sentences making their way into the sentencing guidelines have resulted in the confinement of more violent criminals. The truth is that violent criminals make up less than half of the total prison population and represent less of the total than they did in 1980. The major reason: the steep rise in the number of drug offenders committed to prison. Figure 13.12 depicts the shifting distribution of prisoners according to the crimes for which they were convicted.

Figure 13.12

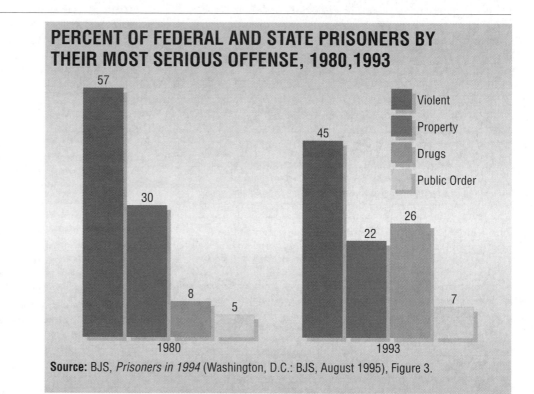

PERCENT OF FEDERAL AND STATE PRISONERS BY THEIR MOST SERIOUS OFFENSE, 1980, 1993

Violent
Property
Drugs
Public Order

Source: BJS, *Prisoners in 1994* (Washington, D.C.: BJS, August 1995), Figure 3.

Length of Imprisonment

mandatory release *time of release based on time off for good behavior or other statutory and administrative sentence reduction mechanisms.*

Time actually spent in prison varies according to the region of the country and according to conviction offense. Due to early release because of parole; **mandatory release** based on time off for good behavior or other statutory sentence reduction mechanisms; commutation; and pardons, prisoners serve less actual time than that prescribed by their sentences. Despite sharp increases in sentences prescribed by new legislation and tougher sentencing practices by judges, the average length of time actually served has only moderately increased in state prisons since 1985, when it was 20 months; in 1992, it was 22 months. The picture in federal prisons is different. There, the average time served rose from 15 months to 24 months. Most of that increase was due to the longer time served by drug offenders. The actual time served by drug offenders rose from 22 to 33 months, compared to an increase from 50 to 56 months by violent offenders.[95]

Several factors affect the length of time prisoners serve. Judges have considerable discretion both in sending people to prison and in deciding how long they will stay once they are there. In some states, parole boards' discretionary powers can lead to the release of prisoners almost as soon as they enter prison. Other states have eliminated parole boards or curtailed their powers. All states but Hawaii, Michigan, Missouri, and Pennsylvania have **good time laws** that allow prisoners to reduce their sentences by at least one-third, that is, one day for every three days served on good behavior. In some states, the rate of good time is as much as one-half. Prisoners can also earn good time for donating blood and for participating in education, treatment, or other programs.[96]

Prisoners also get credit for time spent in jail without bail, during trial, and after conviction waiting for sentences. Convicted murderers earn an average of 20 months for time spent in jail. For other crimes, the time earned is usually less: about 11 months for attempted murder and voluntary manslaughter, 9 months for rape, 7.6 for robbery, 5.7 for aggravated assault, 4.8 for burglary, and 4 for larceny. Increasingly, the heavy rise in prison admissions, mandatory minimum sentences, and crowded prisons have led to the controversial practice of early release. In other words, judges are sentencing more offenders to prison, but prisons, trying to cope with large populations, are releasing them early. The *You Decide,* "Is 'Lock 'em up' good public policy?" examines the problems arising from increased use of imprisonment.[97]

You Decide   Is "Lock 'em Up" Good Public Policy?

"Lock 'em Up" Is Good Public Policy

Most of the public, whatever their gender, race, or ethnic background, believe that violent and repeat offenders belong in prison. A group of academics and professionals representing such organizations as The Sentencing Project and the National Council on Crime and Delinquency, on the other hand, advocates the greater use of alternatives to imprisonment in some cases. According to John DiIulio, imprisonment is worth the cost. DiIulio and Anne Piehl analyzed prisoner self-report surveys that showed that the typical prisoner commits about twelve crimes a year. Crime depresses local business development and erodes local economic activity. According to some estimates, each street crime costs victims and society at least $2,300 in pain, suffering, and economic loss. At the average of twelve street crimes a year, that amounts to $27,600 per year. That means it is cheaper in most states to lock street criminals up than to allow them to be free on the street, according to DiIulio.[98]

Moreover, imprisonment may also reduce crime, according to Patrick A. Langan, a statistician for the Bureau of Justice Statistics. Langan examined admissions and re-

leases to U.S. prisons to explain the steep rise in prison populations. He found that the increase in mandatory sentencing laws and the rise in the crime-prone age group population of the baby-boom era only partially explained the rise. More than half the increase, Langan found, was due to the increased use of imprisonment by sentencing judges. He also noted a decrease in crimes measured by victim surveys during the same period. Langan concluded:

> Whether rising incarceration rates have reduced crime . . . cannot be said with certainty. What is clear is that, since 1973, per capita prison incarceration rates have risen to their highest levels ever while crime rates measured in the National Crime Survey . . . have gradually fallen to their lowest levels ever. The changing age structure apparently does not explain most of the declines. Whatever the causes, in 1989, there were an estimated 66,000 fewer rapes, 323,000 fewer robberies, 380,000 fewer assaults, and 3.3 million fewer burglaries . . . between 1973 versus those of 1989. If only one-half or even one-fourth of the reductions were the result of rising incarceration rates, that would still leave prisons responsible for sizable reductions in crime. That possibility must be seriously weighed in debates about America's prisons.[99]

"Lock 'em Up" Is Bad Public Policy

The National Council on Crime and Delinquency examined the strategy to reduce crime by increasing the probability and the length of imprisonment, particularly for drug offenses. The research focused on Florida. According to researcher James Austin, "More than any state, Florida has dramatically followed this course of increasing the use of imprisonment for drug crimes." Florida has increased the use of imprisonment most dramatically—by over 300 percent from 1980 to 1989 (see Figure 13.13). Despite the increase in both prison building and the number of prison admissions, the Florida prison system has released prisoners at an even greater rate during the same period, as shown in Figure 13.13. The result— shorter prison terms, dropping from an average of 24 months in 1980 to 9 months in 1989 (again see Figure 13.13).

According to the NCCD researchers:

- Based on the theories of deterrence and incapacitation, the sharp and huge rise in imprisonment should have produced a reduction in the crime rate. Instead, the crime rate rose 5 percent during the period. In fact, the steepest rise in crime accompanied the greatest rise in imprisonment, namely, between 1986 and 1989 (see Figure 13.13).
- The war on drugs has not produced a reduction in drug offenses. Admissions to prison for drug offenses rose by 1,825 percent over the decade, compared to an overall admission increase of 381 percent. For female

drug offenders, the rise was even greater—more than 3,000 percent. According to present data, the number of drug offenses continues to rise, not fall, despite the huge increase in prison admissions for drug offenses (see Figure 13.13).

- The explosion in the prison population creates a risk to public safety. Mandatory sentencing requires some prisoners to remain in prison, but it also forces the early release of ordinary prisoners. In one case, Charles Street, convicted of a violent crime, was released a year early. Following his early release, he murdered two Miami police officers. In another case, Robert and Harry Lebo were convicted for "molesting a crawfish trap." After their release, they were convicted of lobster theft. Under the habitual offender law, correctional authorities had to release two prisoners to make room for the Lebos. According to the researchers, "It is the worst of both worlds when nonviolent petty offenders are sentenced inappropriately to prison while dangerous criminals are released early."

Questions

What is the evidence for and against a tougher imprisonment policy? Is the case for imprisonment stronger or weaker than the case against it, as presented here? Is it possible that both are correct? Is Florida perhaps an exception to the national data that Langan and DiIulio present?

Figure 13.13

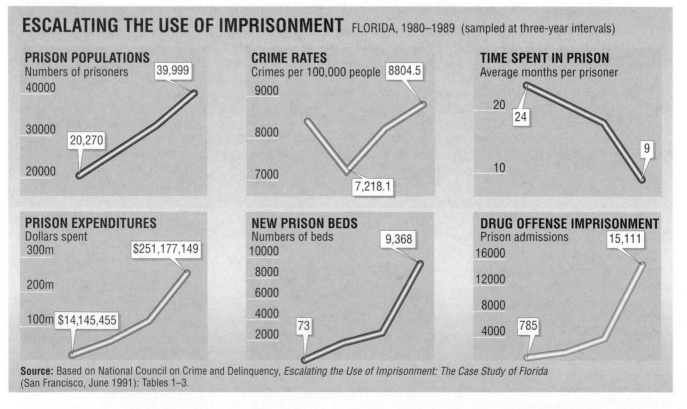

ESCALATING THE USE OF IMPRISONMENT FLORIDA, 1980–1989 (sampled at three-year intervals)

PRISON POPULATIONS Numbers of prisoners — 39,999; 40000; 30000; 20,270; 20000

CRIME RATES Crimes per 100,000 people — 8804.5; 9000; 8000; 7000; 7,218.1

TIME SPENT IN PRISON Average months per prisoner — 20; 24; 10; 9

PRISON EXPENDITURES Dollars spent — 300m; $251,177,149; 200m; 100m $14,145,455

NEW PRISON BEDS Numbers of beds — 10000; 9,368; 8000; 6000; 4000; 2000; 73

DRUG OFFENSE IMPRISONMENT Prison admissions — 15,111; 16000; 12000; 8000; 4000; 785

Source: Based on National Council on Crime and Delinquency, *Escalating the Use of Imprisonment: The Case Study of Florida* (San Francisco, June 1991): Tables 1–3.

Returning to Prison

Most prisoners are **recidivists,** or repeat offenders. Depending on the researcher, recidivism has a variety of meanings. It can include all crimes including juvenile offenses; all prior arrests; all criminal charges; all convictions; or only prior commitments to prison or jail. Nearly 85 percent of prisoners are not first-time offenders. Some time prior to their present imprisonment, they have been sentenced to either probation or incarceration as adults or juveniles. More than a fifth of all prisoners have been convicted six or more times. More than 60 percent have already spent time incarcerated for prior offenses. More than half have been convicted of at least one violent crime.[100]

The longer former prisoners remain out of prison, the less likely they are to return. Recidivism varies according to offense. Property offenders return to prison (36.8 percent) more frequently than violent offenders (31.5 percent). Burglars return most frequently, robbers next most frequently. Drug-related crimes, forgery, embezzlement, and sexual assault follow; homicide has the lowest recidivist rates. The more times prisoners are confined, the greater the likelihood they will return to prison. About a quarter of all prisoners with no prior record will return to prison; 37 percent of all prisoners with one or two prior prison terms will return; and 42.7 percent of those with three or more prior terms will be back in prison. Eighty percent of state prisoners in 1991 had previously served sentences either of probation or incarceration.[101]

Recidivism also varies with age, gender, and race. The younger prisoners are on release, the more likely they are to return to prison. In Massachusetts, for example, 31 percent of prisoners under age 25 will return to prison; between the ages of 25 and 29, 28 percent recidivate. At 30 and older, only 17 percent return to prison. Gender also affects recidivism. Men recidivate at substantially higher rates than women. In New York State, for example, 36 percent of released men return to prison; 12.1 percent of women return. Women are less likely to recidivate when support services are available in the community. Most imprisoned women have "serious economic, medical, mental health, and social difficulties which are often overlooked and frequently intensified" in prison. Community programs more effectively enable women to lead law-abiding lives than does imprisonment. In Pennsylvania, for example, the Program for Women Offenders found that its services reduced recidivism. In a random sample of more than a thousand clients, 3.2 percent recidivated. Intermediate sanctions such as home confinement and intensive supervision may also provide alternatives to imprisonment, if they include direct services. Whites recidivate at significantly lower levels than other races. In California, for example, 27.9 percent of released whites returned to prison. Blacks returned at a rate of 33.5 percent.[102]

Recidivism has three other critical characteristics. First, nearly 60 percent of all prisoners admitted to prison for the first time have been convicted before, but were sentenced to probation instead of prison. In fact, 27 percent of all prisoners were on probation when they were sentenced to their first prison term. Second, nearly 46 percent would still have been in prison when presently admitted if they had completely served out a prior maximum prison term. Third, more than a third of released prisoners are sent back to prison after completing the supervision period following release.

The incidence of recidivism has led to questions about the effectiveness of probation over prison, rehabilitation programs in prison, and community-based parole systems that facilitate ex-prisoners' reentry into the community. The information about high recidivism rates has resulted in several major changes affecting prison policy: mandatory prison terms, sentence enhancements for repeat offenders, the determinate sentence, sentencing guidelines, and parole guidelines. To some extent, these changes reflect a general hardening in public attitudes toward crime; they also stem from increased knowledge about how much recidivism actually occurs. As a result, imprisonment has become the dominant form of punishment.[103]

Women prisoners are committed for similar offenses as men. However, a higher proportion of women prisoners are committed for murder and property offenses than the percentages for men. The proportion of women committed for drug offenses has also risen, while the proportion of women committed for violent crimes has declined. Seventy percent of women prisoners have not finished high school; half had unskilled jobs or were unemployed prior to entering prison; 90 percent come from poor families; nearly three-quarters are nonwhite. Half have dependents.[104]

Summary

More than 1,000,000 people in the United States are confined in jails and prisons on any given day. The United States incarcerates more people per 100,000 of its population—and imprisons them longer—than any other country in the world, except for Russia. Furthermore, these numbers and rates are sharply rising in the United States while they are declining in other Western countries. The increases stem from a combination of causes. Public opinion demands harsher penalties; judges exercise discretion to sentence more offenders to longer imprisonment; legislatures have passed mandatory sentencing laws; sentencing guidelines have resulted in longer terms of imprisonment; and new drug laws have increased the penalties and reduced the discretion of judges in sentencing drug offenders. Half the prisoners in American prisons have been convicted of violent offenses; the other half consist of a mixture of property, public order, and— increasingly—drug law violators. Men outnumber women prisoners 90 to 1. Most prisoners are young, poorly educated, inadequately trained, and unemployed or underemployed. More than half are African Americans, Native Americans, Asian Americans, and Hispanics. About half have spouses and/or children. Most came from—and themselves represent—weak families. Two-thirds will return to prison; 85 percent have been convicted before.

Prisons represent a late development in the history of punishment. Capital punishment, corporal punishment, shaming, fines, and restitution made up the principal punishments until the nineteenth century. Prisons were introduced as a reform to ameliorate the harshness of the penalties of death, mutilation, and shaming. The eighteenth- and nineteenth-century prisons were based on the idea that through quiet reflection, hard work, and the development of industriousness, sobriety, and morality, prisoners could become responsible citizens. Both the Pennsylvania system based on solitary confinement and the Auburn system based on congregate work were supposed to reform prisoners. However, most nineteenth-century prisons shifted from an emphasis on reform to a concentration on custody—from reformatories to warehouses. Most nineteenth-century prisons held mainly poor people and immigrants.

Incarceration today takes place in three primary types of facilities: locally governed jails, state- operated prisons, and privately contracted and publicly operated community-based facilities. Many jails provide only minimum services beyond security. Some, on the other hand, are clean, safe, humane, effectively managed, modern institutions. Half the nation's jail prisoners have not yet been convicted; the other half consist of convicted misdemeanants serving jail sentences and convicted felons awaiting either sentencing or space in crowded prisons. Frequently, due to security demands and budgetary restraints, defendants and convicted offenders receive the same treatment. The courts have intervened to supervise jail conditions, but recently the U.S. Supreme Court has placed limits on the extent to which courts can intervene in the management of local jails. Reasonable measures taken to ensure security do not constitute punishment, even if pretrial detainees suffer the same deprivations imposed on convicted prisoners.

Prisoners are divided according to their security risk and dangerousness into three security-level prisons—maximum, medium, and minimum. Maximum security prisons hold the most dangerous offenders; they focus on security. A few "super" maximum security prisons in the federal prison system, namely Alcatraz and its successor, the United States prison at Marion, Illinois, house the worst of the worst prisoners. Many maximum security prisons are old; some were built more than a century ago. New-generation maximum security prisons focus on providing humane, safe, secure, efficiently managed facilities. Medium security prisons, newer and less forbidding than the old fortress-type prisons, concentrate on security, but not as exclusively as maximum security prisons. Minimum security facilities focus on rehabilitation and preparing prisoners for return to the community. Prisoners in minimum security prisons live with less supervision, in less austere surroundings, and may have private, locked rooms.

Women's prisons provide for all security levels in one facility. These prisons are often located in rural areas, lacking the visible signs of security such as walls and fences that are frequently seen in men's prisons. The prevalence of cottage architecture and single rooms contributes to a less forbidding facility than the old fortress prisons for men.

Prisons are managed according to a variety of styles that vary greatly from place to place and from administration to administration. The control model that stresses hierarchy, rules, and obedience fits the description of a formal management system. The responsibility model, although allowing prisoners considerable freedom, also relies on written rules and their enforcement. The consensus model, which tries to balance control and responsibility, too, relies on rules and their enforcement. All prison management systems attempt to provide an orderly, secure, humane confinement society. Personal styles informally modify the reality of these descriptions. Correctional officers traditionally suffered from poor pay and working conditions. Today, they increasingly find better training, better pay, and improved conditions. Particularly in new-generation prisons and well-managed prisons, correctional officers can find satisfying, challenging professional lives.

The constraints on public budgets and the severely crowded conditions in many prisons and jails have led to the search for alternatives to existing prison funding, construction, and operation. The belief in the efficiency, economy, and imagination of free enterprise has led increasingly to calls for private enterprise to fund, build, and operate correctional facilities. Although historically, prisons have contracted services and some facilities to private providers, only recently has private enterprise entered the jail and prison market. At least one state prison and a few jails are now privately operated. Controversy surrounds the idea; too recent for evaluation, the promise and the fulfillment of privatization remain to be revealed.

Review Questions

1. Compare numbers, rates, and lengths of U.S. prison populations with those of other countries.

2. Trace the major developments in the history of U.S. prisons.

3. Identify, describe, and explain the purposes of the three major types of U.S. prisons.

4. Compare and contrast women's with men's prisons in the U.S.

5. Identify, describe, explain the philosophy of, and assess the costs and benefits of new-generation prisons.

6. Identify, explain, and evaluate the principal management styles that prison research has revealed.

7. List and describe the critical functions of corrections officers.

8. Identify and describe the hierarchy of correctional officers.

9. Compare the work of corrections officers in traditional and new maximum security prisons.

10. Explain the extent of and the effectiveness of women corrections officers.

11. Explain the extent of and the effectiveness of minority corrections officers.

12. Describe the training for corrections officers.

13. Why does the future look brighter for corrections officers?

14. Identify the major types of jail inmates.

15. What role do the courts have in jail management?

16. Briefly describe and assess the effectiveness of programs available to jail inmates.

17. Briefly trace the history of private corrections, describe the extent of private prisons and jails today, and explain the debate over privatization of corrections.

18. Describe the changing nature of American prisoners.

19. What is the distribution of offenses and convictions of U.S. prisoners?

20. Describe the demographic characteristics of U.S. prisoners.

21. What is the nature and extent of chemical abuse among U.S. prisoners?

22. Explain the extent and nature of recidivism in U.S. prisons.

23. Contrast actual time spent in prison with sentence lengths, and explain the discrepancy.

Notes

1. BJS, *Prisoners, 1925-1981* (Washington, D.C.: Bureau of Justice Statistics, 1982); BJS, *Prisoners in 1994* (Washington, D.C.: Bureau of Justice Statistics, 1995); Elliott Currie, *Confronting Crime* (New York: Pantheon Books, 1985), 28-29; Georgia figure quoted in Joan Petersilia, "Georgia's Intensive Probation: Will the Model Work Elsewhere?" in *Intermediate Punishments,* Belinda R. McCarthy, ed. (Monsey, N.Y.: Willow Tree Press, 1987), 22.

2. BJS, *Prisons and Prisoners in the United States* (Washington, D.C.: Bureau of Justice Statistics, 1992), 12; BJS, *Correctional Populations in the United States— 1990* (Washington, D.C.: Bureau of Justice Statistics, 1992), Table 4.20.

3. David A. Ward, "Alcatraz and Marion: Confinement in Super Maximum Custody," in *Escaping Prison Myths: Selected Topics in the History of Federal Corrections,* John W. Roberts, ed. (Washington, D.C.: American University Press, 1994), 91-92.

4. Norval Morris, "Foreword," *Escaping Prison Myths,* vii.

5. Lee H. Bowker, *Corrections: The Science and the Art* (New York: Macmillan and Company, 1982).

6. Adam Jay Hirsch, *The Rise of the Penitentiary* (New Haven: Yale University Press, 1992), 11.

7. David Rothman, *The Discovery of the Asylum* (Boston: Little, Brown, 1971); Gerald Grob, *Mental Institutions in America* (New York: Free Press, 1973).

8. Quoted in A. W. Pisciotta, "Scientific Reform: The 'New Penology' at Elmira, 1876-1900," *Crime and Delinquency* 29 (1983): 621.

9. David Rothman, *Conscience and Convenience: The Asylum and Its Alternatives in Progressive America* (Boston: Little, Brown, 1980).

10. John Irwin, *Prisons in Turmoil* (Boston: Little, Brown, 1980), chap. 2.

11. Willard Gaylin et al., *Doing Good: The Limits of Benevolence* (New York: Pantheon, 1981); American Friends Society, *Struggle for Justice: A Report on Crime and Punishment in America* (New York: Hill and Wang, 1971); Michael Sherman and Gordon Hawkins, *Imprisonment in America: Choosing the Future* (Chicago: University of Chicago Press, 1981); Norval Morris, *The Future of Imprisonment* (Chicago: University of Chicago Press, 1974); Robert Johnson, *Hard Time: Understanding and Reforming the Prison* (Monterey, Calif.: Brooks/Cole, 1987).

12. Johnson, *Hard Time,* 43.

13. Robert Johnson and Hans Toch, *The Pains of Imprisonment* (Beverly Hills: Sage, 1982), 41.

14. Prisoners quoted in Irwin, *Prisons in Turmoil,* 181-213; Robert Blecker, "Haven or Hell? Inside Lorton Central Prison: Experiences of Punishment Justified," *Stanford Law Review,* 42 (1990): 1162.

15. Richard G. Singer, "Prisons: Typologies and Classifications," in *Encyclopedia of Crime and Justice* (New York: Free Press, 1983), 3:1202-4.

16. Ibid.

17. BJS, *Report to the Nation on Crime and Justice,* 2d. ed., 107; Singer, "Prisons: Typologies and Classifications," 1204.

18. Federal Bureau of Prisons, Office of Public Affairs, "Florence Fact Sheet," (June 16, 1993), 1.

19. Federal Bureau of Prisons, Office of Public Affairs, "Florence Background Paper," (June 16, 1993), 1.

20. T. D. Bingham, "Maximum Transfer from Marion to Florence," *Prison Life* (n.d.), 25.

21. Pete Earley, *The Hot House* (New York: Bantham Books, 1992), 30; Ward, "Alcatraz and Marion," 81, 90.

22. David A. Ward and Kenneth F. Schoen, eds., *Confinement in Maximum Custody* (Lexington, Mass.: Lexington Books, 1981), chaps. 9-11.

23. Ibid., Singer, "Prisons: Typologies and Classifications," 1204.

24. Singer, "Prisons: Typologies and Classifications," 1203-4; Earley, *The Hot House,* 30.

25. Isabel C. Barrows, "The Reformatory Treatment of Women in the United States," in *Penal and Reformatory Institutions,* vol. 2, Charles R. Henderson, ed. (New York: Russell Sage Foundation, 1910), 129-67.

26. John DiIulio, *Governing Prisons* (New York: Free Press, 1987), 105.

27. Ibid.

28. Ibid., 107.

29. Quoted in DiIulio, *Governing Prisons,* 112.

30. Steve J. Martin and Sheldon Ekland-Olson, *Texas Prisons: The Walls Came Tumbling Down* (Austin: Texas Monthly Press, 1987) recounts much of this history.

31. Quoted in DiIulio, *Governing Prisons,* 119-20.

32. Quoted in DiIulio, *Governing Prisons,* 124.

33. Quoted in DiIulio, *Governing Prisons,* 127.

34. Ibid.

35. David A. Ward, "Control Strategies for Problem Prisoners in American Penal Systems," in *Problems of Long-Term Imprisonment,* Anthony E. Bottoms and Roy Light, eds., (Brookfield, Vt.: Gower Publishing Company, 1987).

36. Mark S. Fleisher, *Warehousing Violence* (Newbury Park, Calif.: Sage, 1989).

37. Bowker, *Corrections,* 208-209.

38. Ibid., 206-208.

39. Gordon Hawkins, *The Prison: Policy and Practice* (Chicago: University of Chicago Press, 1976), 105; James B. Jacobs and Harold Gretsky, "Prison Guard," *Urban Life* 4 (April 1975): 5-27; James B. Jacobs and Norma Crotty, "The Guard's World," in *New Perspectives on Prisons and Imprisonment,* James B. Jacobs, ed. (Ithaca, N.Y.: Cornell University Press, 1983), 133-41.

40. Quoted in Jacobs and Crotty, "The Guard's World," 135.

41. Jacobs, *New Perspectives,* 115-32.

42. Robert R. Ross, *Prison Guard/Correctional Officer: The Use and Abuse of the Human Resources of the Prison* (Toronto: Butterworths, 1981), part I.

43. Hans B. Toch, "Is a 'Correctional Officer,' By Any Other Name, a 'Screw'?" *Criminal Justice Review* 3 (1978): 19-37.

44. Jacobs and Gretsky, "Prison Guard," 9.

45. *Pugh v. Locke,* 406 F.Supp. 318 (D. Ala. 1976).

46. Hawkins, *The Prison,* 81; Jacobs and Gretsky, "Prison Guard," 10.

47. Ibid; Jacobs and Gretsky, "Prison Guard," 10.

48. Hawkins, *The Prison,* 96, 98.

49. Lynne E. Zimmer, *Women Guarding Men* (Chicago: University of Chicago Press, 1986), 1.

50. Susan M. Hunter, "On the Line: Working Hard with Dignity," *Corrections Today* 48, no. 4 (1986): 12-13; James B. Jacobs, "Female Guards in Men's Prisons," *New Perspectives,* 178-201.

51. Quoted in Jacobs, *New Perspectives,* 187-88.

52. Barbara A. Owen, "Race and Gender Relations Among Prison Workers," *Crime and Delinquency* 31 (1985): 158.

53. Craig Haney, Curtis Banks, and Philip Zimbardo, "Interpersonal Dynamics in a Simulated Prison," *International Journal of Criminology and Penology* 1 (1973): 163. Hawkins, *The Prison,* 101.

54. Hawkins, *The Prison,* 101.

55. Quoted in Hawkins, *The Prison,* 105.

56. I am grateful to Leanne Phinney, Human Research Director, Oak Park Heights Correctional Facility, for these figures.

57. Minnesota Correctional Facility, Oak Park Heights, *Inmate Handbook,* 2-3.

58. Ross, *Prison Guard/Correctional Officer,* stresses these positive dimensions to guards and their work. I am grateful to Professor David Ward, Chairman, Department of Sociology, University of Minnesota; Warden Gordon Wood; Penny Nelson at the warden's office at Oak Park Heights; the BBC special segment about Oak Park Heights; and to Dan Crutchfield, former correctional counselor at Oak Park Heights, for this information.

59. Bureau of Justice Statistics, *Jails and Jail Inmates 1993-1994* (Washington, D.C.: Bureau of Justice Statistics, April 1995), 2.

60. Ibid; Belinda R. McCarthy, "The Use of Jail Confinement in the Disposition of Felony Arrests," *Journal of Criminal Justice* 17 (1989): 241-51.

61. BJS, *Jail Inmates 1987.*

62. Ronald Goldfarb, *Jails: The Ultimate Ghetto* (New York: Archer Press, 1975); *Jails and Jail Inmates 1993-94,* 2.

63. *Jails and Jail Inmates 1993-94,* 3.

64. Advisory Commission, *Jails, Intergovernmental Dimensions of a Local Problem* (Washington, D.C.: Advisory Commission on Intergovernmental Relations, 1984), 14.

65. Ibid., 21.

66. Goldfarb, *Jails: The Ultimate Ghetto.* 27.

67. Ibid.

68. Ibid., 21.

69. Quoted in Goldfarb, *Jails: The Ultimate Ghetto,* 32.

70. Stephen H. Gettinger, *New Generation Jails: An Innovative Approach to an Age-Old Problem* (Washington, D.C.: National Institute of Corrections, March 1984), 1.

71. Richard Weiner, William Frazier, and Jay Farbstein, "Building Better Jails," *Psychology Today* (June 1987), 40.

72. Weiner, Frazier, and Farbstein, "Building Better Jails," 42.

73. Gettinger, *New Generation Jails,* 20-21; Weiner, Frazier, and Farbstein, "Building Better Jails," 42.

74. Weiner, Frazier, and Farbstein, "Building Better Jails," 42.

75. Gettinger, *New Generation Jails,* 5.

76. Patrick G. Jackson and Cindy A. Stearns, "Gender Issues in the New Generation Jail," *Prison Journal* 75 (1995): 205-206.

77. Ibid., 206.

78. Ibid., 215.

79. Charles H. Logan and Gerald G. Gaes, "Meta-Analysis and the Rehabilitation of Punishment," *Justice Quarterly* 10 (1993): 256-257.

80. Douglas C. McDonald, "Private Penal Institutions," *Crime and Justice: A Review of Research,* vol. 16 (Chicago: University of Chicago Press, 1992), 380.

81. GAO *Prison Crowding* (Washington, D.C.: U.S. General Accounting Office, November 1989), 27.

82. Joan Mullen, *Corrections and the Private Sector* (Washington, D.C.: National Institute of Justice, 1984).

83. David Shichor, *Punishment for Profit* (Thousand Oaks, Calif.: Sage Publications, 1995).

84. Marc Mauer and Tracy Huling, "Young Black Americans and the Criminal Justice System: Five Years Later" (Washington, D. C.: The Sentencing Project, October 1995), 3; Blecker, "Haven or Hell?" 1154; Peter C. Kratcoski and George A. Pownall, "Federal Bureau of Prisons Programming for Older Inmates," *Federal Probation* 53 (1989): 28-35;

85. BJS, *Sourcebook of Criminal Justice Statistics—1988* (Washington, D.C.: Bureau of Justice Statistics, 1989); BJS, *Prisons and Prisoners in the United States,* 13.

86. BJS, *Report to the Nation on Crime and Justice,* 2d ed., 48.

87. Quoted in Fleisher, *Warehousing Violence,* 22.

88. Jane R. Chapman, *Economic Realities and the Female Offender* (Lexington, Mass.: Lexington Books, 1980), 21-75; Barbara Owen and Barbara Bloom, "Profiling Women Prisoners: Findings from National Surveys and a California Sample," *Prison Journal* 75 (1995): 166; Russ Immarigeon and Meda Chesney-Lind, *Women's Prisons: Overcrowded and Overused* (San Francisco: National Council on Crime and Delinquency, 1992), 2-3, 6; American Correctional Association, *The Female Offender: What Does the Future Hold?* (Washington, D.C.: St. Mary's Press, 1990).

89. Immarigeon and Chesney-Lind, *Women's Prisons,* 3.

90. Studies cited in Immarigeon and Chesney-Lind, *Women's Prisons,* 9.

91. Jacobs, *New Perspectives,* 82-83.

92. *The Special Management Inmate* (Washington, D.C.: National Institute of Justice, March 1985).

93. BJS, *Sourcebook of Criminal Justice Statistics—1988;* NIJ, *Drugs and Crime 1990: Annual Report* (Washington, D.C.: National Institute of Justice, 1991), 5.

94. BJS, *Report to the Nation on Crime and Justice: The Data,* 37.

95. BJS, *Report to the Nation on Crime and Justice,* 100; BJS, *Prison Admissions and Releases, 1982* (Washington, D.C.: Bureau of Justice Statistics, 1985), Table 11; BJS, *Prisoners in 1994* (Washington, D.C.: BJS, August 1995), Tables 15, 16.

96. James B. Jacobs, "Sentencing by Prison Personnel: Good Time," *UCLA Law Review* 30 (1982): 226.

97. Koppel, *Time Served in Prison* (Washington, D.C.: Bureau of Justice Statistics, 1986).

98. John DiIulio, Jr., "The Value of Prisons," *Wall Street Journal,* 13 May 1992.

99. Patrick A. Langan, "America's Soaring Prison Population," *Science* 251 (1991): 1568, 1573.

100. Lawrence A. Greenfield, *Examining Recidivism* (Washington, D.C.: Bureau of Justice Statistics, 1985), 1; BJS, *Profile of State Prison Inmates, 1986* (Washington, D.C.: Bureau of Justice Statistics, January 1988); Allen J. Beck, *Recidivism of Prisoners Released in 1983* (Washington, D.C.: Bureau of Justice Statistics, 1989).

101. John F. Wallerstedt, *Returning to Prison* (Washington, D.C.: Bureau of Justice Statistics, 1984), 2-3; BJS, *Prisons and Prisoners in the United States,* 16; Immarigeon and Chesney-Lind, *Women's Prisons.*

102. John F. Wallerstedt, *Returning to Prison* (Washington, D.C.: Bureau of Justice Statistics, 1984), 5.

103. Greenfield, *Examining Recidivism,* 1; Wallerstedt, *Returning to Prison,* 5.

104. Josefina Figueira-McDonough et al., *Females in Prison in Michigan, 1968-1978: A Study in Commitment Patterns* (Ann Arbor: University of Michigan, Institute for Social Research, 1981), 77-98.

14 Imprisonment

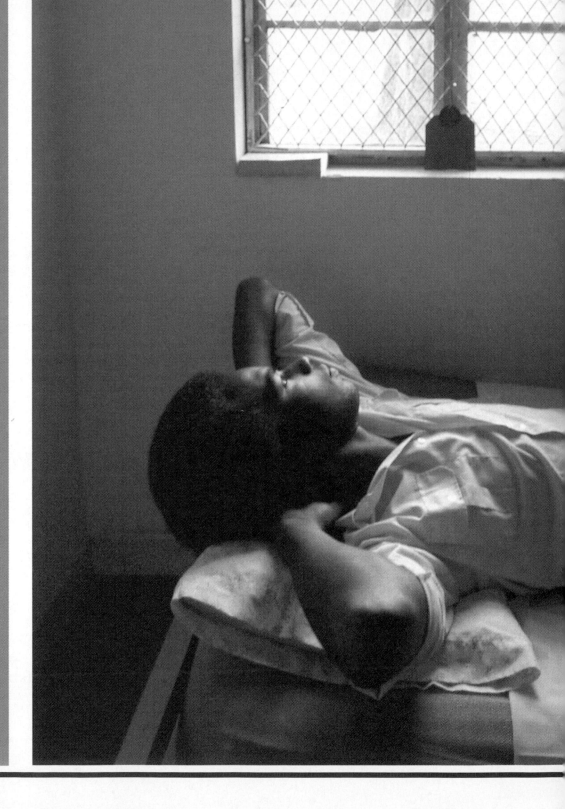

CHAPTER MAIN POINTS

1. Prisoner subculture depends on influences from both inside and outside prison.

2. Prisoners adopt a number of lifestyles in order to adapt to life in prison: some identify with the world outside prison, others identify with the world inside prison; some want to retain the identity they brought with them to prison; others want to change their life patterns.

3. Prisons operate not only according to the formal rules of the prison but also according to an informal inmate code of right and wrong behavior.

4. Prisoners are supposed to live a life of poverty but through hustling they can obtain comforts not allowed within the formal prison economy of supposed enforced poverty.

5. Softening the pains of confinement by hustling causes problems, but it also contributes to reducing management problems by keeping prisoners more comfortable.

6. Harsher sentences have contributed to making prisons more crowded and dangerous by confining younger and more violent criminals.

7. The majority of prisoners in U.S. prisons are members of racial and ethnic minorities, and their numbers are sharply increasing.

8. Life in women's prisons is less violent, more harmonious, and less destructive than life in men's prisons.

9. Racial and ethnic conflict is a serious problem in many prisons; most prison gangs are organized along racial and ethnic lines.

10. Prison gangs not only operate within prisons, but they frequently have close ties to gangs outside prisons.

11. Prison violence, including sexual assault, has always been a part of prison society, but prison gangs, race and ethnic hostility, and the shifting prison populations have increased the problem.

12. Violence is directed not only at other inmates but also against corrections officers and other staff.

13. Collective violence in the form of riots has occurred throughout the history of prisons, but experts cannot agree on a number of popular theories that are supposed to explain why riots occur.

14. Crowding in prisons is a common problem that contributes not only to violence, riots, and racial and ethnic hostility, but also to the difficulty of managing prisons.

15. Prison crowding has led to a policy debate over whether to build more prisons or find alternatives to imprisonment.

16. Boredom and monotony are the most pervasive aspects of life in prison.

17. The purposes of prison programs include not only rehabilitation but also humane punishment, economy, effective management, education for its own sake, religious expression, and recreation.

18. Rehabilitation has motivated many programs and generated enormous controversy.

19. The effectiveness of rehabilitation programs in changing prisoners is decidedly mixed, according to existing empirical research.

20. Rehabilitation programs may be more successful as management tools to keep prisoners busy, keep them out of trouble, and provide humane punishment than they are in turning offenders into law-abiding people.

21. Prisoners retain, to an extremely limited degree, the rights of access to courts; due process of law; equal protection of the laws; freedom of religion, association, and speech; and against cruel and unusual punishment and unreasonable searches and seizures.

22. The restrictions on the rights of prisoners, especially on their liberty, privacy, and property, are both part of their punishment and necessary to maintain the safety, discipline, and efficient management of prisons.

23. Prisoners win few lawsuits when they allege that prison rules and actions by prison officials violate their rights.

24. Prisoners are entitled to limited due process rights in internal prison disciplinary proceedings.

25. Prisoners rarely prevail in internal prison disciplinary proceedings.

I
mprisonment is the most popular and simplest response to crime. It is also the most expensive. What should imprisonment be like? Talk to most people on the street and they will answer, "Torture, misery, horrible! Let them rot in the worst 'hell holes' we can build!" Listen to most politicians and they will follow the lead of most people on the street. Talk to corrections officers and prison officials and you will likely get a quite different answer. They will remind you that most people locked up in prison will eventually get out. Will this torture, misery, and deprivation that the public and politicians prescribe make them less dangerous and more productive when they get out? Will it turn them from lawbreakers who live off the rest of us into people who will work hard, play by the rules, and pay their own way? Corrections professionals will probably also ask you about the lives of corrections officers—the "other prisoners"—who spend most of their days in prison too, associating with prisoners. What do you think their lives should be like? Does it matter that corrections professionals also have to spend their time in the "hell holes" that you recommend for prisoners? Does it concern you that if the prisoners are miserable, that makes the work of the professionals harder, too?

Unfortunately, the state of our empirical knowledge does not help us to answer the question about whether brutal punishment makes prisoners more criminal or punishes them into becoming law-abiding, responsible people. Nor does the empirical evidence tell us that programs intended to rehabilitate prisoners "work." We do know, however, that safe, secure, humane imprisonment makes the lives of corrections officers better, and that in safe, secure, humane prisons the level of disorder, violence, and gang activity is lower. This is the reason that many enlightened corrections professionals, who know a lot more than the rest of us about criminal justice, are recommending that we send offenders to prison not *for* punishment but *as* punishment. Spartan, disciplined, safe, secure, orderly confinement *is* punishment, even if it is *humane.* Punishment does not require brutal, filthy, unsafe, disorderly conditions added to confinement.

This chapter examines some aspects of imprisonment in general, and some aspects of life in prison specific to the turn of the twenty-first century—prisoner subcultures and adaptive lifestyles; the prison economy; prison programs designed to educate, train, and rehabilitate prisoners; the work life of prisoners; and recreation and religious activities. Prison society, like that of the outside world, has rules both in the form of law and of the United States Constitution, along with administrative rules inside prison. But part of punishment is a severe restriction on rights, and an informal inmate code that governs much of the behavior in prison has little to do with formal rules.

Prisoner Subculture

Life in prison has provided fertile subject matter for fiction and sociology throughout the twentieth century. It was in the 1930s, however, that a sociologist first identified a distinct prison subculture in a maximum security prison. Quickly, the idea of a "foreign" culture inside prisons with its own rules, customs, and language captured the way penologists thought about life in prison.

Indigenous or Imported?

Sociologists have developed two basic theories to explain prison society: the indigenous theory and the importation theory. According to the **indigenous theory** of prison society, conditions inside prisons themselves shape the nature of prison society. Donald Clemmer introduced the concept of **prisonization** in his 1940 classic, *The Prison Community.* Clemmer was a former staff member of Menard Penitentiary in Illinois. Based on his detailed observations, Clemmer concluded that prisonization is the process by which inmates adapt to the customs of the prison world.[1]

Since the 1960s, however, prisons have lost much of their isolation from the "free world." With these changed conditions, and perhaps also because of a recognition that prison society was never so distinct from the society outside as the indigenous theory maintained, a new theory of prison society appeared—the **importation theory.** Along with the special conditions in prison to which prisoners must adapt, society outside the prison shapes life inside prison. Television, magazines, music, visitors, lawsuits, friends, and gangs have all contributed to a closer relationship between prison society and society as a whole.

According to the importation theory, prison society has roots in criminal and conventional cultures outside prison. Former inmate turned sociologist John Irwin and the distinguished sociologist Donald Cressey found that the values held by prison newcomers affected prison society as much as the values acquired by inmates in prison. Irwin and Cressey found three inmate subcultures—thief, straight, and convict. Only the convict was indigenous; the thief and the straight are imported. "Convicts" accept life in prison as their normal life and try to obtain power and privileges within the prison community. They are mainly **state-raised youth,** having spent most of their lives in orphanages, reform schools, and other state-operated institutions. "Professional thieves" keep to themselves, waiting to get out and resume their former lives. "Straight" prisoners do not consider themselves criminals at all, at least not "real criminals." White-collar offenders, for example, try to retain in prison legitimate elements of their former lives.[2]

Adaptive Prisoner Lifestyles

The choice of which subculture to join faces all inmates. According to Irwin in his book *The Felon,* based on interviews with convicts in Soledad men's prison in California, all new inmates must ask themselves: "How shall I do my time?" Or, "What shall I do in prison?" A few cannot cope; they either commit suicide or sink into psychosis. Irwin found that those who can cope fit into two basic groups:

1. Those who identify with the world outside prison.
2. Those who identify primarily with the prison world. This is called **jailing.**[3]

Jailers "who do not retain or . . . never acquired any commitment to outside social worlds tend to make a world out of prison." One such inmate told Mark Fleisher, who studied life in the maximum security federal penitentiary at Lompoc, California:

Beating the system is the best game in town. Middle-class Americans will never understand it. You know, I feel "extracultural." I live on the same planet you do. We speak the same language, but that's where our similarity ends. That's right, I live outside this culture. This is your culture. This is your prison. You have to live with all the f——— rules in this society. I don't. You have to obey the rules, Mark. That's how you live. But, I don't have to obey anybody's f——— rules. The worst that can happen to me is that they put me back in prison. And who gives a f—-! When they do that, you got to pay for me. I win. If this is all this society can do to me, then I'm gonna do whatever I want to do. How you going to stop me? I'm invincible.[4]

Convicts who identify with the outside world fall into two further divisions, according to Irwin:

a. Those who for the most part wish to maintain their former life patterns and identities. This is called **doing time.**

b. Those who desire to make significant changes in life patterns and identities and see prison as a chance to do this. This is called **gleaning.**[5]

Time-doers try to get through their prison terms with "the least amount of suffering and the greatest amount of comfort." They avoid trouble, find activities to occupy their time, secure a few luxuries, and make a few friends. The gleaners follow a sometimes detailed plan of self-improvement. According to one gleaner:

> I got tired of losing. I had been losing all of my life. I decided that I wanted to win for a while. So I got on a different kick. I knew that I had to learn something so I went to school, got my high school diploma. I cut myself off from my old . . . buddies and started hanging around with some intelligent guys who minded their own business. We read a lot, a couple of us paint. We play a little of bridge and talk, a lot of time about what we are going to do when we get out.[6]

Deciding whether to be a time-doer, a gleaner, or a jailer is not always easy, and it carries with it important consequences. Irwin cites the example of inmate Piri Thomas, who was forced to decide whether to participate in a riot. Thomas said:

> I stood there watching and weighing, trying to decide whether or not I was a con first and an outsider second. I had been doing time inside yet living every mental minute I could outside; now I had to choose one or the other. I stood there in the middle of the yard. Cons passed me by, some going west to join the boppers, others going east to neutral ground. . . . I had to make a decision. *I am a con. These damn cons are my people. Your people are outside the cells, home, in the streets. No! That ain't so. . . . Look at them go toward the west wall. Why in hell am I taking so long in making up my mind?*[7]

The Inmate Code

Just as people do in the larger society outside prison, prisoners have a code. This **inmate code** is the informal system of rules that determines what is right and wrong and what is good and bad within inmate society. This code should not be confused either with formal prison rules or their informal adaptations of the written rules of the prison to the lives of prisoners. (These are discussed later in this chapter in the section on prisons and the law.) The two cardinal principles of the inmate code are:

1. Do your own time.

2. Never inform on another inmate.

Gresham Sykes, in his classic study of life in a New Jersey prison during the 1950s, *The Society of Captives,* stated these fundamental principles of the inmate code in five graphic rules:

1. *Don't interfere with inmate interests:* Never rat on a con, don't be nosy, don't have a loose lip, don't put a guy on the spot.

2. *Don't quarrel with fellow inmates:* Play it cool, don't lose your head, do your own time.

3. *Don't exploit inmates:* Don't break your word, don't steal from cons, don't sell favors, don't welsh on bets.

4. *Maintain yourself:* Don't weaken, don't whine, don't cop out, be tough, be a man.

5. *Don't trust the guards or the things they stand for:* Don't be a sucker, guards are hacks and screws, the officials are wrong and the prisoners are right.[8]

No single inmate code, of course, can exist for all prisons. These rules derived from maximum security prisons for men, and they stem from the 1950s. Much has changed since then. Prisoners are younger, they are more violent, they are members of racial and ethnic gangs, and they are less tied to codes of any kind. All these changes make the management of prisons, particularly maximum and minimum security prisons for men, more difficult.

The Prison Economy

Punishment by confinement in prison is not only about deprivation of liberty and privacy. Punishment is also about the deprivation of material comforts. Prisoners are supposed to live a life of enforced poverty. They are not supposed to be comfortable in confinement. This means that the state provides only the bare essentials of plain, simple food, clothing, and shelter. In the words of Virgil L. Williams and Mary Fish, prisons were intentionally designed as "island[s] of poverty" in an outside world sea of abundance.[9]

Of course, nearly everyone has seen pictures and heard stories demonstrating that prisons are not entirely "islands of poverty." They see television sets in prison cells and prisoners working out in well-equipped exercise rooms. They hear of "country club" minimum security prisons where "prisoners" play golf. They read of prisoners who are drunk or high on drugs. How does it happen that such comforts exist in these "islands of poverty"? Some are obtained legally; prisoners are allowed to receive gifts from friends and relatives so long as they are on the approved list of items allowed in the prison. Prisoners can also buy some items from the prison commissary. These purchases are not made with money—currency is not allowed—but with scrip or on credit drawn on accounts supplied with money from the outside or that prisoners have earned in prison. (How prisoners make money while they are in prison is discussed later in this chapter in the section on prison programs.)

The approved list of gifts and the stock of items in the commissary are hardly enough to satisfy the wants of most prisoners. Prisoners are well aware of all the comforts of life they are not allowed or cannot obtain legitimately. Like many other Americans, they find it hard to satisfy their desires with available resources and within the enforced poverty that is part of punishment by confinement. According to Susan Sheehan, most of the men she studied in a New York prison were there "precisely because they were not willing to go without on the street. They are no more willing to go without in prison, so they hustle to obtain what they cannot afford to buy."[10]

Hustling contraband goods and services—mainly food, clothing, weapons, drugs, and prostitution—both violates the rules of prisons and frustrates the goal of punishment by enforced poverty. Deprived of luxuries, prisoners nonetheless seek them. Obtaining them not only helps ease the pain of imprisonment but also contributes informally to prison stability. Because these contraband goods and services contribute to stability and therefore make prisons and prisoners easier to manage, they are tolerated by the authorities to some extent. Prisoners put great stake in these amenities; trouble arises when they do not receive them. Equally important, trouble brews when prisoner leaders lose the profits from and control of contraband goods and services. In some prisons, prisoner leaders who control the contraband business form symbiotic relationships with correctional officers. Both have an interest in maintaining stability, so they make trade-offs: Officers allow some illegal trafficking, usually in "non-serious" contraband such as food; prisoner leaders, in return, maintain peaceful cell blocks.[11]

The Impact of Harsher Penalties

The public demand for harsher penalties for violent crimes and drug offenses has substantially affected prison society, mostly for the worse. Richard Lawrence examined the effects of the increased penalties for drug law violations enacted by the Minnesota legislature in 1989. The dramatic increase in prisoners that resulted—increases that exceeded the state's usually accurate projections of prison populations—altered the proportion of prisoners convicted for drug law violations (see Figures 14.1 and 14.2).

Stiffer penalties for violent crimes have also put more violent offenders in the prisons. Interviews with prison personnel at St. Cloud Prison in Minnesota revealed a number of concerns:

- Prison crowding has resulted from the stiffer penalties.
- More assaults on officers have resulted from more violent prisoners.
- Increased numbers of violent and drug offenders have disrupted the balance between maximum and medium security prisoners and require policies and practices consistent with higher security and safety.
- The high percent of gang members convicted of assault and drug offenses has brought more street gang members to St. Cloud, making gangs in prison stronger and more cohesive. Gang members "tend to be assaultive and to display negative and disorderly conduct."[12]

Figure 14.1

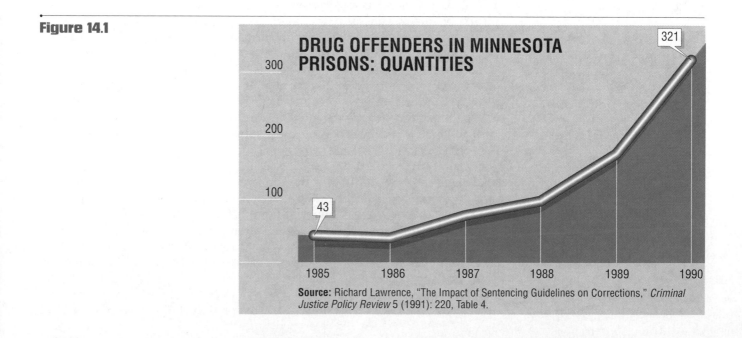

DRUG OFFENDERS IN MINNESOTA PRISONS: QUANTITIES

Source: Richard Lawrence, "The Impact of Sentencing Guidelines on Corrections," *Criminal Justice Policy Review* 5 (1991): 220, Table 4.

Figure 14.2

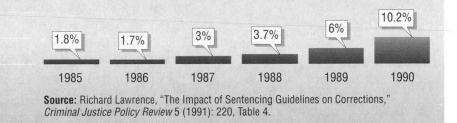

DRUG OFFENDERS IN MINNESOTA PRISONS: PROPORTIONS

Drug offenders as a percent of prison population

1.8%	1.7%	3%	3.7%	6%	10.2%
1985	1986	1987	1988	1989	1990

Source: Richard Lawrence, "The Impact of Sentencing Guidelines on Corrections," *Criminal Justice Policy Review* 5 (1991): 220, Table 4.

Race and Ethnicity

The events of the 1960s dramatically changed prison society. During that decade and the early 1970s, enhanced racial and ethnic consciousness, assertiveness, confrontation, solidarity, and, finally, violence took hold of society in general. These developments did not bypass prisons; instead, they left prisons "fragmented, tense, and often extremely violent." Prison populations were also changing: by the late 1970s, African Americans, Chicanos, Puerto Ricans, Native Americans, and other minorities in the general population became the majority population in American prisons. Stateville, Illinois's maximum security prison just outside Chicago, for example has 80 percent African American prisoners.[13]

Racial hatred has also increased in prisons holding large numbers of urban prisoners. Prisoners tend to restrict their relationships to small friendship groups, cliques, and, increasingly, gangs in which individuals band together according to race. To be sure, other shared experiences, such as committing similar crimes, coming from the same neighborhood, doing time in another state prison or institution, and just living in the same cell block or working in the same prison workshop, contribute to cohesion. But race is the overriding element in much of today's prisoner society.[14]

Race relations were not prominent in early research about prisons. In *The Prison Community*, Donald Clemmer never mentioned race relations, even though he reported that more than 25 percent of the prisoners in his research were African Americans. Nor did John Irwin and Donald Cressey mention race as part of their importation theory in "Thieves, Convicts and Inmate Culture." Any theory that hopes to describe prison society fully as it exists at the turn of the twenty-first century must account for race relations. The most powerful social groupings in prisons today have a racial basis, and the most volatile dynamic within prisons is the hatred between white and African American prisoners. African American prisoners are not only more numerous, but they are also more assertive than they were in the past. According to one African American prisoner at Stateville Prison in Illinois:

> In the prison, the black dudes have a little masculinity game they play. It has no name, really, but I call it whup a white boy—especially the

white gangsters or syndicate men, the bad juice boys, the hit men, etc. The black dudes go out of their way to make faggots out of them. And to lose a fight to a white dude is one of the worst things that can happen to a black dude. And I know that, by and far, the white cats are faggots. They will drop their pants and bend over and touch their toes and get had before they will fight.[15]

According to another:

Every can I been in that's the way it is. It's gettin' even I guess. You guys been cuttin' our b—-s off ever since we been in this country. Now we're just gettin' even.[16]

White prisoners either become bigoted or become even more bigoted if they were already racially prejudiced before coming to prison. According to a white California prisoner:

After 10:30, the voice dropped a decibel or two, and from the morass of sound Ron began to recognize certain voices by timbre and catch snatches of conversation. Above him, perhaps on the second tier, he picked up a gumboed black voice saying he'd like to kill all white babies, while his listener agreed it was the best way to handle the beasts—before they grew up. A year earlier, Ron would have felt compassion for anyone so consumed by hate and whenever whites casually used "nigger" he was irked. Now he felt tentacles of hate spreading through himself—and half an hour later, he smiled when a batch of voices began chanting: "Sieg Heil! Sieg Heil!"[17]

Besides African Americans and whites, prisoners include Chicanos, Puerto Ricans, Native Americans, Asian Americans, and others. According to James B. Jacobs, author of the major study of Stateville Prison:

Afro-American, Caucasian-American and Mexican-American inmates lived side by side but maintained three distinct ethnic cultures. Inmates did not eat at the same table, share food, cigarettes or bathroom facilities with individuals of other ethnic groups. They would not sit in the same row while viewing television or even talk for more than brief interchanges with members of a different ethnic group.[18]

Life in Women's Prisons

Women in prison have attracted considerable media attention, but a paucity of research. Enough research exists, however, to demonstrate that women cope with prison life differently than men. David A. Ward and Gene G. Kassebaum's path-breaking study of the California Institution for Women focused on the role of homosexuality in structuring prison relationships. But, unlike in men's prisons, female prisoners did not coerce their partners.[19]

Rose Giallombardo's study of the Federal Reformatory for Women concluded that women reproduced outside family relationships in prison— father, mother, daughter, sister. Unlike the subculture of men's prisons, women's prison subculture, according to Giallombardo, fostered mutuality and harmony, not competition and dissension. Esther Heffernen found a heterogeneous population in the women incarcerated in the District of Columbia's Reformatory. For women who grew up in foster homes, prison became the center of their lives. They continuously struggled with staff and other inmates for control of their lives and to obtain illegal food, drugs, clothing, and letters. Women imprisoned for situational offenses, such as murder of an abusive husband, rejected any criminal self-identification, attempting to recreate conventional life inside prison and maintain contacts outside. These prisoners accepted rules and regulations and identified with

The subculture in women's prisons—unlike that of men's prisons—fosters mutuality and harmony according to researchers.

the staff. Professional criminals tried to keep busy to pass time quickly, and avoided trouble in order to get released as soon as possible to their former lives of crime.[20]

Gangs

In many men's prisons, violent cliques and gangs form along ethnic and racial lines. Gang members routinely rob, assault, and otherwise prey on each other and retaliate when possible against their attackers. Prisons have always had violent prisoners, generally youths recently "graduated" from juvenile prison as well as unskilled, lower- and working-class criminals. Prior to the 1960s, a strong normative consensus against violence among most other prisoners kept such men in check. Since then, however, the number of tough young prison graduates and unskilled prisoners has greatly increased. As their numbers and assertiveness have grown, they have taken over some of the largest men's prisons. The director of the Illinois Department of Corrections estimated that between 80 and 90 percent of Illinois prisons were affiliated with street gangs.[21]

In California, for example, a tightly knit Chicano clique of youths, who knew each other from the Los Angeles streets and other prisons, began to take over San Quentin in 1967. Known as the "Mexican Mafia," they gained a reputation for toughness, enhanced by rumors that to become a member, initiates had to kill another prisoner. For decades, hostility had existed between Los Angeles Chicanos and those from small towns in California and Texas. These other Chicano prisoners, fueled by rumors of the bloody initiation ritual of the Mexican Mafia, consolidated into a rival gang, La Nuestra Familia. The rivalry between the two gangs grew so deadly that the state segregated them in two prisons—San Quentin for the Mexican Mafia, and Soledad for La Nuestra Familia.[22]

Gang-initiated robbery, assault, rape, and even murder consolidated and expanded black and white groups. Whites formed the Aryan Brotherhood; African Americans, the Black Guerrilla Family. Amid escalating racial tension, the Aryan Brotherhood formed an alliance with the Mexican Mafia, and the Black Guerrillas allied with La Nuestra Familia. Although an uneasy truce prevailed for some time, violence is still common and fear is widespread.

In Illinois, too, gangs have taken over the largest state prison, Stateville. The African American inmate population in Stateville increased from 47 percent in 1953 to 75 percent in 1974. By 1980, 80 percent of Stateville's prisoner population was African American. Prisoner turnover has greatly increased, so a stable prison population is no longer the norm. Changes in Chicago's inner city, which sends so many prisoners to Stateville, profoundly affected its prison society. During the 1960s, Chicago gangs outside prison became politicized, thus raising their demands and expectations inside prisons. Ethnic and racial populations grew more sensitive to injustices, much more willing to oppose and challenge them, and much more sophisticated about tactics.[23]

Unlike older, more traditional prisoners, gang members have a belligerent attitude toward all authority and its institutions when they enter prison. Little rewards, like sneaking extra cups of coffee, do not satisfy gang members as they did older prisoners. Gang members are preoccupied with status and gang rivalry. Challenging authority has become commonplace. According to James Jacobs in his study of Stateville Prison outside Chicago,

> when a lieutenant was called to "walk" an inmate, he was often confronted with ten or twelve of the inmate's fellow gang members surrounding him, challenging his authority. One Stateville guard explained: "The inmate will say, 'I'm not going.' Then a group of his gang will gather around him. I'll have to call a lieutenant. Sometimes one of the leaders will just come over and tell the member to go ahead."[24]

Most challenges to prison authority arise spontaneously, but planned boycotts, strikes, and even riots do occur. Combined, the challenges to authority and inter-gang fighting have created serious control problems for prison administration. At Stateville, prison peace and smooth management depend on four major street gangs—three African American and one Latin. These well-organized and tightly knit groups have enormous group solidarity. Unlike whites, who are unused to grouping together on the basis of race, African Americans especially have long identified themselves by their race in order to survive racism in American society. This solidarity, along with their greater numbers, has produced African American hegemony in Stateville Prison. Whiteness, on the other hand, "simply possesses no ideological significance in American society, except for racist fringe groups." The obvious power of the leading African American gangs led a new prison administration in Stateville to share some authority with them.[25]

> In exchange for their cooperation in keeping things cool, [gangs] were shown deference and given some informal voice in lower-level decision making. For a time this formed the basis for maintaining order in the prison. But cooperation with the gangs was an unstable strategy. First, it was anathema to the [older administrators] and intensified their alienation [from the new strategy of shared authority]. Second, the more established the gangs became, the more precarious became the life of non-gang members, especially whites. Third, there was no assurance that the gangs would not turn against one another.[26]

Despite administration attempts to accommodate gangs in some prisons, violent cliques and gangs pursuing "loot, sex, respect, or revenge will attack any outsider." The close confinement and limited space in prisons make it impossible to ignore gang and clique threats. Prisoners who want to circulate beyond their own cells must join a clique or gang for protection. Today's new prison hero is tough. He can take care of himself in the prison world where attacks are frequent and unprovoked. Toughness also means "having the guts to take from the weak."[27]

Prison, in the eyes of the new prisoner, is the ultimate test of manhood. A man in prison is able to secure what he wants and protect what he has: "In here, a man gets what he can," "nobody can force a man to do something he don't want to," are key elements of their belief system. Any prisoner who does not meet these standards is not a man, "has no respect for himself," and is therefore not entitled to respect from others.[28]

Evidence indicates that the influence of prison gangs is extending beyond individual prisons. In more than half the states, prison gangs have counterparts on the streets. In some of these states, prisons act as bases for criminal gang activity in the community. In California, the Black Guerrilla Family is allied with a gang of younger African American prisoners called "Crips" (after their reputation for crippling their victims), most of whom have been convicted of violent street crimes. According to law enforcement officers, "leaders of the Black Guerrilla Family are directing a growing effort to take over part of Southern California's lucrative cocaine trade by using Crips as their soldiers." The Crips, they say, are recruited in prison. After being paroled they are attempting, often with violence, to push out other cocaine dealers from the predominantly African American South-Central area of Los Angeles. "Investigators say [they have] fresh evidence of the influence of prison gangs beyond prison walls," a problem that a former attorney general of the United States called "serious and spreading."[29]

According to Craig Trout, chief of the intelligence section of the Federal Bureau of Prisons' Correctional Services Branch, gang members in prison

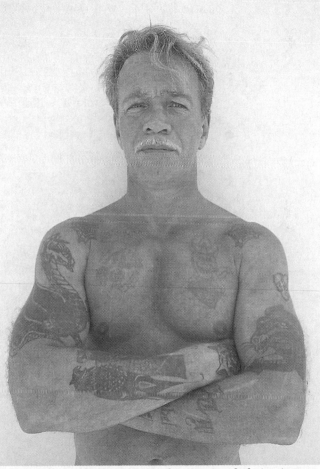

The spread of prison gangs onto the street and of street gangs into prison has blurred the line between prison and street gang membership.

expect gang members released from prison "under penalty of death to continue working for their fellow members inside." Conversely, according to Trout, "street gang members from groups such as Crips or Bloods tend to stick together when they enter prison, forming quasi-prison gangs."[30]

The spread of prison gangs onto the street and of street gangs into prisons has blurred the line between street gangs and prison gangs, creating a challenge to prison management. In addition, the numbers of gangs and gang members are rising rapidly. Also, both the federal and state prison systems are faced with "ever-increasing numbers of highly sophisticated drug groups such as the Medellin . . . and North Atlantic drug cartels," according to Trout. Because of their "extraordinary resources and paramilitary support structures, they far exceed any security threat even imagined with prison gangs."[31]

Throughout the 1980s, the Federal Bureau of Prisons followed a strategy of identifying prison gang members and immediately separating them by disbursing them throughout the federal prison system. In the face of the new challenges, this strategy no longer works. The Bureau of Prisons has now moved toward a strategy of identifying not simply gang members but "security threat groups." According to Trout, this strategy allows the Bureau to track

> rapidly emerging groups such as the Latin Kings or Asian street gangs regardless of whether or not they fit the classic definition of a prison gang. The litmus test simply becomes whether there is documented current illicit activity or a compelling projection of potential threat activity.[32]

Violence

Prison gangs foster not only robbery, assault, and murder, but also fears of rape and other unwanted sexual activity, particularly the role of "insertee" or "punk." Prison rape reflects more an expression of power and dominance than it does a sexual act. Young white prisoners have most to fear from sexual aggression. Most targets of rape and other aggressive sex are white, as many as 83 percent, in contrast to 16 percent of African Americans and 2 percent of Hispanics. Most aggressors are African American (80 percent), some are Hispanic (14 percent), and a few are white (6 percent).[33]

Daniel Lockwood, in his study *Prison Sexual Violence*, maintains that the following three statements explain the preceding figures:

1. Whites are considered weak.
2. Whites are objects of race hatred.
3. Whites are poorly organized, unlike blacks who usually know someone and join a clique or gang for protection.

According to one African American prisoner in a New York State prison:

> If you come in here alone then they [black prisoners] will try to crack on you for something. But if they know that you know people that have been here for awhile, then they know better. They try to pick on some of the weak ones. They like to pick on them.[34]

White prisoners tend to be less organized, less likely to know other whites in prison, and less willing to band together for protection. Class divisions among white prisoners are also much greater than they are among blacks. Middle-class whites look down not only on black prisoners but also on white prisoners they believe to be their social inferiors. Some do not consider themselves criminals at all, which isolates them and makes them more vulnerable to attacks from violent cliques and gangs.[35]

Since the toughness image is so important to the new prison hero, dominating a young white prisoner only enhances prestige. Whites who do not respond violently to unwanted sexual approaches, according to the prison's norm of violence, become victims:

You see a young pretty dude who doesn't come in here on a violent record. Now, he is probably in the worst situation than the guy that comes in here on a violent record. Because if you know that a guy has murdered someone on the street, and has taken a life, and is in here for life, you are going to think three or—not just once but three or four times—before you go up against him.

Somebody that shows he's timid, who is real quiet. That is basically it. Someone who is real quiet and withdrawn and looks scared. He looks frightened you know. He is most apt to be approached.[36]

Whites are seen as weak and vulnerable to attack because they have no group behind them and are less likely to respond violently to threats. Furthermore, a higher percentage of African American prisoners are incarcerated for violent offenses than are whites. These factors, combined with African American prisoners' pent-up rage against what they perceive as white oppression outside prison, make imprisoned whites prime victims. Again according to Daniel Lockwood, from his study of sexual violence in prison,

it is surprising that, viewed as a whole, sexual aggression in prisons is not more widespread. Women rarely sexually assault other women prisoners. Women tend to join groups similar to families, where mother, father, and spousal roles are adopted, engendering strong support and protection for members. Even in men's prisons where sexual violence is most concentrated, estimates of the incidence of sexual assault run as low as less than 1 percent. In some prisons, of course, the numbers are higher. In New York State, 28 percent of the prisoners reported some form of aggression—threats, propositions, and some physical contact. Even here, however, only one prisoner reported actually being raped.[37]

Sexual assault is not the only form of prison violence. Economic victimization occurs when violence or threats of it accompany the involvement of prisoners in gambling, frauds, loan sharking, theft, robbery, protection rackets, con games, delivery of misrepresented contraband (or non-delivery of contraband), and so on. When promised commodities are not delivered—or are not as promised—victims may retaliate. Drug trafficking is a good example. To get drugs into prisons requires sophisticated smuggling operations. Violence results if drugs are stolen, misrepresented, overpriced, or not delivered. Prisoners use violence to prevent these distribution irregularities from happening in the first place, or to retaliate for them if they do take place.[38]

Prisoners attack not only each other but, especially since the 1960s, increasing numbers of correctional officers. Attacks on officers are sometimes spontaneous and sometimes planned in advance. Officers take great risks in attempting to break up fights, manage intoxicated prisoners, and escort prisoners to punitive segregation. Predictably, these situations provoke assaults. Much worse are the random violent acts that cannot be predicted, such as throwing dangerous objects at officers or dropping items from catwalks above as officers patrol the cell blocks below.[39]

Officers also attack prisoners. According to Todd R. Clear and George F. Cole,

Unauthorized physical violence against inmates by officers to enforce rules, uphold the officer-prisoner relationship, and maintain order is a fact of life in many institutions. Stories abound of guards giving individual prisoners "the treatment" outside the notice of their superiors. Many guards view physical force as an everyday operating procedure and legitimize its use.[40]

In Texas, more than 200 employees were terminated or reprimanded for abusing prisoners. A famous case, *Ruiz v. Estelle,* has documented such attacks

concentration model *putting the most violent criminals in one prison to facilitate their management.*

on prisoners, in which the beatings are routine and the intimidation regular and severe.[41]

The most violent American prison used to be the federal prison at Marion, Illinois, which houses the most dangerous prisoners from the federal prison system and a considerable number from state prisons as well. Marion presents a perplexing problem for prison administrators and criminal justice policymakers: how to control violent prisoners. Most prisons segregate violent prisoners in special units. In small- and medium-size prisons, violent prisoners can stay in these units for short periods of time with no serious management problems. However, large prisons, especially ones like Marion with many "dangerous" prisoners, pose a greater problem. Predatory prisoners go through the special units in a revolving door fashion. Because not all violent prisoners are in the special units at the same time, some prisons are operated as if every prisoner is about to explode into violence.[42]

In the 1930s, the Federal Bureau of Prisons adopted a **concentration model,** putting the most violent prisoners in one prison to facilitate their management. The famous Alcatraz, a former military prison, became home to the worst prisoners from the federal maximum security prisons, including Leavenworth and Atlanta. They were transferred to Alcatraz not for rehabilitation, but for incapacitation and punishment. In 1962 Alcatraz was closed, a victory for reformers who sought rehabilitation in imprisonment. Most inmates were returned to Leavenworth and Atlanta for rehabilitation. As racial tension and violence increased in the 1960s and rehabilitation received more vocal criticism, the then-new federal prison at Marion's Control Unit became the most used holding center for the nation's most dangerous prisoners.

In 1978, the Federal Bureau of Prisons reformed its traditional classification system based on three levels of security—maximum, medium, and minimum—replacing it with six security levels. Marion became the first "level six" or highest security federal prison in the country, until the opening of the new supermaximum federal prison as part of the federal prison complex in Florence, Colorado in 1994 discussed in Chapter 13. The purpose of Marion was the same as that of its predecessor Alcatraz—to "provide long-term segregation within a highly controlling setting" for inmates from throughout the federal system who:

- Threatened or injured other inmates or staff.
- Possessed deadly weapons or dangerous drugs.
- Disrupted "the orderly operation of a prison."
- Escaped or attempted to escape in those instances in which the escape involved "injury, threat of life or use of deadly weapons."

Several reasons lie behind the decision to convert Marion to a super maximum security prison, including a series of gang-related killings at Atlanta Penitentiary, the growing power of gangs in other prisons, creation of "assassination squads" under gang auspices in a number of prisons, an increase in the number of assaults on inmates and staff in level 4 and 5 prisons, the violent deaths of three Marion prisoners, and the stabbings of the Marion associate warden and food service steward in the inmate dining room. During the late 1970s when the prison population was declining, assaults at Marion increased sharply: homicides rose 8.5 percent, assaults on inmates 15.3 percent, and assaults on officers 78.4 percent.

Assaults on staff and inmates at Marion increased sharply again in the early 1980s. Along with some group disturbances were 54 serious inmate-on-inmate assaults, eight prisoner killings, and 28 serious assaults on staff. During 1983, the frequency and seriousness of assaults on staff increased. On July 8, 1983, two prisoners armed with knives stabbed a guard they had taken

Figure 14.3

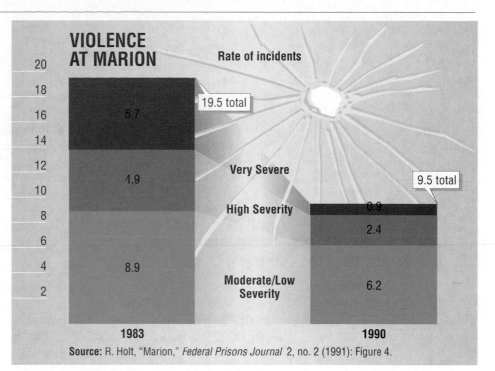

VIOLENCE AT MARION

Rate of incidents

19.5 total

5.7

Very Severe

1.9

High Severity

9.5 total

0.9

2.4

8.9

Moderate/Low Severity

6.2

1983

1990

Source: R. Holt, "Marion," *Federal Prisons Journal* 2, no. 2 (1991): Figure 4.

hostage. The next week, prisoners stabbed five times a **general population inmate** with more privileges than the ordinary level 6 prisoners. Several days later, while prisoners were returning to their cells from the dining hall, two prisoners attacked two guard escorts, stabbing one officer twelve times.

Following this stabbing, the prison was put on **lockdown** status—the temporary suspension of all activities, including recreation. Prisoners received sack lunches in their cells for breakfast, lunch, and dinner. When these restrictions were lifted, one prisoner was stabbed, staff were threatened, and the lockdown was reinstated. This pattern continued, more or less, after 1983—lockdowns, some letup followed by prisoner violence, and then a reinstated lockdown.[43]

Violence at Marion sharply declined with the implementation of a concentration management model (see Figure 14.3). Under the model, prisoners can participate in programs and receive services, but only under a strictly controlled movement system. Prisoners start their sentences at Marion by spending most of their time in their cells or in the cell house. As they demonstrate non-dangerous behavior by compliance with the rules, they progress through a graduated work and housing plan that allows more personal activities. If they continue to progress, prisoners gain more freedom and privileges. The long-term lockdown and close confinement of Marion prisoners have turned them from engaging in physical violence to fighting the conditions of their confinement in federal courts. Impressed with the success of lockdown as a mechanism to control violence, prison managers now speak of "marionizing" their prisons.[44]

Riots

Prison violence sometimes takes the form of collective action; the prison riot is the most feared. Riots, like individual violence, are sometimes spontaneous outbursts; others are planned in advance. A highly organized inmate force held together by racial solidarity and political consciousness planned and executed the famous Attica riot in 1971. To a considerable extent that riot was a product of the 1960s—a political protest against what was considered white oppression. Other riots, such as the New Mexico riot in 1980, were spontaneous, disorganized outbursts.[45]

According to its historian, Mark Colvin, the New Mexico prison riot was the most brutal, destructive, and disorganized riot in American penal history. In 36 hours, prisoners killed 33 fellow prisoners and beat and raped as many as 200 others. After drinking too much homemade whiskey, several drunk prisoners overpowered four guards. Seven guards were taken hostage, beaten, stabbed, or sodomized before being released by their captors. Without any plan, the prisoners took over the entire prison. By chance, they stumbled on an open dormitory door, an open security grill, and blow torches accidentally left behind by renovation crews. Storming through the prison, rioters tortured 12 inmates with blow torches, set them on fire, and mutilated them. They beheaded one with a shovel. Their victims were suspected "snitches" (prisoners who inform on other prisoners' misbehavior), child rapists, and "mentally disturbed" prisoners whose screaming kept their killers awake at night.[46]

Prisoners riot for complicated reasons. It has been argued that riots break out when prison administrations take actions that disrupt existing prison society. This is particularly true when administrations try to alter accommodations existing between staff and prisoners in which prisoners share power with staff, gain status based on that, and reap material benefits to the extent possible inside prison walls. According to Colvin, these administrative disruptions generally arise out of three situations:

1. *Discovering and exposing corruption,* such as narcotics traffic inside prisons.
2. *Policy conflicts,* such as those between reformist, rehabilitation-oriented administrators and old-line, security-oriented staff.
3. *Policy changes* brought about by new prison administrations, such as wardens who decide they are going to "crack down" on minority prisoner assertiveness.[47]

If all three conditions occur simultaneously, trouble is almost certain to follow. Cohesion arising out of power, status, and wealth badly erodes. Conflict between prisoners' social structure and administration's control structure erupts in various forms. Prisoner protests and strikes are organized to reinstate denied privileges. If privileges are restored, order returns.

Sometimes, however, administrations do not respond by restoring lost privileges. Instead, for political or ideological reasons, administrations meet protest with still more restrictions. Prisoners' resentment grows; administrators find it increasingly difficult to restore lost privileges. Mutual hostility between guards and prisoners escalates; administrations change and guard turnover increases. None of these actions restore order. On the contrary, they only raise tensions. As administrative staff divide into warring bureaucratic camps, prisoners' social structure disintegrates into self-protective, hostile cliques. Eventually, rioting breaks out.

Burt Useem and Peter Kimball, in their stimulating study of prison riots, list the following popular theories of the causes of prison riots:

- Violent, depraved prisoners.
- Prison conditions.
- Liberal judges giving prisoners too many rights.
- Radical prisoner organizations stirring up trouble.
- Prisoners crowded as if in cages.
- Racism.
- Gang plots.
- Prisoners' "cry for help."[48]

The *You Decide,* "Why Did New Mexico Prisoners Riot?" elaborates on these and other explanations for one riot.

Scholars have carefully examined the brutal New Mexico prison riot in 1980, one of the worst in United States history. They have given conflicting interpretations of its outbreak. Summarized here are the principal explanations:

- *Security lapses.* Poor security in the prison caused the riot. The open doors and grills prisoners used to start the riot were cited as evidence. Staff and prisoners both, however, testified that security levels were in some ways better when the riot broke out than they were in 1976. In that year, special training in security was adopted, a pass system was instituted, and special wire was placed on perimeter fences. None of these measures stemmed the growing tide of violence and escapes in the prison.
- *Food and services.* Food was never good, according to prisoners. Medical services had improved somewhat, so it was not deterioration in these services that prompted the riot.
- *Overcrowding.* Prison population fluctuated prior to the riot. In 1978, the prison held 1,272 prisoners, well over its designed capacity of 950 prisoners. However, at the time of the riot, the population was near the 950 capacity level, although in the months just before the riot, population suddenly increased by 200. Furthermore, following the riot, when population was at 700 (a record low), six prisoners and two guards were murdered in the prison.
- *Disorganization.* "The system's worst problem was not overcrowding. It was acute disorganization. Beginning about 1975, the state corrections system was subjected to repeated organizational shocks, restructuring rivalries, and massive turnover high and low, which ruined the system's internal control, discipline, and general ability to function."[49]
- *Conspiracies.* An entrenched administrative clique, in defiance of top officials, had been conspiring in corruption, brutality, arbitrary discipline, and cover-ups, and these conspiracies caused the riots. However, such misbehavior was not peculiar to the period in which the riot occurred. It had been common in the prison for years.
- *New-breed prisoners.* A "new breed" of violent criminal populated prisons. They were characterized as psychopaths and even as "genetically violent" and hard to control. Proponents of this position argued that these especially violent criminals began to inhabit the prison about 1975 or 1976. The records show, however, that in proportion to total population, these new-breed prisoners were decreasing; the increases in prison population were due to an influx of mainly property and other nonviolent offenders.
- *Changes in the structure of control and inmate society.* Until 1975, two powerful inmate groups were accommodated by prison administration. One group dominated inmate programs, including a college program, a "college prep" program, an adult education program, a computer keypunch shop, and several other programs involving contact with the outside. The second power group controlled contraband drug trafficking. The administration did not merely tolerate this trafficking; several prison staff were active in the drug trade themselves.

These powerful groups and administrative tolerance of them operated during a time when prison escapes and violence were low. Fewer than 5 percent of the inmates were in solitary confinement during this period. Prisoners controlled other prisoners without violence because they controlled what prisoners wanted—contraband and programs.

After 1975, all of this changed. Determined to remake the existing arrangement, in which the "inmates were running the place," a new administration tried to "wrest control of the prison from the inmates." The administration removed all prisoners from administrative positions in programs, tightened restrictions on prisoner movements, and terminated outside-contact programs. At the same time, they stepped up drug searches and tried to close off possible conduits for drugs. The effect was to end nonviolent prisoner control and its accommodation.

Organized protests followed quickly. Six hundred of the prison's 912 prisoners participated in a work strike to protest the changed policies. The administration did not accept the demands. Instead, it broke up the strike by force. "We are finally showing them who is in charge," said one officer. Strike leaders were put in solitary confinement, and the organized protest was crushed. The number of prisoners in solitary confinement rose from 5 percent to 20 percent of the prison population. Two prisoners in disciplinary segregation filed a class-action suit against the prison. Negotiations over the suit dragged on, with no satisfaction to the inmates. Breaking the strike and the frustratingly long legal battle ended hopes for collective, nonviolent restoration of prisoner power.

The vacuum created by the failure of collective nonviolent action was quickly filled by new-breed prisoners. They waged struggles for control determined by reputations for violence. Prisoners were forced to choose between equally unsatisfactory alternatives for survival, particularly for protection against sexual assaults. They could either turn to new-breed prisoners—no single one of whom dominated the prison, since many were vying for the upper hand—or they could look to officials, who could not adequately protect them either.

As a result, a new ideology, based on the willingness to engage in violence, advocated a struggle between weakness and strength. Strength was measured by brutality against other prisoners, effectively confronting guards, and toughing it out in solitary confinement. About 75 prisoners fit this definition that set the tone of prisoner society—they were its "heroes." Several cliques warred against each other. The most notorious centered on three prisoners who beat another prisoner to death with a baseball bat.

New Mexico prisoner society became increasingly fragmented, divided into small and insecure self-protection units. Because informal control was no longer possible in the prison, informants, or "snitches," became important to administrators. Snitches were given added privileges and were concentrated in one cell block. They were also considered perfect targets on which new-breed criminals could prove their capacity for and willingness to use violence: as objects of great hostility, snitches were perfect scapegoats.

The circumstances that triggered the riot—drunk new-breed prisoners, and open doors and grates—were only triggers. They were not the ammunition that exploded into the gory violence that followed. That ammunition was removing nonviolent prisoner control and administration accommodation to it.[50]

Questions

If you were asked to give the reason, or reasons, why New Mexico prisoners rioted, how would you answer? Defend your answer, using information and arguments presented above.

Overcrowding

Crowding exacerbates hostile race relations, gangs, and violence. According to experts, crowding is "the most critical administrative problem facing the United States criminal justice system." For reasons outlined in Chapter 13, American prison populations have skyrocketed from less than 300,000 to more than a million since 1980. Projections show no diminution in these increases.[51]

It is difficult to assess exactly how these numbers affect crowding because uniform standards defining prison capacity do not exist. The American Correctional Association Commission on Accreditation for Corrections defines capacity standards as follows:

> There is one inmate per room or cell, which has a floor area of at least sixty square feet, provided inmates spend no more than ten hours per day locked in, exclusive of counts; when confinement exceeds ten hours per day, there are at least eighty square feet of floor space.[52]

At the end of 1994, state prisons were operating at between 17 percent and 29 percent above capacity; the federal system was operating at 25 percent above capacity. Twenty-three jurisdictions reported a total of 48,949 state prisoners held in local jails or other facilities because state prisons were too crowded to hold them. Only 15 percent of federal prisoners and 21 percent of state prisoners have cells or rooms to themselves. Thirty-eight percent live in dormitories.[53]

Several developments have caused crowding, but increasing crime rates is *not* one of them. Crime rates had not increased dramatically during the decade that produced the greatest increase in prison populations. Crime rates are age-sensitive. As a generation passes out of its late teens—the age of highest criminality—the crime rates ought to decline. However, peak *arrest* age—16 to 18—is younger than peak *imprisonment* age—the mid-twenties. Few people under 18 go to prison; instead, they receive probation or diversion out of the criminal justice system into community programs. By the time they reach their middle twenties, these youthful criminals have accumulated enough convictions to send them to prison. As a generation passes through the high-imprisonment age bracket, it will affect prison crowding.[54]

Shifting attitudes toward punishment and prison also affect crowding. Rehabilitation is rapidly losing ground to retribution and incapacitation as justifications for criminal punishment. As a result, prison sentences have grown in frequency and length. For a decade, the number of prisoners admitted to prisons has significantly exceeded the number released. Judges have not ignored public opinion demanding more punishment. Increased admissions to prison at a time when street-crime rates have fallen (despite increased reporting of offenses) reflect, in part, the public demand for harsher punishment.

Exacerbating the demographic shift and public demand for harsher punishment is public unwillingness (and in some cases government inability) to pay for additional facilities. Some say that the public and even government officials in some jurisdictions are content to "allow inmates to pile up in prisons until the pressure they create is relieved by a federal court order or a riot focuses public attention on the problem."[55]

Building more prisons provides only one policy option to reduce prison crowding. The easiest short-term alternative is to do nothing, an approach that permits prosecutors to demand harsh prison penalties, judges to respond to those demands, and wardens to pile prisoners two to a cell. This approach, however, has risks. Crowding almost always leads to diminished control by prison administrators and increased control by inmates, usually the most violent. This transfer of control demoralizes staff and leaves unprotected the prisoners who most need protection. Since prisoners and guards have little, if any, political clout, the situation ordinarily remains in check, but not always. The courts could intervene, declaring the conditions unconstitutional, or prisoners might riot, in which case the public might demand changes in the do-nothing approach.[56]

Selective incapacitation combines the demand for more effective crime control with the need to reduce crowding. Identifying the most serious offenders—those who commit the worst crimes, do so most frequently, and are likely to do so in the future—and reserving scarce and costly prison space for them is an attractive idea with many pitfalls. It is difficult to predict who will commit future serious crimes. Research suggests that such predictions might discriminate racially; blacks tend to fall into the high-risk categories much more frequently than whites. Existing research on prediction of criminal potential, sketchy and preliminary, must be tested carefully before individuals are confined in maximum security prisons for extended periods.[57]

Peter Greenwood, who conducted the most thorough study to date of selective incapacitation, makes only limited claims for its use. He reminds us that the theory "might" provide a means to utilize scarce prison space, and

Crowded and unpleasant prison conditions are hailed by some as part of the punishment prisoners should expect.

that selective incapacitation strategies "may" lead to reduced crime rates. Greenwood also cautions that predictive criteria are imprecise and can lead to wrong predictions. Researchers have not independently verified the results.[58]

Rudy A. Haapenan investigated the patterns of officially recorded criminal behavior over a period of nine to fifteen years for 1,300 men committed to California Youth Correctional facilities during the 1960s. Haapenan focused on changes in criminal behavior as the young men moved through their twenties and into their thirties. Race affected the kinds and rates of arrest, and both declined with age. Social influences related to ethnicity or age affected whether and how long offenders engaged in criminal careers, and the year-to-year nature and intensity of careers. According to Haapenan, the instability of and measurement problems with official data greatly reduce the ability to predict which offenders will recidivate at higher rates. Furthermore, selective incapacitation would not have prevented a significant amount of crime in the sample and seems to offer only minimal potential for reducing crime in society. These difficulties suggest that selective incapacitation requires further evaluation before being adopted as a major strategy to reduce prison crowding.[59]

Crowding can be reduced either by not sending people to prison in the first place, a **front-door strategy,** or by releasing them early once imprisoned, a **back-door strategy.** Front-door population decreases come about when first-time property offenders and other so-called marginal offenders are channeled into alternative programs to incarceration. Probation is the most common front-door practice, but there are others. First-time property offenders, for example, might be assigned to a restitution program whereby, in promising to pay back the victim, they avoid going to prison. In recent years, the alternatives to incarceration have grown in richness and variety to include a variety of intermediate punishments.

Back-door strategies attempt to release prisoners earlier than the prescribed time when their sentences expire. Much recommends the use of back-door strategies to reduce prison populations. Research has demonstrated convincingly that sentence certainty is far more important to the prisoner than sentence severity. Thus, it seems wise to send more people to prison for shorter periods than a few for long periods. Prisoners who are incarcerated for long periods show no better rehabilitation rates than those imprisoned for short periods. Nor does long-term imprisonment assure that, when released, prisoners will not return to crime. People seem to retire from criminal careers at about the same rate, whether they are imprisoned or not. These conclusions call for policies aimed at early release from prison, such as the commonly exercised time off for good behavior and parole.[60]

Jurisdictions have adopted three approaches to adjusting admissions and releases to alleviate prison crowding. One ties sentencing to prison population. For example, in Minnesota, by legislative mandate, sentencing guidelines have to take prison capacity into account. The sentencing guidelines are devised according to a certain prison capacity. Sentences must not overload the prisons; to date, they have not. Whether other states will replicate this self-discipline remains uncertain. Even in Minnesota, present legislation will substantially increase prison capacity to allow for growth.[61]

A second strategy is a **safety-valve policy,** such as that adopted by Michigan's legislature in 1981. A commission monitors prison population. If it exceeds capacity, the governor receives the mandate to reduce prison population by reducing the minimum sentences of all prisoners by up to 90 days. This increases the number of prisoners eligible for parole and eliminates automatic release, thereby retaining the parole board's authority and discretion to decide which eligible prisoners should be released. Of course, capacity has to have some meaningful definition if the population control measures based on it are to work. If its definition can be changed to mean two or three prisoners to a cell, for instance, strategies based on it will not make much sense.

cell rationing *the assignment of a certain number of prison cells to each judicial district.*

By May 1984, under Michigan law, the governor had used the safety-valve policy to order eight sentence reductions in both men's and women's prisons. By 1985, more than 2,000 prisoners had been released under the law, at which point Governor Blanchard began to balk because it was becoming increasingly difficult to avoid releasing violent criminals. Public support for the law seriously eroded when, in October 1984, a convicted murderer was released early under the law and later charged with killing a police officer.[62]

Connecticut has proposed a third strategy, called **cell rationing.** Judges and prosecutors in each district are assigned a certain number of cells in the state's prisons. When they have used up their ration and wish to send another convicted defendant to prison, they must designate which of the cells assigned to them they want vacated in order to make room for this proposed new prisoner.[63]

Programs

More than violence and fear, gangs and riots, race relations, and crowded conditions, sheer boredom and monotony most pervades the lives of prisoners. Anyone who visits a prison cannot help but notice how many inmates are either sleeping or sitting around doing nothing. It seems that the one thing inmates have plenty of is—time. Nothing could more clearly demonstrate the meaning of the saying "time on our hands" than the lives of prisoners. Commenting on research on prison society, Samuel Walker writes:

> For the most part, inmates have little to do, even in the form of make-work. Some have jobs, but they tend to be menial and occupy only a few hours at the most. In general, inmates don't do anything, much less anything of a productive or vocational nature.[64]

The lack of meaningful programs is a disappointing aspect of the history of prison reform. From the Elizabethan Houses of Corrections to the modern prison runs a constant refrain: prisoners should work, and they should work hard. In 1900, the Industrial Commission of the House of Representatives said:

> The most desirable system for employing convicts is one which provides primarily for the punishment and reformation of the prisoners and the least competition with free labor, and, secondarily, for the revenue of the state.[65]

In 1950, F. Flynn wrote:

> The modern concept of prisons as institutions for treatment does not contemplate the "busy prison factory" or the self-supporting prison as a goal. Nevertheless, in any well-rounded program directed toward the needs of those confined, some employment projects have their place.[66]

And in 1982, then Chief Justice of the Supreme Court, Warren Burger, said:

> We can continue to have largely human "warehouses," with little or no education and training, or we can have prisons that are factories with fences around them . . . to accomplish the dual objective of training inmates in gainful occupations and lightening the enormous load of maintaining the prison system of this country.[67]

Why should we have prison programs? For a variety of reasons, including

- Work is a cure for what ails prisoners.
- Work can reduce the cost of imprisonment.
- Work can provide training for life outside prison.
- Work can keep prisoners out of trouble.
- Work can produce goods and services for the state.[68]

historical note

The Queen's most Excellent Majesty . . . remembering how many penalties . . . of her laws sundry of her . . . subjects be fallen . . . Her Highness therefore coveting rather by reasonable pity and princely clemency to win her loving subjects to good order of life and obedience to her laws, than otherwise by severe execution of justice, hath thought it meet . . . with her general and free pardon, to deliver and discharge her said subjects from some part of such great pains, penalties, and forfeitures wherewith they stand now burdened by reason of their offenses.

Proclamation of Queen Elizabeth I, 1576

Most prison programs have focused on four main problems that most prisoners face:

1. Inadequate academic education.
2. Insufficient vocational training.
3. Sketchy industrial employment.
4. Deficient social and psychological treatment.

Important as these problems may be, only 10 percent of institutional budgets go toward rehabilitation programs. Prison programs fall into several categories:[69]

- Education.
- Rehabilitation.
- Prison work.
- Recreation.
- Religious.

We tend to think all prison programs have the purpose of rehabilitating prisoners. The National Academy of Sciences defines rehabilitation programs as "any planned intervention that reduces an offender's further criminal activity." But not all programs have rehabilitation as their goal, and even those that do have purposes beyond rehabilitation. The purposes of correctional programs include:[70]

- Rehabilitation.
- Humane punishment.
- Economy.
- Successful prison management.
- Education for its own sake.
- Recreation.
- Religious expression.

Education

Most prisoners enter prison with less than a ninth-grade education. Although it is widely agreed that academic education for prisoners is highly desirable, too many prisons have insufficient programs. There are exceptions: Minnesota and Texas, for example, have highly innovative computer-assisted instructional programs that are regarded as significant contributions to adult prisoner education. Insight Incorporated, Minnesota's private, no-profit corporation founded by two prisoners independently studying for college, provides post-secondary education for prisoners. Prisoner telemarketing and computer services industries support the cost of the program. Any prisoner who passes a battery of tests can enroll in courses while maintaining at least a C average. Fewer than 15 percent of former students have returned to prison. During Insight Incorporated's first 13 years of existence, 40 men at Stillwater Prison earned bachelor's degrees, two obtained master's degrees, and prisoners earned more than 23,000 quarter credit hours.[71]

One purpose of education programs is, of course, rehabilitation. But education serves other purposes as well. Education in our society is valued for its own sake. Among the public and most criminal justice professionals, it also enjoys wide support as part of humane punishment. Furthermore, it contributes to smooth prison management because it gives prisoners something worthwhile to do with their time.

Rehabilitation

Rehabilitation programs cover a wide spectrum—from vocational training to individual psychotherapy. Furthermore, rehabilitation, like education, serves

Most prisoners lack both an adequate academic education and vocational training.

purposes in addition to "reduc[ing] an offender's further criminal activity." These programs, too, contribute to better prison management, help to accomplish the mission of meting out humane punishment, and give prisoners something to do. We discuss here only some of the many programs aimed at the rehabilitation of offenders, including

- Vocational training.
- Work release.
- Financial assistance.
- Prison industries.
- Treatment.

Vocational Training A powerful logic supports the implementation of vocational training. Most prisoners have few, if any, skills qualifying them for legitimate work. Since at least 1870, vocational training has been recognized as central to rehabilitation. But as rehabilitation, according to John P. Conrad, the results of actual programs are disappointing:

> Some excellent training programs have achieved remarkable results, but they are isolated examples. For the most part, vocational training is conducted with inadequate or obsolete equipment, and instructors are poorly prepared. Too often the training is intended to meet institutional maintenance needs rather than the formal requirements of an apprenticeship.[72]

Vocational training fails for several reasons. Equipment is expensive, and prison budgets cannot support purchasing sufficient quantities of it. Many unions do not accept workers who finished apprenticeships in prison. Most prisoners are not imprisoned long enough to complete apprenticeships, or their training is too often interrupted. However, vocational training has other purposes than preparing inmates for life outside prison. It also gives prisoners something to do and satisfies the aims of humane punishment. Furthermore,

principle of less eligibility
prisoners cannot earn as much as people working outside prison.

vocational training enjoys perhaps even more public support than academic education programs. Rightly or wrongly, the public believes vocational training is "useful" whereas academic learning is not.[73]

Work Release Some rehabilitation programs show more promise. An economist, Ann D. Witte, studied work release in North Carolina. Prisoners who participated in work-release programs were less likely to commit serious crimes than prisoners who did not. According to Witte:

> There seems to be a number of possible ways in which work release might affect the seriousness of criminal activity. First, it provides a man with a stable work record and job experience. Second, it allows a man to support his dependents while in prison and hence could aid in keeping his family together. Third, it might provide new job skills. Fourth, it provides a man with money at the time of release and often with a job. Fifth, it allows a man to maintain contacts with the free community and limits at least somewhat his immersion in the prison community. Finally, it may change a man's attitude toward himself and toward society.[74]

Although the results of the North Carolina experiment did not support all these possibilities, Witte concluded that

> work release should be considered a successful program: successful in the sense that men who have been on the work-release program decrease the seriousness of the criminal offenses which they commit after release from prison. This project found most support for work release effecting this decrease in seriousness of criminal activity by improving the work performance and the attitudes of men who participate in the program.[75]

Financial Assistance Providing offenders released from prison with financial assistance in the form of employment compensation also suggests some positive results. An experiment in Georgia and Texas, the Transitional Aid Research Project (TARP), gave an experimental group of released prisoners small weekly payments, while control groups received no such payments. Released prisoners who received the aid were arrested less frequently and were also able to obtain better jobs than those who did not receive aid.[76]

Prison Industries Prison industries show some promise, but major obstacles stand in the way of their success. Prison industries cannot compete with free industry; labor unions and small businesses secured legislation restricting prison industries in every state, and finally in the federal government as well. Another attitude that is difficult to change because it is so firmly entrenched in the public mind is the belief that prisoners should never have a standard of living even slightly better than the poorest free citizens. This basic tenet of penal philosophy has been dominant for centuries: prisoners are supposed to suffer, not make as much money as people working outside. This is called the **principle of less eligibility.**[77]

One idea for prison industry, currently adopted in Minnesota, Kansas, and some other states, is called Free Venture. Its basic idea is to bring free enterprise to prisons. Prisoners work in businesses managed by private entrepreneurs. Such businesses, like their counterparts outside, have to make money. Employees are paid competitive wages. Businesses compete on the open market; if quality declines, so does business, and employees are laid off. This acquaints prisoners with reality in business. Prisoners who are "fired" or laid off return to the prison's general population. Working gives prisoners something productive to do while they are serving prison sentences.

Prison is still prison, and security considerations impair true competition. If there is a lockdown, Free Venture is not exempted from it. Furthermore,

Treatment in German and Japanese Prisons

According to Japanese criminologist Hisao Katoh, the objectives and the reality of prison and treatment contrast in Germany and Japan. Katoh writes:

> By law, the aim of imprisonment is identical in both Japan and West Germany. In both countries the objective is to enable the convict to lead a socially responsible life without crime, after his/her release. However, the term "resocialisation" has different meanings in Japan and West Germany. The reason for this can be found in the different social structures of the two countries. While Japanese society is still very much a strict hierarchy, in Germany these strict structures no longer exist. The one "closed" society has been replaced by an "open" society. Consequently, the content of the term "resocialisation" results in different objectives. The aim in Japan is that the prisoner should be helped to voluntarily take the place reserved for him/her in society, once he/she has served the sentence. In Germany the aim is that the prisoner should be aided to become responsible enough to find his/her own place in the "open" society. In Japanese prison practice there is no meaningful treatment, or real therapeutic activity. Work is forced labor and at the same time serves the security of the institution. In 1972, 16,915 people were employed in Japanese prisons. In 1985, the number had only risen to 16,932. Meaningful work and career supportive measures should be the prime objective. Wages are only seen as rewards for work done.[78]

Free Venture is at present a small, experimental program in only a few places. Minnesota's Stillwater Data Processing, for example, employs only 16 prisoners. However, pessimistic conclusions of the 1970s that "nothing works" in rehabilitating prisoners definitely seem in need of revision. Evidence suggests more that rehabilitation has not been tried than that it does not work.[79]

Florida's prison industry programs, currently operated by PRIDE (Prison Rehabilitative Industries and Diversified Enterprises), a nonprofit corporation, show great promise, according to an evaluation done for the Florida House of Representatives. According to the report, PRIDE's 1987 profits, $4,052,508, doubled the profits of correctional industry programs for the past twenty years. PRIDE employs fewer than half the available workers, but has increased prisoner employment more than 70 percent since eliminating profitless enterprises. Prison recommitment rates were lower for participants than for nonparticipants. PRIDE has reduced the cost to the state by paying more than $4,122,195 into the state's general revenue for housing prisoner workers.[80]

Timothy J. Flanagan and his associates at the Prison Industry Research Project investigated the impact of prison industry employment on offender behavior. Data were collected on 692 prisoners who had worked in prison shops in one of seven facilities for at least six continuous months, and on a comparison group of 742 prisoners in the same facilities who were not employed in prison shops. Recidivism rates were virtually identical between the two groups. However, participants had lower rates of disciplinary infractions inside prison, even when controlling for low, medium, and high risks for prison misconduct among prisoners in both groups.[81]

Treatment Treatment programs in prison fall into two broad categories:

1. Psychological treatment.
2. Behavior modification.

Prison work both saves taxpayers' money and they contribute to prison discipline.

All psychological treatment programs in prison assume that the cause of criminal behavior is an underlying emotional problem or problems. These programs are of several types. Psychotherapy consists mainly of talking. In **individual psychotherapy,** the therapist and the "patient," by means of one-on-one conversation more or less guided by the therapist, try to get to the core of the assumed emotional "illness" that presumably caused the offender to commit crimes. **Group therapy** is based on the idea that since people are "social animals," they can effectively work through their emotional problems by talking in groups. Offenders come together with a therapist who guides their interaction regarding their "problems."

Reality therapy is much more commonly used as a prison psychological treatment program. Reality therapy rests on the straightforward notion that the best therapy is to act more responsibly. Problems arise when people fail in their responsibilities in life—to work hard according to the rules and to treat other people the way they are supposed to be treated, whatever that means. The job of the reality therapist is to repeatedly get offenders to see the consequences—especially the negative consequences—of irresponsible behavior. Reality therapy is popular in prisons for three reasons:

1. It accepts the proposition that the rules of society are inescapable.
2. Its techniques are easy for therapists to learn and apply.
3. The method can be applied in the short term.[82]

Behavior modification treatment programs focus not on individual emotional illness but on how people respond to their environment, particularly how they respond in social situations that get them "in trouble." What needs rehabilitation or reform is not the *feelings* of offenders, but their *actions.* The method operates in two stages:

1. Identify the conditions that cause the "acting out" problem.
2. Change the conditions so that the behavior will change also.

The **token economy** is one popular form of behavior modification therapy. In order to get benefits, such as a television set, inmates have to purchase them with tokens earned by responsible behavior, like going to work or getting good grades. Resembling reality therapy, the token economy brings inmates into constant contact with the way the real world is supposed to work—responsible behavior is rewarded and irresponsible behavior punished.

Work

Prisons have to provide all the basic services that most communities in the outside world have to provide—and more. These include:

- Utilities—sewer and water, electricity, telephones, and so on.
- Restaurants.
- Laundry and dry cleaning.
- Bakeries.
- Hospitals.
- Mail delivery.
- Fire protection.
- Safety.
- Record keeping.
- Janitorial services.

Prisoners do most of the work required to provide these services. Obviously, the resources of prisoner labor and time are in great supply in prisons. Jobs in these services not only get the work of maintaining prisons done, but they also tell a lot about the prestige of the prisoners who hold them. The most prestigious are those jobs closest to the decision makers. Record keeping is the most prestigious because it puts inmates in charge of a valuable commodity—information, such as who is eligible for release or reclassification to lower or higher security prisons. Desk jobs are also desirable because they provide access to administrators and perhaps an opening to better food and other amenities; so are jobs that allow access to the commodities that prisoners can sell in the prison economy. The lowest prestige job is also the most available—janitorial work. This work is menial, like mopping floors, and there is virtually no access to information, goods, and services.[83]

Prison jobs are important for two reasons. First, they save taxpayers' money by using prison labor to do required work that would cost much more if it were hired out. Second, prison jobs contribute to enforcing prison discipline by providing a system of rewards and punishment, and a hierarchy of prestige.[84]

Recreation

Time that is not spent working, in treatment, school, or vocational training, or just "killing time," prisoners devote to recreation. Most prisons have athletic teams; many prisoners work out in prison exercise rooms; virtually all watch movies; some participate in drama, music, art, and journalism. Recreation is an important—and of course desirable—part of prison life, filling some of prisoners' abundant time. Furthermore, recreation programs allow prisoners to maintain some of their individuality by getting together and doing things with others who share their interests. In addition, recreation also serves the interests of rehabilitation by teaching social skills, such as fair competition and working together, and by building self-esteem. Moreover, recreation programs are part of the reward and punishment system that helps to enforce prison discipline. Few inmates want to lose the privilege of recreation.

Finally, recreation definitely fits in with the philosophy of humane punishment. Perhaps nothing more humanizes prisons than allowing prisoners to participate in social activities that they really enjoy. Of course, recreation programs also create safety risks. Fights can—and do—erupt during competitive sports, for example.

Religious

The scholarly literature gives little attention to religious programs in prison, but they exist almost everywhere. In the first place, the First Amendment guarantees freedom of religion and therefore requires prisons to provide religion programs. Second, like most other prison programs, religious programs help prisoners fill time, are supposed to aid in rehabilitation, and contribute to a humane punishment. Todd Clear and his colleagues conducted one of the few national studies of religion in prison. Interviews with inmates indicated the following reasons why religion helps prisoners:

● It provides both a psychological and physical "safe haven."
● It enables inmates to maintain ties with family and with religious volunteers.

The study also found that participation in religious programs contributed both to helping prisoners adjust to prison and to reducing disciplinary infractions.[85]

Evaluation of Prison Programs

Education, vocational training, prison work, and religious programs attract a broad consensus across the political and ideological spectrum and so arouse little controversy. Recreation programs stir up some controversy over whether prisoners who are sent to prison *for* punishment instead get to "work out," compete in sports, and watch movies. However, rehabilitation programs have aroused the greatest amount of controversy, both from an ideological perspective—*Should* we rehabilitate prisoners?—and from a practical standpoint—*Can* we rehabilitate prisoners? The ideological commitment to or against rehabilitation has definitely—and unfortunately—interfered with the evaluation of rehabilitation programs. Robert Martinson, perhaps not intentionally, caused an enormous stir in a spin-off article to a major evaluation in

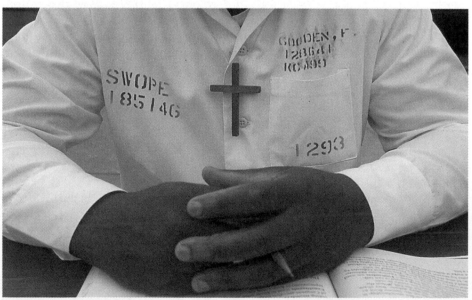

Religious programs exist in virtually every prison in the United States.

1974 of rehabilitation studies. The title of Martinson's article, which appeared prior to the final release of the study, was "What Works?" However, the article quickly was distorted into "nothing works," although Martinson never said that; in fact, 48 percent of the programs surveyed showed positive outcomes.[86]

In an influential survey of the evaluation studies of rehabilitation, the admittedly pro-rehabilitation scholar Ted Palmer reviewed a wide range of prison programs. He found that 25 to 35 percent of the programs "work," meaning they reduce recidivism. But they do not work spectacularly. Some programs that combine treatment with external control reduce recidivism somewhat under some circumstances. Palmer's research suggests that like the 1960s optimism that treatment was a panacea, the deep pessimism that "nothing works" is equally unwarranted. Furthermore, a strong sense that prisons should do more than warehouse prisoners has run throughout the history of American prisons—witness the term *corrections.* As the public's disillusion with the "lock them up and throw away the key" approach of the 1980s grows, rehabilitation has returned to a more favorable place. But practitioners and policymakers hold a more hard-headed attitude toward it.[87]

Charles H. Logan of the University of Connecticut and Gerald G. Gaes of the Federal Bureau of Prisons dismiss Palmer's study and other **meta-analyses** (studies of studies) of rehabilitation programs. Because of a host of definitional, methodological, and other complicated problems, and due to the ideological bias in favor of rehabilitation possessed by most of the meta-analysis scholars, the studies of studies of rehabilitation cannot be trusted, according to Logan and Gaes.[88]

Perhaps the fairest summary of the state of our knowledge about this controversial subject is that the results of the studies evaluating rehabilitation programs are decidedly mixed—decidedly mixed, that is, if we are simply evaluating whether the programs *rehabilitate the offender.* But rehabilitation programs serve other purposes than preparing offenders to "work hard and play by the rules" when they leave prison. Rehabilitation programs keep prisoners busy and keeping them busy keeps them out of trouble, even if it does not turn them into law-abiding people. Furthermore, "constructive" activity is consistent with an orderly, safe, humane confinement. Finally, according to Logan and Gaes:

> "Constructive" activity is not defined here as "contributing to the betterment of inmates" but as activity that is, on its face, consistent with the orderly, safe, secure, and humane operation of a prison. Idleness and boredom can be considered wrong from a work ethic standpoint, or as unnatural because human beings are not meant to be idle, or as so fundamentally related to mischief as to be undesirable for that reason. In any case, prison programs can be defended as forms of constructive and meaningful activity and as antidotes to idleness, without invoking claims of rehabilitative effectiveness. This is not to say that it does not matter whether the programs have any rehabilitative effects; it would be fine if they did so. But when we say that the primary purpose of the prison is to punish through confinement, we become more interested in the operation of these programs inside the prison gates and less concerned about their effects beyond.[89]

The Constitution in Prison

Conviction for a crime and a sentence of imprisonment work a fundamental change in a person's legal status. The Thirteenth Amendment to the U.S. Constitution dramatically states this change:

> Neither slavery nor involuntary servitude, *except as a punishment for crime whereof the party shall have been duly convicted,* shall exist within the United States. (Emphasis added.)

In other words, convicted persons may expect both severe restrictions on liberty and forced labor without either violating the Constitution. An often-cited case from Virginia following the Civil War made clear what the Thirteenth Amendment meant to prisoners. In *Ruffin v. Commonwealth,* the Virginia court held:

> For the time being, during his term of service in the penitentiary, he is in a state of penal servitude to the State. He has, as a consequence of his crime, not only forfeited his liberty, but all his personal rights except those which the law in its humanity accords to him. He is for the time being the slave of the State.
>
> The bill of rights is a declaration of general principles to govern a society of freemen, and not of convicted felons and men civilly dead. Such men have some rights it is true, such as the law in its benignity accords to them, but not the rights of freemen. They are the slaves of the State undergoing punishment for heinous crimes committed against the laws of the land. While in this state of penal servitude, they must be subject to the regulations of the institution of which they are inmates, and the laws of the State to whom their service is due in expiation of their crimes.[90]

The U.S. Supreme Court has gone so far as to say that "prison brutality . . . is part of the total punishment to which the individual is being subjected for his crime." However, prisoners are not totally without rights. The Court has extended some rights—with severe limitations—to prisoners.[91]

"Hands Off" Prisons

Until the 1960s, courts rarely interfered with prison life. How prisons were run and the way prisoners were treated inside them were considered matters for prison administrators, and courts kept their "hands off." This approach was called the **"hands-off" doctrine** of prison law. According to the hands-off doctrine, the law did not accompany prisoners inside the prison; it left them at the prison gate. Prison conditions and prison society were matters properly left wholly to administrative discretion; they were not the courts' business.

The main justification for this hands-off doctrine was that judges were not qualified to run prisons. They were untrained in prison administration and far from the conditions administrators were expected to manage. It made no sense for judges to substitute their own opinions for those of the experts, the prison administrators and line officers. Another argument in favor of the hands-off doctrine was the retributive nature of prisons. Prisons are for punishment; they are supposed to be unpleasant. Finally, the hands-off doctrine was necessary for prison security. Prisoners' rights backed up by judicial intervention could become an avenue for prison unrest and even riot.[92]

During the 1960s—paralleling many other movements for the rights of the dispossessed—a prisoners' rights movement arose. From that time, the courts have recognized and are willing to enforce some constitutional standards in a severely limited fashion. In defining these rights, the courts balance the limited rights of prisoners against strong needs for security, order, and discipline in prison.

A combination of forces in the 1960s put limits on the hands-off doctrine. The civil rights movement extended to the rights of prisoners. Prisoners, especially African American and Hispanic prisoners, took their grievances about prison conditions and the treatment of minority prisoners to court. Moreover, disillusionment with rehabilitation led to a shift from an emphasis on the *needs* of prisoners to a focus on their *rights*. A viable prisoners' rights movement, however, required a forum. The judicial activism of reform-minded judges gave prisoners that forum, permitting them to bring grievances to the courts. Having so respected a grievance forum as the nation's courts generated great solidarity among prisoners, and this prisoner solidarity itself enhanced the prisoners' rights movement. However, without the support of a new breed of prison lawyers, specialists who knew how to voice complaints and frame grievances in legal and constitutional terms, the prisoners' rights movement would have probably come to naught. According to James B. Jacobs, a leading scholar of prisons and the rights of prisoners:

> A platoon, eventually a phalanx, of prisoners' rights lawyers, supported by federal and foundation funding, soon appeared and pressed claims. They initiated, and won, prisoners' rights cases that implicated every aspect of prison governance. In many cases the prisoners' attorneys were more dedicated and effective than the overburdened and inexperienced government attorneys who represented the prison officials.[93]

Overview of Prisoners' Rights

The product of the prisoners' rights movement was the establishment of some general definition of the limited rights of prisoners. Three general principles govern the rights of prisoners:

1. Prisoners do not forfeit all their rights, because they are still citizens.
2. Prisoners have fewer rights than free citizens because (a) restriction on rights is a perfectly appropriate part of punishment and (b) because the restriction of rights is necessary in order to maintain the safety and security of prisons.
3. Courts grant wide discretion to prison officials in determining what restrictions punishment, security, and safety require.[94]

Limited by these principles, prisoners retain the following rights, although to much more limited degree than ordinary citizens:

- Access to the courts.
- Due process of law.
- Equal protection of the laws.
- First Amendment rights.
- The Eighth Amendment right against "cruel and unusual punishment."
- Fourth Amendment rights against unreasonable searches and seizures.

Access to the Courts Prisoners have the right of access to the courts, the most basic right of all Americans. Access to the courts includes access to challenge the legitimacy, duration, and conditions of confinement; access to attorneys; the right to a **jailhouse lawyer** (prisoners who help ignorant, illiterate, or otherwise incompetent fellow prisoners); access to law libraries; and access to transcripts of their cases, to typewriters, and to other writing implements they need to present their claims.

Due Process of Law The Fifth and the Fourteenth Amendments guarantee that neither the federal government nor state governments can "deprive any person of life, liberty, or property without due process of law." (See Chapter 3.) In determining whether state officials have deprived prison inmates of life, liberty, or property without due process of law, the Supreme Court looks at:

1. How severe in degree or kind the deprivation is.
2. The procedures followed to deprive inmates of life, liberty, or property.

The amount of process "due" to prisoners is considerably less than that due to law-abiding people outside prisons. The Court divides deprivations into three categories for the purposes of determining whether they violate due process rights:

1. Deprivations so trivial that they clearly do not deprive prisoners of life, liberty, or property.
2. Deprivations so serious that they clearly deprive prisoners of life, liberty, or property.
3. Deprivations that are not either clearly trivial or clearly in violation of the rights of prisoners.[95]

The Court has found that taking away "good time" clearly invades the liberty of prisoners. Therefore, prison administration cannot take away good time without following procedures that will insure "due process of law." Prison administrators can, however, move prisoners from medium to maximum security facilities where the restrictions are much greater.[96]

Assuming that states have invaded a right, how much process are prisoners due? The Supreme Court has ruled that prisoners are clearly not entitled to the "full panoply of rights due" an ordinary citizen in a criminal trial. The state can follow a more flexible procedure that balances the rights of inmates and the needs of the prison. The state can satisfy the requirements of due process by providing:

1. Prison administrators must provide written notice to inmates of disciplinary charges no less than 24 hours prior to disciplinary proceedings that deprive inmates of their rights.
2. Inmates are entitled to impartial disciplinary proceedings.
3. Decision makers must provide inmates with a written statement of the facts relied on and the reasons for the decision.
4. Inmates should be allowed to call witnesses and present evidence.
5. Inmates have no constitutional right to confrontation and cross-examination in disciplinary proceedings.
6. Inmates have no right to retained or appointed counsel in disciplinary proceedings.[97]

Equal Protection of the Laws The Fourteenth Amendment guarantees all citizens, including prisoners, equal protection of the laws. The most common equal protection claim that prisoners make is against racial discrimination. Although the Constitution prohibits outright racial discrimination, it does not prevent differential treatment on racial grounds. Therefore, according to the Supreme Court, prison administrators have "the right, acting in good faith and in particularized circumstances, to take into account racial tensions in maintaining security, discipline, and good order."[98]

Free Speech, Association, and Religion Prisoners retain First Amendment rights to expression, association, and religion to the extent that such rights do not either conflict with their status as prisoners or interfere with the objectives of the correctional system. Courts strike a balance between prisoners' rights and prison administrative needs in this area. Hence, prison administrators can censor the correspondence of prisoners for legitimate security purposes. In *Procunier v. Martinez,* the Supreme Court ruled that California's prison censorship rules were constitutional because they were designed to enhance security, order, and rehabilitation; and because First Amendment freedoms were restricted only enough to ensure security, order, and rehabilitation.[99]

Right Against Cruel and Unusual Punishment The Eighth Amendment prohibits "cruel and unusual punishments." This prohibition, according to the Supreme Court, was "designed to protect those convicted of crimes."

However, the Eighth Amendment does not extend to "every government action affecting the interests or well-being of a prisoner." According to the Court,

> only the unnecessary and wanton infliction of pain constitutes cruel and unusual punishment forbidden by the Eighth Amendment. . . . It is obduracy and wantonness, not inadvertence or error in good faith, that characterize the conduct prohibited by the Eighth Amendment clause, whether that conduct occurs in connection with establishing conditions of confinement, supplying medical needs, or restoring official control over a tumultuous cellblock. The infliction of pain in the course of a prison security, therefore, does not amount to cruel and unusual punishment simply because it may appear in retrospect that the degree of force authorized or applied for security purposes was unreasonable. . . .[100]

The Court applied this interpretation in *Whitley v. Albers*. During a riot at the Oregon State Penitentiary, prisoners took a correctional officer hostage and held him in the upper tier of a two-tier cellblock. Prison officials developed a plan to free the hostage. According to the plan, the prison security manager entered the cellblock unarmed. Armed prison officials followed him. The security manager ordered one of the officers to fire a "warning shot and to shoot low at any inmates climbing the stairs to the upper tier since he would be climbing the stairs to free the hostage." Assistant Warden Harol Whitley, after firing the warning shot, shot inmate Gerald Albers in the knee when Albers tried to climb the stairs. Albers contended that shooting him was cruel and unusual punishment. Even though the Court agreed that, viewing the incident in retrospect, the use of deadly force was probably excessive, the action was not "cruel and unusual punishment." As long as the action was taken in "good faith," it was not an "intentional and wanton infliction of pain."[101]

Right Against Unreasonable Searches and Seizures The Fourth Amendment protects against unreasonable searches and seizures by any agent of the government (see Chapter 6). But the right of *prisoners* against unreasonable searches and seizures is extremely limited. (Some critics say that for all practical purposes prisoners have *no* rights against unreasonable searches and seizures.) Surveillance, cell and strip searches, monitored visits, censored mail, and other restrictions on privacy are basic parts of prison life, justified on the grounds that prisoners are in prison for punishment and that such intrusions are necessary to secure safe and orderly prisons.

In the leading case on the Fourth Amendment rights of prisoners, *Hudson v. Palmer*, the Supreme Court ruled that the Fourth Amendment search and seizure clause does not protect prisoners' right to privacy in their prison cells. The *You Decide* considers the decision in *Hudson v. Palmer*.

You Decide   Do Prisoners Have a Right against Unreasonable Searches and Seizures?

The following is extracted from the United States Supreme Court's opinion in *Hudson v. Palmer*, 468 U.S. 517 (1984).

Facts

Respondent Palmer is an inmate at the Bland Correctional Center in Bland, Va., serving sentences for forgery, uttering, grand larceny, and bank robbery convictions. On September 16, 1981, petitioner Hudson, an officer at the Correctional Center, with a fellow officer, conducted a "shakedown" search of respondent's prison locker and cell for contraband. During the "shakedown," the officers discovered a ripped pillowcase in a trash can near respondent's cell bunk. Charges against Palmer were instituted under the prison disciplinary procedures for destroying state property. After a hearing, Palmer was found guilty on the charge and was ordered to reimburse the State for the cost of the material destroyed; in addition, a reprimand was entered on his prison record.

Opinion

We have repeatedly held that prisons are not beyond the reach of the Constitution. No "iron curtain" separates one from the other. Indeed, we have insisted that prisoners be accorded those rights not fundamentally inconsistent with imprisonment itself or incompatible with the objectives of incarceration. For example, we have held that invidious racial discrimination is as intolerable within a prison as outside, except as may be essential to "prison security and discipline."

However, while persons imprisoned for crime enjoy many protections of the Constitution, it is also clear that imprisonment carries with it the loss of many significant rights. These constraints on inmates, and in some cases the complete withdrawal of certain rights, are "justified by the considerations underlying our penal system." The curtailment of certain rights is necessary, as a practical matter, to accommodate a myriad of "institutional needs and objectives" of prison facilities, chief among which is internal security. Of course, these restrictions or retractions also serve, incidentally, as reminders that, under our system of justice, deterrence and retribution are factors in addition to correction.

We have not before been called upon to decide the specific question whether the Fourth Amendment applies within a prison cell. . . . [W]e hold that society is not prepared to recognize as legitimate any subjective expectation of privacy that a prisoner might have in his prison cell and that, accordingly, the Fourth Amendment proscription against unreasonable searches does not apply within the confines of the prison cell. The recognition of privacy rights for prisoners in their individual cells simply cannot be reconciled with the concept of incarceration and the needs and objectives of penal institutions.

Prisons, by definition, are places of involuntary confinement of persons who have a demonstrated proclivity for anti-social criminal, and often violent, conduct. Inmates have necessarily shown a lapse in ability to control and conform their behavior to the legitimate standards of society by the normal impulses of self-restraint; they have shown an inability to regulate their conduct in a way that reflects either a respect for law or an appreciation of the rights of others.

The administration of a prison, we have said, is "at best an extraordinarily difficult undertaking." But it would be literally impossible to accomplish the prison objectives identified above if inmates retained a right of privacy in their cells. Virtually the only place inmates can conceal weapons, drugs, and other contraband is in their cells. Unfettered access to these cells by prison officials, thus, is imperative if drugs and contraband are to be ferreted out and sanitary surroundings are to be maintained.

Determining whether an expectation of privacy is "legitimate" or "reasonable" necessarily entails a balancing of interests. The two interests here are the interest of society in the security of its penal institutions and the interest of the prisoner in privacy within his cell. The latter interest, of course, is already limited by the exigencies of the circumstances: A prison "shares none of the attributes of privacy of a home, an automobile, an office, or a hotel room."

We strike the balance in favor of institutional security, which we have noted is "central to all other corrections goals." A right of privacy in traditional Fourth Amendment terms is fundamentally incompatible with the close and continual surveillance of inmates and their cells required to ensure institutional security and internal order. We are satisfied that society would insist that the prisoner's expectation of privacy always yield to what must be considered the paramount interest in institutional security. We believe that it is accepted by our society that "[l]oss of freedom of choice and privacy are inherent incidents of confinement."

Dissent

Prison guard Hudson maliciously took and destroyed a quantity of Palmer's property, including legal materials and letters, for no reason other than harassment. Measured by the conditions that prevail in a free society, neither the possessions nor the slight residuum of privacy that a prison inmate can retain in his cell can have more than the most minimal value. From the standpoint of the prisoner, however, that trivial residuum may mark the difference between slavery and humanity.

Personal letters, snapshots of family members, a souvenir, a deck of cards, a hobby kit, perhaps a diary or a training manual for an apprentice in a new trade, or even a Bible—a variety of inexpensive items may enable a prisoner to maintain contact with some part of his past and an eye to the possibility of a better future. Are all of these items subject to unrestrained perusal, confiscation or mutilation at the hands of a possibly hostile guard? Is the Court correct in its perception that "society" is not prepared to recognize any privacy or possessory interest of the prison inmate—no matter how remote the threat to prison security may be?

It is well-settled that the discretion accorded prison officials is not absolute. A prisoner retains those constitutional rights not inconsistent with legitimate penological objectives. There can be no penological justification for the seizure alleged here. There is no contention that Palmer's property posed any threat to institutional security. Hudson had already examined the material before he took and destroyed it. The allegation is that Hudson did this for no reason save spite; there is no contention that under prison regulations the material was contraband. The need for "close and continual surveillance of inmates and their cells," in no way justifies taking and destroying non-contraband property; if material is examined and found not to be contraband, there can be no justification for its seizure.

Questions

Which opinion do you support, the majority (which is regarded as "the law of the land") or the dissent? If you were deciding the law, what would you decide, and what reasons would you give?

Prisoners' Rights in Germany

Formerly—as was true in the United States—prison authorities in Germany had almost unlimited discretion regarding prisoners. German courts, like those in the United States, followed the "hands-off" doctrine to prison administration. Now, the German Code on the Execution of Prison Sentences requires prison authorities to seek expert advice concerning prison labor, health care, and prisoner rehabilitation. The code also guarantees prisoners a number of other privileges and rights, including the right to receive mail, telephone calls, and visitors; to receive permission to leave the institution for up to 21 days; and to petition the courts for grievances.

The code restricts prison administrators to the following disciplinary measures when prisoners violate prison rules:

- Warnings.
- Restrictions on entertainment, such as watching television or sports events.
- Limits on visits by family and friends.
- Solitary confinement for up to four weeks.

Special courts supervise German prison authorities. Prisoners can file complaints whenever they believe prison authorities have violated their rights. The right to file a complaint and have a court hear the complaint is considered fundamental to the rule of law in Germany, despite complaints by prison administrators that prisoners file too many frivolous complaints.[102]

Prisoners' Rights in Operation

Beginning in the late 1970s and continuing through the 1990s, the Supreme Court placed limits on prisoners' rights, returning much—though by no means all—of the discretion enjoyed by prison administrators during the "hands-off" era. Typical of this move to return discretion to prison administrators and to limit the rights of prisoners is the important case of *Bell v. Wolfish,* in which the Court ruled that prisoners had no right to a single cell. Justice Rehnquist wrote:

> The deplorable conditions and draconian restrictions of our Nation's prisons are too well known to require recounting here, and the federal courts rightly have condemned these sordid aspects of our prison systems. But many of these same courts have, in the name of the Constitution, become increasingly enmeshed in the minutiae of prison operations. Judges, after all, are human. They, no less than others in our society, have a natural tendency to believe that their individual solutions to often intractable problems are better and more workable than those of the persons who are actually charged with the running of the particular institution under examination. But under the Constitution, the first question to be answered is not whose plan is best, but in what branch of government is lodged the authority to initially devise the plan. This does not mean constitutional rights are not to be scrupulously observed. It does mean, however, the inquiry of federal courts into prison management must be limited to the issue of whether a particular system violates any prohibition of the Constitution, or in the case of a federal prison, a statute. The wide range of "judgment calls"

that meet constitutional and statutory requirements are confined to officials outside the Judiciary Branch of Government.[103]

Not only has the Supreme Court restricted the rights of prisoners and returned discretionary judgment to prison officials. Most prisoners fail in their lawsuits even when the Court has accepted that they have rights against discretionary decision making by prison administrators. Most prisoner cases never get beyond the earliest stages of the proceedings. In California, for example, the court terminated 80.4 percent of prisoner cases shortly after filing and before the court registered any response by the defendant prison administrations. Nationwide, 68 percent of all prisoner cases were dropped at this early stage. Due to early dismissal, only 4.2 percent of all cases filed ever get to trial. However, Jack E. Call found that prisoners meet with greater success in prison crowding cases. Courts issued favorable rulings in 73.8 percent of all cases, 80 percent in federal district courts, and 66 percent in courts of appeals. According to Call, many courts have made it clear that prison administrative discretion in managing prisons will not shield prisons from litigation involving "gruesome living conditions."[104]

Even when prisoners succeed in getting their cases into court, they practically never "win." In one 664-case sample, only three court orders were issued regarding confinement conditions; only two prisoners were awarded minimal money damages. In a few more cases, seven temporary restraining orders and five preliminary injunctions were issued. Prisoners who win their cases almost certainly have lawyers, because cases rarely go to trial unless prisoners have attorneys. In the two cited cases awarded damages, the prisoner with a lawyer received $200; the one without a lawyer got only $6![105]

Although prisoners win few victories in lower federal courts, court cases still have an impact on prisons. Even a lost case can lead to prison reform. Prison administrators do not want courts to intrude into their domain, so they sometimes make changes in order to avoid the intrusions. Jim Thomas, in his analysis of prisoner litigation, quotes one prison administrator on the effects of prisoner lawsuits:

> Where only a few years ago prisons operated without written rules and with only the most rudimentary record keeping systems, today prison authorities are engulfed in bureaucratic paper. There are regulations, guidelines, policy statements, and general orders; there are forms, files, and reports for virtually everything.[106]

Litigation has also increased centralization and oversight by correctional administrations. Although in the short term, court orders may reduce staff morale and even cause prison violence, court restrictions on crowding have increased prison and jail construction, according to Malcolm Feeley and Roger Hanson. Court orders have also mitigated the most extreme abusive conditions in prisons. A detailed study of four major prison conditions cases found that compliance, although grudging, slow, and incomplete, led all four states to spend substantial amounts of money responding to court orders. In some cases, new prisons were built following litigation. It is unlikely that this would have occurred had prisoners not sued their keepers.[107]

Internal Grievance Mechanisms

Lawsuits are not the only redress for prisoners who have grievances against prison administration. Virtually every prison provides for internal grievance proceedings. Elaborate rules formulated by administrations with legal assistance govern grievance proceedings. Prison officers and sometimes outside participants, including former prisoners on occasion, operate such grievance mechanisms. Although not totally supported by either prisoners or prisons' critics, internal grievance proceedings play a significant part in prison governance and life. In the past 15 years, a spectacular growth in prison internal grievance mechanisms has taken place. In every adult correctional system in the country, some procedures exist for resolving prisoners' grievances without going to court.[108]

No two states have exactly the same grievance system, but all systems have some basic similarities. Most possess broad mandates to hear prisoner grievances. Illinois, for example, opens its Institutional Inquiry Board (IIB) to any prisoner who wants "resolution to complaints, problems, and grievances which [he or she has] not been able to resolve through other avenues available at the institution or facility."[109]

Common Grievances and Disciplinary Violations

In Illinois, the most common grievances are

- Claims for early release.
- Charges that guards issued disciplinary "tickets" improperly.
- Complaints that work or program assignments were not right.
- Claims that prisoners were classified wrong.
- Charges that property was lost, stolen, or confiscated.

Common disciplinary actions against prisoners include "tickets" for:

- "Dangerous disturbances."
- "Disobeying a direct order."
- "Unauthorized movement."
- "Assaulting another prisoner or an officer."
- "Destroying or damaging property."
- "Possessing dangerous contraband."
- "Sexual misconduct."[110]

Minnesota supplies prisoners in all facilities with a written list of their rights, out of which come most grievances. The rights include:

- A published list of the charges and penalties.
- A prompt and full statement of the nature of the alleged violation not later than five days after the prisoner is charged with a prison rule violation.
- The right to adequate notice prior to the hearing.
- The opportunity for a prisoner to appear in person before the disciplinary hearing board and be heard.
- The right to bring witnesses and present evidence to the hearing.
- The right to an impartial hearing board.
- The right to counsel or substitute counsel throughout the process.
- A written notice of the board's findings.
- The right to appeal to the warden or another designated person.
- The right to a record of the proceedings at the hearing for review and appeal.[111]

Prisoners most often challenge disciplinary tickets when they affect vital prisoner interests, such as good time and classification. In Illinois, for example, prisoners get a one-day sentence reduction for every day of good time served. Discipline infractions can reduce this good time. Also in Illinois, prisoners are classified either A, B, or C. Grade A entitles prisoners to maximum freedom and privileges; C means maximum security and the least freedom. Disciplinary tickets might lead to downgrading in security level. A challenge to a disciplinary ticket might, therefore, be grounds to grieve reduced good time and security reclassification. For example, according to Illinois prison rules, forced sexual contacts carry maximum penalties that reduce good time by 360 days and that downgrade prisoners to grade-C security for 360 days.[112]

Denying requests for protective custody also provides a ground to file a grievance. Protective custody means that prisoners—often at their own request—are put in the segregation unit, where movement is restricted in order to avoid danger. One grievance arose when prison officials denied a request for protective custody against African American gang members to a six foot, four inch white man weighing 210 pounds. Prison officials stated that someone of the prisoner's size ought to be able to protect himself.[113]

The property of prisoners accounts for another group of grievances. Most commonly, these arise because the administration has confiscated property on the ground that it is either unauthorized or contraband. Other common cases involve lost or stolen prisoner property. According to the prisoner, the administration did not carry out its responsibility either to protect the property or to compensate for its loss. Even though property cases do not ordinarily involve items worth a lot of money, they are important. First, they make up a considerable number of grievances filed. Second, items such as photographs, jewelry, and jackets may have sentimental value to the prisoner. These items may be all that provides individuality in an otherwise very impersonal and regulated place.

Grievance Procedures and Their Effects

Decisions regarding these grievances are generally two-tiered. Members of a local grievance committee, drawn entirely from within the prison, initially decide for or against the prisoner. Prisoners can appeal adverse decisions to a board drawn from outside the prison, sometimes one with private citizens as well as correctional administrators on it. The mechanism is self-contained; that is, the local board is a local prison body, and the appeals board is a statewide corrections department body.

Proceedings in grievance bodies are formal, governed by written rules and regulations. Prisoners have basic due process rights, usually including the right to be present at the hearing, sometimes the right to have witnesses and to challenge adverse evidence, and the right to have a decision in writing within a specified time period. This written decision must set forth the reasons supporting the board's ruling. Sometimes, prisoners must go through the whole grievance procedure inside the prison before taking any of their complaints to courts, in a requirement called "exhausting administrative remedies."

Prisoners rarely win their grievance cases. One prisoner overestimated the win ratio when he said, "You don't win more than one in ten." In fact, it is considerably less. One survey reviewed grievances in several cell blocks and showed that prisoners won only one case out of 12 in one block, one of 19 in a second, one of 25 in a third, and only one in 28 in a fourth. On appeal to a review board, the results were also low. In one maximum security prison, prisoners "won" 17 percent of the appeals and lost 75 percent. Another 7 percent had mixed results.[114]

Grievance procedures in prisons have several aims:

● They improve prison management and help to identify problems.
● They reduce inmate frustration and prison violence.
● They aid in prisoner rehabilitation.
● They reduce the number of cases prisoners take to the courts.
● They bring "justice" to prisons.

Existing grievance mechanisms may or may not substantiate these justifications. Research has raised several questions. To improve prison management by identifying problems, the first aim, prison administrations have to take the time periodically to review caseloads to determine what kinds of grievances prisoners have. Only by reviewing the grievances can something be done about them. This takes time and resources that most prisons simply do not have. To achieve this aim might require prisoners to bring grievances more selectively; instead of using grievance procedures to express "rights consciousness" or harassment, prisoners may have to make their complaints more "pure." According to prison litigation expert Jan Brakel:

> The message to inmates should be that abusing the procedures for frivolous, repetitive grievances harms the chances of other inmates, and ultimately their own, of having important things changed.[115]

Few prison officials go so far as to say that grievance procedures eliminate violence from prisons. They may provide a "safety valve" for prisoner discontent and thereby "keep the lid on" violent prison outbreaks, but there is little or no proof that this is true. No correlation seems to exist between violence levels and prison grievance mechanisms. Through grievance procedures, isolated inmates might develop more respect for, and willingness to abide by, regular procedures, thereby becoming "rehabilitated," more ready to live in society without breaking its rules. However, most prisoners do not view grievance mechanisms positively. In many cases they seem only to confirm prisoners' ideas that institutions rig decisions to maintain the establishment against dissidents; in this case, prison officials against prisoners.[116]

Proving that grievance mechanisms reduce the load of cases in courts is also difficult. Many things influence these caseloads, and it is impossible to say that grievance procedures determine them. Grievance mechanisms may even increase litigation because prisoners who are more conscious of their rights are more apt to demand them. If they do not feel satisfied at the administrative level, then they will carry on their fight in the courts.

Finally, it is not clear that grievance mechanisms bring justice to the prisons. For that to be the case, according to Jan Brakel, administrators and prisoners must use them to best advantage,

> instead of playing games with them, games of power, games of psychology, harassment games, legalistic games, passing time games, and so forth. At neither Vienna nor Stateville were the procedures used to full advantage—the staff failed to maximize both the problem-identification and the problem-disposition potential of the process, and far too many of the inmates abused the process with groundless or frivolous claims.[117]

Several recommendations attempt to bring the reality of grievance mechanisms closer to the claims made for them. One suggests changing the composition of the grievance body. Prisoners and other critics commonly complain that prison officials dominate grievance mechanisms. They call for more outside participation, either by citizens or prisoners. However, although outsiders may be impartial, they are also naive and ignorant of prison society, and can therefore be "conned" by both prisoners and administration. Prisoners do not make feasible members, either. They can be partial and subject to intimidation and physical danger if they rule against another prisoner.

Other reformers demand that procedures be made more formal. They ought to generate more documentation, and they should be more bound by precedent. Some believe, however, that there already is enough paper; the real problem is how to use the documentation to achieve fair and just results. Demands for more investigation, more listening to the prisoners' side of the story, and so on accomplish little if they merely add to an already heavily burdened grievance body.[118]

Perhaps the severest criticism is that too many frivolous and trumped-up grievances, or ones brought only to harass, are filed. Grievances must be screened more carefully, but the problem of how to do this remains. How does anyone decide, before hearings begin, whether a complaint has merit or is a farce—something "cooked up to obstruct the system, harass the staff, pass dead time?" Once proceedings begin, however, frivolous claims often come to light. At that point, they could be penalized, and such penalties might take several forms. Privileges such as movies, television, or visits to the commissary could be taken away. Refiling restrictions could be imposed if present grievances are decided to be frivolous or spurious. Extreme cases might even call for the levy of fines.[119]

Summary

Prisons are structures with which all of us are familiar—usually at a distance and in pictures, not by first-hand experience. But inside the walls of prisons exists a society that has both a structure and a process. Prison society, like societies outside prisons, has both its formal and informal dimensions. The rules of the prison, the statutes enacted by legislatures, the decisions of courts, and the provisions of the state and federal constitutions define the formal structure and process of life in prison. But these formal rules cannot regulate the whole of prison life. An inmate social structure operates within prisons, and this structure does not always conform to formal rules. Discretion allows values other than the legal and bureaucratic to shape prison society and life. Management styles, custodial staff relations with each other and with prisoners, and particularly noncustodial staff operate substantially along nonhierarchical, informal, discretionary lines, not mechanically according to rules, statutes, and court decisions. Finally, prison society is not divorced totally from the society outside. In a real sense, prisons are part of, interact with, and reflect the larger society.

The connections between the outside world and the world inside prisons cannot remove a central reality of prison life—the entire daily existence of prisoners takes place inside prison walls, a situation fundamentally different from ordinary society. The basic social arrangement in modern society is to "sleep, play, and work" in different places, under different authorities. Prisoners work, play, and sleep in prison, under prison authority. They do almost everything in blocks or groups, not as individuals. They eat, work, recreate, shower, and move about together, not alone. The days of prisoners are tightly organized and controlled. When one activity ends, another begins immediately according to schedules imposed by prison officials. Prisoners perform all these activities under close supervision. Because they are watched as closely as the reality of supervision allows, they have minimal, if any, privacy.[120]

The formal aims of order, safety, and security justify block movements, tight schedules, limited privacy, and other features of total institutions. Furthermore, these aims conform to the major purpose of prisons—to punish convicted offenders. According to modern standards, the purpose of prison is confinement without the luxuries of life, but of course with the provision of the basics—food, shelter, clothing, medical care, safety, security, and the opportunity to participate in positive programs. It is commonly said among today's academics and professionals in penology that convicted offenders are sent to prison *as* punishment, not *for* punishment. In other words, the loss of liberty—the freedom to come and go as you please—and privacy—to be free from the watchful eyes of the government in the form of prison staff—is the punishment. Punishment does not require—nor should it allow—that prisoners experience brutality by prison staff; fear of sexual or other violent assault from other prisoners; and overcrowded, unhealthy conditions, in addition to their confinement.

The informal aim of administering prisons in an efficient, effective manner also requires the routine associated with life in total institutions. Routine enhances the safety, well-being, and harmony among uniformed and other staff, and it keeps outside interference to a minimum. Nevertheless, tensions between the formal goals of security, safety, punishment, rehabilitation, and humane treatment, and the informal goals of efficiency, effectiveness, and harmony among prison staff make it difficult to manage prisons with total harmony. Everyone agrees that confinement, as a means of punishment, is justified. Everyone also agrees that punishment should be unpleasant. However, no matter how justified and humane the punishment, no matter how harmonious, efficient, and effective the operation, life in prison negatively affects prisoners. It undermines the value of prisoners' work (an important rehabilitative objective) because the primary incentive to work (earning money to spend as its recipients wish) conflicts with outside political pressures that oppose prisoners being in job competition with law-abiding, working people. Prison life may also conflict with internal pressures to keep order and to manage the prison efficiently. The family life of prisoners also suffers because of the needs of prison management. It is often difficult, if not impossible, for people who eat, sleep, work, and play in groups to maintain traditional family relationships. The privacy and individuality such relationships require conflict with efficient, effective prison management. The individual responsibility for making decisions also suffers. Every decision common to daily life—getting up, eating, taking a bath, going to the bathroom, working, working out, relaxing, and going to sleep—is made for prisoners in the interest of safe, efficient management.

No matter how humane or deserved the punishment, prisoners naturally attempt to minimize its discomforts. Some of these efforts are legitimate, others are not. Participating in prison programs, and to a limited extent maintaining ties with family, lawyers, and others outside prison, are legitimate. "Hustling," that is, obtaining unauthorized goods and services, forming cliques and joining gangs, striking, protesting, and rioting are not. The purposes and realities of confinement, prisoners' attempts to avoid or minimize them, and the problems arising out of them pose challenges to prison administration. Management responses affect how successfully prisons can fulfill the goal of humane, safe confinement. Restricted budgets, increased prison populations, and the influx of large numbers of young, violent, gang-affiliated prisoners add to the burdens of prison management. Safe, secure, and orderly prisons not only punish prisoners by humane confinement but they also provide interested prisoners with an opportunity to participate in programs and, not least important, benefit staff by improving working conditions.

Courts had traditionally kept their "hands off" prisons, leaving them to the largely unreviewed and unreviewable control of prison administrators and guards. Offenders left their constitutional rights at the prison gate. In the wake of the civil rights movement, some activist judges, a band of civil rights lawyers, and militant minority prisoners brought an end to the "hands-off" doctrine and subjected nearly all aspects of prison life and society to judicial scrutiny. Prisoners were extended limited constitutional rights enjoyed by law-abiding citizens. Most prisoner lawsuits alleging violations of their rights have never gotten very far in the courts, however, even in the heyday of the prisoners' rights movement of the 1960s. Prisoner petitions are usually dismissed shortly after the courts receive them, and often no judge ever sees the complaint registered. Most prisoners lose if their cases get further into the legal process.

Virtually all prisons have internal mechanisms for hearing prisoner grievances. If disciplinary actions involve the deprivation of fundamental rights, such as liberty, prison disciplinary procedures must operate according to the basic fairness required by due process of law—notice, hearing, presentation of evidence, decisions based on evidence, and written records of the proceedings.

Review Questions

1. Identify and explain the two basic theories used to explain prison society.

2. Identify and explain the adaptive prisoner lifestyle groups into which John Irwin divides prisoners.

3. Identify the two cardinal principles of the inmate code and state the five rules that Gresham Sykes found to reflect these principles.

4. Why are prisons designed as "islands of poverty?"

5. What are the main types of material comforts inmates try to obtain? How and why do inmates obtain these comforts?

6. What are the problems associated with "hustling" for added comforts, and why do prison administrations permit inmates to "hustle"?

7. Describe the impact of harsher sentences on prison society.

8. Describe the racial and ethnic make-up of prisons today and describe the state of race relations in prison.

9. Contrast life in women's prisons with that in men's prisons.

10. Describe the nature and operation of gangs in prisons.

11. Explain the part that race and sex plays in prison violence.

12. What is the nature of and extent of violence against corrections officers and other staff?

13. Identify and explain the major theories explaining prison riots.

14. Describe the extent and effects of overcrowding.

15. Identify the policy options regarding the solution to the problem of prison crowding and summarize the arguments in favor of and against these options.

16. Identify the most pervasive feature in the lives of prisoners.

17. Identify the reasons for having prison programs.

18. Identify the four main problems of inmates that prison programs are aimed to address.

19. What is the state of most prisoners' education? Identify the major purposes of prison education programs.

20. What is the logic behind vocational training programs, and why do the programs fail?

21. Explain the findings and the importance of the economist Ann Witte's work-release study in North Carolina.

22. Explain the financial assistance program TARP, and summarize its results.

23. Describe the promise of prison industries and summarize the obstacles to the success of these industries.

24. Identify and describe the major types of treatment programs.

25. Identify the major services that prisons provide that require the labor of prisoners.

26. Explain how and why prison jobs say a lot about the prestige of prisoners.

27. State the two reasons why prison work is important.

28. List the reasons why recreation programs are an important part of prison life.

29. Summarize the results of Todd Clear's and his colleagues' national study of prison religious programs.

30. Summarize the state of our knowledge about rehabilitation programs. Identify the purposes, other than the reform of prisoners, that rehabilitation programs serve.

31. Identify the "hands-off" doctrine and state the major reasons that justified it.

32. State the three general principles governing the rights of prisoners.

33. List the major reasons why the rights of prisoners are much more limited than the rights of ordinary citizens.

34. Identify the major rights of prisoners. Explain the extent of each.

35. How has the Supreme Court altered the state of prisoners' rights since the 1970s?

36. Summarize the results of prisoners claiming in lawsuits that prison rules and operations have violated their constitutional rights. Explain these results.

37. List the common grievances that prisoners make and the common disciplinary violations they commit.

38. Identify and briefly explain the major aspects of the process that prisoners are "due" in internal disciplinary hearings.

39. How often do prisoners "win" in internal disciplinary proceedings? What explains these results?

Notes

1. Donald Clemmer, *The Prison Community* (New York: Holt, Rinehart, and Winston, 1940).

2. *Social Problems* 10 (1962): 142-55.

3. John Irwin, "The Prison Experience: The Convict World," in *Criminal Justice,* George S. Bridges, Joseph G. Weis, and Robert D. Crutchfield, eds. (Thousand Oaks, Calif.: Pine Forge Press, 1996), 426.

4. Fleisher, *Warehousing Violence,* 28-29.

5. John Irwin, "The Prison Experience: The Convict World," in *Criminal Justice,* George S. Bridges, Joseph G. Weis, and Robert D. Crutchfield, eds. (Thousand Oaks, Calif.: Pine Forge Press, 1996), 426.

6. Ibid., 430-431.

7. Irwin, "The Prison Experience," 426.

8. Gresham M. Sykes, *The Society of Captives: A Study of a Maximum Security Prison* (Princeton, N.J.: Princeton University Press, 1958), quoted in Todd R. Clear and George F. Cole, *American Corrections,* 3d. ed. (Belmont, Calif.: Wadsworth Publishing Co., 1994), 259.

9. Virgil L. Williams and Mary Fish, *Convicts, Codes, and Contraband* (Cambridge, Mass.: Ballinger, 1974), 40.

10. Susan Sheehan, *A Prison and a Prisoner* (Boston: Houghton Mifflin, 1978), 91, as quoted in Clear and Cole, *American Corrections,* 266.

11. David B. Kalinich, *Power, Stability, and Contraband* (Prospect Heights, Ill.: Waveland Press, 1986).

12. Richard Lawrence, "The Impact of Sentencing Guidelines on Corrections," *Criminal Justice Policy Review* 5 (1991): 220.

13. John Irwin, *Prisons in Turmoil* (Boston: Little, Brown, 1980), 181; Samuel Jan Brakel, "Administrative Justice in the Penitentiary: Report on Inmate Grievance Procedures," *American Bar Foundation Research Journal* (1982): 113.

14. Irwin, *Prisons in Turmoil,* 182.

15. Billy "Hands" Robinson, "Love: A Hard Legged Triangle," *Black Scholar* (September 1971): 29.

16. Quoted in James B. Jacobs, "Race Relations and the Prisoner Subculture," in *Crime and Justice: An Annual Review of Research,* Norval Morris and Michael Tonry, eds. (Chicago: University of Chicago Press, 1980), I, 16.

17. Edward Bunker, *Animal Factory* (New York: Viking Press, 1977), 92.

18. Quoted in Jacobs, "Race Relations," 13-14.

19. David A. Ward and Gene G. Kassebaum, *Women's Prison: Sex and Social Structure* (Chicago: Aldine Publishing Company, 1965).

20. Rose Giallombardo, *Society of Women: A Study of a Women's Prison* (New York: Wiley, 1966); Esther Heffernen, *Making It in Prison: The Square, the Cool, and the Life* (New York: Wiley Interscience, 1972).

21. Irwin, *Prisons in Turmoil,* 189; figures for Illinois cited in George W. Knox, *An Introduction to Gangs* (Berrien Springs, Mich.: Van de Vere Publishing Ltd., 1991), 283.

22. Irwin, *Prisons in Turmoil,* 189-90.

23. James Jacobs, *Stateville: The Penitentiary in Modern Society* (Chicago: University of Chicago Press, 1977), 160.

24. Ibid., 161.

25. Jacobs, "Race Relations," 17-18.

26. Ibid., 173.

27. Irwin, *Prisons in Turmoil,* 192-93.

28. Quoted, ibid., 193-94.

29. *New York Times,* 2 June 1985.

30. Craig H. Trout, "A New Look at Gangs," *Corrections Today* (July 1992), 64.

31. Ibid., 66.

32. Ibid.

33. Daniel Lockwood, *Prison Sexual Violence* (New York: Elsevier/North Holland, Inc., 1980), 29.

34. Ibid.

35. Ibid., 30.

36. Quoted in Lockwood, *Prison Sexual Violence,* 33-34.

37. Ibid.

38. Lee H. Bowker, "Prisons: Problems and Prospects," in *Encyclopedia of Crime and Justice,* Sanford H. Kadish, ed. (New York: Free Press, 1983), 3:1230-31.

39. Bowker, "Prisons: Problems and Prospects," 1231.

40. Clear and Cole, *American Corrections,* 275-276.

41. "Texas Copes with the Cost of Criminals," *New York Times,* 30 June 1985; *Ruiz v. Estelle,* 503 F.Supp. 1265 (S.D. Texas 1980).

42. This account of Marion draws heavily on *The United States Penitentiary, Marion, Illinois, Consultants Report Submitted to Committee on the Judiciary, U.S. House of Representatives, Ninety-eighth Congress, Second Session* (Washington, D.C.: U.S. Government Printing Office, 1985).

43. Conversation with David A. Ward, 30 March 1990, about his research on prison management.

44. Ibid.; Raymond Holt, "Marion: Separating Fact from Fiction," *Federal Prisons Journal* 2, no. 2 (1991): 33-34.

45. Mark Colvin, "The 1980 New Mexico Prison Riot," *Social Problems* 29 (June 1982): 449.

46. Mark Colvin, *The Penitentiary in Crisis: From Accommodation to Riot in New Mexico* (Albany: State University of New York Press, 1992).

47. Colvin, "The 1980 New Mexico Prison Riot," 450.

48. Burt Useem and Peter Kimball, *States of Siege: U.S. Prison Riots, 1971-1986* (New York: Oxford University Press, 1989), 3-4.

49. Ibid., 90.

50. See Richard A. Cloward, "Social Control in Prison," in *Theoretical Studies in Social Organization of the Prison,* Richard A. Cloward et al., eds. (New York: Social Science Research Council, 1960), 20-48, for a general theoretical perspective supporting this interpretation.

51. Alfred Blumstein, "Prisons: Population, Capacity, and Alternatives," in *Crime and Public Policy,* James Q. Wilson, ed. (New Brunswick, N.J.: Transaction Books, 1983), 229; Bureau of Justice Statistics, *Prisoners in the United States, 1994* (Washington, D.C.: BJS, August 1995).

52. Quoted in Joan Mullen, *American Prisons and Jails* (Washington, D.C.: National Institute of Justice, 1980), 1:53.

53. BJS, *Prisoners in the United States, 1991* (Washington, D.C.: Bureau of Justice Statistics, 1992); BJS, *Prisoners in the United States, 1994.*

54. Blumstein, "Prisons," 230.

55. Ibid., 229.

56. Ibid., 242-43.

57. Peter Greenwood, *Selective Incapacitation* (Santa Monica: Rand Corporation, 1982).

58. Ibid., xix-xx.

59. Rudy A. Haapenan, *Selective Incapacitation and the Serious Offender: A Longitudinal Study of Criminal Career Patterns* (New York: Springer-Verlag, 1990).

60. Garry, *Options to Reduce Prison Crowding,* 5-12.

61. Ibid., 13.

62. Ibid., 14-16; *Criminal Justice Newsletter* (June 1, 1984), 7; *Criminal Justice Newsletter* (January 2, 1985), 1.

63. Blumstein, "Prisons," 247.

64. Samuel Walker, *Sense and Nonsense About Crime,* 2d ed. (Pacific Grove, Calif.: Brooks/Cole Publishing Company, 1989), 183.

65. Quoted in Timothy J. Flanagan, "Prison Labor and Industry," in *The American Prison: Issues in Research and Policy,* Lynne Goodstein and Doris Layton MacKenzie, eds. (New York: Plenum Press, 1989), 135.

66. Ibid.

67. Ibid.

68. Ibid., 137-40.

69. Walker, *Sense and Nonsense About Crime,* 182.

70. Michael Welch, "Rehabilitation: Holding Its Ground in Corrections," *Federal Probation* (December 1995): 3.

71. John P. Conrad, "Correctional Treatment," *Encyclopedia of Crime and Justice*, 1:274; "Insight Incorporated Fact Sheet" (mimeographed, Stillwater State Prison, Minnesota).

72. Conrad, "Correctional Treatment," 275.

73. Ibid.

74. Ann Dryden Witte, *Work Release in North Carolina: An Evaluation of Its Post-Release Effects* (Chapel Hill: The University of North Carolina, 1975), 99.

75. Ibid., 100.

76. Peter H. Rossi, Richard A. Berk, and Kenneth J. Lenihan, *Money, Work, and Crime: Experimental Evidence* (New York: Academic Press, 1980).

77. Gordon Hawkins, "Prison Labor and Prison Industries," in *Crime and Justice: An Annual Review of Research* (Chicago: University of Chicago Press, 1983), 5:98-103.

78. Hisao Katoh, "The Development of Delinquency and Criminal Justice in Japan," in *Crime and Control in Comparative Perspectives*, Hans-Gauunther Heiland, Louise I. Shelley, and Hisao Katoh, eds. (Berlin: Walter de Gruyter 1991), 78-79.

79. Walker, *Sense and Nonsense About Crime*, 184.

80. Florida House of Representatives, *Oversight Report on PRIDE (Prison Rehabilitative Industries and Diversified Enterprises)* (Tallahassee, Fla., 1988).

81. Timothy J. Flanagan et al., *The Effect of Prison Industry Employment on Offender Behavior: Final Report of the Prison Industry Research Project* (Albany, N.Y.: Hindelang Criminal Justice Research Center, SUNY at Albany, 1988).

82. Clear and Cole, *American Corrections*, 334.

83. Ibid., 369-370.

84. Ibid., 370.

85. Todd R. Clear et al., *Prisoners, Prison, and Religion* (final report, Rutgers University, 1992), as discussed in Clear and Cole, *American Corrections*, 361.

86. Welch, "Rehabilitation," 3.

87. Ted Palmer, *The Re-Emergence of Correctional Intervention* (Newbury Park, Calif.: Sage, 1992), 1-11.

88. Charles H. Logan and Gerald G. Gaes, "Meta-Analysis and the Rehabilitation of Punishment," *Justice Quarterly* 10 (1993): 247.

89. Ibid., 261.

90. *Ruffin v. Commonwealth*, 62 Va. 790 (1871).

91. *Ingraham v. Wright*, 430 U.S. 651, 669 (1977).

92. Donald P. Baker et al., "Judicial Intervention in Corrections: The California Experience—An Empirical Study," *UCLA Law Review* 20 (1973): 454.

93. Jacobs, *New Perspectives on Prison*, 39.

94. James J. Gobert and Neil P. Cohen, *Rights of Prisoners* (New York: McGraw-Hill, 1981); *Bell v. Wolfish*, 441 U.S. 520, 547 (1979).

95. *Sandin v. Connor*, 115 S.Ct. 2293 (1995).

96. *Wolff v. McDonnell*, 418 US 539; *Meachum v. Fano*, 427 US 215.

97. *Wolff v. McDonnell; Sandin v. Connor*, 115 S.Ct. 2293 (1995).

98. *Lee v. Washington*, 390 U.S. 333 (1968), 334.

99. *Procunier v. Martinez*, 416 U.S. 396 (1974).

100. *Whitley v. Albers*, 475 US 312 (1986), 319.

101. Ibid., 313.

102. Joachim Herrmann, "The Federal Republic of Germany," in *Major Criminal Justice Systems: A Comparative Study*, 2d ed., George F. Cole, Stansilaw J. Frankowski, and Marc G. Gertz, eds. (Newbury Park, Calif.: Sage Publications, 1987), 130-32.

103. *Bell v. Wolfish*, 441 U.S. 520 (1979).

104. Jack E. Call, "Lower Court Treatment of Jail and Prison Overcrowding Cases: A Second Look," *Federal Probation* 52 (1988): 34-41.

105. Jim Thomas, "The 'Reality' of Prisoner Litigation: Repackaging the Data," *New England Journal on Criminal Law and Civil Confinement* 15 (1989): 27-54.

106. Ibid.

107. Malcolm Feeley and Roger Hanson, "What We Know, Think We Know and Would Like to Know About the Impact of Court Orders on Prison Conditions and Jail Crowding," in *Prison and Jail Crowding: Workshop Proceedings*, Dale K. Sechrest, Jonathan D. Caspar, and Jeffrey A. Roth, eds. (Washington, D.C.: National Academy of Sciences, 1987); Harris and Spiller, *After Decision*.

108. Samuel Jan Brakel, "Ruling on Prisoners' Grievances," *American Bar Foundation Research Journal* (1983): 393-425, 394, from which most of this section is derived.

109. Ibid., 117.

110. Ibid.

111. Minnesota Department of Corrections, *Inmate Discipline Regulations* (1988).

112. Brakel, "Ruling on Prisoners' Grievances," 412.

113. Ibid., 414-15.

114. Brakel, "Administrative Justice," 124-26.

115. Ibid., 129.

116. Ibid., 130.

117. Ibid., 133.

118. Ibid., 136-37.

119. Ibid., 139.

120. Erving Goffman, *Asylums: Essays on the Social Situation of Mental Patients and Other Inmates* (Garden City: Anchor Books, 1961), 5-6. This section is based on Goffman's first chapter, "Characteristics of Total Institutions."

Returning to Socie

CHAPTER MAIN POINTS

1. Most prisoners eventually return to society.

2. Prisoners are released either outright or conditionally.

3. The number of prisoners conditionally released is growing, but the resources devoted to supervising them in the community is decreasing.

4. Discretionary conditional release is the principal way that prisoners return to society, but mandatory release is an increasing phenomenon.

5. Conditional release from prison is an old practice.

6. Conditional release has always served several purposes, including rehabilitation, punishment, protection of public safety, and the relief of prison crowding.

7. Conditional release is a release from incarceration but not from custody.

8. Parole boards perform a range of functions, including deciding to release prisoners on parole, setting the conditions of release, and revoking parole status.

9. The discretion of parole boards to release prisoners is limited by determinate sentencing and the use of parole guidelines to structure decision making.

10. Parole guidelines focus mainly on a combination of the seriousness of the offense and the risk to the community of the offender in the decision to release.

11. Parole guidelines are supposed to reduce the subjective element in decision making, thereby making the decision to release offenders more rational, safer for the community, and fairer to offenders.

12. Researchers have demonstrated that the predictive capacity of parole guidelines are weak, that they do not transfer well from one population to another, and that they give rise to legal problems.

13. In mandatory conditional release, prisoners know at the time they are sentenced how much time they will serve, minus "good time."

14. Adjustment to society after leaving the highly structured life of prison is difficult for most conditionally released prisoners.

15. The conditions of release restrict the freedom of offenders and subject them to the monitoring of their movements, activities, and associations.

16. Most conditional release programs are supposed to help offenders reintegrate into society.

17. The role of parole officers combines helping released prisoners reintegrate into society with monitoring their movements and associations in order to protect public safety.

18. The surveillance aspect of the parole officer role has predominated for the past two decades.

19. The effects of the supervision of released offenders, measured by the return to criminal behavior, is decidedly mixed, according to empirical research.

20. About 25 percent of parolees leave parole each year to return to prison because of new criminal behavior or because they have violated the conditions of their parole.

21. The Supreme Court has ruled that revocation of parole denies parolees of liberty, and therefore revocation is subject to the due process clauses of the Fifth and Fourteenth Amendments.

22. The process due to parolees is less than that to which criminal defendants and those not suspected or charged with crimes are entitled.

23. Due process requires a preliminary hearing and a revocation hearing to assure that parolees have in fact violated the conditions of their parole, to give notice to parolees, and to give reasons for the decision to revoke parole.

Almost all the talk about corrections these days, at least on television, radio talk shows, and among the general public, is about prisons. Virtually all the increased public spending authorized for corrections is earmarked for building more prisons. We hear of harsher laws, tougher sentences, and the resulting overcrowded prisons. Too many of us hope that this crackdown on crime and criminals will result in sending criminals to prison—and keeping them there. Reality belies this hope.

The reality is that only a few prisoners *never* leave prison—and this is probably the way it should be. A handful of prisoners are executed, and a few thousand are either murdered or otherwise die before their sentences expire. The vast majority, however, eventually return to society. In 1993, over 450,000 of the 900,000 men and women in prison were released into society. Some had served their full sentences. In rare instances, governors and presidents exercised their powers of executive clemency and released prisoners before their terms expire. But the greatest number of prisoners are conditionally released from prison before they have served out their entire sentence. These are prisoners on **parole.** That is, they are released from incarceration before the end of their sentences, but they remain in state custody with restrictions on their liberty and privacy. In 1993, the latest year for which numbers were available when this book went to press, more than 670,000 men and women were on parole. If the figures depicted in Figure 15.1 continue, these numbers will continue to grow. However, despite the increase in the numbers of prisoners released conditionally, the resources devoted to supervising them has decreased.[1]

Release from Prison

The United States sentences more people to prison and keeps them there longer than almost all major countries in the world except for Russia (see Chapter 13). But, despite harsher penalties, sharply increasing prison populations, and the building of new prisons in almost every state and in the federal system, most prisoners convicted of felonies serve less than two years of their sentences before their first release from prison. Release from prison does not mean that prisoners have completed their sentences. They still have to serve the remainder of their sentence under the supervision of parole officers. Parolees are not incarcerated, but they are still in the custody of the state. Virtually all prisoners obtain release in one of three ways:

1. Discretionary release. Discretionary decisions by parole boards determine the date of release from prisons within the limits of maximum, minimum, and good time set by statutes. Prisoners are released conditionally and remain in state custody until the expiration of their full sentence.

2. Mandatory release. Offenders are released conditionally into the community by provisions of determinate sentencing laws and parole guidelines. Legislatures and judges, not correctional authorities, determine sentences. Prisoners remain in state custody until the expiration of their terms.

3. Expiration release. In a few states, such as Maine and Connecticut, parole has been abolished. In these jurisdictions, prisoners are released uncondition-

Figure 15.1

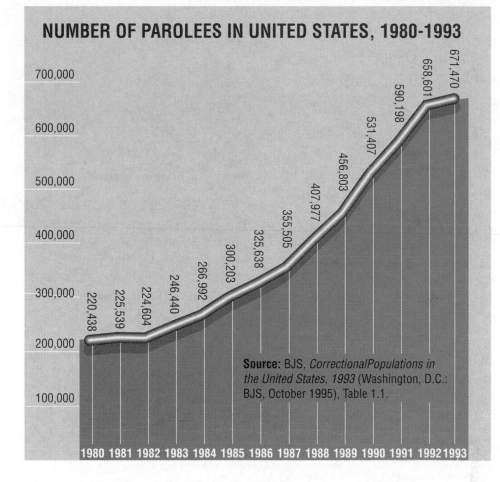

NUMBER OF PAROLEES IN UNITED STATES, 1980-1993

700,000

600,000

500,000

400,000

300,000

200,000

100,000

220,438 225,539 224,604 246,440 266,992 300,203 325,638 355,505 407,977 456,803 531,407 590,198 658,601 671,470

Source: BJS, *CorrectionalPopulations in the United States, 1993* (Washington, D.C.: BJS, October 1995), Table 1.1.

1980 1981 1982 1983 1984 1985 1986 1987 1988 1989 1990 1991 1992 1993

ally at the end of their terms, less good time; they are released not only from incarceration but also from state custody at the time they leave prison.[2]

Until the 1970s, virtually all prisoners were released at the full discretion of parole boards, who decided when and under what conditions prisoners were ready to reenter society. The adoption of determinate sentencing by means of mandatory sentencing laws and sentencing guidelines (discussed in Chapter 11), and the abolition of parole boards markedly changed this practice. Mandatory release sharply reduced the discretionary decision making of some parole boards and eliminated it altogether in a few states. Despite this trend toward mandatory release mechanisms, most people still leave prison when parole boards decide to conditionally release them into the community while they are still under state custody. Furthermore, except in the few states with expiration release, most people remain under the supervision of parole authorities of some kind until the final expiration of their sentences. (See Figure 15.2.)

History of Parole

The practice of releasing prisoners before the end of their terms is ancient. It goes back at least as far as the sixteenth century when the Tudor monarchs issued general pardons releasing all people convicted of certain crimes in the hope that the act of mercy would "reform" them. The practice of conditional release was common throughout Europe in the nineteenth century, but Alexander Maconochie, a captain in the British Royal Navy, has generally received credit for beginning our modern practice of parole. Maconochie was put in charge of the infamous English penal colonies in New South Wales in 1840.

Figure 15.2

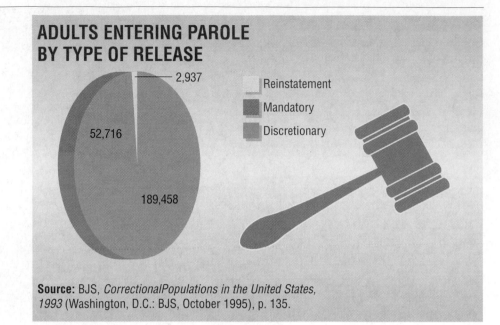

ADULTS ENTERING PAROLE BY TYPE OF RELEASE

2,937

52,716

189,458

Reinstatement

Mandatory

Discretionary

Source: BJS, *CorrectionalPopulations in the United States, 1993* (Washington, D.C.: BJS, October 1995), p. 135.

"ticket of leave" *a document that allowed prisoners to remain free as long as they kept the conditions of release attached to the ticket.*

Maconochie believed that many prisoners were capable of reform. Therefore, he developed a plan to gradually prepare prisoners for their eventual return to society. He divided prisoners into three grades, each of which was progressively more like life outside prison. Prisoners could earn promotion through the grades by labor, study, and good behavior. In other words, advance toward freedom was tied to success in prison programs that were intended to improve and reform prisoners. The third grade in Maconochie's system was what today we call parole—conditional liberty with a **"a ticket of leave."** This document allowed prisoners to remain free as long as they observed the conditions of release attached to the ticket. Violating the rules of release meant returning to prison and starting all over again through the ranks. So conditional liberty, like the grades inside prison, was tied to success in living according to the rules outside prison walls.[3]

Sir Walter Crofton, director of Irish Convict Prisons, took over and developed Maconochie's idea. Named the Irish System, prisoners passed through similar stages to those designed by Maconochie. The "ticket of leave" under the Irish System was a form of conditional release. According to the ticket, prisoners were required to report to the chief of police of their home towns as soon as they arrived, and once a month thereafter until the expiration of their sentences. Conditions were attached to the ticket. Any of the following violations could lead to immediate arrest and return to prison:

1. "Idle or dissolute living."
2. Association with "notoriously bad characters."
3. "Lack of visible means of support."[4]

In other words, during a prisoner's period of conditional liberty, living outside prison depended on working hard, playing by the rules, and living a clean, sober life.

Dr. S. G. Howe of Boston has received credit for the first use of the word 'parole.' "I believe," Dr. Howe told the Prison Association of New York in 1846, "there are many who might be so trained as to be left upon their parole during the last period of their imprisonment with safety." Parole is a French word, literally meaning "word," but defined by Webster in Dr. Howe's time as "word of honour." In military terms, parole meant the promise of prisoners of war to fulfill certain conditions upon their release. It is that meaning that more closely captured Howe's notion of parole. According to Howe, parole meant

> a method by which prisoners who have served a portion of their sentences are released from penal institutions under the continued custody of the state upon conditions which permit their reincarceration in the event of misbehavior.[5]

Hence, parole came to include three major aspects:

1. Conditional release from incarceration before the expiration of the sentence.
2. Supervision under state custody until the end of the sentence.
3. Revocation for violations of the conditions of the release.

At first, parole was slow to catch on in American jurisdictions. Only three states had provided for parole by 1880. From 1880 to 1889, nine more did so. During the Progressive Era in the early twentieth century, most other states adopted parole. But it was not until 1940, when Mississippi created its parole system, that every jurisdiction in the United States, including the federal government, had some form of conditional release. Today, all states and the federal government continue to have some form of conditional release. However, those states that have replaced discretionary parole-board decision making with mandatory release have severed the tie between the initial decision to release and the success of prisoners in prison programs.[6]

This pedophile asked to be castrated when he was released on parole so that he would not molest children.

Throughout its history, parole has generated controversy—usually heated controversy. Clair Wilcox, in his masterful survey of parole in Pennsylvania in the 1920s, surveyed newspapers and magazine articles about parole. He found headlines like "Turning the Criminals Loose" and "Uplifters and Politicians Free Convicts." He quotes the writer of one article, typical of those he surveyed:

> "The organized efforts of well-meaning sentimentalists who are unable to see anything but the welfare of the individual criminal and are interested only in the reform of the criminal to the exclusion of any consideration of his victims or of society as a whole" have caused "desperate criminals, convicted of serious offenses and sent to prison for long terms" to be set free "wholesale" again "to prey upon society."[7]

Criticism of parole was not limited to Pennsylvania. Even former president William Howard Taft joined in the attacks. During his term as Chief Justice of the Supreme Court, Taft took the opportunity to tell an interviewer for the highly popular *Collier's Weekly* magazine:

> Paroles have been abused and should be granted with greater care. It is discouraging to read of the arrest and prosecution of one charged with a new felony who had committed some prior offense, had secured parole after a short confinement and then had used his release to begin again his criminal life.[8]

These criticisms come from the 1920s, but they could have come from any decade—including the 1990s. Criticisms of this nature are timeless. Every time a parolee commits a serious crime, it is major news. The reality, like so much else in criminal justice, is more complex than these criticisms of parole suggest. This chapter introduces you to the complexities—and, hopefully some of the reality—of the three major functions of parole listed earlier: conditional release, supervision until final release, and revocation.

Missions of Parole

The decisions made in releasing and supervising parolees and in revoking their parole are made for a variety of reasons, most of which are tied to the missions that parole is intended to accomplish. Among the general public, it is widely believed that the mission of parole is leniency, that parole was dreamed up by bleeding hearts who care more about criminals than about their victims, society, and justice. To the slightly more sophisticated, the mission of parole is seen not so much as pure leniency—although it may well involve some measure of leniency—but as a means toward the rehabilitation of offenders so they can return to society willing and able to earn a living and obey the law. In reality, parole—like police, courts, and prisons—is supposed to accomplish a number of complex and conflicting missions. The missions of parole include the following:

1. Punishment.
2. Rehabilitation.
3. Public safety.
4. Prison management.

Offenders on parole are released from incarceration but not from custody. From its early days—and certainly today—proponents of parole have had to defend it against the attack that it allowed criminals to avoid punishment for their crimes. As early as 1916, Warren F. Spalding, in an address to the American Prison Association, found it necessary to remind his audience that parole was part of punishment:

> A parole does not release the parolee from custody; it does not discharge him from the penal consequences of his act; it does not mitigate

parole boards *agency that decides when to conditionally release prisoners before the end of their sentences.*

his punishment; it does not wash away the stain or remit the penalty. . . . Unlike a pardon, it is not an act of grace or mercy, of clemency or leniency. The granting of parole is merely permission to a prisoner to serve part of his sentence outside the walls of the prison. He continues to be in the custody of the authorities, both legally and actually, and is still under restraint. The sentence is in full force and at any time when he does not comply with the conditions upon which he was released, or does not conduct himself properly, he may be returned, for his own good and in the public interest.[9]

"For his own good" points to perhaps the best known mission of parole—the rehabilitation of offenders. As we have seen from its brief history, parole was based on the idea that prisoners could reform. Parole was the last stage in the process of proving that prisoners had in fact changed from criminals into law-abiding citizens. The proof that prison programs have "worked" is in the behavior of parolees. If they find jobs and keep them, and if they obey the law, then the programs have worked. If, on the other hand, parolees cannot adapt to the outside world by "working hard and playing by the rules," then parole has not accomplished its reformative mission.

The "playing by the rules" part of reformation points to a third mission of parole—the protection of public safety. This mission involves predicting before release and ensuring by supervision during release that offenders do not commit crimes or otherwise "misbehave" while they are in custody on conditional release. Furthermore, it means revoking and possibly returning to incarceration parolees who violate the conditions of their parole that forbid them to endanger public safety.

Parole has throughout its history also performed missions that aid in the management of prisons. Parole can support the prison discipline system by denying release to "troublemakers" who repeatedly break prison rules. It can also promote order in prison by only paroling prisoners who have served the "average amount of time" for people convicted of the same offense. Probably the most constant management mission of parole is its use in controlling prison populations. Since at least the nineteenth century, when prisons became "warehouses for the poor," releasing prisoners has been a mechanism to relieve prison crowding. The relief from prison overcrowding continues to remain one mission—if largely unstated—of parole. The record numbers of prisoners (see Chapter 13), the lag between prison construction and population growth (see Chapter 14), and the limits of public budgets have all placed pressure on release as a mechanism to reduce prison populations. Parole, by releasing prisoners before the end of their term, makes room for new prisoners who are waiting in jail or elsewhere to be transferred to prison.

As in all other parts of criminal justice, these varied goals are not always in harmony. Releasing more prisoners may well reduce prison populations, but perhaps at the risk of public safety. Close supervision outside prison may enhance public safety, but at the risk of interfering with rehabilitating offenders. Allowing the flexibility of rehabilitation may endanger public safety. These conflicting missions indicate the complexity and difficulty of decision making about conditional release, supervision during conditional release, and either final release from or revocation of parole.

historical note

The principal information placed before the community today . . . mostly in the form of headlines, is that a crime has been committed, that a paroled man has committed it, and then follows . . . a stinging criticism on the abuse of the parole system.

Hugo Pam, 1919

Parole Authorities

The authority to grant parole varies greatly from jurisdiction to jurisdiction. As mentioned, two states—Maine and Connecticut—have abolished parole. These states have no parole authority except for prisoners sentenced before the abolition of conditional release. Others have retained the indeterminate sentence. In most of these states, **parole boards** decide when to conditionally release prisoners before the end of their sentences. Nearly all parole authorities are part of the executive branch of government. They are ordinarily quite small agencies, but they have considerable power.

The Powers of Parole Boards

Parole boards not only determine the date of release in the majority of jurisdictions, but also whether parolees have violated the conditions of their parole, and they decide whether to revoke and return parolees to prison. But the power of most parole boards extends beyond release and revocation. Depending on the jurisdiction, parole boards also have the following powers:

- Rescinding a parole date that is already set.
- Issuing warrants and subpoenas.
- Setting the conditions of supervision.
- Restoring the civil rights of offenders.
- Granting final discharge from state custody.
- Ordering payment of restitution to victims.
- Ordering payment of part of the fees of prisoners' supervision.
- Granting furloughs to prisoners.
- Granting or recommending pardons and commutations of sentences.[10]

Parole Board Membership

The powers of parole boards are obviously extensive, as the previous section demonstrates. Statutes and, in a few cases, state constitutions determine the size and the basic qualifications of parole board membership. These are important, but *who* sits on the board obviously plays a large role in how parole is administered. Most jurisdictions provide for five- to seven-member parole boards. Over half limit the terms of members to either four or six years. The average length of actual service on parole boards is a little more than four and a half years. Most jurisdictions prescribe minimum requirements for parole board membership. About half of the states require "some experience" in criminal justice. Seven states require a bachelor's degree.

The power of parole boards is extensive and *who* sits on parole boards affects *how* parole is administered.

Figure 15.3

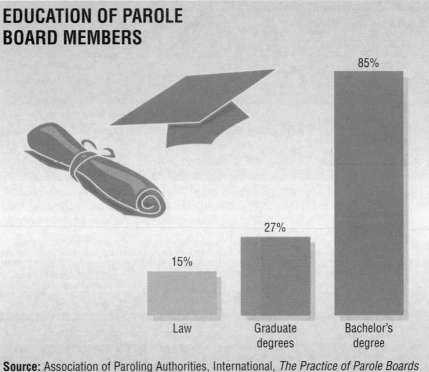

EDUCATION OF PAROLE BOARD MEMBERS

85%

27%

15%

Law   Graduate   Bachelor's
       degrees   degree

Source: Association of Paroling Authorities, International, *The Practice of Parole Boards* (Lexington, Ky.: Association of Paroling Authorities, 1994), p 30.

Twenty-three jurisdictions have no statutory requirements for board membership. Despite either the total lack of statutory requirements or the minimum requirements specified, parole board members tend to be well educated. Their average age is 53; nearly three-quarters are men; most are white.[11] (See Figure 15.3 and Figure 15.4.)

The minimal requirements specified by statute give state governors—the central figures in the appointment of parole board members—enormous

Figure 15.4

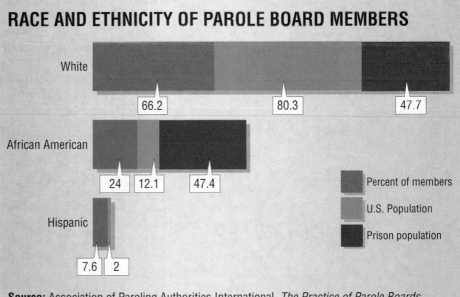

RACE AND ETHNICITY OF PAROLE BOARD MEMBERS

White   66.2   80.3   47.7

African American   24   12.1   47.4

Hispanic   7.6   2

Percent of members

U.S. Population

Prison population

Source: Association of Paroling Authorities International, *The Practice of Parole Boards* (Lexington, KY.: Association of Paroling Authorities, 1994), p. 30

hearing officers *special examiners who conduct parole hearings and interview inmates eligible for parole.*

power to shape the administration of parole in individual states. Governors appoint parole board members in 44 states, and in 36 states, governors also have the power to appoint board chairs. In 11 states, either the attorney general or the state judiciary appoints the chair and members of parole boards. The President of the United States appoints both the chair and the members of the United States Parole Board.[12]

Parole Release

The decision to release prisoners takes place according to two basic mechanisms—mandatory release and discretionary parole board decisions. Mandatory release was common until the 1890s, when parole boards with discretionary power to release prisoners were introduced. Discretionary release by parole boards was the almost exclusive mechanism for release from prison until the revival of determinate sentences during the 1970s. (See Chapter 11.) States with determinate sentencing laws have sharply curtailed the discretionary powers of parole boards; a few have abolished parole entirely.

The process of parole begins when judges sentence defendants. In states with indeterminate sentences and traditional parole boards, judges sentence defendants to a minimum and maximum term, such as 5 to 10 years. After inmates have served a portion of this term, less credit earned for good behavior and the performance of prison duties, they are *eligible* for parole. Parole boards decide whether to release eligible prisoners onto parole. In states with determinate sentencing, whether in the form of mandatory minimum sentencing laws or sentencing guidelines, conditional release is mandatory. That is, parole authorities must release inmates onto parole when they have served a specified portion of their sentence.

Parole Board Release

Since the 1970s, critics have mounted serious challenges to the discretionary release of prisoners by parole boards. Linked with both the general hardening of public attitudes toward crime and demands for harsher punishment, the challenges to parole board discretionary release have resulted in considerable restrictions on discretionary release. Although they have received by far the most public attention, mandatory minimum sentence laws—especially the "three-strikes-and-you're-out" variety—are only one mechanism devised to limit or remove altogether the discretion of parole boards to release prisoners. Sentencing guidelines have had a similar effect, particularly when their adoption is accompanied by the abolition of discretionary parole board release. However, despite the publicity surrounding mandatory minimum sentences and sentencing guidelines, parole boards remain the predominant mechanism for conditionally releasing prisoners from incarceration. (See Figure 15.5.)

Parole Release Hearing In most jurisdictions, parole boards interview inmates in prison before granting or denying them parole. These hearings are usually brief and cursory, lasting between 15 and 30 minutes. In states where parole boards do not personally interview inmates, the decision to grant or deny parole is made in a variety of ways. In some jurisdictions, the board reviews the case materials and acts on the recommendation of **hearing officers,** special examiners who conduct hearings and interview inmates eligible for parole. In others, the board personally interviews only inmates imprisoned for specific crimes. In some states, boards only review inmate files and related information, such as risk assessment scores that form part of parole guidelines discussed below.[13]

Figure 15.5

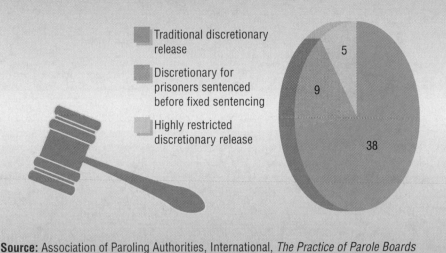

NUMBER OF STATES AND TYPE OF DISCRETIONARY PAROLE

Traditional discretionary release

Discretionary for prisoners sentenced before fixed sentencing

Highly restricted discretionary release

Source: Association of Paroling Authorities, International, *The Practice of Parole Boards* (Lexington, Ky.: Association of Paroling Authorities, 1994), p 7.

risk assessment instruments *used to put inmates in a particular group according to the risk of committing further crimes.*
parole guidelines *risk assessment instruments based on the seriousness of the offense and the risk of the offender to public safety.*

Jurisdictions vary significantly as to how many votes it takes to grant or deny parole. However, most states require either a majority of the entire board or a majority of a quorum of the board. In one state, Oregon, denying parole requires a unanimous vote of the full parole board. Iowa, on the other hand, requires a unanimous vote of a quorum of the board to grant parole.[14]

The United States Supreme Court has consistently ruled that parole is a privilege, not a right. Therefore, states have wide leeway in establishing the privileges that parolees enjoy at parole hearings. In some states, inmates can bring lawyers to the hearings; in others, they cannot. In some states, they can present witnesses in their behalf, but not in others. Some jurisdictions require that parole boards give written reasons for their decisions to grant or deny parole. Most states have established rules for determining when prisoners are eligible for parole. In some states, prisoners are eligible when they have served the minimum sentences; in some, they are eligible when they have served one-third of the maximum sentence; in some, eligibility depends on the number of prior felony convictions; and in some, parole is restricted for specific offenses such as murder, kidnapping, and aggravated rape.[15]

Parole Guidelines Parole boards rely on a wide range of information to assist them in release decisions. Since the 1970s, parole boards have relied on various **risk assessment instruments** as a means to predict the likelihood of parolees committing crimes while on parole. Twenty-six states—exactly half—rely on risk assessment instruments. These instruments *guide* release decision making; they do not *determine* it. The instrument merely puts inmates in a particular group according to the risk of committing further crimes. If the board finds grounds to override the instrument-based prediction, it can do so. In other words, parole boards retain the ultimate power to grant or deny parole.[16]

Trying to predict the success of parolees during conditional release began in the 1920s, but the development of current risk assessment instruments called **parole guidelines** began in the 1970s. The National Council of Crime and Delinquency and the United States Parole Commission proposed to study parole decision making and turned to social scientists for help. Don Gottfredson and Leslie Wilkins became the pioneers in parole (and, by example, in

Salient Factor Score (SFS) *number that states the probability that a parolee will succeed on parole.*

bail and sentencing guidelines as well) when they headed up the Parole Decision-Making Project in the early 1970s. Relying on social science methods, Gottfredson and Wilkins examined the criteria parole boards used in their decision making. Parole boards themselves used the findings to facilitate an evaluation of the appropriateness and the effectiveness of these criteria. This collaboration between researchers and parole board members led to the development of parole guidelines.[17]

Parole guidelines place offenders into categories according to two criteria:

1. The seriousness of their offense. (See Figure 15.6.)
2. Their salient factor score (SFS). (See Figure 15.7.) **Salient Factor Score (SFS)** is a number that states the probability that a parolee will succeed on parole.

These categories form the two parts of the guidelines grid depicted in Figure 15.6. Along the left side of the grid are listed eight categories of offense seriousness. Along the top of the grid are listed the four parole probability prognoses (Very good, Good, Fair, and Poor), based on the SFS of prospective parolees. Parole boards award points according to these salient factors. Figure 15.7 depicts the salient factors included in the United States Parole Commission's guidelines and the points that parolees can earn for them. They can earn up to a maximum of 10 points depending on their prior record of criminal behavior, prior commitments, age, and dependence on drugs. The

Figure 15.6

FEDERAL PAROLE GUIDELINES

Offense Severity: Severity of Offense Behavior	Salient	Factors	1981	
	Very Good (10–8 points)	Good (7–6 points)	Fair (5–4 points)	Poor (3–0 points)
Category One (formerly "Low Severity")	6 months	6–9 months	9–12 months	12–16 months
Category Two (formerly "Low Moderate Severity")	8 months	8–12 months	12–16 months	16–22 months
Category Three (formerly "Moderate Severity")	10–14 months	14–18 months	18–24 months	24–32 months
Category Four (formerly "High Severity")	14–20 months	20–26 months	26–34 months	34–44 months
Category Five formerly "Very High Severity")	24–36 months	36–48 months	48–60 months	60–72 months
Category Six (formerly "Greatest I Severity")	40–52 months	52–67 months	67–78 months	78–100 months
Category Seven (formerly part of "Greatest II Severity	52–80 months	64–92 months	78–110 months	100–148 months
Category Eight (formerly part of "Greatest II Severity")	100 months	120 months	150 months	150 months

Figure 15.7

**SALIENT FACTOR
SCORE (SFS)**

A. Prior Convictions/Adjudications (Adult or Juvenile)
    None   = 3 points
    One   = 2 points
    Two   = 1 points
    Three   = 0 points

B. Prior Commitments of more than 30 days (Adult or Juvenile)
    None   = 2 points
    One or two   = 1 points
    Three or more   = 0 points

C. Age at current offense/prior commitments
    26 years of age or more   = 2 points*
    20–25 years of age   = 1 point*
    19 years of age or less   = 0 points
    *Exception: If five or more prior commitments of more than 30 days (adult or
    juvenile) place an x here____and score this item   = 0 points

D. Recent Commitment-free period (3 years)
    No prior commitment of more than 30 days (adult or juvenile), or released to the
    community from last such commitment at least 3 years prior to the commence-
    ment of the current offense   = 1 point
    Otherwise   = 0 points

E. Probation/Parole/Confinement/Escape Status violator this time
    Neither on probation or parole, confinement, or escape status at the time of the
    current offense; nor committed as probation, parole, confinement, or escape
    status violator this time   = 1 point
    Otherwise   = 0 points

F. Heroin/Opiate dependence
    No history of heroin or opiate dependence   = 1 point
    Otherwise   = 0 points

salient factor score translates into the eight risk categories shown in Figure 15.6. The cells in the grid indicate the presumptive range of months offenders must serve before they are conditionally released.[18]

The grid demonstrates that the decision to conditionally release offenders from prison depends on a combination of the seriousness of the offense for which they are incarcerated and on the probability of their success if they are released. So a prisoner serving time for a "Category One" (least serious) offense who has a "very good" SFS presumptively has to serve up to 6 months before parole. On the other hand, a prisoner who is doing time for a "Category Eight" (most serious) offense who has a "poor" SFS has to serve 150 months before release. Hence, as we have seen throughout this text, both the seriousness of criminal behavior and the probable dangerousness of individual offenders are important in decision making in criminal justice.

To their supporters, parole guidelines are appealing for a number of reasons. First, they appear to be objective. Both the seriousness of the offense and the salient factor scores derive from measurable criteria that reduce the subjective element in decision making. Second, because they are objective, they are also fairer, particularly because they reduce or eliminate unacceptable criteria such as gender, race, and class from the decision to release offenders on parole. Third, they are economical. Maintaining prisoners costs more than supervising parolees. The guidelines ranking keeps the highest-risk offenders who have committed the most serious offenses in expensive prisons longer. On the other hand, the ranking allows the less expensive release on parole of less serious offenders with the lowest risk to the community. Finally, reliance on the salient factor score releases the offenders most likely to succeed on parole. As a result, the kind and amount of supervision on parole depends on the degree of risk of the parolee.[19]

Researchers have challenged these conclusions about the advantages of devices that predict the risk of failure of convicted offenders living outside prison. Kevin N. Wright, Todd R. Clear, and Paul Dickson studied a risk-assessment instrument developed for Wisconsin that the National Institute of Corrections called a "model system" and that a number of other states adopted. Wright and his associates conducted a validation study of the system by choosing a sample of closed cases from New York, a state that had adopted the Wisconsin model. Although the instrument ranked *probationers* as to their "potential risk to the community, thus permitting closer supervision of those who are most likely to offend again," the risk is similar to ranking parolees. The researchers concluded that their "analysis raises serious questions about the state-of-the-art of risk prediction." They found that risk assessment instruments developed for one population do not necessarily work with other populations. Furthermore, Wright and his colleagues confirmed other studies that showed that no matter what the instrument used, all predictions are "fairly weak."[20]

Furthermore, the degree of sophistication of the device does not appear to improve the accuracy of the predictions. Stephen D. Gottfredson and Don M. Gottfredson compared five different prediction methods of varying levels of sophistication used to predict the success of 4500 parolees released from federal prisons. They found that simpler and easy-to-understand prediction methods worked as well as complex schemes based on advanced statistical techniques.[21]

Parole guidelines can also create legal problems. The Florida Parole Commission, for example, reported that civil litigation by adult male prisoners rose 450 percent following the introduction of parole guidelines. The increase in litigation forced the Parole Commission to increase its legal staff from two to seven lawyers during the first year of the guidelines. Civil litigation usually involved four issues:

1. Errors in computing salient factor scores.
2. Complaints about placement in offense severity levels.
3. Claims that parole examiners illegally elevated cases of aggravation.
4. Claims that the parole commission failed to consider mitigating factors.[22]

Mandatory Conditional Release

Parole guidelines restrict—but do not eliminate—the discretionary decision making of parole boards. As we saw in Chapter 11, both conservatives and liberals joined the public in demanding fixed sentences for convicted offenders during the 1970s. Along with this came the demand to restrict the discretionary power of parole boards to return prisoners to society; so the determinate sentencing statutes shifted the responsibility for fixing the release date to judges and legislatures. Determinate sentencing is based on the idea that judges—at the time of sentencing—should assign a specific amount of time the offender should serve. This replaced the indeterminate sentencing system in which judges sentenced offenders to a minimum and maximum amount of time, such as "from 1 to 20 years," leaving it to parole boards to determine the exact date of release within that range.

States vary as to how much discretion judges have. In determinate sentencing, at the time they enter prison, all offenders know how much time they have to serve. Release does not depend on participating in prison programs or on the degree of rehabilitation. Instead, prisoners are released at the end of the term fixed by the judge. This transfer of authority from parole boards to judges has not left corrections departments with no effect on release. All determinate sentencing states allow the deduction of "good time" from the time that prisoners are required to serve in prison. Most have also provided corrections officials with generous amounts of good time to allocate.

Of course, statutes regulate both the rate of good time accumulation and the amount that officials can take away for "bad time." However, prison officers and staff have considerable discretion in interpreting the rules, in establishing procedures for the revocation of good time (see Chapter 14), and in utilizing good time to reduce prison crowding.[23]

Parole Supervision

A common error among the general public is believing that when prisoners leave prison they have "paid their debt to society" and are free to come and go as they please. That is not true of the more than two-thirds of a million men and women who are conditionally released from prison. According to the United States Sentencing Commission's *Federal Sentencing Guidelines Manual,* for example, judges are required to

> order a term of supervised release to follow imprisonment when a sentence of imprisonment of more than one year is imposed. . . .

The period of supervised release ranges from five years for the most serious felonies to one year for the least serious offenses.[24]

Parolees are released into programs that vary according to types of parolees and that require different levels of custody. Parolees remain in the legal custody of corrections authorities and are subject to a wide range of conditions that restrict their movements, activities, associations with other people, and employment.[25]

Returning to society after serving time in prison is not easy, whether the release is conditional or outright (as when prisoners have served out their maximum term). People leave prison with clothes, a little cash, a list of the conditions of their parole, the name and address of their parole officer, and the *promised* job. Most are unskilled or have only minimal job skills, and they move from the regimented, controlled life of prison to life on the "outside," with all its difficulties and temptations. Todd R. Clear and George F. Cole list the following handicaps of released prisoners:

- Long absence from family and friends.
- Legal and practical limits on employment.
- Suspiciousness and uneasiness of acquaintances.
- Strangeness of everyday living.[26]

According to Clear and Cole:

> No matter what the intentions of others, the former inmate always faces the cold fact that no truly "clean start" is possible. The change in status is from convict to former convict; the new status is nearly as stigmatizing as the old, and in many ways is more frustrating. In the former convict's mind, he or she is "free." Yes, the crime was a big mistake, but the prison time has paid for it and now there is a chance to turn over a new leaf. Yet most people look at the parolee askance and treat him or her as though there is still something to prove. . . .[27]

The Conditions of Release

In addition to the practical and legal problems of adjustment and the obligation to obey the law, parolees have the added responsibility of complying with the specific conditions of their release. These conditions restrict their freedom, subjecting them to the monitoring of their movements, activities, and associations. Supervision of activities, movements, and associations is based on the reasonable assumption that supervision is part of punishment, required by both parolees and society: society to provide public safety, parolees to avoid a return to bad habits and activities.

Among the many conditions of parole are the prohibitions against the excessive use of alcohol and the total prohibition against other habit forming drugs without a doctor's prescription.

parole contract an agreement between the state and the offender in which the state promises to release the offender and the offender agrees to abide by the conditions of release.

certificate of parole document that specifically sets out the conditions of the parole contract.

The conditions of release are an essential part of a **parole contract,** an agreement between the state and the offender. As its part of the contract, the state promises to release the offender on specific conditions. The offender, the other party to the contract, promises to abide by the conditions. If the offender fails to keep any of the conditions in the agreement or commits a new crime, the offender is in breach of the parole contract and the state can revoke it. (See the section on revocation later in this chapter.) The conditions of the parole contract are usually set out specifically in the contract or the **certificate of parole.** Each jurisdiction determines its own conditions, and each individual agreement may have its own special conditions. However, most conditions resemble those included in the United States Parole Commission's certificate of discharge, issued to every parolee from the federal prison system. These conditions are:

1. You shall go directly to the district showing on this CERTIFICATE OF PAROLE (unless released to the custody of other authorities). Within three days after your arrival you shall report to your parole advisor if you have one, and to the United States Probation Officer whose name appears on this certificate. If in any emergency you are unable to get in touch with your parole advisor, or your probation officer or his office, you shall communicate with the United States Board of Parole, Department of Justice, Washington, D.C. 20537.

2. If you are released to the custody of other authorities, and after your release from physical custody of such authorities, you are unable to report to the United States Probation Officer to whom you are assigned within three days, you shall report instead to the nearest United States Probation Officer.

3. You shall not leave the limits of this CERTIFICATE OF PAROLE without written permission from the probation officer.

4. You shall notify your probation officer immediately of any change in your place of residence.

5. You shall make a complete and truthful written report (on a form provided for that purpose) to your probation officer between the first and third day of each month, and on the final day of parole. You shall also report to your probation officer at other times as he directs.

6. You shall not violate any law. Nor shall you associate with persons engaged in criminal activity. You shall get in touch immediately with your probation officer or his office if you are arrested or questioned by a law enforcement officer.

7. You shall not enter into any agreement to act as an "informer" or special agent for any law enforcement agency.

8. You shall work regularly, unless excused by your probation officer, and support your legal dependents, if any, to the best of your ability. You shall report immediately to your probation officer any change in employment.

9. You shall not drink alcoholic beverages to excess. You shall not purchase, possess, use, or administer marijuana or narcotic or other habit forming or dangerous drugs, unless prescribed or advised by a physician. You shall not frequent places where such drugs are illegally sold, dispensed, used, or given away.

10. You shall not associate with persons who have a criminal record unless you have the permission of your probation officer.

11. You shall not have firearms (or other dangerous weapons) in your possession without the written permission of your probation officer, following prior approval of the United States Board of Parole.

12. You shall, if ordered by the Board pursuant to Section 4203, Title 18, U. S. C., as amended October 1970, reside in and/or participate in a treatment program of a Community Treatment Center operated by the Bureau of Prisons, for a period not to exceed 120 days.[28]

Parole Programs

Most parolees are required to participate in some kind of activity as a condition of their release. This may be no more than filing regular reports with parole agencies. It can also include living in special housing, performing community service, working, going to school, getting vocational training, or participating in drug, alcohol, sex, and other treatment programs. Many of these programs resemble those in which probationers participate (see Chapter 12). In fact, probationers and parolees are often in the same programs together, and the same correctional officers act as both probation and parole officers. But parolees differ from probationers in some important respects. Parolees have lived in confinement, sometimes for a long time. The effects of prison life put them in special circumstances requiring major adjustment to living outside prison. (See Chapter 14 on life in prison.) Also, parolees are sometimes more serious offenders than probationers. For both these reasons, parolees generally require more intense supervision than do probationers.[29]

Halfway Houses Some inmates are released to transitional residences called **halfway houses.** Halfway houses vary enormously. Some provide no more than shelter on a voluntary basis. At the other extreme, some provide mandatory confinement with curfew. Some provide extensive services, such as drug and alcohol treatment complete with hospitalization on the premises, employment assistance, and other counseling services. The basic idea is to gradually reintegrate released prisoners into society by providing a residence in the community. Offenders are frequently assigned to halfway houses for a prescribed amount of time, during which they receive at least the basic necessities of food, shelter, and clothing. They also receive employment in order to pay at least part of the cost of these necessities. Dean Champion compiled the following list of halfway house missions and functions:

1. Reintegration of offenders into the community.
2. Counseling parolees.
3. Job placement and employment assistance.
4. Medical treatment.
5. Emergency legal aid.
6. Vocational training.
7. Crisis management services.
8. Pre- and post-natal care.
9. Monitoring offenders.
10. Assistance in rehabilitation.[30]

Furloughs Several thousand prison inmates participate in furlough programs. **Furloughs** are authorized leaves from confinement for specified time periods and for specific purposes. The major mission of furloughs, as with halfway houses, is to aid in the reintegration of prisoners into society. Furloughs can ease reintegration in a number of ways. Some are intended to help families by getting inmates and their family members used to each other again. Study release, either academic or vocational, prepares inmates for school and employment.

Work Release Several thousand prisoners also participate in work release programs. **Work release** is any program that allows inmates to leave prison in order to work in the community; occurs under minimum or no supervision; and pays inmates adequate wages for their labor. According to Dean Champion, work release has all of the following missions that working in the community can help to achieve:

Figure 15.8

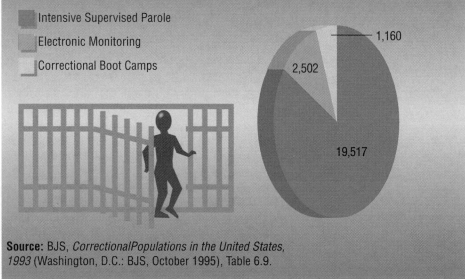

NUMBERS OF CONDITIONALLY RELEASED PRISONERS IN INTERMEDIATE PUNISHMENTS, 1993

Intensive Supervised Parole

Electronic Monitoring

Correctional Boot Camps

1,160

2,502

19,517

Source: BJS, *CorrectionalPopulations in the United States, 1993* (Washington, D.C.: BJS, October 1995), Table 6.9.

1. Reintegration into the community.
2. Opportunity to learn, develop, and practice new skills.
3. Means to pay restitution to victims and to the community.
4. Chance to help support inmates and their families.
5. Help corrections authorities predict the likelihood of success on parole.
6. Improve self-image and responsibility by having inmates assume full responsibility in an unsupervised environment.[31]

Intermediate Sanction Release Over 20,000 prisoners are released into intensive supervised parole, electronic monitoring, and correctional boot camps (see Figure 15.8). These programs, the same to which probationers are assigned, are discussed in detail in Chapter 12.

Parole Officers

Parole officers are responsible for the supervision of the vast majority of parolees during the period of their conditional release. As we have seen throughout this text, most criminal justice professionals have always had to play conflicting roles to suit the multiple and conflicting missions of criminal justice. In this respect, parole officers are much like professionals in courts and police departments. Former corrections commissioner and penal reformer David Fogel succinctly described the conflict between two basic—and conflicting—roles of parole officers, as counselors and law enforcement officers:

> [A] parole officer can be seen going off to his/her appointed rounds with Freud in one hand and a .38 Smith and Wesson in the other hand. It is by no means clear that Freud is as helpful as the .38 in most areas where parole officers venture. . . . Is Freud backup to the .38? Or is the .38 carried to support Freud?[32]

Supervising parolees has always meant both surveillance, to protect society, and treatment, to rehabilitate individual parolees. But since the 1970s, with the tougher attitude toward crime and the accompanying shift in emphasis from rehabilitation to incapacitation and punishment, the law enforcement role of parole officers has taken precedence.

The treatment mission arose from the social work approach to corrections. Social work adopts a **casework model** of treatment, in which supervision provides the basis for a treatment plan in which individual parolees are the cases. **Welfare parole officers** use all the information they can get about individual parolees ("cases") in order to diagnose their needs and design a treatment plan. This plan is supposed to rehabilitate parolees, which usually means reintegrate them into the community as people who "work hard and play by the rules." Or, as the President's Task Force on Corrections put it,

> developing the offender's effective participation in the major social institutions of the school, business and the church . . . which offer access to a successful career.[33]

The National Conference on Parole offered a definition of the surveillance role of parole officers:

> Surveillance is that activity of the parole officer which utilizes watchfulness, checking, and verification of certain behavior of a parolee without contributing to a helping relationship with him.[34]

Law enforcer parole officers see themselves as the guardians of middle-class morality. To safeguard ordinary, law-abiding people, such parole officers have to watch parolees to make sure they follow the rules and do not victimize innocent people. (See Chapter 12 on types of probation officers.)

The law enforcer and welfare roles do not necessarily conflict. According to Richard McCleary's *Dangerous Men,* a study of parole officers at work, parole officers sort through their caseload to identify the "dangerous men." This means identifying those parolees who "do not demonstrate willingness to accept the PO as a therapist." These parolees become candidates for surveillance instead of treatment. So parole officers "rehabilitate the offenders who are amenable to treatment, while simultaneously protecting society from those who prove to be dangerous."[35]

Daniel Glaser identified another type of parole officer—the passive officer. **Passive parole officers** are just doing a job, putting in only the minimum effort required, doing only enough to get by in order to keep their jobs. Charles L. Erickson offered the following satirical advice to passive officers who want to "fake" their way to a "trouble-free caseload."

> "I'm just so busy—never seem to have enough time." A truly professional execution of this ploy does require some preparation. Make sure that your desktop is always inundated with a potpourri of case files, messages, memos, unopened mail, and professional literature. . . . Have your secretary hold all your calls for a few days and schedule several appointments for the same time. When, after a lengthy wait, the . . . [parolee] is finally ushered into your presence, impress him (or her) with the volume of your business. . . . Always write while conversing with the subject, and continue to make and receive telephone calls. Interrupt your dialogue with him to attend to other important matters, such as obtaining the daily grocery list from your wife or arranging to have your car waxed. Apologize repeatedly and profusely for these necessary interruptions and appear to be distracted, weary, and slightly insane. Having experienced the full treatment, it is unlikely that the probationer will subsequently try to discuss with you any matters of overwhelming concern. He could even feel sorrier for you than he does for himself. You should henceforth be able to deal with him on an impersonal basis, if indeed he tries to report anymore at all.[36]

Parole supervision has always suffered from criticism, as has any criminal justice policy that seems to "coddle criminals." But since the 1970s, the attacks have become especially severe. Crime control supporters have—as always—attacked parole as "soft on crime." Due process advocates have hammered it for being arbitrary and unfair. Rehabilitation proponents have denounced the lack of meaningful programs to help parolees. These attacks have led to a shift in the focus of parole in general, and of parole supervision in general, to the missions of punishment and public safety. So, although the welfare role still exists and the passive officer will always be with us, it is the law enforcer who predominates in conditional release at the end of the twentieth century.[37]

The predominance of the law enforcement mission of parole has allowed a shift in resources from the *needs* of parolees to the *risks* they pose for the community. According to Cheryl L. Ringel, Ernest L. Cowles, and Thomas C. Castellano, who traced the shift,

> The shift in emphasis from offender treatment needs to offender risk meant that scarce resources could be directed away from treatment programs without damage to the integrity of the model. No longer was there a strong implicit assumption that the correctional agencies providing such supervision had to provide extensive programs to bring about offender change. Such treatment became more the offender's responsibility, as program participation became less often a condition of supervision and offenders were also more frequently called upon to pay the costs of such programs.[38]

The Effectiveness of Conditional Release

recidivism *return to criminal behavior.*

The shift in emphasis in parole from the needs of offenders to the risks they pose to public safety raises the important public policy question: How effective is conditional release? In corrections, "effective" usually means lack of **recidivism,** that is, the return to criminal behavior. Recidivism means different things to different researchers. Usually, it consists of three measures:

1. *New criminal event.* The new criminal event can mean *arrest* for a new crime; *conviction* for a new crime; or *revocation* of parole for the new crime.
2. *Duration until return to criminal behavior.*
3. *Seriousness of the new criminal behavior.*

The effectiveness of parole varies depending on the definition of recidivism selected. For example, effectiveness will be dramatically less if you define (as many do) recidivism as the arrest for any offense, however minor, at any time after release from prison. Effectiveness will increase dramatically if you define recidivism (as some researchers do) as the return to prison for the commission of a felony within one or two years. For a long time, the numbers have indicated that more than half of all prisoners released on parole return to prison—*eventually.* (See Figure 15.9.) But empirical research is decidedly mixed as to what parole supervision has to do with these numbers.

A Connecticut court decision provided a unique opportunity for researchers Howard R. Sacks and Charles H. Logan to study the effect of parole release on recidivism. In *Szawarak v. Warden,* the Connecticut Supreme Court declared that the legislature had violated the Connecticut constitution by authorizing sentences of more than one year for Class D felonies (less serious felonies such as unarmed robbery, burglary, and possession of drugs). The court ordered the discharge of all prisoners who had already served more than one year for these felonies. Ordinarily, all of these prisoners eventually would have been granted parole. This group of offenders discharged outright became the experimental group in a natural experiment. The control group consisted of similar prisoners who were released on parole. After the first year, the researchers found that parole had only modest effects on recidivism.

Figure 15.9

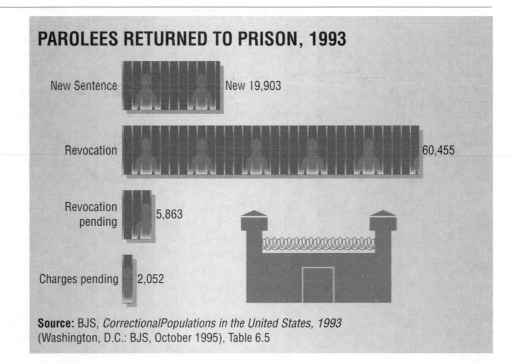

PAROLEES RETURNED TO PRISON, 1993

New Sentence — New 19,903

Revocation — 60,455

Revocation pending — 5,863

Charges pending — 2,052

Source: BJS, *CorrectionalPopulations in the United States, 1993* (Washington, D.C.: BJS, October 1995), Table 6.5

Parolees did avoid conviction at a slightly higher rate (about 7 percent) than the discharged prisoners in the experimental group. The researchers found that parole had no significant effect on the seriousness of the offenses committed.[39]

Moreover, the modest positive effects of parole supervision on recidivism were short-lived. According to Sacks and Logan,

> parole had no preventive effects after two (or three) years following release. Parole seems to affect recidivism while the parolee is on parole (and for a short period thereafter) but these effects soon begin to dissipate and tend to disappear by the time parolees have finished two years in the community.[40]

Nor, as mentioned, did the researchers find any significant differences between parolees and those discharged outright in terms of the seriousness of the offenses they committed following release. However, parolees remained in the community slightly longer—about 6 months—than discharged offenders before they committed new crimes. In other words, "parole does not prevent a return to crime, but it does delay it."[41]

Some research suggests that the success of parole depends on the kind of supervision parolees receive. Mark Jay Lerner evaluated parole in the state of New York. There, although the social work mission is recognized, never is helping parolees to take precedence over the law enforcement mission of protecting society. According to the statement of the New York State Department of Correctional Services:

> The Parole officer is a professional caseworker who at no time is permitted to put the rights of the individual parolee ahead of the rights of society. He protects society by helping the parolee become a productive member of society but at all times he takes every precaution to insure the parolee's activities are not a threat to society.[42]

In keeping with this law enforcement orientation, parole officers are "armed with .38 caliber revolvers [and] have even more extensive investigative and surveillance powers than those of policemen." This led the Citizens' Inquiry on Parole and Criminal Justice to conclude that

> in New York, the designation of parole officers as peace officers—arming them with guns, using technical violations of parole rules as a basis for return to prison, and encouraging surveillance activities—were indicators of a higher emphasis on law enforcement than is found in other parole systems.[43]

Lerner sampled 195 misdemeanant parolees. About half were in the control group of inmates released at the end of their sentences; the other half were inmates released on parole. Using the electronic retrieval system in New York State, Lerner collected arrest information for two years following the release of the 195 inmates in his sample. He found that "parole supervision reduces criminal behavior of persons released from local correctional institutions." Figure 15.10 shows the results of Lerner's study. Although Lerner concedes that his study did not try to explain why parole reduced recidivism, he speculated that the "effect is probably due to the deterrent or law-enforcement effect of parole supervision and not to the popular notions of rehabilitation."[44]

Two evaluations of different levels of supervision of parolees in California confirm neither Lerner's findings about the success of parole nor his speculation that the law enforcement orientation of parole reduces recidivism. Deborah Star reported the results of two surveys of the effectiveness of parole supervision in California. In the first, a group of felons (excluding inmates convicted of murder, rape, and some other serious offenses) was randomly assigned to either an experimental group of parolees who received reduced

Figure 15.10

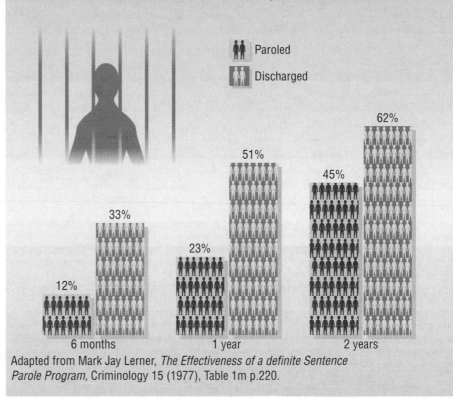

NUMBER OF PRISONERS PER 100,000 RESIDENTS

Paroled

Discharged

12%
33%
23%
51%
45%
62%

6 months   1 year   2 years

Adapted from Mark Jay Lerner, *The Effectiveness of a definite Sentence Parole Program,* Criminology 15 (1977), Table 1m p.220.

levels of supervision, or a control group that received regular parole. The experimental group had significantly fewer face-to-face contacts initiated by parole officers for the purpose of checking up on parolees than the control group on regular parole. After six months, the researchers found no significant difference in either the frequency or the severity of criminal activity between the control group on regular parole and the experimental group on reduced supervision. A follow-up study after one year confirmed the researchers' conclusions that reduced supervision had no significant effect on either the frequency or the severity of criminal activity.[45]

In a second study, Star reported the results of the High Control Project, another parole experiment conducted by the California Department of Corrections. This study evaluated the effects of increased surveillance and investigation of parolees to control their criminal activities. The High Control Project differed from regular parole in the following important ways:

1. It emphasized control of, not service to, parolees.

2. It placed primary emphasis on conducting investigation of parolees' possible criminal activities *before* arrest. Traditional parole supervision focuses on investigation after arrest. (See below on parole revocation.)

3. It targeted a group of parolees selected by agents as "high risk" cases.

4. It used specialized units of parole officers who specialized in law enforcement.[46]

The High Control Project relied on two law enforcer tactics to test the effectiveness of high levels of control. The first tactic, criminal investigation, utilized high control parole officers to conduct short-term investigations of parolees suspected of current involvement in illegal activities. The purposes of the investigations were to verify the involvement, apprehend the suspected parolees, and aid in successfully prosecuting them. The second tactic, intensive supervision, utilized parole officers with reduced caseloads to closely monitor parolees with serious prior criminal records. The purpose of the close surveillance was to prevent parolees from returning to criminal activities.[47]

Using a quasi-experimental design, high control parolees were compared to regular parolees. The evaluation that followed showed that neither enhanced investigation nor intensive supervision significantly affected either the frequency or the severity of criminal behavior. The researchers concluded that "there was nothing readily apparent about intensive supervision which would suggest that a close watch may deter parolees from returning to criminal activity and thereby reduce recidivism rates." However, researchers did find that criminal investigation in the High Control Project was more successful than regular parole in *verifying* criminal behavior once it had occurred, even if it did not significantly affect the frequency and severity of that behavior.[48]

The *You Decide,* "Should We Spend More Money on Parole Supervision?" deals with some of the implications of this research.

You Decide — "Should We Spend More Money on Parole Supervision?"

[The following is an excerpt from the respected criminal justice researcher and past president of the American Society of Criminology, Joan Petersilia. In "A Crime Control Rationale for Reinvesting in Community Corrections," Petersilia suggests some policies for community corrections generally, and for parole especially. These suggestions are based on recent empirical research and stem from the debate over whether to spend our tax dollars on building more prisons or on crime prevention and supervision of offenders in the community.]

Last year Congress passed the most ambitious crime bill in our nation's history, the Violent Crime Control and Law Enforcement Act of 1994. It allocated $22 billion to expand prisons, impose longer sentences, hire more police, and to a lesser extent, fund prevention programs. But as part of the Republicans' "Contract with America," the House significantly revised the Act, and the money allocated to prevention programs was eliminated. The amended bill—whose price tag rose to $30 billion—shifted nearly all of the $5 billion targeted for prevention programs into prison construction and law enforcement. As a *Los Angeles Times* op-ed concluded of the whole matter: "what started out last legislative season as a harsh and punitive bill has gotten downright Draconian."

While such tough-on-crime legislation has political appeal, it finds almost no support among criminal justice practitioners and scholars. They are uniformly agreed that such efforts—which endorse an "enforcement model" to the sacrifice of all else—will do little to curb crime. In recent months, organizations as diverse as the International Association of Chiefs of Police (IACP), the U.S. Conference of Mayors, the American Bar Association (ABA), National Governors Association, the League of Cities, The RAND Corporation, the National Council on Crime and Delinquency (NCCD), the Campaign for an Effective-Crime Policy (CECP), and the National Research Council have all voiced opposition to the approach.

Even prison wardens (who stand to benefit from an enforcement model) uniformly reject the crime-fighting solutions coming out of Washington. In a recent national survey of prison wardens, 85 percent of those surveyed said that elected officials are not offering effective solutions to America's crime problem. Chase Riveland, Washington State Director of Corrections, said that focusing only on prisons and ignoring the rest of the system is "drive-by legislation, at best." And Jerome Skolnick, President of the American Society of Criminology (ASC), spoke of the federal efforts in his 1994 Presidential Address and entitled it, "What *Not* to Do About Crime."

What is wrong with the current proposals? Some argue that they are racist, others argue that they cost too much, but nearly everyone agrees they have two major flaws: 1) they fail to prevent young people from entering and continuing a life of crime; and 2) they leave the vast majority of criminals, who are serving sentences on probation and parole rather than prison or jail, unaffected.

Criminologists have long observed that age 18 is the year of peak criminality. Analysis recently completed by Alfred Blumstein at Carnegie-Mellon showed that today we have the smallest cohort of 18-year-olds we will see for at least the next 15 years. Next year, the number is going to start going up, and the biggest growth will occur in the number of African American children who are now four to nine years old. Blumstein (1994) recently observed:

These young people are being less well educated and socialized, and as a result are easy recruits for the booming crack cocaine industry, where weapons are a business accessory for an increasing number of youths. The result will be a steep increase in juvenile and young adult violent crime, unless we begin investing in community-based programs to better socialize kids when their parents are not doing so. This is a population crying out for our attention, and, as a society, we need to find a means to divert them from becoming as violent as their big brothers.

As more young people are recruited into and retained in a criminal lifestyle, the ability of back-end responses (such as imprisonment) to increase public safety is severely limited because of the replenishing supply of young people who are entering into criminal careers.

The second, and equally important reason that current federal efforts will fail, is that they focus exclusively on prisons as a corrections strategy, ignoring the fact that most criminals are serving probation and parole sentences. In 1993 there were just under five million adult (convicted) criminals—or about one in every 39 Americans. Seventy-two percent of all identified criminals were not in prison, but serving sentences in the community on probation or parole supervision. Even though we have quadrupled the number of prisoners in the past decade, prisoners are still less than $1/5$ of the convict population, and the vast majority of offenders remain in the community amongst us (Bureau of Justice Statistics 1995). If we are to effectively control crime—as opposed to exacting retribution and justice—we must focus our efforts where the offenders are, which is in the community reporting to probation and parole officers.

Despite the fact that both crime bills were touted by their proponents as comprehensive approaches to the crime problem, neither the 1994 Crime Act or the 1995 "Taking Back Our Streets" proposal *even mentions* probation or parole, much less provides funding or direction for revising programs or practices. Moreover, the federal bill will likely take money away from community corrections budgets, which are already at a dangerously low level, to fund the expanded prison space required to comply with federal mandates requiring state prisoners to serve 86 percent of their sentence (so called "truth in sentencing").

This article addresses the public safety consequences of current probation and parole practices. It contends that current crime policies are neither comprehensive nor will they be effective unless we focus on the needs and risks posed by probationers and parolees. Whether we are able to control the crime propensities of *these* offenders is critical to the effectiveness of any anti-crime program.

Who Is On Probation and Parole? A Profile of the Population

The public misunderstands the safety risks and needs posed by offenders currently under community supervision. . . . To gauge the public safety risks of probationers and parolees, it is useful to consider the population as a whole in terms of conviction crimes. . . . [A]bout 16 percent of all adult probationers were convicted of violent crimes, as were 26 percent of parolees. This means that on any given day in the U.S. in 1991, there were an estimated 435,000 probationers and 155,000 parolees residing in local communities who have been convicted of violent crime—or over a half million offenders. If we compare that to the number of violent offenders residing in prison during the same year, we see that there were approximately 372,500 offenders convicted of violent crime *in* prison, and approximately 590,000 *outside* in the community on probation and parole! Overall, we can conclude that nearly three times as many violent offenders (1.02 million) were residing in the community as were incarcerated in prison (372,000). These numbers make painfully clear why a failure to provide adequate funding for community corrections invariably places the public at risk. . . .

Despite the unprecedented growth in probation populations and their more serious clientele, probation budgets have not grown. From 1977 to 1990 prison, jail, parole, and probation populations all about tripled in size. Yet only spending for prisons and jails had accelerated growth in overall government expenditures. In 1990 prison and jail spending accounted for two cents of every state and local dollar spent—twice the amount spent in 1977. Spending for probation and parole accounted for two-tenths of one cent of every dollar spent in 1990 — unchanged from what it was in 1977. Today, although nearly *three fourths* of correctional clients are in the community, only about *one tenth* of the correctional budget goes to supervise them.

The increase in populations, coupled with stagnant or decreasing funding, means that caseloads (the number of offenders an officer is responsible for supervising) keep increasing. . . .

But neglect in funding has had serious consequences. As caseloads rise, there is less opportunity for personal contact between officer and offender, limiting any ability of the officer to bring about positive change in the offender, or refer the offender to appropriate community-based resources and programs (which incidentally are also being reduced). Court-ordered fines and restitution don't get paid, and community service doesn't get performed. . . .

What Can We Do? A Proposal to Develop an Integrated Treatment/Control Program for Drug Offenders

The grim situation described above is known to most of those who work in the justice system or study it. Until we curb the criminal activities of the three-fourths of criminals who reside in the community, real reductions in crime or prison commitments are unlikely. But just as there is growing agreement about the nature of the problem, there is also an emerging consensus about how to address it.

We need to first regain the public's trust that probation and parole can be meaningful, credible sanctions. During the past decade, many jurisdictions developed "intermediate sanctions" as a response to prison crowding. These programs (e.g., house arrest, electronic monitoring, and intensive supervision) were designed to be community-based sanctions that were tougher than regular probation, but less stringent and expensive than prison. The program models were good and could have worked, except for one critical factor: they were usually implemented without creating an organizational capacity to ensure compliance with the court-ordered conditions. Intermediate sanctions were designed with smaller caseloads enabling officers to provide both services and monitoring for new criminal activity, but they never were given the resources needed to enforce the sanctions or provide necessary treatment. . . .

But not all programs have had this experience. In a few instances, communities invested in intermediate sanctions and made the necessary treatment and work programs available to offenders. And, most importantly, the programs worked: in programs where offenders both received surveillance (e.g., drug tests) and participated in relevant treatment, recidivism was reduced 20-30 percent. Recent program evaluations in Texas, Wisconsin, Oregon, and Colorado have found similarly encouraging results. Even in BJS's national probation follow-up study, it was found that if probationers were participating in or making progress in treatment programs, they were less likely to have a new arrest (38 percent) than either those drug offenders who had made no progress (66 percent) or those who were not ordered to be tested or treated (48 percent).

There now exists rather solid empirical evidence that ordering offenders into treatment and getting them to participate, reduces recidivism. So, the first order of business must be to allocate sufficient resources so that the designed programs (incorporating both surveillance and treatment) can be implemented. Sufficient monetary resources are essential to obtaining and sustaining judicial support, and achieving program success.

Once we have that in place, we need to create a public climate to support a reinvestment in community corrections. Good community corrections costs money, and we should be honest about that. We currently spend about $200 per year, per probationer, for supervision. It is no wonder that recidivism rates are so high. Effective treatment programs cost at least $12,000–$14,000 per year. Those resources will be forthcoming only if the public believes the programs are both effective and punitive.

Public opinion is often cited by officials as the reason for supporting expanded prison policies. According to officials, the public demands a "get tough on crime" policy, which is synonymous with sending more offenders to prison for longer terms. We must publicize recent evidence showing that offenders—whose opinion on such matters is critical for deterrence—judge some intermediate sanctions as *more* punishing than prison. Surveys of offenders in Minnesota, Arizona, New Jersey, Oregon, and Texas reveal that when offenders are asked to equate criminal sentences, they judge certain types of community punishments as *more* severe than prison.

One of the more striking examples comes from Marion County, Oregon. Selected nonviolent offenders were given the choice of serving a prison term or returning to the community to participate in the Intensive Supervision Probation (ISP) program, which imposed drug testing, mandatory community service, and frequent visits with the probation officer. About a third of the offenders given the option between ISP or prison chose prison. When Minnesota inmates and corrections staff were asked to equate a variety of criminal sentences, they rated three years of Intensive Supervision Probation as equivalent in punitiveness to one year in prison.

What accounts for this seeming aberration? Why should anyone prefer imprisonment to remaining in the community—no matter what the conditions? Some have suggested that prison has lost some of its punitive sting, and hence its ability to scare and deter. For one, possessing a prison record is not as stigmatizing as in the past because so many of the offenders' peers (and family members) also have "done time." A recent survey shows that 40 percent of youths in state training schools have parents who have been incarcerated. Further, about a quarter of all U.S. black males will be incarcerated during their lives, so the stigma attached to having a prison record is not as great as it was when it was relatively uncommon. And the pains associated with prison—social isolation, fear of victimization—seem less severe for repeat offenders who have learned how to do time.

In fact, far from stigmatizing, prison evidently confers status in some neighborhoods. Jerome Skolnick of U.C. Berkeley found that for drug dealers in California, imprisonment confers a certain elevated "home boy" status, especially for gang members for whom prison and prison gangs can be an alternative site of loyalty. And according to the California Youth Authority, inmates steal state-issued prison clothing for the same reason. Wearing it when they return to the community lets everyone know they have done "hard time.". . .

The length of time an offender can be expected to serve in prison has also decreased—the latest statistics show that the average U.S. prison term for those released to parole is 17 months. But more to the point, for less serious offenders, the expected time served can be much less. In California, for example, more than half of all offenders entering prison in 1995 are expected to serve six months or less. Offenders on the street seem to be aware of this, perhaps because of the extensive media coverage such issues are receiving.

For convicted felons, freedom, of course, is preferable to prison. But the type of program being advocated here—combining heavy doses of surveillance and treatment—does not represent freedom. In fact, as suggested above, such community-based programs may have more punitive bite than prison. Consider a comparison between Contra Costa (California) County's Intensive Supervision Program (ISP) for drug offenders, which was discontinued in 1990 due to a shortage of funds, with what drug offenders would face if imprisoned.

ISP: Offenders were required to serve at least one year on ISP. In addition to twice weekly face-to-face contacts, ISP included a random drug testing hotline, Saturday home visits, weekly Narcotics Anonymous meetings, special assistance from police to expedite existing bench warrants, and a liaison with the State Employment Development Department. To remain on ISP, offenders had to be employed or in treatment, perform community service, pay victim restitution, and remain crime- and drug-free.

Prison: A sentence of 12 months will require that the offender serve about half of that. During his term, he is not required to work nor will he be required to participate in any training or treatment, but may do so if he wishes. Once released, he will probably be placed on routine parole supervision, where he might see his officer once a month.

It is important to publicize these results, particularly to policymakers, who say they are imprisoning such a large number of offenders because of the public's desire to get tough on crime. But it is no longer necessary to equate criminal punishment solely with prison. The balance of sanctions between probation and prison can be shifted, and at some level of intensity and length, intermediate punishments can be the more dreaded penalty. . . .

Assume you are on the staff of a legislator. You receive a copy of this article by Joan Petersilia. On the basis of the article, how would you advise your legislator to vote on a proposal to spend more of the taxpayers' money on corrections? Support your advice with specific information and arguments from this article. If you cannot decide what advice to give, what questions do you want answered and what further information do you need before you advise your legislator? In giving your advice, how would you use the mixed results of the empirical research discussed in the section of the text called "The Effectiveness of Conditional Release?"

Parole Revocation

parole revocation *cancellation of conditional release and return to prison.*
technical violations *violations of conditions of parole other than the commission of new crimes.*

"The enforcement leverage that supports the parole conditions derives from the authority to return the parolee to prison to serve out the balance of his sentence if he fails to abide by the rules," wrote Chief Justice Warren Burger in the landmark parole revocation case, *Morrissey v. Brewer* (excerpted in the *You Decide*, "What Process Is 'Due' to Parolees?") that appears later in this chapter. If Chief Justice Burger is right, then that enforcement leverage fails in almost half the cases. Somewhat less than half of all parolees who leave parole every year do so because they have successfully completed their parole and are discharged from state custody. Approximately 25 percent return to prison either because they are convicted or charged with a new crime or because they have had their parole revoked or revocation is pending. Figure 15.9 depicts the breakdown of these numbers for 1993.[49]

Parole revocation can occur for two reasons:

1. Parolees commit new crimes.
2. Parolees commit **technical violations,** that is, they violate any of the conditions of their release that are not defined as crimes in the criminal codes of their jurisdictions.

Notice that revocation *can* occur for these two reasons. Parole officers possess considerable discretion in reporting violations and in calling for revocation when they occur. Accurate figures concerning the reasons for revocation are difficult to determine. However, revocation probably rarely occurs for a single technical violation. From what is known, revocation occurs only if parolees:

1. Are arrested on serious criminal charges.
2. Repeatedly violate the conditions of their parole.
3. Abscond or cannot otherwise be found.
4. Abuse alcohol or other drugs.
5. Carry weapons.[50]

Revocation is not automatically carried out; parole officers have the discretionary authority to decide if it should take place. The United States Supreme Court has ruled that the revocation of parole denies parolees liberty. The Fourteenth Amendment provides that "No state shall deprive any person of life, liberty, or property without due process of law." Parole officers and parole boards are agents of the state. As such, they cannot revoke parole "without due process of law." But what process is "due" to parolees? Not the full, impressive array of rights afforded criminal defendants not yet convicted of crimes, and certainly not the rights afforded people who are not even suspected of committing crimes. (See Chapters 2, 6, 9, and 10 for discussions of these rights.) According to the Supreme Court,

> what is needed is an informal hearing structured to assure that the finding of a parole violation will be based on verified facts and that the exercise of discretion will be informed by an accurate knowledge of the parolee's behavior.[51]

Parole cannot be revoked without due process of law, according to the U.S. Supreme Court.

The United States Code has provided for the following two-stage procedure to guarantee the due process rights of parolees in the revocation of their parole:

§ 4214. Revocation of parole

. . . [A]ny alleged parole violator summoned or retaken under section 4213 shall be accorded the opportunity to have—

(A) *a preliminary hearing* at or reasonably near the place of the alleged parole violation or arrest, without unnecessary delay, to determine if there is probable cause to believe that he has violated a condition of his parole; and upon a finding of probable cause a digest shall be prepared by the Commission setting forth in writing the factors considered and the reasons for the decision, a copy of which shall be given to the parolee within a reasonable period of time; except that after a finding of probable cause the Commission may restore any parolee to parole supervision if:

(i) continuation of revocation proceedings is not warranted; or
(ii) incarceration of the parolee pending further revocation proceedings is not warranted by the alleged frequency or seriousness of such violation or violations;
(iii) the parolee is not likely to fail to appear for further proceedings; and
(iv) the parolee does not constitute a danger to himself or others.

(B) upon a finding of probable cause under subparagraph (1)(A), *a revocation hearing* at or reasonably near the place of the alleged parole violation or arrest within sixty days of such determination of probable cause, except that a revocation hearing may be held at the same time and place set for the preliminary hearing.

(2) Hearings held pursuant to subparagraph (1) of this subsection shall be conducted by the Commission in accordance with the following procedures:

(A) notice to the parolee of the conditions of parole alleged to have been violated, and the time, place, and purposes of the scheduled hearing;
(B) opportunity for the parolee to be represented by an attorney (retained by the parolee, or if he is financially unable to retain counsel, counsel shall be provided pursuant to section 3006A) or, if

he so chooses, a representative as provided by rules and regulations, unless the parolee knowingly and intelligently waives such representation.

(C) opportunity for the parolee to appear and testify, and present witnesses and relevant evidence on his own behalf; and

(D) opportunity for the parolee to be apprised of the evidence against him and, if he so requests, to confront and cross-examine adverse witnesses, unless the Commission specifically finds substantial reason for not so allowing.

For the purposes of subparagraph (1) of this subsection, the Commission may subpoena witnesses and evidence, and pay witness fees as established for the courts of the United States. If a person refuses to obey such a subpoena, the Commission may petition a court of the United States for the judicial district in which such parole proceeding is being conducted, or in which such person may be found, to request such person to attend, testify, and produce evidence. The court may issue an order requiring such person to appear before the Commission, when the court finds such information, or testimony directly related to a matter with respect to which the Commission is empowered to make a determination under this section. Failure to obey such an order is punishable by such court as a contempt. All process in such a case may be served in the judicial district in which such a parole proceeding is being conducted, or in which such person may be found.

(b)(1) Conviction for any criminal offense committed subsequent to release on parole shall constitute probable cause for purposes of subsection (a) of this section. In cases in which a parolee has been convicted of such an offense and is serving a new sentence in an institution, a parole revocation warrant or summons issued pursuant to section 4213 may be placed against him as a detainer. Such detainer shall be reviewed by the Commission within one hundred and eighty days of notification to the Commission of placement. The parolee shall receive notice of the pending review, have an opportunity to submit a written application containing information relative to the disposition of the detainer, and, unless waived, shall have counsel as provided in subsection (a)(2)(B) of this section to assist him in the preparation of such application.

. . .

(d) Whenever a parolee is summoned or retaken pursuant to section 4213, and the Commission finds pursuant to the procedures of this section and by a preponderance of the evidence that the parolee has violated a condition of his parole the Commission may take any of the following actions:

(1) restore the parolee to supervision;

(2) reprimand the parolee;

(3) modify the parolee's conditions of the parole;

(4) refer the parolee to a residential community treatment center for all or part of the remainder of his original sentence; or

(5) formally revoke parole or release as if on parole pursuant to this title.

. . .

(e) The Commission shall furnish the parolee with a written notice of its determination not later than twenty-one days, excluding holidays, after the date of the revocation hearing. If parole is revoked, a digest shall be prepared by the Commission setting forth in writing the factors considered and reasons for such action, a copy of which shall be given to the parolee.

(f) Notwithstanding any other provision of this section, a parolee who is found by the Commission to be in possession of a controlled substance shall have his parole revoked.[52]

The *You Decide*, "What Process Is 'Due' to Parolees?" excerpts the landmark case of *Morrissey v. Brewer*.

You Decide   "What Process Is 'Due' to Parolees?"

Morrissey v. Brewer, 408 U.S. 471 (1972)

Mr. Chief Justice BURGER delivered the opinion of the Court.

FACTS

. . . Petitioner Morrissey was convicted of false drawing or uttering of checks in 1967 pursuant to his guilty plea, and was sentenced to not more than seven years' confinement. He was paroled from the Iowa State Penitentiary in June 1968. Seven months later, at the direction of his parole officer, he was arrested in his home town as a parole violator and incarcerated in the county jail. One week later, after review of the parole officer's written report, the Iowa Board of Parole revoked Morrissey's parole, and he was returned to the penitentiary located about 100 miles from his home. Petitioner asserts he received no hearing prior to revocation of his parole.

The parole officer's report on which the Board of Parole acted shows that petitioner's parole was revoked on the basis of information that he had violated the conditions of parole by buying a car under an assumed name and operating it without permission, giving false statements to police concerning his address and insurance-company after a minor accident, obtaining credit under an assumed name, and failing to report his place of residence to his parole officer. The report states that the officer interviewed Morrissey, and that he could not explain why he did not contact his parole officer despite his effort to excuse this on the ground that he had been sick. Further, the report asserts that Morrissey admitted buying the car and obtaining credit under an assumed name, and also admitted being involved in the accident. The parole officer recommended that his parole be revoked because of 'his continual violating of his parole rules.'. . .

After exhausting state remedies, . . . petitioner filed [a] habeas corpus petition in the United States District Court for the Southern District of Iowa alleging that [he] had been denied due process because [his] parole had been revoked without a hearing. The State responded by arguing that no hearing was required. The District Court held on the basis of controlling authority that the State's failure to accord a hearing prior to parole revocation did not violate due process. . . . The Court of Appeals, dividing 4 to 3, held that due process does not require a hearing. . . . Iowa law provides that a parolee may be returned to the institution at any time. . . .

Opinion

. . . The enforcement leverage that supports . . . parole conditions derives from the authority to return the parolee to prison to serve out the balance of his sentence if he fails to abide by the rules. In practice, not every violation of parole conditions automatically leads to revocation. Typically, a parolee will be counseled to abide by the conditions of parole, and the parole officer ordinarily does not take steps to have parole revoked unless he thinks that the violations are serious and continuing so as to indicate that the parolee is not adjusting properly and cannot be counted on to avoid antisocial activity. The broad discretion accorded the parole officer is also inherent in some of the quite vague conditions, such as the typical requirement that the parolee avoid 'undesirable' associations or correspondence. Yet revocation of parole is not an unusual phenomenon, affecting only a few parolees. It has been estimated that 35%–45% of all parolees are subjected to revocation and return to prison. Sometimes revocation occurs when the parolee is accused of another crime; it is often preferred to a new prosecution because of the procedural ease of recommitting the individual on the basis of a lesser showing by the State. . . . If a parolee is returned to prison, he usually receives no credit for the time 'served' on parole. Thus, the returnee may face a potential of substantial imprisonment.

We begin with the proposition that the revocation of parole is not part of a criminal prosecution and thus the full panoply of rights due a defendant in such a proceeding does not apply to parole revocations. Parole arises after the end of the criminal prosecution, including imposition of sentence. Supervision is not directly by the court but by an administrative agency, which is sometimes an arm of the court and sometimes of the executive. Revocation deprives an individual, not of the absolute liberty to which every citizen is entitled, but only of the conditional liberty properly dependent on observance of special parole restrictions.

We turn, therefore, to the question whether the requirements of due process in general apply to parole revocations. . . . Whether any procedural protections are due depends on the extent to which an individual will be 'condemned to suffer grievous loss.' The question is . . . whether the nature of the interest is one within the contemplation of the 'liberty or property' language of the Fourteenth Amendment. Once it is determined that due process applies, the question remains what process is due. It has been said so often by this Court and others as not to require citation of authority that due process is flexible and calls for such procedural protections as the particular situation demands. . . .

We turn to an examination of the nature of the interest of the parolee in his continued liberty. The liberty of a parolee enables him to do a wide range of things open to persons who have never been convicted of any crime. The parolee has been released from prison based on an evaluation that he shows reasonable promise of being able to return to society and function as a responsible, self-reliant person. Subject to the conditions of his parole, he can be gainfully employed and is free to be with family and friends and to form the other enduring attachments of normal life. Though the State properly subjects him to many restrictions not applicable to other citizens, his condition is very different from that of confinement in a prison. He may have been on parole for a number of years and may be living a relatively normal life at the time he is faced with revocation. The parolee has relied on at least an implicit promise that parole will be revoked only if he fails to live up to the parole conditions. In many cases, the parolee faces lengthy incarceration if his parole is revoked.

We see, therefore, that the liberty of a parolee, although indeterminate, includes many of the core values of unqualified liberty and its termination inflicts a 'grievous loss' on the parolee and often on others. It is hardly useful any longer to try to deal with this problem in terms of whether the parolee's liberty is a 'right' or a 'privilege.' By whatever name, the liberty is valuable and must be seen as within the protection of the Fourteenth Amendment. Its termination calls for some orderly process, however informal.

Turning to the question what process is due, we find that the State's interests are several. The State has found the parolee guilty of a crime against the people. That finding justifies imposing extensive restrictions on the individual's liberty. Release of the parolee before the end of his prison sentence is made with the recognition that with many prisoners there is a risk that they will not be able to live in society without committing additional antisocial acts. Given the previous conviction and the proper imposition of conditions, the State has an overwhelming interest in being able to return the individual to imprisonment without the burden of a new adversary criminal trial if in fact he has failed to abide by the conditions of his parole.

Yet, the State has no interest in revoking parole without some informal procedural guarantees. Although the parolee is often formally described as being 'in custody,' the argument cannot even be made here that summary treatment is necessary as it may be with respect to controlling a large group of potentially disruptive prisoners in actual custody. Nor are we persuaded by the argument that revocation is so totally a discretionary matter that some form of hearing would be administratively intolerable. A simple factual hearing will not interfere with the exercise of discretion. . . .

This discretionary aspect of the revocation decision need not be reached unless there is first an appropriate determination that the individual has in fact breached the conditions of parole. The parolee is not the only one who has a stake in his conditional liberty. Society has a stake in whatever may be the chance of restoring him to normal and useful life within the law. Society thus has an interest in not having parole revoked because of erroneous information or because of an erroneous evaluation of the need to revoke parole, given the breach of parole conditions. And society has a further interest in treating the parolee with basic fairness: fair treatment in parole revocations will enhance the chance of rehabilitation by avoiding reactions to arbitrariness.

Given these factors, most States have recognized that there is no interest on the part of the State in revoking parole without any procedural guarantees at all. What is needed is an informal hearing structured to assure that the finding of a parole violation will be based on verified facts and that the exercise of discretion will be informed by an accurate knowledge of the parolee's behavior.

We now turn to the nature of the process that is due, bearing in mind that the interest of both State and parolee will be furthered by an effective but informal hearing. In analyzing what is due, we see two important stages in the typical process of parole revocation.

(a) Arrest of Parolee and Preliminary Hearing. The first stage occurs when the parolee is arrested and detained, usually at the direction of his parole officer. The second occurs when parole is formally revoked. There is typically a substantial time lag between the arrest and the eventual determination by the parole board whether parole should be revoked. Additionally, it may be that the parolee is arrested at a place distant from the state institution, to which he may be returned before the final decision is made concerning revocation. Given these factors, due process would seem to require that some minimal inquiry be conducted at or reasonably near the place of the alleged parole violation or arrest and as promptly as convenient after arrest while information is fresh and sources are available. Such an inquiry should be seen as in the nature of a 'preliminary hearing' to determine whether there is probable cause or reasonable ground to believe that the arrested parolee has committed acts that would constitute a violation of parole conditions.

In our view, due process requires that after the arrest, the determination that reasonable ground exists for revocation of parole should be made by someone not directly involved in the case. It would be unfair to assume that the supervising parole officer does not conduct an interview with the parolee to confront him with the reasons for revocation before he recommends an arrest. It would also be unfair to assume that the parole officer bears hostility against the parolee that destroys his neutrality; realistically the failure of the parolee is in a sense a failure for his supervising officer. However, we need make no assumptions one way or the other to conclude that there should be an uninvolved person to make this preliminary evaluation of the basis for believing the conditions of parole have been violated. The officer directly involved in making recommendations cannot always have complete objectivity in evaluating them. *Goldberg v. Kelly* found it unnecessary to impugn the motives of the caseworker to find a need for an independent decision maker to examine the initial decision.

This independent officer need not be a judicial officer. The granting and revocation of parole are matters traditionally handled by administrative officers. In *Goldberg,* the Court pointedly did not require that the hearing on termination of benefits be conducted by a judicial officer or even before the traditional 'neutral and detached' officer; it required only that the hearing be conducted by some person other than one initially dealing with the case. It will be sufficient, therefore, in the parole revocation context, if an evaluation of whether reasonable cause exists to believe that conditions of parole have been violated is made by someone such as a parole officer other than the one who has made the report of parole violations or has recommended revocation. A State could certainly choose some other independent decision maker to perform this preliminary function.

With respect to the preliminary hearing before this officer, the parolee should be given notice that the hearing will take place and that its purpose is to determine whether there is probable cause to believe he has committed a parole violation. The notice should state what parole violations have been alleged. At the hearing the parolee may appear and speak in his own behalf; he may bring letters, documents, or individuals who can give relevant information to the hearing officer. On request of the parolee, the person who has given adverse information on which parole revocation is to be based is to be made available for questioning in his presence. However, if the hearing officer determines that an informant would be subjected to risk of harm if his identity were disclosed, he need not be subjected to confrontation and cross-examination.

The hearing officer shall have the duty of making a summary, or digest, of what occurs at the hearing in terms of the responses of the parolee and the substance of the documents or evidence given in support of parole revocation and of the parolee's position. Based on the information before him, the officer should determine whether there is probable cause to hold the parolee for the final decision of the parole board on revocation. Such a determination would be sufficient to warrant the parolee's continued detention and return to the state correctional institution pending the final decision. As in *Goldberg,* 'the decision maker should state the reasons for his determination and indicate the evidence he relied on . . .' but it should be remembered that this is not a final determination calling for 'formal findings of fact and conclusions of law.' No interest would be served by formalism in this process; informality will not lessen the utility of this inquiry in reducing the risk of error.

(b) The Revocation Hearing. There must also be an opportunity for a hearing, if it is desired by the parolee, prior to the final decision on revocation by the parole authority. This hearing must be the basis for more than determining probable cause; it must lead to a final evaluation of any contested relevant facts and consideration of whether the facts as determined warrant revocation. The parolee must have an opportunity to be heard and to show, if he can, that he did not violate the conditions, or, if he did, that circumstances in mitigation suggest that the violation does not warrant revocation. The revocation hearing must be tendered within a reasonable time after the parolee is taken into custody. A lapse of two months, as respondents suggest occurs in some cases, would not appear to be unreasonable.

We cannot write a code of procedure; that is the responsibility of each State. Most States have done so by legislation, others by judicial decision usually on due process grounds. Our task is limited to deciding the minimum requirements of due process. They include (a) written notice of the claimed violations of parole; (b) disclosure to the parolee of evidence against him; (c) opportunity to be heard in person and to present witnesses and documentary evidence; (d) the right to confront and cross-examine adverse witnesses (unless the hearing officer specifically finds good cause for not allowing confrontation); (e) a 'neutral and detached' hearing body such as a traditional parole board, members of which need not be judicial officers or lawyers; and (f) a written statement by the fact finders as to the evidence relied on and reasons for revoking parole. We emphasize there is no thought to equate this second stage of parole revocation to a criminal prosecution in any sense. It is a narrow inquiry; the process should be flexible enough to consider evidence including letters, affidavits, and other material that would not be admissible in an adversary criminal trial.

We do not reach or decide the question whether the parolee is entitled to the assistance of retained counsel or to appointed counsel if he is indigent.

We have no thought to create an inflexible structure for parole revocation procedures. The few basic requirements set out above, which are applicable to future revocations of parole, should not impose a great burden on any State's parole system. Control over the required proceedings by the hearing officers can assure that delaying tactics and other abuses sometimes present in the traditional adversary trial situation do not occur. Obviously a parolee cannot relitigate issues determined against him in other forums, as in the situation presented when the revocation is based on conviction of another crime. . . .

We reverse and remand to the Court of Appeals for further proceedings consistent with this opinion. Reversed and remanded.

Concurring Opinion

Mr. Justice BRENNAN, concurring in the result.
. . . The Court . . . states that it does not now decide whether the parolee is also entitled at each hearing to the assistance of retained counsel or of appointed counsel if he is indigent. *Goldberg v. Kelly,* 397 U.S. 254, 90 S.Ct. 1011, 25 L.Ed.2d 287 (1970), nonetheless plainly dictates that he at least 'must be allowed to retain an attorney if he so desires.' As the Court said there, 'Counsel and help delineate the issues, present the factual contentions in an orderly manner, conduct cross-examination, and generally safeguard the interests of' his client. The only question open under our precedents is whether counsel must be furnished the parolee if he is indigent.

Dissent

Mr. Justice DOUGLAS, dissenting in part.
. . .

Under modern concepts of penology, paroling prisoners is part of the rehabilitative aim of the correctional philosophy. The objective is to return a prisoner to a full family and community life. . . . That status is conditioned upon not engaging in certain activities and perhaps in not leaving a certain area or locality. Violations of conditions of parole may be technical, they may be done unknowingly, they may be fleeting and of no consequence. The parolee should, in the concept of fairness implicit in due process, have a chance to explain. Rather, under Iowa's rule revocation proceeds on the ipse dixit of the parole agent; and on his word alone each of these petitioners has already served three additional years in prison. The charges may or may not be true. Words of explanation may be adequate to transform into trivia what looms large in the mind of the parole officer.

'(T)here is no place in our system of law for reaching result of such tremendous consequences without ceremony—without hearing, without effective assistance of counsel, without a statement of reasons.' Parole, while originally conceived as a judicial function, has become largely an administrative matter. The parole boards have broad discretion in formulating and imposing parole conditions.

Parole is commonly revoked on mere suspicion that the parolee may have committed a crime. Such great control over the parolee vests in a parole officer a broad discretion in revoking parole and also in counseling the parolee—referring him for psychiatric treatment or obtaining the use of specialized therapy for narcotic addicts or alcoholics. Treatment of the parolee, rather than revocation of his parole, is a common course. Counseling may include extending help to a parolee in finding a job. A parolee, like a prisoner, is a person entitled to constitutional protection, including procedural due process. At the federal level, the construction of regulations of the Federal Parole Board presents federal questions of which we have taken cognizance. At the state level, the construction of parole statutes and regulations is for the States alone. . . .

It is only procedural due process, required by the Fourteenth Amendment, that concerns us in the present cases. Procedural due process requires the following.

If a violation of a condition of parole is involved, rather than the commission of a new offense, there should not be an arrest of the parolee and his return to the prison or to a local jail. Rather, notice of the alleged violation should be given to the parolee and a time set for a hearing. The hearing should not be before the parole officer, as he is the one who is making the charge and 'there is inherent danger in combining the functions of judge and advocate.' Moreover, the parolee should be entitled to counsel. As the Supreme Court of Oregon said in *Perry v. Williard,* 'A hearing in which counsel is absent or is present only on behalf of one side is inherently unsatisfactory if not unfair. Counsel can see that relevant facts

are brought out, vague and insubstantial allegations discounted, and irrelevancies eliminated.'

The hearing required is not a grant of the full panoply of rights applicable to a criminal trial. But confrontation with the informer may . . . be necessary for a fair hearing and the ascertainment of the truth. The hearing is to determine the fact of parole violation. The results of the hearing would go to the parole board—or other authorized state agency—for final action, as would cases which involved voluntary admission of violations.

The rule of law is important in the stability of society. Arbitrary actions in the revocation of paroles can only impede and impair the rehabilitative aspects of modern penology. 'Notice and opportunity for hearing appropriate to the nature of the case,' are the rudiments of due process which restore faith that our society is run for the many, not the few, and that fair dealing rather than caprice will govern the affairs of men.

I would not prescribe the precise formula for the management of the parole problems. We do not sit as an ombudsman, telling the States the precise procedures they must follow. I would hold that so far as the due process requirements of parole revocation are concerned:

(1) the parole officer—whatever may be his duties under various state statutes—in Iowa appears to be an agent having some of the functions of a prosecutor and of the police; the parole officer is therefore not qualified as a hearing officer;

(2) the parolee is entitled to a due process notice and a due process hearing of the alleged parole violations including, for example, the opportunity to be confronted by his accusers and to present evidence and argument on his own behalf; and

(3) the parolee is entitled to the freedom granted a parolee until the results of the hearing are known and the parole board—or other authorized state agency   acts.

Questions
What "liberties" do parolees have that entitles them to due process when their parole is revoked? Why is less process "due" to parolees than to defendants and people not charged with crimes? What process exactly is "due" to parolees in revocation of their parole? If you were writing the rules regarding the revocation of parole, would you write the ones recommended by the majority of the Court as set out by Chief Justice Burger, or those of Justice Douglas in his dissent? Should parolees have a right to counsel at their revocation hearings? Defend your answer. Should parole officers have the authority to take parolees into custody and have them detained in jail without a hearing prior to the detention? Defend your answer.

Summary

Most of the public attention and most of the public's tax dollars spent on corrections are going to prisons. But, except for a few prisoners who stay in prison until the expiration of their sentence, most offenders serve only part of their sentence in prison, usually about two years. They serve the remainder of their sentence in the community. Release from prison for these prisoners ordinarily does not mean release from custody. It means release with conditions that require supervision by the state for the period of time that is left of their sentence. Far more people are supervised in the community than are in prison, and these numbers are growing. Yet, despite these large and growing numbers, the budgets of parole agencies are decreasing.

The conditional release of prisoners is an old practice. For more than four centuries, keepers have released prisoners for a combination of sometimes conflicting reasons. These reasons range from the punishment of offenders and their rehabilitation, to the protection of public safety and the relief of prison crowding. Supporters of parole have always had to defend it against attacks that it is soft on crime and criminals and that it threatens the safety of society.

Parole consists of three major aspects—conditional release from incarceration before the end of the sentence; supervision until the expiration of the sentence; and revocation of parole for the violation of the conditions of parole or the commission of new crimes. The decision to release varies according to jurisdiction, but generally it is either discretionary and made by parole boards or mandatory and determined by legislatures and judges. Parole boards not only control the date of release of prisoners but also a wide range of actions related to the conditions of release, the revocation of parole, and the final discharge of offenders from state custody. Most states set only minimum requirements for parole board membership.

Until the 1970s, parole boards had wide discretion in making the decision to release onto parole. Since then, two changes have sharply curtailed parole board discretion in about half the states. First, when determinate sentences of various types were reintroduced in a number of states during the 1970s and 1980s, mandatory release of prisoners became more common. In fact, a few states, like Maine, abolished parole. Prisoners knew at the time they were sentenced the date of their release, modified only by the accumulation of good time. Second, parole guidelines focused parole board release decisions on objective criteria—the seriousness of the offense and the risk to the community of releasing offenders. The release of offenders was tied to specific recommended times based on these criteria. Although guidelines and determinate sentences are praised for their objectivity and fairness, empirical research has concluded that their predictive capacity is weak. Furthermore, parole guidelines have led to legal wrangling between offenders and releasing authorities over classification of offenses and the calculation of risk factors.

Parolees are released from *incarceration,* not from *custody.* Parole is a contract between parolees and the state in which the state agrees to allow them to remain free as long as they comply with a range of specific conditions that limit what they do, who they associate with, and where they go. These conditions are justified as part of punishment, necessary to protect public safety, and necessary to gradually reintegrate offenders into society. Parolees are required to work, go to school, or participate in some other kind of program, such as treatment for alcohol or other drug abuse.

Parole officers are responsible for the supervision of offenders conditionally released from prison. They perform several conflicting missions related to protecting society from the criminal acts and other misbehavior of released offenders and helping parolees reintegrate into society as law-abiding, self-supporting members of their community. Depending on how they view their roles and how they classify the parolees they supervise, parole officers may emphasize one mission over another. Criticism of parole, hardening public attitudes toward crime, and the concomitant disenchantment with rehabilitation have led to an increased focus on the public safety mission.

The effectiveness of supervision in protecting society by preventing parolees from committing new crimes is decidedly mixed. Some research in some places has found that closer supervision of parolees has reduced recidivism. Other research in other places has found that the amount of supervision has little or nothing to do with the number of crimes parolees commit. In fact, some research has demonstrated that people released without any supervision at all do about as well as parolees supervised during their release. However, there is some reason to believe that parole supervision *delays*, even if it does not *prevent*, future criminal behavior.

Parole revocation can occur when parolees either commit new crimes or commit technical violations involving the specific conditions of their parole. However, in practice revocation occurs only when parolees are arrested for serious crimes, repeatedly commit technical violations, run away, abuse alcohol and other drugs, or carry weapons. The Supreme Court has ruled that the revocation of parole denies parolees of liberty because of the freedoms that parolees enjoy under their contract of parole. As a result, parolees are protected by the due process clauses of the Fifth and Fourteenth Amendments. Neither the federal nor state authorities can deny them this liberty "without due process of law." The process due to parolees is less than that due to defendants in criminal trials. Parolees are entitled to a two-staged hearing, one to make sure that the parole violation is based on fact and the other to make sure that the revocation of parole is fair.

Review Questions

1. What proportion of prisoners eventually return to society?
2. What is the trend in numbers of inmates released conditionally from prison?
3. How much time do most prisoners spend in prison?
4. Identify and explain the three principal ways prisoners are released from prison.
5. Explain the effect of determinate sentencing on the way prisoners are released from prison.
6. Briefly trace the history of parole.
7. Explain the significance of Alexander Maconochie and Sir Walter Crofton in the history of parole.
8. Identify the four major elements of parole.
9. Explain why parole has generated controversy throughout its history.
10. Identify and describe the four major missions of parole.
11. Identify the major powers of parole boards.
12. Describe the size and characteristics of parole boards, and the qualifications for parole board membership.
13. Identify and explain the two basic mechanisms for releasing prisoners.
14. Contrast release in states with determinate and indeterminate sentencing laws.
15. What are the principal arguments of critics of parole board release?
16. Describe a parole board release hearing.
17. How have parole guidelines influenced release decision making by parole boards?
18. Into what two categories do parole guidelines put offenders?
19. What is a salient factor score and what are its main elements?

20. Describe the reasons why parole guidelines appeal to their supporters.
21. In what ways have researchers challenged the conclusions of supporters of parole guidelines?
22. Identify the four main issues in the civil litigation that parole guidelines create.
23. Describe the origin of mandatory release and contrast it with discretionary release.
24. Identify and describe some of the difficulties released prisoners face when they return to society.
25. Describe how parole release is a contract.
26. List the most common conditions of parole.
27. Identify and list the missions of the major parole programs.
28. Identify and describe the multiple and conflicting roles of parole officers.
29. How have the missions of parole shifted from the 1970s?
30. How is the effectiveness of parole supervision measured? What definitional problems arise in this measure?
31. Summarize the results of the empirical research regarding the effectiveness of parole supervision.
32. What are the two principal reasons that *can* lead to the revocation of parole? What are the four major reasons parole is *actually* revoked?
33. According to the U.S. Supreme Court, why are parolees entitled to due process in their revocation hearings?
34. Exactly what process is "due" to parolees in the revocation of their parole?

Notes

1. BJS, *Correctional Populations in the United States, 1993* (Washington, D.C.: BJS, October 1995), Tables 5.11b, 5.12a; Joan Petersilia, "A Crime Control Rationale for Reinvesting in Community Corrections," *Spectrum* (Summer 1995): 16–27.

2. BJS, *Prisoners in 1994* (Washington, D.C.: BJS, August 1995), 12, and Table 15.

3. Joel Samaha, "Hanging for Felony," *Historical Journal* (1979); Clair Wilcox, *Parole from State Penal Institutions*

(Philadelphia: Pennsylvania State Parole Commission, 1927), 5–6.

4. Wilcox, *Parole,* 6.

5. Ibid., 3.

6. Harry Elmer Barnes and Negley K. Teeters, *New Horizons in Criminology,* 3d. ed. (Englewood Cliffs, N.J.: Prentice-Hall, 1959), 567.

7. Wilcox, *Parole,* 1.

8. Quoted in Wilcox, *Parole,* 2.

9. Ibid., 21.

10. John C. Runda, Edward E. Rhine, and Robert E. Wetter, *The Practice of Parole Boards* (Lexington, Ky.: Association of Paroling Authorities, 1994), 1–7.

11. Ibid., 28.

12. Ibid.

13. Ibid., 9.

14. Ibid.

15. *Greenholtz v. Inmates of the Nebraska Penal and Correction Complex,* 99 S.Ct. 2100 (1979).

16. Ibid.

17. John S. Goldkamp, "Prediction in Criminal Justice Policy Development," in *Prediction and Classification: Criminal Justice Decision Making,* Don M. Gottfredson and Leslie T. Wilkins, eds. (Chicago: University of Chicago Press, 1987), 106.

18. Kevin N. Wright, Todd R. Clear, and Paul Dickson, "Universal Applicability of Probation Risk-Assessment Instruments," *Criminology* 22 (1984): 113.

19. John H. Lombardi and Donna M. Lombardi, "Objective Parole Criteria: More Harm than Good?" *Corrections Today* (February 1986): 86–87; Donald Atkinson, "Parole Can Work!" *Corrections Today* (February 1986): 54–55.

20. Wright, Clear, and Dickson, "Risk-Assessment Instruments," 122–123.

21. Stephen D. Gottfredson and Don M. Gottfredson, "Screening for Risk Among Parolees: Policy, Practice, and Method," in *Prediction in Criminology,* David P. Farrington and R. Tarling, eds. (Albany, N.Y.: State University of New York Press, 1985).

22. Lombardi and Lombardi, "Objective Parole Criteria," 87.

23. Todd R. Clear and George F. Cole, *American Corrections,* 3d ed. (Monterey, Calif.: Wadsworth Publishing, 1994), 412–413.

24. U.S. Sentencing Commission, *Federal Sentencing Guidelines Manual* (St. Paul: West Publishing Company, 1995), § 5D1.1, 2.

25. Dean J. Champion, *Probation and Parole in the United States* (Columbus, Ohio: Merrill Publishing Company, 1990), 173.

26. Clear and Cole, *American Corrections,* 428.

27. Ibid.

28. U.S. Department of Justice, United States Parole Commission, *Parole Commission Rules* 28 C.F.R. §2.39, 2.40 (November 12, 1991).

29. Champion, *Probation and Parole,* 316.

30. Ibid., 175.

31. Ibid., 186.

32. Quoted in Harry E. Allen et al., *Probation and Parole in America* (New York: Free Press, 1985), 127.

33. Quoted in Allen et al., *Probation and Parole,* 128.

34. Ibid.

35. Cited and discussed in Allen et al., *Probation and Parole,* 129.

36. Quoted in Allen et al., *Probation and Parole,* 130.

37. Cheryl L. Ringel, Ernest L. Cowles, and Thomas C. Castellano, "Changing Patterns in Parole Supervision," in *Critical Issues in Criminal Justice,* Albert R. Roberts, ed. (Thousand Oaks, Calif.: Sage Publications, 1994), 299.

38. Ibid., 306.

39. Howard R. Sacks and Charles H. Logan, *Does Parole Make a Difference?* (Storrs, Conn.: The University of Connecticut Law School Press, 1979).

40. Howard R. Sacks and Charles H. Logan, *Parole: Crime Prevention or Crime Postponement* (Storrs, Conn.: The University of Connecticut Law School Press, 1980), 14–15.

41. Ibid., 15–17, 20.

42. Quoted in Mark Jay Lerner, "The Effectiveness of a Definite Sentence Parole Program," *Criminology* 15 (1977): 215.

43. Ibid.

44. Ibid., 220.

45. Deborah Star, *Summary Parole* (California Department of Corrections, 1979), 2–3, 52, 132.

46. Deborah Star, *Investigation and Surveillance in Parole Supervision: An Evaluation of the High Control Project* (California Department of Corrections, 1981), i.

47. Ibid., i–ii.

48. Ibid., 168, 251, 257.

49. *Morrissey v. Brewer,* 408 US 471 (1972); BJS, *Correctional Populations in the United States, 1989–1993* (Washington, D.C.: BJS, 1990–1995), Table 6.5 in each year.

50. Champion, *Probation and Parole,* 172.

51. *Morrissey v. Brewer,* 484.

52. 18 United States Code Annotated, §4214.

PART FIVE

Juvenile Justice

Juvenile Justice

CHAPTER MAIN POINTS

1. *The dual system of justice provides one system for adults and one for juveniles.*

2. *Juvenile justice deals with crimes and status offenses.*

3. *Most juveniles commit status or minor property offenses.*

4. *Juvenile justice, until recently, was predominantly an informal process.*

5. *Historically, the law does not treat juveniles as criminals, and has emphasized reform and help, not incapacitation and punishment. Juvenile proceedings have become more formal since the 1960s.*

6. *Juvenile corrections emphasize community corrections.*

7. *Reforms in juvenile justice concentrate on decriminalization, diversion, deinstitutionalization, due process, and certification.*

8. *Evaluations of juvenile justice reforms have produced mixed results.*

9. *Recent trends focus on punishment and safety of the community particularly for older juveniles who have committed what in adults would be considered serious crimes.*

A 12-year-old-boy attacks a woman walking down the street and grabs her purse. A 16-year-old boy does the same thing to another woman on another street. A 19-year-old young man attacks a third woman and takes her purse. The police arrest all three. Do their ages make a difference in what happens to them following arrest? Yes. In all American jurisdictions, age determines which institutions will process these cases, what procedures govern their process, and what policies shape their disposition. The United States has a dual justice system: one set of institutions, procedures, and goals governs juveniles and another governs adults. This dual criminal justice system has roots deep in history.

The agencies that deal with juveniles have traditionally served multiple formal and informal purposes. Among their formal purposes are meeting juveniles' needs for supervision, protection, and support—often referred to, sometimes negatively, as the child-saving purpose; protecting society from juveniles who commit crimes or otherwise threaten social stability; and protecting juveniles' constitutional rights. Informally, juvenile justice agencies are organizations whose goals are shaped by work-group relationships; ambitions and attitudes of personnel within particular agencies; and political, economic, and social influences from the community outside. Despite shifting emphases and conflict, the purposes of American juvenile justice encompass service to children's needs and rights and general social control on the formal level, and organizational goals at the informal level.

Contemporary juvenile justice confronts difficult and controversial issues in defining who juveniles are and what needs exist for their support, supervision, and protection, as well as in determining what rights juveniles have. Once juveniles are defined, the major steps in the process to determine which of them need supervision, support, and protection involve several agencies: namely, the police, the juvenile court and its supporting staff, corrections officers, and lawyers. This process reflects the multiple, and often conflicting, formal and informal purposes of juvenile justice. Once it is determined which juveniles need supervision, support, or protection, then the processes of meeting these needs involve a range of agencies and groups, including juvenile training schools, probation officers, and community social service agencies. These agencies, too, might serve multiple and conflicting roles in juvenile justice.

The primary issues in juvenile justice, hotly debated today, include (1) Which is paramount—juveniles' needs or rights or society's need for security? (2) What is the proper scope of authority for juvenile justice? (3) What is the proper process for juveniles? (4) Do existing juvenile justice programs actually achieve their goals in acceptable measure? and (5) What reforms might improve juvenile justice for the remainder of the century and beyond?

History of Juvenile Justice

In early English history, both criminal and civil law treated children differently from adults. Children under 7 were considered not legally competent to form the requisite intent to commit crimes. Children over 14 were treated as adults, that is, as if they had the capacity to form criminal intent. Between the ages of 7 and 14, children enjoyed the presumption that they could not form intent, but evidence showing such capacity could rebut this presumption. Even when formally treated as adults, however, children were rarely punished as harshly as adults by criminal court judges and juries.

In civil law, according to the **doctrine of *parens patriae,*** the Crown could intervene in family life to protect children's estates from dishonest guardians. This principle expanded over time to include the power to intervene to protect children's welfare in general against parental neglect, incompetence, and abuse. The *parens patriae* doctrine and the presumptions against children's capacity to form criminal intent came to America with the English colonists.[1]

 **You Decide**   ## "Should the Boys Be Charged with Attempted Murder and Burglary?"

On April 23, 1996, two eight-year-old twin boys tearfully described a burglary and assault on a four-week-old baby that they had committed the day before in a "rough, working-class neighborhood" of Richmond, California. Police were led to the three boys by a relative of the infant who recognized the tricycle they stole and took it away from them as they fled the apartment. During an interview with police, the twins admitted that they and a six-year-old boy had entered the apartment after they found the door open and had made their way to a bedroom, where the baby, Ignacio Bermudez, was sleeping. They had entered the apartment to steal the tricycle. During the Monday burglary, the infant's bassinet was kicked over and the baby was attacked with fists, kicked in the head, and possibly struck on the head with a stick, according to Richmond Police Sgt. Michael Walter. The infant is in "critical condition on life support at the Chil-

dren's Hospital in Oakland, according to hospital officials. Doctors said he likely will have permanent brain damage."

The six-year-old boy was charged with attempted murder in the beating of the baby. According to Dennis Murphy, a senior deputy district attorney for Contra Costa County, "the juvenile's strained relations with the baby's family was only 'the tip of the iceberg' of reasons prosecutors thought they could pursue an attempted murder charge." Juvenile court referee Stephen Easton ordered the boy "to remain in a juvenile detention hall." The twins were charged with burglary.

Experts are divided over whether the justice system can cope with offenders so young. Leslie Bialik, the public defender for the six-year-old, told Easton that she did not think the detention hall was "set up to deal with someone of this age." In a telephone interview, Deputy District Attorney Howard Jewett said, "The state has a responsibility to say this conduct is not okay." Jewett said that "with a crime of this severity, I don't think we can look the other way. When you're talking about another person's death, society must assign legal responsibility if the law permits it to." Deputy District Attorney Murphy said videotapes of police questioning the boy showed he clearly understood that the assault was wrong. "This is not to punish the child but to control the situation and remedy it," he said. "This is the route that has to be taken to get wardship." If the referee determines the allegations are true, the boys would become wards of the court. They could be placed in a foster home, rehabilitation home, or a stricter juvenile detention facility, said officials.

The Associated Press reported that the six-year-old's mother and grandparents attended today's hearing and that he hugged his grandparents but ignored his mother.

Crimes this vicious are so rarely committed by children so young that the justice system does not have facilities to house them. All three youngsters have been kept separated from the general population at the juvenile hall, where the next-youngest resident is 13, according to Terrence Starr, chief probation officer. J. P. Trembly of the California Youth and Corrections Agency said the agency is not equipped to care for offenders younger than 11 years old. "We do not have the staffing and training to deal with these kids who are this young," he said.

Patricia Puritz, director of the American Bar Association's Juvenile Justice Center, said a child so young shouldn't have been charged. "Charging a six-year-old with anything is beyond what a civilized society should do, even if that child is behaving in an uncivilized way." Shannan Wilber, a staff attorney at the San Francisco-based Youth Law Center, a child advocacy organization, said, "There's really no benefit to prosecuting this child. You don't need to prosecute to access services like counseling for him or his family and that's clearly what's needed here."

In juvenile court, prosecutors must prove their case beyond a reasonable doubt. For attempted murder, they also must show intent to kill, which experts say could prove difficult given the boy's age. "We don't know if he understands the consequences of his actions," said Wilber. "Does he know that if he hits someone over the head, he'll die? Does he even know what death is?"

Questions

What are the arguments for and against charging these boys with attempted murder and burglary? If you were the prosecutor, what would be your decision? Defend your answer, particularly arguing what would be the benefits of your decision to society, to the victim, and to the boys.

Based on Kathryn Wexler, "Prosecutors Pursue Case Against 6-Year-Old Suspect," *The Washington Post,* 27 April 1996.

During the reform movements that swept through the country during the nineteenth century, a romantic concern arose for children generally, and a "child-saving" movement directed at children in need and trouble grew out of that general concern. Since the general institutionalization of America took place at around the same time, the child-saving movement began saving children by means of the house of refuge and the reform school. Both children's institutions were based on the contemporary idea that children's environments made them bad. Removing youths from poor homes and unhealthy associates and placing them in special homes and schools would make them give up their evil habits. These refuges and schools would, in fact, reform children.[2]

During the Progressive Era, the second reform era affecting children and criminal justice, attention focused again on children in hopes of improving their plight. The Progressives believed children were not inherently bad, but were made bad by their environment, particularly their home life if parents did not bring them up properly. "Proper" meant according to middle-class values: the virtues of hard work, thrift, temperance, and deference to established authority. Families who did not have these values—particularly immigrants, whose numbers were increasing at what, to the Progressives, were alarming rates—should be replaced by more favorable influences that the Progressives themselves would supply.

The Progressives had great confidence both in the state and in experts. Hence, they called on the state, in its *parens patriae* capacity, to supply a battery of experts to exert a healthy influence to "save" children by "curing" their "unhealthy" home lives. The Progressives distrusted traditional, or what to them were outdated, institutions that operated according to archaic formal rules. They turned away from the criminal courts that emphasized criminal conduct. They created a new institution, the juvenile court, that focused on what children needed to make them responsible, law-abiding citizens. The juvenile court was supposed to differ from adult courts. Judges did not sit on benches above the child, but next to them. Proceedings were informal. Their aim was not to affix blame, but to find out what caused children to "go wrong" so that something could be done about it. Any and all information about children's home life, past behavior, health, and so on was relevant to determine what was wrong. To prescribe a cure, a diagnosis was first necessary, and a proper diagnosis required adequate information as a basis.

The Progressives developed the **medical model** of crime, that is, that crime is a disease that societal intervention can treat and cure. The Progressives optimistically believed that the government could supply experts who, armed with sufficient discretion and not hampered by formal rules, could attend to children's needs and make them law-abiding, responsible citizens. Chicago established the first juvenile court in 1899; by 1925 nearly every jurisdiction in the country had them.[3]

The emphasis on informality, discretion, and experts to operate state agencies empowered to meet children's needs prevailed until the 1960s, when another reform wave introduced two other dimensions to the public response to crime by youths. Reflecting both the civil rights fervor during that era and growing skepticism about the government's capacity to meet children's needs, the emphasis shifted to children's rights. The increase in the fear of street crime in particular and disorder in general that characterized that turbulent era led critics to attack juvenile justice generally and juvenile court specifically.

In 1967, the President's Commission on Law and Enforcement and the Administration of Justice concluded:

> The juvenile court has not succeeded significantly in rehabilitating delinquent youth, in reducing or even stemming the tide of juvenile criminality, or in bringing justice to the child offender. Uncritical and unrealistic estimates of what is known can make expectation so much greater than achievement and serve to justify extensive official action, and to mask the fact that much of it may do more harm than good. Official action may help to fix and perpetuate delinquency in the child—the individual begins to think of himself as a delinquent and proceeds to organize his behaviors accordingly. The undesirable consequences of official actions are heightened in programs that rely on institutionalization of the child. The most informed and benign institutional treatment, even in well designed and staffed reformatories and training schools, thus may contain within it the seeds of its own frustration, and itself may often feed the very disorder it is designed to cure.[4]

Several landmark Supreme Court decisions restricted the informal, discretionary powers of the juvenile court and other agencies dealing with juveniles by extending several constitutional protections afforded to adult criminal defendants to juveniles who came in contact with the state. In *Kent v. United States,* a case involving a 16-year-old charged with housebreaking, robbery, and rape, the Supreme Court ruled that juvenile court proceedings must afford juveniles basic due process rights to a fair hearing.[5]

The following year, the Court extended to juvenile court proceedings an elaborate and detailed list of requirements associated with due process. *In re Gault* involved proceedings against a 15-year-old Arizona boy that resulted in committing him to a training school because he made lewd remarks to an elderly woman on the telephone. The Court ruled that to satisfy due process requirements in a juvenile proceeding that resulted in commitment to a correctional facility, the juvenile must receive adequate written notice that a hearing was scheduled and advice about the right to counsel and the right to confront and cross-examine witnesses. In *In re Winship,* a 12-year-old boy was charged with taking money from a woman's purse. The Court ruled that the due process clause required that juvenile proceedings provide proof beyond a reasonable doubt in order to classify juveniles as delinquent in juvenile court proceedings.[6]

The Court did not, however, go to the logical extreme of ruling that due process required that juvenile proceedings must proceed exactly like adult criminal court proceedings. In *McKeiver v. Pennsylvania*, the Court concluded that juveniles did not have the right to jury trial in delinquency proceedings in juvenile court. By 1970, therefore, juveniles had gained some of the constitutional protections of adults, but not all. In the Court's words:

> We do not mean to indicate that the hearing must be held to conform with all the requirements of a criminal trial but we do hold that the hearing must measure up to the essentials of due process and fair treatment.[7]

During the 1970s, the rising fear of street crime and youth rebellion coincided with the juvenile rights movement and the disillusionment with the juvenile justice system's capacity to reform and rehabilitate juveniles in a humane, fair, and objective manner. Both contributed to a harsher public attitude toward youth crime. The general disillusionment with rehabilitation was replaced with renewed confidence in retribution and punishment as responses to street crime. A growing consensus among both criminal justice professionals and the public generally demanded that juveniles be tried as adults: if they were old enough to commit crimes, then they were old enough to take the consequences. By 1980, in the amalgam of children's needs, children's rights, and society's demand for order that makes up juvenile justice policy and practice, society's needs were clearly in the ascendancy.

Defining and Measuring Delinquency

States vary considerably in their definitions of who are juveniles for purposes of juvenile justice jurisdiction. Most states do not make anyone younger than eight years old subject to juvenile justice jurisdiction. States differ about the upper age, some using 16 and others 18 as the dividing line between juvenile and criminal justice jurisdiction. In most states, "older" juveniles, those within a year or two of the upper age limit, qualify either as juveniles or adults, depending on circumstances discussed later.

Juvenile justice, depending on the jurisdiction, processes several types of juveniles: the needy, the dependent, the neglected, the delinquent, and the deviant. This chapter focuses mainly on the delinquent and, to a lesser extent, on the deviant. **Delinquency** means conduct that would be criminal if an adult engaged in it. **Status offenses** include conduct that is illegal only if children engage in it, such as truancy, curfew violations, running away, and incorrigibility. The term **juvenile delinquent** can mean youths who have committed either crimes or status offenses, or both. The term is so broad that the late Paul Tappan noted that "delinquency has little specific behavioral content either in law or in fact," and that a "juvenile delinquent is a person who has been adjudicated as such by a court of proper jurisdiction."[8]

The California Welfare and Institutions Code captures the broad scope of the meaning of delinquency in the nation's most populous state:

> Any person who is under the age of eighteen when he violates any law of this state or the United States or any ordinance of any city or county of this state defining crime other than an ordinance establishing a curfew based solely on age, is within the jurisdiction of the juvenile court. Any person under the age of eighteen years who persistently or habitually refuses to obey the reasonable and proper orders or directions of his parents, guardian, or custodian, or who is beyond the control of such person, or who is under the age of 18 years when he violates any ordinance of any city or county of this state establishing a curfew based solely on age is within the jurisdiction of the juvenile court.[9]

Juvenile delinquency includes everything from violent crime to curfew violations.

Juvenile delinquency, therefore, can include everything from serious violent crime to staying out too late at night. Clearly, for criminal justice purposes, serious crime is more important than curfew violations. Juveniles are capable of committing—and do commit—horrible crimes. In one three-month period, an 11-year-old killed a companion who annoyed her at a video arcade, a 15-year-old stabbed a classmate to death following an argument over a pencil, and a 16-year-old shot his parents to death because they grounded him.[10]

These are shocking events, but are they typical? As is the case with measuring adult crime, statistics concerning delinquency are not complete. Most criticisms regarding crime statistics generally apply also to measures of juvenile delinquency. In fact, these measures stem mainly from the same sources: the Uniform Crime Reports, the National Crime Survey, court records, and self-reports of one type or another.

Despite difficulties in measuring delinquency, several facts stand out. First, youths are substantially more "crime-prone" than adults. The juvenile arrest rate for serious property crimes exceeds the adult rate by about six to one, and for violent crimes by about two to one. Second, the majority of youth arrests are for property crimes, such as theft and burglary, and youth-only offenses, such as truancy, runaway, and curfew. Indications are that juveniles commit fewer violent crimes and more crimes against property.[11]

Third, most juveniles commit crimes in groups, not alone. Younger offenders commit crimes in groups of four or more five times more often than adults. Of the total juvenile crimes charged in New York City, 90 percent of the robberies, 86 percent of the burglaries, 78 percent of the homicides, 60 percent of the assaults, and 50 percent of the rapes were committed in groups. Finally, serious juvenile crime is concentrated in urban minority group males, a population group that is increasing.[12]

Finally, youths are frequently armed. Three sociologists at Tulane University, James Wright, Joseph Sheley, and M. Dwayne Smith, interviewed male juveniles serving sentences and male students attending inner-city schools. They found that city youths can easily acquire handguns, and almost a third have owned a gun at one time or another. They get them from friends, family, and street sources. Most guns were stolen and purchased at prices well below their retail value. Most youths claimed that they carried guns for

Figure 16.1

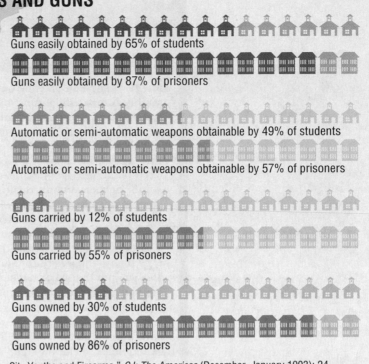

YOUTHS AND GUNS

Guns easily obtained by 65% of students

Guns easily obtained by 87% of prisoners

Automatic or semi-automatic weapons obtainable by 49% of students

Automatic or semi-automatic weapons obtainable by 57% of prisoners

Guns carried by 12% of students

Guns carried by 55% of prisoners

Guns owned by 30% of students

Guns owned by 86% of prisoners

Source: "Inner City Youths and Firearms," *CJ: The Americas* (December–January 1993): 24.

certification *treating juveniles as adults for criminal prosecution.*

protection. Figure 16.1 depicts the percent of the two groups answering yes to questions of obtaining guns, the type of gun obtained, whether they carry guns, and whether they own guns.[13]

Juvenile Justice System

The main agencies dealing with juvenile delinquency are legislatures, police, prosecutors, defense attorneys, courts, probation offices, detention centers, correctional facilities, treatment centers, halfway houses, and a range of social service agencies. Legislatures define the scope of these agencies' legal authority, particularly what age span and what conduct falls within the jurisdiction of the juvenile justice system. They also determine when older juveniles can be transferred to the criminal justice system as adults, in a procedure called **certification.** Legislatures determine the budgets each agency receives to administer juvenile justice.[14]

Police and Juveniles

Most large-city police departments have special units to handle juveniles. They keep records on juveniles, investigate cases involving them, and initiate referrals to the juvenile court. Police also have the power to detain some juveniles in secure facilities for brief periods. Although these special youth divisions are responsible for juveniles, patrol officers encounter most juveniles and make the critical decisions whether to investigate, arrest, or otherwise detain them. How police handle juveniles depends on a combination of internal and external influences that differ from department to department and even among individuals within departments, making generalization risky. Departments adopting a community-service approach

Juvenile Delinquency in Japan

MOST JAPANESE juvenile offenders are from the middle class. They mainly commit shoplifting, bicycle theft, glue sniffing, and assaults against teachers and parents, particularly against mothers. In 1986, Japanese students committed 1,376 violent crimes; almost half were committed against teachers. Japanese youths are better integrated into society than youths in most industrial countries. Japan stresses education; its best schools and universities are open to all students who can meet the entrance requirements. Schools and universities provide the opportunity for the best positions in business and society. Students compete fiercely for the few available spaces in the best schools and universities.

Violence against mothers and teachers is on the rise in Japan. Youths who fail to meet their own, their parents, their schools, and Japanese society's high standards "lose their self-respect and fall into juvenile crime." Mothers are the major target of the frustrations of their children, because mothers are primarily responsible for raising their children. Frustrated, angry youths who are not doing well in school attack teachers and fellow students and vandalize school property. The pressures on Japanese youth have also led to an increase in aggression not classified as violent crime or delinquency, including "bullying and cruelty towards weaker juveniles."

SOURCE: Hisao Katoh, "The Development of Delinquency and Criminal Justice in Japan," Hans-Günther Heiland, Louse I. Shelley, and Hisao Katoh, eds., *Crime and Control in Comparative Perspectives* (Berlin: Walter deGruyter, 1992), 76–77.

emphasize helping juveniles, while departments stressing the crime-fighting role view rehabilitation very differently. As one officer put it:

> I don't want to sound like a hardass, but we have some really bad young hoodlums on the streets in L.A. These aren't the nickel and dime kid shoplifters; they are hardcore. Some of them have dozens of arrests, but they're still out there ripping off people. These pukes are into juvenile hall and out twenty minutes later; seriously, some of these hoodlums are back on the street before I finish the paperwork. If you are going to correct kids they have to get their hands whacked the first time they put them in the cookie jar, not six months later. Juvenile justice is slow. Jesus, the rights these kids have got. They have more rights than I have. I'm not talking about the Mickey Mouse cases; I mean the serious hoodlums.[15]

The general policies and outlooks that departments and officers espouse also affect the way police exercise their discretion in processing juveniles. The general formalization of the criminal process has affected police discretion in processing juveniles, but not so much as it has their dealings with adults. The police have a range of options in deciding what to do with juvenile lawbreakers. Their four major choices are to (1) ignore them, (2) counsel and release them, (3) divert or refer them to other agencies, and (4) process them further into the juvenile justice system. Which of these four options officers choose—that is, how they exercise their discretion in processing juveniles—depends mainly on the nature of the encounter between the police and juvenile and the seriousness of the offense the officer detects or suspects.

If, for example, officers encounter juveniles together in a situation where the officers "sense something is wrong," they may simply pass by or stop for a brief conversation. They may go further and ask the juveniles their names, addresses, and what they are doing or where they are going. Officers may go still further and search them. They may tell the juveniles to break up the group and move on, or they may take them home and warn their parents to keep them off the street. Alternatively, they may take them to the station for further questioning, without formal arrest. In a considerable number of cases, the police take juveniles to the station house and call in their parents. If the parents seem amenable, the police then warn them and the juveniles of the consequences of further bad conduct and send them home. None of these choices involves formal police action, because the police did not make any arrests.[16]

According to the police, all these alternatives fall very loosely within the "counsel-and-release" category, or, as it is sometimes more vaguely labeled, "handled within the department." Individual departments vary widely in how many juvenile cases they handle within the department at this stage. Some informally dispose of as many as 90 percent of the juvenile cases, others as few as 10 percent. On the average, about 50 percent of juveniles are "counseled and dismissed," which might mean considerably more than the words imply. In some cases, police treat this option as an informal probation system. If juveniles who are counseled and dismissed commit further offenses, police will formally arrest them. Police also use the informal counsel-and-release option as a trade for information about other juveniles.[17]

Driving while intoxicated is a serious offense whether committed by juveniles or adults.

Only partial information exists on the extent to which police refer juveniles to other social service agencies, a practice called **diversion.** Available information indicates that even during diversion's "heyday" in the 1970s, police referrals to social service agencies ranged from a high of 4.8 percent to a low of 2.9 percent. Whether police exercise the formal option to refer depends on several factors, the main factors being type of offense, character and attitude of the juvenile, degree to which the department emphasizes social service, the availability of youth social services in the particular community, and the confidence police have in the services' effectiveness.[18]

Police do not arrest most juveniles who are either counseled and released or diverted to social service agencies. Hence, no formal action has been taken against them. The remaining juveniles who come in contact with the police are either arrested and then released or diverted, or are processed further into the juvenile justice system, meaning they are formally referred to juvenile court. According to most estimates, about 50 percent of the juveniles who come in contact with police are referred to juvenile court, but this figure varies according to department. The police also have the authority to detain juveniles until the intake process begins. Although they release most juveniles during this period, they detain about one-third.[19]

What enters into the police decision to dismiss, divert, or process cases further into the juvenile justice system? The most important factor, according to research findings, is the seriousness of the offense. The police are almost certain to arrest and refer to juvenile court juveniles suspected of serious crimes, such as murder, rape, or major theft. They are much more likely to dismiss or divert juveniles they suspect have committed less serious offenses, particularly status offenses.[20]

Citizen complaints affect police decisions to arrest. Police acquire most of their information concerning juveniles in the same way they do for adults—from citizens. If citizen complainants are present and demand action short of arrest, police comply; if they ask for leniency, police grant it; if they demand formal arrest and processing, the officers usually accede. Hence, citizens' presence and their wishes influence whether juveniles are counseled and released, diverted to social service agencies, or arrested. Department policy also affects what action police take. The numbers of arrested juveniles police refer to juvenile court vary widely. Some departments refer less than 10 percent, others as many as 80 percent. In a legalistic department, to use James Q. Wilson's typology, impersonal legal standards are applied and more arrests will take place. In more service-oriented departments, or those that are less formalized, officers exercise wider discretion in releasing and diverting.

Demographic characteristics of juveniles who come in contact with police also affect police discretion. First is gender. Although most research shows that female delinquents commit fewer delinquent acts, in the main they commit the same kinds of offenses as males. They drink, shoplift, skip school, destroy property, steal, and burglarize. The police, however, use a double standard in dealing with male and female delinquents. Police are much less likely to arrest females for these offenses than males. However, if females violate what are considered traditional expectations—if they run away from home, disobey their parents, are sexually active—police are much more likely to take them into custody. In Honolulu, for example, only 6.1 percent of the females who committed serious criminal offenses were referred to juvenile court, while 33.7 percent of those arrested for status offenses were referred. Nationwide, 75 percent of the female delinquents referred to juvenile court were arrested for status, not criminal, offenses.[21]

Racial minorities and the poor are overrepresented in the arrest statistics for juveniles, just as they are for adults. To what extent this overrepresenta-

All individuals whether adult or juvenile have a right against "unreasonable searches and seizures".

tion is due to outright prejudice or to deep structural features in American society and economy is not clear, although both certainly play a part. Naturally, inner-city dwellers and the police see matters very differently.[22] James Baldwin, African American novelist and commentator on racism, wrote about the police in the inner cities:

> Their very presence is an insult, and it would be, even if they spent their entire day feeding gum drops to children. They represent the force of the white world, and that world's criminal profit and ease, to keep the black man corralled up here, in his place. The badge, the gun in the holster, and the swinging club make vivid what will happen should his rebellion become overt.[23]

For the other side, criminologist James Q. Wilson writes:

> The patrolman believes with considerable justification that teenagers, Negroes, and lower income persons commit a disproportionate share of all reported crimes; being in those population categories at all makes one, statistically, more suspect than other persons; but to be in those categories and to behave unconventionally is to make oneself a prime suspect. Patrolmen believe they would be derelict in their duty if they did not treat such persons with suspicion, routinely question them on the street, and detain them for longer questioning if a crime has occurred in the area. To the objection of some middle-class observers that this is arbitrary or discriminatory, the police are likely to answer: "Have you ever been stopped or searched? Of course not. We can tell the difference; we have to tell the difference in order to do our job. What are you complaining about?"[24]

Juvenile Court

The combination of conflicting ideology, competing goals, and a colorful history infuses the juvenile court with particular vigor. Former juvenile judge H. Ted Rubin writes:

> This court is a far more complex instrument than outsiders imagine. It is law, and it is social work; it is control, and it is help; it is the good parent and, also, the stern parent; it is both formal and informal. It is concerned not only with the delinquent, but also with the battered child, the runaway, and many others. The juvenile court has been all things to all people.[25]

To fulfill its competing goals (help children in need, treat or punish juveniles who commit crimes, and protect society from juvenile criminality), work within its traditions, and balance conflicting ideologies, the juvenile court uses a three-step process: intake, adjudication, and disposition. All involve screening those juveniles who will be processed further into the juvenile justice system from those who will either be released or referred to other social service agencies.

The rate at which juveniles are referred to juvenile court has risen steadily since the 1950s, from 20 per 1,000 to nearly 40 by the late 1970s. The police refer most cases; but parents, relatives, schools, and welfare agencies also bring juveniles to juvenile court attention. **Intake** is the process following police referrals to juvenile court during which several important decisions are made, including (1) whether to detain juveniles during case investigation, (2) whether to file a petition for a formal court hearing, and (3) whether to dismiss cases entirely or divert them to social service agencies. Since the juvenile court's creation, probation officers have most often done intake screening (the decisions made during the intake process), although sometimes juvenile court judges, especially in smaller courts, screen cases at intake. Probation officers also supervise juveniles following court action or disposition. Judge Richard Tuthill, an early reform juvenile judge, captured the high hopes held for probation officers by the court's founders when he described probation as "the cord upon which all the pearls of the juvenile court are strung. Without it, the juvenile court could not exist."[26]

At intake, probation officers, or judges if they do the screening, have five options:

- They can transfer the juvenile to criminal court for trial as an adult. Called either certification or judicial waiver, this option is increasingly heralded as the answer to rising juvenile street crime.
- They can refer to an intake or prejudicial conference where, if the charge is not serious and the juvenile admits wrongdoing, the case is most often dropped. An intake conference also continues the case pending fulfillment of specified conditions, such as drug treatment, restitution, or psychological counseling.
- They can refer cases to a juvenile conference committee (JCC). Juvenile conference committees comprise citizens appointed by juvenile courts to recommend dispositions for juveniles in nonserious cases. These JCC's are not common, and they apply only to first-time petty offenders.[27]
- The probation officer or judge can dismiss the case, simply dropping it without any further action.
- Probation officers can recommend adjudication, or court hearing. Since about 1950, only half of all court referrals result in adjudication.[28]

In one study of several hundred juvenile courts, the researchers conclude:

The most typical pattern is either to dismiss the case or to counsel, warn, and release the youth. Only a small fraction are put on informal probation (16 percent) or referred to other social service agencies. In other words, most courts seem to cope with the inflow of cases through very minimal intervention which may, at most, produce a court record, but no significant action by court staff.[29]

Status offenses and property offenses account for most referrals to juvenile court. Only a minor proportion are crimes against persons, and most of the crimes against persons are lesser assaults. Most research has demonstrated that the decision to dismiss, divert, or adjudicate primarily depends on the seriousness of the offense. Hence, the evidence does not support the conventional wisdom that juvenile courts adhere mainly to their original purpose: to look at juveniles, not their crimes, and consider rehabilitating them, not punishing them. Nor does it support the current complaint that juveniles are treated leniently—many offenses are either not crimes, or, if they are, are property offenses, not violent crimes.[30]

According to some experts, the evidence has another conclusion. Because status and property offenders make up about 70 percent of the cases referred to adjudication, and only juveniles who commit serious crimes against persons are certain to go forward to adjudication, Lamar T. Empey believes:

Such findings reflect in a striking way the persistence of the benevolent assumption that the moral and social condition of the child is more

Underage drinking is one of the many acts of juvenile delinquency.

important than the act he or she commits. When intake personnel encounter children who are out of parental control, who are persistently truant from school, or who are habitual runaways, they often feel that formal action is required.[31]

Adjudication, following intake, is the legal process that judges conduct in juvenile court with probation officers' assistance. Judges determine if the allegations in the petition are proven. If they are, the juveniles are formally delinquent. In the early juvenile court days, these proceedings were supposed to be informal affairs whose major purpose was to determine what caused the delinquency in order to "save" delinquents, not to affix blame and punish them. Juvenile court judges' selection rested more on their knowledge of child psychology and social problems than on their legal expertise. Judges did not, nor were they expected to, operate juvenile courts according to formal rules, such as those in effect in criminal courts for adults. Juvenile court judges shunned such formal practices. They did not keep written records or allow attorneys to prosecute and defend juveniles. Affording juveniles constitutional protections was not necessary because the proceedings were intended to help or "save" juveniles from their environment, not to punish them for their wrongdoing. One early juvenile court judge described court proceedings this way:

> The judge excludes all newspaper reporters and all other persons having only a general interest in the proceedings. The sheltered location of the room, the absence of decoration, the dispensing with attendants, and the exclusion of outsiders give the simplicity which is necessary to gain the undivided attention of the child and give the quiet which is indispensable for hearing clearly what the child says and speaking to him in the calmest tone.
>
> When the judge is ready to hear a case, the probation officer brings in the child from the waiting room. The child does not stand in front of the desk, because that would prevent the judge from seeing the whole of him, and the way a child stands and even the condition of his shoes are often useful aids to a proper diagnosis of the case. The child stands at the end of the platform, where the judge can see him from top to toe, and the judge sits near the end, so he is close to the child and can reassure him if necessary by a friendly hand on the shoulder. The platform is just high enough to bring the average child's eye about on a level with the eye of the judge.[32]

Until the 1960s, this description proved typical of most juvenile courts throughout the country. Since the Supreme Court opinions reviewed at the beginning of this chapter, the juvenile court's proceedings have been formalized considerably. Juveniles are notified of the pending delinquency charges, lawyers are more often present, evidence standards are stricter, and proceedings are more like criminal courts. However, it would be an exaggeration to conclude that juvenile proceedings are just like criminal proceedings for adults, or that juvenile courts are uniformly more formal. Regional and local differences are significant, and even the Supreme Court—as do many others—accepts what it believes is the need for separate and different procedures for adults, where the focus is on affixing guilt for criminal behavior and punishing for it, and for juveniles, where determining delinquent status and "curing," or reforming, is the uppermost goal.

Juvenile justice expert Lamar Empey noted signs of change in juvenile court, indicating that formal proceedings are replacing the informal. He concluded nevertheless that

> it is only in a minority of courts where attorneys and due process procedures are uniformly present. As more courts begin to adhere to this model, however, it seems likely that less attention will be paid to the

disposition hearings *determine what should follow finding of delinquency.*
continuance in contemplation of dismissal *case in abeyance pending good behavior.*

moral condition of the child and more to the evidence in support of the charge. It is likely, moreover, that resistance will grow to the formal trials of status offenders, not only because they are not charged with crimes, but because status offenses are more difficult to prove.[33]

Once juveniles have been adjudicated delinquent, judges usually adjourn cases and schedule **disposition hearings** in which they decide how best to resolve delinquency cases. In the meantime, probation officers conduct background investigations to assist judges in their disposition decisions. Disposition hearings resemble sentence hearings in adult criminal courts. Juvenile court judges have wide discretion to choose from a broad range of alternative dispositions, ranging from outright dismissal to commitment to secure correctional facilities resembling adult prisons.

Judges may order cases held in abeyance, or **"continuance in contemplation of dismissal."** If delinquents do not get into further trouble with the law within a specified period—often between six months and a year—judges will dismiss their cases without further action. Abeyance allows judges to keep open their option for further action if juveniles do not obey the law. Judges might continue cases until the fulfillment of specified conditions, including taking required diagnostic tests and treatment for disturbances stemming from emotional problems, substance abuse, and physical illness; observing curfew; paying restitution to victims; and providing community service. Delinquents usually receive a time period of one to six months to fulfill these conditions.[34]

If given probation, juveniles live in the community under probation officers' supervision for a period of about one to three years, in a situation that very much resembles adult probation. Juveniles can also be committed to juvenile correctional facilities. For less serious delinquency, perhaps status offenses and minor property crimes, such facilities probably mean training schools or camps for delinquent children, or they might even mean community-based programs, such as foster care, youth development centers, or independent living arrangements. For serious delinquency, juvenile corrections mean secure facilities very much like adult prisons.

Most juvenile cases are handled informally before a disposition hearing ever occurs. Of those adjudicated cases in which formal disposition takes place, most result in probation, only a few terminate in commitment to juvenile facilities, and an insignificant number are certified to adult criminal courts. Juvenile court judges exercise wide discretion in choosing among these alternatives. Some observers believe juveniles are not treated fairly, that is, that inappropriate factors weigh in judges' disposition decisions. Anthony Platt concluded that the Progressive "child savers" used dispositions to impose middle-class values on lower-class youth:

> The child saving movement had its most direct consequences on the children of the urban poor. The fact that "troublesome" adolescents were depicted as "sick" or "pathological," were "imprisoned for their own good," and were addressed in a paternalistic vocabulary, and exempted from criminal law processes did not alter the subjective experiences of control, restraint and punishment. The "invention" of delinquency consolidated the inferior social status and dependency of lower-class youth.[35]

Sociologist Edwin Schur concurred:

> The philosophy of the juvenile court ensures that stereotypes will influence judicial dispositions. Sending the child who comes from a "broken home" in the slums to a training school, while giving probation to a youngster from a "good family" may not strike the judge as an exercise in stereotyping. [H]owever, such stereotypes tend to be self-confirming. Children from "broken homes" are likely to be committed to institutions

because they are believed to be delinquency-prone; yet these very commitments, in turn, serve to reinforce that belief.[36]

Neither Platt nor Schur based their findings on solidly based empirical evidence. Lawrence E. Cohen made an effort to measure empirically the influences on juvenile court dispositions. He gathered information about nearly 13,000 juveniles who appeared before juvenile courts in three counties in Colorado, Tennessee, and Pennsylvania. Cohen measured the effects of juveniles' age, sex, ethnicity, socioeconomic status, family situation, seriousness of offense, number of prior referrals to juvenile court, referral agent, whether juveniles were in detention prior to hearings, and whether there were formal petitions against juveniles or informal dispositions. The jurisdictions varied considerably. In Colorado, the seriousness of offense was most important. In Tennessee, offense seriousness was also most significant but was followed closely by whether the police referred the juveniles, and whether they were in detention prior to adjudication. In Pennsylvania, the most important factors were whether juveniles were idle, from broken homes, and referred by agencies other than police.[37]

Other investigators have found that minority youth—Hispanics, Native Americans, African Americans, and others—are more likely to be incarcerated and less likely to be put on probation. Barry Krisberg and others took data collected nationally in a semiannual survey conducted by the U.S. Bureau of the Census, called Children in Custody, or CIC, and compared the populations in juvenile correctional facilities with the arrest statistics in the Uniform Crime Reports. They found that in 1982, for example, black youths were incarcerated at a rate of 8.6 per 100 compared with 5.1 per 100 for whites, a ratio 69 percent higher. For Native Americans, the ratio is even higher—14.5. The researchers concluded that the reasons for this higher incarceration rate are not due to offense seriousness.[38]

Offense seriousness is an appropriate reason for incarceration, but race and ethnicity clearly are not. Equally inappropriate are idleness and broken homes, criteria that demonstrate that juveniles are incarcerated according to attitudes prejudicial to those who are not from traditional, middle-class families.[39]

Juvenile Corrections

Several responses to juvenile crime have been employed throughout most of American history. Colonial Americans assumed people were basically prone to do wrong and were, therefore, more forgiving toward juveniles who had done so, often permitting young, convicted offenders to return to the community after warning, shaming, or corporal punishment. Toward the end of the eighteenth century, the Enlightenment philosophy worked a change in this approach. Relying on the assumption that criminals chose to commit crimes out of their own free will, deterring crime through effective law enforcement, followed by certain and swift punishment, became fashionable. Corporal punishment, hard labor, and similar tactics reinforced the idea that basic human nature did not lead inevitably to crime, but rather individuals chose to commit crimes because they did not suffer sufficient pain to offset the pleasure derived from committing crimes.[40]

During the 1830s—the Jacksonian era—another shift occurred. The unsettled society that resulted from deep changes in the American way of life led to the conclusion that rapidly accelerating urbanization, industrialization, and immigration caused crime. As a solution, society proposed to remove criminals from it until they could be reformed and returned to lead law-abiding lives and withstand the evils spawned by urban, industrial America. Hence, a great building spree produced adult prisons, reformatories for older youthful offenders, and industrial training schools for younger delinquents where reform could take place away from the evils afflicting general society.

Correctional boot camps are becoming an increasingly popular form of correctional instutition.

Within a few years, the great hopes for institutional correction were clearly not realized. Early alternatives to institutional corrections, the roots of modern probation and parole, were created. John Augustus, a Boston boot-maker, took young children from courts and placed them under his direct care in his home (Chapter 12). If they remained free from further delinquency during the period in which they would have been incarccrated, they were released. Augustus's efforts began what would be a series of shifts between institutional and community corrections.

Shifting emphases between institutional corrections and various community alternatives to it, as well as efforts to "improve" them both, characterized the century from 1850 to 1950. In the 1950s, a great interest arose in community-based alternatives to large, state-run institutions for delinquents, exemplificd in the growth of local institutions, residential youth centers, group homes, and specialized probation services. From the late 1960s to the 1970s, in a second phase of this development, diversion and deinstitutional-ization programs proliferated and were touted as the panacea to youth crime and delinquency. These community-based corrections rested on the convic-tion that state reformatories failed to prevent delinquency and, in fact, exacerbated it by stigmatizing youths exposed to it: such youths became part of a "state youth subculture" heavily involved in patterns of both state dependence and criminality that were very difficult, if not impossible, to break.[41]

During the 1970s, the rise in reported street crime, heavy emphasis on juvenile crime, growing empirical literature questioning rehabilitation's effec-tiveness, the perception that retribution is the most effective response to crime, and growing public demand for retributive punishment led to a return to demands to incarcerate delinquents. The trend has produced additional demands for other reforms that generally emphasize punishment and community safety in juvenile justice. Informally, punishment and community protection have always been juvenile justice goals to some extent, even if they are not explicitly articulated. Despite changes that have brought them to a closer resemblance to adult corrections, juvenile corrections are still quite distinct. Juvenile corrections continue to emphasize rehabilitation and have a considerably richer variety of institutions and alternatives than adult corrections.

Community Corrections The definition of community corrections is very broad, and the distinction between community and institutional corrections for juveniles is often blurred. The Task Force on Corrections, National Advisory Commission on Criminal Justice Standards and Goals, defines community corrections as

> all correctional activities that take place in the community. The community base must be an alternative to confinement of an offender at any point in the correctional system.[42]

Sociologist Paul Lerman notes:

> In practice, the term has been treated as elastic, stretching to cover institutional "communities" in Texas housing Illinois children, institutional communities in western Massachusetts housing youths from eastern Massachusetts, a youth service bureau in a youngster's neighborhood, a residential treatment facility in a distant county, a secure mental hospital ward in a state hospital, and a group home on the grounds of a large hospital.[43]

James O. Finckenauer offers perhaps the best working definition of community-based corrections for juveniles:

> Community corrections must include, at a minimum, regular access to school or a job in the community, regular access to home, family, and friends, and regular access to recreation in the community.[44]

Perhaps nothing more clearly demonstrates the difference between adult and juvenile corrections than the heavier commitment to, and the greater variety of, community corrections as an alternative to institutions following disposition.

Probation surpasses all other types of community juvenile corrections. Probation and parole for juveniles strongly resemble the same practices for adults (see Chapter 12). Both probation and parole are types of community supervision. Probation is community supervision in place of incarceration in an institution; parole is community supervision following a period of incarceration. Juvenile probation is informal probation supervised by the police. Juveniles are usually required to report periodically to police departments and to follow police-established conditions for behavior.[45]

Institutional Corrections Juvenile correctional institutions cover a broad spectrum, from small, short-term, nonsecure facilities to long-term, highly secure facilities serving large areas. Foster homes—small, nonsecure facilities that are supposed to be real family substitutes—are used at all stages in the juvenile justice process. Police might temporarily place arrested juveniles who cannot be returned to their homes in foster homes instead of detention facilities. Courts might also assign juveniles to foster homes before, or after, adjudication. The National Advisory Commission (NAC) recommends foster care as the primary placement for minor delinquency. However, due to inadequate—and sometimes totally lacking—accreditation and monitoring, some persons convicted of child abuse have received or retained foster home licenses.[46]

Shelters, nonsecure residential facilities, hold juveniles temporarily assigned, usually in lieu of detention or returning home following arrest, or after adjudication while awaiting more permanent placement. Shelters are reserved primarily for status offenders and are not intended for either treatment or punishment.

Group homes, also nonsecure, relatively open community-based facilities, mainly hold juveniles adjudicated delinquent. Group homes are larger and less family-like than foster homes. Small group homes serve from four to eight; large group homes, from eight to twelve. Residents range in age from 10 to 17, but most are between 13 and 16. Group homes permit more independent living in a more permanent setting, and they are more treatment-oriented than shelters. Group home residents usually attend school—in the home or in the community—or they work. They also participate in individual and group counseling and recreation. Group homes are intended to provide support and structure in nonrestrictive settings that facilitate reintegration into the community.[47]

Halfway houses, large, nonsecure residential centers, hold residents placed either by court commitment or as a condition of probation. They provide a structured living environment with personal and social services. The typical halfway house serves from twelve to twenty residents, but some large programs serve as many as forty residents. Residents' ages range from 14 to 18. "Halfway houses provide a range of services and emphasize normal group living, school attendance, securing employment, working with parents to resolve problems and general participation in the community."[48]

Camps and ranches are nonsecure facilities, almost always located in rural and remote areas. Juveniles adjudicated delinquent are generally placed in camps as an alternative to the more secure training schools. The healthful setting, small numbers of residents, and close contact between staff and juveniles are supposed to develop good work and living habits that will facilitate rehabilitation. Ranches and camps emphasize outside activity, self-discipline, and the development of vocational and interpersonal skills. Juveniles assigned to them are not only supposed to develop good work habits, but they are also to perform "useful and necessary" work that benefits the community.[49]

Like shelters, **detention centers** are temporary custodial facilities. However, unlike shelters, detention centers are secure institutions—lockups—that hold juveniles both before, and after, adjudication. Formally, only three purposes justify locking juveniles up in detention centers: (1) to secure their presence at court proceedings, (2) to hold those who cannot be sent home, and (3) to protect them from harming themselves or others or disrupting juvenile court processes. Juveniles who have committed more serious offenses are sent to detention centers, while those who have committed less serious ones are sent to shelters.[50]

Prior to adjudication, juveniles may stay in detention centers anywhere from a day to more than two weeks, raising the troubling question of the fairness of detention prior to proven delinquency. Detention is also sometimes used as informal punishment. Judges lock juveniles up to scare them, to show them what might happen to them, or to "teach them a lesson and give them a taste of jail." Some jurisdictions have formalized detention centers as jails for children. New Jersey, for example, permits sentencing juveniles who have been adjudicated delinquent for "repetitive disorderly persons offenses" to up to sixty days in detention centers.[51]

Not all juveniles go to juvenile detention centers. Some are housed in adult jails—a situation criticized for more than a century. James O. Finckenauer visited one of these jails in Tyler, Texas, and reported the following:

> This author visited one such all purpose jail. On the upper floor of this jail (on a very humid day in late June, with the temperature soaring

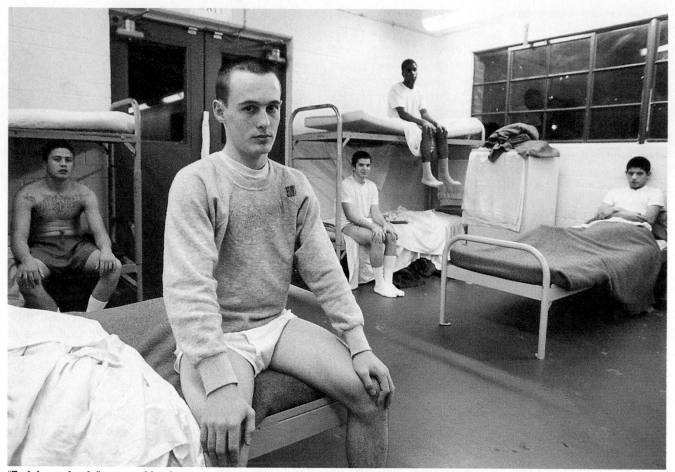

"Training schools" are used in almost every state to confine some juveniles adjudicated as delinquents.

training schools *secure detention facilities.*

into triple figures) approximately a dozen juveniles were confined in a large bullpen cell. This cell was literally a "hot box," dark and without ventilation. Some of the juveniles were from out of the state, and the average stay for most was somewhere around forty-five days. Because these youth were confined in an adult facility, and because the sheriff was attempting to maintain physical separation of juveniles and adults, the youth had no place to go and nothing to do for just about the entire duration of their incarceration. The NAC referred to the jailing of juveniles as a "disconcerting phenomenon." This is certainly an understatement, to say the very least. Because they are intended to be temporary holding facilities, jails and detention centers offer little or nothing in the way of correctional treatment.[52]

Training schools exist in every state except Massachusetts, which abolished them in the 1970s. They vary greatly in size, staff, services, programs, ages, and types of residents. Most, however, house from one to several hundred juveniles committed by juvenile courts. Some training schools resemble adult prisons, with congregate-style living and emphasis on security and order, while others are relatively open facilities that focus on treatment and rehabilitation. Training schools are the instrument of last resort in the juvenile correctional system. They contain the most serious delinquents: those who are security risks, have substantial prior records, or have exhausted other juvenile court dispositions. Almost all training schools are state-operated and controlled, unlike the other facilities discussed. Most legislation requires training schools to provide both safe custody and rehabilitative treatment.[53]

According to corrections expert Kenneth Wooden:

I found basically two types of training schools. The first is a miniature penitentiary with high walls surrounding the grounds. All the buildings and cell block wings therein are interlocked by long corridors. Not only are individual cell doors secured, but each wing is also locked at all times. There is almost always a self-sufficient industrial complex on the grounds—laundry, hospital, maintenance shop and any other facility needed to keep strangers out and the children in. Dubious educational and religious services are available to the children, along with the standbys of solitary confinement and of bloodhounds to locate any who run away. The second and more common type of training school is the cottage system. Its concept was introduced in 1856 to give children the closest thing to some form of home life. Those in charge are "house parents" rather than "guards." The outside area is usually quiet and pleasant and bears little semblance to a penal facility. The cottages are usually small, aesthetically pleasing, dormlike structures. Unfortunately, those I have seen have no back or side doors, or if they do, the doors are always chained and locked. The windows are also secured with heavy wire. The cottage system always reserves one building for secure treatment, solitary confinement. Any child who acts up in solitary cottage is further isolated in a special single room for indefinite periods of time.[54]

Juvenile Justice Reform

Since at least the nineteenth century, critics have found much wrong with almost every dimension of juvenile justice, and reformers, much to recommend for improvement in the public policy and practice concerning "troublesome" juveniles. The most recent wave of criticism and reform started in the 1960s and has continued until the present. During the 1970s, critics and reformers summarized their concerns as the "four D's": decriminalization, diversion, deinstitutionalization, and due process.

By the 1980s, critics were demanding criminalization of juveniles' acts and punishment by incarceration for juvenile offenders. Critics and reformers very much reflected the ideological shifts from liberal thought dominant during the 1960s among academics and some politicians (although never very strong among criminal justice practitioners and the public) to the more conservative thinking during the 1980s that believed punishment and incapacitation a more proper response to juvenile crime than rehabilitation. At the same time, this shift in thinking has affected academics whose research has questioned the efficacy of liberal juvenile justice reforms.

Decriminalization of Status Offenses

Some reformers advocate removing the status offenses as grounds for legal intervention; others recommend making acts committed by juveniles into crimes if the acts would be criminal had adults committed them. Hence, **decriminalization** removes status offenses from both juvenile and criminal justice, and criminalization transfers serious juvenile criminal behavior to criminal justice.[55]

Traditional juvenile justice stemmed from the theory that criminality was a developmental process that began with child neglect and led to incorrigibility, minor offenses, and finally to serious crime. According to that theory, children who committed crimes were not "bad," and even children who had not yet committed crimes might still need help. As a result, juvenile delinquency leading to state intervention did not deserve, nor would it lead to, stigma and negative consequences. State intervention offered a benign, helping process to change wayward children into responsible adults. Hence, early juvenile delinquency legislation had broad interpretations in order to "help" as many children as possible.

By 1960, these premises were badly shaken. Adjudication of a youth as "delinquent" had indeed become a stigma with harmful social consequences. Although formally confidential, in fact, juvenile court proceedings became known to a variety of other agencies, such as schools, employers, and other social service agencies that denied "delinquents" access to education, employment, vocational training, and other benefits. Attitudes toward youth crime were hardening. In 1960, for example, one commentator wrote:

> It is clear that these children are not so much at war with themselves as with their parents. It is equally valid, legally and behaviorally, to say that their parents are at war with them.[56]

At the same time, labeling theory claimed that it was not only unfair but also dangerous to attach the label *delinquent* to children. According to labeling theorists, the label *delinquent* promoted future criminal conduct, because it acted as a self-fulfilling prophecy. Delinquents treated like delinquents soon begin to act like delinquents. Putting such youths with other delinquent youth places them all in a delinquent subculture that further strengthens their delinquent behavior. Legislatures came under the influence of labeling theory beginning in the 1960s. By the late 1970s, about half of the states had separated status from delinquency jurisdiction. Status offenders came to be called Persons in Need of Supervision (PINS). By 1980, only a handful of states retained delinquency definitions that included status offenders. This relatively conservative response to criticism of status offenses does not satisfy some critics, who advocate eliminating status offense jurisdiction altogether.[57]

Diversion

In 1967, the President's Crime Commission recommended that

> communities should establish neighborhood youth serving agencies, youth service bureaus, located if possible in comprehensive neighborhood community centers and receiving both delinquent and nondelinquent youth.[58]

In 1973 the NAC followed suit, by recommending diversion in its standards. By 1974, diversion was firmly entrenched as a federal and state policy supported by public funding. So widespread did diversion programs become that Malcolm Klein, noted juvenile justice expert, referred to it as the "explosion of diversion programs."[59]

Most programs were instituted without an evaluation of the effectiveness of existing programs. Such evaluation for effectiveness requires knowing the goals of diversion in order to determine whether, or to what extent, they have been realized. Diversion programs attempted to correct existing juvenile justice evils, including (1) the denial of due process to juveniles, (2) backlogs in juvenile courts, (3) failure of juvenile justice to reduce recidivism, (4) the labeling and stigmatization of youth, and (5) the community's failure to assume responsibility for juveniles.

When diversion programs were evaluated, as they have increasingly been since the mid-1970s, they produced conflicting and mixed results at best. Many studies focused on the evils produced by labeling and the resulting stigma from involvement with juvenile justice. Some labeling theorists even went so far as to consider contacts with juvenile justice as causes of delinquency:

> The idea that the label "delinquent" can be a cause of delinquent behavior is at best crude and naive; but unfortunately it is an all-too-common application of labeling theory, furthered by the use of mechanical

cause-effect models to research the question. Our knowledge has not moved much beyond a starting assumption that the effect of exposure to arrest and court hearings on juveniles' self-conception and behavior is variable particularly when the exposure happens but once.[60]

Most labeling theorists, however, claimed only that once labeled, the stigma attached to delinquency leads to further delinquency, difficulty in changing delinquent behavior, and unfavorable school, vocational, and employment opportunities. Other research, however, shows that labeling does not always have negative consequences. When police, for example, made it clear to older juveniles that they would commit them to the California Youth Authority if they were arrested again, the label worked to deter them from further arrests. Hence, labeling might well deter further delinquency, or at least lead to changing behavior to avoid contacts with the police.[61]

This is not to deny the potential negative impact of involvement in juvenile justice. The juvenile justice system might add new rules that, if broken, lead to further action. It might interrupt school; if such interruptions occur often enough and for long enough periods of time, they can lead to dropping out. This, in turn, can lead to difficulty in finding employment and, finally, to isolation from the community so severe that reintegration becomes very difficult. Labeling, stigma, and contact with the juvenile justice system, therefore, can have both negative and positive effects that will vary among individuals and communities.

Diversion does not necessarily mean less state social control over juveniles. It has instead had the negative consequence of transferring state power from juvenile court to police and probation departments. In some cases, police have set up diversion projects in their own departments, hired their own personnel, and programmed cases to fit law enforcement needs, a development opposed to diversion's purpose to lessen state power in the control of juveniles. Such police programs diminish the juvenile court's power over juveniles while augmenting police discretionary power. Police also influence where juveniles are referred: they not only directly control referral at intake, but they also sit on boards empowered to fund diversion projects. They have even established diversion projects outside police departments, most often in schools.[62]

Diversion does not always direct youth away from the juvenile justice system. Numerous studies demonstrate that it more often expands control over juveniles who otherwise would not come into contact with the system at all, a phenomenon called **net widening.** Cases selected for diversion ordinarily include large numbers of juveniles who would be dismissed outright or counseled and released, younger juveniles without prior records who have committed trivial offenses, females, and status offenders. Since police release about half the juveniles they encounter, diversion provides them with the opportunity to "do something about the other half." This might mean referring them to diversion projects by labeling them status offenders or, if necessary, relabeling them delinquents.[63]

That many youths who are diverted are not free from the heavy hand of the juvenile justice system is highlighted when diversion is made conditional. A frequent condition for referral to a diversion program is the juvenile's admission of an offense. In reality, this is an outgrowth of police discretion, in which contrition is a prerequisite for leniency. Parents and even siblings may be required to participate in counseling, in order for the youth to be diverted. If juveniles perform well in the program, no further legal action is taken; but if they are uncooperative, they may be returned to court for further processing. Some of the methods used in police diversion programs, such as weekly reporting by juveniles and official "tracking" of youths' activities, are reminiscent of old-style informal police probation, now grown large and strengthened by official sanction.[64]

This is not a criticism of police efforts. The police have clear and definable responsibilities: controlling crime, preserving public order, and serving the community. Treating juveniles receives lower priority than these more workable goals. Police also emphasize social control over treatment simply by virtue of their training and orientation. Many police react to treatment tasks with apathy—sometimes hostility—and they frequently distort treatment into another crime control or peacekeeping instrument.[65]

One national evaluation of diversion projects reported mixed results. It found that, compared both to regular justice processing and outright release, diversion programs did not reduce stigma or succeed any better in reducing delinquent acts or antisocial behavior. However, significant numbers of delinquents were referred to diversion projects; hence, diversion projects were not simply net-widening devices. Diversion projects are less coercive, less controlling, and more helpful than justice agencies, and they did mean less penetration into the juvenile justice system.[66]

Deinstitutionalization

The treatment of delinquents in the community instead of in institutions was supposed to reduce the numbers of juveniles in detention centers, training schools, and jails. **Deinstitutionalization** has the same three rationales as diversion and community corrections generally: (1) It is more humane, (2) it is cheaper, and (3) it is more effective in reducing delinquency.

One of the most studied community treatment programs is California's Community Treatment Project (CTP), a special parole unit in the California Youth Authority (CYA). The project was specifically designed to provide individually programmed, intensive treatment services, instead of commitment to a CYA facility. Its experimental research design randomly allocated eligible juveniles to an experimental or traditional correctional program. Control youths spent about eight months in an institution; the youths in the experimental group were released to community placement. Preliminary assessments praised the CTP's success in reducing recidivism at significantly less cost than training schools. As a result of these preliminary findings, in 1967 the President's Commission on Law Enforcement and the Administration of Justice recommended that community treatment replace juvenile correctional facilities, that is, deinstitutionalization. Community corrections proliferated after that until the late 1970s.[67]

Subsequent evaluations of CTP did not produce results as favorable as the initial ones. Paul Lerman reexamined the CTP data more critically than it had initially been examined. He found that CTP was not any less expensive to operate than training schools. Furthermore, community treatment led to considerable loss of liberty. CTP experimental subjects experienced considerably more detention stays than juveniles in regular correctional parole and control group members in CTP. Probation officers were more likely to put experimentals in temporary detention for technical violations and minor infractions because they violated treatment expectations. Other reasons for the excess detention included the probation officers' accommodation to community complaints, administrative convenience, and attempts at preventing "acting out." Perhaps Lerman's most damning finding is that after allowances for administrative tasks, paperwork, and other duties, very little time was spent on actual treatment.[68] Lerman writes:

> In a quantitative sense, it is possible to define intensive treatment as consisting of a worker's devoting, on the average, two hours a week to direct service to each ward and family.[69]

Experimentals not only spent more time in temporary confinement than did juveniles in the control group, but they also spent more time in temporary detention than they did in treatment. What were supposed to be treatment issues—attendance, cooperation, task performance, and so on— were often used more as social control measures. Often, treatment meant little more than a euphemism for social control. Lerman concluded that

> the evidence indicates that the new correctional policy implemented in California modified—but did not entirely exclude—the type, degree, duration, and even the scheduling of negative sanctions administered by official agencies of the state. The evidence appears to be at odds with the ideal conception of community treatment, whereby reliance on traditional forms of incarceration were to be avoided. Community treatment, in practice, has involved intermittent doses of short-term detention that bears a marked resemblance to aspects of traditional correctional policy.[70]

Formally, community corrections offers an alternative to institutional confinement, in which treatment predominates over social control, coercion, and loss of liberty. Informally, however, it is more like traditional corrections, in which social control is paramount. Perhaps not surprisingly when these findings are taken into account, Lerman concluded that there was no significant difference in behavior between the control group and the experimentals. Juveniles who went through traditional youth institutions and those treated in the community returned to delinquency at about the same rates.

Certification

Every jurisdiction in the United States operates two separate systems for responding to criminal conduct, one for juveniles and one for adults. Different laws, procedures, and terminology govern each system. Furthermore, historically they operated according to distinct policies regarding the people who came before them. Age determines which system has authority to determine cases before it. Depending on the laws of a given state, for a criminal suspect younger than 16, 17, or 18, juvenile court handles the case; adult criminal courts manage the others.

This division of authority, the **dual system of justice,** has received careful scrutiny. How does this dual (or "two-track") system affect the sentencing of offenders who, while legally juveniles, have demonstrated a sustained commitment to serious predatory crime, or who have just crossed the age boundary between juvenile court and criminal court? A number of commentaries assert that these youthful offenders receive more lenient treatment than their older peers. Some people question whether such leniency is appropriate, given that sentencing criteria in the adult courts are moving away from rehabilitation and more toward punishment and community protection.[71]

This debate is not simply academic. Many jurisdictions are looking at a variety of reforms that would change the way in which serious youthful offenders are treated. They include:

- Reducing the juvenile court's maximum age limit from 18 to 16, so that older juveniles must be tried in adult courts.
- Increasing the use of juvenile records, particularly in adult courts, to help identify high-risk offenders and treat them accordingly.
- Replacing the juvenile court's rehabilitation philosophy with a get-tough policy in which the sentencing objective becomes punishment that fits the crime.
- Mandatory sentencing of juveniles charged with specific, violent crimes.
- Special programs for prosecuting juvenile career criminals.

- Replacing the two-track system with a three-track system that would include (1) a family court for neglected and dependent youths under 14 years of age, (2) a juvenile court for 14- to 18-year-olds whose crimes are not particularly serious, and (3) a criminal court to handle offenders over 18 and juveniles whose crimes are serious.[72]

The Rand Corporation explored how youthful offenders, ages 16 to 21, are treated during that time when legal responsibility for dealing with their criminal behavior is shifting from juvenile to adult court. They found a positive relationship between age and average crime seriousness for young offenders, prompting Rand to conclude that aggregate arrest figures probably exaggerate the amount of serious crime attributable to this age group. This exaggeration also appears to inflate the leniency with which these offenders are treated. Their analysis of case disposition patterns disclosed a wide degree of variation among jurisdictions, both between offenders of the same age across sites and in the relative severity with which different age groups are treated within sites. The sentencing patterns across these sites could not be fully attributed to organizational or legal differences between them.[73]

You Decide — How Should Criminal Justice Treat Juveniles Who Murder?

Andre, who was born and lives in New York City, is the product of a broken home. There was never enough money at home, and he was left to fend for himself. He tried selling crack when he was 12 but found that it was too dangerous, so he turned to mugging. "I would go up to somebody and tell them to give me money. If they tried to hit me, my friends would jump in. We hardly ever used a weapon. Sometimes, my friends had a razor." By the time he was 14, Andre had pulled off more than 120 muggings. "It was fun," he said. "It's like getting away with something. It's like a high, excitement." Did he think it was wrong? "Not really," he said. "I didn't think much about it. It was like I was going through a stage."

Andre first held a gun when he was 13. He had cut school and a friend let him hold the gun in the hallway of an apartment building. When he was 14, Andre fired a friend's gun in the air at a birthday party. One afternoon, while Andre was talking to two girls, about a dozen boys rode up on bicycles and one hit Andre with a baseball bat and another punched him in the face. The next morning, Andre went to a friend who was a crack dealer and bought a chrome-plated Smith & Wesson .32. Later that day he ran into the boys from the previous day. One boy accused Andre of roughing up the boy's cousin. He danced around Andre like a prize fighter, jabbing a hand in Andre's face. Andre warned him to back away or "he would have to shoot." The boy said, "If you shoot me, you better kill me, because I'll get you." Andre fired the gun into the boy's face, turned, and ran away, dodging traffic as he tried to avoid the victim's friends. "I didn't intend to kill him. I just wanted to scare him. I didn't know it would go off so easily."

Andre is one of an increasing number of teenagers who have murdered with guns. In 1982, 10 to 15 percent of teenagers who got into serious trouble in New York City were carrying guns. In 1992, 60 to 65 percent were carrying guns. Researchers at the Federal Center for Disease Control reported that shootings by teenagers contributed significantly to the rising homicide rate in the early 1990s. The National Crime Analysis Project at Northeastern University found that the number of 17-year-olds arrested for murder climbed 121 percent from 1985 through 1991. The number of 16-year-olds rose 158 percent. But the biggest increase—217 percent—was in the arrest of 15-year-olds. Even the number of arrests of boys 12 and under rose 100 percent.

According to James Alan Fox, dean of the College of Criminal Justice at Northeastern University, "Murder is plunging to a much younger age group. What is so dangerous about this is that a 15-year-old with a gun in his hand is a much more volatile individual than a 40-year-old or even an 18-year-old." Fox predicted that the United States is on the verge of a "vast new epidemic of murder." "What we've seen in the past few years is nothing compared with what we'll see in the . . . next century as the resurging adolescent population mixes with changes in our society, our culture, and our economy." The reason is the expected increase in the numbers of adolescents in the population.

Experts point to a number of reasons for the sharp increase in killings by younger boys, including

- The drug epidemic among the urban poor.
- The growing number and firepower of guns.
- The eroding quality of public schools.
- The glorification of violence on television and in the movies.

More important, according to Alfred Blumstein, dean of the Heinz School of Public Policy and Management at Carnegie-Mellon University and president of the American Society of Criminology, is the continued breakdown of the American family. Blumstein said that many young people are poorly socialized and are more vulnerable to drugs, violence on television, and the easy availability of guns. "The glorification of violence on television has little effect on most folks, but it has a powerful effect on kids who are poorly socialized. It dehumanizes them and becomes a self-fulfilling process." Blumstein says change requires "a considerable investment in the socialization process, which we have heretofore left to the family." This is expensive and intrusive and, therefore, unpopular, he added.

James Alan Fox is skeptical of the current policy of imprisonment. "People say, 'Let's just try these kids who kill as adults and lock them up.' But that won't work. They don't care. They don't think about the consequences, and they don't have a long-term perspective. They face death every day on the street and even at school, so why should they be afraid that maybe the police will catch them and maybe they will be executed?"

According to Marvin Wolfgang, professor of criminology and law at the University of Pennsylvania, and director of the Sellin Criminology Center, "What we're seeing is the loss of childhood. These kids are growing up too fast into the subculture of violence. They are learning at an ever younger age that violence is not only tolerated, but often expected and sometimes required. If you don't respond aggressively to a slur on your mother or your manhood, you're a coward."

The story of Andre and the comments of Fox, Blumstein, and Wolfgang point to teenagers murdering with guns in slums of large cities. However, George Butterfield, deputy director of the National School Safety Center at Pepperdine University in Malibu, California, sees a clear migration of guns to the suburbs, much the way that drugs and gangs have come to the middle class. "Teen age shootings and weapons incidents have increased across the board. It's just that in the suburbs you have a lot more denial. All over the country, people tell me, 'This was an isolated incident.'" In Westport, Connecticut, for example, a 16-year-old was charged with fatally shooting a classmate. The newspapers were deluged by critical letters when it reported on widespread drunkenness at the high school homecoming game, and on a teenage party where a youth had brandished a 9mm pistol. "We believe Westport suffers from the disease of denial," responded an editorial in the local newspaper.

Questions

What is the best policy to reduce the increase in murder by teenagers? Lock them up? Execute them? Intervene in the family and socialization process? Improve schools? Pass gun control legislation? After reading the comments of Blumstein, Fox, and Wolfgang, what would you recommend specifically for Andre? Consider the comments of Butterfield regarding the increase of shootings in suburbs. What are your recommendations for long-term policy to deal with teenage murderers? Do you recommend the same policies for urban slums and affluent suburbs? Explain your answer.

Sources: Based on Fox Butterfield, "Seeds of Murder Epidemic: Teen-Age Boys with Guns," *New York Times*, 19 October 1992; Joseph B. Treaster, "Teen-Age Murderers: Plentiful Guns, Easy Power," *New York Times*, 24 May 1992; Ellen Graham, "Mainstream America Finds It Isn't Immune to Kids Killing Kids," *Wall Street Journal*, 7 February 1992.

Summary

For centuries the law has treated juveniles differently from adults. Under the *parens patriae* doctrine, the state has acted as a protector of children's interests. The idea became entrenched in early English history, when the king protected wealthy wards from unscrupulous guardians who wasted minors' estates (as well as the king's own interests in the estate). In addition, the law limited minors' criminal liability. During the nineteenth century, separate institutions for needy, dependent, and delinquent juveniles were created. In the early twentieth century, the establishment of the juvenile court resulted in an American dual system of justice: one for youths, called juvenile justice, and the other for adults, called criminal justice.

Juvenile justice has consistently emphasized helping and protecting youths. Its other not-so-visible aims include protecting society and punishing juveniles who commit crimes. While the idea of helping children has predominated during most of the twentieth century, during the 1980s, public demands to protect society and punish juveniles came to the fore.

The jurisdiction of juvenile justice extends to three kinds of juveniles: children who need financial support, children who need supervision, and children who commit crimes. The lines between the three classes are not always clearly drawn. Often, children who need financial support also need supervision because they commit crimes. The vast majority of juvenile cases involve status offenses and minor crimes. Only a few have to do with serious crimes against persons.

Juvenile justice operates through three major institutions: the police, the juvenile court, and juvenile corrections. Most large police departments have separate juvenile units. These units—and, to a large extent, patrol officers—

decide whether juveniles will enter the formal juvenile justice system. The police either dismiss outright or counsel and dismiss most juveniles they encounter. A few are diverted into social service agencies or informally put on police probation. The police formally refer the remaining few to juvenile court. These agencies all operate according to both formal and informal goals. Helping children in need, protecting society, punishing young criminals, satisfying work group and other organizational needs, and attending to ideological and personal pursuits all influence the decision-making process within the juvenile justice system.

Most juveniles are not detained while waiting for the juvenile court's decision whether to proceed further in the case, but some are sent to juvenile detention centers or, less frequently, to jails to await their adjudication or other court disposition. The juvenile court conducts three principal operations: intake, adjudication, and disposition. At intake, probation officers and sometimes juvenile court judges decide whether to dismiss, divert, certify to adult criminal courts, or adjudicate cases that the police—and, to a lesser extent, schools, parents, and social service agencies—refer to them. Most cases are either dismissed or diverted to other agencies for further action. A few youths are transferred to adult courts, and about half are scheduled for adjudication, or formal juvenile court proceedings. Following adjudication, the juvenile court disposes of cases. Dispositions include dismissal, probation, diversion, commitment to juvenile correctional facilities, or some combination of these. Most juveniles are either put on probation or, until recently, diverted or assigned to community treatment corrections. A minority are sent to training schools or other correctional facilities.

Juvenile corrections has two primary divisions, community correction and institutional correction. Community correction consists mainly of probation and diversion projects in which social service agencies treat juveniles within the community in nonrestrictive settings, where they can live at home, go to school, work, and be with their friends. Community correction also includes some institutions of a noncoercive nature, such as foster homes and group homes. Institutional correctional facilities mainly include large state training schools and reform schools. Some are very much like prisons for adults; others are relatively open, campus-like places that combine treatment with considerable freedom.

The juvenile justice system has received much criticism that has led to several demands for reform. The reform demands stem primarily from disillusionment with the effectiveness of juvenile justice in reducing juvenile crime, the lack of due process and other constitutional protections in juvenile court, and the public demand for more punishment and deterrence and less rehabilitation. The many reform demands are summarized in the "four D's": (1) decriminalization of status offenses, (2) due process in juvenile court proceedings, (3) deinstitutionalization of juvenile corrections in favor of community corrections, and (4) diversion of some juvenile offenders, either from state supervision or into public and private social service agencies.

Review Questions

1. What is the dual system of justice in America? How did it come into existence?

2. What main types of juveniles come under juvenile justice jurisdiction?

3. What is the difference between a status offense and delinquency?

4. What are the major steps in the juvenile justice process?

5. What are the principal alternatives open to juvenile court justices in disposing of juveniles adjudicated delinquent?

6. What constitutional rights do juveniles have in the juvenile justice process?

7. What are the main differences between community and institutional juvenile corrections?

8. What are the "four D's"?

9. What are the main reforms proposed in juvenile justice? Which do you favor? Why?

Notes

1. Stephen Schlossman, *Love and the American Delinquent: The Theory and Practice of "Progressive" Juvenile Justice, 1825–1920* (Chicago: University of Chicago Press, 1977).

2. Anthony Platt, *The Child Savers: The Invention of Delinquency* (Chicago: University of Chicago Press, 1969).

3. David J. Rothman, *Conscience and Convenience: The Asylum and its Alternatives in Progressive America* (Boston: Little, Brown, 1980); Ellen Ryerson, *The Best Laid Plans: America's Juvenile Court Experiment* (New York: Hill and Wang, 1978); Platt, *Child Savers.*

4. President's Commission on Law Enforcement and the Administration of Justice, *The Challenge of Crime in a Free Society* (Washington, D.C.: U.S. Government Printing Office, 1967).

5. *Kent v. United States,* 383 U.S. 541 (1966).

6. *In re Winship,* 387 U.S. 1 (1967); 397 U.S. 358 (1970).

7. *McKeiver v. Pennsylvania,* 403 U.S. 528 (1970), 533–34.

8. H. Ted Rubin, *Juvenile Justice: Policy, Practice and Law* (Santa Monica, Calif.: Goodyear Press, 1979), 40; Tappan quoted in Malcolm W. Klein, ed., *Western Systems of Juvenile Justice* (Beverly Hills: Sage Publications, 1984), 20.

9. Department of Youth Authority, 1981, secs. 601, 602.

10. Richard J. Lundman, *Prevention and Control of Juvenile Delinquency* (New York: Oxford University Press, 1984), 4.

11. Robert A. Mathias, Paul DeMuro, and Richard S. Allinson, eds., *Violent Juvenile Offenders: An Anthology* (San Francisco: National Council on Crime and Delinquency, 1984), 8; National Institute for Juvenile Justice and Delinquency Prevention, *Reports of the National Juvenile Justice Assessment Centers: A National Assessment of Serious Crime and the Juvenile Justice System* (Washington, D.C.: Law Enforcement Assistance Administration, April 1980), 59.

12. Franklin E. Zimring, "Kids, Groups and Crime: Some Implications of a Well-Known Secret," *Journal of Criminal Law and Criminology* 72 (1981):867–85; Franklin E. Zimring, *Confronting Youth Crime—Report of the Twentieth Century Fund Task Force on Sentencing Policy toward Young Offenders: Background Paper* (New York: Holmes and Maier, 1978), 38.

13. *CJ: The Americas,* December-January 1993, reporting on a study by James Wright, Joseph Sheley, and M. Dwayne Smith, "Where and How Kids Get Guns."

14. Lamar T. Empey, *American Delinquency: Its Meaning and Construction* (Homewood, Ill.: The Dorsey Press, 1978), 403–484; Robert M. Carter, "The United States," in Klein, *Western Systems of Juvenile Justice,* 17–38; Jay S. Albanese, *Dealing with Delinquency: An Investigation of Juvenile Justice* (Lanham, Md.: University Press of America, 1985).

15. Robert M. Carter, "The Police View of the Justice System," in *The Juvenile Justice System,* Malcolm W. Klein, ed. (Beverly Hills: Sage Publications, 1976), 124.

16. Carter, "United States," 27.

17. Ibid., 29.

18. Ibid.

19. Empey, *American Delinquency,* 432; Patricia M. Harris, "Is the Juvenile Justice System Lenient?" *Criminal Justice Abstracts* 18 (1986):107.

20. Harris, "Is the Juvenile Justice System Lenient?" 107.

21. Empey, *American Delinquency,* 426–27.

22. Ibid., 427–28.

23. James Baldwin, *Nobody Knows My Name* (New York: Dell Publications, 1962), 66.

24. James Q. Wilson, *Varieties of Police Behavior* (Cambridge, Mass.: Harvard University Press, 1978), 40–41.

25. H. Ted Rubin, *The Courts: Fulcrum of the Justice System* (Pacific Palisades, Calif.: Goodyear Publishing Company, 1976), 66.

26. Empey, *American Delinquency,* 445, 451, 453.

27. Albanese, *Dealing with Delinquency,* 85.

28. Ibid., 454.

29. Yeheskel Hasenfield, "Youth in the Juvenile Court: Input and Output Patterns," in *Brought to Justice? Juveniles, the Courts and the Law,* Rosemary Sarri and Yeheskel Hasenfield, eds. (Ann Arbor: National Assessment of Juvenile Corrections, University of Michigan, 1976), 70.

30. Harris, "Is the Juvenile Justice System Lenient?" 111.

31. Empey, *American Delinquency,* 455.

32. Harvey H. Baker, "Procedure for the Boston Juvenile Court," *Preventive Treatment of Neglected Children,* Hastings Hart, ed. (New York: Charities Publications Committee, 1910), 319.

33. Empey, *American Delinquency,* 457–58.

34. Albanese, *Dealing with Delinquency,* 89.

35. Platt, *Child Savers,* 176–78.

36. Edwin Schur, *Radical Non Intervention: Rethinking the Delinquency Problem* (Englewood Cliffs, N.J.: Prentice-Hall, 1973), 44.

37. Lawrence E. Cohen, *Delinquency Dispositions: An Empirical Analysis of Processing Decisions in Three Juvenile Courts* (Washington, D.C.: U.S. Government Printing Office, 1975).

38. Barry Krisberg et al., *The Incarceration of Minority Youth* (Minneapolis: University of Minnesota, Hubert H. Humphrey Institute of Public Affairs, 1986), 23.

39. Albanese, *Dealing with Delinquency,* 91.

40. Thomas G. Blomberg, *Juvenile Court and Community Corrections* (Lanham, N.Y.: University Press of America, 1984), 1–3; Alden D. Miller and Lloyd E. Ohlin, *Delinquency and Community* (Beverly Hills: Sage Publications, 1985), 11–22.

41. Richard A. Cloward and Lloyd E. Ohlin, *Delinquency and Opportunity: A Theory of Delinquent Gangs* (New York: Free Press, 1960).

42. National Advisory Commission on Criminal Justice Standards and Goals, *Corrections* (Washington, D.C.: U.S. Government Printing Office, 1973), 222.

43. Paul Lerman, "Trends and Issues in the Deinstitutionalization of Youths in Trouble," *Crime and Delinquency* 26 (1980):295.

44. James O. Finckenauer, *Juvenile Delinquency and Corrections: The Gap Between Theory and Practice* (Orlando: Academic Press, 1984), 126.

45. Thomas R. Collingwood et al., "Juvenile Diversion: The Dallas Police Department Youth Services Program," in *Effective Correctional Treatment*, Robert R. Ross and Paul Gendreau, eds. (Toronto: Butterworths, 1980), 93–100.

46. Finckenauer, *Juvenile Delinquency*, 151.

47. National Institute of Corrections, *Standards for Juvenile Community Residential Facilities* (Washington, D.C.: National Institute of Corrections, 1983), xvii.

48. Ibid., xvi.

49. National Advisory Committee, *Standards for Administration of Juvenile Justice* (Washington, D.C.: Government Printing Office, 1980), 487–91.

50. Finckenauer, *Juvenile Delinquency*, 152.

51. Ibid; New Jersey P.L. 1982, chap. 77, sec. 24; American Correctional Association, *Standards for Juvenile Training Schools*, 2d ed. (Washington, D.C.: National Institute of Justice, 1983), xvii.

52. Finckenauer, *Juvenile Delinquency*, 132.

53. American Correctional Association, *Standards for Juvenile Training Schools*, xvii.

54. Kenneth Wooden, *Weeping in the Playtime of Others* (New York: McGraw-Hill, 1976), 28–29.

55. Brooke E. Spiro, "Abolishing Court Jurisdiction Over Status Offenders: Anticipating the Unintended Consequences," in *Juvenile Justice Policy: Analyzing Trends and Outcomes*, Scott H. Decker, ed. (Beverly Hills: Sage Publications, 1984), 77–93, 83.

56. Sol Rubin, "Legal Definition of Offenses by Children and Youths," *University of Illinois Law Forum* (1960):512–23, 514.

57. Lee E. Teitelbaum, "Juvenile Status Offenders," in *Encyclopedia of Crime and Justice*, Sanford H. Kadish, ed. (New York: Free Press, 1983), 3:987.

58. President's Commission on Law Enforcement and the Administration of Justice, *The Challenge of Crime in a Free Society* (Washington, D.C.: U.S. Government Printing Office, 1967), 83.

59. Edwin M. Lemert, "Diversion in Juvenile Justice: What Hath Been Wrought," *Journal of Research in Crime and Delinquency* 18 (1981):34–46, 36.

60. Ibid., 36.

61. Ibid., 38.

62. Ibid., 40.

63. Ibid., 41.

64. Ibid.

65. Ibid.

66. Finckenauer, *Juvenile Delinquency*, 135.

67. Paul Lerman, *Community Treatment and Social Control: A Critical Analysis of Juvenile Correctional Policy* (Chicago: University of Chicago Press, 1975).

68. Ibid., 34.

69. Ibid.

70. Ibid., 7.

71. Rand Corporation, *Age, Crime, and Sanctions: The Transition from Juvenile to Adult Court* (Santa Monica: Rand Corporation, 1980).

72. Ibid.

73. Ibid.

Appendix A
Careers in Criminal Justice

According to the *Monthly Labor Review's* projections of occupational employment, the total number of jobs will continue to grow between 1988 and 2000, but at half the rate of the previous twelve-year period. Jobs that require special education and training will foreclose a growing and attractive segment of the job market to those with low educational attainment or specific practical skills. Much of the growth in employment until the year 2000 will be in the service industries, which includes the criminal justice occupations. So, criminal justice is an area of job growth for those with the education and training to compete for the jobs. This appendix describes the range of positions in criminal justice. An excellent source for more details concerning these and other positions related to criminal justice, a description of the specific qualifications for the jobs described here, and general information on how to prepare a résumé and get ready for an interview is J. Scott Harr and Kären M. Hess, *Seeking Employment in Law Enforcement, Private Security, and Related Fields.*

Law Enforcement: Federal Agencies

Career opportunities are available in the following agencies of the federal government:

United States Bureau of Alcohol, Tobacco, and Firearms

The Bureau of Alcohol, Tobacco, and Firearms has a unique opportunity to deter crime because of its diversified jurisdictions. Enforcement of possession laws in the areas of alcohol, tobacco, and firearms are the bureau's main concern. Investigation of arson-for-profit schemes is also an important function of ATF. Irregular hours and rigorous training are common for special agents.

- *Salary schedule:* Special agents begin at a salary level usually between $18,340 and $22,717. Employees then progress along the General Schedule for federal employees with income potential well above $60,000.
- *Educational qualifications:* A college degree or at least three years of general experience is necessary with an additional year of specialized experience often preferred.

- *Benefits:* Early retirement as early as 50, premiums on income potential as high as an additional 25 percent, group health and life insurance programs, and paid holidays are only a few of the benefits enjoyed by ATF employees.
- *Do you want to know more?*
  Contact Bureau of Alcohol, Tobacco, and Firearms
  Personnel Division–Employment Branch
  Washington, D.C. 20226
  Phone: (202) 927-8610

Central Intelligence Agency

Many diverse careers are available upon appointment to a position in the CIA. There is a current need for intelligence analysts and overseas analysts within the CIA. Employment can be exciting and rewarding but employees are expected to work many odd hours and days. Employees must also be able to relocate.

- *Salary schedule:* Employees earn their salary according to the General Schedule with beginning salaries dependent upon the appointment.
- *Educational qualifications:* A college degree is necessary for appointment and fluency in a foreign language is definitely preferred. A 6–9 month application process must be completed as well as polygraph, medical, and physical examinations.
- *Benefits:* Employees enjoy many benefits comparable to other Federal agencies such as accumulated vacation time, health insurance, life insurance, and a quality retirement plan.
- *Do you want to know more?*
  Contact Central Intelligence Agency
  Recruitment Office
  Philadelphia, PA 12330
  Phone: (800) 562-7242

United States Department of Justice: Federal Bureau of Investigation

A wide range of employment opportunities exist within the Federal Bureau of Investigation. Careers such as special agents as well as computer programmers, laboratory technicians, and electronics technicians illustrate the diversity of opportunities within the bureau. Employees often are required to relocate many times throughout their careers in order to undertake new, challenging, and exciting assignments.

- *Salary schedule:* Employees are salaried on the General Schedule pay rates. Entry level positions offer salaries between $18,340 and $27,789 with many employees earning over $50,000 annually.
- *Educational qualifications:* Most positions require a four-year college degree from an accredited institution.
- *Benefits:* Employees enjoy benefits equivalent to many programs in the private sector with vacation days, paid sick days, federal holidays, and more. It is important to note that the holidays and vacation days are often not the same as other federal employees, as careers in the FBI often require hours other than a typical 9:00 A.M. to 5:00 P.M. shift, Monday–Friday.
- *Do you want to know more?*
  Contact U.S. Department of Justice
  Federal Bureau of Investigation
  Office of Public Affairs
  10th Street and Pennsylvania Avenue, N.W.
  Washington, D.C. 20535
  Phone: (202) 324-5611

United States Department of Justice: Federal Bureau of Prisons

Within the Federal Bureau of Prisons a wide range of opportunities are available with careers in areas such as accounting and marketing analysis as well as jobs for correction officers and administrators. As many "prisoner contact" positions exist as well as behind the scenes careers where employees may never even meet a prisoner.

- *Salary schedule:* Correctional Treatment Specialists earn $27,789 in their first year alone with potential to earn $33,623 in their second year. Other careers begin at various salaries with advancement opportunities abundant.
- *Educational Qualifications:* Almost all careers require a bachelor's degree with a master's being preferred in some areas.
- *Benefits:* Employees enjoy low-cost life insurance programs, family health plans, 13–26 days of annual paid leave (based on length of employment), early retirement, and more.
- *Do you want to know more?*
  Contact U.S. Department of Justice
  Federal Bureau of Prisons
  Human Resource Management Division
  National Recruitment Office
  320 First Street, N.W., Room 446
  Washington, D.C. 20534
  Phone: (202) 307-3026, (202) 307-3204,
  or (202) 514-6089

United States Department of Justice: Immigration and Naturalization Service

Careers as criminal investigators, immigration inspectors, immigration examiners, deportation officers, and detention enforcement officers are some of the more common opportunities available within the INS. These are exciting and demanding careers that enforce the United States immigration laws. Hours are abnormal depending on the employee's appointment within the bureau.

- *Salary schedule:* Employees earn competitive salaries based on appointment with many earning $30,000 in their first year alone.
- *Educational qualifications:* While qualifications may vary from department to department, law-enforcement experience, investigative experience, fluency in a foreign language, and a college degree may be beneficial.
- *Benefits:* Life and health insurance, early retirement, paid vacations, and sick leave are only a few of the many benefits the INS affords its employees.
- *Do you want to know more?*

Contact	**Eastern Region**	**Southern Region**
	INS	INS
	70 Kimball Avenue	7701 North Stemmons Freeway
	South Burlington, VT 05403-6813	Dallas, TX 75247
	Western Region	**Northern Region**
	INS	INS
	24000 Avila RD	Bishop Henry
	P.O. Box 30080	Whipple Bldg.
	Laguna Niguel, CA 92607-8080	Room 400
		1 Federal Drive
		Ft. Snelling, MN 55111-4007

United States Department of Justice: Probation Office

This division of the government enforces sentencing guidelines set forth by the courts. Probation is also in charge of the supervision of federal offenders as well as conducting investigations into the backgrounds of individuals. Careers are considered to be somewhat hazardous due to daily contact with criminals.

- *Salary schedule:* Employees earn excellent salaries with most beginning at approximately $27,000 and progressing to more than $52,000.
- *Educational qualifications:* A bachelor's degree with an emphasis in the social sciences is preferred and experience in related fields is desirable.
- *Benefits:* Employees enjoy early retirement, accumulated vacation time, and medical and life insurance benefits comparable to many private sector employees.
- *Do you want to know more?*
  Contact U.S. Department of Justice
  Probation
  1 Columbus Circle
  Washington, D.C. 20544
  Phone: (202) 273-1610

United States Department of Justice: United States Marshals

United States Marshals help transport federal prisoners, accompany them to court appearances, protect judges, and play a major role in the witness protection program. Marshals are, in a way, the security guard of the government.

- *Salary schedule:* Employees generally begin earning $22,717, with progression up the General Schedule.

- *Educational qualifications:* A bachelor's degree is preferred, but three years of related experience may qualify an applicant.
- *Benefits:* Marshals enjoy the same benefits as other federal employees with opportunities for early retirement. Employees must be willing to relocate.
- *Do you want to know more?*
  Contact United States Marshals
  Recruitment Center
  600 Army–Navy Drive
  Arlington, VA 22202

Department of Health and Human Services: Social Security Administration

Careers within the Social Security Administration offer a wide range of opportunities. Positions in areas of claims examination as well as "public contact" positions are always available in various locations throughout the United states.

- *Salary schedule:* Employees are salaried on the General Schedule pay rates. Most entry-level careers pay between $16,393 and $22,717 per year with top salaries exceeding $100,000 annually.
- *Educational qualifications:* A bachelor's degree or three years of progressively responsible experience or a combination of both is generally required.
- *Benefits:* Employees enjoy benefits that are comparable to if not better than those earned by employees in the private sector with 11 paid federal holidays, 13 vacation days annually with increases based upon service, 13 days of paid sick leave annually with unlimited accumulation, as well as numerous other benefits.
- *Do you want to know more?*
  Contact Department of Health and Human Services
  Regional Personnel Office
  105 West Adams
  Chicago, Illinois
  Phone: (312) 353-5175

United States Post Office: Division of Postal Inspectors

Postal Inspectors are responsible for regulating the mails, regulating pornography and contraband when they are sent through the mail, and investigating mail fraud, internal theft within the post office, and external theft of the mails.

- *Salary schedule:* Postal inspectors can earn up to $70,000 annually with most starting at $47,000.
- *Educational qualifications:* Any non-postal employee must have a professional degree, preferably with an emphasis in law, accounting, or computer science, and it is desirable for applicants to be fluent in a second language.
- *Benefits:* Employees enjoy excellent retirement plans, health insurance, and can accumulate sick and vacation time.
- *Do you want to know more?*
  Contact Recruitment Program Manager
  United States Postal Inspection Service
  William F. Bolger Management Academy
  9600 Newbridge Drive
  Potomac, MD 20858-4328
  Phone: (301) 983-7340

Department of the Treasury: Internal Revenue Service

Employing over 120,000 people nationwide in careers in areas such as revenue officers, special agents, tax auditors, and computer specialists, the IRS has a wide range of career opportunities available. Enforcement of tax laws, decisions on liability of taxes, and investigation of criminal and civil violations of Internal Revenue laws are some of the main functions of the IRS.

- *Salary schedule:* Employees earn competitive salaries on the General or Special Schedules based on employment. Typical starting salaries are around $20,000 with quick progression along the schedules for dedicated employees.
- *Educational qualifications:* A bachelor's degree in accounting, liberal arts, computer science, public administration, or business is preferred.
- *Benefits:* Employees enjoy co-op educational programs in which the IRS shares the cost, retirement plans, ten paid holidays annually, 26 days of vacation each year, and more.
- *Do you want to know more?*
  Contact the District Director or IRS Recruitment Coordinator in your area.

Law Enforcement: State Agencies

The following state government agencies offer criminal justice career opportunities:

- *State Bureaus of Investigation and Apprehension.* Many states have an agency that places investigators throughout the state to help county and municipal law enforcement agencies investigate major crimes, organized crime, and illegal drug trafficking. In addition to investigation, they provide scientific examinations of crime scenes and laboratory analysis of evidence, maintain criminal justice information and telecommunications systems, and conduct training courses for law enforcement officers.
- *State Fire Marshal Division.* State fire marshals investigate suspicious fire origins, fire fatalities, and fires that cause major losses. They also tabulate fire statistics and provide training programs for fire prevention.
- *State Departments of Natural Resources.* Conservation officers investigate complaints about nuisance wildlife, misuse of public lands and waters, violations of state parks rules, and unlawful taking of state timber. Conservation officers also issue fishing, hunting, and boat licenses.
- *Departments of Human Rights.* Departments of Human Rights enforce the states' laws that prohibit discrimination on the bases of race, religion, ethnicity, and gender in employment, education, housing, and public accommodations and services.
- *State Police and Highway Patrol.* Some state police agencies are responsible for enforcing all the laws of the state, such as crimes committed on the highways of the state. Others enforce only the traffic laws on state highways and freeways.

Law Enforcement: County Agencies

County agencies offer these criminal justice opportunities:

● *County Sheriff.* Sheriffs appoint deputies who are responsible for a range of law enforcement duties, including (1) keeping the peace; (2) executing civil and criminal process, such as warrants; (3) staffing and maintaining the county jail; (4) preserving order and dignity in the courts; and (5) enforcing court orders.
● *Coroner or Medical Examiner.* The main duties of the coroner are to determine the cause of death in cases of "suspicious" deaths and to take care of the remains and the personal effects of deceased persons.

Law Enforcement: Local Agencies

At the local level, municipal police are by far the most numerous and best known of all the law enforcement agencies and personnel. The duties of the more than 12,000 local police departments include law enforcement, order maintenance, crime prevention, service, and civil rights and liberties protection.

Law Enforcement: Private Security

The rapidly expanding private security industry includes two basic types of entry-level positions. Private security guards control access to private property, and protect, enforce rules, and maintain order regarding private property. Private patrol officers move from location to location on foot or in vehicles, protecting property and preventing property losses. Mid-level jobs include private investigators, detectives, armed couriers, central alarm experts, and security consultants. The top jobs in private security include managing private security companies or heading security divisions in large companies.

Courts

Career opportunities in the courtroom include the following:

● *Lawyers.* The three leading professionals in the courts are the judges, prosecutors, and defense attorneys. Judges and prosecutors all have law degrees, and most are elected to their positions. Defenders are either hired by clients who can afford to pay, are appointed by some selection system, or are employed by public defender systems. Prosecutors manage cases for the government from the time the police bring them to their attention to final disposition. Defense attorneys represent the interests of their clients from the time that either a client hires them or they are assigned a case by the court or the public defender's office. Judges preside over all of the formal proceedings in court.
● *Court Administrator.* Court administrators are in charge of running the court system. They manage cases and resources.
● *Paralegals.* Paralegals work as legal secretaries, court reporters, legal assistants to judges, prosecutors, and defense attorneys. According to the *Monthly Labor Review,* paralegals will be the fastest-growing occupation in the 1990s. The *Review* projects a 75 percent increase in the number of paralegals between 1988 and 2000.

Corrections

Career opportunities in corrections include the following:

● *Probation Officers.* Probation officers supervise offenders who are released into the community following their convictions. They act as both counselors and law enforcement officers, making sure that offenders do not commit new offenses or violate the conditions of their probation.
● *Correctional Officers.* Correctional officers spend most of their time guarding prisoners. But increasingly, they work with prisoners in such tasks as recreation, vocational training, and education. They help prisoners adjust to incarceration and prepare for release back into society. According to the *Monthly Labor Review,* the demand for correctional officers will continue to be strong throughout the 1990s. The *Review* projects an increase in correctional officers of 40 percent from 1988 to 2000.
● *Parole Officers.* Parole officers supervise prisoners following their release from prison. They help them find jobs, continue their education, and deal with family problems. They also act as law enforcement officers in preventing the violation of parole conditions and the commission of new crimes.

Research and Teaching

Career opportunities in research and teaching include the following:

● *Research.* Researchers contribute to the basic knowledge of criminal justice and to the assessment of the effectiveness of criminal justice policies. Many private research groups referred to in the text conduct both types of research. The federal government, some state governments, most universities, and many colleges have strong research units that provide opportunities for those who are interested in criminal justice research.
● *Teaching.* More than 600 criminal justice programs require instructors to teach the courses offered in the programs. Some are specialized criminal justice schools and departments; others are offered in connection with sociology, political science, or other social science departments. Criminal justice programs exist at all levels, including graduate programs, four-year universities and colleges, two-year junior colleges and vocational-technical schools. Even a number of high schools offer criminal justice courses.

---

[1]This appendix is based on J. Scott Harr and Kären M. Hess, *Seeking Employment in Law Enforcement, Private Security, and Related Fields* (St. Paul: West Publishing Company, 1992); George Silvestri and John Lukasiewicz, "Projections of occupational employment, 1988–2000," *Monthly Labor Review,* November 1989, 42–65.

Appendix B
Constitution of the United States

Preamble

We the People of the United States, in Order to form a more perfect Union, establish Justice, insure domestic Tranquility, provide for the common defence, promote the general Welfare, and secure the Blessings of Liberty to ourselves and our Posterity, do ordain and establish this Constitution for the United States of America.

Article I
Section 1

All legislative Powers herein granted shall be vested in a Congress of the United States, which shall consist of a Senate and House of Representatives.

Section 2

The House of Representatives shall be composed of Members chosen every second Year by the People of the several States, and the Electors in each State shall have the Qualifications requisite for Electors of the most numerous Branch of the State Legislature.

No Person shall be a Representative who shall not have attained to the Age of twenty five Years, and been seven Years a Citizen of the United States, and who shall not, when elected, be an Inhabitant of that State in which he shall be chosen.

Representatives and direct Taxes shall be apportioned among the several States which may be included within this Union, according to their respective Numbers, which shall be determined by adding to the whole Number of free Persons, including those bound to Service for a Term of Years, and excluding Indians not taxed, three fifths of all other Persons. The actual Enumeration shall be made within three Years after the first Meeting of the Congress of the United States, and within every subsequent Term of ten Years, in such Manner as they shall by Law direct. The Number of Representatives shall not exceed one for every thirty Thousand, but each State shall have at Least one Representative; and until such enumeration shall be made, the State of New Hampshire shall be entitled to choose three, Massachusetts eight, Rhode Island and Providence Plantations one, Connecticut five, New York six, New Jersey four, Pennsylvania eight, Delaware one, Maryland six, Virginia ten, North Carolina five, South Carolina five, and Georgia three.

When vacancies happen in the Representation from any State, the Executive Authority thereof shall issue Writs of Election to fill such Vacancies.

The House of Representatives shall choose their Speaker and other Officers; and shall have the sole Power of Impeachment.

Section 3

The Senate of the United States shall be composed of two Senators from each State, chosen by the Legislature thereof, for six Years; and each Senator shall have one Vote.

Immediately after they shall be assembled in Consequence of the first Election, they shall be divided as equally as may be into three Classes. The Seats of the Senators of the first Class shall be vacated at the Expiration of the second Year, of the second Class at the Expiration of the fourth Year, and of the third Class at the Expiration of the sixth Year, so that one third may be chosen every second Year; and if Vacancies happen by Resignation, or otherwise, during the Recess of the Legislature of any State, the Executive thereof may make temporary Appointments until the next Meeting of the Legislature, which shall then fill such Vacancies.

No Person shall be a Senator who shall not have attained to the Age of thirty Years, and been nine Years a Citizen of the United States, and who shall not, when elected, be an Inhabitant of that State for which he shall be chosen.

The Vice President of the United States shall be President of the Senate, but shall have no Vote, unless they be equally divided.

The Senate shall choose their other Officers, and also a President pro tempore, in the Absence of the Vice President, or when he shall exercise the Office of President of the United States.

The Senate shall have the sole Power to try all Impeachments. When sitting for that Purpose, they shall be on Oath or Affirmation. When the President of the United States is tried, the Chief Justice shall preside: And no Person shall be convicted without the Concurrence of two thirds of the Members present.

Judgment in Cases of Impeachment shall not extend further than to removal from Office, and disqualificationto hold and enjoy any Office of honor, Trust, or Profit under the United States: but the Party convicted shall nevertheless be liable and subject to Indictment, Trial, Judgment, and Punishment, according to Law.

Section 4

The Times, Places and Manner of holding Elections for Senators and Representatives, shall be prescribed in each State by the Legislature thereof; but the Congress may at any time by Law make or alter such Regulations, except as to the Places of choosing Senators.

The Congress shall assemble at least once in every Year, and such Meeting shall be on the first Monday in December, unless they shall by Law appoint a different Day.

Section 5

Each House shall be the Judge of the Elections, Returns, and Qualifications of its own Members, and a Majority of each shall constitute a Quorum to do Business; but a smaller Number may adjourn from day to day, and may be authorized to compel the Attendance of absent Members, in such Manner, and under such Penalties as each House may provide.

Each House may determine the Rules of its Proceedings, punish its Members for disorderly Behavior, and, with the Concurrence of two thirds, expel a Member.

Each House shall keep a Journal of its Proceedings, and from time to time publish the same, excepting such Parts as may in their Judgment require Secrecy; and the Yeas and Nays of the Members of either House on any question shall, at the Desire of one fifth of those Present, be entered on the Journal.

Neither House, during the Session of Congress, shall, without the Consent of the other, adjourn for more than three days, nor to any other Place than that in which the two Houses shall be sitting.

Section 6

The Senators and Representatives shall receive a Compensation for their Services, to be ascertained by Law, and paid out of the Treasury of the United States. They shall in all Cases, except Treason, Felony and Breach of the Peace, be privileged from Arrest during their Attendance at the Session of their respective Houses, and in going to and returning from the same; and for any Speech or Debate in either House, they shall not be questioned in any other Place.

No Senator or Representative shall, during the Time for which he was elected, be appointed to any civil Office under the Authority of the United States, which shall have been created, or the Emoluments whereof shall have been increased during such time; and no Person holding any Office under the United States, shall be a Member of either House during his Continuance in Office.

Section 7

All Bills for raising Revenue shall originate in the House of Representatives; but the Senate may propose or concur with Amendments as on other Bills.

Every Bill which shall have passed the House of Representatives and the Senate, shall, before it become a Law, be presented to the President of the United States; If he approve he shall sign it, but if not he shall return it, with his Objections to the House in which it shall have originated, who shall enter the Objections at large on their Journal, and proceed to reconsider it. If after such Reconsideration two thirds of that House shall agree to pass the Bill, it shall be sent together with the Objections, to the other House, by which it shall likewise be reconsidered, and if approved by two thirds of that House, it shall become a Law. But in all such Cases the Votes of both Houses shall be determined by Yeas and Nays, and the Names of the Persons voting for and against the Bill shall be entered on the Journal of each House respectively. If any Bill shall not be returned by the President within ten Days (Sundays excepted) after it shall have been presented to him, the Same shall be a Law, in like Manner as if he had signed it, unless the Congress by their Adjournment prevent its Return in which Case it shall not be a Law.

Every Order, Resolution, or Vote, to which the Concurrence of the Senate and House of Representatives may be necessary (except on a question of Adjournment) shall be presented to the President of the United States; and before the Same shall take Effect, shall be approved by him, or being disapproved by him, shall be repassed by two thirds of the Senate and House of Representatives, according to the Rules and Limitations prescribed in the Case of a Bill.

Section 8

The Congress shall have Power To lay and collect Taxes, Duties, Imposts and Excises, to pay the Debts and provide for the common Defence and general Welfare of the United States; but all Duties, Imposts and Excises shall be uniform throughout the United States;

To borrow Money on the credit of the United States;

To regulate Commerce with foreign Nations, and among the several States, and with the Indian Tribes;

To establish an uniform Rule of Naturalization, and uniform Laws on the subject of Bankruptcies throughout the United States;

To coin Money, regulate the Value thereof, and of foreign Coin, and fix the Standard of Weights and Measures;

To provide for the Punishment of counterfeiting the Securities and current Coin of the United States;

To establish Post Offices and post Roads;

To promote the Progress of Science and useful Arts, by securing for limited Times to Authors and Inventors the exclusive Right to their respective Writings and Discoveries;

To constitute Tribunals inferior to the supreme Court;

To define and punish Piracies and Felonies committed on the high Seas, and Offenses against the Law of Nations;

To declare War, grant Letters of Marque and Reprisal, and make Rules concerning Captures on Land and Water;

To raise and support Armies, but no Appropriation of Money to that Use shall be for a longer Term than two Years;

To provide and maintain a Navy;

To make Rules for the Government and Regulation of the land and naval Forces;

To provide for calling forth the Militia to execute the Laws of the Union, suppress Insurrections and repel Invasions;

To provide for organizing, arming, and disciplining, the Militia, and for governing such Part of them as may be employed in the Service of the United States, reserving to the States respectively, the Appointment of the Officers, and the Authority of training the Militia according to the discipline prescribed by Congress;

To exercise exclusive Legislation in all Cases whatsoever, over such District (not exceeding ten Miles square) as may, by Cession of particular States, and the Acceptance of Congress, become the Seat of the Government of the United States, and to exercise like Authority over all Places purchased by the Consent of the Legislature of the State in which the Same shall be, for the Erection of Forts, Magazines, Arsenals, dock-Yards, and other needful Buildings;—And

To make all Laws which shall be necessary and proper for carrying into Execution the foregoing Powers, and all other Powers vested by this Constitution in the Government of the United States, or in any Department or Officer thereof.

Section 9

The Migration or Importation of such Persons as any of the States now existing shall think proper to admit, shall not be prohibited by the Congress prior to the Year one thousand eight hundred and eight, but a Tax or duty may be imposed on such Importation, not exceeding ten dollars for each Person.

The privilege of the Writ of Habeas Corpus shall not be suspended, unless when in Cases of Rebellion or Invasion the public Safety may require it.

No Bill of Attainder or ex post facto Law shall be passed.

No Capitation, or other direct, Tax shall be laid, unless in Proportion to the Census or Enumeration herein before directed to be taken.

No Tax or Duty shall be laid on Articles exported from any State.

No Preference shall be given by any Regulation of Commerce or Revenue to the Ports of one State over those of another: nor shall Vessels bound to, or from, one State be obliged to enter, clear, or pay Duties in another.

No Money shall be drawn from the Treasury, but in Consequence of Appropriations made by Law; and a regular Statement and Account of the Receipts and Expenditures of all public Money shall be published from time to time.

No Title of Nobility shall be granted by the United States: And no Person holding any Office of Profit or Trust under them, shall, without the Consent of the Congress, accept of any present, Emolument, Office, or Title, of any kind whatever, from any King, Prince, or foreign State.

Section 10

No State shall enter into any Treaty, Alliance, or Confederation; grant Letters of Marque and Reprisal; coin Money; emit Bills of Credit; make any Thing but gold and silver Coin a Tender in Payment of Debts; pass any Bill of Attainder, ex post facto Law, or Law impairing the Obligation of Contracts, or grant any Title of Nobility.

No State shall, without the Consent of the Congress, lay any Imposts or Duties on Imports or Exports, except what may be absolutely necessary for executing its inspection Laws: and the net Produce of all Duties and Imposts, laid by any State on Imports or Exports, shall be for the Use of the Treasury of the United States; and all such Laws shall be subject to the Revision and Control of the Congress.

No State shall, without the Consent of Congress, lay any Duty of Tonnage, keep Troops, or Ships of War in time of Peace, enter into any Agreement or Compact with another State, or with a foreign Power, or engage in War, unless actually invaded, or in such imminent Danger as will not admit of delay.

Article II
Section 1

The executive Power shall be vested in a President of the United States of America. He shall hold his Office during the Term of four Years, and, together with the Vice President, chosen for the same Term, be elected, as follows:

Each state shall appoint, in such Manner as the Legislature thereof may direct, a Number of Electors, equal to the whole Number of Senators and Representatives to which the State may be entitled in the Congress; but no Senator or Representative, or Person holding an Office of Trust or Profit under the United States, shall be appointed an Elector.

The Electors shall meet in their respective States, and vote by Ballot for two Persons, of whom one at least shall not be an Inhabitant of the same State with themselves. And they shall make a List of all the Persons voted for, and of the Number of Votes for each; which List they shall sign and certify, and transmit sealed to the Seat of the Government of the United States, directed to the President of the Senate. The President of the Senate shall, in the Presence of the Senate and House of Representatives, open all the Certificates, and the Votes shall then be counted. The Person having the greatest Number of Votes shall be the President, if such Number be a Majority of the whole Number of Electors appointed; and if there be more than one who have such Majority, and have an equal Number of Votes, then the House of Representatives shall immediately choose by Ballot one of them for President; and if no Person have a Majority, then from the five highest on the List the said House shall in like Manner choose the President. But in choosing the President, the Votes shall be taken by States, the Representation from each State having one Vote; A quorum for this Purpose shall consist of a Member or Members from two thirds of the States, and a Majority of all the States shall be necessary to a Choice. In every Case, after the Choice of the President, the Person having the greater Number of Votes of the Electors shall be the Vice President. But if there should remain two or more who have equal Votes, the Senate shall choose from them by Ballot the Vice President.

The Congress may determine the Time of choosing the Electors, and the Day on which they shall give their Votes; which Day shall be the same throughout the United States.

No person except a natural born Citizen, or a Citizen of the United States, at the time of the Adoption of this Constitution, shall be eligible to the Office of President; neither shall any Person be eligible to that Office who shallnot have attained to the Age of thirty five Years, and been fourteen Years a Resident within the United States.

In Case of the Removal of the President from Office, or of his Death, Resignation or Inability to discharge the Powers and Duties of the said Office, the same shall devolve on the Vice President, and the Congress may by Law provide for the Case of Removal, Death, Resignation or Inability, both of the President and Vice President, declaring what Officer shall then act as President, and such Officer shall act accordingly, until the Disability be removed, or a President shall be elected.

The President shall, at stated Times, receive for his Services, a Compensation, which shall neither be increased nor diminished during the Period for which he shall have been elected, and he shall not receive within that Period any other Emolument from the United States, or any of them.

Before he enter on the Execution of his Office, he shall take the following Oath or Affirmation: "I do solemnly swear (or affirm) that I will faithfully execute the Office of President of the United States, and will to the best of my Ability, preserve, protect and defend the Constitution of the United States."

Section 2

The President shall be Commander in Chief of the Army and Navy of the United States, and of the Militia of the several States, when called into the actual Service of the United States; he may require the Opinion, in writing, of the principal Officer in each of the executive Departments, upon any Subject relating to the Duties of their respective Offices, and he shall have Power to grant Reprieves and Pardons for Offenses against the United States, except in Cases of Impeachment.

He shall have Power, by and with the Advice and Consent of the Senate to make Treaties, provided two thirds of the Senators present concur; and he shall nominate, and by and with the Advice and Consent of the Senate, shall appoint Ambassadors, other public Ministers and Consuls, Judges of the supreme Court, and all other Officers of the United States, whose Appointments are not herein otherwise provided for, and which shall be established by Law; but the Congress may by Law vest the Appointment of such inferior Officers, as they think proper, in the President alone, in the Courts of Law, or in the Heads of Departments.

The President shall have Power to fill up all Vacancies that may happen during the Recess of the Senate, by granting Commissions which shall expire at the End of their next Session.

Section 3

He shall from time to time give to the Congress Information of the State of the Union, and recommend to their Consideration such Measures as he shall judge necessary and expedient; he may, on extraordinary Occasions, convene both Houses, or either of them, and in Case of Disagreement between them, with Respect to the Time of Adjournment, he may adjourn them to such Time as he shall think proper; he shall receive Ambassadors and other public Ministers; he shall take Care that the Laws be faithfully executed, and shall Commission all the Officers of the United States.

Section 4

The President, Vice President and all civil Officers of the United States, shall be removed from Office on Impeachment for, and Conviction of, Treason, Bribery, or other high Crimes and Misdemeanors.

Article III
Section 1

The judicial Power of the United States, shall be vested in one supreme Court, and in such inferior Courts as the Congress may from time to time ordain and establish. The Judges, both of the supreme and inferior Courts, shall hold their Offices during good Behavior, and shall, at stated Times, receive for their Services a Compensation, which shall not be diminished during their Continuance in Office.

Section 2

The judicial Power shall extend to all Cases, in Law and Equity, arising under this Constitution, the Laws of the United States, and Treaties made, or which shall be made, under their Authority;—to all Cases affecting Ambassadors, other public Ministers and Consuls;—to all Cases of admiralty and maritime Jurisdiction;—to Controversies to which the United States shall be a Party;—to Controversies between two or more States;—between a State and Citizens of another State;—between Citizens of different States;—between Citizens of the same State claiming Lands under Grants of different States, and between a State, or the Citizens thereof, and foreign States, Citizens or Subjects.

In all Cases affecting Ambassadors, other public Ministers and Consuls, and those in which a State shall be a Party, the supreme Court shall have original Jurisdiction. In all the other Cases before mentioned, the supreme Court shall have appellate Jurisdiction, both as to Law and Fact, with such Exceptions, and under such Regulations as the Congress shall make.

The Trial of all Crimes, except in Cases of Impeachment, shall be by Jury; and such Trial shall be held in the State where the said Crimes shall have been committed; but when not committed within any State, the Trial shall be at such Place or Places as the Congress may by Law have directed.

Section 3

Treason against the United States, shall consist only in levying War against them, or, in adhering to their Enemies, giving them Aid and Comfort. No Person shall be convicted of Treason unless on the Testimony of two Witnesses to the same overt Act, or on Confession in open Court.

The Congress shall have Power to declare the Punishment of Treason, but no Attainder of Treason shall work Corruption of Blood, or Forfeiture except during the Life of the Person attainted.

Article IV
Section 1

Full Faith and Credit shall be given in each State to the public Acts, Records, and judicial Proceedings of every other State. And the Congress may by general Laws prescribe the Manner in which such Acts, Records and Proceedings shall be proved, and the Effect thereof.

Section 2

The Citizens of each State shall be entitled to all Privileges and Immunities of Citizens in the several States.

A Person charged in any State with Treason, Felony, or other Crime, who shall flee from Justice, and be found in another State, shall on Demand of the executive Authority of the State from which he fled, be delivered up, to be removed to the State having Jurisdiction of the Crime.

No Person held to Service or Labour in one State, under the Laws thereof, escaping into another, shall, in Consequence of any Law or Regulation therein, be discharged from such Service or Labor, but shall be delivered up on Claim of the Party to whom such Service or Labor may be due.

Section 3

New States may be admitted by the Congress into this Union; but no new State shall be formed or erected within the Jurisdiction of any other State; nor any State be formed by the Junction of two or more States, or Parts of States, without the Consent of the Legislatures of the States concerned as well as of the Congress.

The Congress shall have Power to dispose of and make all needful Rules and Regulations respecting the Territory or other Property belonging to the United States; and nothing in this Constitution shall be so construed as to Prejudice any Claims of the United States, or of any particular State.

Section 4

The United States shall guarantee to every State in this Union a Republican Form of Government, and shall protect each of them against Invasion; and on Application of the Legislature, or of the Executive (when the Legislature cannot be convened) against domestic Violence.

Article V

The Congress, whenever two thirds of both Houses shall deem it necessary, shall propose Amendments to this Constitution, or, on the Application of the Legislatures of two thirds of the several States, shall call a Convention for proposing Amendments, which, in either Case, shall be valid to all Intents and Purposes, as part of this Constitution, when ratified by the Legislatures of three fourths of the several States, or by Conventions in three fourths thereof, as the one or the other Mode of Ratification may be proposed by the Congress; Provided that no Amendment which may be made prior to the Year One thousand eight hundred and eight shall in any Manner affect the first and fourth Clauses in the Ninth Section of the first Article; and that no State, without its Consent, shall be deprived of its equal Suffrage in the Senate.

Article VI

All Debts contracted and Engagements entered into, before the Adoption of this Constitution shall be as valid against the United States under this Constitution, as under the Confederation.

This Constitution, and the Laws of the United States which shall be made in Pursuance thereof; and all Treaties made, or which shall be made, under the Authority of the United States, shall be the supreme Law of the Land; and the Judges in every State shall be bound thereby, any Thing in the Constitution or Laws of any State to the Contrary notwithstanding.

The Senators and Representatives before mentioned, and the Members of the several State Legislatures, and all executive and judicial Officers, both of the United States and of the several States, shall be bound by Oath or Affirmation, to support this Constitution; but no religious Test shall ever be required as a Qualification to any Office or public Trust under the United States.

Article VII

The Ratification of the Conventions of nine States shall be sufficient for the Establishment of this Constitution between the States so ratifying the Same.

Amendment I [1791]

Congress shall make no law respecting an establishment of religion, or prohibiting the free exercise thereof; or abridging the freedom of speech, or of the press; or the right of the people peaceably to assembly, and to petition the Government for a redress of grievances.

Amendment II [1791]

A well regulated Militia, being necessary to the security of a free State, the right of the people to keep and bear Arms, shall not be infringed.

Amendment III [1791]

No Soldier shall, in time of peace be quartered in any house, without the consent of the Owner, nor in time of war, but in a manner to be prescribed by law.

Amendment IV [1791]

The right of the people to be secure in their persons, houses, papers, and effects, against unreasonable searches and seizures, shall not be violated, and no Warrants shall issue, but upon probable cause, supported by Oath or affirmation, and particularly describing the place to be searched, and the persons or things to be seized.

Amendment V [1791]

No person shall be held to answer for a capital, or otherwise infamous crime, unless on a presentment or indictment of a Grand Jury, except in cases arising in the land or naval forces, or in the Militia, when in actual service in time of War or public danger; nor shall any person be subject for the same offence to be twice put in jeopardy of life or limb; nor shall be compelled in any criminal case to be a witness against himself, nor be deprived of life, liberty, or property, without due process of law; nor shall private property be taken for public use, without just compensation.

Amendment VI [1791]

In all criminal prosecutions, the accused shall enjoy the right to a speedy and public trial, by an impartial jury of the State and district wherein the crime shall have been committed, which district shall have been previously ascertained by law, and to be informed of the nature and cause of the accusation; to be confronted with the witnesses against him; to have compulsory process for obtaining witnesses in his favor, and to have the Assistance of Counsel for his defence.

Amendment VII [1791]

In Suits at common law, where the value in controversy shall exceed twenty dollars, the right of trial by jury shall be preserved, and no fact tried by jury, shall be otherwise re-examined in any Court of the United States, than according to the rules of the common law.

Amendment VIII [1791]

Excessive bail shall not be required, nor excessive fines imposed, nor cruel and unusual punishments inflicted.

Amendment IX [1791]

The enumeration in the Constitution, of certain rights, shall not be construed to deny or disparage others retained by the people.

Amendment X [1791]

The powers not delegated to the United States by the Constitution, nor prohibited by it to the States, are reserved to the States respectively, or to the people.

Amendment XI [1798]

The Judicial power of the United States shall not be construed to extend to any suit in law or equity, commenced or prosecuted against one of the United States by Citizens of another State, or by Citizens or Subjects of any Foreign State.

Amendment XII [1804]

The Electors shall meet in their respective states, and vote by ballot for President and Vice-President, one of whom, at least, shall not be an inhabitant of the same state with themselves; they shall name in their ballots the person voted for as President, and in distinct ballots the person voted for as Vice-President, and they shall make distinct lists of all persons voted for as President, and of all persons voted for as Vice-President, and of the number of votes for each, which lists they shall sign and certify, and transmit sealed to the seat of the government of the United States, directed to the President of the Senate;—The President of the Senate shall, in the presence of the Senate and House of Representatives, open all the certificates and the votes shall then be counted;—The person having the greatest number of votes for President, shall be the President, if such number be a majority of the whole number of Electors appointed; and if no person have such majority, then from the persons having the highest numbers not exceeding three on the list of those voted for as President, the House of Representatives shall choose immediately, by ballot, the President. But in choosing the President, the votes shall be taken by states, the representation from each state having one vote; a quorum for this purpose shall consist of a member or members from two-thirds of the states, and a majority of all states shall be necessary to a choice. And if the House of Representatives shall not choose a President whenever the right of choice shall devolve upon them, before the fourth day of March next following, then the Vice-President shall act as President, as in the case of the death or other constitutional disability of the President.— The person having the greatest number of votes as Vice-President, shall be the Vice-President, if such number be a majority of the whole number of Electors appointed, and if no person have a majority, then from the two highest numbers on the list, the Senate shall choose the Vice-President; a quorum for the purpose shall consist of two-thirds of the whole number of Senators, and a majority of the whole number shall be necessary to a choice. But no person constitutionally ineligible to the office of President shall be eligible to that of Vice-President of the United States.

Amendment XIII [1865]
Section 1

Neither slavery nor involuntary servitude, except as a punishment for crime whereof the party shall have been duly convicted, shall exist within the United States, or any place subject to their jurisdiction.

Section 2

Congress shall have power to enforce this article by appropriate legislation.

Amendment XIV [1868]
Section 1

All persons born or naturalized in the United States, and subject to the jurisdiction thereof, are citizens of the United States and of the State wherein they reside. No State shall make or enforce any law which shall abridge the privileges or immunities of citizens of the United States; nor shall any State deprive any person of life, liberty, or property, without due process of law; nor deny to any person within its jurisdiction the equal protection of the laws.

Section 2

Representatives shall be apportioned among the several States according to their respective numbers, counting the whole number of persons in each State, excluding Indians not taxed. But when the right to vote at any election for the choice of electors for President and Vice President of the United States, Representatives in Congress, the Executive and Judicial officers of a State, or the members of the Legislature thereof, is denied to any of the male inhabitants of such State, being twenty-one years of age, and citizens of the United States, or in any way abridged, except for participation in rebellion, or other crime, the basis of representation therein shall be reduced in the proportion which the number of such male citizens shall bear to the whole number of male citizens twenty-one years of age in such State.

Section 3

No person shall be a Senator or Representative in Congress, or elector of President and Vice President, or hold any office, civil or military, under the United States, or under any State, who having previously taken an oath, as a member of Congress, or as an officer of the United States, or as a member of any State legislature, or as an executive or judicial officer of any State, to support the Constitution of the United States, shall have engaged in insurrection or rebellion against the same, or given aid or comfort to the enemies thereof. But Congress may by a vote of two-thirds of each House, remove such disability.

Section 4

The validity of the public debt of the United States, authorized by law, including debts incurred for payment of pensions and bounties for services in suppressing insurrection or rebellion, shall not be questioned. But neither the United States nor any State shall assume or pay any debt or obligation incurred in aid of insurrection or rebellion against the United States, or any claim for the loss or emancipation of any slave; but all such debts, obligations and claims shall be held illegal and void.

Section 5

The Congress shall have power to enforce, by appropriate legislation, the provisions of this article.

Amendment XV [1870]
Section 1

The right of citizens of the United States to vote shall not be denied or abridged by the United States or by any State on account of race, color, or previous condition of servitude.

race / color   ←→

Section 2

The Congress shall have power to enforce this article by appropriate legislation.

Amendment XVI [1913]

The Congress shall have power to lay and collect taxes on incomes, from whatever source derived, without apportionment among the several States, and without regard to any census or enumeration.

Amendment XVII [1913]
Section 1

The Senate of the United States shall be composed of two Senators from each State, elected by the people thereof, for six years; and each Senator shall have one vote. The electors in each State shall have the qualifications requisite for electors of the most numerous branch of the State legislatures.

Section 2

When vacancies happen in the representation of any State in the Senate, the executive authority of such State shall issue writs of election to fill such vacancies: Provided, That the legislature of any State may empower the executive thereof to make temporary appointments until the people fill the vacancies by election as the legislature may direct.

Section 3

This amendment shall not be so construed as to affect the election or term of any Senator chosen before it becomes valid as part of the Constitution.

Amendment XVIII [1919]
Section 1

After one year from the ratification of this article the manufacture, sale, or transportation of intoxicating liquors within, the importation thereof into, or the exportation thereof from the United States and all territory subject to the jurisdiction thereof for beverage purposes is hereby prohibited.

Section 2

The Congress and the several States shall have concurrent power to enforce this article by appropriate legislation.

Section 3

This article shall be inoperative unless it shall have been ratified as an amendment to the Constitution by the legislatures of the several States, as provided in the Constitution, within seven years from the date of the submission hereof to the States by the Congress.

Amendment XIX [1920]
Section 1

The right of citizens of the United States to vote shall not be denied or abridged by the United States or by any State on account of sex.   *sex*

Section 2

Congress shall have power to enforce this article by appropriate legislation.

Amendment XX [1933]
Section 1

The terms of the President and Vice President shall end at noon on the 20th day of January, and the terms of Senators and Representatives at noon on the 3d day of January, of the years in which such terms would have ended if this article had not been ratified; and the terms of their successors shall then begin.

Section 2

The Congress shall assemble at least once in every year, and such meeting shall begin at noon on the 3d day of January, unless they shall by law appoint a different day.

Section 3

If, at the time fixed for the beginning of the term of the President, the President elect shall have died, the Vice President elect shall become President. If the President shall not have been chosen before the time fixed for the beginning of his term, or if the President elect shall have failed to qualify, then the Vice President elect shall act as President until a President shall have qualified; and the

Congress may by law provide for the case wherein neither a President elect nor a Vice President elect shall have qualified, declaring who shall then act as President, or the manner in which one who is to act shall be selected, and such person shall act accordingly until a President or Vice President shall have qualified.

Section 4

The Congress may by law provide for the case of the death of any of the persons from whom the House of Representatives may choose a President whenever the right of choice shall have devolved upon them, and for the case of the death of any of the persons from whom the Senate may choose a Vice President whenever the right of choice shall have devolved upon them.

Section 5

Sections 1 and 2 shall take effect on the 15th day of October following the ratification of this article.

Section 6

This article shall be inoperative unless it shall have been ratified as an amendment to the Constitution by the legislatures of three-fourths of the several States within seven years from the date of its submission.

Amendment XXI [1933]
Section 1

The eighteenth article of amendment to the Constitution of the United States is hereby repealed.

Section 2

The transportation or importation into any State, Territory, or possession of the United States for delivery or use therein of intoxicating liquors, in violation of the laws thereof, is hereby prohibited.

Section 3

This article shall be inoperative unless it shall have been ratified as an amendment to the Constitution by conventions in the several States, as provided in the Constitution, within seven years from the date of the submission hereof to the States by the Congress.

Amendment XXII [1951]
Section 1

No person shall be elected to the office of the President more than twice, and no person who has held the office of President, or acted as President, for more than two years of a term to which some other person was elected President shall be elected to the office of President more than once. But this Article shall not apply to any person holding the office of President when this Article was proposed by the Congress, and shall not prevent any person who may be holding the office of President, or acting as President, during the term within which this Article becomes operative from holding the office of President or acting as President during the remainder of such term.

Section 2

This article shall be inoperative unless it shall have been ratified as an amendment to the Constitution by the legislatures of three-fourths of the several States within seven years from the date of its submission to the States by the Congress.

Amendment XXIII [1961]
Section 1

The District constituting the seat of Government of the United States shall appoint in such manner as the Congress may direct:

A number of electors of President and Vice President equal to the whole number of Senators and Representatives in Congress to which the District would be entitled if it were a State, but in no event more than the least populous state; they shall be in addition to those appointed by the states, but they shall be considered, for the purposes of the election of President and Vice President, to be electors appointed by a state; and they shall meet in the District and perform such duties as provided by the twelfth article of amendment.

Section 2

The Congress shall have power to enforce this article by appropriate legislation.

Amendment XXIV [1964]
Section 1

The right of citizens of the United States to vote in any primary or other election for President or Vice President, for electors for President or Vice President, or for Senator or Representative in Congress, shall not be denied or abridged by the United States, or any State by reason of failure to pay any poll tax or other tax.

Section 2

The Congress shall have power to enforce this article by appropriate legislation.

Amendment XXV [1967]
Section 1

In case of the removal of the President from office or of his death or resignation, the Vice President shall become President.

Section 2

Whenever there is a vacancy in the office of the Vice President, the President shall nominate a Vice President who shall take office upon confirmation by a majority vote of both Houses of Congress.

Section 3

Whenever the President transmits to the President pro tempore of the Senate and the Speaker of the House of Representatives his written declaration that he is unable to discharge the powers and duties of his office, and until he transmits to them a written declaration to the contrary, such powers and duties shall be discharged by the Vice President as Acting President.

Section 4

Whenever the Vice President and a majority of either the principal officers of the executive departments or of such other body as Congress may by law provide, transmit to the President pro tempore of the Senate and the Speaker of the House of Representatives their written declaration that the President is unable to discharge the powers and duties of his office, the Vice President shall immediately assume the powers and duties of the office as Acting President.

Thereafter, when the President transmits to the President pro tempore of the Senate and the Speaker of the House of Representatives his written declaration that no inability exists, he shall resume the powers and duties of his office unless the Vice President and a majority of either the principal officers of the executive department or of such other body as Congress may by law provide, transmit within four days to the President pro tempore of the Senate and the Speaker of the House of Representatives their written declaration and the President is unable to discharge the powers and duties of his office. Thereupon Congress shall decide the issue, assembling within forty-eight hours for that purpose if not in session. If theCongress, within twenty-one days after receipt of the latter written declaration, or, if Congress is not in session, within twenty-one days after Congress is required to assemble, determines by two-thirds vote of both Houses that the President is unable to discharge the powers and duties of his office, the Vice President shall continue to discharge the same as Acting President; otherwise, the President shall resume the powers and duties of his office.

Amendment XXVI [1971]

Section 1

The right of citizens of the United States, who are eighteen years of age or older, to vote shall not be denied or abridged by the United States or by any State on account of age.

Section 2

The Congress shall have power to enforce this article by appropriate legislation.

Glossary

Actual Offense Behavior: the offense actually committed, not the offense charged.

Actus Reus: the physical element, or the criminal act.

Adjudication: court proceedings.

Adjudication: proceedings in court.

Administrative Sentencing Model: legislatures and judges prescribe boundaries, but administrative agencies determine the actual length of sentence.

Admissable Evidence: information that justifies government intrusions and deprivations.

Adversarial Proceedings: disposition of cases by argument in court presided over by judges.

Adversary Process: view of criminal justice as a contest between the government and the individual.

Affirmative Defense: defendant proves the elements in the defense.

Aggregate Crime Rates: number of crimes per 100,000 of the general population.

Aggressive Field Investigation: police take initiative in checking out suspicious circumstances, places, and persons.

Allocution: the defendant's addressing of the court before sentencing.

Anomie: the weakening of social norms.

Appellate Courts: courts of appeal jurisdiction.

Arraign: bring defendant before a court to hear and answer charges.

Arraignment: bringing defendants to court to hear criminal charges and plead to them.

Arrest: a detention that amounts to a Fourth Amendment seizure.

Attempt: taking substantial steps toward committing a crime.

Attrition of Cases: cases dropped at various stages in the criminal process.

Back-Door Strategy: reducing prison population by the early release of prisoners.

Back-End Alternative: sanctions following incarceration.

Background Forces: psychoanalytic, biological, and sociological causes of crime.

"Bark-and-Bite" Sentencing: sentence of judges modified by actions of parole boards.

Bench Trials: trials without juries.

Bifurcated Trials: trials in two stages, the first to determine guilt and the second to decide on the death penalty.

Bind Over: a judge's order to send a defendant on to trial.

Building-Tender System: relying on prisoners to assist officers in managing prisons.

Capital Felonies: crimes punishable by death or life imprisonment.

Career Criminals: criminals who devote their lives to crime.

Career-Criminal Units: prosecutors who specialize in the prosecution of repeat offenders.

Case System: prosecutors manage a case throughout the criminal process.

Case-Load Pressure Hypothesis: the high number of cases requires plea negotiation to keep the system working.

Causation: one thing produces a result.

Cell Rationing: assigning a certain number of cells in state prisons to individual judicial districts.

Certification: treating juveniles as adults for criminal prosecution.

Challenge for Cause: objections to jurors based on showing bias.

Charge: initiate formal criminal court proceedings.

Charge Bargaining: plea negotiations over the charge the government will file.

Citation: an order to appear in court.

Civilian Review Boards: commissions set up outside the police department to hear and review citizen complaints against the police.

Colloquy: the formal discussion between judge and defendant to determine if defendants have pleaded knowingly and voluntarily.

Commercial Bail: the private business of bail bonding.

Common Law: custom translated into law.

Community Policing: citizen participation in setting police priorities and police operations.

Community Service Internships: field experiences offering officers opportunities to gain broad perspectives on crime and criminal law enforcement.

Community-Based Corrections: sentence served outside prison or jail under supervision and with conditions attached.

Commute: executive authority to reduce a sentence.

Concentration Model: putting the most violent prisoners in one prison.

Conflict Perspective: conflict, not agreement, is the normal state of society.

Consensus Perspective: general agreement of values in society.

Consensus Prison Management: a balance of control and responsibility management.

Consent Search: search conducted with knowing and voluntary consent.

Conspiracy: the agreement to commit a crime.

Constructive Intent: the conscious or unconscious creation of risk of harm.

Contingent Fees: compensation for lawyers determined by a per cent of the damages recovered by plaintiffs in civil actions.

Continuance in Contemplation of Dismissal: case in abeyance pending good behavior.

Control Model of Management: prison management emphasizing obedience, work, and education of prisoners.

Correctional Boot Camps: shock incarceration for youthful first-time nonviolent offenders.

Correlation: an association not necessarily causal.

Courthouse Work Group: lawyers who form a courtroom elite whose primary goal is the efficient and harmonious disposition of cases.

Courts of Last Resort: courts of final appeal.

Courts of Record: courts that keep a formal written record of their proceedings.

Crime Control: the value or goal of reducing crime, emphasizing informal discretionary decision making.

Crime Control Model: values discretion to quickly sort out factually innocent from factually guilty.

Crimes Cleared by Arrest: crimes known to the police but removed from police records.

Criminal Event: the commission of a specific crime.

Criminal History: record of prior offenses.

Criminal Involvement: process of getting involved, continuing, and stopping criminal behavior.

Criminal Justice System: a loose confederation of agencies, including police, courts, and corrections.

Criminal Negligence: unconscious creation of a high risk of harm.

Criminal Procedure: the law prescribing how the government enforces criminal law.

Criminal Process: sorting individuals for further action or removing them from the criminal justice system.

Criminal Recklessness: conscious creation of a high risk of harm.

Criminogenic Forces: causes of crime in the society.

Crowded Prisoners: prisoners who live in less than 60 square feet of floor space.

Cycle of Violence Hypothesis: childhood abuse creates a predisposition to later violent behavior.

D.A.R.E. (Drug Abuse Resistance Education): specially trained police officers go to schools to teach drug prevention.

Damages: money awarded in noncriminal lawsuit for injuries.

Dark Figure in Crime: the number of crimes committed but not discovered.

Dead-Bang Cases: cases in which conviction is almost certain.

Decriminalization: removing status offenses from juvenile jurisdiction.

Defenses of Excuse: admit to the wrongfulness of crime but deny responsibility.

Defenses of Justification: admit to the crime but assert that it was right to do it.

Deferred Release Decisions: the setting of release after the determination that prisoner has reformed.

Deinstitutionalization: community-based noninstitutional treatment.

Delinquency: behavior that would be criminal in adults.

Density: number of square feet of floor space per prisoner.

Descriptive Guidelines: sentencing ranges based on actual past sentence practices.

Detention Centers: secure, temporary holding facilities.

Differential Association: criminal behavior depends on associations.

Differential Response: police response to routine calls differs from that to emergency calls.

Diminished Capacity: mental impairment less severe than insanity.

Direct Information: facts known by direct knowledge.

Direct Supervision: officers residing in living units in contact with the prisoners they supervise.

Dirty Harry Problem: the need for police officers to resort to "dirty" means to catch criminals.

Discretion: decision making without laws and other written rules.

Disposition Hearings: determine what should follow finding of delinquency.

Diversion: removal from juvenile justice system to alternative programs.

Diversion: transferring defendants into some alternative to criminal prosecution.

Dual System of Justice: separate systems for adults and juveniles.

Due Process: the value of formal rules and procedures to limit the power of government and protect the rights of individuals.

Due Process Clause: guarantee of fair procedures and protection of life, liberty, and property.

Due Process Model: emphasizes formal legal adversary process at the heart of the criminal process.

Due Process of Law: government can act only according to rules.

Due Process Revolution: the expansion by the Supreme Court during the 1960s of the rights of criminal defendants and the application of the rights to state proceedings.

Duress: committing a crime under coercion.

Entrapment: induced by the government into committing a crime.

Equal Protection of the Laws: prevents unreasonable classifications.

Ethnographic Study: research by intensive field observation and interviews.

Ex Post Facto Laws: retroactive laws.

Exclusionary Rule: prohibiting the use of illegally obtained evidence to prove guilt.

Exclusive Jurisdiction: the sole authority to hear and decide cases.

Executive Clemency or Pardon: the authority of presidents and governors to eliminate a sentence.

Express Bargaining: a direct meeting to decide concessions.

Factual Guilt: defendant has actually committed a crime.

Factual Guilt: knowledge of guilt but not necessarily provable in court.

Family Crime: crimes against people known to the offender.

Federalism: division of power between federal and state governments.

Felonies: crimes punishable by one year or more in prison.

First Appearance: brief proceedings to read charges, set initial bail, and assign attorneys.

First Appearance: proceedings to read charges against defendants, set bail, and assign an attorney.

Fixed or Determinate Sentence: a specific penalty determined by the seriousness of the crime.

Foreground Forces: the immediate lure of crime.

Formal Criminal Justice: the law and other written rules that determine the outer boundaries of action in criminal justice.

Formalization: replacing discretion with rules.

Frankpledge: every male over 12 years obligated to keep peace.

Front-Door Strategy: reducing prison populations by diverting convicted offenders from prison.

Front-End Alternative: sanctions prior to incarceration.

Full Enforcement: enforce all laws with equal vigor.

Fundamental Fairness Doctrine: due process definition focusing on substantive due process.

Funnel Effect: the fewer individuals remaining at successive stages in the criminal process resulting from sorting decisions.

Furlough: temporary release from prison.

General Deterrence: to prevent crime in general population by threatening punishment.

General Intent: the intent to commit the actus reus.

General Jurisdiction: the authority to hear and decide all criminal cases.

General Population Inmate: prisoners without special problems.

General Principles of Criminal Law: the broad general rules that provide the basis for other rules.

Goal Displacement: rehabilitation as a rationalization for crime control.

Going Rate for Guilty Pleas: the penalty that accords with local practice.

Good Time: days deducted from prison terms based on good behavior of prisoners.

Good Time Laws: reduction of sentence length by one third or one half based on behavior in prison.

Grand Jury: citizens who test the government's case.

Gross Misdemeanors: crimes punishable by jail terms of 30 days to a year.

Group Home: relatively open, community-based facility.

Guided Discretion Statutes: laws requiring juries to use guidelines on mitigating and aggravating circumstances.

Halfway House: institutions in the community for parolees and probationers.

Halfway Houses: large, nonsecure, community-based residential centers.

"Hands-off" Doctrine: prison management left to discretion of prison administrators.

Hawthorne Principle: the creation of a new and closely watched project produces temporary positive results.

Hearsay: information acquired through a third person.

Hearsay Evidence: evidence offered by someone who does not know its truth first-hand.

Home Confinement: sentence to detention at home except for work, study, service, or treatment.

Hostile Witnesses: witnesses favorable to the other side in a trial.

Huber Law: statute permitting prisoners in county jails to work outside but return at night and for weekends.

Implicit Bargaining: the assumption that a guilty plea will result in a concession.

Importation Hypothesis: prison society has its roots in the criminal and conventional societies outside the prison.

Incapacitation: to prevent crime by incarceration, mutilation, or capital punishment.

Incident Reports: patrol officer's description of a crime, witnesses, and suspects.

Incident-Based Reporting: report each crime separately whether part of the same event or not.

Incident-Driven Strategies: isolated event determines response by police.

Incorporation Doctrine: due process focusing on procedural regularity.

Indeterminate Sentence: an open-ended penalty tailored to individual offenders.

Indictment: formal accusation of a crime by a grand jury.

Indigenous Theory: conditions inside the prison shape prison society.

Indigent Defendants: defendants too poor to afford a lawyer.

Inducement Test: entrapment focusing on government actions.

Informal Criminal Justice: the reality of criminal justice in action.

Information: formal accusation of a crime by a prosecutor.

Initial Case Screening: prosecutors reviewing whether to charge, divert, or dismiss a case.

Insanity: legal term excusing criminal liability not synonymous with mental illness.

Institutional Support: prisoners who work in maintaining the jail to pay part of the expenses of incarceration.

Intake: early juvenile court process.

Intensive Probation Supervision: closely supervised probation stressing retribution, incapacitation, and economy.

Intermediate Appellate Courts: courts that hear initial appeals.

Intermediate Punishment: sanctions somewhere between the extremes of incarceration and straight probation.

Intermittent Incarceration: incarceration at night and on weekends with release for school, work, treatment, or community service.

Internal Affairs Unit: units created to investigate, report, and recommend with respect to civilian complaints against police officers.

Internal Grievance Mechanisms: procedures inside prisons for dealing with grievances.

Interrogation: questioning suspects.

Irresistible Impulse Test: insanity definition focusing on impairment of will.

Jailhouse Lawyer: prisoners who give legal advice to other prisoners.

Judicial Sentencing Model: judges prescribe sentences within boundaries prescribed by legislatures.

Jury Instructions: the judge's explanation of the law to juries.

Jury Nullification: the power of juries to decide cases according to extralegal considerations.

Jury Trials: proceedings in which juries decide the facts.

Justice Model: focus on deserts, rights, and rules in corrections.

Justice Model: justice demands punishment for the crime committed.

Juvenile Delinquent: youth who has committed either status or delinquency offense.

Kansas City Preventive Patrol Experiment: tested the effectiveness of preventive patrol and found it wanting.

Knock-Down Force: enough use of force by the police to bring a suspect to the ground.

Labeling Theory: society's response to crime defines some people as criminals.

Lawlessness in Sentencing: the wide discretion in sentencing allowed judges in some jurisdictions.

Leading Questions: questions that steer witnesses to a desired answer.

Legal Guilt: proof beyond a reasonable doubt by admissible evidence.

Legal Guilt: sufficient admissible evidence to prove guilt in court.

Legalistic Style: emphasis on criminal law enforcement and formal rules.

Legislative Sentencing Model: legislatures set penalties for offenses.

Liberation Hypothesis: close cases allow jurors to decide according to their own values.

Limited Jurisdiction: courts limited to hearing and deciding minor offenses and preliminary proceedings in felonies.

Local Legal Culture: the attitudes, values, and expectations toward law and legal practice in specific communities.

Local Legal Culture: the values and customs making up the environment of courtrooms.

Lockdown: the suspension of all activities with prisoners confined to their cells.

Lower Criminal Courts: courts of limited jurisdiction.

Mala In Se: crimes wrong in themselves.

Mala Prohibita: crimes wrong because a statute defines them as wrong.

Management-of-Demand (MOD) System: handling noncritical calls by alternatives to sending a patrol car.

Mandatory Minimum Sentence Legislation: the requirement that judges must sentence offenders to a minimum time in prison.

Mandatory Parole Release Statutes: laws requiring the release of prisoners at specified times.

Mandatory Release: release based on good behavior and other sentence-reducing devices.

Material Elements: the parts of a crime that prosecution must prove beyond a reasonable doubt in order to convict.

Material Evidence: evidence that tends to prove the elements of a crime.

Maximum Security Prisons: prisons that focus on preventing prisoners from escaping or hurting themselves or others.

Measured Capacity: one prisoner per cell.

Medical Model: view crime as illness and criminals as sick.

Medical Model: views crime as a disease that requires treatment to cure.

Medium Security Prisons: prisons that focus less on security and allow prisoners greater freedom of movement.

Mens Rea: the mental element in crime, or criminal intent.

Merit System: the selection of judges by a governor from a list drawn up by a commission of citizens, lawyers, and judges.

Middle-Range Offenders: those not requiring imprisonment but demanding more than ordinary probation.

Minimum Security Prisons: prisons containing prisoners who do not pose security problems and that emphasize trust and a normal life-style.

Ministers: officers mechanically enforcing rules.

Misdemeanors: crimes punishable by one year or less in jail.

Mistake of Fact: ignorance or error concerning facts.

Mistake of Law: ignorance or mistake concerning the law.

Modified Retribution Theory: date of release fixed at sentencing, but actual release depends on conditions.

National Crime Victim Survey (NCVS): national sample of victims surveyed about their victimization.

National Institute of Justice: the research arm of the U. S. Department of Justice.

Negotiated Plea: a plea of guilty in exchange for a concession by the government.

Net Widening: expanding jurisdiction.

Net Widening: sentencing borderline cases to intermediate punishments instead of straight probation.

New Generation Jails: jails that combine architecture, management, and training to provide safe, humane confinement.

New Generation Prisons: combines management and architecture to provide safe, secure confinement for maximum security prisoners.

Nolle-Prosequi: voluntarily dropping charges by a prosecutor.

Nolo Contendere: no contest to the charges.

Occupancy: the number of prisoners for each unit of confinement.

Occupational Crime: crimes committed in the course of employment.

Opportunity Theory: criminal behavior depends on the available criminal opportunities.

Order Maintenance: settle disputes now using discretion.

Organization Crime: crimes committed to illegally benefit organizations.

Original Jurisdiction: the authority to initiate proceedings.

Paradigm: a model or pattern of analysis.

Parens Patriae: government acts as parent.

Parish Constable-Watch System: every parish appointed two constables.

Parole: a conditional release from prison.

Parole Board: panels of civilians and experts that determine the release from prison to parole.

Particularity: the detailed description in a warrant of the object of a search.

Pendulum Swing: the alternating emphasis on crime control and due process in the history of criminal justice.

Peremptory Challenge: objection to jurors without showing cause.

Persons Arrested: a wide variety of serious and minor offenses reported in raw numbers.

Petty Misdemeanors: crimes punishable by fine or up to 30 days in jail.

Plain-View Search: object of seizure discovered inadvertently where officer has a right to be.

Podular Design: allows greater security and opportunity for surveillance of fewer numbers of prisoners.

Point System: determine community ties by points for employment, resi-

dence, and relationships in the community.

Police "War Stories": socialization by means of episodes related by experienced officers to police recruits.

Police Academy: training school where police socialization begins.

Police Corruption: form of occupational crime in which officers use their authority for private gain.

Police Defensiveness: distrust of outsiders.

Police Depersonalization: treating violence and other unpleasant experiences as matter-of-fact.

Police Misconduct: range of behavior including brutality, constitutional violations, corruption, and unfair treatment of citizens.

Police Stress: negative pressures associated with police work.

Police Working Personality: character traits of police officers revealed in their work.

Police-Prosecutor Teams: police officers and prosecutors working together from investigation to conviction.

Posttraumatic Stress Syndrome: mental impairment caused by stress during battle.

Pre-Sentence Investigation: the gathering of information about offenders in order to sentence them.

Pre-Trial Settlement Conferences: the negotiation of pleas in the presence of judges, defendants, victims, and police officers.

Predatory Crime: crimes committed for property or money.

Predisposition Test: entrapment focusing on defendant's intent.

Preliminary Hearings: public proceeding to test the government's case.

Premenstrual Syndrome (PMS): an excuse to crime based on mental impairment due to hormonal changes during menstruation.

Prescriptive Guidelines: sentencing ranges prescribing new practices.

Presumption of Guilt: to treat individuals in the criminal process as probably guilty.

Presumption of Innocence: to treat all individuals as innocent until proven guilty according to legally correct proceedings.

Presumptive Guidelines: legally mandated ranges within which judges can prescribe specific sentences.

Presumptive Sentencing: allows judges discretion to sentence within a narrow range of penalties.

Preventive Detention: the detention of defendants prior to trial in order to protect public safety.

Preventive Patrol: moving through the streets to intercept and prevent crime.

Principle of Less Eligibility: prisoners should earn less than free citizens doing the same work.

Prisoners' Rights: constitutional rights that survive incarceration.

Privatization: private management of correctional facilities.

Pro Bono Assistance: the representation of criminal defendants without a fee.

Pro Se Filings: court proceedings in which prisoners file their own papers.

Proactive Police Operations: police initiate operations.

Probable Cause: the quantum of proof required to search or arrest.

Probation: a sentence in place of incarceration.

Problem-Oriented Policing: drawing on community resources and expertise to solve a broad range of problems.

Procedural Due Process: limits on criminal procedure.

Proof Beyond a Reasonable Doubt: enough facts to convict a criminal defendant.

Protective Custody Units: units devoted to the protection of prisoners with special problems.

Protective Officers: stresses the balance of interests between society and probationers.

Public Order Offenses: minor crimes of public annoyance.

Public Works Crew: prisoners who work in groups performing public services.

Punitive Officers: stresses the control of probationers.

Quality Arrests: those resulting in conviction.

Quantum of Proof: the amount of evidence that justifies government action.

Quasi-Judicial Proceedings: proceedings that mix formal rules and discretionary judgments.

Quasi-Military Lines: form bureaucracy with a hierarchical authority structure.

Rational Choice Perspective: focuses on the rational element in criminal behavior.

Rational Decision Making: decisions based on defined goals, alternatives, and information.

Reactive Police Patrol: police mobilize when citizens ask for service.

Reasonable Suspicion: the quantum of proof required for a stop and frisk.

Recidivist: repeat offenders.

Rehabilitation: to prevent crime by changing behavior of individual offenders.

Relative Deprivation: feelings of deprivation when compared to others doing better.

Release on Recognizance: the release of defendants on their promise to appear.

Relevant Evidence: evidence that relates to the elements of a crime.

Reported Capacity: the number of prisoners that a jurisdiction decides is the capacity of a facility.

Response Time: the time it takes for the police to respond to citizen calls.

Responsibility Management: management stressing the responsibility of prisoners for their own actions.

Restitution: repayment by offenders for the injuries their crime caused.

Retribution: looks back in order to punish for the crime committed.

Revocation: the retraction of parole.

Right-Wrong Test: insanity definition focusing on impairments of reason.

"Rotten Apple" Theory: single bad officer who does not reflect a departmental problem.

Rule of Law: limits on the discretionary power of government.

Rule of Law: the principle that rules, not discretion, govern decisions in criminal law and procedure.

Safety-Valve Policy: reducing the minimum sentence of prisoners when prisons exceed capacity.

Saturation Patrol: assigning large numbers of officers to a specific location.

"Scottsboro Case": case announcing the fundamental fairness doctrine.

Search: examining person or property in order to discover evidence, weapon, or contraband.

Search Incident to Arrest: search without a warrant conducted at the time of arrest.

Section 1983 Actions: legal actions brought under the Ku Klux Klan Act permitting citizens to sue government officials for the violation of civil rights.

Selective Enforcement: enforce some laws some of the time.

Selective Hypothesis Fallacy: choosing subjects for research that favor a particular outcome.

Selective Incapacitation: imprisoning offenders who commit the most crimes.

Self-Reports: asking samples of the population if they have committed crimes.

Sentence Bargaining: plea negotiations over the sentence the judge will grant.

Sentencing Discrimination: the determination of sentences by unacceptable criteria, such as race.

Sentencing Disparity: persons who commit similar offenses under similar circumstances do not receive similar sentences.

Sentencing Guidelines: ranges within which judges prescribe specific sentences.

Separation of Powers: the three branches of government—legislative, executive, and judiciary—stay separate and perform their own functions without interference from the others.

Service Style: reliance on bureaucracy to provide service to the community.

Shelters: temporary, nonsecure, community-based holding facilities.

Shock Probation: indeterminate period of incarceration followed by probation.

Sinister Defendants: defendants who create fear due to extralegal factors.

Slow Pleas: pleas of guilty following trials that are not really contested.

Social Conflict Theories: power structure of society creates crime.

Social Control Theory: obedience to rules depends on institutions to keep desire to break the rules in check.

Social Structure of the Case: extralegal or sociological influences on decisions.

Social Structure Theory: links crime to criminogenic forces in society.

Solicitation: asking another to commit a crime.

Solvability Factors: information that leads to the solution of crimes.

Special Management Inmates: prisoners in need of special care.

Specific Intent: the intent to do something in addition to the criminal act.

Split Sentence: part of sentence served in jail, remainder served on probation.

Split-Sentence Probation: sentence to specified term of incarceration followed by a specified time on probation.

Status Offenses: behavior that only juveniles commit.

Stop and Frisk: less intrusive seizures and searches protected by the Fourth Amendment.

Straight Plea: a plea of guilty without plea negotiations.

Strain Theory: pressures in the social structure cause crime.

Street Crimes: one-on-one crimes against strangers.

Strict Liability: criminal liability without a criminal intent.

Subculture of Competition: goal of success more important than the means of gaining it.

Subculture of Violence: a subculture that condones violence.

Subpoena: a court order to a witness to appear in court.

Substantial Capacity Test: insanity definition focusing on impairments of either or both reason and will.

Substantial Justice Approach: decide according to the justice of individual cases.

Summons: notification of proceedings against defendants and requirements of their appearance in court.

Substantive Due Process: limits on criminal law.

"Sweet Deals": the acceptance of a guilty plea for a lesser crime in weak cases.

Systems Paradigm: the decision-making perspective that treats the criminal justice agencies as an integrated whole.

Ten Percent Bond Program: payment to a court which is returned if defendants appeal.

Tithing: group of ten sworn to keep peace.

Tort: noncriminal legal wrong.

Training Schools: secure detention facilities.

Transferred Intent: intent to cause one harm results in causing harm to another.

Trial Courts: courts of general jurisdiction.

Trials De Novo: retrial by a trial court of cases heard in lower criminal courts.

Uniform Crime Reports (UCR): summary of information provided by local police agencies to the FBI.

Utilitarian Punishment: looks forward to preventing crime in the future.

Vehicle Search: search of vehicles without a warrant but without probable cause.

Victimless Crimes: crimes without complaining victims.

Violations: punishable by a small fine without a criminal record.

Violent Predators: career criminals who commit a range of street crimes.

Violent Prison: modern prisons inhabited increasingly by young members of gangs.

Void for Vagueness: statutes must define crimes precisely.

Voir Dire: the examination of prospective jurors.

Voluntary Guidelines: suggested ranges of sentences that are not legally binding on judges.

Walling: building walls for protection.

Wariness: measures to protect against suspicious strangers.

Warrant: document issued by a magistrate that the Constitution requires for a search or arrest.

Watching: keeping a lookout for suspicious persons and circumstances.

Watchman Style: focus on order maintenance and discretionary decision-making.

Welfare Officers: stresses the welfare of the client.

White-Collar Crime: crimes committed by "respectable" people.

"Wild Beast" Test: insanity measured by total destruction of reason and will.

Work Release: programs allowing prisoners to leave confinement to work.

Work-Release: allowing prisoners to leave prison or jail to work during the day.

Writ of Habeas Corpus: order to review the lawfulness of detention.

Writ of Certiorari: order to review the proceedings of a lower court.

Zone System: prosecutors manage a particular stage of the criminal process.

Table of Cases

Name Index

Subject Index

Fifth Amendment, 113, 133–135, 226–227, 249–252, 256, 260, 402, 422, 472, 603
Final revocation hearing, 499–500
Finland, intermediate punishments, 505
Financial assistance for released offenders, 596
Fines, 449, 514–515, 643
First Amendment, 399, 600, 604
First appearance, 366
Fixed sentencing, 436–438
Fleeing felon doctrine, 233–235
Florence Administrative Maximum security penitentiary, 532–533
Follow-up investigation, 205–207
Foot patrol, 194–196
Force,
    abuse of, 290–295
    deadly, 292–298
    excessive, 292
    legitimate use of, 290
    necessary, 292
    policies and practices, 302–303
    reasonable, 292
    types and amounts of, 292–293
    use of and arrest, 232–235
    use of by police, 396–397
    violent, 292
Foreground forces in crime, defined, 83
Formal and informal policing, 146–147
Formal criminal justice,
    defined, 9
    informal criminal justice and, 9–10
    source of rules of, 9
Formalization,
    defined, 227
    of stop and frisk, 243–244
Fortress prison, 530
Foster homes, 674
Fourteenth Amendment, 113, 133–135, 227, 256, 260, 395, 422, 472, 603–604, 645, 648–649, 651
Fourth Amendment, 134–136, 227–248, 260, 262, 499–502, 605–606
Frankpledge, 148
Free Venture, 596–597
Freedom of religion, prisoners' rights to, 604
Freedom of speech, prisoners' rights, 604
Frisk, stop and, 243–249
Front-door strategy, 592
Full cash bonds, 377
Full enforcement, 162
Functions of criminal courts, 331–335
    bureaucratic, 334
    crime control, 333–334
    due process, 332–333
    organizational, 334
    social service, 334–335
Fundamental fairness doctrine, 134–135
Funnel effect, 19
    international gender differences and, 20–21
Funnel, Criminal justice, 18–20
Furloughs, 636

Gangs, prison, 533, 581–584
Gender
    bail and, 383
    crime rates by race and, 68

juveniles, 666
    model of police attitudes, 282
    police attitudes and, 282–283
General deterrence, 444–445
General intent, 116
General population inmate, 587
General principles of criminal liability and specific crimes, 118
General warrants, 235–236
Geography of crime, 64
German Code on the Execution of Prison Sentences, 607
German Criminal Code, 451
Germany,
    guilty pleas in, 428
    police in, 174
    prisoners' rights in, 607
    prisons, treatment in, 597
Ghetto poverty theory, 172
Gleaning, 576
Going rate for guilty pleas, 409
Good behavior bond, 489
Good time laws, 563
Grand juries, 384–386
Grievances, prison, 609–610
Gross misdemeanors, 131
Group home, 675
Group therapy, 598
Guardian Angels, 209
Guided discretion death penalty statutes, 472
Guilty defendants, and defense counsel, 347–348
Guilty plea, 406–430
    Constitution and, 422–425
    defense counsel and, 416–419
    in Germany, 428
    innocent defendants and, 423–424
Gun Control Act, Massachusetts, 466

Habeas corpus, writs of, 330–331
Habitual felon laws, 470
Halfway houses, 635–636, 675
Halo effect, 395
Hands-off doctrine, 602–603
Harsher penalties, impact of, 578
Hawthorne principle, defined, 204
Hearing officers, 628
Hearsay, 231
Hearsay evidence, 404
High control project, 641–642
High-speed chases, 298–301
Highway patrols, state, 155
Hiring quotas, 285–287
Home confinement, 509–511
    benefits, 509
    constitutional issues, 509–510
    evaluation of, 511
    history, 509
    net widening, 511
Homes, entering and arrest, 232–233
Hostile witnesses, 403
Hot spot patrol, 198
Hot spots, 98
Houses of Corrections, Elizabethan, 593
Hydraulic effect, 15

Identification, 252–259
    Constitution and, 256–257

mistaken, dangers of, 253–255
    race and, 254
Immigration and Naturalization Service (INS), 153
Implicit bargaining, 409
Importation theory of prisoner subculture, 575
Imprisonment,
    length of, 562–564
    punitive power, 518–519
Inmate code, 576–577
Incapacitation, 445
Incarceration, 449
    costs of, 527
    intensive supervised probation and, 507
    intermittent, 494
    rates, 525–527
    shock, 494
Incident report, 204
Incident-based reporting, 52
Incorporation doctrine, 135–136
Incorrigible prisoners, 439
Indeterminate sentencing, 438–439
    defined, 436
Index crimes, 57–59
Indictment, 384–386
Indigenous theory of prisoner subculture, 575
Individual psychotherapy, 598
Inducement test of entrapment, 127
Influences on the decision to charge, 360–366
    extralegal, 362–364
    legal, 361
    relationship, 365–366
    sociological, 362
Informal and formal policing, 146–147
Informal criminal justice, 10–12
    defined, 10
    formal criminal justice and, 9–10
    range of, 10
Informal functions of defense counsel, 348–351
Informal rules, police, 271–272
Informality and speed in criminal cases, 332
Information, 384–385
Initial case screening, 359
Initial probable cause hearing, 498–499
Injunctions, 306
Insanity, 127–129
    burden of proof and, 129
    tests of, 128–129
Insight Incorporated, 594
Institutional corrections, juvenile, 674–677
Institutional support, 547
Institutionalization, 659
    of prisons, 529
Instrumentalist radical theory, 138–139
Intake conference, 668
Intake, 668
Intensive Probation Supervision, Georgia, 508–509
Intensive supervised parole, 637
Intensive supervised probation, 505–509, 644
    aims of, 506
    defined, 506
    evaluations, 507–509

Minneapolis Domestic Violence Study, 168–171
Minneapolis Hot Spots Patrol Experiment, 198
Minnesota Multiphasic Personality Inventory, 274
Minnesota Sentencing Guidelines, 458–460
Minority
    corrections officers, 541–543
    judges, 338–340
    police officers, 283–287
Miranda warnings, 249–251
    defined, 249
    reactions to, 250–251
Misconduct, accountability for, 305–318
Misdemeanor, 130–131
    defined, 16
Missouri Bar Plan, 338
Mistake of fact, 124
Mistake of law, 124
Mistake, defense of, 124
Model Code of Pre-Arraignment Procedure, 230–231
Model Penal Code, 129
Moral entrepreneurs, 139–140
Motor patrol, 190–194
Municipal police departments, 155–156
Murder, Inc., 474
Mutilation, 445

Narcotic Control Act of 1956, 464
National Council on Crime and Delinquency, 440
National Crime Victimization Survey (NCVS), 48, 52–55
    defined, 52
    juvenile crime, 662
    limitations of, 54–55
    summary reports, 53
National Prison Congress, 438
Negotiated pleas,
    abolishing, 426–427
    benefits of, 425
    criticisms of, 425–426
    defense counsel and, 417–418
    defined, 407
    judges and, 419–422
    offender seriousness, 414–415
    offense seriousness, 414–415
    prosecutor's influence, 415–416
    prosecutors and, 410–416
        decision to negotiate, 411–412
        determining bargain, 412–413
        police relations, 411
    reform, 425–430
    strength of government's case, 413–414
    types of, 409
Neighborhood Defender Service of Harlem, 372
Neighborhood Watch programs, 208
Net widening,
    home confinement, 511
    intensive supervision probation, 509
    juveniles and, 679–680
Neurosis, 89
New generation maximum security prisons, 533–534
    corrections officer in, 544–545
New Mexico prison riot, 588–590

New-generation jails, 549–552
    women offenders and, 552
    women officers and, 551
Nolle prosequi, 360
Nolo contendere, 386
Nordic countries, intermediate punishments, 505
Norway, intermediate punishments, 505

Oak Park Heights (Minnesota) prison, 534, 538, 544–545
Objective basis, 226
Occupancy, 548
Occupational crime, 70–72
    defined, 70
    measuring, 56–57
Offender seriousness and negotiated pleas, 414–415
Offender surveys, defined, 47
Offender-victim relationship, 65–66
Offense seriousness and negotiated pleas, 414–415
Officers of the court, prosecutors, 344
Official immunity, doctrine of, 307
Old age, as excuse, 125
Opening statements, 401–402
Operation Clean Sweep, 247–249
Operation Safe Streets, 245
Opportunity theory, 91
Order maintenance, 166–167
Organization crime, and strain theory, 91
Organizational functions of criminal courts, 334
Original jurisdiction, 330
Overcrowding, 590–593
    causes of, 590–591
    jails, 548
    parole and, 625
    responses to, 591–593

Pardon, 442
Parens patriae, doctrine of, 658
Parish-constable watch system, 148
Parole,
    authorities, 625–628
    conditions of release, 633–635
    contract, 634
    defined, 620
    determinate sentencing and, 628
    distinguished from probation, 488–489
    due process rights, 648–651
    federal guidelines, 630–631
    guidelines, 629–632
    guidelines, evaluation of, 632
    history of, 621–624
    juvenile, 674
    missions of, 624–625
    officers, 637–638
    prison crowding and, 625
    probation and, 635
    programs, 635–637
    release hearing, 628–629
    release, 628–633
    revocation of, 645–651
    revocation, defined, 645
    supervision of, 633–637
    supervision, 641–645
    United States Code, 645–648

Parole board,
    defined, 625
    influence on sentencing, 442
    membership, 626–628
    powers of, 626
    release, 628–633
Parole Decision Making Project, 630
Part I offenses, 48
Part II offenses, 60–64
    defined, 49
Particularity of the warrant, defined, 237
Passive parole officers, 638
Patrol
    discretion and, 189–190
    mobilization, 189–190
    strategies, 189–197
    types of, 190–198
Penalties, impact of harsher, 578
Penitentiary, 529
Pennsylvania system of prisons, 529
Perception, 253–254
Peremptory challenges, 399
Petty misdemeanors, 131
Photographic identification, 257–258
    defined, 253
Plain-view searches, 242–243
Plaintiffs, 306
Plea bargaining,
    abolishing, 426–427
    benefits of, 425
    criticisms of, 425–426
    judges and, 419–422
    offender seriousness, 414–415
    offense seriousness, 414–415
    prosecutor's influence, 415–416
    prosecutors and, 410–416
        decision to negotiate, 411–412
        determining bargain, 412–413
    reform, 425–430
    strength of government's case, 413–414
Police,
    community service, 172–175
    courts and, 224–225
    criminal law enforcement, 162–166
    detectives, 205–207
    discretion, 162–163
    education, 275–277
        innovations in, 279–280
    field training, 279
    functions of, overlap of, 177
    influence on sentencing, 441–442
    informal rules and, 271–272
    juveniles and, 663–667
    law enforcement, myths of, 224
    management styles, 159–160
    minority officers, 283–287
    order maintenance, 166–167
    organization, 157–159
    professional force, elements of, 149–150
    private, 156–157
    promotion, 272–280
    prosecutors and,
        cooperation with, 343–344
        negotiated pleas, 411
    recruitment, 272–280
    response, categories of, 160
    roles of, 160–181
        drug laws and, 177–181